Modern Auditing & Assurance Services

Gurdarshan S. Gill
MONASH UNIVERSITY

Graham Cosserat
NOTTINGHAM TRENT UNIVERSITY

Philomena Leung
RMIT UNIVERSITY

Paul Coram
UNIVERSITY OF WESTERN AUSTRALIA

John Wiley & Sons Australia, Ltd

Sixth edition published 2001 by
John Wiley & Sons Australia, Ltd
33 Park Road, Milton, Qld 4064

Offices also in Sydney and Melbourne

First edition 1985
Second edition 1989
Third edition 1993
Fourth edition 1996
Fifth edition 1999

Authorised adaptation of W. G. Kell & W. C. Boynton,
Modern Auditing, 6th edition.

Typeset in 10.5/12pt Times

National Library of Australia
Cataloguing-in-Publication data

Modern auditing and assurance services

6th ed.
Bibliography.
Includes index.
ISBN 0 471 42244 4.

1. Auditing. I. Gill, Gurdarshan Singh
II. Title: Modern auditing. 5th ed.

657.45

Printed in Singapore by
Kyodo Printing Co (S'pore) Pte Ltd

10 9 8 7 6 5 4 3 2

Preface

Modern Auditing and Assurance Services is written for introductory courses in auditing and assurance at undergraduate, postgraduate and professional levels. This text is more than just a manual of auditing, and the practice of auditing is explained in the context of auditing theory and concepts, with appropriate reference to Auditing Standards.

The practice of auditing is changing and traditional audit services are becoming a diminishing proportion of the services offered by accounting firms. Assurance services are expected to be the primary growth area for auditors in the twenty-first century. To reflect these changes in accounting practice, in this edition we focus on assurance services more than in prior editions. In addition, the new 'Professional environment' vignettes throughout the text illustrate current changes and developments in professional practice. However, at this time the core assurance service for most accounting firms is the traditional financial report audit, so it is this assurance service that receives the most attention throughout this textbook.

The internationalisation of Auditing and Accounting Standards is an ongoing development in global accounting practice. The importance of international Auditing (and Accounting) Standards is expected to increase over the coming years; for this reason, and for non-Australian readers, this textbook includes references to international as well as Australian Standards wherever appropriate. The cross-referencing of these Standards is of particular benefit to readers in Asia and the Pacific rim, and to overseas students studying at Australian universities.

Significant changes from the previous edition

In preparing this edition, we have acknowledged a number of recent developments, particularly (1) the growing importance of assurance services to the accounting profession, (2) changes in information technology and the growth of e-commerce, (3) the internationalisation of auditing practice and Standards, (4) amendments to the Corporations Law and the changes to Auditing Standards, and (5) the interest of an increasing number of international students undertaking Australian degrees and professional courses. We have also amended the structure of the book to improve further the readability and the logical flow of topics covered.

Organisation

How to use this book. This three-page graphic feature assists readers to see at a glance how they can make best use of the key features of this text.

Chapter openers. This double-page spread presents a summarised account of the main elements in each chapter, the learning outcomes and the relevant professional statements, thus providing readers with a broad contextual base from which to approach each chapter. To maximise relevance for other than Australian readers, both the relevant Australian professional statements and any corresponding international statements are listed.

Learning objectives. The learning objectives are linked to the relevant section of the text by use of a restatement of the objective within the margin.

Learning check. The learning checks have been summarised into two blocks within each chapter, summarising the major points covered. These checks are to reinforce student learning and provide a basis for subsequent revision.

Professional environment vignettes. Within each chapter are one or two professional environment vignettes that highlight changes in the professional audit environment. These vignettes are to keep students up to date with recent trends, new developments, and changes in technology that have an impact on auditing and assurance services.

Glossary. The key terms, bolded in the text and listed at the end of each chapter, are defined in a glossary at the end of the text. This enables readers to clarify quickly the meaning of technical or unusual terms throughout the text.

Content

In summary, we have made the following changes to the content of this edition:

- There is a greater focus on the assurance services offered by the accounting profession.
- There is greater consideration of current developments in audit and assurance practice, particularly through the use of the 'Professional environment' vignettes.
- The increasing importance of international Accounting and Auditing Standards is reflected throughout the text.
- The application of audit procedures within a computerised information system is now discussed throughout the text where appropriate, rather than in an individual chapter.
- Issues associated with the growth in e-commerce are discussed in a separate chapter.
- Ongoing changes arising from the Corporate Law Economic Reform Program are discussed.
- Significant changes to the function and profession of internal auditing are discussed.
- The ongoing controversial debate over audit independence is explored in more detail.
- The end-of-chapter questions are extensively revised, with numerous professional application questions and case studies drawn from the professional examination papers of Australian and international accounting bodies.

Part 1: The auditing and assurance environment

Part 1 now better illustrates the impact of assurance services on the audit environment. This is reflected in the change of title from 'The audit environment' to 'The auditing and assurance environment'.

Chapter 1 now includes in the title 'assurance' to reflect the broader auditing and assurance environment. A new section is included on the assurance engagement framework, which is now a Standard issued by the International Federation of Accountants. An expanded section has been introduced to discuss why and how the auditing paradigm has been shifted, and the implications of this shift for the perception of audit independence and auditor liability. We have updated the discussion of the types of audit service offered by accounting firms to reflect some of the current types of assurance service being provided.

The major change to **Chapter 2** relates to the recent changes to the rules on independence, including the recent debate over audit independence (which has primarily occurred in the United States) and the developments leading to the changes in the US Securities and Exchange Commission's rules on audit independence. (This topic is also dealt with in Chapter 18.) The discussion on corporate governance is expanded to account for the latest Australian practices and the implications of the UK Turnbull Report.

Chapter 3 on auditor's legal liability remains substantially unchanged, but reflects changes to the role of the Australian Securities and Investment Commission and updates of the Corporations Law through the Corporate Law Economic Reform Program. However, no major legal judgements have significantly affected the common law in relation to auditors since the previous edition.

Part 2: Audit planning

Chapter 4 has been significantly restructured to improve the logical flow and readability. The chapter is now more clearly focused on why there is a demand for auditors, their duties and the main parties with whom they have a relationship.

Substantial revision has been made to Chapters 5 and 6, compared with the equivalent Chapters 5, 6 and 7 in the previous edition. **Chapter 5** now introduces the core concepts underlying the determination of an audit strategy and the planning of a particular engagement. These are the concepts of risk, materiality, assertions and evidence. **Chapter 6** now explains the application of these concepts in planning for a particular audit engagement, in addition to explaining the process of accepting an engagement and recording the evidence gathered and the decisions made in performing that engagement.

The application of audit procedures within a computerised information system is now explained within the relevant chapters dealing with audit procedures. Thus, **Chapter 7** now explains the effect of computerisation on the internal control structure, considers the implications of computerisation in evaluating the design effectiveness of internal controls, and explains the use of computer-assisted audit techniques in testing the operating effectiveness of internal controls.

Part 3: Audit testing methodology

Chapter 8 now includes further clarification of the difference between statistical and non-statistical sampling techniques. There is also greater emphasis on non-statistical sampling techniques to reflect their common use in audit practice. The discussion of factors considered in selecting the size of the sample has been expanded to include some of the guidelines outlined in the Auditing Standard. There is also greater consideration of specific types of attribute and variable sampling plans.

The structure of **Chapter 9** remains predominantly the same. To help explain the audit risk model, the chapter now includes a diagrammatic representation and discussion of the 'rain cloud' analogy. Given that the audit procedures within a computerised information system are now referred to throughout the text, the impact of computer-assisted audit techniques as substantive procedures has been included in this chapter. The section on special audit requirements has been expanded to include a consideration of related parties, confirmation of receivables, and the existence and valuation of inventory.

Part 4: Auditing transactions and balances

Chapters 10–13 have been updated to reflect the application of audit procedures within a computerised information system (which were considered in a separate chapter in the previous edition).

Chapter 10 considers the design of both manual and computerised information for recording sales and receivables transactions and balances. It explains the application of computer-assisted audit technniques in evaluating control risk over sales and receivables assertions. It further explains the use of computer-assisted audit techniques in the design of substantive audit procedures applicable to sales and receivables. A similar approach is followed in **Chapters 11, 12** and **13** on the audit of specific transaction classes and account balances, applying the techniques described in Chapter 10. However, the more specialised areas of e-commerce and on-line auditing are considered in Chapter 16.

In addition to these changes, the material in this part has been updated to reflect changes in Auditing and Accounting Standards, and the text has been carefully revised to improve its readability. Otherwise, the content and organisation of these chapters remains close to that in the previous edition.

Part 5: Completing the audit, reporting and other services

Chapter 14 has been significantly restructured to improve the logical sequencing of topics covered and to more closely align the material to the sequence of steps in practice. As part of this change, the discussion of post-audit responsibilities in the previous edition has now been incorporated in the section 'Undertaking a subsequent-events review'. The increased importance of the audit committee in the corporate governance structure of an entity is given greater emphasis, with a section covering the auditor's reporting responsibilities to the audit committee.

Chapter 15 has been amended to reflect the increased importance of both International Auditing (and Accounting) Standards in reporting on financial statements. A couple of new diagrams have been added to assist readers in (1) choosing between the various qualified audit opinions when an unqualified opinion is not appropriate, and (2) deciding on the most appropriate reporting options when there are questions about the going-concern basis for preparing the accounts.

Chapter 16 is a new chapter on e-commerce. Audit issues associated with e-commerce were introduced in Chapter 20 of the previous edition. However, the growth in e-commerce over the past few years has resulted in its increased importance for auditors. This chapter considers a number of issues associated with e-commerce, including (1) the development of the information economy and a framework for e-commerce, (2) strategic and functional implications for assurance service providers, (3) risks and safeguards in e-commerce, and (4) considerations in auditing the transaction cycles.

The major change to **Chapter 17** relates to the substantial changes to internal auditing as a function and a profession undertaken by the Institute of Internal Auditors. These changes have had a significant impact on the definition, scope and objectives of internal auditing, as well as on its ethics framework. The material relating to operational and public sector audits is still relevant and has not been substantially changed.

Part 6: Future directions

This part, consisting of a single chapter, was introduced in the previous edition. In this edition, 'assurance' has been included in the **Chapter 18** title because it is one of the most important issues affecting the auditing profession at the moment. As would be expected for a chapter of this nature, it has been significantly revised for the current edition. E-commerce has been moved to a separate chapter (Chapter 16) and replaced with a section discussing the mobile Internet.

A section on current issues in the profession has been added, addressing the topical debate over auditor independence and considering issues associated with changes in the structures of accounting firms. Also, value reporting has been added as a major stream of business reporting development that is shaping the growth of environmental auditing.

End-of-chapter questions

The end-of-chapter questions have been significantly revised, and over half the questions are new. A new feature is the inclusion of discussion questions that are designed to raise broader issues to enhance understanding of the material covered. In the professional application questions and case studies, extensive use has been made of questions drawn from the Institute of Chartered Accountants, former Professional Year Programme. Questions have also been drawn from examinations of the Association of Chartered Certified Accountants and the American Institute of Certified Public Accountants. The end-of-chapter material includes review questions, discussion questions, professional application questions and case studies. Both of the latter have been graded in terms of difficulty. The material provides ample opportunities for self-study and for use in assignments, seminars and the classroom. The discussion questions, in particular, provide opportunities for group work within seminars and the classroom.

We would like to thank all of our colleagues for their input and interest in the review process. In particular, we would like to thank Robyn Cameron from Griffith University. Writing a textbook is a team effort and, in addition to the feedback from our academic colleagues, we would especially like to thank the excellent editorial, production and management team at John Wiley & Sons Australia, Ltd.

How to use this book

Modern Auditing and Assurance Services has been designed with you — the student — in mind. The design is our attempt to provide you with a book that both communicates the subject matter and facilitates learning. We have tried to accomplish these goals through the following elements.

The double-page chapter opener displays, at a glance, the chapter's content and regulatory framework, and expected learning outcomes.

Learning objectives are clearly stated and linked to subsequent discussion in the chapter.

The overview provides a brief summary of the topics, processes and procedures developed within the chapter.

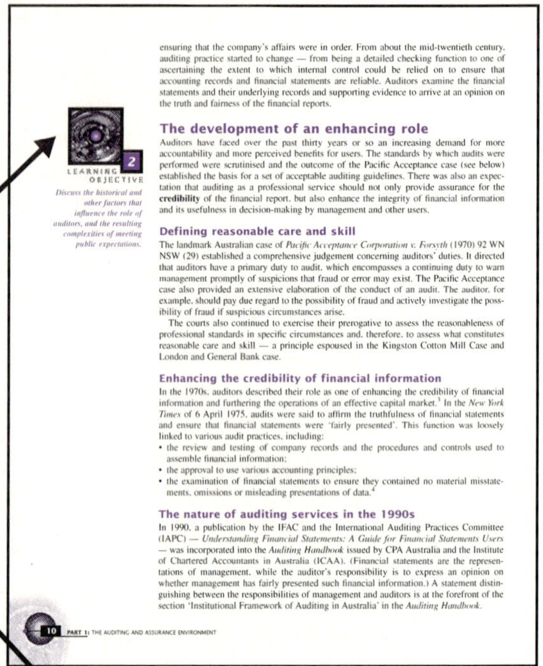

ensuring that the company's affairs were in order. From about the mid-twentieth century, auditing practice started to change — from being a detailed checking function to one of ascertaining the extent to which internal control could be relied on to ensure that accounting records and financial statements are reliable. Auditors examine the financial statements and their underlying records and supporting evidence to arrive at an opinion on the truth and fairness of the financial reports.

2 LEARNING OBJECTIVE

Discuss the historical and other factors that influence the role of auditors, and the resulting complexities of meeting public expectations.

The development of an enhancing role

Auditors have faced over the past thirty years or so an increasing demand for more accountability and more perceived benefits for users. The standards by which audits were performed were scrutinised and the outcome of the Pacific Acceptance case (see below) established the basis for a set of acceptable auditing guidelines. There was also an expectation that auditing as a professional service should not only provide assurance for the **credibility** of the financial report, but also enhance the integrity of financial information and its usefulness in decision-making by management and other users.

Defining reasonable care and skill

The landmark Australian case of *Pacific Acceptance Corporation v. Forsyth* (1970) 92 WN NSW (29) established a comprehensive judgement concerning auditors' duties. It directed that auditors have a primary duty to audit, which encompasses a continuing duty to warn management promptly of suspicions that fraud or error may exist. The Pacific Acceptance case also provided an extensive elaboration of the conduct of an audit. The auditor, for example, should pay due regard to the possibility of fraud and actively investigate the possibility of fraud if suspicious circumstances arise.

The courts also continued to exercise their prerogative to assess the reasonableness of professional standards in specific circumstances and, therefore, to assess what constitutes reasonable care and skill — a principle espoused in the Kingston Cotton Mill Case and London and General Bank case.

Enhancing the credibility of financial information

In the 1970s, auditors described their role as one of enhancing the credibility of financial information and furthering the operations of an effective capital market.[3] In the *New York Times* of 6 April 1975, audits were said to affirm the truthfulness of financial statements and ensure that financial statements were 'fairly presented'. This function was loosely linked to various audit practices, including:

- the review and testing of company records and the procedures and controls used to assemble financial information;
- the approval to use various accounting principles;
- the examination of financial statements to ensure they contained no material misstatements, omissions or misleading presentations of data.[4]

The nature of auditing services in the 1990s

In 1990, a publication by the IFAC and the International Auditing Practices Committee (IAPC) — *Understanding Financial Statements: A Guide for Financial Statements Users* — was incorporated into the *Auditing Handbook* issued by CPA Australia and the Institute of Chartered Accountants in Australia (ICAA). (Financial statements are the representations of management, while the auditor's responsibility is to express an opinion on whether management has fairly presented such financial information.) A statement distinguishing between the responsibilities of management and auditors is at the forefront of the section 'Institutional Framework of Auditing in Australia' in the *Auditing Handbook*.

10 PART 1: THE AUDITING AND ASSURANCE ENVIRONMENT

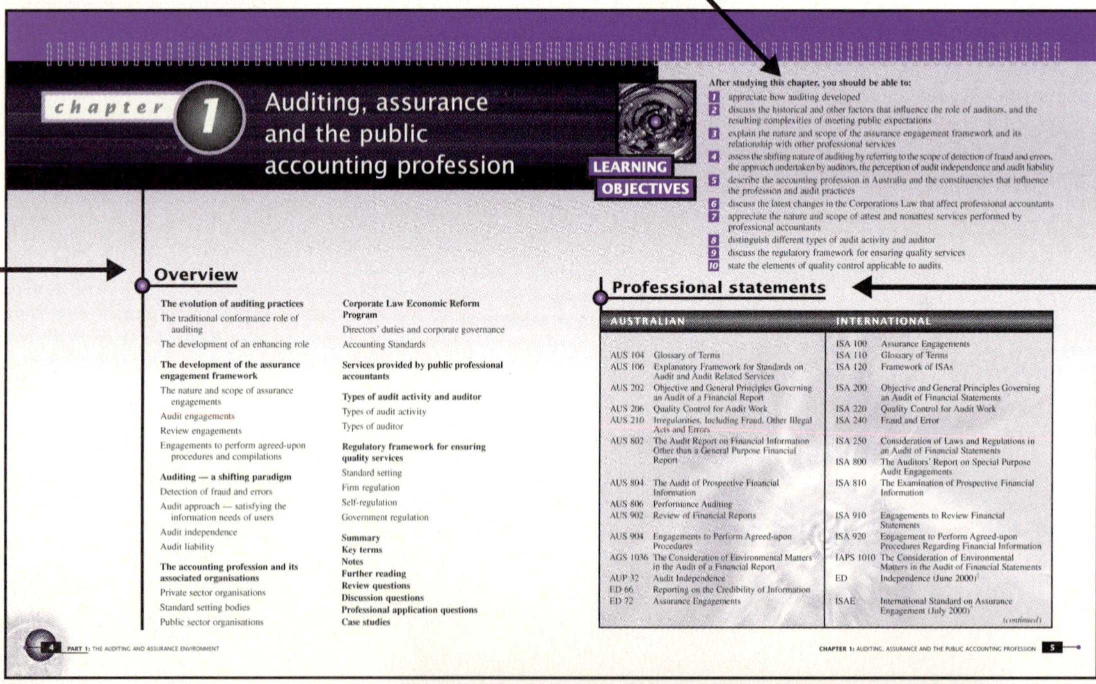

chapter 1

Auditing, assurance and the public accounting profession

LEARNING OBJECTIVES

After studying this chapter, you should be able to:

1. appreciate how auditing developed
2. discuss the historical and other factors that influence the role of auditors, and the resulting complexities of meeting public expectations
3. explain the nature and scope of the assurance engagement framework and its relationship with other professional services
4. assess the shifting nature of auditing by referring to the scope of detection of fraud and errors, the approach undertaken by auditors, the perception of audit independence and audit liability
5. describe the accounting profession in Australia and the constituencies that influence the profession and audit practices
6. discuss the latest changes in the Corporations Law that affect professional accountants
7. appreciate the nature and scope of attest and nonattest services performed by professional accountants
8. distinguish different types of audit activity and auditor
9. discuss the regulatory framework for ensuring quality services
10. state the elements of quality control applicable to audits.

Overview

Professional statements

AUSTRALIAN		INTERNATIONAL	
		ISA 100	Assurance Engagements
AUS 104	Glossary of Terms	ISA 110	Glossary of Terms
AUS 106	Explanatory Framework for Standards on Audit and Audit Related Services	ISA 120	Framework of ISAs
AUS 202	Objective and General Principles Governing an Audit of a Financial Report	ISA 200	Objective and General Principles Governing an Audit of Financial Statements
AUS 206	Quality Control for Audit Work	ISA 220	Quality Control for Audit Work
AUS 210	Irregularities, Including Fraud, Other Illegal Acts and Errors	ISA 240	Fraud and Error
AUS 802	The Audit Report on Financial Information Other than a General Purpose Financial Report	ISA 250	Consideration of Laws and Regulations in an Audit of Financial Statements
		ISA 800	The Auditors' Report on Special Purpose Audit Engagements
AUS 804	The Audit of Prospective Financial Information	ISA 810	The Examination of Prospective Financial Information
AUS 806	Performance Auditing		
AUS 902	Review of Financial Reports	ISA 910	Engagements to Review Financial Statements
AUS 904	Engagements to Perform Agreed-upon Procedures	ISA 920	Engagement to Perform Agreed-upon Procedures Regarding Financial Information
AGS 1036	The Consideration of Environmental Matters in the Audit of a Financial Report	IAPS 1010	The Consideration of Environmental Matters in the Audit of Financial Statements
AUP 32	Audit Independence	ED	Independence (June 2000)
ED 66	Reporting on the Credibility of Information		
ED 72	Assurance Engagements	ISAE	International Standard on Assurance Engagement (July 2000)

(continued)

4 PART 1: THE AUDITING AND ASSURANCE ENVIRONMENT

CHAPTER 1: AUDITING, ASSURANCE AND THE PUBLIC ACCOUNTING PROFESSION 5

The list of Professional Statements identifies the Australian and international regulatory context and the issues discussed in each chapter.

Learning checks identify and reinforce the key issues raised, and occur at the end of each main section. Their simple format makes them ideal for reviewing chapter content and for revision.

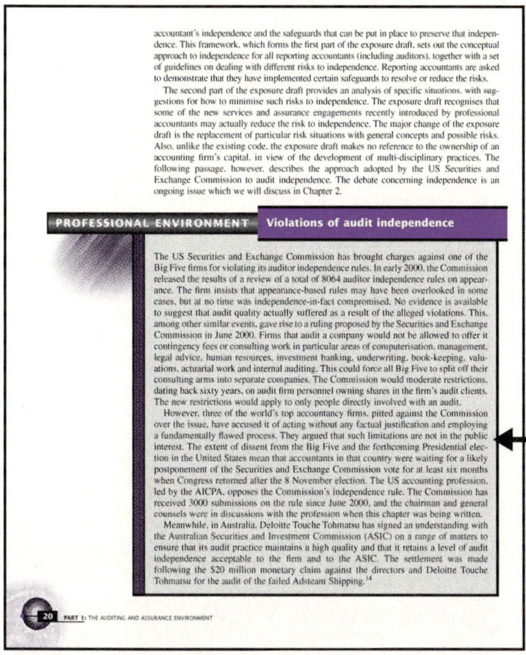

accountant's independence and the safeguards that can be put in place to preserve that independence. This framework, which forms the first part of the exposure draft, sets out the conceptual approach to independence for all reporting accountants (including auditors), together with a set of guidelines on dealing with different risks to independence. Reporting accountants are asked to demonstrate that they have implemented certain safeguards to resolve or reduce the risks.

The second part of the exposure draft provides an analysis of specific situations, with suggestions for how to minimise such risks to independence. The exposure draft recognises that some of the new services and assurance engagements recently introduced by professional accountants may actually reduce the risk to independence. The major change of the exposure draft is the replacement of particular risk situations with general concepts and possible risks. Also, unlike the existing code, the exposure draft makes no reference to the ownership of an accounting firm's capital, in view of the development of multi-disciplinary practices. The following passage, however, describes the approach adopted by the US Securities and Exchange Commission to audit independence. The debate concerning independence is an ongoing issue which we will discuss in Chapter 2.

PROFESSIONAL ENVIRONMENT **Violations of audit independence**

The US Securities and Exchange Commission has brought charges against one of the Big Five firms for violating its auditor independence rules. In early 2000, the Commission released the results of a review of a total of 8064 auditor independence rules on appearance. The firm insists that appearance-based rules may have been overlooked in some cases, but at no time was independence-in-fact compromised. No evidence is available to suggest that audit quality actually suffered as a result of the alleged violations. This, among other similar events, gave rise to a ruling proposed by the Securities and Exchange Commission in June 2000. Firms that audit a company would not be allowed to offer it contingency fees or consulting work in particular areas of computerisation, management, legal advice, human resources, investment banking, underwriting, book-keeping, valuations, actuarial work and internal auditing. This could force all Big Five to split off their consulting arms into separate companies. The Commission would moderate restrictions, dating back sixty years, on audit firm personnel owning shares in the firm's audit clients. The new restrictions would apply to only people directly involved with an audit.

However, three of the world's top accountancy firms, pitted against the Commission over the issue, have accused it of acting without any factual justification and employing a fundamentally flawed process. They argued that such limitations are not in the public interest. The extent of dissent from the Big Five and the forthcoming Presidential election in the United States mean that accountants in that country were waiting for a likely postponement of the Securities and Exchange Commission vote for at least six months when Congress returned after the 8 November election. The US accounting profession, led by the AICPA, opposes the Commission's independence rule. The Commission has received 3000 submissions on the rule since June 2000, and the chairman and general counsels were in discussions with the profession when this chapter was being written.

Meanwhile, in Australia, Deloitte Touche Tohmatsu has signed an understanding with the Australian Securities and Investment Commission (ASIC) on a range of matters to ensure that its audit practice maintains a high quality and that it retains a level of audit independence acceptable to the firm and to the ASIC. The settlement was made following the $20 million monetary claim against the directors and Deloitte Touche Tohmatsu for the audit of the failed Adsteam Shipping.[14]

20 PART 1: THE AUDITING AND ASSURANCE ENVIRONMENT

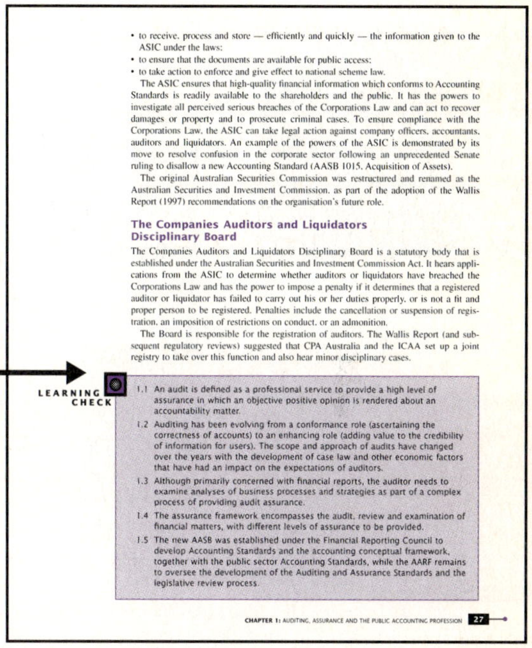

- to receive, process and store — efficiently and quickly — the information given to the ASIC under the laws;
- to ensure that the documents are available for public access;
- to take action to enforce and give effect to national scheme law.

The ASIC ensures that high-quality financial information which conforms to Accounting Standards is readily available to the shareholders and the public. It has the powers to investigate all perceived serious breaches of the Corporations Law and can act to recover damages or property and to prosecute criminal cases. To ensure compliance with the Corporations Law, the ASIC can take legal action against company officers, accountants, auditors and liquidators. An example of the powers of the ASIC is demonstrated by its move to resolve confusion in the corporate sector following an unprecedented Senate ruling to disallow a new Accounting Standard (AASB 1015, Acquisition of Assets).

The original Australian Securities Commission was restructured and renamed as the Australian Securities and Investment Commission, as part of the adoption of the Wallis Report (1997) recommendations on the organisation's future role.

The Companies Auditors and Liquidators Disciplinary Board

The Companies Auditors and Liquidators Disciplinary Board is a statutory body that is established under the Australian Securities and Investment Commission Act. It hears applications from the ASIC to determine whether auditors or liquidators have breached the Corporations Law and has the power to impose a penalty if it determines that a registered auditor or liquidator has failed to carry out his or her duties properly, or is not a fit and proper person to be registered. Penalties include the cancellation or suspension of registration, an imposition of restrictions on conduct, or an admonition.

The Board is responsible for the registration of auditors. The Wallis Report (and subsequent regulatory reviews) suggested that CPA Australia and the ICAA set up a joint registry to take over this function and also hear minor disciplinary cases.

LEARNING CHECK

1.1 An audit is defined as a professional service to provide a high level of assurance in which an objective positive opinion is rendered about an accountability matter.

1.2 Auditing has been evolving from a conformance role (ascertaining the correctness of accounts) to an enhancing role (adding value to the credibility of information for users). The scope and approach of audits have changed over the years with the development of case law and other economic factors that have had an impact on the expectations of auditors.

1.3 Although primarily concerned with financial reports, the auditor needs to examine analyses of business processes and strategies as part of a complex process of providing audit assurance.

1.4 The assurance framework encompasses the audit, review and examination of financial matters, with different levels of assurance to be provided.

1.5 The new AASB was established under the Financial Reporting Council to develop Accounting Standards and the accounting conceptual framework, together with the public sector Accounting Standards, while the AARF remains to oversee the development of the Auditing and Assurance Standards and the legislative review process.

CHAPTER 1: AUDITING, ASSURANCE AND THE PUBLIC ACCOUNTING PROFESSION 27

'Professional environment' boxes amplify the chapter content and profile topical industry issues and developments in Australia and internationally.

The summary outlines the core issues explored in the chapter and reinforces key points. Where relevant, it also provides links to other chapters.

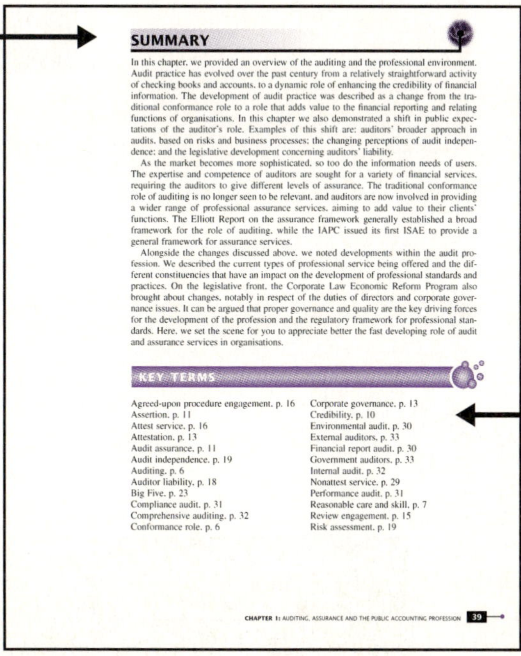

SUMMARY

In this chapter, we provided an overview of the auditing and the professional environment. Audit practice has evolved over the past century from a relatively straightforward activity of checking books and accounts, to a dynamic role of enhancing the credibility of financial information. The development of audit practice was described as a change from the traditional conformance role to a role that adds value to the financial reporting and relating functions of organisations. In this chapter we also demonstrated a shift in public expectations of the auditor's role. Examples of this shift are: auditors' broader approach in audits, based on risks and business processes; the changing perceptions of audit independence; and the legislative development concerning auditors' liability.

As the market becomes more sophisticated, so too do the information needs of users. The expertise and competence of auditors are sought for a variety of financial services, requiring the auditors to give different levels of assurance. The traditional conformance role of auditing is no longer seen to be relevant, and auditors are now involved in providing a wider range of professional assurance services, aiming to add value to their clients' functions. The Elliott Report on the assurance framework generally established a broad framework for the role of auditing, while the IAPC issued its first ISAE to provide a general framework for assurance services.

Alongside the changes discussed above, we noted developments within the audit profession. We described the current types of professional service being offered and the different constituencies that have an impact on the development of professional standards and practices. On the legislative front, the Corporate Law Economic Reform Program also brought about changes, notably in respect of the duties of directors and corporate governance issues. It can be argued that proper governance and quality are the key driving forces for the development of the profession and the regulatory framework for professional standards. Here, we set the scene for you to appreciate better the fast developing role of audit and assurance services in organisations.

KEY TERMS

Agreed-upon procedure engagement, p. 16	Corporate governance, p. 13
Assertion, p. 11	Credibility, p. 10
Attest service, p. 16	Environmental audit, p. 30
Attestation, p. 13	External auditors, p. 33
Audit assurance, p. 11	Financial report audit, p. 30
Audit independence, p. 19	Government auditors, p. 33
Auditing, p. 6	Internal audit, p. 32
Auditor liability, p. 18	Nonattest service, p. 29
Big Five, p. 23	Performance audit, p. 31
Compliance audit, p. 31	Reasonable care and skill, p. 7
Comprehensive auditing, p. 32	Review engagement, p. 15
Conformance role, p. 6	Risk assessment, p. 19

CHAPTER 1: AUDITING, ASSURANCE AND THE PUBLIC ACCOUNTING PROFESSION 39

Key terms are bold in the text at first mention and defined in the glossary at the end of the book.

Review questions test understanding of the material presented in the chapter, and encourage considered comment.

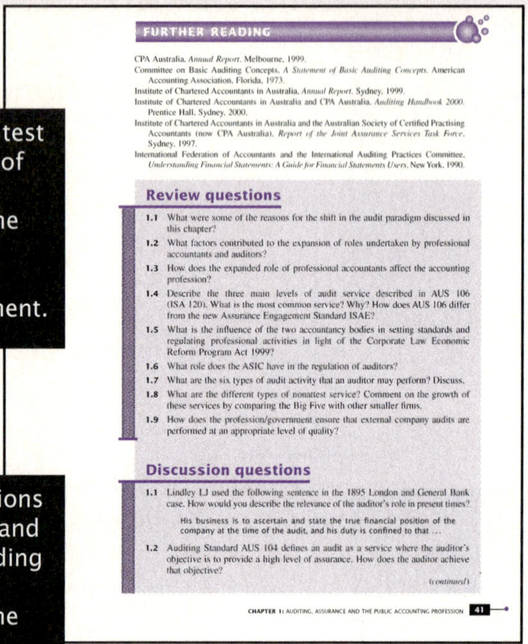

FURTHER READING

CPA Australia, *Annual Report*, Melbourne, 1999.

Committee on Basic Auditing Concepts, *A Statement of Basic Auditing Concepts*, American Accounting Association, Florida, 1973.

Institute of Chartered Accountants in Australia, *Annual Report*, Sydney, 1999.

Institute of Chartered Accountants in Australia and CPA Australia, *Auditing Handbook 2000*, Prentice Hall, Sydney, 2000.

Institute of Chartered Accountants in Australia and the Australian Society of Certified Practising Accountants (now CPA Australia), *Report of the Joint Assurance Services Task Force*, Sydney, 1997.

International Federation of Accountants and the International Auditing Practices Committee, *Understanding Financial Statements: A Guide for Financial Statements Users*, New York, 1990.

Review questions

1.1 What were some of the reasons for the shift in the audit paradigm discussed in this chapter?

1.2 What factors contributed to the expansion of roles undertaken by professional accountants and auditors?

1.3 How does the expanded role of professional accountants affect the accounting profession?

1.4 Describe the three main levels of audit service described in AUS 106 (ISA 120). What is the most common service? Why? How does AUS 106 differ from the new Assurance Engagement Standard ISAE?

1.5 What is the influence of the two accountancy bodies in setting standards and regulating professional activities in light of the Corporate Law Economic Reform Program Act 1999?

1.6 What role does the ASIC have in the regulation of auditors?

1.7 What are the six types of audit activity that an auditor may perform? Discuss.

1.8 What are the different types of nonattest service? Comment on the growth of these services by comparing the Big Five with other smaller firms.

1.9 How does the profession/government ensure that external company audits are performed at an appropriate level of quality?

Discussion questions

1.1 Lindley LJ used the following sentence in the 1895 London and General Bank case. How would you describe the relevance of the auditor's role in present times?

> His business is to ascertain and state the true financial position of the company at the time of the audit, and his duty is confined to that ...

1.2 Auditing Standard AUS 104 defines an audit as a service where the auditor's objective is to provide a high level of assurance. How does the auditor achieve that objective?

(continued)

CHAPTER 1: AUDITING, ASSURANCE AND THE PUBLIC ACCOUNTING PROFESSION 41

Discussion questions help to develop and refine understanding of the issues presented in the chapter.

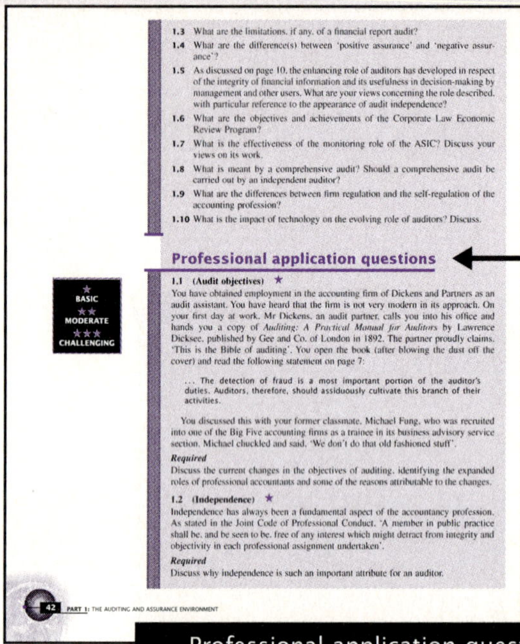

1.3 What are the limitations, if any, of a financial report audit?

1.4 What are the difference(s) between 'positive assurance' and 'negative assurance'?

1.5 As discussed on page 10, the enhancing role of auditors has developed in respect of the integrity of financial information and its usefulness in decision-making by management and other users. What are your views concerning the role described, with particular reference to the appearance of audit independence?

1.6 What are the objectives and achievements of the Corporate Law Economic Review Program?

1.7 What is the effectiveness of the monitoring role of the ASIC? Discuss your views on its work.

1.8 What is meant by a comprehensive audit? Should a comprehensive audit be carried out by an independent auditor?

1.9 What are the differences between firm regulation and the self-regulation of the accounting profession?

1.10 What is the impact of technology on the evolving role of auditors? Discuss.

Professional application questions

★ BASIC
★★ MODERATE
★★★ CHALLENGING

1.1 (Audit objectives) ★

You have obtained employment in the accounting firm of Dickens and Partners as an audit assistant. You have heard that the firm is not very modern in its approach. On your first day at work, Mr Dickens, an audit partner, calls you into his office and hands you a copy of *Auditing: A Practical Manual for Auditors* by Lawrence Dicksee, published by Gee and Co. of London in 1892. The partner proudly claims, 'This is the Bible of auditing'. You open the book (after blowing the dust off the cover) and read the following statement on page 7:

> ... The detection of fraud is a most important portion of the auditor's duties. Auditors, therefore, should assiduously cultivate this branch of their activities.

You discussed this with your former classmate, Michael Fung, who was recruited into one of the Big Five accounting firms as a trainee in its business advisory service section. Michael chuckled and said, 'We don't do that old fashioned stuff'.

Required

Discuss the current changes in the objectives of auditing, identifying the expanded roles of professional accountants and some of the reasons attributable to the changes.

1.2 (Independence) ★

Independence has always been a fundamental aspect of the accountancy profession. As stated in the Joint Code of Professional Conduct, 'A member in public practice shall be, and be seen to be, free of any interest which might detract from integrity and objectivity in each professional assignment undertaken'.

Required

Discuss why independence is such an important attribute for an auditor.

42 PART 1: THE AUDITING AND ASSURANCE ENVIRONMENT

Professional application questions are drawn, in many instances, from the examination papers of Australian and international professional associations. They encapsulate 'real world' auditing scenarios and are graded according to difficulty. The questions are designed to develop professional skills in analysing, interpreting, evaluating, communicating and reporting auditing information.

Case studies, graded according to their difficulty, encourage detailed evaluation of the audit scenarios presented. These challenging exercises are ideal for group discussion and build professional communication skills.

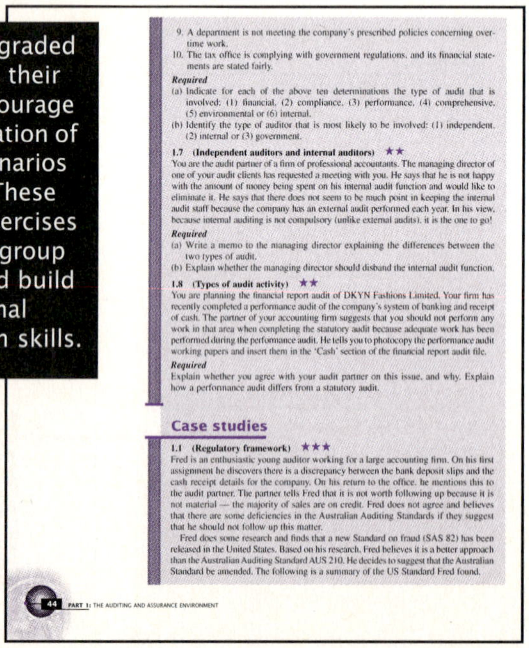

9. A department is not meeting the company's prescribed policies concerning overtime work.
10. The tax office is complying with government regulations, and its financial statements are stated fairly.

Required

(a) Indicate for each of the above ten determinations the type of audit that is involved: (1) financial, (2) compliance, (3) performance, (4) comprehensive, (5) environmental or (6) internal.

(b) Identify the type of auditor that is most likely to be involved: (1) independent, (2) internal or (3) government.

1.7 (Independent auditors and internal auditors) ★★

You are the audit partner of a firm of professional accountants. The managing director of one of your audit clients has requested a meeting with you. He says that he is not happy with the amount of money being spent on his internal audit function and would like to eliminate it. He says that there does not seem to be much point in keeping the internal audit staff because the company has an external audit performed each year. In his view, because internal auditing is not compulsory (unlike external audits), it is the one to go!

Required

(a) Write a memo to the managing director explaining the differences between the two types of audit.

(b) Explain whether the managing director should disband the internal audit function.

1.8 (Types of audit activity) ★★

You are planning the financial report audit of DKYN Fashions Limited. Your firm has recently completed a performance audit of the company's system of banking and receipt of cash. The partner of your accounting firm suggests that you should not perform any work in that area when completing the statutory audit because adequate work has been performed during the performance audit. He tells you to photocopy the performance audit working papers and insert them in the 'Cash' section of the financial report audit file.

Required

Explain whether you agree with your audit partner on this issue, and why. Explain how a performance audit differs from a statutory audit.

Case studies

1.1 (Regulatory framework) ★★★

Fred is an enthusiastic young auditor working for a large accounting firm. On his first assignment he discovers there is a discrepancy between the bank deposit slips and the cash receipt details for the company. On his return to the office, he mentions this to the audit partner. The partner tells Fred that it is not worth following up because it is not material — the majority of sales are on credit. Fred does not agree and believes that there are some deficiencies in the Australian Auditing Standards if they suggest that he should not follow up this matter.

Fred does some research and finds that a new Standard on fraud (SAS 82) has been released in the United States. Based on his research, Fred believes it is a better approach than the Australian Auditing Standard AUS 210. He decides to suggest that the Australian Standard be amended. The following is a summary of the US Standard Fred found.

44 PART 1: THE AUDITING AND ASSURANCE ENVIRONMENT

Brief contents

Contents

Acknowledgements

We take this opportunity to express our sincere appreciation to individuals who have made significant contributions to *Modern Auditing and Assurance Services*, particularly to those adopters of the previous edition who were kind enough to provide us with comments and suggestions. We gratefully acknowledge the permission given by the American Institute of Certified Public Accountants, the Chartered Institute of Management Accountants, the Institute of Internal Auditors and CPA Australia to use material from their publications, including their professional examinations. We express particular appreciation to the Institute of Chartered Accountants in Australia and the Association of Chartered Certified Accountants for permission to adapt and use an extensive number of their professional examination questions. This has enabled us to change substantially the end-of-chapter material in this edition. Together with the publisher, we specifically acknowledge the following copyright holders, organisations and individuals for their assistance and permission to reproduce copyright material in this book.

Text

Questions and case studies: The Association of Chartered Certified Accountants for permission to reproduce questions and case studies from ACCA Audit Framework Papers and The Institute of Chartered Accountants in Australia (ICAA) for permission to reproduce questions and case studies from various Accounting 2 and Advanced Audit Modules; tables 1.2, 2.1, 7.1, 8.1, 8.2, pp. 305–6, 514 (professional environment), 543, 581: reproduced with permission of CPA Australia and the Institute of Chartered Accountants of Australia; pp. 94–5 (professional environment): Carl Pacini and David Sinason, *American Business Law Journal*, Spring 1999. Reproduced with permission from the authors and the Academy of Legal Studies in Business; p. 151 (professional environment): Copyright © April 2000 from the *Journal of Accountancy* by the American Institute for Certified Public Accountants, Inc. Opinions of the authors are their own and do not necessarily reflect policies of the AICPA; table 5.1: Copyright © 1991 by the American Institute of Certified Public Accountants, Inc. Reprinted with permission; p. 194 (professional environment): excerpt adapted from David Coderre, *Fraud Detection: Using Data Analysis Techniques to Detect Fraud*, Global Audit Publications; table 8.3: Copyright © 2000 by the American Institute of Certified Public Accountants, Inc. Reprinted with permission; pp. 335–6 (professional environment): Copyright © September 2000 from the *Journal of Accountancy* by the American Institute for Certified Public Accountants, Inc. Opinions of the authors are their own and do not necessarily reflect policies of the AICPA; pp. 340–1 (professional environment), 420 (professional environment), 555 (professional environment): reproduced with permission of CPA Australia; pp. 409 (10.7), 526 (13.2), 527 (13.6), 558–9 (14.1, 14.2), 594–5 (15.7), 597 (15.2): Material adapted from the Uniform CPA Examination Questions. Copyright © 1961 through 1994 by the American Institute of Certified Public Accountants, Inc., adapted with permission; p. 477 (professional environment): © Accountancy Age www.accountancyage.com; p. 551 (professional environment): reproduced with permission from CA magazine, published by the Canadian Institute of Chartered Accountants, Toronto, Canada.

Figures

Fig. 1.1: adapted from *Assurance Engagements: A Schematic of Assurance and Related Services*, International Standard of Assurance Engagement; figs 1.3, 15.8: reproduced with permission of CPA Australia and the Institute of Chartered Accountants of Australia; figs 6.2, 14.2, 15.1, 15.3–15.7: reproduced with permission of CPA Australia and the Institute of Chartered Accountants of Australia; figs 7.5, 7.8: Copyright © 1991 by the American Institute of Certified Public Accountants, Inc. Reprinted with permission; pp. 308–9: from 'Introducing Audit Sampling' by Margaret Stewart and John Dunn, *The Auditor's Report*, Vol. 23, No. 3, Summer 2000. © American Accounting Association.

Every effort has been made to trace the ownership of copyright material. Information that will enable the publisher to rectify any error or omission in subsequent editions will be welcome. In such cases, please contact the Permissions Section at John Wiley & Sons Australia, Ltd, which will arrange for payment of the usual fee.

Abbreviations

AAA	American Accounting Association
AARF	Australian Accounting Research Foundation
AASB	Australian Accounting Standards Board
ACCA	Association of Chartered Certified Accountants
AFROSAI	African Organisation of Supreme Audit Institutions
AGM	Annual general meeting
AGS	Auditing Guidance Statement (Australian)
AICPA	American Institute of Certified Public Accountants
ANAO	Australian National Audit Office
APS	Miscellaneous Professional Statement (Australian)
AR	Audit risk
ASIC	Australian Securities and Investment Commission
ASOSAI	Asian Organisation of Supreme Audit Institutions
ASX	Australian Stock Exchange
AuASB	Auditing and Assurance Standards Board
AUP	Auditing Practice Statement (Australian)
AUS	Auditing Standard (Australian)
BSI	British Standard Institution
B2B	Business to Business
B2C	Business to Consumers
CAAT	Computer-assisted audit technique
CAPA	Confederation of Asian and Pacific Accountants
CEO	Chief executive officer
CERES	Coalition for Environmentally Responsible Economics
CFO	Chief financial controller
CIA	Certified internal auditor
CICA	Canadian Institue of Chartered Accountants
CIS	Computer information system
CJ	Chief Justice
CLERP	Corporate Law Economic Reform Program
CLERPA	Corporate law Economic Reform Program Act
CMS	Credit management system
COSO	Committee of Sponsoring Organisations (of the Treadway Commission)
CPA	Certified Practising Accountant
CPA Australia	CPA Australia, formerly the Australian Society of Certified Practising Accountants
CR	Control risk
DBMS	Database management system
DR	Detection risk
EAM	Embedded audit modules
E-commerce	Electronic commerce
E-tailing	Electronic retailing
ED	Auditing Exposure Draft (Australian)
EDI	Electronic data interchange
EFT	Electronic funds transfer
EMAS	Environmental management accounting system
EMS	Environmental management system
EUROSAI	European Organisation of Supreme Audit Institutions
GAAP	Generally Accepted Accounting Principles (US)
GRN	Goods received note
IAPC	International Auditing Practices Committee
IAPS	International Auditing Practice Statement
IASB	Internal Auditing Standards Board
IASC	International Accounting Standards Committee
ICAA	Institute of Chartered Accountants in Australia
ICC	International Chamber of Commerce
ICQ	Internal control questionnaire
ICS	Internal control structure
IFAC	International Federation of Accountants
IFMAC	International Financial and Management Accounting Committee
IIA	Institute of Internal Auditors
IIAA	Institute of Internal Auditors — Australia
INCOSAI	International Congress of Supreme Audit Institutions
INTOSAI	International Organisation of Supreme Audit Institutions
IPSC	International Public Sector Committee
IR	Inherent risk
ISA	International Standard on Auditing
ISAE	International Standard of Assurance Engagements
ISO	International Organisation for Standardisation
ITF	Integrated test facility
JCPAA	Joint Committee of Public Accounts and Audit
LAN	Local area network
LJ	Lord Justice
MDP	Multidisciplinary practice
MINCO	Ministerial Council for Corporations

PAAC Act	*Public Accounts and Audit Committee Act 1951* (Cwlth)
POS	Point of sale
PPS	Probability-proportional-to-size
PSA	*Professional Standards Act 1974* (NSW)
PSASB	Public Sector Accounting Standards Board
PSPR	Professional Standards Practice Release
PY	Professional year
RAM	Random access memory
SCARF	Systems control audit review file
SIAS	Statement on Internal Auditing Standards
SPPIA	Standards for the Professional Practice of Internal Auditing
UIG	Urgent Issues Group
VFM audit	Value-for-money audit
WAN	Wide area network
WDV	Written-down value

PART 1 The auditing and assurance environment

PART 1

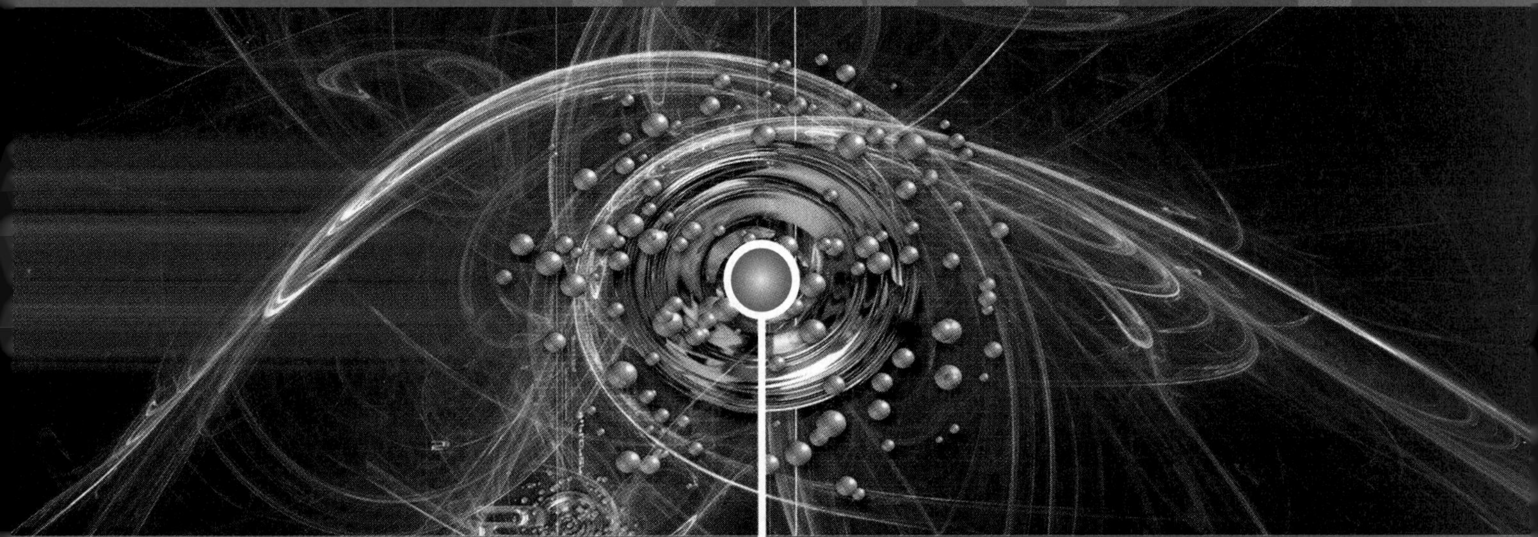

A large number of students will graduate to join the accounting profession. The first part of this book introduces the changing professional environment, reflecting the role of auditors (Chapter 1), the expectations of a professional accountant (Chapter 2) and the legal framework that has an impact on the accountant in practice (Chapter 3).

Chapter 1 demonstrates how the nature of auditing has evolved to become part of a global shift in a wide range of assurance services offered by accountants and auditors. Alongside the shift, professional bodies need to review the duties, standards and professionalism that underpin their outlook and operations, as explained in **Chapter 2**. **Chapter 3** offers a further insight into the significant influence of the legal environment on the development of the role and duties of accountants and auditors.

At the end of Part 1, students should be able to appreciate the development of the nature of auditing, the changing role of auditors and accountants, and the standards of behaviour expected of them.

chapter 1 Auditing, assurance and the public accounting profession

Overview

LEARNING OBJECTIVES

After studying this chapter, you should be able to:

1. appreciate how auditing developed
2. discuss the historical and other factors that influence the role of auditors, and the resulting complexities of meeting public expectations
3. explain the nature and scope of the assurance engagement framework and its relationship with other professional services
4. assess the shifting nature of auditing by referring to the scope of detection of fraud and errors, the approach undertaken by auditors, the perception of audit independence and audit liability
5. describe the accounting profession in Australia and the constituencies that influence the profession and audit practices
6. discuss the latest changes in the Corporations Law that affect professional accountants
7. appreciate the nature and scope of attest and nonattest services performed by professional accountants
8. distinguish different types of audit activity and auditor
9. discuss the regulatory framework for ensuring quality services
10. state the elements of quality control applicable to audits.

Professional statements

AUSTRALIAN		INTERNATIONAL	
		ISA 100	Assurance Engagements
AUS 104	Glossary of Terms	ISA 110	Glossary of Terms
AUS 106	Explanatory Framework for Standards on Audit and Audit Related Services	ISA 120	Framework of ISAs
AUS 202	Objective and General Principles Governing an Audit of a Financial Report	ISA 200	Objective and General Principles Governing an Audit of Financial Statements
AUS 206	Quality Control for Audit Work	ISA 220	Quality Control for Audit Work
AUS 210	Irregularities, Including Fraud, Other Illegal Acts and Errors	ISA 240	Fraud and Error
AUS 802	The Audit Report on Financial Information Other than a General Purpose Financial Report	ISA 250	Consideration of Laws and Regulations in an Audit of Financial Statements
		ISA 800	The Auditors' Report on Special Purpose Audit Engagements
AUS 804	The Audit of Prospective Financial Information	ISA 810	The Examination of Prospective Financial Information
AUS 806	Performance Auditing		
AUS 902	Review of Financial Reports	ISA 910	Engagements to Review Financial Statements
AUS 904	Engagements to Perform Agreed-upon Procedures	ISA 920	Engagement to Perform Agreed-upon Procedures Regarding Financial Information
AGS 1036	The Consideration of Environmental Matters in the Audit of a Financial Report	IAPS 1010	The Consideration of Environmental Matters in the Audit of Financial Statements
AUP 32	Audit Independence	ED	Independence (June 2000)‡
ED 66	Reporting on the Credibility of Information		
ED 72	Assurance Engagements	ISAE	International Standard on Assurance Engagement (July 2000)*

(continued)

Miscellaneous Professional Statements (Australian only)

APS 1, Conformity with Accounting Standards and UIG Consensus Views; APS 1.1, Conformity with Auditing Standards; APS 4, Statement of Quality Control Standard; APS 5, Quality Control Policies and Procedures — General Guidelines; APS 6, Statement of Taxation Standards; APS 7, Statement of Insolvency Standards; APS 8, Statement of Management Consulting Services Standards; APS 9, Statement of Compilation of Financial Reports.

[*] The International Federation of Accountants (IFAC) released its first International Standard on Assurance Engagements (ISAE) in August 2000.

[‡] IFAC's Ethics Committee issued the Exposure Draft on Independence in June 2000, with a response due date of 15 September 2000.

Auditing plays a vital role in business, government and our economy. The fact that all of the following bodies are required to have an annual audit demonstrates its importance:

- all public and large proprietary companies;
- Commonwealth and state government departments, statutory authorities, government companies and business undertakings and municipalities;
- 'not-for-profit' organisations, including educational institutions.

Auditing services have been changing rapidly over the past decade. Audit practices have been evolving in response to growing public expectations of accountability and to the complexities in economic and technological advancements occurring in corporations. The auditing profession has responded positively in terms of broadening its scope of services and developing an assurance framework, with auditing being part of the assurance services that firms provide. As a vocation, therefore, auditing offers the opportunity for challenging and rewarding careers in a dynamic business environment, and the chance to develop a thorough understanding of professional services, primarily serving the interests of users of financial information.

In this chapter we will trace the conceptual development of auditing and assurance over the years. We will also provide a broad overview of the accounting and auditing profession and its related associations, a discussion of the assurance framework recently considered by the profession, a description of the general types of audit activity, and a review of the system of quality procedures generally prescribed for the profession.

THE EVOLUTION OF AUDITING PRACTICES

1 LEARNING OBJECTIVE

Appreciate how auditing developed.

Auditing has developed from primarily a check of the accounting for stocks and revenues by authorised officers into a sophisticated professional assurance service performed by independent accountants for the interests of their clients and other users of the financial reports. This section describes the development of the role of auditing over the years, with particular reference to the nature and objectives of auditing, the responsibilities of auditors, and the evolution of the accounting and auditing profession. This historical perspective is particularly relevant given the current debate concerning the shifting relationships of auditors and clients, and the perceived impact on traditional accounting and auditing services of professional firms offering a broad spectrum of assurance services.

The traditional conformance role of auditing

The traditional **conformance role** of auditing first appeared in the United Kingdom during the 1800s. Such a role was debated, however, in major case decisions in the late 1800s and was further elaborated through court decisions in the United States. The development of the auditing role is very much an outcome of court cases, as is seen in the following sections.

Auditing in the United Kingdom — early functions

The word 'auditing' comes from the Latin word *audire*, meaning 'to hear'. In the late Middle Ages in Britain, both accounts of revenue (tax receipts) and expenditure for manors and estates were 'heard' by an auditor, whose task was to examine such accounts. After the introduction of Luca Pacioli's 'double-entry book-keeping' in 1494, associations of accountants were formed and auditing gradually established an important role.

Auditing as we know it today can be linked to the development of joint-stock corporations in the United Kingdom during the Industrial Revolution in the mid-1800s. The increasing use of the company form of business organisation led to the growth of a professional class of managers who handled large sums of capital on behalf of shareholders. Recognising the need for periodic reporting by managers to shareholders, the *Joint Stock Companies Registration and Regulations (Joint Stock Companies Act) 1844* (UK) stipulated that 'Directors shall cause the Books of the Company to be balanced, and a full and fair Balance Sheet to be made up'. The Act provided for the appointment of auditors who were empowered to examine the accounts of the company.

Regulation 94 of the *UK Companies Act 1862* (UK) required the auditors to state in their report:

> ... whether, in their opinion, the Balance Sheet is a full and fair Balance Sheet, containing the particulars required by these Regulations, and properly drawn up so as to exhibit a true and correct view of the State of the Company's Affairs ... such Report shall be read, together with the Report of the Directors, at the Ordinary Meeting.

In 1900, the annual presentation of the balance sheet to the shareholders and the carrying out of a statutory audit (i.e. an audit carried out in accordance with the provisions of the Act) were made mandatory for companies registered under the Act. English and Scottish investors began to send their own professional auditors to check on the condition of US companies in which they had invested. These early audits focused on finding errors in balance sheet accounts and stemming the growth of fraud associated with the increasing phenomenon of professional managers and absentee owners.

Lawrence R. Dicksee, for example, noted in his book *Auditing*: *A Practical Manual for Auditors* (1892)[1] that the objective of an audit was three-fold: (1) the detection of fraud, (2) the detection of technical errors, and (3) the detection of errors of principle.

The influence of case law on auditing

While 'hearing' the accounts and checking records were then the predominant functions of auditors, two major audit cases in the late 1800s helped to establish the fundamental principles of auditing. In the first of these, *London and General Bank* (1895) 2 Ch. 673, Lindley LJ described the auditor's duty in the following terms:

> His business is to ascertain and state the true financial position of the company at the time of the audit, and his duty is confined to that. But then comes the question, how is he to ascertain that position? The answer is by examining the books of the company. But he does not discharge his duty by doing this without inquiry and without taking any trouble to see that the books themselves show the company's true position. He must take reasonable care to ascertain that they do so.
>
> An auditor, however, is not bound to do more than exercise **reasonable care and skill** in making inquiries and investigations. He is not an insurer, he does not guarantee that the books do correctly show the true position ... He does not even guarantee that the balance sheet is accurate ... His obligation is not as onerous as this. Such I take to be the duty of the auditor: he must be honest, that is, he must not certify what he does not believe to be true, and he must take reasonable care and skill before he believes that what he certifies is true. What is reasonable care in any particular case must depend on the circumstances of that case.

The last sentence of the judgement emphasises the fact that what is proper conduct in any set of circumstances is inevitably a subjective question which the court determines with hindsight. In the second case, *Kingston Cotton Mill Co.* (1896) 2 Ch. 279, Lopes LJ delivered the now well known passage on the auditor's duty. It is still relevant today.

> It is the duty of an auditor to bring to bear on the work he has to perform that skill, care and caution which a reasonably competent, careful and cautious auditor would use. What is reasonable skill, care and caution must depend on the particular circumstances of each case. An auditor is not bound to be a detective, or, as was said, to approach his work with suspicion, or with a foregone conclusion that there is something wrong ... He is a watchdog, but not a bloodhound ... If there is anything calculated to excite suspicion, he should probe it to the bottom but, in the absence of anything of that kind, he is only bound to be reasonably cautious and careful ... Auditors must not be made responsible for not tracking out ingenious and carefully laid schemes of fraud, when there is nothing to arouse their suspicion ...

The complexity of the accounting and the business environment makes it impossible for auditors to detect all aspects of fraudulent activity in an organisation. Thus, the auditor's responsibility for detecting fraud and errors continues to be a much debated issue. Following these two landmark cases the primary duties of auditors were subsequently confirmed in legislation.

Auditing in the United States — further developments

In 1931 the Ultramares case in the United States prompted the accounting profession to clarify that the auditor was expressing an opinion, not giving a guarantee, and that the 'balance sheet and the related statement of income and surplus present fairly'. In responding to severe criticism of the financial community and corporate management, the Congress of the United States passed the *Securities Act 1933* (USA) and the *Securities Exchange Act 1934* (USA). These Acts contained the requirements for the audit of financial statements of corporations seeking to issue securities and corporations wanting to register with the commission for the public trading of securities. The Acts placed a significant responsibility on professional accountants and increased their authority.

The hearings held by the Securities and Exchange Commission into the McKesson & Robbin fraud case in 1939 and the findings released the following year had an impact not only on audit procedures, but also on the development of Auditing Standards and the content of the auditor's report. The confirmation of receivables and the observation of inventory-taking procedure were made mandatory.

Robert H. Montgomery identified in his book *Auditing Theory and Practice* (1912)[2] the change in audit objectives as follows:

> In what might be called the formative days of auditing, students were taught that the chief objects of an audit were:
> (1) the detection and prevention of fraud;
> (2) the detection or prevention of errors;
> but in recent years there has been a decided change in the demand and in the service ... The relative position of the present-day purposes are:
> (1) to ascertain the actual financial condition and earnings of an enterprise ...
> (2) the detection of fraud and errors.

Auditing in Australia — a historical profile

Following the example set by the legislators in the United Kingdom, the Australian states passed Companies Acts requiring audits of all publicly held companies. The statutory requirements of the audit were similar to those that applied in the United Kingdom. These state Acts, for the period 1863–1896, were largely a verbatim reproduction of the English Acts. They stipulated the method of appointment and remuneration of the auditor, the eligibility and disqualification criteria, and the auditor's rights and duties.

The *Companies Act 1896* (Vic.) dealt with a number of matters pertaining to an audit. It stipulated that only a qualified accountant, licensed by what is now the Companies Auditors and Liquidators Disciplinary Board, could be appointed as an auditor. The Act emphasised the independence of the auditor and recognised the professional accounting bodies that existed at that time. A number of features pertaining to an audit have been retained to this day in Corporations Law (a body of legislation which includes the *Corporations Act 1989* (Cwlth)). The following features were stipulated in Victoria's Act of 1896:

- The appointed auditors were to certify the correctness or otherwise of the balance sheet of the company.
- The auditor's stipulated duties were to:
  - use reasonable diligence with a view to ascertaining that the books of the company have been properly kept;
  - examine the shareholders' balance sheet and any accounts presented to the members of the company;
  - report in writing to the members of the company whether, in the auditor's opinion, the accounts have been drawn up in accordance with the provision of the relevant Companies Act and, when taken together with any explanations attached thereto, present a correct view of the state of the company's affairs, and whether all their requisitions as auditors have been complied with.
- In addition, the auditor's report was to be read at the general meeting.

An auditor wilfully certifying a false or fraudulent balance sheet or account was liable to imprisonment and, if negligently certifying a false or fraudulent balance sheet, was liable to a fine. During the twentieth century, the Australian states continued to enact their own companies legislation, notably in Victoria. A significant amendment to Victoria's Companies Act in 1938 recognised university qualifications as an alternative to passing examinations to the satisfaction of the Companies Auditors and Liquidators Board. Following the enactment of the *Uniform Companies Act 1961* (Cwlth), the National Companies and Securities Commission (NCSC) was established in 1979, with overall power to administer the National Companies and Securities Industries Legislation of which the *Companies Act 1981* (Cwlth) was a part. Most of the functions and powers were delegated to the existing states and territories. Given continuing variations in audit and other requirements, the Commonwealth Government enacted the *Australian Securities Commission Act 1989* (Cwlth). This Act established the former Australian Securities Commission (now the Australian Securities and Investment Commission (ASIC)). The centrepiece of the Act is the Corporations Law. The Commission is now the only administering authority of the Corporations Law in Australia.

Under the Corporations Law, the financial statements of all companies (except exempt proprietary companies) must be audited for the protection of the shareholders. For consistency, the Corporations Law sets out the form and content of the financial statements and additional disclosure requirements on which the auditor is required to report. It also establishes the rights and responsibilities of the auditor.

From its early beginnings through to its role by the mid-twentieth century, auditing can be argued to have been fulfilling a conformance role, directly geared to satisfying the needs of investors. The conformance role relates to the auditor's function in ensuring that the organisation conforms to policies, procedures and statutory matters. In this role, the auditor examined books and records to ensure their correctness, reported on the accounts in accordance with statutory requirements, and generally adopted a 'watchdog' role in ensuring that the company's affairs were in order. From about the mid-twentieth century, auditing practice started to change — from being a detailed checking function to one of ascertaining the extent to which internal control could be relied on to ensure that accounting records and financial statements are reliable. Auditors examine the financial statements and their underlying records and supporting evidence to arrive at an opinion on the truth and fairness of the financial reports.

2 LEARNING OBJECTIVE

Discuss the historical and other factors that influence the role of auditors, and the resulting complexities of meeting public expectations.

The development of an enhancing role

Auditors have faced over the past thirty years or so an increasing demand for more accountability and more perceived benefits for users. The standards by which audits were performed were scrutinised and the outcome of the Pacific Acceptance case (see below) established the basis for a set of acceptable auditing guidelines. There was also an expectation that auditing as a professional service should not only provide assurance for the **credibility** of the financial report, but also enhance the integrity of financial information and its usefulness in decision-making by management and other users.

Defining reasonable care and skill

The landmark Australian case of *Pacific Acceptance Corporation v. Forsyth* (1970) 92 WN NSW (29) established a comprehensive judgement concerning auditors' duties. It directed that auditors have a primary duty to audit, which encompasses a continuing duty to warn management promptly of suspicions that fraud or error may exist. The Pacific Acceptance case also provided an extensive elaboration of the conduct of an audit. The auditor, for example, should pay due regard to the possibility of fraud and actively investigate the possibility of fraud if suspicious circumstances arise.

The courts also continued to exercise their prerogative to assess the reasonableness of professional standards in specific circumstances and, therefore, to assess what constitutes reasonable care and skill — a principle espoused in the Kingston Cotton Mill Case and London and General Bank case.

Enhancing the credibility of financial information

In the 1970s, auditors described their role as one of enhancing the credibility of financial information and furthering the operations of an effective capital market.[3] In the *New York Times* of 6 April 1975, audits were said to affirm the truthfulness of financial statements and ensure that financial statements were 'fairly presented'. This function was loosely linked to various audit practices, including:

- the review and testing of company records and the procedures and controls used to assemble financial information;
- the approval to use various accounting principles;
- the examination of financial statements to ensure they contained no material misstatements, omissions or misleading presentations of data.[4]

The nature of auditing services in the 1990s

In 1990, a publication by the IFAC and the International Auditing Practices Committee (IAPC) — *Understanding Financial Statements: A Guide for Financial Statements Users* — was incorporated into the *Auditing Handbook* issued by CPA Australia and the Institute of Chartered Accountants in Australia (ICAA). (Financial statements are the representations of management, while the auditor's responsibility is to express an opinion on whether management has fairly presented such financial information.) A statement distinguishing between the responsibilities of management and auditors is at the forefront of the section 'Institutional Framework of Auditing in Australia' in the *Auditing Handbook*.

In August 1997, the IAPC issued a proposed framework of reporting on the credibility of information, which was adopted in Australia as Exposure Draft ED 66, Framework for Reporting by Professional Accountants on the Credibility of Information. ED 66 recognises the need for authoritative professional guidance to support the expanding role for assurance providers to enhance the credibility of information on a wide range of subject matters. The IAPC has devoted considerable resources to reviewing the exposure draft and it published a revised exposure draft in March 1999. This is incorporated in Australia as ED 72, Assurance Engagements. The IAPC subsequently published its first International Standard on Assurance Engagements (ISAE) as ISA 100 in July, 2000. This ISAE (discussed later on page 13) provides an overall framework for assurance engagements intended to provide a high or moderate level of assurance. It establishes the basic principles and essential procedures for professional accountants in public practice to perform engagements intended to provide a high level of assurance.

Through the application of audit practices, the auditor is intended to render a professional opinion on the truth and fairness of the financial statements. However, the process also suggests that the expertise and knowledge needed to conduct an audit properly require the exercise of professional judgement.[5] In a critical review of the definitions of the auditor's responsibilities, Young[6] criticises both the auditing profession's attempt to impose a limited obligation on auditors to detect fraud and other illegal acts, and the lack of incentives to satisfy public expectations regarding corporate failures. Young argues that the profession has attributed such failures to the public's lack of understanding of the auditor's role. (The concept of 'the audit expectation gap' is discussed in Chapter 2.)

For the purposes of this text, Auditing Standard AUS 104 (International Standard on Auditing ISA 110), Glossary of Terms defines an audit as a service where the auditor's objective is to provide a high level of assurance through:

(a) the issue of a positive expression of an opinion that enhances the credibility of a written **assertion**(s) about an accountability matter ('attest audit');
(b) the provision of relevant and reliable information and a positive expression of opinion about an accountability matter where the party responsible for the matter does not make a written assertion(s) ('direct reporting audit').

THE DEVELOPMENT OF THE ASSURANCE ENGAGEMENT FRAMEWORK

3 LEARNING OBJECTIVE

Explain the nature and scope of the assurance engagement framework and its relationship with other professional services.

The previous paragraphs demonstrate the significance of audit quality and audit expertise in providing a high level of assurance to users regarding the credibility of financial information. However, the concept of **audit assurance** services, together with the whole notion of traditional financial reporting, has been criticised in that these services have failed to meet users' needs sufficiently. In 1991, the American Institute of Certified Public Accountants (AICPA) formed a special committee, the Jenkins Committee, to assess the needs of the users of financial information and recommend improvements to the financial reporting framework. One recommendation of the Committee was that business reporting should provide more forward-looking information. However, such recommendations were a conundrum for the world of financial reporting and the accounting profession in particular.[7] There was justifiable demand for improvement in financial reporting, yet any change in that direction would, where the profession had assured the presentations of financial data, potentially increase the profession's exposure to liability/litigation. It is in this context that the AICPA formed another special committee on assurance services — the Elliott Committee.

The charge of the Elliott Committee was to:

> ... analyse and report on the current state and future of the audit/assurance function and the trends shaping the audit/assurance environment, focusing on the current and changing needs of users of decision-making information and other stakeholders in the audit/assurance process, and how best to improve the related services.

The Elliott Committee recognised the need for the profession to diversify its product potential away from traditional financial report audit and related services, in the light of declining demand for these services. It recommended that this be achieved by embracing and significantly expanding the 'assurance services' provided by the profession to consolidate its existing markets and capitalise on its competitive advantages in the emerging information markets.[8] Furthermore, it recommended that the audit/attestation function should evolve into the assurance function, with a movement towards broader-based assurance services.[9] The need for reassessment and redirection by the profession is a vision shared by reports produced in Canada and the United Kingdom. The Australian accounting profession also recognises the significant changes needed for the profession to remain relevant to the public.

Within the context of the broad range of assurance services, there is a growing demand in both the public and private sectors for professional accountants to provide assurance on a variety of subject matter by expressing a conclusion regarding its relevance, reliability or context. The IAPC of the IFAC developed (in March 1999) and subsequently published (in August 2000) the ISAE to meet the demand for services that increase the value of information for decision-making. The new Standard has major implications for the services provided by professional accountants. Although the ISAE does not supersede existing ISAs, it formally brings auditing within the assurance engagement framework, with the intention that future standards will be revised to incorporate the expanded roles of a professional accountant.

Meanwhile, the AICPA's Special Committee on Assurance Services also published its deliberations on the definitions and interpretive summary of assurance services, with a model that links new assurance services to clients' business value chain. The frameworks put forward by the AICPA and the ISAE differ, but the codification of the assurance engagement framework by the IFAC has become a milestone in the development of the profession. In this section we will summarise this development and its relationship with auditing.

A financial report is a means of communication by management to shareholders and other stakeholders of an organisation. It reports on how resources are used, and how the business achieves its goals. This accountability relationship may be jeopardised, however, if the report produced by the responsible party (the management) is biased, perhaps due to that party pursuing its self-interests. The credibility of such a report can be enhanced by having an independent professional person provide an assurance report based on an examination of the subject matter, in accordance with some predetermined criteria. The objective of an assurance engagement is for a professional accountant to evaluate or measure subject matter that is the responsibility of another party against identified criteria, and to express a conclusion that provides the intended user with a level of assurance about that subject matter. The level of assurance provided by the professional accountant's conclusion conveys the degree of confidence that the intended user may place in the credibility of the subject matter.

The nature and scope of assurance engagements

Auditing Standard AUS 106, Explanatory Framework for Standards on Audit and Audit Related Services (International Standard on Auditing ISA 120, Framework of ISAs) defines assurance as satisfaction with the reliability of information provided. The degree of satisfaction (or confidence) achieved is determined by the nature and extent of procedures performed by the assurance provider, the results of the procedures and the objectivity of the evidence obtained.

Assurance engagements may include any combination of the following:

- engagements to report on a broad range of subject matters covering financial and non-financial information;
- engagements intended to provide high or moderate level of assurance;
- **attestation** and direct reporting engagements;
- engagements to report internally and externally; and
- engagements in the private and public sector.

The ISAE excludes the following engagements from the assurance engagements framework:

- agreed-upon procedures;
- the compilation of financial or other information;
- the preparation of tax returns where no conclusion is expressed;
- management and tax consulting;
- other advisory services.

Assurance engagements may be the result of various types of accountability relationship. Such a relationship exists when one party is answerable to and/or responsible to another for a subject matter, either as a result of an agreement or legislation, or when one voluntarily chooses to report to another party on a subject matter. An accountability responsibility may also arise when a user is expected to have an interest in how the responsible party has discharged its responsibility for a subject matter.

The elements of an assurance engagement are:

- a subject matter;
- a three-party relationship involving a professional accountant or a professional firm, a responsible party and an intended user;
- a set of suitable criteria;
- an engagement process; and
- a conclusion.

The broad schematic framework of assurance engagements and their scope of services (which include auditing and attestation) is provided in Figure 1.1 on the next page.

The subject matter of an assurance engagement can take many forms — data, systems or processes, or behavioural matters. The data can include financial or non-financial information, relevant historical or prospective information, and statistical or performance measures. Systems or processes can include internal or hired systems for electronic commercial transactions, control criteria, system integrity measures and the value chain of an organisation. Behavioural matters can include risk management, **corporate governance**, compliance, human resources, and social and environmental issues.

The three parties involved in an assurance engagement are the professional accountant, the responsible party and the intended user. The ISAE recognises that professional accountants, including auditors, who are responsible for the assurance engagements should comply with the Code of Ethics for Professional Accountants issued by the IFAC.

The ethical principles that govern their work are primarily integrity, objectivity, professional competence and due care, confidentiality, professional behaviour and the application of relevant technical standards. Professional accountants in public practice undertaking assurance engagements should be, and should appear to be, free of any interest that might be regarded, whatever its actual fact, as being incompatible with integrity, objectivity and independence.

The responsible party is the person or group of persons who are responsible for the subject matter. They may or may not be the party who engages the professional accountant. In a financial report audit engagement (which is one type of assurance engagement), for example, the management is the responsible party for the preparation of financial statements and the implementation of internal control within the organisation, while the auditors are engaged by the members or shareholders of the organisation.

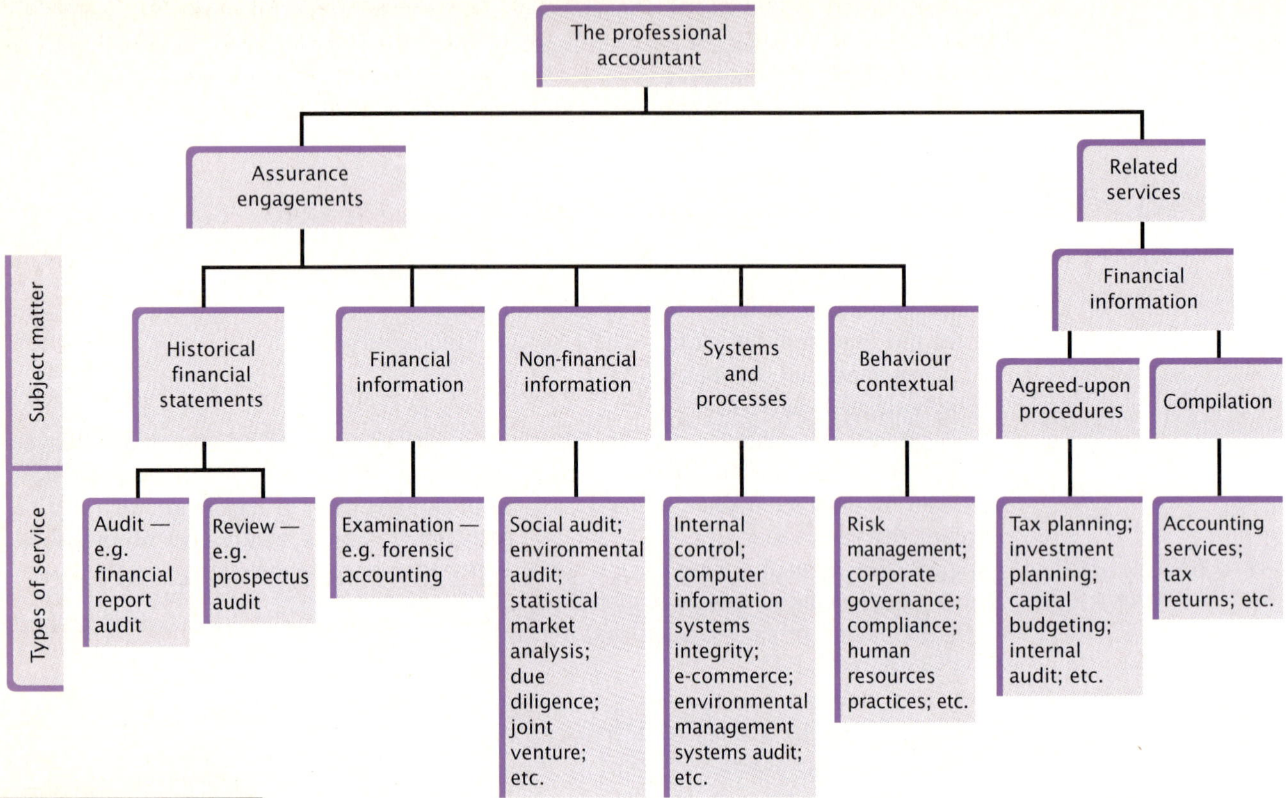

FIGURE 1.1 (Source: Adapted from the ISAE, the International Federation of Accountants, July 2000)

Assurance engagements — a schematic framework

The intended user is the person or groups of persons expected to use the professional accountants' report. The responsible party may be an intended user. Intended users are normally the addressees of the report and may impose restrictions on or requirements for an assurance engagement. In a special purpose financial report audit, for example, the professional accountant may consider restricting the access of the report to only identified users. However, other intended users may have no involvement in defining the scope of an assurance engagement.

The criteria used in an assurance engagement are the standards or benchmarks used to measure and evaluate the subject matter for the purpose of the report. They form the basis on which conclusions are drawn and they set the frame for individual interpretation of the report prepared by the professional accountant.

The process of engagement involves the professional accountant and the appointing party agreeing to the terms of the engagement (subject to the provisions of the legal regulations). Within that context, the professional accountant considers the appropriate approaches in terms of materiality, engagement risk, the application of professional judgement in planning, and the conduct of collecting and evaluating evidence. The professional accountant normally adopts a systematic method that requires a specialised set of knowledge and skill base. He or she must ensure proper documentation for all processes, with sufficient evidence to support a conclusion that provides a level of assurance about the subject matter.

In an attest engagement, the professional accountant's conclusion relates to an assertion by the responsible party. In a direct reporting engagement, the professional accountant expresses a conclusion on the subject matter regardless of whether the responsible party has made a written assertion. The accountant must demonstrate that his or her conclusions concerning the reliability of the subject matter are based on acceptable criteria, the results of the engagement process, and the quality and scope of the evidence evaluated.

Figure 1.2 shows the parties involved in an assurance engagement.

FIGURE 1.2

Assurance engagement relationships

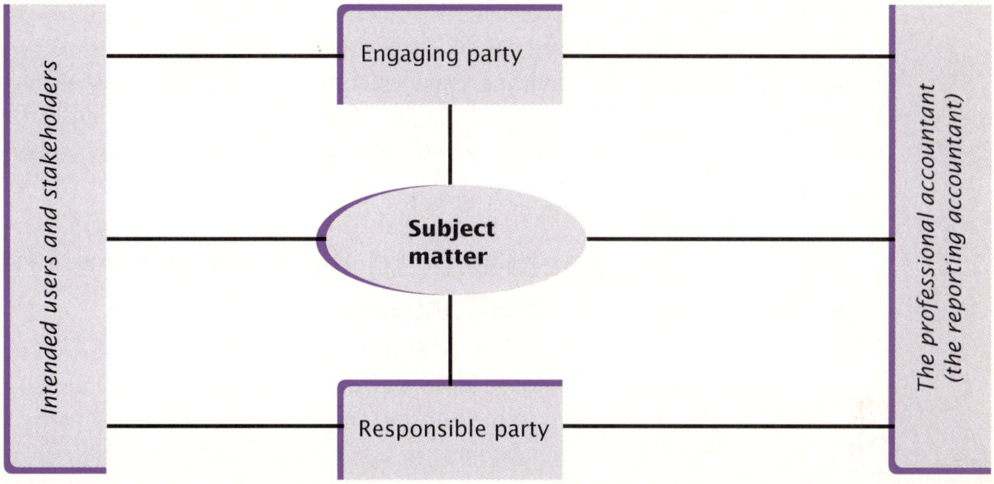

Notes:
1. The engaging party may also be the responsible party (e.g. the governing body of the responsible party).
2. Relationships defined by the lines are subject to the terms of engagements.

Audit engagements

According to AUS 106 (ISA 120), an audit engagement is designed to provide a high but not absolute level of assurance on an accountability matter. The professional accountant designs the engagement process so as to reduce to a low level the risk of an inappropriate conclusion that the subject matter does not conform, in all material respects, with suitable criteria. The accountant or the auditor obtains sufficient and relevant evidence through procedures such as inspection, observation, inquiry, confirmation, computation and analysis. Given inherent limitations such as those in control systems and testing procedures, absolute assurance is rarely attainable. The auditor obtains persuasive rather than conclusive evidence, and uses his or her professional judgement in gathering information and drawing conclusions. The expression 'high level of assurance' refers to the highest reasonable level of assurance that a professional accountant can provide concerning a subject matter.

Review engagements

A **review engagement** is designed to provide a moderate level of assurance and thus is less extensive in scope than an audit. The professional accountant designs the engagement process so as to reduce to a moderate level the risk of an inappropriate conclusion that the subject matter does not conform, in all material respects, with suitable criteria. The conclusion will be expressed in a clear manner, indicating the conformity of the subject matter with the criteria. It may be expressed as a statement on whether anything has come to the professional accountant's attention that causes him or her to believe non-conformity exists (negative assurance).

An audit or review can be further divided into an **attest service** or a direct reporting engagement. In an attest engagement, the professional accountant provides a conclusion about the assertion by the responsible party or about the subject matter in a form similar to the assertion made by the responsible party. A general purpose financial report audit is an example of an attest audit. In a direct reporting engagement, the professional accountant expresses a conclusion on the subject matter based on suitable criteria, regardless of whether the responsible party has made a written assertion on the subject matter. Examples of direct reporting engagements are audit reports issued on the adequacy of an internal control structure or issued to the governing body of an entity regarding compliance with environmental laws and regulations. We will further explain the conduct of an audit in Chapter 4.

Engagements to perform agreed-upon procedures and compilations

An **agreed-upon procedure engagement** does not enable the professional accountant to express assurance. Normally, the accountant is engaged to undertake certain requested procedures to meet the information needs of the engaging party and to provide a report on his or her factual findings in accordance with client requirements. The accountant does not determine the nature and extent of the procedures, so no assurance is expressed. The ISAE also specifically excludes from its scope any engagements to perform agreed-upon procedures. However, it also recognises that there should be some flexibility in such exclusion. If the professional accountant intends to provide a conclusion to indicate a high or moderate level of assurance, then such an engagement is included as an assurance engagement. Examples of agreed-upon procedures are operational investigations conducted into matters such as the integrity of computer-generated records or suspected fraudulent activities. Compilation engagements, on the other hand, do not meet the requirements for an assurance engagement.

It is worth noting that the AICPA, which first researched in the area of assurance services, adopts a broad-based assurance framework. It defines assurance services as independent professional services that improve the quality of information or its context for decision-makers. The AICPA regards assurance independence as the absence of interests that create an unacceptable risk of material bias with respect to the quality or context of information that is the subject matter of an assurance engagement. It also emphasises that the goal of assurance services is information improvement. The AICPA includes engagements to perform agreed-upon procedures as part of attestation. However, unlike the ISAE, the AICPA framework includes both compilation and agreed-upon procedure engagements as assurance services. Figure 1.3 shows a framework of audit and related services provided in AUS 106.

In summary, from the Jenkins Committee in 1991, to the establishment of a formalised ISAE by the IAPC in 2000, auditing has become part of a broad framework of assurance engagements. This development recognises the changing nature and scope of services provided by professional accountants, and identifies areas where accountants add value in the public interest. The ISAE defines an assurance engagement and its elements. The skills and procedures in auditing — such as those related to planning, examining systems, obtaining evidence, determining risk and materiality, documenting and reporting — are all part of the systematic method used in assurance engagement. The professional accountant makes a judgement on the appropriate level of assurance to be provided.

FIGURE 1.3

Explanatory framework for standards on audit and related services

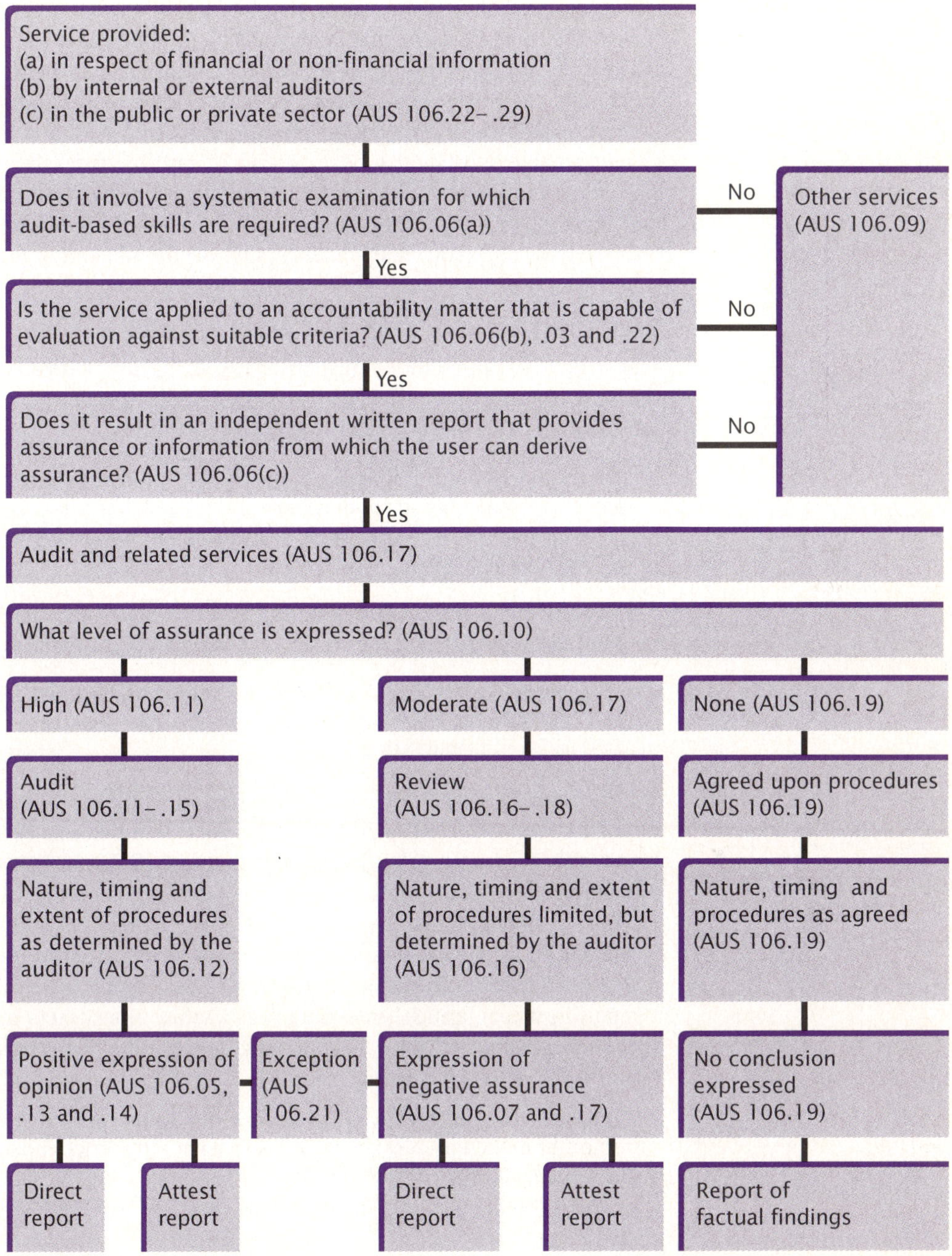

(Source: AUS 106, Appendix 1)

4 LEARNING OBJECTIVE

Assess the shifting nature of auditing by referring to the scope of detection of fraud and errors, the approach undertaken by auditors, the perception of audit independence and audit liability.

AUDITING — A SHIFTING PARADIGM

From the previous sections, it is clear that the role of auditing has evolved through a number of stages. The relevance of auditing was established through its historical value in ensuring the correctness of the accounts, detecting fraud and errors, and providing an independent opinion on the truth and fairness of the financial statements for users. Nowadays, to address the complexity of the information needs of users, auditors are expected not only to enhance the credibility of financial reports, but also to provide value-added services, such as reporting on irregularities, identifying business risks and advising management of internal weaknesses. Alongside the changes in audit expectations is the increasingly competitive audit environment, in which traditional audit services are blurred with non-audit services. The paradigm of independent auditing can be argued to be shifting, redefining the auditor's role. Here, we will discuss consequential changes in major aspects of the auditing environment — namely, (1) its scope in the detection of fraud and errors, (2) the audit approach used, (3) the characteristics of audit independence, and (4) the sustaining factor of **auditor liability**.

Detection of fraud and errors

The extent of the auditor's responsibility in terms of detection of fraud and errors has changed over the years. In Coopers & Lybrand's *Manual of Auditing*, the auditor's role in the detection of fraud or errors is described as follows:

> The examination of the accounting records, which the auditor undertakes in order to assess whether the accounts show a true and fair view, is not primarily or specifically designed, and cannot be relied upon, to disclose errors, defalcations and similar irregularities.[10]

Issued in 1993, the revised Auditing Practice Statement AUP 16 (the old AUP 16 issued by the Australian Accounting Research Foundation (AARF)) stated:

> . . . that the auditor's role is not to prevent irregularities; rather it is to exercise skill and care so as to have a reasonable expectation of detecting material misstatements arising from irregularities.

Five years later, the new codified statement Auditing Standard AUS 210, Irregularities, Including Fraud, Other Illegal Acts and Errors (International Standard on Auditing ISA 240, Fraud and Error) states that its purpose is to establish standards and provide guidance on:

- planning and conducting an audit to detect misstatements that have an impact on the financial report of an entity arising from irregularities, including fraud, other illegal acts and errors;
- procedures to be performed when circumstances cause the auditor to suspect that irregularities (including fraud, other illegal acts and errors) have occurred;
- reporting irregularities (including fraud, other illegal acts and errors) to the governing body or an appropriate level of management, users of financial reports and third parties.

AUS 210.01 also states that:

> The auditor should plan and conduct the audit so as to have a reasonable expectation of detecting misstatements that have a material impact on the financial report arising as a result of irregularities, and should report irregularities discovered during the course of the audit as appropriate in the circumstances.

Audit approach — satisfying the information needs of users

Over the years, there has also been a shift in audit approaches. The changes include:

- the use of selective audit sampling to replace detailed verification of balance sheet accounts;
- the development of techniques for the design of audit testing using a risk model;
- from a system-based audit approach, the development of a broad-based risk analysis of business processes.

These changes enable the auditor to focus on those areas of the audit that require the highest level of assurance. While the professional bodies reassess their position regarding audit and assurance services, the professional firms continue to address the complexity of the changing needs of users and the rapid growth of information technology. In a 1997 publication by KPMG Peat Marwick LLP, William Kinney Jr, Director of Assurance Services, announces that business viability and profitability assessments are essential parts of financial statement auditing today.[11] He refers to the need to establish, formally, strategy analyses, the evaluation of business processes, the development of key indicators necessary to monitor business performance, and **risk assessment** as key audit steps. The viability of the business strategy, the reasonableness of business plans and the effectiveness of internal controls are all essential matters about which decisions need to be made in determining audit procedures. Thus, auditing practices are evolving to yet another level — an enhancing role of adding value to business reporting.

As the global economy, the business organisations operating within it, and organisations' business strategies become increasingly complex and interdependent, more attention needs to be paid to the development of audit methods and procedures that focus on assertions at the entity level — that is, methods and procedures that promise greater power to detect material misstatements because they allow the auditor to ground key judgements in a more critical and holistic understanding of the client's systems dynamics. Further, today's complex economic world requires a break from the auditing traditions that have evolved from the early balance sheet audit — traditions under which the auditor's attention is focused at the sub-unit level primarily, and his or her views on evidence are heavily skewed towards tangibility (i.e. the physical existence of assets, the existence of tangible documentation supporting transactions, etc.). When forming an opinion about the validity of financial statement assertions, today's auditor must place more weight on knowledge about the client's business, industry and interactions with its environment.[12]

Audit independence

Auditors provide assurances on the credibility of the financial report, so the concept and practice of audit independence — the cornerstone of auditing — is also subject to debate. Independence underpins the success and credibility of the accounting profession, and its service to the public. It helps to provide the objectivity that permits the profession to perform effectively its attestation and monitoring functions. The paradigm for addressing independence issues has historically been based on the belief that allowing auditors to perform non-audit functions for audit clients, or to engage in management activities, presents the greatest potential for conflict. Those espousing this view would argue that auditors should do little non-audit work for audit clients. Auditing Practice Statement AUP 32, Audit Independence (issued in 1992) refers to considerations concerning actual and perceived independence. However, as pointed out by Wallman,[13] this approach of **audit independence** may seem reasonable, but fails in a number of respects and may well be contrary to the public interest. It is perceived to have failed to recognise the complexity of audit practices, the sophisticated business environment and the acute competition in which accounting firms now operate. In Australia, AUP 32 has been slow to respond to criticism (during the codification process), pending the re-examination of the issue in the light of the current auditing environment. The Joint Code of Professional Conduct issued by CPA Australia and the ICAA in early 1998 incorporates the requirement for audit independence.

As professional accountants in public practice are increasingly being asked to provide assurance on different types of information, including non-financial information, debates about whether such additional professional services may threaten the independence of the professional accountant continue. Recognising the need for more detailed guidance on independence issues, the Ethics Committee of the IFAC released the Exposure Draft ED, Independence — Proposed Changes to the Code of Ethics for Professional Accountants in June 2000. The current rules, which are adopted in AUP 32, describe a series of circumstances in which a reporting accountant's independence may be at risk. The new rules proposed in the exposure draft take a different approach. They set out a framework describing the factors that could threaten a reporting accountant's independence and the safeguards that can be put in place to preserve that independence. This framework, which forms the first part of the exposure draft, sets out the conceptual approach to independence for all reporting accountants (including auditors), together with a set of guidelines on dealing with different risks to independence. Reporting accountants are asked to demonstrate that they have implemented certain safeguards to resolve or reduce the risks.

The second part of the exposure draft provides an analysis of specific situations, with suggestions for how to minimise such risks to independence. The exposure draft recognises that some of the new services and assurance engagements recently introduced by professional accountants may actually reduce the risk to independence. The major change of the exposure draft is the replacement of particular risk situations with general concepts and possible risks. Also, unlike the existing code, the exposure draft makes no reference to the ownership of an accounting firm's capital, in view of the development of multi-disciplinary practices. The following passage, however, describes the approach adopted by the US Securities and Exchange Commission to audit independence. The debate concerning independence is an ongoing issue which we will discuss in Chapter 2.

PROFESSIONAL ENVIRONMENT Violations of audit independence

The US Securities and Exchange Commission has brought charges against one of the Big Five firms for violating its auditor independence rules. In early 2000, the Commission released the results of a review of a total of 8064 auditor independence rules on appearance. The firm insists that appearance-based rules may have been overlooked in some cases, but at no time was independence-in-fact compromised. No evidence is available to suggest that audit quality actually suffered as a result of the alleged violations. This, among other similar events, gave rise to a ruling proposed by the Securities and Exchange Commission in June 2000. Firms that audit a company would not be allowed to offer it contingency fees or consulting work in particular areas of computerisation, management, legal advice, human resources, investment banking, underwriting, book-keeping, valuations, actuarial work and internal auditing. This could force all Big Five to split off their consulting arms into separate companies. The Commission would moderate restrictions, dating back sixty years, on audit firm personnel owning shares in the firm's audit clients. The new restrictions would apply to only people directly involved with an audit.

However, three of the world's top accountancy firms, pitted against the Commission over the issue, have accused it of acting without any factual justification and employing a fundamentally flawed process. They argued that such limitations are not in the public interest. The extent of dissent from the Big Five and the forthcoming Presidential election in the United States mean that accountants in that country were waiting for a likely postponement of the Securities and Exchange Commission vote for at least six months when Congress returned after the 8 November election. The US accounting profession, led by the AICPA, opposes the Commission's independence rule. The Commission has received 3000 submissions on the rule since June 2000, and the chairman and general counsels were in discussions with the profession when this chapter was being written.

Meanwhile, in Australia, Deloitte Touche Tohmatsu has signed an understanding with the Australian Securities and Investment Commission (ASIC) on a range of matters to ensure that its audit practice maintains a high quality and that it retains a level of audit independence acceptable to the firm and to the ASIC. The settlement was made following the $20 million monetary claim against the directors and Deloitte Touche Tohmatsu for the audit of the failed Adsteam Shipping.[14]

Audit liability

Another aspect of the changing auditing environment is the shifting nature of auditor liability. In an audit conducted in accordance with the Corporations Law, the auditor is liable under statute and common law to the shareholders — who made the appointment and to whom auditors report — for any negligent performance of statutory duties. These duties cannot be restricted or reduced. The auditor's liability to the organisation being audited is contractual and stems from having undertaken to perform an audit, with due care, for the purpose of expressing an opinion on the financial report. A considerable body of case law has built up over the years with respect to the duty of care that an auditor owes to the auditee and the owners of the entity. In the Pacific Acceptance case, Moffitt J held that auditors may not be excused from negligence on the grounds that the client's directors or employees were also negligent. However, in the case of *AWA Ltd v. Daniels t/a Deloitte Haskins & Sells & Ors* (1992) IO ACLC 933, the principle of contributory negligence was established, whereby the company was held to be proportionately liable with the auditors concerned.

Also, the auditor may be considered, in certain circumstances, to assume a duty of care towards third parties. The common law concerning the auditor's liability to third parties is complex and has been subject to broad interpretation. The landmark case of *Caparo Industries PLC v. Dickman* (1990) 1 All ER 568 redefined the concept of proximity and subsequently used it to limit the auditor's liability for economic loss suffered by potential investors and individual shareholders.

The liability issue was further developed from the judgement in *Esanda Finance Corporation v. Peat Marwick Hungerfords* (1994) 12 ACLC 199, where the auditor's liability was found to not have existed because it was argued that compliance with the Accounting Standards cannot be used to enlarge the area of legal duty by creating a legal duty of care to persons to whom it would not otherwise be owed. Auditors in some countries are now permitted to practise under a limited liability organisational structure.

The development of auditing practices over the years suggests a shift in the auditor's conformity role into a far more dynamic role of enhancing the value of financial reporting. Although the fundamental principle of audit assurance has not changed explicitly, one can envisage the development of an expansion of attest services within the audit function. On the other hand, there have been fundamental changes in the business environment within which auditors' professional services are required. The increasing expectations of business entities and the high level of accountability required of the auditors give rise to a change in the audit framework. It may be too early to predict the auditing practice of the twenty-first century; however, it is apparent that the audit paradigm is changing from a conformative attestation to the enhancing role of a value-added service.

THE ACCOUNTING PROFESSION AND ITS ASSOCIATED ORGANISATIONS

5 LEARNING OBJECTIVE

Describe the accounting profession in Australia and the constituencies that influence the profession and audit practices.

The development of the accounting profession and statutory audits in the United Kingdom considerably influenced corresponding developments in Australia. Accounting associations first began to appear in Australia in the mid-1880s. Accounting bodies have influenced the development of the profession and audit practice by:

- maintaining standards of qualifications achieved through accredited courses, examinations and practical experience for accountants seeking to become members;
- furthering standards of practice achieved through research and the issue of standards, professional education and the establishment of rules of professional conduct for members;
- ensuring professional conduct and effective self-regulation of quality of service.

The accounting profession in Australia is influenced by a number of professional and regulatory organisations that either function within the profession or directly influence the profession through their standard setting and regulatory activities. These organisations represent both the private and public sectors.

Private sector organisations

The public accounting profession in Australia is represented directly by the two prominent accountancy bodies in the country — CPA Australia and the ICAA. Membership of either of these two bodies is voluntary but nevertheless important. Membership is necessary, for example, to satisfy the registration qualification for auditors and liquidators, and is a requirement for those conducting an audit under various state Acts in Australia. Self-regulation within the profession in setting competency standards is enforced among members. This is in the public interest.

CPA Australia and the ICAA provide a broad range of services to their respective members to ensure that they serve the public interest in performing quality professional services. The two accounting bodies cooperate in handling some of the important aspects of the profession's activities, such as standard setting, submissions to government and international representations.

The Australian accountancy profession is also active internationally. The work carried out by the international technical committees forms a valuable part of the process of developing Australian Accounting Standards and Auditing Standards. Australia is represented on the International Accounting Standards Committee (IASC), the IFAC and the three IFAC committees — the International Auditing Practices Committee (IAPC), the International Public Sector Committee (IPSC) and the International Financial and Management Accounting Committee (IFMAC). The profession is also represented on the Confederation of Asian and Pacific Accountants (CAPA).

CPA Australia

CPA Australia is one of the largest professional accountancy bodies in the world. The antecedent body, the Institute of Accountants of Victoria, was formed in 1886 by forty-five practitioners who were dedicated to raising the standard of the profession. Subsequently, in 1952, the Australian Society of Accountants was established through a merger of the Commonwealth Institute of Accountants in Australia and the Federal Institute of Accountants. It became the largest professional body in Australia in 1953. On 1 July 1990, the Australian Society of Accountants changed its name to the Australian Society of Certified Practising Accountants. Its membership of over 90 000 was represented in branches as widely distributed as the Northern Territory, Hong Kong, Singapore, Malaysia, New Zealand and the United Kingdom. Approximately 20 per cent of its members were then engaged in public practice and 52 per cent worked in commerce and industry. The remaining members were employed in the public sector or in academia.[15] On 13 April 2000, the Society changed its name to CPA Australia.

CPA Australia issues professional and technical statements, has a code of ethics (the Joint Code of Professional Conduct, shared with the ICAA), conducts continuing professional development, provides a professional schedule for obtaining the designation of Certified Practising Accountant (CPA), and holds annual congresses. It maintains libraries and publishes a monthly journal (*Australian CPA*) and a *Members' Handbook*. It also provides an update service for the handbook.

The Institute of Chartered Accountants in Australia

The ICAA is the professional accounting organisation incorporated by Royal Charter in 1928. Until recently, it recruited primarily educated and trained members in public practice. However, it is now encouraging commerce and industry to participate in the training of chartered accountants. A significant number of commercial organisations are now accredited for this purpose. The ICAA is also exporting its education program into Asia, particularly to Hong Kong, Malaysia and Singapore.

At the time of publication, the ICAA had approximately 30 000 members who worked in public practice (50 per cent), the business community (39 per cent) and academia and government organisations.[16]

The services that the ICAA provides to its members include professional and technical standards and continuing professional education, including the education of future members through the CA Program (previously the Professional Year (PY) Program), which now offers specialist options and training in commerce. The ICAA maintains a library, information service and bookshop for its members. Its publications include a monthly journal (*Charter*) and the *Members' Handbook*, which is updated twice per year. Members who hold public practice certificates are subject to the ICAA's practice review program.

Practice entities

The public accounting profession comprises a large number of individual practitioners who may operate within firms as sole practitioners or in partnership. These firms are generally classified into four groups: international, national, regional and suburban.

International firms have offices in the major cities throughout the world. These firms dominate the practice of public accountancy and they have the critical resource mass needed to service multinational companies. The largest firms in the group are known as the **Big Five**, following the merger of Coopers & Lybrand and Price Waterhouse (before which these firms were known as the Big Six). In 2000 these firms audited approximately 86 per cent (up from 68 per cent in 1998) of the top 1000 entities in Australia. Selected data for these large firms (and others) are presented in Table 1.1.

TABLE 1.1

Who audits the top 1000 in 1999–2000?

Audit firm	No. of audits	Audit fee ($m)	Other fees ($m)	Total fees ($m)
KPMG	173.5	67.72	100.63	168.34
PricewaterhouseCoopers	233.0	65.28	91.82	157.09
Ernst & Young	105.5	41.44	68.13	109.58
Deloitte Touche Tohmatsu	99.0	28.66	31.13	59.79
Arthur Andersen	76.5	29.61	21.71	51.32
Auditors-general	176.0	29.33	2.62	31.95
Non-Big Five	113.5	8.09	4.05	12.14
Not available/no audit	23.0	–	–	–
Total	1000.0	270.13	320.09	590.21

(Source: Tony Thomas, 'Big Five Insist Low Audit Fees Are Not Baits', *Business Review Weekly* (7 July 2000), p. 83)

The position of the non-Big Five firms (i.e. national firms not among the Big Five) has been steadily slipping in terms of fee incomes. Although they increased their number of audits from 109.5 of the top 1000 entities in 1998–99 to 113.5 in 1999–2000, their audit fees dropped from $10.76 million to only $8.09 million over the same period — an 18.5 per cent reduction. The main strength of these second-tier firms is in the private and family company sector. It is believed that these firms face an increasing handicap in audit work because they lack the extensive knowledge-management technology (e.g. consulting arrangements) of the global Big Five, which clients now demand.[17] The Big Five firms are continually engaged in innovative strategies to deliver the range of professional services demanded by clients. The growth of consulting and assurance services in tax, electronic commerce and technology is pushing the profession to develop continuous or 'live' audits, and to engage in a wider range of information-based management services. In the three years to June 1996, the consulting service revenue of Australian accounting firms increased by 70 per cent (up 19.8 per cent per year), compared with an increase of only 18.7 per cent in accounting services. It is argued that accountants and auditors will need to be 're-skilled' to meet the dynamic growth in business advisory and consulting services. Underpinning this point, the 'other fees' received by the Big Five (except Arthur Andersen) in 2000 were nearly one and a half times the audit fees they received.

Second-tier firms have offices in the major cities in Australia. These firms serve mainly medium-sized and small clients. Many have some form of association with smaller firms in other countries to handle the international needs of their clients. Regional firms have offices within a limited geographic area and usually serve smaller clients relative to the size of those served by international and national firms. Suburban firms may consist of a sole practitioner or a relatively small partnership. These are by far the most common form of practice unit. Such firms serve small entities and individual clients. Some of the smaller regional and suburban firms have flourished by developing their own specialities, such as specific aspects of tax practice, superannuation consulting, litigation support and business advisory services.

In summary, the expertise and experience of the practitioner and the size and resources of the practice entity dictate the range of services that a firm is able to offer. Vigorous competition has encouraged the growth of multi-service practice entities. The Big Five accountancy firms are able to provide a broad range of services to their clients, while the medium-sized to smaller firms tend to be more localised and specialised in the nature of the services they offer.

The Australian Stock Exchange

The Australian Stock Exchange (ASX) was established in 1987 through the amalgamation of six independent stock exchanges in Australia. It was demutualised in 1996 and listed under the revised legislation of the Australian Parliament. The change of status took place on 13 October 1998 and the ASX commenced operation as a public company, operating as the primary national stock exchange for equities, derivatives and fixed interest securities. It facilitates capital raisings for unlisted companies, uses advanced computer systems for trading (CHESS), settlement and capital matching, and provides comprehensive market data and information to a range of users.

Pursuant to s.769 of the Corporations Law, the ASX makes or adopts listing rules in the interest of the public (with the latest being revised in July 2000). The listing rules provide prerequisites for the admission and continuation of listing. The continuing listing rules supplement the disclosure requirements of the Corporations Law. A company whose securities are listed on the ASX is regarded as a listed disclosing entity (s.111AL). Over 1250 entities are listed on the ASX, including more than sixty overseas entities. With 7.6 million Australians who own shares directly or through managed funds, the ASX continues to provide up-to-date market information and services to the public. Recently, the ASX All Ordinaries Index was revamped, with the addition of the ASX100, ASX200 and ASX300 indices. The new All Ordinaries Index has 500 stocks instead of the 266 stocks in the old index. The ASX also plays a useful role in directing the attention of the accounting profession to important financial reporting issues.

Standard setting bodies

The two predominant accountancy bodies discussed in the previous section (CPA Australia and the ICAA) have been actively involved in setting standards and regulating professional activities in accounting in Australia. They have jointly undertaken these activities through the AARF and its constituent boards.

The Australian Accounting Research Foundation

The AARF was originally established in 1966 by CPA Australia and the ICAA, then reorganised in 1974 to act as the research arm of the accounting profession. The objectives of the AARF are to:

- improve the quality of financial reporting and auditing in Australia;
- contribute to the international development of financial report auditing;
- contribute to the development of commercial law and practice in Australia.

The AARF is responsible to CPA Australia and the ICAA through their Joint Standing Committee, which comprises the executive committee of each accounting body. Following the *Corporate Law Economic Reform Program Act 1999* (Cwlth), the AARF now operates chiefly through the following two functional boards.

- The Auditing and Assurance Standards Board (AuASB) has an overall objective to improve the quality of auditing in Australia. It develops and promulgates standards and practice guidance for audit and related services. In meeting its responsibilities, the AuASB seeks to ensure that appropriate consideration is given to theory, practice and reasonable community expectations. Its work is integrated with that of the IAPC.
- The Legislation Review Board reviews all existing and proposed Commonwealth legislation (other than taxation legislation), official Commonwealth reports and other documents to identify matters directly relevant to the accounting profession, and takes appropriate action where this is considered necessary or desirable.

Other functional segments (the Public Sector Accounting Standards Board and the Urgent Issues Group (UIG)) of the AARF were transferred into the new Australian Accounting Standards Board (AASB) in 2000.

Public sector organisations

The public sector organisations that directly influence the public accounting profession are the Financial Reporting Council, the AASB and the ASIC. Here, we will explain their principal activities.

Following the Corporate Law Economic Reform Program Act 1999 (CLERPA) the Commonwealth Government's proposal for standard setting reform — outlined in CLERP Paper no. 1, *Accounting Standards: Building International Opportunities for Australian Business* (September 1997) — was formally legislated on 24 November 1999, commencing on 13 March 2000. CLERPA establishes the Financial Reporting Council (s.225) and the AASB (s.226, with its functions in s.227), and interprets the roles of Accounting Standards (s.228).

The Financial Reporting Council

Section 225 of CLERPA lists the functions of the Financial Reporting Council. They include overseeing the setting of Accounting Standards in Australia; appointing members of the AASB (other than the chair); giving directions to the AASB on matters of general policy and procedures; and monitoring the operation of Accounting Standards to assess their continued relevance and effectiveness in achieving their objectives. The Council does not have the power to direct the AASB in the development of a particular Standard, nor is it able to veto a Standard formulated and recommended by the AASB; however, it monitors the development of international Accounting Standards in which Australia plays a part. The members of the Financial Reporting Council are appointed by the Minister for Finance, who receives an annual report on its operations and the operations of the AASB.

The Australian Accounting Standards Board

Now separate from the AARF, the AASB's functions and powers include making Accounting Standards and developing a conceptual framework for the purpose of evaluating Accounting Standards. CLERPA confers on the AASB the function of contributing to the development of a single set of Accounting Standards for worldwide use, giving regard to the interests of Australian corporations. The AASB can make or formulate an Accounting Standard by issuing or amending the text of an international Accounting Standard.

The Australian Securities and Investment Commission

The ASIC is one of the three Commonwealth Government bodies that regulate financial services and the single national regulator of Australia's 1.1 million companies. The scope of activities overseen by the ASIC include the advising, selling and disclosure of financial products and services to consumers so they have adequate information and are treated fairly with adequate avenues for redress. As a corporate watchdog, the ASIC is expected to develop policy and guidance on the laws below; monitor compliance and licensing; protect consumer interests and market integrity; enforce relevant laws; and provide comprehensive and accurate company information.

Enacted under the *Australian Securities and Investment Commission Act 1989* (s.1(2)), the ASIC has the role of maintaining, facilitating and improving the performance of the financial system. It administers the following legislation:

- the Corporations Law and Corporations Act 1989;
- the Australian Securities and Investment Commission Act;
- the *Insurance (Agents and Brokers) Act 1984*;
- the *Insurance Contracts Act 1984*;
- the *Superannuation (Resolution of Complaints) Act 1993.*

It also exercises consumer protection related functions under the *Superannuation Industry (Supervision) Act 1993*, the *Retirement Savings Accounts Act 1997*, the *Insurance Act 1973* and the *Life Insurance Act 1995.*

The ASIC is an authority accountable to the Commonwealth Parliament through the Attorney-General. Its objectives (s.1(2)), are:

- to maintain, facilitate and improve the performance of companies, the securities markets and the futures markets;
- to promote the informed and confident participation of investors and consumers in the financial system;
- to achieve uniformity of administration of the Corporations Law throughout Australia;
- to administer the laws that confer functions and powers on it effectively and with a minimum of procedural requirements;

- to receive, process and store — efficiently and quickly — the information given to the ASIC under the laws;
- to ensure that the documents are available for public access;
- to take action to enforce and give effect to national scheme law.

The ASIC ensures that high-quality financial information which conforms to Accounting Standards is readily available to the shareholders and the public. It has the powers to investigate all perceived serious breaches of the Corporations Law and can act to recover damages or property and to prosecute criminal cases. To ensure compliance with the Corporations Law, the ASIC can take legal action against company officers, accountants, auditors and liquidators. An example of the powers of the ASIC is demonstrated by its move to resolve confusion in the corporate sector following an unprecedented Senate ruling to disallow a new Accounting Standard (AASB 1015, Acquisition of Assets).

The original Australian Securities Commission was restructured and renamed as the Australian Securities and Investment Commission, as part of the adoption of the Wallis Report (1997) recommendations on the organisation's future role.

The Companies Auditors and Liquidators Disciplinary Board

The Companies Auditors and Liquidators Disciplinary Board is a statutory body that is established under the Australian Securities and Investment Commission Act. It hears applications from the ASIC to determine whether auditors or liquidators have breached the Corporations Law and has the power to impose a penalty if it determines that a registered auditor or liquidator has failed to carry out his or her duties properly, or is not a fit and proper person to be registered. Penalties include the cancellation or suspension of registration, an imposition of restrictions on conduct, or an admonition.

The Board is responsible for the registration of auditors. The Wallis Report (and subsequent regulatory reviews) suggested that CPA Australia and the ICAA set up a joint registry to take over this function and also hear minor disciplinary cases.

LEARNING CHECK

1.1 An audit is defined as a professional service to provide a high level of assurance in which an objective positive opinion is rendered about an accountability matter.

1.2 Auditing has been evolving from a conformance role (ascertaining the correctness of accounts) to an enhancing role (adding value to the credibility of information for users). The scope and approach of audits have changed over the years with the development of case law and other economic factors that have had an impact on the expectations of auditors.

1.3 Although primarily concerned with financial reports, the auditor needs to examine analyses of business processes and strategies as part of a complex process of providing audit assurance.

1.4 The assurance framework encompasses the audit, review and examination of financial matters, with different levels of assurance to be provided.

1.5 The new AASB was established under the Financial Reporting Council to develop Accounting Standards and the accounting conceptual framework, together with the public sector Accounting Standards, while the AARF remains to oversee the development of the Auditing and Assurance Standards and the legislative review process.

LEARNING OBJECTIVE 6

Discuss the latest changes in the Corporations Law that affect professional accountants.

CORPORATE LAW ECONOMIC REFORM PROGRAM

Announced by the federal Treasurer in March 1997, the Corporate Law Economic Reform Program (CLERP) is a comprehensive initiative to improve six key areas of Australia's business and company regulation as part of the Commonwealth Government's drive to promote business, economic development and employment. The six proposals for policy reform are:

1. *Accounting Standards*: building international opportunities for Australian business;
2. *fundraising*: undertaking capital-raising initiatives to build enterprise and employment;
3. *directors' duties and corporate governance*: facilitating innovation and protecting investors;
4. *takeovers*: monitoring corporate control to create a better environment for productive investment;
5. *electronic commerce*: cutting cybertape — that is, conducting business by facilitating changes in market activity and making greater use of technology;
6. *financial markets and investment products*: promoting competition, financial innovation and investment by reassessing securities and futures market regulation to facilitate the development of new financial products and competition.

The House of Representatives passed the Corporate Law Economic Reform Bill (a new version) on 3 June 1999 and the Senate passed it (with amendments) on 18 October 1999. The Bill was subsequently approved on 24 November 1999. The key elements of the CLERPA are legislation in the areas of fundraising, directors' duties and corporate governance, Accounting Standards and takeovers. In May 2000, Mr Alan Cameron, Chairman of the ASIC, released the details of CLERP 6 in *Developments in the Financial Services Industry: Investor Protection in the New Economy and CLERP 6.*

Directors' duties and corporate governance

The key features of the CLERPA that relate to directors' duties and corporate governance are described below:

- It introduces a business judgement rule which offers directors a safe harbour from personal liability for breaches of the duty of care and diligence in relation to honest, informed and rational business judgements.
- It introduces a statutory derivative action which enables shareholders or directors of a company to bring an action on behalf of the company, for a wrong done to the company, where the company is unwilling or unable to do so.
- It rewrites the duty to exercise care and diligence under s.232(4) of the Corporations Law to clarify that the standard of care required by the duty must be assessed by reference to the particular circumstances of the officer concerned. A breach of the duty of care and diligence will give rise to civil consequences only and will no longer provide a basis for an offence under the law. Criminal liability will continue to apply to breaches of the duty to act honestly.
- It expressly allows directors to rely on the advice or information provided by experts when making decisions, so long as the director believes on reasonable grounds that the expert is reliable and competent in relation to the matters concerned.
- It clarifies the duty of directors in situations of conflict of interest to permit directors who serve on wholly owned subsidiaries to take into account the interest raised by the nominating company in certain circumstances. The common law obligation to disclose conflicts of interest remains.

The clarification of directors' duties and corporate governance issues reinforce the auditors' position in their value-enhancing role.

Accounting Standards

The key features of the CLERPA that have implications for Accounting Standards are described below:

- It establishes the Financial Reporting Council as an advisory body with responsibility for the broad oversight of the Australian Accounting Standard setting process, and for providing reports and advice to the minister. The minister appoints members of the council with specific functions, including appointing the members of the standard setter (the AASB), approving and monitoring the standard setter's priorities, and monitoring the development of international Accounting Standards with harmonisation priorities.
- It reconstitutes the standard setter, the AASB, as a body corporate.
- It facilitates interpretation of Accounting Standards by setting out the objectives of Accounting Standard setting in the legislation, providing that Accounting Standards are to be interpreted in accordance with those objectives.
- It requires a cost–benefit analysis of the impact of a proposed Accounting Standard.
- It assigns power to the minister to give the AASB a direction about the role of international Accounting Standards in the Australian Accounting Standard setting system. The council will be required to provide a report about the desirability of such a direction.

SERVICES PROVIDED BY PUBLIC PROFESSIONAL ACCOUNTANTS

7 LEARNING OBJECTIVE

Appreciate the nature and scope of attest and nonattest services performed by professional accountants.

Accountants in public practice provide a variety of services. Traditionally, services provided by public accounting firms can be classified as either attest or nonattest services. Attest services include audit, review and sometimes agreed-upon procedures. Attest services are normally those in which a professional accountant issues a written communication that expresses a conclusion about the reliability of a written assertion that is the responsibility of another party. The principal types of **nonattest service** rendered by public accountants are those in respect to traditional accounting and taxation, management consulting or advice, insolvency and business recovery services. The common characteristic of these services is that they do not result in the expression of an opinion, negative assurance, a summary of findings or any other form of assurance by the public accountant.

With the fast growing demand for professional and financial services, accounting firms have diversified into providing a wide range of services and products. The assurance services identified by the AICPA include engagements for risk assessment, business performance measurement, information systems reliability, electronic commerce, health care performance measurement and Eldercare. The *Report of the Joint Assurance Services Task Force*, released by CPA Australia and the ICAA, was largely drawn from the *Report of the Special Committee on Assurance Services* (the Elliott Report) prepared by the AICPA. It recognises that the expanded assurance services are in areas in which accountants do not have a legislative monopoly, and that these services are performed by other professional groups. The Elliott Report highlighted the issue of accountants operating in a competitive market for assurance services:

> By virtue of their knowledge and training, and reputation for integrity and objectivity, accountants are acknowledged as quintessential information professionals. They are equipped to provide independent assurance on, and navigation through, the massive information overload that businesses and individuals experience every day in making decisions.

The report also cited ISO 9000 (five universal standards for quality assurance systems) and ISO 14000 (maintenance of an environmental management system) as examples of where accountants have not competed in the market for new services.

One can identify the following types of service and product by browsing through the web sites of the Big Five accounting firms:

- assurance;
- business and information risk management;
- electronic commerce;
- corporate governance and corporate recovery;
- actuarial and legal services;
- managed investment, superannuation, financial planning and tax services;
- business transformation and arbitration;
- financial advisory, outsourcing and global resource solutions.

TYPES OF AUDIT ACTIVITY AND AUDITOR

8 LEARNING OBJECTIVE

Distinguish different types of audit activity and auditor.

AUS 106 (ISA 120) defines and differentiates between the range of audit and related service engagements according to the level of assurance to be provided. While audit firms are normally appointed as independent external auditors, they are sometimes also engaged to undertake internal audit functions. The range of audit-related services provided varies according to client needs.

Types of audit activity

Audits are generally classified into different types of activity — namely, financial report, compliance, performance, comprehensive and **environmental audits**. We will also describe internal auditing — a category of audit activity that relates to any audit service carried out within an organisation — in the following section.

Financial report audit

Auditing Standard AUS 202, Objective and General Principles Governing an Audit of a Financial Report (International Standard on Auditing ISA 200, Objective and General Principles Governing an Audit of Financial Statements) states that the objective of a **financial report audit** is to enable the auditor to express an opinion as to whether the financial report is prepared, in all material respects, in accordance with an identified financial reporting framework. The financial report audit involves obtaining and evaluating evidence about an entity's financial affairs so as to establish the degree of correspondence between the management's assertions and the established criteria, such as legal requirements and Accounting Standards (applicable Accounting Standards and UIG Consensus Views — see Chapter 2). This type of audit is performed by independent auditors appointed by the shareholders of the company, or by equivalent proprietors of non-incorporated entities whose report is being audited. The auditor must be qualified and able to exercise his or her skills in an independent and objective manner. The nature and extent of the audit examination are functions of the requirements of these entities in terms of the audit mandate. Division 3, ss.307–313 of the Corporations Law, provides guidelines for an audit stipulated by the Corporations Law. We will further explain in Chapter 2.

Compliance audit

A **compliance audit** involves obtaining and evaluating evidence to determine whether certain financial or operating activities of an entity conform to specified conditions, rules or regulations. The established criteria in this type of audit may come from a variety of sources. Management, for example, may prescribe policies (or rules) pertaining to overtime work, participation in a superannuation plan, and conflict of interests. Compliance audits based on criteria established by management may be undertaken frequently during the year. This type of audit is usually carried out by company employees who perform an internal audit function.

Business enterprises, not-for-profit organisations, government units and individuals are required to prove compliance with a myriad of regulations. In many instances, the audit opinion issued under the requirements of the Corporations Law has elements of a compliance audit, where the auditor is required to express an opinion on the company's compliance with the provisions of the Corporations Act. Corporate and individual taxpayers comply with the *Income Tax Assessment Act 1936* (Cwlth), as amended, in filling out their annual tax returns.

In the public sector, the term 'regularity audit' is used to denote an examination that reports on the legality and control of operations and the probity of those dealing with public funds, including the expression of an opinion on an entity's compliance with statutory requirements, rules, ordinances or directives that govern its activities.

Findings related to a compliance audit are generally reported to the authority that established the criteria and may include a summary of findings or an expression of assurance as to the degree of compliance with those criteria.

Performance audit

A **performance audit** involves obtaining and evaluating evidence about the efficiency, economy and effectiveness of an entity's operating activities in relation to specified objectives. This type of audit activity may also be referred to as a value-for-money (VFM), operational or management audit. The term 'performance audit' is usually applied in the public sector, with some application in the private sector; the other terms are common to both private and public sectors. Auditing literature provides strong support for equating the conceptual definitions of VFM, performance, operational and management auditing. In a business enterprise, the scope of a performance audit (management audit) may encompass all the activities of a division or a function that applies across a number of business units. The Australian National Audit Office (ANAO) defines a performance audit as:

> . . . an independent and systematic examination of an organisation, program or function for the purposes of:
>
> - forming an opinion about:
>   — whether the organisation, program or function is being managed in an economical, efficient and effective manner; and
>   — the adequacy of internal procedures for promoting and monitoring economy, efficiency and effectiveness; and
> - suggesting ways by which management practices, including procedures for monitoring performance, might be improved.

Auditing Standard AUS 806, Performance Auditing defines 'economy' (a resource acquisition concept) as the acquisition of financial, human, physical and information resources of appropriate quality and quantity at the lowest reasonable cost (e.g. bulk buying for cost reduction). Efficiency, on the other hand, is the use of a given set of resource inputs to maximise outputs; essentially, it is a resource use concept (e.g. minimisation of duplication of labour). Effectiveness focuses on the achievement of an intended outcome (e.g. a reduction in the incidence of work-related accidents). The auditor in a performance audit task provides a report on the extent to which predetermined goals have been achieved economically and efficiently.

Comprehensive auditing

Comprehensive auditing occurs when an auditor undertakes a range of audit and related services within an audit mandate for a client — a scenario that is more common in the public sector. A comprehensive audit encompasses the elements of a financial report audit, a compliance audit and a performance audit. It entails, for example:

- an independent examination of books and records for the purpose of expressing a positive opinion on financial reports;
- a communication of moderate to negative assurance concerning compliance with legal and regulatory matters;
- a statement on the adequacy of control of operations;
- the auditor's opinion on the economy, efficiency and effectiveness of the entity's performance based on certain objectives.

Environmental audit

Environmental matters may have an impact on the financial statements. Some examples of environmental matters affecting financial statement accruals, the impairment of assets, disclosures or the basis of preparation include:

- a pollution prevention system, of which the cost may be accrued for remediation costs;
- liability relating to transportation of, or contamination by, hazardous waste;
- the obsolescence of inventory due to environmental laws and regulations.

Auditors are required to carry out their audit with an attitude of professional skepticism, recognising that the audit may reveal conditions and events that would lead to questioning whether the entity is complying with relevant environmental laws and regulations. Auditing Guidance Statement AGS 1036, The Consideration of Environmental Matters in the Audit of a Financial Report (International Auditing Practice Statement IAPS 1010, The Consideration of Environmental Matters in the Audit of Financial Statements) lists factors that the auditor should consider when obtaining knowledge of the business and when identifying the risk and internal control structure in respect to environmental matters. The environmental audit is a recent trend and normally involves a review or an agreed-upon procedures engagement.

Internal audit

While the previous audit activities are classified according to the outcome of the activity, an **internal audit** merely refers to any of the above audit activities carried out by audit professionals who are employees of the entity being audited. Organisations use the internal audit as a management tool to enhance internal control. The role of an internal auditor varies. It may involve complex systems review, straightforward internal checking, intensive forensic investigations, internal appraisals of operations and financial planning or, in some cases, a financial report audit.

The independent auditor may be able to work with the internal auditor in some aspects of the work, where objectives are similar. Internal audit professionals are sometimes qualified accountants. The Institute of Internal Auditors, which was formed in the United States in 1941, operates in chapters worldwide. The Australian chapter was formed in 1986 and offers professional development services to its members.

With the growth of consultancy and audit-related services demanded by clients, independent audit firms have engaged themselves in internal audit tasks. The outsourcing of the internal audit function, whereby the expertise of an accounting firm is employed to carry out an audit-related assurance service of an internal audit nature, is a recent trend. We will discuss the topic further in Chapter 17.

Types of auditor

Individuals who are engaged to audit economic actions and events for individuals and legal entities are generally classified into three groups: independent auditors, internal auditors and **government auditors**.

Independent auditors

Independent auditors, frequently referred to as **external auditors**, are either individual practitioners or members of public accounting firms who render professional auditing services to clients. By virtue of their education, training and experience, independent auditors are qualified to perform each of the types of audit previously described. The clients of independent auditors may include profit-making business enterprises, not-for-profit organisations, government agencies and individuals.

Like members of the medical and legal professions, independent auditors work on a fee basis. There are similarities between the role of an independent auditor in a public accounting firm and that of a solicitor who is a member of a law firm. However, there is also a major difference — that is, the auditor is expected to be independent of the client in making an audit and reporting the results, whereas the solicitor is expected to be an advocate for the client in rendering legal services.

Audit independence involves both conceptual and technical considerations (see Chapter 2). It is enough to say at this point that an auditor, to be independent, should be without bias in respect of the client under audit and should appear to be objective to those relying on the results on the audit.

Only independent auditors registered with the ASIC through the Companies Auditors and Liquidators Disciplinary Board can perform the audit of reporting entities in Australia. The purpose of registration is to set minimum standards of competence, integrity and accountability. Various state Acts also stipulate that only a registered company auditor may audit real estate agents' trust accounts, solicitors' trust accounts, etc. The criteria for registration of auditors is stipulated in s.1280 of the Corporations Law, which prescribes that a person applying for registration must be:

- ordinarily resident in Australia;
- a member of the ICAA or CPA Australia or another approved body such as the Association of Chartered Certified Accountants (ACCA);
- a graduate or diplomate of a prescribed university or other prescribed institution in Australia who has passed the examinations in such subjects as the university or other institution certifies to the ASIC to represent a course of study in accountancy (including auditing) of not less than three years duration and in commercial law (including company law) of not less than two years duration, or who has other equivalent qualifications acceptable to the ASIC.

In addition, the person must have sufficient experience in auditing and must be a fit and proper person to be registered as an auditor.

A working party established by the Commonwealth Attorney-General to review the requirements for the registration and regulation of auditors has proposed that the accounting bodies take on the responsibility for registering and supervising auditors. It also recommends that the accounting bodies undertake investigation and disciplinary procedures for breaches of professional rules, including the breaches of Auditing Standards. Another suggestion is that the title 'Registered Independent Auditor' replace the current 'Registered Company Auditor' to reflect that auditing services are provided to a wider range of entities.

Internal auditors

Internal auditors are employees of the entities they audit. This type of auditor is involved in an independent appraisal activity (called internal auditing) within an organisation, as a service to the organisation. The objective of internal auditing is to assist the management of the organisation in the effective discharge of its responsibilities (see Chapter 17).

Government auditors

Government auditors are employed in the ANAO and the offices of the auditors-general of the Australian states and territories and various local authorities. The ANAO audits government departments, departmental commercial undertakings, statutory authorities, and Commonwealth-owned companies and their controlled entities. The federal auditor-general bears ultimate responsibility for the audit of the Australian Commonwealth public sector. As an external auditor, the federal auditor-general reports to the Commonwealth Parliament on the financial statements prepared by the federal Minister for Finance. The enabling Acts are the *Auditor-General Act 1997* (Cwlth), the *Commonwealth Authorities and Companies Act 1997* (Cwlth) and the *Financial Management and Accountability Act 1977* (Cwlth), the Corporations Law and other legislation under which the authorities have been established. The auditors-general of the Australian states and territories report to their respective parliaments on the financial operations of government departments and statutory bodies. By virtue of their office, the auditors-general are registered company auditors.

As noted previously, this text deals primarily with financial report audits performed by independent auditors practising as members of the public accounting profession. We will learn more about financial report audits in Chapter 4. For now, we will turn our attention to some important background information about the public accounting profession.

REGULATORY FRAMEWORK FOR ENSURING QUALITY SERVICES

LEARNING OBJECTIVE 9

Discuss the regulatory framework for ensuring quality services.

Every profession is concerned about the quality of its services, and the public accounting profession is no exception. Quality audits are essential to ensure that the profession meets its responsibilities to clients, to the general public and to regulators who rely on independent auditors to maintain the credibility of financial information. To help assure quality audits, the profession and the regulators have developed a multi-level regulatory framework. This framework encompasses many of the activities of the private and public sector organisations associated with the profession (described earlier in this chapter). For the purpose of describing the framework, these activities may be organised as follows:

- *Standard setting*: The AASB, the AARF (through its functional boards — the PSASB, the AuASB and the UIG), the IACC and CPA Australia establish standards for financial reporting, auditing, quality control and ethical practice (the Joint Code of Professional Conduct) to govern the conduct of accountants and practice entities.
- *Firm regulation*: Each public practice entity adopts policies and procedures to ensure that practising accountants adhere to professional standards.
- *Self- or peer regulation*: The accounting profession has implemented a comprehensive program of self-regulation (including mandatory continuing professional education) and a program of quality control and practice reviews.
- *Government regulation*: Only qualified professionals are licensed to practise, and the ASIC and the courts monitor and regulate auditor conduct.

Standard setting

In previous sections in this chapter we noted the role of the AASB and the AARF and its constituent boards in setting Standards for the various types of attest and nonattest services. The accounting bodies (the ICAA and CPA Australia) also establish rules of professional conduct for accountants (see Chapter 2). All these professional pronouncements provide guidance for individual practitioners who aspire to do high quality work for their employers and clients.

10 LEARNING OBJECTIVE

State the elements of quality control applicable to audits.

Quality control standards

The pursuit of quality practice must occur at the firm level as well as the individual level. To assist firms in achieving this goal, the ICAA and CPA Australia have made the following specific pronouncements relating to quality control standards:

- Miscellaneous Professional Statement APS 1, Conformity with Accounting Standards, which is a mandatory statement of responsibilities for members involved in the preparation, presentation or audit of financial reports;
- Miscellaneous Professional Statement APS 1.1, Conformity with Auditing Standards, which is an authority statement for the Australian Auditing Standards and the Auditing Guidance Statements. It establishes auditors' responsibilities in relation to compliance with Australian Auditing Standards;
- Miscellaneous Professional Statement APS 4, Statement of Quality Control Standard, which is a statement that includes ten elements of quality control that apply to a practice as a whole — namely, professional independence, the assignment of personnel to engagements, guidance and assistance, supervision, employment, professional development, promotion, client evaluation, inspection and review, and the allocation of administrative and technical responsibilities;
- Miscellaneous Professional Statement APS 5, Quality Control Policies and Procedures — General Guidelines, which is a statement that guides the establishment of policies and procedures for the elements of quality control stated in APS 4.

Other Miscellaneous Professional Statements are:

- APS 6, Statement of Taxation Standards;
- APS 7, Statement of Insolvency Standards;
- APS 8, Statement of Management Consulting Services Standards;
- APS 9, Statement of Compilation of Financial Reports.

These standards include the basic principles governing the professional responsibilities to be exercised by practices rendering services in those particular areas.

The quality of auditing services rendered by a firm depends on Auditing Standards for each engagement, and on quality control policies and procedures for the firm's auditing practice as a whole. The statement directly relevant to audit practice as a whole is Auditing Standard AUS 206 (International Standard on Auditing ISA 220), Quality Control for Audit Work.

This statement describes the elements of quality control relevant for individual audits, as well as general quality controls applicable to the audit practice as a whole. The general quality controls included in this statement are the policies and procedures that should, if adopted by a firm, provide reasonable assurance that all audits conducted by the firm are being carried out in accordance with the Auditing Standards. Seven quality control elements are identified in this statement. These controls and examples of related policies and procedures are shown in Table 1.2 on the next page.

TABLE 1.2 *Quality control — elements, policies and procedures*

Element	Policy	Procedures
Professional independence	Personnel in the firm are to adhere to the principles of independence, integrity, objectivity, confidentiality and professional behaviour.	Assign responsibility in the practice to provide guidance and to resolve questions on matters of integrity. Communicate to staff any policies and procedures relating to independence. Monitor compliance with policies and procedures relating to independence.
Employment	The firm is to be staffed by personnel who attain and maintain the technical standards and professional competence required to enable them to fulfil their responsibilities with due care.	Plan for personnel needs, establish hiring objectives, and determine requisite qualifications. Establish qualifications for evaluating potential personnel to be hired at each professional level. Establish guidelines and requirements for continuing professional education. Make available to personnel any information about new professional pronouncements. Establish the qualifications necessary for each level of responsibility in the firm.
Assignment of personnel	Audit work is to be assigned to personnel who have the degree of technical training and proficiency required in the circumstances.	Plan staff level requirements for the firm as a whole and for individual practice offices. Designate an appropriate person to assign personnel to audits. Provide for the auditor to approve the scheduling and staffing of the audit.
Supervision	There is to be sufficient direction, supervision and review of work at all levels to provide reasonable assurance that the work performed meets appropriate standards of quality.	Establish procedures for planning audits. Provide procedures for maintaining the firm's quality standards. Provide on-the-job training.
Guidance and assistance	Whenever necessary, consultation within or outside the audit firm is to occur with those who have appropriate expertise.	Identify areas and specialised situations where consultation is required. Inform personnel of the firm's consultation policies. Specify areas of expertise. Maintain access to adequate reference materials. Designate individuals as specialists for consultative processes. Specify the extent of documentation for the results of the consultation.
Client evaluation	Evaluate prospective clients and conduct a review on an ongoing basis of existing clients.	Establish criteria for evaluating prospective clients. Establish review procedures for continuing to service a client.
Allocation of administrative and technical responsibilities	Monitor the adequacy and effectiveness of quality control policies and procedures.	Define the scope and content of the monitoring program. Provide the findings of monitoring to appropriate management levels in the firm.

(Source: AUS 206)

The first element in Table 1.2 pertains to the performance of attest services only. We will discuss the rationale for (and rules pertaining to) independence at length in Chapter 2. The next five elements help assure quality in rendering professional services. The seventh element requires a periodic internal review to determine that the quality assurance program is functioning as intended.

Firm regulation

Firm regulation occurs within the public accounting firm. A prime example is implementing a system of quality control as mandated by quality control standards discussed in the preceding section. This means that the firm's day-to-day actions will comply with the policies and procedures pertaining to quality control elements. To assist staff in meeting professional standards, for example, firms generally provide on-the-job training and require their professionals to participate in continuing professional education courses. Personnel whose work is substandard should be counselled and, if rapid improvement is not forthcoming, their employment should be terminated. (Individuals who perform are rewarded.) Motivation also results from the desire to avoid the expense and damage to a firm's reputation that accompanies litigation and other actions brought against the firm for alleged non-compliance with professional standards. We will discuss auditors' exposure to litigation in Chapter 3.

Self-regulation

The ICAA and CPA Australia independently undertake quality assurance practice reviews. To continue to hold a Certificate of Public Practice, members have to demonstrate compliance with quality control standards. Members are obliged to give an annual signed assurance that the quality control requirements are being met. Reviewers appointed by the ICAA and CPA Australia visit all practices on a cyclical basis over five years. Reviews are based on the requirements of APS 4 and APS 5 as they affect the practice as a whole. Findings from the reviews are confidential. The reviewed practice is given an assessment by the reviewer. If findings are unsatisfactory, the practitioner is required to take remedial action and will be subject to further review within an agreed time frame. Serious deficiencies are dealt with through disciplinary procedures. The primary focus of practice reviews, or self-regulation, is educational.

Government regulation

The primary objective of government regulation is to protect the investing public from substandard financial reporting and auditing practice. It is basically punitive in nature. Government regulation is exercised through the ASIC. The ASIC has instituted an Accounts Examination Program which involves the scrutiny of all aspects of the financial statements of listed and some non-listed Australian public companies. The objective of this surveillance process is to ensure compliance with mandatory Accounting Standards. The ASIC's Accounts Examination Program is supplemented by an auditors' review program and a liquidators' review program. Where necessary, breaches in the Corporations Law by auditors and liquidators are referred to the Companies Auditors and Liquidators Disciplinary Board. This Board can cancel the registration of auditors under powers conferred by the Corporations Law, s.1292(1). The Board also monitors the minimum educational and experience requirements and the ethical and professional considerations relevant to the registration of auditors and liquidators.

A significant, additional regulatory mechanism occurs through the courts, whereby an accountant may face a lawsuit for negligence and incur costs and damages for failure to comply with the profession's standards of practice (see Chapter 3). All these forms of regulation are important. They are interrelated and aspire to the objective of improving the quality of audit practice. The following 'Professional environment' demonstrates the government regulatory system.

PROFESSIONAL ENVIRONMENT Examples of the ASIC's surveillance

In March 1999, the ASIC released the results of its surveillance of company financial reports for the 1998 calendar year. The reports of 180 listed public companies were examined, as well as matters arising from complaints received in the course of other ASIC activities. An area of particular concern was the lack of disclosure of plans and progress on the Year 2000 issue and non-compliance with new disclosure requirements in relation to financial instruments. Other areas of non-compliance were those requirements pertaining to the acquisition of assets, events occurring after the balance sheet date, and corporate governance issues.

In terms of AASB 1015, Accounting for the Acquisition of Assets, the ASIC has encountered various cases of auditors accounting for the liability for restructuring costs of the acquiring entity in the determination of goodwill, rather than treating the costs as an expense. A well publicised example of ASIC's work in this area was when St George Bank agreed to write down the goodwill recognised in its acquisition of Advance Bank to comply with the Standard.

Another significant issue is the recording of acquisitions on the basis of legal form rather than the substance of the transactions. An example is the artificial breaking down of acquisition transactions into separate transactions separated by a short period of time such that the consideration for the acquisition appears to be less and the goodwill on an acquisition is minimised. These events have subsequently led to the Senate's disallowance of the Standard.

On AASB 1024, Consolidated Accounts, the ASIC found cases of entities recording the profits of newly acquired entities prior to the date of obtaining control. Overstating goodwill is also a concern. There were also cases where profit was misstated owing to events that were recorded that did not relate to conditions that existed at the end of the prior period. Moreover, 24 per cent of the listed companies' annual reports did not include the corporate governance statements required by the ASX Listing Rules.

LEARNING CHECK

1.6 The latest legislation, the CLERPA, reinforces the importance of the duties of directors and corporate governance, and of compliance with Accounting Standards in financial reports.

1.7 Auditors are engaged to carry out a variety of tasks: attest services involve providing an opinion on written assertions (audit, review and agreed-upon procedures), while nonattest services are all other types of professional advisory service that require the expertise and competence of the auditor or accountant.

1.8 The different types of audit include the financial report audit, the compliance audit, the performance audit, the comprehensive audit and the environmental audit. Internal audit refers to all types of audit activity carried out by internal employees of the organisation.

1.9 Independent auditors are those auditors who practise audit and other services for the public, and who are independent of the auditees. Internal auditors are employees of the organisations who are appointed to carry out certain types of audit or review function within the organisation. Government auditors are employees of the government who are employed to carry out different types of public sector audit.

1.10 Regulatory controls exist within firms; in the profession's own regulatory procedures for memberships, standards, behaviour and quality; and through government bodies such as the ASIC.

SUMMARY

In this chapter, we provided an overview of the auditing and the professional environment. Audit practice has evolved over the past century from a relatively straightforward activity of checking books and accounts, to a dynamic role of enhancing the credibility of financial information. The development of audit practice was described as a change from the traditional conformance role to a role that adds value to the financial reporting and relating functions of organisations. In this chapter we also demonstrated a shift in public expectations of the auditor's role. Examples of this shift are: auditors' broader approach in audits, based on risks and business processes; the changing perceptions of audit independence; and the legislative development concerning auditors' liability.

As the market becomes more sophisticated, so too do the information needs of users. The expertise and competence of auditors are sought for a variety of financial services, requiring the auditors to give different levels of assurance. The traditional conformance role of auditing is no longer seen to be relevant, and auditors are now involved in providing a wider range of professional assurance services, aiming to add value to their clients' functions. The Elliott Report on the assurance framework generally established a broad framework for the role of auditing, while the IAPC issued its first ISAE to provide a general framework for assurance services.

Alongside the changes discussed above, we noted developments within the audit profession. We described the current types of professional service being offered and the different constituencies that have an impact on the development of professional standards and practices. On the legislative front, the Corporate Law Economic Reform Program also brought about changes, notably in respect of the duties of directors and corporate governance issues. It can be argued that proper governance and quality are the key driving forces for the development of the profession and the regulatory framework for professional standards. Here, we set the scene for you to appreciate better the fast developing role of audit and assurance services in organisations.

KEY TERMS

Agreed-upon procedure engagement, p. 16
Assertion, p. 11
Attest service, p. 16
Attestation, p. 13
Audit assurance, p. 11
Audit independence, p. 19
Auditing, p. 6
Auditor liability, p. 18
Big Five, p. 23
Compliance audit, p. 31
Comprehensive auditing, p. 32
Conformance role, p. 6
Corporate governance, p. 13
Credibility, p. 10
Environmental audit, p. 30
External auditors, p. 33
Financial report audit, p. 30
Government auditors, p. 33
Internal audit, p. 32
Nonattest service, p. 29
Performance audit, p. 31
Reasonable care and skill, p. 7
Review engagement, p. 15
Risk assessment, p. 19

NOTES

1. L. R. Dicksee, *Auditing: A Practical Manual for Auditors*. Gee and Co., London, 1892.
2. R. H. Montgomery, *Auditing Theory and Practice*, 3rd edn. Ronald Press, New York, 1912.
3. D. R. Carmaichael, 'The Assurance Function — Auditing at the Crossroads', *Journal of Accountancy* (September 1974), pp. 64–72.
4. E. J. Silverman, 'Practitioner's Forum: Why Have an Audit?', *Journal of Accountancy* (April 1971), pp. 80–1.
5. M. Power, 'From Common Sense to Expertise: Reflections on the Prehistory of Audit Sampling', *Accounting, Organisations and Society* (1992), pp. 37–62.
6. Joni J. Young, 'Defining Auditors' Responsibilities', *Accounting Historians Journal* (Vol. 24, No. 2, December 1997), pp. 3–4.
7. R. I. Miller & M. R. Young, 'Financial Reporting and Risk Management in the 21st Century', *Fordham Law Review* (April 1997), pp. 1–5.
8. P. Schelluch & G. Gay, 'Assurance Services and the Profession', *Communique* (October 1997), p. 4.
9. M. W. Uzumeri & R. H. Tabor, 'Emerging Management Metastandards: Opportunities for Expanded Attest Services', *Accounting Horizons* (Vol. 11, No. 1, March 1997), pp. 54–66.
10. Coopers & Lybrand, *Manual of Auditing*, 4th edn. 1984, p. 2. The detection of errors and defalcations was said to be the secondary objective of an audit, not the primary objective.
11. T. Bell, F. Marrs, I. Solomon & H. Thomas, *Auditing Organisations through a Strategic Systems Lens: The KPMG Business Measurement Process*. KPMG Peat Marwick LLP, Illinois, 1997.
12. This quote was taken from the 'Foreword' to the research monograph cited in Note 10. William R. Kinney Jr (Charles and Elizabeth Prothro Regents Chair in Business and Price Waterhouse Auditing Fellow, Graduate School of Business, University of Texas, Austin) made the comment about the new scope of work involved in financial statement audits as a result of changes in information technology and the extensive acceptance of non-financial dimensions of business reporting.
13. Steven M. H. Wallman, 'The Future of Accounting, Part III: Reliability and Auditor Independence', *Accounting Horizons* (Vol. 110, No. 4, 1997), pp. 76–97.
14. This is a snapshot summarised from articles from the *Australian Financial Review* and the *Age* concerning audit independence. The Chairman of the Securities and Exchange Commission, Arthur Levitt, issued a ruling on audit independence ordering audit firms to discontinue the provision of consulting services to their audit clients. This ruling has an impact on the Big Five operations in Australia, and the implications of similar regulatory treatment are issues that face the profession in Australia. To further complicate the issues, the ASIC and Deloitte Touche Tohmatsu entered a settlement on 2 November 2000 concerning a range of audit matters, including audit independence standards to be observed by the firm. This was reported in an ASIC media release on 2 November 2000 and commented on by Tom Ravlic on 7 November in the 'Business comment' column of the *Age*.
15. Details sourced from CPA Australia, *Annual Report 1997*. Melbourne, 1998, and the CPA web site http://www.cpaonline.com.au.
16. Details sourced from the ICAA web site http://www.icaa.org.au.
17. T. Thomas, 'Auditors and Consultants Blur the Edges of Objectivity', *Business Review Weekly* (27 April 1998), pp. 122–6.

FURTHER READING

CPA Australia, *Annual Report*. Melbourne, 1999.

Committee on Basic Auditing Concepts, *A Statement of Basic Auditing Concepts*. American Accounting Association, Florida, 1973.

Institute of Chartered Accountants in Australia, *Annual Report*. Sydney, 1999.

Institute of Chartered Accountants in Australia and CPA Australia, *Auditing Handbook 2000*. Prentice Hall, Sydney, 2000.

Institute of Chartered Accountants in Australia and the Australian Society of Certified Practising Accountants (now CPA Australia), *Report of the Joint Assurance Services Task Force*, Sydney, 1997.

International Federation of Accountants and the International Auditing Practices Committee, *Understanding Financial Statements: A Guide for Financial Statements Users*. New York, 1990.

Review questions

1.1 What were some of the reasons for the shift in the audit paradigm discussed in this chapter?

1.2 What factors contributed to the expansion of roles undertaken by professional accountants and auditors?

1.3 How does the expanded role of professional accountants affect the accounting profession?

1.4 Describe the three main levels of audit service described in AUS 106 (ISA 120). What is the most common service? Why? How does AUS 106 differ from the new Assurance Engagement Standard ISAE?

1.5 What is the influence of the two accountancy bodies in setting standards and regulating professional activities in light of the Corporate Law Economic Reform Program Act 1999?

1.6 What role does the ASIC have in the regulation of auditors?

1.7 What are the six types of audit activity that an auditor may perform? Discuss.

1.8 What are the different types of nonattest service? Comment on the growth of these services by comparing the Big Five with other smaller firms.

1.9 How does the profession/government ensure that external company audits are performed at an appropriate level of quality?

Discussion questions

1.1 Lindley LJ used the following sentence in the 1895 London and General Bank case. How would you describe the relevance of the auditor's role in present times?

> His business is to ascertain and state the true financial position of the company at the time of the audit, and his duty is confined to that ...

1.2 Auditing Standard AUS 104 defines an audit as a service where the auditor's objective is to provide a high level of assurance. How does the auditor achieve that objective?

(continued)

1.3 What are the limitations, if any, of a financial report audit?

1.4 What are the difference(s) between 'positive assurance' and 'negative assurance'?

1.5 As discussed on page 10, the enhancing role of auditors has developed in respect of the integrity of financial information and its usefulness in decision-making by management and other users. What are your views concerning the role described, with particular reference to the appearance of audit independence?

1.6 What are the objectives and achievements of the Corporate Law Economic Review Program?

1.7 What is the effectiveness of the monitoring role of the ASIC? Discuss your views on its work.

1.8 What is meant by a comprehensive audit? Should a comprehensive audit be carried out by an independent auditor?

1.9 What are the differences between firm regulation and the self-regulation of the accounting profession?

1.10 What is the impact of technology on the evolving role of auditors? Discuss.

Professional application questions

★ BASIC
★★ MODERATE
★★★ CHALLENGING

1.1 (Audit objectives) ★

You have obtained employment in the accounting firm of Dickens and Partners as an audit assistant. You have heard that the firm is not very modern in its approach. On your first day at work, Mr Dickens, an audit partner, calls you into his office and hands you a copy of *Auditing: A Practical Manual for Auditors* by Lawrence Dicksee, published by Gee and Co. of London in 1892. The partner proudly claims, 'This is the Bible of auditing'. You open the book (after blowing the dust off the cover) and read the following statement on page 7:

> ... The detection of fraud is a most important portion of the auditor's duties. Auditors, therefore, should assiduously cultivate this branch of their activities.

You discussed this with your former classmate, Michael Fung, who was recruited into one of the Big Five accounting firms as a trainee in its business advisory service section. Michael chuckled and said, 'We don't do that old fashioned stuff'.

Required

Discuss the current changes in the objectives of auditing, identifying the expanded roles of professional accountants and some of the reasons attributable to the changes.

1.2 (Independence) ★

Independence has always been a fundamental aspect of the accountancy profession. As stated in the Joint Code of Professional Conduct, 'A member in public practice shall be, and be seen to be, free of any interest which might detract from integrity and objectivity in each professional assignment undertaken'.

Required

Discuss why independence is such an important attribute for an auditor.

1.3 (Standard setting) ★

Auditors perform audit attestation to enhance the credibility of the financial statements. However, it is quite impossible for the auditors to provide an absolute assurance regarding the subject matter on which they express their opinion.

Required

(a) Comment on an auditor's ability and methods in attesting the credibility of financial statements prepared by the governing party of an organisation.
(b) Explain what type of assurance an auditor should provide in a financial report audit.

1.4 (Regulatory framework) ★

The accounting profession's commitment to achieving high quality in rendering professional services is demonstrated by the breadth and effectiveness of its multi-level regulatory framework.

Required

(a) One component of this framework is standard setting, which occurs primarily in the private sector. Identify the types of standard included in this component, along with the private sector bodies that establish them.
(b) Identify and briefly describe the other three components of the regulatory framework.

1.5 (Organisations associated with the profession) ★

Several private and public sector organisations are associated with the public accounting profession. Listed below are activities pertaining to these organisations:

1. Issue certificates of public practice to members.
2. Promulgate Accounting Standards and Statements of Accounting Concepts.
3. Promulgate Auditing Standards and Audit Guidance Statements.
4. Regulate the distribution and trading of securities offered for public sale.
5. Establish a code of professional ethics.
6. Impose mandatory continuing education on members.
7. Issue statements of Auditing Standards.
8. Take punitive action against an independent auditor.
9. Establish accounting principles for state and local government entities.
10. Establish quality control standards for audit work.
11. Undertake investigation of perceived breaches of the Corporations Law.
12. Provide timely guidance on urgent financial reporting issues.

Required

Indicate the organisation(s) associated with each activity.

1.6 (Types of audit and auditor) ★★

After performing an audit, the auditor determines the following facts:

1. The Department of Transport is in violation of an established government employment practice.
2. The supervisor is not carrying out the responsibilities that have been assigned.
3. A company's tax return does not conform with tax regulations.
4. The accounts clerk has not been stealing from the company.
5. A company's receiving department is inefficient.
6. The company's financial statement presents a true and fair view.
7. The company has an adequate provision to fill the mine pit at the expiration of the lease term.
8. Controls over the sales invoicing system are operating effectively.

(*continued*)

9. A department is not meeting the company's prescribed policies concerning overtime work.
10. The tax office is complying with government regulations, and its financial statements are stated fairly.

Required

(a) Indicate for each of the above ten determinations the type of audit that is involved: (1) financial, (2) compliance, (3) performance, (4) comprehensive, (5) environmental or (6) internal.

(b) Identify the type of auditor that is most likely to be involved: (1) independent, (2) internal or (3) government.

1.7 (Independent auditors and internal auditors) ★★

You are the audit partner of a firm of professional accountants. The managing director of one of your audit clients has requested a meeting with you. He says that he is not happy with the amount of money being spent on his internal audit function and would like to eliminate it. He says that there does not seem to be much point in keeping the internal audit staff because the company has an external audit performed each year. In his view, because internal auditing is not compulsory (unlike external audits), it is the one to go!

Required

(a) Write a memo to the managing director explaining the differences between the two types of audit.

(b) Explain whether the managing director should disband the internal audit function.

1.8 (Types of audit activity) ★★

You are planning the financial report audit of DKYN Fashions Limited. Your firm has recently completed a performance audit of the company's system of banking and receipt of cash. The partner of your accounting firm suggests that you should not perform any work in that area when completing the statutory audit because adequate work has been performed during the performance audit. He tells you to photocopy the performance audit working papers and insert them in the 'Cash' section of the financial report audit file.

Required

Explain whether you agree with your audit partner on this issue, and why. Explain how a performance audit differs from a statutory audit.

Case studies

1.1 (Regulatory framework) ★★★

Fred is an enthusiastic young auditor working for a large accounting firm. On his first assignment he discovers there is a discrepancy between the bank deposit slips and the cash receipt details for the company. On his return to the office, he mentions this to the audit partner. The partner tells Fred that it is not worth following up because it is not material — the majority of sales are on credit. Fred does not agree and believes that there are some deficiencies in the Australian Auditing Standards if they suggest that he should not follow up this matter.

Fred does some research and finds that a new Standard on fraud (SAS 82) has been released in the United States. Based on his research, Fred believes it is a better approach than the Australian Auditing Standard AUS 210. He decides to suggest that the Australian Standard be amended. The following is a summary of the US Standard Fred found.

SAS 82 — February 1997

The new Standard articulates the independent auditor's responsibility — that is, to plan and perform the audit to obtain reasonable assurance about whether the financial statements are free of material misstatement, whether caused by error or fraud.

The AICPA's Auditing Standards Board has issued the new standard to enhance auditor performance and to provide auditors with additional operational guidance on the consideration of material fraud in conducting a financial statement audit. Specifically, the Standard describes two types of fraud — fraudulent financial reporting and misappropriation of assets — that are relevant to the auditor's consideration of fraud in a financial statement audit.

The Standard requires the auditor to specifically assess the risk of material misstatement due to fraud on every audit and provides categories of fraud risk factors that the auditor should consider in making that assessment. It provides examples of fraud risk factors that might, when present, indicate the presence of fraud. It also:

- provides guidance on how the auditor responds to the results of the assessment;
- provides guidance on the evaluation of test results as they relate to the risk of material misstatements due to fraud;
- requires the auditor to document risk factors identified as present and any related response.

Required

(a) If it was found that the fraud was material, explain what regulatory problems would face the audit partner.

(b) Discuss the main differences between AUS 210 and SAS 82.

(c) Outline what procedures Fred would follow and what organisations he would need to contact to attempt to achieve these changes (as suggested in SAS 82) to AUS 210.

1.2 (Quality control and ethics) ★★★

Mr Skate is one of the partners of a small firm of public accountants. He is responsible for the audits within the firm. He received a phone call from the managing director of Slick Software Limited, Ms Jones, who said that her company would like an audit performed within a month because the company's bank required audited financial statements. She offered Mr Skate a fixed fee, plus a bonus if the audit was completed within a month. Mr Skate immediately accepted the assignment.

On returning to the office, Mr Skate realised that all of his audit staff were unavailable for the next month. Knowing that the tax section of the firm was quiet, he requested the services of a tax graduate for the next month. The partner in the tax section allowed him to use a young graduate, Thomas, who had been working with the firm for three months and had never performed an audit.

Mr Skate called Thomas into his office and spent an hour briefing him on the fundamental principles of auditing. He explained that he required the audit to be completed on time and that he did not want Thomas wasting time testing controls. Mr Skate said Thomas was to perform a detailed analytical review and, from those results, substantiate unusual balances — this would be the main part of the audit.

After three weeks, Thomas returned to the office and gave Mr Skate the financial statements (without notes or a directors' statement). Mr Skate gave the figures a careful review and, when he was satisfied they appeared reasonable, signed the audit report.

Required

(a) Explain whether Mr Skate breached any of the quality control guidelines outlined in AUS 206 (ISA 220).

(b) Describe any ethical issues raised in this case study.

chapter 2

Professional ethics and conduct

Overview

LEARNING OBJECTIVES

After studying this chapter, you should be able to:

1. explain the role of a professional accountant
2. state the objectives and implications of professional ethics for accountants
3. explain the key principles of the Joint Code of Professional Conduct
4. identify the key principles and rules of professional independence
5. state the importance of audit quality and the standards for technical competence
6. discuss auditors' responsibilities for fraud, irregularities and illegal acts
7. explain the current audit environment affecting the auditor's ethical behaviour
8. discuss the implications of and recommendations for bridging the audit expectation gap
9. explain the concept of corporate governance as it relates to auditors
10. describe the essential disciplinary measures for auditors.

Professional statements

AUSTRALIAN		INTERNATIONAL	
US 206	Quality Control for Audit Work	ISA 220	Quality Control for Audit Work
AUS 210	Irregularities, Including Fraud, Other Illegal Acts and Errors	ISA 240	Fraud and Error
Joint Code of Professional Conduct		Code of Ethics for Professional Accountants (also proposed changes, June 2000)	
APS 1	Conformity with Accounting Standards and UIG Consensus Views		
APS 1.1	Conformity with Auditing Standards		
APS 2	Engagement Letters to Clients		
APS 4	Statement of Quality Control Standard		
APS 5	Quality Control Policies and Procedures — General Guidelines		
APS 6	Statement of Taxation Standards		
APS 7	Statement of Insolvency Standards		
APS 8	Statement of Management Consulting Services Standards		
APS 9	Statement of Compilation of Financial Reports		
APS 10	Client Money and the Maintenance and Audit of a Member's Trust Account		
AUP 32	Audit Independence		

Note: See 'Further reading' for details of the most pertinent parts of the codes.

One of the distinguishing characteristics of any profession is the existence of a code of professional conduct or ethics for its members. In Chapter 1, we noted that CPA Australia and the Institute of Chartered Accountants in Australia (ICAA) have established a Joint Code of Professional Conduct. We also noted that the regulatory activities under the Code make up an important part of the profession's multi-level regulatory framework and are significant in addressing the issue of the **audit expectation gap**.

However, ethical behaviour requires consideration of more than just a few regulatory activities and rules of conduct. No professional code of ethics or regulatory framework can anticipate all the situations for which a personal judgement on ethical behaviour is required. Accordingly, we will begin this chapter with a brief discussion of the role of professional accountants. We will then examine the profession's code of ethics, with an emphasis on the organisation of a public accounting practice.

Given its significance, professional **independence** is treated as a stand-alone topic, considered separately from the rules of ethical conduct. To understand the significance of the ethical values of accountants, we will discuss the key principles of the Joint Code of Professional Conduct and the main elements in the ethics environment. We will also highlight some of the implementation by CPA Australia and the ICAA of the recommendations of the Australian Working Party on Bridging the Audit Expectation Gap (including providing an overview of corporate governance). The chapter concludes with a discussion of the ethics enforcement procedures (such as investigation and discipline), quality assurance and the auditor's duty in respect to **irregularities**.

Students should study this chapter in conjunction with the detailed provisions of the Joint Code of Professional Conduct; only key principles of **professional ethics** are covered in this chapter. For the purpose of understanding professional ethics and conduct, the term 'professional accountants' includes auditors and the term 'professional independence' includes the concept of audit independence (unless otherwise stated).

THE ROLE OF A PROFESSIONAL ACCOUNTANT

1 LEARNING OBJECTIVE
Explain the role of a professional accountant.

This section describes the role of an accountant in society as a professional and an individual. Firstly, we will discuss the concept of a profession to identify some characteristics and skills that differentiate professionals from non-professionals, and to provide a context for understanding the role of a professional accountant. The fiduciary relationships involved in the performance of professional services (accounting, auditing and assurance) are examined, with the altruistic purpose of benefiting society as a whole. In this section we will further discuss accountants' duties and examine the significance of the ethical values raised.

The concept of a profession

A lot has been written about the professionalism of accountants.[1] To distinguish professional occupations from those that are not, Greenwood[2] outlines five attributes of a profession: (1) a systematic body of theory, (2) authority, (3) community sanction, (4) ethical codes and (5) a culture. Greenwood stresses, however, that the true difference between a professional and a non-professional is not a qualitative difference but a quantitative one, because non-professionals also possess these five attributes to a lesser degree. The various occupations in society can be said to distribute themselves along a continuum, with the well organised and undisputed professions at one end, displaying these identified attributes to the maximum extent.

The skills that characterise a profession flow from, and are supported by, a body of knowledge which has been organised into systematic theories or propositions that underpin and rationalise complex operations. Preparation for a profession requires not only intellectual cultivation, but also practical experience. This preparation takes the form of formal education in an academic setting. In Australia, accounting degrees are accredited by the two professional accounting bodies and satisfy the body of knowledge required for the profession to discharge its social role. However, society in general is subordinate to a professional's expertise, providing the professional with a monopoly of judgement and authority in specific spheres. This means the professional is subject to only peer scrutiny.

The professional authority expresses itself in the client–professional relationship, although there are ramifications. A profession strives to obtain community sanction within certain spheres in the form of a series of powers and privileges, reinforced from time to time by the community's regulatory power. The powers and privileges sanctioned by the community include the profession's control over its accrediting process, its control over its licensing system, and the privileges of confidentiality and a relative immunity from community judgement on technical matters. The profession continues to assure society of its benefits, to maintain its authority and monopoly. A profession's benefit to society is demonstrated by its superior performance in fulfilling a highly competent and sophisticated role in the society.

The monopoly enjoyed by a profession vis-a-vis its clients and the community is fraught with hazards; for example, a monopoly may be abused as a result of self-interest. To counter the hazards, a profession normally has a built-in regulatory code to compel ethical behaviour on the part of its members. A profession's ethical code is partly formal and partly informal. The formal part is the written code by which the individual usually swears to abide on admission to the profession. Through its ethical code, the profession's commitment to social welfare becomes a matter of **public interest**, thereby helping to ensure the continued confidence of society. **Self-regulatory** codes are characteristic of all occupations. However, a professional code is more explicit, systematic and binding; it possesses altruistic overtones and is more public-service oriented. The specifics of ethical codes are generally described in terms of both client–professional and colleague–colleague relations. Also, a profession generally enforces observation of its ethical code through controlling measures designed to engender self-discipline. Professional associations exercise these controls.

Every profession operates through a network of formal and informal groups. The formal groups include the organisations within which the profession performs its services (e.g. the professional firms), the organisations that supply the talent and expand the body of knowledge (e.g. the universities and research centres), and the professional bodies that emerge as a focus of common interests and aims. The informal groups are all the other affiliations, selective and specific subgroups and units to which the professional is attached. The interactions of social roles required by these formal and informal groups generate a social configuration unique to the profession — namely, a professional culture. A professional culture distinguishes itself from a non-professional culture through its values, norms and symbols of practice. The professional value is the belief that the profession provides a service to society as a social good which benefits the community. The norms of a professional group form for its members both guides to behaviour in social situations and role definitions. The controlling values, behavioural norms and symbols of practice distinguish the profession from non-professional occupations.

The concept of a profession thus evolves around the above five elements. In relation to this concept, Brooks[3] identifies the duties of a profession as including the maintenance of (1) competence in the field of expertise and knowledge, (2) integrity in client dealings,

(3) objectivity in the offering of services, (4) confidentiality in client matters and (5) discipline over members who do not discharge these duties according to public expectations. These duties are vital to the quality of service provided by the professional in maintaining a proper fiduciary relationship with clients. The client, in turn, trusts or relies on the professional's judgement and expertise. The maintenance of such trust or credibility inherent in the fiduciary relationship is fundamental to the role of a professional person.

The duties of a professional accountant

The credibility of an accountant's services is founded on the values, norms and symbols displayed by accountants in the performance of their duties. Such duties involve not only the exercise of competence in the technical aspects of financial services, but also, more importantly, integrity and objectivity in discharging these services.

Consistent with Greenwood's proposition, the accounting profession has features that accord with each of the five attributes he identified. It has an established body of knowledge in financial theories and conceptual framework; it has organised bodies to exercise its authority in the discharge of services to the public; it maintains community sanction concerning its control over membership and accreditation; it constitutes a self-regulatory framework through its pronouncements and ethical codes; and it attains a high image in society through its professional culture. A professional accountant, whether engaged in auditing or management, or as an employee or a consultant, is expected to be both an accountant and a professional. That means professional accountants are expected to have special technical expertise associated with accounting and an understanding of related fields (such as law, management, economics, taxation, information technology, systems development and quantitative methods) that exceeds that of the lay person. In addition, they are expected to adhere to the general professional duties and values described above, as well as to those specific standards established by the professional body to which they belong. Sometimes an isolated deviation from these expected norms can result in a lack of credibility for, or confidence in, the entire profession. In the past decade or so, the spate of corporate collapses and the considerable number of allegations made against accountants (and auditors) have resulted in a credibility crisis for the profession, triggering public inquiries into the affairs of the profession in general. Such was the case with the Treadway Commission[4] in the United States, the Macdonald Commission[5] in Canada, and the inquiries concerning the audit expectation gap in both these countries and Australia. (We will further discuss the audit expectation gap later in the chapter.)

Brooks considers that the accounting profession has the duties, rights and values detailed below — each of which is also attributable to a professional accountant.

- Duties to sustain a fiduciary relationship:
  - displaying behaviour that espouses responsible values;
  - paying continual attention to the requirements of clients and other stakeholders;
  - acquiring and maintaining the required skills and knowledge;
  - maintaining a credible reputation for the profession;
  - maintaining an acceptable personal reputation.
- Rights allowed:
  - represent oneself as a professional;
  - be involved in the development of accounting and audit practice;
  - establish entrance standards and examine candidates;
  - require self-regulation and discipline of members of the profession based on specified codes of conduct;
  - have access to certain or all areas of accounting and auditing activity.

- Values required to carry out duties and maintain rights:
  - — honesty;
  - — integrity;
  - — wish to exercise due care;
  - — objectivity;
  - — confidentiality;
  - — competence;
  - — a commitment to put the needs of the public, the client, the profession and the employer ahead of any self-interest.

PROFESSIONAL ETHICS AND THE ACCOUNTANT

2 LEARNING OBJECTIVE

State the objectives and implications of professional ethics for accountants.

Ethics is concerned with the evaluation of choices where the options are not clear or where there is no absolute right or wrong answer. The study and practice of ethics is important to enable an accountant to examine critically a situation in which there is a conflict of loyalties and interests, involving issues that relate to roles and responsibilities, both as an individual and a professional. Minz[6] goes one step further in his perception of ethics. He sees it as a system or code of conduct based on moral duties and obligations that include how one should behave; this code deals with the ability to distinguish right from wrong and the commitment to do what is right. He also defines professionalism as the conduct, aims or qualities that characterise a professional person. The fundamental ethical characteristics required of professional accountants are competence, objectivity and integrity. While professional ethics may largely refer to the written code of ethics put forward by a professional body, the practice of ethical behaviour requires (1) an understanding of ethical issues, (2) a framework within which a responsible decision can be made, and (3) an awareness of the consequences of such decisions.

The nature of ethics

The word 'ethics' is derived from the Greek word *ethos*, meaning 'character'. While morality focuses on the 'good' and 'bad' of human behaviour, ethics focuses on what is 'right' and 'wrong', and how and why people act in a certain manner. It focuses on a study of choices, standards and behaviour.

Ethics entails a number of moral philosophies or normative ethical theories, including the following:

- ***Deontology***: This doctrine holds that actions and motivations are inspired by a sense of moral obligation, such as duty, justice, rights and fairness.
- *Egoism*: This doctrine holds that all behaviour is ultimately directed by individual self-interest.
- *Relativism*: This theory posits that all judgements are relative and that they vary according to circumstances and different individuals.
- ***Teleology***: This doctrine holds that actions are seen as right or wrong only in terms of their ability to bring about desired ends. What matters is the consequence, not the intention.
- ***Utilitarianism***: This doctrine holds that actions should be directed towards providing the greatest good for the greatest number of people.

Moral philosophy refers to the set of principles that individuals use to decide what is right or wrong. These philosophies present some guidelines for resolving conflicts and optimising the mutual benefit of individuals in a group. Businesspeople are guided by various moral philosophies as they formulate business strategies and resolve ethical issues, but they do not necessarily use the same philosophy to do so. Some of the principles discussed earlier are specifically relevant to accountants; for example, the concept of professionals serving the public interest, the rights and duties of auditors and shareholders, and some of the realisation concepts in accounting can be said to correspond to utilitarianism, deontology and teleology respectively.

Individuals develop their ethical beliefs through a complex process of socialisation in formal and informal groups such as the family, schools, universities, clubs, etc. These are moral communities which have their own values, rules and norms. The moral knowledge acquired while in these communities tends to be intuitive and, as a result, individuals may display inconsistent ethical behaviour and make different decisions under different circumstances. Ethics provides a framework of beliefs and a reasoned and systematic analysis of decisions to help individuals acquire the skills and insights necessary for ethical decision-making.

The new CA Program of the ICAA[7] (to be effective from 2001) includes a CA Foundation module. The CA Foundation module is structured around a framework that enables graduates not only to develop essential competencies in business strategy and information management, but also to appreciate their role in the profession and demonstrate a comprehensive understanding of the importance of ethics as it applies to the professional activities of a chartered accountant. Incorporating the ICAA's former Ethics Professional Year (PY) Programme, the CA Foundation module emphasises the responsibilities of a professional accountant and the demands of a diverse role. It also covers the application of ethics to professional activities, and focuses on the significance of ethical decision-making.

CPA Australia has also embarked on a new CPA program, with a foundation unit that centres on ethics, professionalism and corporate governance. In addition to various normative ethical theories and cognitive concepts, this foundation unit — 'Reporting and professional practice' — encompasses the relationship between the accountant's role and the application of ethics and judgement, both in the professional and corporate environments. Both bodies offer a much broader knowledge base in their professional programs than previously offered, in order to address the expanding role of an accountant and its increasing complexity. In particular, both bodies regard ethics as the underpinning for well founded decisions and responsible behaviour. Thus, ethical decision-making models take an important part in these educational programs.

Ethical decision-making models are systematic procedures designed to help individuals to arrive at well informed and ethical decisions under different circumstances. Where individuals face an ethical problem or dilemma, such models will assist them to address issues such as duties, consequences and priorities, and to assess alternative actions. The professional programs have introduced different decision-making models or tools. The most commonly used model is that by Rockness and Langenderfer, which is also known as the AAA (American Accounting Association) model.[8] This model accounts for the facts of the matter, the values and principles that one has to consider, evaluating issues relating to the matter against one's values and principles, identifying alternative courses of action, and responsibly making the decision that aligns with the most important value.

Professional ethics for accountants

Professional ethics extend beyond principles. They include standards of behaviour for a professional person that are designed for both practical and idealistic purposes. As outlined in the 'Introduction' (A1) to the Joint Code of Professional Conduct, professional ethics for accountants refer to the objectives of the accountancy profession to work to the highest standards of professionalism, to attain the highest levels of performance and, generally, to meet the public interest requirement. A professional accountant acts as both a responsible individual and a professional person who is bound to operate within a set of professional norms and values. A professional code of ethics may be designed, in part, to encourage ideal behaviour and it must be both realistic and enforceable.

The Joint Code of Professional Conduct of the ICAA and CPA Australia identifies four basic needs to be met by the profession:

1. There is a need for credibility in the information systems.
2. The professional needs to demonstrate professionalism that distinguishes him or her from non-professionals.
3. There is a need for assurance that all services provided by a professional accountant are carried out to the highest degree of competence and standards of performance.
4. Users of professional services should be confident that a framework of professional ethics exists which governs the quality and delivery of such services.

3 LEARNING OBJECTIVE

Explain the key principles of the Joint Code of Professional Conduct.

The Joint Code of Professional Conduct

The Joint Code of Professional Conduct is designed to provide accountants with authoritative guidance on minimum acceptable standards of professional conduct. It deals with essential matters of principle and is not to be taken as a definitive statement on all matters. It stresses that members of the profession should be guided not merely by the terms of the Code, but also by its spirit. Compliance with its provisions is mandatory for all accountants who are members, their affiliates and registered graduates of the two bodies. Non-compliance can lead to disciplinary proceedings. The main issues covered in the Code include (1) the fundamental principles of professional conduct applicable to all members, (2) matters applicable to all members and (3) matters applicable to those in public practice. The Code also stipulates how statements, by-laws and so on are applicable, and includes a number of professional statements.

Fundamental principles of professional conduct applicable to all members

The fundamental principles of professional conduct applicable to members of the accounting profession are described below:

- *The public interest*: Members must at all times safeguard the interests of their clients and employers, provided that those interests do not conflict with their duties and loyalties owed to the community and its laws.
- *Integrity*: Members must be straightforward, honest and sincere in their approach to professional work.
- *Objectivity*: Members must be fair and must not allow prejudice, conflict of interest or bias to override their objectivity. When reporting on financial statements that come under their review, they must maintain an impartial attitude.
- *Independence*: Members must be, and should be seen to be, free of any interest that may be regarded, whatever its actual effect, as being incompatible with integrity and objectivity. Professional Statement 1 elaborates the norms for independence.
- *Confidentiality*: Members must respect the confidentiality of information acquired in the course of their work and must not disclose any such information to a third party without specific authority, unless there is a legal or professional duty to disclose it. Professional Statement 5 gives guidance on this issue.
- *Technical and professional standards*: Members must carry out their professional work in accordance with the technical and professional standards relevant to the work.

- *Competence and due care*: Members must perform professional services with due care, competence and diligence. A member has a continuing duty to maintain professional knowledge and skill to a level required to ensure that a client or employer receives the advantage of a competent professional service based on up-to-date developments in practice, legislation and techniques. Professional accountants should refrain from performing any services that they are not competent to carry out, unless they obtain advice and assistance to ensure the services are performed satisfactorily.
- *Ethical behaviour*: Members must conduct themselves in a manner consistent with the good reputation of their profession and refrain from any conduct that may bring discredit to their profession. A distinguishing feature of a profession is acceptance of its responsibility to the public. The notion of safeguarding the public interest is paramount to ethical conduct.

Matters applicable to all members

Section C of the Code refers to matters that are applicable to all members and that are scenarios that accountants (especially those in employment) will encounter. If a member performs some services in a foreign country, for example, then the code of professional ethics issued by the International Federation of Accountants (IFAC) applies whenever the local standard is seen to be less strict. An employed accountant is prohibited from providing public practice services in his or her own name for an employer that is not a public practice entity, or undertaking legal work similar to that of a legal practitioner. Accountants have a duty to maintain an adequate level of competence throughout their career and must take care in signing confidentiality agreements.

Matters applicable to those in public practice

Section D of the Code deals with matters that are mainly applicable to all members in public accounting practice. These matters are addressed so as to assure clients of the quality, objectivity and integrity of the service provided by members and member firms of the professional accountancy bodies. Some matters dealt with in this section include the following.

Professional fees

Fees must reflect fairly and equitably the value of work performed, accounting for the skill and knowledge required for the type of work, the level of training and the experience of the personnel necessarily engaged, the degree of responsibility applicable, and the time required by all persons engaged on the work. Before undertaking an assignment, the accountant must advise the client of the basis on which fees are charged and clearly define the billing arrangement. An accountant is not allowed to make a representation that specific professional services in future periods will be performed for either a stated fee, an estimated fee or a fee range if, at the time of the representation, such fees will be (or are likely to be) substantially increased. The client should also be informed in writing if the accountant is provided with an agency fee or a commission earned from a third party. An accountant must not enter into a **contingency fee** arrangement for professional services requiring independence and objectivity; however, members may charge a client a fee for advisory services and/or may receive commissions from third parties for advisory services provided to a client. Full disclosure should be made to the client regarding the form of arrangement, the identity of the third party, the method of calculating of the agency fee or commission, and any other benefit directly or indirectly provided to the member.

Professional appointments

Professional appointments are governed by professional etiquette such as communicating with the outgoing accountant before accepting an appointment, and accepting referrals without impairing the position of others. Also, members of the profession may advertise or seek publicity for their services provided that the content or nature of such advertising is not false, misleading or deceptive. Soliciting of professional work is allowed; however, accountants in public practice must ensure that communications are terminated if so requested by the recipient.

Other matters also require members to comply with certain prescriptive procedures so as to ensure quality and objectivity. These include keeping records for clients' monies held in trust by the accountant and not engaging in incompatible businesses while providing professional services.

4 LEARNING OBJECTIVE

Identify the key principles and rules of professional independence.

PROFESSIONAL INDEPENDENCE

Independence is the cornerstone of the auditing profession. Ethical situations exist when accountants are faced with situations in which they may compromise their professional integrity in response to outside pressures. An auditor may be pressured by management to compromise his or her objectivity in deciding on an accounting policy, for example, or an accountant may be instructed by a superior to amend financial statements so as to show a profitable return. Many of the ethical situations faced by accountants and auditors involve professional judgement, objectivity and independence.

Without independence, the auditor's opinion is suspect. In relation to auditing and other attestation services, independence has two facets — the fact of independence (also called actual independence) and the appearance of independence (also called perceived independence). The fact of independence depends on the auditor's integrity, objectivity and strength of character, which are defined as follows:

- *Integrity* implies the observance of accepted standards of honesty which must underpin all professional decisions and actions.
- *Objectivity* implies that a fair and impartial attitude must be maintained, with bias not being allowed to influence one's judgement.
- *Strength of character* refers to one's ability to withstand pressure and maintain one's integrity and objectivity.

The greatest potential threat to the independence of the auditor is the auditor's relationship with the directors. Directors' remuneration, the value of the shares they hold and even their position within the company may all depend on the financial performance of the company. The opinion of the auditor is vital to the credibility of financial reports. Recognising this connection, directors may seek to influence the auditor. Without the strength of character to withstand such pressure, the auditor may be unable to express an independent opinion.

The fact of auditor independence is not always readily visible to those relying on the auditor's opinion; situations in which a reasonable person might consider the auditor's independence to be impaired have been criticised in the past. To ensure independence is more visible, the Joint Code of Professional Conduct's Professional Statement F1 on Professional Independence and Auditing Practice Statement AUP 32, Audit Independence stipulate principles, rules and guidelines that emphasise the need for the appearance of independence.

Rules of independence

Professional Statement F1 on Professional Independence prescribes both the principles of professional independence and the rules for reporting, client relationships and dealing with other conflicts. Professional independence is fundamental to the accounting profession. It requires accountants both to be persons of integrity and to adopt an objective approach to their professional work.

The key principles of professional independence are that:

- accountants in public practice must both be, and be seen to be, free of any interest that is incompatible with objectivity. The criterion is whether a reasonable person, having knowledge of the relevant facts and accounting for the conduct of an accountant and his or her behaviour under the circumstances, could conclude that the accountant had placed himself or herself in a position in which objectivity would or could be impaired;
- an accountant not in public practice has a duty to be objective in carrying out professional work, whether or not the appearance of professional independence is attainable. Accountants performing professional work in commerce, industry and public service must recognise the problems created by personal relationships or financial involvements that may threaten (by reason of their nature or degree) their objectivity.

The rules cover the following situations with respect to audit or other professional services provided to clients: prohibited financial interests, incompatible duties and other conflicts.

Prohibited financial interests

Prohibited financial interests include:

- having an interest in the shares of a client, whether beneficially or as trustee or nominee, which is material either to the equity capital of the client or to the assets of the individual (or trust);
- accepting, making or guaranteeing loans from or to clients except at arm's length in the ordinary course of the client's business, and then with due regard to the outward appearance of the transaction;
- accepting commissions that could impair professional independence;
- accepting goods or services on favourable terms or conditions;
- accepting hospitality or gifts on a scale not commensurate with normal social courtesies.

These prohibitions also extend (except for the acceptance of commissions) to near relatives, who are defined as the spouse and any relative financially dependent on either the person in the practice or the spouse.

Incompatible duties

The following stipulations apply in respect to incompatible duties:

- No partner or employee of an audit practice shall be an officer of an audit client (for example, the company secretary).
- No partner or employee shall be a director of a company that exerts a significant influence over an audit client.
- Any partner or employee who used to be associated with an audit client in such a way as to impair his or her independence (for example, as an officer or in a commercial relationship) shall not personally be involved in the audit of that client for a financial period commencing within a year of the severance of the association.

Other conflicts

Other conflicts can arise that may impair the auditor's independence. These may involve:

- the practice or a member of the practice in conflict with a client; or
- clients in conflict with each other.

The practice may be a tenant of an audit client, for example, and a dispute may arise over the terms of the lease. Alternatively, two clients may be in dispute over royalty payments. In either case, the client may feel uncomfortable about the auditor having access to information relating to both sides of the dispute, and may fear that the auditor's independence or objectivity will be impaired. In such situations, the client should be advised of the conflict and the auditor's position in regard to it. Where a client wishes to continue the professional relationship, the auditor must be satisfied that it is possible to do so without prejudice to the interests of the client or the objectivity of the audit.

Conflict may also arise over the provision of both audit and **non-audit services** to the same client, particularly the provision of management consultancy services. There has been much debate about whether auditors should provide management consultancy services to audit clients; however, it is now generally accepted that the two services are an integral part of the practice of public accounting, and that their forcible separation would impair the efficiency of both. The auditor has substantial knowledge of an entity's business, which facilitates the provision of management consultancy services. Furthermore, evidence suggests that economies are obtained by using one accounting firm to provide all these services.[9] Recognising this reality, the rules of independence require that a practice must avoid becoming involved in executive decision-making on behalf of an audit client when it is providing management consultancy services. It is not sufficient that the management consultancy services are provided by a different department or different members of the firm or practice.

Guidelines

Professional Statement F1 on Professional Independence also includes advisory guidelines on the following matters: fees, personal and business relationships, and the preparation of books. The fact that these matters have been addressed in terms of guidelines rather than rules reflects the complexity of the issues and the difficulty of framing workable rules. In no way does it suggest that these issues are of only secondary importance.

Fees

Public accountants depend on fees for their livelihood, so a practice could conceivably be reluctant to displease an audit client — by qualifying the audit report, for example — for fear of losing income. This argument is especially pertinent if the audit practice depends on the client for a significant proportion of its fee revenue. The guidelines, while refraining from quoting the commonly regarded benchmark that no more than 15 per cent of fees should be obtained from the one client, nevertheless advise firms to be aware of the possible effects on apparent objectivity of one client (or group of connected clients) providing a substantial part of the practice's gross revenue, or one client being significant to a partner's position within a firm. It is recommended, in such instances, that adequate quality control procedures be implemented, including an involvement by a review partner or the adoption of some form of consultative process and independent review of audit decisions.

Personal and business relationships

By its very nature, an audit brings members of the accounting practice into close contact with management and employees of clients over a period of years. Cordial relationships are usually desirable and facilitate the effective conduct of the audit. The guidelines use, as an example, the effect on independence of the establishment of a mutual business interest between audit practice employees and client employees; but, in the context of independence, the mere existence of a cordial relationship is of equal concern because it could adversely influence an auditor's judgement when he or she is confronted with evidence of a fraud.

To overcome this problem, some practices rotate audit staff among engagements every few years. Another option is to rotate audits among firms; however, the high initial cost of taking on a new audit client means mandatory audit rotation is not widely favoured.

One method of enhancing auditor independence with respect to both fee dependence and personal relationships is to establish **audit committees** of non-executive directors. We will consider the role and functions of audit committees later in this chapter (see page 77).

Preparation of books

It is common practice for auditors to provide a compilation service — that is, to keep the books and prepare the financial statements for smaller audit clients. In such cases, clients must be made aware that they accept full responsibility for the books, and care must be taken to ensure that the write-up work does not require anyone in the practice to make executive decisions on behalf of the client. Audit firms may adopt the practice of not involving personnel in the audit function if they have kept books and prepared the financial statements of an audit client. Except in exceptional circumstances, as permitted by the rules, write-up services should not be provided for public company audit clients.

Statutory provisions enhancing auditors' independence

As we indicated in Chapter 1, statutory law recognises the need for audit independence. As with the Joint Code of Professional Conduct, these statutory provisions establish an appearance of auditor independence.

The Corporations Law provides that companies have the power, in general, to appoint (s.327) or remove (s.329) auditors. Directors may appoint the first auditor and fill casual vacancies, but such appointments are in force only until the conclusion of the next annual general meeting of members. This is intended to protect the auditor from intimidation by the directors.

Section 331 of the Corporations Law entitles the auditor to reasonable fees. Disclosure of these is required in the published accounts. Theoretically, the shareholders have the power to set fees, but negotiations are usually delegated to the directors. Low fees could be an indication of '**low-balling**' to gain market share. Conversely, high fees could be an extraction of quasi-rent as a result of incumbency.

The statutory rights and responsibilities of the auditor, embodied in several provisions of the Corporations Law, are intended also to allow the auditor's independence of action in the conduct of the audit. These provisions relate to:

- access to accounting records (s.310);
- the right to information and explanations from the company and its controlled entities (s.310).

Section 1289 affords qualified privilege to an auditor if he or she makes a statement, orally or in writing, in the course of his or her duties as auditor.

There are also statutory provisions which make certain categories of people ineligible for appointment as auditors on the grounds that they lack independence. In accordance with s.324(1), a person is ineligible for appointment as a company's auditor if he or she is:

- an officer of the company;
- a partner, employer or employee of an officer of the company;
- a partner or employee of an employee of an officer of the company;
- indebted to the company or related corporation for more than $5000 or holding a substantial interest (as defined in s.708) in a corporation that is so indebted. An exception is when the debt is incurred in the company's ordinary course of business for the acquisition of the auditor's principal place of residence.

Fear of losing an audit client in the event of a disagreement with management stems largely from an awareness that management (and not those to whom the audit report is addressed and by whom the auditor appointment is ostensibly made) exerts the strongest influence on the choice of auditor. In companies, this situation arises because few members actually attend general meetings of the company. Furthermore, most of the votes cast at such meetings are proxy votes held by directors, and these proxy votes usually represent only a fraction of the company's issued share capital. Naturally, the directors must approve all resolutions that the board has put on the agenda, including resolutions as to a change of auditor.

Shareholders need to be apprised of any serious matters affecting their interests vis-a-vis those of management in the event of a proposed change of auditor before abrogating their voting rights on such a proposal. To this end, the Corporations Law (s.329(3)) affords some protection. When there is a motion before a general meeting for the replacement of the auditor, that company is required, if the auditor so requests, to circulate to all shareholders a statement by the auditor as to why he or she should not be replaced. The auditor also has the right to be heard at the general meeting.

The Corporations Law, s.329(4) and (6), requires any auditor proposing to resign to seek approval of the Australian Securities and Investment Commission (ASIC). The application to the ASIC should detail reasons for the resignation and any disagreements with the company. As a matter of policy, the ASIC will not consent to the auditor's application if it considers that the auditor is being pressured by management and that his or her independence is being threatened. The ASIC is also unlikely to agree to the auditor's resignation if it is mid-audit or if the scope of the auditor's work is being limited by management's refusal to provide adequate information and explanations.

These procedures are designed to protect the auditor's independence and the interests of the shareholders.

The independence debate

Professional accountants in public practice are increasingly being asked to provide assurance on different types of information, including non-financial information. This could threaten their independence. In early 2000, Arthur Levitt, chairman of the Securities and Exchange Commission of the United States, made a speech entitled 'Renewing the Covenant with Investors' at New York University. While recognising the broad reorganisations of some large accounting firms which, according to Levitt, were designed to monetise the firms' consulting businesses, he reiterated the fundamental concept that the public must perceive the accountant as independent if investors are to maintain their confidence in the quality of the audit. Levitt lamented the emerging culture of 'gamesmanship' in which short-term expectations dominate the public interest. He pledged for a full plan of action to address the apparent loss of professional independence. He recommended:

- that the profession should seek to establish 'broad principles' of independence, make greater public disclosure of the types and amounts of service offered by the professional firms, or prohibit the firms from engaging in professional services considered inconsistent with an independent public audit;
- a request to the Public Oversight Board (which is an entity engaged with the oversight of the profession) to undertake a special review of firms' compliance with the Securities and Exchange Commission and professional independence rules.

The Securities and Exchange Commission ordered the split between the consulting and audit arms of professional accounting firms, because firms were perceived to have violated the rules of independence by being engaged in many different types of professional activity with their clients, including financial interests. Levitt also called for a new independence framework for accountants.

The IFAC issued an exposure draft on independence in June 2000, with an invitation to comment until 15 September 2000. The IFAC's proposed changes on independence in the Code of Ethics for Professional Accountants encompass the following:

- The redefinition of the reporting accountant accounts for those ultimately responsible for the outcome of the assurance engagement, along with those who supervise the assurance engagement, have direct management responsibility for the assurance engagement or provide technical consultation, quality control or other oversight of partners and staff in the assurance engagement.
- A different approach to independence is proposed in a framework describing the factors that could threaten a reporting accountant's independence and the safeguards that can be implemented to preserve that independence.
- Instead of a list of prohibitions, specific cases and suggestions for how to minimise the risk to independence are presented.
- The scope of professional independence covered by the proposed exposure draft deals with professional accountants in public practice, which includes auditors. Definitions used in the exposure draft are based on the expanded roles of accountants; for example, the entity is described as the assurance client, while professional services engagements are included in assurance engagement. Furthermore, 'close relative' and 'immediate family' are defined.
- The exposure draft makes it clear that national laws on independence are not superceded and that the reporting accountant should comply with both national and IFAC guidelines.
- The following definition for 'independence' is proposed:

> Independence of a reporting accountant is: (a) the state of mind that permits the provision of an opinion without being affected by influences that impair professional judgement (sometimes referred to as independence of mind), and (b) the ability to demonstrate that risks to independence of mind have been eliminated or limited to such clearly insignificant matters that an informed third party would not reasonably question the reporting accountant's objectivity (sometimes referred to as independence of appearance).

It is not certain how much of the above recommendations will be adopted in Australia; on the other hand, both professional bodies in Australia are members of the IFAC, which makes it clear that its amendment to the Code will be enforceable in its member bodies in the world. The approach undertaken by the Securities and Exchange Commission has rekindled academic and professional discussions on independence, calling for further research. An example is given in the following 'Professional environment' (page 61) in which the concept is reviewed.

While the independence debate continues, professional firms continue to develop. During the past five years or so, the Big Five have defined their niche in a broad range of assurance and consulting services, while a large number of medium-sized and smaller firms have evolved into consolidated practices to strengthen their competitiveness. On the other hand, there is the development of multidisciplinary practices where, for example, lawyers are brought into a practising accounting firm to provide added service to clients. Thus, the debate on professional independence encompasses approaches to maintaining credibility through impartiality, as well as the ability of accountants to add value as a business partner to clients. In Chapter 18 we will review this contemporary phenomenon in more detail.

PROFESSIONAL ENVIRONMENT Independence — the US approach

A number of factors have given a distinct economic advantage to large practice units that, in turn, have raised questions regarding the utility of existing independence Standards. The SEC (Securities and Exchange Commission) has recognised the need for reassessment of those Standards through its involvement in the creation of the Independence Standards Board (ISB).

The... growth of the Big Five, particularly in consulting services, prompted American Express and other commercial organisations to acquire accounting practices with the aim of developing a national accounting practice to sell a broad range of business and tax consulting services to mid-sized businesses ...

The ISB has identified two possible approaches to providing financial statement users with confidence as to an auditor's independence. The first approach is to require the disclosure of all relationships with the client enterprise that might be felt to impair the auditor's independence and to let the user assess how much reliance it is willing to place upon the auditor's report.

Through this process, if the client feels that financial statement users might be reluctant to rely on the auditor's report, it could simply insist upon the elimination of the condition or retain an audit firm that does not have the relationship that is causing an independence question. The advantage of this approach is that it does not require that the threshold for impairing independence be determined in advance and out of context. The problem is that it may require a lot of detailed disclosure, which would obscure more than clarify.

The second approach is to create a series of requirements for independence that are generally known to the public and simply have the audit firm attest that it has met those requirements. This is the system currently in use, and it has the advantage of not miring the financial statement user in a sea of secondary disclosure ... [T]he problem with this approach is that it requires that criteria for determining independence be established in advance ... In short, the independence rules make no allowance for a firm's hard-earned reputation for honesty and integrity or for its well honed internal quality control systems.

The [American Institute of Certified Public Accountants] has proposed a variation on this approach under which each audit firm would be authorised to establish its own rules for safeguarding auditor independence, rules which would be established under ISB guidelines and would be subject to advance review and periodic compliance checks ...

Even after the ISB decides upon an approach to safeguarding audit independence, it must still develop standards addressing the wide variety of consulting services being provided to other clients and the nontraditional firm structures being used by American Express and other consolidators. It is difficult, at best, to assess the overall impact of consulting services on the independence of an accounting firm.

There is a natural tendency to believe an auditor cannot be wholly objective in assessing financial data of a company that her firm has advised on ways to improve efficiency or profitability. No objective evidence, however, exists to support this hypothesis and there is no evidence that the number or percentage of audit failures increases where such services have been performed. Perhaps equally important, the public has shown no reluctance to rely on the financial statements of companies whose auditors perform such services. ...

To be sure, there are many trade-offs suggesting that the performance of consulting services has an overall positive impact. These trade-offs include the audit firm's greater understanding of the client's operations and accounting systems; profitability, which enables it to hire more qualified individuals and provide those individuals with better training and supervision; and exposure to the client's management, which enables it to better assess the integrity of management and the economic pressures placed upon it. ...

Because of these concerns, a more flexible approach to independence would seem to be called for; one which is capable of focusing on the class of services being provided, the extent to which those services might affect the client's operations or the audit firm's objectivity, and the presence of other factors that might mitigate any such adverse effects.

The current 'all or nothing' approach to audit independence seems rigid and inappropriate.

(Source: Extracted from Dan L. Goldwasser, 'Is it Possible to Achieve? Independence in a Changing Accounting Profession', *CPA Journal* (Vol. 69, No. 10, 1999), pp. 46–51)

LEARNING OBJECTIVE 5

State the importance of audit quality and the standards for technical competence.

AUDIT QUALITY

Discharging responsibilities with due professional care and adequate competence in the public interest is a characteristic of a professional person. When auditors face pressures (from management or time constraints), the audit quality may be compromised. In this section we will examine a number of proposals intended to improve both the quality of audit services and the public's perception of that quality. Matters considered are (1) quality reviews of audit practices, (2) proposed improvements to the quality standards that were introduced in Chapter 1, (3) arrangements for setting Auditing and Accounting Standards, and (4) arrangements for monitoring alleged departures from Accounting Standards. We will conclude by considering the debate about whether it is appropriate for the accounting profession to regulate the performance of its members or whether this role should be entrusted to an independent body.

Technical standards

The professional accountant must comply with various Accounting Standards, Auditing Standards and those relating to specific professional services covered by a range of Miscellaneous Professional Statements (specifically APS 1, 1.1, 2 and 4–10 — see page 35 for further details). Non-compliance represents unacceptable professional conduct.

Accounting concepts and Standards

APS 1.10, Client Money and the Maintenance and Audit of a Member's Trust Account imposes the following requirement:

> ... that in the context of the preparation and presentation of a general purpose financial report for a reporting entity or where an entity which is not a reporting entity elects to prepare a general purpose financial report, application of the standards set out in Accounting Standards is mandatory as are the Consensus Views set out in UIG Abstracts.

Additionally, those responsible for preparing and presenting auditing reports (i.e. management) must take all reasonable steps within their power to ensure that the Accounting Standards and Urgent Issues Group (UIG) Consensus Views are consistently applied and that any departures (together with the reasons for departure, and the financial effects) are properly disclosed and explained in the general purpose financial report.

Similarly, auditors are required to take all reasonable steps within their power to ensure compliance with Accounting Standards and UIG Consensus Views or otherwise issue a qualified audit opinion. Members can refer to the Statements of Accounting Concepts for guidance if no Accounting Standard deals with an accounting treatment or a disclosure issue. Compliance with APS 1, Conformity with Accounting Standards and UIG Consensus Views is mandatory, however, for members of either professional body.

Auditing Standards and Auditing Guidance Statements

Compliance with Auditing Standards is required of members of CPA Australia and the ICAA when performing an audit or an audit-related service. Auditing Guidance Statements do not have the same status as Auditing Standards.

Standards for taxation, insolvency and management consulting services

Standards for taxation, insolvency and management consulting services, which are also mandatory for members, are not directly relevant to the provision of auditing services except insofar as they assist in maintaining the reputation and standing of the profession. It is pertinent, however, that their subject matter is closely related to the fundamental concepts of independence, objectivity, integrity and competence. The following paragraphs from APS 6, Statement of Taxation Standards emphasise this relationship:

> A member shall not associate himself with any arrangement which involves documents or accounting entries that are intended to misrepresent the true nature of a transaction or which depend upon lack of disclosure for its effectiveness.
>
> A member shall not promote, or assist in the promotion of, any schemes or arrangements which have no commercial justification other than the avoidance of tax through exploitation of the revenue laws.

Compliance with Standards

Although Accounting Standards are now being developed within the framework of the Statements of Accounting Concepts, there is no generally agreed **conceptual framework for auditing**. This has led to the accusation that Auditing Standards tend to codify rather than lead practice, such that auditing is what auditors do, rather than what users require. This point was made in the Pacific Acceptance case, in which the auditors were found to have been negligent, despite having followed accepted practices of the day. Research is needed to design a framework that supports the development of more effective Auditing Standards.

Auditing Standards are currently set by the Auditing and Assurance Standards Board (AuASB) of the Australian Accounting Research Foundation (AARF). In the United Kingdom, the Auditing Practices Board was reconstituted in 1991 to include equal numbers of practitioners and non-practitioners, and was given the authority to set standards in its own name without the need to obtain approval from the professional bodies. Such a development could enhance public confidence in the Auditing Standard setting process in Australia.

The quality of an audit performed on a general purpose financial report is constrained by the quality of financial reporting standards. To demonstrate the independence and objectivity of the Standard setting process for accounting, it has been recommended that the Australian Accounting Standards Board (AASB) be appointed, funded and overseen by an independent overseeing board.[10] This would bring Australian practice into line with that in the United States and the United Kingdom, and remove concern that Accounting Standards were unduly influenced by accounting firms and their corporate clients. This recommendation was implemented through the 1999 Corporate Law Economic Reform Program (explained in Chapter 1).

One of the complaints against auditors is that they tolerate accounting practices that are not specifically prohibited by Accounting Standards, even though they may be inconsistent with the spirit underlying the concept of fair presentation. Such practices are often referred to as 'creative accounting'. Groups such as the Australian Stock Exchange, the ASIC and the Accounting Practices Group of the ICAA have mounted surveillance activities. The Australian Commonwealth Government is still reviewing the various initiatives. One proposition — that this surveillance be transferred to a single **financial reporting review panel**, as was done successfully in the United Kingdom — was still under consideration when this textbook went to print. Such a panel would liaise with (1) the AASB and the UIG on setting Accounting Standards to eliminate undesirable practices, and (2) the professional bodies when the work of a registered auditor or principal financial officer fails to meet professional standards.

Quality assurance

The ASIC's auditor surveillance program has identified four categories of audit deficiency: two relate to the performance of the audit and two relate to the opinion. The deficiencies in the audit performance are (1) the tendency to accept management's representations without adequate verification and (2) the inadequate documentation of audit work. The reporting deficiencies are (1) the failure to report any departures from Accounting Standards and (2) the uncritical acceptance of questionable accounting practices.[11]

In Chapter 1 we explained the current provision for ensuring the quality of audit work performed — notably, the requirements of APS 4, Statement of Quality Control Standard; APS 5, Quality Control Policies and Procedures — General Guidelines; and Auditing Standard AUS 206 (International Auditing Standard ISA 220), Quality Control for Audit Work. The **quality assurance programs** of the professional bodies monitor compliance with these standards.

Quality control Standards

The Australian Working Party on the Audit Expectation Gap[12] made three suggestions for improving quality within a firm. Firstly, although many firms already appoint a **review partner** (or a **concurring partner**) on each audit engagement, Auditing Standards should require this practice. Both the engagement and review partner should sign the audit report. Secondly, no partner should be responsible for the audit of an entity for longer than seven years, whether as the engagement or concurring partner. This is considered to be a sufficient period to overcome the initial cost of the learning curve on undertaking a new assignment. If the partner is engaged for longer, he or she may either become complacent or so familiar with the entity's management that his or her objectivity and professional scepticism may become impaired. Finally, each firm should establish an overseeing body, similar to an audit committee, to monitor its quality control practices. In 1997, the Task Force which reviewed the recommendations of the Australian Working Party recommended merging the accounting bodies' quality review programs into one program, so as to facilitate administration, method, training and marketing.

FRAUD AND ILLEGAL ACTS

In its early days, the primary objective of the independent audit was the detection of fraud and error; now, the primary objective is to determine whether the financial report is presented fairly in accordance with Accounting Standards, and whether the financial report provides reasonable assurance that it is free of material misstatement. Nevertheless, surveys of users find that many still believe **fraud** detection is the primary objective of the audit. This belief even extends to fraud that is not material to the financial report as a whole.

The Institute of Chartered Accountants of Scotland identified several users' expectations regarding audit assurance. The Institute found that user expectations are excessive, with the general public tending to regard an unqualified opinion as a clean bill of health for a company. Public expectations tend to be that:

- there has been no fraud;
- the company has acted within the law;
- they (the auditors) will be responsible for reporting to a third party if they suspect that the directors are involved in fraud or other **illegal acts**.

In this section we will explain the current responsibilities of auditors for the detection and reporting of fraud and illegal acts as laid down by Auditing Standards. We will consider the argument that the profession is not doing enough to meet user expectations, and will discuss suggestions for reducing the expectation gap by reducing the incidence of fraud and improving the profession's detection and reporting procedures.

LEARNING OBJECTIVE

Discuss auditors' responsibilities for fraud, irregularities and illegal acts.

Current responsibilities for detecting and reporting irregularities

Irregularities comprise:
- fraud, which is any act involving the use of deception to obtain an illegal advantage;
- other illegal acts that involve non-compliance with laws and regulations;
- other acts that contravene the constitution of an entity;
- intentional but not fraudulent or illegal misstatements;
- **errors**, which are unintentional mistakes.

Paragraph 7 of Auditing Standard AUS 210, Irregularities Including Fraud, Other Illegal Acts and Errors provides the following examples of irregularities:
- manipulation, falsification, forgery or alteration of records or documents;
- suppression or omission of the effects of transactions from records or documents;
- recording of transactions without substance;
- intentional false accounting or misapplication of accounting policies;
- misappropriation of assets;
- non-compliance with legislation such as the Corporations Law and associated regulations;
- non-compliance with other legislation or regulations (for example, equal employment opportunity, occupational health and safety, and environmental protection legislation).

The distinction between errors and other irregularities is one of intent. This is not always easy to determine, especially in matters involving judgement. AUS 210.06 provides the following examples of errors:
- arithmetical, data entry, programming and clerical mistakes in the underlying records and accounting data;
- oversight or misinterpretation of facts;
- unintentional misapplication of accounting policies and disclosure requirements.

An error is accidental and the individual responsible for the error neither expects nor realises any personal gain. In contrast, a fraudulent or other illegal act is premeditated and the perpetrator usually hopes to achieve personal gain or some specific objective. Whether an irregularity is a fraudulent or other illegal act is a matter for the courts to determine. With the advancement of technology and electronic commercial transactions, auditors' responsibilities regarding fraudulent activities are complex and will be covered in more detail in Chapter 18. The auditor's primary concern is with suspected rather than proven fraud or other illegal acts.

Prevention and detection of irregularities

The prevention and detection of fraud and error is primarily the responsibility of management. Auditors also have a professional duty under AUS 210 (ISA 240) to plan and conduct an audit in such a way that there is a reasonable expectation of detecting material misstatements arising from irregularities. This assurance will be obtained through the use of audit procedures as required by Auditing Standards. This duty is not the same as a duty to discover all material irregularities. It means that auditors, in planning and executing an audit program, should be aware of the possibility of irregularities.

When auditors believe that material irregularities exist, they should extend the scope of their examination to either dispel their beliefs or determine that the irregularity has been corrected or properly reflected in the financial report. Consequently, the use of an unqualified opinion on a financial report implicitly means, in the auditor's opinion, that the financial report is not materially misstated as a result of irregularities.

However, an examination in accordance with Auditing Standards cannot guarantee the detection of all material irregularities because an audit involves only the selective testing of transactions and balances. It is possible, therefore, that any fraud or error might not have been a part of the evidence examined. In particular, the perpetrators of fraudulent and other illegal acts are likely to have taken steps (such as forgery or collusion) to conceal the evidence of their acts from auditors and others. Whether it should have been detected will depend on the auditor's adherence to Auditing Standards and the adequacy of the auditing procedures undertaken in the circumstances.

AUS 210 (ISA 240) identifies conditions or events that increase the risk of fraud or error as being (1) doubt as to the integrity or competence of management, (2) unusual pressures within an entity, (3) unusual transactions and (4) problems in obtaining sufficient appropriate audit evidence. Three examples of each condition or event are provided in Table 2.1, although there are many others.

TABLE 2.1 *Examples of conditions or events that increase the risk of irregularities*

Category	Examples
Integrity or competence of management	• One person (or a small group) dominates management and there is no effective overseeing board or committee. • There is a continuing failure to operate key controls or to attend to major weaknesses in the internal control structure that are able to be corrected. • There are frequent changes in key accounting and financial personnel and in legal counsel and auditors.
Unusual pressures within an entity	• Declining profits or rapid expansion have caused an inadequacy in working capital. • The entity has a significant investment in an industry or product line that is noted for changing quickly. • Accounting personnel are pressured to complete the financial reports in an unusually short time period.
Market pressures	• The industry is declining and failures are increasing. • The industry is subject to specific or complex legislation. • The industry is volatile, with numerous corporate takeovers or mergers.
Unusual occurrences and/or transactions	• Unusual transactions occur, especially near the balance date, that have a significant effect on profit. • Payments for services (e.g. payments to lawyers) appear excessive. • There is evidence of falsified documents.
Unsatisfactory records and/or problems in obtaining sufficient appropriate audit evidence	• Accounting records are inadequate (e.g. incomplete files, excessive adjustments to accounts). • Documentation of transactions is inadequate (e.g. lack of proper authorisation, alteration to documents). • There are an excessive number of differences between accounting records and third party confirmations, conflicting audit evidence, and inexplicable changes in operating ratios.

(Source: AUS 210, Appendix 2 — adapted extract)

Management fraud

During an examination, the auditors will not assume that management is either dishonest or honest, but will apply professional scepticism in planning and performing the audit. In particular, it should not be forgotten that management can render the system of internal control ineffective in three ways:

- by overriding controls that would prevent similar fraud by other employees;
- by directing subordinates to record transactions incorrectly or to conceal them;
- by suppressing information about transactions.

The 1999 KPMG Fraud Survey[13] identified that $239 million ($104 million in 1997) had been lost through fraud, with the majority of fraud perpetuated internally (21 per cent by management and 57 per cent by non-management employees). Management overriding controls was the largest single factor attributed to the occurrence of fraud. Other factors were poor internal controls and collusion between the employees and third parties. Fraud perpetuated by management included, in descending order of frequency, purchases for personal use, conflicts of interest, misuses of expense accounts, kickbacks, unnecessary purchases, false financial statements, credit card fraud and the diversion of sales and information. Computer-related crime was experienced by 12 per cent of the 1800 respondents, with a total reported loss of over $16 million. Also, more than $14 million was reported lost as a result of international fraud.

The 1999–2000 Ernst & Young's International Fraud Survey[14] endorses the view that computer-related fraud is the greatest concern of all respondents. Computer-related fraud includes the manipulation of data records held on a computer to disguise the true nature of transactions (a concern of 98 per cent of respondents), hacking into an organisation's system to manipulate records (94 per cent), manipulation of computer programs (96 per cent), personal use of an organisation's hardware or software (91 per cent) and unauthorised electronic transfer of funds (95 per cent). Sixty-five per cent of Australian respondents had suffered fraud in the twelve months prior to the survey, with just over one in ten suffering more than fifty frauds. Twenty-seven per cent of Australian bankers surveyed had suffered more than fifty frauds in the twelve-month period, compared with the international survey average of just 14 per cent. The single worst fraud suffered by all Australian respondents during the twelve months was an estimated loss of $20 million. The auditor should consult with the client's management about fraud control and the assessment of inherent fraud risks and internal control risks.

The auditor should take note of anything that indicates that management's good faith cannot be relied on — for example, the presence of conditions as detailed in Table 2.1. In a new engagement, the auditor should ask the previous auditors (if there were any) and the business community about the reputation of the owners and management. For continuing engagements, experience from previous examinations is likely to enable the auditor to assess the reasonableness of the assumption of good faith. Significant changes in either ownership or management would normally require a reassessment of this position.

If there are suspicions that any members of management are associated with fraudulent activities, then further investigation should be made to find out more about the circumstances. If the auditors are unable to confirm the absence of fraud, then they should advise senior management. In such circumstances, the auditors may find that it is not possible to complete the audit and they should seek legal advice about their responsibilities and their future course of action. An auditor is not an insurer of good faith and reliability on the part of management.

Discovery of illegal acts

Many lay people believe that an audit must surely detect all illegal acts committed by an entity. However, this is not necessarily the case. An audit may result in the detection of illegal acts, but it cannot be relied on to do so, for two reasons:

1. The determination of whether an act is illegal involves matters of law that may be beyond the auditor's competence.
2. Illegal acts may pertain to aspects of the company's operations that are generally unrelated to the financial report.

Furthermore, management may be able to conceal effectively the occurrence of illegal acts, and limitations in the auditing process may permit illegal acts to remain undiscovered. For audit purposes, the three principal categories of illegal act are:

1. those pertaining to the form, content and preparation of the financial report;
2. those having a fundamental effect on operations, of which a breach would jeopardise the viability of the entity or a major part of it;
3. others.

Auditors should plan the audit so they have a reasonable expectation of detecting illegal acts in the first category. While planning, they should also identify any other illegal acts that could have a fundamental effect on an entity's operations and assess the risk of material misstatements arising from these acts. Auditors are not responsible, however, for searching for other illegal acts that are not expected to result in material misstatements.

Reporting of irregularities

All irregularities (whether discovered or suspected) should be reported to an appropriate level of management, regardless of materiality, so parties can agree on the future course of action. Care must be exercised to ensure that the manager to whom the matter is reported is unlikely to be implicated in the irregularity. If top management is suspected to be involved in fraudulent or other illegal acts, then the auditor's findings should be reported to a level of authority high enough to take appropriate action. This may be the audit committee or, in some cases, the board of directors. If appropriate action is not forthcoming, the auditor should seek legal advice and consider severing any further business relationship with the entity. In extreme cases where the entity's governing body is believed to be implicated, it may be necessary to seek direct legal advice, so as not to provide the governing body with the opportunity to destroy or conceal the evidence.

If the irregularity is clearly immaterial, then no further action need be taken. However, failure to report a fraud, no matter how immaterial, and failure to ensure management take appropriate action may lead the client to sue the auditor for damages (as in the case of *WA Chip & Pulp Co. Pty Ltd. v. Arthur Young* (1987) 12 ACLR 25).

If the irregularity is possibly material, then further investigation is necessary to confirm or dispel suspicions and to determine materiality. In evaluating the materiality of an irregularity, particularly an illegal act, the auditor should consider related fines, penalties, damages and possible loss contingencies, such as expropriation of property and forced discontinuance of operations. When the presence of a material irregularity is confirmed, the auditor needs to consider such matters as:

- the effect on the financial report or audit report;
- an evaluation of internal control, the possibility of the occurrence or recurrence of similar irregularities, and the need for further audit procedures;
- management's proposed actions to prevent the recurrence of the irregularity;
- public interest implications of the irregularity.

Reporting of illegal acts to regulatory authorities

The auditor's contractual obligation to observe client confidentiality prevents the reporting of any aspect of the client's affairs to a third party. Notifying other parties of the occurrence of irregularities is the responsibility of management. The auditor has no obligation or right to notify other parties except:

- under the Corporations Law (s.311), which requires the auditor to notify the ASIC in writing if he or she has reasonable grounds for suspecting that the law has been contravened, and if he or she considers that commenting on that suspicion in the auditor's report or drawing it to the attention of directors will not see the contravention adequately dealt with;
- in the public interest, which represents a common law duty that overrides the auditor's duty of confidentiality to the client. It arises where the illegal act or intended illegal act could result in great social harm. In such cases, the auditor should consult legal advisers as to whether he or she should report the matter to the authorities.

Meeting public expectations for detecting and reporting irregularities

The Australian Working Party on the Audit Expectation Gap considered that it was unreasonable of users to expect that the principal objective of an audit is the detection of fraud. The cost of performing the extensive audit procedures needed to detect all material fraud, along with the resultant delay in completing the audit, would be disproportionate to the benefits to users.

The legal responsibility is uncertain. Most recent court cases involving the failure of auditors to detect fraud were settled out of court. Critics argue that auditors have a legal duty to detect fraud, and that AUS 210 (ISA 240) and its predecessor, Auditing Practice Statement AUP 16, represent improper attempts by the profession to persuade courts and the public to accept a lower standard of responsibility for fraud.

User expectations may be difficult to shift. Every time a fraud is perpetrated and not discovered by the auditor — no matter how skilfully it might have been concealed or how senior the level of management responsible — the competence of the whole audit will be called into question. The Australian Working Party considered that improved communication offers the best prospect for reducing the gap in this area. It proposed an expanded audit report, a signed **management responsibility statement** and a further statement by management as to the effectiveness of internal control. The management responsibility statement is aimed at reminding company management of their responsibility for internal control and the prevention and detection of fraud and irregularities.

Reducing the incidence of undetected irregularities

Despite the reluctance of auditors to accept greater responsibility for detecting and reporting fraud, a number of initiatives could reduce the extent of losses through fraud. Not least among these initiatives are proposals to improve the effectiveness of internal control structures and to emphasise management's responsibility for undertaking such improvement. We will discuss these proposals in the section on **corporate governance** (see page 76). The establishment of an audit committee would help communication between the auditor and the entity where top management fraud is suspected; in the absence of an audit committee, the auditor cannot be sure which executive members of the board are not party to the fraud. There may not be anyone to whom the auditor can present his or her suspicions.

Many auditing firms have developed expertise in forensic audits, entailing an in-depth assessment of an entity's arrangements to minimise fraud and investigations into any apparent areas of weakness. Such exercises are costly, especially if conducted as part of the independent audit, and the auditor accepts full responsibility for any fraud that evades detection. However, if performed separately, or even if undertaken by internal audit (without the consultant or auditor carrying the same degree of risk), forensic audits would be less costly and management could be persuaded to commission such investigations in fulfilling its responsibility for internal control.

The training and education of auditors could also be extended to incorporate aspects of behavioural and forensic audits. Top management fraud often involves powerful, plausible individuals, and many frauds (undetected by experienced auditors for years) have continued because the auditor has been the subject of clever persuasion and manipulation. Recognising behavioural patterns and knowing some of the methods used in previously investigated frauds could help auditors reduce the extent to which they are deceived by perpetrators of fraud.

Other regulatory bodies and individuals investigate aspects of an entity's affairs and, therefore, can become aware of irregularities. However, as yet, there is no requirement for these bodies and individuals to communicate any suspicions of irregularities to the independent auditor. The Australian Working Party proposed that parties such as management, solicitors, other advisers and regulators be required to inform auditors of suspected fraud or manipulation.

In the reporting of fraud, auditors often complain that they are in an impossible situation. They do not have the investigative powers of law enforcement agencies and, at best, have suspicions rather than proof of the occurrence of fraud. If their suspicions prove to be unfounded, then premature revelation of those suspicions could result in an action for defamation. Moreover, auditors have a duty of confidentiality to the entity. If top management is believed to be implicated in a fraud, then auditors have no right to inform the appropriate authorities unless required to do so in the 'public interest'. This is clearly an ill-defined concept. Timeliness of reporting is vital in such matters and rarely allows the auditor time to seek legal advice. The Australian Working Party has proposed legislation that would indemnify auditors against claims for breach of confidentiality or defamation where those auditors have reported suspicions of irregularities in good faith to an appropriate regulatory body.

These measures would reduce the incidence of irregularities, increase the likelihood of detecting irregularities, and ensure that all suspicions of irregularities are properly reported and investigated.

LEARNING CHECK

2.1 An accountant is regarded as a professional person who possesses knowledge, authority and community sanction; complies with an ethical code; and belongs to and practises within the culture and rules of a professional body. Accountants' complex roles involve extensive duties and relationships, and distinctive rights under a regulatory framework, and they require the practice of certain values.

2.2 Ethics concerns the study of choices in situations in which there are conflicting duties, rights and interests. Professional ethics examines ethical situations in a professional setting, where accountants are guided by a professional code of ethics and other moral standards and norms.

2.3 The Joint Code of Professional Conduct lays down fundamental principles for accountants' roles and detailed prescriptive rules in areas such as fees, appointments and technical competence. Accountants are required to serve the public interest with due professional care, objectivity, integrity and the skills and competence appropriate for the circumstances.

2.4 Independence is the cornerstone of auditing. It is a state of mind characterised by appearance. Independence in fact refers to the objectivity and integrity possessed by accountants at all times, and AUP 32 and the Joint Code of Professional Conduct stipulate detailed requirements to enhance the appearance of independence. The concept of independence is critically reviewed, and the US Securities and Exchange Commission and the IFAC have proposed alternative approaches.

2.5 To act in the public interest and with due professional care means accountants must maintain a high quality and standard in behaviour and the professional services they offer. Accountants and auditors must comply with both technical standards and other quality assurance requirements.

2.6 Ethical dilemmas are complex situations in which the accountant is faced with competing interests. In cases of irregularities such as fraud and illegal acts, auditors must plan and conduct audits with a reasonable expectation of detecting material misstatements. Fraud detection and prevention are not the primary objectives of an audit, yet they are often misunderstood by the public in terms of the auditor's duties.

7 LEARNING OBJECTIVE

Explain the current audit environment affecting the auditor's ethical behaviour.

THE SIGNIFICANCE OF ETHICAL VALUES FOR AUDITING

Threats to independence are frequently encountered by auditors and accountants in public practice and are complex issues. Some of the threats are a direct consequence of the audit–client relationship (such as management pressure) and the phenomenon of accountants in public practice providing non-audit services which may have an impact on the appearance of audit independence. The accountants' and auditors' decisions depend on their ability to identify and prioritise various conflicting interests and duties, while maintaining professional competence and independence. How independent these decisions are in reality often depends on how successfully the auditor deals with issues such as those discussed below.

The environment affecting professional conduct

Auditors often face pressure situations that present them with an ethical dilemma — one in which they have to choose between unclear alternatives, of which some may compromise their integrity. Not all of these situations are easily defined and the auditor may need to look beyond the requirements of the Joint Code of Professional Conduct for guidance. Here, we will examine some of these situations.

Management pressure on audit appointment

Under the Corporations Law, the auditor is normally appointed by the shareholders of the company at the annual general meeting. Ownership of large public companies is diverse, with financial institutions such as banks and insurance companies holding a majority of the shares. Such shareholders generally do not intervene in the running of the company and usually assign their voting rights to the directors. This gives rise to a practice known as '**opinion shopping**': an audit client invites another firm of accountants to offer a second opinion on a disagreement between the client's management and the auditor over a proposed accounting treatment. This puts pressure on the auditor to issue an unqualified audit report, so as not to lose the audit to the second firm.

One proposed solution to such problems is to restrict the total fee income that an audit firm may derive from one reporting entity from both audit and non-audit services (e.g. a cap of 15 per cent). The loss of an audit, therefore, would not cause the audit firm to lose substantial revenue, thus encouraging the auditor to adopt a firmer attitude in disagreements with management.

A more fundamental solution is to eliminate management's ability to control the audit appointment. The profession has proposed amending the Corporations Law to entrust the appointment, dismissal and remuneration of auditors to a committee of shareholders unconnected with management. The UK auditing profession, however, is concerned that management could still capture the power of appointment to such a committee; it proposes empowering the audit committee to appoint the auditor.

A more radical proposal is **audit rotation**. Under this arrangement, auditors are appointed for a fixed term of five or seven years during which they cannot be removed from office. At the end of this term, they must be replaced by another firm. The profession rejects this proposal on the grounds that it increases the incidence of 'new' audits, with their high start-up costs and increased risk of audit failure during the learning phase. There is also concern, for larger entities, that audit rotation would reduce competitiveness among the Big Five audit firms. Even more extreme proposals have been suggested more recently, such as the direct appointment of auditors by the government and the establishment of an audit review court.

Non-audit services

As explained in Chapter 1, firms of public accountants provide a range of services in addition to audits. The auditor of a particular entity has a competitive advantage over other accounting firms in providing non-audit services to that client. Firstly, knowledge gained during the audit reduces the cost of providing other services (e.g. preparing tax returns). Secondly, the audit provides the firm with a chance to identify opportunities for selling other services to the entity. However, because the revenue from non-audit services often exceeds that from audit services, this situation can result in 'low-balling' (see page 58).

The practice of low-balling raises issues that potentially affect audit quality. Firstly, auditors may be reluctant to dispute management over audit matters lest the disagreement prejudice their access to contracts for non-audit services. If, for whatever reason, the auditing firm does not secure contracts for the supply of non-audit services, then it will lose money on the audit and thus may be tempted to reduce the loss by lowering audit quality. Even without low-balling, the fact that an auditor provides non-audit services to management may be seen as conflicting with that auditor's independence and his or her duty of care to shareholders.

There is a vigorous debate as to whether auditors should provide non-audit services at all. Professional bodies in Australia and overseas see nothing wrong with the practice, subject to ethical safeguards to ensure that independence is not prejudiced. These parties argue that entities should be free to choose their professional advisers and may prefer to use an auditing firm in which they have confidence and which may be able to provide a service at a lower cost than another service provider. Furthermore, they would argue, the performance of non-audit work enhances the audit by adding to the auditor's knowledge of the business. Disclosure of fees from non-audit services in the annual report provides a market control over the extent of the provision of these services. Such disclosure enables the securities market to determine whether the extent of non-audit service provision could threaten the auditor's independence and thus the reliability of the audited financial report. In such a case, the share price would fall, thus signalling to management that it should reduce the number of other services that the audit firm provides.

The alternative viewpoint is that auditors of public companies and similar entities should be banned from providing other services to the entity so as to assure public confidence in the auditor's independence from the influence of management. It was found in the United Kingdom, for example, that companies facing potentially high agency costs in management tend to require fewer non-audit services from the auditors, because such service provision by the auditor is perceived to jeopardise the desired appearance of independence of the auditors.[15]

Independence — the cornerstone of traditional auditing — is becoming an increasingly problematic issue for the contemporary auditing profession. Recent publications have called for 'a fresh look at this issue'.[16] The profession has been urged to consider a proposal for full and fair disclosure of information that may affect investors' or public perceptions about the auditor's independence from the auditee's management. Acknowledging the importance of auditor independence to the reliability of accounting information, Steven Wallman[17] (the then Commissioner at the Securities and Exchange Commission in the United States in 1996) argues that the current paradigm for assessing independence issues needs to be made both more comprehensive and more comprehensible to advance the public interest. He asserts that the current approach does not adequately address independence concerns related to traditionally accepted audit and related activities, while it precludes, without good reason, various non-traditional services, including those that may advance the public interest. Wallman advocates an alternative model that focuses not on auditor independence, but on auditor *dependence*. He believes that such a measure would change people's thinking about independence issues — from a preoccupation with public duty, to a concern for what is best in the public interest.

Professional judgement in accounting and auditing

Although accounting and auditing are based on relatively systematic techniques, few financial allegations result from methodological errors. Rather, many are cases of judgements about the appropriate use of a technique or standard. Some may be errors of judgement, while others may result from a misinterpretation of the problem; a lack of awareness due to complexity; or a failure to observe the ethical values of honesty, integrity, objectivity, due care, confidentiality and a commitment to the public interest. An accounting treatment in accordance with an Accounting Standard may be biased, for example, if it is based on inadequate or incomplete information that is wrongly judged to be sufficient to support it. A non-disclosure of an accounting item may not be a question of competence, but of misplaced loyalty to management, a client or one's self-interest, rather than to the public who rely on the information.

Auditing and Accounting Standards, although a sound basis for professional practice, will not cover every contingency. In complex situations in which the course of action is not clearly prescribed, accountants must be able to maintain integrity and objectivity in making a judgement. When a professional accountant finds a problem that exceeds his or her expertise, it is the professional's ethical values that will compel him or her to recognise such limitations, seek advice, remain objective and disclose the relevant facts. This is necessary to maintain the trust within a fiduciary relationship. There are cases, however, where Accounting Standards and technical guidelines are insufficient (due to the complexity of business transactions) to provide an objective basis for accounting treatment. Consequently, while technical feasibility may govern the short-term solutions, ethical considerations such as the potential consequences of such accounting problems should dominate in the longer term.

Priority of duty and loyalty

Given that the role of professional accountants is to provide fiduciary services to society as a whole, the performance of such services involves choices between the interests of various parties — the client or the employer of such services, the management of the client or employing organisation, the current and prospective investors of the business being examined, other stakeholders, employees, the government, etc. Auditors are appointed by the shareholders or members of the client to examine the financial affairs of the organisation. The underlying principle in this engagement is to protect the interest of the resource providers against the possible pursuit of self-interests by management. To the extent that the stakeholders mentioned above are considered to be the 'public', the auditor has a fiduciary relationship with the public that requires the exercise of the same duties and values that would apply in a more direct contractual relationship. The choice of accounting and auditing methods and treatments that maximise a current benefit at the expense of future income would therefore breach the trust required for the fiduciary arrangement with the public. Accordingly, the loyalty to the public should not be less than the loyalty owed to existing shareholders or owners. Defining the legal liability of auditors in this respect has been complex. The establishment of auditors' relationships with various parties has broadened the strict privity of contract in terms of liability (see Chapter 3).

Accountants employed within an organisation have no contractual relationship with shareholders or the public. However, in performing their duties to their employers, accountants are required to adhere to the values expected of a professional person by considering their responsibility to others who may be disadvantaged by an act at the request of their superior. Accountants employed in this capacity need, therefore, to consider the accuracy and reliability of their work for the benefit of the end-user (that is, the public as the stakeholders). This situation is complex, entailing consideration of such debatable issues as confidentiality to one's employer and the ethical premises for 'whistleblowing' (that is, disclosing unethical deeds to parties outside of an organisation). Recently, for example, professional accountants were given certain privilege to disclose information required by law to third parties such as the ASIC.

The code of a profession endeavours to provide guidelines to follow in difficult ethical situations, yet accountants often have to rely on personal integrity and values to make the 'right' decision. One viewpoint[18] is that a professional accountant facing a difficult choice should consider that loyalty is owed to affected stakeholders in the following order: the public, the profession, the client/employer and, finally, the individual.

Professional competence

The ethical provisions in the Joint Code of Professional Conduct Code deal with mainly business matters that relate to public accounting, but ethical responsibility also extends to technical competence. Competence is the product of education and experience. Education begins with preparation for entry into the profession and extends to continuing professional education throughout the member's career. Experience involves on-the-job training and the acceptance of increased responsibilities during a member's professional life.

The Code states that (1) members have a duty to maintain their level of competence throughout their professional career, and (2) public accountants should undertake only work in which they are competent. Minimum annual hours of continuing professional education are prescribed for all members, affiliates and members holding a certificate of public practice. Compliance with these rules is monitored by requiring members to keep a personal record of time spent on continuing professional education and to certify compliance at the time they pay their annual subscription. Now, there is an increasing emphasis in the professional programs on also developing competence in dealing with ethical conflicts.

8 LEARNING OBJECTIVE

Discuss the implications of and recommendations for bridging the audit expectation gap.

The audit expectation gap

Over the past few decades, there has been public concern for accountability and an increasing demand by stakeholders for value-added services. The professional accountant who serves the often conflicting interests of different stakeholders must not only be aware of the public expectations for business, but also exercise professional integrity and demonstrate a high standard of competence in dealing with all facets of business decisions. The public expectations for business behaviour can be classified into those related to (1) the physical environment of the business activities (e.g. environmental concerns such as pollution and waste), (2) community pressures for equity and fairness in dealings, (3) the demands for professionalism as a result of financial scandals, (4) economic objectives that must be achieved for survival, (5) the maintenance of competitive advantages to combat global pressures, and (6) the development of synergy among businesses, government and other operations (e.g. institutional reinforcement and codification). A survey conducted by Epstein and Geiger of US investors found that over 70 per cent of investors expected absolute assurance that auditors would detect material misstatement due to fraud, while over 47 per cent expected auditors to be able to discover errors. Epstein and Geiger suggested that the audit profession needs to expand services and undergo a fundamental change of attitude from self-defending self-preservation to meeting society's expectations.[19]

The expectation gap is arguably one of the major issues confronting the profession in recent years. Financial report users, such as investors, expect auditors to provide assurance concerning material fraud, irregularities and the viability of the business and its management. When entities fail through fraud or mismanagement, there is a tendency to blame the auditor for not having given adequate warning of the problems. Until recently, the profession has argued that the problem is that users fail to understand the role of the auditors and the limitations of financial reporting. Figure 2.1 on the next page illustrates the nature of the expectation gap. The gap is partly due to the unreasonable expectations of users, and it is being addressed by the initiatives described in the previous paragraph. In recent years, however, the profession has come to recognise the need to undertake active measures to improve the quality of financial reporting, so as to reduce any part of the gap caused by inadequate performance. Some of these measures relate to the audit function directly — for example, improving the quality of audit work performed and enhancing the independence of the auditor.

The 1993 report of the Australian Working Party on Bridging the Audit Expectation Gap encapsulated key recommendations on quality control, perfecting the existing financial reporting and auditing scope, and audit environmental considerations. These recommendations encompassed a wide range of issues, such as quality assurance; auditor independence; the continued development of a conceptual framework for financial reporting; the introduction of a management responsibility statement; a mandatory fee limit of 15 per cent for any one client; the criteria for designing, assessing and evaluating internal controls; and the promotion of audit committees. Some recommendations have already been implemented; for example, to perfect the existing auditing scope, the long-form audit report has been introduced, the 'subject to' form of qualification has been eliminated and Auditing Standards have been codified. Other recommendations, such as the development of Statements of Accounting Concepts, are beyond the scope of this text.

FIGURE 2.1

Components of the audit expectation gap

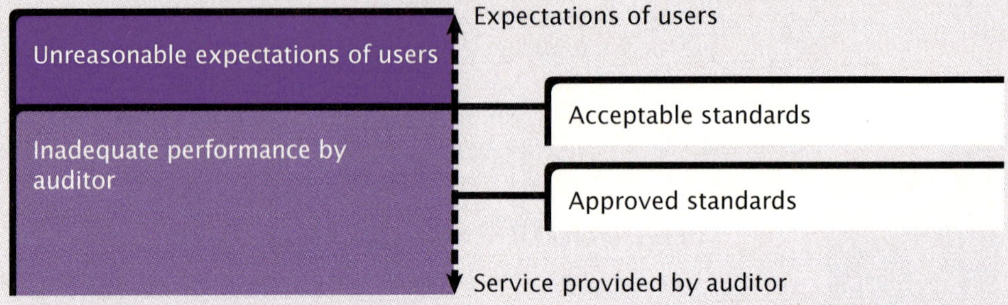

Note: Dotted line shows the performance range of auditors. Performance above acceptable standards to meet the expectations of users is prompted by unreasonable user expectations. Performance below acceptable standards reflects a perceived inadequacy of audit performance.

As part of due process by the accounting bodies, a Task Force was commissioned in 1996 to consider the recommendations of the Australian Working Party, along with the submissions made on the research study. Major recommendations were identified in the Task Force report, encompassing the categories of corporate governance, financial reporting and auditing. Key recommendations that affect the auditor include:

- promoting the importance of internal control and internal audit;
- making audit committees mandatory for all listed companies;
- having audit committees be responsible for recommending the appointment, removal and remuneration of auditors (to enhance auditor independence);
- defining the limitations of audit liability;
- establishing a Financial Reporting Review Board to advise on standards and accounting practice;
- establishing a single quality review program to ensure audit quality;
- supporting auditors' right to a knowledge of the business;
- allowing auditors to be unrestricted in carrying out other services for the entity, because these services may contribute to the auditor's knowledge of the business.

Professional accounting bodies in other countries have also conducted inquiries into reducing the audit expectation gap, and many recommendations of the Australian Working Party were derived from studies of overseas developments.

9 LEARNING OBJECTIVE

Explain the concept of corporate governance as it relates to auditors.

Corporate governance in reducing the expectation gap

Corporate governance refers to the role of directors in discharging their duties. Corporate best practice is demonstrated by various studies, such as the Treadway Report and the Cadbury Report.[20] The findings of these studies were incorporated and further developed in Australia by a working party, whose 1993 report identified various features of corporate governance that it recommended.[21] Key features are listed below:

- The board should include outside or non-executive directors.
- Audit committees are strongly recommended as a part of corporate governance, offering independent advice and expertise on matters such as internal controls, management fraud, etc.
- Directors should disclose financial and non-financial information.

Since the issue of this report, it has been a growing practice for outside directors to form an audit committee of the board, with special responsibility for overseeing the financial reporting process and ensuring auditor independence. Corporate governance has emerged as one of the best vehicles for reducing the expectation gap. The proposals in the report require the governing bodies of entities to adopt improved structures and to undertake additional reporting responsibilities in cooperation with the independent auditors. Not being interested parties, members of the audit committee are well placed to resist board pressure and maintain the auditor's independence. This arrangement helps to minimise conflict between directors and auditors.

Despite demands, only listed companies in Australia are required to report if they have audit committees. In contrast, the United Kingdom, the United States and Canada, for example, have all legislated for audit committees. Consideration of corporate governance issues (e.g. a board's duties and responsibilities) helped to ensure that the roles of auditors and directors are clearly and separately explained and that no misunderstandings or excessive expectations arise. Corporate governance recently received further attention in the United Kingdom when the London Stock Exchange endorsed the Turnbull Report (see the 'Professional environment' below).

PROFESSIONAL ENVIRONMENT — Corporate governance in the new millennium

The first stage in the process of increasing the transparency and accountability of UK boardrooms began in 1991 with the issue of the Cadbury Committee report on the financial aspects of corporate governance, followed by a report by Greenbury and Hampel. The London Stock Exchange compressed all these recommendations in 1998 into what is now known as the 'Combined Code'.

More recently, the call for standardised, transparent corporate reporting on environmental and social performance has become more strident. Report users (such as investors and non-government organisations) have voiced concerns over their inability to compare companies based on factors other than financial performance — factors such as the blend of economic, environmental and social aspects that comprise sustainability.

The latest link in the UK corporate governance chain is *Internal Control: Guidance for Directors on the Combined Code* (1999), otherwise called the Turnbull Report after the chairman Nigel Turnbull (Executive Director of Reed PLC). Turnbull's guidance is based on a board's adoption of a risk-based approach to establishing a sound system of internal control and reviewing its effectiveness. A company should incorporate this approach within its normal management and governance processes. The span of internal control contemplated by Turnbull stretches wider than financial controls, to encompass social and environmental issues — matters that have come to be grouped under the generic heading of 'reputational risk'.

Throughout the history of the corporate governance debate there have been many calls for companies and financial institutions to adopt a wider notion of corporate governance — that is, a view that goes beyond board level structures and executive pay issues, to embrace the full range of risks facing an enterprise, including risks arising from non-conventional sources such as the environmental, social, ethical, human rights and child labour issues.

(*continued*)

The appendix to the Turnbull Report provides explicit guidance on risk assessment procedures. The matters most relevant to this chapter are:

- an ongoing basis for assessing significant internal and external operational, financial, compliance and other risks. These risks include those related to market, credit, liquidity, technological, legal, health, safety, environmental, reputation and business probity issues.
- the communication to employees of the scope of freedom to act on areas such as customer relations, outsourcing activities, service levels and environmental protection;
- an established channel of communication for individuals to report suspected breaches of laws or regulations;
- specific arrangements for management to report and monitor on risk and control matters (including actual or suspected fraud and other irregularities) or matters that may affect the company's reputation or financial position.

Compliance with the Turnbull Report will require a board to consider all these matters. Readers may like to visit the web site www.kpm.co.uk to find a review on Turnbull's recommendations on internal control.

In Australia, a Corporate Code of Conduct Bill 2000 was presented in the Senate of the Parliament in August 2000. This Bill contains standards to be imposed on the conduct of Australian corporations that undertake business activities in other countries, and for related purposes. The scope of the proposed standards includes environmental, health and safety, employment and human rights issues, the duty to observe tax laws, and consumer protection and trade practices. These standards, put forward by the opposition (the Labor Party), were regarded as a stepping stone towards the global improvement of ethical standards in businesses. Auditors of a multinational company may find such standards helpful in evaluating risks for businesses.

10
LEARNING OBJECTIVE

Describe the essential disciplinary measures for auditors.

PROFESSIONAL DISCIPLINE

The value of an auditor's opinion is significantly enhanced by the public's recognition of the high standards of practice and professional conduct of the auditor. This recognition comes in three ways:

1. high entry standards for professional membership;
2. high standards of performance and conduct required of members;
3. the power to discipline and, in extreme cases, to dismiss from membership those whose performance falls short of required standards.

The investigative and disciplinary powers of the ICAA and CPA Australia over their members are contained in the Supplemental Royal Charter and the Articles of Association respectively. Article 26 of CPA Australia's Articles of Association confers on the National Council the right to impose forfeiture of membership, suspension from membership, fines, censure and/or admonishment on any member of CPA Australia who, in the opinion of the Council:

(a) has been guilty of any breach of the Memorandum, Articles, By-Laws or Pronouncements of CPA Australia;
(b) has been guilty of dishonourable practices or conduct derogatory to the profession of an accountant or conduct that is not in the best interests of CPA Australia or its members;
(c) has failed to observe a proper standard of professional care, skill or competence;
(d) has become an insolvent under administration.

The Supplemental Royal Charter of the ICAA confers similar powers on that body, with the additional right to discipline any member found by any court to be guilty of any felony, misdemeanour or fraud.

Disciplinary procedures

The Articles of Association of CPA Australia provide for establishing an Investigation Committee and a Disciplinary Committee in each state. Complaints against members are first referred to the Investigation Committee, which will interview the member and obtain information from any source considered necessary. The Investigation Committee then advises the Disciplinary Committee whether there is a case to answer. If there is a case, the Disciplinary Committee will require the member to appear before it, with legal representation if the member so desires. The member also has the right of appeal to an Appeals Committee at a national level. Penalties imposed against the member shall be made public as appropriate, such as by publication in CPA Australia's journal.

The ICAA has similar procedures. Its investigation committees, which function at the state level, have the authority to consider minor cases. Minor cases are those that do not require, in the opinion of the state investigation committees, the imposition of a sanction greater than (1) a reprimand, (2) an order for the payment of costs associated with the hearing, (3) an order that the member obtain and implement advice on the conduct of his or her practice, (4) a requirement that a member attend specified professional development activity, or (5) a fine not exceeding $5000.

The National Disciplinary Committee of the ICAA has the authority to impose sanctions as for minor cases. Additional punitive measures that it can impose include exclusion from membership, suspension from membership for up to five years cancellation of a certificate of public practice, a declaration that a member is ineligible for a certificate of public practice for up to five years, and a fine not exceeding $100 000. There is a right of appeal (except for minor cases) to the National Appeals Committee.

Both the National Disciplinary Committee and the National Appeals Committee comprise senior members of the profession, state or national councillors, Fellows of the ICAA of at least fifteen years standing and lay representatives. Thus, the person subject to discipline faces the elders of the profession and members of the public. To ensure the objectivity of deliberations, committee members can serve on only one of these committees at any one time.

In addition to investigation and disciplinary procedures exercised by the profession, the Companies Auditors and Liquidators Disciplinary Board has the power to cancel or suspend the registration of an auditor who:

- has failed to adequately and properly perform the duties of an auditor;
- is not a fit and proper person to remain registered as an auditor (s.1292(1), Corporations Law).

LEARNING CHECK

2.7 Auditors need to appreciate the current audit environment, which may present threats to auditors' independence, quality of work and objectivity. Features of the audit environment include competition, potential management pressure, the provision of non-audit services and the discharge of professional judgement in interpreting and applying standards. Auditors must be aware of duty and loyalty priorities when making difficult decisions to uphold their objectivity, integrity and ethical and professional standards. An auditor's decision may affect a number of stakeholders, and the responsibility to serve the public interest should prevail.

(*continued*)

2.8 Latest developments in the audit expectation gap investigations demonstrate the professional bodies' support for strengthening audit independence, while recognising the scope of the directors' and auditor's work in the interest of the public.

2.9 Auditors need to appreciate the current audit environment, which may present threats to auditors' independence, quality of work and objectivity. Features of the audit environment include competition, potential management pressure, the provision of non-audit services and the discharge of professional judgement in interpreting and applying standards. Auditors must be aware of duty and loyalty priorities when making difficult decisions to uphold their objectivity, integrity and ethical and professional standards. An auditor's decision may affect a number of stakeholders, and the responsibility to serve the public interest should prevail.

2.10 Latest developments in the audit expectation gap investigations demonstrate the professional bodies' support for strengthening audit independence, while recognising the scope of the directors' and auditor's work in the interest of the public.

2.11 Corporate governance refers to the systems and governing mechanisms used by the board of directors to pursue the interests of a company while satisfying its stakeholders. It promotes concepts such as the optimal size and structure of the board, compensation systems and a much broader role of internal control. The introduction of an audit committee is recommended to enhance the independence of the auditor. Corporate governance also assists the auditor to add value to the company by making sure that the board practises an adequate degree of accountability, transparency and social responsibility.

2.12 A characteristic of a profession is the ability to self-regulate. One feature of self-regulation is the establishment and monitoring of disciplinary procedures to ensure that members of a professional body comply with a minimum set standard of behaviour. The investigative and disciplinary powers of the ICAA and CPA Australia are contained in the Supplementary Royal Charter and the Articles of Association respectively.

SUMMARY

In this chapter we discussed the professional foundations on which the role and behaviour of accountants are based. By defining what a profession encompasses, we explained the objectives and implications of professional ethics. Professional ethics are an abstract concept, but the Joint Code of Professional Conduct espouses the basic principles and expectations of behaviour to which members of the accounting profession must adhere. Although the Code addresses the issue of professionalism by outlining fundamental principles and prescribing practical and enforceable standards, such standards evolve over time and reflect changes in the profession and in the expectations of society. We specifically illustrated the significance and debates over the concept of independence — a cornerstone of auditing. Furthermore, we discussed the requirements of auditors in terms of the quality of their work, the standards for technical competence and their responsibilities in dealing with fraud and irregularities. Given that the ethical environment in which accountants and auditors operate is complex, users have had some unrealistic expectations of auditors — a situation that is known as the audit expectation gap. In response, the profession has recently investigated improvements in financial reporting, thus reducing the number of instances where users are dissatisfied. Auditors have involved other parties in this process, including the governing bodies of the entities being audited, the government, and Accounting and Auditing Standard setters. Consequently, auditors and corporate management are increasing their role in the corporate governance structure of organisations, while accountants are subject to an ongoing effort to achieve better quality and more rigorous self-regulatory procedures.

KEY TERMS

Audit committees, p. 58
Audit expectation gap, p. 48
Audit rotation, p. 72
Conceptual framework for auditing, p. 63
Concurring partner, p. 64
Contingency fee, p. 54
Corporate governance, p. 69
Deontology, p. 51
Errors, p. 65
Financial reporting review panel, p. 63
Fraud, p. 64
Illegal acts, p. 64
Independence, p. 48
Irregularities, p. 48
Low-balling, p. 58
Management responsibility statement, p. 69
Non-audit services, p. 57
Opinion shopping, p. 72
Professional ethics, p. 48
Public interest, p. 49
Quality assurance programs, p. 64
Review partner, p. 64
Self-regulatory, p. 49
Teleology, p. 51
Utilitarianism, p. 51

NOTES

1. The distinctions between a professional and a non-professional are the key issues discussed in A. Abbot, 'Professional Ethics', *American Journal of Sociology* (Vol. 88, No. 5, 1988), pp. 855–85. The literature has identified five major characteristics possessed by a professional: theoretical knowledge, authority to practise, the community's sanction in terms of regulation and disciplines, an enforceable code of ethics or conduct, and a self-defined culture.
2. E. Greenwood, 'Attributes of a Profession', *Social Work* (July 1957), pp. 45–55.
3. Leonard J. Brooks, *Professional Ethics for Accountants*. West Publishing, Toronto, 1999. This text identifies facets of the professional ethical issues faced by auditors.
4. Treadway Commission, *Report of the National Commission on Fraudulent Financial Reporting*. A report by Sir James Treadway, Chairperson, National Commission on Fraudulent Financial Reporting, US Government Printing Office, Washington DC, 1987. This report advocates the exercising of ethics in business, internal control and corporate governance.
5. The Macdonald Commission (1988) took a similar approach in its report to the approach of the Treadway Commission (see Note 4). Canadian accounting bodies commissioned it to conduct research into business and professional ethics — specifically, to study the public's expectations of audits.
6. Steven M. Mintz, *Cases in Accounting Ethics and Professionalism*, 2nd edn. McGraw-Hill, New York, 1992.
7. The Institute of Chartered Accountants in Australia conducted a Professional Year (PY) Programme to train accountants. A new program entitled the CA Program was introduced in 1999–2000. Ethics is one of the topics of the CA Foundation module.

8. The American Accounting Association (AAA) model originates from H. Q. Langenderfer & J. W. Rockness,'Integrating Ethics into the Accounting Curriculum — Issues, Problems and Solutions', *Issues in Accounting Education* (Vol. 4, 1989), pp. 58–69, who introduced a seven-step decision-making model. These steps are to (1) determine the facts, (2) define the ethical issue, (3) identify the major principles, rules and values involved, (4) specify alternatives, (5) compare the values and alternatives, and see if a clear decision emerges, (6) assess the consequences, and (7) make a decision.
9. Wanda A. Wallace, *The Economic Role of the Audit in Free and Regulated Markets*. Touche Ross & Co., New York, 1980.
10. This recommendation was made by both the Task Force on the Audit Expectation Gap and a working party of the Ministerial Council for Corporations (in July 1997) in reviewing the requirements for the registration and regulation of company auditors.
11. K. Cheung, 'Auditing the Auditors', *Australian Accountant* (October 1994), p. 37.
12. In 1993, the Australian Working Party on the Audit Expectation Gap (set up by the ICAA and CPA Australia) produced a report entitled *A Research Study on Financial Reporting and Auditing — Bridging the Expectation Gap*. The Working Party put forward over 100 recommendations on requirements for financial reporting and auditing. In 1996, as part of due process by the accounting bodies, a Task Force was formed to consider these recommendations further and to review the submissions made on the research study. The Task Force supported some of the submissions and recommendations.
13. KPMG conducts a fraud survey of Australian organisations biannually. The latest survey results published in 1999 reflect a pattern of fraud in Australian businesses similar to the pattern found in previous years.
14. Ernst & Young International Fraud Group, *Fraud — the Unmanaged Risk*. London, 2000. This report of the 1999–2000 international survey on fraud and its effect on business is published on the Ernst & Young web site www.ey.com.
15. M. Firth, 'The Provision of Non-audit Services by Accounting Firms to their Audit Clients', *Contemporary Accounting Research* (Vol. 14, No. 2, Summer 1997), pp. 1–21.
16. Schuetze, J., then Chair of the Securities Exchange Commission in the United States, quoted in H. Falk, V. Frucot & T. van Zijl, 'Auditor Independence'. Working paper, Rutgers University, Canada, 1995.
17. Steven M. H. Wallman, 'The Future of Accounting, Part III: Reliability and Auditor Independence', *Accounting Horizons* (Vol. 10, No. 4, December 1996).
18. L. Brooks (see Note 3).
19. M. J. Epstein & M. A. Geiger, 'Investor Views of Audit Assurance: Recent Evidence of the Expectation Gap. What do Investors Expect from an Audit?', *Journal of Accountancy* (January 1994), pp. 60–6. This article highlighted some of the expectations that users have about various aspects of financial report issues and auditors in particular — namely, that auditors are expected to provide absolute assurance on material misstatements of accounts and to discover errors.
20. The full title of the Cadbury Report is the *Report of the Committee on the Financial Aspects of Corporate Governance*. (A small supplement to the report is subtitled *The Code of Best Practice*). The Financial Reporting Council (UK), the London Stock Exchange and UK accountancy bodies set up the Committee in May 1991 to consider the issues of the responsibilities of executive and non-executive directors; audit committees; the links between shareholders, boards and auditors; and other matters. The report was issued in December 1992.
21. Business Council of Australia, *Corporate Practices and Conduct*, 3rd edition. Information Australia, Melbourne, 1991. This working party led by Henry Bosch was made up of representatives from the Australian Institute of Company Directors, CPA Australia, the Business Council of Australia, the Law Council of Australia, the ICAA and the Securities Institute of Australia.

FURTHER READING

CPA Australia and the Institute of Chartered Accountants in Australia, *A Research Study on Financial Reporting and Auditing — Bridging the Expectation Gap*, 1993.

Australian Society of Certified Public Accountants and the Institute of Chartered Accountants in Australia, Joint Code of Professional Conduct: A1 Introduction; A2 Compliance; A3 Definitions; A4 Format of the Code of Professional Conduct; A5 Assistance to Members; B1 The Public Interest; B2 Integrity; B3 Objectivity; B4 Independence; B5 Confidentiality; B6 Technical and Professional Standards; B7 Competence and Due Care; B8 Ethical Behaviour; C1 Members Practising or Employed Overseas; C2 Members in Outside Employment; C3 Preparation of Legal Documents; C4 Professional Competence; C5 Confidentiality; D1 Professional Fees; D2 Advisory Services — Fees and Commissions; D3 Funds held in Trust and Clients' Monies; D4 Advertising, Publicity and Solicitation; D5 Changes in Professional Appointments; D6 Referrals; D7 Incompatible Business; D8 Stationery and Signboards; D10 Attention to Correspondence and Enquiries; F1 Professional Independence; F2 Prospectuses and Reports on Profit Forecasts; F3 Changes in Professional Appointments; F4 Referrals; F5 Opinion Requests; F6 Professional Fees; F7 Incompatible Business.

English, L., 'Closing the Audit Expectation Gap', *Australian Accountant* (December 1989), pp. 54–64.

Goldwasser, Dan L., 'Is it Possible to Achieve? Independence in a Changing Accounting Profession', *CPA Journal*, (October 1999).

Institute of Chartered Accountants in England and Wales, *Internal Control: Guidance for Directors on the Combined Code* (Turnbull Report), London, 1999.

Institute of Chartered Accountants in Australia, *Members' Handbook*, Vol. 1. Sydney, 'Supplemental Royal Charter', 'By-Laws', 'Rules of Ethical Conduct' and 'Miscellaneous Professional Statements'.

International Federation of Accountants, Code of Ethics for Professional Accountants: Paras 1–8, Introduction; Preface to the Code; Paras 17–18, The Code; Paras 9–13, The Public Interest; Para. 16, Part A, s.1, Integrity and Objectivity; Part B, s.8, Independence; Para. 16, Part A, s.4, Confidentiality; Para. 16, Technical Standards; Para. 16, Professional Competence and Due Care; Para. 16, Professional Behaviour; Part A, s.3, Professional Competence; Part A, s.4, Confidentiality; Part B, s.10, Fees and Commissions; Part B, s.12, Clients' Monies; Part B, s.14, Advertising and Solicitation; Part B, Relations with Other Professional Accountants in Public Practice; Part C, s.15, Conflict of Loyalties; Part B, s.8, Independence; Part B, s.14, Advertising and Solicitation; Part B, s.10, Clients' Monies; Part C, s.15, Incompatible Business.

McDonald, M., 'The Canadian Research Strategy for Applied Ethics: A New Opportunity for Research in Business and Professional Ethics', *Journal of Business Ethics* (Vol. 11, No. 8, August 1992), pp. 569–83.

Parker, L. D., 'An Historical Analysis of Ethical Pronouncements and Debate in the Australian Accounting Profession', *Abacus* (Vol. 23, No. 2, September 1987), pp. 122–40.

Review questions

2.1 How do 'professional ethics' apply to accountants?

2.2 What fundamental principles of professional conduct apply to all members of the Australian accounting profession? Discuss.

2.3 What is the difference between independence in fact and independence in appearance? What are some of the difficulties faced by an auditor in applying professional independence?

2.4 Professional Statement FI includes separate guidelines on fees, personal and business relationships, and the preparation of books. What are the main elements of these guidelines?

2.5 What procedures are to be followed in the event of allegations of unprofessional conduct by a member of the profession?

2.6 What are the main ways in which the profession ensures the quality of audit services?

2.7 What are some factors that would make an auditor increase his or her assessment of the potential risk of irregularities for an audit client?

Discussion questions

2.1 What is the significance of the concept of audit independence in the accounting profession? Discuss the recent development of this concept.

2.2 Why is ethics important to accountants? Explain, with examples, the complexity of the roles of accountants in terms of their responsibilities and relationships with others. How do you think ethics may assist accountants in these roles?

2.3 What are the responsibilities of the auditors in the detection and prevention of fraud and the discovery of illegal acts?

2.4 What are the detailed quality assurance processes that an audit firm may adopt in ensuring quality standards in its audit work? Discuss, providing examples.

2.5 What are the implications of the audit expectation gap? Can the gap be reduced? If so, how?

2.6 What is the meaning of corporate governance? How does corporate governance relate to the auditor of a large multinational company?

2.7 'The notion of ethics is far too abstract. Professionals should just follow their code of ethics because, after all, they are professionals.' Do you agree with this contention? Why?

2.8 Which statutory provisions are aimed at reinforcing auditors' independence? Discuss.

2.9 What are the ethical implications of the following terms: (a) low-balling; (b) opinion shopping; and (c) creative accounting? Discuss each practice.

2.10 How can an audit committee effectively enhance the independence of the auditor?

BASIC ★
MODERATE ★★
CHALLENGING ★★★

Professional application questions

2.1 (Professionalism) ★

Frank Fong, who just completed his chartered accountant examinations, is given for the first time a lead role in the audit of a small chemical company. Frank is excited but concerned that he does not know much about chemical products. He is puzzled about the nature of some of the accounts prepared by the client. Furthermore, he does not dare ask the company's controller, Thomas Kahn, who is known to be rude to auditors. As Frank's supervisor, you notice that Frank is uneasy when you inquire about the audit progress.

Required

Explain to Frank the importance of professionalism, using the Joint Code of Professional Conduct and particularly referring to its guidance on dealing with a difficult client and a complex audit. What would you suggest to Frank?

2.2 (Ethical decision-making) ★

As an audit senior for a long standing client, you discover some discrepancies in the accounts prepared by its financial controller, Craig. Furthermore, it appears that Craig has been spending large sums of the company's money to entertain his family and friends. Recently Craig bought an expensive painting for his own lounge room in his country resort. Craig maintains a very good relationship with your audit partner, Richard, because both play golf every Friday afternoon. You are not sure if you should raise the matter with Craig. You are increasingly concerned about the integrity of the accounts and Richard, the audit partner, is also earnestly waiting to complete the audit before he goes on leave.

Required

Analyse the ethical issues you confronted. How would you resolve the issues? What principles should you consider? Use the skills in ethical decision-making identified on pages 51–2 to reach a solution.

2.3 (Ethical issues) ★

The following situations involve Lola Payne, an audit senior with the accounting firm of Joyce & Mark. She is involved with the audit of Dockland Ferries Limited (Dockland).

1. The assistant accountant of Dockland resigned six months ago and has not been replaced. As a result, Dockland's transactions have not been recorded and the books are not up to date. To comply with the terms of a loan agreement, Dockland needs to prepare interim financial statements but cannot do so until the books are posted. The managing director of Dockland wants Lola to help them out because she performed the audit last year. The audit partner of Joyce & Mark allows Dockland to use her for one month before the start of the annual audit.
2. During the annual audit of Dockland, Lola discovers Dockland had materially understated net income on the previous year's tax return. The client is unwilling to take corrective action. Lola decides to inform the taxation office.
3. On completion of the fieldwork of the audit of Dockland, Lola is offered six free ferry tickets by the managing director. He tells her this gesture is meant to show his appreciation of a job well done. Lola accepts the tickets.
4. The partner of Joyce & Mark is not pleased with the time Dockland is taking to pay its audit fee for the year. He decides to take $5000 out of a trust fund that Joyce & Mark holds for Dockland. He intends to replace it as soon as the company pays its audit fee.

(continued)

Required

For each of the above four situations (a) identify the ethical issues involved, and (b) discuss whether there has been any violation of ethical conduct. Support your answers by reference to the relevant professional statements.

2.4 (Ethical issues) ★

Steven, a trainee auditor, is undertaking part-time university studies. While auditing the books of Oval Park Health Club, he discovers certain financial and management information that he believes will assist him in completing one of his university assignments. He copies the information and uses it in his assignment, carefully removing all reference to the name of the club to preserve the client's confidentiality.

Required

Discuss the ethical issues involved in this situation.

(Professional Year Programme of the ICAA — 1997, Accounting 2 Module — adapted)

2.5 (Joint Code of Professional Conduct) ★★

The following circumstances raise questions about an auditor's ethical conduct.

1. An auditor accepts an engagement knowing that he or she does not have the expertise to do the audit.
2. An auditor quotes a client a fee but also states that the actual fee will be contingent on the amount of work done.
3. A public accounting firm states in a newspaper that it has had fewer lawsuits than have had its principal competitors.
4. An auditor discloses confidential information about a client to a successor auditor.
5. A public accountant pays a commission to a solicitor to obtain a client.
6. A public accountant agrees to be the committee chairperson for a local fund-raising activity.
7. An auditor accepts a Christmas gift from a client.
8. An auditor accepts a commission from an insurance company for recommending it to one of its audit clients.
9. An auditor has a bank loan with a bank that is an audit client.
10. An auditor retains a client's records as a means of enforcing payment of an overdue audit fee.

Required

(a) Indicate in each of the above ten circumstances whether the effect on professional ethics is (i) a violation, (ii) not a violation or (iii) indeterminate.

(b) Identify the rule that is at issue in each case. Give reason(s) for your answer.

2.6 (Independence) ★★

Polo Babywear Limited was formed on 30 August 20X0 and its first financial year will end on 30 June 20X1. The audit firm of Ross, Young & Partners has tendered for and won the audit for the first financial year. After signing the audit engagement letter, Mr Ross is approached and asked to act as the company secretary for a period of six months because the company has had difficulty in obtaining staff. The role would be primarily to sign documents and to satisfy the ASIC that the company had a complete set of officers. Mr Ross would have no financial interest in the company through share ownership or otherwise, would receive no salary, would not keep the books, and would not give any advice that is different from what he would normally give in his duties as a public accountant.

Mr Ross decides to accept the offer, conditional on the appointment being definitely completed before the rendering of the audit opinion on the financial report.

Required

Discuss Mr Ross's acceptance of the dual roles as company secretary and auditor.

(AICPA — adapted)

2.7 (Independence) ★★

The accounting firm of Michael Lewis & Associates has been performing the audit of Versatile Fittings Limited for a number of years. The firm decides to review some relationships with the company as part of its efforts to ensure independence. These are outlined below.

1. The audit manager in charge of the audit of Versatile holds 1000 $1 ordinary shares in the company (total shares on issue — $100 000). The audit partner holds no shares.
2. An audit partner of Michael Lewis & Associates is a personal friend of the chief accountant of Versatile. The chief accountant is not a director of the company and the audit partner is not responsible for the audit work of Versatile.
3. The audit fee from Versatile for the year was $200 000. The total fee income from the audit section of the firm was $1 600 000.
4. The audit partner responsible for Versatile is also responsible for the audit of Hill's Hardware Limited. Versatile has tendered a contract with Hill's Hardware for the supply of a material quantity of fixtures over the next few years. Hill's Hardware has asked the audit partner to advise on the matter.

Required

Comment on each of the four situations above in the context of audit independence. State the principles involved.

(ACCA — adapted)

2.8 (Incompatible duties) ★★

Warren Nickel has been requested by an audit client to perform a non-recurring engagement involving the implementation of a computer information system. The client requests that Warren, in setting up the new system and during the period before converting to the new system:

- advise on the potential expansion of business activity plans;
- search for and interview new personnel;
- hire new personnel;
- train personnel.

In addition, the client requests that Warren, during the three months after the conversion:

- supervise the operation of the new system;
- monitor client-prepared source documents and make changes in basic computer information system-generated data as he may deem necessary without the concurrence of the client.

Warren says that he may perform some of the services requested, but not all of them.

Required

(a) Nominate which of these services Warren Nickel may perform.

(b) Before undertaking this engagement, Warren should inform the client of all significant matters related to the engagement. Nominate these matters.

2.9 (Audit quality) ★★

John Doyle is the financial controller for a large retail company. Every year the auditors visit the company for about four weeks (usually during August) to perform the annual audit. The team usually comprises an audit senior and two audit assistants. This year John notices that the audit lasted only about two weeks and that there was only one audit senior and one audit assistant on the job. He had not seen either of these two people before and he was surprised that they asked only a few questions. After the audit was finished, an unqualified audit report was given on the company, as usual. However, John felt his company had not been audited properly. He decided to ring the audit partner, Jenny Jones, and advise her of his concern. Jenny said that the reason for the shorter time period was that auditing technology had improved. John was not convinced.

Required

(a) Explain how John Doyle could determine whether the auditors had performed adequate work.

(b) Discuss some of the proposals to improve audit quality that may alleviate John Doyle's concerns.

2.10 (Fraud) ★★

You are a partner in an auditing firm. You have just received notification that one of your audit clients is suing your firm for negligence. It has discovered that its accounts receivable clerk has been misappropriating funds received from customers for the past year. Although a substantial amount of money was involved, it was not material compared with total cash receipts. The audit client has evidence that your firm found a discrepancy during the audit in testing accounts receivable. It also knows that your firm brought the discrepancy to the attention of the accounts receivable clerk.

You decide to locate the audit file to review what the audit senior recorded in his working papers. You note that the audit senior felt that the accounts receivable clerk had given a satisfactory explanation and that no further action was deemed necessary.

Your client believes your firm should have reported the matter to a more senior person within the organisation and followed it up more thoroughly.

Required

(a) Prepare a defence based on auditors' obligations for detecting and reporting irregularities.

(b) Do you think you will win the case? Explain.

Case studies

2.1 (Ethical issues) ★★★

Noreen Parke has been working at Tony Young & Associates for three years. Noreen and her husband Tom are both interested in environmental issues and have participated in community work concerning the environment. During a pharmaceutical company's annual audit for the financial year ended 30 June 20X1, Noreen notices the company had recently changed its contractor for waste management to Dumpound Limited. Noreen happens to know, through her community activities, that Dumpound is being investigated by the local council for the level of toxic waste at one of its sites.

The waste management contract between Dumpound and the pharmaceutical company does not specify damages and has not been signed by Dumpound. The contract is for a substantial amount and valid for three years, and Noreen is concerned about the implications. The local council carries out strict inspections and imposes heavy fines for toxic dumping.

Noreen raises the issue with Tony, the partner in charge of the audit. 'This is reality, Noreen,' Tony says sternly. 'As far as I am concerned, we are responsible for the correctness of its financial report, and nothing else. Besides, you do not have the qualification to judge if a company is a good corporate citizen or not. We are not concerned with the business management.' Noreen is told to mind her audit without raising any fuss.

Required

(a) Explain the ethical issues involved here.

(b) Recommend a course of action for Noreen.

2.2 (Independence) ★★★

You are an audit supervisor at Flack Mitchell — a large, reputable accounting firm with offices across Australia. Your client is Newbuild Limited — a large and diversified group operating in the housing sector. Your firm recently won a competitive tender to provide extensive internal auditing services to Newbuild. The fee quoted in the tender was 50 per cent of standard charge rates. Flack Mitchell also performs internal auditing work for Jensons Limited, which is Newbuild's major competitor.

Flack Mitchell operates distinctly separate internal and external audit divisions. The objectives and scope of Newbuild's internal audit were set by its audit committee after detailed advice from Flack Mitchell. The work performed by the internal audit division of your firm began two months before the end of the financial year and was extensive. It included:

- reviewing controls surrounding all major transaction flows and reporting to the audit committee on improvements;
- performing creditors' circularisation and preparing a list of adjusting journals for processing by accounts payable staff;
- rewriting branch stocktake instructions and attending branch stocktakes.

Your audit senior on the external audit was seconded to the internal audit division for the first two months of the engagement. This occurred because she has extensive knowledge of the housing sector and of Newbuild's operations in particular. She recently purchased roofing materials for her house from Newbuild at staff discount prices.

Required

(a) From the perspective of a small shareholder of Newbuild, discuss whether Flack Mitchell is independent in fact and appearance.

(b) Identify the specific independence issues that Flack Mitchell needs to address. Recommend a course of action for the firm for each issue.

(Professional Year Programme of the ICAA — 1997, Advanced Audit Module — adapted)

chapter 3

Auditor's legal liability

Overview

LEARNING OBJECTIVES

After studying this chapter, you should be able to:

1. comprehend the impact of the changing legal environment on the profession
2. explain the auditor's liabilities to shareholders and auditees
3. describe the concept of due care owed by auditors to those entitled to rely on their services
4. explain the circumstances giving rise to negligence in the conduct of audit and compliance
5. identify the issues and rulings of legal cases with respect to the auditor's liability to third parties
6. enumerate the precautions the auditor should take to avoid litigation
7. describe the types of and rationale for legal reform concerning auditor liability.

Professional statements

AUSTRALIAN		INTERNATIONAL
AAS 5	Materiality in Financial Statements	–
AGS 1014	Privity Letter Requests	
APS 1	Conformity with Accounting	

Note: The above statements have no equivalent international auditing statements.

Auditors are accountable in law for their professional conduct. This responsibility may arise under **common law** or statute law. Responsibility under common law may be under contract to clients or, in certain circumstances, to third parties to whom a legal duty of care is owed. Also of interest is the extent of liability in terms of:

- the determination of damages awarded by the courts where **negligence** is proved;
- defences that may be offered by the auditor in full or part mitigation of his or her responsibility.

Here we will illustrate these issues by referring to decided cases. We will also describe the extent of auditors' statutory responsibilities. The vulnerability of the auditing profession to negligence lawsuits has been brought to notice in recent years by two sets of events: firstly, the litigation crisis, and secondly, arising out of the Cambridge Credit and AWA cases, the debate over the limitation of company auditors' exposure to liability.

THE LEGAL ENVIRONMENT

LEARNING OBJECTIVE 1

Comprehend the impact of the changing legal environment on the profession.

Throughout its history, the public accounting profession has had an extremely low percentage of **alleged audit failures** relative to the total number of audits conducted. In recent years, both the volume and cost of litigation related to alleged audit deficiencies have caused some concern to the profession. This can be attributed, in part, to several widely reported business failures that resulted in significant losses to investors. However, not all business failures can be equated with audit failures. There is a growing concern that too often following a business failure and alleged fraudulent financial reporting, the plaintiffs and their legal representatives prey on the auditor regardless of degree of fault, simply because the auditor may be the only party left with sufficient financial resources to indemnify the plaintiffs' losses (the so-called **deep pockets theory**).

The requirement to hold a practising certificate imposes an obligation on auditors to carry **professional indemnity insurance** for possible liability to their clients and members of the public. This source of compensation creates a perception that auditors have 'deep pockets' and, arguably, it contributes to the extent of claims filed against them. There is a presumption that the courts, finding this source of compensation to be a means of spreading loss, are easily influenced by the arguments of the plaintiffs' solicitors.

On the other hand, accountants should be aware of the trap generally known as the **'no transaction' claim**. A typical example is when a client enters into a risky venture, supported by funding from a financier. For a minimal fee, the accountant provides advice on a certain aspect of the venture. If the venture fails, the client, the financier or both may sue the accountant. The basis for their case is that the venture would not have proceeded if not for the accountant's negligent advice and, consequently, the accountant should compensate the client or the financier for all losses following the failed venture. This argument ignores the fact that the negligent advice in question may have caused only a small part of the total loss. The loss may be due to a combination of factors, including bad business decisions by the client, the financier's breaching of its own prudential standards or external influences such as economic downturn.

In Australia, the courts have generally accepted the 'no transaction' argument, except in the case of *Trust Company of Australia v. Perpetual Trustees of WA*. Assuming that the courts accept 'no transaction' claims, the test for adequacy of an accountancy practice's limit of indemnity ought not to be the level of fees earned. Rather, it should be a value based on the transactions undertaken by the clients, which is difficult to estimate. Therefore, how much professional indemnity is enough is impossible to estimate.[1]

The settlement of claims by insurance companies leads to increases in future premiums. Consequently, professional indemnity insurance is becoming increasingly expensive and almost unacceptably high.[2] A figure of $60 000 per partner per year for the Big Five firms has been quoted. The 2000 Practice Comparison Survey by the Institute of Chartered Accountants in Ireland shows a major difference in professional indemnity insurance premiums borne by accounting firms, even though the firms had not suffered any claims. Sole practitioners took a minimum cover of 65 per cent of their annual billings, with the annual average premium at a minimum of 3.5 per cent of turnover. Partnerships were insured for at least 1.6 times the annual average billings per partner, with the annual premium at a minimum of 5 per cent of the average turnover per partner.[3] Insurance premiums can vary substantially, depending on the firm's claims, experience and risk profile. A benchmark of around 1–2 per cent of turnover has been quoted.[4] Furthermore, the cover that can be obtained often falls well short of meeting the claims. This coverage gap between the potential liability and available insurance cover exposes auditors to the risk of significant personal liability. Many argue that this risk represents a real threat to the viability of the profession.

A further influence on litigation against auditors is the increasing **internationalisation of the profession**. International firms practising in Australia may well be caught up directly in lawsuits originating overseas. Australian firms auditing controlled entities or branches of multinational companies with overseas creditors and ownership interest could find themselves being sued in overseas courts.

The recent debate in the United States concerning multi-disciplinary practices (commonly called MDPs) further complicates the issue of professional liability. A multi-disciplinary practice is a partnership, professional corporation or other association or entity that includes lawyers and non-lawyers, and delivers legal services to clients as one, but not all, of its purposes. In June 1999, the American Bar Association MDP Commission issued its recommendation to the House of Delegates in support of multi-disciplinary practices, proposing that the Association allow attorneys to share legal fees with non-attorneys and provide legal services to clients through such practices. Changes to the ethical rules (the Model Rules of Professional Conduct) were also proposed. The rule changes would allow accounting firms to employ attorneys who could offer, subject to certain restrictions, a full array of legal services to their clients. The rule changes would also allow accountants and lawyers to share fees and be partners under one roof. Proponents of fee sharing from both the legal profession and the accountancy profession note that multi-disciplinary practices already exist in other countries.

The blurring lines between the legal and accounting professions have led to the creation of mega-professional services firms in multi-disciplinary partnerships, capable of providing a multitude of products and services. This recent trend became apparent in the accounting profession in 1999 when the Big Five firms expanded their legal arms and recruited 'big dollar' lawyers, aiming to offer services as one-stop shops. Although the Securities and Exchange Commission in the United States has put forward strict new regulatory proposals on professional practices, Australian accountants appear ready to embark on the challenge. Following a decision by the New South Wales Government, there is pressure on state governments to allow the incorporation of law firms in Australia. Western Australia revealed in August 2000 that it would follow New South Wales and introduce legislation allowing for multi-disciplinary practices. Given this emerging trend, more complex issues concerning the auditor liability debate can be expected, because the structure of such practices may impose further constraints on the joint and several liability of a partnership and, to some extent, would heighten the risks of conflicts of interest situations. In Australia, for example, both KPMG and Arthur Andersen have been active in recruiting top lawyers from large legal firms to provide their assurance engagement clients with a one-stop shop. On the other hand, large legal firms have been seen to be recruiting marketing and software personnel from accounting firms to enable their expansion into the financial services market. However, the noticeable turnover of legal personnel in the past twelve months in the Big Five firms may suggest that the change is still very much at an early stage.

The litigation crisis

On 22 January 1998 the *Australian Financial Review* reported that the accountancy industry had survived the $7.5 billion litigation tidal wave that had threatened to swamp the profession after the corporate collapses of the 1980s and early 1990s. The number and size of claims that have been mounted against auditors over the past fifteen years or so indicate the seriousness of the current legal environment for the auditing profession. Claims lodged over this time were as high as $3.1 billion, with settlement amounts being as high as $136 million. The claims alleged a range of defaults, including negligence, breach of contract, incorrect placement of a company in receivership, failure to account for loans and transactions properly, and failure to give a true and fair view of company accounts. Consequences of these alleged defaults were the near collapse or failure of banks, losses on investments and foreign exchange deals, overstated profits and aborted sales of companies.

Litigation against auditors is argued to be having an adverse effect. Firms are retreating from serving high-risk clients, and some smaller firms are shying away from audits — a trend that is counter to the public interest. It is also argued that intense competition for fees accelerated the breakdown of traditionally stable relationships between firms and their clients. Furthermore, the litigation crisis is causing professional staff to question their continued association with audit firms and deterring new graduates from entering into public practice.

How can a profession with a multi-level regulatory framework, including technical, ethical and quality control standards and a system of quality or practice reviews, find itself in such a predicament? Certainly, some audits have not measured up to existing standards. Some litigation can also be attributed to the audit expectation gap discussed in Chapter 2. Furthermore, with advanced technology and the push for electronic commerce, large accounting firms have become concerned about the potential risks of liability in respect of the increasing assurance services they provide (see the 'Professional environment' below). In this chapter, we will also examine the problem of auditor liability in relation to client companies and to third parties, and introduce recommendations for legal reform.

PROFESSIONAL ENVIRONMENT

Auditor liability for electronic commerce transaction assurance

The American Institute of Certified Public Accountants (AICPA) and the Canadian Institute of Chartered Accountants (CICA) have developed a new and promising assurance service for certified practising accountants/chartered accountants (CPAs/CAs) to offer clients — the WebTrust. A WebTrust seal of assurance is issued by a licensed CPA or CA who has been hired by a business web site owner to render the WebTrust assurance service. Once a seal is obtained, the entity will be able to continue displaying it on its web site provided the CPA or CA WebTrust provider updates the assurance examination at least once every three months. Consumers will be able to access the web site owner's business policies and the auditor's opinion regarding business practice disclosures, transaction integrity and information protection by clicking on the WebTrust seal of assurance on the web page.

The WebTrust is one example of a movement towards the emergence of a business reporting system in which the primary vehicle for transmission of business information is a computer network such as the Internet. Former Securities and Exchange Commission Commissioner Steven Wallman predicted a movement away from 'substance attestation' towards 'process attestation'. Process attestation means providing some type of assurance about the integrity or reliability of the business reporting system a client employs, rather than about the integrity of the information produced by such a system.

The development and deployment by CPAs and CAs of any new assurance service, such as the WebTrust, are carried out in a high litigation risk environment. The litigation crisis that has confronted the accounting profession during the last twenty-five years ... [has seen accountants and auditors] becoming defendents in lawsuits filed by aggrieved shareholders or creditors. The potential liability of assurance providers is staggering given that a WebTrust seal on a business web site can be accessed by virtually anyone who owns or has access to a computer. No US legal case has yet been reported which addresses directly the liability of accountants to non-clients for disseminating misleading financial or business information over a computer network. The rule that can be distilled from several related legal cases is that one who negligently disseminates misleading financial or other business information on a public medium will be immune from a negligence claim. However, the current US legal environment is characterised by a high level of uncertainty. Several risk management strategies may be adopted by WebTrust providers to minimise litigation risk.

(Source: Adapted from Carl Pacini and David Sinason, 'Auditor Liability for Electronic Commerce Transaction Assurance: The CPA/CA WebTrust', *American Business Law Journal* (Spring 1999), pp. 479–514)

LIABILITY TO SHAREHOLDERS AND AUDITEES

2 LEARNING OBJECTIVE

Explain the auditor's liabilities to shareholders and auditees.

For audits conducted in accordance with the Corporations Law, the auditor is liable under statute and common law to the shareholders for any negligent performance of statutory duties. These duties cannot be restricted or reduced.

Auditors are also liable in the same manner as any other citizen for cases of fraud or defamation. The Corporations Law stipulates that auditors, in cases of irregularities, are required to report to the Australian Securities and Investment Commission (ASIC) if they have 'reasonable grounds to suspect' any contravention of the law.

One of the major problems in accepting greater responsibility for reporting suspected fraud to a regulatory body is that the auditor, if he or she is mistaken, may be liable to a defamation action by the party identified by the auditor as perpetrating the fraud. Also, negligence, if proven to be wilful, may constitute a conspiracy with management to defraud the company or other parties. Auditors in the United Kingdom and the United States have found themselves in court on the criminal charge of fraud after issuing unqualified reports on financial statements subsequently found to be misleading.

In respect of the provision of auditing services, an auditor is liable to compensate a plaintiff if:

- a duty of care is owed to the plaintiff;
- the audit is negligently performed or the opinion is negligently given;
- the plaintiff has suffered a loss as a result of the auditor's negligence (where the causal relationship is reasonably foreseeable);
- the loss is quantifiable.

Due care

3

LEARNING OBJECTIVE

Describe the concept of due care owed by auditors to those entitled to rely on their services.

We will examine the development of the concept of **due care**, as applied to the performance of an auditor's duties, by referring to cases decided in UK and Australian courts. We will then consider the relevance of professional standards — namely:

- Auditing Standards in determining the adequate performance of audit work;
- Accounting Standards in determining the basis for expressing an opinion on fairness of presentation.

The classic statement on the extent of auditor responsibility in examining the accounts to be reported on is contained in the Kingston Cotton Mill Co. case of 1896 (see box below). An equally famous case dealing with the auditor's responsibility for reporting on the accounts is the 1895 London and General Bank case (see box on page 97).

KINGSTON COTTON MILL CO. (No. 2) (1896) 2 Ch. 279

***Facts of the case*:** For several years the manager of Kingston Cotton Mill had been exaggerating the quantities and values of the company's stocks so as to fraudulently overstate the company's profits. This came to light when the company was unable to pay its debts and its true financial position was revealed. The auditor relied on a certificate signed by the manager and ensured that the amount appearing in the accounts was consistent with that certificate. The valuation of stocks was described in the accounts as being as 'per manager's certificate'. In line with contemporary practice, the auditor did not physically observe stocks or attempt to verify the valuation of individual items. Neither did the auditor reconcile stocks with the opening balance and purchases and sales during the year, all of which would have put the auditor upon notice that something was amiss.

***Judgement*:** As regards stocks, Lopes LJ had the following to say:

> I confess that I cannot see that their omission to check his [the manager's] returns was a breach of their duty to the company. It is no part of the auditor's duty to take stock. No-one contends that it is. He must rely on other people for details of the stock-in-trade in hand. In the case of a cotton mill he must rely on some skilled person for the materials necessary to enable him to enter the stock-in-trade at its proper value in the balance sheet.

In relation to the auditor's responsibilities in general, but particularly with respect to the detection of fraud, the following points from the judgement of Lopes LJ are important:

> It is the duty of an auditor to bring to bear on the work he has to perform that skill, care and caution which a reasonably competent, careful and cautious auditor would use. What is reasonable skill, care and caution must depend on the particular circumstances of each case. An auditor is not bound to be a detective, or, as was said, to approach his work with suspicion or with a foregone conclusion that there is something wrong. He is a watchdog, but not a bloodhound. He is justified in believing tried servants of the company in whom confidence is placed by the company. He is entitled to assume that they are honest, and to rely upon their representations, provided he takes reasonable care. If there is anything calculated to excite suspicion, he should probe it to the bottom but, in the absence of anything of that kind, he is only bound to be reasonably cautious and careful.
>
> The duties of auditors must not be rendered too onerous. Their work is responsible and laborious, and the remuneration moderate.

> Auditors must not be made responsible for not tracking out ingenious and carefully laid schemes of fraud, when there is nothing to arouse their suspicion and when those frauds are perpetrated by tried servants of the company and are undetected for years by the directors. So to hold would make the position of an auditor intolerable.

The Kingston Cotton Mill case laid down some fundamental auditing principles such as the 'watchdog' role and the notion of taking reasonable skill and care.

LONDON AND GENERAL BANK (No. 2) (1895) 2 Ch. 673

***Facts of the case*:** The bank made loans to customers for which it held inadequate security. Interest due on the loans was accrued but not received, yet dividends were paid out of profits arising from such interest. The auditor made a full report to the directors in respect to the valuation of these loans and the need for a provision for bad debts against both the loan and the accrued interest. However, in his report to the shareholders, the auditor merely qualified his opinion with the following sentence: 'The value of the assets as shown on the balance sheet is dependent upon realisation'.

***Judgement*:** As regards the auditor's responsibility for reporting, Lindley LJ observed:

> It is no part of an auditor's duty to give advice either to directors or shareholders as to what they ought to do.
>
> It is nothing to him whether the business of the company is being conducted prudently or imprudently, profitably or unprofitably; it is nothing to him whether dividends are properly or improperly declared, provided he discharges his own duty to shareholders. His business is to ascertain and state the true financial position of the company at the time of the audit and his duty is confined to that.
>
> He is not an insurer; he does not guarantee that the books do correctly show the true position of the company's affairs; he does not guarantee that the balance-sheet is accurate according to the books of the company. If he did, he would be responsible for an error on his part, even if he were himself deceived, without any want of reasonable care on his part — say, by the fraudulent concealment of a book from him. His obligation is not so onerous as this.
>
> Such I take to be the duty of the auditor: he must be honest — that is, he must not certify what he does not believe to be true, and he must take reasonable care and skill before he believes that what he certifies is true.

As to the specific issues of the case, however, Lindley LJ noted the following:

> It is a mere truism to say that the value of loans and securities depends upon their realisation. We are told that a statement to that effect is so unusual that the mere presence of those words is enough to excite suspicion. But, as already stated, the duty of an auditor is to convey information, not to arouse enquiry, and although an auditor might infer from an unusual statement that something was seriously wrong, it by no means follows that ordinary people would have their suspicions aroused by a similar statement if, as in this case, its language expresses no more than an ordinary person would infer without it.

The judgement also discussed at length the extent of inquiry necessary to enable an auditor to express an opinion on the accounts. This part of the judgement was relied on by Lopes LJ in arriving at his judgement as to the auditor's responsibilities in the Kingston Cotton Mill Co. case.

Implications of the Kingston Cotton Mill Co. case and London and General Bank case

These two cases have formed the basis for most subsequent decisions as to the determination of auditor negligence. The recognition of auditing as a profession is crucial in both instances. The auditor does not guarantee that the financial report is fairly presented any more than a solicitor guarantees to win a case or a doctor guarantees to effect a cure. Neither does an auditor warrant to bring to bear the highest degree of skill in the performance of his or her duties, because there may be more skilful auditors within the profession. Furthermore, the auditor is not necessarily answerable for an error of judgement provided he or she exercises the skill and care of a reasonably competent and well informed member of the profession.

Nevertheless, a too literal interpretation of the Kingston Cotton Mill Co. case has been criticised as retarding the development of improved auditing practices. For sixty years after the case, auditors continued to rely heavily on management representations (such as inventory certificates), notwithstanding developments in auditing techniques (especially in the United States) that enabled the auditor to acquire a significantly higher degree of assurance with relatively little increase in audit effort.

In fraud detection, experience led auditors to anticipate common frauds and to design audit procedures so as to have a reasonable chance of detecting such frauds; nonetheless, they continued to rely on the Kingston Cotton Mill Co. case judgement in denying any legal responsibility for the detection of fraud in those instances where their suspicions were not aroused.

The developments in the United States arose out of criticisms of auditors contained in the Securities and Exchange Commission's report of 1941 into the McKesson and Robbins fraud. From that date, the evaluation of internal control, attendance at stocktaking and the circularisation of accounts receivable became required procedure in that country.

A comparable advance in Australia, following British case law, came about with the observation of Denning L in *Fomento (Stirling Area) Ltd v. Selsdon Fountain Pen Co. Ltd* (1958) 1 WLR 45 at 61 as to an auditor's approach. This observation was that the auditor:

> . . . must come to it with an enquiring mind — not suspicious of dishonesty, I agree — but suspecting that someone may have made a mistake somewhere and that a check must be made to ensure that there has been none.

Auditors hold themselves out as possessing special skills. Consequently, the courts will require a higher standard of care of auditors. Pennyquick J's observation in *Thomas Gerrard & Son Ltd* (1967) 2 All ER 525 at 536 was another advance. He stated that:

> The real ground on which re Kingston Cotton Mill Co. (No. 2) is, I think, capable of being distinguished is that standards of reasonable care and skill are, on the expert evidence, more exacting today than those which prevailed in 1896. I see considerable force in this contention.

The narrow interpretation of the Kingston Cotton Mill Co. case concerning some audit practice was finally laid to rest by the Pacific Acceptance case (see box on page 96). However, the more exacting auditor responsibility prompted by the Pacific Acceptance case showed the changing expectations in respect to the auditor's responsibility, with the standards of reasonable care also being altered.

One feature of the case was the willingness of the audit staff to allow themselves to be persuaded by the perpetrator of the fraud to accept his or her representations on matters where corroborative evidence was available, but not sought. This lack of objective independence was also a feature of the Cambridge Credit case. UK Department of Trade inspectors investigating corporate failures have been critical of auditors for failing to stand up to company chairpersons with strong personalities.

PACIFIC ACCEPTANCE CORPORATION LTD V. FORSYTH
(1970) 92 WN (NSW) 29

***Facts of the case*:** A branch manager of Pacific Acceptance made loans to a real estate speculator on the strength of security confirmed by a solicitor introduced by the speculator. In fact, most of the security offered in the form of title deeds, registered charges and mortgages was worthless, being either forged or improperly drawn up. Numerous auditing deficiencies were alleged, such as the assignment of insufficiently experienced audit staff, lack of adequate supervision, excessive reliance on management representations instead of examination of documentary evidence, and a failure to identify irregularities and to follow up those discovered during the audit.

***Judgement*:** In finding the auditor liable, Moffit J had the following to say about the auditor's level of skill of care:

> The legal duty, namely, to audit the accounts with reasonable skill and care, remains the same, but reasonableness and skill in auditing must bring to account and be directed towards the changed circumstances referred to. 'Reasonable skill and care' calls for changed standards to meet changed conditions or changed understanding of dangers, and in this sense standards are more exacting today than in 1896. This the audit profession has rightly accepted, and by change in emphasis in their procedures and in some changed procedures has acknowledged that due skill and care calls for some different approaches.

The judgement was wide ranging and covered the following procedures and practices which it was held should exist in a normally competent audit:

- Pay due regard to the possibility of material fraud or error in framing or carrying out audit procedures so the auditor has a reasonable expectation that the fraud or error will be detected.
- Promptly report fraud or warn of suspicion of fraud, whether material or not.
- Closely supervise and review the work of inexperienced staff.
- Properly document audit procedures in a written audit program which is to be amended as necessary as the audit progresses.
- Audit the whole of the year, not just the year-end balances; the duty to audit encompasses the client's financial affairs throughout the period of appointment and is not confined to reporting on the year-end balances as presented in the accounts.
- Carry out proper objective auditing procedures; reliance on independent sources or client personnel is an aid but not a substitute for the auditor's own procedures.
- Do not shirk reporting to shareholders on the pretext that some detriment would arise if the matter were revealed.

This catalogue of recommendations, arising largely out of deficiencies in the defendant's audit work, reveals how lax audit procedures appear to have been compared with today's requirements. One of the defences offered was the testimony of expert witnesses that the audit procedures applied by the defendants were those of a normally competent auditor. Not surprisingly, the judge commented that it was for the courts to determine whether prevailing standards are met in a particular engagement (see Chapter 2). This prompted the profession's leaders to persevere with the recently introduced program of codifying Auditing Standards to persuade all auditors to recognise the need for uniformly higher standards.

Negligence

LEARNING OBJECTIVE 4

Explain the circumstances giving rise to negligence in the conduct of audit and compliance.

Negligence has been defined as any conduct that is careless or unintentional in nature and entails a breach of any contractual duty or duty of care in **tort** owed to another person or persons. The auditor's duty of care to a client arises either in contract or in the tort of negligence. If the auditor has been negligent, then the client may sue the auditor for breach of an implicit term of the contract to exercise reasonable care and skill, so as to recover any consequential loss suffered. The client may sue the auditor in the tort of negligence to obtain **damages** sufficient to restore the client to its original position. The case of negligence, however, depends on the court's judgement under the circumstances of the case. Compliance with Accounting Standards, Auditing Standards and guidelines provides a certain degree of assurance that the auditor has exercised reasonable care and skill.

In making a report, the auditor expresses an opinion as to whether the financial report fairly presents the financial position of the entity and its operations for the period. In most of the cases so far described, the plaintiff has alleged that the auditor's investigation was flawed, thus preventing the auditor from being in a position to express an opinion. There have been very few cases against the auditor solely on the grounds that the financial report did not present the entity's financial position fairly or, as in the London and General Bank case, that any qualification in the auditor's report was not sufficiently informative as to the extent of the financial report's failure to present the financial position fairly. In the 1970s, when high inflation prevailed, it was argued that financial reports based on the historical cost convention were misleading, yet financial reports based on this convention continued to be prepared and reported on by auditors as presenting a true and fair view.

Although the Corporations Law (s.296) now requires financial reports to be prepared in accordance with applicable Accounting Standards, the auditor must still exercise judgement in applying standards to the specific circumstances of the entity on which he or she is reporting. Judgement must also be exercised in those rare circumstances envisaged by the Corporations Law (ss.295(3), 297) where compliance with Accounting Standards would not give a true and fair view, and where additional information and explanations must be added. A true and fair override is no longer applicable.

In the United States, the right of the auditor to rely on Generally Accepted Accounting Principles (GAAPs) is also subject to an overriding requirement for fair presentation. GAAPs are those principles laid down by the Financial Accounting Standards Board and its predecessor bodies, along with other accounting practices for which there is substantial authoritative support. In *Continental Vending (United States) v. Simon* (1969) 425 F 2d 796, it was held that the requirement to report on fairness is separate from the requirement to report on compliance with GAAPs. The US profession has challenged this finding by issuing an Auditing Standard requiring fairness to be determined within the framework of GAAPs. Australia's 'true and fair override' (enacted in 1991) followed the same principle — that accountants must comply with Accounting Standards in the discharge of their reporting duties.

Subsequent to the Pacific Acceptance case, the Australian accounting bodies issued more comprehensive and specific Auditing Standards and Practice Statements concerning the conduct of the audit. Disputes may still arise and will continue to be settled by the courts as to whether, in a specific engagement, an auditor has complied with the standards and thus has a good defence against an action for damages on the grounds of negligence. In the 1992 AWA case (see box on page 103), for example, the court considered whether the auditor had complied with the requirement of paragraph 28 of the former Auditing Practice Statement AUP 12 that 'the auditor should make management aware on a timely basis of material weaknesses which have come to his attention'. In this case, it was held that the auditor had been negligent. With the codification of Auditing Standards, the courts may be expected to be able to determine, to a certain degree, whether the auditor has complied with the required concept of due care.

Privity of contract

The term **privity of contract** refers to the contractual relationship that exists between two or more contracting parties. In a typical auditing relationship, an audit (or audit-related service) is assumed to be performed in accordance with professional standards unless the contract (engagement letter) contains specific wording to the contrary. Remember, also, that where an auditor is appointed under s.327 of the Corporations Law, then under s.241 of that law any contractual reduction of the auditor's liability is void.

There is sometimes misunderstanding as to the parties to the contract in an audit under the Corporations Law where the auditor's report is addressed to the members. The term 'members' is used collectively and does not indicate responsibility to individual shareholders or others entitled to receive copies of the accounts. Under contract, only the directors or, more commonly, the liquidator or receiver may sue the auditor in respect of losses incurred by the company arising from the auditor's negligence. Monies recovered by way of damages from the auditor are then applied to meet the prior claims of creditors first; only the residue, if any, is available for the shareholders. Individual shareholders, creditors, employees, directors and others have no claim against the auditor under contract. The issue of auditors' responsibility to existing and future shareholders and creditors is demonstrated in Figure 3.1.

FIGURE 3.1

Liability of auditors at one and two stages removed

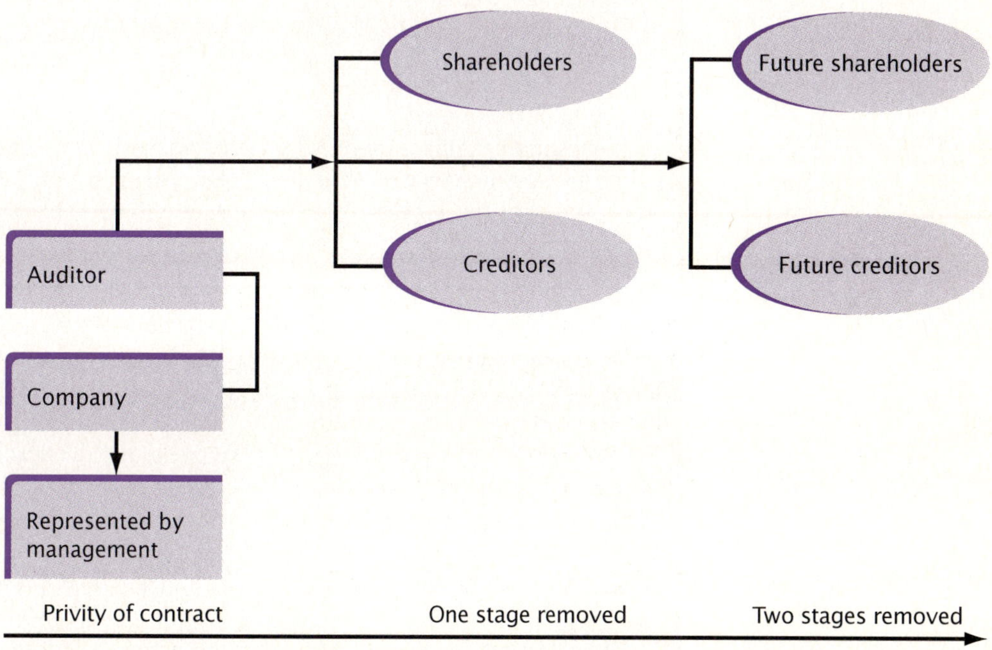

An Australian case brought by a company against its auditors for failing in their contractual duty to the company was that of *WA Chip & Pulp Co. Pty Ltd v. Arthur Young* (1987) 12 ACLR 545. In this case, a senior employee obtained loans from the company that were not properly authorised and eventually became irrecoverable. The auditors were aware of the loans and expressed concern at their size but relied on verbal assurance from the person authorising the loans that he had authority to do so. At no time did the auditors bring their concern to the attention of the general manager of the company because the amounts were not material. It was held that the auditors had been negligent.

Causal relationship

A **causal relationship** (illustrated by the two cases in the boxes below) exists between the breach of duty by the defendant and the loss or harm suffered by the plaintiff. This relationship must have been reasonably foreseeable and it must be proven that the loss suffered is attributable to the negligent conduct of the auditor in a negligent case. In *Caparo Industries Pty Ltd v. Dickman & Others* (1990) 1 All ER 568 in the United Kingdom (see box on page 110), Bridge L stated:

> In advising the client who employs him, the professional man owes a duty to exercise that standard of skill and care appropriate to his professional status and will be liable both in contract and in tort for all losses which his client may suffer by reason of any breach of that duty.

SEGENHOE LTD V. AKINS & ORS (1990) 8 ACLC 263

***Facts of the case*:** In this Australian case, Segenhoe argued that it, as a separate legal entity and distinct from its shareholders, had suffered loss by wrongly paying an amount to its shareholders that would otherwise not have been paid. It claimed the loss was due to the negligence of the auditor and should be recovered from the auditor.

***Judgement*:** The court held that where an auditor has been negligent and the company has been induced to pay a dividend out of capital — relying on an incorrectly audited profit and loss account — the auditor is liable for the loss incurred. Further, the right of the company to recover from shareholders' dividends paid out of capital is a question of mitigation of loss; the company is not required to undertake complicated litigation against shareholders. The court supported the view that where auditors are negligent, ultimately, they are likely to be liable for the full amount of loss while the corporate veil is retained.

GALOO LTD V. BRIGHT GRAHAM MURRAY (1994) BCC 319

***Facts of the case*:** For the purposes of appreciating the development of audit liability, a recent decision of the English Court of Appeal in the Galoo Ltd v. Bright Graham Murray case has reaffirmed the causation relationship requirement to establish the liability of the auditor. Galoo had incurred losses of approximately \$55 million between 1986 and 1990, and had paid a dividend of \$1.1 million in 1988. Galoo sued the auditor for breach of its contractual duty to exercise reasonable care and skill, arguing that the trading losses were attributable to the continued existence of the company, which in turn was due to reliance on the allegedly negligent audit opinions.

***Judgement*:** The court of appeal held that there was no causal connection between the alleged negligence and the losses incurred. The financial reports may have allowed the company to continue trading, but the company's existence was not the cause of its losses. The claim against the auditor was struck out.

Contributory negligence

Contributory negligence relates to the failure of the plaintiff to meet certain required standards of care. Together with the defendant's negligence, it contributes to bringing about the loss in question. The judgement in the AWA case (see box below) is the landmark decision on contributory negligence in an auditor–client relationship.

AWA LTD V. DANIELS T/A DELOITTE HASKINS & SELLS & ORS
(1992) 10 ACLC 933

***Facts of the case*:** This case provides a landmark for the principle of contributory negligence. Under the established principle that the auditor's duty has to be evaluated in the light of the standards of today, the auditor was held to have been negligent in failing to warn management of internal control weaknesses discovered during the course of the audit, even though that was not the principal purpose of the audit. An important development, however, was that the company was held to be guilty of contributory negligence through not establishing adequate controls in the first place. This reverses a finding of the Pacific Acceptance case in which it was held that the extent of an auditor's responsibility was not diminished by failings of management that contributed to the losses.

***Judgement*:** In the AWA case, the court accepted that the directors have a duty to establish a sound system of internal control to safeguard the company's assets. Their failure to do so was held to be contributory negligence. In the words of the judgement:

> . . . the primary complaints of the plaintiff are failure on the part of the auditors to report on the insufficiency and inappropriateness of the plaintiff's internal controls. Now that was not the principal purpose of the audit. It was something that the auditors discovered in the course of preparing to do their audit. I am of the view that AWA should be held to have been guilty of contributory negligence . . . Contributory negligence is a plaintiff's failure to meet the standard of care to which it is required to conform for its own protection and which is a legally contributing cause, together with the defendants' default, in bringing about the loss.

In May 1995, the New South Wales Court of Appeal reduced the auditor's share of the damages, placing further responsibility on AWA management. The court upheld the notion of proportionate liability. As a result, AWA management shared 20–33.3 per cent of the loss, the auditor's liability was reduced from 72 per cent to 66.6 per cent, and the chief executive officer's responsibility was reduced from 8 per cent to zero.

Damages

Where auditors fail in their duty to act with reasonable care and skill, whether under contract or in tort, a plaintiff is entitled to recover any economic loss arising out of such breach of duty. Two issues need to be considered here. Firstly, what is the purpose of accounts that may give rise to reliance reasonably being placed on them? Secondly, to what extent may responsibility for any loss be assigned on the one hand to the auditor's negligence and, on the other, to other causes and other parties?

The Cambridge Credit case (1985 and 1987) provides a suitable basis for examining some of these issues. Cambridge Credit Corporation failed in 1974 and it was determined that the audit of the 1971 accounts had been negligently performed. Had the auditor's report been appropriately qualified, the amended view of the company's financial position would have required the trustee for the debenture holders to appoint a receiver. It was alleged that the company, through the auditor's negligence, was allowed to remain in business for a further three years, incurring further losses before a receiver was finally appointed in 1974. Damages were claimed in the amount of losses incurred by virtue of the company being liquidated in 1974 instead of 1971.

The law is much clearer on the purpose of accounts than is most accounting theory. Accounts form the basis for the determination of legal relationships between the company and other parties; for instance, where dividends are paid out of capital (contrary to the provisions of the Companies Acts) as a result of an overstatement of profits, the auditors are liable to the extent of such dividends. In the Cambridge Credit case, the debenture trust deed provided that if the company's gearing ratio as per the audited accounts exceeded a given amount, then the debenture trustee would be entitled to appoint a receiver. Due to an overstatement of profits undetected by the auditor, the gearing ratio appeared sufficient to support the level of borrowing. In this case, the receiver sued the auditor for losses arising from the failure to appoint a receiver in 1971.

At this point we must consider the issue of the extent of loss caused by the auditor's negligence. The original verdict in the 1985 Cambridge Credit case determined damages in an amount based on the losses of the company incurred through its continued trade over a further three years. However, the auditor appealed on the grounds that he could not have foreseen the economic downturn that caused the losses to reach the level they did, and that he did not have control over the actions of management (notably, its decisions to expand borrowings and real estate investments when the real estate market was being affected by the economic decline) that may have contributed to the extent of the actual losses. The court of appeal agreed that there was no causal connection between the auditor's negligence and the losses eventually sustained by the company, and upheld the principle that the auditors are not liable for all the consequences of their negligence, only those they cause directly.

As was explained in the AWA case, damages may also be reduced in the event of contributory negligence by the company. However, that case involved the reporting of internal control weaknesses to management. Where the matter involves the auditor's report on the financial report issued by the directors (for the purpose of helping members to oversee the directors' conduct), the members, as a class, cannot be held to have contributed to the loss, notwithstanding any negligence by the directors in preparing the report. The judgement in the AWA case does not appear to be in dissent with this view, although courts are now likely to consider the possibility of contributory negligence instead of dismissing it as in the past.

LIABILITY TO THIRD PARTIES

5
LEARNING OBJECTIVE
Identify the issues and rulings of legal cases with respect to the auditor's liability to third parties.

Action for damages may also be brought against an auditor under tort, outside of any contractual relationship. In *Donoghue v. Stevenson* (1932) AC 562 it was held that a duty of care is owed to **third parties** in the absence of a contract where the plaintiff has suffered physical injury. The case related to a woman who drank a bottle of ginger ale (bought by her sister) which appeared to have the remains of a snail at the bottom. She was taken ill and later sued Stevenson, the soft-drink manufacturer. Atkins LJ, in defining the limits of when a duty of care is owed, stated:

> You must take reasonable care to avoid acts or omissions which you can reasonably foresee would be likely to injure your neighbour. Who, then, in law is my neighbour? The answer seems to be — persons who are so closely and directly affected by my act that I ought reasonably to have them in contemplation as being so affected when I am directing my mind to the acts or omissions which are called in question.

From this case, it became evident that a duty of care can be owed to a third party through negligent acts. Liability to third parties for financial injury is still confused. Since the 1964 Hedley Byrne case, a number of such actions have been brought against auditors, but rarely successfully. The UK House of Lords verdict in the Caparo Industries case makes it doubtful that any third party claim under the Corporations Law (s.331A) against an auditor in respect of his or her report would succeed.

Prior to the Hedley Byrne case (see box on page 105), the precedent was derived from such cases as *Ultramares Corporation v. Touche Niven & Co.* (1931) 255 NY in the United States and *Candler v. Crane Christmas & Co.* (1951) 1 All ER 426 in the United Kingdom. In the Ultramares case, Cardozo CJ found for the defendant accountants on the grounds that:

> If liability for negligence exists, a thoughtless slip or blunder, the failure to detect a theft or forgery beneath the cover of deceptive entries may expose accountants to a liability in an indeterminate amount for an indeterminate time to an indeterminate class.

In adopting Cardozo CJ's view, the courts simply denied liability for negligence in making statements. If the plaintiff suffered an economic loss as a result of statements made by a defendant, then the plaintiff would recover damages only if the defendants had been guilty of fraud, as in *Derry v. Peek* (1889) 14 App Cas 337 and the Candler case.

In the Candler case, it was found that the defendants owed no duty to the plaintiffs in the absence of any contractual relationship and that the negligence claim could not be sustained. Denning LJ, however, passed a dissenting judgement:

> [Accountants] owe a duty, of course, to their employer or client, and also, I think, to any third person to whom they themselves show the accounts, or to whom they know their employer is going to show the accounts so as to induce him to invest money or take some other action on them. I do not think, however, the duty can be extended still further to include strangers of whom they have heard nothing and to whom their employer without their knowledge may choose to show their accounts. Once the accountants have handed their accounts to their employer, they are not, as a rule, responsible for what he does with them without their knowledge or consent ... [This duty] extends, I think, only to those transactions for which the accountants knew their accounts were required.

The UK House of Lords upheld this view in reaching its decision in the Hedley Byrne case. The majority decision in the Candler case was expressly overruled and Denning LJ's dissenting judgement was upheld as correctly stating the law.

Under the Hedley Byrne principle, auditors' liability to third parties to whom they owe a duty of care is no different from their liability to clients in that (1) they must have been negligent in the performance of their duties, (2) the plaintiff must have suffered an economic loss arising directly from that negligence and (3) the loss must be quantifiable. The problem lies in determining to whom that duty of care is owed. The Hedley Byrne case identified a number of relevant factors and emphasised that different factors would have different weights in different types of case. The issue has come to be known as one of **proximity**. The Pandora's box envisaged by Cardozo CJ in the Ultramares case has not been opened.

The Hedley Byrne case is a landmark case for professional liability to third parties. Readers will often refer to it.

HEDLEY BYRNE & CO. LTD. V. HELLER & PARTNERS
(1963) 2 A11 ER 575

Facts of the case: The Hedley Byrne case involved not an auditor but a bank. The bank (Heller & Partners) was approached by Hedley Byrne, an advertising agency, for a credit reference on a potential client, Easipower Limited, which was a customer of the bank. The reference was supplied by the bank without making a careful check of its records. The negligence of the bank in supplying the reference was not disputed. On the strength of the reference, the advertising agency incurred costs on behalf of its client, which went into liquidation before the costs were recovered. The bank's first defence was that it owed no duty of care to the plaintiff in the absence of any contractual or fiduciary relationship with the advertising agency. The bank's duty of care was owed to its client. The second defence was the presence of a disclaimer at the foot of the reference supplied.

Judgement: In reaching a decision, the House of Lords upheld the minority judgement of Denning LJ in the Candler case. Reid L, in his judgement, said in relation to the limits of duty:

> I can see no logical stopping place short of all those relationships where it is plain that the party seeking information or advice was trusting the other to exercise such a degree of care as the circumstances required, where it was reasonable for him to do that, and where the other gave the information or advice when he knew or ought to have known that the inquirer was relying on him. I say 'ought to have known' because in questions of negligence we now apply the objective standard of what the reasonable man would have done.

The verdict, however, was in favour of the defendant on the grounds that the disclaimer of liability was a good defence, notwithstanding that a duty of care existed.

Proximity

As a result of the reluctance of professional indemnity insurers to allow cases to come to court for reasons explained earlier in this chapter, there have been very few decided Australian cases of significance involving claims by third parties against auditors. There have been only a few such cases overseas, and examination of these cases demonstrates the law's confusion about the matter. Most of these cases involve action being brought by companies relying on audited accounts in making a takeover bid for another company. Proximity is held to arise through the fact that where a company's financial condition is such that it is a likely takeover target, auditors should be aware that potential suitors will rely on the accounts and that a duty of care thus arises. Proximity is generally meant to be interpreted as the person injured physically or financially being within that class that could reasonably be considered as being affected by the act.

The Australian High Court applied the doctrine of negligent misrepresentation in the Evatt case (see box on page 107) in 1968. The expertise of the defendant was crucial to the decision.

MUTUAL LIFE AND CITIZENS ASSURANCE CO. LTD V. EVATT
(1968) 122 CLR 556

***Facts of the case*:** Evatt was a policyholder in Mutual Life and Citizens Assurance Co. Limited (MLC Assurance). MLC Assurance was a subsidiary of MLC Limited. Evatt approached MLC Assurance and sought advice on the financial stability of H. G. Palmer Limited (Palmer). Palmer was also a subsidiary of MLC Limited. He also inquired whether investment in Palmer was a sound decision. Evatt claimed that he approached MLC because it had a special relationship with Palmer. Acting on that advice, the plaintiff invested in Palmer, which subsequently failed. The plaintiff claimed that MLC's negligent advice had caused his loss.

***Judgement*:** The High Court of Australia held that the defendant did owe the plaintiff a duty to take care in giving advice. It was held that the fact that the defendant was not in the business of giving investment advice did not affect the existence of duty to take reasonable care in giving such advice. Barwick CJ said:

> The elements of special relationship to which I have referred do not require either the actual possession of skill or judgement on the part of the speaker or any profession by him to possess the same. His willingness to proffer the information or advice in the relationship which I have described is, in my opinion, sufficient.

MLC Assurance appealed to the Privy Council (see *Mutual Life and Citizens Assurance Co. Ltd v. Evatt* [1971] AC 793). The Privy Council reversed the decision of the High Court on the basis that MLC Assurance was not in the business of giving investment advice, and nor did it claim expertise in the giving of investment advice.

Thus, the Privy Council accepted that negligent misrepresentation was part of the law of Australia but restricted its application, insofar as advisers are concerned, to situations in which the advice was given by a person who was in the business of giving advice of that nature.

The decision of the Privy Council in the Evatt case in 1971 was rejected by a majority of the High Court in the Shaddock case (see box below).

SHADDOCK & ASSOCIATES PTY LTD V. PARRAMATTA CITY COUNCIL (1981) 55 ALJR 713

***Facts of the case*:** Shaddock & Associates was a land developer with an interest in buying a parcel of land in Parramatta. It enquired of the Parramatta City Council whether there were any proposals for road widening that might affect the property. The Council said that there was not, so Shaddock purchased the land. In fact, the Council did have a proposal to compulsorily acquire a part of the said property for road-widening purposes. The plaintiff (Shaddock) was unable to sue for breach of contract and so sued for tort of negligent misstatement.

(*continued*)

***Judgement*:** In summing up the circumstances in which a duty of care will apply, Mason J said:

> Whenever a person gives information or advice to another upon a serious matter in circumstances where the speaker realises, or ought to realise, that he is being trusted to give the best of his information or advice as a basis for action on the part of the other party and it is reasonable in the circumstances for the other party to act on that information or advice, the person giving the information or advice is under a duty to take reasonable care that the information or advice is accurate.

The High Court held that the Council owed a duty of care to the plaintiff. It was further held that the Council had breached its duty and was therefore liable to compensate the plaintiff. This gives a determinative role to reliance as the cornerstone of proximity in cases of negligent misstatements.

In the New Zealand case of *Scott Group Ltd v. McFarlane* (1978) 1 NZLR 553, two out of three appeal court judges held that the auditor owed a duty of care to the plaintiff, but only one judge thought that any loss had been suffered as a result of reliance on the negligently audited accounts, and the quantum of loss (if any) could not be determined.

In the JEB Fasteners case (see box below), Woolf J held that the auditor owed a duty of care, but that the plaintiff's loss had not arisen out of reliance on the audited accounts.

JEB FASTENERS LTD V. MARKS, BLOOM & CO. (1981) 2 AER 289

***Facts of the case*:** Marks, Bloom & Co. was the auditor of BG Fasteners. Marks, Bloom & Co. was aware that BG Fasteners was in financial difficulty. A company, JEB Fasteners, previously unknown to the auditor, took over BG Fasteners. Subsequently, JEB Fasteners sued the auditor for negligence on the grounds that inventories of the company were overstated. It was alleged that JEB Fasteners paid more for the acquisition than it would have, had it known the true facts.

***Judgement*:** The test applied was one of reasonable foreseeability that the company would use the audited accounts to obtain financial support, or be a subject of a takeover. It was held that there was sufficient degree of 'proximity or neighbourhood', thus a duty of care was owed to the plaintiff. No damages were awarded because the plaintiff's purpose for taking over the company was to obtain the services of two directors of BG Fasteners. The causal relationship between the auditor's negligence and economic loss was not established.

In the Twomax case (see box on page 109), a third party was successful in recovering losses suffered through reliance on negligently audited accounts. The essential elements in a negligence action that must be proven to the satisfaction of the courts are shown in Figure 3.2 (page 109).

TWOMAX LTD V. DICKSON, McFARLANE & ROBINSON
(1983) Scots Law Times Reports 98

***Facts of the case*:** Dickson, McFarlane & Robinson was the auditor of Kintyre Knitwear. Kintyre reported losses of $33 000 and $12 000 for the years ending 31 March 1971 and 1972 respectively. A profit of $20 000 was reported for the 1973 year. Relying on the 1973 audited accounts, Twomax and two other investors acquired a controlling interest in Kintyre. Subsequently, for the year ended 31 March 1975, the audited accounts showed a loss of $88 000. The company went into liquidation and the investors lost their entire investment. It was alleged that the profits reported in 1973 were a myth, and litigation was commenced against the auditor.

***Judgement*:** The precedent set in the JEB Fasteners case was upheld. Stewart J, in his judgement, concentrated on the principle of foreseeability. Given the financial condition of Kintyre, the probability of a takeover was reasonably foreseeable. The potential investors were owed a duty of care. The auditor, however, did not meet the required standard of care: the audit was negligently performed; there were errors in the accounts; overseas commissions were underestimated; and there was under-provision for bad and doubtful debts. The auditor 'made no attempt to circularise any debtors for the 1973 audit or even to go through the list of debtors for bad or doubtful debts'. Lord Stewart awarded damages to the plaintiff.

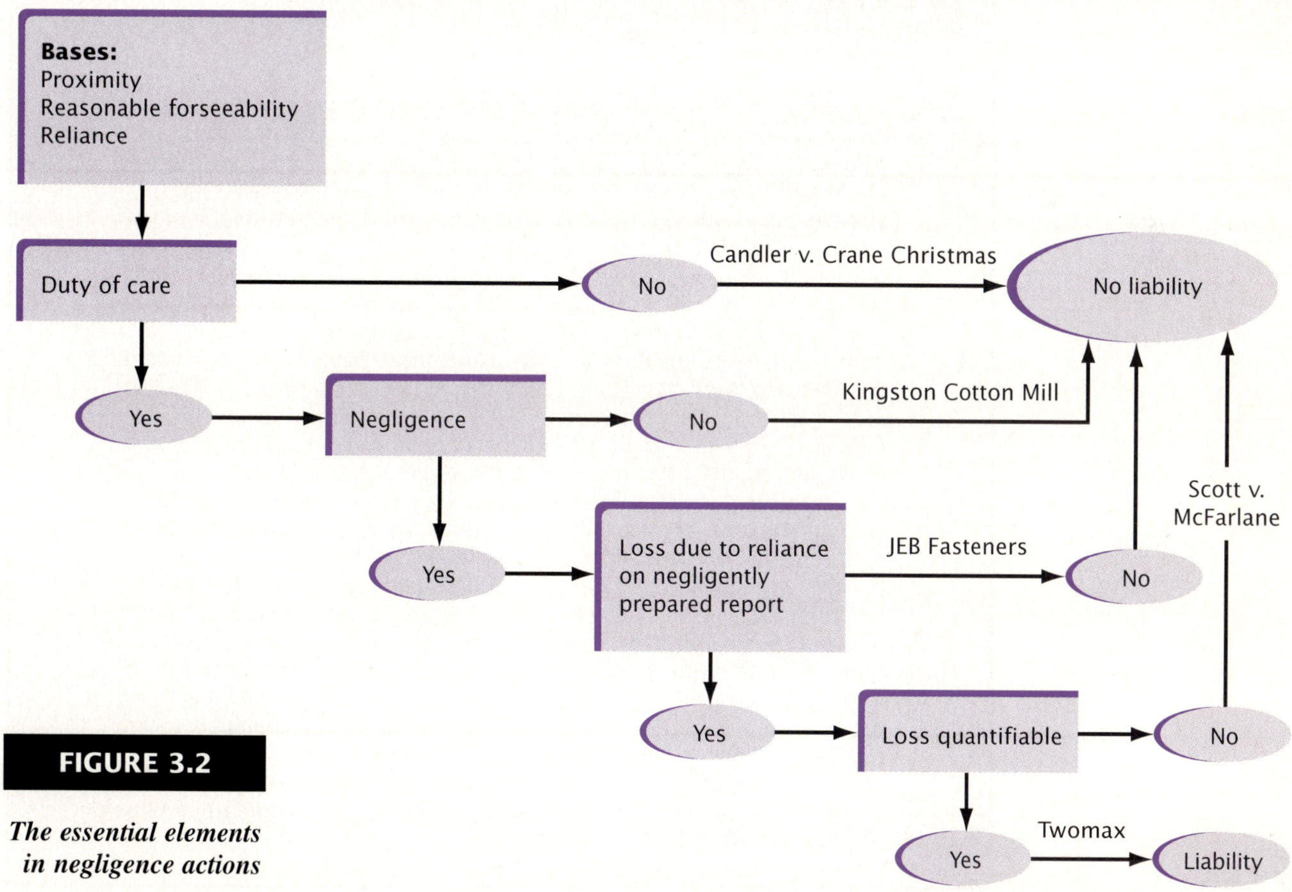

FIGURE 3.2

The essential elements in negligence actions

The UK Court of Appeal hearing of the Caparo case was later reversed in the House of Lords. In a majority verdict, two of the judges held that a duty of care was owed to only third parties who were existing shareholders that the auditors knew would receive and rely on their report. This reversed the findings in the three previous cases which all held that a duty of care was owed to those relying on the accounts for the purposes of making a take-over bid, regardless of whether they were already shareholders. The third judge upheld the High Court's finding that no duty of care was owed.

CAPARO INDUSTRIES PTY LTD V. DICKMAN (1990) 1 A11 ER 568

***Facts of the case*:** Caparo Industries relied on the audited accounts of Fidelity PLC in making a successful takeover bid for that company. The audited accounts for Fidelity showed a profit for the year ended 31 March 1984 of £1.2 million. After taking Fidelity over, Caparo discovered that the result should have been a loss of over $400 000 and alleged that the auditors had been negligent in auditing the accounts. The trial was of a preliminary issue as to whether the auditors owed a duty of care to the plaintiff. The issue of negligence was not an issue to be determined then.

The High Court judge found that no duty of care was owed to the plaintiff. This verdict was overturned by a majority verdict in the Court of Appeals but, as explained above, on different grounds from that of previous cases. Given the importance of the matter, leave was given for a final appeal to the House of Lords, which is the highest court in the United Kingdom.

***Judgement*:** Their Lordships reached their verdict by identifying the statutory purpose for the audit:

> The structure of the corporate trading entity, at least in the case of public companies whose shares are dealt with on an authorised stock exchange, involves the concept of more or less widely distributed holding of shares rendering the personal involvement of each individual shareholder in the day-to-day management of the enterprise impracticable, with the result that management is necessarily separated from ownership. The management is confided to a board of directors which operates in a fiduciary capacity and is answerable to and removable by the shareholders who can act, if they act at all, only collectively and only through the medium of a general meeting, hence the legislative provisions requiring the board annually to give an account of its stewardship to a general meeting of the shareholders. This is the only occasion in each year on which the general body of shareholders is given the opportunity to consider, to criticise and to comment on the conduct of the board of the company's affairs, to vote on the directors' recommendation as to dividends, to approve or disapprove the directors' remuneration and, if thought desirable, to remove and replace any or all of the directors. It is the auditors' function to ensure, so far as possible, that all the financial information as to the company's affairs prepared by the directors accurately reflects the company's position in order, first to protect the company itself from the consequences of undetected errors or, possibly wrongdoing (by, for instance, declaring dividends out of capital) and, second, to provide shareholders with reliable intelligence for the purpose of enabling them to scrutinise the conduct of the company's affairs and to exercise their collective powers to reward or control or remove those to whom that conduct has been confided. (Lord Oliver)

On this basis it was argued that it would be unreasonable:

> ... to widen the area of responsibility ... and to find a relationship of proximity between the advisor and third parties to whose attention the advice may come in circumstances in which the reliance said to have given rise to the loss is strictly unrelated either to the intended recipient or to the purpose for which the advice was required. (Lord Oliver)

And neither was it the intention of the Act:

> For my part, however, I can see nothing in the statutory duties of a company's auditors to suggest that they were intended by Parliament to protect the interests of investors in the market. (Lord Oliver)

In summary, therefore, the House of Lords argued that the purpose of the financial statement on which auditors express an opinion is to assist the shareholders in their collective function of scrutinising the company's affairs. It would be unreasonable, therefore, to hold the auditors responsible for their use, by shareholders or others, for any other purpose.

Preceding the Caparo case, of the cases in which the courts held that the auditors owed a duty of care to those relying on the accounts in making a takeover bid, in only the Twomax case did the court find that any loss arose from that reliance. In the Scott Group and JEB Fasteners cases, the courts found no direct link between reliance on the accounts and any loss suffered; they recognised not only the limitations of general purpose financial reports as a basis for investment decision-making, but also the reliance by investors on many other sources of information.

Reaction to the Caparo case verdict

Reaction to the House of Lords verdict in the Caparo case has generally been unfavourable. The general view of the legal profession is that the verdict appears to treat auditors more favourably than it treats other experts on whom third parties place reliance. There is also concern that it appears to reverse what is seen as a socially desirable development in law of holding experts liable for the consequences of negligent advice.

Even auditors are divided in their reaction. Many accept that audited financial reports provide investors with a reliable source of information. The value of auditors' services are seen, therefore, to be diminished. One response by third party users of financial reports (such as investors, lenders and suppliers of goods and services) has been to request a letter from the auditor in which the auditor acknowledges the user's reliance on the audited financial report, thereby establishing a relationship with the required **foreseeability** and proximity. Such letters are known as privity or comfort letters. (Auditing Guidance Statement AGS 1014, Privity Letter Requests provides guidance to auditors who are asked to provide such a letter.)

In reaching its verdict, the House of Lords implied that it is up to the UK Parliament to introduce legislation whereby auditors' statutory responsibilities could be extended to meet directly the interests of investors.

The Caparo case was followed by a majority verdict of the Victorian Supreme Court in the Lowe Lippmann Figdor & Franck case (see box on page 112).

LOWE LIPPMANN FIGDOR & FRANCK V. AGC (ADVANCES) LTD
(1992) 2 VR 671

***Facts of the case*:** AGC (Advances) was a finance company and the main creditor of Lyvetta. Lowe Lippmann was the auditor. Lyvetta created a false set of stock sheets, which led to an overstatement of stocks as at 30 June 1981 by $228 000. This converted what would have been a loss of $205 000 for that year into a profit of $23 000. Lyvetta's auditor knew of the stock sheets that disclosed the true position, but signed a report on the 1981 accounts which was unqualified. Lyvetta requested an increase in its credit facilities from AGC. Before making advances, AGC wished to examine an audited copy of Lyvetta's financial reports.

An officer of AGC telephoned the auditor and requested the audited accounts 'for review purposes'. The officer also asked the auditor whether the profit was $100 000 as had been stated by Lyvetta. The auditor replied that the profit would be a lesser sum.

In this case the auditor failed to detect that the value of closing stocks and, thus, profit was overstated in the company's 1981 accounts. Its negligence in this regard was not denied. The company derived a substantial portion of its finance from AGC, which extended its credit on the strength of the company's 1981 audited results. On the subsequent collapse of the company, AGC sued the auditor for its losses on the grounds that it was owed a duty of care.

***Judgement*:** The Supreme Court finding, which was reversed on appeal, held that the test of proximity was satisfied and that the auditor did owe a duty of care in tort to AGC. The principal grounds for reaching this verdict were that AGC had made direct contact with the auditor by telephone, indicating its interest in receiving the audited accounts as quickly as possible.

On appeal, however, it was held that the expression of interest by AGC in the audited accounts for the purpose of reviewing its position did not create a special relationship with the auditor. The interest of a major creditor in the audited accounts is only to be expected. The auditor was not aware that the accounts were produced for the special purpose of inducing AGC to act in a certain way. As the judgement states:

> The auditor who supplies his report to the company in the usual way cannot be liable unless his purpose, or one of his purposes, in making the statement in question is to induce the plaintiff, or a class which includes the plaintiff, to act on it.

The court referred to the Caparo case, and its acceptance of the limitations of the purpose of an auditor's report delivered under the Companies Act (as it then was) appears to have been influenced by that judgement. The judgement also cites, as precedent, *San Sebastian Pty Ltd v. The Minister* (1986) 162 CLR 340 — an Australian case involving reliance by a property developer on planning scheme documents issued by a local authority.

Post-Caparo case developments

Limits to the applicability of the Caparo case have been established in the UK Court of Appeal case of *Morgan Crucible Co. PLC v. Hill Samuel Bank Ltd and Others* (1991) 1 AER 148. In a contested takeover of First Castle Electronics by Morgan Crucible Co., the directors of First Castle Electronics issued circulars to their shareholders advising them not to accept Morgan Crucible's offer. Consequently, Morgan Crucible increased its offer and was eventually successful. The circulars issued by First Castle Electronics included the results revealed by the most recent audited accounts, as well as interim accounts for the first half of the current financial year and a profit forecast for the year.

In a letter to the directors of First Castle Electronics, the auditor reaffirmed its opinion as to the truth and fairness of the audited accounts and stated that the accounting policies that were adopted in compiling the interim accounts and profit forecast were in accordance with generally accepted accounting practices in the United Kingdom and consistent with those that were normally adopted by the group. The court held that the auditor should have known that its representations, although related to circulars issued by First Castle Electronics, would be relied on by Morgan Crucible in making its offer. By its actions the auditor established a duty of care to Morgan Crucible by implying the relevance of its representations to the purposes of the takeover bid.

In the Columbia Coffee & Tea case (1992), a purchaser of shares sued the auditor for negligence in respect of the value of the shares. The Supreme Court of New South Wales did not follow the decision in the Caparo case or the Lowe Lippmann Figdor & Franck case.

Rolfe J of the New South Wales Supreme Court focused on the fact that the audit manual of the defendent auditor acknowledged that the persons interested in its reports extended beyond those to whom the reports were addressed. Rolfe J held that this amounted to the auditor assuming responsibility for a class of persons beyond just the company and its shareholders. Thus, according to Rolfe J, the auditor could owe a duty of care to a purchaser of shares who:

- relied on the audited accounts and audit report;
- suffered economic loss as a result.

On the facts in the Columbia Coffee case, Rolfe J found that the prospective investor had not actually relied on the audited accounts in any way, so the action failed as a result of a lack of causation.

ESANDA FINANCE CORPORATION V. PEAT MARWICK HUNGERFORDS (1994) 12 ACLC 199

***Facts of the case*:** Peat Marwick Hungerfords was the auditor of Excel for the year ended 30 June 1989. Esanda Finance Corporation alleged that it, relying on the audited accounts, lent money to companies associated with Excel, accepting a guarantee from Excel, and purchased debts from Excel upon terms that included an indemnity from Excel against a shortfall. Excel was subsequently placed in receivership. This resulted in a loss to Esanda. In a statement of claim, Esanda did not plead that the auditors intended it to rely on the audited accounts.

***Judgement*:** King CJ outlined (at 201) that since the introduction into law of the concept of legal liability for negligent misstatement in the Hedley Byrne case:

> ... there have been difficulties in defining the circumstances giving rise to a duty of care in relation to statements and the class of persons to whom the duty is owed. The concept of reasonable foreseeability of harm which had served adequately in relation to physical acts was found to be no longer adequate, standing alone, by reason of the spectre of, to use the famous words of Cardozo J in *Ultramares Corporation v. Touche* (1931) 174 NE 441, 'liability in an indeterminate amount for an indeterminate time to an indeterminate class'. This has led to a revival of recognition of the notion of proximity, found in the seminal speech of Lord Atkin in *Donoghue v. Stevenson* (1932) AC 562 at 578 et seq., but rather submerged in subsequent cases, as an essential requirement, together with foreseeability of harm, for the imposition of a duty of care.

(*continued*)

It was indicated that the auditor was a member of the Institute of Chartered Accountants in Australia and, as such, bound by the Australian Accounting Standards. Reference was made to Miscellaneous Professional Statement APS 1, Conformity with Accounting Standards and Urgent Issues Group (UIG) Consensus Views which, in substance, provides that the Australian Accounting Standards are mandatory for members and lays down the principles to be followed by members. The failure by a chartered accountant to observe the provisions of APS 1 may be regarded as failure to observe a proper standard of professional care, skill or competence. Specific reference was made to Australian Accounting Standard AAS 5, Materiality in Financial Statements. The test of materiality requires consideration as to who are likely to be the prime users of financial statements. It was indicated that the present and potential providers of equity or loan capital, and creditors are an important group of users of financial statements. This was an attempt to demonstrate that a duty of care was owed to the plaintiff.

King CJ put this matter to rest:

> I am unable to see how membership of the body responsible for the promulgation of those Standards can give rise to a duty of care to persons to whom a duty would not otherwise be owed. Apart from any other consideration, the Standards themselves do not purport to create such a duty. They are not concerned with the legal duty but with the content of financial statements. The concept of materiality is developed for the purpose of determining what should be included in financial statements. The reference to providers of loan capital and creditors as users of financial statements occurs in the context of determining what is material for inclusion in such statements. It does not imply any assumption of legal responsibility to such users to exercise care.

King CJ, referring to the Columbia Coffee & Tea case, stated that the *Auditor's Audit Manual* is not of similar status, purpose and language to the Accounting Standards. He added that reasoning underlying the Columbia Coffee & Tea case is inconsistent, in his view, in relation to the significance of the Accounting Standards.

King CJ stated (at 204) that:

> It seems to be that in a case of alleged auditor's liability to persons other than the client or members of the client company, the assumption of responsibility necessary to dispense with the need for an intention to induce reliance will exist only where there is a clear indication of a willingness to be responsible to the particular plaintiff, or to a class of which he is a member, for the careful auditing of the financial statements. I do not think that a mere inclusion in a manual or set of standards of an acknowledgement of a professional responsibility to have the interests of users other than the client in mind in determining what is to be included in the accounts or in carrying out the audit can have the effect of enlarging the area of legal duty by creating a legal duty of care to persons to whom it would not otherwise be owed.

The case was further appealed to the High Court, which ruled in favour of the auditor in an unreported judgement delivered on 18 March 1997. The judgement upheld the earlier decision of the Supreme Court of South Australia.

Brennan CJ stated that it was not possible, based on the facts, for the third party to rely on the report prepared by the auditor. He held that for a third party to succeed in such circumstances, the following would have to be established:

1. The report was prepared on the basis that it would be conveyed to a third party.
2. The report would be conveyed for a purpose that was likely to be relied upon by that third party.
3. The third party would be likely to act in reliance on that report, thus running the risk of suffering the loss if the statement was negligently prepared.

It was suggested that liability could exist if someone in Esanda's position suffered loss. However, there was nothing to suggest that Esanda was unable to have accountants assess Excel's true financial position on its behalf, as a condition to entering into a financial transaction with Excel. There was nothing to suggest that it was reasonable for Esanda to act on the audited reports without further enquiry.

The outcome in the Esanda Finance Corporation case (1994) (see box on page 113) provided some comfort to the auditor. This outcome was the result of an appeal against the decision of Bollen J in *Esanda Finance Corporation v. Peat Marwick Hungerfords* (1993) 11 ACLC 908. The Full Court of the Supreme Court of South Australia held that the defendant did not owe the plaintiff a duty of care. The Court endorsed the approach of the House of Lords in the Caparo case and indicated that the decision in the Columbia Coffee & Tea case was wrong.

Thus, the judgement of the Esanda case appears to support the view of Justice Cardozo in the Ultramares case that to allow third parties to sue in such a case would be to expose auditors to 'liability in an indeterminable amount for an indeterminable time to an indeterminable class of persons'.

In Australia, the common law concerning the nature and extent of an auditor's duty of care to third parties remains complex because judgements contain differences of judicial opinion and interpretation. However, the judgement in Esanda was a positive development for auditors because the Court rejected the contention that liability could be based on foreseeability of reliance alone. The High Court found that there had to be circumstances establishing a relationship of proximity between the auditor and the third party before a duty of care could be said to exist. This indicates that the auditor has to come into a real relationship with the third party for liability to arise, rather than just know of the third party's existence as a theoretical possibility.

6 LEARNING OBJECTIVE

Enumerate the precautions the auditor should take to avoid litigation.

Avoidance of litigation

The following precautions may be taken by auditors wishing to avoid or minimise the consequences of litigation.

- *Use engagement letters for all professional services.* Engagement letters are of particular importance on non-audit engagements (such as those described in Chapter 4) where misunderstanding may arise as to the nature of the public accountant's association with the financial report. They are also important on audit engagements where there may be some misunderstanding as to the extent of an auditor's responsibilities, particularly as to the detection of fraud. The new Statement of Auditing Standards No. 83 in the United States (issued in 1997) — Engagement Letter — details the auditor's responsibility for the conduct of the audit and suggests other matters that may be included in the letter: arrangements regarding the conduct of the engagement such as timing and assistance required; fees; and limitations regarding the liability of the auditor or the client, such as indemnification of the auditor for liability arising from management's misrepresentations to the auditor. The following 'Professional environment' illustrates how an engagement letter is used as a defensive tool.

PROFESSIONAL ENVIRONMENT Using the engagement letter as a defence

A recent case in California demonstrates the importance of drafting the engagement letter so as to minimise potential legal liability. In *Software Design v. Price Waterhouse*, investors in Embrace Systems Corporation sued the company's auditor, Price Waterhouse, for its alleged inaccurate audit report, contending that they were third party beneficiaries of the engagement contract. The California Court of Appeals concluded that the plaintiffs were not third party beneficiaries based on the unambiguous terms of the engagement letters. The investors were not identified or even alluded to in the engagement letters signed by Price Waterhouse and acknowledged by Embrace.

(Source: Extracted from Michael J. Garrison and James D. Hansen, 'Accounting and Auditing Update', *Ohio CPA Journal* (July–September 1999), pp. 59–62)

- *Investigate prospective clients thoroughly.* Establishing a policy on client acceptance is seen as a means of reducing exposure to litigation. Litigation tends to follow corporate collapse. It can be limited by avoiding clients that are in poor financial health or managed by directors whose business ethics or competence is suspect as a result of past association with failed corporations.
- *Comply fully with professional pronouncements.* Strict adherence to Auditing Standards is essential. An auditor must be able to justify any material departures from established guidelines.
- *Recognise the limitations of professional pronouncements.* Professional guidelines are not all encompassing. In addition, it should be recognised that the courts and regulatory agencies will use subjective tests of reasonableness and fairness in judging the auditor's work. The auditor must use sound professional judgement during the audit and in the issue of the audit report.
- *Establish and maintain high standards of quality control.* The dominant objective of quality control is the assurance that all of the firm's work complies with required professional standards. Recent cases have emphasised the particular importance of:
  — the assignment of appropriately competent staff to engagements and their proper supervision;
  — adequate documentation of all audit procedures;
  — compliance with independence guidelines, especially in terms of personal relationships with clients.
- *Maintain adequate professional indemnity cover.* Professional indemnity insurance has been the cause of misunderstanding. Some argue that it protects auditors against their legal responsibilities, encouraging a less than desirable standard of care, because any losses can be claimed against insurance. A contradictory view is that the possession of indemnity insurance encourages lawsuits on the grounds that the insurance company will have to pay. It is generally held, however, that responsible public accountants need to carry such insurance for the protection of their clients. Professional indemnity insurance is required to obtain a certificate of public practice.

- *Be prepared to issue a privity letter, on request.* Following the Caparo decision, auditors may be asked to acknowledge the third party's reliance on an audited financial report (the privity letter). The purpose of the letter is to establish a relationship with required foreseeability and proximity, and thus a duty of care by the auditor to the third party. Auditing Guidance Statement AGS 1014, Privy Letter Requests was issued in 1991 to guide auditors if requested to produce a privity letter. AGS 1014.5 states that a decision to provide such a letter is an individual business risk and management decision.

LEARNING CHECK

3.1 Auditors have been facing a litigation crisis following the corporate collapses of the 1980s, which may be a result of the deep pocket theory, the expectation gap and the possible erosion of audit quality.

3.2 Under statute and common law, auditors are liable to the auditee company if the following factors exist: (1) a duty of care is owed to the plaintiff; (2) negligence has been proven; (3) a causal relationship is established for financial or other loss suffered by the plaintiff; and (4) the losses are identifiable and quantifiable.

3.3 Contributory negligence is applicable where management is found to be liable for a failure of internal control, leading to injury to the plaintiff.

3.4 An auditor's liability to third parties is established if (1) they owe a duty of care to the party (based on the criteria of proximity, reliance and reasonable foreseeability); (2) negligence has been proven in the performance of the auditor's duties; (3) economic loss has been suffered as a consequence of the negligence; and (4) the loss is quantified.

3.5 The landmark cases of Caparo and Esanda establish that the duty of care of auditors is owed to a body of shareholders as a whole, unless at the time of the audit, the auditor had knowledge of the third party and that there would be reliance on the audit report and financial statements.

3.6 Auditors should avoid litigation by: (1) complying with auditing standards; (2) ensuring a clear understanding of the engagement is conveyed through the engagement letter; (3) under certain circumstances, giving consideration to issuing a privity letter; and (4) adhering to proper quality controls.

TRADE PRACTICES LEGISLATION

In addition to the legislative rulings discussed earlier, the *Trade Practices Act 1974* (Cwlth) and the state Fair Trading Acts provide further rights for individual investors and shareholders. Section 52 of the Trade Practices Act prohibits misleading and deceptive conduct, and has been used as a basis for several successful actions by investors against promoters of businesses and others in respect of misleading statements. Investors can also make use of the Trade Practices Act to take actions under common law for deceit and negligence. Similarly, the state Fair Trading Acts offer a further channel for redress to shareholders and investors. In the Esanda case, in ruling out the claim that 'the auditor's duty to report is statutory, and is merely incidental to the provision of accounting and auditing services for reward, and [does] not give rise to trade or commerce,' Bollen J argued that:

> ... the words 'trade or commerce' are to be given a wide import. The lending of money is surely in trade or commerce. Accountants assist those who lend money. Auditors work for those who lend money. It may be held in the end that an auditor is right in the middle of trade or commerce.

Therefore, the Esanda case is a very important case for the future of auditors' liability to third parties. One can note, too, that a litigation under the Trade Practice Act does not require the various factors of foreseeability and proximity as do cases under tort of negligence.

LEARNING OBJECTIVE 7

Describe the types of and rationale for legal reform concerning auditor liability.

THE NEED FOR LEGAL REFORM

The potential claims against auditors reporting on entities responsible for many millions of dollars of assets and liabilities are astronomical, as has been indicated in the early part of this chapter. The damages awarded against the auditors can be far in excess of their ability to pay, either from their own resources or through their professional indemnity cover. The award is likely to be totally unrelated to the audit fee received for the work performed, as is exemplified by the initial award of $145 million in the case of *Cambridge Credit Corporation Ltd and Anor v. Hutcheson & Ors* [1985] ACLR 545. The possible collapse of an accounting firm as a result of litigation is a reality; it has already happened to Levanthal & Horwath and Spicer & Oppenheim in the United States. The well capitalised and well managed firms may survive, but they and their partners are increasingly at risk. The liability system is regarded as a risk transfer mechanism and the auditors are the prime transferees.

The judgement in the Cambridge Credit case provided the momentum for the accounting profession to seek legal reforms that are likely to curb unwarranted litigation. The momentum for reform was accelerated by the comments made by Rogers CJ in *AWA v. Daniels, t/a Deloitte, Haskins & Sells & Ors* (1992) 10 ACLC 933 (at 1022):

> The scope for injustice occasioned by solidary liability is self apparent ... In brief, a well insured defendant, who may perhaps be responsible for only a minor fault, in comparison with the fault of other persons, may nonetheless be made liable, at least in the first instance, for the entirety of the damage suffered by the plaintiff. The defendant may indeed seek contribution from other persons responsible for the major damage. Why should the whole of the burden of a possibly insolvent wrongdoer fall entirely on a well insured, or deep pocket defendant?

The Auditors' Legal Liability Task Force of the International Federation of Accountants (IFAC) produced a report in June 1995 analysing the worldwide situation regarding auditors' legal liability.[5] The legislative reforms recommended by the IFAC are:

- eliminating joint and several liability in favour of a system of proportionate liability;
- allowing auditing firms more organisational options;
- adopting a statutory limitation or 'cap' on professional liability for negligence;
- providing disincentives for plaintiffs filing frivolous lawsuits;
- adopting a statutory requirement for professional advisers and directors of companies to have adequate insurance cover;
- limiting auditor responsibilities to third parties;
- strengthening privity standards;
- reducing the statute of limitations.

Proportionate liability

A suggestion is that some form of **proportionate liability** be introduced whereby the plaintiff's loss is divided among the defendants according to their share of responsibility. As a result of the law of joint and several liability, even if an auditor commits a small degree of fault, the auditor must bear the entire financial burden of damages. Under proportionate liability, defendants are required to pay only in proportion to their involvement in any wrongdoing. This essentially enables the courts to assess awards that reflect the degree of responsibility of each defendant. Seven states in the United States abolished the doctrine of **joint and several liability** in favour of proportionate liability. Proportionate liability rules also apply in Denmark and France. Currently, the New Zealand Law Commission is examining the issues and support for such reform.

In Australia, the July 1994 report of the Inquiry into the Law of Joint and Several Liability detailed several alternatives of proportionate liability: proportionate liability in all circumstances; proportionate liability when the plaintiff is partly at fault; proportionate division of the insolvent defendant's share; and proportionate liability and the defendant's degree of fault.[6] Here, we will describe each in turn.

Proportionate liability in all circumstances

Each defendant bears the proportion of the loss suffered by the plaintiff that is equal to his or her level of responsibility. Legislation in Victoria, South Australia and the Northern Territory abolishes joint and several liability for those who may be found responsible for defective building work, and imposes proportionate liability in all circumstances without regard to whether the plaintiff has also been in any way to blame for the loss. It has the advantage of holding each defendant responsible 'to the extent to which the act or default of that defendant contributed to the damage or loss' (*Development Act 1993* (SA), s.72). This legislation obviously relates to building trades. Nevertheless, it is a move away from joint and several liability, and sets a precedent for other trades and professions.

Proportionate liability when the plaintiff is partly at fault

Proportionate liability is applied when there is contributory negligence on the part of the plaintiff. This approach extends the principle of apportionment of the liability between the plaintiff and the defendant to all defendants and the plaintiff in proportion to the degree of fault of each. This method of apportionment is law in British Columbia, for example.

Proportionate division of the insolvent defendant's share

This method is practised in Ireland and is proposed in New Zealand. If a defendant turns out to be insolvent or untraceable, his or her share of the loss or damage is divided rateably among all other parties, including the plaintiff, in proportion to their respective share of responsibility. The risk of an insolvent defendant is thereby spread among all remaining parties.

Proportionate liability and the defendant's degree of fault

This type of proportionate liability has been introduced in some jurisdictions in the United States. A defendant's liability is proportionate if the degree of fault is less than a specified percentage or less than that of the plaintiff. It has the disadvantage of an arbitrary stipulation of the percentage ceiling. The National Joint Limitation of Liability Task Force of the Institute of Chartered Accountants in Australia (ICAA) and the Australian Society of Certified Practising Accountants (now CPA Australia) was of the opinion that the introduction of proportionate liability, in association with a statutory cap on liability, will be a valuable reform. The Inquiry into the Law of Joint and Several Liability (in its second report issued in January 1995) recommended proportionate liability in all circumstances.

More organisational options for auditing firms

Auditors need flexibility in selecting forms of practice that can help them to maximise their business opportunities, but minimise their personal risk. Many countries limit practice options for auditors and, as a result, subject them to greater liability exposure — much more so than even their own clients. By allowing accounting firms to take advantage of organisational forms such as limited liability companies and limited liability partnerships (as well as permitting them to incorporate), the personal assets of partners not involved in malpractice wrongdoing may be protected from unsatisfied malpractice claims against the firm.

The accounting profession's codes of ethics prohibit the incorporation of services that require members to hold a certificate of public practice, such as those provided for auditing, taxation, liquidation and trustee in bankruptcy. This prohibition ensures that members accept 'full responsibility and full liability for negligence . . . [which is not limited] in any way by practising through a corporate structure'. However, certain activities permitted by law, and with the consent of the National Council, may be provided through service, administrative or practice entities. Given these constraints, public practitioners operate either as sole practitioners or through partnerships with unlimited liability.

In some jurisdictions of the United States, limited liability partnerships and limited liability corporation statutes have been enacted. It is expected that all states in the United States eventually will adopt some form of similar legislation that does not limit liability resulting from an individual's own substandard work. However, such legislation would limit an individual's liability (arising from the substandard work of other partners or shareholders in the professional firm) to the individual's capital investment in the firm. Thus, a partner or shareholder would not need to fear losing his or her home and other personal assets as a result of shortcomings in another's work. Incorporation of audit practices is also permitted in the United Kingdom, although, at the time of publication, only PriceWaterhouse had announced its intention to incorporate. The profession is seeking the adoption of similar practices in Australia.

In seeking these reforms, the profession argues that it is not asking to be held harmless when at fault. Rather, it is asking that it be granted equity in the judicial process and that it not be hindered by unwarranted liability claims that arise from providing a service essential to the public. For its part, the profession, through self-regulation, has been improving Auditing Standards and practices, and is continuing to monitor compliance with these standards.

Incorporation is already common practice for firms in France, Germany, Switzerland, Japan and some provinces in Canada. There is no evidence in these countries that incorporation has negatively affected the quality of the auditor's work.

Limiting the auditor's liability and the statutory cap issue

The issue of limited liability has been debated for some years. In September 1986 the Companies and Securities Law Review Committee recommended the introduction of a statutory cap on auditor's liability, being a multiple of the audit fee. The statutory cap (as a multiple of the audit fee) introduces a direct correlation between the nature and size of the audit engagement (as reflected in the fees) and the potential liability. It is argued that such a scheme, together with a requirement for compulsory indemnity insurance and risk management strategies, can provide appropriate protection to users and some guarantee of payments to claimants.

This recommendation was rejected by the government, however, on the grounds that it would represent an unwarranted intrusion by the state and may lead other professions to seek similar concessions. At the time, the preferred approach was to ensure that auditors carry adequate indemnity insurance such that the cost of audit failure is equitably distributed and not borne by those whose legitimate claims against the auditor are unsatisfied through the operation of the statutory cap. However, the professional bodies are continuing to push for some kind of ceiling on auditors' liability. In 1993 the Commonwealth Attorney-General released a report, *Professional Liability in Relation to Corporations Law Matters*, prepared by the Ministerial Council for Corporations (MINCO). The report observed that capping of liability was the preferred option of professional bodies, yet there were more preferred alternatives for limiting the liability of auditors and other professionals under the Corporations Law. These alternatives included:

- permitting the incorporation of audit practices as limited liability companies;
- replacing the rules relating to joint and several liability with proportionate liability;
- amending s.241 of the Corporations Law to permit companies to pay the insurance premiums for (or indemnify) auditors and officers. This option was taken up in the *Corporation Law Reform Act 1994* (Cwlth).

MINCO's second option was considered in 1994 when the Attorneys-General of the Commonwealth Government and the New South Wales Government set up an inquiry into the law of joint and several liability.

There has been some success at the state level, particularly in New South Wales, which enacted the *Professional Standards Act 1994* (NSW). (Similar legislation is expected to be passed in Western Australia.) The Act (often referred to as the PSA) seeks to limit the liability for members of approved professional and other occupational associations to a capped amount, referred to as a 'limitation amount'. The maximum amount is determined by either a multiple of the fee charged or a specific amount backed by professional indemnity insurance and/or business assets (s.23). The maximum liability of accountants is \$50 million. Capping is to apply to only claims of \$500 000 or more. Compulsory insurance, risk management schemes and a complaints system are also stipulated in the Act.

The scheme described in the Act is unusual for something embodied in legislation in that it is not imposed on any particular profession. Rather, individual professional bodies determine whether they will participate and they then seek a specific scheme for their members. While the accounting profession is of the view that this Act will be effective, some argue that it will not achieve the desired result and that a national uniform approach should be adopted.

Some professionals argue that the Act is substantially hindered in three ways — each probably stemming from the fact that the Act's aims do not have support at a national level.[7] The three scenarios in which the Act is seen to have been undermined are described below:

1. *Forum shopping*: While only some jurisdictions may seek to cap liability, there is a potential for forum shopping, whereby plaintiffs shape and pursue their claims so as to be governed by jurisdictions where liability remains unlimited.
2. *Liability under the Trade Practices Act*: Negligence claims against professionals are typically coupled with allegations of breaches of the Trade Practices Act, while the statutory liability for negligence is sometimes ignored or remains unaffected. One should also note that the quantum of damages recoverable under the Trade Practices Act is much less than the expectation damages flowing from statute.
3. *Directors' and officers' position*: Although directors can be included as an occupational association, the provision in the PSA excludes directors and officers so as to limit their level of liability arising from statutory breaches of their obligations under the Corporations Law.

Any agreement between the auditor and the company attempting to indemnify the auditor against any liability for negligence or breach of duty is made void by s.241(1) of the Corporations Law.

On the other hand, legislation penalising those who initiate frivolous suits can help deter opportunistic litigation. The United Kingdom, for example, already has a rule requiring that the loser of a lawsuit pay the defendants' legal costs. Also, some countries (such as

Norway) have introduced legislation to increase the requirements for proof of an adequate link between auditors' culpable behaviour and the damages incurred. As a result, auditors have had far fewer claims awarded against them. Privity standards determine when non-client third parties, such as clients' creditors, have the right to sue an auditor for malpractice. Strong privity standards limit the circumstances under which third parties may sue auditors for malpractice. Another measure has been the recommendation to establish a reasonable period during which one can bring a suit to court (to help accounting firms keep their liability exposure and liability insurance fees under control).

The issue of auditor liability and the recommendations for related legal reform have also been subject to other external influences, such as political agendas.

LEARNING CHECK

3.7 The legal reforms proposed to limit auditors' liability for negligence include: introducing statutory limitation or capping; changing joint and several liability into proportionate liability; and providing flexibility for more organisational options for accounting firms such as incorporation.

3.8 The statutory capping of liabilities has been introduced by the Professional Standards Act in New South Wales. Complications arise, however, when a prospective plaintiff shops for the 'best' forum in seeking damages against the auditor, using either the Trade Practices Act or different state laws.

3.9 Proportionate liability can be shared on the basis of attributable fault, responsibility or contributory negligence with other parties.

3.10 Auditors are advised to strengthen privity standards and establish proofs of the link between the damage suffered and the alleged negligence.

SUMMARY

Litigation has had a significant impact on the public accounting profession and it seems reasonable to expect that it will continue to do so in the foreseeable future. In this chapter we examined the changing legal environment concerning auditors, highlighting some of the issues that have arisen as a result of case law and the corporate collapses of the 1980s. Auditors can be liable for negligence or breach of duties under the Corporations Law. We discussed auditors' liability to shareholders and auditees, with particular reference to the concept of due care and negligence. A number of case decisions over the past few decades have highlighted the importance of the criteria in establishing auditor liability in court — namely, reliance by the plaintiff on the auditor's report, proven breach of negligence by the auditor, a causal relationship between the negligence and the loss suffered by the plaintiff, and the existence of a duty of care.

The concepts of proximity and foreseeability provide some guidance for examining whether a duty of care exists. In this chapter we also discussed the concept of contributory negligence (as a result of case law) where the conduct of directors and auditors is found to be 'contributing' to the damage suffered by the plaintiff. However, the issue of auditor liability is very much an unresolved matter. The case law concerning auditors' liability to third parties is inconsistent and the applications of the tests for proximity and reasonable foreseeability have been inconclusive.

The complexity of the issue has led to calls for legal reforms. We discussed the debates concerning different types of reform in Australia and overseas. So far, reforms affecting auditor liability have been slow and, to some extent, ineffective as a result of a number of factors.

KEY TERMS

Alleged audit failures, p. 92
Causal relationships, p. 102
Common law, p. 92
Contributory negligence, p. 103
Damages, p. 100
Deep pockets theory, p. 92
Due care, p. 96
Foreseeability, p. 111
Internationalisation of the profession, p. 93
Joint and several liability, p. 119
Negligence, p. 92
'No transaction' claim, p. 92
Privity of contract, p. 101
Professional indemnity insurance, p. 92
Proportionate liability, p. 118
Proximity, p. 105
Third parties, p. 104
Tort, p. 100

NOTES

1. An information article for accountants (*Charter* (June 1998), pp. 70–4) published by MMI General Insurance Limited, Australia.
2. Submission of the National Joint Limitation of Liability Task Force of the Institute of Chartered Accountants in Australia and the Australian Society of Certified Practising Accountants (now CPA Australia) to the Inquiry into the Law of Joint and Several Liability, established by the Federal Attorney-General and the New South Wales Attorney-General, 1994, p. 3.
3. The Institute of Chartered Accountants in Ireland's Practice Comparison Survey 2000 was cited by John McCarthy, 'Live Long and Prosper!', *Accountancy Ireland* (October 2000), pp. 4–5. Much variation in the cost of professional indemnity insurance was found.
4. Quoted by Mark Lawson (financial journalist), 'The Writ Stuff: Accountancy Weathers $7.5 billion storm', *Australian Financial Review* (22 January 1998).
5. In the report, *Auditors' Legal Liability in the Global Marketplace: A Case for Limitation*, the International Federation of Accountants analyses some of the causes and developments in auditors' liability issues, and recommends legislative reforms.
6. Justice Davis, *Inquiry into the Law of Joint and Several Liability: Report of Stage One*. Commonwealth of Australia, Canberra, July 1994, pp. 27–9.
7. Mark Buchanan, Partner, Blake, Dawson and Waldron, *Corporate Risk Magazine on Limiting Liability* (January 1996).

FURTHER READING

Anonymous, 'Auditor Liability Evokes Wider Concerns', *CMA* (July–August 1998), p. 31.
Anonymous, 'Moderating Auditor Liability', *The Internal Auditor* (August 1998), pp. 12–13.
Baker, J., Hanson, R. & Smith, J., 'Multidisciplinary Practice: Big Changes Brewing for the Accounting Profession', *CPA Journal* (June 2000), pp. 14–18.
Baxt, Bob, 'Time Bomb', *Charter* (May 1995), pp. 22–3.
Davis, Justice, *Inquiry into the Law of Joint and Several Liability: Report of Stage Two*. Commonwealth of Australia, Canberra, July 1995.
Ford, H. A. J., Austin, R. P. & Ramsay, I. M., *An Introduction to the CLERP Act 1999 — Australia's New Company Law*. Butterworths, Sydney, 2000.
Garrison, M. J. & Hansen, J. D., 'Accounting and Auditing Update', *Ohio CPA Journal* (July–September 1999), pp. 46–8.

Government of New South Wales, *Professional Standards Act 1994* (NSW), No. 81.
Gwilliam, D. R., 'Apportionment in Actions against Auditors', *Abacus* (Vol. 24, No. 1, 1988), pp. 37–54.
Gwilliam, David, 'The Auditor's Liability to Third Parties', in Michael Sherer & Stuart Turley (eds), *Current Issues in Auditing*. Paul Chapman Publishing, London, 1991, pp. 60–75.
Livanes, George, 'Fair Enough', *Charter* (August 1990), pp. 56–60.
Livanes, George, 'When the Numbers Fall', *Charter* (October 1992), pp. 34–5.
Livanes, George, 'A U-Turn by the Courts?', *Charter* (February 1993), pp. 46–8.
Livanes, George, 'The Overseas Trend', *Charter* (July 1993), pp. 38–40.
Malcolm, David, 'So You Thought You Were Just a Watchdog?', *Charter* (March 1991), pp. 28–32.
Murray, G., 'Auditors' Liability: A Comforting Decision', *Charter* (February 1995), p. 40.
Pacini, Carl & Sinason, David, 'Auditor Liability for Electronic Commerce Transaction Assurance: The CPA/CA WebTrust', *American Business Law Journal*, (Spring 1999), pp. 479–514.
Pacini, Carl, Martin, Mary Jill & Hamilton, Lynda, 'At the Interface of Law and Accounting: An Examination of a Trend toward a Reduction in the Scope of Auditor Liability to Third Parties in the Common Law Countries', *American Business Law Journal* (Winter 2000), pp. 171–235.
Small, Bill (Task Force Chair), 'Review of the Law of Joint and Several Liability'. Submission by the National Joint Limitation of Liability Task Force, Canberra, May 1994.
Temple, N., 'Professional Liability', *Australian Accountant* (July 1988), pp. 50–6.

Review questions

3.1 When would an auditor be regarded as being negligent? Has the interpretation of negligence been subject to the court's decisions over time?

3.2 What matters must be proved against an auditor by a plaintiff to the satisfaction of the court before a claim for loss from the auditors can succeed?

3.3 What key principles of law in relation to the 'due care' required from an auditor arose from the Kingston Cotton Mill Co. case and the London and General Bank case? Discuss.

3.4 What is the significance of the judgement by Moffitt J in the Pacific Acceptance case (1970) regarding the conduct of an audit?

3.5 What do the courts perceive to be the relationship between the Auditing Standards and the standards of performance of an audit?

3.6 What factors should the court consider in determining the level of damages to be paid by an auditor to a successful plaintiff? Discuss.

3.7 What are the contributions of (a) the Caparo case (1990), (b) the AGC Advances case (1992), (c) the Columbia Coffee case (1992) and (d) the Esanda Finance case (1994), with respect to the auditor's duty of care to third parties?

3.8 How should an auditor attempt to minimise the risks of litigation?

3.9 What legal reforms in relation to audit legal liability have been implemented in Australia?

Discussion questions

3.1 What is meant by the 'deep pocket theory'? How does it affect auditors?

3.2 How do the Caparo case and the Esanda case differ in terms of the application of liability claims against the auditor? How are they similar in this regard?

3.3 Should auditors' liability be limited? Discuss the liability issue, given your understanding of the 'joint and several' structure of a firm or partnership.

3.4 What are the implications of multi-disciplinary practices for the accounting profession? Discuss.

3.5 Following the IFAC research, many argue in favour of legal reform for auditor liability to safeguard the public interest. What are possible arguments for and against legal reform?

3.6 What is a privity letter? How should the auditor respond to a request for a privity letter?

3.7 What are the implications of liability with respect to the wide range of assurance services provided by an accounting firm?

3.8 How may an auditor be liable under Australia's Trade Practices Act?

3.9 What are the different ways in which an audit firm may avoid litigation?

3.10 What is meant by 'negligence'? How is negligence established in civil liability cases?

Professional application questions

★ BASIC
★★ MODERATE
★★★ CHALLENGING

3.1 (Negligence, duty to detect irregularities) ★

Moreland Shipping transports all types of goods between Australia and Asia. Its auditor, John Brown and Partners, usually had to rely on shipping documentary confirmations with suppliers and customers to ascertain Moreland's liability. In the past few months, shipping documents were found to be incomplete and two shipments were missing, with the consequence that Moreland had to repay over $1.5 million of compensation to the suppliers. John Brown and his audit team were uncomfortable with the fact that millions of dollars of contracts were reported based on some internal memos and correspondence between Moreland's shipping manager and a few overseas suppliers and customers. It appeared to the auditors that some defalcations could be taking place, and the effect on the financial statements was unknown. John Brown, however, felt that they should still submit an unqualified opinion on the financial statements because he was not convinced that it was the auditor's job to uncover management fraud.

Required

Explain the legal implications of these facts as they relate to the role and liability of John Brown and Partners in the audit of Moreland Shipping.

3.2 (Due care) ★★

As the audit senior for Lockerparts Hardware Limited, you are happy with the smoothness of the audit for the year ended 30 June 20X1. Today, your audit partner tells you that Lockersparts has just gone into liquidation. The financial controller was diverting company funds into a Swiss bank account and has left the country to live in Majorca. The lawyers for the creditors of Lockerparts are taking action against the partner for not performing an appropriate audit. They believe that a properly conducted audit should have detected such a fraud.

(*continued*)

The fraud was substantial; however, it was not material from the company's point of view. You explain to the partner that the audit was performed in accordance with all Auditing Standards and nothing was found to arouse suspicion during the audit. The audit took the same amount of time as last year's, and all appropriate work steps were performed. Your work was reviewed by a manager and the entire file was reviewed by the audit partner.

The audit partner is still concerned. He rings an audit partner in an associated office of your accounting firm and asks her to review the audit file. She agrees and spends a day reviewing the file. After completing her review, she is satisfied that the audit was performed properly.

Required

(a) Explain whether your accounting firm has acted with due care. What do you think will be the court's decision if the case goes to trial?

(b) Even if the partner is convinced he acted with due care, explain why he may offer Lockerparts a substantial settlement amount.

3.3 (Negligence, duty to report) ★★

Martin is a trainee audit staff member engaged in the audit of Antique Clocks Limited. On the day of the stocktake, James, the audit supervisor, was taken ill. James told Martin that he could not attend the stocktake: 'There should not be any problem. The stores people are pretty good and figures in the stocksheets have always been properly prepared.' Martin attended the stocktake alone and thought everything went well, at least for his first time. The stocksheets were prepared and stocks were stated at $700 000. James reported the figure as correct and the accounts were signed off as showing a true and fair view. Three months later, Antique Clocks announced bankruptcy because it was unable to pay its bank on its mortgaged property. The liquidator discovered that the majority of the stock held by Antique Clocks comprised either broken or counterfeit clocks, and the real value of the entire stock was adjusted to $130 000. Moreover, the liquidator questioned the conduct of the audit which had just been completed.

Required

Discuss the legal problems of the accounting firm as a result of the above facts.

3.4 (Negligence, liability to third parties) ★★

Western Limited purchased the assets of Green Limited. The financial report of Green was audited by Donaghue Partners, registered company auditors. While performing the audit Donaghue Partners discovered that Green's accounts clerk had embezzled $500. Donaghue Partners also had some evidence of other embezzlements by the bookkeeper. However, the auditor decided that the $500 was not material and that the other suspected embezzlements did not require further investigation. Donaghue Partners did not discuss the matter with Green's management. Unknown to the auditor, the accounts clerk had, in fact, embezzled large sums of cash from Green. In addition, the accounts receivable were significantly overstated. Donaghue Partners did not detect the overstatement because it had inadvertently failed to follow its audit program.

Despite the foregoing, Donaghue Partners issued an unqualified opinion on Green's financial report and furnished a copy of the audited financial statements to Western. Unknown to the auditor, Western required financing to purchase Green's assets and gave a copy of Green's audited financial report to City Bank to obtain approval of the loan. Based on Green's audited financial report, City Bank loaned Western $600 000.

Western paid Green $750 000 to purchase its assets. Within six months, Western began experiencing financial difficulties and later defaulted on the City Bank loan. City Bank commenced legal action against Donaghue Partners, citing negligence on the part of the auditor for its failure to discover the fraud and the overstatement of accounts receivable.

Required

Explain whether City Bank will succeed in its action against Donaghue Partners.

3.5 (Negligence, liability to third parties) ★★

In performing the audit of Telstar Electronics Limited, Greg (the audit senior) found some significant deficiencies in the internal controls over the company's foreign exchange operations. This concerned Greg because he knew that foreign exchange operations were a high risk area for many companies. Greg reported these deficiencies to the partner of the engagement, Ken Stokes. Ken agreed that the matter was one of high importance and decided to report it to Telstar Electronics' manager of foreign exchange operations, Felicity Leeson. The matter was reported to Felicity who agreed with the conclusions of the auditors about the poor controls in foreign exchange. She assured Ken that the problem would be remedied before the next audit. Ken was convinced that she realised the significance of the problem and would act promptly. He decided not to report the matter to the board of directors.

Six months later, Ken received information that Telstar Electronics was about to go into liquidation. It appeared that a decline in the value of the Australian dollar resulted in substantial losses on unhedged futures currency contracts held by the company. Holding of these contracts was a breach of the company's policies and should not have occurred if the controls in the foreign exchange area were operating effectively. Felicity had not implemented the recommendations for improvements to controls over the foreign exchange system.

Ken Stokes was also notified that he was being sued by the shareholders and an investor who lent the company money after reading the audited financial statements.

Required

(a) Explain whether Ken Stokes was negligent.
(b) Explain whether a duty of care existed to (i) the shareholders, and (ii) the investor who lent money after reading the audited financial statements.
(c) If the legal action was successful, nominate whether Ken would have to shoulder the full responsibility.

3.6 (Negligence, liability to third parties) ★★

Excregrow Limited was a successful fertiliser company operating in New South Wales. The company had large inventories of fertiliser held in different locations throughout the state and Queensland. The annual audit for 30 June 20X1 was completed by Detmold Forster, a firm of chartered accountants. It signed the audit report on 25 August 20X1. Manuremate Limited made a successful takeover offer of Excregrow during September 20X1.

However, when some of the financial staff of Manuremate began to have a look at the financial statements of Excregrow, they found that the inventory was substantially overvalued. This overvaluation of inventory resulted in Manuremate having offered a higher value for the company than it would have otherwise. Manuremate took court action against Detmold Forster for the losses it had incurred due to this overstatement.

(*continued*)

In the subsequent court case, it was found that inventory had been overvalued because Detmold Forster relied on management's representations about the value. It appeared that a large amount of the inventory was worthless because it contained some damaging weeds. The review of the auditor's working papers also discovered that its staff had not attended the stock count in Queensland, because the majority of the stock was in New South Wales. From the working papers it was discovered that 40 per cent of the stock was held in Queensland.

Required

(a) Prepare a case against Detmold Forster to prove it acted in a negligent way (referring to Auditing Standards and cases where appropriate).

(b) Explain whether you think Manuremate would win the case.

3.7 (Liability to third parties, privity letters) ★★★

You have been the auditor of SHF Limited for several years. The audit report for the year ended 30 June 20X1 was unqualified. In August 20X1 SHF obtained a large loan from a finance company, LRB Limited, to provide additional working capital. The company experienced severe trading problems and was placed in receivership in May 20X2.

Your firm has been notified by legal representatives of LRB that it is taking action against your firm based on the audit of the 30 June 20X1 accounts. It claims that the cause of SHF's failure related to both the inadequate provision for doubtful debts and a fall in the value of inventories on hand, and that these problems were apparent earlier than June 20X1, but had not been adequately dealt with in the financial statements. LRB also claims that it would not have given the loan to SHF had those accounts been qualified.

Required

(a) Outline your defence to the action taken by LRB. Provide specific case references to support your answer.

(b) Explain whether you would change your answer for part (a) if LRB had written to your firm telling you that it intended to make a loan to SHF and was relying on the audited financial statements to assist it in making its decision.

(Professional Year Programme of the ICAA — 1998, Advanced Audit Module — adapted)

3.8 (Negligence, liability to third parties) ★★★

Newsday Marketing's financial statements for the year ended 30 June 20X1 were audited by Brian Leung and Partners. The unqualified auditor's report was published alongside the directors' statements on 20 August 20X1. Stephen Maine, a tycoon in the publishing industry, put forward a bid to take over Newsday at $2.50 per share, based on the net asset value of the audited accounts (which also showed a net profit for the year of $18 million). The takeover was finalised on 30 September 20X1. In October it was leaked to the press that the financial statements of Newsday Marketing had excluded a significant legal liability on a case, for a claim of $5 million. The case was being appealed by Newsday in June 20X1. The outcome of the damages claim caused the company's share price to plummet. Stephen Maine was extremely annoyed, partly because he had examined the accounts but overlooked the lawsuit. He decided to sue Brian Leung for negligence and a compensation for not including an estimate for the likely damages.

Required

Analyse Brian Leung's legal liability and the likelihood that Stephen Maine may succeed in the action.

Case studies

3.1 (Negligence, contributory negligence) ★★★

You are the external auditor of Kiwi Tours, a company which promotes New Zealand tours to Australia and owns a chain of duty free shops. You have been auditing the company since it was listed on the Australian Stock Exchange ten years ago. Although the accounts have never been qualified, you are aware that the company has been making losses for the past three years as a result of short-term cash flow difficulties. The company has no long-term loans and the bank overdraft is near its limit at the end of the financial year.

During the financial year, the company upgraded its accounting system to a computer database. A consultant was hired to aid in the correct changeover of files for this system. At year end, this new system had been in place for six months, and the directors report they are happy with the way in which it is operating. You do not have the expertise to review and evaluate the database management system, so you ask an independent expert to undertake this role. This person concludes that the system appears reliable and that the changeover was correctly carried out. You have never before audited this type of system, so you attend some courses to familiarise yourself with its features. Your firm has a standard work program that you use to test the controls operating within the system.

In your review of the minutes of the board of directors' meetings, you become aware that the New Zealand parent company (which owns 40 per cent of the shares of the company) is considering making an offer for the remaining shares. This is because the company's share price is trading well below its net asset backing.

After your audited 30 June 20X0 financial reports were published, the takeover offer from the New Zealand parent company proceeds on the basis of an offer price equivalent to the net asset backing of $1.10 per share (as determined from the financial reports). The takeover results in acceptances of 96 per cent of the issued capital, and compulsory acquisition proceedings have been instituted for the other 4 per cent.

While these compulsory acquisition proceedings are being instituted, it is discovered that there were errors in the changeover of the computer system, which resulted in inventory at the duty free stores being materially misstated. After the subsequent write-down of inventory, a new asset backing of $0.70 per share is established. The New Zealand parent company is suing you for alleged negligence for its loss of $0.40 per share.

Required

(a) Decide what major questions must be addressed to determine whether you have been negligent. You should support your answer by referring to case law and the Auditing Standards.

(b) Outline the major issues to be determined to decide whether the company is guilty of contributory negligence.

(c) Assuming you were negligent, explain whether you owe a duty of care to the New Zealand parent company.

(Professional Year Programme of the ICAA — 1996, Advanced Audit Module — adapted)

3.2 (Liability to shareholders and the company) ★★★

Lookbest Limited is a newly established public dot.com company. Its main business is to buy and sell published information, music, books, compact discs, etc. through the Internet. It maintains a web site with listings of all types of publication for sale. As auditor for Lookbest's first year's financial statements for the year ended 30 June 20X1, you note that the accounts of Lookbest show a turnover of about $10 million, shareholders' funds of $3 million, and a profit before tax of $250 000. During the course of your audit you discover that the balance on the sales ledger control account is $500 000 and that about 80 per cent of the accounts receivables are from new customers who bought items on line without full details of the banking particulars. You further discover that all on-line transactions were reported and executed without proper security checks. Moreover, half of the items listed as stocks for sale cannot be located. The share price of the company stands at $1.50. You raise the issue with the director of Lookbest and he tells you that this is not uncommon with this type of e-business and that he is only concerned that the Australian Stock Exchange allows it to go on trading. He assures you that nothing major will happen; an unqualified auditor's report is all that is necessary. However, you are worried about your own liability.

Required

Discuss the potential liability of the auditor to:

(a) the shareholders;

(b) the company.

You may refer to any relevant case law in your answer.

chapter 4

PART 2 Audit planning

PART 2

Often considered the most crucial part of the audit, planning is the starting point for any audit. Planning should begin from when the auditor is appointed, which is discussed in **Chapter 4**. Chapter 4 also gives an overview of why financial report audits exist and the responsibilities and duties of auditors.

The evaluation of audit risk (which comprises inherent, control and detection risk) and materiality are discussed in **Chapter 5**. These are the first major issues that need to be considered as part of audit planning. The actual development of the audit plan — which includes obtaining an understanding of the entity's business and industry to gain some idea about the level of inherent risk, which consequently has an impact on the audit strategy — is discussed in **Chapter 6**. Chapter 6 also discusses the types of evidence that need to be accumulated over the course of the audit to support the audit opinion.

To conclude our discussion on the planning phase of the audit, **Chapter 7** discusses how the auditor should obtain an understanding of internal controls when planning the audit, and the types of test that he or she should perform when users are to rely on these controls.

chapter 4

Overview of the financial report audit

Overview

LEARNING OBJECTIVES

After studying this chapter, you should be able to:

1. explain why a demand exists for financial report audits
2. describe the benefits and limitations of financial report audits
3. discuss the legal and professional issues in appointing independent auditors
4. state the statutory and other duties of the independent auditor
5. indicate the current Auditing Standards and their major concepts
6. explain the importance of Auditing Standards for the profession
7. describe the auditor's relationship with the shareholders, audit committee and other important groups
8. explain the interrelationship between management's and the auditor's responsibilities
9. prepare an audit report and explain its basic elements
10. indicate the types of modified audit report and when use of each is appropriate.

Professional statements

AUSTRALIAN		INTERNATIONAL	
AUS 202	Objective and General Principles Governing an Audit of a Financial Report	ISA 200	Objective and General Principles Governing an Audit of Financial Statements
AUS 204	Terms of Audit Engagements	ISA 210	Terms of Audit Engagements
AUS 206	Quality Control for Audit Work	ISA 220	Quality Control for Audit Work
AUS 210	Irregularities, Including Fraud, Other Illegal Acts and Errors	ISA 240	Fraud and Error
AUS 212	Other Information in Documents Containing Audited Financial Reports	ISA 720	Other Information in Documents Containing Audited Financial Statements
AUS 520	Management Representations	ISA 580	Management Representations
AUS 604	Considering the Work of Internal Auditing	ISA 610	Considering the Work of Internal Auditing
AUS 702	The Audit Report on a General Purpose Financial Report	ISA 700	The Auditor's Report on Financial Statements
AUS 710	Communication to Management on Matters Arising from an Audit	ISA 1007	Communications with Management
AGS 1004	Transitional Arrangements on Changes in Audit Appointments under the Corporations Law		
AGS 1016	Audit and Review Reports on Half-Year Accounts and Consolidated Accounts		
APS 1.1	Conformity with Auditing Standards		
APS 2	Engagement Letters to Clients		
APS 9	Statement of Compilation of Financial Reports		
AUP 32	Audit Independence		

As noted in Chapter 1, financial report audits play an important role in a free market economy. This textbook outlines the basic principles of auditing and assurance with a focus on financial report audits. This chapter is intended to give an overview of financial report audits. We will begin by examining several fundamentals of financial report audits. We will then examine issues surrounding the appointment of independent auditors, duties of independent auditors and important auditor relationships — issues that collectively underpin the conduct of financial report audits. We will also identify the sources and form of the Auditing Standards that guide the performance of audits. Then, we will consider a number of the auditor's relationships with others — particularly the relationship between the auditor and management and an associated issue — and the interrelationship between accounting and auditing. To provide an understanding of the end product of the financial report audit, we will introduce the audit report and **general purpose financial reports** together, presenting several alternative types of report and the circumstances in which each is appropriate.

FUNDAMENTALS OF FINANCIAL REPORT AUDITS

We will begin this section by examining some of the reasons for a demand for auditing, then reviewing the main benefits associated with a financial report audit. However, there are limitations as well as benefits, so we will also consider some of the inherent limitations of a financial report audit.

LEARNING OBJECTIVE 1

Explain why a demand exists for financial report audits.

Demand for financial report audits

The separation of ownership from control in entities is considered one of the main reasons for a demand for auditing. This assertion has been difficult to confirm through research, because the majority of audits are conducted in response to a statutory requirement, which has made it difficult for researchers to observe characteristics of entities that may have demanded an audit in an unregulated environment. Here, we will discuss some explanatory theories that have been the subject of research (see Wallace)[1] — namely:

- **agency theory** (**stewardship** monitoring hypothesis);
- **information hypothesis**; and
- **insurance hypothesis**.

Watts and Zimmerman[2] took a historical perspective to establish whether a demand exists for auditing in the absence of a regulatory requirement. They reviewed the practice of using auditors in merchant guilds, regulated companies and joint-stock companies when there were no legal requirements for an audit (over the period 1200–1844). They note the following about the introduction of the first legislative requirement for an audit:

> Thus, when the *UK Companies Act 1844* required directors to keep accounts and required those accounts to be audited by persons other than the directors (or their clerks), Parliament was merely incorporating into the law a version of practice that had existed for six hundred years.
>
> The hypothesis advanced here is that [auditors] survived because they were an efficient method of monitoring contracts between managers and those supplying capital.[3]

In conclusion, they state that:

> Overall, the evidence suggests that the existence of the independent auditor is not the direct result of government fiat.[4]

Agency theory

This theory has generally been considered in the research literature as the primary reason for a demand for financial statement audits. Jensen and Meckling[5] are considered to be the first ones to develop agency theory in the context of financial reporting. In an agency relationship, investors (as principals) entrust their resources to managers (as agents). There is a behavioural assumption that all parties involved in the relationship will act rationally and will attempt to maximise their benefits. The agent's self-interest is expected to diverge from the principals' interest, giving rise to agency costs which Jensen and Meckling divide into:

- monitoring costs;
- bonding costs; and
- residual loss.

The cost of monitoring is associated with obtaining an external auditor to verify the assertions made by **management** in the financial reports. A monitoring mechanism in the form of regular reports is important to provide an account for the agent's performance. Investors are then able to take certain action on the basis of the reports. If investors anticipate misuse of funds, then they are able to protect themselves by raising the cost of capital provided; this behaviour is generally called 'price protection'. As a corollary, management recognises the desirability of an audit and will incur additional costs for an audit if these costs are less than the related increase in the value of the company's capital stock. Agency theory postulates that the demand for monitoring will increase as ownership in companies becomes less concentrated. The level of direct share ownership in Australia is now over 40 per cent,[6] which would suggest that the demand for monitoring would be quite high even if there were no regulatory requirement for audits.

Bonding costs are associated with the costs of schemes to align management's interests with those of shareholders, such as bonus schemes, share options, etc. The residual loss occurs because the costs of monitoring and bonding make it impossible to identify or stop all self-interested behaviour by managers.

Information hypothesis

Investors demand audited financial information because it is useful for decision-making. An audit is a means of improving the quality of the financial information. Investors require information to assess the expected returns and risks associated with their investment. An audit is also valued as a means of improving financial data for internal decision-making; it can detect errors and motivate employees to exercise more care in preparing records in anticipation of an audit.

There is some degree of overlap of the information hypothesis with agency theory. Information that is useful in monitoring an agent's performance is also useful for making investment decisions. According to agency theory, the agent is the source of demand for audits; the information hypothesis stresses the increase in the reliability of information as an input to decision-making.

Insurance hypothesis

This is a more recent explanation of the demand for auditing. Insurance is an important contributing factor in the litigation crisis (see Chapter 3). Wallace describes the insurance hypothesis as follows:

> The ability to shift financial responsibility for reported data to an auditor lowers the expected loss from litigation or related settlements to managers, creditors, and other professionals involved in the securities market. As potential litigation awards increase, this insurance demand for an audit from managers and professional participants in financial activities can be expected to grow.[7]

Wallace identifies four reasons for managers and professionals' use of auditors as insurance:

1. An audit function is well accepted by society. Professionals and managers can substantiate that they exercised reasonable care by using auditing services.
2. Auditors have developed in-house legal expertise and may provide more efficient insurance coverage as a co-defendant than an insurance company could provide as a third party.
3. While an insurance company will make a cost–benefit choice of legal defence versus settlement out of court based on monetary loss, the common interests of the auditor and manager ensure a proper consideration of the effects of litigation on the reputation of the parties.
4. The courts view auditors as a means of socialising risk; that is, because auditors are held responsible for business failures, they shift this cost firstly to clients through higher fees and then to society through higher prices and lower returns on investment. Risks otherwise faced by investors are borne by society.

Another dimension of the insurance hypothesis is the incentive of politicians to require audits. Whenever there are notable corporation failures — for example, the financial failures of Tricontinental, the Pyramid Building Society and the Bank of South Australia — it is often convenient for the politicians/legislators to make auditors the scapegoats. The usual question in these situations is: 'Why didn't the auditor discover and disclose the problem?'. Wallace notes:

> Political benefits are derived from mandating audits, increasing liability exposure of auditors to provide greater remedies to individual investors who lose money in the market, and focusing attention on audit failure which places auditors in the defendant's chair.[8]

Government regulators and politicians can insure themselves against blame by requiring that reporting entities be audited by public accounting firms.

2 LEARNING OBJECTIVE

Describe the benefits and limitations of financial report audits.

Benefits

Irrespective of the view held or the dominance of any particular explanatory theory, a number of benefits arise from having a financial report audit. These benefits can also create a demand for auditing services. Examples of possible benefits are described in the following sections.

Access to capital markets

Public companies must satisfy statutory audit requirements in accordance with the Corporations Law. The Australian Stock Exchange imposes its requirements for listing securities. Without audits, companies may be denied access to these capital markets. These requirements are designed to ensure some protection for investors in the capital markets (particularly small investors). (Refer to http://www.asic.gov.au/ and http://www.asx.com.au/ for more information.)

The lower cost of capital

Small companies often have financial report audits to obtain bank loans or more favourable borrowing terms. Often, banks require audited financial reports before lending any funds; sometimes, they will also require audit reports of compliance with debt covenants.

Given the reduced information risk resulting from audited financial reports, potential creditors may offer low interest rates and potential investors may be willing to accept a lower rate of return on their investment. In short, audited financial reports improve an entity's credibility and therefore reduce risk for investors and creditors. This benefit is associated with the agency theory of auditor demand.

A deterrent to inefficiency and fraud

Financial report audits can be expected to have a favourable effect on employee efficiency and honesty. Knowledge that an independent audit is to be performed is likely to result in fewer errors in the accounting process and reduce the likelihood of employee misappropriation of assets. Similarly, the auditor's involvement in an entity's financial reporting process is a restraining influence on management. The fact that its financial report assertions are to be verified reduces the likelihood that management will engage in fraudulent financial reporting. It should be noted that an audit is not designed to detect fraud. Auditing Standard AUS 210, Irregularities, Including Fraud, Other Illegal Acts and Errors (International Standard on Auditing ISA 240, Fraud and Error) states that the auditor's duty to investigate and report irregularities arises in only circumstances in which suspicions are aroused.

Control and operational improvements

Based on observations made during a financial report audit, the independent auditor can suggest how controls could be improved and how greater operating efficiencies within the entity's organisation may be achieved. This is especially valuable to small and medium-sized entities. Weaknesses in controls and suggestions for improvement are usually outlined in the **management letter** (see page 161 and Chapter 14) prepared by the auditor at the end of the audit.

Limitations

Traditionally, the financial report has been regarded as being primarily for the benefit of the members of a company. By receiving full and accurate information on the financial affairs of their company, members are able to assess better the performance of management. A financial report audit performed in accordance with **Auditing Standards** provides an objective assurance of the credibility of the assertions by management. However, the financial report audit is subject to a number of inherent limitations. Some of these limitations are described in the following sections.

A time lapse

A common criticism of the audit function (and also of financial accounting reporting practices) is that the lapse of time between the balance sheet date and the presentation of the audit report may be up to four months. The auditor is required to review for subsequent events under Auditing Standard AUS 706, Subsequent Events (International Auditing Standard ISA 560), but this does not create a full 'up-to-date' financial report as of the audit report date. The Enhanced Disclosure Scheme, a result of the *Corporate Law Reform Act 1994* (Cwlth), provides investors with more up-to-date information about a company by requiring the ongoing or continual disclosure of information that a reasonable person could expect would have a material effect on the value of the investment. Also, the scheme requires all disclosing entities to prepare and lodge half-yearly financial statements. It is expected that both financial reporting and auditing will soon move to become more 'real time' to maintain relevance.[9] Many consider continuous assurance to be a natural evolution of the role of the auditor. The Canadian Institute of Chartered Accountants (CICA) and the American Institute of Certified Public Accountants (AICPA) commissioned a report on issues associated with continuous assurance (see the 'Professional environment' on the following page).

PROFESSIONAL ENVIRONMENT **Continuous auditing**

The research report *Continuous Auditing* defines a continuous audit as: 'a methodology that enables independent auditors to provide written assurance on a subject matter using a series of auditors' reports issued simultaneously with, or a short period of time after, the occurrence of events underlying the subject matter'.

The report concluded that continuous audits are viable, provided certain, interrelated conditions are met.

- The short time frames for reporting would result in the need for a high degree of automation of the processes [that] entities use to capture, manipulate and store data and to report information related to the subject matter being audited.
- The automated processes would need to be highly reliable in producing information about a subject matter soon after the occurrence of events underlying that subject matter. Increased emphasis on the use of automated preventive controls would be essential.
- Highly automated audit procedures would need to be implemented to provide most of the required audit evidence. The audit tools would be integrated, to varying degrees, with the entity's system and controls.
- The auditors need to be quickly informed of the results of automated procedures, when the process has identified anomalies or errors requiring follow-up procedures to be performed personally by audit personnel.
- Auditors' reports would need to be produced automatically and safeguarded against unauthorised changes. Such reports could include short interval reports (e.g. reports issued daily or weekly), 'evergreen' reports (i.e. reports that are always available to users and dated as at the time of user access) and 'reports on demand' (i.e. reports that are available when specifically requested by a user and dated as at the time of request).
- Auditors would have to be technically proficient enough to handle the circumstances of the engagement. In most cases, that would require a high level of expertise in various aspects of information technology.

(Source: Extracted from the Canadian Institute of Chartered Accountants and the American Institute of Certified Public Accountants, *Continuous Auditing*. Toronto, 1999)

Audit testing on selective samples

Results of audit selective testing may involve either using the scientific sampling method to obtain representative data or exercising an element of judgement based on the auditor's understanding of the business. Audit testing based on selective samples has limitations due to sampling risk (which is the risk that a sample drawn from a population may not be representative of that population). The advantage of scientific sampling is that this sampling risk can be quantified. Refer to Chapter 8 for a more detailed discussion of some of the risks and limitations associated with sampling.

Assessment of materiality

The assessment of **materiality** is a part of the audit process that requires a high degree of **professional judgement**. It requires both quantitative and qualitative considerations. There are no universally agreed-upon guidelines for quantitative measures of materiality.

Guidelines that attempt to establish a quantitative threshold are necessarily arbitrary, thereby requiring significant professional judgement. Qualitative considerations of materiality relate to an assessment of the impact of the causes of the misstatements rather than just the amount of the impact. This qualitative assessment also requires a significant degree of professional judgement by the auditor. Refer to Chapter 5 for a more detailed discussion on materiality.

Highly specialised areas

Auditors may be required to form a professional judgement on areas that are highly specialised or that are not dealt with adequately by the Accounting Standards or Auditing Standards. For example, there are many questions concerning the valuation of intangible assets or environment-related accounting items (i.e. Auditing Guidance Statement AGS 1036, The Consideration of Environmental Matters in the Audit of a Financial Report), and audit judgement can be influenced by a number of factors.[10] Substantial disagreements between auditors and management during the course of an audit often relate to specialised areas or contentious accounting issues.

Report format limitations

Finally, the auditor is required to report within a **standard format of audit reports**, as prescribed by Auditing Standard AUS 702, The Audit Report on a General Purpose Financial Report (International Auditing Standard ISA 700, The Auditor's Report on Financial Statements). The audit report and the body of the financial statements are subject to interpretation. The standard format of the audit report may not reflect fully the complexities involved in the audit process and the decision of the audit opinion. Despite these limitations, a financial report audit adds credibility to the financial information. As a result, this type of audit has become an indispensable part of our society. A study by Anderson and Epstein[11] of Australian shareholders found that many wanted annual reports to be audited more carefully.

There are many other 'perceived' limitations to audit reports due to the fact that users think auditors are giving more assurance than they actually are. Some of these perceived assurances are outlined by Porter:[12]

- that auditors are guarantors of the accuracy of a company's financial statements and/or its solvency;
- that auditors give early warning of company failure;
- that auditors detect and report to shareholders any fraud and other illegal acts.

Generally, auditors do not give the above assurances because they are not within the requirements of current Auditing Standards. Thus, the commonly known 'audit expectation gap' arises (see Chapter 2).

3
LEARNING OBJECTIVE

Discuss the legal and professional issues in appointing independent auditors.

THE APPOINTMENT OF AN INDEPENDENT AUDITOR

The Corporations Law governs the appointment of the independent auditor. In this section, we will outline the basic principles of auditor appointment, as well as the applicable statutory provisions, the procedures for the registration of auditors, and the procedures for the removal and resignation of auditors.

Principles of the appointment of auditors

As a general rule, the members of a company (i.e. shareholders with voting rights) appoint the auditor. A company (except for a small proprietary company) must have its financial report audited in accordance with s.301 of the Corporations Law. (*Note*: Hereafter, any sections of legislation referred to in this chapter are sections of the Corporations Law unless otherwise specified.)

Directors of public and large proprietary companies are required to appoint an auditor within one month after the company is incorporated, unless the members have appointed one at a general meeting (s.327(1)). As a result of changes made by the *First Corporate Law Simplification Act 1995* (Cwlth), small proprietary companies are generally not required to appoint an auditor (s.301(2)). However, the directors of a small proprietary company are required to appoint an auditor if either the Australian Securities and Investment Commission (ASIC) or shareholders holding at least 5 per cent of the voting shares request the company to prepare audited financial statements for a particular year. In addition, a small proprietary company must comply with s.327 and appoint an auditor if it is a disclosing entity or if it is controlled by a foreign company and its accounts are not consolidated with its foreign controller.

The ASIC issued Class Order 98/1418, which under certain circumstances relieves a company from preparing full audited financial statements when it is a wholly owned entity. The main requirement for meeting this provision is a Deed of Cross Guarantee between the wholly owned entity and the holding entity.

The duration of the first appointment is only until the first annual general meeting, during which the members appoint an auditor (s.327(3)). Once an auditor is appointed, the company is liable to pay the auditor's reasonable fees and expenses in carrying out the audit (s.331). An auditor holds office until his or her death, removal or resignation (s.327(4)). The removal or resignation of an auditor (see page 143) is governed by the Corporations Law. An auditor also ceases to hold office after a company goes into liquidation (s.330).

A person may be appointed to act as the auditor of a company only if he or she has consented to the appointment in writing before the appointment (s.327(7)). Appointment without such consent is of no effect and constitutes an offence by the company and any officer in default (s.327(9)).

The registration of auditors

The Corporations Law requires auditors to be competent. To this end, they are required to have a certain level of training and experience. To be suitably qualified, the person must:

- be a member of the Institute of Chartered Accountants in Australia (ICAA), CPA Australia or other prescribed body;
- hold a degree, diploma or certificate from a university or other prescribed body in Australia, and have passed a course of study in accountancy of not less than three years duration and a course of study in commercial law of not less than two years duration;
- have such practical experience in auditing as prescribed;
- be capable of performing the duties of an auditor and be a fit and proper person to be registered as an auditor.

The practical experience required is specified in the Corporations Regulations as:

- work experience in company auditing under the direction of a registered company auditor;
- at least one year's experience in the supervision of audits of companies.

Those persons who satisfy the above criteria may apply to the ASIC to be registered under s.1279. The Corporations Law also ensures the independence of the auditor in s.324(1) by prohibiting or disqualifying any person who is an officer of the company, a partner of the company, an employer or employee of an officer of the company, or a partner or employee of an employee or an officer of the company. An auditing firm cannot act as auditor of a company unless at least one member of the firm is registered as a company auditor and is ordinarily a resident in Australia. No member of the audit firm can be indebted to the company for an amount in excess of $5000. No officer of the company may receive payment from the auditing firm for acting as a consultant on accounting or auditing matters.

There are benefits for a registration procedure for company auditors. The ASIC maintains a list of registered company auditors for public reference. Registration provides an assurance of the qualification, level of competence and experience of the auditor concerned. Alongside the registration requirements are conditions that require the accounting bodies to maintain and monitor a comprehensive and mandatory code of ethics and other rules, and to continue the professional development of members.

The cancellation and suspension of registration of auditors and liquidators are governed by ss.1290–1298. Under these provisions, the Companies Auditors and Liquidators Disciplinary Board, on application to the ASIC, has the power to hold hearings and decide whether to cancel or suspend the registration of an auditor. It also has the power to impose penalties (including a reprimand) or to require the auditor to undertake or refrain from a certain conduct.

The removal and resignation of auditors

An auditor may be removed from office only by resolution of the company at a general meeting, for which special notice under s.329(1A) has been given at least two months before the meeting is held. When a company receives special notice of a resolution to remove an auditor, it must send a copy of the notice to the auditor and lodge a copy with the ASIC as soon as possible (s.329(2)). The auditor is then given seven days to make representation in writing, with copies of the representation being sent to all members entitled to attend the meeting (s.329(3)). The auditor also has the right to be heard at the meeting. Where an auditor is removed from office at a general meeting, the company may appoint another auditor at that meeting by a resolution passed by at least a three-quarter majority, or at an adjourned meeting (s.327(10)(a)).

These provisions regarding the removal of an auditor have the effect of strengthening the auditor's independence. The auditor can therefore qualify the accounts or argue an accounting position without the potential threat of immediate dismissal by the directors.

For auditors of a company other than a proprietary company to resign, they must apply to the ASIC for consent to resign, stating their reasons. The company must be notified in writing of the application (s.329(5)). If the ASIC gives its consent, then the auditor may resign after giving written notice to the company (s.329(9)). The resignation of an auditor of a proprietary company does not require consent from the ASIC. The auditor who resigns also has the protection that such statements made by the auditor in relation to his or her resignation are not admissible in evidence in any proceedings, nor may they be used for any action against the auditor (s.329(7)).

If the auditor resigns or is removed, then notice of that resignation or removal must be lodged with the ASIC within fourteen days and a copy of the notice must be sent to the trustee of the company (if one is appointed) (s.329(11)).

4 LEARNING OBJECTIVE

State the statutory and other duties of the independent auditor.

DUTIES OF AN INDEPENDENT AUDITOR

When an auditor accepts an appointment, he or she enters into a **contractual relationship** with the company. The audit engagement letter, agreed to and signed by the auditor and the client, details some of the duties of an auditor for a company (Miscellaneous Professional Statement APS 2, Engagement Letters to Clients). There are express or implied terms in such contracts that the auditor will:

- exercise a reasonable degree of care and skill;
- be independent of the company;
- report to members his or her opinion, based on the audit, as to whether the financial statements are properly drawn up so as to give a true and fair view of the company's financial position, in accordance with the Corporations Law and applicable Accounting Standards;
- comply with Auditing Standards and other professional standards.

The duty to use reasonable care and skill

The duty to use reasonable care and skill is subject to interpretation of the circumstances of each case. The duty to use reasonable care and skill was established in *Re London and General Bank Ltd* (No. 2) (1895) 2 Ch. 673, which was one of the earliest legal cases to discuss auditors' duties. Lindley LJ said of auditors that '[they] must take reasonable care and skill before [they] believe that what [they] certify is true'.

An auditor is under an obligation to use reasonable care and skill at all times in carrying out the audit and forming the audit opinion. The interpretation of 'reasonable care and skill' is a matter of professional judgement, whereby the auditor considers his or her priorities of duties and rights under specific circumstances. However, the ultimate test of what constitutes 'reasonable care and skill' is decided by the courts when legal action is taken against the auditor.

The duty to be independent

The Corporations Law reinforces the requirement that the auditor for a company must be independent by disqualifying certain categories of person (s.324(1)) or firm (s.324(2)) connected with the company (see page 143). Professional Statement F1 on Professional Independence (of the ICAA and CPA Australia's Joint Code of Professional Conduct) and Auditing Practice Statement AUP 32, Audit Independence state principles, rules and guidelines that emphasise that the auditor must not only be independent but also be *seen* to be independent. Auditors are entitled to seek assistance from the company's directors, officers and accountants in carrying out their function. However, they should not rely on information obtained in this manner without exercising reasonable care and diligence, applying their own tests and independent judgement as required. Independence is discussed in more detail in Chapter 2.

Statutory duties to report to members and the Australian Securities and Investment Commission

The auditors are required to provide an audit report to the members (i.e. shareholders with voting rights) of the company concerning the financial statement audit. The format of the audit report is governed by AUS 702 (ISA 700), while the matters on which the auditor must express his or her opinions are specified by statute. Auditors are also required to disclose and report on other regulatory matters under certain circumstances.

The audit opinion

The auditor must express an opinion on whether the financial report is in accordance with the Corporations Law, complies with Accounting Standards (s.296) and gives a true and fair view (s.297).

The opinions expressed in an auditor's report must be in accordance with AUS 702 (ISA 700). The audit opinion can be either unqualified or qualified. A qualified opinion should be expressed as:

- an 'except for' opinion;
- an adverse opinion; or
- an inability to form an opinion.

An audit report that contains either an unqualified or a qualified opinion may, in certain cases, include an **emphasis of matter** section.

The duty to report

An auditor is under a statutory duty to report to members on the company's financial statements for an accounting period and on the accounting records relating to those financial statements (s.308). A copy of the auditor's report must be laid before the annual general meeting of a public company and must be furnished to the directors in sufficient time to reach members by the earlier of either twenty-one days before the annual general meeting after the end of the financial year or four months after the end of the financial year (s.315).

Section 308 sets out the matters that must be contained in an auditor's report. The report must state whether, in the auditor's opinion, the financial statements are properly drawn up:

- so as to give a true and fair view of the financial affairs of the company;
- in accordance with the Corporations Law;
- in accordance with applicable Accounting Standards and the Corporations Regulations.

Section 308(3) also requires the report to describe any defect or irregularity in the financial reports. The auditor must report on the following implied conditions if there is any deficiency or failure to comply:

- whether the auditor has obtained all the information, explanation and assistance required;
- whether proper financial records have been maintained;
- whether other records or registers have been maintained as required by the Corporations Law.

If, in the auditor's opinion, the financial statements are not drawn up in accordance with a particular applicable Accounting Standard or an Urgent Issues Group (UIG) Consensus View, then the report must give particulars of the qualified financial effect on the financial statements of non-compliance.

The duty to report to the Australian Securities and Investment Commission

The auditor conducting a financial report audit must notify the ASIC as soon as possible if there are reasonable grounds to suspect a contravention of the Corporations Law. This is required unless the auditor believes the contravention will be adequately dealt with by commenting on it in the auditor's report or bringing it to the attention of the directors (s.311).

Professional duties

The auditor, as a member of the accounting profession, also has professional responsibilities. Members involved in the audit of a general purpose financial report of a reporting entity are required to take all reasonable steps within their power to ensure that Accounting Standards and UIG Consensus Views are consistently applied in the preparation and presentation of the report (Miscellaneous Professional Statement APS 1.1, Conformity with

Accounting Standards and UIG Consensus Views, paragraph 11). Members involved in audits of financial reports are also required to comply with all Auditing Standards (APS 1.1, paragraph 5) in addition to any ethical and legal requirements (see Chapter 2 and Chapter 3 respectively).

LEARNING CHECK

4.1 The Corporations Law requires financial report audits for certain types of company. However, a demand for audits would probably exist without regulation because the audit is seen as an efficient way in which to reduce agency costs, provide useful information and provide insurance against company failure.

4.2 There are many benefits associated with having a financial report audit — for example, informed access to capital markets, the potentially lower cost of capital, a deterrent to inefficiency and fraud, and a means of improving control and operations.

4.3 Financial report audits can be limited by such factors as the lapse of time before the audited financial statements are published, the inherent limitations in the audit tests, technical uncertainties and the prescribed format of audit reports.

4.4 The statutory duties of auditors are stipulated in the Corporations Law and the Corporations Regulations. These include the duty to report to members in accordance with legislative requirements and the duty to report to the ASIC on certain matters.

4.5 Auditors also have duties to exercise reasonable care and skill, be independent of the company and comply with professional standards.

AUDITING STANDARDS

LEARNING OBJECTIVE 5

Indicate the current Auditing Standards and their major concepts.

In discharging their responsibilities, auditors rely on a codified set of Auditing Standards prepared by the Auditing and Assurance Standards Board (AuASB), an arm of the Australian Accounting Research Foundation (AARF). The Auditing Standards originate from two sources: (1) the AuASB and (2) the International Auditing Practices Committee (IAPC). The AuASB identifies an emerging issue and uses its own resources and those of the AARF and/or a contractor to initiate and develop the Standards. The IAPC, a standing committee of the International Federation of Accountants (IFAC), has the objective of developing and issuing International Standards on Auditing (ISAs) which provide a degree of uniformity in auditing practice throughout the world. The Australian accounting profession is committed to the broad objectives of the international organisation. The AuASB's work program therefore integrates the work of the IAPC.

Both the AuASB and the IAPC employ an extensive due process in the development of Auditing Standards. The AuASB adapts the ISAs to Australian conditions and issues an exposure draft subject to the due process. Prior to 1995, there was a single Auditing Standard — AUS 1 — supplemented by guidance contained in Auditing Practice Statements (AUPs). Following the completion of a codification and revision project, these have been reissued as a range of Auditing Standards (AUSs). This follows the direction taken by the IAPC in redesignating all International Auditing Guidelines (IAGs) as ISAs. Commencing in September 1993, the AuASB issued a series of exposure drafts containing the proposed Auditing Standards. The process was completed in October 1995.

The Auditing Standards contain:

- the basic principles and essential procedures with which the auditor is required to comply in the planning, conduct and reporting of an audit;
- explanatory and other material to assist the auditor in interpreting and applying the basic principles and essential procedures.

The basic principles and essential procedures are identified separately in bold type (black lettering) in each of the Auditing Standards. The statements in the Standards that are set in bold type must be complied with whenever a financial report audit is conducted. They must also be applied (with adaptation as necessary) to audits of other financial and non-financial information and audit-related services. Any departure from the basic principles and procedures must be explained in the auditor's report (APS 1.1.05).

Auditing Guidance Statements (AGSs) have been issued to guide the application of Auditing Standards. These are not mandatory.

It can be argued that auditing pronouncements tend to codify what is generally accepted practice. There is no conceptual basis to support a particular practice, and many academics and practitioners believe that an auditing conceptual framework is needed to counter misconceptions about the role and practice of auditing.

The structure of the series of Auditing Standards (as well as the ISA equivalents) is reproduced in Figure 4.1. The Standards are arranged in a logical order based on subject matter. Hereafter, Auditing Standards will be referred to by only their respective acronyms.

FIGURE 4.1

Auditing Standards and Auditing Guidance Statements

100–999 AUDITING STANDARDS		INTERNATIONAL AUDITING PRACTICE STATEMENTS
100–199 Introduction		
AUS 102	Foreword to Australian Auditing Standards and Guidance Statements	ISA 100
AUS 104	Glossary of Terms	ISA 110
AUS 106	Explanatory Framework for Standards on Audit and Audit Related Services	ISA 120
200–299 Responsibilities		
AUS 202	Objective and General Principles Governing an Audit of a Financial Report	ISA 200
AUS 204	Terms of Audit Engagements	ISA 210
AUS 206	Quality Control for Audit Work	ISA 220
AUS 208	Documentation	ISA 230
AUS 210	Irregularities, Including Fraud, Other Illegal Acts and Errors	ISA 240
AUS 212	Other Information in Documents Containing Audited Financial Reports	ISA 720
AUS 214	Auditing in a CIS Environment	ISA 401
300–399 Planning		
AUS 302	Planning	ISA 300
AUS 304	Knowledge of the Business	ISA 310
AUS 306	Materiality	ISA 320
400–499 Internal Control		
AUS 402	Risk Assessments and Internal Controls	ISA 400
AUS 404	Audit Implications Relating to Entities Using a Service Entity	ISA 402

(*continued*)

FIGURE 4.1

Auditing standards and Auditing Gui8dance Statements *(continued)*

100–999 AUDITING STANDARDS (CONTINUED)		INTERNATIONAL AUDITING PRACTICE STATEMENTS
500–599 Audit Evidence		
AUS 502	Audit Evidence	ISA 500
AUS 504	External Confirmations	ISA 501 (Pt B)
AUS 506	Existence and Valuation of Inventory	ISA 501 (Pt A)
AUS 508	Inquiry Regarding Litigation and Claims	ISA 501 (Pt C)
AUS 510	Initial Engagements — Opening Balances	ISA 510
AUS 512	Analytical Procedures	ISA 520
AUS 514	Audit Sampling and Other Selective Testing Procedures	ISA 530
AUS 516	Audit of Accounting Estimates	ISA 540
AUS 518	Related Parties	ISA 550
AUS 520	Management Representations	ISA 580
AUS 522	Audit Evidence Implications of Externally Managed Assets of Superannuation, Provident or Similar Funds	
AUS 524	The Auditor's Use of the Work of the Actuary and the Actuary's Use of the Work of the Auditor in Connection with the Preparation and Audit of a Financial Report	
600–699 Using the Work of Others		
AUS 602	Using the Work of Another Auditor	ISA 600
AUS 604	Considering the Work of Internal Auditing	ISA 610
AUS 606	Using the Work of an Expert	ISA 620
700–799 Audit Conclusions and Reporting		
AUS 702	The Audit Report on a General Purpose Financial Report	ISA 700
AUS 704	Comparatives	ISA 710
AUS 706	Subsequent Events	ISA 560
AUS 708	Going Concern	ISA 570
AUS 710	Communication to Management on Matters Arising from an Audit	ISA 1007
800–899 Specialised Areas		
AUS 802	The Audit Report on Financial Information Other than a General Purpose Financial Report	ISA 800
AUS 804	The Audit of Prospective Financial Information	ISA 810
AUS 806	Performance Auditing	
AUS 808	Planning Performance Audits	
AUS 810	Special Purpose Reports on the Effectiveness of Control Procedures	
900–999 Related Services		
AUS 902	Review of Financial Reports	ISA 910
AUS 904	Engagements to Perform Agreed-upon Procedures	ISA 920

	1000–1999 AUDITING GUIDANCE STATEMENTS	INTERNATIONAL AUDITING PRACTICE STATEMENTS
AGS 1002	Bank Confirmation Requests	
AGS 1004	Transitional Arrangements on Changes in Audit Appointments under the Corporations Law	
AGS 1006	Expression of an Opinion on Internal Control	
AGS 1008	Audit Implications of Reserve Bank Prudential Reporting Requirements	
AGS 1010	Audit Obligations of the Financial Institutions Scheme	
AGS 1014	Privity Letter Requests	
AGS 1016	Audit and Review Reports on Half-Year Financial Reports	
AGS 1018	CIS Environments — Stand-alone Microcomputers	ISA 1001
AGS 1020	CIS Environments — On-line Computer Systems	ISA 1002
AGS 1022	CIS Environments — Database Systems	ISA 1003
AGS 1024	Life Insurance Act 1995 — Audit Obligations	
AGS 1026	Superannuation Funds — Auditor Reports on Externally Managed Assets	
AGS 1028	Uncertainty	
AGS 1030	Derivatives in a Corporate Environment	
AGS 1032	The Audit Implications of Accounting for Investments in Associates	
AGS 1034	Implications for Management and Auditors of the Year 2000 Systems Issue	ISA 1011
AGS 1036	The Considerations of Environmental Matters in the Audit of a Financial Report	ISA 1010
AGS 1038	Access to Audit Working Papers	
AGS 1040	Franchising Code of Conduct — Auditor's Report	
AGS 1042	Reporting on Control Procedures at Outsourcing Entities	
AGS 1044	Audit Reports on Information Provided Other than in a Financial Report	
AGS 1046	Responding to Questions at an Annual General Meeting	
AGS 1048	Special Considerations in the Audit of Small Entities	ISA 1005
AGS 1050	Audit Issues Relating to the Electronic Presentation of Financial Reports	
AGS 1052	Special Considerations in the Audit of Compliance Plans of Managed Investment Schemes	
AGS 1054	Auditing Revenue of Charitable Entities	
AUP 32	Audit Independence	

LEARNING OBJECTIVE 6

Explain the importance of Auditing Standards for the profession.

The importance of Auditing Standards

Auditing Standards (AUSs) set a minimum standard of technical proficiency in auditing, codifying current best practice. They are applicable in each financial report audit (subject to the exceptional circumstances departure provision) that an independent auditor undertakes, regardless of the size of the entity, the form of business organisation, the type of industry or whether the entity is for profit or not for profit. Shareholders and other users are informed in the 'Scope' section of the audit report that the audit has been conducted in accordance with Auditing Standards.

The professional accounting bodies are the source of the Standards, which have authority with respect to members of the accountancy profession because the National Councils of Accounting Bodies approve them. APS 1.1 stipulates that compliance with Auditing Standards is mandatory — that is, the Standards are enforceable under the Joint Code of Professional Conduct of the ICAA and CPA Australia. The Code stipulates that non-compliance will be investigated and appropriate actions will be taken.

Within each Auditing Standard, the basic principles and essential procedures identified in bold type are mandatory and are to be complied with in the planning, conduct and reporting of audit and audit-related services. The explanatory text and other information provide guidance and practical examples to assist the auditor in the conduct of the audit. Auditing Guidance Statements (AGSs) do not establish new principles or amend existing standards, and they are not mandatory.

Compliance with the Auditing Standards may provide adequate defence against actions for malpractice, because the Standards indicate the minimum level of care required in performing an audit. Ultimately, however, the courts determine whether the level of care provided is adequate. As the comments of Moffitt J in *Pacific Acceptance Corporation Ltd v. Forsyth* (1970) 92 WN (NSW) 29 (at 75) indicate:

> When the conduct of an auditor is in question in legal proceedings, it is not the province of the auditing profession itself to determine what is the legal duty of auditors or to determine what reasonable skill and care requires to be done in a particular case, although what others do or what is usually done is relevant to the question of whether there has been a breach of duty.

The courts may decide that auditors should review and update their practices and procedures to meet changing business conditions and expectations. Moffit J (at 74) commented:

> It is not a question of the court requiring higher standards because the profession has adopted higher standards. It is a question of the court applying the law, which by its content expects such reasonable standards as will meet the circumstances of today, including modern conditions of business and knowledge concerning them ... it might be said that the modern procedures call for more sophistication and higher standards on the part of those who perform the work.

It is argued that the Standards enhance the reputation of the profession. In constantly updating old Standards and issuing new Standards, the accounting bodies are seen to be responding to difficult problems and endeavouring to meet the changing needs of society. However, no matter how comprehensive or current Auditing Standards are, they will not improve the reputation of the profession if there is a lack of compliance with those Standards (see the 'Professional environment' on page 151).

PROFESSIONAL ENVIRONMENT

Consistent application of international Accounting Standards

Although the IFAC has developed a comprehensive set of International Auditing Standards (ISAs), there is some concern that these Standards have not been consistently applied over international boundaries. A new initiative between the IFAC and seven major transnational accounting firms is aimed at strengthening international accounting and auditing practices. The following was reported in the *Journal of Accountancy*:

> The IFAC hopes firms in the alliance, by uniformly applying standards developed by the International Accounting Standards Committee (IASC), and its own International Auditing Practices Committee (IAPC), will help the world's nations increase the transparency, reliability and consistency of their financial statements. And that, the IFAC thinks, will encourage investors to move more public and private capital across international borders.
>
> The IFAC alliance, known as the Forum of Firms, so far consists of the Big Five firms plus Grant Thornton LLP and BDO Seidman, LLP, but the IFAC said firms of any size can apply for membership. In order to qualify, applicants must have, or anticipate working with, clients that conduct business in two or more international jurisdictions.
>
> 'The classic example of such a client is Coca-Cola, which operates all around the world, but, of course, there are smaller ones,' said Peter Johnston, the IFAC's director.
>
> Member firms also are required to establish, and train their staffs to observe, internal policies and practices that comply with international accounting standards (IASs), international standards on auditing (ISAs) and the IFAC code of ethics.
>
> 'It's possible, at first, that few transnational firms will qualify for membership,' Johnston acknowledged to the JofA. Firms that gain admission to the group must submit to quality control and monitoring and ensure that all their offices — domestic and international — consistently use adequate standards. Other requirements include supporting the establishment of professional bodies and international standards in developing countries.

(Source: Extracted from Robert Tie, 'IFAC, Firms to Apply International Standards Consistently', *Journal of Accountancy* (April 2000), p. 20)

INDEPENDENT AUDITOR RELATIONSHIPS

7 LEARNING OBJECTIVE

Describe the auditor's relationship with the shareholders, audit committee and other important groups.

In a financial report audit, the auditor maintains professional relationships with four important groups: (1) the shareholders, (2) the board of directors and audit committee, (3) internal auditors and (4) management.

Shareholders

The shareholders of the company are the primary beneficiaries of the audit function — a point that is emphasised in the audit report title, which is usually: 'Independent Auditor's Report to the Members (or Shareholders) of XYZ Limited'.

Shareholders rely on the audited financial report for assurance that management has properly discharged its stewardship responsibility. The auditor, therefore, has an important responsibility to shareholders of the company. During the course of an audit engagement, the auditor is unlikely to have direct personal contact with shareholders, who often are not officers, key employees or directors of the entity. Yet, the auditor's appointment, removal or resignation are ultimately determined by (or influenced by) the shareholders. In theory, the directors' powers to appoint the auditor are limited; in practice, the members of the company generally accept the recommendations of the directors.

The board of directors and audit committee

The board of directors of an entity is responsible for seeing that the entity operates in the best interests of the shareholders. The auditor's relationship with the directors largely depends on the composition of the board. Thus, when the board consists primarily of entity or executive officers, the auditor's relationship with the board may be the same as his or her relationship with management. When the board has a number of outside or non-executive directors, a different relationship is possible. Outside members are not officers or employees of the entity, so the board in such cases — composed exclusively or primarily of outside members of the board — can serve as an intermediary between the auditor and management, and may have oversight responsibilities for the financial reporting and auditing process.

Irrespective of the structure of the board of directors, companies are encouraged to have an **audit committee**. Audit committees can play a key role in assisting boards of directors to fulfil their corporate governance and oversight responsibilities. Usually, neither the independent auditor nor the internal auditor is a member of the audit committee. However, both meet with the audit committee to discuss matters pertaining to the audit.

In recent years there has been a marked increase in the number of audit committees in Australia. In 1995, Deloitte Touche Tohmatsu conducted a survey of chief executive officers and internal audit managers of a broad range of companies and organisations in Australia.[13] The study reported that 72 per cent of the organisations had established audit committees at that time. Australian Stock Exchange listing rule 4.10.2 requires disclosure of the existence of an audit committee.

Audit committees have an important role in corporate governance. In 1997 the AARF issued *Audit Committees: Best Practice Guide* to assist companies in setting up audit committees. In the guide it makes the following statement about the usefulness of an audit committee:

> An audit committee is unique in that it provides a forum where directors, management and auditors can deal together with issues relating to the management of risk and with financial reporting obligations.[14]

The guide also outlines the objectives and benefits of an effective audit committee, including:

- to improve the credibility and objectivity of the accountability process (including financial reporting);
- to assist the board of directors to discharge its responsibility to exercise due care, diligence and skill;
- to improve the effectiveness of the internal and external audit functions and the communication between the board of directors and the external and internal auditors;

- to facilitate the maintenance of the independence of the external auditor;
- to strengthen the role and influence of non-executive directors.[15]

It is important that the terms of reference of the audit committee be clearly defined in a formal charter, so the committee's role does not overlap that of management. This charter should ensure that the audit committee has adequate resources and the authority necessary to meet its objectives. The majority of audit committee members should be independent, non-executive directors and at least one member should have significant financial experience. The chairperson of the board of directors should not be the chairperson of the audit committee.

Appendix 1 of AUS 710, Communication to Management on Matters Arising from an Audit guides independent auditors on matters arising from a financial report audit that may be communicated to an audit committee. When an effective audit committee is in place, it provides an effective mechanism for the auditor to communicate with management about issues relating to the nature and scope of the audit, and to report significant issues arising from the audit. We will discuss this process in more detail in Chapter 14.

Internal auditors

An independent auditor often has a close working relationship with the entity's **internal auditor**. From the perspective of the independent auditor, internal auditing is a component of the entity's control environment. As an independent unit within the entity, the internal auditor examines, evaluates and monitors the adequacy and effectiveness of the internal control structure. The work of the internal auditor in conducting tests of control is likely to influence the nature, timing and extent of the independent auditor's audit procedures. AUS 604, Considering the Work of Internal Auditing (ISA 610) requires the independent auditor to assess the work of the internal auditor for the purpose of planning the audit and developing an effective audit approach.

The internal auditor's work cannot be used as a substitute for the independent auditor's work, but it can be an important complement. AUS 604 (ISA 610) requires the independent auditor, in determining the effect of such work on the audit, to consider: (1) the organisational status, (2) the scope of work, (3) the technical training and proficiency of internal auditors and (4) due professional care observed in the work of internal auditors. We will discuss internal auditing further in Chapter 18.

Management

The term 'management' is a collective reference to individuals who actively plan, coordinate and control the operations and transactions of the entity. In an auditing context, 'management' refers to the entity officers, controller and key supervisory personnel.

During the course of an audit, there is extensive interaction between the auditor and management. To obtain the evidence needed, the auditor often requires confidential data about the entity, so a relationship based on mutual trust and respect is an imperative. An adversarial relationship will be counterproductive. The typical approach of the auditor towards management's assertions may be characterised by professional scepticism. This means the auditor should neither disbelieve management's assertions nor thoughtlessly accept them without concern for their truthfulness. Rather, the auditor should recognise the need to evaluate objectively the conditions observed and evidence obtained during the audit. The auditor should also consider AUS 520 (ISA 580),

Management Representations when considering management representations during an audit. As stated in AUS 520.08 (ISA 580.07), 'Representations by management cannot be a substitute for other evidence that the auditor could reasonably expect to be available.' Generally, it will be only in exceptional circumstances that alternative evidence is not reasonably expected to be available. The auditor should ensure that he or she does not rely on management representations for the sake of convenience when alternative evidence is available.

8 LEARNING OBJECTIVE

Explain the interrelationship between management's and the auditor's responsibilities.

MANAGEMENT AND THE AUDITOR — RESPONSIBILITIES

In this section, we will describe in more detail the division of responsibility between an entity's management and the auditor in the financial reporting process. An important aspect of this division is associated with the relationship between accounting and auditing.

The relationship between accounting and auditing

There are significant differences in the accounting process by which financial reports are prepared and the audit of these reports. Each process has different objectives and methods, and the parties responsible for each are not the same.

Accounting methods involve identifying the events and transactions that affect the entity, and then measuring, recording, classifying and summarising these items in the accounting records. The outcome of this process is the preparation and distribution of financial reports in accordance with an identified financial reporting framework. The ultimate objective of accounting is the communication of relevant and reliable financial information that will be useful for decision-making. An entity's employees are involved in the accounting process and the entity's directors have ultimate responsibility for the financial report.

The audit of financial reports involves obtaining and evaluating evidence on management's financial report assertions. Auditing culminates in the issue of an audit report that contains the auditor's opinion on whether the financial information is presented fairly in accordance with an identified financial reporting framework. The auditor is responsible for adhering to Auditing Standards both in gathering and evaluating evidence, and in issuing an audit report that contains the auditor's conclusion. This conclusion is expressed in the form of an opinion on the financial information. Rather than creating new information, auditing adds credibility to the financial report prepared by management.

The relationship between accounting and auditing in the financial reporting process is illustrated in Figure 4.2.

Sometimes an auditor may be asked to assist in the preparation of an entity's books, which is clearly part of the accounting process. Professional Statement F1 on Professional Independence prohibits this involvement with public company audit clients, other than in exceptional circumstances. Such involvement is allowed with other clients, provided the need for professional independence is considered, the client accepts responsibility for the books, and the auditor makes no executive decisions.

FIGURE 4.2

Relationship between accounting and auditing

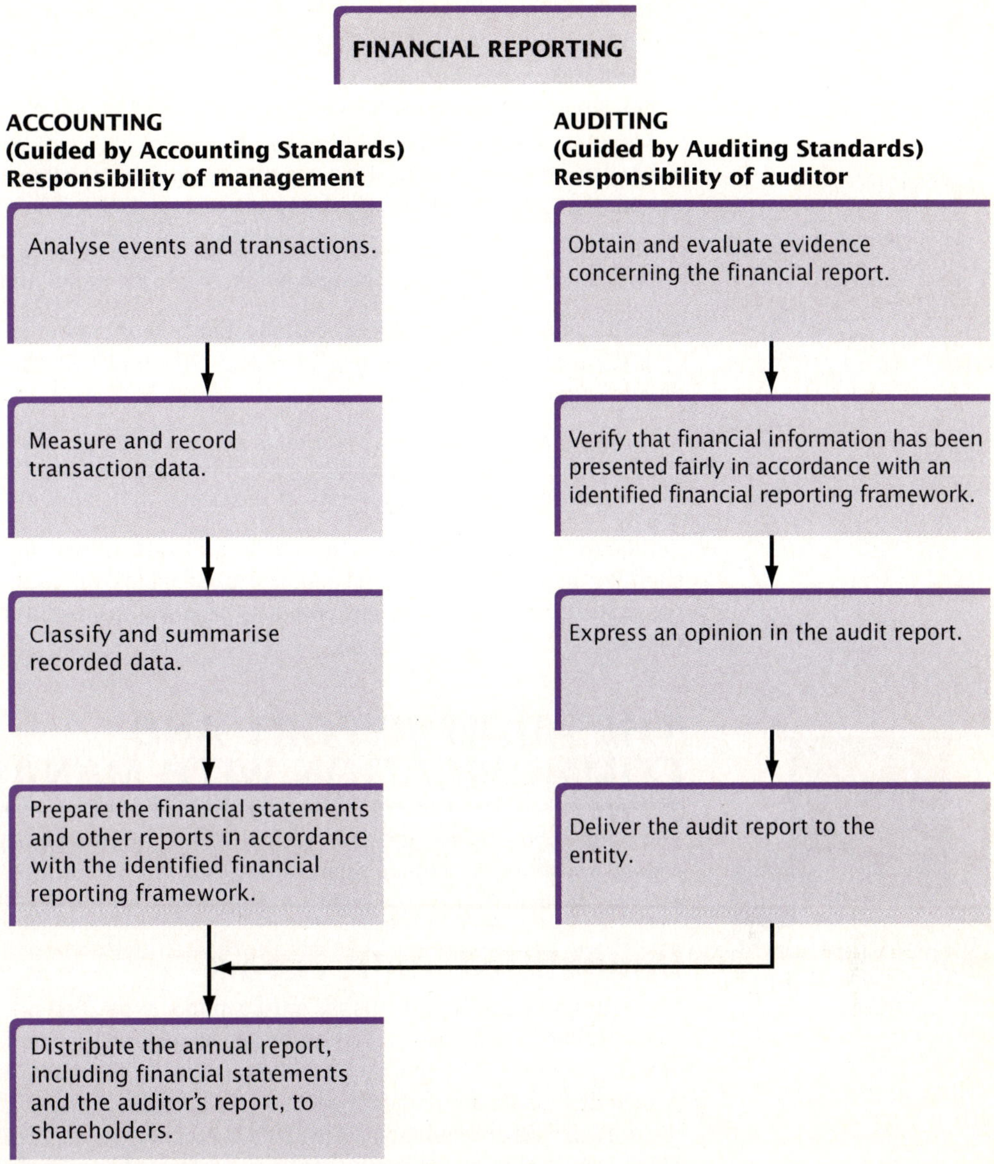

The division of responsibility

Fundamental to a financial report audit is the division of responsibility between management and the independent auditor. AUS 202, Objective and General Principles Governing an Audit of a Financial Report (ISA 200, Objective and General Principles Governing an Audit of Financial Statements) states:

> The responsibility for the preparation and presentation of the financial report is that of the management of the entity. The audit of the financial report does not relieve management of its responsibilities.

The Corporations Law (s.294(4)) stipulates that directors must make a declaration that states:

- that the financial statements and notes comply with Accounting Standards;
- that the financial statements and notes give a true and fair view;

- that the financial statements comply with the Corporations Law;
- that there are reasonable grounds to believe that the company will be able to pay its debts as and when they fall due.

An example of a directors' declaration is shown in Figure 4.3 on page 158.

The division of responsibility is not clear when legal responsibility is to be allocated for errors that have been found within a company's financial statements. Historically, the view was as outlined by Moffitt J in *Pacific Acceptance Corporation v. Forysth* (1970) 92 WN (NSW) 29:

> To excuse an auditor because the directors or management were also at fault ... , would be to negate a fundamental reason for the appointment of the auditor.

The allocation of responsibility shifted slightly in the more recent *AWA Limited v. Daniels (trading as Deloitte Haskins & Sells) and Others* (1992) 10 ACLC 933; 7 ACSR 759, in which Rogers CJ stated:

> I cannot accept that a corporation is entitled to abdicate all responsibility for proper management of the financial aspects of its operation and then, when loss is suffered, to seek to attribute the entirety of the blame to its auditors.

'Shades of grey' will still exist in determining directors' and auditors' respective responsibilities. In practice, most legal action is taken against the auditors because they have greater resources from which damages could be paid. We discussed these issues in more detail in Chapter 3.

THE AUDIT REPORT AND COMMUNICATION WITH MANAGEMENT

9 LEARNING OBJECTIVE

Prepare an audit report and explain its basic elements.

The audit report is the auditor's formal means of communicating to interested parties a conclusion about the audited financial information. In issuing an audit opinion on a general purpose financial report, the auditor must comply with AUS 702 (ISA 700).

Unqualified audit report

An **unqualified audit report** is the most common type of report issued. It contains an unqualified opinion that the financial report presents fairly, in all material respects, the financial position and the results of operations and cash flows of the entity in accordance with applicable Accounting Standards, other mandatory professional reporting requirements, and relevant statutory and other regulations. This conclusion may be expressed only when the auditor has formed an opinion on the basis of an audit performed in accordance with Auditing Standards.

A basic understanding of the form and content of the audit report is essential. The objective of the standard report format is to communicate better to users of an audited financial report the work done by the auditor and the character and limitations of an audit. The second objective is to differentiate clearly between the responsibilities of management and the independent auditor in the financial report audit. The third objective is to state clearly the level of assurance provided by the auditor's opinion.

An example of an audit report from a large listed Australian company is presented in Figure 4.3 (page 158). Each element in the report is prescribed in AUS 702 (ISA 700). The two main elements of the report are the Scope and Opinion sections, each of which is explained in the following sections.

Scope section

The introductory paragraph in the Scope section of the report contains three factual statements. A primary objective of this paragraph is to distinguish clearly between the responsibility of the governing body and the auditor. From the example in Figure 4.3, the wording of this paragraph is presented below:

> We have audited the financial report of CSR Limited for the financial year ended 31 March 2000 as set out on pages 38 to 66.

This states that the auditor has audited a specific financial report of CSR Limited. It also clearly states which pages in the annual report have been audited, because a large amount of other information is included in the annual report (such as performance highlights, the chairperson's overview and the growth strategy). The auditor does not audit this 'other' information but must ensure that it is not inconsistent with the financial report.

To acknowledge that the responsibility for the financial report rests with the company's directors and to refute the notion that the auditor develops the representations underlying the financial report, the following statement is made:

> The company's directors are responsible for the financial report.

The following sentence indicates the auditor's responsibility. The auditor's role is to perform an audit and to express an opinion based on the findings. When read in conjunction with the sentence that precedes it, there is a clear differentiation between the responsibility of the directors and the responsibility of the auditor.

> We have conducted an independent audit of the financial report in order to express an opinion on it to the members of the company.

The second paragraph of the Scope section describes the nature and scope of the audit. It satisfies the reporting Standard (AUS 702.02; ISA 700.02) that requires the auditor to give a clear indication of the character of the audit. The paragraph also identifies several limitations of an audit. The wording is as follows:

> Our audit has been conducted in accordance with [Australian] Auditing Standards to provide reasonable assurance whether the financial report is free of material misstatement.

The above sentence asserts that the auditor has met the requirements of the Auditing Standards. In rare and exceptional circumstances when departures occur, 'details of the particular basic principle(s) or essential procedure(s) that has been departed from together with the justification for the departure' should be provided (AUS 702.17(e)). The sentence also identifies a limitation of an audit — that is, that the auditor seeks only reasonable rather than absolute assurance. Thus, the aim is a high level of assurance, which is not a guarantee. The concept of materiality is also introduced. An audit is planned and performed to discover material, but not all, misstatements in the financial report.

> Our procedures included examination, on a test basis, of evidence supporting the amounts and other disclosures in the financial report, and the evaluation of accounting policies and significant accounting estimates.

The above sentence further explains the nature of an audit. 'Test basis' indicates that less than 100 per cent of the evidence is examined. Furthermore, it implies a risk that evidence not examined may be important in assessing the fairness of the overall financial report presentation and disclosures. The sentence also indicates that judgement is required in assessing the appropriateness of accounting policies and amounts of accounting estimates.

> These procedures have been undertaken to form an opinion whether, in all material respects, the financial report is presented fairly ...

The phrase 'in all material respects' informs users that the auditor's opinion does not attest to the absolute accuracy of the financial report. This limitation is stated as a result of the test basis of an audit and the inclusion of significant estimates in the financial report.

FIGURE 4.3

Directors' declaration and independent audit report

DIRECTORS' DECLARATION

Declaration by directors on the financial statements and notes thereto set out on pages 38 to 65

The directors declare that the financial statements and notes thereto:
(a) comply with Accounting Standards;
(b) give a true and fair view of the financial position and performance of the company and consolidaed entity;
(c) are, in the directors' opinion, in accordance with the Corporations Law.

In the directors' opinion, there are reasonable grounds to believe that the company will be able to pay its debts as and when they become due and payable.

Signed in accordance with a resolution of the directors made pursuant to s.295(5) of the Corporations Law.

IAN BURGESS
Chairman

PETER KIRBY
Managing Director
15 May 2000

INDEPENDENT AUDIT REPORT TO THE MEMBERS OF CSR LIMITED

Scope

We have audited the financial report of CSR Limited for the financial year ended 31 March 2000 as set out on pages 38 to 66. The financial report includes the consolidated financial statements of the consolidated entity comprising the company and the entities it controlled at the year's end or from time to time during the financial year. The company's directors are responsible for the financial report. We have conducted an independent audit of the financial report in order to express an opinion on it to the members of the company.

Our audit has been conducted in accordance with Australian Auditing Standards to provide reasonable assurance whether the financial report is free of material missatement. Our procedures included examination, on a test basis, of evidence supporting the amounts and other disclosures in the financial report, and the evaluation of accounting policies and significant accounting estimates. These procedures have been undertaken to form an opinion whether, in all material respects, the financial report is presented fairly in accordance with Accounting Standards and other mandatory professional reporting requirements and statutory requirements so as to present a view which is consistent with our understanding of the company's and the consolidated entity's financial position, and performance as represented by the results of their operations and their cash flows.

The audit opinion expressed in this report has been formed on the above basis.

Audit opinion

In our opinion, the financial report of CSR Limited is in accordance with:
(a) the Corporations Law, including:
  (i) giving a true and fair view of the company's and the consolidated entity's financial position as at 31 March 2000 and of their performance for the year ended on that date; and
  (ii) complying with Accounting Standards and the Corporations Regulations; and
(b) other mandatory professional reporting requirements.

DELOITTE TOUCHE TOHMATSU

HARLEY McHUTCHISON
Partner
Chartered Accountants
15 May 2000

The liability of Deloitte Touche Tohmatsu is limited by, and to the extent of, the Accountants' Scheme under the *Professional Standards Act 1994* (NSW).

(Source: CSR Limited, *CSR Annual Report 2000*. Sydney, 2000)

Opinion section

The Opinion statement satisfies the reporting Standards. From the CSR example on page 158 (Figure 4.3), the wording of the Opinion section is as follows.

> In our opinion, the financial report of CSR Limited is in accordance with: ...

In interpreting the meaning and significance of these words, it is proper to conclude that the opinion is being expressed by a professional, experienced and expert person (or persons). It is incorrect, however, to conclude that this phrase means, 'We certify', 'We guarantee' or 'We are certain (or positive)'.

> ... (a) the Corporations Law, including:
> (i) giving a true and fair view of the company's and the consolidated entity's financial position ...

The intended connotation of the words 'true and fair' is that the financial report is presented reasonably and without bias or distortion. The auditor's opinion on fairness pertains to each component of the financial report taken as a whole. It does not apply to the accuracy or correctness of individual accounts. An unqualified opinion expresses the auditor's belief that the financial report accomplishes the stated purpose by presenting a true and fair view of the entity's financial position (balance sheet), its results of operations (profit and loss) and its cash flows. An unqualified opinion also means that any differences between management and the auditor on accounting matters have been resolved to the auditor's satisfaction.

The Corporations Law stipulates that the accounts presented give a 'true and fair view' of the financial position of the company and the results of its operations. However, AUS 702.23 requires that the auditor use the following phrase wherever possible:

> ... presents fairly in accordance with applicable Accounting Standards and other mandatory professional reporting requirements ...'

While under Australian Auditing Standards, the choice of phrase does not affect the auditor's responsibilities, the standard setters believe that the phrase 'presents fairly in accordance with applicable Accounting Standards' provides a more effective communication of the auditor's opinion. It emphasises that the concept of fairness is too broad to be capable of meaningful interpretation and must be linked with a set of standards to provide a framework within which judgement can be exercised, honestly and responsibly, to report the entity's economic condition and performance. ISA 200.17 allows the auditor the choice of 'true and fair view' or 'presented fairly' in reporting on a set of financial statements. ISA 200.18 states that the two phrases are equivalent.

Disclaimer

A disclaimer at the bottom of the audit report in Figure 4.3 states that:

> The liability of Deliotte Touche Tohmatsu is limited by, and to the extent of, the Accountants' Scheme under the *Professional Standards Act 1994* (NSW).

A limitation of liability exists for members of the accountancy profession in New South Wales only. The maximum liability of accountants is $50 million (see Chapter 3).

Modified audit report

10 LEARNING OBJECTIVE

Indicate the types of modified audit report and when use of each is appropriate.

A **modified audit report** is issued when the audit opinion is qualified or when it is appropriate for the auditor to draw attention to or emphasise a matter that is relevant to users.

Qualified opinion

A **qualified audit opinion** is issued when any of the following circumstances occur:
- a disagreement with management regarding the financial report;
- a conflict between applicable financial reporting frameworks;
- a limitation on the scope of the audit.

An auditor may disagree with management when, in the auditor's opinion: (1) an inappropriate accounting policy is selected; (2) an accounting policy is misapplied; (3) the appropriateness of an accounting estimate is questioned; or (4) there is failure to make adequate or appropriate disclosures required by Accounting Standards and relevant statutory and other requirements.

A conflict between applicable financial reporting frameworks results when:
- the application of accounting policies required or allowed by relevant statutory and other requirements has not resulted in a fair presentation in accordance with applicable Accounting Standards; or
- the accounting policies applied are contrary to those required by relevant statutory and other requirements.

In the event of a disagreement with management or a conflict between applicable financial reporting frameworks, the auditor may express an 'except for' opinion or an adverse opinion. Adverse opinions are expressed only when disagreements with management or the conflict between financial reporting frameworks have extremely material effects and the auditor concludes that the overall usefulness of the financial report taken as a whole is impaired.

In a scope limitation, the auditor is unable to obtain sufficient appropriate evidence regarding one or more of management's material assertions in the financial report. In the event of scope limitations, the auditor expresses an 'except for' opinion or an inability to form an opinion. An inability to form an opinion is used only for scope limitations that pertain to matters that have an extremely material effect.

The position indicated by the differing opinions is as follows:
- An 'except for' opinion states that except for the effects of the matter(s) to which the qualification relates, the financial report presents fairly . . . in accordance with applicable Accounting Standards and other mandatory professional reporting requirements, and relevant statutory and other requirements.
- An adverse opinion states that the financial report does not present fairly . . . in accordance with applicable Accounting Standards and other mandatory professional reporting requirements, and relevant statutory and other requirements.
- An inability to form an opinion states that the auditor is not in a position to, and does not, express an opinion on the financial report.

When other than an unqualified opinion is expressed, the reason(s) for the opinion should be explained in a separate Qualification section. The Qualification precedes the Opinion section. The Opinion section of the audit report should be headed 'Qualified audit opinion'. The opinion refers to the reason(s) for the qualification and is followed by wording appropriate to the type of opinion being expressed.

A summary of the types of audit report discussed in this chapter, and the circumstances when each is appropriate, is presented in Table 4.1. Additional consideration is given to audit reports on audited financial reports in Chapter 15.

TABLE 4.1

Types of qualified audit opinion

Circumstances	Effects of the matter: Material	Effects of the matter: Extremely material
Disagreements with management (including inherent uncertainty not adequately disclosed)	'Except for' opinion	Adverse opinion
Conflict between applicable financial reporting frameworks	'Except for' opinion	Adverse opinion
Scope limitation	'Except for' opinion	Inability to form an opinion

Emphasis of matter

An audit report may be modified as a result of an emphasis of matter. The distinguishing characteristic of this category of report is that the Opinion section continues to express an unqualified opinion. This is followed by an emphasis of matter paragraph to draw the reader's attention to the specific circumstances. The circumstances in which an emphasis of matter paragraph is to be used are:

- additional disclosures that are contrary to the requirements of Accounting Standards;
- inherent uncertainties, including those involving a going-concern question that are adequately disclosed;
- inconsistent other information;
- subsequent-event results in a new audit report.

We will discuss this type of modification further in chapter 15.

Management letter

The product of the audit is usually a communication to management in the form of a letter that is usually described as a 'management letter'. This letter usually contains recommendations for improving the efficiency and effectiveness of matters noticed during the audit, and advises management of weaknesses in their internal control structures. AUS 710, Communication to Management on Matters Arising from an Audit (ISA 1007, Communications with Management) provides guidance on the content of management letters (see Chapter 14).

LEARNING CHECK

4.6 Auditing Standards are set by the AuASB of the AARF. They are important for maintaining quality service and safeguarding the auditor when called on to justify his or her opinion. Shareholders and other users of audit reports can also be assured of the minimum standards employed by the auditor in arriving at the audit opinion.

4.7 Shareholders of the company are the primary reason for the audit function. However, they typically have little contact with the auditor.

4.8 The independent auditor must retain a degree of professional scepticism when dealing with the management of the organisation, while maintaining objectivity and mutual respect.

4.9 Management is primarily responsible for the preparation and presentation of financial reports.

4.10 There are two types of audit report: unqualified and modified. Unqualified audit reports signify a 'clean' opinion. Modified audit reports can be further divided into those that are qualified and those with an emphasis of matter. Qualified audit reports refer to certain matters on which the auditor is unable to form an opinion or with which he or she disagrees.

SUMMARY

In this chapter, we provided an overview of the financial report audit, firstly considering some of the fundamentals of financial report audits. These fundamentals outline some of the reasons for the use of independent audits, along with the benefits and limitations of these reports.

Although there would be a demand for audits without regulation, most financial report audits are conducted under a statutory mandate, which in Australia is the Corporations Law. We discussed details of the regulations relating to the audit, auditor appointment and auditor responsibilities under the Corporations Law. We also discussed other professional duties, including the duty to use reasonable care and skill (see Chapter 3) and the duty to be independent (see Chapter 2).

Auditing Standards provide the primary guidance for the auditor in the conduct of an audit. The AuASB prepares the Australian Auditing Standards which are issued jointly by the ICAA and CPA Australia. Users of a financial report look to the auditors for assurance that the financial information meets the qualitative characteristics of relevance and reliability, and that the financial statements taken as a whole are presented fairly in accordance with an identified financial reporting framework. Financial report audits provide a high but not absolute level of assurance. (We discussed the levels of assurance provided by other assurance engagements in Chapter 1.)

In the course of the audit, the auditor maintains professional relationships with four important groups: the shareholders, the entity's board of directors and audit committee, the internal auditors (see Chapter 18) and the entity's management. The relationship between accounting and auditing in the financial reporting process involves a basic division of responsibilities between the management of an entity and its independent auditors. Management is responsible for preparing the financial report in accordance with an identified financial reporting framework, and the auditor is responsible for expressing an opinion on the financial report in an audit performed in accordance with Auditing Standards.

The audit report on a general purpose financial report clearly distinguishes the responsibilities of management and the auditor, explains the character and limitations of an audit, and expresses the auditor's opinion as to whether the financial report is presented fairly. Modified audit reports are used when circumstances require the issue of a qualified opinion or an emphasis of matter.

KEY TERMS

Agency theory, p. 136
Audit committee, p. 152
Auditing Standards, p. 139
Contractual relationship, p. 144
Emphasis of matter, p. 145
General purpose financial reports, p. 136
Information hypothesis, p. 136
Insurance hypothesis, p. 136
Internal auditor, p. 153
Management, p. 137
Management letter, p. 139
Materiality, p. 140
Modified audit report, p. 160
Professional judgement, p. 140
Qualified audit opinion, p. 160
Standard format of audit reports, p. 141
Stewardship, p. 136
Unqualified audit report, p. 156

NOTES

1. Wanda A. Wallace, *The Economic Role of the Audit in Free and Regulated Markets*, Touche Ross & Co., New York, 1980.
2. Ross L. Watts & Jerold L. Zimmerman, 'Agency Problems, Auditing and the Theory of the Firm: Some Evidence', *Journal of Law and Economics* (Vol. 26, 1983), pp. 613–33.
3. See Note 2, p. 626.
4. See Note 2, p. 633.
5. Michael C. Jensen & William H. Meckling, 'Theory of the Firm: Managerial Behaviour, Agency Costs and Ownership Structure', *Journal of Financial Economics* (Vol. 3, 1976), pp. 305–60.
6. Andrew White, 'Shares Hold Our Dreams', *Australian* (9 February 2000), p. 18.
7. See Note 1, p. 21.
8. See Note 1, p. 23.
9. J. P. Percy, 'Auditing and Corporate Governance — A Look forward into the 21st Century', *International Journal of Auditing* (Vol. 1, No. 1, 1997), pp. 3–12.
10. K. T. Trotman, *Research Methodology for Judgement and Decision-making Studies in Auditing*, Coopers & Lybrand and the AAANZ, Melbourne, 1996.
11. Ray Anderson & Marc Epstein, 'The Usefulness of Annual Reports', *Australian Accountant* (April 1995), pp. 25–8.
12. Brenda A. Porter, 'Narrowing the Audit Expectation–Performance Gap: A Contemporary Approach', *Pacific Accounting Review* (Vol. 3, No. 1, 1991), pp. 1–36.
13. C. M. H. Matthews, B. J. Cooper & P. Leung, *A Profile of Internal Audit in Australia*. Deloitte Touche Tohmatsu and RMIT University, Melbourne, 1995.
14. Australian Accounting Research Foundation, the Australian Institute of Company Directors & the Institute of Internal Auditors, *Audit Committees: Best Practice Guide*. Melbourne, 1997, p. 2.
15. See Note 14, p.4

FURTHER READING

Azoor Hughes, S. D., 'Adding Value through Continuous Assurance', *Charter* (November 1999), pp. 70–1.

Canadian Institute of Chartered Accountants & the American Institute of Certified Public Accountants, *Continuous Auditing*. Toronto, 1999.

Clarke, F. L., Dean, G. W. & Oliver, K. G., *Corporate Collapse: Regulatory, Accounting and Ethical Failure*. Cambridge University Press, Melbourne, 1997.

CPA Australia & the Institute of Chartered Accountants in Australia, *Auditing Handbook 2000*. Prentice Hall, Sydney, 2000.

International Federation of Accountants, *IFAC Handbook 2000 — Technical Pronouncements*. New York, 2000.

Lipton, P. & Herzberg, A., *Understanding Company Law*, 7th edn. LBC Information Services, New South Wales, 1998.

Power, M., *The Audit Society — Rituals of Verification*. Oxford University Press, London, 1997.

Sherer, M. & Turley, S., *Current Issues in Auditing*. Paul Chapman Publishing, London, 1997.

Simplification Task Force, Attorney-General's Department, *Accounts and Audit: Proposal for Simplification, Corporations Law Simplification Program*. Australian Government Publishing Service, Canberra, 1995.

Review questions

4.1 What factors underpin the need for financial report audits?

4.2 What are the main limitations of an external audit?

4.3 What are the main Corporations Law requirements with regard to the appointment, removal and registration of auditors?

4.4 What is the interrelationship between the Auditing and Assurance Standards Board and the International Auditing Practices Committee?

4.5 What are the responsibilities of the auditor compared with those of management?

4.6 What circumstances are required for use of each of the three different types of qualified audit report?

Discussion questions

4.1 Would the audit function exist in an unregulated environment? Discuss.

4.2 What are the benefits of a financial report audit?

4.3 What is the most significant limitation of financial report audits in your view?

4.4 Can an auditor be removed for issuing a qualified audit opinion? Discuss.

4.5 Why is independence crucial for an external auditor?

4.6 Why are auditing standards important?

4.7 How does the relationship that independent auditors have with shareholders compare to their relationship with management?

4.8 What are some of the benefits of an effective audit committee?

4.9 What is the difference between accounting and auditing?

4.10 What main limitations are outlined in the 'Scope' section of a financial report audit? Discuss.

Professional application questions

★ BASIC
★★ MODERATE
★★★ CHALLENGING

4.1 (Financial report audits) ★

You are an employee of a small proprietary company in the accounting department. The company has always had a financial report audit of its yearly financial statements to 30 June, because it was considered an important deterrent to fraud within the company. It is approaching September, which is normally the time for the annual audit. The managing director calls you to a meeting, and says: 'I am sick of wasting money on auditors! I think that it is time to stop having an annual audit. They never find any fraud and they never have anything useful to tell us about how to improve the running of our business. Section 301(2) of the Corporations Law states that we do not need to have an audit, so I think it is time to stop. Can you write a letter to the auditors telling them that we do not require their services this year?'.

You feel unsure about this request because you have always had a good relationship with the company's auditors.

Required

Write a memo to the managing director, detailing why the company should continue to have an audit.

4.2 (Audit committees) ★

The following was reported in *Chartered Accountant* in Australia (Vol. 48, No. 3, April 1977), p. 7:

> The subject of audit committees is relatively unknown in Australia. The writer is aware of only two major listed companies which have formed audit committees. No doubt there are others but these are likely to be very few.

Required

(a) Define 'audit committee'.

(b) Identify the reasons for the formation of audit committees.

4.3 (Audit report) ★

Independent audit report

To the members of Highbury Limited

Matters relating to the electronic presentation of the audited financial statements

This audit report relates to the financial statements of Highbury Limited for the year ended 30 June 2001 included on the Highbury Limited web site. The company's directors are responsible for the integrity of the Highbury Limited web site. We have not been engaged to report on the integrity of the Highbury Limited web site. The audit report refers only to the statements named below. It does not provide an opinion on any other information which may have been hyperlinked to/from these statements. If users of this report are concerned with the inherent risks arising from electronic data communications they are advised to refer to the hard copy of the audited financial statements to confirm the information included in the audited financial statements presented on this web site.

Scope

We have audited the financial statements of Highbury Limited for the financial year ended 30 June 2001 as set out on pages 1 to 35. The company's directors are responsible for the financial statements. We have conducted an independent audit of these financial statements in order to express an opinion on them to the members of the company.

Our audit has been conducted in accordance with Auditing Standards to provide reasonable assurance whether the financial statements are free of material misstatement. Our procedures included examination, on a test basis, of evidence supporting the amounts and other disclosures in the financial statements, and the evaluation of accounting policies and significant accounting estimates. These procedures have been undertaken to form an opinion whether, in all material respects, the financial statements are presented fairly in accordance with Accounting Standards, other mandatory professional reporting requirements and statutory requirements so as to present a view which is consistent with our understanding of the company's financial position, and performance as represented by the results of its operations and its cash flows.

The audit opinion expressed in this report has been formed on the above basis.

(continued)

Audit opinion

In our opinion, the financial statements of Highbury Limited are in accordance with:

(a) the Corporations Law, including:

(i) giving a true and fair view of the company's financial position as at 30 June 2001 and of its performance for the year ended on that date; and

(ii) complying with Accounting Standards and the Corporations Regulations; and

(b) other mandatory professional reporting requirements.

GMPK	**Brad Johns**
Chartered Accountants	Partner

Dated at Melbourne this 15th day of September 2001

Required

(a) Nominate whether the above report is a qualified or unqualified audit report.

(b) Explain the following components of the audit report and discuss why they are important:

(i) title; (ii) scope; (iii) audit opinion; (iv) date;

(c) Explain how this report differs from the one shown on page 158.

4.4 (Appointment of auditors) ★★

Revglow Limited, a large proprietary company, was incorporated on 1 July 20X2. A short time later, one of the non-shareholding directors, Fred Bile, approached his tax agent, Gina Rogers, to ask her to be Revglow's auditor. Ms Rogers is a chartered accountant, but had not performed any audits and was hesitant about accepting the engagement. Mr Bile said the appointment would be only temporary until proper documentation could be prepared and the audit work put out to tender. Ms Rogers said she would accept this arrangement and Mr Bile prepared a letter confirming the appointment on 21 July 20X2.

At its first meeting on 1 September 20X2, the board decided to confirm Ms Rogers as the auditor of Revglow for a period of three years. They were impressed with the recommendation given by Mr Bile and decided that requesting tenders would be a timely and inefficient process.

Required

Discuss whether Corporations Law requirements have been followed in the above scenario.

(Professional Year Programme of the ICAA — 1998, Accounting 2 Module — adapted)

4.5 (Removal of an auditor) ★★

On 31 March 20X3, Black and Black (a firm of certified practising accountants [CPAs]) completed the audit of E-Wine Pty Limited for the year ended 31 December 20X2. E-Wine is a wine store that operates solely on the Internet. On 15 May 20X3, Tom Black (the audit partner responsible for E-Wine) received a phone call from the financial controller of E-Wine, Ms Chong, who was very angry. Ms Chong said that their accounts receivable clerk suddenly resigned a month ago. This sudden departure raised suspicions and, after an investigation of the accounting records, it was discovered that $200 000 was missing. Subsequently, the board met and decided Black and Black was almost entirely to blame. As a result, Ms Chong said the board had decided to dismiss Black and Black as auditors, effective immediately. Black and Black would receive written confirmation in the next week and legal action would probably follow.

Required

(a) Explain whether E-Wine has taken the proper action to remove an auditor.

(b) Explain why restrictions are placed on removing auditors.

4.6 (Statutory and professional duties) ★★

You are an audit senior working in a Big 5 accountancy practice in Australia. It is April and not long until the 'busy' season, which generally starts from about May. A number of audit managers and seniors will come from the United Kingdom on secondment for the Australian busy season.

Your audit partner notes that you do not have much work at the moment and he suggests that you prepare a memo for the new UK arrivals to assist with their acclimatisation into the Australian audit environment. He wants the following outlined in the memo:

1. statutory duties to report, as outlined in the Corporations Law;
2. a discussion of the purpose of Australian Auditing Standards.

Required

Prepare the memo as requested by the audit partner.

4.7 (Management and auditor responsibilities) ★★

The following statement is from the *Auditing Handbook 2000*, in the section 'Understanding Financial Statement Audits — A Guide for Financial Statement Users':

> Management is responsible for establishing an accounting system to identify, measure, record, and adequately disclose an entity's transactions and other events that affect its financial position and results of operations. In addition, management is responsible for selecting accounting principles that appropriately reflect events that occur and for making other accounting estimates and judgements. This responsibility is not lessened by an independent audit.

Required

If management is responsible for all of the above, explain the role of the audit.

4.8 (Audit report) ★★

Ms Ryan was concerned about the results of the audit of her footwear company, Performance Feet Limited, for the year ended 30 June 20X1. The bank recently contacted her, wanting to obtain the company's audited financial statements for the year. Ms Ryan was worried about the results of the audit and was concerned that a qualified audit report would result in the bank calling in its loan. She rang the audit partner on the engagement, Mr Tomney, and asked him about the result of the annual audit of Performance Feet. He said that they had decided to issue a modified audit report, because they had had problems in obtaining all of the financial records. Ms Ryan said, 'Thank goodness it is not qualified!', then hung up the telephone.

Required

Discuss whether Ms Ryan should be confident in going to the bank with this 'modified' audit report.

Case studies

4.1 (Audit committees) ★★

You are the chief internal auditor of IKIA Limited, which is a large manufacturing company listed on the stock exchange. At the last board meeting, one of the items discussed was the establishment of an audit committee. Some members of the board did not support the idea of having another committee, especially when they already have a well established internal audit function that has been in operation for the past three years. These particular directors feel that there is too much money being spent on the monitoring process, considering the resources already allocated to both the internal and external audit functions, and that this is eating into profits that could be redistributed to the shareholders in the form of higher dividends. They argue that investors place their money with them in the hope of high returns, not just to have it spent on checking and rechecking transactions. There have been no major problems uncovered by internal audit since its inception, and the external auditors have never qualified the audit report.

Although you have read only a little about the functions of an audit committee, you feel uncomfortable in the other directors' dismissive attitude, and request that the board consider the matter further. As a result, you are asked to research the subject of audit committees further and report back at the next board meeting whether IKIA should establish an audit committee.

Required

Prepare your report for the Board, covering the following matters.

(a) Address the directors' concerns about the amount of resources being allocated to the monitoring process.
(b) Outline the objectives of an audit committee.
(c) Recommend terms of reference for the committee.
(d) Identify who should comprise the committee.
(e) Discuss the interaction between the audit committee and both the internal and external audit functions.

(Professional Year Programme of the ICAA — 1999, Advanced Audit Module — adapted)

4.2 (Management and auditor responsibilities) ★★★

Elektra Company is a publicly held corporation that manufactures a line of home appliances. The comments below were included in Elektra's 20X2 annual report to its shareholders:

1. The integrity of the financial information reported by Elektra Company is the responsibility of Elektra's management. Fulfilling this responsibility requires the preparation of a financial report in accordance with applicable Accounting Standards.
2. Elektra uses an established system of accounting and internal controls in gathering and processing financial data. Management believes that internal control is sufficiently maintained by the established business policies and procedures and the ongoing review of operations by Elektra's internal audit department.
3. Dicksee & Son, an independent auditing firm, is engaged to issue an opinion on the financial report of Elektra Company. The opinion is based on the firm's audit of Elektra's financial report in accordance with Auditing Standards.

4. The audit committee of Elektra's board of directors reviews the audit report submitted by the external auditing firm, including the audited financial report. The external auditing firm has full and free access to the audit committee.

Required

(a) Judgement and estimates are necessary in the application of the Accounting Standards. Explain whose judgement and estimates are reflected in the financial report of Elektra Company.

(b) Explain the extent of the audit of Elektra's financial report in accordance with Auditing Standards by the independent auditors, Dicksee & Son.

(c) Assume that the independent auditors, Dicksee & Son, have issued an unqualified opinion on Elektra's financial report. Describe what inferences, if any, can be made from the opinion of Dicksee & Son about:

 (i) the soundness of the decisions made by the management of Elektra Company;

 (ii) the financial report of Elektra Company.

(CIMA — adapted)

chapter 5 Audit risk and audit evidence

Overview

LEARNING OBJECTIVES

After studying this chapter, you should be able to:

1. explain the importance of the concept of audit risk and its three components
2. describe the relationship between audit risk and audit evidence
3. define the concept of materiality used in auditing
4. state how the auditor arrives at judgements about materiality at the financial report level and at the individual account balance level
5. describe the relationship between materiality and audit evidence
6. state the categories of management's financial report assertions
7. derive specific audit objectives from the categories of assertions
8. indicate the factors that affect the sufficiency and appropriateness of audit evidence
9. identify the types of corroborating information available to the auditor
10. enumerate and describe the types of auditing procedure that may be used in an audit
11. describe the three classifications of auditing procedure and their purpose.

Professional statements

AUSTRALIAN		INTERNATIONAL	
AUS 202	Objective and General Principles Governing an Audit of a Financial Report	ISA 200	Objective and General Principles Governing an Audit of Financial Statements
AUS 306	Materiality	ISA 320	Audit Materiality
AUS 402	Risk Assessments and Internal Controls	ISA 400	Risk Assessments and Internal Control
AUS 502	Audit Evidence	ISA 500	Audit Evidence
AUS 504	External Confirmations	ISA 505	External Confirmations
AUS 520	Management Representations	ISA 580	Management Representations
AUS 606	Using the Work of an Expert	ISA 620	Using the Work of an Expert
AAS 5	Materiality	Framework for the Preparation and Presentation of Financial Statements	
AASB 1031	Materiality		

Now that we have considered the environmental factors pertaining to auditing, we will begin to explain the nature of the investigation that an auditor undertakes to arrive at an opinion as to the fairness of the financial report. In this chapter we will look at the fundamental issues relating to the audit process, namely:

- the risks that the financial report may not be fairly presented;
- the threshold of materiality that the auditor uses in identifying misstatements that could materially affect the decisions and judgements of users placing reliance on the financial report;
- the different types of assertion that combine to ensure the financial report is fairly presented and that underpin the objectives of the audit process;
- the types of evidence available to the auditor;
- the procedures used by auditors in obtaining the different types of evidence.

In the next chapter, we will examine the application of these issues in planning and performing specific audit engagements.

To begin, it is necessary to consider the nature of the financial report being subject to audit examination. The report is made up of the elements of assets, liabilities, revenues and expenses — or, in accounting terminology, **account balances**. Account balances are built up from entries in the accounting records, which arise mostly from transactions such as purchases and cash receipts. Thus, the account balance, accounts payable, is the difference between purchase transactions creating the liability and cash payment transactions decreasing the liability. In verifying the balance, the auditor may investigate the balance directly, such as by examining suppliers' statements. Alternatively, the auditor can verify the **transactions** that make up the balance, such as by examining purchase transactions and cash payment transactions. By the use of such tests the auditor can substantiate the correctness of the amounts recorded as account balances. Such procedures are referred to as **substantive procedures**. As we will explain in this and subsequent chapters, auditors also use other types of procedure.

Entities are aware of the importance of maintaining reliable accounting records and design information systems intended to reduce the likelihood of errors. The use of double-entry bookkeeping is itself a means of self-checking the accuracy of the records by its use of the balancing process. The sum of the procedures that entities use to ensure the reliability of their accounting records is known as the **internal control structure**. We will describe the components of this structure in detail in Chapter 7.

AUDIT RISK

1 LEARNING OBJECTIVE

Explain the importance of the concept of audit risk and its three components.

Audit risk is the risk of the auditor giving an inappropriate opinion on the financial report (AUS 402.03; ISA 400.03). This arises when the auditor expresses the opinion that the financial report is fairly presented when it is materially misstated. It also arises when the auditor incorrectly expresses an opinion that the financial report is other than fairly presented; however, this is unlikely because the auditor would perform additional procedures if initial procedures suggest the need for such a qualification.

The more certain the auditor wants to be of expressing the correct opinion, the lower will be the audit risk that he or she is willing to accept. In setting the desired audit risk the auditor seeks an appropriate balance between the costs of an incorrect audit opinion and the costs of performing the additional audit procedures necessary to reduce audit risk.

The default presumption is that every transaction in a transaction class and every item in an account balance is potentially misstated and that substantive procedures must be sufficient to reduce the risk that material misstatements remain undetected. However, experience teaches auditors that most transactions and account balance items are correctly stated, but that the actual level of misstatements varies from one entity to another. Experience also suggests that the principal causes of variation lie in the nature of the entity and the effectiveness of its internal control structure. In many cases, therefore, the auditor can reduce audit risk by investigating and assessing the likelihood that the financial report is misstated.

The first step involves obtaining an understanding of the entity's business and industry, its management, the intended users of its financial information, its legal and financial stability, and its operations. The auditor then considers the effect these factors could have on the fairness of the financial report. If the auditor assesses the entity as being well managed and financially sound, for example, then he or she may reduce the overall assessment of audit risk.

The auditor may also obtain an understanding of the internal control structure that the entity adopts to guard against the likelihood of errors occurring or remaining undetected in its accounting records and causing misstatements in its financial report. If the auditor assesses these procedures as being effective, then he or she may reduce the overall assessment of audit risk. Conversely, if the auditor considers the entity to be in financial difficulty or to have an inadequate internal control structure, then he or she may assess audit risk as being higher, requiring a more extensive audit investigation.

Audit risk components

Audit risk is commonly assessed within three components: inherent risk, control risk and detection risk. We will discuss each component in the following sections.

Inherent risk

Inherent risk is the possibility that a material misstatement could occur (AUS 402.09; ISA 400.04). At this level the auditor does not consider the presence of control procedures that may detect the misstatement.

The assessment of inherent risk requires consideration of both matters that may have a pervasive effect on the entity as a whole and matters that may affect only specific accounts.

The inherent risk of material misstatement is greater for some industries than for others. Entities operating in the gas and oil exploration or insurance industries, for example, have unique accounting problems compared with merchandising or manufacturing entities. The existence of related parties, foreign exchange dealings and other complicated contracts also presents opportunities for misstatements to occur.

Further, inherent risk may be greater for some accounts or transactions than for others. Cash, for example, is more susceptible to misstatement through misappropriation than are plant assets. Similarly, the valuation of assets held under a finance lease is more susceptible to misstatement (as a result of the complex nature of finance lease calculations) than is the valuation of similar assets owned outright. (Matters that may have a pervasive effect on the entity and matters that may pertain to specific accounts only are shown in Table 5.1 on page 174.)

Inherent risk exists independently of the audit of a financial report. Thus, the auditor cannot change the *actual* level of inherent risk. However, he or she can forgo attempting to assess inherent risk for a particular audit component and simply assume that it is at a maximum — that is, at 100 per cent. This is a conservative approach but the auditor may choose this option when he or she concludes that the effort required to evaluate inherent risk for a particular account balance or class of transactions would exceed the potential reduction (derived from assessing inherent risk as being less than 100 per cent) in the extent of auditing procedures required. However, the auditor should gain an understanding of the inherent risk factors at the entity level when he or she is determining the overall audit strategy. This understanding may enable the auditor to reduce the assessment of inherent risk below 100 per cent.

TABLE 5.1 *The audit risk concept*

	Examples of attributes considered by the auditor		Response by the auditor
	Inherent risk	**Control risk**	**Detection risk**
Matters pervasive to many account balances or transaction classes	• Profitability relative to the industry • Sensitivity of operating results to economic factors • Going-concern problems • Nature, cause and amount of known and likely misstatements detected in previous audits • Management turnover • Management reputation • Management accounting skills	• Business planning, budgeting and monitoring of performance • Management attitude and actions regarding financial reporting • Management consultation with auditors • Management concern about external influences • Audit committee • Internal audit function • Personnel policies and procedures • Effectiveness of the accounting system	• Overall audit strategy – Number of locations visited – Significant balances or transaction classes • Degree of professional scepticism • Staffing — levels of supervision and review
Matters pertaining to specific account balances or transaction classes	• Accounts or transactions that are difficult to audit • Contentious or difficult accounting issues • Susceptibility to misappropriation • Complexity of calculations • Extent of judgement related to assertions • Sensitivity of valuations to economic factors • Nature, cause and amount of known and likely misstatements detected in previous audits	• Effectiveness of the accounting system, personnel policies and procedures • Adequacy of accounting records • Segregation of duties • Adequacy of safeguards over assets and records (including software) • Independent checks on performance	• Substantive analytical procedures and tests of details – Nature of tests – Timing of tests – Extent of tests

(Source: AICPA Control Risk Audit Guide Task Force, *Audit Guide: Consideration of the Internal Control Structure in a Financial Statement Audit*, 1990, p. 210)

As defined by Auditing Standards, inherent risk is confined to the risk of misstatements. Many auditors additionally consider the business risks that may cause an entity to suffer unexpected losses or some other catastrophe. They then look at the entity's risk management procedures for identifying and managing such risks. Not only does this direct the auditor's attention to matters that could affect the ability of the entity to survive as a going concern, it also enables the auditor to use his or her risk management skills to alert management of the entity to shortcomings in their approach to risk. For this reason, the approach is sometimes referred to as an 'added value audit' (see the 'Professional environment' on the next page).

PROFESSIONAL ENVIRONMENT The information revolution and audit risk

The information revolution is changing the process of communicating information and even the nature of business, and thus is influencing the development of financial reporting and auditing. In the past products had lengthy life cycles and profits generated from investment in productive tangible assets could be expected to continue. Increasingly, however, profits are determined by investment in intangible assets such as reputation, employee skills, research and development, etc. Product life cycles are short, innovation is continually in demand, and past performance is increasingly irrelevant. In response, the accounting profession is experimenting with new forms of financial reporting, emphasising the process of value creation, rather than past performance.

Accounting firms are aware that the real audit risk in such an environment is unexpected business failure. Arthur Andersen notes on its web site that 'traditional auditing was designed to detect errors, not anticipate them. Today, problems arise quickly, often with devastating impact. When the greatest risk to value is not what has gone wrong, but what could go wrong, you need a forward-looking, risk-based approach to provide reliable assurances.' That firm is targeting its audit effort at management processes to obtain assurance that a company is properly managed.

Auditing Standard setters are currently reviewing the need to revise existing requirements on audit risk.

Control risk

Control risk is the risk that a material misstatement could occur and not be prevented or detected on a timely basis by the entity's internal control structure (AUS 402.06; ISA 400.05).

Control risk is a function of the effectiveness of the internal control structure. Effective internal controls reduce control risk. Control risk can never be zero, because internal controls cannot provide complete assurance that all material misstatements will be prevented or detected. Controls may be ineffective, for example, as a result of human failure due to carelessness or fatigue. Factors that influence the auditor's considerations of control risk are depicted in Table 5.1.

The auditor cannot change the level of control risk. He or she can *influence* control risk by recommending improvements in internal controls, but this influence is more likely to affect future periods and then only to the extent that the entity's management implements the suggestions. As with inherent risk, the auditor can choose not to assess control risk or to perform only a limited assessment and assume it to be 100 per cent (or close thereto). This decision would be appropriate where the cost of assessing control risk is likely to exceed the benefits to be obtained from the reduction in the level of substantive procedures. This applies where the auditor reasonably suspects that control risk is likely to be high (as with many small entities), or where other factors restrict the opportunities for cost saving (as with transaction classes involving few entries or account balances made up of few items). The cost of substantive procedures is likely to be low in such cases.

Where the auditor chooses to assess control risk, the procedure is to obtain an understanding of the internal control structure so as to assess its potential effectiveness. The auditor then performs further tests to determine whether the internal control structure is operating effectively. We will explain these procedures in detail in Chapter 7.

Auditors, while being unable to control inherent and control risk, can assess these risks and design substantive procedures to produce an acceptable level of detection risk, thus reducing audit risk to an acceptable level (AUS 402.59; ISA 400.42).

Detection risk

Detection risk is the risk that the auditor's substantive procedures will not detect any misstatements that occur and are not prevented or detected by the internal control structure (AUS 402.07; ISA 400.06).

Detection risk is a function of the effectiveness of substantive procedures and their application by the auditor. Unlike inherent and control risk, the actual level of detection risk is controllable by the auditor through:

- appropriate planning, direction, supervision and review;
- variation in the nature, timing and extent of audit procedures (AUS 402.59; ISA 400.42);
- effective performance of the audit procedures and evaluation of their results.

We will explain the determination of audit strategy once inherent and control risk have been assessed, along with the procedures for properly planning and controlling the audit process, in Chapter 6. A summary of the components of audit risk is presented in Figure 5.1.

FIGURE 5.1

Summary of audit risk components

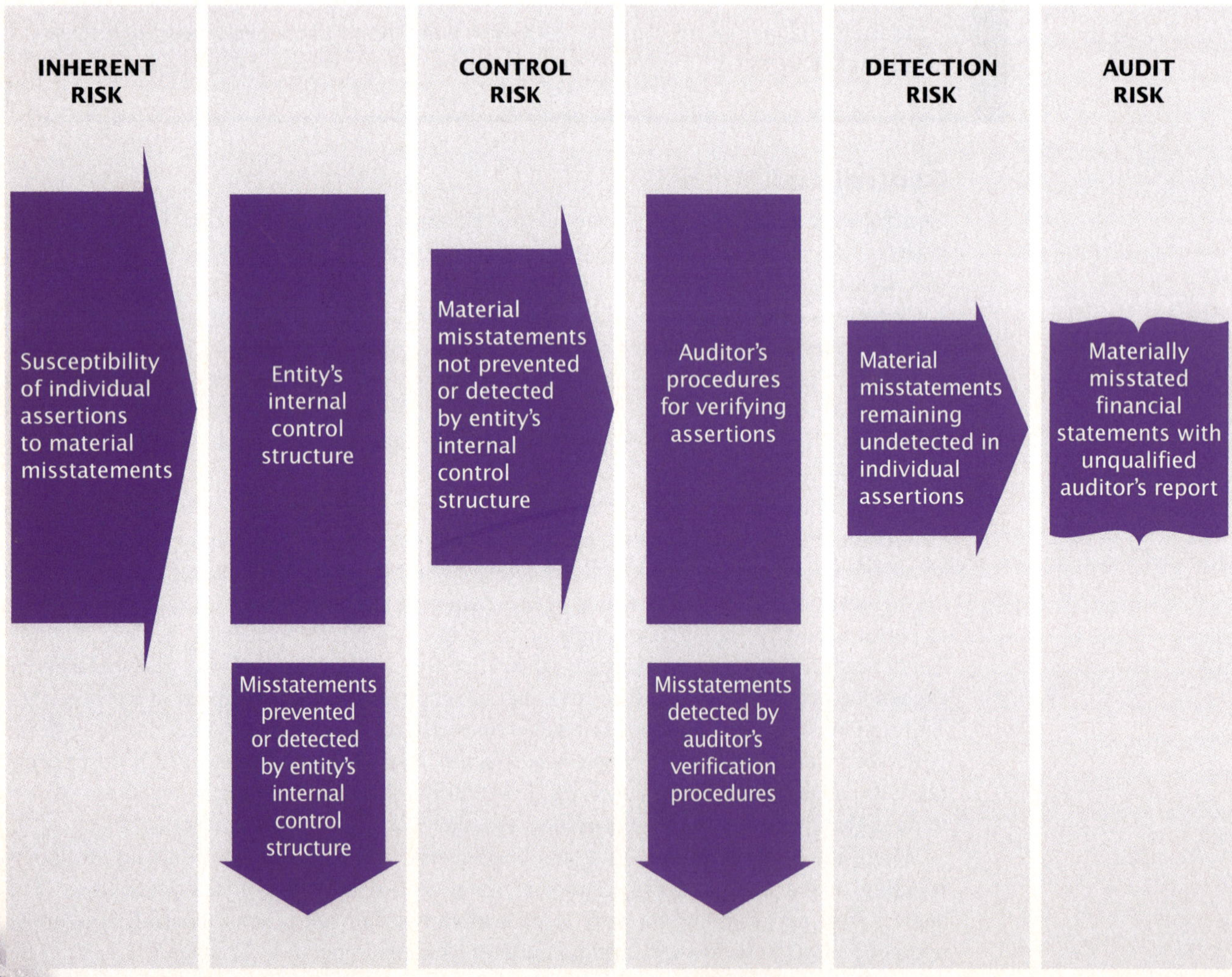

2

LEARNING OBJECTIVE

Describe the relationship between audit risk and audit evidence.

The relationship among risk components

Given that the auditor's objective is to achieve as low a level of audit risk as is practicable, and recognising the cost of performing audit procedures, there is an inverse relationship between the assessed levels of inherent and control risks and the level of detection risk that the auditor can accept. Thus, if inherent and control risks are assessed as being low, the auditor can tolerate a higher level of detection risk, enabling a reduction in the extent of substantive procedures he or she must undertake. Table 5.2 provides guidance as to the acceptable level of detection risk. (The light shaded area represents detection risk.)

In relating the components of audit risk, the auditor may express each component in quantitative terms (such as percentages) or non-quantitative terms (such as low, medium and high). In either case, the auditor must understand the relationships expressed in the **audit risk model** in determining the planned acceptable level of detection risk.

TABLE 5.2

Acceptable detection risk matrix

		Auditor's assessment of control risk is		
		High	**Medium**	**Low**
Auditor's assessment of inherent risk is	**High**	Lowest	Lower	Medium
	Medium	Lower	Medium	Higher
	Low	Medium	Higher	Highest

(Source: AUS 402; IAS 400)

Quantified audit risk model

The audit risk model expresses the relationship among the audit risk components as follows:

$$AR = IR \times CR \times DR.$$

The acronyms represent audit risk (AR), inherent risk (IR), control risk (CR) and detection risk (DR). To illustrate the use of the model, assume the auditor has made the following risk assessments for a particular transaction class or account balance — that IR and CR both equal 50 per cent. Now, assume the auditor has specified an overall AR of 5 per cent. Detection risk can be determined by solving the model for DR as follows:

$$DR = \frac{AR}{IR \times CR} = \frac{0.05}{0.5 \times 0.5} = 20 \text{ per cent.}$$

If the auditor decides that IR cannot be assessed, or that the effort to do so will exceed the benefits of a lower assessment, then he or she can take the conservative approach of assessing IR at 100 per cent. In this case, the model yields a DR of 10 per cent — that is, $0.05 \div (1.0 \times 0.5)$. If the auditor also assesses CR at 100 per cent, then DR becomes 5 per cent — that is, $0.05 \div (1.0 \times 1.0)$.

The model assumes that inherent and control risks are independent of each other. However, management responds to inherent risk by designing an internal control structure to prevent or detect misstatements (see Figure 5.1). As a result, in many instances inherent and control risks may be interrelated. In these circumstances a separate assessment of inherent and control risks would be inappropriate (AUS 402.57; IAS 400.40), and the auditor will arrive at a joint assessment.

It is important to be aware that the numerical values attached to risks do not have any real meaning but are used to facilitate consistency in the application of judgement. An assessment of control risk at 50 per cent, for example, does not mean that the control system will not detect 50 per cent of errors. Similarly, when auditors assign a value of 5 per cent to overall audit risk, it does not mean that an incorrect audit opinion is given on one audit in every twenty.

Few auditors attempt to quantify each of the risk components. However, even when the risk assessment is not solved mathematically, familiarity with the model makes the following relationship clear: given that the aim is to hold audit risk to a specified level, the higher the assessed levels of inherent and control risks, the lower will be the acceptable level of detection risk.

Risk components matrix

The auditor may use non-quantitative expressions for risk, such as the risk components matrix shown in Table 5.2. The matrix is consistent with the quantified audit risk model in that the acceptable levels of detection risk are inversely related to the assessments of inherent and control risks.

If the auditor's assessment of control and inherent risks is at a maximum, then the acceptable level of detection risk will have to be very low — that is, the risk that the auditor's substantive procedure will not detect misstatement will need to be low.

Audit risk at the financial report and account balance levels

The auditor specifies an overall audit risk level to be achieved for the financial report as a whole. In contrast, the assessed levels of inherent and control risk and the acceptable level of detection risk can vary for each account balance and transaction class.

MATERIALITY

Materiality underpins the application of Auditing Standards and thus it has a pervasive effect in a financial report audit. The auditor should consider materiality in planning the audit and evaluating the fair presentation of the financial report.

3 LEARNING OBJECTIVE

Define the concept of materiality used in auditing.

The concept of materiality

In relation to information, materiality means:

> . . . that information which if omitted, misstated or not disclosed has the potential to adversely affect decisions about the allocation of scarce resources made by users of the financial report or the discharge of accountability by the management, including the governing body of the entity. (AASB 1031, Materiality)

Material information means information that matters, is important or is essential. In the measuring or disclosing of accounting information, the emphasis is on the needs of users. In auditing, materiality pertains to the extent of misstatements (uncorrected errors, erroneous disclosures or omissions) that exist in the financial report. The auditor plans and executes an audit with a reasonable expectation of detecting material misstatements. The assessment of what is material is a matter of the auditor's professional judgement of the needs of the reasonable person relying on the information.

The auditor considers materiality when:

- determining the nature, timing and extent of audit procedures;
- evaluating the effect of misstatements on the fair presentation of the financial report (AUS 306.08; ISA 320.08).

4 LEARNING OBJECTIVE

State how the auditor arrives at judgements about materiality at the financial report level and at the individual account balance level.

Materiality at the financial report level

Financial reports are materially misstated when they contain errors or irregularities that act, individually or in aggregate, to prevent the statements from being presented fairly in accordance with Accounting Standards. In this context, misstatements may result from misapplication of applicable Accounting Standards, departures from fact, or omissions of necessary information.

More than one level of materiality may relate to the financial report. For the profit and loss statement, materiality could be related to revenue or profit. For the balance sheet, materiality could be based on shareholders' equity, assets or liability class totals.

In making a judgement about materiality, the auditor should use the smallest aggregate level of misstatement considered to be material to any one of the financial statements. This decision rule is appropriate because the financial statements are interrelated and many audit procedures pertain to more than one statement. The audit procedure to determine whether year-end credit sales are recorded in the proper period, for example, provides evidence about both accounts receivable (balance sheet) and sales (profit and loss statement).

Materiality judgements involve an assessment of both the amount (quantity) and the nature (quality) of the misstatements. Materiality considerations may be influenced by legal and statutory requirements; for example, disclosures pertaining to audit fees and directors' remuneration must be made irrespective of the amounts involved.

Quantitative guidelines

In assessing the quantitative importance of a misstatement, the auditor needs to relate the dollar amount of the error to the financial report under examination. There is no agreed guideline for determining this relationship but, in the absence of evidence or a convincing argument to the contrary:

- an amount that is equal to or greater than 10 per cent of profit is presumed to be material;
- an amount that is equal to or less than 5 per cent of profit may be presumed not to be material;
- whether an amount between 5 per cent and 10 per cent is material is a matter of judgement. (AASB 1031 (4.1.6))

Materiality judgements relating to profit and loss should ordinarily exclude the effect of unusual items or abnormal fluctuations, exceptional events or transactions, and discontinued operations. Therefore, in relation to profit and loss, an amount as referred to above should be an amount after allowing for any income tax effect where the base amount has been determined after allowing for any income tax effect (AASB 1031 (4.1.7)).

In determining whether an amount or aggregate of an item is material, the auditor should compare the item with the more appropriate of the base amounts described below:

- *for items relating to the balance sheet*:
  - — equity or the appropriate asset or liability class total;
- *for items relating to the profit and loss account*:
  - — operating profit or loss for the current financial year; or
  - — average operating profit or loss for a number of years (including the current financial year);
- *for items relating to cash flows*:
  - — net cash provided by or used in the operating, investing, financing or other activities, as appropriate for the current financial year; or
  - — average net cash flows provided by or used in the operating, investing, financing or other activities, as appropriate for a number of years (including the current financial year).

Some of the commonly used bases and materiality thresholds (expressed as a percentage of that base) are as follows:

Base	Materiality threshold (%)
Turnover	0.5
Gross profit	2.0
Profit before tax	5.0
Total assets	0.5
Equity	1.0

Sometimes auditors use the blended method — that is, combining the five thresholds listed above with equal weights, and computing an average of the sum.

Qualitative considerations

In planning the examination, the auditor generally is concerned only with misstatements that are quantitatively material. The errors are not yet known, so their qualitative effect can be considered only as evidence becomes available.

Qualitative considerations relate to the causes of misstatements or to misstatements that do not have a quantifiable effect. A misstatement that is quantitatively immaterial may be qualitatively material. This may occur, for instance, when the misstatement is attributable to a control weakness, an irregularity or an illegal act by the entity. Discovery of such an occurrence could lead the auditor to conclude there is a significant risk of additional similar misstatements. Other examples of qualitative misstatements include:

- an inadequate or improper description of an accounting policy;
- a failure to disclose the breach of regulatory requirements;
- a change in accounting method which is likely to affect materially the results of subsequent financial years;
- a related party transaction or event requiring disclosure;
- a probability of a breach of a financial covenant; for example, a loan agreement may require the entity to maintain a specified minimum current ratio as at the balance sheet date. The company may be tempted to overstate current assets or understate current liabilities. For this reason auditors might choose to use a lower materiality threshold for current assets and current liabilities.

Although it is suggested that the auditor should be alert for misstatements that could be qualitatively material, ordinarily it is not practical to design procedures to detect them.

Materiality at the account balance level

Account balance materiality is the minimum misstatement that can exist in an account balance for it to be considered materially misstated. Misstatement up to that level is known as **tolerable error**. The recorded balance of an account generally represents the upper limit on the amount by which an account can be overstated. Thus, accounts with balances smaller than materiality are sometimes said to be immaterial in terms of the risk of overstatement. However, there is no limit on the amount by which an account balance could be understated. Thus, accounts with immaterial balances could still be materially understated.

In making judgements about materiality at the account balance level, the auditor must plan the audit to detect misstatements that, although immaterial individually, may be material to the financial report taken as a whole when aggregated with misstatements in other account balances.

Allocating financial report materiality to accounts

When the auditor's preliminary judgements about financial report materiality are quantified, a preliminary estimate of materiality for each account may be obtained by allocating financial report materiality to the individual accounts. The allocation may be made to both balance sheet and profit and loss statement accounts. However, because most profit and loss statement misstatements also affect the balance sheet, and because there are fewer balance sheet accounts, many auditors make the allocation on the basis of the balance sheet accounts.

To illustrate the allocation, assume that the total assets of Hart Company consist of the following:

	Balance	Per cent
Cash	$ 500 000	5
Accounts receivable	1 500 000	15
Inventories	3 000 000	30
Plant assets	5 000 000	50
Total	$10 000 000	100

Assuming the preliminary estimate of financial report materiality is 1 per cent of total assets, or $100 000, consider the following alternative allocation plans:

	Materiality allocation			
Account	**Plan A**	**Per cent**	**Plan B**	**Per cent**
Cash	$ 5 000	5	$ 2 000	2
Accounts receivable	15 000	15	18 000	18
Inventories	30 000	30	50 000	50
Plant assets	50 000	50	30 000	30
Total	$100 000	100	$100 000	100

In Plan A, materiality has been allocated proportionately to each account. It is a conservative approach and inefficient in terms of audit effort. In Plan B, the allocation is based on the auditor's subjective judgement of the inherent risk relative to size and of the probability of misstatements. The largest materiality allocation is made to plant and machinery where few misstatements are expected and, particularly with regard to the depreciation provision, users do not expect the recorded amounts to be precise. The lowest allocation is to cash where users expect the amount to be correct and where a slight misstatement could affect assessment of liquidity.

The allocation of the preliminary estimate of materiality may be revised as the audit progresses. Under Plan B, if, after auditing accounts receivable, the auditor estimates that the maximum misstatement in that account is $8000, then the $10 000 unused portion of materiality for this account can be reallocated to inventories.

Although the foregoing example suggests a certain degree of precision in allocating overall materiality to accounts, in the final analysis the process heavily depends on the subjective judgement of the auditor.

Preliminary judgements about materiality

The auditor's preliminary judgements about materiality may be made several months before the balance sheet date. Thus, the judgements may be based on interim financial report data. Alternatively, they may be based on prior years' financial results adjusted for current changes, such as the general condition of the economy and industry trends. This assessment, often referred to as **planning materiality**, may ultimately differ from the materiality levels used at the conclusion of the audit in the evaluation of the audit findings because the surrounding circumstances may change and additional information about the entity will have been obtained during the course of the audit. As a result of errors discovered during the audit, for example, the auditor may know that the entity's financial position is worse than he or she presumed when planning the audit. In such cases, the materiality level used in evaluating the audit findings may be lower than the planning level of materiality.

In planning an audit, the auditor should assess materiality at the following two levels:

- the financial report level (overall materiality), because the auditor's opinion on fairness extends to the financial report taken as a whole;
- the account balances and class of transactions level (testing materiality), because the auditor verifies account balances in reaching an overall conclusion on the fairness of the financial report.

The overall level of materiality and the nature of account balances enable the auditor to determine which account balances to audit and how to evaluate the effects of misstatements in financial information as a whole. Materiality at the account balance and class of transactions level assists the auditor in determining which items in a balance or transaction class to audit and which audit procedures to undertake (for example, whether to use sampling or analytical procedures).

The relationship between materiality and audit evidence

5 LEARNING OBJECTIVE

Describe the relationship between materiality and audit evidence.

Materiality, like risk, is a key factor that affects the auditor's judgement about the sufficiency of audit evidence. It is generally correct to say, for example, that the lower the materiality level, the greater the amount of evidence that is needed (an inverse relationship). This is the same as saying that it takes more evidence to obtain reasonable assurance that any misstatement in the recorded inventory balance does not exceed $100 000 than it does to be assured the misstatement does not exceed $200 000. It is also generally correct to say that the larger or more significant an account balance is, the greater the amount of evidence that is needed (a direct relationship). This is the same as saying that more evidence is needed for inventory when it represents 30 per cent of total assets than when it represents 10 per cent.

Using materiality to evaluate audit evidence

If there are misstatements in the accounts, then the auditor may perform additional audit procedures or request that management correct the errors. If uncorrected errors exceed materiality and management refuses to make adjustments, then the auditor may consider issuing a qualified audit opinion. The uncorrected aggregated misstatements that the auditor needs to examine when considering whether they misstate the financial report include:

- uncorrected errors specifically identified during the audit (known misstatements);
- projected errors where audit components have been tested by sampling techniques (likely misstatements);
- the net effect of uncorrected likely misstatements from a prior period that affect the current period's financial report. (AUS 306.13; ISA 320.13)

The auditor reviews the aggregate of the total misstatements and considers the need to approach management about having these corrected. The auditor may issue a modified audit report if aggregated uncorrected misstatements exceed materiality (AUS 306.15; ISA 320.15).

In this chapter our focus is planning materiality. We will explain making a final assessment of materiality in Chapter 14.

LEARNING CHECK

5.1 The auditor's objective in planning and performing the audit is to reduce audit risk to an appropriately low level to support an opinion as to whether the financial report is fairly presented.

5.2 Audit risk is the risk that the auditor may give an inappropriate audit opinion when the financial report is materially misstated. The three components of audit risk are inherent risk, control risk and detection risk.

5.3 For a specified level of audit risk, there is an inverse relationship between the assessed levels of inherent and control risks and the level of detection risk that the auditor can accept.

5.4 Materiality pertains to the amount of misstatements that could affect decisions by the users of the financial report.

5.5 For planning purposes the auditor uses the smallest aggregate level of misstatements considered to be material to any one of the financial statements.

AUDIT OBJECTIVES

The *overall* objective of a financial report audit is 'to enable the auditor to express an opinion whether the financial report is fairly prepared, in all material respects, in accordance with an identified financial reporting framework' (AUS 202.02; ISA 200.02). To meet this objective, it is necessary to identify *specific* audit objectives for each transaction class and account balance. In preparing the financial report the management of the entity can be said to be making a set of assertions about each transaction class and account balance — referred to as **financial report assertions**.

The auditor formulates an opinion on the financial report as a whole on the basis of evidence obtained through the verification of assertions related to individual account balances or transaction classes. The objective is to restrict audit risk at the account balance level so, at the conclusion of the audit, the audit risk in expressing an opinion on the financial report as a whole will be at an appropriately low level. Thus, the overall audit risk is disaggregated to each account balance or transactions class.

6 LEARNING OBJECTIVE

State the categories of management's financial report assertions.

Management's financial report assertions

Management's financial report assertions are both explicit and implicit. AUS 502 (ISA 500), Audit Evidence presents a classification of these financial report assertions. Some of these assertions are applicable to account balances only, some to transactions and others to both account balances and transactions. These are defined in Table 5.3.

TABLE 5.3

Definitions of financial report assertions

Assertion	Definition
Account balances	
Existence	Assets and liabilities of the entity exist at a given date.
Rights and obligations	Assets are rights of the entity and liabilities are the obligations of the entity at a specified date.
Valuation	Assets or liabilities are recorded at appropriate carrying value.
Transactions	
Occurrence	Recorded transactions or other events occurred during the relevant period and pertain to the entity.
Balances and transactions	
Completeness	There are no unrecorded assets, liabilities, transactions or other events, or undisclosed items.
Measurement	A transaction or event is recorded at the proper amount and revenue or expense is allocated to the proper period.
Disclosure	Particular components of the financial report are properly disclosed, classified and described.

It is possible to group the assertions of existence and occurrence, and the assertions of valuation and measurement. The existence of an asset or liability can only be the consequence of the occurrence of a transaction. On initial recognition the appropriate carrying value of an account balance item is determined by a transaction that is recorded at the proper amount.

For a snapshot understanding of some of these assertions, consider the following balance sheet component:

Current assets:
Cash $252 900

In reporting this item in the balance sheet, management makes the following explicit assertions:

- Cash exists (existence).
- The correct amount of cash is $252 900 (valuation).

Management also makes the following implicit assertions:

- All cash that should be reported has been included (completeness).
- All the reported cash is owned by the entity (ownership rights).
- There are no restrictions on the use of cash (disclosure).

The last assertion follows from the presentation of cash in current assets and the absence of any reference to footnote disclosures. If any of these assertions is a misrepresentation, then the financial report could be misstated.

In the following sections, we will first describe each category of assertion and provide examples. We will then illustrate specific audit objectives for cash derived from each category of assertion.

Existence or occurrence

Existence applies to accounts with physical substance, such as cash and inventories, as well as to accounts without physical substance, such as accounts receivable and accounts payable. In the above example, this assertion refers to the existence of items included in cash, such as petty cash funds, undeposited receipts and bank accounts. It does not extend to whether $252 900 is the correct amount for these items. The latter relates to the valuation assertion, as we will explain.

Management also asserts that the revenues and expenses shown in the profit and loss statement are the results of transactions and events that occurred during the reporting period, and are properly recognised by the entity. Again, this **occurrence** assertion extends only to whether transactions and events occurred, not to whether the amounts reported are correct. This assertion would be misrepresented if reported sales transactions were fictitious or occurred after the end of the period, or if reported expenses include personal expenses improperly charged to the entity.

The auditor's principal concern about this assertion relates to the possible overstatement of financial report balances through the inclusion of items that do not exist, the effects of transactions that did not occur or the improper inclusion of transactions that do not pertain to the entity.

Completeness

For each account balance presented in the financial report, management implicitly asserts that all related transactions and events have been included. Management asserts, for example, that the cash balance of $252 900 includes the effects of all cash transactions and all the cash funds mentioned above. The **completeness** assertion for cash would be misrepresented if a bank balance was omitted or cash receipts transactions that occurred were not recorded until the next period.

The auditor's concern about completeness assertion relates primarily to the possible understatement of financial report balances through the omission of items that exist or of the effects of transactions that occurred. If omissions are identified, then the issue of the correct dollar amounts at which they should be included relates to the valuation or measurement assertion.

This assertion is the most difficult for the auditor to verify because the starting point of the inquiry is what ought to be recorded, not what is recorded. It is also the audit objective that causes the greatest difficulty for students.

Rights and obligations

The **rights** and **obligations** assertion deals with assets and liabilities, unlike the other assertions, which relate to revenue and expenditure accounts as well. This assertion refers to rights constituting a degree of control over future economic benefits sufficient for recognition as an asset, and to obligations (legal or constructive) sufficient to require recognition as a liability. Management implicitly asserts, for example, that it controls the cash and other assets reported in the balance sheet and that accounts payable and other liabilities are the obligations of the entity.

Valuation or measurement

The reporting of an account balance at an appropriate amount means that the amount has been determined in accordance with applicable Accounting Standards and is free of mathematical or clerical errors. The determination of amounts in accordance with applicable Accounting Standards includes the proper **valuation** of assets, liabilities, revenues and expenses through:

- proper **measurement** at cost on initial recognition and proper valuation at net realisable value, market value or present value on subsequent remeasurement;
- the reasonableness of management's accounting estimates;
- consistency in the application of accounting policies.

Thus, for example, accounts receivable are reported at net realisable value; inventories are reported at lower of cost or net realisable value; and investments, depending on their characteristics, are reported at cost or fair value. Accounting estimates, such as bad debt provisions and net realisable values of inventory, should be reasonable. Where applicable, the valuation requirements of Accounting Standards should be consistently applied across periods except when a change is justified.

Mathematical correctness refers to such matters as the clerical accuracy of journal entries, postings to ledger accounts and the determination of account balances. It also applies to the correctness of computations for such items as accruals and depreciation. Continuing our cash illustration from page 184, mathematical errors in adding the cash receipts or payment journals, or clerical errors made in recording the amount of a transaction or posting the journal totals to the general ledger account for cash, would cause a misstatement in the valuation or measurement assertion for cash.

Disclosure

In the financial report, management implicitly asserts that the financial information is properly presented and that accompanying **disclosure** is adequate. In the cash example, it would be a misrepresentation of this assertion if the use of cash was restricted and the notes included in the financial report did not indicate this fact.

7 LEARNING OBJECTIVE

Derive specific audit objectives from the categories of assertions.

Specific audit objectives

The auditor develops specific audit objectives for each account balance using the financial report assertions. Table 5.4 illustrates the derivation of specific audit objectives for cash. Specific audit objectives are tailored to fit the circumstances of each audit entity, such as the nature of its economic activity and its accounting policies and practices. From the evidence accumulated, the auditor reaches a conclusion as to whether any of management's assertions are misrepresentations. Subsequently, the auditor combines conclusions about the individual assertions to reach an opinion on the fairness of the financial report as a whole.

TABLE 5.4 *Specific audit objectives for cash*

Assertion category	Specific audit objective
Existence	The petty cash funds, undeposited receipts, bank accounts and any other items reported as cash exist at the balance sheet date.
Completeness	Reported cash includes all petty cash funds, undeposited receipts, and other cash on hand. Reported cash includes all bank account balances.
Rights and obligations	All items included in cash are controlled by the entity at the balance sheet date.
Valuation	The items comprising cash have been correctly totalled. Cash receipts and payment journals are mathematically correct and have been properly posted to the general ledger. Cash on hand has been correctly counted. Bank account balances have been properly reconciled.
Disclosure	All items included in cash are unrestricted and the cash is available for operations. Required disclosures (such as compensating balance agreements) have been made.

AUDIT EVIDENCE

Audit evidence is a fundamental concept in auditing by which the auditor achieves the objective of reasonable assurance that none of management's assertions is materially misstated. Audit evidence consists of:

- underlying accounting data;
- all corroborating information available to the auditor.

Examples of each type of evidence in each category and the relationship of the categories to the Auditing Standard are shown in Figure 5.2. In a computer information system (CIS) environment, the underlying accounting data may consist of machine-readable media (such as disks) and may also be available in hard copy or printed form.

FIGURE 5.2

Categories and types of audit evidence

NATURE OF AUDIT EVIDENCE	RELATIONSHIP TO AUDITING STANDARDS
Underlying accounting data • Books of original entry • General and subsidiary ledgers • Related accounting manuals • Informal and memorandum records, such as worksheets, computations and reconciliations ***Corroborating information*** • Documents such as cheques, invoices, contracts etc. • Confirmations and other written representations • Information from inquiry, observations, inspection and physical examination • Other information obtained or developed by the auditor	SUFFICIENT AND APPROPRIATE AUDIT EVIDENCE

Both categories of evidence are required in making an audit in accordance with Auditing Standards. **Underlying accounting data** are indispensable, for they provide the basis for the entity's financial report. However, it is imperative that the auditor obtains supportive or corroborative evidence of the reliability of the financial records. Much of this evidence is available within the entity, but recourse to sources outside the entity (such as customers and independent experts) is also necessary.

The process of identifying specific sources of evidence to meet specific audit objectives for individual account balances is covered extensively in later chapters of this book. In this chapter, we will establish a general framework for identifying the types of evidence and the financial report assertions to which they relate.

8 LEARNING OBJECTIVE

Indicate the factors that affect the sufficiency and appropriateness of audit evidence.

The Auditing Standard pertaining to evidence

AUS 502.02 (ISA 500.02) states that:

> The auditor should obtain sufficient appropriate audit evidence to be able to draw reasonable conclusions on which to base the audit opinion.

The Standard specifies that 'sufficient' (enough) 'appropriate' (relevant and reliable) audit evidence should be obtained to provide a 'reasonable' (rational) basis for an opinion. If sufficient appropriate evidence is not available, then the scope of the audit is restricted, which may prevent the auditor from giving an unqualified opinion. The audit evidence required to support an opinion is a matter for the auditor to determine in the exercise of professional judgement after a careful study of the circumstances of the specific audit engagement. We will discuss considerations that may influence the auditor's judgement in the following sections.

Sufficiency of audit evidence

Sufficiency relates to the quantity of audit evidence. Factors that may affect the auditor's judgement of sufficiency include:
- materiality and risk;
- economic factors;
- the size and characteristics of the population.

Materiality and risk

In general, more evidence is needed for accounts that are material to the financial report. Thus, in the audit of a manufacturing company, the quantity of evidence needed in support of the audit objectives for inventories will be greater than the quantity needed for the audit objectives for prepaid expenses.

Similarly, more evidence is normally required for accounts that are likely to be misstated than for accounts that are likely to be correct. Normally, for example, there is a higher risk of error in the valuation of inventory than in the valuation of land used as a factory site. The required degree of assurance (conversely, audit risk) has an impact on the sufficiency of evidence. The auditor will obtain evidence to reduce the level of audit risk to an acceptably low level.

Economic factors

Auditors work within economic limits that dictate that sufficient evidence must be obtained within a reasonable time and at a reasonable cost. Thus, auditors are frequently faced with a decision as to whether the additional time and cost will produce commensurate benefits in terms of both the quantity and quality of the evidence obtained. To verify the existence of inventory at each of an entity's twenty-five branches, for example, the auditor can visit each branch. A less costly alternative is to visit five of the branches and rely on the reports of the entity's internal auditors for the other twenty.

Population size and characteristics

The size of a population refers to the number of items that comprise the total — for example, the number of credit sales transactions or the number of customer accounts in the accounts receivable ledger. The size of the accounting populations underlying many financial report items makes sampling a practical necessity in gathering evidence. We will explain the nature of audit sampling in Chapter 8.

Appropriateness of audit evidence

Appropriateness refers to the quality of audit evidence. For evidence to be appropriate, it must be relevant and reliable.

Relevance

Relevance means that evidence must be sufficient with respect to each of the auditor's objectives. An auditor may determine, for example, the existence of inventory through inspection, but must also perform tests of pricing of inventory to provide evidence for valuation.

Reliability

The reliability of evidence is influenced by factors such as the source and nature of the information, and its timeliness and objectivity. The importance of these factors is illustrated by the following examples.

Source and nature of the information

Evidence may be oral or written and may be created by the auditor, obtained from sources outside of the entity or obtained from sources within the entity. AUS 502.15 (ISA 500.15) recognises the following presumptions about the effects of the source of the information on the reliability of audit evidence.

- Audit evidence from external sources is more reliable than that obtained from the entity's records.
- Audit evidence obtained from the entity's records is more reliable when the related internal control structure operates effectively.
- Evidence obtained directly by the auditor is more reliable than evidence obtained by or from the entity.
- Evidence in the form of documents and written representations is more reliable than oral representations.
- Original documents are more reliable than photocopies or facsimiles.

Suppose that you, as an auditor, seek evidence concerning the amount of cash on hand and the amount owed by customer X. You conclude that the cash should be counted, but by whom — you or the entity? If you count it, you have direct personal knowledge of the amount on hand; if the entity makes the count and gives you a report, you have indirect knowledge. Clearly, the former provides more appropriate evidence. For the customer's balance, you can examine evidence within the entity (such as the duplicate sales invoice) or ask the customer to confirm the balance owed. In this case, the latter is considered to be the more reliable evidence because the customer is a third party who is independent of the entity.

Timeliness

Timeliness relates to the date to which the evidence is applicable. The timeliness of the evidence is especially important in verifying current asset, current liability and related profit and loss balances. For these accounts, the auditor seeks evidence that the entity has made a proper cut-off of cash, sales and purchase transactions at the balance sheet date. This task is facilitated when appropriate auditing procedures are applied at or near that date. Similarly, evidence obtained from physical counts at the balance sheet date provides better evidence of quantities on hand at that date than counts made at other times.

Objectivity

Evidence that is objective in nature is generally considered more reliable than evidence that is subjective. Evidence of the existence of tangible assets, for example, can be ascertained with a substantial degree of conclusiveness through physical inspection.

In contrast, evidence in support of management's estimates of inventory obsolescence and product warranties may be largely subjective. In such cases the auditor should:

- consider the expertise and integrity of the individual making the estimate;
- assess the appropriateness of the processes followed by the entity in arriving at the estimate.

Reasonable basis

The auditor is not expected or required to have an absolute, certain or guaranteed basis for an opinion. In arriving at his or her professional judgement of reasonable assurance, the auditor is guided by the persuasiveness of the evidence.

Professional judgement

Given that professional judgement is involved, different auditors will not always reach identical conclusions about the quantity and quality of evidence needed to reach an opinion on a financial report. However, several factors contribute to achieving a uniform application of the reasonable basis requirement.

Auditing Standards contain many specific requirements about audit evidence and provide guidance about ways in which to meet these requirements. Auditors are required to justify any departure from the requirements and must consider carefully the desirability of not complying with the guidance.

The practice of auditing involves two counterbalancing forces. On the one hand, the auditing firm is well aware that an inadequate basis for an opinion may result in lawsuits by those harmed by reliance on an incorrect auditor's report. On the other hand, competition tends to make each firm cost and fee conscious. Accordingly, the firm is restrained from obtaining an inordinately high degree of assurance in a specific engagement because other firms may be able to perform the audit at less cost.

Professional scepticism

Management is responsible for the financial report and also in a position to control much of the corroborating evidence and underlying accounting data that support the report. Professional scepticism is about achieving an appropriate balance between distrusting management and placing complete trust in the integrity of management. In conducting the audit the auditor must be alert to any suspicious circumstances that may require a greater degree of scepticism than would otherwise be appropriate.

9 LEARNING OBJECTIVE

Identify the types of corroborating information available to the auditor.

Types of corroborating information

The auditing student should already be familiar with the basic components of underlying accounting data identified in Figure 5.2 (i.e. journals, ledgers, worksheets, reconciliations, etc.). In this section we will identify and elaborate on the principal types of **corroborating information**. For each type, we will consider its nature, reliability and the categories of assertion to which it is most relevant.

Analytical evidence

Analytical evidence involves comparisons of current period entity data, such as total revenues or return on assets, with expected values. The normal expectation is that the values will be similar to prior period values. Alternatively, the auditor may expect current values to be related to budgeted amounts, industry data or specially developed values based on known changes in the period. The comparisons are then used to draw inferences about the fairness of specific financial report balances in terms of existence, completeness and valuation.

When several related financial variables all conform to expectations, the reliability of this type of evidence is enhanced. When recorded sales, cost of sales, gross profit margin and accounts receivable and inventory turnover rates all conform to expectations, for example, the analytical evidence may be viewed as supporting the existence, completeness and valuation assertions for sales and cost of sales balances. The existence and effectiveness of controls influence the reliability of analytical evidence. When controls are effective, the auditor has greater confidence in the reliability of the information and therefore the results of analytical procedures.

Confirmations

Confirmations are direct written responses made by knowledgeable third parties to specific requests for factual information. Table 5.5 shows the items that are frequently confirmed.

TABLE 5.5

Frequently confirmed items and their sources

Item	Knowledgeable respondent
Cash in bank	Bank
Accounts receivable	Individual customers
Inventory stored in public warehouse	Warehouse custodian
Accounts payable	Creditors
Debentures payable	Trustee
Lease terms	Lessor
Ordinary shares issued	Registrar
Insurance coverage	Insurance company

AUS 504 (ISA 505), External Confirmations provides guidance on the use of confirmations that are generally considered to have a high degree of reliability. It is normal practice for the auditor to obtain confirmation evidence for accounts receivable whenever it is practical and reasonable to do so, and it is standard practice to obtain confirmations for bank balances. The use of confirmations in other applications depends on the relative cost and reliability of alternative forms of evidence that may be available to the auditor. However, the effort involved in preparing and sending confirmation requests and in analysing the responses can be quite time consuming, often making this a costly form of evidence.

This type of evidence may support any of the assertions, but it is primarily related to the existence or occurrence assertion.

Documentary evidence

Documentary evidence includes documents relating to transactions such as invoices and requisitions, as well as such items as minutes of the board of directors, lease agreements and bank statements. Documents, which may be generated externally or internally, are usually contained in entity files and are available for the auditor's inspection on request.

Examples of externally generated documents include customer order forms, suppliers' invoices, tax assessments and bank statements. Externally generated documents are considered to be reliable because they originate from independent third parties. However, they may be altered by an employee at the entity before being shown to the auditor. This risk is particularly high if the auditor is offered a photocopy or facsimile. The reliability of externally generated documents can be enhanced when the auditor obtains copies directly from the external party. Thus, while the auditor normally examines the copy of the bank statements held by the entity, he or she may request the entity to have the bank send a statement as of a particular date directly to the auditor for use in verifying cash balances.

Examples of internally generated documents include sales order forms, sales invoices, purchase orders and receiving reports. Given that it is possible for entity employees to create internal documents to support fictitious transactions, the reliability of internally generated documents is enhanced when they bear evidence of having been circulated to external parties before being placed in the entity's files. A delivery note prepared by the entity but signed by the customer to acknowledge receipt of the goods, for example, provides strong evidence that the transaction occurred. Similarly, a deposit slip receipted by the bank provides strong evidence that a deposit was actually made. In contrast, duplicate file copies of sales invoices and purchase requisitions that bear no evidence of external circulation may be less reliable. Figure 5.3 summarises the effects of circulation on the reliability of documentary evidence.

FIGURE 5.3

Effects of circulation on the reliability of documentary evidence

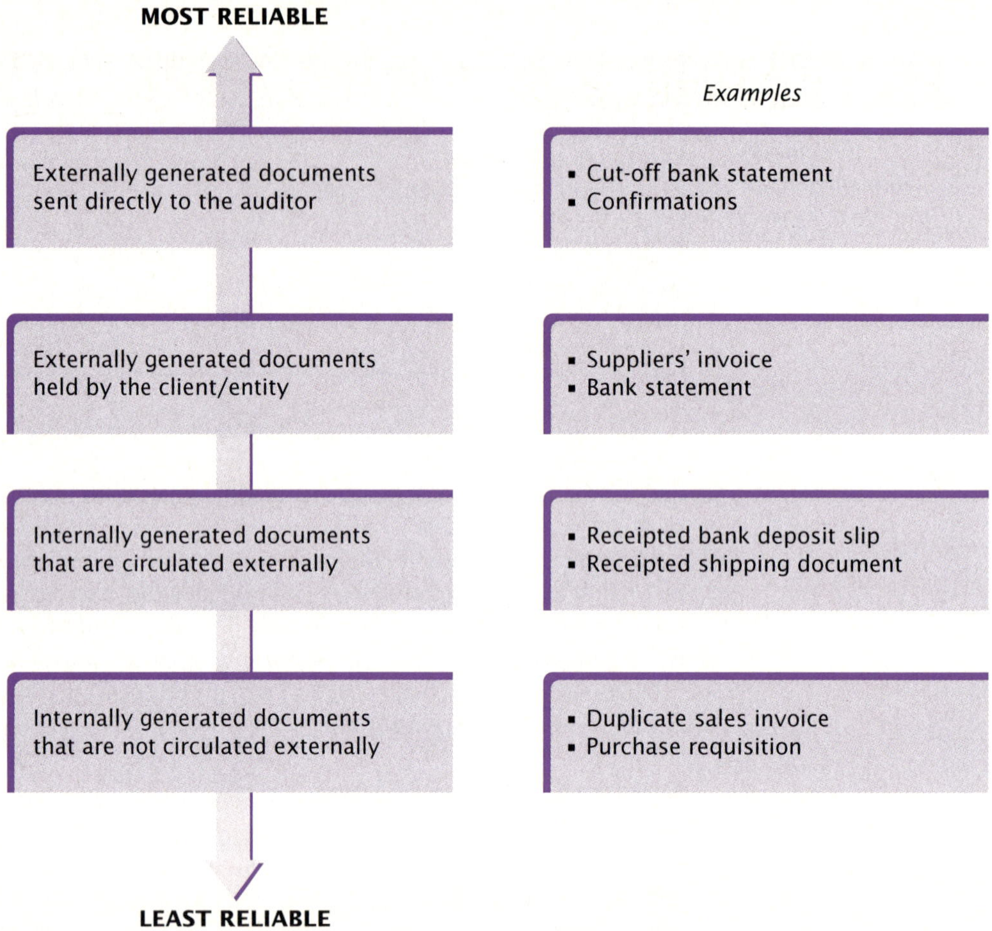

The physical characteristics of documents may also affect their reliability. Special papers, pre-numbered documents and machine-imprinted data, for example, are designed to be more difficult to alter documents or to create phony documentation.

Documentary evidence is used extensively in auditing and may pertain to any of the categories of management assertion. There are two special classes of documentary evidence: (1) confirmations, which we have already discussed, and (2) written representations, which we will discuss in the next section.

Written representations

Written representations are responses to inquiries by the auditor by responsible and knowledgeable individuals. They may be differentiated from confirmations in two ways: (1) they may originate either from within the entity's organisation or from external sources, and (2) they may contain subjective information or an individual's opinion about a matter, rather than factual information.

AUS 520 (ISA 580), Management Representations requires the auditor to obtain certain written representations from management. Commonly presented in the form of a letter, such representations are designed to document management's replies to inquiries made by the auditor during the audit. These representations may reveal information that is not shown in the accounting records, such as the existence of contingencies that may require investigation. We will explain the use of a management representation letter in Chapter 14.

During the course of an audit, the auditor may also request written representations from outside experts. The independent auditor is not expected to possess the expertise of a geologist in estimating the quantity of ore in a mine or of a lawyer in evaluating litigation pending against the entity. When such evidence is needed, AUS 606 (ISA 620), Using the Work of an Expert states that the auditor may use the work of a specialist. A relatively high degree of reliance may be placed on this type of evidence, especially when the response validates other information that has come to the auditor's attention. Written representations may pertain to any of the assertions.

Mathematical evidence

Mathematical evidence results from recomputations by the auditor and a comparison of those results with entity computations. This may involve the results of: (1) routine tasks such as checking the additions of journals, ledgers and supporting schedules, and (2) complicated recalculations such as reconciliations. Mathematical evidence generated by the auditor is reliable, has a relatively low cost and contributes to the basis for the auditor's conclusions about valuation or measurement assertions.

Oral evidence

During an audit, an auditor will make frequent oral inquiries of officers and key employees of the entity. **Oral evidence** is rarely reliable by itself. Its primary value lies in directing the auditor to other sources of evidence, corroborating other types of evidence and disclosing matters that may merit further investigation and documentation.

When oral evidence plays a key role in an audit decision, the source, nature and date of the evidence should be documented in the working papers. When obtained from management, the auditor may request that such evidence be reaffirmed in writing in management's representation letter. Oral evidence may pertain to any of the categories of financial report assertions.

Physical evidence

Physical evidence is obtained from physical inspection of tangible assets. For example, the auditor will acquire direct personal knowledge of the existence of undeposited cash receipts or inventories by inspecting them.

Physical evidence is also helpful in determining the quality (or condition) of an asset that may relate to the valuation assertion. In some cases, the auditor may not be qualified to determine quality, condition or value based on the physical evidence, so may engage an expert to examine the physical evidence. The auditor would then rely on the expert's written representation, together with the physical evidence.

Electronic evidence

Electronic evidence is any information produced or maintained by electronic means, that is used by an auditor. 'Electronic' means the use of computers, scanners, sensors, magnetic media and other electronic devices associated with the creation, manipulation, transmission and reception of electronic data.

When transactions are conducted over computer networks, many traditional accounting documents are eliminated. An entity's computer may be used, for example, to: (1) determine when an inventory item needs to be reordered, (2) generate and electronically transmit the order to a supplier's computer, (3) receive shipping and invoicing information directly from the supplier's computer, and (4) initiate the electronic transfer of funds from the entity's bank account to the supplier's bank account to pay for the order.

In such cases, the auditor must use the electronic evidence of the transactions. The reliability of such evidence is a function of the controls over the creation, alteration and completeness of such data, and the competence of the tools (audit software) that the auditor uses to access the electronic evidence.

The impact of technology on other traditional forms of evidence also poses new opportunities and challenges, such as the faxing of confirmations. Again, the auditor must consider controls related to the origin, transmission and receipt of faxed information in assessing the reliability of the evidence.

Electronic evidence may substitute for several of the traditional types of evidence discussed previously and may pertain to any of the categories of assertions (see the 'Professional environment' below).

PROFESSIONAL ENVIRONMENT **Computer-assisted techniques for fraud detection**

Computer technology gives auditors a new set of techniques for examining the automated business environment. In fact, the detection of fraud is a perfect application for computer-assisted audit tools and techniques. ...

Audit software permits auditors to obtain a quick overview of the business operations and drill down into the details of specific areas of interest. The audit program can also be extended to perform a 100 per cent verification of certain transactions and a recalculation of important ratios and figures.

Audit software can highlight those individual transactions that contain characteristics often associated with fraudulent activity. With audit software, millions of files can be examined, previous years data can be used to identify anomalies, and comparisons can be made between different locations. Also, computer-based data analysis tools can prove invaluable when addressing suspected fraud situations.

The techniques and types of data interrogations in modern audit software are almost unlimited. For example, audit software has many commands that support the auditor's requirement to review transactions for fraud such as the existence of duplicate transactions, missing transactions, and anomalies. ...

Audit software can be used to interrogate a company's data files and identify data patterns associated with fraud. Patterns such as negative entries in inventory received fields, voided transactions followed by 'No Sale', or a high percentage of returned items may indicate fraudulent activity. Auditors can use these data patterns to develop a 'fraud profile' early in their review of operations. The patterns can function as auditor-specified criteria, and transactions fitting the fraud profile can trigger auditor review. Systems can even be built to monitor transactions on an ongoing basis. Continuous monitoring is a proactive approach to the early detection of fraud.

(Source: Extracted from David Coderre, 'Computer-Assisted Techniques for Fraud Detection', *The CPA Journal* (August 1999), pp. 57–8)

AUDITING PROCEDURES

Auditing procedures are methods and techniques used by the auditor to gather and evaluate audit evidence. Each procedure has a particular advantage for obtaining evidence for an assertion. In selecting a procedure, the auditor must take care to balance the potential effectiveness of the procedure in meeting specific objectives against the cost of performing the procedure. Below, we will discuss some of these procedures.

10 LEARNING OBJECTIVE

Enumerate and describe the types of auditing procedure that may be used in an audit.

Types of auditing procedure

Auditing procedures include analytical procedures, inspecting (documents and assets), confirming, inquiring, counting, observing, reperforming and computer-assisted audit techniques.

Analytical procedures

Analytical procedures involve comparing recorded accounting data with historical information, budget expectations or external benchmarks. These procedures enable the auditor to assess the overall reasonableness of account balances and they produce analytical evidence. We will discuss these procedures in detail in Chapter 6.

Inspecting

Inspecting involves careful scrutiny or detailed examination of documents and records, and physical examination of tangible resources. This procedure is used extensively in auditing.

Inspecting documents provides a means for evaluating documentary evidence. Through inspection the auditor can assess the authenticity of audit evidence or detect the existence of alterations or questionable items. Inspection of documents also permits the auditor to determine the precise terms of invoices, contracts and agreements. Inspection may involve *tracing* (see below), *vouching* (see below) or *scanning*. Scanning involves the less careful scrutiny of documents and records.

Inspecting tangible resources provides the auditor with direct personal knowledge of their existence and physical condition.

Tracing

Tracing involves inspecting documents created when transactions were executed and determines that information from the documents was properly recorded in the accounting records. The direction of the testing is from the documents to the accounting records, thus retracing the original flow of the data through the accounting system. This procedure provides assurance that data from source documents were ultimately included in the accounts, so it is especially useful for detecting understatements in the accounting records. Thus, it is an important procedure in obtaining evidence pertaining to completeness assertions.

The effectiveness of tracing is enhanced when the entity uses serially pre-numbered documents and the auditor combines this procedure with counting to verify the completeness of the numerical sequence.

Vouching

Vouching involves selecting entries in the accounting records and inspecting the documentation that served as the basis for the entries, so as to determine the propriety and validity of the recorded transactions. In vouching, the direction of the testing is opposite to that used in tracing.

Vouching is used extensively to detect overstatements in the accounting records. Thus, it is an important procedure in obtaining evidence pertaining to existence or occurrence assertions. Vouching pertains to documentary evidence. Figure 5.4 (page 196) shows the principal differences between vouching and tracing.

Both tracing and vouching provide evidence as to measurement and rights or obligations. Measurement is confirmed by a comparison of the amount on the document with the accounting record. Rights or obligations are confirmed where the information on the document confirms the transaction as creating a right or obligation pertaining to the entity.

FIGURE 5.4

Differences between vouching and tracing

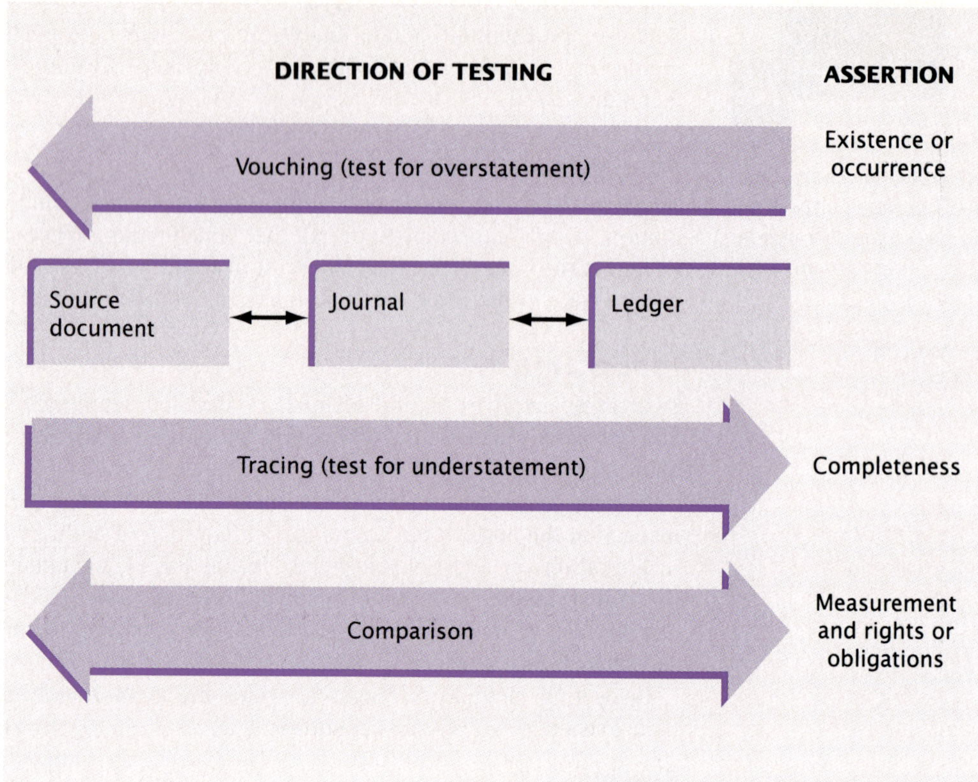

Confirming

Confirming is a form of inquiry that enables the auditor to obtain information directly from an independent source outside the entity. Normally, the entity makes the request of the outside party in writing, but the auditor controls the mailing of the inquiry. The request should ask the recipient to send the response directly to the auditor. This auditing procedure produces confirmation evidence.

Inquiring

Inquiring involves either oral or written inquiry by the auditor. Such inquiries may be made internally to management or employees, as in the case of questions pertaining to the obsolescence of inventory items and the collectibility of receivables, or externally, as in inquiries to lawyers concerning the probable outcome of litigation. Inquiry produces either oral evidence or evidence in the form of written representations.

Counting

The two most common applications of the **counting** procedure are the physical counting of tangible resources (such as the amount of cash or inventory on hand) and accounting for all pre-numbered documents. The first provides physical evidence of the quantity on hand.

The second may be used by the auditor to obtain documentary evidence of the completeness of the accounting records.

Observing

Observing pertains to watching or witnessing the performance of some activity or process. The activity may be the manner in which cash is safeguarded or the care taken by the entity in counting inventory. The subject matter of such observation is personnel, procedures and processes. From these observations, the auditor obtains direct personal knowledge of the activities in the form of physical evidence. Observation of procedures provides highly reliable evidence as to their performance at a given time but not necessarily as to their performance at other times. For this reason auditors often perform observation procedures on a surprise basis.

Reperforming

A major application of **reperforming** is to check calculations and reconciliations made by the entity. Amounts computed for depreciation and accrued interest may be recalculated. In addition, the auditor will usually verify the accuracy of totals on supporting schedules and reconciliations. Mathematical evidence is produced by this procedure. The auditor may also reperform selected aspects of the processing of selected transactions to determine that the original processing conformed to prescribed control policies and procedures. The auditor may reperform, for example, the customer credit check for a sales transaction to determine that the customer did indeed have sufficient credit available when the transaction was processed.

Computer-assisted audit techniques

When the entity's accounting records are maintained on electronic media, the auditor may use **computer-assisted audit techniques** in performing several of the procedures described in the preceding sections. The following are examples of how the auditor can use computer audit software:

- to perform the calculations and comparisons used in analytical procedures;
- to select a sample of accounts receivable for confirmation;
- to scan a file to determine that all documents in a series have been accounted for;
- to compare data elements in different files for agreement (such as the prices on sales invoices with a master file containing authorised prices);
- to reperform a variety of calculations, such as totalling the accounts receivable subsidiary ledger or inventory file.

The relationships among auditing procedures, types of evidence and assertions

During the course of an audit, in meeting the numerous specific audit objectives derived from management's financial report assertions, the auditor will use all the auditing procedures and all the types of evidence described in this chapter. Some examples of the relationships among auditing procedures, types of evidence and assertions are depicted in Figure 5.5 (page 198). From this figure we can see that tracing, vouching and inspecting involve the use of documentary evidence. The procedure of inspecting may involve the use of physical evidence, as do the procedures of counting and observing. Also, the procedure of inquiring may produce either written representations or oral evidence, depending on the nature of the inquiry and the response.

FIGURE 5.5

Relationships among auditing procedures, types of evidence and specific audit objectives

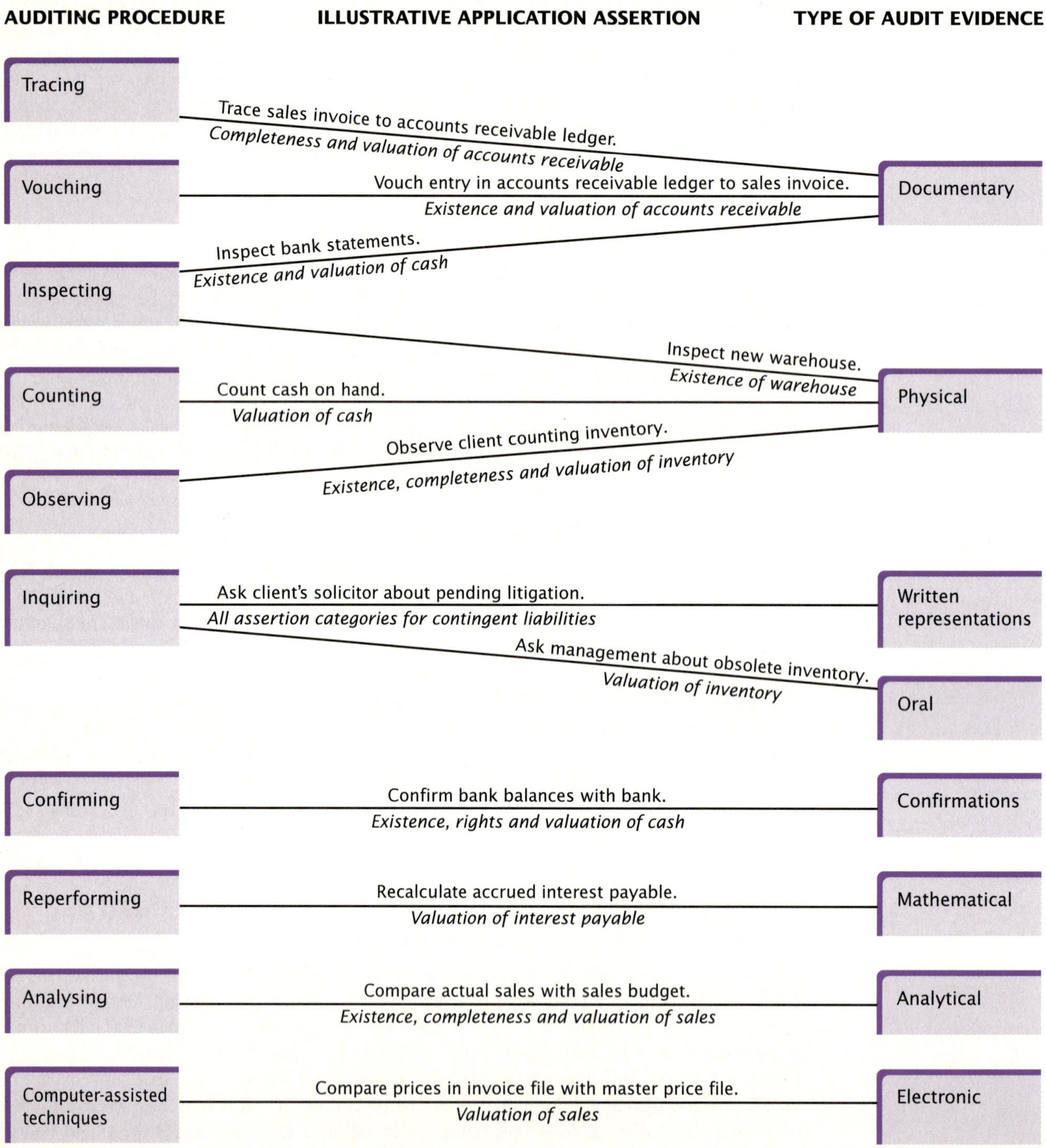

11 LEARNING OBJECTIVE

Describe the three classifications of auditing procedure and their purpose.

Classification of auditing procedures

Auditing procedures are usually classified by purpose into the following three categories:

1. procedures to obtain an understanding of the internal control structure;
2. tests of control;
3. substantive procedures.

Procedures to obtain an understanding

Auditing Standards require the auditor to obtain an understanding of the entity's internal control structure sufficient to plan the audit. To do this, the auditor may inquire of management about internal control policies and procedures, and inspect accounting manuals and flow charts of the accounting system. In addition, the auditor may obtain knowledge about the internal control structure by observing the entity's activities and operations. In performing these procedures, the auditor is concerned with the design of the entity's internal control structure — that is, how it is supposed to work.

Tests of control

Tests of control are made to provide evidence about the effectiveness of the design and operations of internal control structure policies and procedures. Assume, for example, that the control procedure provides for depositing cash in the bank daily. The auditor can test the effectiveness of the control by observing actual deposits being made or by inspecting duplicate deposit slips. Tests of control also include an inquiry of employees as to their performance of control procedures and a reperformance of control procedures by the auditor. The performance of tests of control in a financial report audit depends on the strategy adopted by the auditor, which we will explain in Chapter 6.

Substantive procedures

Substantive procedures provide direct evidence as to the fairness of management's financial report assertions. This category of auditing procedure consists of:

- analytical procedures;
- tests of details of transactions;
- tests of details of balances.

Analytical procedures involve the use of comparisons to assess fairness — for example, a comparison of an account balance with the prior year's balance or a budgeted amount.

Tests of details of transactions involve examining support for the individual debits and credits posted to an account (for example, vouching the debits in accounts receivable to entries in the sales journal and supporting sales invoices). Similarly, tracing the details from source documents to journals and the affected ledger accounts constitutes a test of details of transactions.

Tests of details of balances involve examining support for the closing balance directly (for example, confirming accounts receivable directly with the customer).

The three types of substantive procedures are complementary. The extent to which each type is used on a given account can vary based on such factors as the relative effectiveness for that account and the cost.

In some cases the auditor may perform tests of transactions to determine that:

- laid down procedures were followed in processing the transactions (tests of control);
- the transactions were accurately journalised and posted to the ledger accounts (substantive test of details of transactions).

When both purposes are served by the same test, it is called a **dual-purpose test**.

Evaluation of evidence obtained

To have a reasonable basis for an opinion on the financial report, the auditor needs a preponderance (i.e. a consensus or majority) of persuasive evidence for each financial report assertion that is material. When the auditor lacks a reasonable basis for an opinion, he or she expresses an inability to issue an opinion. When a reasonable basis for an opinion has been obtained, the auditor should issue either an unqualified, 'except for' or adverse opinion, depending on the degree of correspondence of the assertions established by the evidence obtained with the concept of fairness.

The process of obtaining and evaluating audit evidence and determining the effects on the auditor's report is summarised in Figure 5.6.

FIGURE 5.6

Obtaining and evaluating audit evidence

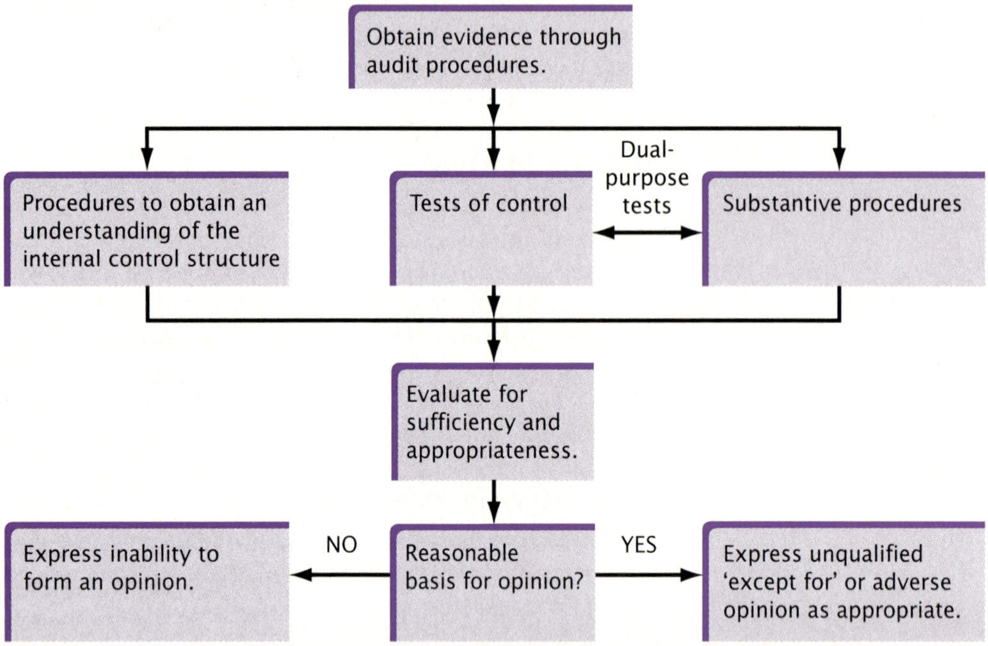

LEARNING CHECK

5.6 Management's financial report assertions are a useful starting point in developing specific audit objectives for each account balance or class of transactions. If any of these assertions is a misrepresentation, then the financial report could be materially misstated.

5.7 Audit evidence comprises underlying accounting data and corroborating information, and it needs to be sufficient and appropriate to afford a reasonable basis to form an opinion.

5.8 The principal types of corroborating information consist of analytical evidence, confirmations, documentary evidence, written representations, and mathematical, oral, physical and electronic evidence.

5.9 Audit procedures are the techniques used to obtain evidence. They include: analysing, inspecting, confirming, inquiring, counting, tracing, vouching, observing, reperforming and computer-assisted audit techniques.

5.10 Auditing procedures can be classified by their purpose into three categories: (1) procedures to obtain an understanding of the internal control structure; (2) tests of control; and (3) substantive procedures.

SUMMARY

Audit risk consists of three components. The inherent and control risk components are beyond the auditor's control, and the auditor merely assesses these risks. Detection risk is inversely related to the other components. The auditor keeps audit risk to an appropriately low level by controlling detection risk. Audit risk may be expressed in either quantitative or non-quantitative terms and has an inverse effect on the amount of evidence needed.

Materiality is considered at both the financial report and account balance levels, and may be expressed in either quantitative or non-quantitative financial report terms. There is an inverse relationship between materiality levels and the level of evidence needed.

The auditor achieves his or her overall objective of rendering an opinion on general purpose financial reports by collecting and evaluating evidence pertaining to numerous specific audit objectives. These objectives are derived from the management assertions contained in the components of the financial reports. The five categories of management assertions are: (1) existence or occurrence, (2) completeness, (3) rights or obligations, (4) valuation or measurement, and (5) disclosure.

In performing the audit, the auditor exercises professional judgement in selecting from a variety of auditing procedures and types of evidence to meet the numerous specific audit objectives. He or she also exercises judgement at the conclusion of the audit in evaluating whether sufficient appropriate evidence has been obtained to afford a reasonable basis for the opinion on the overall financial report.

We will explain the application of considerations of risk, materiality and types of audit evidence in planning an audit engagement in Chapter 6. In Chapter 7 we will describe the process of assessing control risk, while in Chapter 9 we will explain the use of audit evidence and procedures for obtaining evidence in the development of specific audit programs.

KEY TERMS

Account balances, p. 172
Analytical evidence, p. 190
Analytical procedures, p. 195
Audit evidence, p. 187
Audit risk, p. 172
Audit risk model, p. 177
Auditing procedures, p. 194
Completeness, p. 185
Computer-assisted audit techniques, p. 197
Confirmations, p. 191
Confirming, p. 196
Control risk, p. 175
Corroborating information, p. 190
Counting, p. 196
Detection risk, p. 176
Disclosure, p. 186
Documentary evidence, p. 191
Dual-purpose test, p. 199
Electronic evidence, p. 193
Existence, p. 184
Financial report assertions, p. 183
Inherent risk, p. 173
Inquiring, p. 196
Inspecting, p. 195
Internal control structure, p. 172
Materiality, p. 178
Mathematical evidence, p. 193
Measurement, p. 185
Obligations, p. 185
Observing, p. 197
Occurrence, p. 185
Oral evidence, p. 193
Physical evidence, p. 193
Planning materiality, p. 182
Reperforming, p. 197
Rights, p. 185
Substantive procedures, p. 172
Tests of control, p. 199
Tests of details of balances, p. 199
Tests of details of transactions, p. 199
Tolerable error, p. 180
Tracing, p. 195
Transactions, p. 172
Underlying accounting data, p. 187
Valuation, p. 185
Vouching, p. 195
Written representations, p. 192

FURTHER READING

Alderman, C. Wayne & Tabor, Richard H., 'The Case for Risk-Driven Audits', *Journal of Accountancy* (March 1989), pp. 55–61.

American Institute of Certified Public Accountants (AICPA) Control Risk Audit Guide Task Force, *Audit Guide: Consideration of the Internal Control Structure in a Financial Statement Audit*. AICPA, New York, 1990.

Dusenbury, Richard et. al., 'The Audit Risk Model: An Empirical Test for Conditional Dependencies among Assessed Component Risks', *Auditing: A Journal of Practice and Theory* (Fall 2000), pp. 105–17.

Dutta, Saurav K. & Graham, Lynford E., 'Considering Multiple Materialities for Account Combinations in Audit Planning and Evaluation: A Cost Efficient Approach', *Journal of Accounting, Auditing and Finance* (Vol. 13, No. 2, Spring 1998), pp. 151–71.

Flint, D., *The Philosophy and Principles of Auditing*. Macmillan Education, Hampshire, 1988, Chapter 6, pp. 104–15.

Hadnot, B. L., 'Audit Evidence — What Kind and How Much?', *The CPA Journal* (October 1979), pp. 23–9.

Hatherley, David, 'Is the Risk Driven Audit Too Risky', *Accountancy* (August 1998), p. 86.

Hellier, C., Lyon, R., Monroe, G. S., Ng, J. & Woodliffe, D. R., 'UK Auditors' Perceptions of Inherent Risk', *British Accounting Review* (March 1996), pp. 45–72.

Holstrum, Gary L. & Mock, Theodore J., 'Audit Judgement and Evidence Evaluation', *Auditing: A Journal of Practice and Theory* (Fall 1985), pp. 101–8.

Iselin, Errol R. & Iskandar, Takiah M., 'Auditors' Recognition and Disclosure Materiality Thresholds: Their Magnitude and the Effects of Industry', *British Accounting Review* (September 2000), pp. 289–309.

Jennings, Marianne, Kneer, Dan C. & Reckers, Philip M. J., 'A Re-Examination of the Concept of Materiality: Views of Auditors, Users and Officers of the Court', *Auditing: A Journal of Practice and Theory* (Spring 1987), pp. 104–15.

Leslie, Donald A., *Materiality, the Concept and Its Application to Auditing*. Canadian Institute of Chartered Accountants, Toronto, 1985.

McKee, Thomas E. & Eilifsen, Aasmund, 'Current Materiality Guidance for Auditors', *The CPA Journal* (July 2000), pp. 75–9.

Marchant, Garry, 'Analogical Reasoning and Hypothesis Generation in Auditing', *Accounting Review* (July 1989), pp. 500–13.

Mautz, R. K. & Sharaff, Hussein A., *The Philosophy of Auditing*, Monograph No. 6. American Accounting Association, Sarasota, Florida, 1961, Chapter 5, pp. 68–110.

Messier, William F. & Austen, Lizabeth A., 'Inherent Risk and Control Risk Assessments: Evidence of the Effect of Pervasive and Specific Risk Factors', *Auditing: A Journal of Practice and Theory* (Fall 2000), pp. 119–31.

Moeckel, Cindy L. & Plumlee, R. David, 'Auditors' Confidence in Recognition of Audit Evidence', *Accounting Review* (October 1989), pp. 653–66.

Pany, Kurt & Wheeler, Stephen, 'A Comparison of Various Materiality Rules of Thumb', *The CPA Journal* (June 1989), pp. 62–3.

Perrin, Sarah, 'Spot the Difference', *Accountancy* (June 1998), pp. 84–5.

Seidler, Lee J., 'The Old Ways Don't Hold Water: Materiality Decisions in the Computer Age', *CPA Journal* (May 1999) pp. 22–4.

Whittington, R., Zulinski, M. & Ledwith, James W., 'Completeness — The Elusive Assertion', *Journal of Accountancy* (August 1983), pp. 89–92.

Yardley, J., 'Explaining the Conditional Nature of the Audit Risk Model', *Journal of Accounting Education* (Vol. 7, 1989), pp. 107–14.

Review questions

5.1 Audit risk is said to be a function of inherent risk, control risk and detection risk. Explain audit risk. Define and differentiate between each of its components.

5.2 What is the audit risk model? Explain both its quantitative and non-quantitative forms.

5.3 Explain the term 'materiality' in the context of financial reporting. What is the audit significance of the concept of materiality?

5.4 Why may planning materiality differ from the materiality level used in evaluating audit findings?

5.5 How may the auditor determine tolerable error when testing a specific account balance or transaction class?

5.6 Discuss the differences between 'quantitative' and 'qualitative' in terms of materiality.

5.7 What is the overall objective of a general purpose financial report audit? How does the auditor usually meet this objective?

5.8 Identify the separate financial report assertions, each of which must be properly stated if the financial report is not to be misstated.

5.9 Discuss the interrelationship between assertions and the specific audit objectives developed for a client.

5.10 What factors should the auditor consider when developing specific audit objectives? Can there be more than one specific audit objective for a particular account for each category of assertion? Explain.

5.11 What factors are important in determining the sufficiency and appropriateness of corroborating information?

5.12 Identify the types of auditing procedure that may be used to obtain evidence. For each procedure indicate one type of audit evidence that it obtains.

Discussion questions

5.1 Compare and contrast the concept of inherent risk at the entity level, with guidance provided in AUS 210, Irregularities, Including Fraud, Other Illegal Acts and Errors (Appendix 2) (see Table 2.1, page 66).

5.2 Because management usually address the inherent risks at the account balance and class of transactions level by implementing appropriate control procedures, is it practicable for auditors to assess inherent risk at this level separately from control risk?

5.3 Most guidance provided to auditors on materiality addresses its quantitative aspect. Is there a risk that auditors could fail to detect misstatements that are small but qualitatively material?

5.4 One of the major weaknesses in audit practice is the absence of any logical basis for determining the extent of testing materiality at the level of each account balance or transaction class. Explain why this is a problem.

(*continued*)

5.5 The occurrence assertion has two aspects. Firstly, there is the issue of whether the recorded transaction actually occurred. Secondly, there is the issue of whether it is a transaction that may legitimately be recorded as a transaction of the entity. Discuss this distinction.

5.6 Professional scepticism is an important quality for auditors to possess when interpreting evidence. Explain what is meant by professional scepticism. Suggest problems that may arise in achieving an appropriate level of scepticism.

5.7 In their theoretical examination of auditing, *The Philosophy of Auditing*, Mautz and Sharaf distinguish between those assertions for which compelling evidence is available and those for which compelling evidence is not available. (They use the term 'assertion' in the context of types of corroborating information.) Discuss the validity of this distinction.

Professional application questions

★ BASIC
★★ MODERATE
★★★ CHALLENGING

5.1 (Assertions) ★

In planning the audit of a client's non-current assets, an auditor derived the following specific objectives from the five categories of management's financial report assertions:

1. Non-current assets are not valued greater than recoverable amount in accordance with an applicable Accounting Standard.
2. All non-current assets were on hand at year end.
3. Non-current assets include all purchases made during the financial year.
4. Mortgages over non-current assets are properly disclosed in the financial statements.
5. All non-current assets on hand are owned.
6. Obsolete non-current assets have been identified and revalued or written off as appropriate.
7. Non-current assets have been properly classified in the balance sheet.
8. All non-current assets under lease have been identified separately.
9. Depreciation on non-current assets has been properly calculated.
10. The fixed asset register has been totalled and the totals agree with the figures in the general ledger.

Required

For each of the specific audit objectives in items 1–10, identify the category of management assertion from which it was derived.

5.2 (Audit evidence) ★

Corroboratory evidence inspected by an auditor in the course of an audit includes:

1. a letter from the bank confirming the company's bank balance, which is sent directly to the auditor;
2. the creditor's monthly statement from the company's files;
3. copies of sales invoices sent to customers from the company's files;
4. delivery notes, sent with goods, receipted by customers, and held in the company's office;
5. title deeds for the company's properties, which are held at the company's safe deposit box at the bank;
6. a bank statement from the client's files;
7. material requisitions filed in the storeroom;
8. a board minute authorising purchase of new equipment.

Required
For each item, comment on its reliability as audit evidence.

5.3 (Substantive procedures and audit evidence) ★
An auditor may perform the following three types of substantive procedures: (a) tests of details of transactions; (b) tests of details of balances; and (c) analytical procedures. Below are specific audit procedures that fall within one of these categories:

1. Inspect new machine purchased during the year.
2. Vouch purchases with suppliers' invoices.
3. Confirm amounts owed with customers.
4. Calculate inventory turnover ratios and compare with industry data.
5. Reconcile bank accounts at year end.
6. Test count inventory of supplies on hand at year end.
7. Inspect purchase invoices recorded after the year end to see if any relate to goods purchased before the year end
8. Calculate the gross profit ratio and compare it with the previous year's ratio.

Required
For each procedure, explain which of the three types it belongs to.

5.4 (Materiality) ★★
You have just completed audit testing on the 30 June 20X2 accounts of JJJ Limited, a manufacturing firm. Extracts from the draft financial report are given below.

	$'000
Current assets	12 095
Non-current assets	8 297
Current liabilities	5 630
Non-current liabilities	4 500
Shareholders' equity	10 262
Operating profit before tax	2 857
Operating profit after tax	2 333

The audit manager has asked you to review the summary of audit differences working paper to determine if there are any material errors in the financial report. This working paper is set out below.

Details of error found	**Amount ($)**
1. Non tax-deductible fine incurred due to breaches of safety regulations; not taken up as at 30 June 20X2	250 000
2. Incorrect prices on sales invoices issued in June (customers overcharged)	25 000
3. Unrecorded liabilities due to 30 June 20X2 stock purchases not being taken up (cut-off error)	71 000
4. Interest receivable on bank deposit not taken up	175 000

Required
(a) Discuss the differences in the purpose, method of calculation and relative use of judgement of:
  (i) materiality as used at the planning stage of the audit.
  (ii) materiality as used at the final review stage of the audit.
(b) Outline the materiality guidelines as described in AASB 1031.

(continued)

(c) Under what circumstances might an error be judged to be material as a result of its nature rather than its amount? Give examples.

(d) Are any of the errors in items 1–4 material? In each case explain how you reached your conclusion.

(Professional Year Programme of the ICAA — 1998, Accounting 2 Module — adapted)

5.5 (Audit objectives, procedures and evidence) ★★

You are an audit senior and your firm audits Extractwell Limited, a large mining company that operates all over Australia. Consider the following situations that have arisen during the audit.

1. Extractwell has a number of highly specialised fixed assets held at various remote regions across the country. Your firm has engaged an expert to carry out a fixed assets stocktake at each location and to perform an independent valuation of each material asset.
2. You are auditing the trade debtors of Extractwell. The majority of Extractwell's customers are in South-East Asia. Due to communication difficulties, direct confirmation of debtors' balances is unlikely to give satisfactory results.
3. You are auditing the investments of Extractwell. It owns several parcels of shares in related, unlisted companies.

Required

(a) Identify the key assertion(s) at risk in relation to the balances described in each of the three situations described.

(b) Describe the audit procedures you would perform to gather sufficient appropriate audit evidence on each of these assertions.

(Professional Year Programme of the ICAA — 1997, Accounting 2 Module — adapted)

5.6 (Auditing procedures and evidence) ★★

Specific auditing procedures for obtaining audit evidence are listed below.

1. Send debtor's confirmation letters to a number of the client's customers.
2. Recompute depreciation charges.
3. Compute gross profit rates for the current year and preceding year.
4. Discuss the potential obsolescence of stock with the management.
5. Examine registration certificates for motor vehicles purchased during the year.
6. Use the computer to scan a file to determine that all documents in a numbered series have been accounted for.
7. Learn about a possible lawsuit in conversation with the financial controller.
8. Obtain a valuation of land held by the company interstate.
9. Observe the year-end stock count.
10. Select a sample of repairs and maintenance expenses and check whether any should have been capitalised.

Required

Indicate (a) the type of evidence obtained by each procedure and (b) the assertion or assertions to which it pertains.

5.7 (Audit risk, components of audit risk) ★★★

Elliott Limited operates a road maintenance company. Consider the following information.

1. Your firm has just been appointed auditor of Elliott at its annual general meeting. During your planning of the audit, you notice that Elliott is an unlisted public company and its directors do not consider it to be a reporting entity. Elliott has prepared special purpose financial reports for the past five years. It has significant bank debts and is required to lodge audited accounts with its bankers within ninety days of year end.
2. Elliott recently won a substantial contract to perform road maintenance work for the Queensland Government for the next three years. As a result of winning the contract, to meet the increased demands and satisfy the specialised nature of the work for the government, Elliott purchased additional machinery. The machinery has an expected life of ten years.
3. Elliott is also involved in the manufacture of backyard water tanks. A revolutionary process developed a couple of years ago has enabled Elliott to build a far superior tank than any of its competitors, at half the price. It has therefore dominated the market over the past few years. However, you were recently reading a weekend newspaper in which you saw an article previewing Elliott's main competitor's new tank. It is made of a new material called Lycrafon, and it will be superior to Elliott's tanks and cost 25 per cent less.

Required

(a) Discuss why each of the three situations represents a risk.

(b) Identify the main account or group of accounts affected by these risks and how the specific aspects of the audit plan would be affected by these risks.

(Professional Year Programme of the ICAA — 1997, Advanced Auditing Module — adapted)

5.8 (Assertions and evidence) ★★★

You are finalising the audit of ABC Pty Limited, a large proprietary company with a 30 June year end. Control risk was assessed as being high, so you performed a fully substantive audit.

You have just completed your review of the working papers prepared by the audit assistant, and you have made the following notes on the work performed:

1. *Trade creditors*

   The assistant has:
   - selected a sample of creditors from the year end creditors' ledger;
   - vouched each creditors' balance selected to invoices and subsequent cash payments;
   - agreed the total of the creditors' ledger to the trial balance and general ledger.
2. *Payroll expense*

   The assistant has:
   - selected a sample of individual pays from monthly payroll listings of May and June;
   - vouched the pay rates used to the related industrial awards;
   - checked the calculations of each pay;
   - traced any annual, sick and other leave to authorised forms;
   - agreed the balance of the payroll listings for May and June to the general ledger.

(*continued*)

3. *Sales*
   The assistant has:
   - selected a sample of customer orders from throughout the year;
   - traced each order to the related sales invoice;
   - checked the adds and extensions of each sales invoice;
   - agreed prices on the invoices to an authorised price list;
   - traced each invoice to the debtors and general ledger.
4. *Fixed assets*
   The assistant has:
   - selected a sample of fixed asset additions from the register;
   - agreed each addition selected to creditors' invoices; and
   - agreed the total of additions throughout the year to the trial balance and general ledger.

Required

(a) Explain to which audit assertion each of the procedures performed by the assistant is directed.

(b) Identify the assertions on which you believe the assistant should perform further testing. Ignore disclosure issues.

(Professional Year Programme of the ICAA — 1998, Accounting 2 Module — adapted)

Case studies

5.1 (Materiality) ★★★

You are nearing completion of the 31 December 20X2 audit of ABC Wholesalers Limited (ABC). The following figures have been extracted from the final draft financial report:

	$'000
Operating profit before income tax	5 722
Operating profit after income tax	3 541
Total revenue	718 635
Current assets	253 881
Non-current assets	216 752
Total assets	470 633
Current liabilities	103 333
Non-current liabilities	132 760
Total liabilities	236 093
Shareholders' equity	234 540

During your review of the audit files, you note the following items recorded on the summary of audit differences.

1. ABC has been involved in a long-running dispute with the taxation authorities in relation to the amount of sales tax payable on certain lines of merchandise. The case was resolved this year in favour of the taxation authorities. The court ruled that ABC, as well as paying the outstanding taxes, must pay a non-tax-deductible fine of $420 000.
2. Sales cut-off at one of ABC's stores was incorrect, resulting in a large sale of stock made early in January 20X3 being recorded in the 31 December 20X2 year end. The cost price of the inventory sold was $250 000. ABC marks up inventory by 40 per cent.

3. Purchases cut-off at the same store was also incorrect, resulting in a large purchase of stock made in late December not being recorded until January 20X3. The invoice price of the inventory purchased was $5 950 000.

You also note that the planning materiality level was set by the audit manager at $200 000.

Required

(a) Consider items 1–3 independently. State whether the amounts involved would be considered material for the purpose of issuing an audit report. Give reasons.

(b) Explain the relevance, if any, of the planning materiality level to your decisions in (a).

(Professional Year Programme of the ICAA — 1999, Advanced Audit Module — adapted)

5.2 (Audit risk, components of audit risk) ★★★

Audrey Pearce is an audit partner of Pearce Green, a firm of accountants. She is considering audit risk at the overall financial statement level in planning the audit for the finance company Homes South Limited (HS) for the year ending 30 June 20X2. This risk is influenced by a combination of factors related to management, the industry and the entity. Audrey has gathered the following information concerning HS's environment.

1. HS has been consistently more profitable than the industry average by marketing mortgages on properties in a prosperous rural area, which has experienced considerable growth in recent years. HS packages and sells mortgages to large investment trusts. Despite recent volatility of interest rates, HS has been able to continue selling its mortgages as a source of new lendable funds.
2. HS's board of directors is controlled by George Watson, the majority shareholder, who also acts as the chief executive officer. Management at the company's branch offices has authority for directing and controlling HS's operations, and is compensated according to branch profitability. The internal auditor reports directly to Henry Stevenson, a minority shareholder, who is chairman of the audit committee.
3. The accounting department has experienced little turnover in personnel during the five years for which Audrey has audited HS. HS's formula constantly underestimates the allowance for loan losses, but its financial controller has always been receptive to Audrey's suggestions to increase the allowance.
4. During 20X1, HS opened a branch office in a metropolitan area 30 kilometres from its principal place of business. Although this branch is not yet profitable (as a result of competition from several well-established banks), management believes it will be profitable by 20X3.
5. During 20X2, HS increased the efficiency of its operations by installing a new computer system.

Required

Based only on the information above, indicate the factors that would affect the risk of material misstatement and explain why.

chapter 6

Accepting the engagement and planning the audit

Overview

LEARNING OBJECTIVES

After studying this chapter, you should be able to:

1. identify the phases of a financial report audit
2. state the steps involved in accepting an audit engagement
3. state the purpose and content of an engagement letter
4. explain the components of an audit plan
5. describe the procedures used in obtaining an understanding of the entity's business and industry
6. explain the role of analytical procedures in audit planning
7. differentiate alternative audit strategies
8. explain the purpose and function of audit working papers
9. apply the essential techniques of good working paper preparation.

Professional statements

AUSTRALIAN		INTERNATIONAL	
AUS 106	Explanatory Framework for Standards on Audit and Audit Related Services	ISA 100	Assurance Engagements
AUS 202	Objective and General Principles Governing an Audit of a Financial Report	ISA 200	Objective and General Principles Governing an Audit of Financial Statements
AUS 204	Terms of Audit Engagements	ISA 210	Terms of Audit Engagements
AUS 206	Quality Control for Audit Work	ISA 220	Quality Control for Audit Work
AUS 208	Documentation	ISA 230	Documentation
AUS 302	Planning	ISA 300	Planning
AUS 304	Knowledge of the Business	ISA 310	Knowledge of the Business
AUS 512	Analytical Procedures	ISA 520	Analytical Procedures
AUS 518	Related Parties	ISA 550	Related Parties
AUS 606	Using the Work of an Expert	ISA 620	Using the Work of an Expert

In Chapter 5 we described the factors determining the approach to any particular audit, the assessment of the risks, the concept of materiality, the identification of the objectives of the audit, and the types of evidence available. In this chapter we will explain the application of these matters to a specific audit engagement. Firstly, we will discuss the steps involved in completing the initial phase of an audit — that is, accepting the engagement. Secondly, we will identify the steps involved in the planning phase of the audit, then provide an in-depth coverage of the first two steps in the planning phase — namely, obtaining an understanding of the entity's business and industry and performing analytical procedures. Thirdly, we will describe the types of audit strategy and explain their application under specific circumstances. Finally, we will explain the importance of documenting all phases of the audit, giving guidance as to how to set about preparing working papers and accumulating them into audit files.

It is common practice to refer to the business, which is the subject of the audit, as the 'entity'. This reflects the fact that the auditor's duty of care, in a financial report audit, is to the shareholders or other owners of the business, not to the business or its management. In this chapter we will also use the term 'client' in connection with the engagement, because it reflects the contractual relationship between the auditor and the entity subject to audit. The distinction may appear sometimes confusing, especially given that the term 'client' is still widely used to refer to the management and directors. The current view, however, is that use of the term 'client' to refer to management and directors may lead auditors to overlook the fact that their ultimate responsibility is to the shareholders. For other assurance engagements it is also important that the auditor or reporting accountant is clear as to which party or parties a duty of care is owed. To avoid confusion you should also be aware that the term 'firm', in auditing, refers to the audit firm and should not be confused with the entity that is the subject of the audit.

The procedures that we will describe in this chapter apply principally to the acceptance and planning of a financial report audit engagement that results in the issue of an audit report meeting the requirements of the Corporations Law. Similar requirements apply to the acceptance and planning of other assurance engagements, subject to the specific nature of the proposed service.

ACCEPTING THE AUDIT ENGAGEMENT

1 LEARNING OBJECTIVE

Identify the phases of a financial report audit.

The following four **phases of an audit** can be identified:

- accepting the audit engagement;
- planning the audit;
- performing audit procedures;
- reporting the findings.

In each phase, the auditor should be mindful of the environment in which audits are performed, as described in the preceding chapters. Environmental factors include the impact of regulation, the public's expectations, exposure to litigation, and the need to comply with professional standards.

The initial phase of a financial report audit involves a decision to accept (or decline) the opportunity to become the auditor for a new client or to continue as auditor for an existing client. In most cases, the decision to accept (or decline) is made several months before the client's fiscal year end.

An auditor is not obliged to perform a financial report audit for any entity that requests it. In accepting an engagement an auditor takes on professional responsibilities to the public, the client and other members of the public accounting profession. The client's best interests must be served with competence and professional concern. In relation to other members of the profession, the auditor has a responsibility to enhance the stature of the profession and its ability to serve the public. An auditor wishing to avoid legal liability would not associate with clients that pose a high risk of litigation. Thus, a decision to accept a new client or continue a relationship with an existing client should not be taken lightly.

The decision to accept an audit engagement depends on the client evaluation and ethical considerations. Client evaluation involves (1) a consideration of the integrity of management and (2) the identification of any special circumstances and unusual risks associated with the entity. Ethical considerations relate to whether the audit firm is able to meet independence criteria, complete the engagement with professional competence and perform the audit with due care. If the audit firm is of the opinion that the audit can be completed in accordance with professional standards, then the firm prepares an engagement letter to confirm the auditor's responsibility.

2 LEARNING OBJECTIVE

State the steps involved in accepting an audit engagement.

Client evaluation

Client evaluation is an important element of quality control. AUS 206 (ISA 220) Quality Control for Audit Work states that:

> ... prospective clients are evaluated and existing clients are reviewed on an ongoing basis. In making a decision to accept or retain a client, the audit firm's independence and ability to serve the client properly and the integrity of the client's management are considered. AUS 206.06(f) (ISA 220.06(f))

Section F, in the Appendix to AUS 206 (ISA 220), details the following procedures that will assist the auditor in complying with the client evaluation policy:

- obtaining and reviewing available financial information on the prospective client;
- making inquiries of third parties, such as bankers, as to information that may influence the evaluation of the prospective client;
- communicating with the existing auditors with the view to evaluating the integrity of the client's management;
- identifying circumstances that require special attention or that carry unusual risks;
- evaluating the audit firm's independence and whether the firm is able to properly serve the client;
- establishing that acceptance of the client would not violate codes of professional ethics.

The series of steps involved in the evaluation process is shown diagrammatically in Figure 6.1.

FIGURE 6.1

Considerations in accepting an audit engagement

CLIENT EVALUATION	ETHICAL CONSIDERATIONS	ENGAGEMENT
Evaluate integrity of management.	Evaluate independence.	Prepare engagement letter.
Identify special circumstances and unusual risks.	Assess competence to perform audit.	
	Determine ability to use due care.	

Evaluating the integrity of management

In undertaking a client evaluation, the auditor seeks reasonable assurance that an entity's management can be trusted. When management lacks integrity, there is a greater likelihood that material errors and irregularities may occur in the accounting process from which the financial report is prepared. For a new client, the **successor auditor** may obtain information about the integrity of management by communicating with the **predecessor auditor**, if applicable, and by making inquiries of other third parties. For an existing client, the auditor should consider previous experience with the client's management.

Communicating with existing auditors

Statement F3 of the Joint Code of Professional Conduct of the Institute of Chartered Accountants in Australia (ICAA) and CPA Australia requires that an auditor invited to take on a new audit client communicate with the existing auditor, if the client is already being audited. The communication should be made with the client's permission and the client should be requested to authorise the existing auditor to respond fully to the inquiries. Authorisation is required because the profession's code of ethics prohibits an auditor from disclosing confidential information obtained in an audit without the client's permission. If the client refuses to permit the existing auditor to disclose information, then the prospective auditor should not accept the appointment.

In communication with the predecessor auditor, the prospective auditor should make specific and reasonable inquiries regarding matters that may affect the decision to accept an engagement. AUS 206 (ISA 220) suggests that inquiries should address questions such as the integrity of management, disagreements with management about accounting policies and audit procedures, and the existing auditor's understanding of the reasons for the change of auditor.

The existing auditor is expected to respond promptly and fully, assuming the client gives consent. If the existing auditor does not respond, then it may be assumed there are no matters to be communicated. On occasions, the existing auditor may prefer to communicate orally, such as where they have unconfirmed suspicions of unlawful acts by the client. Whatever the reply, the prospective auditor alone must decide whether to accept the appointment.

The previous auditor's working paper files are a valuable source of information about a new client. The new auditor may, therefore, ask to review these files. The previous auditor is under no obligation to consent to such a review, but many audit firms will consent to a supervised review, given the client's permission.

Making inquiries of other third parties

The auditor may also obtain information about a client management's integrity from knowledgeable persons in the community. AUS 206 (ISA 220) suggests that the proposed auditor may direct inquiries to:

> . . . the prospective client's bankers, legal advisers, investment banker, and others in the financial or business community who may have such knowledge.

Other potential sources of information include news items in the financial press on changes in senior management.

Reviewing previous experience with existing clients

Before making a decision to continue an engagement with an existing audit client, the auditor should carefully consider prior experiences with the entity's management — for example, any material errors or irregularities and illegal acts discovered in prior audits. During an audit, the auditor makes inquiries of management about such matters as the existence of contingencies, the completeness of all minutes of board of directors' meetings, and compliance with regulatory requirements. The truthfulness of management's responses to such inquiries in prior audits should be carefully considered in the evaluation of the integrity of management.

In the Appendix to AUS 206, Section F2 (ISA 220, Section F2) suggests the auditor should regularly evaluate clients in respect to the occurrence of specified events to determine whether to continue a relationship with that client. These events include:

- the expiration of a period of time, such as every three years;
- a significant change since the first evaluation (for example, a change in management, financial condition, litigation status or the nature of the client's business);
- the existence of conditions that would lead the auditor to reject a client had they existed at the time of the initial acceptance of audit engagement.

Identifying special circumstances and unusual risks

This step in accepting an engagement includes identifying the intended users of the audited financial report, making a preliminary assessment of the prospective client's legal and financial stability, and evaluating the entity's auditability.

Identifying intended users of the audited financial report

In Chapter 3 we noted that the auditor's legal responsibilities in an audit may vary based on the intended users of the financial report. Thus, the auditor should consider (1) the prospective client's status as a private or public company, (2) any named beneficiaries or foreseen or foreseeable third parties to whom the potential for liability exists under common law, and (3) what, if any, statutes apply in the circumstances. The auditor should also consider whether a general purpose financial report will meet the needs of all intended users or whether any special reports will be required. Added reporting requirements may mean additional competency requirements, add to audit costs and broaden the auditor's legal liability exposure.

For assurance engagements, other than a financial report audit, it may be necessary to restrict the report to specific identified users.

Assessing a prospective client's legal and financial stability

If an entity experiences legal difficulties, and if plaintiffs can find any pretext for claiming reliance on the financial report, then such litigation will probably also involve the auditors, who are often thought to have 'deep pockets'. Thus, auditors may incur the financial and other costs of defending themselves, no matter how professionally they performed their services.

For this reason, auditors should attempt to identify and reject prospective clients that pose a high risk of litigation. These may include entities whose operations or principal products are the subjects of either material lawsuits or investigations by authorities, the outcome of which could adversely affect the viability of the business. Clients to reject may also include entities already known to be experiencing financial instability, such as an inability to meet debt payments or to raise needed capital. The auditor can identify such matters by inquiring of management; reviewing credit agency reports; and analysing previously issued audited or unaudited financial reports, and, if applicable, previous annual returns with regulatory agencies.

Evaluating the entity's auditability

Before accepting an engagement, the auditor should evaluate whether other conditions exist that raise questions as to the prospective client's auditability. Such conditions may include the absence or poor condition of important accounting records; management's disregard of its responsibility to maintain other elements of an adequate internal control structure; or restrictions imposed by the prospective client on the conduct of the audit. In such cases, the auditor should decline the engagement or make clear to the client the possible effects of such conditions on the auditor's report.

Ethical considerations

In conducting an audit, the auditor should comply with the ethical requirements of the profession's Auditing Standards, legislation and regulation and, where appropriate, the terms of the audit engagement (as specified in AUS 202, Objective and General Principles Governing an Audit of a Financial Report (ISA 200, Objective and General Principles Governing an Audit of Financial Statements)).

Evaluating independence

Statement F1 of the Joint Code of Professional Conduct of the ICAA and CPA Australia requires that 'members in public practice must both be and be seen to be free of any interest which is incompatible with objectivity'. Quality control standards and the Corporations Law require the observance of this rule.

Thus, before accepting a new audit client, the firm must evaluate whether there are any circumstances that would compromise its independence. One procedure is to circulate the name of a prospective client to all professional staff to identify any financial or business relationships inconsistent with independence. If such relationships exist, then they should be discontinued where practicable — such as by sale of the shares — or the engagement should be declined. In addition, the firm should determine that acceptance of the client engagement would not result in any conflict of interest with other clients.

For a continuing audit, a professional independence questionnaire may be completed annually for each client to ensure ongoing compliance with the firm's quality control policies and procedures on independence. Some firms require the engagement partner to provide a written representation to this effect.

Assessing competence to perform the audit

The quality control policy on employment in AUS 206.06(b) (ISA 220.06(b)) states:

> The firm is to be staffed by personnel who have attained and maintain the technical standards and professional competence required to enable them to fulfil their responsibilities with due care.

The audit firm will rely on its quality control procedures on personnel (such as on hiring, continuing professional development and advancement) to ensure compliance with the above policy. For a prospective client, the firm will have to identify an **audit team** that will match the staffing needs of the engagement. The typical audit team consists of:

- a **partner**, who has both overall and final responsibility for the engagement;
- an **audit manager**, who coordinates and supervises the execution of the audit program;
- one or more seniors, who may oversee the conduct of the audit with specific responsibility for work in complex areas;
- staff assistants, who perform many of the required procedures under the supervision of the seniors.

The team may also need the assistance and guidance of **experts**, such as computer audit specialists. If the audit firm does not have the required skills, it may engage external consultants to provide the necessary expertise. An auditor is not expected to have the expertise of a person trained for, or qualified to engage in, the practice of another profession or occupation. AUS 606 (ISA 620), Using the Work of an Expert recognises that the auditor may use the work of experts to obtain sufficient appropriate audit evidence. Examples are the use of:

- appraisers to provide evidence about the valuation of assets such as property, plant and equipment, works of art and precious stones;
- geologists and engineers to determine the quantities of mineral and petroleum reserves and remaining useful life of plant and equipment;
- actuaries to determine amounts used in accounting for a superannuation plan;
- lawyers to assess the probable outcome of pending litigation, interpretations of agreements, statutes and regulations;
- computer specialists to assist in evaluating database management systems.

Before using an expert, the auditor is expected to become satisfied as to the professional qualifications, reputation and objectivity of the expert. The auditor should consider, for example, whether the expert has appropriate professional qualifications, relevant experience in the matters in question, adequate standing within the profession, and any relationship with the client that may impair his or her objectivity.

Determining ability to use due care

Ethical principles require that the auditor exercise due care in performing the audit and preparing the report. The auditor should decline an engagement if due professional care cannot be exercised throughout the audit. Determination of due care may involve a review of both the work done and the judgements exercised by those assisting in the audit.

The audit team and consultants must be available to perform the proposed engagement during the relevant period. Consequently, audit work is scheduled. The detailed schedule for completing an engagement may not be finalised until several steps in the audit planning phase have been completed. Nonetheless, the probable impact of accepting a new client on the firm's overall work schedule must be considered prior to accepting the engagement. A limiting factor for many audit firms is the requirement to be present at many clients at, or close to, their financial year end to observe inventory, count cash, etc.

Preliminary work on a **time budget** for the audit is often done as part of the scheduling considerations. The development of a time budget involves estimating the hours expected to be required at each staff level (partner, manager, senior and so on) for each part of the audit. These time estimates may then be multiplied by the charge-out rates for each staff level to arrive at an estimate of total costs for the engagement. The audit firm may use these estimates as the basis for discussions with the prospective client about fee arrangements. Although some audits are carried out on a fixed-fee basis, the use of daily charge-out rates plus expenses is the more typical arrangement.

If the engagement is accepted and the appointment is properly confirmed, such as by the members of the company, then details of the time budget and scheduling of the audit will be further developed as additional steps in the planning phase are performed. Then, as work on each area of the audit progresses, the audit firm can monitor actual hours and compare them with the budget to help to control overall audit costs.

The use of client personnel can also have an impact on staffing and scheduling and, thus, on audit cost. The work of internal auditors in obtaining an understanding of the internal control structure and in performing tests of control and substantive procedures may (subject to evaluation of the effectiveness of internal audit) reduce the extent of independent audit work in certain areas. Other client personnel can be used to perform tasks such as preparing schedules of insurance policies in force, notes receivable, and plant asset additions and disposals. To demonstrate that the audit was undertaken with due care, the auditor must plan to review and test all such work.

Preparing an engagement letter

As a final step in the acceptance phase, in compliance with Auditing Standards and good professional practice, it is important to confirm the terms of each engagement in an **engagement letter**, as in Figure 6.2. (*Note*: ISA 210 does not refer to any quality control issues.)

3 LEARNING OBJECTIVE

State the purpose and content of an engagement letter.

FIGURE 6.2

Auditor's engagement letter as per AUS 204 (ISA 210)

To [the governing body (e.g. the board of directors) or the appropriate representative of senior management]:

Scope

You have requested that we audit the financial report of [entity] as of and for the year ending [date]. We are pleased to confirm our acceptance and our understanding of this engagement by means of this letter. Our audit will be conducted pursuant to the [relevant statutory and other requirements][1] with the objective of expressing an opinion on the financial report.

We will conduct our audit in accordance with Australian Auditing Standards to provide reasonable assurance as to whether the financial report is free of material misstatement. Our procedures will include examination, on a test basis, of evidence supporting the amounts and other disclosures in the financial report, and the evaluation of accounting policies and significant accounting estimates. These procedures will be undertaken to form an opinion whether, in all material respects, the financial report is presented fairly in accordance with Accounting Standards and other mandatory professional reporting requirements [and relevant statutory and other requirements][2] so as to present a view which is consistent with our understanding of the [entity's] financial position, the results of its operations and its cash flows.

The work undertaken by us to form an opinion is permeated by judgement, in particular regarding the nature, timing and extent of the audit procedures for gathering of audit evidence and the drawing of conclusions based on the audit evidence gathered. In addition, there are inherent limitations in any audit, and these include the use of testing, the inherent limitations of any internal control structure, the possibility of collusion to commit fraud, and the fact that most audit evidence is persuasive rather than conclusive. As a result, our audit can only provide reasonable — not absolute — assurance that the financial report is free of material misstatement.

In addition to our report on the financial report, we expect to provide you with a separate letter concerning any material weaknesses in the internal control structure that come to our notice.

Our audit procedures are designed to gather sufficient appropriate audit evidence to form an opinion on the financial report. Unless otherwise agreed with you, we assume no responsibility to design audit procedures to identify matters that may be appropriate to report to you. However, if we encounter matters during the course of our audit that we believe should be brought to your attention for consideration or further action, we will communicate these matters to you. If no such matters come to our attention, we will report accordingly.

You should not assume that any matters reported to you, or that a report that there are no matters to be communicated, indicates that there are no additional matters, or matters that you should be aware of in meeting your responsibilities.

We remind you that the responsibility for the preparation of the financial report, including adequate disclosure, is that of the governing body of the [entity]. This includes the maintenance of adequate accounting records and internal control structure, the selection and application of accounting policies, and the safeguarding of the assets of the [entity]. As part of our audit process, we will request from management written confirmation concerning representations made to us in connection with the audit.

Presentation of audited financial report on the Internet[3]

It is our understanding that [the entity] intends to publish a hard copy of the audited financial report and audit report for members, and to electronically present the audited financial report and audit report on its Internet web site. When information is presented electronically on a web site, the security and controls over information on the web site should be addressed by [the entity] to maintain the integrity of the data presented. The examination of the controls over the electronic presentation of audited financial information on the entity's web site is beyond the scope of the audit of the financial report. Responsibility for the electronic presentation of the financial report on the entity's web site is that of the governing body of [the entity].

Quality control

The conduct of our audit in accordance with Australian Auditing Standards means that information acquired by us in the course of our audit is subject to strict confidentiality requirements. Information will not be disclosed by us to other parties except as required or allowed for by law or professional standards, or with your express consent. Our audit files may, however, be subject to review as part of the quality control review program of [*insert* CPA Australia and/or the Institute of Chartered Accountants in Australia *as appropriate*] which monitors compliance with professional standards by its members. We advise you that by signing this letter you acknowledge that, if requested, our audit files relating to this audit will be made available under this program. Should this occur, we will advise you. The same strict confidentiality requirements apply under this program as apply to us as your auditor.

Fees

We look forward to full cooperation with your staff and we trust that they will make available to us whatever records, documentation and other information are requested in connection with our audit. Our fees, which will be billed as work progresses, are based on the time required by the individuals assigned to the engagement plus out-of-pocket expenses. Individual hourly rates vary according to the degree of responsibility involved and the experience and skill required.

Other

This letter will be effective for future years unless we advise you of its amendment or replacement, or the engagement is terminated.

Please sign and return the attached copy of this letter to indicate that it is in accordance with your understanding of the arrangements for our audit of the financial report.

Yours faithfully,	Acknowledged on behalf of [entity] by
(signed)	(signed)
....	....
Name and Title, Date	Name and Title, Date

1. Cite relevant statutory and other requirements where appropriate.
2. Cite relevant statutory and other requirements where appropriate.
3. For further guidance on this issue, refer to AGS 1050, Audit Issues Relating to the Electronic Presentation of Financial Reports.

The form and content of the letter may vary for different clients, but should generally include the following:

- a reminder to management that it is responsible for preparing the financial report and providing the auditors with access to the accounting records and other related information;
- the objective or purpose of the audit;
- reference to professional standards (e.g. Auditing Standards) to which the auditor will adhere (and, if applicable, to statutes such as the Corporations Law or any other governing legislation or regulations);
- an explanation of the nature and scope of the audit and the auditor's responsibilities;
- a statement to the effect that weaknesses in the entity's accounting system identified in the course of the audit will be brought to management's attention but may not be provided to third parties;
- an indication that management will be asked to provide certain written representations to the auditor;
- a requirement to sight all other disclosures to be issued with the financial report;
- a statement that management are responsible for safeguarding the entity's assets and that the audit should not be relied on for detecting all material misstatements;
- a description of any other services provided by the auditor;
- the basis on which fees will be computed and any billing arrangements;
- a request for the client to confirm the terms of the engagement by signing and returning a copy of the letter to the auditor.

To eliminate the need to prepare a new letter each year, the letter normally includes a statement that it continues in force until replaced. A new letter may be appropriate on the occurrence of events such as a change in management, ownership, nature and/or size of the entity's business or legal requirements.

Auditors appointed in accordance with the provisions of the Corporations Law must fulfil their statutory responsibilities. However, they may assume additional responsibilities if that is the desire of both parties. When auditors are appointed by an entity not incorporated under the Corporations Law — for example, a partnership or a tertiary education institution — it is even more important to confirm the nature of duties and responsibilities through an engagement letter.

An engagement letter constitutes a legal contract between the auditor and the client. By clearly stating the nature of services to be performed and the responsibilities of the auditor, such letters may help the auditor to avoid becoming involved in litigation. The letter in Figure 6.2 (pages 218–19) is for use as a guide, in conjunction with the considerations outlined in AUS 204 (ISA 210), Terms of Audit Engagements, and will need to be varied according to individual requirements and circumstances.

4 LEARNING OBJECTIVE

Explain the components of an audit plan.

PLANNING THE AUDIT

The second phase of the audit requires the development of a plan for the conduct and scope of the audit. Planning is crucial to a successful audit engagement because it enables auditors to meet their professional responsibilities at a reasonable cost. **Audit planning** is usually carried out three to six months prior to the entity's fiscal year end. We will explain the components involved in audit planning in this and the next two chapters.

Some pre-planning would have been accomplished when the auditor decided to accept the engagement. However, more detailed planning is required for an effective and efficient audit. AUS 302 (ISA 300), Planning states:

> The auditor should plan the audit work so as to perform the audit in an effective manner. AUS 302.02 (ISA 300.02)

Audit planning involves the development of an overall plan for the conduct and scope of the audit. Adequate planning helps to ensure that appropriate attention is given to important areas of the audit, that problems are identified properly, and that work is completed expeditiously (AUS 302.04; ISA 300.04). It is also necessary in coordinating the work done by other auditors and experts. The audit should be planned with a degree of professional scepticism in relation to matters such as the integrity of management, errors and irregularities, and illegal acts. The amount of planning required in an engagement will vary with the size and the complexity of the entity, and the auditor's knowledge of the business and experience with the entity. Considerably more effort is needed to plan an initial audit than a recurring audit. It should be recognised, too, that planning is continual throughout the engagement.

Steps in planning the audit

Planning starts with an understanding of the entity's business and industry. **Analytical procedures** add to the auditor's understanding. Planning also involves (1) setting materiality levels, (2) assessing audit risk and its components, (3) obtaining an understanding of the internal control structure and (4) developing a preliminary audit strategy for significant assertions. We explained the first two steps in Chapter 5. In all but the smallest engagements, the auditor will make a preliminary visit to the entity, usually before its financial year end. This visit is referred to as the **interim audit**. During the interim audit, the auditor obtains an understanding of the internal control structure and assesses control risk. (We will consider the concepts pertaining to this step in Chapter 7.) An audit program is then developed on the basis of a final determination of detection risk for each assertion, consistent with the overall level of audit risk and materiality levels (see Chapter 9). The steps in planning the audit are shown in Figure 6.3.

FIGURE 6.3

Steps in planning the audit

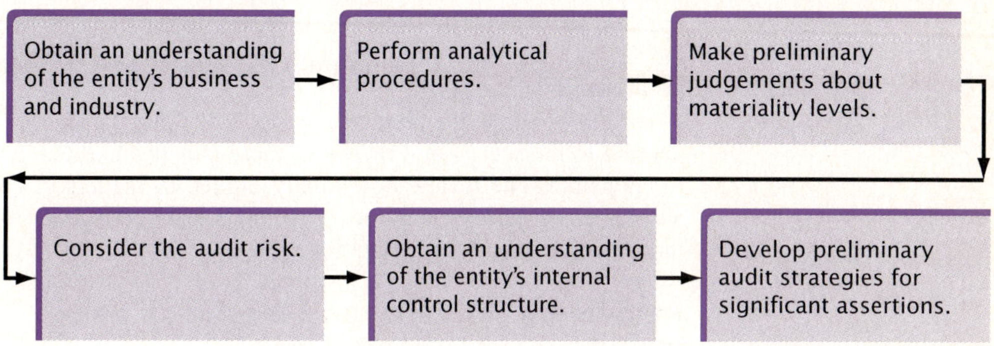

5 LEARNING OBJECTIVE

Describe the procedures used in obtaining an understanding of the entity's business and industry.

Obtaining an understanding of the entity's business and industry

To plan an audit, the auditor should obtain sufficient knowledge of the entity's business to understand events, transactions and practices that may have a significant effect on the financial report. This understanding provides a framework for planning an overall audit approach that responds to the unique characteristics of the entity. In recurring engagements, the auditor's emphasis is on evaluating new developments in the entity's business and industry. Changes may be gradual or sudden, and may increase the likelihood of errors of audit importance or alleviate audit problems.

The auditor needs knowledge of the economy and industry within which the entity operates. More detailed knowledge is required of the operations of the entity. Specifically, the auditor may need knowledge about:

- the type of industry and its vulnerability to changing economic conditions, and major industry policies and practices;
- the type of business, types of product and service, entity locations and operating characteristics of the entity, such as its production and marketing methods;
- the existence of related party transactions;
- the entity's internal control structure;
- government regulations that affect the entity and its industry;
- the nature of reports to be filed with regulatory agencies.

AUS 304 (ISA 310), Knowledge of the Business identifies sources for obtaining knowledge of the industry and the entity. These include:

- previous experience with the entity and its industry;
- visits to the entity's premises and plant facilities;
- discussions with people within the entity;
- discussions with other auditors, legal and other advisers, and other people who have provided services to the entity;
- discussions with knowledgeable people outside the entity;
- publications relating to the industry;
- legislation and regulations that significantly affect the entity;
- documents produced by the entity relating to its business and financial performance;
- professional literature giving industry-specific guidance.

We will discuss the procedures with the widest application in the following sections.

Reviewing the prior year's working papers

In a recurring audit engagement, the auditor can review the prior year's audit working papers for knowledge about the entity. In addition, the working papers may indicate problem areas in prior audits that may be expected to continue in the future; for example, they may reveal that the entity has ongoing internal control weaknesses or complicated profit-sharing bonus plans.

For a new client, the previous auditor's working papers may be helpful. The client must consent to the successor's review of these papers and the previous auditor must be willing to cooperate. The review is normally limited to matters of continuing audit significance, such as analyses of balance sheet accounts and contingencies. During the review, the previous auditor may be available for consultation.

Reviewing industry and business data

The Appendix to AUS 304 (ISA 310) lists a broad range of matters that an auditor may consider in seeking knowledge of general economic factors, the industry and the entity. Information on the industry and economic conditions can be obtained from trade journals, industry statistics compiled by government or private agencies, data accumulated by the audit firm, and professional guidance statements where available.

To obtain knowledge of the entity's business, the auditor may examine the entity's legal documents, minutes of directors' and shareholders' meetings, and significant contracts. The principal legal documents of the company are the **memorandum of association** and the **articles of association**. The memorandum of association is the constitution of the company. It contains information on the name, objectives and powers of the company; the types and amount of share capital authorised; the liability of members; and the subscribers to the company's capital. The articles regulate the internal management of the company, particularly in relation to the allotment of shares; the calling of general meetings; the powers, duties and appointment of directors; the secretary and the company seal; and how dividends are declared and reserves are provided.

Auditors must have a knowledge of pertinent legal documents to determine that the financial report is properly presented. The disclosures pertaining to shareholders' funds and the declaration of dividends must be in accordance with these documents.

Minutes of meetings of directors are important to the audit. Information contained in minutes provides corroborative evidence for the company's significant transactions and for practices such as:

- authorisations for capital expenditures;
- new business undertakings;
- long-term loans;
- officers' remuneration;
- important contracts;
- approval for pledging assets;
- the opening and closing of bank accounts (and the specification of persons authorised to operate those accounts).

Important continuing contracts may relate to such matters as loan agreements, leases and superannuation plans. Auditors need an understanding of the contracts to determine the correctness of the terms of the transactions and to ensure that disclosures in the financial report are appropriate.

Other sources of information on the entity are the internal documents prepared by the entity's internal auditors and other consultants. These documents include annual and interim financial statements, tax returns, reports to regulatory agencies and other special reports prepared by management or internal auditors for internal decision-making.

The auditor should document the information obtained and retain it in a permanent file for use in subsequent audits.

Touring operating facilities and offices

A tour of the operating facilities and offices is a significant help to an auditor in obtaining knowledge about a new client's operating characteristics. During a tour of the factory, the auditor should become familiar with the factory layout, the manufacturing process, storage facilities and potential trouble spots such as unlocked storerooms, obsolete materials and excessive scrap.

During a tour of the office, an auditor should become knowledgeable about the work habits of personnel and the types and locations of accounting records and computer-processing facilities. An important by-product of both tours is the opportunity to meet personnel who occupy key positions within the organisation. The auditor should document the information obtained from the factory and office tours.

In a recurring engagement, audit personnel new to the engagement should be expected to tour the operating facilities.

Making inquiries of management

For both new and recurring engagements, discussions with management may reveal current business developments affecting the entity that may have audit significance. In addition, management should be knowledgeable about new industry and government regulations that affect the entity. In some cases, areas of particular audit interest to management — such as a new division or a controlled entity — may be discussed.

Inquiries of management may also concern the extent and timing of entity personnel's involvement in preparing schedules and analyses for the auditor. In addition, the auditor can inquire about the internal audit function and matters pertaining to corporate accountability, such as codes of conduct, potential conflicts of interest and possible illegal payments.

Making inquiries of the audit committee

The audit committee of the board of directors may provide the auditor with special insights into the entity's business and industry. The committee may have information about, for example, the strengths and weaknesses of the company's internal controls in a specific division or in a newly implemented computer information system. The committee may also be able to inform the auditor of significant changes in the entity's management and organisational structure. In some cases, the audit committee may request additions or modifications to the auditor's planned audit.

Determining the existence of related parties

Management is responsible for identifying and disclosing related parties and **related party transactions**. Auditing Standards require that the auditor obtain sufficient appropriate evidence to ensure adequate disclosure of related parties.

The concern about related party transactions results from the realisation that 'arm's length' bargaining of terms and conditions of transactions between such parties may not apply. Alternatively, related parties may conspire to enter into transactions intended to obscure financial or other business problems that would otherwise be reflected in the financial report. Thus, the auditor will ordinarily require more appropriate evidence for related party transactions than for transactions between unrelated parties. To ensure that such evidence is obtained, the auditor must take steps in the planning phase to determine the existence of related parties.

Certain related party transactions may be clearly evident, such as those between a controlling and a controlled entity, between or among entities under common control, or between an entity and its executive officers. AUS 518 (ISA 550), Related Parties indicates that specific audit procedures, including the following, should be used to determine the existence of other related parties.

- Inquire of management.
- Review the prior year's working papers for names of known related parties.
- Inquire as to the names of all superannuation and other trusts established for the benefit of employees and the names of their management and trustees.
- Inquire as to the affiliation of management with other entities.
- Review shareholder records to determine the names of principal shareholders.
- Inquire of other auditors involved in the audit or predecessor auditors as to their knowledge of additional related parties.
- Review the entity's tax returns and other information supplied to regulatory agencies.
- Review the entity's procedures for identifying related parties.
- Review minutes of the meetings of shareholders, the board of directors and other important committees, as well as other relevant statutory records such as the register of directors' interests.

A list of identified related parties is usually maintained in the permanent audit file. These parties should be made known to all members of the audit team so they can be alert to evidence of transactions with these parties.

Considering the impact of applicable accounting and auditing pronouncements

Although all auditors are knowledgeable about Accounting Standards and Auditing Standards, special accounting principles and audit procedures may apply in certain industries or to certain types of business activity. The auditor may refer to audit and accounting guides, if available, that describe distinctive characteristics of the industry or activity covered, alert the auditor to unusual problems, and explain regulations and other special factors to take into account. These guides may illustrate financial report treatment and the form and wording of audit reports whenever applicable.

The auditor should also consider the impact of applicable pronouncements of regulatory agencies such as the Australian Securities and Investment Commission (ASIC) and the stock exchanges. Finally, consideration should be given during the planning phase of the audit to the impact of any newly effective Accounting Standards and Auditing Standards.

6 LEARNING OBJECTIVE

Explain the role of analytical procedures in audit planning.

Performing analytical procedures

Analytical procedures involve a study and comparison of relationships among data to identify expected or unexpected fluctuations and other unusual items. The common types of analytical procedure involve a comparison of the entity's financial information with:

- comparable information for a prior period or periods;
- anticipated results such as budgets and forecasts;
- industry averages.

Analytical procedures also include the study of relationships:

- among elements within the financial statements, such as a study of gross margin percentages;
- between financial information and relevant non-financial information, such as a study of payroll costs for a number of employees.

Such procedures are performed during the planning phase to:

- enhance the understanding of the entity's business;
- identify unexpected fluctuations and unusual relationships.

Unexpected fluctuations and unusual relationships indicate areas of greater risk of misstatements, so the auditor plans to perform extended procedures on these amounts. When results of analytical procedures are as expected, the possibility of a misstatement or an irregularity is minimal. The auditor may, therefore, reduce the level of substantive tests of details performed in support of these amounts.

Generally, analytical procedures performed during the planning phase use highly aggregate entity-wide data which are based on year-to-date or expected annual data. However, for entities with diverse operations, some disaggregation by product line or division may be necessary. In other cases, such as a company with seasonal business, it may be desirable to perform the analysis on monthly or quarterly data rather than on year-to-date or annual data.

Determining effects on audit planning

Unexplained significant differences are ordinarily viewed as an increased risk of misstatement in the accounts involved. In such cases, the auditor will usually plan to perform more substantive tests of details of those accounts. By directing the auditor's attention to areas of greater risk, analytical procedures may contribute to performing a more effective and efficient audit.

Analytical procedures are also used as a substantive procedure. We will explain their use for this purpose in Chapter 9. They are also used in the overall review of the financial report immediately prior to the issue of the auditor's report. We will explain this use in Chapter 14.

LEARNING CHECK

6.1 The four phases of an audit are: (1) accepting the audit engagement, (2) planning the audit, (3) performing audit procedures and (4) reporting the findings.

6.2 The decision to accept an audit engagement depends on evaluating the client by inquiring of the existing auditor and other parties about the integrity of management and by identifying special circumstances and unusual risks associated with the entity.

6.3 The decision to accept an audit also depends on ethical considerations which relate to the firm's ability to meet the independence criteria and to complete the audit with competence and due care.

6.4 The steps in audit planning are: (1) obtaining an understanding of the entity's business and industry, (2) performing analytical procedures, (3) making preliminary judgements about materiality levels, (4) considering audit risk, (5) developing preliminary audit strategies and (6) obtaining an understanding of the internal control structure.

6.5 The widely accepted procedures for obtaining an understanding of the entity's business and industry include: (1) reviewing the prior year's working papers, (2) reviewing industry and business data, (3) touring the entity's operational facilities and offices, (4) making inquiries of the audit committee, (5) determining the existence of related parties and (6) considering the impact of applicable accounting and auditing pronouncements.

6.6 Analytical procedures enhance the auditor's understanding of the entity's business and help to identify unusual relationships and unexpected fluctuations.

AUDIT STRATEGIES

7 LEARNING OBJECTIVE

Differentiate alternative audit strategies.

Given the interrelationships among evidence, materiality and the components of audit risk, the auditor may choose from among alternative audit strategies in planning the audit of individual assertions or groups of assertions. In this section we will identify the components of audit strategies, describe two alternative strategies and explain their application to transaction classes and account balances.

Developing the audit strategy

The process of developing the audit strategy commences with obtaining an understanding of the internal control structure. This is a requirement of all audits, whatever strategy is to be adopted.

The default presumption is that all of the evidence will come from the performance of substantive procedures — sometimes referred to as the **predominantly substantive approach**. Substantive procedures are those that substantiate the amounts recorded in the financial statements. They are normally costly to perform. A more efficient audit can be performed if controls are judged to be sufficiently effective to enable a reduction in the level of substantive procedures undertaken. This is illustrated in Figure 6.4 (page 229). Furthermore, in certain situations, substantive procedures may be unable to provide sufficient evidence and a more effective audit could be performed if the auditor could rely on certain controls. The completeness of cash receipts is an obvious example; unless controls over the receipt of cash are effective, it may be impossible to determine, through the use of substantive procedures, that all cash to which the entity is entitled has been properly recorded.

An audit strategy that relies on internal controls to support using a reduced level of substantive procedures is sometimes referred to as a **lower assessed level of control risk approach**. This is not a single strategy, but a range of strategies determined by the relative effectiveness of applicable control procedures (combined with assessments of inherent risk and materiality). The auditor must make four separate decisions before adopting such a strategy, and each decision (except the first) must be supported by relevant evidence.

1. Is it cost-effective to adopt a lower assessed level of control risk strategy?
2. Are control procedures effectively designed?
3. Are control procedures effectively operated?
4. Do the results of substantive procedures confirm the assessment of control risk?

In many situations it is apparent to the auditor during the course of planning the audit that there is nothing to be achieved by assessing control risk, such as when:

- the entity is small, such that controls are unlikely to be effective;
- the understanding of the internal control structure reveals that controls are inadequate;
- prior audits have revealed inadequate controls;
- there are few transactions in a transaction class or items making up an account balance, such that substantive procedures are unlikely to be costly.

In such situations the auditor would proceed to plan an audit consisting entirely of substantive procedures. In all other situations the auditor would make a preliminary assessment of control risk.

In the planning phase the auditor is concerned with the design of control procedures. In evaluating design effectiveness the auditor identifies the presence of the control procedures that are likely to reduce control risk for a particular assertion. Based on this preliminary assessment, the auditor will plan the audit, incorporating both tests of control and substantive procedures. The tests of control are designed to verify that control procedures are actually operating as laid down. The level of use of planned tests of control depends on the assessed level of control risk to be confirmed: that is, the lower the assessed level of control risk, the more extensive the tests of control required to confirm that assessment and, conversely, the lower the planned level of substantive procedures.

In some respects it may be better if the auditor waits until completing tests of control before planning substantive procedures. However, experience has shown that the results of tests of control usually confirm the assessed level of control risk and, thus, the planned audit strategy. By designing substantive procedures at this stage, the auditor can commence detailed planning of the final audit. Moreover, tests of control are typically performed during the interim audit, simultaneously with substantive tests of details of transactions, sometimes as dual-purpose tests. Given that both tests are applied to the same records, it is more efficient to draft the audit program so as to incorporate all tests to be conducted on the same records simultaneously.

If the tests do not confirm the operation of the control as planned, then the auditor will need to reconsider the audit strategy and increase the level of use of substantive procedures as appropriate.

We will explain procedures employed in assessing control risk in Chapter 7. These procedures include methods of obtaining the understanding of the internal control structure and of assessing the design effectiveness of controls, the design of tests of control and the interpretation of the results of tests of control in making the final assessment of control risk.

Effect of the assessment of control risk on substantive procedures

In considering the effect of the assessment of control risk on the level of substantive procedures necessary to achieve the desired level of detection risk, the auditor may vary the nature, timing or extent of such procedures.

The nature of substantive procedures may vary between tests of details and analytical procedures. Because they examine individual transactions and items making up an account balance, tests of details are far more persuasive than analytical procedures, which consider only the reasonableness of recorded totals. However, where a relatively high level of detection risk may be tolerated, analytical procedures may be sufficient. In such cases the use of analytical procedures would be the preferred option because they are less costly than tests of details to perform.

The timing of substantive procedures refers to the distinction between those performed at the balance sheet date and those performed prior to that date. Performance of procedures prior to the year end reduces pressure on the auditor and enables the audit to be completed earlier. Where controls over inventory records are effective, for example, reliance may be placed on a physical inventory prior to the year end updated by transactions in the intervening period. Where controls are particularly effective, attendance at perpetual inventory alone may be sufficient.

PROFESSIONAL ENVIRONMENT Auditing planning and fraud

The auditor complying with Australian and international Auditing Standards is currently required to:

> ... plan and conduct the audit so as to have a reasonable expectation of detecting misstatements that a material impact on the financial report arising as a result of irregularities ... (AUS 210, Irregularities Including Fraud, Other Illegal Acts and Errors; ISA 240, Fraud and Error)

The American Institute of Certified Public Accountants Panel on Audit Effectiveness recently called for all audits to contain a mandatory forensic phase aimed specifically at the detection of fraud. Ian Plaistowe, a UK partner with Arthur Andersen, has expressed the following concern at the proposed US development:

> As the world moves towards harmonising auditing standards — based on the work of the International Auditing Practices Committee (IAPC) — and as the EU is considering the issue of a recommendation on the use of international auditing standards, changes to US auditing standards will influence international standards, especially as the IAPC seeks the endorsement of International Commission of Securities Organisations. It is important that those outside the United States provide their input into major US developments. Otherwise, there is a danger that what happens in the United States will, without debate, end up being required in the United Kingdom. ...
>
> I suggested that the United States participate in the work of the IAPC which . . . is about to review its core auditing standards. This would provide an opportunity to move auditing standards forwards on a global basis and avoid the risk of regulatory divergence.
>
> The most controversial recommendation of the panel is that there should be a mandatory forensic phase on all audits. This would add significantly to the cost of audits. The research that the Auditing Practices Board (APB) has conducted shows that most frauds that have a material impact on financial statements involve directors and senior management and frequently involve complex mechanisms and collusions designed to prevent detection. Many such frauds are extremely difficult for a normal audit to detect in a cost-effective manner.
>
> (Source: Extracted from Ian Plaistowe, 'The Audit of Audits', *The Times* (17 August 2000), p. 27)

It should be recognised, however, that it is inappropriate under Auditing Standards for the auditor to conclude that inherent and control risks are so low that it is unnecessary to perform any substantive procedures for all assertions pertaining to an account. Some evidence must always be obtained from substantive procedures for each significant account balance, although not necessarily for each financial report assertion (AUS 402.61; ISA 400.45). The design of substantive procedures is explained in more detail in Chapter 9.

The 'Professional environment' on page 228 introduces the debate about whether the auditor, in planning the audit, needs to have specific regard to the possibility of fraud.

The relationship between strategies and transaction classes

The strategies are not intended to characterise the approach to an entire audit. Rather, they represent alternative approaches to auditing individual assertions. Frequently, however, a common strategy is applied to groups of account balance assertions affected by the same transaction class. The rationale is that many internal controls focus on the processing of a single type of transaction. Double entry means that each transaction class affects two or more account balances. Sales transactions relate to accounts receivable in the balance sheet and to sales in the profit and loss statement. Thus, the assessed control risk for the occurrence assertion for sales transactions will apply to the existence assertion in the audit of both sales and accounts receivable balances. Because the accounts receivable balance is affected by cash receipts and sales adjustment transactions as well as sales transactions, the auditor also considers the assessment of control risks for all three transaction classes in developing the audit strategies for accounts receivable assertions.

FIGURE 6.4

Preliminary audit strategies for material financial report assertions

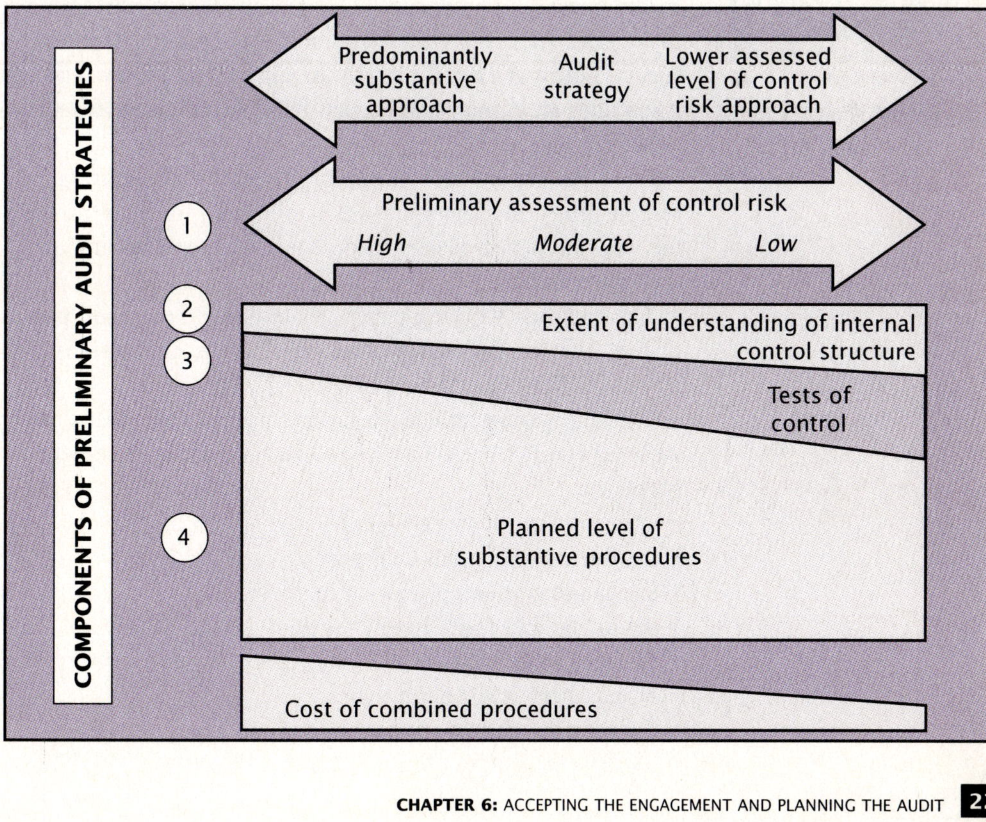

WORKING PAPERS

Evidence collected in support of an audit opinion (for example, worksheets and check lists) is recorded in the **working papers**. The term 'audit working papers' is used to include all documentation stored in paper, film or electronic media.

Types of working paper

Types of working paper prepared during an audit include:

- a working trial balance;
- schedules and analyses;
- audit memoranda and documentation of corroborating information;
- adjusting and reclassifying entries;
- audit programs.

Working papers may be prepared manually or using software developed for microcomputers. Figure 6.5 (page 232) is an example of a microcomputer-generated working paper. The use of electronic working papers provides several advantages: auditors can obtain more information on their own from the entity's system; data can be instantaneously retrieved; the audit team can share information with members who are not on site; and review can take place at any time and anywhere.

8 LEARNING OBJECTIVE

Explain the purpose and function of audit working papers.

The purpose and function of working papers

Working papers are the subject of AUS 208 (ISA 230), Documentation. Properly prepared working papers demonstrate that the audit was performed in accordance with Auditing Standards. They show that the audit was properly planned and carried out, that adequate supervision was exercised, that an appropriate review was made of the audit work undertaken and, most importantly, that the evidence is sufficient and appropriate to support the audit opinion.

Working papers also serve to monitor the progress of the audit, especially where responsibility for separate tasks is allocated to different staff members. When completed, the working papers also provide a guide to the planning and performance of audits in subsequent periods.

The auditor's working papers should record the audit plan; the nature, timing and extent of the audit procedures performed; and the conclusions drawn from the audit evidence obtained (AUS 208.05, 06; ISA 230.05, 06).

Working papers should be tailored to meet the needs of the specific audit engagement. AUS 208.08 (ISA 230.08) states that the form and content of the working papers is influenced by:

- the nature of the engagement;
- the form of the auditor's report.
- the nature and complexity of the business;
- the nature and condition of the entity's internal control structure;
- the need in the particular circumstances for direction, supervision and review of the work of members of the audit team;
- the specific method and technology the auditor uses.

Working paper files

Working papers are generally filed under one of two categories: (1) a permanent file and (2) a current file.

Permanent file

A **permanent file** contains data that are expected to be useful to the auditor on many future engagements with the entity. Items typically found in a permanent file are:

- extracts or copies of the memorandum and articles of association. These describe, among other matters, the objectives of the company, the number and types of share authorised for issue, their par value, the rights of shareholders and the duties of directors.
- copies of important long-term operating agreements or contracts such as leases, superannuation plans, profit-sharing and bonus agreements, and labour contracts;
- analysis of accounts that are important to the audit each year (such as shareholder fund accounts and long-term debt);
- analytical review schedules from prior years, including ratios and percentage analysis or trend statements for various items. A review of these schedules enables the auditor to focus on unusual changes in the current year's account balances compared with those for previous periods;
- a description of the entity's internal control structure. This may consist of the description of the control environment, control policies and procedures, internal control questionnaires, flow charts, decision tables, and a chart of accounts and sample forms to aid in obtaining an understanding of the company's procedures;
- information relevant to audit planning, such as the master copy of the audit program, information on accounts (bank accounts or cost centres) or locations (controlled entities or branches) tested on a rotation basis.

Current file

The **current file** contains evidence gathered in the performance of the current year's audit program.

Working trial balance

A partial working trial balance is illustrated in Figure 6.5. Note that columns are provided for the current year's ledger balances (before audit adjustments and reclassifications), adjustments, adjusted balances, reclassifications and final (audited) balances. Including the final (audited) balances for the prior year facilitates the performance of certain analytical procedures.

The working trial balance may be prepared by the entity or the auditor. When the former occurs, the auditor verifies the trial balance by adding the columns and tracing the account balances to the general ledger. A working trial balance is of paramount importance during the conduct of the audit because it:

- provides a basis for controlling all the individual working papers;
- serves as a connecting link between the entity's general ledger and the general purpose financial report;
- identifies the specific working papers containing the audit evidence for each financial report item.

Figure 6.5 (page 232), for example, indicates that the amount reported in the financial report for marketable securities is based on general ledger account 150 and that the evidence used by the auditor to evaluate management's assertions about marketable securities can be found in a section of the working papers with a reference or index of B. The absence of an account number for cash in Figure 6.5 indicates that this financial report item is the aggregate of several general ledger cash accounts. In such cases, the initial working paper of the section referenced on the working trial balance (A in this case) should contain a group schedule showing which general ledger accounts have been combined for this financial report item. The link between the cash line item in the working trial balance for Omni Co. Limited (working paper AA–1) and Omni's balance sheet presentation of cash is illustrated in the bottom portion of Figure 6.6.

FIGURE 6.5 *Partial working trial balance working paper*

Omni Co. Limited
Working trial balance — Balance sheet
31 December 20X1

W/P ref. AA–1
Prepared by: _______ Date: _____
Reviewed by: _______ Date: _____

W/P ref	Acc. no.	Description	Final balance 31.12.X0	Ledger balance 31.12.X1	Adjustments AJE ref.	Adjustments Debit (Credit)	Adjusted balance 31.12.X1	Reclassifications RJE ref.	Reclassifications Debit (Credit)	Final balance 31.12.X1
		Assets								
		Current								
A		Cash	392 000	427 000	(1)	50 000	477 000			477 000
B	150	Marketable securities	52 200	62 200			62 200			62 200
C		Receivables (net)	1 601 400	1 715 000	(1)	(50 000)	665 000	(A)	10 000	1 675 000
D	170	Inventories	2 542 500	2 810 200	(2)	133 000	943 200			2 943 200
E		Prepaid expenses	24 900	19 500			19500			19 500
		Total current	4 613 000	5033 900		133 000	5 166 900		10 000	5 176
				190 000						900
F	240	Long-term investments	3 146 500				190 000			190 000
		Property, plant and								
G		equipment (net)		3 310 900			3 310 900			3 310 900
		Total	7 759 500	8 534 800		133 000	8 667 800		10 000	8 677 800
		Liabilities and shareholders' equity								
		Current liabilities								
M	400	Notes payable	750 000	825 000			825 000			825 000
N	410	Accounts payable	2 150 400	2 340 300	(2)	(133 000)	2 473 300	(A)	(10 000)	2 483 300
O	420	Accrued payables	210 600	189 000			189 000			189 000
P	430	Income taxes payable	150 000	170 000			170 000			170 000
		Total current	3 261 000	3 524 300		(133 000)	3 657 300		(10 000)	3 667 300
R	500	Debentures payable	1 000 000	1 200 000			1 200 000			1 200 000
S	600	Ordinary shares	2 400 000	2 400 000			2 400 000			2 400 000
T	700	Profit and loss appropriation	1 098 500	1 410 500			1 410 500			1 410 500
		Total	7 759 500	8 534 800		(133 000)	8 667 800		(10 000)	8 677 800

Schedules and analyses

The terms 'working paper schedule' and 'working paper analysis' are used interchangeably to describe the individual working papers that contain the evidence supporting the items in the working trial balance. Working papers are normally filed by balance sheet item, with a further section for the profit and loss account. The first schedule for each item is referred to as a **lead schedule**. This schedule groups the general ledger accounts that are combined for reporting purposes and identifies the individual working paper schedules or analyses that contain the audit evidence obtained for each account comprising the group. The middle portion of Figure 6.6 illustrates the use of a cash lead schedule for Omni Co. Limited (working paper A) and how it is linked both to the cash line of the working trial balance (working paper AA–1) and the supporting working papers for the two general ledger cash accounts listed on the lead schedule (i.e. working paper A–1 for A/C 100 Petty cash and working paper A–2 for A/C 101 Cash in bank).

FIGURE 6.6

Integrated working papers for cash

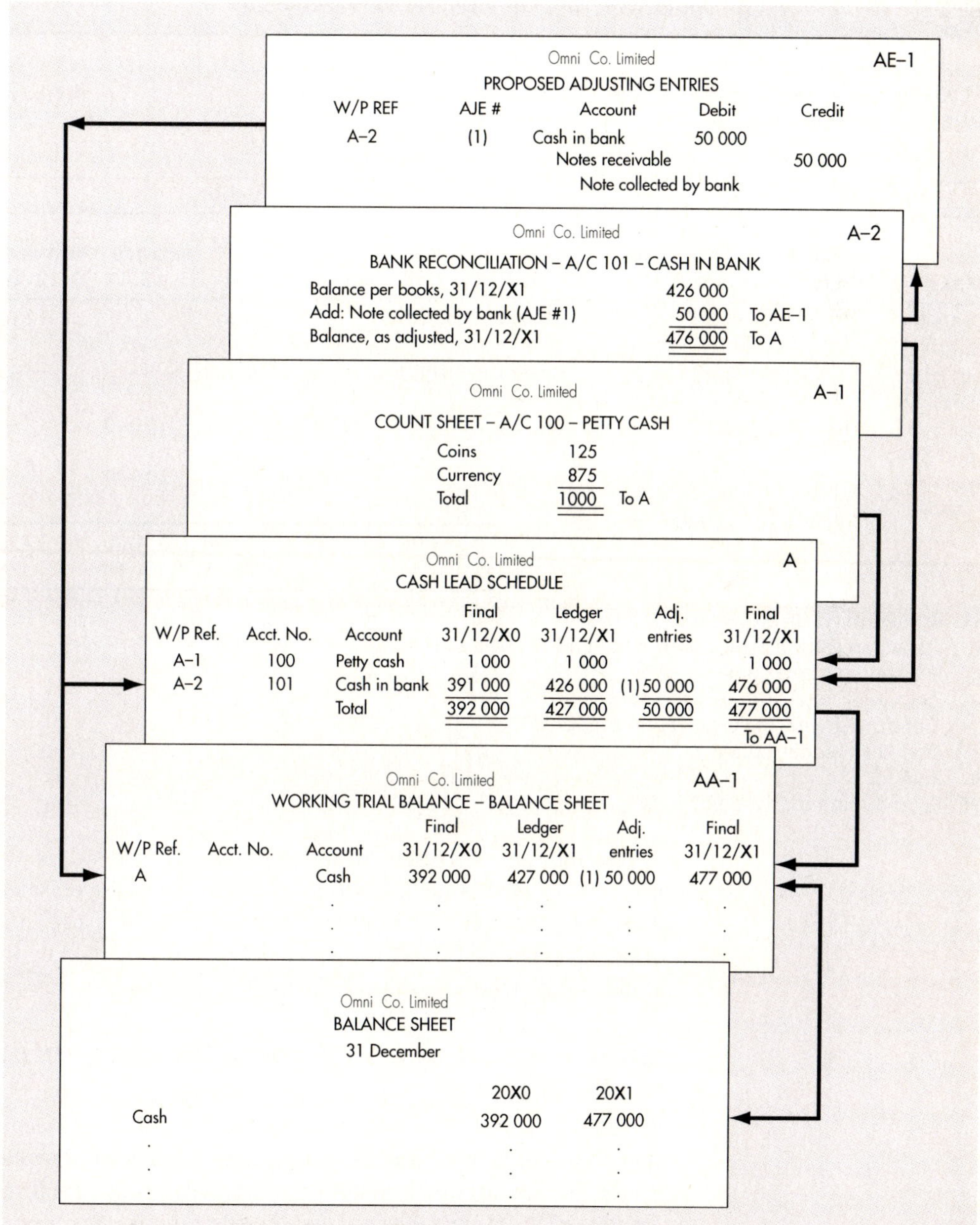

Individual schedules or analyses often show the composition of an account balance at a particular date, as in working paper A–1 of Figure 6.6. Other examples would include a list of customer balances comprising the accounts receivable control account balance and a list of investments comprising the marketable securities account balance. A working paper schedule may also show the changes in one or more related account balances during the period covered by the financial report, as illustrated in Figure 6.7. In some cases, the auditor uses schedules prepared by the entity, which is indicated by the letters 'PBC' for 'prepared by client'. Such schedules need to be checked against the accounting records to ensure their accuracy. Audit work performed is indicated by the tick marks and related explanations on the working paper, as illustrated in Figure 6.7.

FIGURE 6.7 *Notes receivable and interest working paper*

Omni Co. Limited
Notes receivable and interest
31 December 20X1

W/P ref. C–4
Prepared by: ________ Date: _____
Reviewed by: ________ Date: _____

Accts 160, 161, 450

				Notes receivable					Interest			
Maker	**Made**	**Date due**	**Interest rate (%)**	**Face amount**	**Balance 31.12.X0**	**Debits**	**Credits**	**Balance 31.12.X1**	**Accrued 31.12.X0**	**Earned 20X1**	**Collected 20X1**	**Accrued 31.12.X1**
Coffman inc.	1/7/X0	30/6/X1	10	25 000	25 000		25 000 C	—	1250 ✗	1250 ϕ	2500 C	—
Morrison Bros.	1/11/X0	31/10/X1	10	30 000	30 000		30 000 C	—	500 ✗	2500 ϕ	3000 C	—
Shirley and Son	1/4/X1	31/3/X2	12	40 000 ✓	—	40 000 ⋌		40 000	—	3600 ϕ	—	3600
Warner Corp.	1/10/X1	30/9/X3	12	20 000 ✓	—	20 000 ⋌		20 000	—	600 ϕ	—	600
					55 000 ✗ F	60 000 F	55 000 F	60 000 ^ FF	1750 ✗ F	7950 F	5500 F	4200 ^ FF

✗ Agreed to 31.12.X0 working papers.
C Traced collections to cash receipts and deposit slips.
ϕ Verified computations.
✓ Examined note during cash count.
⋌ Confirmed with maker — no exceptions.
^ Traced to ledger balance.
F Footed.
FF Footed and cross-footed.

Schedules are of particular importance where evidence is obtained from the examination of a sample. The schedule should indicate the basis of selection and the specific items selected for sampling, enabling performance of the audit to be replicated if any query arises. It is also useful if documents and records sampled by the auditor are also marked to establish the proper conduct of the audit in the event of any inquiry.

Audit memoranda and corroborating information

Audit memoranda refer to written data in narrative form prepared by the auditor. Memoranda may include comments on the performance of auditing procedures and conclusions reached from the auditing work performed. Documentation of corroborating information includes extracts of minutes of the board of directors meetings, confirmation responses, written representations from management and outside experts, and copies of important contracts.

Proposed adjusting and reclassifying entries

It is important to distinguish between adjusting entries and reclassifying entries. Audit adjusting entries are corrections of entity errors of omission or misapplication of Accounting Standards. Thus, adjusting entries ultimately deemed to be material (individually or in the aggregate) are expected to be recorded by the entity. In contrast, reclassifying entries pertain to the proper financial report presentation of correct account balances. Assume, for example, that the accounts receivable balance includes some customer accounts with credit balances pertaining to customer advances. Although it is not necessary for the entity to record the reclassifying entry on its books, for reporting purposes an entry should be made on the working trial balance in which accounts receivable is debited to offset the customer advances and a liability account is credited. This is illustrated in Figure 6.5 (page 232) and will result in the reclassification being reflected in the financial report. As with adjusting entries, only reclassifications that have a material effect need be made.

In the working papers, each entry should be shown on (1) the schedule or analysis of the account, (2) the lead schedules, if any, (3) the summary of proposed adjusting or reclassifying entries and (4) the working trial balance. This is illustrated in Figure 6.6 (page 233).

The summaries of adjusting and reclassifying entries are initially designated as 'proposed' entries because (1) the auditor's final judgment as to which entries must be made may not occur until the end of the audit and (2) the entity must approve them. The disposition of each proposed entry should ultimately be recorded on the working papers. If the entity declines to make adjusting or reclassifying entries that the auditor feels are necessary, then the auditor's report must be appropriately modified.

Audit program

An audit program is a listing of the auditing procedures to be performed. Audit programs are used for the evaluation of internal controls and for substantive procedures. We include examples of these audit programs throughout this textbook, particularly in Chapters 10–13.

Preparing working papers

9 LEARNING OBJECTIVE

Apply the essential techniques of good working paper preparation.

A number of basic techniques are used widely in preparing a working paper. These pertain to the mechanics of working paper preparation and include the following essential points.

Heading

Each working paper should contain the name of the entity, a descriptive title identifying the content of the working paper (such as 'Bank Reconciliation — National Bank'), and the balance sheet date or the period covered by the audit.

Index numbers

Each working paper is given an index or reference number — such as A–1, B–2 and so on — for identification purposes. Indexing facilitates the organisation and review of working papers. Most audit firms have standardised referencing systems so the organisation of audit files is consistent throughout the firm.

Cross-referencing

Data on a working paper that are taken from another working paper or that are carried forward to another working paper should be cross-referenced with the index numbers of those working papers, as illustrated in Figure 6.6 (page 233).

Evidence

The paper should document the evidence examined and the audit procedures applied to that evidence. A common practice is the use of tick marks (symbols such as check marks) to identify the different procedures applied. A legend on the working paper should explain the nature and extent of the work represented by each tick mark, or provide the additional information applicable to the items marked. Most firms use standardised tick marks to indicate common procedures such as adding columns and posting totals to ledgers.

Where the evidence is in the form of documents and records, it is usual to leave a trail of tick marks on those documents and records. This enables the work of the auditor to be traced back to the evidence if necessary.

Conclusion

The results of audit procedures should be summarised, indicating whether they confirm the particular assertion being tested.

Signature and dates

Upon completing their respective tasks, both the preparer and reviewer of a working paper should initial and date it. This establishes responsibility for the work performed and the review.

The partial working papers in Figure 6.6 (page 233) do not show all of these essential elements because that figure was designed primarily to illustrate indexing and cross-referencing. Figure 6.7 (page 234), however, illustrates all the above elements.

Reviewing working papers

There are several levels in the review of working papers within an audit practice. The first-level review is made by the preparer's supervisor, such as a manager. This review occurs when the work on a specific segment of the audit has been completed. The reviewer is primarily interested in the work done, the evidence obtained, the judgement exercised and the conclusions reached by the preparer of the working paper.

The working papers undergo other reviews when the audit has been completed. We will explain these reviews in Chapter 14.

Ownership and custody of working papers

The property rights of working papers rest with the auditor if he or she is acting as an independent 'contractor'. This was established in *Chantrey Martin & Co. v. Martin* (1953) 3 WLR 459. Working papers prepared at the auditor's request by the entity's staff also belong to the auditor. In certain circumstances an auditor may be acting as an agent for other auditors. In the absence of any agreement to the contrary, the working papers belong to the principal auditors. In non-audit situations (for example, when the auditor is making representations on behalf of the client to the Australian Taxation Office), the auditor owns the audit working papers but not the working papers relating to the representations to the Taxation Office.

The auditor's ownership rights, however, are subject to constraints imposed by the auditor's own professional standards. The fundamental principles of professional conduct of the accounting bodies (as outlined in CPC B5) stipulate that:

> . . . members must respect the confidentiality of information acquired in the course of their work and should not disclose any such information to a third party without specific authority or unless there is a legal or professional duty to disclose it.

Similarly, AUS 208.13 states:

> The auditor should adopt appropriate procedures for:
> (a) maintaining the confidentiality and safe custody of the working papers; and
> (b) retaining the working papers for a period sufficient to meet the needs of the practice and in accordance with legal and professional requirements of record retention.

A successor auditor may have access to the working papers of the predecessor auditor, with client approval. Working papers may also be made available during a practice review.

Physical custody of the working papers rests with the auditor, and he or she is responsible for their safekeeping. Working papers included in the permanent file are retained indefinitely; current working papers should be retained for as long as they are useful to the auditor in servicing an entity or needed to satisfy legal or professional requirements for record retention.

LEARNING CHECK

6.7 Two alternative audit strategies are (1) the predominantly substantive approach and (2) the lower assessed level of control risk approach. The auditor determines the strategy separately for each assertion for each major account balance.

6.8 The decision to adopt the lower assessed level of control risk approach depends on the desirability in terms of audit efficiency and on the likelihood of being able to assess control risk as being less than high.

6.9 Working papers contain the evidence that the auditor collects to assist in performing the audit and reviewing the work of assistants, to use as a guide to subsequent audits, and to show that the audit was carried out in accordance with Auditing Standards.

6.10 Working paper files are classified into permanent or current files. The permanent file contains information of a continuing nature. The current file contains information relevant to the current period's audit.

SUMMARY

Prior to accepting an audit engagement, the auditor should ascertain that it could be completed in accordance with all applicable professional standards, including Auditing Standards and professional ethics. Important steps in accepting the engagement include evaluating the integrity of management, identifying any special circumstances and unusual risks, assessing competence, evaluating independence, determining that the engagement can be completed with due care, and issuing an engagement letter.

Proper planning is crucial in performing an efficient, effective audit. Planning steps include obtaining an understanding of the entity and the industry, performing analytical procedures, making preliminary judgements about materiality levels, considering audit risks, obtaining an understanding of the entity's internal control structure, and developing preliminary audit strategies for significant assertions. In the next chapter we will explain in more detail the procedures to be followed in obtaining the understanding of the internal control structure and in assessing control risk. In Chapter 9 we will explain the design of substantive procedures and the development of an audit program setting out the nature, timing and extent of audit procedures required to implement the audit plan.

The procedures performed, the evidence obtained and the auditor's evaluation of that evidence should be fully documented in working papers, which should provide the support for the auditor's report and evidence of the auditor's compliance with Auditing Standards.

KEY TERMS

Analytical procedures, p. 221
Articles of association, p. 222
Audit manager, p. 216
Audit planning, p. 220
Audit team, p. 216
Current file, p. 231
Engagement letter, p. 218
Experts, p. 216
Interim audit, p. 221
Lead schedule, p. 233
Lower assessed level of control risk approach, p. 227
Memorandum of association, p. 222
Minutes of meetings, p. 223
Partner, p. 216
Permanent file, p. 231
Phases of an audit, p. 212
Predecessor auditor, p. 214
Predominantly substantive approach, p. 226
Related party transactions, p. 224
Successor auditor, p. 214
Time budget, p. 217
Working papers, p. 230

FURTHER READING

CPA Australia and the Institute of Chartered Accountants in Australia, Professional Statement F3 — Changes in Professional Appointments, *Joint Code of Professional Conduct.*

Callahan, Patrick S., Jaenicke, Henry R. & Neebes, Donald L., 'SASs Nos 56 and 57: Increasing Audit Effectiveness', *Journal of Accountancy* (October 1988), pp. 56–68.

Flesher, D. L. & de Magalhaes, R., 'Electronic Workpapers', *Internal Auditor* (August 1995), pp. 38–43.

Fraser, I. A. M., Hatherley, D. J. & Lim, K. Z., 'An Empirical Investigation of the Use of Analytical Review by External Auditors', *British Accounting Review* (March 1997), pp. 35–48.

Harper, Robert M., Strawser, Jerry R. & Twang, Kwei, 'Establishing Investigation Thresholds for Preliminary Analytical Procedures', *Auditing: A Journal of Practice & Theory* (Fall 1990), pp. 115–33.

Holder, W. W., 'Analytical Review Procedures in Planning the Audit: An Application Study', *Auditing: A Journal of Practice & Theory* (Spring 1983), pp. 100–07.

Hull, Rita P. & Mitchem, Cheryl, 'Practitioners' Views on Communications between Predecessor and Successor Auditors and Accountants', *Accounting Horizons* (June 1987), pp. 61–9.

Mcallister, John P. & Dirsmith, Mark W., 'How the Client's Business Environment Affects the Audit', *Journal of Accountancy* (February 1982), pp. 68–74.

Trotman, K., *Analytical Review, Audit Monograph 1*, Australian Accounting Research Foundation, 1990.

Perkins, Andrew, 'Put it in Writing', *Accountancy (International Edition)* (April 1996), p. 68.

Van Son, W. Peter, Guy, Dan M. & Betts, J. Frank, 'Engagement Letters: What Practice Shows', *Journal of Accountancy* (June 1982), pp. 72–80.

Van Son, W. Peter & Winters, Alan J., 'The Pre-Audit Conference: A Communication Tool', *Journal of Accountancy* (November 1982), pp. 86–93.

Wright, Arnold & Ashton, Robert H., 'Identifying Audit Adjustments with Attention-Directing Procedures', *Accounting Review* (October 1989), pp. 710–28.

APPENDIX 6A

Key financial ratios used in analytical procedures

Users of general purpose financial reports can obtain valuable insights into a company's financial condition and performance through analysis of key financial ratios. The same analysis performed by auditors provides them with a better understanding of the entity.

Given that auditors already have some knowledge of the entity from other planning procedures, analytical procedures can also play a different role in the audit. Using prior knowledge, auditors can develop expectations as to whether current year ratios are expected to differ from those in prior years or from industry norms. When comparisons reveal unexpected fluctuations, or when expected fluctuations do not occur, the auditor will generally want to investigate whether the aberration is due to the misstatement of one or more variables used in calculating the ratio.

In this appendix we explain the calculation of ten common ratios. In addition, we comment on the purpose of each ratio and how it is interpreted. The comments on interpretation are general in nature and should be tailored according to a particular entity's circumstances, such as its recent experience and the industry in which it operates.

RATIO	CALCULATION	PURPOSE AND INTERPRETATION
Solvency		
Quick ratio	$\frac{\text{Cash + Accounts receivable + Current asset investments}}{\text{Current liabilities}}$	To reveal protection afforded by cash or near-cash assets to short-term creditors — the larger the ratio, the greater the liquidity
Current ratio	$\frac{\text{Total current assets}}{\text{Total current liabilities}}$	To measure the degree to which current liabilities are covered by current assets — the higher the ratio, the greater the assurance that current liabilities can be paid in a timely manner
Debt to equity	$\frac{\text{Total liabilities}}{\text{Shareholders equity}}$	To measure the extent to which a company is using its debt financing capacity. In general, this ratio should not exceed 100 per cent because in such cases creditors will have more at stake than owners will.
Times interest earned	$\frac{\text{Operating profit before interest and tax}}{\text{Interest expense}}$	To measure the number of times a company can meet its fixed interest charges with earnings
Efficiency		
Accounts receivable turnover	$\frac{\text{Sales}}{\text{Accounts receivable}}$	To measure the number of times receivables are collected during the period. When used in analytical procedures, some auditors prefer to use the ending receivables balance rather than average receivables, which would make a misstatement more difficult to detect. A variation, *the collection period*, is found by dividing the turnover ratio by 365. This ratio may be useful in evaluating the adequacy of the provision for doubtful debts.

(continued)

RATIO	CALCULATION	PURPOSE AND INTERPRETATION
Inventory turnover	$\frac{\text{Cost of sales}}{\text{Inventory}}$	To indicate how rapidly inventory turns over. When using this calculation in analytical procedures, some auditors prefer to use the ending inventory balance rather than average inventories, which would make a misstatement more difficult to detect. Although the ratio varies widely among industries, low values may indicate excessively high inventories and slow-moving items; conversely, extremely high values may reflect insufficient merchandise to meet customer demand, resulting in lost sales.
Asset turnover	$\frac{\text{Sales}}{\text{Total assets}}$	To measure the efficiency with which a company uses its assets to generate sales. For the reasons noted above, some auditors prefer using ending rather than average assets to calculate this ratio.
Profitability		
Return on sales	$\frac{\text{Operating profit}}{\text{Sales}}$	To reveal profits earned per dollar of sales. This ratio indicates ability to earn satisfactory profits for owners, as well as the entity's ability to withstand adverse conditions such as falling prices, rising costs and declining sales.
Return on assets	$\frac{\text{Operating profit}}{\text{Total assets}}$	To indicate profitability based on total assets available. Companies efficiently using assets will have a high ratio; less efficient companies will have a low ratio
Return on shareholders' equity	$\frac{\text{Operating profit after tax}}{\text{Ordinary shareholders equity}}$	To reveal management's ability to earn an adequate return on capital invested by owners. Generally, a minimum of 10 per cent is considered desirable to provide funds for dividends and growth.

Review questions

6.1 Explain the procedures to follow in evaluating a prospective audit client.

6.2 Identify three matters about which the proposed auditor should direct inquiries to the previous auditor.

6.3 Identify applicable ethical considerations in accepting a new audit engagement.

6.4 Why is it important for an auditor to evaluate competence in deciding whether to accept a new client?

6.5 State the matters to be included in an audit engagement letter.

6.6 When may it be necessary to reissue the audit engagement letter?

6.7 Discuss the steps involved in the audit planning process.

6.8 What is the purpose of touring operating facilities and offices?

6.9 How can analytical procedures assist the auditor in audit planning?

6.10 Define the term 'working papers' and indicate their principal function in auditing.

Discussion questions

6.1 Discuss the suggestion that if all auditors reject, as clients, entities identified as being too risky, those entities most in need of an audit will be unable to secure the services of an auditor. As professionals, should auditors be required to provide their services to any entity requiring an audit?

6.2 Identify factors that need to be considered in evaluating the auditor's ability to service a client.

6.3 Discuss the contention that the engagement letter understates the auditor's legal responsibilities so as to discourage litigation.

6.4 Would you agree with the argument that adoption of the lower assessed level of control risk audit strategy is driven by competitive pressures on auditors seeking cost savings, and that it exposes auditors to excessive risks of audit failure?

6.5 Should the detailed audit program be drafted for both tests of control and substantive procedures on completion of the planning phase? Or, should the program of substantive procedures be drawn up only after control risk has been assessed?

6.6 In the planning phase auditors use analytical procedures in much the same way as investors do; however, the auditor knows the financial position and performance that the analysis should show as a substantive procedure, and uses analytical procedures to detect possible misstatements in the financial report. Explain.

6.7 Discuss the argument that time budgets put pressure on audit staff members to give priority to completing the audit within the budget at the expense of audit quality.

6.8 Discuss the role of working papers and tick marks on entity records in providing an evidence 'trail' of the proper performance of the audit.

6.9 Discuss the respective merits of (1) using standardised documentation (such as pre-printed audit programs) and (2) tailoring all documentation for each separate audit engagement.

6.10 Explain why it may be important for the audit firm to retain custody of audit working papers.

Professional application questions

★ BASIC
★★ MODERATE
★★★ CHALLENGING

6.1 (Working papers) ★

The senior partner has asked you to explain the contents and importance of audit working papers to unqualified audit staff who have recently joined your audit firm. It has been explained that audit working papers are divided into the permanent audit file and the current audit file.

Your audit firm has a standardised method of organising and referencing working papers within each audit file.

(*continued*)

Required

(a) List and briefly describe the contents of the permanent audit file and the current audit file.

(b) Suggest a system for referencing the different sections of the audit working papers and explain why it is important for the audit firm to use a standard referencing system.

(c) Describe three types of check list (excluding audit programs) that are commonly included in the audit working papers.

(d) Describe why auditors use working papers to record their work. Explain whether it is necessary for auditors to record all their audit work.

(from ACCA Audit Framework — Paper 6(U), June 1998)

6.2 (Accepting the audit engagement) ★★

The audit partner of an accounting firm has just advised you that he has been approached to accept appointment as the auditor for One Armed Limited, a manufacturer of gaming machines. One Armed was named in a recent anti-corruption inquiry as having offered incentives to state government members to support a proposed bill that would allow an increased number of gaming machines in licensed premises. No charges have yet been laid against One Armed or any of its employees. The audit partner explains to you that One Armed's auditors were reappointed for the current financial year at the annual general meeting held two months ago. However, One Armed's managing director is unhappy with the existing auditing firm because the audit partner assigned to One Armed has been changed.

Required

(a) The audit partner is unsure whether to accept the appointment and has asked you to outline any ethical or other factors he should consider in his decision.

(b) Explain what information he should obtain from the previous auditor.

(Professional Year Programme of the ICAA — 1997, Advanced Audit Module — adapted)

6.3 (Planning the audit) ★★

Your client is Gigabight Limited, a large family-owned company which imports and sells computer hardware products. You are planning the 30 June 20X1 audit and have obtained the following information from your inquiries of management.

1. In January 20X1, Gigabight applied for and was granted a new loan. The submission made to the bank stated that:
   - the current ratio was 0.90;
   - gross profit was up by 25 per cent compared with that at the same time last year;
   - the debt-to-equity ratio was 0.40.
2. The bank agreed to the new loan but did enter into a loan covenant with Gigabight. The covenant required that the company should not breach certain ratios, and placed certain restrictions on dividends.

From audits you have conducted in previous years, you are suspicious about the validity of the ratios discussed in the submission. You hear from one of Gigabight's accounting staff that the figures had been 'gently massaged' to obtain the required ratios.

Required

Discuss (referring to specific areas of the audit) the implications of this information on your planning of the audit.

6.4 (Planning) ★★

Your firm has been the auditor of Bridgford Products, a listed company, for a number of years. The engagement partner has asked you to describe the matters you would consider when planning the audit for the year ending 31 January 20X2.

During a recent visit to the company you obtain the following information.

1. The management accounts for the ten months to 30 November of the previous year show sales of $130 million and profit before tax of $4 million. Assume that sales and profits accrue evenly throughout the year. In the year ended 31 January Bridgford Products had sales of $110 million and profit before tax of $8 million.
2. The company installed a new computerised inventory control system which has operated from 1 June 20X1. Given that the inventory control system records inventory movements and current inventory quantities, the company is proposing:
   - to use the inventory quantities on the computer to value the inventory at the year end; and
   - not to carry out an inventory count at the year end.
3. You are aware there have been reliability problems with the company's products, which have resulted in customers making legal claims against the company and refusing to pay for the products.
4. The sales increase in the ten months to 30 November 20X1 was achieved by attracting new customers and offering extended credit. The new credit arrangements allow customers three months credit before their debt becomes overdue, rather than the one-month credit period previously allowed. As a result of this change, the receivables age has increased from 1.6 months to 4.1 months.
5. The chief financial officer and purchasing manager were dismissed on 15 August 20X1. A replacement purchasing manager has been appointed, but a new chief financial officer is not expected to be appointed before the year end of 31 January 20X2. The chief accountant will be responsible for preparing the financial statements for audit.

Required

(a) Describe why it is important that auditors should plan their audit work.

(b) Describe the matters you will consider in planning the audit and the further action you will take concerning each of the five matters listed above.

(ACCA Audit Framework — Paper 6(U), December 1998 — adapted)

6.5 (Reliance on experts) ★★

Your client, FNP Limited, engaged the services of Z Limited, a firm of real estate valuers, to perform a valuation of all real estate held by FNP. This revaluation led to property values on the balance sheet being significantly increased, resulting in a material increase in net asset backing per share.

(*continued*)

Required

(a) Describe the audit procedures that would be required with respect to the valuations performed by Z.

(b) Explain whether the procedures identified in (a) would change if the valuations had been performed in house.

(c) Assuming that you are dissatisfied with the results of procedures performed, describe alternative procedures that could be performed.

(Professional Year Programme of the ICAA — 1999, Advanced Audit Module — adapted)

6.6 (Planning the audit, analytical review) ★★

You are the auditor of Hills Wholesale Limited and you are auditing the financial statements for the year ended 31 June 20X2. You have carried out an analytical review on the profit and loss account and are concerned that there has been a significant fall in the gross profit margin, as shown by the following statement. (20X2 figures are from the draft accounts and figures for the previous year, 20X1, are from the audited accounts.)

Year ended 30 June	20X2 $'000	20X1 $'000
Sales	2514	3126
Opening stock	441	426
Purchases	2067	2214
	2508	2640
Closing stock	412	441
Cost of goods sold	2096	2199
Gross profit	418	927
Gross profit %	16.6%	29.7%

The company does not maintain book stock records, and stock quantities were found from a physical stocktake at 30 June 20X2. The company prepares only annual accounts. Assume that the accounts for the year ended 30 June 20X1 are correct.

Required

Discuss the implications for specific aspects of your audit plan of the fall in gross profit margin noted in your analytical review.

(ACCA Audit Framework — Paper 6, December 1994 — adapted)

6.7 (Planning the audit) ★★★

Alice is an audit senior for the accounting firm of Shark and Partners. In Alice's planning of the audit of Shrimp Limited for the year ended 30 June 20X2, she asked to review the minutes of board of directors meetings for the year to date. From her review, she noted the following information.

Shark and Partners **Shrimp Limited** **Planning**	P–7 Prepared by: Alice Date: 28/5/X2

Notes from board of directors meetings for year to May 20X1:

16/8/X1	The board agreed to revalue land and buildings in its financial report in accordance with a property valuation recently undertaken at the company's request. The effect would be to increase their value by 50 per cent.
17/10/X1	The company took over one of its major customers during the year. This was not expected to alter its trading relationship.
15/12/X1	It was agreed that a new 'bonus scheme' would be implemented. This scheme would award directors a bonus of a percentage of the profits for this year if they could exceed last year's profit figure by 20 per cent.
16/2/X2	It was agreed that construction should begin on a new factory for processing tuna. A construction contract was approved and it was expected the work on the new factory would commence before the end of March, at least three months before the end of the financial year.
17/5/X2	The board agreed to make a large loan to one of the company's subsidiaries in Fiji one month before the end of the financial year. The loan did not have any security and no interest was charged.

Required

Discuss the effect that each of the above five items in the minutes of the board of directors meeting will have on specific aspects of the audit plan.

Case studies

6.1 (Working papers) ★★★

You are the audit partner of the accounting firm Cooper, Young and Partners. You are reviewing the work of an audit senior, Emily Tan, on your client Browns Limited. You find the following working paper in relation to testing of sales invoices.

(*continued*)

Cooper, Young and Partners **Browns Limited** **Sales Testing**	R–7 Prepared by: ET Date 3/8/X2

Objective

To ensure that a sales invoice is properly raised for all orders processed

Sample

Selected the thirty sales orders for the month of June.

Work done

1. Traced orders selected to dispatch docket.
2. Traced to invoice prepared.
3. Checked that all quantities match.
4. Ensured that prices were correctly calculated and were from an approved price list.

Matters arising

1. Two dispatch dockets did not result in the production of an invoice — accept as not material. ET
2. There were a number of prices that were not as per the price list. Discussed with the accounts clerk who said that they were discounts that were negotiated with the customers to ensure their continued business — accept explanation as reasonable. ET
3. The quantity for all orders delivered did not always match the quantity on the invoice. Staff in the delivery area said that this was due to companies receiving extra stock to replace damaged stock that had been sent — accept. ET

Conclusion

From the work performed, management's assertions in relation to sales have been validated.

Required

Review the above working paper (*Note*: It is the only documentation on file that relates to this test performed by Emily Tan.) Comment on the adequacy of the working paper, the level of documentation, the matters arising and the conclusion reached.

6.2 (Analytical procedures) ★★★

You are the audit manager of a medium-sized firm and have just received a package from Ms P, the financial controller of OMF Limited, a toy manufacturer. This is your firm's first year as auditor of OMF. The information was prepared for a board meeting and Ms P felt it might be useful to you in preparation of the forthcoming audit for the year ended 31 December 20X3.

During a brief telephone call with Ms P you have also made the following notes.

1. One of the conditions of the long-term loan is that the company is not to exceed a debt-to-equity ratio of 2:1 at any time. The loan is reviewed each year on 31 December.
2. Provision against inventory obsolescence is provided for at a flat rate of 10 per cent. The amount provided in prior years was 20 per cent. Ms P said that the company believes it has been overly conservative in prior years and 5 per cent is a more realistic level, given the nature of its products.
3. The long-term loan receivable is from a company that is involved in the development and production of computer software, and that is owned by one of the directors.

Balance sheet	20X3 $'000	20X2 $'000	20X1 $'000
Current assets			
Cash	1 586	1 743	830
Inventory	16 498	11 731	7 197
Trade debtors	12 134	10 700	9 323
Total current assets	30 218	24 174	17 350
Non-current assets			
Property, plant and equipment	14 606	12 840	9 572
Long-term loan receivable	5 200	3600	3 300
Total non-current assets	19 806	16 440	12 872
Total assets	50 024	40 614	30 222
Current liabilities			
Trade payables	9 012	6 288	2 021
Provisions	4 875	3 821	4 577
Total current liabilities	13 887	10 109	6 598
Non-current liabilities			
Long-term loan payable	20 000	16 000	12 000
Total liabilities	33 887	26 109	18 598
Net assets	16 137	14 505	11 624
Shareholders' equity			
Share capital	2 000	2 000	2 000
Retained earnings	14 137	12 505	9 624
Total shareholders' equity	16 137	14 505	11 624
Statement of profit and loss			
Sales	72 945	74 927	89 735
Cost of goods sold	51 840	51 765	63 066
Gross profit	21 105	23 162	26 669
Depreciation	5 595	4 332	2 796
Inventory obsolescence	1 650	2 346	1 439
Marketing expense	1 345	1 980	2 548
Administration expense	8 925	8 727	11 516
Interest expense	1 040	1 275	1 140
Total expenses	18 555	17 660	19 439
Net profit	2 550	4 502	7 230
Tax expense	918	1 621	2 386
Net profit after tax	1 632	2 881	4 844

Required

(a) Suggest possible sources of information that would help you gather sufficient knowledge of the business to perform the audit of OMF.

(b) Perform preliminary analytical procedures using the information provided. Identify the key areas that would require special attention during the audit of the 31 December 20X3 financial report.

(c) Outline ways in which the analytical procedures performed could be extended using the information collected in (a).

(d) Suggest ways of using analytical procedures as a substantive test during the audit of OMF.

(Professional Year Programme of the ICAA — 1999, Advanced Audit Module — adapted)

chapter 7

Internal control and control risk assessment

Overview

LEARNING OBJECTIVES

After studying this chapter, you should be able to:

1. appreciate the importance of internal control to an entity and to its independent auditors
2. describe the components of the internal control structure
3. state the inherent limitations of the internal control structure
4. indicate the procedures to obtain and document an understanding of the internal control structure
5. explain the purpose of making a preliminary assessment of control risk
6. describe the approach to evaluating the design effectiveness of control procedures
7. state the purpose of tests of control and the nature of such tests
8. describe how the work of internal auditing may be used in tests of control
9. explain the process of assessing control risk and documenting the conclusion.

Professional statements

AUSTRALIAN		INTERNATIONAL	
AUS 402	Risk Assessments and Internal Controls	ISA 400	Risk Assessments and Internal Control
AUS 604	Considering the Work of Internal Auditing	ISA 610	Considering the Work of Internal Auditing
AUS 710	Communication to Management on Matters Arising from an Audit	ISA 1007	Communications with Management

One of the most important tasks in planning an audit engagement is obtaining an understanding of the entity's internal control structure. This structure consists of:

- the control environment;
- the information system;
- control activities.

The understanding must be at least sufficient to enable the auditor, firstly, to design procedures for obtaining evidence applicable to the separate assertions described in Chapter 5 and, secondly, to make a preliminary assessment as to the probable effectiveness of controls. If the control structure appears to reduce the likelihood of errors occurring or remaining undetected, then the auditor could consider adopting the lower assessed level of control risk audit strategy described in Chapter 6. If this strategy is adopted, then it must be supported by more extensive tests of control.

In this chapter we will describe the nature of an entity's **internal control structure** and explain the auditor's responsibility for obtaining an understanding of that structure. We will then describe how the auditor tests the design effectiveness of the internal control structure to form a preliminary assessment of the level of control risk. Where that preliminary assessment is other than high, the auditor plans and performs further tests of control to support (or otherwise) that preliminary assessment, as we will explain later in the chapter.

INTERNAL CONTROL

We will begin by explaining the importance of internal control within an entity, and then describe the nature of an entity's information system and the control activities within that system. These procedures, together with the control environment, make up the internal control structure.

LEARNING OBJECTIVE 1

Appreciate the importance of internal control to an entity and to its independent auditors.

The importance of internal control

The importance of internal control has been recognised in the professional literature for half a century. As early as 1947 a US publication entitled *Internal Controls* cited the following factors as contributing to the expanding recognition of the significance of internal control:

- The scope and size of the business entity has become so complex and widespread that management must rely on numerous reports and analyses to effectively control operations.
- The checks and reviews inherent in a good system of internal control afford protection against human weaknesses and reduce the possibility that errors or irregularities will occur.
- It is impracticable for auditors to audit most companies within economic fee limitations without relying on the client's system of internal control.

The incidence of creative and even fraudulent accounting in the 1980s by large companies has led to internal control being elevated from a private concern of management and auditors to a matter of public interest. In Australia, the Institute of Chartered Accountants in Australia (ICAA) and CPA Australia published a report in 1993 entitled *A Research Study on Financial Reporting and Auditing — Bridging the Expectation Gap*, recommending that management be required to report publicly on the adequacy of its internal control.

The United States has taken the lead in this matter. In 1987, the National Commission on Fraudulent Financial Reporting (the Treadway Commission) re-emphasised the importance of internal control in reducing the incidence of fraudulent financial reporting. The Commission's final report included the following recommendation:

> All public companies should maintain internal controls that will provide reasonable assurance that fraudulent financial reporting will be prevented or subject to early detection.

In implementing this recommendation, the Committee of Sponsoring Organisations (COSO) of the Treadway Commission issued a report in 1992 entitled *Internal Control — Integrated Framework*. According to COSO, the two principal purposes of its efforts were to:

- establish a common definition of internal control that served the needs of different parties;
- provide a standard against which businesses and other entities could assess their control systems and determine how to improve them.

The COSO report defines **internal control** as:

> ... a process, effected by an entity's board of directors, management and other personnel, designed to provide reasonable assurance regarding the achievement of objectives in the following categories:
> - reliability of financial reporting;
> - compliance with applicable laws and regulations;
> - effectiveness and efficiency of operations.

The COSO report especially emphasises the following fundamental concepts that are embodied in the foregoing definition:

- Internal control is a *process*. It is a means to an end, not an end in itself. It consists of a series of actions that are pervasive and integrated with, not added onto, an entity's infrastructure.
- Internal control is effected by *people*. It is not achieved merely by having policy manuals and forms, but by the actions and attitudes of people at every level of an organisation, including the board of directors and management.
- Internal control can be expected to provide only *reasonable assurance*, not absolute assurance, for an entity's management and board. This is because limitations are inherent in all internal control systems and because the entity must consider the relative costs and benefits of establishing controls.
- Internal control is geared to the achievement of *objectives* in the overlapping categories of financial reporting, compliance and operations.

Internal controls relevant to an audit

In this chapter we are primarily concerned with controls that have the objective of achieving reliable financial reporting. Other objectives and related controls may also be relevant if they pertain to data that the auditor uses in applying audit procedures, such as:

- non-financial data used in analytical procedures — for example, the number of employees, the volume of goods manufactured, and other production and marketing statistics;
- financial data developed for internal purposes — for example, budgets and performance data that the auditor uses to obtain independent evidence about amounts in the financial report.

As explained in Chapter 2, auditors have certain responsibilities for detecting errors and irregularities (including management and employee fraud) and particular illegal acts. Thus, any entity objectives and controls related to these matters are also relevant to the auditor. Where non-compliance could have a direct and material effect on the financial report, controls over 'compliance with applicable laws and regulations' are particularly relevant.

Operational effectiveness and efficiency controls that are designed to reduce the risk of bad operating decisions — such as selling a product at too low a price or failing to order replacement inventory in time — are not usually considered relevant to a financial report audit. Exceptions are controls that relate to the safeguarding of assets against unauthorised acquisition, use and disposition when these controls help to ensure that the entity's financial report properly reflects related losses (such as from theft).

LEARNING OBJECTIVE 2

Describe the components of the internal control structure.

Internal control structure

The elements of the internal control structure identified by AUS 402 (ISA 400), Risk Assessments and Internal Controls are:

- the **information system**;
- **control procedures**;
- the **control environment**.

(In ISA 400 the internal control structure is referred to as 'accounting and internal control systems' and the information system is referred to as the 'accounting system'.)

Information system

Before commencing an audit on an entity's financial report, the auditor must have a thorough understanding of its information system, as stated in AUS 402:

> The auditor should obtain an understanding of the internal control structure sufficient to plan the audit and develop an effective audit approach.

AUS 402 defines the information system as:

> ... the methods and records established to identify, assemble, analyse, calculate, classify, record and report transactions and other events that affect an entity, and to maintain accountability for assets, liabilities, revenues and expenditures.

It is not only as auditors, however, that accountants need to have an understanding of information systems. As accountants, their prime function is to establish and maintain such a system to ensure that the financial reports they produce, whether for management or external parties, are accurate and reliable.

The focus of the information system is on transactions. **Transactions** consist of exchanges of assets and services between an entity and outside parties, and the transfer or use of assets and services within an entity. A major focus of controls in the information system is to ensure that transactions are initiated and processed in a way that prevents misstatements in financial report assertions. An effective information system should:

- identify and record *only the valid* transactions of the entity that occurred in the current period;
- identify and record *all* valid transactions of the entity that occurred in the current period;
- ensure that recorded assets and liabilities are the result of transactions that produced rights to, or obligations for, those items;
- measure the value of transactions in a way that allows their proper monetary value in the financial report to be recorded;
- capture sufficient detail of transactions to allow their proper classification and disclosure in the financial report.

For the first two requirements for an effective information system, the time period in which transactions occurred must be determined so as to allow them to be recorded in the proper accounting period — that is, a proper cut-off must be established.

An entity's information system should provide a complete **audit trail** for each transaction. An audit trail is a chain of evidence provided by coding, cross-references and documentation that connects account balances and other summary results with original transaction data. Audit trails are essential to both management and auditors; for example, management uses the trail in responding to inquiries from customers or suppliers concerning account balances and auditors use the trail in vouching and tracing transactions. In computer information systems the audit trail may exist in electronic format only and sometimes may be deleted once the transaction has been verified (for example, when the personal identification number (PIN) is read and verified at the initiation of a credit or debit card transaction). Special audit techniques are required to verify the audit trail, such as the use of embedded audit facilities that trace the operation of controls electronically.

Control procedures

Control procedures are detailed procedures that management establishes to ensure, as far as possible, that specific entity objectives will be achieved. Control procedures that are relevant to a financial report audit may be categorised in many different ways, including as follows:

- information processing controls;
  - — general controls;
  - — application controls;
- segregation of duties;
- physical controls;
- performance reviews.

We will explain these categories in the following sections.

Information processing controls

Of particular relevance to an audit are **information processing controls** that address risks related to the authorisation, completeness and accuracy of transactions. Most entities, regardless of size, now use computers for information processing in general and for accounting information in particular. In such cases, information processing controls are often further categorised as **general controls** and **application controls**.

General controls

General controls are those controls that apply to computer information systems (CIS) as a whole and include controls related to such matters as data centre organisation, hardware and systems software acquisition and maintenance, and backup and recovery procedures. Figure 7.3 on pages 263–4 lists the more important general controls.

Application controls

Application controls are those controls that apply to the processing of specific types of transaction, such as invoicing customers, paying suppliers and preparing payroll. Whether they are in a computerised or a manual environment, application controls may be further classified into the following categories:

- proper authorisation;
- documents and records;
- independent checks.

Proper authorisation procedures ensure that transactions are authorised by personnel acting within the scope of their authority. Authorisations may be general or specific. General authorisation relates to the general conditions under which transactions are authorised, such as standard price lists for products and credit policies for charge sales. Specific authorisation is granted on a case-by-case basis and may apply in both non-routine transactions (such as major capital expenditures) and routine transactions that exceed the limits provided by the general authorisation (such as requisitioning goods or services other than replacement of inventory).

Authorisation procedures are also important in limiting access to assets, documents and records, as well as to computer equipment, programs and files. We will explain these procedures in the section on physical controls (see page 255).

Documents and **records** are source documents, journals and ledgers. In computerised systems, some documents and records may exist only in electronic format. Documents provide evidence of transactions that have occurred and of the applicable price, nature and terms. Invoices, cheques and time tickets illustrate common types of document. When duly signed or stamped, documents also provide a basis for establishing responsibility for the execution and recording of transactions. Documents should be designed to encourage the capture of all relevant information and to provide for the required signatures and initials of those responsible for executing and recording the transaction. Employees are more likely to perform their duties reliably if their responsibility is evidenced on the document.

Pre-numbered documents are useful in maintaining control and accountability by providing a means for ensuring that:

- all transactions are recorded;
- no transactions are recorded more than once.

Records include the primary accounting records (i.e. journals and ledgers) as well as other records of accumulated data, such as employee earnings records (which show cumulative payroll data for each employee) and perpetual inventory records.

Independent checks involve the verification of work performed by other individuals or departments, or the proper measurement of recorded amounts. The following are examples of independent checks.

- A dispatch clerk verifies the agreement of goods received from the warehouse with the details on a duplicate copy of the approved sales order before shipping the goods.
- A sales supervisor checks prices on invoices prepared by invoicing clerks against an authorised price list before mailing them.
- A treasurer compares the amounts on cheques prepared by the accounts department with amounts on supporting documentation before signing the cheques.
- A routine in a computer program compares a computer-generated total of credits posted to the receivables master file with a manually prepared batch total keyed in at the beginning of the computer run, and prints the result.

Performance of independent checks should be evidenced in writing.

Segregation of duties

Segregation of duties ensures that individuals do not perform incompatible duties. Duties are considered incompatible when it is possible for an individual to commit an error or irregularity and then be in a position to conceal it in the normal course of his or her duties. An individual who processes cash remittances from customers, for example, should not also have authority to approve and record credits to customers' accounts for sales returns and bad debt write-offs. In such a case, the individual could steal a cash remittance and cover the theft by recording a fictitious sales return or by writing off the balance. This reasoning supports segregation of duties in the following situations.

- *Responsibility for executing a transaction, recording the transaction and maintaining custody of the assets resulting from the transaction should be assigned to different individuals or departments.* As an example, purchasing department personnel should initiate purchase orders, goods inward personnel should record the goods received, and storeroom personnel should assume custody of the goods. Before recording the purchase, accounting personnel should ascertain that the purchase was authorised and that the goods ordered were received. The accounting entry, in turn, provides an accountability basis for the goods in the storeroom.
- *The various steps involved in executing a transaction should be assigned to different individuals or departments.* Thus, in executing a sales transaction, the entity should assign responsibility for authorising the sale, filling the order, shipping the goods and invoicing the customer to different individuals.
- *Responsibility for certain accounting operations should be segregated.* In a manual information system, for example, different personnel should maintain the general ledger and the accounts receivable subsidiary ledger, and personnel involved in recording cash receipts and payments should not reconcile the bank accounts.

When duties are segregated such that the work of one individual automatically provides a cross-check on the work of another, the entity has the added benefit of an independent check. It should be noted that while an independent check always involves segregating duties, segregating duties does not always involve an independent check. The following are examples of how segregation of duties affects the control risk.

- Separating the custody of assets from the maintenance of the accounting record of assets reduces the risk of theft because the perpetrator will not have an opportunity to cover up the theft by eliminating the record of the assets.
- Segregation of duties for processing cash payment transactions and reconciling the bank accounts reduces the risk of unrecorded payments by cheque. Whereas the cash payment clerk may wish to conceal his or her error by falsifying the reconciliation, an independent person would have no such incentive.
- Segregating responsibility for approving credit from initiating sales orders reduces the risk of bad debts that may result from sales made to bad credit risks to achieve sales targets or to boost commissions.

Physical controls

Physical controls limit access to assets and important records. Such controls may be direct or indirect. Direct controls include initiating measures for the safekeeping of assets, documents and records (such as fireproof safes and locked storerooms) and restricting access to storage areas to authorised personnel only. Indirect controls apply to the preparation or processing of documents (such as sales orders and payment vouchers) that authorise the use or disposition of assets. They involve the use of mechanical and electronic equipment such as cash registers, which help to assure that all cash receipt transactions are rung up and which provide locked-in summaries of daily receipts.

To be effective, physical controls must include periodic counts of assets and comparisons with the amounts shown on control records. Examples include petty cash counts and physical inventory checks.

Access controls, both physical and electronic, are particularly important in a computer information system. They should provide assurance that transactions being entered into the computer systems are appropriately authorised and that access to data and programs is restricted to authorised personnel.

Access to computer hardware should be limited to authorised individuals. Physical safeguards include housing the equipment in an area restricted by security guards, or using keys, badges or other automated security devices.

Access to data files and programs should be designed to prevent unauthorised use of such data. All computer users should have passwords, whether for access to the mainframe computer, to terminals or to a microcomputer system. Each user may have restricted access to specific programs and files. Access may be further designated as 'read only' or 'read and write'. The computer should also be programmed to record the name of all users who access the computer for the purposes of adding, altering or deleting data. If passwords are to provide for the security of data files and programs, then they should be changed regularly, not easily guessed, and secured by both the user and the system.

In systems with on-line entry of data, many users have direct access through remote input devices. Access often extends beyond the entity's employees to customers and suppliers through remote terminals such as automated teller machines or even via the Internet. To provide the necessary control, each user of a remote input device is provided with a key, code or card that identifies the holder as an authorised user.

Security packages can also provide access security. They can define the relationships of different types of user to the programs and data files stored in the computer. The software can detect access violations by logging all abortive access attempts.

Performance reviews

Examples of performance reviews include management review and analysis of:

- reports that summarise the detail of account balances such as an aged trial balance of accounts receivable or reports of sales activity by region, division, salesperson or product line;
- actual performance compared with budgets, forecasts or prior period amounts.

Control environment

The control environment means management's overall attitude, awareness and actions regarding internal control and its importance in the entity. Numerous factors comprise the control environment, including:

- integrity and ethical values;
- a commitment to competence;
- management's philosophy and operating style;
- organisational structure;
- the assignment of authority and responsibility;
- internal audit;
- the use of information technology;
- human resource policies and practices;
- the board of directors and audit committee.

We will discuss these factors in the following sections.

Integrity and ethical values

Increasingly, constituents of businesses — such as employees, customers, suppliers and the public — are demanding that business management exhibit integrity and ethical values. Managers of well-run entities are increasingly accepting the view that 'ethics pays' — that is, that ethical behaviour is good business.

To emphasise the importance of integrity and ethical values among all personnel of an organisation, the chief executive officer and other members of top management should:

- *set the tone by example*, by demonstrating integrity and practising ethical behaviour;
- *communicate* to all employees, verbally and through written policy statements and codes of conduct, that the same behaviour is expected of them, that each employee has a responsibility to report known or suspected violations to a higher level in the organisation, and that violations will result in penalties;
- *reduce or eliminate incentives and temptations* that may lead individuals to engage in dishonest, illegal or unethical acts. Incentives for undesirable negative behaviour include placing undue emphasis on short-term results or on unrealistic performance targets, and offering bonus and profit-sharing plans that may, in the absence of necessary controls, encourage fraudulent financial reporting practices.

A commitment to competence

Personnel at every level in the organisation must possess the knowledge and skills needed to perform their jobs effectively. Meeting financial reporting objectives in a large publicly held company generally requires higher levels of competence on the part of chief financial officers and accounting personnel than would be needed for such personnel in a small, privately held company.

Management's philosophy and operating style

Characteristics that form part of a management's philosophy and operating style and that have an impact on the control environment include the management's:

- approach to taking and monitoring business risks;
- reliance on informal face-to-face contacts with key managers versus a formal system of written policies, performance indicators and exception reports;
- attitudes and actions towards financial reporting;
- conservative or aggressive selection of accounting principles from available alternatives;
- conscientiousness and conservatism in developing accounting estimates;
- attitudes towards information processing and accounting functions and personnel.

The last four characteristics are particularly significant to an assessment of the control environment for financial reporting.

Organisational structure

An organisational structure contributes to an entity's ability to meet its objectives by providing an overall framework for planning, executing, controlling and monitoring the entity's activities. Developing an organisational structure for an entity involves determining the key areas of authority and responsibility and appropriate lines of reporting.

The assignment of authority and responsibility

The assignment of authority and responsibility is an extension of the development of an organisational structure. It includes the particulars of how and to whom authority and responsibility are assigned, and should enable each individual to know:

- how his or her actions contribute to the achievement of the entity's objectives;
- for what he or she will be held accountable.

Internal audit

The establishment of an internal audit function strengthens the control environment. To be effective, internal audit personnel need to:

- be sufficiently skilled;
- possess integrity;
- have appropriate access to the board of directors and the audit committee, and to the independent auditor.

The use of information technology

The use of information technology should be appropriate to the entity's size and complexity. The framework of overall control established by management should ensure that the general controls over information processing described above are achieved.

Human resource policies and practices

A fundamental concept of internal control is that it is effected or implemented by people. Thus, for the internal control structure to be effective, human resource policies and practices must ensure that entity personnel possess the expected integrity, ethical values and competence. Such practices include:

- developing appropriate recruiting policies;
- screening prospective employees;
- orienting new personnel to the entity's culture and operating style;
- developing training policies that communicate prospective roles and responsibilities;
- exercising disciplinary action for violations of expected behaviour;
- evaluating, counselling and promoting people based on periodic performance appraisals;
- implementing compensation programs that motivate and reward superior performance while avoiding disincentives to ethical behaviour.

Board of directors and audit committee

The composition of the board of directors and the audit committee, along with the manner in which they exercise their governance and oversight responsibilities, has a major impact on the control environment. Influential factors include:

- the proportion of non-executive directors and the establishment of an audit committee;
- the experience and stature of directors;
- the extent of their involvement with and scrutiny of management's activities;
- the degree to which they raise and pursue difficult questions with management;
- the nature and extent of their interaction with internal and independent auditors.

Internal control and corporate governance

Corporate governance codes recognise the importance of management maintaining and demonstrating a responsible attitude to control. The 'Professional environment' below describes recent developments in the United Kingdom.

PROFESSIONAL ENVIRONMENT

Corporate governance and internal control

The UK Combined Code on Corporate Governance, which forms part of the London Stock Exchange's Listing Agreement, requires directors to conduct an annual review of the effectiveness of their system of internal control and to report to shareholders that they have done so. A committee chaired by Nigel Turnbull on behalf of the Institute of Chartered Accountants in England & Wales has developed guidelines for implementing this requirement — the Turnbull Guidelines. The following paragraphs from these guidelines (*Internal Control, Guidance for Directors on the Combined Code*, 1999) state the importance of internal control and risk management:

> 10. A company's system of internal control has a key role in the management of risks that are significant to the fulfilment of its business objectives. A sound system of internal control contributes to safeguarding the shareholders' investment and the company's assets.
>
> 11. Internal control facilitates the effectiveness and efficiency of operations, helps ensure the reliability of internal and external reporting and assists compliance with laws and regulations.
>
> 12. Effective financial controls, including the maintenance of proper accounting records, are an important element of internal control. They help ensure that the company is not unnecessarily exposed to avoidable financial risks and that financial information used within the business and for publication is reliable. They also contribute to the safeguarding of assets, including the prevention and detection of fraud.
>
> 13. A company's objectives, its internal organisation and the environment in which it operates are continually evolving and, as a result, the risks it faces are continually changing. A sound system of internal control therefore depends on a thorough and regular evaluation of the nature and extent of the risks to which the company is exposed. Since profits are, in part, the reward for successful risk-taking in business, the purpose of internal control is to help manage and control risk appropriately rather than to eliminate it.

3
LEARNING OBJECTIVE
State the inherent limitations of the internal control structure.

Limitations of control

One of the fundamental concepts identified earlier in the chapter is that internal control can provide only reasonable assurance regarding the achievement of an entity's objectives. Reasons for this include the following **inherent limitations** in an entity's internal control structure:

- *Costs versus benefits*: The cost of an entity's internal control structure should not exceed the benefits that are expected to ensue. Because precise measurement of both costs and benefits is not usually possible, management must make both quantitative and qualitative estimates and judgements in evaluating the cost–benefit relationship.

- *Management override*: Management can overrule prescribed policies or procedures for illegitimate purposes, such as personal gain or enhanced presentation of an entity's financial condition (e.g. inflating reported earnings to increase a performance bonus or the market value of the entity's shares). Override practices include making deliberate misrepresentations to auditors and others, such as by issuing false documents to support the recording of fictitious sales transactions.
- *Mistakes in judgement*: Occasionally, as a result of inadequate information, time constraints or other pressures, management and other personnel may exercise poor judgement in making business decisions or performing routine duties.
- *Collusion*: Individuals acting together may evade the planned segregation of duties to perpetrate and conceal an irregularity (e.g. collusion among three employees from the personnel, manufacturing and payroll departments to initiate payments to fictitious employees, or 'kickback' schemes arranged between an employee in the purchasing department and a supplier, or between an employee in the sales department and a customer).
- *Breakdowns*: Breakdowns in established controls may occur because personnel misunderstand instructions or make errors as a result of carelessness, distractions or fatigue. Temporary or permanent changes in personnel, systems or procedures may also contribute to breakdowns.

Application to smaller entities

The information system, control procedures and the control environment are applicable to entities of all sizes. However, the degree of formality and the manner in which the components are implemented may vary considerably for practical and sound reasons.

Smaller entities are less likely to have written codes of conduct, external directors, formal policy manuals, sufficient personnel to provide for optimal segregation of duties, or internal auditors. However, they can mitigate the absence of these safeguards by developing a culture that emphasises integrity, ethical values and competence. In addition, owner-managers can assume responsibility for certain critical tasks such as approving credit, signing cheques, reviewing bank reconciliations, monitoring customer balances and approving write-offs of bad debts. Moreover, the familiarity that managers of smaller entities can have with all critical areas of operation, and the simpler and shorter lines of communication, can obviate the need for the formalised control activities that are essential in larger entities.

Control in computer information systems

The general principles of control are the same in both computerised and manual information systems, but the effect of technology on the internal control structure must be recognised. Generally, computer information systems (CISs) are:

- more consistent;
- more efficient;
- able to review and act on more transactions;
- designed to identify and deal with exceptions.

As the use of CISs becomes more common, their operation is becoming increasingly free of human intervention and greater reliance is being placed on them. Table 7.1 indicates that a well-designed CIS can significantly reduce errors. However, if the system is not well designed, then the impact of error is much greater.

TABLE 7.1 *Information technology (IT) systems versus manual processes*

Attributes of IT systems	Attributes of manual processes	Benefits of IT system processes	Potential risks of IT system processes
More consistent processing	No real assurance as to consistency	Once right, always right; potentially fewer errors	If wrong, consistently wrong for that logical process; difficulty in detecting small but possibly significant individual discrepancies spread over a large volume of transactions
Often limited flexibility unless incorporated in design (which may change)	High dependence on individuals; high flexibility		Presumption by users that systems are right without sufficient review and testing Major effort required for changes (e.g. new products) Where flexibility is incorporated in IT system design, potential for error arising from the increased complexity
Increased efficiency (in capacity and volume), because the volume of transactions that can be handled is increased	Effect of an increase in volume on timeliness and need for resources	Easier to maintain delivery, accuracy and timeliness requirements as volumes increase Easier to maintain costs in the face of increasing volumes Reduced ongoing operational costs	Higher up-front costs
Use of user-controlled parameters or key data for multiple transactions and calculations	Similar use of key data but needs to be examined for each transaction (e.g. the price list)	Use of data in this way, but data still examined each time, so as to ensure consistency of application (e.g. the consistent use of interest rates)	If key data are wrong or manipulated, potential effect on numerous transactions
Ability to review all transactions and report only exceptions	Only a sample of transactions reviewed Possibility that the review may be limited to a scrutiny for reasonableness	Reduced number of items that require follow-up (increased efficiency) Ability to deal with all details of a transaction	Detection of potential problems only if programmed to do so Possible inability to identify or deal with unexpected real or potential errors Reliance on effective and timely manual follow-up of potential errors
Minimal manual interpretation or review	Need for detailed human knowledge of the process	Reduced cost Reduced likelihood of disruption Reduced reliance on operational staff	Possibility that users may no longer understand how the system works and, thus, may not be able to identify or deal with errors or operate without the system Increased impact of disruption The possibility that reduced intervention may reduce the levels of authorisation and increase exposure to fraud
Minimal visible evidence of the process that has been followed	Normally, physical evidence of the action taken	A reduced amount of information that is required to be reviewed manually	Possible difficulty in identifying the nature and extent of errors where they do arise Reliance on the system documentation to define how the process works

(Source: Adapted from Margaret Wright, *Audit Guide No. 5: Auditing in an IT Systems Environment*, Table 2.1. AARF, Melbourne, 1999)

LEARNING OBJECTIVE 4

Indicate the procedures to obtain and document an understanding of the internal control structure.

PROCEDURES TO OBTAIN AN UNDERSTANDING

This section explains how the auditor meets his or her responsibility for obtaining and documenting an understanding of the information system and internal control environment.

Obtaining an understanding

The procedures necessary to obtain an understanding consist of:
- reviewing previous experience with the entity;
- inquiring of appropriate management, supervisory and staff personnel;
- inspecting documents and records;
- observing entity activities and operations.

In a repeat engagement, the previous year's working papers contain a great deal of information relevant to the current year's audit. The auditor can use the previous year's recorded understanding and assessment of control risk as the starting point, making inquiries as to the changes that may have occurred in the current year. The working papers should also contain information about the types and causes of misstatements found in prior audits. The auditor can follow up on this information to determine whether management has taken corrective actions.

The auditor should also inspect relevant documents and records of the entity, such as organisation charts, policy manuals, the chart of accounts, accounting ledgers, journals and source documents. These inspections will inevitably lead to additional inquiries about specific controls and changes in conditions.

To reinforce his or her understanding of the information system and control procedures, the auditor performs a **transaction walk-through review** by tracing one or a few transactions within each major class through the transaction trail to confirm the documented understanding.

Documenting the understanding

Documenting the understanding of the information system is a requirement for all audits. Documentation may take the form of completed questionnaires, flow charts and/or narrative memoranda. In an audit of a large entity, involving a combination of audit strategies, all three types of documentation may be used for different parts of the understanding. In an audit of a small entity, a single memorandum may suffice to document the auditor's understanding of all the components. In a repeat engagement, it may be necessary only to update documentation from the prior year's working papers. Only those parts of the information system that are relevant to the audit need to be documented.

Questionnaires

An **internal control questionnaire** (ICQ) consists of a series of questions about accounting and control policies and procedures that the auditor considers necessary to prevent material misstatements in the financial report. The questions are usually phrased in such a way that a 'yes' answer indicates a favourable condition. Space is also provided on the questionnaire for comments such as who performs a control procedure and how often.

Standardised questionnaires are used for many audits. Some firms use quite different questionnaires for large versus small entities or for particular industries.

Excerpts from three questionnaires are illustrated in Figures 7.1, 7.2 and 7.3. These relate to parts of the control environment, to the cash payment activities of an information system and to general controls over a computer information system respectively. In Figure 7.2, the questions relate to several possible categories of control activity: questions 1 and 4 relate to authorisation procedures; questions 2 and 6 relate to documents and records; questions 5, 8 and 9 relate to independent checks; question 3 relates to physical controls; and questions 7(a) and (b) relate to segregation of duties.

FIGURE 7.1

Excerpts from an internal control questionnaire — control environment

CLIENT Amalgamated Products Limited — BALANCE SHEET DATE 31/12/X1
Completed by: RSC Date: 12/9/X1 — Reviewed by: GEY Date: 29/10/X1

Internal Control Questionnaire Component: Control Environment

Question	Yes, No, N/A	Comments
Integrity and ethical values		
1. Does management set the 'tone at the top' by demonstrating a commitment to integrity and ethics through both its words and deeds?	Yes	Management is conscious of setting an example. Entity does not have a formal code of conduct.
2. Have appropriate entity policies regarding acceptable business practices, conflicts of interest, and codes of conduct been established and adequately communicated?	Yes	Expectations of employees included in a policy manual distributed to all employees.
3. Have incentives and temptations that might lead to unethical behaviour been reduced or eliminated?	Yes	Profit-sharing plan monitored by audit committee.
Board of directors and audit committee		
1. Are there regular meetings of the board and are minutes prepared on a timely basis?	Yes	Board has nine inside members, three of whom serve on the audit committee. Considering adding three outside members to the board who would comprise the audit committee.
2. Do board members have sufficient knowledge, experience and time to serve effectively?	Yes	
3. Is there an audit committee composed of outside directors?	No	
Management's philosophy and operating style		
1. Are business risks carefully considered and adequately monitored?	Yes	Management is conservative about business risks.
2. Is management's selection of accounting principles and development of accounting estimates consistent with objective and fair reporting?	Yes	
3. Has management demonstrated a willingness to adjust the financial statements for material misstatements?	Yes	Management has readily accepted all proposed adjustments in prior audits.
Human resource policies and practices		
1. Do existing personnel policies and procedures result in the recruitment or development of competent and trustworthy people needed to support an effective internal control structure?	Yes	Formal job descriptions are provided for all positions.
2. Do personnel understand the duties and procedures applicable to their jobs?	Yes	
3. Is the turnover of personnel in key positions at an acceptable level?	Yes	Normal 'turnover'.

FIGURE 7.2

Excerpts from an internal control questionnaire — cash payments

CLIENT Amalgamated Products Limited		BALANCE SHEET DATE 31/12/X1
Completed by: RSC Date: 12/9/X1		Reviewed by: GEY Date: 29/10/X1

Internal Control Questionnaire Component: Cash Payments

Question	Yes, No, N/A	Comments
Cash payments transactions		
1. Is there an approved payment voucher with supporting documents for each cheque prepared?	Yes	
2. Are pre-numbered cheques used and accounted for?	Yes	Safe in treasurer's office.
3. Are unused cheques stored in a secure area?	Yes	
4. Are only authorised personnel permitted to sign cheques?	Yes	Only treasurer and assistant treasurer can sign.
5. Do cheque signers verify agreement of details of cheque and payment voucher before signing?	Yes	
6. Are vouchers and supporting documents cancelled after payment?	Yes	Vouchers and all supporting documents are stamped 'Paid'.
7. Is there segregation of duties for:		
(a) approving payment vouchers and signing cheques?	Yes	
(b) signing cheques and recording cheques?	Yes	
8. Are there periodic independent reconciliations of cheque accounts?	Yes	Performed by assistant controller.
9. Is there an independent check of agreement of daily summary of cheques issued with entry to cash payments?	No	Comparison now made by assistant treasurer; will recommend it be made by assistant controller.

FIGURE 7.3

Internal control questionnaire — computer information system (CIS) general controls

CONTROLS	YES	NO	COMMENTS
Organisational controls			
1. Are the following duties segregated within the CIS department?			
(a) Systems design			
(b) Computer programming			
(c) Computer operations			
(d) Data entry			
(e) Custody of systems documentation, programs and files			
(f) Data control			
2. Are the following duties performed only outside the CIS department?			
(a) Initiation and authorisation of transactions			
(b) Authorisation of changes in systems, programs and master files			
(c) Preparation of source documents			
(d) Correction of errors in source documents			
(e) Custody of assets			

(continued)

CONTROLS	YES	NO	COMMENTS
Systems development and maintenance controls 1. Is there adequate participation by users and internal auditors in new systems development? 2. Is proper authorisation, testing and documentation required for systems and program changes? 3. Is access to systems software restricted to authorised personnel? 4. Are there adequate controls over data files (both master and transaction files) during conversion to prevent unauthorised changes?			
Access controls 1. Is access to computer facilities restricted to authorised personnel? 2. Does the librarian restrict access to data files and programs to authorised personnel? 3. Are computer-processing activities reviewed by management?			
Other controls 1. Is there a disaster contingency plan to ensure continuity of operations? 2. Is there off-site storage of backup files and programs? 3. Are sufficient generations of programs, master files and transaction files maintained to facilitate recovery and reconstruction of CIS processing? 4. Are there adequate safeguards against fire, water damage, power failure, power fluctuations, theft, loss, and intentional and unintentional destruction?			

Some auditing firms have automated their internal control questionnaires. The staff auditor enters the responses into a notebook computer as the information is obtained, using software that analyses the pattern of responses across related questions and guides the auditor through subsequent steps in assessing control risk and designing substantive audit procedures.

Some auditing firms also provide special training for staff in the interviewing skills needed to administer questionnaires. By being alert to non-verbal signals given by interviewees (such as a hesitancy to respond, an apparent lack of familiarity with controls, or undue nervousness during the interview), for example, the auditor can significantly enhance his or her understanding.

As a means of documenting the understanding, questionnaires offer a number of advantages. They are developed by experienced professionals and provide guidance for less experienced staff who may be assigned to obtain the understanding on a particular audit. They are relatively easy to use and reduce the possibility that the auditor may overlook important internal control matters. Their disadvantage is that to cater for the varied types of information system, they may be long and unwieldy.

Flow charts

A **flow chart** is a schematic diagram that uses standardised symbols, interconnecting flow lines and annotations to portray the steps involved in processing information through the information system. Flow charts are prepared to depict the processing of individual classes of transaction, such as sales, cash receipts, purchases, cash payments, payroll and manufacturing.

Flow charts should depict:

- all operations performed in processing the class of transactions;
- the methods of processing (manual or computerised);
- the extent of segregation of duties (by identifying each operation with a functional area, department or individual);
- the source, flow and disposition of the documents, records and reports involved in processing.

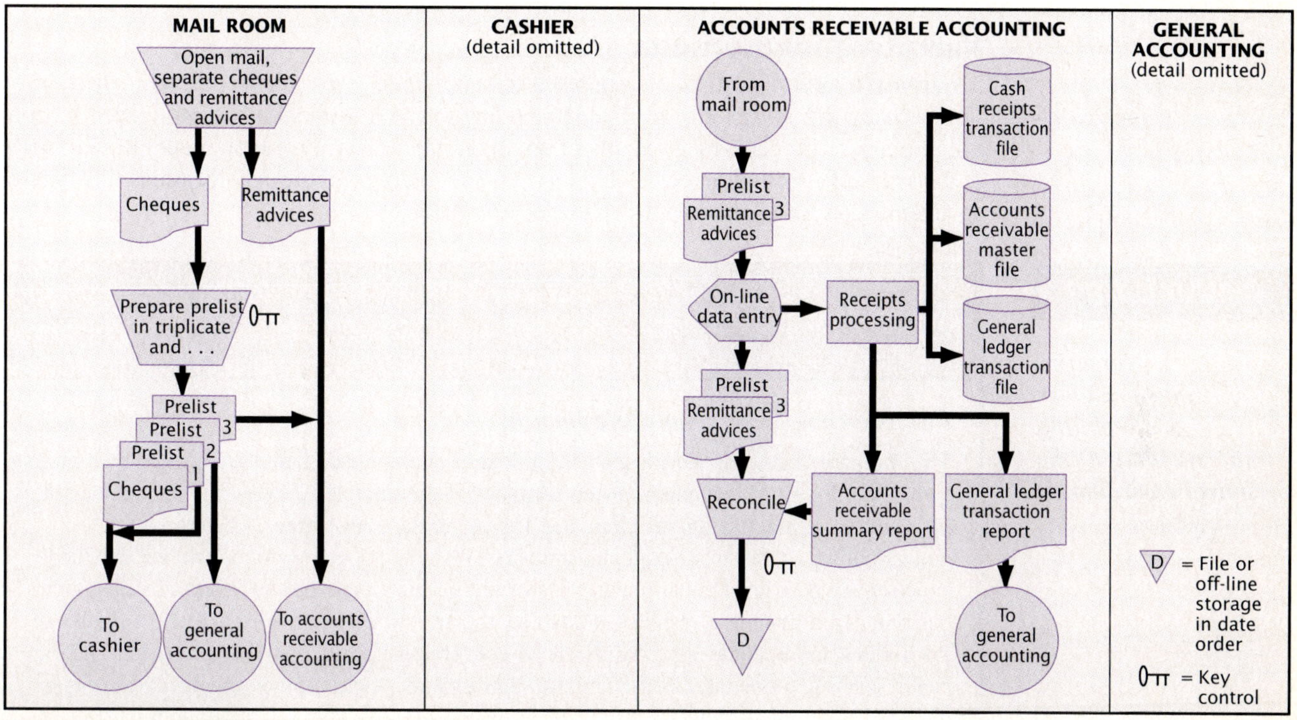

FIGURE 7.4

Partial flow chart for the processing of mail receipts transactions

These essential components are illustrated in Figure 7.4, which is a partial flow chart of a system for processing cash (cheques) and accompanying remittance advices received from customers. (An example of a remittance advice is the portion of a telephone account or credit card statement that the customer returns with the payment.) The flow chart in Figure 7.4 displays four operations. The first two take place in the mail room — namely, (1) opening the mail and separating the cheques and remittance advices, and (2) preparing a prelist (in triplicate) of the cheques (to show the amount of each remittance and the grand total). The other two operations take place in accounts receivable accounting — namely, (3) entering the remittance data into the computer for processing, and (4) reconciling a computer-generated summary with the input documents. The first, second and fourth operations involve manual processing, which is indicated by the use of a trapezoidal shaped symbol. The third operation is represented in the flow chart by the symbol labelled 'On-line data entry' and the rectangular symbol labelled 'Receipts processing', which, together, indicate computer processes. The segregation of duties is indicated by the division of the flow chart into four vertical partitions, representing the four departments involved with the cash receipts processing. (The details of only two of these departments are shown, so as to keep the illustration simple.) Finally, the figure shows the source, flow and disposition of the following documents and records:

- the remittance advices and cheques received in the mail;
- the three copies of the prelist of cheques prepared in the mail room;
- the two computer-generated reports that are produced when the remittance data are entered into the computer in accounts receivable accounting.

The flow chart also shows that the computerised receipts processing results in the updating of three computer files maintained on disk (the symbols in the accounts receivable accounting partition that look like cans).

A more complete illustration of flow charting is presented in Appendix 7A. As well as extending the illustration of the system shown in Figure 7.4 (page 265), Appendix 7A includes an explanation of additional standardised flow charting symbols and some helpful guidelines for preparing flow charts.

Narrative memoranda

A **narrative memorandum** may be used to supplement other forms of documentation by summarising the auditor's overall understanding of the information system or specific control policies or procedures. In audits of small entities, a narrative memorandum may serve as the only documentation of the auditor's understanding. Figure 7.5 illustrates this type of documentation for a small owner-managed company.

FIGURE 7.5

Narrative memorandum documenting understanding of the control environment

CLIENT Ownco Pty Limited	BALANCE SHEET DATE 31/12
Completed by: m/w Date: 30/9/X1	Reviewed by: i/p Date: 02/11/X1
Updated by: m/w Date: 15/9/X2	Reviewed by: i/p Date: 29/10/X2

Understanding of the control environment

The company manufactures plastic fishing worms at one location and is managed by its sole owner, Ed Jones. Management of the company is dominated by Jones, who is responsible for marketing, purchasing, hiring and approving major transactions. He has a good understanding of the business and the industry in which it operates. Jones believes that hiring experienced personnel is particularly important because there are no layers of supervisory personnel and thus, as a result of limited segregation of duties, few independent checks of employees' work. Jones has a moderate-to-conservative attitude to business risks. The business has demonstrated consistent profitability and, because Jones considers lower taxes to be as important as financial results, he has a conservative attitude to accounting estimates.

Jones and Pat Willis, the bookkeeper, readily consult with our firm on routine accounting questions, including the preparation of accounting estimates (tax accrual, inventory obsolescence or bad debts). Our firm also assists in assembling the financial report.

The company's board of directors is composed of family members. The board is not expected to monitor the business or the owner-manager's activities.

Most of the significant accounting functions are performed by Willis, the bookkeeper, and Jones's secretary, Chris Ross. Willis was hired by the company in 20X0 and has a working knowledge of accounting fundamentals, and we have no reason to question her competence. Willis regularly consults with our firm on unusual transactions, and past history indicates that it is rare for adjustments to arise from errors in the processing of routine transactions.

Jones made the decision to purchase a microcomputer and a turnkey accounting software package. The source code is not available for this software. Access to the computer and computer files is limited to Willis, Ross and Jones, who effectively have access to all computer files.

The owner–manager carefully reviews computer-generated financial reports, such as reports on receivable ageing, and compares revenues and expenses with prior years' performance. He also monitors the terms of the long-term debt agreement that requires certain ratios and compensating balances.

(Source: AICPA, *Audit Guide: Consideration of the Internal Control Structure in a Financial Statement Audit*, 1990, pp. 117–18)

LEARNING CHECK

7.1 AUS 402 (ISA 400) focuses on the internal control structure, which incorporates the information system, control procedures and the control environment.

7.2 The information system processes and records transactions to ensure that financial reports are accurate and reliable. Management establishes control procedures to ensure achievement of entity objectives, including the reliability of financial reports and compliance with applicable laws and regulations. The control environment relates to the attitude of management towards the importance of internal controls.

7.3 Control procedures relating to the information system consist of information processing controls, the segregation of duties, physical controls and performance reviews.

7.4 Internal control provides only reasonable assurance, being subject to inherent limitations. In smaller entities controls are likely to be less formal and to depend on the direct supervision of management.

7.5 In obtaining an understanding of the information system, the auditor calls on previous experience with the entity, the outcomes of inquiries of personnel, the inspection of documents, personal observation and a final walk-through to confirm the understanding.

7.6 The auditor documents the internal control structure:
- using internal control questionnaires (prepared at the time of obtaining the understanding), which may be completed by inexperienced staff but have the disadvantage of being lengthy;
- in the form of flow charts, which are useful for complex systems and in establishing the segregation of functions, but which require experience in their preparation and interpretation;
- as a narrative, which is simple to prepare and suitable for smaller entities.

PRELIMINARY ASSESSMENT OF CONTROL RISK

LEARNING OBJECTIVE 5

Explain the purpose of making a preliminary assessment of control risk.

In this section we will explain the role of the **preliminary assessment of control risk** and the nature of evidence used in making the assessment. The process of assessing control risk and its role in determining the audit strategy are shown in Figure 7.6 on the following page.

The purpose of the preliminary assessment

Assessment of control risk is conducted in two phases. The preliminary phase is to enable design of the detailed audit procedures. In drawing up a detailed audit program, it is cost-effective for the auditor to perform the tests of control and the substantive procedures (based on the same evidence sources, such as examination of documents) concurrently. The preliminary assessment is made to obtain a reasonable expectation of the effectiveness of controls, such that the detailed audit program can be designed in accordance with the appropriate audit strategy. The second phase occurs on completion of all tests of control. If these tests do not support the preliminary assessment of control risk, then the auditor must perform additional substantive procedures, adding to the cost of the audit. In most instances, however, the preliminary assessment is sufficiently reliable (especially for repeat engagements), such that the need to extend substantive procedures after completion of tests of control rarely arises.

In all audits, the auditor can normally identify, on the basis of experience, those transactions and assertions for which a strategy based on a lower assessed level of control risk will rarely be cost-effective. Such a conclusion may be reached where transactions are few or where previous experience indicates that controls are unlikely to be effective. In such circumstances the auditor makes litle or no effort to assess control risk. For audit purposes, the auditor assesses control risk as being 100 per cent and plans a predominantly substantive audit strategy.

In computer information systems, the use of computer-assisted audit techniques (CAATs) may enable the auditor to perform extensive substantive testing as cheaply as less extensive testing. This applies where all of the testing can be computerised, enabling the auditor to draw conclusions based on exceptions reported by the computer; for example, it may be possible for the auditor to use a computer program to check the pricing of all sales invoices. Assessment of control over invoice pricing is, therefore, unnecessary.

FIGURE 7.6

The process of risk assessment and its effect on audit strategy

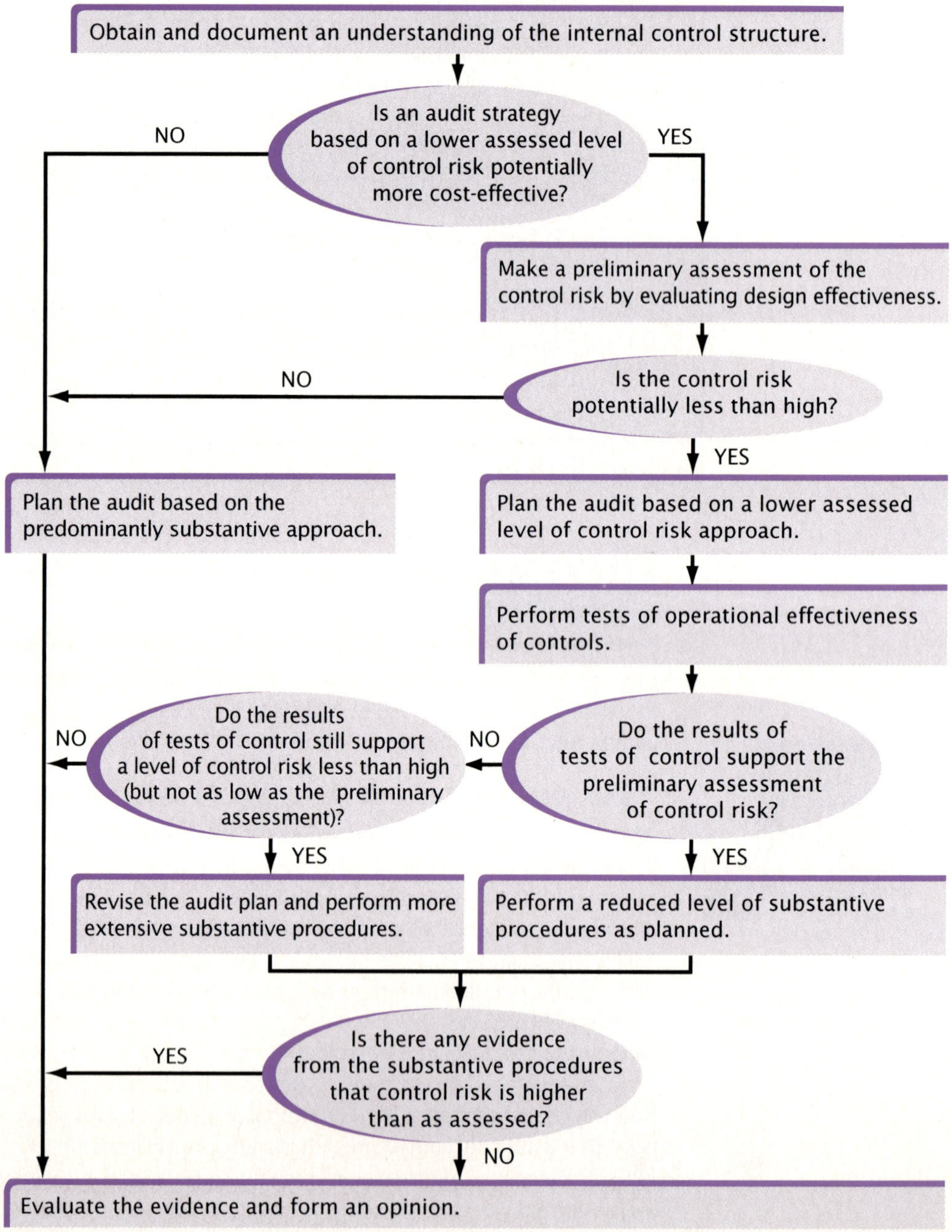

The process of assessing control risk

Assessing control risk is the process of evaluating the effectiveness of the design and operation of an entity's internal controls in preventing or detecting material misstatements in the financial report.

The first step is to assess the control environment. A weak control environment can undermine the internal control structure. Strong individual control procedures cannot compensate for a weak control environment. Assessment of the control environment is a matter for professional judgement, and is common to all assertions for all transaction classes.

6 LEARNING OBJECTIVE

Describe the approach to evaluating the design effectiveness of control procedures.

The second step is to assess the **design effectiveness of control procedures** and the ability of such procedures to prevent or correct misstatements. The effectiveness of a control is ultimately limited by its design. Control risk is assessed in terms of individual financial report assertions. Because the information system focuses on the processing of transactions, and because many control procedures pertain to the processing of a particular type of transaction, the auditor commonly begins by assessing control risk for transaction class assertions, such as the occurrence, completeness and measurement assertions for cash receipts and cash payment transactions. It is important to keep in mind that control risk assessments are made for individual assertions, not for the information system as a whole.

The final step is to assess whether the controls were effectively applied throughout the period under audit. This stage of tests of control is normally deferred until after the preliminary assessment and performed only where the auditor adopts a lower assessed level of control risk strategy.

In evaluating design effectiveness in order to make a preliminary assessment of control risk for an assertion, the auditor has to:

- identify *potential misstatements* that could occur in the entity's assertion;
- identify the *necessary controls* that would be likely to prevent or detect the material misstatements;
- evaluate the evidence and *make the assessment.*

Identifying the potential misstatements

If the auditor's understanding of the system has been obtained through the use of internal control questionnaires, then the 'yes' answers indicate the presence of effective controls and the 'no' answers indicate weaknesses. Some auditing firms use computer software to link responses to specific questions in computerised questionnaires to potential misstatements for particular assertions. However, most auditing firms have developed **internal control evaluation check lists** that enumerate the types of potential misstatement that could occur in specific assertions. Using either the computer software aid or check lists and the understanding of the entity's information system, the auditor identifies the potential misstatements applicable to specific assertions, given the entity's circumstances. Examples of potential misstatements for several assertions pertaining to cash payments transactions are shown in the first column of Table 7.2 (page 270).

Identifying the necessary controls

Whether by using computer software that processes internal control questionnaire responses or by manually analysing check lists, the auditor can identify the **necessary controls** that would be likely to prevent or detect specific potential misstatements. The second column in Table 7.2 illustrates a list of such controls.

TABLE 7.2 *Potential misstatements, necessary controls, tests of control — cash payments transactions*

Potential misstatement/ assertion	Necessary controls	Tests of operating effectiveness
A cash payment may be made for an unauthorised purpose (occurrence of valid transaction).	• An approved supplier's statement, with matching supporting documents (supplier's invoice, receiving report and approved purchase order), is required for each payment transaction. • Only authorised personnel are permitted to sign cheques. • The duties of approving suppliers' invoices and signing cheques are segregated.	• For a sample of cash payment transactions, determine the existence of the approved supplier's invoice and matching supporting documents for each payment. • Observe individuals signing cheques and identify them as authorised signatories. • Observe the segregation of duties.
An invoice may be paid twice (occurrence of valid transaction).	• The invoice and supporting documents are stamped 'Paid' when the cheque is issued.	• Observe documents being stamped and/or inspect a sample of paid documents for the presence of the 'Paid' stamp.
A cheque may be issued for the wrong amount (measurement).	• Signers verify the agreement of the cheque and invoice details before signing.	• Observe cheque signers performing an independent check of the agreement of details and/or reperform an independent check.
A cash payment transaction may not be recorded (completeness) or it may be recorded for the wrong amount (measurement).	• All payment transactions are to be made by cheque. • All cheques are to be pre-numbered and accounted for. • Unused cheques are to be stored in a secure area. • An independent check is to be made of the agreement of the daily summary of cheques issued with the entry in the cash payments journal. • Periodic independent bank reconciliations are to be performed.	• Inquire about methods of making cash payments and/or inspect paid cheques for a sample of payment transactions. • Examine evidence of use of, and accounting for, pre-numbered cheques and/or scan the sequence of cheque numbers in the cheque register or the cash payments journal. • Observe the handling and storage of unused cheques. • Observe the performance of an independent check and/or reperform an independent check. • Observe the performance of bank reconciliations and/or inspect bank reconciliations.

Several controls may pertain to a given potential misstatement; in other instances, a single control may apply. In addition, a single control may pertain to more than one type of potential misstatement; for example, the control 'periodic independent bank reconciliations' (shown at the bottom of the second column in Table 7.2) may detect unrecorded cheques (completeness assertion) or cheques made out for the right amount but recorded in the cash payments journal at an incorrect amount (measurement assertion).

We recommend that you compare the information listed in the first and second columns of Table 7.2 with the questions presented in Figure 7.2 (page 263). Comparison of the two illustrates how a questionnaire that a staff auditor may be asked to administer can be developed by more experienced staff to facilitate analysis of potential misstatements and necessary controls. (*Note*: The questions in Figure 7.2 do not necessarily appear in the same order as the controls listed in Table 7.2 because some controls pertain to more than one assertion.)

Specifying necessary controls also requires judgement and a consideration of circumstances. Where there is a very high volume of cash payment transactions, for example, it may be critical to conduct an independent check of the agreement of a daily summary of cheques issued with the entry in the cash payments journal. In this way, errors will be quickly detected. When the volume of cash payments is light and timely detection of errors is not so essential, periodic independent bank reconciliations may compensate for the lack of a daily independent check. In such a circumstance, the bank reconciliation could be seen as a compensating control.

Where transactions are processed by a computer information system, Table 7.3 provides an outline of the assessment of the design effectiveness of controls over the computerised application.

TABLE 7.3 *Control risk assessment considerations for application controls in a computerised information system (CIS)*

Potential misstatement/ assertion	Necessary controls	Possible tests of control
Input controls		
Data for unauthorised transactions may be submitted for processing (completeness).	Authorisation and approval of data in user departments, and screening of data by data control group	Examine source documents and batch transmittals for evidence of approval; observe data control group.
Valid data may be incorrectly converted to machine-readable form (occurrence, completeness, measurement).	Computer editing and use of control totals	Observe data verification procedures; use test data to test edit routines; examine control total reconciliations.
Errors on source documents may not be corrected and resubmitted (occurrence, completeness, measurement).	Maintenance of error logs; return to user department for correction; follow-up by data control group	Inspect logs and evidence of follow-up by data control group.
Processing controls		
Wrong files may be processed and updated (disclosure).	Use of external and internal file labels	Observe use of external file labels; examine documentation for internal file labels.
Data may be lost, added, duplicated or altered during processing (occurrence, completeness, measurement).	Use of control totals; limit and reasonableness checks; sequence tests	Examine evidence of control total reconciliations and use of test data.
Output controls		
Output may be incorrect (occurrence, completeness, measurement).	Reconciliation of totals by data control group and user departments	Examine evidence of reconciliations.
Output may be distributed to unauthorised users.	Use of report distribution control sheets; data control group monitoring	Inspect report distribution control sheets; observe data control group monitoring.

Making the assessment

The auditor can make a preliminary assessment of control risk from the knowledge acquired from (1) procedures to obtain an understanding and (2) the identification of potential misstatements and the necessary controls to prevent or detect those misstatements. The auditor's assessment must also consider the assessment of the control environment and the extent to which the design of the control procedures is likely to be effective. The preliminary assessment is based on the presumption that further tests of control will provide evidence of the effective operation of the control.

7 LEARNING OBJECTIVE

State the purpose of tests of control and the nature of such tests.

TESTS OF CONTROL

As explained previously, **tests of control** are auditing procedures performed to determine the effectiveness of the design and operation of internal controls. Tests of control pertaining to design are concerned with whether the control is suitably designed to prevent or detect misstatements in a specific financial report assertion. The auditor may conclude, for example, that management's plan to store inventory in locked warehouses should prevent or significantly reduce the risk of misstatements in the existence assertion for inventories. Tests of control pertaining to the **operating effectiveness of the control procedures** are concerned with whether controls are actually working. In the inventory example, observing whether inventory is actually stored in locked warehouses would provide a test of the effectiveness of operation. Tests of operating effectiveness focus on three questions:

1. How was the control applied?
2. Was it applied consistently during the year?
3. By whom was it applied?

A control is operating effectively when it has been properly and consistently applied during the year by the employee(s) authorised to apply it. In contrast, failure to apply a control properly and consistently, or application of that control by an unauthorised employee, indicates ineffective operation. Such failures are referred to as **deviations**. This terminology is preferable to the term 'error' because a failure in performance indicates only that there may be an error in the accounting records. The failure, for example, of a second employee to verify the accuracy of a sales invoice is a deviation, but the document could still be correct if the first employee prepared it correctly.

Tests of control sufficient to make a preliminary assessment of control risk are performed at the planning stage concurrently with obtaining the understanding. If this preliminary assessment of control risk is less than high, and the auditor chooses to perform a reduced level of substantive procedures, then the auditor will perform further tests of control during interim work.

Tests of design effectiveness

Tests of the design effectiveness of controls are usually performed at the time of obtaining an understanding, and the auditor uses the results in making the preliminary assessment of control risk. We have already described the performance of such tests.

Tests of operating effectiveness

These tests of control are included in the audit program that is drawn up once the appropriate audit strategy is determined. They are mainly performed during the interim audit, but the auditor may conduct further tests at the final audit on significant controls for the period after the interim audit. These tests provide evidence of the proper and consistent application of a control throughout the year under audit, and support the preliminary assessment of control risk as being moderate or low and the corresponding planned level of substantive procedures.

Designing tests

In designing tests of the operating effectiveness of controls the auditor must decide their nature, timing and extent. The design may also be affected where there is no visible evidence of the performance of control procedures applied by computer to transactions processed by a computer information system.

Nature of tests

The auditor's choices in terms of the nature of tests of control are:

- *inquiring* of personnel about the performance of their duties;
- *observing* personnel perform their duties;
- *inspecting* documents and reports indicating performance of controls;
- *reperforming* the control.

In performing the tests, the auditor selects the procedure that will provide the most reliable evidence about the effectiveness of the control.

Inquiring is designed to determine:

- an employee's understanding of his or her duties;
- how that employee performs those duties;
- the frequency, cause(s) and disposition of deviations.

Unsatisfactory answers by an employee may indicate improper application of a control.

Observing the employee's performance provides similar evidence. Ideally, this procedure should be performed without the employee's knowledge or on a surprise basis. Inquiring and observing are especially useful means of obtaining evidence about the control procedure of segregation of duties. However, evidence obtained from observation has the following limitations:

- The employee may perform the control differently when not being observed.
- The evidence applies only to the time when the observation occurs.

Inspecting documents and records is applicable when there is a transaction trail of signatures and validation stamps that indicate whether the control was performed and by whom. Any document or record that fails to evidence the required performance is a deviation, regardless of whether the document is correct.

Dual-purpose tests

Reperformance is a **dual-purpose test** in that it provides evidence as both a test of control and a substantive test of detail. Where such a test reveals an error, it suggests the failure of controls intended to prevent such errors. Assume, for example, that the control procedure of independent checks requires a second clerk in the invoicing department to check the correctness of unit selling prices on sales invoices by comparing them to an authorised price list. On doing so, the employee initials a copy of the invoice to indicate performance of the independent check. In testing this control procedure, the auditor inspects invoices for the employee's initials and may reperform the process by comparing selling prices on invoices to the authorised price list. Such a test doubles as both a test of control and a substantive test of details, because any errors detected provide evidence both of a failure to perform the independent check properly and of monetary errors in the transactions recorded. When this type of testing is done, the auditor should exercise care in designing the tests to ensure that evidence is obtained as to both the effectiveness of controls and the monetary errors in the accounts. The auditor should also be careful in evaluating the evidence obtained.

Timing of tests of control

The **timing of tests of control** refers to the part of the accounting period to which they relate. Planned tests of control are performed during interim work, which may be several months before the end of the year under audit. These tests, therefore, provide evidence of the effectiveness of controls only from the beginning of the year to the date of the tests. However, the auditor is required by AUS 402 (ISA 400) to have evidence about effectiveness for the entire year covered by the financial report. Thus, from the standpoint of audit efficiency, the auditor should perform the tests of control as late in the interim period as possible.

The need to perform additional tests of control later in the year depends on:

- the length of the remaining period;
- the occurrence of significant changes in controls subsequent to interim testing, causing the auditor to revise his or her understanding of the internal control structure;
- the decision to perform substantive tests of details on balances prior to the year end (such as confirming accounts receivable one month before the year end), thus requiring assurance that control procedures remained effective in the period between the date of substantive procedures and the year end.

Extent of tests

More extensive tests of control provide more evidence of the operating effectiveness of a control. Asking more than one individual about the same control procedure, for example, will provide more evidence than a single inquiry; similarly, a more extensive inspection of documents for initials or signatures indicating performance of a control procedure provides more evidence than would examining fewer documents.

The **extent of tests of control** is determined by the auditor's planned assessed level of control risk. More extensive testing will be needed for a low assessed level of control risk than for a moderate level. Remember, however, that the assessment of control risk is ultimately limited by the control environment and the design of the control.

Tests of control in a computer information system

A particular problem arises with testing programmed application controls whose performance is invisible. In such situations auditors make use of a variety of computer-assisted audit techniques such as test data, integrated test facility (ITF) and parallel simulation.

Test data

Under the **test data approach**, dummy transactions are prepared by the auditor and processed under auditor control by the entity's software. The test data consist of one transaction for each valid or invalid condition that the auditor wants to test. Payroll test data, for example, may include both a valid and an invalid overtime pay condition. The output from processing the test data is then compared with the auditor's expected output to determine whether the controls are operating effectively. This approach to testing is relatively simple, quick and inexpensive. However, the method has the following audit deficiencies:

- The method is a test only of the presence and functioning of controls in the program tested.
- There is no examination of documentation actually processed by the system.
- Computer operators know that test data are being run, which could reduce the validity of the output.
- The scope of the test is limited by the auditors' imagination and knowledge of the controls within the application.

Integrated test facility

The **integrated test facility** (ITF) approach overcomes some of the limitations of the use of test data. It requires the creation of a small subsystem (a mini-company) within the regular computer accounting system. This may be accomplished by creating dummy master files or appending dummy master records to existing entity files. Test data, specially coded to correspond to the dummy master files, are introduced into the system, together with actual transactions. The test data should include all kinds of transaction errors and exceptions that may be encountered. In this manner, the test data are subjected to the same programmed controls as placed on the actual data. A separate set of outputs is produced for the subsystem of dummy files. The results can be compared with those expected by the auditor.

A disadvantage of the ITF approach is the risk that errors could be created in entity data. In addition, the entity's programs may need to be modified to accommodate the dummy data.

Parallel simulation

Parallel simulation involves reprocessing actual entity data using auditor-controlled software. This method is so named because the software is designed to reproduce or simulate the entity's processing of real data. This approach does not corrupt the entity's files and may be conducted at an independent computer facility. It has the following advantages:

- Because real data are used, the auditor can verify transactions by tracing them to source documents and approvals.
- The size of the sample can be greatly expanded at relatively little additional cost.
- The auditor can independently run the test.

If the auditor decides to use parallel simulation, he or she must take care to determine that the data selected for simulation are representative of actual entity transactions and include errors intended to be detected by the application of programmed controls. This could be a problem where the entity has corrected input data as a result of errors detected in processing.

Audit programs for tests of control

The auditor's decisions regarding the nature, extent and timing of tests of control should be documented in an audit program and related working papers. A sample audit program for tests of control of cash payment transactions is illustrated in Figure 7.7 (page 276). The program lists the procedures to be used in performing the tests for indicated assertions. It also provides columns to indicate:

- cross-references to the working papers in which the test results are documented;
- who performed the tests;
- the date on which the tests were completed.

Details concerning the extent and timing of the tests may be indicated in the audit program or in the working papers, as assumed in Figure 7.7. The tests listed in the formal audit program shown in Figure 7.7 are derived from the possible tests of control listed in column 3 of Table 7.2 (page 270). Some of the tests have been rearranged and grouped by assertions. An alternative approach is to rearrange tests to facilitate their efficient performance — for example, grouping tests 1, 2 and 6 together such that tests on the sample selected in test 1 are performed together.

FIGURE 7.7

Illustrative partial audit program for tests of control

Prepared by:________ Date:________
Reviewed by:________ Date:________

Amalgamated Products Limited
Planned tests of control — Cash payments transactions
Year ending 31 December 20X1

Assertion/test of control	Working paper reference	Auditor	Date
Existence or occurrence			
1. Select a sample of cash payment transactions from the cash payments journal and determine existence of matching approved payment vouchers and supporting documents.			
2. Inspect paid invoices and supporting documents from (1) above for presence of 'Paid' stamp.			
3. Observe segregation of duties for approving suppliers' invoices and signing cheques.			
Completeness			
4. Examine evidence of use of, and accounting for, pre-numbered cheques and scan sequence of cheque numbers in cash payments journal.			
5. Observe handling and storage of unused cheques.			
Valuation or measurement			
6. For transactions selected in (1) above, examine evidence of independent verification of agreement of details of cheques with supporting suppliers' invoices and test by reperformance.			
7. Select a sample of dates and examine evidence of independent check of agreement of daily summary of cheques issued with entry to cash payments and test by reperformance.			
8. Inspect independent bank reconciliations. (*Note*: Steps 7 and 8 also provide evidence of control over completeness.)			

8
LEARNING OBJECTIVE

Describe how the work of internal auditing may be used in tests of control.

Using internal auditors

Companies with many divisions (such as Pacific-Dunlop and News Corporation) or many branches (such as Coles Myer and Westpac) usually employ internal auditors. (We will discuss the internal audit, as a distinct audit activity, in Chapter 18.) Whenever an entity has an internal audit function, the auditor may coordinate his or her audit work with that of the internal auditors and/or use the internal auditors to provide direct assistance in the audit. The 'Professional environment' on page 277 explains the growing importance that businesses attach to the internal audit function.

PROFESSIONAL ENVIRONMENT **Internal audit**

If ever there were a forgotten grouping within the accounting profession it is the internal auditors. This is unfair, but probably inevitable.

The internal auditors suffered from the old idea that accountants were process-driven nerds with an array of differently coloured Biros spreading like military decorations across the tops of their breast pockets. They were the downtrodden of the business hierarchy. They were disliked on all sides. It was their job, after all, to ensure that processes were in place to safeguard the probity and security of the financial systems of the company.

But over the past few years everything has changed. The internal audit function is now seen as being at the heart of the integrity of a business. Two factors have turned their world upside down. The first has been the growing obsession of business with risk management and the second the Turnbull Report.

This set of principles and rules took corporate governance beyond mere financial fields and into virtually every area of corporate activity. It was the report which insisted on systems being set up that would enable boards of directors to understand their responsibilities, their companies and how they worked.

That is not as daft as it may sound. It was always surprising how many directors of companies were quite happy to let responsibilities for corporate rectitude rest with people further down the hierarchy. As Nigel Turnbull said at its launch in April last year: 'Internal control takes governance right into the heart of business. It forces the board of directors to understand the business. So many boards just assume these things happen.'

It was a happy conjunction that saw the Turnbull revolution arrive just as the whole concept of risk management throughout a business was being taken on board. Internal auditors could become risk managers. The cultural downside of being in internal audit could be escaped. Risk management, as any reader of management books knew, was suddenly the sexiest discipline to be in. Everyone wanted to be part of this. The large accounting firms pitched in with serious internal controls and risk management advisory services. Surveys flourished.

(Source: Extracted from Robert Bruce, 'How Internal Auditing Has Become Sexy', *The Times* (Thursday 12 October 2000))

Coordination with internal auditors

Internal auditors will usually monitor the internal control structure in each division or branch as part of their regular duties. The monitoring may include periodic reviews. In such cases, the independent auditor may coordinate work with the internal auditors and reduce the number of entity locations at which they would otherwise perform tests of control. The auditor must first consider the effectiveness of the internal auditors by:

- considering their organisational status:
  - Do they report to the highest level of management?
  - Are they free of operating responsibilities?
  - Are they free to communicate fully with the independent auditor?
- determining the scope of their work and, in particular, whether management acts on their recommendations;
- evaluating their technical competence;
- ensuring that their work is performed with due professional care.

When there is coordination of the work, the auditor should evaluate the quality and effectiveness of the internal auditors' work. AUS 604 (ISA 610), Considering the Work of Internal Auditing requires the independent auditor to confirm that:

- the work is performed by persons having adequate technical training and proficiency as internal auditors;
- the work of assistants is properly supervised, reviewed and documented;
- sufficient appropriate audit evidence is obtained to afford a reasonable basis for the conclusions reached;
- the conclusions reached are appropriate in the circumstances;
- any reports prepared by internal audit are consistent with the results of the work performed;
- any exceptions or unusual matters disclosed by internal auditors are properly resolved.

In coordinating work with internal auditors, the auditor may find it efficient to have periodic meetings with them, review their work schedules, obtain access to their working papers and review internal audit reports.

9 LEARNING OBJECTIVE

Explain the process of assessing control risk and documenting the conclusion.

Final assessment of control risk

The final assessment of control risk for a financial report assertion is based on evaluating the evidence gained from (1) procedures to obtain an understanding of relevant internal control structure components and (2) related tests of control. When different types of evidence support the same conclusion about the effectiveness of a control, the degree of assurance increases. Conversely, when they support different conclusions, the degree of assurance decreases; for example, the initials of an employee may be consistently present on documents, indicating performance of a control procedure, but the auditor's inquiries of the person initialling the documents may reveal that employee's lack of understanding of the control procedure being applied. The oral evidence would reduce the assurance obtained from the inspection of initials on the documents.

The evaluation of evidence involves both quantitative and qualitative considerations. In forming a conclusion about the effectiveness of a control procedure, the auditor often uses guidelines concerning the tolerable frequency of deviations from the proper performance of a control (usually expressed as a percentage). If the results lead the auditor to conclude that the frequency of deviations is less than or equal to the tolerable level, then the operation of the control is considered effective. Before reaching this conclusion, the auditor should also consider the causes of the deviations; for example, the auditor may attach different significance to excessive deviations caused by a vacation replacement than to those caused by an experienced employee. It is also essential in reaching a conclusion about effectiveness to determine whether a deviation is attributable to unintentional errors or to deliberate misrepresentations (irregularities). Evidence of one deviation due to an irregularity may be more important to the auditor than are more frequent deviations caused by errors. When it is concluded that the nature and frequency of deviations exceeds the tolerable level, the preliminary assessed level of control risk is not confirmed. In this case the auditor must revise the audit program for substantive procedures reflecting either a higher level of control risk than originally planned or the adoption of a predominantly substantive strategy for that particular assertion.

Documenting the assessed level of control risk

The auditor's working papers should include **documentation of the control risk**. Where control risk is assessed as high, only this conclusion needs to be documented. Where control risk is assessed as less than high, the basis for the assessment must be documented.

AUS 402 (ISA 400) does not prescribe the form of the documentation required. A common approach is to use narrative memoranda organised by financial report assertions. This approach is illustrated in Figure 7.8 (page 279), which documents the control risk assessments for selected sales transaction assertions.

FIGURE 7.8

Partial documentation of control risk assessments

CLIENT Young Fashions Limited	BALANCE SHEET DATE 30/9/X1
Completed by: CRS Date: 19/05/X1	Reviewed by: RMT Date: 28/05/X1

Control risk assessment for: Sales transactions

COMPLETENESS

Entity internal control structure policies and procedures relevant to completeness relate primarily to the computer listing of unmatched sales orders, bills of lading, packing slips and sales invoices. Based on discussions with sales ledger personnel on 11/5/X1 and with selected shipping personnel at Perth and Adelaide locations on 18/4/X1 and 8/5/X1, respectively, it normally can take up to two weeks between the placing of a sales order and shipment. It is rare, however, for an unmatched bill of lading or packing slip to remain on the unmatched documents report for more than two days. This was corroborated by examining the unmatched documents report for selected days (seeW/P XX–4–2 [not illustrated here]) where the longest period a bill of lading or packing slip was outstanding was two days. Selected transactions on these reports were traced to underlying documents with no exceptions.

Based on this examination of audit evidence, combined with the results of inquiry of sales ledger and shipping personnel and corroborating observations, control risk is assessed as slightly less than high.

RIGHTS AND OBLIGATIONS

Control risk is assessed as high.

(Source: Adapted from the AICPA, *Audit Guide: Consideration of the Internal Control Structure in a Financial Statement Audit*, 1990, p. 145)

Communication of internal control matters

AUS 710, Communication to Management on Matters Arising from an Audit (ISA 1007, Communications with Management) requires auditors to report material control weaknesses that have led to control risk being assessed as high for particular financial report assertions. We will explain the form and content of such reports in Chapter 14.

LEARNING CHECK

7.7 The preliminary assessment of control risk is based on knowledge obtained during the course of obtaining an understanding. It is primarily based on the design effectiveness of controls and involves identifying potential misstatements and identifying control procedures that prevent or detect such misstatements.

7.8 Planned tests of control are performed where the preliminary assessment of control risk is less than high and the auditor has adopted an audit strategy based on a lower assessed level of control risk. Such planned tests are aimed at assessing the operating effectiveness of the controls through inquiry of personnel, observation of procedures, inspection of documents and reperformance of control procedures by the auditor. The purpose of testing is to identify the extent of deviations from laid down controls.

7.9 The extent of testing is determined by the preliminary assessment of control risk. However, the final assessed level of control risk cannot exceed limitations determined by assessment of the control environment or the design effectiveness of individual controls. Where control risk is assessed as being less than high and the auditor proceeds to perform an audit strategy based on a reduced level of substantive procedures, the basis for that assessment must be documented.

7.10 The work of internal audit may be taken into account in performing tests of control, providing the independent auditor is satisfied as to the effectiveness of the internal audit function.

SUMMARY

Internal control is important for the effective operation of entities so, for all but very small entities, control risk for many assertions may be less than high. It is important for the auditor to obtain an understanding of the internal control structure as a basis for planning the audit and for identifying particular problems relating to control risk. As a minimum, the auditor is required to obtain an understanding of the information system and control environment, and to document that understanding. At this point, the auditor may make a preliminary assessment of control risk based primarily on his or her evaluation of the design effectiveness of control procedures.

Where preliminary assessment indicates that control risk for a particular assertion may be less than high, the auditor may choose to adopt a lower assessed level of control risk audit strategy. The auditor then proceeds to test controls as a basis for confirming that assessment and the consequent reduction in the level of substantive procedures. These tests of control are aimed at testing the operating effectiveness of the controls.

An important side effect of tests of control is the opportunity to advise management of significant internal control weaknesses.

KEY TERMS

Application controls, p. 253
Assessing control risk, p. 269
Audit trail, p. 252
Control environment, p. 252
Control procedures, p. 252
Design effectiveness of control procedures, p. 269
Deviations, p. 272
Documentation of the control risk, p. 278
Documenting the understanding, p. 261
Documents, p. 253
Dual-purpose test, p. 273
Extent of tests of control, p. 274
Flow chart, p. 264
General controls, p. 253
Independent checks, p. 254
Information processing controls, p. 253
Information system, p. 252
Inherent limitations, p. 258
Integrated test facility, p. 275
Internal control, p. 251
Internal control evaluation check list, p. 269
Internal control questionnaire, p. 261
Internal control structure, p. 250
Narrative memorandum, p. 266
Necessary controls, p. 269
Operating effectiveness of the control procedures, p. 272
Parallel simulation, p. 275
Physical controls, p. 255
Preliminary assessment of control risk, p. 267
Proper authorisation, p. 253
Records, p. 253
Segregation of duties, p. 254
Test data approach, p. 274
Tests of control, p. 272
Timing of tests of control, p. 274
Transactions, p. 252
Transaction walk-through review, p. 261

FURTHER READING

American Institute of Certified Public Accountants (AICPA) Control Risk Audit Guide Task Force, *Audit Guide: Consideration of the Internal Control Structure in a Financial Statement Audit*. New York, 1990.

Committee of Sponsoring Organisations of the Treadway Commission (COSO), *Internal Control — Integrated Framework*. AICPA, New York, 1992.

D'Aquila, Jill M., 'Is the Control Environment Related to Financial Reporting Decisions?', *Managerial Auditing Journal* (Vol. 13, No. 8, 1998), pp. 472–8.

Kelley, Thomas P., 'The COSO Report: Challenge and Counterchallenge', *Journal of Accountancy* (February 1993), pp. 10–18.

McKillop, G. & Shackall, M., 'Fraud Control: Best Practice in Business', *Australian Accountant* (October 1997), pp. 46–9.

National Commission on Fraudulent Financial Reporting, *Report of the National Commission on Fraudulent Financial Reporting*. Washington DC, 1987.

Spencer-Pickett, K. H., 'Diary of a Control Freak: The Manager's Guide to Internal Control', *Managerial Auditing Journal* (Vol. 13, No. 4/5, 1998), pp. 210–332.

Turpen, R., 'Fraud Prevention and the Management Accountant', *Management Accounting (USA)* (February 1997), p. 34.

Vanasco, Rocco, 'Fraud Auditing', *Managerial Auditing Journal* (Vol. 13, No. 1, 1998), pp. 4–71.

York, David, 'Assessing Risk', *Accountancy* (February 1997), p. 76.

Willingham, John J. & Wright, William F., 'Financial Statement Errors and Internal Control Judgments', *Auditing: A Journal of Practice and Theory* (Fall 1985), pp. 57–70.

Wright, Margaret, *Audit Guide No. 5: Auditing in an IT Systems Environment*, Australian Accounting Research Foundation, Melbourne, 1999.

APPENDIX 7A

Flow charting guidelines

Flow charting is a creative task, making it unlikely that any two people would draw flow charts exactly alike for a given system. The more commonly used flow charting symbols are shown in Figure 7.9 on the next page. Some firms supplement these basic symbols with more extensive sets of special-purpose symbols.

In addition to the four essential components of flow charts listed on page 265, the following guidelines are helpful in preparing useful flow charts:

- Identify the class(es) of transaction to be included in a flow chart.
- Collect information through interviews, observations and the review of documents.
- Visualise an organisational format for the flow chart (e.g. the number and order of columns needed to represent departments, functions or individuals) and prepare a rough sketch.
- Prepare the flow chart, selecting the correct symbols carefully.
- Test the completeness and accuracy of the flow chart by tracing a hypothetical transaction through it.

To illustrate, assume the auditor wishes to prepare a flow chart depicting the Hayes Company's processing of mail cash receipts. The following description of the processing system is based on information obtained through inquiries of entity personnel, observations, and review of documents. (*Note*: This is an extension of the system illustrated in Figure 7.4 on page 265.)

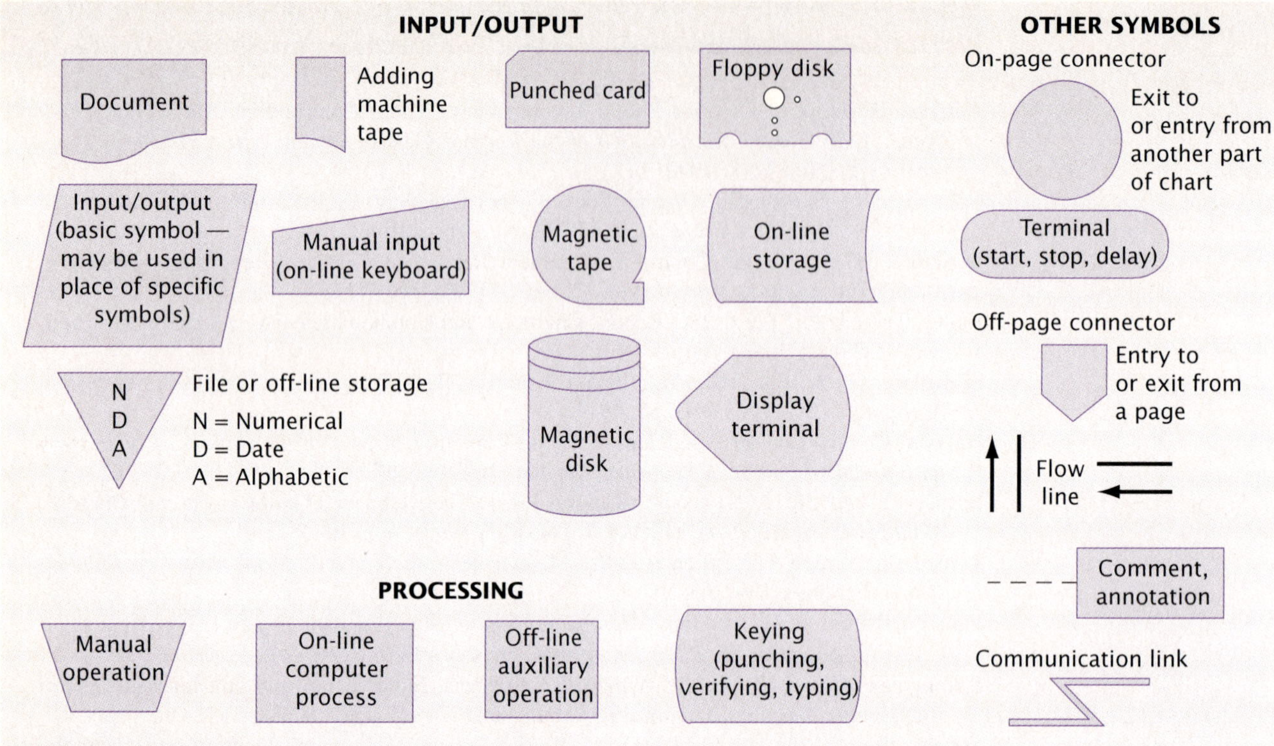

FIGURE 7.9

Flow charting symbols

Hayes Company — mail cash receipts processing

All receipts from customers are received by mail and are accompanied by a pre-printed remittance advice (the bottom portion of the billing originally sent to the customer). In the mail room, the cheques and remittance advices are separated. The cheques are restrictively endorsed (For Deposit Only) and a listing (prelist) of the cheques is prepared in triplicate and totalled. The cheques and one copy of the prelist are then forwarded to the cashier. The remittance advices and a copy of the prelist are sent to accounts receivable accounting, and another copy of the prelist is sent to general accounting.

The cashier prepares a bank deposit slip in duplicate and makes the daily bank deposit. The cashier forwards the validated copy of the bank deposit (slip stamped and dated by the bank) to general accounting and files the prelist by date.

In accounts receivable accounting, the remittances are processed on a computer. The accounts receivable clerk keys the remittance data into a cash receipts transaction file via an on-line terminal. This file is then processed to (1) update the receivables master file and (2) generate an entry in the general ledger transaction file, which is subsequently used to update the general ledger. This processing routine also generates two printed reports. A receivables summary report shows the total credits posted to the receivables master file and is reconciled to the total on the prelist received from the mail room. The remittance advices, prelist and summary report are then filed by date. The general ledger transaction report shows the daily totals for cash, discounts and receivables, and is forwarded to general accounting.

General accounting compares the totals from the prelist received from the mail room, the validated deposit slip received from the cashier and the general ledger transaction report received from accounts receivable accounting, and resolves any discrepancies. The documents are then collated and filed by date.

After considering the information opposite, the auditor envisions a flow chart with the following four columns: mail room, cashier, accounts receivable accounting and general accounting. After first preparing a rough sketch, the auditor prepares the flow chart depicted in Figure 7.10.

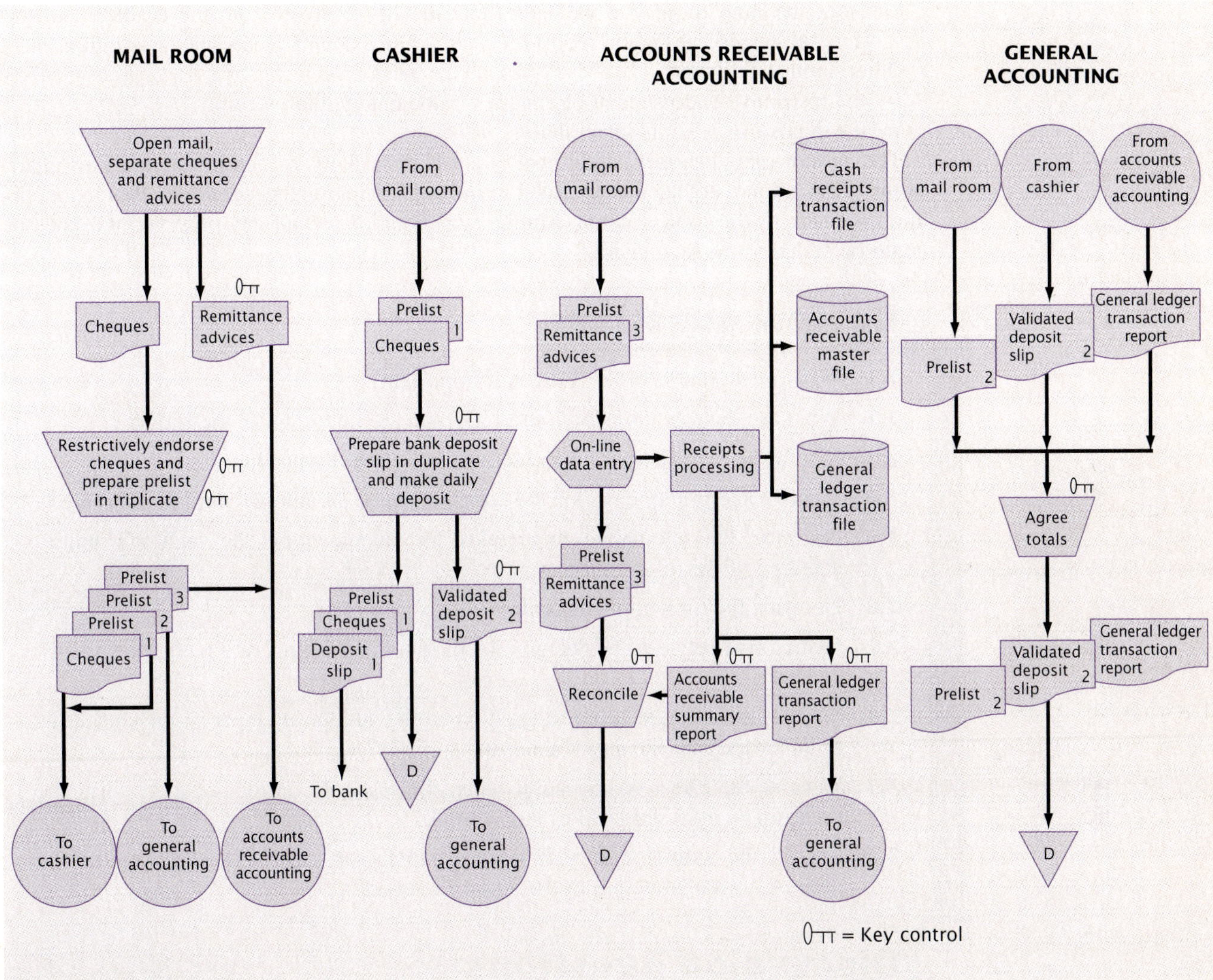

FIGURE 7.10

Flow chart for the processing of mail receipts

A flow chart is a means to an end, not an end in itself. It should enable the auditor to see the relationships that exist among controls and facilitate the identification of key controls related to specific financial report assertions. From studying the flow chart in Figure 7.10 (page 283), you could observe, for example, the following controls (among others):

- Documents and records:
  - — the use of preprinted remittance advices returned by customers with payments;
  - — the preparation of a prelist of cash receipts in triplicate for use in subsequent control;
  - — the retention of a validated (receipted) deposit slip for use in subsequent control;
  - — the generation of a sales summary report and general ledger transaction report for use in subsequent controls;
  - — the segregation of handling cash (mail room and cashier) from accounting for cash and receivables (general accounting and accounts receivable accounting).

- Independent checks:
  - — the reconciliation of the accounts receivable summary report in accounts receivable accounting with the total on the prelist received from the mail room;
  - — the reconciliation by general accounting of amounts reported on the prelist received from the mail room, the validated deposit slip received from the cashier, and the general ledger transaction report received from accounts receivable accounting.
- Other control activities:
  - — the restrictive endorsement of cheques immediately upon receipt;
  - — the deposit of receipts intact daily.

The auditor may document additional controls by making written notes on a flow chart. In this illustration a note could be added to indicate that an independent monthly reconciliation is made of the bank account. Similarly, annotations about any observed weaknesses could be added to the flow chart.

Review questions

7.1 What is internal control? Why is it important?

7.2 What are the categories of control? Which are important to the auditor?

7.3 Identify and explain the four categories of control procedure.

7.4 Identify and briefly describe the components of the internal control structure.

7.5 Describe the alternative techniques for documenting the auditor's understanding of the information system.

7.6 Describe the limitations of control.

7.7 Distinguish between the design effectiveness and the operating effectiveness of control.

7.8 What factors should be considered when the auditor attempts to coordinate his or her work with the entity's internal auditors?

7.9 What is the effect on the audit when the tests of control fail to confirm the preliminary assessed level of control risk?

7.10 Should the auditor comment on the satisfactory review and testing of the internal control structure in the auditor's report?

Discussion questions

7.1 The COSO guidelines on internal control have been described as providing a framework for generally accepted control policies similar to the financial reporting framework provided by Accounting Standards. Discuss the practicalities of prescribing such a framework in the light of the inherent limitations of control described on pages 258–9.

7.2 The auditor is primarily concerned with controls over financial reporting. Consider to what extent the auditor should consider controls over compliance with applicable laws and regulations, and controls over the effectiveness and efficiency of operations.

7.3 The major problems facing the development of e-commerce include those of access controls and security of on-line data. Identify problems that may concern auditors in auditing businesses engaged in e-commerce.

7.4 Describe the control problems faced by a small business, all of whose accounting records are held on a single desktop computer.

7.5 Two problems with the use of internal control questionnaires are:

- the large number of questions to which the answer is 'not applicable';
- 'yes' answers being too readily interpreted as indicating control strengths without adequate consideration being given to qualitative aspects.

Discuss the advantages and disadvantages of internal control questionnaires with particular reference to these two concerns.

7.6 Consider the possibility that an auditor, having adopted a lower assessed level control risk strategy, will be tempted to ignore adverse findings from tests of control as a result of the consequences for the cost and time involved in extending substantive procedures.

7.7 Describe situations in which an auditor may choose to adopt a predominantly substantive approach and make no attempt to make a preliminary assessment of control risk.

7.8 Describe the extent to which auditors are responsible for detecting and reporting control weaknesses as part of a financial report audit. Consider the argument that auditors should accept greater responsibility for detecting control weaknesses and reporting them either to directors or to outside users of financial reports.

Professional application questions

★ BASIC
★★ MODERATE
★★★ CHALLENGING

7.1 (Obtaining an understanding) ★

AUS 402, Risk Assessments and Internal Controls states that 'The auditor should: obtain an understanding of the internal control procedures sufficient to develop the audit plan'.

Required

(a) Explain what knowledge the auditor should obtain about the accounting and internal control systems in obtaining this understanding.

(b) Explain how the auditor obtains the understanding.

7.2 (Control activities and related assertions) ★★

This chapter identified several categories of control activity, using the following categorisation:

A. Information processing controls:
   1. General controls
   2. Application controls:
      (a) Proper authorisation
      (b) Documents and records
      (c) Independent checks
B. Segregation of duties
C. Physical controls
D. Performance reviews.

(*continued*)

The internal control system of the Turnbull Company includes the following control procedures:

1. An approved voucher is required for each cheque issued.
2. Two signatures are required on every cheque.
3. A supervisor makes daily cash register counts.
4. Overtime work must be approved by a supervisor.
5. Pre-numbered sales invoices are used in billing.
6. A second clerk is required to verify the accuracy of each voucher.
7. Employee payroll records are kept in a locked file cabinet.
8. An accounting supervisor reviews journal entries periodically for reasonableness of account classifications.
9. Sales ledger personnel make postings to only the sales ledger.
10. All vouchers must be stamped 'Paid' on payment.
11. Only computer equipment operators are allowed in the computer room.
12. A supervisor reconciles the sales subsidiary ledger with the balance of debtors in the general ledger.

Required

(a) Indicate the category of control activity applicable to each of the above twelve procedures.

(b) Identify an assertion to which each procedure pertains.

7.3 (Assessment of control risk) ★★

Jason Blythe is the audit senior on the audit of Grenache Limited, a wine distributor. The following is an excerpt from an interview between Jason and the sales ledger clerk, Ralph Mitchell.

Jason: What are the controls over the cash receipts our company receives?

Ralph: Good! The receptionist opens the mail each day and makes sure each cheque is crossed. He then gives me all the cheques to post against the sales ledger.

Jason: What happens then?

Ralph: I make a list of all the cheques received — for control purposes. Then, I record each cheque against each customer's record on the sales ledger. After the cheques have accumulated for a couple of days, I give them to the receptionist to bank. The receptionist keeps all banking slips as a record in case there are any queries later.

Jason: Are there ever any differences between the cheque value and the associated invoice?

Ralph: Sometimes there are. Usually it relates to a special discount that has been authorised by me or the sales manager. If the differences are not material, I will normally raise a credit note to write off the difference.

Jason: What about reconciliations?

Ralph: Of course! The cheque listings that I have prepared are reconciled to the cash recorded in the sales subsidiary ledger; this is then reviewed by the financial controller. The main reconciliation of the sales ledger is performed only at the end of each year. This one is, of course, checked by you guys as part of your annual audit. You cannot get a better independent check than that!

Required

(a) Comment on any control strengths or weaknesses in the cash receipts/sales ledger system of Grenache.

(b) Describe your preliminary assessment of control risk on this part of the client's system.

7.4 (Testing of internal controls) ★★

An audit was performed for Daley's Motors. The evidence for the audit of cash receipts and cash payments was based primarily on testing controls. The audit assistant, as part of his interim control testing, noted that all bank reconciliations for the year had been reviewed — a good control. However, he also noted that for the last three months there was a 'net miscellaneous reconciling item' of $42 000.

The audit assistant questioned the accountant about this item and was told the client did not have time to follow up this matter. He was assured that 'it would all come out in the wash by balance date'. Because the reconciling item was immaterial, the audit assistant performed no further work in this area.

Required

(a) Decide whether the audit assistant obtained sufficient evidence to rely on this control.

(b) If you were the audit senior on the engagement, nominate what changes you would make to the year-end work program (if any).

(Professional Year Programme of the ICAA — 1996, Accounting 2 Module — adapted)

7.5 (Assessment of control risk) ★★★

Exotic Adventures is a travel company owned by two directors, Mike and Mal. The following is a summary of their internal controls:

1. Mike and Mal are each responsible for their own booking files. On the back of each file are the accounting records, which form the input for the month-end trust account reconciliation.
2. All manual trust cheques are approved and signed by Mike or Mal for all locations. This year electronic funds transfer (EFT) was introduced to allow agents to pay wholesalers and airlines directly for travel arrangements. Each payment is entered directly into the file by the agent. No hard copies of the EFT transactions are made.
3. Receipts are issued for all moneys received, although they are not pre-numbered or accounted. Banking is done daily, with all cheques and cash from both agents deposited together.
4. All payments that are not client related are made by Mal through a 'general' account. Only Mike and Mal have access to the general account.
5. At the end of each month, a trial balance of the files is prepared and balanced by Mal against the bank account.

Required

(a) Comment on any control strengths or weaknesses in the client's system.

(b) Explain your preliminary assessment of control risk in this part of the client's system.

(Professional Year Programme of the ICAA — 1996, Advanced Audit Module — adapted)

7.6 (Reporting on internal controls) ★★★

You are the manager of a large auditing firm and have recently finalised the audit of MPV Limited, a large, publicly listed company. The audit went smoothly and no major problems were encountered. As in prior years, your firm adopted a controls-based approach to the audit, given the efficient and effective internal control structure that MPV has in place. All of the exceptions that were noted in the testing phase were raised with the appropriate level of management and were not considered serious enough to bring to the attention of the board. All follow-up work as a result of these exceptions has been satisfactorily performed.

(*continued*)

The financial controller, Mr B, has received a request from the overseas parent company that all subsidiaries obtain an opinion on their internal control structure from their external auditors as part of the overall internal audit function of the group. Mr. B has approached your firm for the opinion and has indicated that the opinion, given that the audit has just been satisfactorily completed, could be prepared and signed with no extra audit time required.

Required

How much reliance can be placed on the results of the audit that has just been completed? Give reasons for your answer.

(Professional Year Programme of the ICAA — 1999, Advanced Audit Module — adapted)

Case studies

7.1 (Information systems and internal controls) ★★

Fabulous Fashion Limited (FF) runs four private colleges which provide education and training for people in the fashion industry. Its two-year course includes training in design, textiles and the manufacture and retail of fashion garments. You are conducting the interim audit for the year ended 30 June 20X2. The tangible fixed assets of each college are recorded in an asset register which is maintained at each college location by each college manager. The system operates as described below:

1. In order to obtain new assets, a purchase requisition form is completed and approved by the manager at each college.
2. The requisition is sent to head office, where the purchasing officer checks the requisition for approval and completes a purchase order for the new asset.
3. Assets costing more than $5000 are approved by the financial accountant. All assets over $20 000 require board approval.
4. The purchase order is then sent to the supplier and a copy is sent to the central store at the head office location.
5. The asset is received by the central store where the receiving clerk checks that all the asset details agree with those on the receiving report and the copy of the purchase order. The receiving clerk then issues the asset with its computer-generated sequential barcode number. This barcode is fixed to the asset and written on the receiving report and the supplier invoice.
6. The relevant college manager inputs the new asset details into the asset register using a copy of the purchase order, the original requisition and the asset's barcode.
7. For disposal or write-off of an asset, an asset disposal write-off form is completed by the relevant college manager, signed and sent to head office. Disposals and write-offs are approved by the financial accountant. A copy of the form is filed at head office and the approved original returned to the college manager for action. The college manager then updates the fixed asset register for the subsequent disposal.
8. The asset register is maintained on FAST — a tailored fixed assets computer system — and reconciled to the general ledger by each college manager monthly.
9. The FAST system calculates depreciation automatically each month using the rate input by the college manager at the time the asset was added to the register.

Required

(a) Identify five internal control strengths on which you would rely for your audit.
(b) Design tests of control to evaluate the effectiveness of each control identified.

(Professional Year Programme of the ICAA — 1996, Accounting 2 Module — adapted)

7.2 (Reliance on internal audit) ★★★

Assume you are planning the 31 March 20X2 audit of HP Limited (HP), a large financial planning association based in Melbourne. HP has offices in all capital cities of Australia and established an internal audit department late in the previous financial year. As part of the audit planning process, you had a meeting with the head of the department, Ms T. Your notes from the meeting are documented below.

1. In the first few months of operation, the department reported to the chief financial officer (CFO), to enable it to gain a good understanding of the systems. Once this set-up phase was completed, the organisational structure of the internal audit department changed. The department now reports to the chief executive officer (CEO), who is also chairman of the board of directors.
2. Ms T sets the department's work program after receiving feedback on risk areas from the CFO, the financial controllers of each state and the chairman. Over the past year, about 90 per cent of the work program was achieved; only the internal audit of the Perth office was postponed to the next financial year. This was due to a request from the board that the department allocate resources to investigate a suspected travel claims fraud in Brisbane.
3. Each month, Ms T prepares a report for the CEO, outlining the work planned and performed, and a summary of the results achieved. The CEO presents this report at the board's monthly meeting.
4. Ms T was appointed chief internal auditor in February 20X1 after spending three years as the financial controller in Sydney. Previously she was an audit manager at a Big 5 firm. She has four staff: two graduates undertaking the ICAA commerce program, an ex-public sector auditor and an assistant who is completing his commerce degree part time.
5. Ms T has familiarised herself with the Standards set by the Institute of Internal Auditors. Audit programs are being written as each audit is performed; these programs will be revised and updated as the department develops.
6. Some of the financial controllers have been hostile to Ms T since the department was established. She suspects this is due to professional jealousy, because they had also applied for the chief internal auditor's position.
7. Two of the six board members have yet to be convinced of the value of the internal audit department. They believe that its focus should be on improving operational efficiency, rather than on dealing with compliance matters. As a compromise, the CEO has agreed to ask Ms T to set aside 20 per cent of the department's time to undertake a performance audit of the company's administrative procedures.
8. Ms T and her team have visited each office this year (except Perth), examining the systems and carrying out detailed transactions testing. Many minor control breaches were noted, although none likely to result in major errors or fraud. These breaches were reported in detail to the relevant financial controller.

(continued)

9. The board has been under enormous pressure over the past two months because an offer to buy the business has been received from an international financial planning chain. Accordingly, the internal audit department's reports have received little attention in the monthly board meetings.

At the end of the meeting, Ms T suggests to you that it would be advantageous if the internal and external auditors work together more closely. She notes two advantages: firstly, the audit fee may fall and, secondly, the board will appreciate her contribution to reducing HP's costs.

Required

Prepare a memo to the audit manager, outlining your overall assessment of the internal audit department and your opinion on whether the work of the internal audit department can be relied upon.

(Professional Year Programme of the ICAA — 1999, Advanced Audit Module — adapted)

chapter 8

PART 3 Audit testing methodology

PART 3

Designing the audit testing methodology involves making decisions about a suitable approach to performing a particular audit. The auditor must first consider the appropriate sampling approach (as we will discuss in **Chapter 8**), which is important because it allows the auditor to make an opinion about a population without testing every item within it. The decisions about the type of sampling approach and the size of the sample depend on the type of audit testing being performed and the required level of assurance, which will be different for each audit engagement.

The most significant decisions associated with the audit testing methodology relate to the performance of substantive procedures. The audit risk model states that an appropriate level of substantive procedures needs to be performed to gain the required level of detection risk to ensure that audit risk is kept at a satisfactory level. In **Chapter 9** we will consider issues associated with designing substantive procedures — in particular, how the required level of detection risk affects the nature, timing and extent of substantive procedures.

The principles discussed in this part of the text (and Part 2) apply to all transaction cycles of the audit, which we will explain further in Part 4.

chapter 8 Audit sampling

Overview

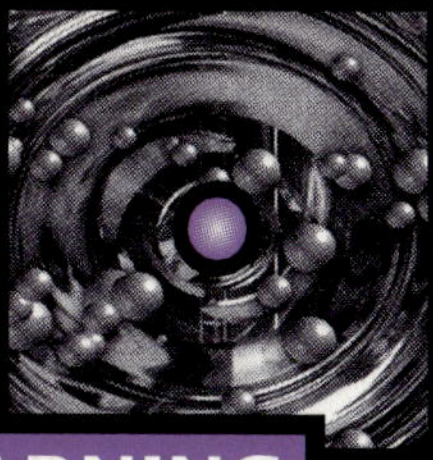

LEARNING OBJECTIVES

After studying this chapter, you should be able to:

1. define audit sampling and discuss its applicability
2. differentiate sampling and non-sampling risks and explain the types of sampling risk
3. differentiate statistical and non-statistical sampling
4. explain the steps in planning a sample test
5. indicate the factors that affect sample size
6. describe the methods of selecting a sample
7. explain the steps in evaluating the results from a sample
8. describe the principal methods of statistical sampling used in auditing
9. explain the circumstances leading to the choice of a specific statistical method
10. indicate why auditors may use non-statistical sampling.

Professional statements

AUSTRALIAN		INTERNATIONAL	
AUS 514	Audit Sampling and Other Selective Testing Procedures	ISA 530	Audit Sampling and Other Selective Testing Procedures

Sampling is well established as an audit procedure, but this was not always the case. A textbook published in 1881 contained the following statement:

> A thorough and efficient Audit should embrace an examination of all the transactions of a Company, and an auditor acting on this principle would ascertain that all had been duly entered and discharged.[1]

However, the changing size and complexity of business was causing this to become an unrealistic approach. Lindley LJ in the London and General Bank case (*Re London and General Bank Ltd* (No. 2) (1895), 2 Ch. 673) accepted sample testing as providing sufficient evidence for audit purposes. He said:

> Where there is nothing to excite suspicion, very little enquiry will be reasonable and quite sufficient; and in practice, I believe, businessmen select a few cases haphazard, see that they are right, and assume that others like them are correct also.

The importance of audit sampling in current practice is underscored by the issuance of AUS 514 (ISA 530), Audit Sampling and Other Selective Testing Procedures. In addition, the Australian Accounting Research Foundation has published a comprehensive audit guide entitled *Audit Guide No. 1: Audit Sampling* (hereinafter referred to as the Audit Sampling Guide) to assist auditors in applying AUS 514 (ISA 530).

In this chapter, we will explain the basic concepts of audit sampling and its application in tests of control and substantive tests of details. The chapter is divided into four sections. In the first section, we will explain how evidence obtained from sample testing introduces the risk that the evidence may not be representative of the population from which the sample is taken. This risk is known as sampling risk. In the second section, we will describe the process of sampling in audit testing from the planning stage, through the selection and testing of the sample, to the evaluation of the results of sample tests. In the third section, we will explain the use of statistical sampling techniques and consider the relative merits of the different types of statistical sampling technique. In the final section, we will consider why many practitioners may choose to use non-statistical sampling rather than statistical sampling.

The four case studies attached as appendices to this chapter illustrate the use of sampling in the performance of auditing procedures. The first case study involves the use of non-statistical sampling while the remaining three illustrate the use of different statistical sampling plans in auditing.

BASIC CONCEPTS OF SAMPLING

1 LEARNING OBJECTIVE

Define audit sampling and discuss its applicability.

Sampling is defined in AUS 514.03 (ISA 530.03) as:

> ... the application of audit procedures to less than 100 per cent of items within an account balance or class of transactions such that all sampling units have a chance of selection.

Sampling may be used in compliance or substantive testing. An example of sampling in tests of control is the examination of a sample of purchase invoices to see that they have been initialled, by the employee responsible, as having been checked against the receiving report. The objective of the test is to confirm compliance with the laid down control procedure. As explained in Chapter 7, the proportion of deviations in the sample enables the auditor to draw conclusions as to the effectiveness of the control procedure, contributing to the assessment of control risk.

An example of sampling in substantive tests of details is the checking of a sample of invoices against receiving reports to verify the occurrence of recorded purchase transactions. The incidence of errors in the sample will enable the auditor to draw conclusions as to the occurrence of recorded purchase transactions.

One of the most important issues for the auditor to consider in audit sampling is the risk of drawing an incorrect conclusion from the sample selected. Another important consideration is the distinction between **statistical sampling** and **non-statistical sampling**.

2 LEARNING OBJECTIVE

Differentiate sampling and non-sampling risks and explain the types of sampling risk.

Sampling risk and non-sampling risk

When sampling is used to obtain audit evidence, uncertainties may result from factors associated directly with the use of sampling (**sampling risk**) and from those unrelated to sampling (**non-sampling risk**).

Sampling risk

Sampling risk is defined in AUS 514.07 (ISA 530.07) as:

> ... the possibility that the auditor's conclusion, based on a sample, may be different from the conclusion reached if the entire **population** were subjected to the same audit procedure.

The following example illustrates this point: if a bag contains eighty red balls and twenty white balls, then a representative sample of ten would contain eight red balls and two white balls. Sampling risk is the risk that a randomly selected sample of ten would not consist of eight red and two white balls. The larger the sample, the more probable it is that it will consist of red and white balls in the same proportion as the population. Sampling risk, therefore, is the risk that the auditor's conclusion about internal controls or the details of transactions and balances based on testing a sample may be different from the conclusion that would result from an examination of the entire population. In performing tests of control and substantive tests of details, the following types of sampling risk — as outlined in AUS 514.07 (ISA 530.07) — may occur (Figure 8.1):

(a) the risk the auditor will conclude, in the case of a test of control, that control risk is lower than it actually is (**risk of overreliance**), or in the case of a substantive test, that a material error does not exist when in fact it does (**risk of incorrect acceptance**). This type of risk affects audit effectiveness and is more likely to lead to an inappropriate audit opinion; and

(b) the risk the auditor will conclude, in the case of a test of control, that control risk is higher than it actually is (**risk of underreliance**), or in the case of a substantive test, that a material error exists when in fact it does not (**risk of incorrect rejection**). This type of risk affects audit efficiency as it would usually lead to additional work to establish that initial conclusions were incorrect.

These risks can have a significant impact on both the effectiveness and efficiency of the audit. The risk of overreliance and the risk of incorrect acceptance relate to audit effectiveness. When reaching either of these erroneous conclusions, the auditor may find that the combined procedures may be insufficient to detect material misstatements, and that he or she may not have a reasonable basis for an opinion. In contrast, the risk of underreliance and the risk of incorrect rejection relate to the efficiency of the audit. When reaching either of these erroneous conclusions, the auditor will increase substantive procedures unnecessarily. However, such effort will ordinarily lead to a correct conclusion, ultimately, and the audit will nevertheless be effective. The sampling risk associated with audit effectiveness is of much greater concern than the sampling risk associated with audit efficiency because it can lead to an inappropriate audit opinion.

Sampling risk in substantive procedures is effectively the same as detection risk for that particular audit procedure (see Chapter 9). The terms 'sampling risk' and 'detection risk' are used interchangeably throughout this chapter. Figure 8.1 is a summary of the types of sampling risk for tests of control and substantive tests of details, and their effects on the audit.

FIGURE 8.1

Sampling risks for tests of control and substantive tests of details

TYPES OF SAMPLING RISK FOR TESTS OF CONTROL

Assessed levels of control risk based on sample	True operating effectiveness of entity's control structure policy or procedure: Adequate for planned assessed level of control risk	True operating effectiveness of entity's control structure policy or procedure: Inadequate for planned assessed level of control risk
Supports preliminary assessment of control risk	Correct decision	Risk of assessing control risk too low (Audit ineffective)
Does NOT support preliminary assessment of control risk	Risk of assessing control risk too high (Audit inefficient)	Correct decision

TYPES OF SAMPLING RISK FOR SUBSTANTIVE TESTS OF DETAILS

Sample estimate of account balance or error in account balance	True state of entity's recorded account balance: Not materially misstated	True state of entity's recorded account balance: Materially misstated
Supports conclusion that recorded balance is NOT materially misstated	Correct decision	Risk of incorrect acceptance (Audit ineffective)
Supports conclusion that recorded balance is materially misstated	Risk of incorrect rejection (Audit inefficient)	Correct decision

Non-sampling risk

Non-sampling risk refers to the component of audit risk that is not due to examining only a portion of the data. Therefore, even if the auditor selected 100 per cent of items within a population for testing, there would still be a risk of drawing an inappropriate conclusion. Sources of non-sampling risk include human mistakes (such as failing to recognise errors in documents, applying auditing procedures that are inappropriate to the audit objective, and misinterpreting the results of a sample) and reliance on erroneous information received from another party. Non-sampling risk can never be mathematically measured. However, proper planning and supervision and adherence to the quality control standards described earlier can hold it to a negligible level.

LEARNING OBJECTIVE

Differentiate statistical and non-statistical sampling.

Statistical and non-statistical sampling

Statistical sampling has the following two characteristics according to AUS 514.10 (ISA 530.10):

1. **random selection** of a sample; and
2. use of probability theory to evaluate sample results, including the measurement of the sampling risk.

Statistical sampling does not replace judgement. It provides a decision model within which the auditor's judgements as to the acceptable level of detection risk, testing materiality and other variables are the inputs. Given the acceptable level of both sampling risk and materiality for the audit procedure, the model specifies the sample size and evaluates the sample results in terms of sampling risk and materiality. The interpretation of the results is, therefore, only as reliable as the values placed on the sampling risk and testing materiality.

Non-statistical sampling is a sampling approach that does not have the above characteristics of statistical sampling. In non-statistical sampling the auditor uses judgement directly, both to determine sample size (given the planned level of detection risk and of testing materiality) and to interpret the results against the audit objective. Historically, non-statistical sampling was called judgement sampling; however, as revealed in the preceding discussion, both approaches require a significant amount of judgement. The main difference between the two is that sampling risk can be quantified when using statistical sampling.

The choice of non-statistical or statistical sampling does not affect the selection of auditing procedures to be applied to a sample. Moreover, it does not affect the appropriateness of evidence obtained about individual sample items or the appropriate response by the auditor to errors found in sample items. These matters require the exercise of professional judgement.

Current practice in Australia

In Australia the majority of audit firms would use some type of audit sampling for most audit clients. A large number of firms employ non-statistical sampling, because it allows the auditor a greater degree of judgement in choosing a sample size and evaluating results based on prior client knowledge. A common approach to sample selection is **haphazard selection**. (*Note*: This method is inappropriate when using statistical sampling.) Methods vary among firms and among clients within firms. Statistical sampling is much more likely, for example, for the audit of a financial institution where the audit approach relies heavily on compliance testing. However, for a predominantly substantive audit of a small manufacturing entity, for example, non-statistical sampling is more likely to be used.

No recent studies have examined the methods of sampling used by Australian auditors; however, Hitzig performed a study of sampling in practice in the United States in 1995 (see the 'Professional environment' below).

PROFESSIONAL ENVIRONMENT

Audit sampling — a survey of current practice

Neal Hitzig performed a study of sampling in audit practice in the United States in 1995. He found that 96 per cent of firms surveyed used some form of audit sampling, and that of these firms, 39 per cent used statistical sampling and 94 per cent used non-statistical sampling. Despite many firms not using statistical sampling, a number employed probability sampling techniques. None of these firms used only block selection and 5 per cent used only haphazard selection.

Methods of sample selection	%
Random	30
Probability proportional to size	27
Systematic	53
Haphazard	39
Block	17

Hitzig also found that a large percentage of firms ignored (or were unaware of) tolerable error, risk and the requirements to project errors to the population as outlined in the Auditing Standard, especially when employing non-statistical sampling.

Non-statistical sampling	%
Projected errors to population?	55
Considered tolerable error?	66
Considered risk of incorrect acceptance?	49

Many firms reported using audit sampling to test controls, but did not rely on those tests to reduce the extent of their substantive procedures. An implication of this finding is that a number of firms may not be giving due consideration to the audit risk model, which suggests that lower control risk can be associated with a higher acceptable level of detection risk.

The results suggest that many firms could benefit from further training on audit sampling.

(Source: Based on N. B. Hitzig, 'Audit Sampling: A Survey of Current Practice', *CPA Journal* (July 1995), pp. 54–7)

Other types of testing

The following two methods of selecting items for audit testing do not constitute 'audit sampling'. The auditor can choose to select all items (100 per cent examination) or select specific items.

Selecting all items

The auditor may decide that it is appropriate to examine the entire population of items that make up the account balance or class of transactions. This decision is unlikely in tests of control but may sometimes occur in substantive testing; for example, in performing the audit of an account balance that is made up of a small number of large-value items, and when inherent and control risks are high, the auditor may find it cost-effective to examine the entire population. This may be a means of reducing sampling risk to zero, but does not constitute audit sampling.

Selecting specific items

Selective testing is the examination of specific items within a population, based on the auditor's knowledge of the business and the characteristics of the population being tested. AUS 514.25 (ISA 530.25) outlines specific items that may be selected using this method:

- *High value or key items.* Individual items may be selected because they are of high value or are suspected to be prone to error, such as overdue accounts receivable. The rest of the population, if material in the aggregate, may be subjected to testing by sampling.
- *All items over a certain amount.* These items may be selected to verify a large proportion of the total amount.
- *Items to obtain information.* The auditor may obtain information about the client's business, nature of transactions, accounting and internal control systems.
- *Items to test procedures.* The auditor may examine a specific item to determine whether a particular procedure is being performed.

Selective testing may be an efficient way in which the auditor can collect audit evidence, but it does not constitute audit sampling. The characteristic that distinguishes selective testing from sampling, whether statistical or non-statistical, is that the results of verification of the selected items provide no information as to the probability of material misstatement in items not tested.

USE OF SAMPLES FOR AUDIT TESTS

Regardless of whether statistical or non-statistical sampling is used, the auditor undertakes some common steps:

- planning the sample;
- selecting and testing the sample; and
- evaluating the results.

4 LEARNING OBJECTIVE

Explain the steps in planning a sample test.

Planning the sample

Once the auditor has decided that examining a sample will yield sufficient evidence on the operation of a control or on the absence of material misstatements in a transaction class or account balance, it is important that he or she then proceeds to plan the sample testing process properly if the results are to be projected to the entire population. Planning the sample involves the following steps:

- determining the objectives of the test;
- defining what errors or deviations are being sought;
- identifying the population and **sampling unit**; and
- deciding the size of the sample.

Determining the objectives of the test

The auditor needs to consider the specific objectives to be achieved and the combination of audit procedures that is most likely to achieve those objectives. Audit sampling is applicable to both tests of control and substantive procedures. However, it is not equally applicable to all the auditing procedures that may be used; for example, audit sampling is widely used in vouching, confirming and tracing, but rarely used in inquiring, observing and analysing.

Tests of control

The overall purpose of tests of control is to evaluate the effectiveness of the design and operation of internal controls. Sampling is applicable in testing the operation of controls only when there is a trail of documentary or electronic evidence of the performance of control procedures. Such control procedures normally fall into the categories of authorisation procedures, documents and records, and independent checks.

Sample testing of the performance of the control procedures is sometimes known as **attribute sampling** because each sample tested will have one of two attributes — either that the control has been properly performed or that it has not. The outcome of testing is known as a **deviation rate**, representing the proportion of transactions tested that have not been processed in accordance with laid down control procedures.

Substantive tests of details

Sampling plans for substantive tests of details may take one of two approaches. The first approach is to obtain evidence that an account balance is not materially misstated (for example, the book value of accounts receivable). The second approach is to make an independent estimate of some amount (for example, to value inventory for which no recorded book value exists). **Variable sampling** is sometimes used in substantive tests of details because it is a statistical technique to estimate the dollar amount of an account balance or some other quantity.

Defining what errors or deviations are being sought

The auditor must consider what constitutes an error by referring to the objectives of the test. In tests of control, the test objective is the identification of 'deviations' from the laid down control procedure. In substantive testing, the test objective is the identification of 'errors or misstatements' in recorded transactions or balances.

The type of error or deviation expected will be related to the objective of the test. However, an audit procedure may also reveal errors that were not specifically being sought. When examining purchase invoices to verify that quantities invoiced agree with those on the receiving report, an auditor may also notice some other defect in the invoice, such as errors in posting prices on the invoices. Sample evidence can be interpreted as evidence of the incidence of errors or deviations in the population as a whole only for those errors or deviations that are being sought. Other errors must be regarded as individual occurrences, which must be separately evaluated. It may be necessary for the auditor to conduct further tests that are designed to determine the extent of such errors; he or she must never neglect an error simply because it was not what was being verified by a particular test. Cleverly concealed frauds are often discovered by such chance events.

Identifying the population and sampling unit

The auditor must carefully identify the population and the sampling unit. In particular, he or she must consider the objective of the audit test to ensure that the population and sampling unit are appropriate.

Population

The first stage in planning the sample test is to identify the relevant population. AUS 514.06 (ISA 530.06) defines a 'population' as:

> ... the entire set of data from which a sample is selected and about which the auditor wishes to draw conclusions.

The auditor must ensure that the population is:

- *appropriate* to the objective of the sampling procedure. When testing for overstatement of accounts payable, for example, the auditor could define the population as the accounts payable listing. However, when testing for understatement of accounts payable, it is inappropriate to use the accounts payable listing; the appropriate population is subsequent payments, unpaid invoices, suppliers' statements and unmatched receiving reports.
- *complete*. Ensuring completeness is important and requires particular care. It is made easier by the use of pre-numbering in recording transactions. For the auditor to be able to make appropriate assessments of the level of monetary errors or of the application of a particular control, the population needs to include all relevant items from throughout the period. A complete population is particularly important when the auditor is using computer-assisted audit techniques to perform sample selection — that is, he or she must use the correct file.

Sampling unit

A sampling unit means the individual items constituting a population — for example, sales invoices, debtors' balances, fixed assets on a register and a listing of suppliers. It will often appear to be self-evident but sometimes requires closer consideration. Accounts payable, for example, may be made up of a population of unpaid invoices or amounts owing to particular suppliers. The auditor will need to consider whether any particular advantage arises out of using a particular sampling unit. Sometimes, customers will be unable to respond to a request for confirmation of the balance owed, but they can confirm individual invoices outstanding; in such cases, the best sampling unit would be the unpaid invoices making up the balance.

When **probability-proportional-to-size sampling** is used, the sampling unit is an individual dollar (or other monetary unit) contained in the population. We will discuss this method later in the chapter (see page 312).

Stratification

A common approach to increasing audit efficiency in sampling is **stratification**. Stratification is defined in AUS 514.11 (ISA 530.11) as:

> ... the process of dividing a population up into sub-populations, each of which is a group of sampling units which have similar characteristics (often monetary value).

The objective of stratification is to focus greater audit work on areas that are of higher inherent risk or potentially materially misstated. Monetary value is the most common method of stratifying a population, particularly for asset balances. The auditor's main risk with asset balances is overstatement, so he or she will want to place more emphasis on testing items of large dollar values. In a fixed asset register, for example, the assets may be split into three strata:

1. balances greater than $2 000 000;
2. balances of $100 000 to $2 000 000;
3. balances less than $100 000.

The auditor may choose to perform tests on a random sample of 50 per cent of items in group 1, on a random sample of twenty items in group 2, and on a random sample of ten items in group 3. When using computer-assisted audit techniques, stratification of the population and sample selection can be performed by most auditing software packages according to whatever criteria are specified by the auditor.

Where individual items are selected for 100 per cent testing on the grounds of materiality or otherwise, the results of testing such items must be separated from the results of sample testing the remaining items in the population.

Stratification is a means of reducing audit costs while increasing the efficiency of the audit. It is a very popular technique to assist in audit sampling, particularly in the audit areas of accounts receivable, inventory and property, plant and equipment.

5 LEARNING OBJECTIVE

Indicate the factors that affect sample size.

Deciding the size of the sample

In determining an appropriate sample size, the auditors' main concern is with reducing sampling risk to an acceptably low level. The level of sampling risk that the auditor is willing to accept will have an inverse relationship with the sample size required. The sample size can be determined by the application of a statistically based formula or through the exercise of professional judgement.

Sampling, as an audit procedure, is valid only if the sample selected for testing is representative of the population from which it is drawn, such that the incidence of errors or deviations in the sample closely approximates the incidence of errors or deviations in the population. The larger the sample, the more representative of the population it is likely to be. However, only a 100 per cent sample will be completely representative. Given that the purpose of sampling is to save time and cost, it would be pointless to audit a larger sample than necessary. Population size, which is the factor most commonly presumed to be the major influence on sample size, has no effect on sample size for populations over 5000. Table 8.1 outlines factors that influence sample size for tests of control, and the Standard extract that follows on page 305 explains each of these factors.

TABLE 8.1

Factors that influence sample size for tests of control

Factor	Effect on sample size
An increase in the auditor's intended reliance on accounting and internal control systems	Increase
An increase in the rate of deviation from the prescribed control procedure that the auditor is willing to accept	Decrease
An increase in the rate of deviation from the prescribed control procedure that the auditor expects to find in the population	Increase
An increase in the auditor's required confidence level (or, conversely, a decrease in the risk that the auditor will conclude that the control risk is lower than the actual control risk in the population)	Increase
An increase in the number of sampling units in the population	Negligible effect

(Source: AUS 514, Appendix 1)

.01 *The auditor's intended reliance on accounting and internal control systems.* The more assurance the auditor intends to obtain from accounting and internal control systems, the lower the auditor's assessment of control risk will be, and the larger the sample size will need to be. . . .

.02 *The rate of deviation from the prescribed control procedure the auditor is willing to accept* ***(tolerable error)***. The lower the rate of deviation that the auditor is willing to accept, the larger the sample size needs to be.

.03 *The rate of deviation from the prescribed control procedure the auditor expects to find in the population* ***(expected error)***. The higher the rate of deviation that the auditor expects, the larger the sample size needs to be so as to be in a position to make a reasonable estimate of the actual rate of deviation. Factors relevant to the auditor's consideration of the expected error rate include the auditor's understanding of the business (in particular, procedures undertaken to obtain an understanding of the accounting and internal control systems), changes in personnel or in the accounting and internal control systems, the results of audit procedures applied in prior periods and the results of other audit procedures. High expected error rates ordinarily warrant little, if any, reduction of control risk, and therefore in such circumstances tests of control would ordinarily be omitted.

.04 *The auditor's required confidence level.* The greater the degree of confidence that the auditor requires that the results of the sample are in fact indicative of the actual incidence of error in the population, the larger the sample size needs to be.

.05 *The number of sampling units in the population.* For large populations, the actual size of the population has little, if any, effect on sample size. Probability theory suggests that once the number of items in a population exceeds 5000, any increase in population size has no significant effect on the size of the sample. For small populations, however, audit sampling is often not as efficient as alternative means of obtaining sufficient appropriate audit evidence.

Table 8.2 outlines factors that influence sample size for substantive procedures.

TABLE 8.2

Factors that influence sample size for substantive procedures

Factor	Effect on sample size
An increase in the auditor's assessment of inherent risk	Increase
An increase in the auditor's assessment of control risk	Increase
An increase in the use of other substantive procedures directed at the same financial report assertion	Decrease
An increase in the auditor's required confidence level (or, conversely, a decrease in the risk that the auditor will conclude that a material error does not exist, when it does exist)	Increase
An increase in the total error that the auditor is willing to accept (tolerable error)	Decrease
An increase in the amount of error the auditor expects to find in the population	Increase
Stratification of the population when appropriate	Decrease
The number of sampling units in the population	Negligible effect

(Source: AUS 514, Appendix 2)

The following Standard extract explains each of the factors listed in Table 8.2:

.01 *The auditor's assessment of inherent risk.* The higher the auditor's assessment of inherent risk, the larger the sample size needs to be. Higher inherent risk implies that a lower detection risk is needed to reduce the audit risk to an acceptably low level, and lower detection risk can be obtained by increasing sample size.

.02 *The auditor's assessment of control risk.* The higher the auditor's assessment of control risk, the larger the sample size needs to be. This is because where the control risk is high to reduce audit risk to an acceptably low level, the auditor needs a low detection risk and will rely more on substantive tests. The more reliance that is placed on substantive tests (that is, the lower the detection risk), the larger the sample size will need to be.

.03 *The use of other substantive procedures directed at the same financial report assertion.* The more the auditor is relying on other substantive procedures (tests of detail or analytical procedures) to reduce to an acceptable level the detection risk regarding a particular account balance or class of transactions, the less assurance the auditor will require from sampling and, therefore, the smaller the sample size can be.

.04 *The auditor's required confidence level.* The greater the degree of confidence that the auditor requires that the results of the sample are in fact indicative of the actual amount of error in the population, the larger the sample size needs to be.

.05 *The total error the auditor is willing to accept (tolerable error).* The lower the total error that the auditor is willing to accept, the larger the sample size needs to be.

.06 *The amount of error the auditor expects to find in the population (expected error).* The greater the amount of error the auditor expects to find in the population, the larger the sample size needs to be in order to make a reasonable estimate of the actual amount of error in the population. Factors relevant to the auditor's consideration of the expected error amount include the extent to which item values are determined subjectively, the results of tests of control, the results of audit procedures applied in prior periods, and the results of other substantive procedures.

.07 *Stratification.* When a population can be appropriately stratified, the aggregate of the sample sizes from the strata generally will be less than the sample size that would have been required to attain a given level of sampling risk had one sample been drawn from the whole population.

.08 *The number of sampling units in the population.* For large populations, the actual size of the population has little, if any, effect on sample size. Probability theory suggests that once the number of items in a population exceeds 5000, any increase in population size has no significant effect on the size of the sample. Thus, for small populations, audit sampling is often not as efficient as alternative means of obtaining sufficient appropriate audit evidence.

The case study in Appendix 8A provides a formula that could be used to determine sample size based on judgements concerned with required assurance, tolerable error and expected error.

Selecting and testing the sample

The test objectives and sample size are often determined during the audit planning and detailed in the audit plan. The staff member responsible is then required to select the required number of individual members of the population for testing, perform the test and evaluate the results.

LEARNING OBJECTIVE 6

Describe the methods of selecting a sample.

Selecting the sample

The fundamental principle in selecting the sample is that each item in the population must have a chance of being selected, but not necessarily an equal chance. Statistical sampling requires random selection so each sampling unit has a known chance of being selected.

A sample can be selected in a number of ways. The selection approaches suggested in AUS 514, Appendix 3 include:

- random;
- systematic;
- haphazard.

Another type of selection is called **block selection**. This is not considered a method of audit sampling because most populations are structured such that items in a sequence can be expected to have similar characteristics. Given this problem, it is difficult to draw valid inferences about the population based on the sample selected. However, this method of selection may be appropriate; for example, if the auditor suspects fraud in accounts payable, then he or she may decide to review all transactions for a particular month.

Random selection

Random selection is generally considered to be the best method of obtaining a sample to evaluate the results statistically. A computer may be used to generate random numbers to test. Alternatively, if computer-assisted audit techniques are being used and the population is on the auditor's computer, then most auditing software packages will allow an audit sample to be selected at random. The advantage of this method is that it does not allow auditor bias to affect the selections of the sample, either knowingly or not. Random selection is generally associated with statistical sampling, but is often used in non-statistical sampling as well. Historically, auditors used random number tables to generate random samples.

Systematic selection

Systematic selection is the process of dividing the number of sampling units in the population by the sample size to give a **sampling interval**. It is generally considered to be the most widely used sample selection technique in auditing.[2] The population — say 8200 — is divided by the sample size — say 40 — to obtain the sampling interval — 205 in this case. Every 205th item is then selected, starting from a randomly selected point between 1 and 205. To be able to evaluate the results statistically, the auditor must randomly select the starting point, not using the haphazard method of selection.

The criticism of systematic selection is that the population may have a fixed pattern; for example, employee numbers of supervisors may always end in 0, such that a sampling interval which is a multiple of 10 will result in a sample of supervisors only, or one that excludes supervisors. The auditor should have sufficient knowledge of the population to make sure this does not happen. When this problem could arise, the auditor should use random selection to select the sample.

Haphazard selection

Haphazard selection is the selection of a sample without following a structured technique. Sometimes, this is the only practical method when the population is not ordered in any numerical sequence, such as postings to the repairs and maintenance expense account in the ledger. The auditor must take care to avoid any bias (such as avoiding the first or last entry on each page of the ledger) particularly conscious bias (such as avoiding difficult-to-locate items). The method is not recommended where other methods are available, because the absence of bias cannot be subsequently evidenced. Haphazard selection is inappropriate when the auditor is using statistical sampling because he or she cannot measure the probability of an item being selected.

An illustration of the problem with unconscious bias is outlined below in the 'Professional environment'.

PROFESSIONAL ENVIRONMENT Introducing audit sampling

Margaret Stewart and John Dunn (University of Strathclyde) conducted the following experiment on a class of 140 auditing students. The purpose of the experiment was to illustrate the inherent problems in haphazard audit sampling.

The students were asked to:

1. Select a number from 1 to 10;
2. Select one of the following invoices:

2360	2240
2480	2420
2670	2660
2590	2380.

The results were as follows:

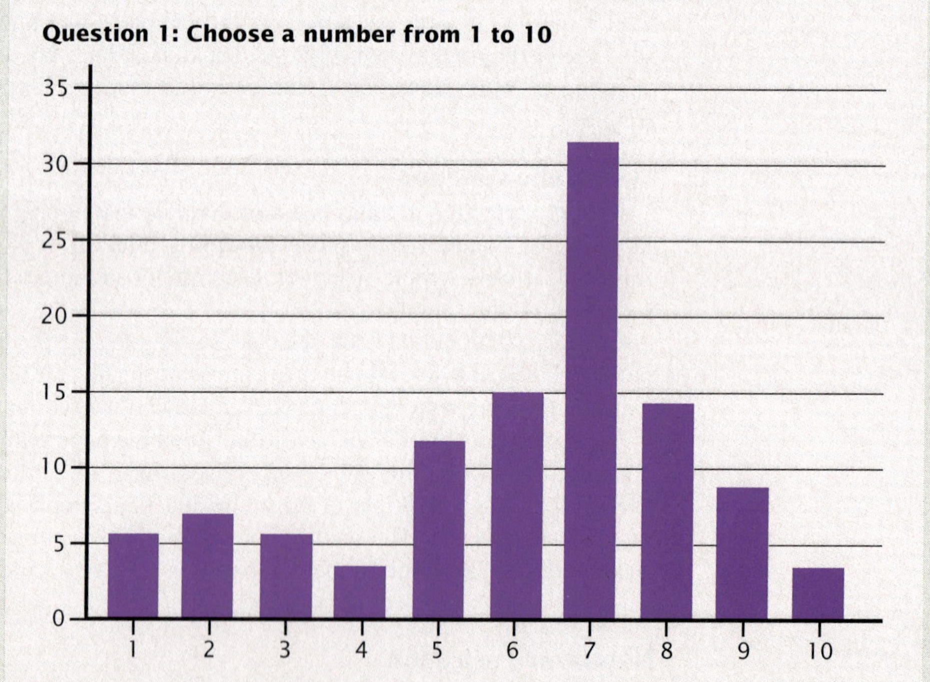

A random selection would have led to one-tenth of the class selecting each number. The results show the human affinity with the number seven. (Our weeks are seven days long; we indulge in seven deadly sins; we drink 7-Up; etc.) Whether the students were aware of this or not, their selection of a random number was significantly biased by this innate affinity.

Question 2: Select an invoice for testing

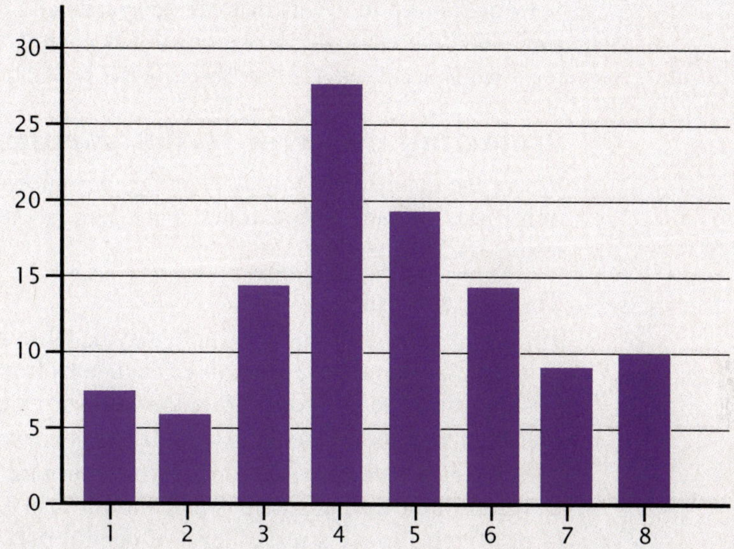

Each invoice should have been picked about 12.5 per cent of the time if it was random. However, a bias towards the transactions in the middle was found to occur because they would appear to be 'more random' than those at either end.

(Source: Based on Margaret Stewart and John Dunn, 'Introducing Auditing Sampling', *The Auditor's Report* (Vol. 23, No. 3, 2000))

Testing the sample

Having drawn the sample, the auditor should then perform audit procedures that are appropriate to the test objective on each item selected. In the case of missing documents or similar difficulties encountered in completing the test, the auditor must consider the item to be misstated or to represent a deviation from laid down controls, and evaluate the sample evidence accordingly.

7 LEARNING OBJECTIVE

Explain the steps in evaluating the results from a sample.

Evaluating the results

Each error or deviation discovered will need to be examined for its implications (i.e. its qualitative aspects). Errors or deviations that appear to be consistent with those anticipated during the procedure's planning can then be projected to consider the effect on the population. Given the planned level of sampling risk, it is assumed that the sample deviation or error rate is representative of the rate of deviation or errors in the population.

Both non-statistical and statistical sampling require the sample results to be projected on the population. The key difference with non-statistical sampling is that sampling risk is not mathematically quantified, but assessed on a more qualitative basis.

Qualitative aspects of errors or deviations

In analysing errors, the auditor must consider whether the error or deviation:

- has an effect on the whole population; or
- is an isolated or localised occurrence.

An error due to posting a sales invoice to the wrong customer's account will not affect the total balance of accounts receivable. Similarly, a control deviation properly authorised by management will not affect the assessed level of control risk.

Errors related to events that can be specifically identified (such as payroll errors occurring when the computer broke down and payrolls had to be prepared manually) may be regarded as localised and not affecting the population as a whole.

Projecting the error to the population

Where the qualitative analysis identifies deviations or errors consistent with the objective of the test, the auditor then draws conclusions about the population, based on the results of testing the sample.

Tests of control

The rate of deviations in the sample may be taken to be the rate of deviations in the population. If, of a sample of sixty, three deviations from laid down control procedures are discovered, then the projected deviation rate (or expected error) for the population can be estimated as 5 per cent ($3 \div 60 = 5$). If this is no worse than the tolerable deviation rate (or tolerable error), then it is appropriate to confirm the preliminary assessment of control risk. However, if the deviation rate is much lower than expected, then this cannot be interpreted as justifying a lower assessed level of control risk. This level of risk has been determined from an evaluation of the overall effectiveness of controls.

If the projected deviation rate exceeds the tolerable deviation rate, then the preliminary assessment of control risk is not confirmed. Depending on qualitative considerations of actual deviations or on the existence of compensating controls, the auditor must reassess control risk at a higher level, thus reducing the acceptable detection risk. This means that the auditor has to revise the audit program to increase the level of substantive procedures.

Substantive tests

The projection of errors in substantive testing depends on whether the object of the test is to estimate (1) the population mean (**mean-per-unit method**) or (2) the relative differences between recorded and audited amounts (**difference estimation**). Each of these methods requires a different projection from sample results to estimated population values. (Both methods are discussed in more detail later in this chapter.)

Where a population has been stratified, the **projected error** must be related to the specific sub-population. Errors in items singled out for selective testing must be omitted from the errors projected to the population.

Where projected error approaches or exceeds tolerable error, the auditor will need to consider carefully whether additional evidence may be necessary. It would normally be appropriate to select a further sample, thus reducing sampling risk. (However, where statistical sampling is employed, certain sampling plans do not provide for extension of the existing sample.) If the further sample confirms the projected results, indicating a substantial error, then the auditor will ask management to revise the recorded amount. If the projected error is only slightly greater than the tolerable error and management is unwilling to make any corrections, then the error will be carried forward to the working paper showing aggregate uncorrected misstatements for evaluation at the end of the audit (see Chapter 14).

LEARNING CHECK

8.1 Sampling is the testing of a representative sample to obtain evidence about a population. It may be used for audit compliance or substantive testing.

8.2 Sampling risk is the risk that evidence derived from testing a sample may not reflect characteristics of the whole population.

8.3 The advantage of statistical sampling is that sampling risk may be quantified. However, many auditors prefer non-statistical approaches. Both approaches require the use of professional judgement.

8.4 Where sample testing is considered appropriate, the auditor must consider the objectives of the test, the appropriate population from which the sample is to be selected, the errors or deviations being sought, and the size of the sample.

8.5 Stratification is a common method of increasing audit efficiency. The auditor subdivides a population into two or more sub-populations based on areas that are of higher inherent risk or potentially materially misstated.

8.6 In selecting a sample the auditor may use the random, systematic or haphazard selection methods. If the auditor is using statistical sampling, then only the random and systematic (with a random start) selection methods are appropriate.

8.7 Once testing is completed the auditor needs to assess the projected error and compare it to the tolerable error. If the projected error is greater than the tolerable error, then the auditor may decide to do more testing. If this is not satisfactory, then for compliance testing the auditor should assess control risk at a higher level; for substantive testing the auditor should ask management to adjust the recorded amount.

8 LEARNING OBJECTIVE

Describe the principal methods of statistical sampling used in auditing.

STATISTICAL SAMPLING TECHNIQUES

The major statistical sampling techniques used by auditors are:

- attribute sampling plans;
- variable sampling plans;
- probability-proportional-to-size sampling.

Attribute sampling plans

Attribute sampling plans refer to three different methods of sampling that are used to test the operating effectiveness of controls by estimating the rate of deviation:

1. *Attribute sampling*. This is the most common attribute sampling plan. It is a statistical sampling plan to estimate the proportion of a characteristic in a population. In relation to testing controls the auditor determines the effectiveness of a control in terms of deviations from a prescribed internal control policy. An example of this method is shown in Appendix 8C.
2. ***Sequential sampling***. This method is used to improve audit efficiency when it is expected that there will be relatively few deviations in the population. The auditor may stop testing as soon as he or she obtains enough assurance to assess that the control being tested is operating effectively.
3. ***Discovery sampling***. This method is used when the expected rate of error occurrence in the population is extremely low and the expected error rate can be set at zero.

Variable sampling plans

The main difference between attribute sampling and variable sampling is that the auditor estimates the error in terms of a quantity rather than an occurrence rate. Variable sampling is generally used in substantive testing to estimate a monetary misstatement in an account balance. The different types of variable sampling plan include the following three plans:

1. *Unstratified mean-per-unit method.* When using this approach the auditor estimates a total population amount by calculating the mean for items in the sample and projecting the mean to the number of items in the population. This method is illustrated in Appendix 8D.
2. *Stratified mean-per-unit method.* This method is essentially similar in approach to the unstratified mean-per-unit, except that the population is stratified into two or more sub-populations. The rationale for adopting this approach is to improve audit efficiency.
3. *Difference estimation.* Using this approach, the auditor calculates the mean difference between audited and recorded amounts of the sample items, and projects the mean difference to the population. The estimated population difference between audited values and recorded (book) values is added or subtracted from the total recorded value to produce an estimate of the true population total.

Probability-proportional-to-size sampling

The most commonly used statistical sampling technique for substantive testing is probability-proportional-to-size (PPS) sampling. This technique is also known as dollar unit sampling. As previously discussed, attribute sampling is used to reach a conclusion about a population in terms of the rate of occurrence. Variable sampling is generally used to reach conclusions about a population in terms of a monetary (dollar) amount. PPS sampling is a hybrid sampling plan that uses characteristics of both because it uses attribute sampling theory to express a conclusion as a monetary (dollar) amount rather than a rate of occurrence.

PPS sampling takes each dollar of the population as the sampling unit and tests whether it is correctly stated, incorrectly stated or tainted. Incorrectly stated and tainted dollars are then projected to the number of dollars recorded as the population to estimate the extent of monetary error in the population. Application of this sampling plan is illustrated in the case study in Appendix 8B.

Explain the circumstances leading to the choice of a specific statistical method.

Choice of statistical sampling method

If statistical sampling is to be used for tests of control, then the auditor must use one of the attribute sampling plans. However, if substantive testing is being done, then there is a choice of either PPS sampling or variable sampling. Here, we will consider the relative merits and drawbacks of each method.

PPS sampling

The advantages of PPS sampling over variable sampling are that:

- it is not affected by variability and, therefore, it is easy to determine sample size;
- it is mathematically simple and, therefore, easy to apply, especially if computer assistance is not available;
- it usually enables conclusions to be drawn on the basis of small sample sizes where the auditor expects no or few errors;
- individually material items are automatically selected for sampling.

The disadvantages of PPS sampling are that:

- it is unsuitable for detecting errors of understatement because understated items, being smaller than they ought to be, are less likely to be selected for sampling. Special considerations are needed where a PPS sample detects understated items;

- if detected errors exceed those expected when the sampling plan is developed, then the auditor is likely to be forced to conclude that the population is materially misstated and to have to conduct further audit work;
- as expected error increases, sample size is likely to exceed that required by variables sampling;
- the required cumulative addition of the population for the purposes of drawing the sample may not be convenient.

Audit situations in which PPS sampling will produce sufficient evidence using smaller sample sizes are those where:

- few errors are expected;
- the auditor is principally concerned with overstatement;
- understatement errors are unlikely;
- it is convenient to obtain a cumulatively added listing of the population.

The technique is most useful for verifying the existence of assets and the occurrence of recorded transactions where sampling risk is moderate to low. Many audit tests where sampling is appropriate fall into this category, such as inventory pricing and accounts receivable circularisation.

Variable sampling

Variable sampling is preferable where:

- errors of understatement are expected or are being sought;
- the population includes zero and negative balances;
- many errors are expected;
- it may be necessary to extend the sample to estimate the population value more reliably.

Difference estimation techniques work reliably only where fifty or more errors are found. Where fewer errors are expected, the choice is between PPS sampling and the mean-per-unit methods of variable sampling.

Variable sampling is most likely to be useful in the audit of large computerised accounting systems with the assistance of computer audit software. This will be the case especially when most of the testing can be performed directly on the computer. In such circumstances, however, the auditor must consider whether the time spent planning and evaluating a sample may be better spent using the computer audit software to perform a 100 per cent test.

NON-STATISTICAL SAMPLING TECHNIQUES

10 LEARNING OBJECTIVE

Indicate why auditors may use non-statistical sampling.

The evidence suggests that non-statistical sampling is much more widely used than statistical sampling. Given that non-statistical sampling is less rigorous than statistical sampling, why would auditors use non-statistical sampling?

Why use non-statistical sampling?

Part of the reason for the prevalence of non-statistical sampling is probably found in AUS 502.17 (ISA 500.17), which states that:

> The auditor needs to consider the relationship between the cost of obtaining audit evidence and the usefulness of the information obtained.

The rationale for non-statistical sampling is often that it is less costly and less time consuming but can be just as effective in satisfying audit objectives. This advantage is explained by the following:

- *The lower training costs of non-statistical sampling*. It usually takes less time to learn non-statistical sampling methods.
- *The ease of implementation of non-statistical sampling*. These methods are less complex, which makes them easier and quicker to apply in the field and also reduces the risk that staff will misuse the method.
- *The impracticality of random selection*. In some cases it is impractical to apply random selection — for example, where the population of source documents is large and unnumbered.
- *Proposed adjustment based on qualitative analysis*. The increased precision of a statistical estimate is often not needed because the proposed audit adjustment is based on the auditor's qualitative analysis of sample results rather than a mathematical calculation.[3]

An example of non-statistical sampling of substantive tests of details is shown in Appendix 8A.

Formal and informal non-statistical sampling

A formal non-statistical sampling plan uses a structured approach to determine the sample size and evaluate sample results. The main differences from a statistical sampling plan is that the selection of sample items may be haphazard and the level of sampling risk is not precisely quantified.

An informal approach is an unstructured approach to determining the sample size and evaluating the results. Sample size and results are determined on an entirely qualitative basis, so any conclusions about the population are also qualitative. Disadvantages with informal non-statistical sampling include the following:

- *Training difficulties*. There is no systematic way to train staff in this approach, which requires experience and, therefore, is problematic for junior staff.
- *The absence of consistency and uniformity*. Auditors in the same circumstances may reach significantly different judgements about the scope of audit work necessary on an engagement.
- *Peer review exceptions (and potential litigation problems)*. There may not be enough documentation to prove that the auditor has complied with Auditing Standards on sampling.
- *Incorrect evaluation of sampling risk*. The unstructured approach increases the likelihood that the auditor will fail to recognise an unacceptable level of sampling risk.[4]

LEARNING CHECK

8.8 Statistical sampling techniques relate to sampling for attributes (as in the case of tests of control) and sampling for variables (as is commonly the case in substantive testing) or probability-proportional-to-size sampling.

8.9 The advantages of statistical sampling are that: samples are determined and evaluated in accordance with probability theory; it provides a uniform framework for making consistent judgements; and it requires explicit consideration of relevant factors.

8.10 The advantages of non-statistical sampling are that: it has lower training costs; it is easy to implement; sometimes random selection is impractical; and adjustments are often based on qualitative analysis anyway.

SUMMARY

The purpose of sampling is to obtain evidence about an account balance or transaction class without examining each individual item or transaction. The risk is that the sample examined might not be representative of the population from which the sample is drawn (such as transactions from a transaction class, or items making up an account balance). Increasing the size of the sample reduces this risk. Sample size in auditing is a function of:

- the risk the auditor is willing to accept, based on the audit risk model;
- the magnitude of control deviations or errors that are considered material;
- the level of expectation that deviations or errors do exist in the population.

Statistics tells us much about how to make sure that our sample is sufficiently large to provide the required level of knowledge about the account balance or transaction class. Auditors sometimes use statistical sampling techniques in their sample tests. However, non-statistical sampling is also commonly adopted, often using the principles of statistical theory in the planning of the sample test.

In selecting the sample from the population, the auditor should adopt a technique that provides reasonable assurance that the sample is representative and unaffected by selection bias. Random sampling is required for statistical sampling, but less rigorous techniques may be applied for non-statistical sampling.

In examining the sample, the auditor must remember that it should be representative of the population and that its purpose is to assess the extent to which deviations or errors could be present in the population from which the sample is drawn. The major statistical sampling techniques used by auditors are attribute sampling plans, variable sampling plans and probability-proportional-to-size sampling. Attribute sampling is used for compliance testing, while the other two techniques are used for substantive testing.

Non-statistical sampling is widely used and, if undertaken properly, provides valid evidence. Reasons for its widespread use include its lower training costs, its ease of use and the fact that the auditor often bases adjustments on a qualitative assessment irrespective of the sampling method employed.

KEY TERMS

Attribute sampling, p. 302
Block selection, p. 307
Deviation rate, p. 302
Difference estimation, p. 310
Discovery sampling, p. 311
Expected error, p. 305
Haphazard selection, p. 299
Mean-per-unit method, p. 310
Non-sampling risk, p. 297
Non-statistical sampling, p. 297
Population, p. 297
Probability-proportional-to-size sampling, p. 303
Projected error, p. 310
Random selection, p. 299
Risk of incorrect acceptance, p. 297
Risk of incorrect rejection, p. 297
Risk of overreliance, p. 297
Risk of underreliance, p. 297
Sampling interval, p. 307
Sampling risk, p. 297
Sampling unit, p. 301
Selective testing, p. 301
Sequential sampling, p. 311
Statistical sampling, p. 297
Stratification, p. 303
Systematic selection, p. 307
Tolerable error, p. 305
Variable sampling, p. 302

NOTES

1. F. W. Pixely, *Auditors: Their Duties and Responsibilities*. Effingham Wilson, London, 1881, Reprinted by Arno Press, New York, 1976, p. 154.
2. N. B. Hitzig, 'Audit Sampling: A Survey of Current Practice', *CPA Journal* (July 1995), p. 56.
3. Dan M. Guy, Douglas Carmichael & O. Ray Whittington, *Audit Sampling: An Introduction*, 3rd edn. John Wiley & Sons, New York, 1998, p. 210.
4. See Note 3, p. 212.

FURTHER READING

Akresh, Abraham D. & Tatum, Kay W., 'Audit Sampling — Dealing with the Problems', *Journal of Accountancy* (December 1988), pp. 58–64.

Australian Accounting Research Foundation, *Audit Guide No. 1: Audit Sampling*. Melbourne, 1983.

Elder, Randal J. & Allen, Robert D., 'An Empirical Investigation of the Auditor's Decision to Project Errors', *Auditing: A Journal of Practice and Theory* (Fall 1998), pp. 71–87.

Epstein, B. J., 'Attributes Sampling: A Local Firm's Experience', *Journal of Accountancy* (January 1986), pp. 130–5.

Felix, William L., Grimlund, Richard A., Koster, Frank J. & Roussey, Robert S., 'Arthur Andersen's New Monetary Unit Sampling Approach', *Auditing: A Journal of Practice and Theory* (Fall 1990), pp. 1–16.

Gillett, Peter, R. & Srivastava, Rajendra, P., 'Attribute Sampling: A Belief-Function Approach to Statistical Audit Evidence', *Auditing: A Journal of Practice and Theory* (Spring 2000), pp. 145–55.

Guy, Dan M., Carmichael, Douglas & Whittington, O. Ray, *Audit Sampling: An Introduction*, 3rd edn. John Wiley & Sons, New York, 1998.

Jones, Peter, *Statistical Sampling and Risk Analysis in Auditing*. Gower Publishing, Hampshire, England, 1999.

Levine, M., 'Probability Proportional to Size Sampling and Its Application to Auditing', *Chartered Accountant in Australia* (August 1985), pp. 53–7.

Manson, Stuart, 'Statistical Sampling', in M. Sherer & S. Turley (eds), *Current Issues in Auditing*, 3rd edn. Paul Chapman Publishing, London, 1997, pp. 234–53.

Robertson, Jack C. & Rouse, Robert, 'Substantive Audit Sampling — The Challenge of Achieving Efficiency along with Effectiveness', *Accounting Horizons* (Spring 1994), pp. 35–44.

Woodhead, A. D., 'The Other Audit Risk: The Impact of False Rejections on Audit Planning', *Managerial Auditing Journal* (Vol. 12, No. 1, 1997) pp. 4–8.

APPENDIX 8A

Non-statistical sampling of substantive test of details

Facts of the case

Objective	Circularisation of accounts receivable to confirm existence
Population	Accounts receivable (excluding credit balances) $4 250 000
Sampling unit	Account balances 1100
Variability	$100 to $140 000

Judgements

Five accounts over $50 000 totalling $500 000 were considered to be individually material, leaving a population of 1095 accounts with a value of $3 750 000 to be sampled.

Tolerable error	$130 000
Control risk assessment	Moderate
Effect on detection risk of other substantive procedures	Analytical procedures provide moderate assurance. Cut-off test provides moderate assurance.
Acceptable level of sampling risk	Moderate
Expected errors	Few or none

Sample size

Using the formula:

$$\frac{\text{Population value}}{\text{Tolerable error}} \times \text{Reliability factor}$$

where the reliability factor is determined using the data in Table 8.3, produces a sample size of:

$$\frac{3\,750\,000}{130\,000} \times 2.3 = 66.$$

TABLE 8.3

Reliability factors for non-statistical sampling

Required level of assurance	Reliability factor: Few or no errors expected	Reliability factor: Some errors expected
Substantial	3.0	6.0
Moderate	2.3	4.0
Little	1.5	3.0

(Source: Adapted from AICPA, *Audit and Accounting Guide: Audit Sampling*, p. 59)

Sample selection

The sample was selected systematically from a listing of accounts receivable balances from the accounts receivable ledger, and had been added and agreed in total to the balance on the control account in the general ledger.

Sample results

Replies were received from the five large customers and from sixty of those sampled. The accounts of the six customers failing to reply were verified by other tests and found to be correctly stated. The reported errors were considered qualitatively. Those considered to reflect errors in the population are detailed in Table 8.4 on the next page.

TABLE 8.4

Errors considered to reflect errors in the population

	Population	Sample		
	Recorded amount ($)	Recorded amount ($)	Audited amount ($)	Overstatement errors ($)
Material items	500 000	500 000	499 000	1000
Sampled items	3 750 000	180 000	177 000	3000

Projected error

Using the ratio method, the projected error is:

$$\frac{\$3\,000}{\$180\,000} \times \$3\,750\,000 = \$62\,500.$$

Conclusion

The entity corrected the $3000 errors found in the sample, but disputed the $1000 error on the large accounts, resulting in a net projected population error of:

$$\$62\,500 - \$3000 + \$1000 = \$60\,500.$$

This is significantly lower than the tolerable error, so the auditor concluded that the recorded existence of accounts receivable is not materially misstated.

APPENDIX 8B

Probability-proportional-to-size sampling

Facts of the case

Objective — To verify that standard costs used in valuing ending inventory have been accurately determined

Population — Inventory, all of which is valued at standard cost, with a recorded value of $1 375 000 and consisting of 320 different items

Sampling unit — Individual dollars of recorded value

Judgements

Tolerable error — $53 500

Internal control — Not assessed because there are no procedures for checking the accuracy of standard costs. Control risk, therefore, is 100 per cent.

Other substantive procedures — The operation of the costing system has been tested, particularly the determination of variances, all of which are immaterial. Analytical procedures confirm that inventory appears to be properly valued. Allowing for reliance on other substantive procedures, detection risk is judged to be 70 per cent.

Inherent risk — Inherent risk, overall, is judged to be low and no material errors have been detected by this test in previous years. Inherent risk is assessed at 70 per cent.

Assurance required Audit risk is set at 5 per cent. Using the audit risk model, risk for this particular test is determined as being:

$$\frac{\text{Audit risk}}{\text{Inherent risk} \times \text{Control risk} \times \text{Detection risk}}$$

$$\frac{0.05}{0.7 \times 1.0 \times 0.7} = 0.102 \text{ or } 10\%.$$

Ninety per cent assurance, therefore, is required from this particular test.

Expected errors Two errors are expected on items not individually material.

Sample size

Using the formula:

$$\frac{\text{Population value}}{\text{Tolerable error}} \times \text{Reliability factor}$$

where the reliability factor is determined as per the data in Table 8.5, sample size is calculated as being:

$$\frac{1\,375\,000}{53\,500} \times 5.33 = 137.$$

The sample interval is $\frac{1\,375\,000}{137} = 10\,036$ (say $10\,000$).

TABLE 8.5

Table of reliability factors for attribute sampling

Number of sample errors	Confidence level 90%	Confidence level 95%
0	2.31	3.00
1	3.89	4.75
2	5.33	6.30
3	6.69	7.76
4	8.00	9.16

(*Note*: Based on Poisson distribution.)

Sample selection

The sample is selected from inventory listings which have been printed from the computer with a running cumulative total. The listing is test-added to verify its completeness and the sample is selected as shown in Table 8.6 (see page 320) for the first twenty items on the list. A random start below $10 000 is selected (say 4000) and every 10 000th dollar is then systematically selected and used as a hook to catch the inventory item containing that dollar.

As can be seen in Table 8.6, the random sample start of $4000 comes within the range of $2000 to $10 000 on the cumulative value column. Within that range lies inventory number 1101 with a value of $8000, thereby resulting in its selection for testing. The second hook to select an item is $14 000 ($4000 + $10 000), resulting in the selection of inventory number 1103.

TABLE 8.6

Details of first twenty items selected

Inventory no.	Qty	Unit cost ($)	Total value ($)	Cumulative value ($)	Hook ($)	Sample ($)
1100	20	100	2 000	2 000		
1101	400	20	8 000	10 000	4 000	8 000
1102	100	5	500	10 500		
1103	1000	7	7 000	17 500	14 000	7 000
1104	10	50	500	18 000		
1105	300	40	12 000	30 000	24 000	12 000
1200	1500	3	4 500	34 500	34 000	4 500
1201	7	1200	8 400	42 900		
1202	300	20	6 000	48 900	44 000	6 000
1203	20	5	100	49 000		
1204	200	5	1 000	50 000		
1205	30	50	1 500	51 500		
1206	20	75	1 500	53 000		
1207	500	4	2 000	55 000	54 000	2 000
1208	11	1200	13 200	68 200	64 000	13 200
2100	300	4	1 200	69 400		
2101	20	10	200	69 600		
2102	50	5	250	69 850		
2103	100	15	1 500	71 350		
2104	50	10	500	71 850		

Sample results and projected error

Three alternative scenarios will be considered:

1. No errors were found.
2. Two errors were found in items with a recorded value less than the sampling interval.
3. Three errors were found, including one error in an item with a recorded value above the sampling interval.

Scenario 1 — no errors

In this scenario, the monetary precision is better than tolerable error. When determining sample size, the auditor expected two errors and used a reliability factor of 5.33. As it turned out, the auditor could have used a reliability factor of 2.31. The extra sample size enables the auditor to conclude, with 90 per cent assurance, that the maximum possible error in the population is:

$$\text{Reliability factor} \times \text{Sampling interval} = \text{Upper error limit}$$

which gives

$$2.31 \times \$10\,000 = \$23\,100.$$

This figure is known as basic error or basic precision.

Scenario 2 — two errors

The upper error limit is determined as being basic error plus the projected error plus the precision gap widening. Basic error is the upper error limit if no errors were found (i.e. $23 100 as above). Projected error is based on the assumption that the dollar being sampled is tainted by the extent of any error in the item of which it forms part. Thus, a $200 error in an item with a recorded amount of $1000 taints the dollar being sampled by 20 per cent. This tainting percentage is then projected to all those dollars of which the dollar is a representative sample (i.e. the sampling interval).

Projected error is calculated as follows:

Book value ($) (BV)	Audited value ($) (AV)	Tainting (%) (TP)*	Sample interval ($) (SI)	Projected error ($) TP × SI
1000	800	20	10 000	2 000
8000	4000	50	10 000	5 000
			Projected error	7 000

$$*TP = \frac{(BV - AV)}{BV}$$

For precision gap widening, the projected errors are ranked and the calculation is as follows:

No. of errors	RF @ 90% (Table 8.5)	Incremental change (IC)	Projected error ($) (PE)	Precision gap widening ($) (IC × PE) – PE
0	2.31			
1st	3.89	1.58	5000	2900
2nd	5.33	1.44	2000	880
				3780

The upper error limit can now be calculated.

Basic errror	$23 000
Projected error	7 000
Precision gap widening	3 780
	$33 880

If both errors were 100 per cent, then:

Projected error would have been:	2 × 100% × $10 000	= $20 000
Precision gap widening would have been:	$10 000 × 0.58 plus $100 000 × 0.44 = $5800 + $4400	= 10 200
Basic error as before:		= 23 100
Upper error limit:	= tolerable error	= $53 300

In other words, if our worst expectations as to expected errors are confirmed, then our sample size would be just sufficient to provide us with the required level of assurance.

Scenario 3 — three errors

The calculation of projected error and precision gap widening for the two errors in items with recorded values below the sampling interval is exactly the same as for scenario 2. The actual error in the item whose recorded value is above the sampling interval is not subjected to a precision gap widening calculation, and is simply added to the other figures in determining the upper error limit.

If an item with a recorded value of $14 000 were found to be overstated by $3000, then the upper error limit would be:

As previously calculated	$33 880
Error in material item	3 000
Upper error limit	$36 880

Conclusion

The auditor would conclude, with 90 per cent confidence, that the inventory is not overstated as a result of errors in standard costs by more than:

- scenario one — $23 100
- scenario two — $33 880
- scenario three — $36 880.

All of these are below the tolerable error for this particular test. Given assurance from other procedures, the auditor has 95 per cent confidence that the inventory is not materially misstated.

APPENDIX 8C

Test of control using attribute sampling

Facts of the case

Objective	To test compliance of invoicing procedures, with laid down controls as a basis for confirming a preliminary assessment of control risk as moderate
Population	8190 credit sale invoices issued in the year
Attributes being tested	1. Authorisation of order 2. Shipment of goods agreed with order 3. Invoices agreed with dispatch note 4. Invoice pricing verified 5. Mathematical accuracy of invoice verified

Judgements

Confidence level	95 per cent
Tolerable deviation	7 per cent (also referred to as the upper rate error limit, or UEL)

Sample size

The auditor can determine sample size in a number of ways.

Sample plan 1

The auditor can estimate the likelihood of deviations being found in the sample. If the auditor expects two deviations, then the required sample size is determined by the formula:

$$\frac{\text{Reliability factor (see Table 8.5)}}{\text{Tolerable deviation rate}} = \frac{6.3}{0.07}$$

$$= 90.$$

This approach is complicated by the fact that, without knowing the sample size, it is difficult to estimate how many deviations it is expected to contain.

Sample plan 2

If the auditor is reasonably confident that no deviations will be found, then he or she can take the minimum sample size possible of $\frac{3}{0.07} = 43$, using the same formula as shown in sample plan 1. This approach is also known as discovery sampling.

Sample plan 3

A third approach is to use a standard sample size (say 75) for all tests of control and determine, retrospectively, what assurance of control effectiveness can be obtained.

Sample selection

Sales invoices for sampling are selected from the sales transaction file on the computer using computer-generated random numbers. The same sample will be used for testing each of the attributes.

Sample results

Two orders not evidenced as being authorised and one invoice not evidenced as being checked for either pricing or mathematical accuracy are found. No other deviations are found.

Projected deviation rate

Sample plan 1

If two deviations are found, the auditor can calculate the upper error limit using the following formula:

$$\frac{\text{Reliability factor}}{\text{Sample size}} = \frac{6.3}{90}$$

$$= 0.07.$$

Given that the sample size was determined on the basis that there is a 95 per cent probability, if no more than two deviations are found, that the upper error limit will not exceed 7 per cent, it is hardly surprising, if two deviations are found, that the auditor can conclude that the level of compliance is just acceptable. For the attributes where one deviation was found, the auditor can conclude that the level of compliance is well within the tolerable range.

Sample plan 2

Given that the discovery sample was based on the expectation that no errors would be found, the finding of even one error means that the auditor must conclude that there is a more than 5 per cent probability that the deviation rate could exceed 7 per cent. Using the above formula, there is a 5 per cent probability that the deviation rate could be as high as:

$$\frac{6.3}{43} = 14.65\%.$$

The calculation is not necessary because the finding of any deviation means that there is a better than 5 per cent probability that the deviation rate exceeds the tolerable rate. The problem with discovery sampling is that it can lead, unless the auditor is confident that no errors will be found, to underreliance being placed on internal control, with consequent over-auditing in substantive procedures.

Sample plan 3

Using the formula, the auditor, finding two deviations in a sample of 75, can determine with 95 per cent assurance that the upper error limit could be $\frac{6.3}{75} = 8.4\%$. However, this approach is relatively informal, so the auditor may consider whether a 90 per cent assurance that the upper error limit does not exceed $\frac{5.33}{75} = 7.1\%$ would be sufficient to support the preliminary assessed level of control risk, or at least an assessed level higher than planned but still less than high.

Conclusion

With the second and probably the third approaches, the auditor would be required to conclude that the preliminary assessment of control risk used in planning the level of substantive procedures on receivables cannot be supported on the basis of the results of tests of those controls. With the second method, discovery sampling, the sample results do not provide sufficient information to support some higher assessed level of control risk. The auditor could always use his or her judgement as to the importance of orders being approved in the overall context of controls over receivables, and may conclude that the final assessed level of control risk is still sufficient to support the planned program of substantive procedures.

APPENDIX 8D

Variable sampling using the mean-per-unit method

Facts of the case

Objectives	Circularisation of loans receivable by a finance company
Population	Loans receivable $1 340 000
Sampling unit	3000 accounts, all below $500

Judgements

Tolerable error	$60 000
Risk of incorrect rejection	This judgement, which is not necesary in dollar unit sampling, allows the auditor to control the risk that the sample results show the population as being misstated when it is not. The trade-off facing the auditor is of increased sample size against reduced possibility of unnecessary audit work if the sample results in incorrect rejection. This risk is typically set at 5 per cent.
Risk of incorrect acceptance	This is the same as the sampling risk in dollar unit sampling and the same as detection risk. Using the audit risk model, this risk is put at 20 per cent.

Sample size

The above factors were fed into a computer program which calculated the required sample size as 184. In the process, the computer estimated standard deviation at $100.

Sample selection

The sample was selected from files held on computer by means of a random number generator.

Sample results

The 184 accounts confirmed had a total audited value of $81 328. Details of the audited value of each account confirmed were fed into the computer program. Given that this is a mean-per-unit sample, the auditor was not interested in errors.

Population projection

The computer calculated population value as being $1 326 000 with an achieved allowance for sampling risk of $37 803.

Conclusion

Given that the recorded value lies within the range of $1 326 000 plus or minus $37 803, the auditor may conclude that the recorded value is confirmed by the sample results.

Review questions

8.1 What is audit sampling? Is selecting all of the items within a population appropriately described as a method of sampling? Explain.

8.2 What is the difference between sampling risk and non-sampling risk?

8.3 What other methods of selecting items for audit testing do not constitute audit sampling?

8.4 What steps are involved in planning the sample?

8.5 What are the different methods available for selecting a sample? What method would auditors normally prefer?

8.6 What are the three main statistical sampling techniques used by the auditor?

Discussion questions

8.1 Discuss the risk of overreliance and its potential implications for an audit.

8.2 Explain the difference between statistical and non-statistical sampling.

8.3 Discuss the benefits to the auditor from using statistical sampling.

8.4 Explain the difference between selective testing and stratification in selecting items for audit testing.

8.5 Discuss the factors that will affect the sample size for tests of control and substantive tests.

8.6 Consider the appropriateness of using haphazard selection for statistical sampling.

8.7 Explain how errors should be projected to the population for tests of control and substantive testing.

8.8 Discuss the advantages and disadvantages of using probability-proportional-to-size sampling rather than variable sampling plans.

8.9 Explain why an auditor may decide to use non-statistical sampling.

8.10 Discuss some of the potential problems associated with using informal non-statistical sampling methods.

★
BASIC
★★
MODERATE
★★★
CHALLENGING

Professional application questions

8.1 (Sample sizes and population selection) ★★

During the audit planning of TKD Limited, a manufacturer of blank video cassettes, the audit team highlighted the following matters:

1. The audit partner wishes to place greater reliance on the control structure of non-current assets, arguing that the control risk assessment can be decreased from medium to low if adequate control testing is performed.
2. Your client has warehouses in both Sydney and Melbourne. In the previous year the audit team attended a stocktake at only the Sydney warehouse. One substantive stocktake procedure involved a selection of fifty items from the inventory report. Three errors were identified and projected over the whole population. This year the manager has suggested testing both sites.
3. A number of stock cut-off errors were noted in the prior year. The planning process has identified that this may be an issue this year.
4. Even though the value has remained constant, the number of debtors' accounts has doubled from 800 to 1600 in the last year.

Required

Discuss the effect of each of the above matters on the auditor's selection of sample size and population for testing.

(Professional Year Programme of the ICAA — 1996, Accounting 2 Module — adapted)

8.2 (Sample selection) ★★

Paul Wong is the auditor of OnePhone Limited, a company that manufactures and sells telephones and answering machines in Brisbane. OnePhone has many branches, which are both local and interstate. During 2002, Paul was asked to complete the audit program based on the following information.

1. Each branch processes its own sales invoices. Each month a sales listing is produced, showing a sequential listing of the invoices used, the date, the customer and the amount. Each branch has a unique series of invoice numbers.
2. Many of OnePhone's stock lines have a twelve-month free replacement warranty. Items are returned to the relevant branch office, which keeps a record of the product details. The warranty provision is determined at year end by a percentage of returns of major sales items over the previous twelve months.

Required

(a) Describe how you would select a sample for testing in each of the above scenarios.
(b) List the information you would require to perform the testing.

8.3 (Use of sampling methods) ★★

You are a senior accountant with Barrington, Taylor and Partners (BT), a four-partner firm operating in Perth. BT was formed two months ago as a result of a merger between Barrington Partners and Taylor Partners. The only major audit client of the merged firm is Hardware Centre Limited (HC), which has twelve hardware stores across Australia and a 30 June year end.

BT's accounting records show significant write-offs on the HC audit over the past few years, mainly due to the performance of extensive testing. To increase audit efficiency and reduce write-offs, the partners have asked you to review the 20X2 planning information and suggest methods of sampling that will reduce the level of work performed without compromising audit effectiveness. The partners have stressed that they still wish to comply fully with audit standards.

The 20X2 planning notes contain the following information.

1. Trade creditors are handled centrally in Perth. Major purchases of products are made through Perth, but each shop also orders about 20 per cent of its stock. Each shop sends all authorised invoices to Perth for processing and payment on a weekly basis. An alphabetical list of all unpaid invoices is produced each month. There are no individually significant creditors. You need to select a sample of creditors to test for existence and a sample to test for completeness.
2. Fifty per cent of the stock is held in the main warehouse in Perth, which is subject to an annual stocktake and maintains perpetual inventory records. The remainder of the stock is held across the twelve branches, with each holding approximately similar quantities. The branches maintain periodic inventory records and are required to perform a stocktake and send the information to Perth every six months. You need to select a sample of stock to test for existence.
3. Although about 70 per cent of total sales are paid for by cash or credit cards, 30 per cent of sales are on account. The Perth head office deals with these accounts and the responsibility for debtor collection. An alphabetical debtors list is produced each month, showing the invoices making up each debtor, payment details and the outstanding balance. The report also shows the ageing details of each debtor. You need to select a sample of debtors to test for existence and a sample to test for valuation.

Required

Describe how you would select the above samples to ensure the audit is performed in an efficient as well as effective manner.

8.4 (Non-statistical sampling) ★★

Lee and Jones are auditing the 31 December 20X2 inventory of Sparks Limited, a distributor of electronic parts. They have already performed procedures to satisfy themselves that (1) a computer print-out listing inventory at the year end in ascending sequence by stock number and lot number is complete; (2) the quantities shown thereon are correct; (3) the extensions of quantity times price are accurate; (4) the listing is properly footed; and (5) the total agrees with the general ledger ending inventory account balance.

As the next step, Lee and Jones decide to use a non-statistical sample to test the pricing of the inventory. They plan to perform this test by checking prices to (1) vendor's invoices and (2) current price lists provided by vendors. The closing inventory consists of 3000 stock items with a total recorded value of $1 900 000. A perpetual inventory record is maintained for each stock item. Additionally, an inventory tag showing the quantity on hand at the year end is on file for each item.

Lee and Jones agree that a misstatement of $85 000 or more in the inventory balance, when combined with misstatements in other accounts, may result in material misstatement of the financial report.

Required

(a) Describe the component of audit risk to which the inventory pricing test relates.

(b) List factors that should influence Lee and Jones's determination of sample size.

(c) State what the sampling unit should be and how the sample items should be selected.

8.5 (Sample selection methods) ★★★

Your audit firm is testing accounts receivable and has stratified the population into five strata, as outlined in the following table. Probability theory has been used to determine the appropriate sample size for a given level of confidence within each stratum. Different methods of sample selection were used for each stratum.

(continued)

Dollar value of accounts ($)	No. of accounts in population	Confidence required (%)	No. of accounts sampled	Sample selection method
>1 000 000	10	100	10	—
100 000 to 1 000 000	53	95	10	Used computer-generated random numbers to select.
10 000 to 100 000	110	90	10	Randomly selected the second account, then every eleventh account.
1000 to 10 000	175	80	10	Chose two accounts from every page of a five-page print-out.
<1000	245	50	10	Selected the ten accounts from Tasmania which were all less than $1000.

Required

(a) Define stratification and the benefits that may arise from using this technique.

(b) For each stratum, define the sample selection method used and whether it would be an appropriate sample selection method for statistical sampling.

(Professional Year Programme of the ICAA — 1996, Advanced Audit Module — adapted)

8.6 (Evaluating sample results) ★★★

Consider each of the following results from compliance testing performed during an audit.

1. *Purchases*: The auditor used judgemental sampling techniques to determine an appropriate sample size of twenty in testing a key control over the proper authorisation of purchases. After randomly selecting twenty purchase transactions, the auditor undertook appropriate testing and identified that three of the twenty transactions were not properly authorised.
2. *Sales*: The auditor used attribute sampling techniques to test a key authorisation control over sales. For a 5 per cent risk of overreliance, a tolerable deviation rate of 10 per cent and an expected population deviation rate of zero, the auditor determined the minimum sample size to be twenty-nine. The auditor selected twenty-nine items using a systematic sampling technique and, on undertaking the audit testing, found that one transaction was not properly authorised.

Required

For both tests performed, discuss the relevant issues in determining whether the auditor can place reliance on the controls.

(Professional Year Programme of the ICAA — 1996, Advanced Audit Module — adapted)

8.7 (Evaluating sample results) ★★★

You are the supervisor on the audit of Acorn Limited, a large and diversified company which has eighteen branches across Australia. A debtors' circularisation was performed at 31 March 20X1. For the purposes of sample selection, the assistant divided the debtors ledger into the following strata:

Strata no.	Strata details ($)	No. of debtors	Amount ($)
1	50 000 and over	8	2 783 214
2	20 000–49 999	12	552 648
3	10 000–19 999	44	1 332 282
4	1000–9999	395	1 930 178
5	Less than 1000	203	181 888
		662	**6 780 210**

In performing the circularisation, the assistant selected all debtors from strata 1 and 2 and a haphazard sample of debtors from strata 3 and 4. Given the insignificance of the amounts in stratum 5, none of these debtors was circularised.

Only one error was found (an error of $51 780), which occurred in stratum 1. The error was lower than the materiality level, so the audit assistant concluded that no further work needed to be performed.

Required

Evaluate the assistant's sample selection and evaluation of results.

(Professional Year Programme of the ICAA — 1999, Advanced Audit Module — adapted)

8.8 (Dollar unit sampling) ★★★

Lucia Toppini, an audit senior, was performing the 30 June 20X1 audit of Liberty & Co. In her initial investigations, she found that the book value of inventory was $1 000 000 (which represented the cumulative value of 4000 stock items). After discussions with the audit partner she decided to employ probability-proportional-to-size (dollar unit) sampling in testing the valuation of physical inventory. The partner and Lucia decided that the maximum tolerable misstatement should be $50 000, with a 10 per cent risk of incorrect acceptance. They are not expecting any errors in the sample.

Lucia selected the sample and performed her audit testing using the above specifications. Her testing indicated that one voucher recorded on the books at $1000 actually had an audit value of $600. Lucia found no other misstatements.

Required

(a) Explain the sample size and sampling interval that Lucia used.

(b) Describe what Lucia's conclusion would have been, based on the above results.

Case studies

8.1 (Sampling — method of selection) ★★★

You are carrying out the audit of All Weather Limited, a company that manufactures roofing tiles and other ceramic products for the building industry. The head office of All Weather is in Melbourne and branches are located in Sydney, Adelaide, Brisbane and Perth. You are about to design sampling plans for various audit file sections. Consider the following scenarios for the organisation of All Weather's accounting records:

1. Computerised sales invoices are issued by each branch on an on-line basis as required. A single sequence of invoices is used — for example, invoice number 100 may be issued by the Perth branch, invoice number 101 by the Melbourne head office, etc. The branches retain all supporting documents. Head office produces a monthly invoice register that lists all invoices issued in numerical order. You need to select a sample of invoices for tests of control.
2. The provision for annual leave is calculated centrally at head office. An annual leave listing is produced, listing each employee and his or her related leave balance. The listing is produced in employee number order; each branch uses a unique range of employee numbers. You need to select a sample of employees and substantively test their annual leave provision.
3. Standard costs for stock are determined centrally in head office. There are about 200 product lines, although stock is held for only about 100 of these at any one time. Five stock lines make up about 40 per cent of the inventory balance at the year end. The following monthly reports are produced: (1) a stock listing that shows all stock held by location (each branch maintains a warehouse) and (2) a catalogue listing that shows all stock lines (whether actually in stock or not) in part number order. You need to select a sample of standard costs and check whether they are reasonable.
4. Each branch maintains its own creditors ledger. Monthly creditors ledgers are produced centrally at head office, listing each creditor in alphabetical order and showing the invoices that make up the creditor's balance. Each branch draws monthly creditors' cheques and produces a cheque listing showing the cheque number, supplier and amount paid. Cheque number sequences are unique to each branch. You need to select a sample of cheque payments for tests of control.
5. The fixed asset register is centrally maintained at head office. Assets are grouped in categories (e.g. computer equipment, furniture and fittings) and listed within each category in date and purchase order. You need to select a sample of fixed asset additions for substantive testing.

Required

(a) List factors that the auditor should consider when designing an audit sample.

(b) Explain how you could select a sample in each of the above situations. List the advantages of the approach you have chosen.

(Professional Year Programme of the ICAA — 1997, Accounting 2 Module — adapted)

8.2 (Sampling — method of selection) ★★★

Freewheel Motors sells car accessories such as seat covers, headlight protectors and towbars from six retail outlets spread across Sydney, Melbourne and Brisbane. The company also has a main warehouse located at head office in Sydney.

Freewheel has about 250 stock lines active at any one time. The value of individual items ranges from 10 cents to $2500. Around 25 per cent of the year-end stock is expected to be held at the warehouse, with the remainder spread relatively evenly across the six retail outlets. A full stocktake will be carried out at all locations at the year end.

The inventory system produces the following reports at the year end:

1. A complete stock listing, showing:
   — stock code
   — total quantity held
   — cost per unit
   — total cost per stock item.

   The report also gives a breakdown of the location(s) of stock items and the total value of items held at each location.
2. An ageing report of all stocklines, showing:
   — stock code
   — total quantity held
   — sales quantity over each of the past three months
   — month-by-month purchase details.

In addition, the system produces a stocksheet report for each location. It lists the description and stock code of each item held at that location per the perpetual records. Quantities are omitted because these are completed by the count team.

Required

(a) Performing test counts at the stocktake helps the auditor gather evidence about the existence and completeness assertions. In general, identify the populations from which samples must be selected to satisfy each of these assertions.

(b) Explain how your test count sample size for a retail outlet would be affected if the following independent events occurred.

   (i) A higher value of stock was held at that outlet compared with the stock at other outlets.
   (ii) Stock thefts had occurred at the outlet over the past few months.
   (iii) Your preliminary assessment of internal controls was that they were very good, but the manager decided no tests of control would be performed.
   (iv) The outlet had a history of only minor difference between the perpetual records and actual stock held compared with the differences at other outlets.
   (v) The branch auditors assigned to the stocktake were new to the job.
   (vi) Three out of five outlet staff, including the manager, had commenced work in the past three months.
   (vii) The number of stock lines held was 500, not 300.

   Briefly explain your answer in each case.

(Professional Year Programme of the ICAA — 1999, Accounting 2 Module — adapted)

chapter 9

Designing substantive procedures

Overview

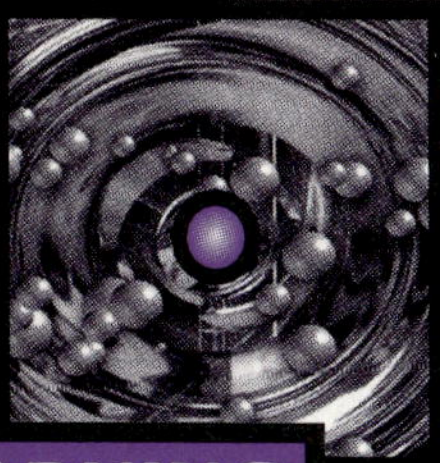

LEARNING OBJECTIVES

After studying this chapter, you should be able to:

1. explain the process for determining the appropriate level of substantive procedures based on the assessment of inherent risk and control risk
2. indicate how the nature of substantive procedures is varied to achieve an acceptable level of detection risk
3. indicate how the timing and extent of substantive procedures are varied to achieve an acceptable level of detection risk
4. explain how computer-assisted audit techniques may be used as substantive procedures
5. explain which substantive procedures may normally be included in an audit program
6. describe and apply a general framework for developing audit programs for substantive procedures
7. indicate special considerations for when designing substantive procedures for selected types of account.

Professional statements

AUSTRALIAN		INTERNATIONAL	
AUS 208	Documentation	ISA 230	Documentation
AUS 402	Risk Assessments and Internal Controls	ISA 400	Risk Assessments and Internal Control
AUS 502	Audit Evidence	ISA 500	Audit Evidence
AUS 504	External Confirmations	ISA 501	Audit Evidence — Additional Considerations for Specific Items (Part B)
AUS 506	Existence and Valuation of Inventory	ISA 501	Audit Evidence — Additional Considerations for Specific Items (Part A)
AUS 510	Initial Engagements — Opening Balances	ISA 510	Initial Engagements — Opening Balances
AUS 512	Analytical Procedures	ISA 520	Analytical Procedures
AUS 516	Audit of Accounting Estimates	ISA 540	Audit of Accounting Estimates
AUS 518	Related Parties	ISA 550	Related Parties

In Chapter 5, we considered how the auditor needs to assess the level of inherent risk within the client at the planning stage of the audit. This assessment may pertain to all assertions for all or many accounts or may pertain to assertions for specific accounts. In Chapter 7, we considered how the auditor (1) obtains and documents an understanding of the internal control structure and (2) assesses control risk for significant transaction class and account balance assertions, based on the understanding of the internal control structure and the results of tests of control.

In this chapter, we will explain how the assessment of inherent risk and the assessment of control risk have an impact on the required level of **detection risk**, which will affect the design of substantive procedures. The acceptable level of detection risk influences the auditor's assessment of the nature, timing and extent of the procedures that need to be performed to gain sufficient appropriate audit evidence.

DETERMINING DETECTION RISK

1 LEARNING OBJECTIVE

Explain the process for determining the appropriate level of substantive procedures based on the assessment of inherent risk and control risk.

The relationship between the assessed levels of inherent risk and control risk and the level of detection risk may be expressed in the following model, which we introduced in Chapter 5:

$$DR = \frac{AR}{IR \times CR}$$

The model shows that for a given level of audit risk (AR) specified by the auditor, detection risk (DR) is inversely related to the assessed levels of inherent risk (IR) and control risk (CR). The auditor normally makes a preliminary assessment of inherent risk and control risk for each financial report assertion, as explained in Chapter 5. The auditor ordinarily assesses the level of control risk as high when the entity's internal control structure is ineffective or where evaluating the effectiveness of internal controls would not be efficient. Where the auditor's preliminary assessment of inherent risk and control risk is high, detection risk must be low if the desired level of audit risk is to be attained. A low level of detection risk requires the auditor to adopt a predominantly substantive audit strategy (as explained in Chapter 6), whereby evidence obtained through the performance of substantive procedures enables the auditor to minimise the risk of failure to detect such material misstatements as might exist.

Assessing control risk as being less than high means that the auditor is confident that the entity's own procedures reduce the likelihood of material misstatement in that particular financial report assertion. The auditor needs to obtain less evidence from substantive procedures to achieve the desired level of audit risk, and adopts a lower assessed level of control risk audit strategy, as explained in Chapter 7. In such situations, the auditor is said to tolerate a higher level of detection risk. Where tolerable or **planned detection risk** is high, the auditor obtains less evidence from substantive procedures than where planned detection risk is low. This can appear confusing, and it is important to understand the logic underlying the terminology of AUS 402 (ISA 400), Risk Assessments and Internal Control. It is important to note that the auditor should perform, regardless of the assessed levels of inherent and control risks, some substantive tests for material balances and transactions. The relationships between the audit strategy, detection risk and the level of substantive procedures that were explained in Chapter 5 are summarised in a rain cloud analogy in Figure 9.1.

FIGURE 9.1

Rain cloud analogy

The raindrops falling from the cloud represent material errors that occur as a result of the nature of the client's business — this is known as the inherent risk of the client. Filter 1 represents the client's internal control system. The assessment of how effectively this filter stops the raindrops (material errors) is the auditor's assessment of the level of control risk. If this assessment of control risk is less than 100 per cent, then the auditor must perform some tests of control. Filter 2 represents the substantive audit procedures performed by the auditor. The assessment of how effectively this filter stops the raindrops (material errors) that have passed through Filter 1 (the internal control system) is the level of detection risk. Audit risk is, therefore, the chance that raindrops (material errors) will pass through both filters and reach the ground (material undetected errors).

PROFESSIONAL ENVIRONMENT

The audit risk model — the interdependence of component risks

Are the risks assessed for the audit risk model judged independently or are they conditional on values of the other risks?

Auditing standards indicate that inherent, control and analytical procedures risks may be combined to determine the extent of substantive, detailed testing. The standards depict each component risk individually; however, the audit risk model will not produce proper results unless the components are considered in relation to each other. That is, knowledge about one component of the risk model must be weighed in order to properly assess the risks associated with another (this relationship is known as being 'conditionally dependent').

(*continued*)

For example, imagine that firm A and firm B have identical control structures with respect to an audit objective or account, but that firm A is inherently riskier than firm B. If auditors consider only features of the internal controls as the basis to assess control risk, then they will assess A's and B's control risk as being the same. However, to use the risk model properly, the assessed control risk of firm A should be higher than the control risk of firm B. To oversimplify, if there is inherently a higher probability of more material misstatements in firm A than in firm B, then the same control structure has a higher risk of failing to detect/correct misstatements in firm A than in firm B. Assessing these component risks interdependently calls for subtle, highly skilled judgement.

In a series of cases, we looked at inherent, control and analytical-procedures risks from auditors in firms where each of these risks was separately assessed. Our research showed that a client factor or behaviour could affect the assessed level of more than one component risk (for example, the aggressiveness of the client firm's management could influence both the inherent and control risks). Next, we found that auditors did base subsequent risk assessments on the prior risk assessment level, as is necessary for proper use of the audit risk model. The implication is that inherent risk need not automatically be set at a maximum (to offset a possibility that risk components will be assessed independently). Instead, auditors appear to be capable of making combined assessments of the component risks to plan the extent of substantive testing.

(Source: R. Dusenbury, J. Reimers & S. Wheeler, 'The Audit Risk Model — the Interdependence of Component Risks', *Journal of Accountancy* (September 2000), p. 103)

Assessing control risk for account balances

The internal control structure usually applies controls at the time the relevant transaction is first recognised and recorded. For many financial report assertions, therefore, control risk is assessed by reference to transaction classes. Where substantive procedures are to be applied to account balances, the assessed level of control risk applicable to the account balance has to be derived from the assessed control risk of the relevant transaction classes. For the balance of accounts payable, for example, this would be controls over purchase and payment transactions. We will now consider the relationship between transaction class control risk and account balance control risk for (1) account balance assertions affected by a single transaction class and (2) for account balance assertions affected by more than one transaction class.

Account balance assertions affected by a single transaction class

The process of assessing control risk for account balance assertions is straightforward for accounts that are affected by a single transaction class. This is the case for most profit and loss statement accounts. The balance on the sales account, for example, is the cumulative effect of credits for sales transactions. Similarly, many expense accounts reflect the cumulative effect of debits for purchase transactions. In these cases, the auditor's control risk assessment for each account balance assertion is the same as the control risk assessment for the related transaction class assertion; for example, the control risk assessment for the occurrence assertion for the sales account balance is the same as the control risk assessment for the occurrence assertion for sales transactions. Similarly, the control risk assessment for the valuation or measurement assertion for many expenses is the same as the control risk assessment for the valuation or measurement assertion for purchases transactions.

Account balance assertions affected by multiple transaction classes

Many balance sheet accounts are affected by more than one transaction class. The cash balance, for example, is increased by cash receipt transactions and decreased by cash payment transactions. In these cases, assessing control risk for an account balance assertion requires consideration of the relevant control risk assessments for each transaction class. Thus, the control risk assessment for the valuation or measurement assertion for the cash balance is based on the control risk assessments for the valuation or measurement assertions for both cash receipt and cash payment transactions.

When the control risk assessments for the relevant transaction class assertions differ, the auditor may judgementally weigh the significance of each assessment in arriving at a combined assessment. The auditor may consider the significance of a transaction class to the balance or, alternatively, whether one of the assessments was less persuasive. Some firms elect to use the most conservative (highest) of the relevant assessments. The existence or occurrence assertion for the cash balance, for example, is affected by the existence or occurrence of cash receipts and the completeness of cash payments. If the control risk for existence or occurrence is assessed as being low, and completeness is assessed as being moderate, then the auditor would assess the control risk for the existence or occurrence of cash as being moderate.

Effects of preliminary audit strategies

Regardless of the audit strategy chosen for a particular part of the audit, the auditor needs to identify types of potential misstatement in the assertions. However, the manner in which the auditor considers factors that affect the risk of misstatements and assesses that risk can vary in several respects, based on the audit strategy chosen.

Predominantly substantive approach

The auditor may assess control risk as being high and adopt the predominantly substantive approach where he or she has reason to suppose that one or more of the following assumptions are appropriate:

- There are no significant control procedures that pertain to the assertion.
- Any relevant control procedures are unlikely to be effective.
- It would not be efficient to obtain evidence to evaluate the effectiveness of relevant control policies or procedures.

In making this decision, the auditor considers the costs of performing the higher level of substantive procedures required by the predominantly substantive approach to be less than the combined costs of performing sufficient tests of control to support a lower assessed level of control risk approach and the reduced level of substantive procedures that would be appropriate, assuming a lower control risk assessment were supported.

This may happen more commonly with small audit clients, because small clients may not have adequate resources to implement all appropriate controls, the controls may not be as effective (often as a result of problems due to a lack of segregation of duties) and the size of the entity may make it inefficient for the auditor to rely on these controls in performing the audit. In these cases, the level of detection risk (i.e. the amount of substantive procedures) is the only part of the audit risk model that the auditor can vary.

Lower assessed level of control risk approach

Use of this approach requires the auditor to plan and perform tests of control. On completion of these tests, the auditor must consider whether the actual assessed level of control risk supports the **planned level of substantive procedures**, determined on the basis of the preliminary assessment. If the results of tests of control do not support the preliminary assessed level of control risk, then the auditor must increase the planned level of substantive procedures. For example, the auditor might have made a preliminary assessment of control risk as being low, resulting in the lowest planned level of substantive procedures. If evidence from tests of control (including **dual-purpose tests**) fails to support the assessment of control risk as being low, then revision of the planned level of substantive procedures to a higher level would be appropriate. This is one of the reasons that compliance testing is usually performed before substantive testing.

The auditor may assess the controls as being low if the controls are operating effectively within the firm and the auditor performs adequate work to support the assessment. However, if the controls are not operating effectively within the firm, then no amount of audit testing can change the assessment of control risk as being high. Thus, the assessed level of control risk is really outside of the auditor's control. The only aspects of the audit risk model that are completely within the auditor's control are the assessment of audit risk and the amount of substantive work performed to vary detection risk.

Detection risk for individual substantive procedures

The term 'detection risk' as used in the preceding sections refers to the risk that all the substantive procedures used to obtain evidence about an assertion will collectively fail to detect a material misstatement. Typically, the auditor will apply **analytical procedures** as early in the audit as practicable as being the most cost-effective substantive procedures. In designing substantive tests of details, the auditor will assume that analytical procedures will fail to reveal unexpected differences. This will reduce the risk of a material misstatement remaining undetected, and it may be appropriate to use a higher level of detection risk for the remaining tests. If analytical procedures do reveal unexpected differences, then tests of details will need to be amended to enable the planned level of detection risk to be achieved. In summary, the lower the risk that analytical procedures will not detect material misstatements, the higher the detection risk can be for the tests of details that follow.

DESIGNING SUBSTANTIVE PROCEDURES

To have a reasonable basis for an opinion on the entity's financial report, the auditor must obtain sufficient appropriate audit evidence as required by AUS 502 (ISA 500), Audit Evidence. Substantive procedures either provide evidence that supports the fairness of each significant financial report assertion or, conversely, reveal monetary errors or misstatements in the recording or reporting of transactions and balances. Designing substantive procedures involves the following considerations as discussed in AUS 402.59 (ISA 400.42):

> The auditor should consider the assessed levels of inherent and control risks in determining the nature, timing and extent of substantive procedures required to reduce audit risk to an acceptable level.

In this section we will explain considerations to be made by the auditor in determining the substantive procedures to be performed.

2 LEARNING OBJECTIVE

Indicate how the nature of substantive procedures is varied to achieve an acceptable level of detection risk.

Nature

The **nature of substantive procedures** refers to the type and effectiveness of the auditing procedures to be performed. When the planned level of detection risk is low, the auditor must use more effective and usually more costly procedures. When the planned level of detection risk is high, less effective and less costly procedures can be used. As explained in Chapter 5, the types of substantive procedure are:

- analytical procedures;
- **tests of details of transactions**;
- **tests of details of balances**.

We will discuss these procedures and their relative effectiveness and cost in the following sections.

Analytical procedures

The use of analytical procedures in audit planning to identify areas of greater risk of misstatement is explained in Chapter 6. AUS 512 (ISA 520), Analytical Procedures suggests that analytical procedures should be used at the planning and overall review stage of the audit. However, it also notes that analytical review may be used at other stages of the audit as a substantive procedure to reduce detection risk. Analytical procedures are often the least costly to perform. Thus, consideration should be given to the extent to which these procedures can contribute to achieving the planned level of detection risk, thus reducing the extent of tests of details. For most assertions, analytical procedures are considered to be less effective than tests of details, so they are used as a supplement to tests of details. However, the opposite is true in a few cases, in which analytical procedures provide most (if not all) of the required evidence. When the results of the analytical procedures are as expected and the planned level of detection risk for the assertion is high, it may not be necessary to perform tests of details.

In the hotel industry, for example, relatively small amounts of revenue are billed to and collected from many customers each month. Tests of details of these high-volume, low-value revenue transactions would be tedious and costly. But, revenues in such cases can often be estimated fairly precisely using independent variables such as the occupancy rate and average room rate. The auditor could multiply the average occupancy rate for each month (probably monthly, given seasonal variations) by the average room rate by the number of rooms to estimate the revenue for every month. The auditor's estimated balance for room revenue can then be compared with the reported balance as part of the evidence used in determining whether revenues are fairly stated. Reasons for substantial differences would need to be discussed with the client to determine whether alternative procedures need to be performed.

In other cases, the auditor may use the expected relationship of one account balance to another. Total sales commission expense, for example, could normally be estimated from total sales revenue, rather than from the details of entries to sales commissions.

AUS 512 (ISA 520) indicates that the extent of reliance on analytical procedures depends on:

- *materiality*: *Ceteris paribus*, the more material a balance is, the less likely it is that the auditor would rely solely on the results of analytical procedures to audit the balance;
- *other audit procedures*: If other audit procedures are directed towards the same audit objective and similar results are found, then more reliance can be placed on the analytical procedures;
- *accuracy of predicted results*: The more accurate the results that can be predicted, the more reliance that can be placed on the analytical procedures. Greater accuracy can be expected, for example, for balances where interrelationships are expected to be constant over time (such as gross profit margin percentages);
- *inherent and control risks*: If these risks are high, then more reliance will be placed on tests of details than on analytical procedures.

PROFESSIONAL ENVIRONMENT

Use and perceived usefulness of analytical procedures by Australian auditors

A study was performed on the use and perceived usefulness of analytical procedures in the Australian audit environment. The sample consisted of fifty-two auditors from both Big 5 and non-Big 5 audit firms.

Subjects were asked to indicate on a five-point Likert scale (1 = never; 5 = always) the frequency of their application of certain analytical procedures. The results are summarised in Table 9.1.

TABLE 9.1 *Use of analytical procedures*

Analytical procedure	Proportion (%)
Scan of data	98
Ratio analysis	89
Regression models	15
Time series models	19
Other	17

Subjects were also asked to indicate on a five-point scale (1 = not at all important; 5 = crucial importance) their perception of the importance of analytical procedures during different stages of the audit. The results are shown in Table 9.2.

TABLE 9.2 *Perception of usefulness of analytical procedures at different stages of the audit*

Stage of audit	Mean	Standard deviation
Planning	3.4	1.0
Detailed substantive testing	3.0	0.9
Final review	3.8	0.8

The final question asked of the subjects was about their expectations for the use of analytical procedures in the next five years. The responses are contained in Table 9.3.

TABLE 9.3 *Perception of future use of analytical procedures*

Future use	Proportion (%)
Decrease substantially	0
Decrease	0
Remain unchanged	32
Increase	60
Increase substantially	8

The researchers made the following comments about the study results:

> The findings indicate that analytical procedures are used extensively by almost all auditors. The most commonly used analytical procedures include the simpler long-established techniques such as scanning the data, simple comparisons and standard ratio analysis. Clearly, their simplicity and therefore cost-effectiveness would play a part in their extensive use. However, auditors indicated a belief that the simpler analytical procedures were very valuable techniques. In addition, most auditors believed that analytical procedures were effective in signalling errors. This belief was supported by the finding that 44 per cent of all financial statement errors encountered by the auditors were detected initially by analytical procedures. ...
>
> The perceived usefulness of analytical procedures extends to all three stages of the audit (planning, detailed substantive testing, and final review). However, most auditors believed that analytical procedures were most useful in the final review process. ...
>
> Finally, there was a strong expectation among most auditors that the use of analytical procedures will increase substantially in the next five years. Such expectations are probably due to the effectiveness of analytical procedures, and also the belief that there is scope for further integration of analytical procedures into most aspects of the audit. It also implies that auditors believe that analytical procedures are a very effective yet defensible form of audit evidence.

(Source: Extracted from G. Smith, J. Psaros & S. Holmes, 'A Research Note of the Use and Perceived Usefulness of Analytical Procedures by Australian Auditors', *Australian Accounting Review* (Vol. 9, No. 2, 1999), pp. 64–72)

Tests of details of transactions

Tests of details of transactions are tests to obtain evidence of a sample (or all) of the individual debits and credits that make up an account to reach a conclusion about the account balance. These tests primarily involve tracing and vouching. These terms are used to describe the direction (in terms of the accounting system) of the testing. Tracing involves following a transaction from source documents through to the accounting records, whereas vouching involves selecting entries in the accounting records and obtaining the documentation to substantiate the transaction.

The details of transactions may be traced, for example, from source documents (such as sales and suppliers' invoices) to entries in accounting records (such as the sales and purchase journals). Or, the details of entries in accounting records (such as the cash payments journal and perpetual inventory records) can be vouched to supporting documents (such as suppliers' invoices). The auditor's focus in performing these tests is on finding monetary errors rather than deviations from controls. As noted in Chapter 5, tracing is useful in testing for understatements, and vouching is useful in testing for overstatements.

In tests of details of transactions, the auditor uses evidence obtained about some (a sample) or all of the individual debits and credits in an account to reach a conclusion about the account balance. These tests generally use documents available in entity files, although sometimes documents will be obtained from external sources. The effectiveness of the tests depends on the particular procedure and documents used. Externally generated documents are more reliable than internally generated documents, for example.

Although tests of details of both transactions and balances may be performed in an audit, the former will provide most of the evidence for account balances affected by few transactions during the year, such as property, plant and equipment or investments. For account balances affected by many transactions, such as cash and accounts receivable, it is more effective to apply tests of details to the balances. Different assertions for the same account may be tested by tests of details of transactions or balances. Often, because the same documentation may be required, tests of details of transactions may be performed in conjunction with tests of control. This dual-purpose testing increases the cost-efficiency of such tests of details of transactions.

Cut-off tests are a special category of tests of details of transactions that are related more to the closing balance than to transactions. It is much more important at balance sheet date to ensure that transactions are recorded on the correct date, given the impact on the financial statements. Because cut-off is critical only once a year, control procedures are rarely effective and are usually monitored directly by senior accounting personnel. The purpose of cut-off tests is to ensure (1) completeness (in that all transactions occurring before the balance sheet date are recorded) and (2) occurrence (in that transactions occurring after the balance sheet date are excluded). Cut-off errors can significantly affect profit; for example, goods received before balance sheet date and included in inventory, but not recorded in purchases until after the year end, will overstate profit by the amount of the purchases.

Cut-off testing is needed for many accruals that will have a direct impact on profit, including electricity, telephone, gas, wages, advertising, etc. Often, the amount of these accruals is not confirmed until the receipt of an invoice, which may take several weeks (or longer) after the balance sheet date.

Tests of details of balances

Tests of details of balances focus on obtaining evidence directly about an account balance rather than the individual transactions that are debited and credited to the account. The auditor may, for example, verify amounts owed by individual customers making up the balance on accounts receivable, by requesting confirmation of balances from the customers. The auditor may also inspect plant assets, observe the entity's inventory taking and perform pricing tests of the closing inventory.

The effectiveness of these tests also depends on the particular procedure performed and the type of evidence obtained. The information in the tabular layout below illustrates how the effectiveness of tests of balances can be tailored to meet different detection risk levels for the completeness assertion for accounts payable.

Detection risk	Test of details of balances
High	Inspect suppliers' statements held by the entity and consider the reasonableness of explanations of differences.
Low	Confirm the amount owing with the suppliers directly and investigate reported differences.

Note in the above explanation that when detection risk is high, the auditor uses documentation held by the entity and performs limited auditing procedures. In contrast, when detection risk is low, the auditor uses documentation obtained from third parties directly and performs extensive auditing procedures.

For many account balances on the balance sheet, tests of details of balances are the most efficient method of collecting audit evidence.

Illustration of the use of substantive procedures

The application of the three types of substantive procedure may be illustrated in the context of the following accounts (see Figure 9.2 on page 343).

Accounts receivable

To simplify Figure 9.2, only one receivables account is shown; in practice, there would typically be a control account backed up by a subsidiary ledger of customer accounts containing the individual debits and credits for transactions affecting each customer. We will assume the opening balance of accounts receivable is fairly stated based on the prior year's audit. To determine that the closing balance of accounts receivable is fairly stated, the auditor may consider obtaining evidence from any of the following substantive procedures:

- analytical procedures, such as:
  - — comparing this year's closing balance in the control account with the prior year's balance, a budgeted amount or other expected value;
  - — using the closing balance to determine the percentage of accounts receivable to current assets for comparison with the prior year's percentage or industry data;
  - — using the closing balance to calculate the accounts receivable turnover ratio for comparison with the prior year's ratio, industry data or other expected value;
- tests of details of transactions, such as:
  - — vouching a sample of the individual debits and credits in customer accounts for the transaction classes indicated to the entries in journals (for example, vouching the debits to the sales journal) and supporting documentation (such as sales invoices);
  - — tracing transactions data from source documents (such as remittance advices) and journals (such as the cash receipts journal) to the corresponding entries in the customer accounts for the transaction classes indicated;
- tests of details of balances, such as:
  - — determining that the closing balances in the individual customer accounts add up to the control account balance;
  - — confirming the balances for a sample of customer accounts with the customers.

FIGURE 9.2

General ledger accounts illustrating the processing of sales transactions to accounts receivable

ACCOUNTS RECEIVABLE			
Opening balance	x		
Credit sales transactions	x	Collections from customers	x
	x		x
		Write-offs	x
			x
		Returns and allowances	x
Closing balance	x		

SALES REVENUE			
		Credit sales transactions	x
			x
			x
			x
		Closing balance	x

COMMISSIONS EXPENSE			
Commissions accrual	x		
	x		
	x		
	x		
Closing balance	x		

Note: The number of entries shown by crosses is arbitrary. In reality, there would be likely to be many more than these.

In the case of accounts receivable, it is common to apply each of the three types of substantive procedure to some extent. For other accounts, only one or two of the types of test may be performed in obtaining sufficient evidence to meet the planned level of detection risk.

Sales revenue

For simplicity, the sales revenue account shown in Figure 9.2 shows the credits representing the individual sales transactions. In practice, the sales revenue account may show only daily, weekly or monthly totals posted from the sales journal. In either case, to determine that sales revenue is fairly stated, the auditor may obtain evidence from any of the following:

- analytical procedures, such as:
  - — comparing the absolute value of the closing balance with the prior year's balance, a budgeted amount or other expected value;
  - — comparing the closing balance with an independent estimate of the closing balance (as illustrated previously for a hotel's revenues — see page 339);
- tests of details of transactions, such as:
  - — vouching the individual credits to the sales journal and to supporting documentation such as sales invoices, shipping documents and sales orders;
  - — tracing transactions data from source documents such as shipping documents, to sales invoices, to the sales journal, and then tracing postings from the sales journal to the sales account;
- tests of details of balances (although this type of test is unlikely to be applicable).

In many cases, both analytical procedures and tests of details are applied to the sales revenue account to achieve the acceptable level of detection risk. In some cases, analytical procedures alone may suffice, as we will discuss in a later section (see page 353).

Commissions expense

The commissions expense account shown in Figure 9.2 (page 343) is a good example of a situation in which analytical procedures alone may be all that is needed to achieve the planned level of detection risk. Examining source documents and recalculating the individual commissions could test the details of the individual debits to the account. However, for this type of account, it may be sufficient simply to obtain evidence by calculating an independent estimate of the total for commissions expense (using an expected relationship with the sales revenue account balance, such as 3 per cent) and then to compare the estimate with the recorded balance for commissions expense.

3 LEARNING OBJECTIVE

Indicate how the timing and extent of substantive procedures are varied to achieve an acceptable level of detection risk.

Timing

Often, many of a firm's audit clients have similar year ends. In Australia a common year end is 30 June. The result is that the months of July to September are commonly referred to as the 'busy season', when resources are often stretched to ensure that all audits are completed on a timely basis. To reduce this pressure auditors will try to perform as much work as possible in the 'quieter' time before the audit busy season. This has the dual advantage of (1) putting less pressure on resources during the busy season and (2) helping to complete audits on a timely basis. The level of detection risk has an impact on the extent to which the auditor can alter the **timing of substantive procedures**.

If detection risk is high, then certain procedures (typically tests of details of balances) may be performed several months before the end of the year. At the end of the year the auditor can conduct **roll-forward testing** to verify the account balance as at the year end, using analytical procedures or tests of details of transactions applied to transactions in the intervening period. In contrast, when detection risk for an assertion is low, all substantive procedures relating to account balances will ordinarily be performed at or near the balance sheet date.

Substantive procedures prior to balance sheet date

Substantive procedures commonly performed prior to the balance sheet date are (1) the confirmation of accounts receivable, (2) the observation of physical inventory and (3) the physical inspection of investments.

Performing substantive procedures prior to the balance sheet date may enable the audit to be more cost effective but only if it does not increase the audit risk that material misstatements existing in the account at the balance sheet date will not be detected by the auditor beyond an acceptable level. This risk becomes greater as the time period remaining between the date of the interim audit and the balance sheet date is lengthened.

The potential increased audit risk can be controlled if:

- the internal control structure during the remaining period is effective;
- there are no conditions or circumstances that may predispose management to misstate the financial report in the remaining period;
- the year-end balances of the accounts examined at the interim date are reasonably predictable as to amount, relative significance and composition;
- the entity's accounting system will provide information concerning significant unusual transactions and significant fluctuations that may occur in the remaining period.

If these conditions do not exist, then the account should be examined at the balance sheet date. In practice, early substantive testing of account balances is not done unless tests of control have provided convincing evidence that the internal control structure is operating effectively. Substantive procedures prior to the balance sheet date do not completely eliminate the need for substantive procedures at the balance sheet date. Such procedures (roll-forward testing) ordinarily should include:

- a comparison of the account balances at the two dates and of the totals of transactions making up the difference to identify amounts that appear to be unusual, and the investigation of such amounts;
- other analytical procedures or other substantive tests of details to provide a reasonable basis for extending the interim audit conclusions to the balance sheet date.

When properly planned and executed, the combination of substantive procedures prior to the balance sheet date and substantive procedures for the remaining period should provide the auditor with sufficient appropriate audit evidence to have a reasonable basis for an opinion on the entity's financial report.

Extent

The auditor can vary the amount of evidence obtained by changing the **extent of substantive procedures** performed. 'Extent' means the number of items or sample size to which a particular test or procedure is applied. More evidence is needed to achieve a low planned level of detection risk than a high planned level of detection risk.

The extent will therefore relate to the size of the samples selected by the auditor. Thus, more extensive substantive procedures are being performed when the auditor confirms 200 accounts receivable rather than 100 accounts, or vouches 100 sales journal entries to supporting documents rather than fifty entries. The sample size to which a particular test is applied can be determined by probability theory or professional judgement. No matter what method is chosen, similar factors should be considered to determine sample size. Some of these factors are outlined in Appendix 2 of AUS 514 (Appendix 2, ISA 530), Audit Sampling and Other Selective Testing Procedures. One consideration is that the higher the assessment of inherent risk and control risk, the larger the sample size needs to be. This is because a lower level of detection risk is required, which means a larger sample size is needed. This topic was discussed in Chapter 8.

Audit risk and choice of substantive procedures

A graphic summary of several important relationships between the audit risk components and the nature, timing and extent of substantive procedures is presented in Figure 9.3. As noted earlier, designing substantive procedures involves determining the nature, timing and extent of substantive procedures for significant financial report assertions. In the next section, we will consider how the auditor relates assertions, specific audit objectives and substantive procedures in developing written **audit programs** for substantive procedures.

FIGURE 9.3

Risk components and the nature, timing and extent of substantive procedures

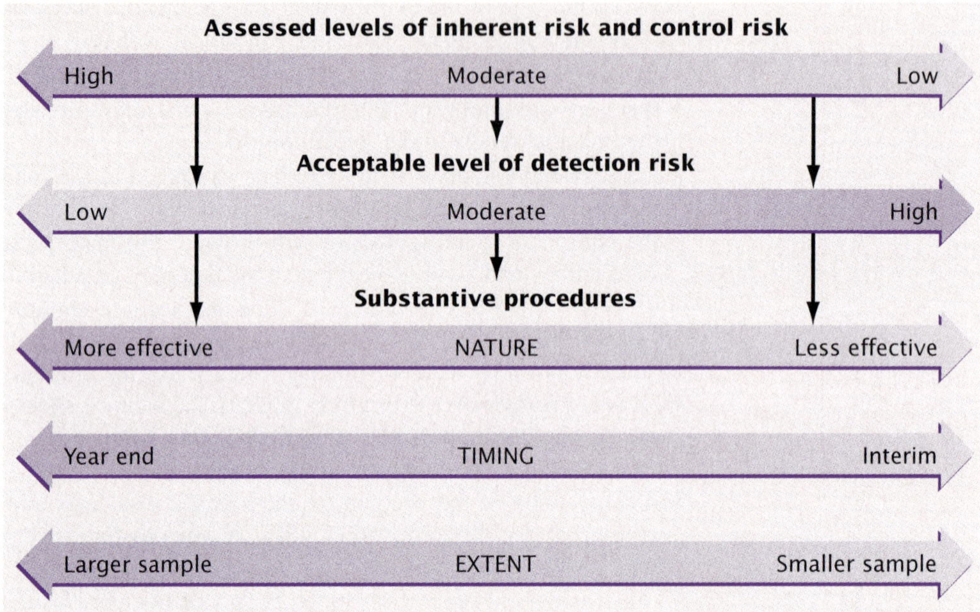

4 LEARNING OBJECTIVE

Explain how computer-assisted audit techniques may be used as substantive procedures.

Computer-assisted audit techniques as substantive procedures

Often the auditor will use computer-assisted audit techniques to assist in performing substantive procedures during the audit. A common type of audit software that can be used in performing substantive procedures is known as **generalised audit software**. Depending on the application, one or more of the following distinct phases may be involved in using audit software packages such as generalised audit software:

- identifying the audit objective and the tests to be performed;
- determining the feasibility of using a software package with the entity's system;
- designing the application, which may include the logic, calculations and form of the output;
- processing the application on actual entity file data and reviewing the results.

The use of generalised audit software enables the auditor to deal effectively with large quantities of data. This may permit the accumulation of either the same quantity of evidence at less cost or more evidence at an economical cost. Often, the main cost is associated with using this type of software on an audit for the first time. The software may be designed to perform nearly any of the auditing procedures that an auditor can perform manually.

Generalised audit software can be used for control and substantive procedures; however, their most common use in practice is for substantive procedures. A couple of the most common substantive procedure applications are outlined in the following sections.

Testing calculations and making computations

Tests of extensions, footings or other computations can be performed on the data. Inventory quantities may be extended by a unit cost, and the amount of the inventory may be recalculated. Individual customer accounts receivable records may be individually footed and a total of all accounts may be prepared. If entity files contain sufficient information, then the recalculation of certain year-end adjusting entries also may be possible. The speed with which computer processing is performed means recomputations can be performed on a more extensive basis than is practicable in a manual system.

Summarising data and performing analyses

The auditor often prefers to have the entity data re-organised in a manner that will suit a special purpose. The auditor may want, for instance, to determine slow-moving inventory items, debit balances in accounts payable or past-due accounts receivable. Similarly, in performing analytical procedures, the auditor may use the computer to compute ratios and other comparative data.

LEARNING CHECK

9.1 Detection risk is determined by considering the assessment of inherent risk and control risk. The level of detection risk determines the amount of substantive procedures required.

9.2 The preliminary assessment of control risk must be reviewed on completion of tests of control. Control risk for most account balance assertions is determined by the control risk of transaction classes making up that account balance.

9.3 The nature of substantive procedures refers to the type and effectiveness of audit procedures performed. The types of substantive procedure are: analytical procedures; tests of details of transactions; and tests of details of balances.

9.4 Analytical procedures are a useful substantive audit procedure to reduce detection risk. They are typically performed first. Planned tests of details are based on the presumption that analytical procedures will fail to detect misstatements.

9.5 The assessment of detection risk will also have an impact on the timing and extent of substantive audit procedures. If the acceptable detection risk is high, then the auditor may perform more testing prior to year end and may reduce the sample sizes of transactions and balances for testing.

DEVELOPING AUDIT PROGRAMS FOR SUBSTANTIVE PROCEDURES

As previously stated, the overall objective of a financial report audit is the expression of an opinion on whether the entity's financial report is presented fairly, in all material respects, in accordance with applicable Accounting Standards. Furthermore, as noted in Chapter 5, it is good audit practice to develop numerous specific audit objectives for each account balance, based on each of the financial report assertions. In designing substantive procedures, the auditor should determine that appropriate procedures have been identified to achieve each of the specific audit objectives pertaining to each assertion. If this is done for each account, then the overall objective will be met.

LEARNING OBJECTIVE 5

Explain which substantive procedures may normally be included in an audit program.

Assertions, audit objectives and substantive procedures

Table 9.4 illustrates the relationships between assertions, specific audit objectives and substantive procedures for the inventories of a manufacturing company. Study of the procedures shown in the second column indicates that a mix of analytical procedures and tests of details of both transactions and balances is included. In some cases, a procedure is listed more than once because the evidence from the procedure relates to more than one specific audit objective or assertion. Table 9.4 is not intended to include a listing of all possible substantive procedures that may be used in auditing inventory, and neither should you infer that all the listed procedures would be performed in every audit. In the next section we will illustrate how these procedures are incorporated into the audit program.

TABLE 9.4 *Relationships between assertions, specific audit objectives and substantive procedures*

Specific audit objective	Examples of substantive procedures
For the existence or occurrence assertion	
Inventories included in the balance sheet physically exist.	Observe and test physical inventory counts.
	Obtain confirmation of inventories at locations outside the entity.
Inventories represent items held for sale or use in the normal course of business.	Review perpetual inventory records and purchasing records for indications of current activity.
	Compare inventories with a current sales catalogue and subsequent sales and delivery reports.
For the rights and obligations assertion	
The entity has legal title or similar rights of ownership to the inventories.	Observe physical inventory counts.
	Obtain confirmation of inventories at locations outside the entity.
	Examine paid suppliers' invoices, consignment agreements and contracts.
Inventories exclude items billed to customers or owned by others.	Examine paid suppliers' invoices, consignment agreements and contracts.
	Test shipping and receiving cut-off procedures.
	Compare inventories with a current sales catalogue and subsequent sales and delivery reports.
For the completeness assertion	
Inventory quantities include all products, materials and supplies on hand.	Observe and test physical inventory counts.
	Account for all inventory tags and count sheets used in making the physical inventory counts.
	Analytically review the relationship of inventory balances to recent purchasing and sales activities.
	Test shipping and receiving cut-off procedures.
Inventory quantities include all products, materials and supplies owned by the company that are stored at outside locations.	Obtain confirmation of inventories at locations outside the entity.

Specific audit objective	Examples of substantive procedures
For the valuation or measurement assertion	
Inventory listings are accurately compiled and the totals are properly included in the inventory accounts.	Trace test counts recorded during the physical inventory observation to the inventory listing.
	Test the clerical accuracy of inventory listings.
	Reconcile physical counts to perpetual records and general ledger balances, and investigate significant fluctuations.
Inventories are properly stated at cost (except when net realisable value is lower).	Examine suppliers' invoicers.
Slow-moving, excess, defective and obsolete items included in inventories are properly indentified.	Inquire of sales personnel concerning possible excess or obsolete inventory items.
	Examine an analysis of inventory turnover.
	Review industry experience and trends.
	Analytically review the relationship of inventory balances to anticipated sales volume.
Inventories are reduced, when appropriate, to net realisable value.	Review estimates of realisable values.
For the disclosure assertion	
Inventories are properly classified in the balance sheet as current assets.	Review drafts of the financial report.
The basis of valuation is adequately disclosed in the financial report.	Compare the disclosures made in the financial report with the requirements of the Corporations Law and applicable Accounting Standards.
The pledge or assignment of any inventories is appropriately disclosed.	Obtain confirmation of inventories pledged under loan agreements.

Illustrative audit program

As required by AUS 208 (ISA 230), Documentation, the auditor's decisions regarding the design of substantive procedures must be documented in the working papers in the form of written audit programs. An audit program is a list of audit procedures to be performed. Contrary to the way they are grouped in Table 9.4, generally the procedures are not listed by assertion or specific audit objective, so as to avoid the duplication of procedures that apply to more than one assertion or objective.

In addition to listing audit procedures, each audit program should have:

- columns for a cross-reference to other working papers detailing the evidence obtained from each procedure (when applicable);
- the initials of the auditor who performed each procedure;
- the date performance of the procedure was completed.

Figure 9.4 (page 350) shows an audit program in this format. The procedures in the program are based on those shown in Table 9.4, except that each procedure is listed only once, and the procedures are listed in a sequence that is logical for the development of the program and/or performance of the procedures.

Details of procedures are given in outline here. Such an outline would form part of an audit firm's standard documentation to be tailored for each engagement. In a tailored audit program, the details would refer to the entity's specific information system and portions of the audit trail applicable to processing the transactions. They would also identify the particular documents and records involved, and may specify the extent of each procedure.

Audit programs should be sufficiently detailed to provide: an outline of the work to be done; a basis for coordinating, supervising and controlling the audit; and a record of the work performed.

The audit program shown in Figure 9.4 is presented to illustrate the format of audit programs for substantive procedures and how they can be developed. We will explain the application of the substantive procedures shown in Chapter 12, which includes the audit of inventories.

FIGURE 9.4 *Illustrative audit program for substantive procedures of inventories*

Prepared by:_______ Date:_______
Reviewed by:_______ Date:_______

XYZ Company Limited
Audit program for substantive procedures of inventories
31 December 20X1

Substantive procedure	W/P ref.	Auditor	Date
1. Verify totals and agreement of inventory balances and records that will be subjected to further testing: (a) Trace opening inventory balances to prior year's working papers. (b) Review activity in inventory accounts and investigate unusual items. (c) Verify totals of perpetual records and other inventory schedules and their agreement with closing general ledger balances. 2. Perform analytical procedures: (a) Review industry experience and trends. (b) Examine an analysis of inventory turnover. (c) Review relationship of inventory balances with recent purchasing and sales activities. (d) Compare inventory balances with anticipated sales volume. 3. Test details of inventory transactions: (a) Vouch additions to inventory records and to suppliers' invoices. (b) Trace data from purchases to inventory records. (c) Test cut-off of purchases (receiving) and sales (shipping). 4. Observe physical inventory count: (a) Make test counts. (b) Look for indications of slow-moving, damaged or obsolete inventory. (c) Account for all inventory tags and count sheets used in the physical count. 5. Test clerical accuracy of inventory records: (a) Recalculate extensions of quantities times unit prices. (b) Trace test counts to records. (c) Vouch items on inventory listings to inventory tags and count sheets. (d) Reconcile physical counts to perpetual records and general ledger balances. 6. Test inventory pricing: (a) Examine supplier's paid invoices for purchased inventory. (b) Obtain market quotations and perform lower of cost or net realisable value test. (c) Review perpetual inventory records and purchasing records for indications of current activity. (d) Compare inventories with current sales catalogue and sales reports. (e) Inquire about slow-moving, excess or obsolete inventories and determine need for write-downs. 7. Confirm inventories at locations outside the entity. 8. Examine consignment agreements and contracts. 9. Confirm agreements for assignment and pledging of inventories. 10. Review disclosures for inventories in drafts of the financial report and determine conformity with the Corporations Law and applicable Accounting Standards.			

6 LEARNING OBJECTIVE

Describe and apply a general framework for developing audit programs for substantive procedures.

Framework for developing audit programs

Referring again to Figure 9.4 and to the previous discussion on designing substantive procedures, we can construct a general framework for developing audit programs for substantive procedures. Such an approach is described in Figure 9.5 (page 352).

The steps listed in the upper portion of Figure 9.5 summarise the application of several important concepts and procedures explained in Chapters 5–7. Note that the first step listed in the lower portion of the figure corresponds to the first step in Figure 9.4. Because subsequent substantive procedures are often performed on the subsidiary records or supporting schedules prepared by the entity, or samples drawn therefrom, it is logical to start by ascertaining that the supporting records do tie in with the general ledger. When applicable, it is also logical to establish the agreement of opening balances with audited amounts in the prior year's working papers, so procedures performed in the current audit can be focused on the effects of transactions that occurred in the current period and the closing balance.

The specification of analytical procedures is considered next because if effective procedures are available, they may reduce or eliminate the need for more expensive tests of details. Note that even though there are several analytical procedures listed in Step 2 of Figure 9.4, in the case of inventories, the normal requirement to observe the physical inventory taking means tests of details cannot be entirely eliminated.

Tests of details of transactions are ordinarily considered next because they are usually performed during the interim audit at the same time as tests of control, often as dual-purpose tests. Finally, the program should specify tests of details of balances, special requirements not previously addressed and procedures to determine that the disclosures pertaining to the assertions covered by the program are in accordance with applicable Accounting Standards. In specifying the latter procedures, the auditor uses knowledge of relevant business practices and financial reporting disclosure requirements such as, in the case of inventories, those pertaining to the method of valuation.

The general framework for developing audit programs described in Figure 9.5 underpins the numerous illustrations of audit programs for substantive procedures presented in subsequent chapters of this text. The auditor generally adopts a consistent approach in developing audit programs for recurring engagements, but there are some special considerations in developing audit programs for **initial engagements**.

Often many of the choices in the preliminary planning part of Figure 9.5 will be input into a computer program designed to assist with developing audit programs. The program will tailor procedures to the audit engagement based on the information entered, reducing the number of decisions required by the auditor in the second part of Figure 9.5, which specifies the substantive procedures.

Audit programs in initial engagements

AUS 510 (ISA 510), Initial Engagements — Opening Balances identifies two matters as requiring special consideration during the design of audit programs for initial engagements. These are:

- determining the fairness of the account balances at the beginning of the period being audited;
- ascertaining the accounting principles used in the preceding period as a basis for determining the consistency of application of such principles in the current period.

The auditor will need to review the audit working papers of the predecessor auditor to ascertain whether he or she can rely on the previous work. If this is not possible, the auditor will need to attempt to gather information on the opening assets and liabilities as part of the current year's audit. If sufficient evidence cannot be gathered, the auditor may need to qualify the audit report based on a limitation of scope.

FIGURE 9.5

General framework for developing audit programs for substantive procedures

GENERAL FRAMEWORK

Complete preliminary planning

1. Develop specific audit objectives for each financial report assertion pertaining to closing inventory balances (as illustrated in Table 9.4 on pages 348–9).
2. Assess inherent and control risk and determine the acceptable level of detection risk for each assertion, consistent with the overall level of audit risk and applicable materiality level.
3. From knowledge acquired from procedures to obtain an understanding of the internal control structure, envision the accounting records, supporting documents, accounting process (including the audit trail), and financial reporting process pertaining to the assertions.
4. Consider options regarding the design of substantive procedures:
   - Alternatives for accommodating varying acceptable levels of detection risk:
     — nature:
       : analytical procedures
       : tests of details of transactions
       : tests of details of balances
     — timing: interim versus year-end
     — extent: sample size;
   - Possible types of corroborating evidence available:

analytical	electronic	physical
confirmations	mathematical	written representations;
documentary	oral	

   - Possible types of audit procedure available:

analytical procedures	counting	reperforming
computer-assisted audit techniques	inquiring	tracing
	inspecting	vouching.
confirming	observing	

Specify substantive procedures to be included in audit program

1. Specify initial procedures to:
   (a) trace opening balances to prior year's working papers (if applicable);
   (b) review activity in applicable general ledger accounts and investigate unusual items;
   (c) verify totals of supporting records or schedules to be used in subsequent procedures and determine their agreement with general ledger balances, when applicable, to establish the tie-in of detail with control accounts.
2. Specify analytical procedures to be performed.
3. Specify tests of details of transactions to be performed.
4. Specify tests of details of balances (in addition to 1(a), (b) and (c) above) to be performed.
5. Consider whether there are any special requirements or procedures applicable to assertions tested in the circumstances, such as procedures required by Auditing Standards (for example, observation of inventories) or by regulatory agencies that have not been included in (3) and (4) above.
6. Specify procedures to determine that disclosure is in accordance with the Corporations Law and applicable Accounting Standards.

7 LEARNING OBJECTIVE

Indicate special considerations for when designing substantive procedures for selected types of account.

SPECIAL CONSIDERATIONS IN DESIGNING SUBSTANTIVE PROCEDURES

The foregoing discussions of assessing detection risk, designing substantive procedures and developing audit programs apply to all accounts. In this section we will note some special considerations relevant to designing substantive procedures for selected types of account.

Profit and loss statement accounts

Traditionally, tests of details of balances have focused more on financial report assertions that pertain to balance sheet accounts than on profit and loss statement accounts. This approach is both efficient and logical because each profit and loss statement account is inextricably linked to one or more balance sheet accounts. Below are examples.

Balance sheet account	Related profit and loss statement account
Accounts receivable	Sales
Inventories	Cost of sales
Prepaid expenses	Various related expenses
Investments	Investment income
Property, plant and equipment	Depreciation expense
Interest-bearing liabilities	Interest expense

The assertions for the accounts are linked as well. Evidence that accounts receivable do not exist, for example, may indicate that sales did not occur (although it could also mean the entity failed to record a payment remitted by the customer). Similarly, if interest-bearing liabilities are not complete, then interest expense may not be complete, and so on. Generally, if there is an error or deliberate misstatement in profit and loss accounts, then there is a higher likelihood that it has occurred towards the end of the year and it will therefore be included in the related balance sheet account.

Given these relationships, evidence obtained through substantive procedures applied to balance sheet accounts also provides much of the evidence required to achieve the desired level of detection risk for profit and loss account balances. For this reason, analytical procedures are frequently the only substantive procedures that must be specifically applied in verifying profit and loss statement accounts.

Analytical procedures for profit and loss statement accounts

Analytical procedures can be a powerful audit tool in obtaining audit evidence about profit and loss statement balances. This type of substantive procedure may be used directly or indirectly. Direct tests occur when a revenue or an expense account is compared with other relevant data to determine the reasonableness of its balance. The ratio of sales commissions to sales, for example, can be compared with the ratios for prior years and with budget data for the current year. Comparisons can also be made with non-financial information, as shown in the following two examples.

Account	Analytical procedure
Hotel room revenue	Number of rooms × occupancy rate × average room rate
Wages expense	Average number of employees per pay period × average pay per period × number of pay periods

Indirect tests occur when evidence concerning profit and loss statement balances can be derived from analytical procedures applied to related balance sheet accounts. Accounts receivable turnover may be used in verifying accounts receivable, for example, and the findings may have an impact on whether bad-debts expense and sales are fairly stated.

Tests of details for profit and loss statement accounts

When the evidence obtained from analytical procedures and from tests of details of related balance sheet accounts does not reduce detection risk to an acceptably low level, direct tests of details of assertions pertaining to profit and loss statement accounts are necessary. This may be the case when:

- inherent risk is high, as in the case of assertions affected by non-routine transactions and management's judgements and estimates;
- control risk is high, such as when related internal controls for non-routine and routine transactions are ineffective, and when the auditor elects not to test the internal controls;
- analytical procedures reveal unusual relationships and unexpected fluctuations;
- the account requires analysis — for example, legal expenses and professional fees, income tax, maintenance and repairs expenses, travel and entertainment expenses, and directors' remuneration.

Accounts involving accounting estimates

An **accounting estimate** is an approximation of a financial report item in the absence of exact measurement. Examples of accounting estimates include depreciation, the provision for bad debts and warranty expense. Management is responsible for making the accounting estimates included in the financial report. These estimates are balances with a greater risk of misstatement because they are often made in conditions of uncertainty about the outcome of events that have occurred or are likely to occur. Due to the use of judgement and, therefore, the subjective nature of these balances, they are often the ones over which the most disputes occur between the auditor and management.

AUS 516.10 (ISA 540.10) suggests that one or a combination of the following approaches should be adopted in the audit of accounting estimates to obtain sufficient appropriate audit evidence.

- *Review and test the processes used by management to develop the estimate.* The auditor could review the data and assumptions used by management in preparing the estimate; test the calculations performed; and compare the accuracy of estimates made by management in prior periods.
- *Use an independent estimate for comparison.* The auditor may make his or her own independent estimate of the balance and compare it with management's estimate.
- *Review subsequent events.* A review of subsequent events after the end of the accounting period may provide evidence as to the accuracy of management's estimate.

Related parties

Related party transactions are a risk area for auditors because very specific disclosure requirements are outlined in AASB 1017 (IAS 24), Related Party Disclosures. Furthermore, these transactions have a higher than average risk of irregularities.[1] The auditor should perform the following specific substantive procedures with respect to the related parties, as outlined in AUS 518 (ISA 550), Related Parties.

- *Existence of related parties.* The auditor should review information provided by management identifying related parties and perform audit procedures to ensure that the risk of related parties remaining undetected is low. These procedures may include reviewing prior period working papers, reviewing shareholder records, and reviewing minutes of shareholders and directors meetings.
- *Transactions with related parties.* The auditor should review information provided by management identifying related party transactions and be alert for other material related party transactions. The auditor will need details of all related parties at the beginning of

the audit so they can identify related party transactions that they encounter. The auditor also needs to be alert for transactions that have abnormal conditions, lack logical reasons for occurrence, have substance that is different from form, or have been processed in an unusual manner.

Balances that have specific audit requirements

Some balances have specific audit requirements, as outlined in the Auditing Standards. This is because they are considered sufficiently important in the audit of a set of financial statements to require more detailed guidance. Here, we will outline the two main examples.

Confirmation of receivables

The audit of receivables requires that a confirmation letter be sent under most circumstances, as per AUS 504, External Confirmations (ISA 501, Additional Considerations for Specific Items, Part B: Confirmation of Accounts Receivable). ISA 501.19 specifically considers accounts receivable and states:

> When the accounts receivable are material to the financial report, and when it is reasonable to expect debtors will respond, the auditor should plan to obtain direct confirmation of accounts receivable or individual entries in an account balance.

The main reasons for this requirement are that a high risk is often associated with accounts receivable and the fact that there is no external evidence within the entity to confirm the balance (unlike accounts payable, for which there will often be suppliers' statements). One reason for it being a high-risk balance is because if fictitious sales are processed by the entity then there is likely to be a corresponding fictitious balance in accounts receivable. We will further discuss the audit of accounts receivable in Chapter 10.

Existence and valuation of inventory

AUS 506, Existence and Valuation of Inventory, (ISA 501, Additional Considerations for Specific Items, Part A: Attendance at Physical Inventory Counting) requires the following of an auditor during the audit of inventory (as discussed in AUS 506.02):

> The auditor should obtain sufficient appropriate audit evidence regarding the existence and valuation of inventory material to the financial report.

The main requirement of the Standard is in relation to existence, as stated in AUS 506.07 (ISA 501.05):

> When inventory is material to the financial report, the auditor should obtain sufficient appropriate audit evidence regarding its existence and condition by attendance at physical inventory counting, unless impracticable.

The Standard also outlines some specific procedures to ensure that inventory is properly valued. The reason for these specific requirements is that a high risk of misstatement is associated with inventory. This risk is due to the often large number of relatively small items that make up the total inventory balance and to the subjectivity associated with the provision for obsolescence. We will discuss further details about the audit of inventory in Chapter 12.

LEARNING CHECK

9.6 The audit program details substantive procedures required to provide sufficient appropriate audit evidence for each material account balance assertion.

9.7 The written audit program is listed in a sequence that is logical for the performance of the audit, instead of by assertion, because many procedures provide evidence pertaining to more than one assertion.

9.8 In developing the audit program, the auditor first identifies the audit objectives, the primary evidence available from the information system and the alternative types of substantive procedure.

9.9 Many profit and loss accounts are inextricably linked to one or more balance sheet accounts. Thus, much of the evidence obtained through substantive procedures on balance sheet accounts provides evidence for profit and loss account balances. This allows more extensive use of analytical procedures in these accounts.

9.10 Due to the nature of accounting estimates and related party transactions, special consideration must be given to them during the design of substantive audit procedures.

SUMMARY

After obtaining an understanding of the internal control structure relevant to an assertion and making a preliminary assessment of control risk, the auditor determines the preliminary audit strategy and the associated acceptable level of detection risk and level of substantive procedures. The auditor then plans specific substantive procedures to achieve the acceptable level of detection risk by exercising judgements about the nature, timing and extent of such procedures. The auditor also relates the tests to specific audit objectives to ensure that he or she meets the overall objective of rendering an opinion on the financial report as a whole.

The types of substantive procedure performed on particular account balances and transaction classes are discussed in more detail in the following chapters:

- Chapter 10 — Auditing sales and receivables;
- Chapter 11 — Auditing purchases, payables and payroll;
- Chapter 12 — Auditing inventories and property, plant and equipment;
- Chapter 13 — Auditing cash and investments.

The auditor's decisions about the design of substantive procedures are documented in the form of written audit programs, which provide an outline of the work to be done and a means for controlling the audit and recording the work performed. A general framework may be used in developing effective and efficient audit programs for substantive procedures tailored to the entity's circumstances. There are special considerations in designing substantive procedures for selected types of account, including profit and loss accounts, accounting estimates and related parties. Ultimately, for most audits the performance of these substantive tests will comprise a large part of the audit evidence that the auditor uses to form an opinion on the financial statements (discussed further in Chapter 15).

KEY TERMS

Accounting estimate, p. 354
Analytical procedures, p. 338
Audit program, p. 346
Cut-off tests, p. 342
Detection risk, p. 334
Dual-purpose tests, p. 338
Extent of substantive procedures, p. 345
Generalised audit software, p. 346
Initial engagements, p. 351
Nature of substantive procedures, p. 339
Planned detection risk, p. 334
Planned level of substantive procedures, p. 338
Related party transactions, p. 354
Roll-forward testing, p. 344
Tests of details of balances, p. 339
Tests of details of transactions, p. 339
Timing of substantive procedures, p. 344

NOTE

1. Related party transactions are mentioned in Appendix 2 of AUS 210, Irregularities, Including Fraud, Other Illegal Acts and Errors as an example of a factor that increases the risk of irregularities.

FURTHER READING

Bell, Timothy B. & Wright, Arnold M., 'When Judgment Counts', *Journal of Accountancy* (November 1997), pp. 73–7.

Biggs, Stanley F., Mock, Theodore J. & Simnett, R., 'Analytical Procedures: Promise, Problems and Implications for Practice', *Australian Accounting Review* (Vol. 9, No. 1, 1999), pp. 42–52.

Blocher, E. & Patterson, George F. Jr, 'Use of Analytical Procedures', *Journal of Accountancy* (February 1996) pp. 53–5.

Colbert, Janet L., 'International and US Standards — Audit Risk and Materiality', *Managerial Auditing Journal* (Vol. 11, No. 8, 1996), pp. 31–5.

Martinov, N., 'Codification and Its Impact on the Integration of Risk', *Charter* (May 1997), pp. 76–7.

Mock, Theodore J. & Wright, Arnold, 'An Exploratory Study of Auditors' Evidential Planning Judgments', *Auditing: A Journal of Practice and Theory* (Fall 1993), pp. 39–61.

Mock, Theodore J. & Wright, Arnold, 'Are Audit Program Plans Risk-Adjusted?', *Auditing: A Journal of Practice and Theory* (Spring 1999), pp. 55–74.

Pogrob, Kenneth R. & Isenberg, G., 'Auditing in a Paperless Society', *The Secured Lender*, (Vol. 55, No. 7, 1999), pp. 126–8.

Srinidhi, B. N. & Vasarhelyi, M. A., 'Auditor Judgment Concerning Establishment of Substantive Tests Based on Internal Control Reliability', *Auditing: A Journal of Practice and Theory* (Spring 1986), pp. 64–76.

Trotman, K., 'Analytical Review', *Audit Monograph No. 1*. Australian Accounting Research Foundation, Melbourne, 1990.

Review questions

9.1 How is detection risk determined from the assessed levels of inherent and control risk?

9.2 What factors would the auditor consider in deciding to adopt a predominantly substantive approach for an audit?

9.3 What should the auditor consider when using analytical review procedures to reduce detection risk?

9.4 What procedures should the auditor perform in roll-forward testing a particular account balance? Describe these procedures.

9.5 What purposes are served by audit programs?

9.6 What are the main steps involved in developing an audit program?

Discussion questions

9.1 Which components of the audit risk model can be controlled by the auditor? Discuss the interrelationships.

9.2 How does the assessed level of detection risk have an impact on the nature, timing and extent of substantive procedures?

9.3 What are possible situations in which analytical procedures may be the only substantive test used by an auditor for a particular balance? Discuss.

9.4 What is the difference between tests of details of balances and tests of details of transactions?

9.5 Why are cut-off tests a special category of tests of details of transactions?

9.6 Why and under what circumstances may an auditor perform substantive procedures prior to the year end?

9.7 What specific audit tests would an auditor be unlikely to perform prior to the year end? Discuss.

9.8 Why may an auditor decide to perform tests of details on profit and loss statement accounts rather than relying on analytical review?

9.9 What steps may the auditor perform in evaluating the reasonableness of accounting estimates?

9.10 Why is the audit of related party transactions a particular risk area for auditors?

Professional application questions

★ BASIC
★★ MODERATE
★★★ CHALLENGING

9.1 (Substantive procedures) ★

Listed below are fifteen substantive procedures,

1. Calculate debtors' turnover and compare to prior year's turnover.
2. Review all invoices received for one month after the year end to ensure that they do not relate to the current year.
3. Ensure that all contingent liabilities have been included in the notes to the accounts.
4. Attend the year-end stock count and perform test counts on a sample of stock items.

5. Send a letter to the bank to confirm a loan taken out by the company during the year.
6. Ensure that interest paid on the bank loan is correct by multiplying the interest rate by the outstanding principal for each month of the year.
7. Review a sample of repairs and maintenance expenditure for the year to ensure that it does not include any items that are capital in nature.
8. Perform a debtors' circularisation.
9. Obtain the company's depreciation rates from the financial statements and check they have been applied correctly.
10. Review the adequacy of the company's provision for doubtful debts.
11. Trace the last inventory received before the year end to the inventory listing.
12. Review the company-prepared bank reconciliation.
13. Select a sample of invoices and ensure that they have been properly recorded in the sales ledger.
14. Review the profit and loss statement for unusual differences in the balances recorded for this year and last year.
15. Select a sample of fixed assets and sight them.

Required

(a) For each test, indicate the type of substantive procedure to which it relates (analytical review, tests of details of balances or tests of details of transactions).

(b) List one assertion to which each test relates.

9.2 (Detection risk) ★★

Tom Capuro was the new audit assistant at the accounting firm of Johnson and Partners, and he was given the planning strategy for his first audit. Tom could see that there was a very low inherent risk and control risk for the audit. The company had a good system of internal control in place, and a large amount of audit work was performed to place reliance on those controls. However, he could not understand why there was still a large amount of substantive testing performed in the audit. His understanding of the audit risk model from studies at university was that a low inherent and low control risk should mean a high allowable detection risk — therefore, no substantive testing. When he raised this issue with Ms Johnson, the audit partner, she suggested that the substantive tests were performed because 'We can't completely rely on internal controls — it would be too risky! The lawyers would have a field day if we were sued!'.

Required

Discuss whether Tom or Ms Johnson is right.

9.3 (Substantive procedures: nature, timing and extent) ★★

Jenni Francis is an audit partner with your firm. She has asked you, as the audit senior on the audit of Freelance Furnishings Limited (FF), to do the substantive audit work on inventory for the firm. You have been provided with the following information.

- Your firm has performed the audit for a number of years and inherent risk has always been low.
- Control risk is assessed as low, and a colleague of yours will perform extensive control testing in the inventory section of this audit.
- Allowable detection risk has been assessed as being high for the inventory section of the audit.
- The main assertion risk is in relation to valuation for inventory.
- There is a tight time limit for completion of the audit.

(continued)

Required

(a) Discuss the implications of this information on the nature, timing and extent of auditing procedures.

(b) Describe one possible test of details of balances to address the main risk assertion associated with inventory.

9.4 (Design of substantive procedures) ★★

You are the audit partner in Miles Jeffrey, a firm of certified practising accountants. For a number of years you have been the partner in charge of Macchiato Limited — a firm that imports and distributes coffee machines and other coffee-related products. You have had no problems with the audit in the past. Macchiato's fiscal year ends on 31 December. This year, the owners of Macchiato request that the audit be completed by 15 February next year because Macchiato's parent company in Italy requires the accounts for consolidation purposes.

You do not believe you will have time to perform all of the audit fieldwork during January. An alternative would be for you to plan the audit so a considerable amount of the substantive testing is performed during the interim audit of Macchiato in November. This testing would be on balances at 31 October, two months before the year end.

Required

(a) Describe the factors that you should consider before applying substantive procedures to Macchiato's balance sheet accounts at 31 October.

(b) Explain what you should do to ensure that the balances at 31 December are fairly stated when much of the work is performed on balances at 31 October.

9.5 (Design of substantive procedures) ★★

John Greening is an audit senior carrying out the planning of the audit of GrowRite Limited, an importer of hydroponic equipment for the market garden industry. The owners of GrowRite complained to the partner on the audit engagement that the audit fee was too high. The audit partner, Kelly Yeo, was concerned about losing this client so she decided to cut 10 per cent off the fee for the audit — an amount of $2000.

Kelly decided that the amount of work performed on the client would have to be reduced to cover this discount, but she felt this was reasonable because the inherent risk and control risk had always been good.

Kelly calls John into her office and says that she wants to avoid performing debtors and creditors circularisations as they have done in prior years. Her reason is that following up non-responses is an expensive and time-consuming task and that it would be more efficient to use alternative audit procedures. She also tells John that the sample size for selecting debtors and creditors balances for testing should be reduced, given that they have had few problems in those parts of the audits in prior years.

Required

(a) List what factors Kelly should have considered in changing the nature and extent of the substantive audit testing.

(b) Discuss any special considerations in relation to the audit procedures that should be performed in auditing debtors and creditors.

9.6 (Analytical review procedures) ★★

You are an audit senior gathering audit evidence on the audit of Grenfold Pty Limited, a large proprietary company. Your manager has asked you to consider the use of analytical procedures in relation to the prepayments and depreciation. Materiality for the audit has been set at $100 000.

Prepayments — $90 000

- Six insurance contracts are each paid in advance for twelve months. Payments are made at various times during the year.
- Rent is paid quarterly in advance on factory premises.
- Control risk is high and inherent risk is low.

Depreciation expense — $755 000

This expense represents depreciation on furniture, fittings, motor vehicles and computer equipment.

- Assets are divided into five categories for depreciation purposes.
- For the sake of simplicity, tax rates are used to calculate depreciation.
- There were no additions or disposals of fixed assets during the year.
- Control risk is medium and inherent risk is low.

Required

(a) Explain how you would verify each balance using analytical procedures. What verification work do you need to perform on the data used in these procedures?

(b) Using the information given, determine how much reliance you would place on the analytical procedures designed in (a). Explain your decision.

(Professional Year Programme of the ICAA — 1999, Accounting 2 Module — adapted)

9.7 (Substantive procedures, accounting estimates) ★★★

Your client ABC Computer International Limited (ABC) has a balance date of 31 December 20X0. ABC is an importer and distributor for a well known US computer manufacturer. It acts as the main Australian distributor for ABC computer products, and keeps a stock of between $10 million and $10.5 million to meet customer orders. Its local policy is to keep only the latest model computers, and it has developed a reputation in the marketplace as being the first to import and distribute the latest computers. It has recently moved into providing consulting services (such as providing advice on installing a local area network), but this area will not be significant at the year end.

Old computers are usually sold at a discount in the period before Christmas, often below cost. ABC has estimated a provision for stock obsolescence of $50 000 at the year end.

Required

(a) Nominate the main financial report assertion that you should be addressing for ABC. Describe what types of substantive procedure you would perform to address this assertion.

(b) Describe whether there are any special considerations you should make as an auditor in auditing an accounting estimate such as the $50 000 provision for obsolescence.

(Professional Year Programme of the ICAA — 1996, Accounting 2 Module — adapted)

9.8 (Analytical review procedures) ★★★

You are an audit senior currently gathering audit evidence on the audit of Maxims Limited, a large listed company. Your manager has asked you to consider the use of analytical procedures in relation to the salaries expense and interest revenue. Materiality for the audit has been set at $250 000.

(continued)

Salaries expense — $2 210 000
- Salaries are paid monthly to the forty salaried staff.
- There are three levels of seniority and each level is paid a different rate. There are no pay variations within levels.
- Promotions occur annually at 1 July.
- Turnover is relatively high. There were fifteen commencements during the year.
- All salaried staff received an increase of 5 per cent on 1 January. There were no other salary increases during the year.
- Both control risk and inherent risk are medium.

Interest revenue — $315 500
This revenue represents interest earned on bank bills.
- A maximum of five bills are in place at any one time. Bills are always placed for four-monthly terms and rolled over at maturity.
- Rates vary according to the market.
- Control risk is high and inherent risk is medium.

Required
(a) Explain how you would verify each balance using analytical procedures. Describe the verification work you need to perform on the data used in these procedures.
(b) Using the information given, determine how much reliance you would place on the analytical procedures designed in (a). Explain your decision.

(Professional Year Programme of the ICAA — 1999, Accounting 2 Module — adapted)

Case studies

9.1 (Internal control assessment, impact on substantive tests) ★★★
You are performing the interim work at Hays Limited which has a 31 December year end. Hays manufactures chocolates that are sold wholesale to charities and community groups, who use them in their fundraising activities.

At the planning stage, the audit manager assessed control risk over sales as being moderate, and he assigned you to perform tests of control on sales. Extracts from the sales audit program are shown below:

Objective	Procedure no.	Details
Occurrence	1	Select a sample of sales invoices from the general ledger from throughout the period and agree to: • sales orders; • sales invoices; • delivery dockets.
Measurement	2	For the sales invoices selected in Procedure 1 above: • check the transaction is within the customer's credit limit; • check the mathematical accuracy of the invoice; • agree prices to approved price lists.
Occurrence/ measurement	3	Select a sample of credit notes issued throughout the period and; • check approved by credit controller; • determine whether reason for issuing credit note seems reasonable; • check mathematical accuracy of credit note; • agree to general and debtors' ledgers.

While performing the listed procedures, you made note of the following issues:

Procedure no.	Details
1	(i) Per the general ledger, invoice 411 was for \$2200; however, the hard copy sales invoice showed \$2020. The difference of \$180 was corrected via a journal entry in the following month. (ii) No sales order or delivery docket could be located for invoice 395. The customer has not yet paid the invoice.
2	(iii) Invoice 510 put the customer \$5000 over their credit limit. The credit controller explained that the managing director authorised this extension of credit, and shows you a file note supporting this. The customer's account has remained below the credit limit at all other times. (iv) Invoices 521 and 527 were issued on the first day the new price list came into force; however, old prices were used on the invoices due to an oversight in the information technology department.
3	(v) Credit note number 71 was not authorised by the credit controller. However, in all other respects it was issued in accordance with company policy and supporting documents exist which validate the claim. (vi) Credit note number 83 was issued on 15 July, but not posted to the general ledger until August. Apparently this was due to a data entry clerk being ill and the temporary replacement not receiving proper instructions as to his duties.

Required

(a) For each of the issues i–vi discuss whether the issue represents an error for the purposes of evaluating the results of tests of controls.

(b) Assume you decide, based on the sample results, that you cannot rely on controls over sales. Discuss what courses of action are open to you to gain sufficient, appropriate audit evidence.

(Professional Year Programme of the ICAA — 1998, Accounting 2 Module — adapted)

9.2 (Substantive procedures, audit work programs) ★★★

Your client is SkyHigh Limited, whose main business is maintaining commercial aircraft. SkyHigh has contracts with several major airlines to carry out maintenance exclusively on their planes when they are in Australia.

Stock items range from screws and wire to more expensive items such as panelling and electronic components. Due to the value of some of the larger items, SkyHigh keeps stock levels to a minimum. The majority of stock is held at the company's warehouse near Sydney Airport.

This is the first year your firm has performed the audit of SkyHigh. Your review of the predecessor auditor's working papers revealed that problems with cut-off were experienced regularly. Problems were also noted in relation to some obsolete stock not being properly identified as part of the stocktake, and to the use of some inexperienced staff on the stocktake resulting in a number of counting errors.

Your firm's standard audit program for inventories is as described in the following box.

(continued)

STANDARD AUDIT PROGRAM FOR INVENTORIES

Stocktake procedures

1. Attend the year-end stocktake and perform the following:
   1.1 Ensure the stocktake is carried out in accordance with client instructions, and that the instructions are reasonable.
   1.2 Tour the warehouse and check to ensure all locations are included in the count.
   1.3 Ensure no movement of stock occurs during the count.
   1.4 Select a random sample of stock items from the floor and agree to count sheets.
   1.5 Select a random sample of stock items from the count sheets and agree to physical stock.
   1.6 Inquire as to how obsolete or damaged stock is identified, and ensure these procedures are followed.
   1.7 Record details of any apparently obsolete stock for later use in auditing the provision for obsolescence.
   1.8 Check cut-off by obtaining details of the last sale pre-stocktake and the first sale post-stocktake. Agree to general ledger. Reperform procedure for goods inwards.
   1.9 Copy a sample of stock sheets for later agreement to final inventory listing.
2. Obtain final inventory listing and then do the following:
   2.1 Check adds, cross-adds and calculations.
   2.2 Agree items from stocktake to listing, ensuring any adjustments are correctly processed.
   2.3 Agree balance to general ledger.
3. Select a sample of items from the final inventory listing and ensure they are valued at the lower of cost and net realisable value.

Provision for obsolescence

4. Obtain a copy of the client's calculation of the provision for obsolescence and then do the following:
   4.1 Check adds, cross-adds and calculations.
   4.2 Check that calculation appears reasonable in the light of our knowledge of the client's business.
   4.3 Agree items noted as obsolete during the stocktake to the provision calculation.
   4.4 Agree balance to the general ledger.

Financial report

5. Review classification and description of inventory balances. Review accounting policies and ensure they are appropriate to the client's business.

Analytical procedures

6. Perform appropriate analytical procedures and compare results to those for prior year and to industry data where applicable (e.g. inventory turnover by product line/location). Ensure results are consistent with our knowledge of the client's business.

Required

(a) For each of the audit steps identified in the audit program, identify the audit assertion(s) it addresses.

(b) List procedures that you would add, amend or delete on your firm's standard audit program for this client.

(c) Explain whether analytical review tests could replace all of the tests of details of balances and tests of details of transactions of balances for this part of the audit. Discuss.

(Professional Year Programme of the ICAA — 1997, Accounting 2 Module — adapted)

chapter 10

PART 4 Auditing transactions and balances

PART 4

Having obtained an understanding of the entity sufficient to develop an audit strategy (as we described in Part 2), the auditor is in a position to apply the audit testing procedures (explained in Part 3) to specific transactions and balances. The chapters in Part 4 are based on the major asset and liability accounts of receivables (**Chapter 10**), payables (**Chapter 11**), inventory, property, plant and equipment (**Chapter 12**), and cash and investments (**Chapter 13**). In the first two chapters we will also consider the transaction classes logically associated with the account balances: sales, sales adjustments and cash receipts in the case of receivables and purchases, cash payments and payroll in the case of payables. We will commence each chapter by describing the nature of information systems and control procedures that entities commonly employ in recording the relevant transaction classes and maintaining the relevant account balances. We will then describe the process of assessing inherent risk and control risk for the relevant transactions and balances — factors the auditor needs to consider in developing the audit strategy and substantive procedures applicable to achieving the planned level of detection risk for each major audit objective.

In performing an audit, the auditor will be required to obtain sufficient appropriate evidence for transactions and balances not specifically described. However, the general principles in this part should be sufficient to enable the reader to determine appropriate audit evidence procedures for any transaction class or account balance.

Although primarily aimed at providing a level of evidence applicable to the expression of an audit opinion, the approach that we will describe can be adapted to enable auditors and accountants to provide other levels of assurance on the applicable transactions and balances.

chapter 10

Auditing sales and receivables

Overview

LEARNING OBJECTIVES

After studying this chapter, you should be able to:

1. identify the audit objectives applicable to sales and receivables
2. describe the functions and control procedures normally found in information systems for processing sales, cash receipts and sales adjustment transactions
3. apply the concepts of materiality and inherent risk to the audit of sales and receivables
4. discuss considerations relevant to determining the audit strategy for sales and receivables
5. design and execute tests of control over sales, cash receipts and sales adjustment transactions to assess control risk
6. indicate the factors relevant to determining an acceptable level of detection risk for the audit of sales and receivables
7. design a substantive audit program for sales and receivables
8. explain the procedures for undertaking a confirmation of receivables balances.

Professional statements

AUSTRALIAN		INTERNATIONAL	
AUS 402	Risk Assessments and Internal Controls	ISA 400	Risk Assessments and Internal Control
AUS 504	External Confirmations	ISA 505	External Confirmations
AUS 514	Audit Sampling and Other Selective Testing Procedures	ISA 530	Audit Sampling and Other Selective Testing Procedures
AUS 516	Audit of Accounting Estimates	ISA 540	Audit of Accounting Estimates
AGS 1020	CIS Environments — On-Line Computer Systems	ISA 1002	EDP Environments — On-Line Computer Systems

In this and the next three chapters, we will apply the procedures explained in the preceding chapters to specific transaction classes and account balances. In this chapter, we will examine the audit of the balance in accounts receivable and of the transaction classes of sales, cash receipts and sales adjustments.

This chapter is organised as follows:

- Firstly, we will identify the audit objectives that apply to the relevant transaction classes and account balances for each of the financial report assertions explained in Chapter 5.
- Secondly, we will describe (1) the procedures involved in sales, cash receipts and sales adjustment transactions, and (2) the information system and control procedures commonly associated with these procedures that will be identified in the course of 'obtaining the understanding' required by AUS 402, Risk Assessments and Internal Controls (ISA 400, Risk Assessments and Internal Control).
- Thirdly, we will consider factors relevant to developing the audit plan, including determining the appropriate audit strategy (see Chapter 6) and, where appropriate, assessing inherent and control risk, including the use of tests of control (see Chapter 7).
- Fourthly, we will explain the design of substantive procedures, including analytical procedures and tests of details of transactions and balances using the methodology introduced in Chapter 9.

LEARNING OBJECTIVE 1

Identify the audit objectives applicable to sales and receivables.

AUDIT OBJECTIVES

The audit objectives for sales and receivables relate to obtaining sufficient appropriate evidence about each significant assertion for the applicable transactions and balances. The principal audit objectives for these transaction classes and account balances are shown in Table 10.1. These objectives are those that would apply to most merchandising entities selling on credit; they are not intended to apply to all entity situations.

To achieve each of these specific audit objectives, the auditor employs a combination of tests of control (as described in Chapter 7) and substantive procedures (as described in Chapter 9) as determined by the audit strategy adopted (as described in Chapter 6). Each audit objective is numbered (**EO1**, **EO2**, **C1**, **VM4** and so on) in Table 10.1. Using this numbering system, we will reference specific controls and audit procedures described in this chapter to the applicable audit objective.

TABLE 10.1

Selected specific audit objectives for sales and receivables

Assertion category	Transaction class audit objectives	Account balance audit objectives
Existence or occurrence	Recorded sales transactions represent goods shipped during the period (**EO1**). Recorded cash receipts transactions represent cash received during the period (**EO2**). Recorded sales adjustment transactions represent authorised discounts, returns and allowances, and bad debts applicable to the period (**EO3**).	Accounts receivable represent amounts owed by customers at the balance sheet date (**EO4**).

Assertion category	Transaction class audit objectives	Account balance audit objectives
Completeness	All sales (**C1**), cash receipts (**C2**) and sales adjustment (**C3**) transactions that occurred during the period have been recorded.	Accounts receivable include all claims on customers at the balance sheet date (**C4**).
Rights and obligations	The entity has rights to the accounts receivable (**RO1**) and cash (**RO2**) resulting from recorded sales transactions.	Accounts receivable at the balance sheet date represent legal claims of the entity on customers for payment (**RO3**).
Valuation or measurement	All sales (**VM1**), cash receipts (**VM2**) and sales adjustment (**VM3**) transactions are correctly journalised, summarised and posted.	Accounts receivable represent gross claims on customers at the balance sheet date and agree with the sum of the accounts receivable subsidiary ledger (**VM4**). The provision for bad debts represents a reasonable estimate of the difference between gross accounts receivable and their net realisable value (**VM5**).
Disclosure	The details of sales (**D1**), cash receipts (**D2**) and sales adjustment (**D3**) transactions support their presentation in the financial report, including their classification and related disclosures.	Accounts receivable are properly identified and classified in the balance sheet (**D4**). Appropriate disclosures have been made concerning accounts receivable that have been factored or otherwise assigned (**D5**).

2 LEARNING OBJECTIVE

Describe the functions and control procedures normally found in information systems for processing sales, cash receipts and sales adjustment transactions.

SALES, CASH RECEIPTS AND SALES ADJUSTMENT TRANSACTIONS

These transactions arise out of the processes of selling goods and services to customers and collecting the revenue in cash. The three principal functions are those of sales, cash receipts and sales adjustments, and their related information systems and control procedures are described in the following sections. Where sales are made on credit, the information system also needs to maintain records of accounts receivable. The use of an accounts receivable ledger will also be described as appropriate. Where applicable, control functions are keyed to the audit objectives identified in Table 10.1 using the bold symbols (such as **EO1**). The discussions and illustrations in this section are based on a company selling goods. However, much of the commentary can easily be adapted to other types of entity.

Credit sales transactions

Sales orders may be taken over the counter, via the telephone, by mail order, through sales representatives, by facsimile or by electronic data interchange. The goods may be picked up by the customer or shipped by the seller. The accounting for sales transactions may be done manually or with a computer — in real time or batch processing mode. We will begin by identifying the separate functions involved in making credit sales transactions; the documents and records that are used in processing the transactions; and the control procedures that are interwoven into each to reduce the risk of misstatements in the financial report. As we explained in Chapter 7, control procedures include information processing controls, physical controls, the segregation of duties and performance reviews. Information processing controls specific to credit sales transactions include, in addition to documents and records, proper authorisation and independent checks.

Functions

The processing of credit sales transactions involves a sequence of steps or credit sales functions as follows:

- accepting customer orders;
- approving credit;
- filling and dispatching sales orders;
- invoicing customers;
- recording the sales.

We will explain these functions and the applicable control procedures in the following sections.

Accepting customer orders

Sales orders need to be checked for their authenticity, the acceptability of terms and conditions, and the availability of inventory. Orders submitted in writing on a **customer order** provide ready evidence of authenticity. Telephone orders from businesses are sometimes authenticated by requiring an order number, even though no written order is submitted. Specification of an order number provides reasonable assurance that the order has been issued in accordance with the customer's purchasing procedures, as we will describe in Chapter 11. Terms and conditions relate to matters such as prices, delivery dates, modifications, etc. Sales clerks will accept only orders that meet the entity's normal terms. In some businesses, it is necessary to check the availability of the goods in inventory before accepting an order. Any orders not meeting the above checks need to be referred to a supervisor with the authority to accept orders that depart from normal entity policy.

Once accepted, the order is recorded on a multi-copy **sales order**, which is a form showing the description of the goods, the quantity ordered and other relevant data. It is signed by the clerk accepting the order and serves as the basis for internal processing of the customer order. Sales orders are commonly pre-numbered in case they are mislaid and thus business is lost. This represents the start of the transaction trail of documentary evidence and confirms the existence of a valid order. It thus relates to audit objectives **EO1** and **RO1** in Table 10.1. Information on open (unfilled) and filled sales orders is usually maintained in hard-copy files in the sales order department and/or in computer files.

The independent auditor has little interest in the acceptance of orders. Potential risks are the loss of business and the acceptance of unprofitable business, which are unlikely to lead to misstatements in recorded transactions.

Approving credit

Order acceptance is normally entrusted to the sales department. However, although the sales department is unlikely to accept unprofitable orders, because they will have an adverse effect on departmental performance, the department may accept orders from customers who are poor credit risks. Debt collection is normally an accounting function; bad debt losses are not recognised until months after the sale, and responsibility for the loss is rarely blamed on the sales department. For these reasons, credit approval is separated from sales order acceptance, and it is the responsibility of an independent credit department. This prevents sales personnel from subjecting the entity to undue credit risks to boost sales.

A credit check is made of any new customer, which may include obtaining a credit report from a rating agency such as Dun & Bradstreet (Australia). The credit supervisor would then determine an appropriate credit limit and record this on a newly created customer record. For existing customers, a credit department employee compares the amount of the order with the customer's authorised credit limit and the current balance owed by the customer. Credit approval would normally be refused if the order would take the balance over the customer's credit limit or if the account were overdue. To indicate approval (or non-approval) of credit, an authorised credit department employee signs or initials the sales order form and returns it to the sales order department.

For an auditor, controls over credit approval reduce the risk of a sales transaction being initially recorded in an amount in excess of the amount of cash expected to be realised, and thus contributes to audit objective **VM1**. The expectations of realisability for some of these amounts will change over time, resulting in the need for a provision for bad debts. Controls over credit approval enable management to make a more reliable estimate of the size of the provision needed (**VM5**).

Filling and dispatching sales orders

A copy of the approved sales order form is usually sent to the warehouse as authorisation to fill the order and release the goods to the shipping department (or dispatch area). Because the order form constitutes the source of credits to inventory records, the issue of goods by the storekeepers without such authorisation will result in an apparent inventory shortage for which they are held accountable. Segregation of the custody of inventory from the maintenance of inventory records and the physical check of verifying recorded accountability reduces the risk of inventory shortages caused by the unrecorded (and possibly unauthorised) release of inventory. We will describe control over inventory in Chapter 12.

Segregating responsibility for dispatch from responsibility for approving and filling orders prevents dispatch clerks from making unauthorised shipments (**EO1**). In addition, dispatch clerks are normally required to make independent checks to determine that goods received from the warehouse are accompanied by an approved sales order form.

The dispatch function involves preparing multi-copy **dispatch notes**. Dispatch notes can be prepared manually on pre-numbered forms or produced by the computer using order information already logged into the computer, with appropriate delivery data added (such as quantities shipped, carrier details, freight charges and so on). In a manual system, the multi-copy sales order documentation may include a copy to act as a dispatch note, thus retaining the same numerical control. In any event, the dispatch note must be pre-numbered. Subsequent checks of the numerical continuity of dispatch notes invoiced ensure completeness of recorded sales transactions (**C1**). Pre-numbering dispatch notes also helps in establishing cut-off at the year end. Gatekeepers are sometimes required to check that drivers of all vehicles leaving the premises possess dispatch notes for the goods in their vehicle, as a double-check against failure to record deliveries.

Dispatch notes provide evidence that goods were shipped and thus of the occurrence of the credit sale (**EO1**), giving rise to a claim against the customer within accounts receivable (**RO1**). Some entities obtain a copy of the dispatch note, signed by the customer on receipt of the goods, as evidence of the claim on the customer.

Invoicing customers

The invoicing function involves preparing and sending **sales invoices** to customers. Applicable control objectives for invoicing are that:

- all deliveries are invoiced to customers;
- only actual deliveries are invoiced (and there should be no duplicate invoices or fictitious transactions);
- deliveries are invoiced at authorised prices and the invoice amount is accurately calculated.

Control procedures designed to achieve these objectives are likely to include the following:

- segregating invoicing from the foregoing functions (**EO1**, **C1**);
- checking the existence of a dispatch note matching the approved sales order before each invoice is prepared (**EO1**);
- using an **authorised price list** in preparing the sales invoices (**VM1**);
- performing independent checks on the pricing and mathematical accuracy of sales invoices (**VM1**);
- comparing control totals for dispatch notes with corresponding totals for sales invoices (**EO1**, **C1**).

File copies of the sales invoices are usually maintained in the invoicing department.

Recording the sales

The primary control objective is to ensure that sales invoices are recorded accurately and in the proper period, which is usually when the goods are shipped.

In a manual system, the recording process involves entering sales invoices in a **sales journal**, posting the invoices to the **accounts receivable subsidiary ledger**, and posting the sales journal totals to the general ledger. It is common practice for invoices to be entered separately in the sales journal and the accounts receivable ledger. The accounts receivable ledger balance is periodically agreed with the general ledger control account (**VM4**). Failure of the balances on the accounts receivable ledger to agree in total with the control account in the general ledger indicates that an error has been made. A further control is the use of prelists, whereby the total of invoices entered in the sales journal is agreed with the total of sales invoices posted to the accounts receivable ledger (**VM1**). Sales invoices should also be entered in numerical sequence and a check should be made on missing numbers (**C1**). A **monthly customer statement** must be sent to each customer to provide the customer with an opportunity to alert a designated accounting supervisor, who is not otherwise involved in the execution or recording of sales transactions, if the balance does not agree with the customer's records (**EO1**, **RO1**).

As indicated above, balances on the accounts receivable ledger should be regularly and independently agreed to the balance on the control account in the general ledger. Periodic performance reviews by sales executives of sales analysed by product, division, salesperson or region, along with comparisons with budgets, contribute to controls over sales transactions.

Computer information systems

In on-line systems, once an order has been entered into the computer, the computer can be programmed to validate the customer credit, check inventory availability and issue the necessary instructions to the dispatch department. On delivery, the dispatch department can enter the necessary shipping details and the computer will automatically produce the invoice and update the **accounts receivable master file**, as well as the related inventory and general ledger files. Additionally, the computer information system will maintain a **sales transactions file** or equivalent data within a database system. AGS 1020, CIS Environments — On-Line Computer Systems (ISA 1002, EDP Environments — On-Line Computer Systems) provides further guidance on applicable control procedures.

Important controls in such a system include access controls, programmed application controls and controls over standing data files.

Access controls should permit read-only access to transaction and master files except for authorised individuals. Those with authority should have prescribed limits to that authority; for example, the credit controller may have the right to override rejections of orders when an order marginally breaches a customer's credit limit, and the sales manager may have the right to amend price or discount rates for individual customers or sales transactions.

Programmed application controls should include checks to ensure that:

- only orders from customers on the accounts receivable master file are accepted;
- only orders for goods in the entity's product range are accepted;
- the numerical continuity of documents is assured;
- transactions are chased at regular intervals;
- duplicate document numbers are rejected;
- unreasonable quantities, amounts and dates are queried.

The correctness of standing data is of particular significance in a computer information system. Standing data in a sales system include authorised customers, their credit limits and product sales prices. Access controls should ensure that only authorised officers can amend standing data: for example, only the credit controller can add new customers and vary the credit limits of existing customers, and only the sales director can amend selling prices. As an added precaution, standing data should be periodically printed out for approval.

Illustrative system for processing credit sales

There are many variations in the systems used to perform the functions involved in processing credit sales transactions. Figure 10.1 (page 376) shows a flow chart of an on-line/batch-entry processing system that incorporates most of the controls discussed in the preceding sections.

In the illustrated system, as orders are received, sales order clerks use on-line terminals and an order program to determine that the customer has been approved and that the order will not cause the customer's balance to exceed the customer's authorised credit limit. The program also checks the inventory master file to determine that goods are on hand to fill the order. If the order is accepted, the computer enters it into an open order file and produces a multi-copy sales order form on a printer in the sales order department. When an order is not accepted, a message is displayed on the terminal, indicating the reason for rejection.

Copies of the approved sales order are forwarded to the warehouse as authorisation to release goods to dispatch. In dispatch, personnel make an independent check on the agreement of the goods received with the accompanying sales order form. They then use their on-line terminals and a dispatch program to retrieve the corresponding sales order from the open order file and add appropriate dispatch data. Next, the computer transfers the transaction from the open order file to a dispatch file and produces a dispatch note on the printer in the dispatch department.

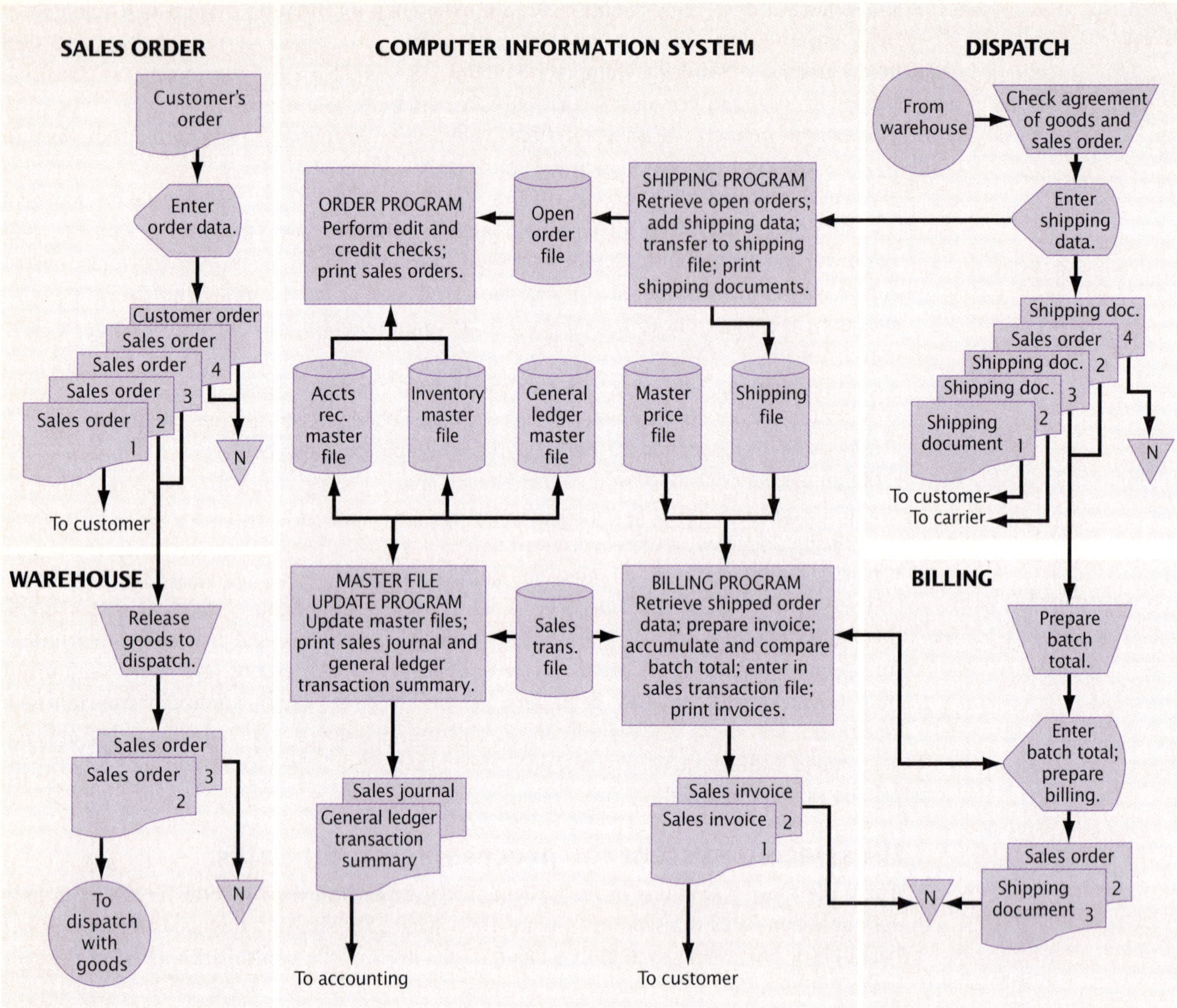

FIGURE 10.1

System flow chart — credit sales transactions

As matching dispatch notes and sales order forms are received in the invoicing department, they are batched and batch totals are manually prepared. Using their on-line terminals and an invoicing program, invoicing department personnel first enter the manually prepared batch totals. Next, they retrieve the previously entered order and dispatch data for each transaction from the dispatch file, and generate a sales invoice using prices from the master price file. As each invoice is completed, the computer enters it into a sales transactions file. After all the transactions in a batch have been processed in this manner, the invoicing program compares a computer-generated batch total with the manual batch total previously entered by the invoicing clerk. Discrepancies are displayed on the terminal and corrected by the invoicing clerks before processing continues. Finally, sales invoices for the batch are printed in the computer department and distributed as shown in the flow chart.

The recording of sales transactions is completed at the end of each day when the computer department runs the master file update program. As shown in Figure 10.1, this program updates three master files and produces a sales journal and a general ledger transaction summary, which are sent to accounting. The use of separate programs to produce monthly customer statements and periodic sales analyses for use in performance reviews is not shown in the flow chart.

Cash receipts transactions

Cash receipts result from a variety of activities. The scope of this section is limited to the information systems for processing and recording cash receipts from cash sales and collections from customers on credit sales.

Functions

The processing of receipts from cash and credit sales involves the following cash receipts functions:

- receiving cash;
- depositing cash in bank;
- recording the receipts.

Receiving cash

A major risk is that cash being paid by customers is stolen before it is recorded. For control purposes, accountability measures must be in place from the moment cash is received, and the cash must be subsequently safeguarded. A second risk is the possibility of errors occurring in the subsequent processing of the receipts.

Over-the-counter receipts

For over-the-counter receipts, the use of a cash register or point-of-sale terminal is indispensable. These devices provide:

- immediate visual display, for the customer, of the amount of the cash sale and the cash tendered;
- a printed receipt for the customer and an internal record of the transaction on a computer file or a tape locked inside the register;
- printed control totals of the day's receipts.

The customer's expectation of a printed receipt and supervisory surveillance of over-the-counter sales transactions helps to ensure that all cash sales are processed through the cash registers or terminals (**C2**). In addition, there should be an independent check of the agreement of cash on hand with the totals printed by the register or terminal (**EO2**, **C2**, **VM2**). The cash is then forwarded to the cashier's department for deposit in the bank, together with the register or terminal-printed totals.

Increasingly, customers pay by use of credit or debit cards. These payments are processed via on-line terminals linked to the bank or other card issuer, which validates the transaction. Staff need to be properly trained in the use of such terminals and in procedures to be followed where the transaction is refused. Procedures must be in place for reconciling card sales with cash register totals as part of the daily agreement of cash on hand. Amounts due from card issuers also need to be recorded and agreed with subsequent payments. The use of credit and debit cards also facilitates the acceptance of mail or telephone orders from customers without the need for creditworthiness checks once the card transaction has been validated. Because no cash handling is involved, such transactions reduce the costs of banking and the risks of misappropriations, and are often preferred despite the commission payable to the card issuer.

Mail receipts

There should always be at least two clerks responsible for mail opening so they would need to be in collusion if they were to misappropriate any cash receipts in the mail. They should immediately restrictively endorse cheques *for deposit only*, which is done by impressing a rubber stamp imprinted with the words 'for deposit to the account of . . .' on the face of the cheques. If it falls into the wrong hands, such a cheque cannot subsequently be endorsed for payment to the person acting fraudulently. All cash received through the mail should be listed, such as in a **rough cash book**. This record then serves for use in independent checks on the completeness and accuracy of processing. All of these procedures ensure that mail receipts are not misappropriated (**C2**).

Most cash receipts will be attached to or accompanied by a **remittance advice** indicating the payee and the particulars of the payment being made. The cheques will be forwarded to the cashier's department for banking, with a copy of the listing made referred to as a prelist. Remittance advices (or other details of the payment enclosed with the cash receipt) are forwarded to accounts receivable for posting to the accounts receivable ledger.

Major suppliers also pay by credit transfer. Such payments may be identified as part of the bank reconciliation process (see Chapter 13). Because this can lead to delays in recording receipts, entities receiving payments this way usually have on-line access to their bank account, linked to the accounts receivable master file which automatically detects credit transfers and updates the accounts receivable records.

Depositing cash in bank

All cash receipts must be deposited intact daily. Intact means *all* receipts should be deposited, not used to make payments. This reduces the risk that cash receipts will not be recorded (**C2**) and the resulting bank deposit record establishes the occurrence of the transactions (**EO2**).

When the cashier receives over-the-counter and mail receipts, he or she should check that the cash agrees with both the accompanying register total and the prelist (**EO2**, **C2**, **VM2**). Details of cash receipts are then entered on a daily cash summary and the bank **deposit slip** is prepared in duplicate. The cash is deposited in the bank and the copy of the deposit slip is receipted by the bank and retained by the cashier. The daily cash summary is forwarded to the general accounting department.

Recording the receipts

To ensure that only valid transactions are entered, access to the accounting records or computer program should be restricted to authorised personnel (**EO2**). In manual systems, the duties of journalising the cash receipt and of posting the receipt to customer accounts are segregated. The daily cash summary is used to enter the **cash receipts journal**, distinguishing between receipts from cash sales and from credit sale customers. Posting the receipts to the accounts receivable ledger may be done in accounts receivable ledger accounting, based on the remittance advices received from the mail room (**VM2**). In computerised processing, it is common for accounts receivable ledger clerks to use a terminal to enter mail receipts into a cash receipts transactions file, which is subsequently used in updating both the accounts receivable and general ledger master files.

To ensure the completeness and accuracy of recording mail receipts, independent checks are made of:

- the agreement of the amounts journalised and posted with the amounts shown in the rough cash book kept by the mail room;
- the agreement of total amounts journalised and posted for over-the-counter and mail receipts with the daily cash summary and receipted deposit slips retained by the cashier (**C2**, **VM2**).

In addition, an employee not otherwise involved in executing or recording cash transactions should perform periodic bank reconciliations.

Computer information systems

Opportunities for automating accounting for cash receipts involving currency and cheques are limited, which is why many companies are moving to on-line banking and direct debit and credit transfer systems. However, the use of point-of-sale cash register terminals provides controls over the pricing of goods sold and over inventory management. The 'Professional environment' below discusses developments in this area.

PROFESSIONAL ENVIRONMENT Automating bill paying

On-line bill payment has become the latest e-business hot spot as companies seek to profit from making a chore a little easier for time-poor households and businesses. Three companies have launched services in the past few months and five more are likely to appear before the end of the year. All agree that the market has potential but are pursuing market share in very different ways.

A recent survey by the Internet research company www.consult shows that bill payment is the single most desired feature of on-line banking. Ramin Marzbani, principal of www.consult, describes it as a breakthrough and says its popularity will continue to grow significantly.

His comments are supported by figures from the on-line bill payment service e-BILL, which estimates that 9 per cent of residential and 42 per cent of business customers who receive bills by post will adopt electronic billing within two years.

Most services allow customers to view and pay bills on-line. Users can elect to pay by credit card or direct debit from a linked bank account. They can pay a bill immediately, on the due date or at a specified time. Some services also offer automatic payment of selected bills.

One of the newest entrants in the market is the consolidation site allmybills.com.au. Launched in April, it manages payment for every bill a customer receives — from telephone bills to rent or even lawn mowing. Chief executive Jason Twydale describes the service as 'total bill management' and says no other company offers an unrestricted service such as this.

Allmybills.com.au is aimed at small businesses and individuals with little spare time. Users redirect their bills to the company's GPO box and the bills are scanned and placed on the Web as a document file. Customers are alerted by e-mail when a new bill arrives, and the biller, amount and the due date are shown. One payment option allows bills up to a certain amount to be paid automatically. Bills are archived for five years.

Allmybills.com.au recently announced a partnership with the application hosting service Peakhour, under which it will provide bill management for Peakhour's accounting and business software. Allmybills.com.au is funded by subscription. Individuals are charged $7.95 a month and small businesses from $19.95 a month. The company hopes to attract 50 000 subscribers in the first year and to be profitable after reaching 65 000 users in the second year.

Two of Australia's largest bill payment services, BPAY and Australia Post, are also planning to introduce on-line bill payment by the end of the year. Australia Post began trials with several billers in April. Neither company is concerned by late entry to the market.

BPAY's national manager, Linda Helmstrom, says on-line bill payment will not reach its market potential for three to five years. 'It definitely has a future, but realistically it will take time for people to learn about it, feel comfortable with it,' she says.

Australia Post is also content to wait. External communications manager Stephen Waters says: 'We want to wait for the best product. We want to offer a full suite of services and we want the most robust system in place.'

(Source: Extracted from Patrice Gibbons, 'Online: Bills, Bills, Bills! Sites Line up to Pay Them', *Business Review Weekly* (2 June 2000))

Illustrative system for processing cash receipts

There are many variations in systems for processing cash receipts. A flow chart for an illustrative system of processing mail receipts is presented in Figure 7.10 on page 283. We suggest that you review this flow chart and the accompanying narrative (pages 283–4) before proceeding further.

Sales adjustment transactions

Sales adjustment transactions involve the following functions:

- granting cash discounts;
- allowing sales returns and allowances;
- determining bad debts.

The number and dollar value of these transactions vary significantly among entities. However, where material, the potential for misstatements resulting from errors and irregularities in the processing of these transactions is considerable. Of primary concern is the possibility of fictitious sales adjustment transactions being recorded to conceal misappropriations of cash receipts. An employee may, for example, conceal misappropriation of cash received from a customer by writing the customer's account off against the provision for bad debts, or by overstating cash discounts or sales returns and allowances. Controls useful in reducing the risk of such frauds focus on establishing the validity of such transactions (**EO3**). They include:

- the proper authorisation of all sales adjustment transactions, such as requiring treasurer's office authority for the write-off of bad debts (**EO3**);
- the use of appropriate documents and records — in particular, an approved **credit memo** for granting credit for returned or damaged goods, and an approved **write-off authorisation memo** for writing off bad debts;
- the segregation of the duties of authorising sales adjustment transactions and of handling and recording cash receipts.

DEVELOPING THE AUDIT PLAN

In this section we will explain how the auditor develops the audit plan for sales and receivables. This requires an assessment of inherent and control risks. Firstly, we will illustrate how the auditor uses the concepts of rationality and inherent risk. Secondly, we will describe factors to be considered by the auditor, in assessing the control environment within which the information system and control procedures operate. Thirdly, we will illustrate the inherent and control risks using tests of design effectiveness and tests of operating effectiveness. Finally, we will explain how the procedures result in the development of the detailed audit program (described in Chapter 6) used in directing audit staff and controlling their work.

3
LEARNING OBJECTIVE
Apply the concepts of materiality and inherent risk to the audit of sales and receivables.

Audit strategy considerations

Audit strategy refers to the mix of tests of control and substantive procedures to be applied in the audit. The main determinants of the mix are the assessed levels of inherent and control risks. Materiality considerations also influence the level of substantive procedures. In this section we will begin by considering the materiality of the relevant transactions and balances. We will then consider factors related to inherent and control risks, and the implications of both materiality and inherent and control risks in determining the audit strategy.

Materiality

Sales transactions are the principal source of operating revenue for most business enterprises. The accounts receivable produced by credit sales transactions are material to the balance sheet for all businesses except those transacting most of their sales for cash. Cash balances at a particular balance sheet date may not be material, but the flow of cash associated with sales transactions is nearly always material. The significance of sales adjustment transactions varies considerably from one entity to another. However, the bad debts expense is often material to the profit and loss of entities that sell to customers on credit. Most of the audit objectives for sales and receivables that are depicted in Table 10.1 (pages 370–1) are important in arriving at an opinion on the financial report as a whole.

Inherent and control risks

In assessing inherent risk for financial report assertions, the auditor should consider pervasive factors that may affect assertions in many transaction classes and account balances, as well as factors that may only pertain to specific assertions affecting sales and receivables. These factors include:

- pressure to overstate sales, so as to report that announced sales or profitability targets were achieved when they were not. Such reporting includes:
  - — recording fictitious sales;
  - — holding the books open to record subsequent period sales in the current year (improper cut-off);
  - — shipping unordered goods to customers near the year end and recording them as sales in the current period only to have them returned in the subsequent period;
- pressure to overstate cash and accounts receivable or understate the provision for bad debts, in order to report a higher level of working capital in the face of liquidity problems or going-concern doubts.

Other factors that could contribute to the possibility of misstatements in sales and receivables assertions include:

- the volume of sales, cash receipts and sales adjustment transactions, resulting in numerous opportunities for errors to occur;
- contentious issues relating to the timing of revenue recognition, such as the effect of purchasers' rights of return;
- susceptibility to misappropriation of liquid assets generated by cash receipts;
- the use of sales adjustment transactions to conceal thefts of cash received from customers by overstating discounts, recording fictitious sales returns or writing off customers' balances as uncollectable.

Recognising these risks, management usually adopts extensive internal controls to address them. Thus, the auditor needs also to consider the extent to which inherent risks are properly addressed by the internal control structure in deciding on the appropriate audit strategy for sales and receivables assertions.

4 LEARNING OBJECTIVE

Discuss considerations relevant to determining the audit strategy for sales and receivables.

Audit strategy

Given the materiality of sales and receivables, the auditor must take care in assessing inherent and control risks, and in determining the audit strategy. The principal inherent risk is that of overstatement of sales revenue and accounts receivable balances. In the audit of transaction classes, this relates to the occurrence and measurement assertions for sales transactions, and to the completeness assertion for cash receipts and sales adjustments. In most entities, controls relative to these assertions for sales and cash receipts are effective and the auditor is able to adopt a lower assessed level of control risk strategy for these transaction classes. Given the variety of sales adjustment transactions in some entities (and their infrequency in others), control risk may be higher for all assertions applicable to such transactions, requiring a predominantly substantive audit strategy.

Although controls over occurrence and completeness assertions of sales transactions are normally effective, this may not extend to the special case of balance sheet date cut-off because this is only of significance at that particular date. A predominantly substantive approach is, therefore, commonly adopted in verifying cut-off. In the design of substantive audit procedures, the large volume of sales and cash receipt transactions means that it is normally cost-effective to obtain most of the evidence from the application of substantive procedures to the accounts receivable balance.

The control environment

The control environment may contain several factors that may mitigate several of the inherent risks discussed earlier in this chapter. In addition, the control environment may enhance or negate the effectiveness of other internal control structure elements in controlling the risk of misstatements in sales and receivables assertions. Management's adoption of and adherence to high standards of *integrity* and *ethical values* is a key control environment factor in reducing the risk of fraudulent financial reporting through the overstatement of sales and accounts receivable. Related aspects include the elimination of incentives for dishonest reporting — such as undue emphasis on meeting sales or profit targets — and of temptations — such as an indifferent or ineffective board of directors and audit committee.

Inherent risks related to contentious accounting issues may be controlled if management has made the appropriate *commitment to competence* on the part of chief financial officers and accounting personnel. In obtaining an understanding of this factor, the auditor will make inquiries of personnel, review personnel files and consider prior experience with the entity.

Management's philosophy and operating style are defined by a number of factors. These include its propensity for either conservative or aggressive selection from alternative accounting policies, and its conscientiousness and conservatism in developing accounting estimates, such as the provisions for bad debts and sales returns.

The control environment is enhanced when the *assignment of authority and responsibility* for all activities in the revenue cycle is clearly communicated through written job descriptions, among other means.

A number of special *personnel policies and practices* are often adopted for employees who handle cash receipts. These include having such employees take mandatory vacations and periodically rotating their duties. The thrust of these controls is to deter dishonesty by making employees aware that they may not be able to conceal their misdeeds permanently. Some embezzlements from banks and other entities, for example, have been traced to the seemingly dedicated employee who held the same job without taking a vacation for ten, twenty or more years so as not to disrupt his or her routine of concealment.

LEARNING OBJECTIVE 5

Design and execute tests of control over sales, cash receipts and sales adjustment transactions to assess control risk.

Assessment of control risk

The procedures described in this section are followed only where the process of obtaining the understanding of the internal control structure leads the auditor to believe that it is both possible and cost-effective to assess control risk as being less than high. Where this is not the case, the auditor notes this conclusion in the working papers and proceeds to obtain the required audit evidence through the performance of a higher level of substantive procedures. This decision is made separately for each financial report assertion, although the same conclusion tends to apply to most, if not all, assertions.

Sales

This section is concerned with credit sales. We will consider the assessment of control risk for cash sales in the next section on cash receipts.

Tests of design effectiveness

Table 10.2 (page 384) contains a partial listing of possible misstatements, necessary controls, potential tests of the operating effectiveness of controls, and the specific transaction class audit objectives for credit sales to which each relates. Using the understanding of the information system the auditor will identify the presence of necessary controls and make a preliminary assessment of control risk.

Where transactions are processed by a computer information system, the auditor will also need to consider the effectiveness of general controls over computer operations. Refer to Figure 7.3, which describes control risk assessment considerations for general controls over computer information systems.

Tests of operating effectiveness

Tests of control designed to provide evidence of operating effectiveness involve a variety of audit procedures, including reperformance of certain control procedures by the auditor. Statistical or non-statistical sampling procedures (see Chapter 8) may be applied in the performance of some tests. In designing tests, the auditor needs to remember that the direction of testing should be *backward* along the audit trail when the objective is to test controls over the occurrence assertion, and *forward* along the audit trail when the objective is to test controls over the completeness assertion. As an example, a sample of invoices from the sales journal would be vouched back to sales orders or shipping documents to test occurrence; to test completeness, a sample of sales orders or shipping documents would be traced to the sales journal to determine that all the transactions were recorded. The auditor must document the tests of controls performed, the evidence obtained and the conclusions reached. A formal audit program that incorporates several of the tests from Table 10.2 is presented in Figure 10.2 (page 386).

As explained in Chapter 7, certain tests of operating effectiveness simultaneously provide substantive evidence as to the correctness of recorded amounts, and these are known as dual-purpose tests. The auditor must be particularly careful in drawing conclusions from such tests. As substantive tests, it may be concluded that misstatements are only significant if material. However, all misstatements suggest that control procedures have not been properly performed. These deviations from prescribed procedures could have caused misstatements in transactions of any size. Therefore, as a test of control, it is the number of misstatements that is important, not their size. Detections of misstatements of any size, therefore, may require the assessment of control risk to be revised.

TABLE 10.2 *Control risk assessment procedures — credit sales transactions*

Function	Potential misstatement	Necessary control	Possible test of operating effectiveness	Relevant transaction class audit objective (from Table 10.1)				
				EO1	C1	RO1	VM1	D1
Accepting customer orders	Sales may be made to unauthorised customers.	Determination that customer is on approved customer list	Observe procedure; reperform.	✓				
		Approved sales order form for each sale	Examine approved sales order forms.	✓				
Approving credit	Sales may be made without credit approval.	Credit department credit check on all new customers	Inquire about procedures for checking credit on new customers.				✓	
		Check on customer's credit limit prior to each sale	Examine evidence of credit limit check prior to each sale.				✓	
Filling sales orders	Goods may be released from warehouse for unauthorised orders.	Approved sales order for all goods released to dispatch	Observe warehouse personnel filling orders.	✓				
Shipping	Goods dispatched may not agree with goods ordered.	Independent check by dispatch clerks of agreement of goods received from warehouse with approved sales order	Examine evidence of performance of independent check.	✓	✓			
	Unauthorised shipments may be made.	Segregation of duties for filling and dispatching orders	Observe the segregation of duties.	✓				
		Preparation of dispatch note for each shipment	Inspect dispatch notes.	✓				
Invoicing customers	Invoices may be made for fictitious transactions, or duplicate invoices may be made.	Matching of dispatch note and approved sales order for each invoice	Vouch invoices to dispatch notes and approved sales orders.*	✓				
	Some shipments may not be invoiced.	Matching of sales invoice with each dispatch note	Trace dispatch notes to sales invoices.*		✓			
		Periodic accounting for all dispatch notes	Observe procedure; reperform.		✓			

Function	Potential misstatement	Necessary control	Possible test of operating effectiveness	Relevant transaction class audit objective (from Table 10.1)				
				EO1	C1	RO1	VM1	D1
Invoicing customers (*continued*)	Sales invoices may have incorrect prices.	Independent check on pricing of invoices	Inspect copy of invoice for evidence of performance.				✓	
			Reperform the check on the accuracy of pricing*.				✓	
Recording the sales	Fictitious sales transactions may be recorded.	Requirement of sales invoice and matching documents for all entries	Vouch recorded sales to supporting documents.*	✓		✓	✓	
	Invoices may not be journalised or posted to customer accounts.	Independent check of agreement of sales journal entries and amounts posted to customer accounts with control totals of invoices	Review evidence of independent check; reperform check; trace sales invoices to sales journal and customer accounts.*		✓		✓	
		Periodic accounting for all sales invoices	Observe procedure; reperform.*		✓			
	Invoices may be posted to the wrong customer account.	Chart of accounts and supervisory review	Observe procedures; reperform.*					✓
		Mailing of monthly statements to customers, with independent follow-up of customer complaints	Observe mailing and follow-up procedures.*	✓	✓	✓	✓	✓

* Sometimes performed as part of dual-purpose tests.

FIGURE 10.2

Partial audit program for tests of control — credit sales

Prepared by: ________ Date: ________

Reviewed by: ________ Date: ________

Amalgamated Products Limited
Planned tests of control — Credit sales transactions
Year ending 31 December 20X2

Assertion/test of control	W/P ref.	Auditor	Date
Occurrence			
1. Observe procedures, including segregation of duties, for: • approving sales orders; • filling sales orders; • dispatching sales orders; • invoicing customers; • mailing monthly statements to customers and following up on customer complaints.			
2. Select a sample of sales transactions from the sales journal and verify transaction dates, customer names and amounts by vouching entries to the following matching supporting documents: • sales invoices; • dispatch notes; • approved sales orders.			
Completeness			
3. Examine evidence of the use of and accounting for pre-numbered sales orders, dispatch notes and sales invoices. Scan the sequence of sales invoice numbers in the sales journal.			
4. Select a sample of approved sales orders and trace to matching: • dispatch notes; • sales invoices; • entries in the sales journal.			
Measurement			
5. For the sample in Step 2 above, examine evidence of: • proper credit approval for each transaction; • an independent check on proper pricing of invoices; • an independent check on the mathematical accuracy of invoices.			
6. For sales invoices processed in batches, examine evidence of an independent check on the agreement of totals for sales journal entries and amounts posted to customer accounts with batch totals.			

Computer information systems

Tests of the operating effectiveness of controls over a computer information system are usually undertaken by **computer-assisted audit techniques** (CAATs). The two main categories of CAAT are:

1. those that test the operation of programs and related programmed application controls directly;
2. those that test data held on computer files.

In the first category, the most common techniques used for testing controls over the processing of sales transactions are the **test data approach** and the use of embedded audit facilities. Test data are composed of simulated transactions. One batch of data will consist of transactions replicating the normal types of transaction processed by the system. A second batch will consist of transactions that should activate those programmed application controls of significance to the audit, such as orders exceeding credit limits. Both batches are processed against a copy of the program, and the results are compared with expected results determined manually. Test data are best suited to batch processing systems where the relevant program can be isolated and a copy can be taken for audit purposes. With real-time processing it is less satisfactory and most such systems incorporate embedded audit facilities. One kind of **embedded audit facility** is the **integrated test facility** (ITF) based on dummy accounts to which test data can be processed on a real-time basis. Another embedded audit facility is a **systems control and audit file** (SCARF). This facility enables auditors to specify parameters of interest, such as orders where credit limits are overridden by the credit controller. The facility will then log all such transactions and record them on a special audit file for subsequent review by the auditors.

For tests applied to sales transactions held on computer files, the auditor can use **generalised audit software** (CCAS) for large computer systems and proprietary database packages for smaller, PC-based systems. Both techniques can be used to access data on computer files according to criteria specified by the auditor and to perform a wide range of mathematical functions on that data. For tests involving the inspection of documents, the software can be programmed to select a sample of documents. If statistical sampling techniques are being used, as described in Chapter 8, the software can be programmed with the sampling parameters, such as the preliminary assessment of inherent and control risk and the tolerable deviation rate. The software will select a suitably random sample and, after testing by the auditor, will calculate the achieved deviation rate. For reperformance, the software can be programmed to perform the entire test. In reperforming invoice pricing, for example, the auditor can program the software to select a sample of invoices and compare unit sales prices on those invoices with sales prices held on the price file, and to report differences.

Cash receipts

Table 10.3 illustrates a partial listing of potential misstatements, necessary controls, possible tests of the operating effectiveness of controls, and related transaction class audit objectives for cash receipt transactions. The particulars of the items listed in this table would vary among entities, based on such factors as the method of data processing used. As we explained for credit sales, the potential misstatements and necessary controls would be the basis of a check list used to assess design effectiveness. Similarly, an audit program for tests of the operating effectiveness of controls for cash receipts transactions can be prepared based on the potential tests of control shown in Table 10.3.

TABLE 10.3 *Control risk assessment considerations — cash receipts*

Function	Potential misstatement	Necessary control	Possible test of operating effectiveness	Relevant transaction class audit objective (from Table 10.1)				
				EO2	C2	RO2	VM2	D2
Receiving cash receipts	Cash sales may not be registered.	Use of cash registers or point-of-sale devices	Observe cash sales procedures.		✓			
		Periodic surveillance of cash sales procedures	Inquire of supervisors about the results of surveillance.		✓			
	Mail receipts may be lost or misappropriated after receipt.	Restrictive endorsement of cheques immediately on receipt	Observe mail opening, including the endorsement of cheques.		✓			
		Immediate preparation of rough cash book or prelist of mail receipts	Observe the preparation of records.	✓	✓		✓	
Depositing cash in the bank	Cash and cheques received for deposit may not agree with the cash count list and prelist.	Independent check of agreement of cash and cheques with register totals and prelist	Examine evidence of independent check.*	✓	✓		✓	
	Cash may not be deposited intact daily.	Independent check of agreement of validated deposit slip with daily cash summary	Reperform independent check.*	✓	✓			
Recording the receipts	Some receipts may not be recorded.	Independent check of agreement of amounts journalised and posted with daily cash summary	Reperform independent check.*		✓			
	Errors may be made in journalising receipts.	Preparation of periodic independent bank reconciliations	Examine bank reconciliations.*	✓	✓	✓	✓	
	Receipts may be posted to the wrong customer account.	Mailing of monthly statements to customers	Observe mailing of monthly statements.	✓	✓		✓	✓

* Sometimes performed as part of dual-purpose tests.

Sales adjustments

Sales adjustment information systems are more diverse than sales and cash receipt systems, so it is not practicable to illustrate typical potential misstatements and necessary controls.

However, tests of control that are likely to be appropriate include:

- recalculating cash discounts and determining that the payments were received within the discount period;
- inspecting credit memoranda for sales returns for indication of proper approval and accompanying receiving reports for evidence of the actual return of goods;
- inspecting written authorisations and supporting documentation (such as correspondence with the customer or collection agencies) for the write-off of bad debts.

Final assessment

Based on the evidence obtained from the procedures to obtain an understanding of the internal control structure and related tests of control, the auditor makes a final assessment of inherent and control risks. For each significant audit objective where assessment of control risk as being less than high is the basis for adopting a lower assessed level of control risk audit strategy, reasons for this assessment must be documented. Figure 7.8 (page 279) illustrates such documentation in the form of a memorandum.

This assessment enables the auditor to plan the level of substantive procedures to be performed. Because many tests of control are dual-purpose tests, providing evidence of errors in amounts as well as deviations from controls, the auditor usually draws up the detailed audit program based on the preliminary assessment of control risk. This improves audit efficiency in that tests of the operating effectiveness of controls that use sources of evidence on which the substantive tests of details are also based are performed simultaneously with those substantive procedures. The auditor must ensure that control deviations are properly identified and that their implications for the assessment of control risk are properly considered in terms of whether further substantive procedures need to be performed.

LEARNING CHECK

10.1 In determining the correct balance for accounts receivable, procedures for recording sales, cash receipts and sales adjustment transactions should ensure that:
- goods are only delivered in respect of approved orders;
- all goods delivered are invoiced;
- all cash received from customers is recorded;
- only genuine sales adjustments are recorded.

10.2 The reconciliation of accounts receivable ledger balances with the general ledger control account, the sending of monthly statements to customers and the comparison of sales with budgets are all important independent checks in ensuring the accuracy of the recording of the related transactions and balances.

10.3 Controls over the completeness of recorded cash receipts are of great importance. For over-the-counter sales, this is achieved by using cash registers; for postal receipts, it is achieved by segregating the mail opening from the recording of cash receipts and posting to the accounts receivable ledger.

10.4 In developing the audit plan, the auditor needs to have (1) obtained the understanding of the information system, control procedures and control environment, (2) assessed inherent risk both for the entity and for the specific transactions and balances, and (3) assessed control risk based on the results of tests of control.

10.5 The greatest inherent risks are the overstatement of sales transactions and the accounts receivable balance and the understatement of cash receipts and the provision for bad debts. The volume of transactions means that most entities ensure that their internal control structure relating to such matters is effective.

(continued)

10.6 The testing of the design effectiveness of controls is achieved by an evaluation of the system with the aid of a list of potential misstatements and suggested control procedures. The testing of the operating effectiveness of controls is achieved by examining evidence of the performance of control procedures.

SUBSTANTIVE PROCEDURES

Our primary consideration here is the gross amount due from customers on credit sales and the related provision for bad debts. To design substantive procedures for these accounts, the auditor must first determine the acceptable level of detection risk for each significant related assertion. Given that the verification of accounts receivable requires consideration of sales, sales adjustment and cash receipts transactions, the procedures also contribute to the profit and loss account balance of sales, and to the balance of cash on hand and at bank in the balance sheet.

6 LEARNING OBJECTIVE

Indicate the factors relevant to determining an acceptable level of detection risk for the audit of sales and receivables.

Determining detection risk

As we explained in Chapter 5, for a specified level of audit risk, detection risk is inversely related to the assessed levels of inherent risk and control risk. Thus, the auditor must consider these assessments when determining the acceptable level of detection risk for each accounts receivable assertion. Several pervasive inherent risk and control environment factors that affect sales and receivables transactions and balances were discussed earlier. The combined effects of these factors, especially those contributing to the risk of credit sales being overstated, may result in assessments of inherent risk as being high for:

- the existence and valuation assertions for accounts receivable;
- the valuation assertion for the related provision account.

Assessments of inherent risk as being lower may be appropriate for the other assertions.

Control risk assessments for accounts receivable assertions depend on the related control risk assessments for the transaction classes (credit sales, cash receipts and sales adjustments) that affect the accounts receivable balance. As we explained in Chapter 9, the assessments for transaction class assertions affect the same account balance assertions for accounts affected by the transactions, with the following exception: control risk assessments for the occurrence and completeness assertions for a transaction class that decreases an account balance affect the assessments for the opposite account balance assertions. Thus, because both cash receipts and sales adjustment transactions decrease the accounts receivable balance, the assessment for the occurrence assertion for these transaction classes affects the assessment for the completeness assertion for the accounts receivable balance. Similarly, the assessment for the completeness assertion for these transaction classes affects the assessment for the existence assertion for the accounts receivable balance.

The audit program will be based on the preliminary assessment of control risk. If tests of control subsequently lead to a revised assessment of control risk, then the design of substantive procedures in terms of their nature, timing or extent will need to be revised. Some auditors use a matrix similar to the one illustrated in Table 10.4 to document and correlate the various risk components that must be considered in the design of substantive procedures for each account balance assertion. The risk levels specified in this matrix are illustrative only and would vary based on the entity's circumstances. Alternatively, when the risk components are quantified, the audit risk model can be solved mathematically for the acceptable levels of detection risk.

TABLE 10.4 *Correlation of risk components — accounts receivable*

Risk component	Existence or occurrence	Completeness	Rights and obligations	Valuation or measurement	Disclosure
Audit risk	Low	Low	Low	Low	Low
Inherent risk	High	Moderate	Low	High	Moderate
Control risk — sales transactions	Low	Low	Moderate	Moderate	Moderate
	↙ ↘ (crossed)		↓	↓	↓
Control risk — cash receipts	Low	Low	Low	Low	Low
Control risk — sales adjustments	Moderate	Low	Moderate	High	Moderate
	↙ ↘ (crossed)		↓	↓	↓
Combined control risk[1]	Low	Moderate	Moderate	High	Moderate
Acceptable detection risk[2]	Moderate	Moderate	High	Low	Moderate

1. This is the most conservative (highest) of transaction class control risk assessments used as the combined risk assessment, as per the method that we discussed in Chapter 9 (page 337).
2. Determined from the risk components matrix shown in Figure 5.2 (page 177), based on the levels of audit risk, inherent risk and combined control risk indicated above for each assertion category.

7 LEARNING OBJECTIVE

Design a substantive audit program for sales and receivables.

Designing substantive procedures

The next step is to finalise the audit program to achieve the specific audit objectives for each account balance assertion. The specific audit objectives addressed here are the ones listed in the 'Account balance audit objectives' column of Table 10.1 (pages 370–1). In Chapter 9 we introduced a general framework for developing audit programs for substantive procedures. Of the steps listed under the heading 'Complete preliminary planning' in Figure 9.5, the application of items 1–4 to accounts receivable has already been considered in this chapter. In this section, we will consider the options for designing the substantive procedures for accounts receivable, following the sequence suggested in the lower portion of Figure 9.5.

Table 10.5 (pages 392–3) lists possible substantive procedures to be included in an audit program developed on this basis. This table does not represent a formal audit program because: it is not tailored to any specific information system; there is no working paper heading; and there are no columns for supporting working paper references, initials and dates.

Instead, for instructional purposes, there are columns to indicate the categories of substantive procedure (referred to in Figure 9.5) and the specific account balance audit objectives from Table 10.1 to which each procedure applies. Several of the procedures apply to more than one audit objective, and each objective is addressed by multiple possible procedures. We will explain each of the procedures in the sections that follow, including comments on how some procedures can be tailored, based on the planned level of detection risk to be achieved.

TABLE 10.5 *Possible substantive procedures for accounts receivable assertions*

Category	Substantive procedure	EO4	C4	RO3	VM#	D#
		Account balance audit objective (from Table 10.1)				
Initial procedures	1. Perform initial procedures on accounts receivable balances and records that will be subjected to further testing. (a) Trace the opening balances for accounts receivable and related provision to the prior year's working papers. (b) Review activity in general ledger accounts for accounts receivable and related provision, and investigate entries that appear unusual in amount or source. (c) Obtain the accounts receivable trial balance and determine that it accurately represents the underlying accounting records by: • adding the trial balance and determining agreement with the total of the subsidiary ledger or accounts receivable master file and the general ledger balance; • testing the agreement of customers and balances listed on the trial balance with those included on the subsidiary ledger or master file.				✓4, 5	
Analytical procedures	2. Perform analytical procedures. (a) Determine expectations. (b) Compare current and prior year balances. (c) Compute significant ratios such as: • gross profit; • days sales in accounts receivable. (d) Obtain explanations for unexpected changes. (e) Corroborate explanations.	✓	✓		✓4, 5	
Tests of details of transactions	3. Vouch a sample of recorded accounts receivable transactions to supporting documentation (see also Step 6(c)). (a) Vouch debits to supporting sales invoices, dispatch notes and sales orders. (b) Vouch credits to remittance advices or sales adjustment authorisation for sales returns and allowances or bad debt write-offs.	✓	✓	✓	✓4	
	4. Perform cut-off tests for sales and sales returns. (a) Select a sample of recorded sales transactions from several days before and the after year end, and examine supporting sales invoices and dispatch notes to determine that sales were recorded in the proper period. (b) Select a sample of credit memos issued after the year end, examine supporting documentation such as dated goods inward notes, and determine that the returns were recorded in the proper period. Also, consider whether the volume of sales returns after the year end suggests the possibility of unauthorised shipments before the year end.	✓	✓			

Category	Substantive procedure	Account balance audit objective (from Table 10.1)				
		EO4	C4	RO3	VM#	D#
	5. Perform cash receipts cut-off test. (a) Observe that all cash received before the close of business on the last day of the financial year is included in cash on hand or deposits in transit, and that no receipts of the subsequent period are included; or (b) Review documentation such as daily cash summaries, duplicate deposit slips and bank statements covering several days before and after the year end date to determine the proper cut-off.	✓	✓			
Tests of details of balances	6. Confirm accounts receivable. (a) Determine the form, timing and extent of confirmation requests. (b) Select and execute a sample and investigate exceptions. (c) For positive confirmation requests for which no reply was received, perform alternative follow-up procedures. • Vouch subsequent payments identifiable with items comprising the account balance at the confirmation date to supporting documentation, as in Step 3(b). • Vouch items comprising the balance at the confirmation date to documentary support, as in Step 3(a). (d) Summarise the results of confirmation and alternative follow-up procedures.	✓		✓	✓4	
	7. Evaluate the adequacy of the provision for bad debts. (a) Add and cross-add the aged trial balance of accounts receivable and agree the total to the general ledger. (b) Test ageing by vouching amounts in ageing categories for sample of accounts to supporting documentation. (c) For past-due accounts: • Examine evidence of collectability, such as correspondence with customers and outside collection agencies, credit reports and customers' financial reports. • Discuss the collectability of accounts with appropriate management personnel. (d) Evaluate the adequacy of the provision component for each ageing category and in the aggregate.				✓5	
Disclosure	8. Compare the report presentation with applicable Accounting Standards. (a) Determine that debtors are properly classified as to type and expected period of realisation. (b) Determine whether there are credit balances that are significant in the aggregate and should be reclassified as liabilities. (c) Determine the appropriateness of presentation and disclosure and accounting for related party or factored debts.				✓4	✓4, 5

Initial procedures

The starting point for verifying accounts receivable and the related provision account is to trace the current period's opening balances to the closing audited balances in the prior year's working papers (when applicable). Next, the auditor should review the current period's activity in the general ledger control account and related provision account for any significant entries that are unusual in nature or amount, and that require special investigation.

An **accounts receivable trial balance** (listing all customer balances) is obtained, usually from the entity. To determine that it is an accurate and complete representation of the underlying accounting records, the auditor should add this listing and compare the total with both the total of the subsidiary ledger from which it was prepared and the general ledger control account balance. The auditor should also compare a sample of the customer details and balances shown on the trial balance with those in the subsidiary ledger, and vice versa. The sample can then serve as the physical representation of the population of accounts receivable to be subjected to further substantive procedures.

An example of an **aged trial balance** of an accounts receivable working paper is presented in Figure 10.3 on the right. This working paper not only provides evidence of performance of the initial procedures just described, but of several of the other substantive procedures we will discuss in subsequent sections. The initial procedures in verifying the accuracy of the trial balance and determining its agreement with the control account in the general ledger relate primarily to the clerical and mathematical accuracy component of the valuation assertion.

Computer information systems

Where accounts receivable data are held on computer files, the auditor can use computer-assisted audit techniques to perform substantive procedures. This is likely to involve the use of computer audit software. Both generalised computer audit software (GCAS) and database packages can be used to print a trial balance directly from the accounts receivable master file, test the ageing of a sample of accounts, and verify the total and its agreement with the control account in the general ledger.

Analytical procedures

Tests of details are usually planned on the basis that the analytical procedures confirm expectations. It is preferable to perform analytical procedures early in the final audit, so any necessary changes to tests of details can be determined prior to the commencement of that part of the audit.

The first stage in applying analytical procedures is to review the understanding of the entity, obtained during the planning phase, as to whether any changes to sales and receivables balances are to be expected.

The second stage is to identify absolute changes in amounts between this year and prior years. This is normally done in the course of preparing the lead schedule for sales and accounts receivable, as we explained in Chapter 6. On this schedule, prior and current year ledger balances making up the financial report disclosures are recorded side by side, making any differences readily apparent.

The third stage involves the use of more sophisticated relationships such as ratios and trends. This procedure can be performed on accounting data held on computer files, using computer audit software. Significant ratios are gross profit and days sales in accounts receivable. If gross profit is higher than expected, it could be that sales have been overstated to boost revenue, such as by a deliberate cut-off error. An increase in days sales in receivables indicates potential problems in collecting receivables, with the consequent need for a greater provision.

Wherever a change in relationships cannot be readily explained, the auditor must seek an explanation from management and corroborate that explanation, usually by performing more tests of details. For accounts receivable and sales, analytical procedures can provide evidence pertaining to the existence or occurrence, completeness, and valuation or measurement assertions.

FIGURE 10.3 *Aged trial balance working paper*

Bates Company
Aged trial balance — Accounts receivable — Trade
31 December 20X1
(PBC)

W/P ref. B–1
Prepared by: A. C. E. Date: 5/1/X2
Reviewed by: P. A. R. Date: 20/1/X2

Account no. 120

Account name	Past due: Over 90 days	Past due: Over 60 days	Past due: Over 30 days	Current	Balance per books 31/12/X1	Adjustments	Balance per audit 31/12/X1
Ace Engineering		2 529.04	2 016.14	11 875.90	16 421.08✓		16 421.08
φ Applied Devices			15 938.89^	27 901.11^	43 840.00✓		43 840.00 C1
φ Barry Manufacturing	1 088.92^	743.12^	3 176.22^	8 993.01^	14 001.27✓		14 001.27 C2
φ Brandt Electonics	501.10^	7 309.50^	30 948.01^	24 441.25^	63 199.86✓		63 199.86 C3
Cermetrics Limited			3 813.76	8 617.30	12 431.06✓		12 431.06
φ Columbia Components				4 321.18^	4 321.18✓		4 321.18
Drake Manufacturing			739.57	2 953.88	3 693.45✓		3 693.45
EMC		1 261.01	1 048.23	16 194.76	18 504.00✓		18 504.00
φ Groton Electric		7 799.36^	20 006.63^	89 017.15^	116 823.14✓		116 823.14 C4
Harvey Industries		1 709.16	6 111.25	18 247.31	26 067.72✓		26 067.72
φ Jed Limited	2 615.87^	12 098.00^	15 434.46^	56 536.88^	86 685.21✓	(9 416.96)	77 268.25 C5
Jericho Electric		1 198.72	13 123.14		14 321.86✓		14 321.86
⋮	⋮	⋮	⋮	⋮	⋮	⋮	⋮
φ W & M Manufacturing Corp.		1 904.65^	2 166.78^	28 389.69^	32 461.12✓		32 461.12 C60
Yancey Corp.	814.98	2 861.05	9 874.13	13 561.80	27 111.96✓		27 111.96
	10 157.46	56 705.59	160 537.28	392 136.41	619 536.74	(9 416.96)	610 119.78
	✓	✓	✓	✓	✓ B	✓ B	✓ B

✓ Added or cross-added
φ Customer name and balance per books agreed to subsidiary ledger
^ Ageing verified by examining transaction dates of related unpaid sales invoices in subsidiary ledger
C Account selected for confirmation — see W/P B–2

Tests of details of transactions

Where balances result from the effects of numerous transactions, it is normally more efficient to concentrate substantive procedures on tests of details of balances, and not tests of details of transactions. The latter are not unimportant, but serve to corroborate tests of details of balances. In the main, the tests of transactions will be performed during the interim audit, commonly in the form of dual-purpose tests. The cut-off tests that we will describe in subsequent sections are always performed as part of year-end work and, although they are tests of transactions, serve to verify the recorded balance at the balance sheet date.

Vouching recorded accounts receivable to supporting transactions

This procedure involves vouching a sample of debits to customers' accounts to supporting sales invoices, and matching documents to provide evidence relevant to the existence, rights and obligations, and valuation or measurement assertions. It also involves vouching a sample of credits to remittance advices and sales adjustment authorisations to provide evidence relevant to the completeness assertion for accounts receivable that reductions in customer balances are legitimate.

Performing sales cut-off test

The **sales cut-off test** is designed to obtain reasonable assurance that:

- sales and accounts receivable are recorded in the accounting period in which the transactions occurred;
- the corresponding entries for inventories and cost of goods sold are made in the same period.

The sales cut-off test is made as of the balance sheet date. Given the greater risk of overstatement, the emphasis is on verifying the occurrence of recorded sales before the year end. The auditor usually records the number of the last issued dispatch note during attendance at the inventory count and agrees it to the cut-off established for inventory purposes. For sales of goods from inventory, the procedure involves comparing a sample of recorded sales from the last few days of the current period with dispatch notes numbered prior to the cut-off number to determine that the transactions occurred before the balance sheet date. A smaller number of sales recorded after the balance sheet date are vouched to dispatch notes numbered subsequently to the cut-off, to ensure that none was delivered before the balance sheet date.

The **sales return cut-off test** is similar and particularly directed towards the possibility that returns made prior to the year end are not recorded until after the year end, resulting in the overstatement of accounts receivable and sales. The auditor can determine the correct cut-off by examining dated receiving reports for returned merchandise and correspondence with customers. The auditor should also be alert to the possibility that an unusually heavy volume of sales returns shortly after the year end could signal unauthorised shipments before the year end to inflate recorded sales and accounts receivable.

Performing cash receipts cut-off test

The **cash receipts cut-off test** is designed to obtain reasonable assurance that cash receipts are recorded in the accounting period in which received. A proper cut-off at the balance sheet date is essential to the correct presentation of both cash and accounts receivable. If the auditor is present at the year end date, then he or she can observe that all collections received prior to the close of business are included in cash on hand or in deposits in transit, and are credited to accounts receivable. An alternative to personal observation is to review supporting documentation such as the daily cash summary and a validated deposit slip for the last day of the year. The objective of the review is to determine that the deposit slip total agrees with the receipts shown on the daily cash summary. In addition, the auditor should determine that the receipts were recorded on the closing date.

Tests of details of balances

As explained above, most of the audit effort on receivables is obtained through tests of details of balances, of which the most important is the confirmation of accounts receivable and related follow-up procedures. Confirmation provides evidence as to existence, rights and valuation. It does not provide evidence of completeness, because customers are unlikely to admit to owing more than their recorded balance. The other major test of details of balances is an evaluation of the adequacy of the provision for bad debts.

8 LEARNING OBJECTIVE

Explain the procedures for undertaking a confirmation of receivables balances.

Confirming accounts receivable

Confirmation of accounts receivable involves direct written communication by the auditor with individual customers. The test is often referred to as an accounts receivable circularisation.

Accepted audit procedure

The confirmation of accounts receivable is an accepted audit procedure when they are material and it is reasonable to presume the debtors will respond (AUS 504 (ISA 505),

External Confirmations). Confirmation is usually the most efficient procedure for obtaining sufficient appropriate audit evidence to support the existence and rights assertions of accounts receivable. There are circumstances, however, in which the auditor concludes that confirmation is unlikely to be effective and that sufficient appropriate audit evidence can be achieved through the performance of alternative audit procedures. Based on the prior year's audit experience on that engagement, the auditor might expect, for example, that responses would be unreliable in the current year or that the response rates would be inadequate. Also, in some cases, customers may be unable to confirm balances if they use voucher systems that show the amount owed on individual transactions, but not the total amount owed to one creditor. This is often true of governmental agencies. The auditor may be able to overcome this problem by confirming individual transactions rather than balances.

As written evidence from third parties, responses to confirmation requests constitute highly reliable evidence. Against this, it must be remembered that:

- where customers are largely small businesses or private individuals, they are less likely to maintain sufficiently accurate accounts payable ledger records to provide a reliable response;
- even larger businesses generally maintain less effective controls over the completeness of liabilities recorded in the accounts payable ledger;
- customers are unlikely to admit to owing more than is shown on the monthly statement, limiting the evidence to that of existence, rights and, to a lesser extent, valuation;
- many trivial differences are likely to be reported as a result of goods and cash in transit;
- the non-response rate may be high.

Given that dealings between the entity and its customers are confidential, the entity must authorise its customers to disclose details of the outstanding balance to its auditors. Occasionally, entities have prohibited auditors from confirming certain accounts receivable. The effect of prohibition should be evaluated on the basis of management's reasons, with the auditor determining whether he or she can obtain sufficient evidence from other auditing procedures. If the auditor regards management's reasons as unacceptable, then there has been a limitation on the scope of the audit that might result in a modified auditor's report.

Form of confirmation

There are two forms of confirmation request:

- the *positive* form, which requires the debtor to respond whether or not the balance shown is correct;
- the *negative* form, which requires the debtor to respond only when the amount shown is incorrect.

The two forms are illustrated in Figures 10.4 and 10.5 (page 398). The positive confirmation request is usually made in the form of a separate letter on entity letterhead, but it may also be printed on the customer's monthly statement. The negative request is usually in the form of a rubber stamp or sticker attached to the statement or a request printed on the statement. The positive form generally produces statistically valid evidence, providing non-responses are verified by other means. With the negative form, it is impossible to determine whether a lack of response indicates agreement with the balance or simply a failure to reply. The positive form is used when detection risk is low or individual customer balances are relatively large. The negative form should be used only when the following conditions apply:

- Detection risk is moderate or high.
- There is a large number of small balances in the population.
- The auditor has no reason to believe that the respondents are unlikely to give the request due consideration.

Frequently, a combination of the two forms is used in a single engagement. In the audit of a public utility, for example, the auditor may elect to use the negative form for residential customers and the positive form for commercial customers. When the positive form is used, the auditor should generally follow up with a second and sometimes an additional request to those accounts receivable that fail to reply.

FIGURE 10.4

Positive confirmation request — letter form

BATES COMPANY

4 Queensland Road

Eastville

Ace Engineering Service
New Road
Westville

6 January 20X3

Dear Sir or Madam,

This request is being sent to you to enable our independent auditors to confirm the correctness of our records. It is not a request for payment.

Our records on 31 December 20X2 showed an amount of $16 421.08 receivable from you. Please confirm whether this agrees with your records on that date by signing this form and returning it directly to our auditors. An addressed envelope is enclosed for this purpose. If you find any difference, then please report details to our auditors directly in the space provided below.

Yours faithfully

Controller

The above amount is correct [ ]. The above amount is incorrect for the following reasons:

____

____

(Individual or company name)

By: ______________________

FIGURE 10.5

Negative confirmation request — stamp form

Please examine this monthly statement carefully
and advise our auditors

Reddy & Abel
Certified Public Accountants
465 City Centre Building
Perth

as to any exceptions.

A self-addressed stamped envelope is
enclosed for your convenience.

THIS IS NOT A REQUEST FOR PAYMENT.

Timing and extent of requests

When the acceptable level of detection risk is low, the auditor ordinarily confirms receivables as at the balance sheet date. Otherwise, the confirmation date may be one or two months earlier. In such case, the auditor must:

- perform analytical procedures on entries to the accounts receivable control account in the period between the date of confirmation and the balance sheet date, and obtain a satisfactory explanation for any unexpected changes;
- perform tests of control in the intervening period to ensure that the assessment of control risk leading to a decision to accept a high level of detection risk continues to apply.

The extent of requests or sample size is determined by the criteria that we described in Chapter 8 on audit sampling. Accounts receivable may be divided into distinct populations for sampling. For example, different categories of debtor — such as wholesale and retail — may be subject to different information systems and control procedures and, thus, different control risks. Also, individually material balances are often confirmed directly and the remainder subdivided into either overdue accounts or other, with a proportionately larger number of the former selected for confirmation as presenting a greater risk of misstatement. Sample size may be determined judgmentally or with the aid of a statistical sampling plan. Apart from the exceptions noted, selection of accounts for confirmation should be effectively random, such as through use of a sequential sampling plan.

Control of the requests

The auditor must control every step in the confirmation process. This means:

- prior to selecting the sample for confirmation, performing the initial procedures described above to ensure the list of balances is complete and accurate;
- drawing up a list of selected accounts and verifying that confirmation requests, prepared and signed by entity management at the auditor's request, are in complete agreement with that list;
- ascertaining that the amount, name and address on the confirmation agree with the corresponding data in the customer's account;
- maintaining custody of the confirmations until they are mailed;
- using the audit firm's own return address envelopes for the confirmations;
- personally depositing the requests in the mail;
- requiring that the replies be sent directly to the auditor.

A working paper should list each account selected for confirmation and the results obtained from each request, cross-referenced to the actual confirmation response (which should also be filed with the working papers). A confirmation control working paper is illustrated in Figure 10.6 (page 400).

Disposition of exceptions

Confirmation responses will inevitably contain some exceptions. Exceptions may be attributable to goods in transit from the entity to the customer, returned goods or payments in transit from the customer to the entity, items in dispute or errors and irregularities. The auditor should investigate all exceptions and record their resolution in the working papers, as illustrated in Figure 10.6.

Computer information systems

Computer audit software may assist the auditor in the process of confirming receivables held on an accounts receivable master file. As explained above in our discussion of initial procedures, the software can be programmed to test the completeness and accuracy of receivables listed on the master file. Software can also be used to select accounts on bases as discussed above, print the letters for circularisation and prepare a working paper for recording responses.

Alternative procedures for dealing with non-responses

When no response has been received after the second (or third) positive confirmation request to a customer, the auditor should perform alternative procedures. The two main alternative procedures are examining subsequent collections and vouching unpaid invoices and supporting documentation comprising customer balances.

The best evidence of existence and collectability is the receipt of payment from the customer. Before the conclusion of the auditor's examination, the entity will receive payments from many customers on amounts owed at the confirmation date. The matching of such cash receipts to unpaid invoices at the confirmation date, evidenced by the remittance advice accompanying the cash receipt, establishes the existence and collectability of the accounts.

Vouching open invoices comprising balances is a variation of Step 3(a) in Table 10.5 (pages 392–3). Preferably, the unpaid item should be traced to a dispatch note signed by the customer acknowledging receipt of the goods, or to a written order from the customer.

FIGURE 10.6 *Confirmation control working paper*

Bates Company
Accounts receivable confirmation control
31 December 20X1

W/P ref. B-2
Prepared by: A. C. E. Date: 28/1/X2
Reviewed by: P. A. R. Date: 31/1/X2

Account no. 120

Conf. no.	Customer	Book value	Confirmed value ∅	Audited value	(Over) Under statement	Subsequent collections examined through 28/1/X2
1	Applied Devices	43 480.00	43 480.00	43 480.00		
2	Barry Manufacturing	14 001.27	NR	14 001.27		14 001.27✓
3	Brandt Electronics	63 199.86	63 199.86	63 199.86		
4	Groton Electric	116 823.14	116 823.14	116 823.14		
5	Jed Limited	86 685.21	77 268.25	77 268.25	(9 416.96)(X1)	
60	W & M Manufacturing Corp.	32 461.12	NR	32 461.12⋀		4 071.43✓
	Totals	470 847.92	414 968.57	461 430.96	(9 416.96)	

Response recap:

	# Items	
Value of confirmations mailed	60	$470 847.92
Value of confirmations received	58	$414 968.57
Response	97%	88%

Summary of results:

	# Items	
Value of account total	300	$619 536.74
Book value of confirmation sample	60	$470 847.92
Coverage of book value		76%
Audited value of sample	60	$461 430.96
Ratio of audited value to book value of sample		98%

∅ Signed confirmation response attached for confirmed values
NR No response — alternative procedures performed
✓ Examined entries in cash receipts journal and related remittance advices for total collections indicated
⋀ Examined supporting documentation for portion of book value remaining uncollected as of 28/1/X2
(X1) Credit memo issued 12/1/X2 for merchandise returned 28/12/X1. Adjusting entry:

Dr. sales returns	9416.96		See W/P B-1 and AE-1
Cr. accounts receivable		9416.96	

Summary and evaluation of the results

The auditor's working papers should contain a summary of the results from confirming accounts receivable. (The lower portion of Figure 10.6 illustrates how such data may be presented.) The auditor may use statistical or non-statistical procedures to project misstatements found in the sample to the population. It must not be forgotten, for a sample test, that it is not sufficient merely to correct errors detected by the confirmation, but that the implications for the entire population of accounts receivable must also be considered.

The auditor evaluates combined evidence from the confirmations, alternative procedures performed on non-responses, and other tests of details and analytical procedures to determine whether sufficient evidence has been obtained to support management's assertions about accounts receivable.

Evaluating adequacy of the provision for bad debts

Most entities determine the provision for bad debts by:

- making a general provision, such as a percentage of balances overdue by more than a specified period;
- making a specific provision, by identifying customers who are known to be in financial difficulty or who are in dispute as to payment.

The provision is an estimate that the auditor will verify in accordance with AUS 516 (ISA 540), Audit of Accounting Estimates. The auditor adopts one or more of the following approaches:

- reviewing and testing the process used by management;
- using an independent estimate;
- reviewing subsequent events.

The auditor usually follows the first approach in verifying the general provision, and it involves:

- ascertaining management's procedures for determining the estimate and considering their reliability;
- ensuring that the procedures have been properly followed and that the estimate has been approved;
- identifying the assumptions underpinning the estimate and considering their reasonableness;
- verifying the reliability of the data (such as the aged analysis of accounts receivable) on which the estimate is based;
- checking the calculations (such as the percentages applied to each overdue category) in determining the general provision;
- considering the reliability of prior year provisions.

The auditor usually applies second and third approaches suggested by AUS 516 (ISA 540) when considering the specific provision. In arriving at an independent estimate, the auditor will examine correspondence with customers and outside collection agencies, review customers' credit reports and financial reports, and discuss the collectability of the account with appropriate management personnel. This review will include a consideration of subsequent events, such as news of a customer's financial difficulties or payment of a disputed amount.

Disclosure

The auditor must be knowledgeable about the report disclosure requirements for accounts receivable and sales under the Corporations Law or other regulatory frameworks. A review of the accounts receivable trial balance may indicate amounts due from employees, officers, other group entities and related parties that should be specifically identified if material. The same source may reveal credit balances in customer accounts that may warrant classification as current liabilities. There should also be disclosure of the pledging, assigning or factoring of accounts receivable. The auditor should be able to obtain evidence of such activities from a review of the minutes of the board of directors meetings and from inquiry of management. As one of the final steps in the audit, the auditor should obtain management's representations on these matters in writing in a representation letter (see Chapter 14).

LEARNING CHECK

10.7 The nature, timing and extent of substantive procedures are determined by the planned level of detection risk which, in turn, is a function of the assessed levels of inherent and control risks.

10.8 Initial procedures ensure the accuracy of the list of receivables balances used as the basis for tests of the receivables balance.

10.9 Analytical procedures require the determination of expectations and the comparison of amounts, trends and ratios, particularly the gross profit ratio and days' sales in receivables ratio.

10.10 Tests of details of transactions are largely dual-purpose tests performed at the interim audit except for cut-off tests of transactions either side of the balance sheet date. The principal test of details of balances is the receivables confirmation which provides third party evidence of the balance. The other major test of details of balances is of the reasonableness of the estimated provision for bad debts.

SUMMARY

Sales and cash receipts from sales are the most important transaction classes for a commercial entity. For businesses selling on credit, maintaining records over the accounts receivable balance is also highly important. In auditing these transactions and the accounts receivable balance, the auditor uses techniques explained in Chapters 5–9.

In this chapter we followed the audit approach required by AUS 402 (ISA 400). We described the information system and related control procedures typically employed by entities in processing the relevant transaction classes. The audit process commences with obtaining the understanding of this system. The auditor also considers issues relating to materiality, inherent risk and the control environment, prior to determining the appropriate audit strategy. For sales and receivables, materiality is invariably high. For audit purposes, the most significant inherent risk is that of overstatement of sales transactions and receivables balances to boost reported profits and assets. For the entity, the greatest inherent risk is that of misappropriation of cash arising from sales transactions. In evaluating the control environment, the auditor considers each of the control environment factors — integrity and ethical values, commitment to competence, management's philosophy and operating style, the assignment of authority and responsibility, and personnel policies and practices — as they relate to sales and receivables

The next stage of the audit is determining the audit strategy, which, for sales and receivables, is likely to be one based on a lower assessed level of control risk. The first stage in assessing control risk is evaluating design effectiveness. In this chapter we illustrated the use of evaluation check lists which hypothesise potential misstatements for each function in the processing of sales and cash receipt transactions. In assessing design effectiveness, the auditor compares the control procedures in the entity's information system with necessary controls identified by the check list. At this point, the auditor drafts the audit program based on the preliminary assessment of control risk, identifying both tests of the operating effectiveness of controls and the reduced level of substantive procedures relevant to the assessed level of control risk. The auditor confirms the assessed level of control risk on completion of the tests of operating effectiveness.

The final stage of the audit is performing substantive procedures. It is usually cost effective to test the balance of receivables rather than the transactions making up that balance. The most important test of transactions is that of cut-off at the year end. The major test of balances is the confirmation of accounts receivable. Given that customers are third parties, such evidence is highly reliable. In this chapter we explained the process of performing the confirmation, procedures to be followed where the test is performed prior to the year end, and alternative procedures for verifying balances where no reply to the request for confirmation is received. Finally, we explained procedures necessary to verify the estimated provision for bad debts.

KEY TERMS

Accounts receivable master file, p. 374
Accounts receivable subsidiary ledger, p. 374
Accounts receivable trial balance, p. 394
Aged trial balance, p. 394
Authorised price list, p. 374
Cash receipts cut-off test, p. 396
Cash receipts journal, p. 378
Computer-assisted audit techniques, p. 387
Credit memo, p. 380
Customer order, p. 372
Deposit slip, p. 378
Dispatch notes, p. 373
Embedded audit facility, p. 387
Generalised audit software, p. 387
Integrated test facility, p. 387
Monthly customer statement, p. 374
Remittance advice, p. 378
Rough cash book, p. 378
Sales cut-off test, p. 396
Sales invoices, p. 374
Sales journal, p. 374
Sales order, p. 372
Sales return cut-off test, p. 396
Sales transactions file, p. 375
Systems control and audit file, p. 387
Test data approach, p. 387
Write-off authorisation memo, p. 380

FURTHER READING

American Institute of Certified Public Accountants, 'Confirmation of Accounts Receivable'. Auditing Procedures Study, New York, 1984.

Bailey, Charles D. & Ballard, Gene, 'Improving Response Rates to Accounts Receivable Confirmations: An Experiment Using Four Techniques', *Auditing: A Journal of Practice and Theory* (Spring 1986), pp. 77–85.

Beran, Denny & Evans, Richard, 'Auditing for Sales Adjustment Fraud', *Internal Auditor* (February 1990), pp. 51–6.

Caster, Paul, 'The Role of Confirmations as Audit Evidence', *Journal of Accountancy* (February 1992), pp. 73–6.

McConnell Jr, Donald K. & Banks, George Y., 'A Common Peer Review Problem', *Journal of Accountancy* (June 1998).

O'Leary, Conor, 'Debtors' Confirmations — Handle with Care', *Australian Accountant* (May 1993), pp. 35–7.

Swearingen, James G., Wilkes, James A. & Swearingen, Sandra L., 'Confirmation Response Differences between Businesses, Clerks and Consumers', *The CPA Journal* (May 1991), pp. 58–60.

Williams, David D. & Ziegler, Teresa J., 'Positive-out Negative-in Confirmations — An Innovative Approach', *The CPA Journal* (July 1987), pp. 78–80.

Review questions

10.1 Explain the importance of credit approval. Describe procedures necessary to ensure proper control over this function.

10.2 Identify programmed application controls and standing data likely to be of significance in a computerised sales system.

10.3 Outline the controls necessary in ensuring the completeness of recorded cash received in the mail.

10.4 Describe inherent risks specific to sales and receivables that the auditor needs to consider.

10.5 Explain how computer-assisted audit techniques are used in testing controls over sales and receivables transactions.

10.6 Why is the control risk assessment of the completeness of cash receipts and sales adjustment transactions associated with control risk over the existence of the accounts receivable balance?

10.7 Why is the auditor likely to adopt a lower assessed level of control risk approach to the audit of accounts receivable wherever practicable? Why are substantive procedures more likely to be based on the accounts receivable balance than on sales, cash receipts and sales adjustment transactions?

10.8 Explain how the auditor verifies cut-off of sales transactions at the year end.

10.9 Outline the procedures involved in performing a receivables confirmation.

10.10 If the auditor does not receive a response after sending a letter to confirm a debtor's balance, what alternative audit procedures may he or she perform?

Discussion questions

10.1 Identify application controls that could be programmed into a computer information system for processing credit sales transactions.

10.2 Discuss situations in which sales adjustments may be necessary. Identify necessary controls to ensure that the accounting system recognises only genuine adjustments.

10.3 Identify situations leading to an inherent risk that an entity may wish to (a) overstate sales revenue and (b) understate sales revenue.

10.4 Explain the kinds of fraud that could be anticipated in sales, cash receipts and sales adjustment transactions in the absence of adequate internal control procedures. Consider the importance of the segregation of duties in preventing such frauds.

10.5 Explain why existence is often regarded as the assertion presenting the greatest degree of inherent risk.

10.6 In the absence of effective controls, consider whether it is possible for the auditor to verify the completeness of cash receipts using substantive procedures. Is there a distinction between the ability to verify the completeness of cash receipts from sales transactions and the ability to verify the completeness of donations to a charity? Discuss.

10.7 Explain what is meant by 'cut-off' and why it is important to auditors in establishing the fairness of financial reports.

10.8 In what situations may the negative form of accounts receivable confirmation be appropriate?

10.9 Consider why management may not wish particular accounts receivable to be circularised. Which of these reasons may the auditor regard as acceptable?

10.10 AUS 514 (ISA 530) distinguishes between sampling and other selective testing procedures. Explain the application of the requirements of this Standard to the selection of accounts receivable balances for confirmation.

Professional application questions

★ BASIC
★★ MODERATE
★★★ CHALLENGING

10.1 (Cash sales system controls) ★

As the internal auditor of the Sellanything Group of companies, you have been asked to investigate the cash sales system of Stationery Limited, one of the subsidiaries. Stationery sells office supplies within the Melbourne area. Its prices are highly competitive and, furthermore, it offers a same-day delivery service for orders telephoned before noon. Costs are kept down by requiring cash on delivery. Sales are made in the following way:

1. The customer phones though an order to the sales department, which raises a pre-numbered multi-copy sales order, two of which (the invoice copies) are priced and totalled.
2. The dispatch department makes up the order and gives the goods to the driver with the invoice copies of the order.
3. The driver delivers the goods, collects the cash and receipts the customer's copy of the invoice.
4. The driver returns and hands over the cash and the second copy of the invoice to the cashier.
5. The cashier records and banks the cash.

Required

(a) State any weaknesses in the cash sales system.
(b) Describe any audit tests you would perform to ensure that there was no material error or fraud within the system.

10.2 (Tests of control — sales transactions) ★★

You have been assigned to perform tests of control on the sales system at EDB Pty Limited as part of the 30 June 20X2 audit. EDB is a wholesaler of bathroom supplies such as vanities, toilets, taps and sinks. During testing, you noted the following errors:

1. Invoice number 54922 issued on 12 December 20X1 was entered twice. The error was discovered when the customer rang to complain about being charged double the agreed amount.
2. Invoice 51839 issued on 25 September 20X1 contained incorrect prices. Three vanity units were charged at $453 each instead of $543, and five sinks were charged at $231 each instead of $321. The error was discovered when the salesperson complained about not receiving the full commission entitlement for the month.
3. No prices were entered on invoice number 56329 issued on 24 January 20X2, resulting in a zero dollar invoice being issued. The error was discovered when accounts receivable staff queried the zero amount appearing on the debtors ledger.

(continued)

4. Invoice number 59328 issued on 18 March 20X2 matched the customer's order. However, the order was only partially filled due to a lack of stock in the warehouse, meaning items which were never delivered were included in the invoice. The error was discovered when the customer rang to complain about being overcharged.
5. Invoice number 61348 issued on 7 May 20X2 was sent to the wrong address. Apparently, the invoice had the correct address on it, but a typing error occurred on the envelope. The error was discovered when the customer rang to complain about the overdue notice they received, stating they had never received the invoice in the first place.
6. Invoice number 62875 issued on 29 June 20X2 was not processed through the usual channels. The details were correct but certain procedures, such as a formal credit check, were not documented. The invoice was a special order for a large building project and amounted to around ten times the value of EDB's average invoices. The sale was personally handled by one of the directors and the invoice was prepared by his assistant.

Required

Treating each of the above errors independently:

(a) Describe application errors (both manual and via the computer information system) that would have prevented or detected the error.

(b) Describe further work you would perform in relation to each of the errors.

(c) Explain the implications of the errors for your substantive testing of debtors.

(d) Briefly discuss how you would present these matters in your year-end management letter.

(Professional Year Programme of the ICAA — 1999, Accounting 2 Module — adapted)

10.3 (Computerised sales system — controls) ★★

Bestwood Limited is planning to replace its computerised sales accounting system. The managing director has asked for your advice on certain matters relating to the new system.

The existing system uses the computer to produce sales invoices from hand-written dispatch notes, posts them to the accounts receivable ledger, records cash received and produces an aged analysis of receivables. The main weaknesses of the existing system are that many documents are still handwritten or typed and that it is possible to deliver goods to customers with poor credit ratings, thus creating excessive debt collection costs and a high level of bad debts.

The managing director suggests that the new system should:

1. produce the order confirmation;
2. produce the dispatch note when the goods are ready for delivery;
3. produce the sales invoice at the same time as the dispatch note, using information from the dispatch note and prices from a standing data file, and post the invoice to the accounts receivable ledger;
4. record receipts of cash from customers on the accounts receivable ledger and in the cash book.

Access to the system will be accessed from terminals and controlled by the use of passwords and by restrictions on the tasks that can be performed from specific terminals.

In view of the large number of orders, the managing director wants the computer to perform credit checks on customers with minimum intervention by the credit controller. The credit checks by the computer will use data input into the system by the credit controller and information on the customer master file. When the programmed criteria decide that goods should not be dispatched to a particular customer, the credit controller may override the computer.

Required

(a) Describe the controls the computer system should exercise before:
  (i) confirming a customer's order;
  (ii) raising a dispatch note authorising the delivery of goods to the customer.
(b) Describe the controls that should be exercised over:
  (i) changing customer details, including adding new customers, amending details of existing customers and deleting customers;
  (ii) changing customer credit limits;
  (iii) changing selling prices of goods;
(c) Describe:
  (i) the credit criteria that the computer system should use to authorise delivery of goods to customers;
  (ii) the manual procedures the credit controller should undertake when overriding the computer.

(ACCA Audit Framework — Paper 6, June 1996 — adapted)

10.4 (Substantive procedures for bad debt provision) ★★

It is common practice for companies to make two provisions for bad debts:

1. The *specific* provision is based on accounts the company has reason to suspect may not be paid.
2. The *general* provision relates to accounts as yet unknown but which experience suggests may not be paid. The likelihood of a debt being unpaid is usually assumed to increase the longer it remains unpaid, and many companies determine a general provision as a percentage of overdue receivables, with an increasing percentage being applied against the longest overdue accounts.

You are aware that AUS 516, Audit of Accounting Estimates is likely to be relevant to the audit of the provision for bad debts.

Required

Describe the procedures you would adopt in verifying:
(a) a general provision for bad debts;
(b) a specific provision for bad debts.

10.5 (Substantive audit program for accounts receivable) ★★★

Your client is BigC Limited, a large private firm with offices in all major cities of Australia. BigC specialises in selling concentrated fruit juices to Australian and overseas buyers. This is the first year your firm will perform the audit. You are currently completing the planning work for the audit of trade debtors for the year ending 30 June 20X2, and have gathered the following information.

(*continued*)

1. The Melbourne office recently won a large contract to supply an overseas department store chain with concentrated orange juice.
2. For the month of January, the Adelaide office ran a sales promotion that allowed new customers double the normal credit terms of thirty days. Several new large customers took advantage of this offer.
3. The Darwin office has been experiencing a higher than usual level of sales returns due to a mould growth being discovered in a batch of the guava juice.

You have calculated the debtors' turnover ratio and debtors-to-total assets ratio for each of the branch offices, as shown in the following tables.

	Debtors' turnover ratio		
Office	**8 months to February 20X2**	**12 months to June 20X1**	**12 months to June 20X0**
Sydney	8.0	9.2	10.1
Melbourne	7.5	9.1	9.2
Hobart	5.2	6.0	7.1
Adelaide	10.1	8.5	9.5
Perth	8.8	9.0	9.0
Darwin	8.5	7.9	7.1
Brisbane	5.9	6.0	6.0

	Debtors' to total assets ratio		
Office	**8 months to February 20X2**	**12 months to June 20X1**	**12 months to June 20X0**
Sydney	0.25	0.12	0.10
Melbourne	0.15	0.15	0.15
Hobart	0.18	0.14	0.12
Adelaide	0.15	0.16	0.17
Perth	0.23	0.16	0.20
Darwin	0.17	0.30	0.15
Brisbane	0.19	0.25	0.22

Required

(a) List the questions you would ask of management in relation to each of the branch office's debtors.

(b) Describe additional audit work you would perform to satisfy yourself that debtors were fairly stated.

(Professional Year Programme of the ICAA — 1997, Accounting 2 Module — adapted)

10.6 (Accounts receivable circularisation) ★★★

Your firm is the external auditor of Southwood Trading Limited and you are auditing the financial statements for the year ended 30 November 20X2. Southwood Trading has a turnover of $25 million and trade debtors at 30 November 20X2 were $5.2 million.

The engagement partner has asked you to consider the relative reliability of evidence from third parties and certain matters relating to a debtors' circularisation.

In relation to part (b)(ii) below, the partner has explained that judgement would be used to select debtors that appear doubtful and those that would not be selected using the dollar unit sampling technique described in part (b)(i).

Required

(a) Consider the relative reliability of the following types of evidence from third parties:
   (i) replies to a debtors' circularisation to confirm trade debtors;
   (ii) suppliers' statements to confirm purchase ledger balances.

(b) In relation to selecting debtors for circularisation:
   (i) explain the use of monetary unit sampling in selecting debtors to circularise;
   (ii) consider the criteria you would use to select individual debtors for circularisation using judgement;
   (iii) discuss the advantages and disadvantages of using monetary unit sampling (in (b)(i)) as compared with judgement (in (b)(ii)) to select the debtors to circularise. Your answer should consider why it is undesirable to use only judgement to select the debtors for circularisation.

(c) Describe the audit work you would carry out in following up the responses to a debtors circularisation where:
   (i) the debtor disagrees the balance and provides a different balance;
   (ii) no reply to the circularisation has been received from the debtor, and all attempts at obtaining a reply have failed.

(ACCA Audit Framework — Paper 6, December 1998 — adapted)

10.7 (Computer-assisted substantive testing for accounts receivable) ★★★

Ally McNeil is conducting the audit of a wholesale electrical goods distributor, Electra Pty Limited. Electra supplies appliances to hundreds of individual customers in the metropolitan area of Perth. It maintains detailed accounts receivable records on a computer system. The customer account master file is updated at the end of each business day. Each customer record in the master file contains the following data:

- customer account number;
- customer address;
- open (unpaid) invoices at the beginning of the month, by invoice number and date;
- sales during the current month, by invoice number and date;
- individual cash receipts during the current month;
- date of last sale;
- date of last cash receipt.

Ally McNeil is planning to confirm selected accounts receivable as at the end of the current month. She will have available a computer file of the data on the accounts receivable master file on the date on which the company sends monthly statements to its customers. Ally has a general purpose software package to assist her in this task.

Required

Detail how Ally McNeil will be able to use the computer software package and accounts receivable master file to assist her in the audit of accounts receivable.

(AICPA — adapted)

Case studies

10.1 (Flow charting and evaluating on-line computer processing) ★★★

Until recently, Optimo Phone Company employed a batch processing system for recording the receipt of customer payments. The following narrative describes the procedures involved in this system.

1. The customer's payment and the remittance advice (a punch card) are received in the treasurer's office. An accounts receivable clerk in the treasurer's office key punches the cash receipt into the remittance advice and forwards the card to the computer information system department. The cash receipt is added to a control tape listing and filed for deposit later in the day. When the deposit slips are received from the computer information system later in the day (at approximately 2.30 p.m. each day), the cash receipts are removed from the file and deposited with the original deposit slip. The second copy of the deposit slip and the control tape are compared for accuracy before the deposit is made, and then filed together.
2. In the computer information system department, the remittance advices received from the treasurer's office are held each day until 2.00 p.m. At that time, the customer payments are processed to update the records on magnetic tape and prepare a deposit slip in triplicate. During the update process, data are read (non-destructively) from the master accounts receivable tape, processed and then recorded on a new master tape. The original and second copy of the deposit slip are forwarded to the treasurer's office. The old master tape (former accounts receivable file), the remittance advices (in customer number order) and the third copy of the deposit slip are stored and filed in a secure place. The updated accounts receivable master tape is maintained in the system for processing the next day.
3. Optimo Phone Company has revised and redesigned its computer system so it has on-line capabilities. The new cash receipts procedures, described below, are designed to take advantage of the new system.
4. The customer's payment and remittance advice are received in the treasurer's office as before. A terminal is located in the treasurer's office to enter the cash receipts. An operator keys in the customer's number and payment from the remittance advice and cheques. The cash receipt is entered into the system once the operator has confirmed that the proper account and amount are displayed on the screen. The payment is then processed on line against the accounts receivable file maintained on magnetic disk. The cash receipts are filed for deposit later in the day. The remittance advices are filed in the order they are processed; these cards will be kept until the next working day and then destroyed. The computer prints out a deposit slip in duplicate at 2.00 p.m. for all cash receipts since the last deposit. The deposit slips are forwarded to the treasurer's office. The cash receipts are removed from the file and deposited with the original deposit slip; the duplicate deposit slip is filed for further reference. At the close of business (5.00 p.m.) each day, the computer information services department prepares a record of the current day's cash receipts activity on a magnetic tape. This tape is then stored in a secure place in the event of a systems malfunction; after ten working days, the tape is released for further use.

Required

(a) Prepare a systems flow chart for Optimo Phone Company's new on-line cash receipts procedures.

(b) Explain whether the new cash receipts procedures, as designed and implemented by Optimo Phone Company, created any internal control structure problems for the company. Explain your answer.

(CIMA — adapted)

10.2 (Controls over cash receipts) ★★★

The head office of Lighttime Limited, wholesalers of electrical equipment, has asked you to review the system of control over cash collection at the Victorian branch because it suspects that irregularities are taking place. The branch is the largest single outlet of the company and has substantial annual sales that are invoiced by the branch.

Inquiries reveal the following procedures for invoicing sales and collecting cash. (Cash refers to currency and cheques.)

1. There are two invoice sets that are used for cash sales and credit sales respectively.
2. When payment for cash sales is received by the cashier, one copy of the invoice is stamped as paid and filed alphabetically, while the other is given to the customer.
3. Credit sales invoices are sent to the customers.
4. Mail is opened by the secretary to the credit controller, who passes any cheques to the credit controller for his review, without recording the amounts received.
5. The credit controller gives the cheques to the cashier by depositing them in a tray on the cashier's desk.
6. The cashier then makes a listing of the cheques which is used by the credit controller for posting to the accounts receivable ledger.
7. The cheques from credit customers and receipts from cash sales are banked daily by the cashier, except for once a week when sufficient currency is retained to reimburse petty cash.
8. The credit controller posts remittances to accounts receivable using a computerised accounting system and verifies the cash discount allowable.
9. The credit controller obtains approval from head office to write off bad debts. Any subsequent remittances received in respect of these accounts are credited to 'sundry income'.

Required

(a) Describe control weaknesses in the accounting for cash receipts.

(b) Suggest improvements in internal control to prevent irregularities in the collection of cash.

(c) Explain substantive audit procedures necessary to determine whether any irregularities have taken place.

chapter 11

Auditing purchases, payables and payroll

Overview

LEARNING OBJECTIVES

After studying this chapter, you should be able to:

1. identify the audit objectives applicable to purchases, payables and payroll
2. describe the functions and control procedures normally found in information systems for processing purchase, payment and payroll transactions
3. apply the concepts of materiality and inherent risk to the audit of purchases, payables and payroll
4. discuss considerations relevant to determining the audit strategy for purchases, payables and payroll
5. design and execute tests of control over purchase, payment and payroll transactions to assess control risk
6. indicate the factors relevant to determining an acceptable level of detection risk for the audit of purchases, payables and payroll
7. design a substantive audit program for purchases, payables and payroll
8. explain the use of suppliers' statements in verifying the completeness of recorded liabilities.

Professional statements

AUSTRALIAN		INTERNATIONAL	
AUS 402	Risk Assessments and Internal Controls	ISA 400	Risk Assessments and Internal Control

In this chapter we will examine the audit of:

- the account balances of accounts payable and of accruals related to payroll;
- the transaction classes of purchases, payments and payroll.

Purchases and payments are for the acquisition of goods and services from outside suppliers, while payroll relates to the acquisition of, and payment for, labour services from employees. Together, they represent the major expenditures of most entities. There are similarities between the two in that both involve the acquisition of resources and payment to the suppliers. However, the nature of the employment contract between the entity and its employees is such that payroll transactions are always processed separately, including the payment of salaries and wages.

This chapter follows a similar structure to that of the previous chapter on auditing sales and receivables. We will begin by identifying the audit objectives for each of the financial report assertions that applies to the transaction classes mentioned above and to the accounts payable and accrued payroll liability balances. In the rest of the chapter we will follow the audit process — from obtaining the understanding of the internal control structure, through the assessment of the inherent and control risks to the design and execution of substantive procedures.

1 LEARNING OBJECTIVE

Identify the audit objectives applicable to purchases, payables and payroll.

AUDIT OBJECTIVES

The audit objectives for purchases, payables and payroll relate to obtaining sufficient appropriate evidence about each significant financial report assertion for the applicable transactions and balances. Table 11.1 lists the primary objectives for each assertion that apply in most audits of these transactions and balances.

TABLE 11.1 *Selected specific audit objectives for purchases, payables and payroll*

Assertion category	Transaction class audit objectives	Account balance audit objectives
Existence or occurrence	Recorded purchase transactions represent goods and services received during the period under audit (**EO1**). Recorded payment transactions represent payments made during the period to suppliers and creditors (**EO2**). Recorded payroll expenses relate to employee services received in the period (**EO3**).	Recorded accounts payable represent amounts owed by the entity at the balance sheet date (**EO4**). Accrued payroll liability balances represent amounts owed at the balance sheet date (**EO5**).
Completeness	All purchase (**C1**) and payment (**C2**) transactions that occurred during the period have been recorded. Recorded payroll expenses include all such expenses incurred during the year (**C3**).	Accounts payable include all amounts owed by the entity to suppliers of goods and services at the balance sheet date (**C4**). Accrued payroll liabilities include all amounts owed in respect of payroll and deductions therefrom at the balance sheet date (**C5**).
Rights and obligations	Recorded purchase (**R1**) and payroll (**R2**) transactions represent the liabilities of the entity.	Accounts payable (**R3**) and accrued payroll liabilities (**R4**) are liabilities of the entity at the balance sheet date.

Assertion category	Transaction class audit objectives	Account balance audit objectives
Valuation or measurement	Purchase transactions (**VM1**), payment transactions (**VM2**) and payroll transactions (**VM3**) are correctly recorded in the information system.	Accounts payable (**VM4**) and accrued payroll liabilities (**VM5**) are stated at the correct amount owed. Related expense balances conform to applicable Accounting Standards (**VM6**).
Disclosure	The details of purchase (**D1**), payment (**D2**) and payroll (**D3**) transactions support their presentation in the financial report, including their classification and disclosure.	Accounts payable (**D4**), accrued payroll liabilities (**D5**) and related expenses (**D6**) are properly identified and classified in the financial report. Disclosures pertaining to commitments, contingent liabilities and related party creditors are adequate (**D7**).

To achieve each audit objective, the auditor employs a combination of tests of control and substantive procedures (as determined by the audit strategy adopted), following the audit planning and testing methods described in Chapters 5–9. The procedures are much the same as those illustrated for sales and receivables in Chapter 10. Each audit objective is numbered in Table 11.1 (e.g. the first objective is numbered **EO1**). Using this numbering system, we will reference controls and audit procedures described in this chapter to the applicable audit objective.

PURCHASE, PAYMENT AND PAYROLL TRANSACTIONS

2 LEARNING OBJECTIVE

Describe the functions and control procedures normally found in information systems for processing purchase, payment and payroll transactions.

In this section we will describe features of internal control structures typically employed by entities in processing and recording purchase, payment and payroll transactions. We will describe information systems likely to be identified by the auditor in obtaining the understanding of the internal control structure. We will also describe control procedures normally found in such systems, referenced to the assertions and audit objectives (identified in Table 11.1) to which they relate. Identifying the presence of these control procedures and evaluating their design effectiveness enables the auditor to make the preliminary assessment of control risk.

Purchase transactions relate to the purchase (from outside entities) of (1) goods (including inventory, plant and equipment, and supplies) and (2) services (such as the supply of utilities and advertising, and the rent of premises). Payment transactions relate to the payment for such goods and services. In this chapter we will presume that most purchases are on credit and that payment is of balances recorded in the accounts payable ledger. Figure 11.1 presents a flow chart that shows the basic features of manual and computer systems for processing purchase and payment transactions. The flow chart is not intended to show every document, record, process or account involved. We will present more detailed flow charts later in the chapter.

Variations in purchase information systems include the use of either a purchase journal or a voucher register for recording purchases. In this chapter we will assume the use of a purchase journal system. Thus, the key accounting records shown in the flow chart in Figure 11.1 (page 416) are the purchase journal (or purchase day book) for recording purchases and the cash book (or cheque register) for recording payments to suppliers. As with sales transactions, recorded purchases occasionally need to be adjusted to take account of claims for credit in respect of returned goods and invoicing errors. Unlike sales adjustments, the extent of such transactions relating to purchases are rarely material, and in this chapter we do not consider such adjustments as a separate class of transaction.

Payroll relates to payment for the services of employees. Most entities have a detailed information system and related internal control procedures for recording labour services (typically in the form of hours worked) and ensuring that payment is only made to current employees in respect of labour services actually provided.

FIGURE 11.1

Overview flow chart — the processing of purchase and payment transactions

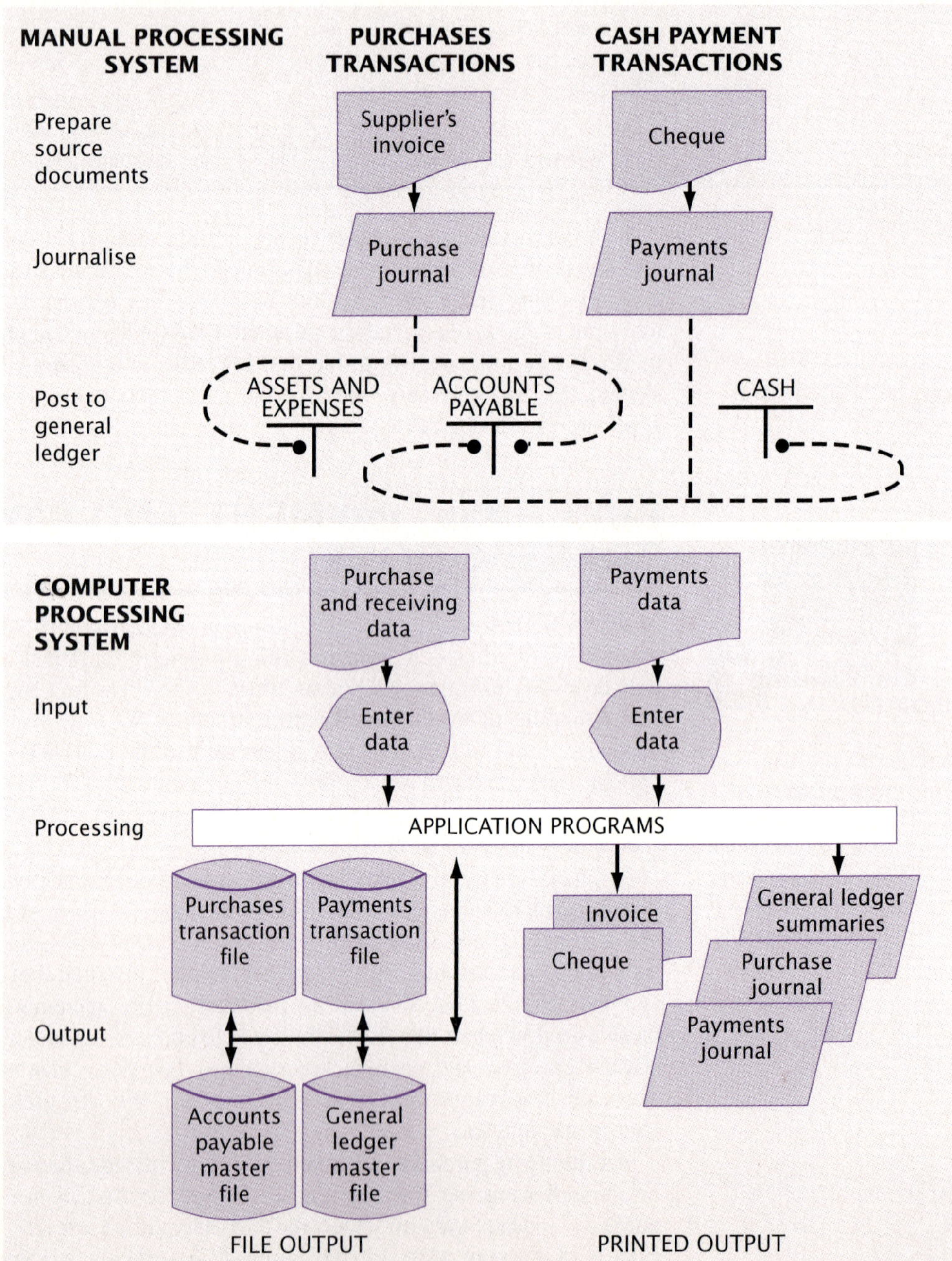

Purchase transactions

We will begin by identifying the separate functions involved in making purchases, the documents and records that are used in processing the transactions, and the control procedures commonly applied to reduce the risk of fraud or error. Among the control activities considered here are information processing controls, the segregation of duties, physical controls and performance reviews.

Functions

The processing of purchase transactions involves the following functions:

- requisitioning goods and services;
- preparing purchase orders;
- receiving the goods;
- storing goods received for inventory;
- checking and approving the supplier's invoice;
- recording the liability.

When practicable, each of these functions should be assigned to a different individual or department. In such cases, the work of one employee or department can provide an independent check on the accuracy of the work of another.

Requisitioning goods and services

Purchase requisitions may originate from stores (the warehouse) for inventory or from any department for other items. For inventory items, computerised inventory records are often programmed to issue requisitions automatically when predetermined re-order levels are reached. For purchases other than inventory replenishment, requisitioning authority is granted to specific individuals. This authority is usually restricted to the value and types of good and service applicable to the individual's function and level of authority. A stationery clerk may requisition sundry stationery supplies, for example, but only the office manager may requisition a photocopier service contract. Special procedures usually apply for requisitioning plant and equipment or for entering into lease contracts.

Purchase requisition forms may be prepared manually or electronically. Manually prepared forms should be signed by a person with the appropriate requisitioning authority. The requisition will normally indicate the general ledger account coding for the purchase, being one over which the person making the requisition has budgetary responsibility.

Purchase requisitions are usually pre-numbered within each originating department as a control over outstanding requisitions to ensure that goods requisitioned are duly ordered and received. The purchase requisition represents the start of the transaction trail of documentary evidence in support of management's assertion as to the occurrence of purchase transactions. Thus, it provides evidence that relates to the specific audit objective coded **EO1** in Table 11.1.

Preparing purchase orders

The purchasing department should issue **purchase orders** only on the receipt of requisitions properly approved by an employee having appropriate requisitioning authority (except for programmed inventory replenishment). Before placing an order, the purchasing department personnel should ascertain the best source of supply and, for major items, should obtain competitive bids.

Segregating requisitioning from ordering achieves two controls. It restricts the opportunity for those making requisitions to issue fraudulent orders, such as for goods for their own use. Purchasing department personnel are less likely to issue improper orders because they do not normally have access to goods delivered. The second control is improved efficiency through the centralisation of purchasing in a specialised department. The purchasing department is better able to negotiate more favourable terms and prices and, by amalgamating orders, can obtain better volume discounts.

Purchase orders should contain a precise description of the goods and services required, quantities, price, delivery instructions and the supplier's name and address. Purchase orders should be pre-numbered and signed by an authorised purchasing officer. The original is sent to the supplier and copies are distributed internally to the receiving department, the accounting department and the requisitioner.

The purchase orders also become part of the transaction trail of documentary evidence that supports the occurrence assertion for purchase transactions (**EO1**). A file of unfilled purchase orders is generally maintained on the computer or as a hard copy. A subsequent independent check on the disposition of purchase orders to determine that the goods and services were received and recorded relates to the completeness assertion for purchase transactions (**C1**).

Receiving the goods

A valid purchase order represents the authorisation for the receiving department to accept goods delivered by suppliers. The quantity ordered is sometimes obliterated to ensure that receiving clerks will make careful counts when the goods are received. Receiving department personnel should compare the goods received with the description of the goods on the purchase order, count the goods and inspect them for damage. Delivery of unordered goods should be refused.

The segregation of receiving from requisitioning and purchase ordering prevents those making requisitions from ordering goods directly from suppliers. It also prevents the purchasing department from gaining access to goods improperly ordered.

A pre-numbered **goods received note** should be prepared for each delivery. In a computer information system, it may be prepared by adding the appropriate receiving data to order details held on file. The goods received note is an important document in supporting the occurrence assertion for purchase transactions (**EO1**). A copy of the goods received note is forwarded to accounts. A subsequent periodic independent check on the sequence of pre-numbered goods received notes (to determine that a supplier's invoice has been recorded for each) relates to the completeness assertion (**C1**).

Storing goods received for inventory

On delivery of the goods to stores or other requisitioning department, receiving clerks should obtain a signed receipt on the copy of the goods received note retained by the receiving department. This provides further evidence for the occurrence assertion for the purchase transaction (**EO1**). The signed receipt also establishes subsequent accountability for the purchased goods. We will consider the physical safekeeping of inventory and the maintenance of records over inventory quantities in Chapter 12.

Checking and approving the supplier's invoice

For goods and services supplied on credit, the supplier is usually instructed by the purchase order to send the invoice directly to the entity's accounting department. Prior to recording **suppliers' invoices**, the department checks and approves them. Procedures applicable to this function include:

- serially numbering suppliers' invoices on receipt so that subsequent checks of numerical continuity can confirm that all invoices are recorded (**C1**);
- establishing the agreement of the details of suppliers' invoices with the related goods received notes and purchase orders to ensure that all invoices relate to valid purchase transactions (**EO1**);
- determining the mathematical accuracy of the suppliers' invoices (**VM1**);

- coding the account distributions on the suppliers' invoices (i.e. indicating the asset and expense accounts to be debited) (**VM1**, **D1**);
- approving the invoices for payment by having an authorised person sign the invoice (**EO1**, **R1**);
- preparing a daily prelist of suppliers' invoices approved for payment (**EO1**, **C1**, **VM1**).

A common practice is to stamp a grid on the supplier's invoice. The grid has boxes in which to record the serial numbers of purchase orders and goods received notes, the account codes and the initials of the clerk performing the check. Invoices, purchase orders and goods received notes are commonly stapled together to support the subsequent payment, then filed by supplier.

Other kinds of supporting documentation (such as copies of contracts) may be required when the invoice relates to certain types of service or to leased assets. In other cases, such as for monthly utility bills, the supplier's invoice alone may suffice because there is no purchase order and goods received note. Other forms of verification will be required, such as a check of utility bills against meter readings recorded in a special register.

Unpaid suppliers' invoices and supporting documentation are held in a file in the accounts department pending their subsequent payment. Properly approved suppliers' invoices provide the basis for recording purchase transactions.

Recording the liability

In manual systems, the approved suppliers' invoices are entered in the **purchase journal**, the monthly totals of which are posted to the accounts payable control account in the general ledger. The approved suppliers' invoices are sent daily, with a prelist, to the accounting department for recording in the **accounts payable ledger**. An accounting supervisor should perform an independent check of the agreement of the total of the invoices recorded by accounting personnel with the daily prelist. Furthermore, a supervisor should check each month that the total of balances on the accounts payable ledger agrees with the control account in the general ledger. A discrepancy will indicate the presence of errors in the recording of suppliers' invoices in either the purchase journal or the accounts payable ledger (**EO1**, **C1**, **VM1**).

In batch processing computer information systems, personnel in the accounts department either send approved suppliers' invoices to the computer department or enter the data via terminals. Programmed edit checks are made for such matters as valid suppliers and the reasonableness of amounts. When the data for a supplier's invoice are accepted by the computer, the **accounts payable master file** for that supplier is updated and the invoice is added to the **purchase transactions file**. Additional controls over the accuracy of the data entry process include the use of batch totals and exception reports (**EO1**, **C1**, **VM1**). The purchase transactions file is used to update the inventory and general ledger master files. The update program produces print-outs of the purchase journal and a general ledger summary showing the amounts posted to general ledger accounts. The print-outs are then sent to accounting. An accounting supervisor determines the agreement of the print-outs with the prelist prepared.

In on-line systems the invoice is entered immediately on receipt, automatically approved by reference to order and receiving details, and coded by reference to information recorded on the order. The accounts payable, inventory and general ledger files are immediately updated. Manual verification is required only if programmed application controls reject the invoice.

Monthly statements received from suppliers should be reconciled with the recorded supplier balances. Periodic performance reviews by management — in the form of comparisons of asset, liability and expense balances with budgeted amounts — can provide a means of both controlling expenditures and detecting misstatements in recorded purchase transactions.

For very small purchases, previously paid for out of petty cash, authorised requisitioners may be supplied with credit cards or purchasing cards (see the 'Professional environment' below). Limits placed on such cards provide a sufficient safeguard against material loss.

PROFESSIONAL ENVIRONMENT **Purchasing card systems**

A purchasing card is an accounts payable mechanism offering predefined cardholder-specific controls on spending and authorisation limits that uses a credit card infrastructure. Designated employees are issued with the purchasing cards and authorised to make purchases directly from the vendors without involving the purchasing department and processing the related paperwork. Vendors generally ship the purchased items directly to the cardholder. The bank sends a monthly statement directly to each cardholder, who is responsible for reviewing, reconciling, and approving the transactions. In turn, these statements are sent to accounts payable, where they are amalgamated and paid using a single cheque or single electronic funds transfer. ...

Purchasing cards are generally used for low-value, high-quantity purchases. ...

The utility of the technology derives partly from the fact that purchasing in companies is typically characterised by an inverse relationship between the volume of transactions and the dollar-size of transactions. ...

Studies suggest that a disproportionate amount of the administrative effort is directed towards only a low portion of the total expenditure. Further, because of the nature of these low-value purchases, companies may acquire a high number of suppliers, many of whom are used infrequently, thus increasing the burden of the maintenance of the supplier database.

Controls

While the purchasing card system bypasses traditional authorisation procedures, it offers management a number of alternative controls. ... Available controls include maximum dollar limits per transaction, maximum monthly transaction dollar limit, specific merchant categories and merchant category groups where the card can be used, time of day and day of week restrictions, specific suppliers where the card can be used and automatic teller machine access. It is these controls which distinguish the purchasing card technology from traditional travel and entertainment (T&E) cards.

(Source: Extracted from Clinton Free, Michael Briers, Wai Fong Chua & Peter Luckett, 'Measuring the Performance Drivers of a Pilot Implementation of a Purchasing Card System', *Australian Accounting Review* (Vol. 9, No. 3, 1999), p. 49)

Illustrative system for purchase transactions

A flow chart of a representative system for processing purchase transactions is shown in Figure 11.2. In this system, the purchasing department prepares purchase orders using on-line terminals. Multi-copy purchase orders are printed and distributed, as shown in the flow chart, and an open purchase order file is maintained on the computer. When goods arrive in the receiving department, a copy of the matching purchase order is pulled from the file. The goods are then counted, inspected and compared against relevant details on the copy of the purchase order. Next, receiving clerks use their computer terminals to retrieve the computer record of the purchase order from the open purchase order file. After a clerk keys in the quantities received, the computer produces a multi-copy goods received note and transfers the record from the open purchase order file to the goods received note file. The copies of the goods received note are distributed as shown in the flow chart.

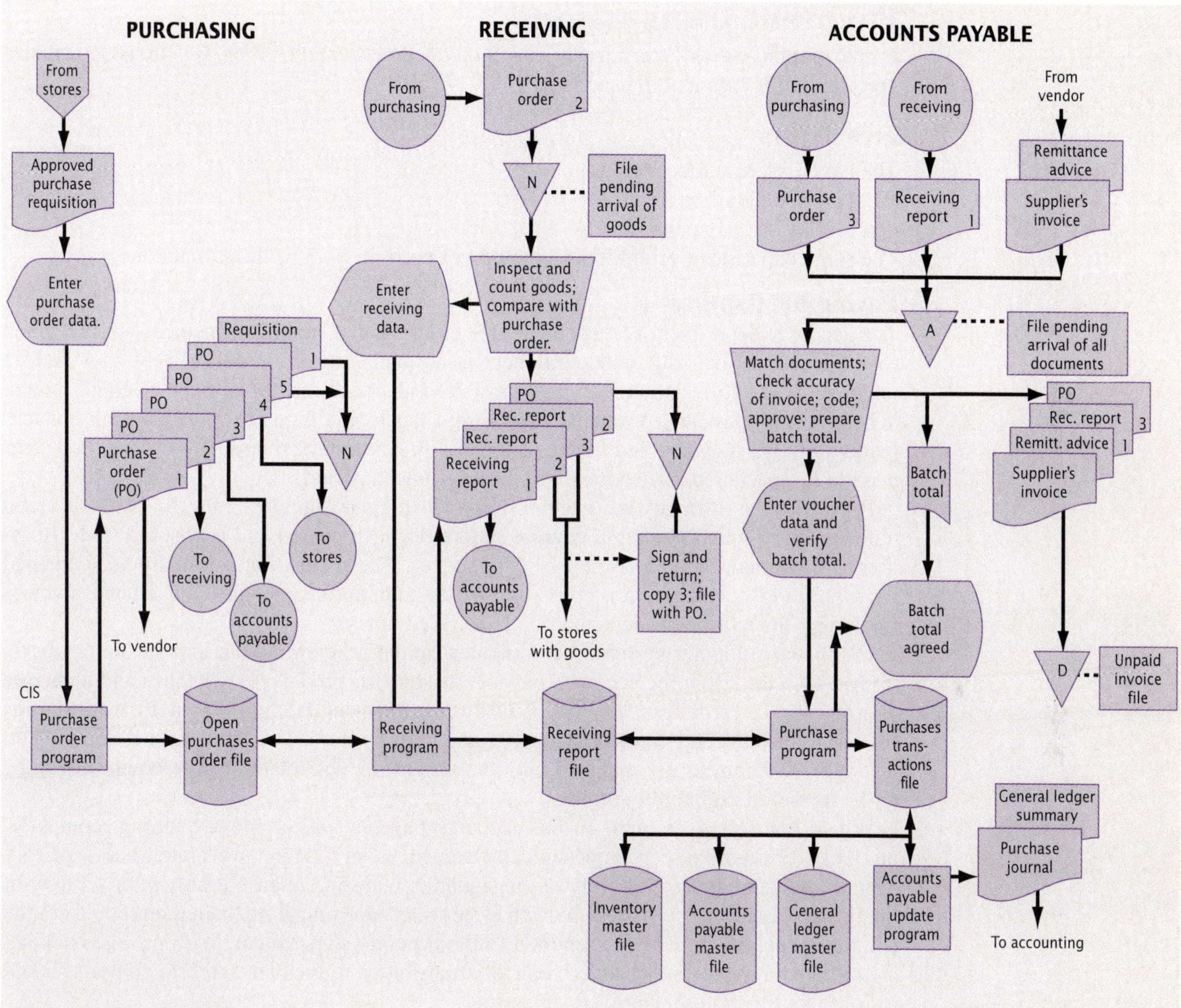

FIGURE 11.2

System flow chart — purchase transactions

Copies of the purchase order and goods received note for each transaction are placed in a holding file in the accounts department pending arrival of the supplier's invoice. Once the supplier's invoice arrives, an accounts clerk checks its mathematical accuracy and compares it with the purchase order and goods received note.

Batches of approved matched documents are assembled and a batch total is calculated manually. Data keyed in from the suppliers' invoices, together with matching data extracted by the computer from the goods received note file, are then used to create the purchase transactions file. The batch total is printed out and compared with the manual batch total in accounts, and any differences are resolved. The unpaid suppliers' invoices are collated with the supporting documents and filed by due date in the accounts department.

The purchase transactions file is subsequently used to update the payables, inventory and general ledger master files. Outputs of that run include a purchase journal listing the newly processed invoices and a general ledger summary showing the totals posted to the general ledger accounts.

Payment transactions

In this section, we will consider the common documents and records, functions and control procedures for payment transactions.

Functions

The two payments functions are:
- paying the liability;
- recording the payments.

The same department or individual should not perform both of these functions.

Paying the liability

The accounts department is responsible for ensuring that suppliers' invoices are processed for payment on their due dates. Payment is normally required within thirty days and, in practice, most entities pay the unpaid payables balance at the end of each calendar month. Where prompt payment discounts are allowed (such as a 2 per cent discount on invoices paid within ten days) — and where it is entity policy to take them up — relevant invoices need to be scheduled for payment within the allowed period.

Payments are normally by cheque, although regular suppliers may be paid by credit transfer. In a manual system, a **cheque requisition** is prepared and forwarded to the treasurer's department for preparation of the cheques. The requisition is usually accompanied by supporting documentation consisting of the supplier's statement and related invoices (including the attached orders and goods received notes).

In a batch computer system, the computer can be programmed to extract the payments due on each day from the accounts payable master file, produce the cheques and a **cheque summary** (or a credit transfer list), and enter the payment data in a **payment transactions file**. The cheques (and credit transfer list) are then forwarded to the accounts department, where they are physically matched with the supporting documents before being forwarded to the treasurer's office for signing.

Where controls over input to the accounts payable master file are strong, computer-produced cheques may be mechanically signed using a signature plate. The signatory should maintain physical custody of the signature plate and release it only after scrutiny of the list of cheques to be signed. In such systems, cheques must be mailed directly from the computer department and not returned to the accounts department. With on-line banking, credit transfer details may be electronically transmitted to the bank. Access controls should restrict this function to approved signatories.

Controls over the preparation and signing of the cheques and related specific audit objectives include the following:
- authorised personnel in the treasurer's department, who otherwise have no responsibility for initiating or processing purchase transactions, should be responsible for signing the cheques (**EO2**);
- authorised cheque signers should determine that each cheque is accompanied by properly approved suppliers' invoices, and that the name of the payee and amount on the cheque agree with details on the invoice (**VM2**);
- the suppliers' invoices and supporting documents should be stamped (or otherwise cancelled) with the date or the cheque number when the cheque is signed to prevent resubmission for duplicate payment (**EO2**);

- the cheque signer should control the mailing of the cheques to reduce the risk of theft or alterations (**EO2**);
- no cheques should be made payable to 'cash' or 'bearer' and no blank cheques should be issued (**EO2**);
- pre-numbered cheques should be used (**C2**);
- access to blank cheques and to signature plates should be limited to authorised personnel (**C2**).

Cheques generally include a perforated attachment known as a **remittance advice** which identifies the serial numbers of the invoice(s) being paid. Alternatively, copies of the supplier's statement or remittance advice provided by the supplier can be enclosed with the cheques mailed to suppliers.

Recording the payments

In manual systems, accounting personnel journalise the payments from the cheques issued to the **payments journal** or the **cheque register**. These personnel should not participate in the execution of purchase transactions such as checking, approving or recording suppliers' invoices, or in the preparation of the cheques. In computer systems, the payment transactions file created when cheques are prepared is used to update the accounts payable master file and general ledger accounts. The update program also produces the payments journal and a general ledger summary, which are forwarded to accounting.

Controls over the recording of payments include:

- an independent check by an accounting supervisor of the agreement of the amounts journalised and posted to the accounts payable ledger with the cheque summary received from the treasurer (**EO2**, **C2**, **VM2**);
- independently prepared bank reconciliations (**EO2**, **C2**, **VM2**).

Payroll transactions

An entity's payroll transactions include salaries, hourly and incentive (piecework) wages, commissions, bonuses and employee benefits (e.g. health insurance, paid holidays and long service leave). In this section we will focus on hourly paid employees. The payroll transactions also record deductions from payroll in determining net pay. These deductions may be statutory (such as taxation) or by agreement (such as employee contributions to a superannuation scheme). Deductions are recorded as liabilities for payment to the appropriate body.

Functions

The relevant functions are those of:

- hiring employees;
- authorising payroll changes;
- preparing attendance and timekeeping data;
- preparing the payroll;
- recording the payroll;
- paying the payroll and protecting unclaimed wages.

Below we will explain each function. Where applicable, we will refer to the flow chart in Figure 11.3, which shows a representative system for processing payroll transactions. In this case, the entity is using on-line entry/on-line processing for payroll authorisation changes and batch entry/batch processing for preparing the payroll.

It is evident from the flow chart that responsibility for executing and recording payroll is spread over several departments. This segregation of duties significantly contributes to reducing the risk of payments to fictitious employees and the risk of excessive payments to actual employees due to inflated rates or hours.

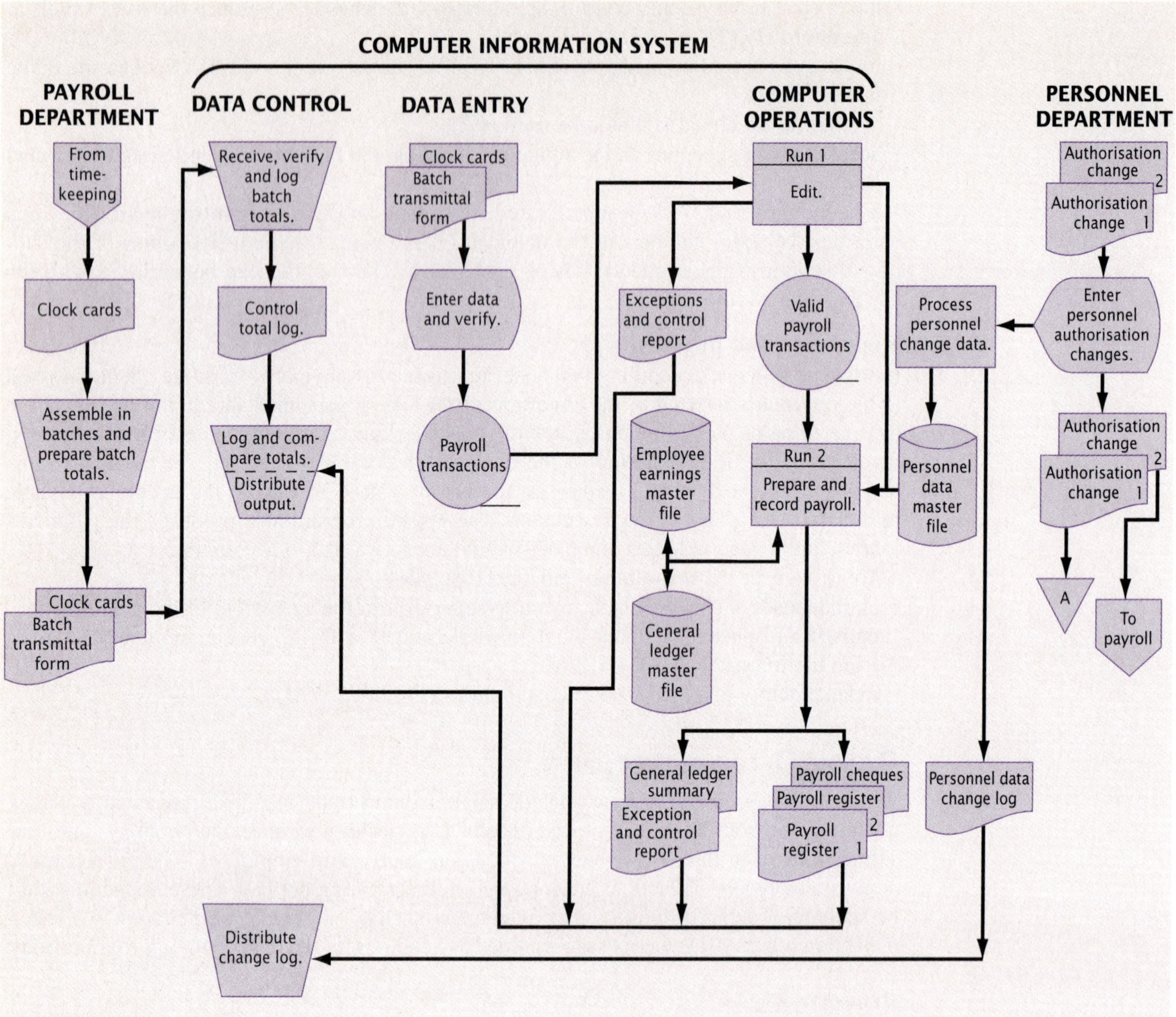

FIGURE 11.3

System flow chart — payroll transactions

Hiring employees

Employees are hired by the personnel department. Details are documented on a **personnel authorisation form** which should indicate the job classification, starting wage rate and authorised payroll deductions. In the system shown in Figure 11.3, data on new employees are entered in the **personnel data master file**. Access to data entry to this file is restricted, by password, to authorised individuals in the personnel department. Periodically, a computer-generated log of all changes to the master file is printed and independently checked by a personnel manager not involved in entering the data into the computer. One copy of the personnel authorisation form is placed in the employee's **personnel file** in the personnel department. Another copy is sent to the payroll department.

Segregating the functions of personnel and payroll reduces the risk of payments to fictitious employees because only the personnel department may add new employees to the personnel master file and only the payroll department may process the payment of wages (**EO3**, **R3**). This segregation of function is also an important control in the next function

— authorising payroll changes. Thus, personnel department employees cannot benefit from falsifying personnel records, while payroll department employees can process payroll only for employees listed in the personnel records and at the wage rates specified therein.

Authorising payroll changes

An employee's supervisor may initiate the request for a change in job classification (or a wage rate increase). However, all changes should be authorised in writing by the personnel department before being entered in the personnel data master file. Other controls over entering the changes in the computer and distributing the change forms are the same as those for new employees. These controls over payroll changes help to ensure the accuracy of the payroll (**R3**, **VM3**).

The personnel department should also issue a **termination notice** on completion of an individual's employment. It is vital that the payroll department is promptly notified of such terminations to prevent payment continuing to be made to employees after they have left (**EO3**).

Preparing attendance and timekeeping data

In many entities, a timekeeping department is responsible for this function for hourly paid employees. Time clocks are frequently used to record time worked. Each employee 'clocks on' and 'clocks off' by inserting a **clock card** or employee badge in the clock. To prevent one employee from 'punching in' for another, the time clock should be located in view of supervisory or security personnel. It may also be used to record direct labour charged to individual jobs within work in progress, thus ensuring the reliability of costing records and inventory valuation.

All time worked that has been recorded on clock cards should be approved in writing by a supervisor, particularly with regard to the authorisation of overtime. The timekeeping department then forwards the clock cards to the payroll department for use in preparing the payroll. These controls ensure that payment is made only for hours worked (**EO3**, **R3**).

Preparing the payroll

Figure 11.3 illustrates typical controls in a basic system for preparing the payroll. Clock cards are batched in the payroll department and a batch total is prepared of hours worked. The documents and a batch transmittal form are then sent to data control in the computer department. Data control verifies the information on the batch transmittal form, enters the batch totals in a control log, and forwards the documents to data entry where they are keyed in to the system. The resulting payroll transactions data are then used in preparing the payroll. In more advanced systems, data on hours worked may be captured directly from time clocks, which are on-line to the computer terminal.

In run 1 (see Figure 11.3), the payroll transactions are subjected to an edit check routine, including a check for a valid employee number and a limit or reasonableness check on the hours worked. The output of this run consists of a valid payroll transactions file and an exceptions and control report that is sent to data control. Data control compares the control totals with the batch control log, informs the payroll department of exceptions discovered by the edit routine, and follows up to see that the payroll department submits corrected data. In the system shown in Figure 11.3, the calculation of the payroll and the preparation of the **payroll register** and payroll cheques occur in run 2. The program uses data from the valid **payroll transactions file**, the personnel data master file and the **employee earnings master file**(s). This run also records the payroll, as we will describe in the next section.

Recording the payroll

Using calculated gross pay, deductions and net pay for each employee from run 2, the program updates the employee earnings master file and accumulates totals for the payroll journal entry that is generated and entered in the general ledger master file at the end of the run. The following printed outputs of this run are sent to data control:

- an exceptions and control report that data control reviews before distributing the other printed output;
- a copy of the payroll register that is returned to the payroll department for comparison with the original batch transmittal data;
- a second copy of the payroll register and pre-numbered payroll cheques that are sent to the treasurer's office (or **pay slips** and a cheque for total net pay if wages are paid in cash);
- a general ledger summary that is sent to accounting, showing the payroll entry generated by the payroll program.

Proper review of each of these outputs by the appropriate personnel contributes to control over misstatements (**EO3**, **C3**, **R2**, **VM3**).

In manual systems, it is common practice for a senior accounting officer to approve the payroll before payroll cheques are prepared. In smaller entities, the authorising officer could verify payroll by reconciling it with the previous period's payroll, allowing for hirings, terminations, changes in hours worked, etc. In any event, the payroll should be independently checked against personnel records at regular intervals.

Paying the payroll and protecting unclaimed wages

These functions are not shown in Figure 11.3. However, in the preceding section we explained that the payroll cheques and a copy of the payroll register are sent to the treasurer's or chief accountant's office where these functions are commonly performed. Applicable controls include the following:

- Treasurer's office personnel should check the agreement of the names and amounts on cheques with payroll register entries (**EO3**, **C3**, **VM3**).
- Payroll cheques should be signed by treasurer's office personnel not involved in preparing or recording the payroll, using cheque-signing machines and signature plates.
- Access to cheque-signing machines and signature plates should be restricted to authorised individuals.
- Payroll cheques should be distributed to employees by treasurer's office personnel not involved in preparing or recording the payroll, who should require proper identification of employees (**EO3**, **VM3**).
- Unclaimed payroll cheques should be stored in a safe or vault in the treasurer's office (**EO3**, **C3**).

Another important control over paying the payroll in many large entities is the use of an imprest payroll bank account on which all payroll cheques are drawn. This account is funded with the amount of net pay. Any errors in preparing payroll cheques or deliberate falsification of payroll cheques would soon be detected because cheques paid in would exceed the account balance, causing the bank to refuse acceptance (**EO3**, **VM3**). Increasingly, entities are paying wages by direct credit transfer to employee bank accounts, eliminating the need for cheques and the associated risks of their misuse.

Some entities pay wages in cash. The payroll system is designed to produce pay slips instead of pay cheques, and a single cheque is produced for the total net pay. The exact amount of cash should be drawn from the bank, and the pay envelopes should be filled and distributed by authorised treasurer's office personnel not involved in preparing or recording the payroll. A preferred system is to arrange for a security company to collect the cash from the bank and make up the pay envelopes, which are then delivered to the entity ready for distribution. Unclaimed wage packets should be returned immediately to a safe in the accounting office and recorded in an unclaimed wages book. If unclaimed by the end of the day, the wages should be rebanked.

LEARNING CHECK

11.1 Purchasing involves the functions of:
- requisitioning;
- storing goods;
- ordering;
- approving the invoice;
- receiving;
- recording the liability.

An important control is the segregation of each of these functions.

11.2 In manual systems, the cheque signer should verify supporting documents and cancel them to prevent reuse. In computer systems, reliance may be placed on controls over the existence of liabilities entered in the accounts payable master file. Cheques are produced by the computer and mechanically signed. It is vital that cheques are not returned to the purchasing and accounts departments.

11.3 Payroll transactions involve the functions of:
- hiring;
- preparing the payroll;
- authorising changes;
- recording the payroll;
- timekeeping;
- distributing pay.

It is important to segregate the personnel functions of hiring and authorising changes from all other payroll functions.

11.4 The greatest risk is of payments to fictitious employees, either through the entry of details of fictitious employees in the records or through the failure to remove details of employees who have left.

DEVELOPING THE AUDIT PLAN

In the previous section, we illustrated features of the internal control structure relating to purchase, payment and payroll transactions typically identified and recorded by the auditor in obtaining the understanding as required by AUS 402, Risk Assessments and Internal Controls (ISA 400, Risk Assessments and Internal Control). The next phase of the audit is to assess inherent and control risk to determine the appropriate level of detection risk for each major assertion. This phase commences with the auditor considering materiality and inherent risk and making a preliminary assessment of control risk based mainly on testing the design effectiveness of the internal control structure. This enables the auditor to determine the audit strategy and to plan an appropriate mix of tests of control and substantive procedures. Tests of control confirm (or otherwise) the auditor's preliminary assessment of control risk by testing operating effectiveness. Results of the tests of control may require a reassessment of control risk and a revision of the planned level of substantive procedures.

LEARNING OBJECTIVE 3

Apply the concepts of materiality and inherent risk to the audit of purchases, payables and payroll.

Audit strategy considerations

As we explained in Chapter 5, materiality relates to the relative importance of the separate financial report components. An assessment of materiality, combined with a consideration of the nature of inherent risk and control risk, enables the auditor to determine an appropriate audit strategy for each financial report assertion.

Materiality

Purchase and payroll transactions account for the major expenses incurred by a business, so are a major component in the determination of net profit. They also relate to the acquisition of major classes of asset (notably, inventories and plant and equipment), which are also individually material. Moreover, the balance on accounts payable produced by credit purchase transactions is nearly always material to the balance sheet. Thus, the auditor seeks to achieve a low level of risk that errors in purchase and payroll transactions could cause material misstatements in the financial report.

Inherent and control risks

In assessing inherent risk for purchase and payroll assertions, the auditor should consider pervasive factors that could motivate management to misstate expenditure. These may include:

- pressures to understate expenses in order to report, falsely, the achievement of announced profitability targets or industry norms;
- pressures to understate payables in order to report a higher level of working capital in the face of liquidity problems or going-concern doubts.

These factors primarily affect the completeness assertion and reduce the acceptable detection risk, particularly in testing for understatement of liabilities. Other factors that may contribute to misstatements include:

- the high volume of transactions, which affects all assertions;
- temptations for employees to make unauthorised purchases and payments, or to misappropriate purchased assets, which relate to the occurrence assertion;
- contentious accounting issues such as whether a cost should be capitalised or expensed (for example, the treatment of repairs and maintenance costs or the classification of a lease as an operating or finance lease), which relate to the valuation assertion;
- the complexity of payroll computations for factory workers whose gross earnings may be based on time and/or productivity, affecting the measurement of payroll costs.

Payroll fraud is a major concern for the auditor. Employees involved in preparing and paying the payroll may process data for fictitious employees or for employees whose services have already been terminated, and then divert the wages for their own use. This affects the auditor's assessment of risk for the occurrence assertion for payroll.

In most well-established entities, management's own risk assessment procedures will have led it to adopt control procedures to reduce the risk of misstatements occurring in the processing and recording of transactions. However, the existence and effectiveness of controls pertaining to different transaction class assertions for purchases, payments and payroll can vary considerably among entities and even among assertions for the same entity. Moreover, the auditor must remain mindful of the inherent limitations of internal control, including the possibility of management override, collusion, errors due to fatigue or misunderstanding, and failure to adapt the control structure for changed circumstances.

4 LEARNING OBJECTIVE

Discuss considerations relevant to determining the audit strategy for purchases, payables and payroll.

Audit strategy

The high volume of transactions, combined with the likely existence of effective control procedures over these transactions, means that it is normally appropriate to adopt an approach based on a lower assessed level of control risk, particularly in respect to the occurrence and measurement assertions. For other assertions, the audit strategy may vary with the preliminary assessment of control risk. The volume of transactions, however, means that the lower assessed level of control risk approach is preferred wherever the assessment of risk can support such a strategy.

Control environment

Factors relating to the control environment that the auditor needs to consider when assessing control risk for purchase, payment and payroll transactions include those described below:

- *Integrity and ethical values* are important because there are numerous opportunities for employee fraud in processing purchase, payment and payroll transactions, and for fraudulent financial reporting by management of expense account balances. Purchasing agents may be subjected to pressures from solicitous suppliers, for example, including offers of 'kickbacks' for transacting more business with those suppliers.
- Management's *commitment to competence* should be reflected in the assignment and training of personnel involved in processing purchasing, payment and payroll transactions. In particular, individuals involved in payroll functions should be knowledgeable about employment laws and regulations, and the applicable provisions of labour contracts.
- The entity's *organisational structure* and management's *assignment of authority and responsibility* over purchase, payment and payroll transactions should be clearly communicated and provide for clear lines of authority, responsibility and reporting relationships. As an example, purchasing, receiving, and stores or warehousing activities may fall under the duties of the production director; accounting may be the responsibility of the finance director; and payments may be supervised by the treasurer. Overall responsibility for personnel matters is often assigned to a director or manager of human or personnel resources. Officers' salaries and other forms of compensation are usually set by the board of directors.

5 LEARNING OBJECTIVE

Design and execute tests of control over purchase, payment and payroll transactions to assess control risk.

Assessment of control risk

Assessment of control risk is normally undertaken in two phases. On obtaining the understanding of the internal control structure, the auditor will normally test the design effectiveness of controls and form a preliminary assessment. Where the design effectiveness of control risk is assessed as being less than high, tests of the operating effectiveness of controls will be included in the audit program to confirm the preliminary assessment. Tests of control for each of the three transaction classes are described below and on pages 430–4.

Purchase transactions

Table 11.2 on the following page contains a partial listing of potential misstatements, necessary controls, potential tests of the operating effectiveness of those controls, and the specific transaction class audit objective for purchases to which each belongs.

Preliminary assessment — design effectiveness

The potential misstatements and necessary controls listed in Table 11.2 form the basis of internal control evaluation check lists. As we explained in Chapter 10 on sales and receivables, the auditor applies this check list to the documented information system and reaches a conclusion as to the effectiveness of controls relative to each potential misstatement. The basis for this conclusion is normally explained on the check list, which thus forms part of the necessary documentation of the assessment of control risk as being less than high. Where the auditor's understanding of the system is obtained and recorded by means of internal control questionnaires, this process simultaneously assesses and documents control effectiveness. Where controls over a particular assertion are judged to be effective, the auditor will incorporate necessary tests of operating effectiveness in drawing up the audit program.

TABLE 11.2 *Control risk assessment considerations — purchase transactions*

Function	Potential misstatement	Necessary control	Possible test of operating effectiveness	Relevant transaction class audit objective (from Table 11.1)				
				EO1	C1	R1	VM1	D1
Requisitioning goods and services	Goods may be requisitioned for unauthorised purposes.	General and specific authorisation procedures	Inquire about procedures.	✓				
Preparing purchase orders	Purchases may be made for unauthorised purposes.	Approved purchase requisition for each order	Examine purchase orders for approved requisitions.	✓				
Receiving goods	Goods received may not have been ordered.	Approved purchase order for each shipment	Examine goods received note for matching purchase order.	✓				
	Incorrect quantities, damaged goods or incorrect items may be received.	Receiving clerks to count, inspect and compare goods received with purchase order	Observe the performance by receiving clerks.	✓				
Storing goods received for inventory	Stores clerks may deny taking custody of purchased goods.	Signed receipt to be obtained on delivery of goods from receiving to stores	Inspect signed receipts.	✓				
Approving the invoice	Invoices may be recorded for goods not ordered.	Matching of purchase order and goods received note with the supplier's invoice	Examine supporting documentation for invoices.*	✓	✓	✓	✓	✓
Recording the liability	Invoices may be recorded incorrectly or not recorded.	Independent check of agreement of prelist against amounts recorded in purchase journal	Examine evidence of independent check; reperform independent check.*	✓	✓		✓	✓
		Periodic accounting for pre-numbered goods received notes and purchase orders	Observe procedure; reperform.		✓			
		Periodic performance reviews by management of reports, comparing actual asset, payable and expense balances with budgeted amounts	Inquire of management about results of performance reviews; inspect reports.*	✓	✓	✓	✓	✓

* Sometimes performed as a part of dual-purpose tests.

Tests of operating effectiveness

The extent of tests of the operating effectiveness of controls will vary inversely with the auditor's preliminary assessment of control risk. Statistical or non-statistical attribute sampling procedures (see Chapter 8) may be applicable to certain tests. Recall that the direction of testing must be compatible with the specific audit objective to which the test relates — vouching for occurrence and tracing for completeness. Evidence applicable to other assertion categories can be obtained from testing in either direction. Also, recall that some tests, particularly those pertaining to checking and approving suppliers' invoices and recording the liability, may be performed as dual-purpose tests. In these tests, evidence is obtained about the effects (measured in dollars) of processing errors on account balances, as well as about the frequency of deviations from controls. These tests are marked with an asterisk in Table 11.2. Based on the evidence obtained from procedures to obtain an understanding of the internal control structure and related tests of control, the auditor makes and documents a final assessment of control risk for each significant assertion related to purchase transactions.

When the processing of purchase transactions is computer assisted, the auditor may use the computer in performing tests of control, using techniques similar to those described for sales transactions in Chapter 10. In particular, tests of effectiveness must be performed for any controls that serve as the basis for a control risk assessment at a reduced level. This includes making inquiries and inspecting documentation concerning general controls over changes to programs and master files used in processing purchase transactions.

Tests of application controls may include the use of test data to determine whether expected results are produced by the entity's program for accepting and recording data for unpaid suppliers' invoices in circumstances such as the following:

- a missing or invalid supplier number;
- a missing or invalid account classification code number;
- a missing or unreasonable amount;
- a missing due date or payment terms;
- alphabetical characters in a numeric field.

Examples of other possible computer-assisted audit tests are:

- using generalised audit software or a database program to perform sequence checks and print lists of purchase orders, goods received notes or invoices whose numbers are missing in designated computer files;
- designing, selecting and evaluating an attribute sample of goods received notes or unpaid invoices.

Payment transactions

Table 11.3 contains a partial listing of potential misstatements, necessary controls, possible tests of the operating effectiveness of those controls, and the specific transaction class audit objective for payments to which each belongs. As explained for purchases, the potential misstatements and necessary controls would be the basis of a check list used to assess design effectiveness. Similarly, an audit program for tests of the operating effectiveness of controls for payment transactions can be prepared, based on the potential tests of control in Table 11.3. Possible computer-assisted tests of control are also similar to those for purchase transactions. Thus, for example, test data can be used to test programmed controls pertaining to the preparation and recording of cheques. Computer assistance can also be used to design, select and evaluate an attribute sample for payments.

TABLE 11.3 *Control risk assessment considerations — payment transactions*

Function	Potential misstatement	Necessary control	Possible test of operating effectiveness	Relevant transaction class audit objective (from Table 11.1)				
				EO2	C2	R2	VM2	D2
Paying the liability	Cheques may be issued for unauthorised purchases.	Cheque signers to review supporting documentation for completeness and approval	Observe cheque signers performing independent check of supporting documentation.	✓		✓		
	An invoice may be paid twice.	'Paid' stamp to be placed on the invoice and supporting documents when a cheque is issued	Examine paid invoices for 'paid' stamp.	✓				
	A cheque may be altered after being signed.	Cheque signers to mail cheques	Inquire about mailing procedures; observe mailing.				✓	
Recording the payment	A cheque may not be recorded.	Use of, and accounting for, pre-numbered cheques	Examine evidence of use of and accounting for pre-numbered cheques.		✓		✓	
	Errors may be made in recording cheques.	Independent check of agreement of the amounts journalised and posted with the cheque summary	Observe procedure; reperform.*	✓	✓		✓	
		Periodic independent bank reconciliations	Examine bank reconciliations.*	✓	✓		✓	✓
	Cheques may not be recorded promptly.	Independent check of dates on cheques with dates recorded	Reperform independent check.	✓	✓			

* Sometimes performed as a part of dual-purpose tests.

Payroll transactions

The process of assessing the control risk for payroll transactions begins, as for purchases and payments, with identifying potential misstatements and necessary controls. These steps are shown in the second and third columns of Table 11.4; possible tests of control are shown in the fourth column.

In computer information systems (CIS), access controls over changes to personnel data are important. In the testing of controls in a CIS, test data can be used to test programmed controls pertaining to the preparation and recording of payroll. Where time recording is computerised, test data can also be used in testing programmed controls over time-keeping.

TABLE 11.4 *Control risk assessment considerations — payroll transactions*

Function	Potential misstatement	Necessary control	Possible test of operating effectiveness	Relevant transaction class audit objective (from Table 11.1)				
				EO3	C3	R3	VM3	D3
Hiring employees	Fictitious employees may be added to the payroll.	Personnel department authorisation for all new hires	Examine authorisation forms for new hires.	✓		✓		
Authorising payroll changes	Employees may receive unauthorised rate increases.	Personnel department authorisation for all rate changes	Inquire about procedures for authorising rate changes.			✓	✓	
	Terminated employees may remain on the payroll.	Personnel department notification to payroll department of all terminations	Examine termination notices in payroll department.	✓				
Preparing attendance and timekeeping data	Employees may be paid for hours not worked.	Use of time clock procedures and supervisory approval of time tickets	Observe time clock procedures; examine time tickets for supervisory approval	✓	✓		✓	✓
Preparing the payroll	Payroll data may be lost during submission to computer department.	Batch totals of hours worked prepared by payroll department and verified by data control	Examine evidence of the preparation and use of batch totals.		✓			
	Payroll transactions file may include incorrectly keyed or invalid data.	Edit checks of data on payroll transactions file	Observe data entry procedures; examine the exceptions and control report.*	✓	✓		✓	✓
Recording the payroll	Processing errors may occur in recording the payroll.	Exceptions and control report to be reviewed by data control	Inquire about the preparation and use of the exceptions and control report.*	✓	✓	✓	✓	✓
	Unauthorised changes may be made to payroll data in computer department.	Payroll department comparison of payroll register with original batch transmittal data	Reperform comparison.*	✓	✓	✓	✓	✓
Paying the payroll and protecting unclaimed wages	Payroll cheques may be distributed to unauthorised recipients.	Employee identification on distribution	Witness distribution of payroll.	✓	✓	✓	✓	✓

*Sometimes performed as a part of dual-purpose tests.

In assessing control risk, the auditor realises that misstatements in payroll may result from unintentional errors or fraud. Of particular concern is the risk of overstatement of payroll through:

- payments to fictitious employees;
- payments to actual employees for hours not worked;
- payments to actual employees at higher than authorised rates.

The first two risks relate to the occurrence assertion. The third risk relates to the measurement assertion.

The risk of understatement (the completeness assertion) is of minimal concern because employees will complain when they are underpaid. Accordingly, many tests of payroll controls are directed at controls that prevent or detect overstatements. The direction of testing for these controls is from the recorded payroll data to source documents; for example, the auditor may vouch data for a sample of employees in a payroll register to approved clock card data and authorised pay rates and deductions.

Two tests of control pertaining to the control risk for the occurrence assertion are the test for terminated employees and witnessing a payroll distribution. The former represents an exception to the normal direction of testing for payroll, in that the auditor selects a sample of termination notices and scans subsequent payroll registers to determine that the terminated employees did not continue to receive pay cheques. In witnessing the distribution of payroll cheques or envelopes, the auditor observes that:

- segregation of duties exists between the preparation and payment of the payroll;
- each employee is identified by a badge or employee identification card;
- each employee receives only one cheque or pay envelope;
- there is proper control and disposal of unclaimed wages.

Final assessment

Based on the evidence obtained from the procedures to obtain an understanding of the internal control structure and related tests of control, the auditor makes a final assessment of inherent risk and control risk. For each significant audit objective where assessment of risk as being less than high is used as the basis for adopting a lower assessed level of control risk audit strategy, the auditor must document reasons for this assessment. This assessment enables the auditor to confirm the level of substantive procedures to be performed. The auditor must ensure that control deviations are properly identified and that their implications for the assessment of control risk are properly considered as to whether further substantive procedures need to be performed.

SUBSTANTIVE PROCEDURES

Accounts payable is usually the largest current liability in a balance sheet and a significant factor in the evaluation of an entity's short-term solvency. Like receivables, it is affected by a high volume of transactions and thus is susceptible to misstatements. However, whereas with receivables the auditor is concerned with overstatement, understatement is the greatest risk with payables. The reason is that management, if motivated to misrepresent payables, would be likely to understate them in order to report a more favourable financial position. Compared with the audit of asset balances, the audit of payables places more emphasis on gathering evidence about the completeness assertion than the existence assertion. Here, we will focus on accounts payable arising from purchase transactions and payroll liabilities arising from payroll transactions.

6

LEARNING OBJECTIVE

Indicate the factors relevant to determining an acceptable level of detection risk for the audit of purchases, payables and payroll.

Determining detection risk

Accounts payable is affected by purchase transactions that increase the account balance and payment transactions that decrease the balance. Thus, detection risk for creditor assertions is affected by the inherent and control risk factors related to both of these transaction classes. The auditor uses the methodology explained in Chapter 9 for combining control risk assessments for transaction class assessments to arrive at control risk assessments for payables balance assertions. The auditor then uses this methodology, involving the audit risk model or a risk matrix, to determine acceptable levels of detection risk in planning the audit. The application of this process for accounts payable is summarised in Table 11.5. The risk levels specified in this matrix are only illustrative and would vary based on the entity's circumstances. Furthermore, note that the acceptable detection risk levels shown in Table 11.5 indicate the need for more persuasive evidence for the completeness, and valuation or measurement assertions than for the other assertions.

TABLE 11.5 *Correlation of risk components — accounts payable*

Risk component	Existence or occurrence	Completeness	Rights and obligations	Valuation or measurement	Disclosure
Audit risk	Low	Low	Low	Low	Low
Inherent risk	Moderate	High	Moderate	High	Low
Control risk — purchase transactions	Low	High	Moderate	High	Moderate
Control risk — payments	Moderate	Low	Low	Low	Low
Combined control risk[1]	Low	High	Moderate	High	Moderate
Acceptable detection risk[2]	High	Low	Moderate	Low	High

1. This is the most conservative (highest) of transaction class control risk assessments used as the combined risk assessment as per the method discussed in Chapter 9 on page 337.
2. Determined from risk components matrix shown in Table 5.2 (page 177), based on the levels of audit risk, inherent risk and combined control risk indicated above for each assertion category.

As we noted above, payroll is subject to high inherent risks for the occurrence and measurement assertions. For this reason, however, controls are usually effective and control risk is low. Substantive procedures for payroll balances are often limited to the application of analytical procedures to the expense accounts and related accruals, and limited tests of details.

LEARNING OBJECTIVE 7

Design a substantive audit program for purchases, payables and payroll.

Designing substantive procedures

The general framework for developing audit programs for substantive procedures that we explained in Chapter 9 and illustrated in Chapter 10 for receivables can also be used in designing substantive procedures for payables and payroll liabilities. Table 11.6 lists possible substantive procedures in an audit program developed on this basis. Note that each test in the table is linked to one or more of the specific account balance audit objectives from Table 11.1. Also note that multiple procedures are keyed to each account balance audit objective.

We will explain each of the procedures in a following section, including comments on how some tests can be tailored based on the acceptable level of detection risk to be achieved.

TABLE 11.6 *Possible substantive procedures for payables assertions*

		Account balance audit objective (from Table 11.1)				
Category	**Substantive procedure**	**EO4**	**C4**	**R4**	**M4**	**D#**
Initial procedures	1. Perform initial procedures on payables balances and records that will be subjected to further testing. (a) Trace the opening balance for payables to prior year's working papers. (b) Review activity in the general ledger account for payables, and investigate entries that appear unusual in amount or source. (c) Obtain a listing of accounts payable at the balance sheet date and determine that it accurately represents the underlying accounting records by: • adding the listing and determining agreement with the total of the subsidiary ledger, or the accounts payable master file and the general ledger control account balance; • testing the agreement of suppliers and balances on the listing with those included in the underlying accounting records.				✓	
Analytical procedures	2. Perform analytical procedures. (a) Determine expectations. (b) Compare current and prior year balances. (c) Compute significant ratios such as: • gross profit; • accounts payable turnover. (d) Obtain explanations for unexpected changes. (e) Corroborate explanations.	✓	✓		✓	
Tests of details of transactions	3. Vouch a sample of recorded creditor transactions to supporting documentation. (a) Vouch credits to supporting suppliers' invoices, goods received notes and purchase orders or other supporting documents. (b) Vouch debits to payments. 4. Perform purchases cut-off test.	✓	✓	✓	✓	✓4
	(a) Select a sample of recorded purchase transactions from several days before and after the year end and examine supporting vouchers, suppliers' invoices and goods received notes to determine that purchases were recorded in the proper period; or (b) Observe the number of the last goods received note issued on the last business day of the audit period, and trace a sample of lower and higher numbered goods received notes to related purchase documents to determine whether transactions were recorded in the proper period.	✓	✓			

Category	Substantive procedure	Account balance audit objective: EO4	C4	RO4	VM4	D#
	(c) Examine subsequent payments between the balance sheet date and the end of fieldwork and, when related documentation indicates the payment was for an obligation in existence at the balance sheet date, trace to the accounts payable listing. (d) Investigate unmatched purchase orders, goods received notes and suppliers' invoices at the year end.					
	5. Perform payments cut-off test by tracing dates cheques were presented for payment on the subsequent period's bank statement to dates recorded.	✓	✓			
Tests of details of balances	6. Reconcile accounts payable to monthly statements received by the entity from suppliers. (a) Identify major suppliers by reviewing the accounts payable ledger or the accounts payable master file. (b) Investigate and reconcile differences.	✓	✓		✓	
	7. Confirm payables with major suppliers whose monthly statements are unavailable.	✓	✓	✓	✓	✓4
	8. Perform a search for unrecorded liabilities. (a) Investigate differences identified by analytical procedures. (b) Review agreements and long-term contracts entered into that require periodic payments for evidence of unrecorded liabilities.		✓			
	9. Recalculate accrued payroll liabilities.				✓	
	10. Verify directors' and officers' remuneration.	✓	✓	✓	✓	✓6
Disclosure	11. Compare financial report presentation with applicable regulations and Accounting Standards. (a) Determine that payables are properly identified and classified as to type and expected period of payment. (b) Determine whether there are debit balances that are significant in the aggregate and that should be reclassified. (c) Determine the appropriateness of disclosures pertaining to related party payables. (d) Inquire of management about existence of undisclosed commitments or contingent liabilities.				✓	✓4, 7

Initial procedures

The starting point for verifying accounts payable is to:

- trace the opening balance to the prior year's working papers, when applicable;
- review activity in the general ledger account for any unusual entries;
- obtain a listing of amounts owed at the balance sheet date.

Usually the listing is prepared by the entity from the accounts payable ledger. The auditor must verify the mathematical accuracy of the listing by adding the total and verifying that it agrees with the underlying accounting records and the general ledger control account balance. In addition, the auditor selectively compares details for suppliers and amounts on the listing with the underlying records to determine that it is an accurate representation of the records from which it was prepared.

Analytical procedures

Tests of details are usually planned on the basis that the analytical procedures confirm expectations. It is preferable to perform analytical procedures early in the final audit so the auditor can determine any necessary changes to tests of details prior to commencing that part of the audit.

As we explained in the case of receivables in Chapter 10, the first stage in applying analytical procedures is to review the understanding of the entity obtained during the planning phase as to whether any changes to payables balances are to be expected. The second stage is to identify absolute changes in amounts between this year and prior years. This is normally done in the course of preparing the lead schedule for payables and payroll balances, as we explained in Chapter 6. The third stage involves the use of more sophisticated relationships such as ratios and trends. As with receivables, the gross profit ratio is important. If it is higher than expected, then one explanation could be an understatement of purchases (such as by a deliberate cut-off error) in order to boost revenues.

Analysis of expense accounts is also important. The auditor usually undertakes this analysis by comparing the ratio of each expense to sales in the current and previous years. In this way, the effect of changes in the level of activity is largely eliminated. An unusually low expense account may indicate unrecorded liabilities such as through cut-off error; for example, if the final quarter's electricity account has neither been paid nor accrued for, then the current year's electricity expense would appear unusually low compared with that for the previous year. Wherever a change in relationships cannot be readily explained, the auditor must seek an explanation from management and corroborate it, usually by conducting additional tests of details.

Analytical procedures are significant in achieving the desired level of detection risk for payroll balances. Particularly useful ratios are those of the average wages per employee, which should not be dissimilar from prior years, subject only to known wage rises, and payroll expenses as a percentage of sales.

Tests of details of transactions

As we explained in Chapter 10 in the case of receivables, balances affected by numerous transactions are more efficiently verified by tests of the closing balance and not of the transactions making up that balance. In the main, the auditor will perform the tests of details of transactions during the interim audit, commonly in the form of dual-purpose tests. For this reason, no substantive tests of details of payroll transactions are described here, because the tests of control described earlier also constitute the primary sources of substantive evidence for payroll transactions. The cut-off tests that we will describe in subsequent sections are always performed as part of year-end work and, although tests of transactions, they serve to verify the recorded balance at balance sheet date.

Vouching recorded payables to supporting documentation

The emphasis of these tests is on vouching purchase transactions to supporting documentation in the entity's files (such as purchase orders, goods received notes and suppliers' invoices) to verify their occurrence as legitimate transactions. It is equally important, however, to test the numerical continuity of purchase orders and goods received notes, and to trace them to suppliers' invoices and accounts payable to verify completeness.

Performing purchases cut-off test

The **purchases cut-off test** involves determining that purchase transactions occurring near the balance sheet date are recorded in the proper period. Most entities hold their books open for a certain period to ensure that purchase transactions are recorded in the correct accounting period. When the books are closed, unmatched goods received notes and purchase orders are scrutinised and, if they relate to the current period, they are recorded by way of journal entry. Unlike receivables, transactions occurring before the balance sheet date may take several weeks before all are invoiced by the suppliers. Because cut-off is significant only at the balance sheet date, most entities do not have effective controls to ensure an accurate distinction between the recording of transactions before and after that date. Acceptable detection risk is likely to be low, and extensive tests of details will be performed. The emphasis is on completeness, which is achieved by tracing goods received notes issued in the days immediately prior to the balance sheet date to purchase journal entries or to the closing journal entry of purchase accruals. This procedure provides evidence that they are recorded in the current accounting period.

Because many purchases do not result in the issue of a goods received note (such as services), after-balance date purchases are vouched to supporting documentation to ensure that they do not relate to goods or services received prior to balance sheet date.

Although the emphasis of the test is on completeness, the auditor also traces some goods received notes issued after the year end to suppliers' invoices, to ensure that they are recorded in the subsequent period's purchase journal. In addition, he or she vouches recorded purchases prior to the balance sheet date to goods received notes dated prior to the balance sheet date, to ensure that no transactions that occurred after the period are recorded prior to the balance sheet date. This provides evidence as to the occurrence assertion. These tests usually cover a period of five to ten business days before the balance sheet date and as long after as appears necessary. In performing this test, the auditor should determine that a proper cut-off is achieved at physical inventory (as we will explain in Chapter 12) as well as in the recording of the purchase transactions. Where inventory is counted other than at the balance sheet date, the auditor needs to check cut-off for purchases of inventory at the physical inventory date as well as at the balance sheet date.

Performing payments cut-off test

A proper cut-off of payment transactions at the year end is essential to the correct presentation of cash and accounts payable at the balance sheet date. The usual method of verifying payments cut-off is to examine the date of presentation of cheques unpresented as at balance sheet date. This test is normally performed as part of the test of the bank reconciliation and the use of the subsequent period's bank statement (see Chapter 13).

Tests of details of balances

The three tests included in this category for payables are:

- reconciling payables to monthly statements received by the entity from suppliers;
- confirming accounts payable;
- searching for unrecorded liabilities.

The two tests for payroll balances are:

- recalculating payroll liabilities;
- verifying directors' and executive officers' remuneration.

8 LEARNING OBJECTIVE

Explain the use of suppliers' statements in verifying the completeness of recorded liabilities.

Reconciling payables with suppliers' statements

In many cases, suppliers provide monthly statements that are available in entity files. As documentary evidence originating outside the entity, suppliers' statements provide reliable evidence as to suppliers' balances. However, because they are obtained from the entity, the auditor needs to be cautious that the statements have not been altered. The auditor should not rely on photocopies and faxed statements. Where there is doubt, he or she should request a copy directly from the supplier or confirm the balance directly with the supplier.

In the selection of accounts for testing, the criterion should be the volume of business during the year, not the balance shown in the entity's accounts payable listing, because the prime concern is that the recorded balance may be understated.

Discrepancies between suppliers' statements and the entity's accounts payable ledger need to be investigated. Most differences are likely to be due to goods and cash in transit and to disputed amounts. This procedure provides evidence as to the existence, completeness and valuation assertions.

Confirming accounts payable

Unlike the confirmation of receivables, the **confirmation of accounts payable** is performed less frequently because:

- confirmation offers no assurance that unrecorded liabilities will be discovered;
- external evidence in the form of invoices and suppliers' monthly statements should be available to substantiate the balances.

Confirmation of accounts payable is recommended (1) when detection risk is low and (2) for suppliers with which the entity undertook a substantial level of business during the current or prior years and that do not issue monthly statements, and for suppliers for which the statement at the balance sheet date is unexpectedly unavailable.

As in the case of confirming receivables, the auditor must control the preparation and mailing of the requests and should receive the responses directly from the supplier. The auditor should use the positive form in making the confirmation request, as illustrated in Figure 11.4. Note that the confirmation does not specify the amount due. In confirming a creditor, the auditor prefers to have the creditor indicate the amount due because that is the amount to be reconciled to the entity's records. Information is also requested regarding purchase commitments of the entity and any collateral for the amount due. This test produces evidence for all assertions relating to payables. However, the evidence provided about the completeness assertion is only limited, given the possible failure to identify and send confirmation requests to suppliers with which the entity has unrecorded obligations.

FIGURE 11.4

Accounts payable confirmation

PO Box 1777
Habitat
Homeland

4 January 20X2

Supplier Limited
2001 Lakeview Drive
Bigtown

Dear Sir or Madam

Will you please send directly to our auditors, Reddy & Abel, an itemised statement of the amount owed to you by us at the close of business on 31 December 20X2. Please also supply the following information:

Amount not yet due $..

Amount past due $ ....

Amount of purchase commitments $ ....

Description of any collateral held ....

....

....

A business reply envelope addressed to our auditors is enclosed. A prompt reply will be very much appreciated.

Yours faithfully

Controller

Searching for unrecorded liabilities

The major procedure for identifying unrecorded liabilities is the examination of the subsequent period's purchase and payment transactions as described earlier under cut-off tests. Analytical procedures may also identify unexpected differences between this year's and the prior year's expense or liability balances, which could indicate the presence of unrecorded liabilities. An analysis of rent expense, for example, may indicate that only three quarterly payments have been made, suggesting that the fourth quarter's rent needs to be accrued. Similarly, a comparison of accruals and prepayments may identify differences due to the failure to make a closing accrual in the current year.

An examination of contractual commitments may also alert the auditor to the existence of liabilities not yet provided for, such as progress payments on long-term contracts, or amounts accrued but not yet due or invoiced under a franchise agreement.

In chapter 14 we will describe procedures known as the subsequent-events review and the review for contingent liabilities. Both of these procedures contribute to the search for unrecorded liabilities.

Recalculating payroll liabilities

It is necessary for many entities to make a variety of accruals at the balance sheet date for amounts owed to officers and employees for salaries and wages, commissions, bonuses, vacation pay and so on, and for amounts owed to government agencies for income tax deductions. Although the auditor's primary concern for payroll expenses for the year is with overstatement, the primary concern for the year-end accruals is with understatement. Also of concern is consistency in the methods of calculating the accruals from one period to the next. In obtaining evidence concerning the reasonableness of management's accruals, the auditor should review management's calculations or make independent calculations. Additional evidence can be obtained by examining subsequent payments made on the accruals prior to the completion of fieldwork. Evidence obtained from these procedures primarily pertains to the valuation assertion.

Verifying directors' and executive officers' remuneration

Directors' and executive officers' remuneration is audit sensitive for the following reasons:

- Directors' remuneration must be disclosed in the financial reports of all companies under the Corporations Law.
- Directors and executive officers may be able to override controls and receive salaries, bonuses, share options and other forms of compensation in excess of authorised amounts.

For these reasons, the auditor should compare the authorisations of the board of directors for directors' and executive officers' salaries and other forms of compensation with recorded amounts. This procedure relates to all assertions.

Disclosure

Each major class of creditors and borrowings must be disclosed. These are likely to include bank overdrafts, bank loans, accounts payable, lease liabilities, taxation and employee entitlements. In addition, disclosure must be made of the amount of each class of liability secured by a charge and the nature of the security. If accounts payable balances include material advance payments for future goods and services, such amounts should be reported as advances to suppliers and classified under current assets.

LEARNING CHECK

11.5 The greatest inherent risks are those of fraudulent purchases for private use by an employee, understatement of credit purchase transactions and the payables balance, and payments to fictitious employees. Given the volume of transactions, most entities ensure their internal control structure relating to such matters is effective.

11.6 Testing the design effectiveness of controls is achieved by an evaluation of the system with the aid of a list of potential misstatements and suggested control procedures. Possible misstatements include payment for goods not ordered or received and payment to fictitious employees.

11.7 Initial procedures ensure the accuracy of the list of accounts payable balances that is used as the basis for tests of the balance.

11.8 Analytical procedures require the determination of expectations and the comparison of amounts, trends and ratios, particularly the gross profit ratio and the analysis of expense accounts. For payroll balances, analytical procedures may be sufficient without the need for further tests of details. An important payroll ratio is that of average wages per employee.

11.9 Tests of details of transactions are largely dual-purpose tests performed at the interim audit, except the cut-off tests of transactions either side of the balance sheet date. Unlike sales, cut-off tests for purchases need to be extended considerably into the subsequent period.

11.10 The principal test of details of balances is the comparison of purchase ledger balances with suppliers' statements. Only if suppliers' statements are unavailable would auditors ordinarily obtain confirmation directly from the supplier.

SUMMARY

Purchase and payroll transactions constitute the major source of expenditure for most entities, and the balance of accounts payable constitutes a major liability. In auditing these transactions and the account balances, the auditor uses techniques that we explained in Chapters 5–9. This chapter follows the audit approach required by AUS 402 (ISA 400). We described the information system and related control procedures typically employed by entities in processing the relevant transactions classes. The audit process commences with obtaining the understanding of this system. The auditor also considers issues relating to materiality, inherent risk and the control environment, prior to determining the appropriate audit strategy. For purchases and payroll transactions, materiality is invariably high. For audit purposes, the most significant inherent risk is that of understatement of purchase transactions and accounts payable balances in order to boost reported profits and enhance liquidity. For the entity, the greatest inherent risk is that of improper purchasing and payments to fictitious employees. In this chapter we illustrated how the control environment factors of integrity and ethical values, commitment to competence, management's philosophy and operating style, assignment of authority and responsibility, and personnel policies and practices apply to the control environment relating to purchases and payroll.

The next stage of the audit is the determination of an audit strategy which, for purchases and payroll, is likely to be one based on a lower assessed level of control risk. The first step in assessing control risk is to evaluate design effectiveness. We illustrated the use of evaluation check lists which hypothesise potential misstatements for each function in the processing of purchases, payments and payroll. The auditor then compares the control procedures in the entity's information system with necessary controls identified by the check list in assessing design effectiveness. At this point, the auditor drafts the audit program based on the preliminary assessment of control risk, identifying both tests of the operating effectiveness of controls and the reduced level of substantive procedures relevant to the assessed level of control risk. The assessed level of control risk is confirmed on completion of the tests of operating effectiveness. The final stage of the audit is the performance of substantive procedures. It is usually more cost effective to test the balance of accounts payable than to test the transactions making up that balance.

The most important test of transactions is that of cut-off at the year end. The major test of balances is the examination of suppliers' statements. As documentary evidence received from third parties, it is moderately reliable; however, the auditor needs to be alert to the possibility that such statements may be forged or altered by the entity.

Finally, in this chapter we explained the importance of verifying directors' and officers' salaries.

KEY TERMS

Accounts payable ledger, p. 419
Accounts payable master file, p. 419
Cheque register, p. 423
Cheque requisition, p. 422
Cheque summary, p. 422
Clock card, p. 425
Confirmation of accounts payable, p. 440
Employee earnings master file, p. 425
Goods received note, p. 418
Pay slips, p. 426
Payment transactions file, p. 422
Payments journal, p. 423
Payroll register, p. 425
Payroll transactions file, p. 425
Personnel authorisation form, p. 424
Personnel data master file, p. 424
Personnel file, p. 424
Purchase journal, p. 419
Purchase orders, p. 417
Purchase requisitions, p. 417
Purchase transactions file, p. 419
Purchases cut-off test, p. 438
Remittance advice, p. 423
Suppliers' invoices, p. 418
Termination notice, p. 425

FURTHER READING

Saunders, George D. & Munter, Paul, 'The Search for Unrecorded Liabilities — The Implications of Maislin', *The CPA Journal* (February 1991), pp. 48–51.

Schwersenz, Jack, 'Accounts Payable Confirmations: Why and How Used', *The CPA Journal* (May 1987), pp. 93–101.

Review questions

11.1 State the main audit objectives for (1) purchases and payroll transactions and (2) accounts payable balances.

11.2 Outline the sequence of events in a purchase transaction, from issuing the requisition to recording the invoice.

11.3 Explain how the segregation of functions within purchasing provides control with respect to the occurrence assertion.

11.4 For both of the functions pertaining to cash payment transactions, indicate two questions that may be used to prepare an internal control questionnaire for this transaction class.

11.5 Explain the importance of segregating the personnel function from wages preparation.

11.6 Explain factors affecting the inherent risk of purchasing transactions, relating to the completeness and occurrence assertions.

11.7 Describe computer-assisted audit procedures that can be used in testing controls over purchasing.

11.8 Describe the procedures for, and explain the objectives of, tests of payroll controls for terminated employees and the observation of payroll distribution.

11.9 Explain why the assessment of control risk over the occurrence of payment transactions affects the assessed level of control risk for the completeness of the accounts payable balance.

11.10 Describe the performance of the purchases cut-off test.

Discussion questions

11.1 Explain how the purchasing function can be fully automated. Explain the process, from identifying the need for inventory replacement through to paying the liability using modern information technology. What manual intervention would still be required in such a fully integrated system?

11.2 It is increasingly common for companies to program their computer information system to print and distribute cheques without further authorisation. As an auditor, describe controls you would expect to find in place over such a system.

11.3 Consider how a payroll fraud may be perpetrated if personnel and payroll functions are not adequately segregated.

11.4 Describe programmed application controls you would expect to find in a computerised payroll system. Explain the audit procedures for testing those controls.

11.5 Explain why an unexpected change in the gross profit ratio leads the auditor to suspect a wide range of possible misstatements in recorded transactions and balances.

11.6 Cut-off procedures can be applied to goods received notes issued before the year end or to liabilities recorded after the year end. Consider the separate merits of each approach in assuring the completeness of recorded liabilities.

11.7 Discuss why auditors rarely confirm accounts payable and yet nearly always confirm accounts receivable.

11.8 Explain why achieving an accurate cut-off of purchase and sale transactions is of critical importance in assuring the fairness of financial statements. Illustrate your explanation with examples of the effect of cut-off errors.

11.9 Describe as many different kinds of unrecorded liability as possible. For each, explain audit procedures you would perform for its detection.

Professional application questions

★ BASIC
★★ MODERATE
★★★ CHALLENGING

11.1 (Purchases and payments controls) ★

Rosedale Limited's newly installed computerised purchases and payables system provides for the automatic print-out of cheques at regular intervals. For cheques under $5000 the computer program imprints a facsimile signature on the cheque as it is printed. Cheques between $5000 and $100 000 are also printed with one facsimile signature, but the company's agreement with the bank requires two signatures on cheques over $5000. The second signature is added manually by an authorised signatory. Cheques over $100 000 are printed unsigned and must be manually signed by two authorised signatories.

Required

Describe controls to ensure that:

(a) only properly approved suppliers' invoices are posted to the accounts payable master file ledger;

(b) cheque payments are only made in respect of properly approved suppliers' invoices.

11.2 (Purchase controls) ★★

Your firm is the external auditor of Bestwood Engineering Limited, which manufactures components for motor vehicles and sells them to motor vehicle manufacturers and wholesalers. It has a turnover of $25 million and a profit before tax of $1 million. The company has a new financial director who has asked your advice on controls in the company's purchasing system.

Bestwood has separate accounts, purchasing and goods received departments. Most purchases are required by the production department, but other departments are able to raise requisitions for goods and services. The purchasing department is responsible for obtaining goods and services for the company at the lowest price that is consistent with the required delivery date and quality, and for ensuring their prompt delivery.

The accounts department is responsible for obtaining authorisation of purchase invoices before they are input into the computer, which posts them to the accounts payable ledger and the general ledger. The accounting records are kept on a microcomputer and the standard accounting software was obtained from an independent supplier. The accounting software maintains the accounts payable ledger, accounts receivable ledger, general ledger and payroll. The company does not maintain inventory records, because it believes the cost of maintaining these records outweighs the benefits.

(*continued*)

The financial director has explained that services include gas, electricity, telephone, repairs and the short-term hire of equipment and vehicles.

Required

(a) Describe the procedures that should be in operation in the purchasing department to control the purchase and receipt of goods.

(b) Describe the controls the accounts department should exercise over obtaining authorisation of purchase invoices before posting them to the accounts payable ledger.

(c) Explain how controls over the purchase of services, from raising the purchase requisition to posting the invoice to the accounts payable ledger, may differ from the procedures for the purchase of goods, as described in your answers to (a) and (b).

(ACCA Audit Framework — Paper 6(U), December 1998 — adapted)

11.3 (Internal control evaluation — cash payments) ★★

Management has requested a review of internal control over cash disbursements for parts and supplies purchased at manufacturing plants. Cash disbursements are centrally processed at head office based on disbursement vouchers prepared and approved at manufacturing plants. Each manufacturing plant purchases parts and supplies for its own production needs.

In response to management's request, a thorough evaluation of internal control over disbursements for manufacturing plant purchases of parts and supplies is being planned. As a preliminary step in planning the engagement, the plant managers have been asked to provide a written description of their respective plant's procedures for processing disbursement vouchers for parts and supplies. Below are nine excerpts from one of the written descriptions.

1. The purchasing department acts on purchase requisitions issued by the stores department.
2. Orders are placed on pre-numbered purchase order forms.
3. A complete purchase order copy is sent to the receiving department.
4. When goods are received, the receiving department logs the shipment in by stamping 'order received' on its purchase order copy and forwards the annotated order to the accounts payable department.
5. Purchase orders, purchase order copies that have been annotated by the receiving department, and supplier invoices are matched by the accounts payable department.
6. Clerical accuracy of supplier invoices is checked by the accounts payable department.
7. A pre-numbered disbursement voucher is prepared and forwarded, along with supporting documentation, to the plant controller who reviews and approves the voucher.
8. Supporting documents are returned to the accounts payable department for filing, and approved disbursement vouchers are forwarded to head office for payment.
9. A report listing cheques issued by head office is received and promptly filed by the accounts payable department.

Required

For each of the disbursement system procedures listed above, state whether it is consistent with good internal control and describe how it strengthens or weakens internal control.

11.4 (Payroll control and audit) ★★

Your firm is the independent auditor of Eastwood Engineering Limited, which has annual sales of $100 million. The head office site includes the manufacturing unit, the accounting functions and main administration. There are a number of sales offices in different parts of the country. Eastwood does not have an internal audit department.

At the interim audit you have been assigned to the audit of the wages system. This will involve obtaining an understanding of the wages system, testing the controls and performing substantive procedures to verify wages transactions.

The wages records are maintained on a computer and all wages information is processed at the head office. Some of the employees in the manufacturing unit are paid in cash and all other employees have their wages paid directly into their bank account. Manufacturing employees are paid their wages a week in arrears. All other employees are paid at the end of each week or month.

Eastwood has a personnel department which is independent of the wages department. The personnel department maintains records of the employees, including their starting date, grade, current wage rate and leaving date (if appropriate).

Previous audits have revealed frauds by wages department staff, which have been facilitated by weaknesses in the controls in the wages system. These frauds have included:

1. paying employees after their appointment but before they commenced work;
2. paying employees after they have left;
3. paying fictitious employees.

A check of current controls in the wages system has revealed that the company has failed to instigate controls to prevent these types of fraud recurring. Thus, the audit program requires extensive substantive procedures to be carried out to ensure that recorded wages transactions have not been misstated by similar frauds taking place in the current year.

The existence of employees at the head office site can be verified by physical inspection. For cost effectiveness, only a small sample of sales offices will be visited. The audit manager has asked you to consider the audit procedures you will carry out to obtain sufficient appropriate evidence of the existence of employees at sales offices that the audit staff do not visit.

The audit manager has explained that 'unclaimed wages' (see part (c) below) arise when manufacturing employees are not present to collect their wages. The unclaimed wage packets are given to the cashier, who records their details in the unclaimed wages book and is responsible for their custody. Any employee who has not received his or her wage packet at the payout can obtain it from the cashier. You have ascertained that there is no system of checking the operation of the unclaimed wages system by a person who is independent of the cashier and the wages department.

Required

(a) Explain how you would verify that employees are not paid before they commenced employment or after they have left (a 'starters and leavers' test).

(b) Describe the audit procedures you would carry out in connection with attending a payout of wages in cash to manufacturing employees.

(c) Describe the substantive procedures you would perform on unclaimed wages.

(d) Explain how you would verify the existence of employees whose wages are paid directly into their bank account, including those employees at sales offices.

(ACCA — Question 3, Paper 6, June 1998 — adapted)

11.5 (Accounts payable — substantive testing) ★★

You are the audit senior for the audit of Grosse Limited and have been given the audit file to review. The balance date is 30 June 20X2 and the materiality for the client has been set at $200 000. You obtained the information listed below from your review of the audit file.

1. The balance noted for accounts payable in the general ledger at 30 June 20X2 is $158 000, which compares with a balance as at 30 June 20X1 of $342 000.
2. The audit assistant noted in the file that 'Because the accounts payable balance is immaterial in the current year, only limited work is necessary.'
3. The only work performed by the audit assistant was to select the three largest payables from the client's detailed purchases ledger (which had been agreed to the general ledger) and agree the balances to photocopies of supplier statements.

Required

(a) Outline any queries you would raise with the audit assistant.

(b) Describe the additional audit procedures you believe should be performed to ensure that the accounts payable balance is fairly stated.

(Professional Year Programme of the ICAA — 1996, Accounting 2 Module — adapted)

11.6 (Computer information system controls — purchasing and cash disbursements) ★★★

You are the auditor of Sofasellers Limited, which buys furniture from manufacturers for sale to the public. You have been asked to audit certain aspects of the computerised purchasing and accounts payable system.

The company comprises a head office, a warehouse and many shops throughout the country. Furniture from manufacturers may be delivered to the warehouse or direct to individual shops. Details of goods received are entered into computer terminals at the warehouse or shop, which are on line with the head office main computer.

The computerised purchasing system involves the following six processes:

1. The user department (shop or warehouse) sends a purchase requisition to the buying department at head office.
2. The buying department issues a purchase order which is sent to the supplier and recorded on the computer.
3. On delivery, the goods are checked by the goods received department in the shop or warehouse and a goods received note is raised, entered into the computer system and allocated against the order.
4. On receipt of the invoice, the head office account department sends it to the user department who authorise it and return it to the accounts department. Invoice details are then recorded on the computer which posts it to the accounts payable ledger.
5. The computer system allows payment only if the system has recorded:
   (a) the purchase order;
   (b) receipt of the goods.
6. When the purchase invoice is due for payment, the computer prints the cheque and remittance advice.

Cheques are automatically produced, so the partner in charge of the audit has asked you to identify controls over authorising purchase invoices and changing suppliers' details on the computer's standing data file. He has explained that 'application controls' comprise controls exercised by the company's staff and by the computer.

Required

(a) Describe the application controls you would expect to find in operation from raising the purchase requisition to the computer accepting the purchase invoice.

(b) Explain the controls that should be exercised over access to the main computer from terminals in the head office and at the shops.

(c) Describe the application controls that should be exercised over changing supplier details on the standing data file on the computer. You should consider:

  (i) why such controls are important and how a fraud could be perpetrated in the absence of effective controls;

  (ii) the controls you would expect to find over changing supplier details and ensuring supplier details are correct. Your answer should include consideration of controls over access to the computer to perform these tasks.

(ACCA Audit Framework — Paper 6(Y), December 1997 — adapted)

11.7 (Payroll control and substantive testing) ★★★

You are reviewing the audit work for On-line Limited, a large Australia-wide company. On-line uses a service bureau to process all award-based wages. Time sheets are authorised by the appropriate supervisor, batched and sent to the service bureau for processing. Detailed payroll reports, as well as the time sheets, are returned to the accountant, who reviews the reports for reasonableness and initials them as evidence of her review.

Your audit assistant performed a month-to-month comparison of wages and found no abnormal trends. The following conclusion was noted on the working paper: 'I have checked that all payroll reports from the period were reviewed and initialled by the client. This, in conjunction with the results of analytical review, led me to conclude that the payroll expense is fairly stated.'

Required

(a) Outline any queries you would raise with the audit assistant.

(b) Describe the additional audit procedures you believe should be performed to ensure that payroll is fairly stated.

(Professional Year Programme of the ICAA — 1997, Accounting 2 Module — adapted)

11.8 (Accounts payable — substantive testing) ★★★

Your firm is the auditor of Newtown Limited, and you have been asked to suggest audit work you will carry out in verifying accounts payable and accruals at the company's year end of 30 June 20X2. You attend the stocktake at the year end.

The company operates from a single site and all raw materials for production are received by the goods inward department. When the materials are received, they are checked for quantity and quality against the delivery note and purchase order, and a multi-copy goods received note is made out and signed by the storekeeper. If there are any problems with the raw materials, then a discrepancy note is raised which gives details of any problems (e.g. incorrect quantities or faulty materials).

(*continued*)

The purchase department receives the suppliers' invoices, checks them against the purchase order and goods received note, and posts them to the purchase ledger. At the end of each month, payments are made to suppliers. The purchases ledger is maintained on a microcomputer. The main sundry creditors and accruals at the year end include:

- wages accruals;
- payroll tax;
- time-dependent accruals, such as loan interest, telephone, heating and lighting, and other expenses that are paid in arrears.

Most employees' wages are paid weekly in arrears.

Required

(a) Describe how you would ensure that purchases cut-off has been correctly performed at the year end.

(b) Describe how you would ensure that sundry creditors and accruals have been correctly stated at the year end.

(ACCA Audit Framework — Paper 6, December 1994 — adapted)

Case studies

11.1 (Purchases – computer information system control and audit) ★★★

You are the audit senior on the MM Limited audit. MM is a distributor of hair care products including shampoos, conditioners and mousses. MM uses an on-line computer system. No goods are manufactured in-house; rather, MM maintains a stock of raw materials and subcontracts the manufacture of its products to third parties. Approximately fifty suppliers and subcontractors are used, and all have proven to be reliable. You have made the following notes about the inventory system:

- Separate systems, staff and warehouses are maintained for both finished goods and raw materials.

Procedures for raw materials

- Purchase orders are automatically generated by the computer when stocks of any raw material fall below 70 per cent of the prior month's usage. The purchase orders contain the date, the supplier's name and address, and the raw material needed. Three copies are produced and distributed as follows:
  1. to the warehouse to enable follow-up of late orders;
  2. to the accounts clerk for filing by date order;
  3. to the supplier.
- When raw materials stock is received, the barcode attached to the delivery boxes by the supplier is scanned into the system. A two-part goods received note is produced:
  1. matched to the warehouse copy of the order by stores staff;
  2. filed by the accounts clerk.
- The scanning process is aborted if the codes do not match those on the master file.

Procedures for finished goods

- Purchase orders are automatically generated when finished goods fall below 60 per cent of the prior month's sales. The production orders contain the date, the subcontractor's name, the raw materials required and the finished goods needed. Two copies are produced and distributed as follows:
  1. to the raw materials store for use as a picking slip, and then packed with the goods and sent to the subcontractor;
  2. to the production controller to be filed in date order.
- When the finished goods stocks are received, the barcodes attached to the delivery boxes by the subcontractor are scanned into the system. A two-part goods received note is produced:
  1. matched to the production controller's copy of the order;
  2. filed by the accounts clerk.
- The scanning process is aborted if the codes do not match those on the master file.

General notes

- The computer automatically selects the supplier/subcontractor of both raw materials and finished goods based on the latest price (as per their most recent invoice) and their delivery times (based on the number of days between the date on which the purchase/production order is raised and the date on which the goods are scanned by the warehouse).

Password access is as follows:

Stores staff (raw materials)	Purchase order printing for raw materials only; goods received note printing for raw materials.
Stores staff (finished goods)	Goods received note printing for finished goods
Production controller	Production order printing; master file amendments
Accounts clerk	Master file amendments

Master file amendments

- The stock master file contains details of existing stock items, including the code and warehouse location, and approved suppliers and subcontractors.
- Orders will be only generated to the suppliers and subcontractors recorded on the master file.
- Master file changes are made by the production controller for both the raw materials inventory and the finished goods inventory. A master file amendment form is completed by the production controller as a record of the changes made.

Required

(a) Identify any weaknesses in the internal controls described. Discuss the implications of each weakness you identifiy.

(b) Assume your computer information system audit division is to perform testing of controls for the inventory systems described. Identify key controls that you would recommend for testing.

(c) Assuming the use of generalised audit software, list the procedures/reports you would request the computer information system auditors to run to assist you in testing the valuation of inventory.

(Professional Year Programme of the ICAA — 1999, Advanced Audit Module — adapted)

11.2 (Accounts payable — substantive testing) ★★★

You are the audit senior in charge of the audit of Black Limited, and you are auditing the company's trade creditors at 30 April 20X2. A junior member of the audit team has been checking suppliers' statements against the balances on the purchase ledger. He is unable to reconcile a material balance, relating to White Limited, and has asked for your assistance and your suggestions on the audit work that should be carried out on the differences. Below is the balance of White on Black's purchase ledger.

Supplier: White Limited

Date	Type	Reference	Status	Dr	Cr	Balance
10.02	Invoice	6004	Paid 1		2130	
18.02	Invoice	6042	Paid 1		1525	
23.02	Invoice	6057	Paid 1		2634	
4.03	Invoice	6080	Paid 2		3572	
15.03	Invoice	6107	Paid 2		1632	
26.03	Invoice	6154	Paid 2		924	
31.03	Payment	Cheque	Alloc. 1	6163		
	Discount		Alloc. 1	126		
14.04	Invoice	6285			2156	
21.04	Invoice	6328			3824	
30.04	Payment	Cheque	Alloc. 2	6005		
	Discount		Alloc. 2	123		
30.04	Balance					5980

Below are the details on White's suppliers' statement.

Customer: Black Limited

Date	Type	Reference	Status	Dr	Cr	Balance
7.02	Invoice	6004	Paid 1	2130		
16.02	Invoice	6042	Paid 1	1525		
22.02	Invoice	6057	Paid 1	2634		
2.03	Invoice	6080	Paid 2	3752		
13.03	Invoice	6107	Paid 2	1632		
22.03	Invoice	6154	Paid 2	924		
10.04	Receipt	Cheque	Alloc. 1		6163	
4.04	Invoice	6210	Alloc. 1	4735		
12.04	Invoice	6285		2156		
18.04	Invoice	6328	Alloc. 2	3824		
28.04	Invoice	6355	Alloc. 2	6298		
30.04	Balance					23447

White's terms of trade with Black allow a 2 per cent cash discount on invoices where White receives a cheque from the customer by the end of the month following the date of the invoice (i.e. a 2 per cent discount will be given on March invoices paid by 30 April).

On Black's purchase ledger, under 'Status', the cash and discount marked 'Alloc. 1' pay invoices marked 'Paid 1' (similarly for 'Alloc. 2' and 'Paid 2'). Black's goods received department checks the goods when they arrive and issues a goods received note. A copy of the goods received note is sent to the purchases accounting department.

Required

(a) Prepare a statement reconciling the balance on Black's purchase ledger to the balance on White's supplier's statement.

(b) Describe the audit work you will carry out on each of the reconciling items you have determined in your answer to (a), to determine the balance that should be included in the financial statements.

(c) In relation to verifying trade creditors:

   (i) consider the basis you will use for selecting suppliers' statements to check against the balances on the purchase ledger;

   (ii) describe what action you will take if you find there is no supplier's statement for a material balance on the purchase ledger.

(ACCA Audit Framework — Paper 6, June 1996 — adapted)

chapter 12 Auditing inventories and property, plant and equipment

Overview

LEARNING OBJECTIVES

After studying this chapter, you should be able to:

1. identify the audit objectives applicable to inventories
2. explain the nature of inventory records
3. describe procedures to be followed at a physical inventory
4. discuss considerations relevant to determining the audit strategy for inventories
5. describe procedures to be followed when observing physical inventory
6. explain the audit procedures for verifying inventory pricing
7. identify the audit objectives applicable to property, plant and equipment
8. discuss considerations relevant to determining the audit strategy for property, plant and equipment
9. design a substantive audit program for property, plant and equipment.

Professional statements

AUSTRALIAN		INTERNATIONAL	
AUS 506	Existence and Valuation of Inventory	ISA 501	Audit Evidence — Additional Considerations for Specific Items, Part A: Attendance at Physical Inventory Counting
AUS 510	Initial Engagements — Opening Balances	ISA 510	Initial Engagements — Opening Balances
AUS 516	Audit of Accounting Estimates	ISA 540	Audit of Accounting Estimates
AUS 602	Using the Work of Another Auditor	ISA 600	Using the Work of Another Auditor
AUS 604	Considering the Work of Internal Auditing	ISA 610	Considering the Work of Internal Auditing
AUS 606	Using the Work of an Expert	ISA 620	Using the Work of an Expert
AAS 2	Inventories	IAS 2	Inventories
AAS 4	Depreciation of Non-current Assets	IAS 16	Property, Plant and Equipment
AAS 17	Accounting for Leases	IAS 17	Accounting for Leases
AAS 38	Revaluation of Non-current Assets		
ED 99	Impairment of Assets	IAS 36	Impairment of Assets

In the first half of this chapter we will deal with the audit of inventories and in the second half we will consider the audit of property, plant and equipment. Audit considerations of the internal control structures of the principal transaction classes affecting both account balances have already been described: purchases in the case of both inventories and property, plant and equipment assets, and also sales in the case of inventories. For this reason, the organisation of the chapter differs from that of the two previous chapters. There is no separate section describing the functions and control procedures for either inventory or property, plant and equipment transactions. For inventory, there is a section describing functions and control procedures associated with the custody of inventory and the maintenance of inventory records. In the section on developing the audit plan, the significance of assessing the effectiveness of controls over inventory records is discussed in the context of determining the audit strategy.

For property, plant and equipment, the auditor adopts a predominantly substantive approach to the audit and rarely considers it necessary to examine controls over fixed asset records. We will describe the nature of such records in the section on developing the audit plan, but there is no assessment of control. Our explanation of the audit of property, plant and equipment then proceeds to the design and execution of substantive audit procedures. Given the complex nature of intangible fixed assets, we do not deal with their audit within this text. The audit of non-current investments is the subject of Chapter 13.

A feature of both classes of asset is the inherent risk as to their valuation. Thus, verification of the valuation assertion for these assets receives special consideration during the audit.

INVENTORY

In a merchandising entity, inventory consists of goods acquired for resale. In a manufacturing entity, inventory can be in one of three stages:

- **raw materials** awaiting processing;
- partly manufactured items known as **work in process** (or work in progress);
- **finished goods** awaiting sale.

Smaller entities, particularly those not engaging in manufacturing, may not maintain inventory records. Instead, inventory is determined at or near the balance sheet date by a count known as a **physical inventory**. The principal audit procedure in such cases is observation of that physical inventory. At the other extreme, large manufacturing entities maintain comprehensive inventory records, with subsidiary inventory ledgers integrated with the general ledger. These records may be used as the basis for determining both the quantity and value of inventory at the balance sheet date. To obtain sufficient audit evidence in such cases, the auditor must perform extensive tests of control over the recording of inventory transactions and the maintenance of inventory records.

Obtaining evidence of the existence of inventory through physical observation is a required audit procedure. The auditor may meet this requirement by observing a number of cyclical counts that the entity undertakes during the year as part of its control procedures over the maintenance of inventory records. Alternatively, where the entity determines inventory by physical count at or close to the year end, the auditor meets the requirement by attendance at that count.

Verifying the valuation assertion for inventory is also an important audit procedure. This involves verifying both cost and net realisable value and the judgement by management as to which basis is relevant for each item of inventory.

Audit objectives

LEARNING OBJECTIVE 1

Identify the audit objectives applicable to inventories.

Table 12.1 lists the primary audit objectives for each assertion, referencing them to specific controls and audit procedures.

Note that, for occurrence and completion, transfer transactions apply to only multi-location entities and manufacturing entities that distinguish between raw materials, work in process and finished goods.

TABLE 12.1

Selected specific audit objectives for inventory

Assertion category	Transaction class audit objectives	Account balance audit objectives
Existence or occurrence	Recorded purchase transactions represent inventories acquired during the period (**EO1**). Recorded transfers represent inventories transferred between locations or categories during the period (**EO2**). Recorded sales transactions represent inventories sold during the period (**EO3**).	Inventories included in the balance sheet physically exist (**EO4**).
Completeness	All purchases (**C1**), transfers (**C2**) and sales (**C3**) of inventories that occurred during the period have been recorded.	Inventories include all materials, products and supplies on hand at the balance sheet date (**C4**).
Rights and obligations	The entity has rights to the inventories recorded during the period (**RO1**).	The entity has rights to the inventories included in the balance sheet (**RO2**).
Valuation or measurement	The costs of materials purchased and of labour and overheads applied have been accurately determined and are in accordance with applicable Accounting Standards (**VM1**).	Inventories are properly stated at the lower of cost or net realisable value, determined in accordance with applicable Accounting Standards (**VM2**).
Disclosure	Transactions relating to inventories have been properly identified and classified in the financial report (**D1**).	Inventories are properly identified and classified in the financial report (**D2**). Disclosures pertaining to the classification, basis of valuation and the pledging of inventories are adequate (**D3**).

Recording inventory transactions

LEARNING OBJECTIVE 2

Explain the nature of inventory records.

We described the process of obtaining evidence relating to purchase and sale transactions in the previous two chapters. For entities that rely entirely on physical inventory at or near the balance sheet date, the auditor will adopt a predominantly substantive approach in obtaining evidence as to the existence and completeness assertions. Where perpetual inventory records are used wholly or partly in determining inventory at the balance sheet date, it is necessary for the auditor to obtain an understanding of the accounting and internal control systems relating to such records. For non-manufacturing entities, the auditor can rely on records of purchase transactions in obtaining sufficient evidence as to valuation and measurement. For manufacturing entities, even where perpetual inventory records are not maintained, the auditor needs to obtain an understanding of the procedures for determining and recording costs of production.

Maintaining inventory records

The increasing use of computer information systems has made it much easier for entities to maintain **perpetual inventory records** which are now relatively common. If the recording of sales and purchases are computerised, it is a relatively simple procedure to extend the system to record the input and removal of goods from inventory. Simpler systems maintain records of quantity only. More sophisticated systems maintain inventory records by quantity and value, which are fully integrated with the accounting records in an **inventory master file**. For merchandising entities, a single inventory record is required, although this may be subdivided by location. Manufacturing entities need to record separate inventories of raw materials, work in process and finished goods, and to establish procedures for recording the movement of goods through production.

An important control over maintaining inventory records is the segregation of this function from the physical custody of the inventory. The custodian will then have no opportunity to conceal an inventory shortage by manipulating the inventory records.

The separate functions are:

- recording the movement of goods into inventory;
- recording the movement of goods from inventory;
- recording transfers of inventory;
- physically comparing inventory with inventory records.

Movement of goods into inventory

In all cases, the initial entry into inventory will be through the purchasing system (see Chapter 11). The storekeeper acknowledges receipt of the goods by initialling a copy of the goods received note. The goods received note then provides the source of entry of the quantity and cost in the appropriate inventory record. These procedures relate primarily to the occurrence and completeness assertions (**EO1**, **C1**), but also contribute to the rights and obligations assertion (**RO1**).

Movement of goods from inventory

When merchandise inventories or finished goods are sold, the dispatch note serves as the basis for authorisation of the release of the goods from inventory, and for the entry in inventory records reducing the quantity on hand. In retail stores, the use of barcodes or security tags scanned at the cash register provides data for reducing recorded inventory. Control procedures as to the occurrence and completeness of sales transactions (see Chapter 10) also relate to the occurrence and completeness of recorded inventory movements (**EO3**, **C3**).

Transfers of inventory

Further procedures are necessary where goods are transferred from one inventory location to another. In manufacturing entities, **production move orders** control the movement of goods from raw materials, through work in process to finished goods. These pre-numbered documents are issued by production control and represent authorisation to issue raw materials and to apply direct labour to process materials to produce the finished goods. Each move order consists of tickets identifying the specific material and labour requirements for the goods to be produced. Initialled copies of tickets represent acknowledgement, by inventory custodians, of the receipt of goods, or evidence of their proper delivery. They also provide the basis for accounting entries, relieving one inventory location and charging the other. Similar procedures, on a less elaborate scale, are required in retailing entities to record and control internal transfers. These procedures relate to the occurrence and completeness assertions for internal inventory movements (**EO2**, **C2**).

Physical comparison of inventory with inventory records

Perpetual inventory records need to be compared with physical inventory at regular intervals. The two functions involved are:

1. an inventory count;
2. a comparison with records.

Inventory count

3 LEARNING OBJECTIVE

Describe procedures to be followed at a physical inventory.

Procedures for physical inventory are similar, whether the purpose is to determine inventory at the balance sheet date or to compare inventory with inventory records at an intermediate date. In this section we will describe procedures applicable to a full physical inventory. Procedures for **cyclical inventory counts** may be less thorough and involve counting only a portion of inventory items. The sample selected for counting may be organised systematically, through different sections of the warehouse or different types of inventory, or by random sampling. A further approach is to count items at the reorder point when inventory levels will be low, thus reducing both the cost of the count and the likelihood of count errors.

The procedures for physical inventory involve:

- assigning and communicating responsibility;
- preparation;
- identification;
- counting;
- checking;
- clearing;
- recording;
- cut-off.

Below we describe these procedures.

- *Assigning and communicating responsibility*: Overall responsibility for the count should be assigned to an individual who has no responsibility for either the custody of inventory or the maintainance of inventory records. Persons involved in the count should also be suitably independent, although storekeepers may be involved if supervised. The area containing inventory should be subdivided, with count teams assigned to specific sections. Inventory-taking instructions should be drawn up, and individual responsibilities should be clearly explained to each person involved.
- *Preparation*: Prior to the count, areas such as the warehouse and shop floor should be tidied, with inventory neatly stacked and items not to be counted (such as scrap or goods held for third parties) removed or clearly marked. Arrangements need to be made to cease production, if possible, and receiving and shipping departments need to be alerted so as to avoid movement of goods to or from these departments during the count. In this way, cut-off errors can be avoided. If an accurate cut-off is not achieved, the physical count may include, for example, goods for which the purchase or production cost is not recorded by the information system until after the count. This could result in an overstatement of inventory.
- *Identification*: Inventory to be counted must be properly identified. This is a particular problem with specialised items or work in process. With work in process, the problem is

with identifying the stage of completion, which determines the costs accumulated against the items. Either the goods must be tagged in advance or count teams knowledgeable in the inventory must be assigned to the count in appropriate sections.

- *Counting*: Count teams usually work in pairs where any lifting or moving of items is necessary to ascertain the quantity. Forklift trucks and weighing scales may also need to be available. Instructions should ensure that count teams understand the unit of measurement (e.g. 25-kilogram bags). The degree of thoroughness also needs to be considered — for example, whether cartons need to be opened at random or weighed to verify that they are full and the contents are as described.
- *Checking*: Sometimes all counts are double-checked and all discrepancies are recounted. Where errors are unlikely, only spot checks need to be performed and only counts by those count teams making errors need to be double-checked.
- *Clearing*: As each item is counted, the count team should leave a mark to avoid duplicating the count. On completion of a section, a supervisor should tour the area to ensure no items appear to be uncounted.
- *Recording*: Control over count sheets is particularly important. Three systems are commonly used. Where inventory items are standardised, pre-printed **inventory count sheets** containing descriptions are issued to the count teams, who then complete the sheets by entering the quantity. Another system is to issue blank, pre-numbered count sheets. The serial numbers issued to each count team must be noted and checked on completion to ensure that no sheets are missing. Half-filled sheets should be ruled off, and unused sheets should be identified as such to prevent items being added after the count. The third method involves attaching pre-numbered, three-part **inventory tags** to each inventory item prior to the count. The count team enters the description and quantity on the first part of the tag and removes it. The checkers do likewise with the second part, which is compared with the first part. The third part, the stub of the tag, remains attached to the item to enable the supervisor to verify completeness of the count. Again, serial numbers should be fully accounted for. In each case, counters and checkers should be required to sign or initial each count sheet or tag.
- *Cut-off*: Serial numbers of the last pre-numbered goods received notes, dispatch notes and production move orders issued prior to physical inventory need to be recorded to ensure that the count is compared with inventory records that are based on the same documents.

Comparison with records

Comparison with records is of greater importance for cyclical counts, where the aims are to ensure the reliability of the inventory records and to ascertain the effectiveness of procedures designed to ensure accountability for custodianship and record-keeping. With counts undertaken at or near the balance sheet date, comparison with the records will assist in identifying any major errors in quantities ascertained by count.

Procedures should require a recount of material differences. If the difference remains, further investigation is required to ascertain if the inventory records are in error and why. A record should be maintained of differences and the cause (if known), and the inventory records should be adjusted to agree with the count. This list of errors provides evidence as to the reliability of the records and the possibility of reliance on book inventory in determining inventory at the balance sheet date, without the need for a further count.

These procedures relate primarily to the existence assertion (**EO4**) but also contribute to the completeness assertion (**C4**).

Determining and recording inventory costs

For merchandise inventory, procedures relating to measurement in the recording of purchase transactions ensure that proper costs are recorded in inventory records. On sale, the cost of sale should be determined in accordance with the appropriate cost flow assumption, which would normally be either first-in first-out or weighted average. Entities recording cost of sales on a continuing basis will usually rely on computer information systems, which should be programmed to determine the appropriate cost.

Costing of manufactured inventory is far more complex. Procedures are required to:

- determine the cost of material entered into raw materials;
- determine the cost of raw materials transferred to work in process at first-in first-out or weighted average cost;
- record costs of direct labour applied to work in process;
- identify abnormal waste or spoilage in the production process;
- identify manufacturing overhead costs and apportion costs to production departments;
- assign overhead costs to work in process using an appropriate absorption rate;
- apportion costs to by-products;
- relieve work in process and charge finished goods on completion of manufacturing, based on costing procedures such as batch or process costing;
- relieve finished goods with the cost of goods sold at first-in first-out or weighted average.

Some entities record inventory at standard cost and identify differences between standard and actual costs as variances.

In obtaining the understanding of the accounting system, the auditor needs to identify the entity's accounting policy and ascertain the procedures for ensuring that costs are recorded in accordance with that policy. It is also necessary for the auditor to ensure that the policy is consistent with the requirements of AAS 2 (IAS 2), Inventories. These procedures relate to the valuation assertion (**VM1**) and contribute to the disclosure assertion (**D1**).

Developing the audit plan

The selected approach to the audit of inventory depends on the availability and reliability of inventory records. Consideration of the internal control structure relating to inventory records, which we described in the previous section, is necessary only where such records exist. In all audits, consideration of the determination of cost records is important.

Materiality and risk

In a manufacturing entity, inventories and cost of goods sold are usually significant to both the entity's financial position and the results of its operations. Moreover, numerous factors contribute to the risk of misstatements in the assertions for these accounts, including those described below:

- The volume of purchase, manufacturing and sale transactions that affect these accounts is generally high, increasing the opportunities for misstatements to occur.
- There are often contentious valuation and measurement issues such as:
  — the identification, measurement and allocation of indirect materials, labour and manufacturing overhead;
  — joint product costs;
  — the disposition of cost variances;
  — accounting for scrap and wastage.
- Special procedures are sometimes required to determine inventory quantity or value, such as geometric volume measurements of stockpiles using aerial photography, and estimation of value by experts.

- Inventories are often stored at multiple sites, leading to difficulties in maintaining physical control over theft and damage, and in accounting for goods in transit between sites.
- Inventories are vulnerable to spoilage, obsolescence and general economic conditions that may affect demand and saleability, and thus their valuation.
- Inventories may be sold subject to right of return and repurchase agreements.

In planning the audit, the auditor will be aware that the inherent risks are greater with respect to the existence and valuation assertions. Management has a greater incentive to overstate inventory being an asset, than to understate it. It may do so by either inflating the quantity or overstating its value. There are numerous instances of such frauds discovered (and not discovered) by auditors. A lack of third party evidence means it is also often easier to overstate inventories than assets such as cash or debtors. Further, inventory is subject to theft both by employees and outsiders. The depletion of inventory as a consequence of shoplifting is well known.

4 LEARNING OBJECTIVE

Discuss considerations relevant to determining the audit strategy for inventories.

Audit strategy

In verifying the existence (and completeness) assertions, the auditor has the choice of three audit strategies — a choice that depends on the entity's own policy for determining inventory quantity. The options are:

1. inventory quantity determined by perpetual inventory records where the entity does not intend to count inventory at or close to the balance sheet date. The audit strategy would require assessing the control risk over inventory records as being low;
2. inventory quantities determined by physical inventory near the balance sheet date, adjusted to balance sheet quantities by reference to perpetual inventory records. This strategy requires assessing the control risk over inventory records, or of purchases and sales, as being less than high;
3. inventory quantities determined by physical inventory at or within a few days of the balance sheet date. This is a predominantly substantive approach in which the auditor would not test control over inventory records, which may not even exist.

A single entity may use all three methods for different categories of inventory or for inventory at different locations. A manufacturing entity may, for example, determine the quantity of raw materials and finished goods at a year-end physical inventory, but rely on perpetual records in determining the work in process inventory.

In developing the audit plan, the auditor will need to discuss the approach that management intends to take. If management intends to rely solely on inventory records, then more extensive tests of control will be necessary to confirm the required assessment of control risk. Moreover, this assessment must be completed before the balance sheet date in the event that tests of control fail to confirm the assessment of control risk as being low, and the auditor is required to advise management to undertake a physical inventory at or near the balance sheet date.

Specialised inventories may require the assistance of experts in determining either the quantity (as in the case of aerial measurement of stockpiles) or value (as in the case of antiques). In accordance with AUS 606 (ISA 620), Using the Work of an Expert, the auditor must discuss use of experts with management to ensure that persons acceptable to both management and the auditor are employed.

For merchandise inventory, a predominantly substantive approach is usually more efficient in verifying the valuation assertion. For manufacturing entities, it is usually necessary for the auditor to have assessed control risk over the maintenance of costing records (used as the basis for costing closing inventory) as being less than high. This is an area that frequently receives insufficient audit attention owing to a reluctance to unravel the complexities of the costing system.

Assessment of control risk

Assessment of control risk over inventory records is important where the entity does not intend to undertake a physical inventory at or close to the year end. In this case, a satisfactory assessment is vital. Otherwise, assessment of control risk over inventory records is unimportant. Assessment of control risk over the cost of inventory is always important for manufacturing entities.

Control risk over inventory records

Table 12.2 (page 464) contains a partial listing of potential misstatements, necessary controls, possible tests of the operating effectiveness of those controls, and the specific audit objective to which each belongs. As explained above, the auditor would assess control risk over perpetual inventory records only where they are used in determining inventory at the balance sheet date. If the preliminary assessment based on the design effectiveness of controls is that control risk is likely to be high, then the auditor would advise management not to rely on the records in determining inventory at the balance sheet date.

If the preliminary assessment supports management's intended reliance on inventory records, then the auditor would proceed to draw up an audit program incorporating possible tests of the operating effectiveness of controls such as those identified in Table 12.2.

Many of these tests are in the form of dual-purpose tests. It is important to remember that AUS 506, Existence and Valuation of Inventory (ISA 501, Audit Evidence — Additional Considerations for Specific Items, Part A: Attendance at Physical Inventory Counting) requires that the auditor, where reliance is placed entirely on perpetual inventory records in determining inventory at the balance sheet date, must additionally perform substantive procedures to:

- verify the physical existence of inventories by inspection and performing test counts, usually in conjunction with observing cyclical counts;
- investigate significant differences between the physical count and the perpetual inventory records, and confirm that the records are properly adjusted.

Close to the balance sheet date, the auditor will need to consider the extent of test counts relative to total inventory, and to review the recorded differences between test counts and inventory records over the year and the explanations of those differences. If the auditor is not satisfied that results of test counts support an assessment of control risk as low, then he or she must discuss with management the need for a complete physical inventory.

Control risk over inventory cost

In a manufacturing entity, assessment of the reliability of the costing system in providing accurate costs of production that are correctly determined in accordance with acceptable Accounting Standards can constitute a substantial component of the interim audit. Manufacturing costs are nearly always determined through the computer information system, and test data can be used to test the accuracy of processing and recording cost information. Where standard costs are intended to be used as the basis for valuing inventories, the tests must extend to the procedures employed in developing standards from the engineering specifications as to:

- the quantities of labour and material required;
- the determination of standard prices for labour and materials.

TABLE 12.2 *Control risk assessment considerations*

Function	Potential misstatement	Necessary control	Possible test of operating effectiveness	Relevant audit objective (from Table 12.1)				
				EO#	C#	RO#	VM#	D#
Recording movement of goods into inventory	Failure to record goods	Use of pre-numbered goods received notes and production move orders	Reperform test of numerical continuity.		✓1, 2			
		Independent reconciliation of inventory records with control account in general ledger	Reperform.*	✓1,2,3	✓1,2,3		✓1	
Recording movement of goods from inventory	Unauthorised removal of goods	Custodian required to acknowledge responsibility for receipt of goods into store.	Inspect goods received notes and production move orders for custodian's initials.	✓1,2				
		Custodian required to obtain receipt for all deliveries from store.	Vouch recorded removals with properly authorised dispatch notes and production move orders.*	✓2,3				
		Physical comparison of inventory with inventory records	Observe. Reperform.*	✓1,2,3	✓1,2,3			
Physical comparison of inventory with inventory records	Unreliable count procedures	Responsibility independent from maintenance of inventory records and custodianship of inventory	Observe.	✓4	✓4			
		Adequate instructions properly issued and followed	Observe. Reperform.*	✓4	✓4			
	Inadequate investigation and correction	Proper record maintained of differences and their correction	Inspect. Reperform.*	✓4	✓4			
	Insufficient extent of comparison	Laid down procedures for systematic counts	Inspect.	✓4	✓4			
Determining inventory costs	Inappropriate basis	Approved by finance director	Enquire. Compare with Accounting Standards.				✓1, 2	✓1, 2
	Improper calculation	Consistent with engineering specification	Inspect. Reperform.*				✓1, 2 ✓1, 2	
		Program controls	Use test data.*					

* Usually performed as part of dual-purpose tests.

Substantive procedures for inventories

Except where perpetual records are used as the basis for determining inventory at the balance sheet date, and for costing records in manufacturing entities, the audit is primarily based on substantive procedures applied to the account balance at balance sheet date. The emphasis is on the assertions of existence and valuation, because the inherent risk of their misstatement is always high. Acceptable detection risk for these two assertions is usually assessed as being low, with detection risk for other assertions being low to moderate.

Designing substantive procedures

A listing of possible substantive procedures to be included in the audit program appears in Table 12.3, with each test referenced to the audit objectives shown in Table 12.1 (page 457).

TABLE 12.3 *Possible substantive procedures for tests of inventory assertions*

Category	Substantive procedure	Relevant audit objective (from Table 12.1)				
		EO4	C4	RO2	VM2	D#
Initial procedures	1. Perform initial procedures on inventory balances and records that will be subjected to further testing. (a) Trace opening inventory balances to the prior year's working papers. (b) Review activity in inventory accounts and investigate entries that appear unusual in amount or source. (c) Verify totals of perpetual inventory records and their agreement with closing general ledger balances.				✓	
Analytical procedures	2. Perform analytical procedures. (a) Review industry experience and trends. (b) Examine an analysis of inventory turnover and gross profit. (c) Review relationships of inventory balances to recent purchasing, production and sales activities.	✓		✓	✓	
Tests of details of transactions	3. Test entries in inventory records to and from supporting documentation.	✓	✓	✓	✓	
	4. Test the cut-off of purchases, inventory transfers and sales.	✓	✓			
Tests of details of balances	5. Observe the entity's physical inventory count. (a) Evaluate the adequacy of the entity's inventory-taking plans. (b) Observe physical inventory and test compliance with laid down procedures. (c) Make test counts. (d) Look for indications of slow-moving, damaged or obsolete inventory. (e) Account for all inventory tags and count sheets used in the physical count. (f) Record cut-off data.	✓	✓	✓	✓	

(*continued*)

TABLE 12.3 *Possible substantive procedures for tests of inventory assertions (continued)*

Category	Substantive procedure	Relevant audit objective (from Table 12.1)				
		EO4	C4	RO2	VM2	D#
	6. Test the clerical accuracy of inventory listings.	✓	✓		✓	
	(a) Recalculate totals and extensions of quantities times unit prices.					
	(b) Trace test counts (from item 5c) to listings.					
	(c) Vouch items on listings to and from count sheets and inventory tags.					
	(d) Compare physical counts to perpetual inventory records.					
	(e) Verify the adjustment of amounts for movements between the date of physical inventory and the balance sheet date.					
	7. Test inventory pricing.				✓	
	(a) Examine suppliers' invoices for purchased inventories.					
	(b) Examine the propriety of costing information, standard costs and the disposition of variances pertaining to manufactured inventories.					
	(c) Perform a lower of cost or net realisable value test.					
	8. Confirm inventories at locations outside the entity.	✓	✓	✓		
	9. Examine consignment agreements and contracts.			✓		✓3
Disclosure	10. Compare report presentation with applicable Accounting Standards.					✓2,3
	(a) Confirm agreements for assignment and pledging of inventories.					
	(b) Review disclosures for inventories in drafts of the financial report and determine conformity with applicable Accounting Standards.					

Initial procedures

In tracing opening inventory balances to prior year working papers, the auditor should make certain that any audit adjustments, agreed upon in the prior year, were recorded. In addition, where perpetual inventory records are maintained, entries to the control accounts in the general ledger should be scanned to identify any postings that are unusual in amount or nature and thus require special investigation. Where perpetual inventory records are to be used as the basis for determining inventory at the balance sheet date, the inventory listing must be test checked to and from the records, added, and agreed with the balance in the control account. We will discuss additional work on inventory listings in a later section on the tests of details of balances.

Analytical procedures

The application of analytical procedures to inventories is often extensive. A review of industry experience and trends may be essential in developing expectations to be used in evaluating analytical data for the entity. Knowledge of an industry-wide fall in turnover, for example, will enable the auditor to expect a fall in the entity's inventory turnover ratio. If the ratio does not show the expected fall, then the auditor may suspect errors as to the existence or occurrence of the inventory balance, or in the completeness of the turnover balance used in calculating the ratio. A review of relationships of inventory balances with recent purchasing, production and sales activities should also aid the auditor in understanding changes in inventory levels. An increase in the reported level of finished goods inventory when purchasing, production and sales levels have remained steady, for example, could indicate misstatements related to the existence or valuation of the finished goods inventory.

Important ratios are those of inventory turnover and gross profit. We previously explained the use of the gross profit ratio with respect to the audits of sales and purchases. An unexpectedly high inventory turnover ratio, or an unexpectedly low gross profit ratio, might be caused by an overstatement of cost of goods sold and a corresponding understatement of inventories. Conversely, conformity of these ratios with expectations provides assurance of the fairness of the data used in the calculations.

Where physical inventory is other than at the year end, the auditor should analyse totals of transactions in the intervening period for reasonableness.

Tests of details of transactions

With the exception of cut-off tests, tests of details of transactions will be performed only where inventory at the balance sheet date is determined wholly or partly from perpetual inventory records.

Testing entries in inventory records

Where inventory at the balance sheet date is determined wholly by reference to perpetual inventory records, the tests of details of inventory transactions will be those described in Table 12.2 as dual-purpose tests. Where inventory at the balance sheet date is determined by count other than at the year end and adjusted by reference to inventory records in the intervening period, such tests of details of transactions may be confined to the period between the date of physical inventory and the balance sheet date.

Testing cut-off of purchase, manufacturing and sales transactions

We explained the purpose and nature of sales and purchases cut-off tests in Chapters 10 and 11 respectively, in connection with the audit of accounts receivable and accounts payable balances. Both tests are important in establishing that transactions occurring near the end of the year are recorded in the correct accounting period. Purchases in transit at the year end, for example, should be excluded from inventory and payables, and inventory in transit to customers at the year end should be included in sales and excluded from inventory. In a manufacturing entity, it must also be determined that entries are recorded in the proper period for the allocation of labour and overhead costs to work in process and for goods moved between raw materials, work in process and finished goods.

In each case, the auditor must ascertain, through inspection of documents and physical observation, that the paperwork cut-off and the physical cut-off for physical inventory are coordinated. If the auditor determines, for example, that an entry transferring the cost of the final completed batch of the period to finished goods has been recorded, then he or she should determine that the goods, even if in transit, were included in the physical inventory of finished goods only — that is, that they were neither counted as part of work in process, nor double-counted, nor missed altogether. During his or her attendance at the count, the auditor should note details of documentation relating to the movement of goods at the date of physical inventory. Where physical inventory is at a date other than at the balance sheet date, the auditor must also check cut-off at the date of physical inventory to ensure that movements between that date and the balance sheet date exclude transactions prior to the count. Evidence from these cut-off tests relates to the occurrence, completeness and measurement assertions for inventory balances.

Tests of details of balances

As already explained, the auditor reduces audit risk to the desired level primarily through the performance of substantive tests of details of balances.

5 LEARNING OBJECTIVE

Describe procedures to be followed when observing physical inventory.

Observing the entity's physical inventory

During the 1930s, audit evidence for inventories was usually restricted to obtaining a certificate from management as to the correctness of the stated amount. In 1938, the discovery of a major fraud in the McKesson & Robbins Company, a major US pharmaceutical firm, caused a reappraisal in the United States of the auditor's responsibilities for inventories. The company's December 1937 financial statements, 'certified' by a national public accounting firm, reported $87 million of total assets. Of this amount, $19 million was subsequently determined to be fictitious: $10 million in inventory and $9 million in receivables. The auditors were exonerated of blame because they had complied with existing Auditing Standards. However, promptly thereafter, US Auditing Standards were changed to include physical observation of inventories.[1]

The observation of physical inventory is now required by AUS 506 (ISA 501) whenever inventories are material to an entity's financial report, and observation is not impracticable. The observation of physical inventory may prove to be inconvenient, time consuming and difficult for the auditor, but it is seldom impracticable. When inventories are material and the auditor does not observe the physical inventory, the auditor may perform alternative procedures, such as verifying sales transactions after the physical inventory date of items included in inventory. However, such procedures may not provide the auditor with sufficient appropriate audit evidence as to applicable assertions.

In observing physical inventory, the auditor has no responsibility to take or supervise the taking of the inventory. From this procedure, the auditor obtains direct knowledge of the reliability of management's physical inventory procedures and, thus, the reliance that may be placed on management's assertions as to the quantities and physical condition of the inventories. In some cases, the entity may hire outside inventory specialists to take inventory. Where the outside inventory specialists have no particular expertise in the type of inventory being counted, the auditor must be present to observe their counts too because, from an auditing standpoint, they are basically the same as entity employees. Where the specialists are experts in the particular type of inventory (such as precious stones), the auditor may be in a position to place a degree of reliance on the work of the expert in accordance with AUS 606 (ISA 620).

As has been explained, the timing of physical inventory is negotiated with management in accordance with the entity's inventory system and the assessment of control risk. Except where reliance is placed wholly on perpetual inventory records, quantities are determined by physical count as of a specific date. The date should be at or near the balance sheet date, and the auditor should be present on the specific date. For a multi-site entity, the auditor may vary locations attended each year, so long as he or she observes a sufficiently sized sample of inventory each year. In such cases, the auditor may consider relying on internal audit for attendance at locations not visited, subject to the requirements of AUS 604 (ISA 610), Considering the Work of Internal Auditing. Such reliance, however, does not replace the requirement for the auditor to undertake sufficient personal observation of inventories. Other firms of auditors may also be engaged to observe physical inventory at inconvenient locations, subject to the requirements of AUS 602 (ISA 600), Using the Work of Another Auditor.

Attendance at physical inventory involves the performance of tests of control over entity procedures and of substantive procedures applied directly by the auditor. Because both procedures are performed simultaneously, both types of audit procedure are usually included within the program of substantive procedures. Moreover, because there is no alternative audit strategy if the entity's physical inventory procedures are found to be inadequate, the auditor should review and evaluate the entity's physical inventory plans well in advance of the counting date. With ample lead time, the entity should be able to respond favourably to suggested modifications in the plans before the count is begun. It is common for the auditor to assist the entity in designing a physical inventory plan that will facilitate both the taking and the observing of the inventory.

Procedures are the same as for test counts in respect of perpetual inventory records (see pages 459 and 460), except that the count is of all inventory, not just a sample thereof.

In observing physical inventory to ensure laid down procedures are being properly followed, the auditor should:

- observe entity employees performing their laid down procedures;
- determine that pre-numbered count sheets or inventory tags are properly controlled;
- be alert to the existence of empty containers and hollow squares (empty spaces) that may exist when goods are stacked in solid formations;
- observe that cut-off procedures are being followed and that the movement of goods, if any, is properly controlled;
- see that all goods are marked as having been counted.

In addition, the auditor should perform substantive procedures, including:

- making test counts and agreeing quantities with the entity's count;
- recording details of serial numbers of count sheets or tags used and unused (or take copies of all used count sheets);
- appraising the general condition of the inventory, noting damaged, obsolete and slow-moving items;
- ensuring that partly used count sheets are ruled off to prevent additional entries being made;
- identifying and noting the last receiving, production and dispatch documents used, and determining that goods received during the count are properly segregated.

The extent of the auditor's test counts partly depends on the nature and composition of the inventory. Prior to physical inventory, the auditor will identify high-value items for test counting in addition to counting a representative sample of other items. In making test counts, the auditor should record the count and give a complete and accurate description of the item (identification number, unit of measurement, location, etc.) in the working papers, as shown in Figure 12.1 (page 470). Such data are essential for the auditor's comparison of the test counts with the entity's counts, and for the subsequent tracing of the counts to inventory summary sheets and perpetual inventory records.

On conclusion of the observation procedure, a designated member of the audit team should prepare a working paper detailing such matters as listed below before reaching a conclusion as to the reliability of the count:

- departures from the entity's physical inventory plan;
- the extent of test counts and any material discrepancies resulting therefrom;
- conclusions on the accuracy of the counts;
- the general condition of the inventory.

In the initial audit of an established entity, it is clearly impracticable for the auditor to have observed the physical inventory at the previous year end that establishes the opening inventory. AUS 510 (ISA 510), Initial Engagements — Opening Balances permits the auditor to verify the inventories by other auditing procedures. When the entity has been audited by another firm of auditors in the prior period, the auditor may review working papers of the predecessor audit firm and consider its competence and independence. If the entity has not been audited previously, the auditor may be able to obtain audit satisfaction by testing prior period transactions, reviewing the records of prior counts or applying analytical procedures.

FIGURE 12.1 *Inventory test counts working paper*

Highlight Company
Raw Materials Test Counts
31/12/X1

Prepared by: L.R.S. Date: 31/12/X1
Reviewed by: B.E.M. Date: 7/1/X2

Tag no.	Inventory sheet no.	Inventory		Count		
		Number	Description	Company	Auditor	Difference
6531	15	1-42-003	Back plate	125 ✓	125	
8340	18	1-83-012	5-mm copper plate	93 ✓	93	
1483	24	2-11-004	Single-end wire	1321 m✓	1325 m	4 m
4486	26	2-28-811	Copper tubing	220 m✓	220 m	
3334	48	4-26-204	Side plate	424 ✓	424	
8502	64	7-44-310	10-mm copper wire	276 m✓	276 m	
8844	68	7-72-460	20-mm copper wire	419 m✓	419 m	
6285	92	3-48-260	Front plate	96 ✓	69	27

Each difference was corrected by the company and the net effect of the corrections was to increase inventory by $840.
Total inventory values for which test counts were made and traced to inventory summaries without exception = $210 460 or 22% of the total. In my opinion, errors were immaterial.
✓ = Traced to company's inventory summary sheets (F-4), noting corrections for all differences.

When sufficient evidence has not been obtained as to the existence of opening inventories, or when the auditor is unable to observe the taking of closing inventory or to obtain sufficient evidence from alternative procedures, he or she is precluded from issuing an unmodified auditor's report. We will consider the specific effects on the auditor's report in Chapter 15. Like the confirmation of accounts receivable, the observation of the entity's physical inventory applies to many assertions. This procedure is the primary source of evidence that the inventory exists. In addition, this procedure relates to the assertions detailed in Table 12.4 on the next page.

TABLE 12.4

Assertions for which attendance at physical inventory provides evidence

Assertion	Application
Completeness	Procedures provide assurance that no items were omitted from the count.
Valuation	Observation of the condition of goods as being damaged, obsolete or apparently slow moving provides evidence as to goods that may need to be valued at net realisable value.
Rights and obligations	Possession of goods on entity premises provides some evidence as to ownership.

Testing clerical accuracy of inventory listings

After the physical inventory, the entity uses the count sheets or inventory tags to prepare a listing of all items counted. The inventory items are then priced to arrive at the total value of the inventory. Because this listing serves as the basis for the recorded inventory balance, the auditor must perform procedures to ensure that the listing is clerically accurate and that it accurately represents the results of the physical count.

To determine that the list accurately represents the results of the count, the auditor:

- tests his or her own test counts to the inventory listings;
- identifies count sheets or tags used in the physical inventory according to records made by the auditor at the time of attendance, and tests items on those count sheets or tags to and from the listings;
- compares the count, on a test basis, with amounts per perpetual records, when applicable, and inquires into any differences noted;
- tests the clerical accuracy by recalculating the extensions of quantities times unit prices on a test basis, and the totals shown on the inventory listings.

Testing inventory pricing

6 LEARNING OBJECTIVE

Explain the audit procedures for verifying inventory pricing.

This procedure involves verifying the cost of inventory and the net realisable value of those items that management has determined need to be written down. It also involves considering whether other items need to be written down whose net realisable value may be below cost. Thus, it relates to the valuation assertion.

Inventory at cost. For merchandise inventory and raw materials valued on a first-in first-out basis, this test involves examining suppliers' invoices covering the quantity in inventory.

For work in process and finished goods inventories, the auditor must test cost against costing records. He or she should have evaluated the entity's costing system during the interim audit, and assessed controls over the determination of product cost. Dual-purpose tests (Table 12.2 on page 464), serving as both tests of control and substantive procedures, should provide sufficient evidence as to the reliability of product cost data. The auditor then vouches the costs that are applied to physical inventory to the costing records.

Where inventory is costed at standard cost, variances for the year need to be analysed. When a variance account has a large balance, the auditor must consider whether fair presentation requires a pro rata allocation of the variance to inventories and to costs of goods sold, instead of charging the entire variance to the cost of goods sold. A large adverse material price variance, for example, may indicate that the true cost of inventory is greater than the standard cost. If the variance is written off, then the cost of inventory is understated.

Inventory at net realisable value. AAS 2 (IAS 2) requires inventory to be written down to net realisable value where below cost. The write-down constitutes an accounting estimate and the auditor must follow the procedures in AUS 516 (ISA 540), Audit of Accounting Estimates.

This requires the auditor to: review and test the process used by management; use an independent estimate; and review subsequent events.

For items priced at net realisable value, the auditor must verify the basis for arriving at that value. In some cases, it will be the actual, current or contracted selling price less an estimate of costs to be incurred in completion and selling. In other cases, a formula may be used, taking into account the age, past movement and expected future movement of the inventory items. The auditor must examine the data and assumptions on which the estimates are based, check the calculations, consider prior period experience, and see that the estimates are properly approved by management.

In view of the inherent risk of understatement of the required write-down, the auditor should also carry out substantive procedures to identify the need for further write-downs. AAS 2 (IAS 2) specifically identifies the following situations in which a write-down may be necessary:

- a fall in selling price;
- physical deterioration of inventories;
- obsolescence;
- a decision to sell at a loss;
- purchasing or production errors.

Specific procedures normally adopted by the auditor include:

- review of sales after the balance date;
- observation of deterioration or obsolescence during the auditor's attendance at physical inventory;
- analysis of inventory holdings relative to recent or future budgeted turnover to identify excessive holdings. This analysis is often performed with the use of generalised computer audit software;
- inquiry of management and of sales and production personnel;
- review of the minutes of the board of directors and executive committees.

Use of an expert. When entity assertions about the value of the inventory pertain to highly technical matters, the auditor may require the assistance of an outside expert. This may occur, for example, in an oil company with different grades of petrol and motor oil, or in a jewellery shop with different carat diamonds. As we explained in Chapter 6, the auditor may use the work of a expert as an auditing procedure to obtain sufficient appropriate audit evidence when he or she is satisfied as to the qualifications and independence of the expert.

Confirming inventories at locations outside the entity

When inventories are stored in public warehouses or with other third parties, the auditor should obtain evidence as to the existence of the inventory by direct communication with the custodian. This type of evidence is deemed sufficient except when the amounts involved represent a significant proportion of current or total assets. When this is the case, the auditor should apply one or more of procedures that include:

- considering the integrity and independence of the third party;
- observing (or arranging for another auditor to observe) physical counts of the goods;
- obtaining another auditor's report on the warehouse's control procedures relevant to physical counting and to custody of goods;
- if warehouse receipts have been pledged as collateral, confirming with lenders the pertinent details of the pledged receipts.

Confirmation of inventories at outside locations also provides evidence about the rights and obligations assertion. In addition, it will result in evidence as to the completeness assertion if the custodian confirms more goods on hand than stated in the confirmation request. It does not provide any evidence about the value of the inventory because the custodian is not asked to report on the condition of the goods stored in the warehouse.

Examining consignment agreements and contracts

Goods on hand may be held for customers, at their request, after a sale has occurred, and goods belonging to others may be held on consignment. A consignment 'sale' is one made on a sale or return basis. Payment for the goods is required only on subsequent sale to a third party. For accounting purposes, such goods are included in the 'seller's' inventory. Thus, management is requested to segregate goods not owned during the physical inventory. In addition, the auditor usually requests a written assertion on ownership of inventories in the representation letter. This letter is illustrated in Chapter 14 (page 547).

The auditor should also inquire whether any of the entity's own goods are held on consignment and included in inventory. If so, the auditor should review the documentation or, if the goods are material, confirm the existence of such goods directly with the other party.

Goods may also be assigned or pledged, usually as security for loans. The auditor must inquire of management as to the existence of such agreements and appropriate disclosure checked in the financial report. The auditor must also consider the possibility of window dressing. Substantial sales immediately prior to the year end, to an unlikely customer, of goods that are not required to be delivered may, in reality, be a loan by the 'customer', secured by the transfer of title to specified goods. Such a 'transaction' enables the entity to reduce its inventories and increase its cash, thus enhancing the quick or acid test ratio. Further inquiry may reveal an agreement, by the entity, to repurchase the goods after the year end. Such a transaction should be accounted for in accordance with its substance: a loan secured by inventory.

Evidence obtained from this procedure relates to the rights and obligations assertion and the disclosure assertion.

Disclosure

It is appropriate to identify the major inventory categories in the balance sheet. In addition, there should be disclosure of the inventory costing method(s) used, the pledging of inventories and the existence of major purchase commitments.

Inquiry of management is used to determine the existence of binding contracts for future purchases of goods. When such commitments exist, the auditor should examine the terms of the contracts and evaluate the fairness of the entity's accounting and reporting. When material losses exist on purchase commitments, they should be recognised in the financial report, together with a disclosure of the attendant circumstances as noted in the discussion of accounts payable in the previous chapter.

The substantive procedures described above provide evidence as to financial report disclosure. Further evidence may be obtained, as needed, from a review of the minutes of board of directors meetings and from inquiries of management. Based on the evidence, and on a comparison of the entity's financial report with the Corporations Law (or other regulatory frameworks) and with applicable Accounting Standards, the auditor determines the fairness of the disclosures.

LEARNING CHECK

12.1 Where perpetual inventory records are used to determine inventory at the balance sheet date, the auditor needs to obtain an understanding of the internal control structure and perform tests of control.

12.2 The most important test of control is evaluation of the design effectiveness of test counts of physical inventory and comparison with the records. The extent and results of such test counts performed by the entity are of critical importance to the assessment of control risk.

12.3 For manufacturing entities, the auditor needs to assess cost accumulation procedures and their reliability as a basis for determining inventory cost.

12.4 Principal inherent risks are those of existence and valuation.

- Management has an incentive to overstate the quantity and/or value of inventories.
- Inventory is subject to theft.
- Valuation of inventory involves judgement, estimation and contentious accounting treatments.

12.5 Physical observation of inventory is a required audit procedure whether by attendance at cyclical counts of perpetual inventory records or at a balance date count, and involves:

- considering the adequacy of management plans;
- observing compliance with laid down procedures;
- performing substantive procedures in the form of inspecting and test counting inventory, noting the use of count sheets and obtaining cut-off information.

12.6 Testing of the pricing of inventory involves testing against costing records, verifying write-downs to net realisable value and considering the need for further write-downs to net realisable value.

PROPERTY, PLANT AND EQUIPMENT

7 LEARNING OBJECTIVE

Identify the audit objectives applicable to plant, property and equipment.

Property, plant and equipment are non-current tangible assets intended to be retained for use in the entity's operations. This category, on the balance sheet, includes land and buildings, plant and equipment, and the related accumulated depreciation. Land and buildings may be freehold or leasehold, and plant and equipment may include assets held under finance leases. The principal related profit and loss accounts are depreciation expense, repairs expense, finance charges on finance leases and rent on operating leases.

The principal transaction class relating to property, plant and equipment balances is that of purchases. We explained the internal control structure relating to purchases in Chapter 11. In this chapter, we shall consider issues relating to developing the audit plan and designing substantive procedures.

Audit objectives

The relevant audit objectives are presented in Table 12.5 on the next page.

TABLE 12.5 *Selected specific audit objectives for property, plant and equipment*

Assertion category	Transaction class audit objectives	Account balance audit objectives
Existence or occurrence	Recorded additions represent property, plant and equipment acquired during the period under audit (**EO1**). Recorded disposals represent property, plant and equipment sold or scrapped during the period under audit (**EO2**).	Recorded property, plant and equipment assets represent productive assets that are in use at the balance sheet date (**EO3**).
Completeness	All additions (**C1**) and disposals (**C2**) that occurred during the period have been recorded.	Fixed asset balances include all applicable assets used in operations at balance sheet date (**C3**).
Rights and obligations	The entity has rights to the property, plant and equipment assets resulting from recorded purchase transactions (**R1**).	The entity owns or has rights to all recorded property, plant and equipment assets at the balance sheet date (**R2**).
Valuation or measurement	Additions (**VM1**) and disposals (**VM2**) are correctly journalised and posted.	Property, plant and equipment are stated at cost or a valuation less accumulated depreciation (**VM3**).
Disclosure	The details of additions (**PD1**) and disposals (**PD2**) of property, plant and equipment support their classification and disclosure in the financial report.	Disclosures as to: • cost or valuation, • depreciation methods and useful lives of each major class, • the pledging as collateral, and • the major terms of finance lease contracts of property, plant and equipment assets are adequate (**PD3**).

Developing the audit plan

Because transactions relating to property, plant and equipment are few and usually individually material, assessment of control risk relating to these transactions is rarely necessary. In this section, we will consider materiality and inherent risk and the development of an appropriate audit strategy. Additionally, we will explain the use of a plant register. Although the auditor rarely assesses controls over recording fixed asset transactions in the register, the existence of the register is a source of evidence used in substantive procedures.

Materiality

Property, plant and equipment often represent the largest category of assets on the balance sheet, and expenses associated with property, plant and equipment are material factors in the determination of net profit.

Inherent risk

There may be significant variations in the inherent risk assessments for assertions pertaining to different property, plant and equipment accounts. Inherent risk for the existence assertion may be low in a merchandising entity, for example, because the plant and equipment are not normally vulnerable to theft. However, it may be moderate or high in a manufacturing entity because scrapped or retired machinery may not be written off the books, or small tools and equipment used in production may be stolen. Similarly, the inherent risk in the valuation or measurement assertions may be low when equipment items are purchased for cash, but high when items are acquired under finance leases. In the same way, the inherent risk may be high for the rights and obligations assertion and disclosure assertion for plant and equipment acquired under finance leases.

8 LEARNING OBJECTIVE

Discuss considerations relevant to determining the audit strategy for property, plant and equipment.

Audit strategy

Although material, the verification of property, plant and equipment typically involves significantly less time and cost than the verification of current assets. Unlike receivables or cash balances, control risk assessments for fixed asset balances are usually less dependent on controls over major transaction classes.

The only transaction class with a significant effect on fixed asset balances is that of purchases, which we considered in Chapter 11. When expenditures for smaller items (such as furniture, fixtures and equipment) are processed as routine purchase transactions, the auditor may elect to use a lower assessed level of control risk approach. In such cases, the auditor's tests of control of purchase transactions should include a sample of such assets. In assessing control risk for the plant and equipment assertions, the control risk assessments for purchase transactions are applicable. Other expenditures for land, buildings and major capital improvements tend to occur infrequently and are not subject to the routine purchasing controls. These transactions may be subject to separate controls, including capital budgeting and specific authorisation by the board of directors. Because such transactions are often individually material, a predominantly substantive approach is often adopted for the property, plant and equipment assets, resulting in the specification of low acceptable levels of detection risk.

In determining detection risk for the valuation assertion for depreciation expense and accumulated depreciation, it should be recognised that inherent risk is affected by both the degree of difficulty in estimating useful lives and residual values, and the complexity of the depreciation methods used. Control risk may be affected by the effectiveness of any controls related to these estimates and calculations.

Plant register

Entities frequently maintain a **plant register** as a subsidiary ledger detailing individual items of plant and equipment. The register records the cost of each asset and of any additions or alterations, and the accumulated depreciation charged against it. Balances in the register reconcile with the written-down value of the plant and equipment account in the general ledger. The register also contains additional information, such as the serial number, the supplier or manufacturer, the insurance cover, the maintenance record and the location, as well as other information relevant to management of the portfolio of plant and equipment. From time to time, the entity may carry out an inventory of plant and equipment, primarily to identify the unrecorded disposals of fully depreciated items.

A number of software packages have recently been developed to enable entities to maintain control over their plant and equipment, as described in the following 'Professional environment'.

Control over maintenance of the register is only of audit significance for assets that are vulnerable to misappropriation. Regular physical inventory of such assets provides evidence as to their existence and may be sufficient to enable the auditor to forgo the need to inspect such assets physically at the balance sheet date. Procedures for understanding the internal control structure and assessment of control risk are similar to those for perpetual inventory records described in the first part of this chapter.

PROFESSIONAL ENVIRONMENT Fixed asset software

With its high reliance on IT and other office equipment, the financial-services sector is one of the most enthusiastic markets for asset-management systems.

Until September 1997, the Royal Bank of Canada's London office used an in-house fixed asset-management system based on a Paradox database. But when the person who wrote the system retired, it became too expensive to run.

'It was an old, antiquated system and we wanted something more user-friendly,' explains John Pelley, a financial analyst at the Royal Bank of Canada in charge of maintaining fixed-asset costs and depreciation each month.

The bank chose Catsoft's AssetPro for Windows and integrated this into its local area network serving around 700 employees.

The fixed-asset software records everything the bank purchases, from company cars to mainframe computers.

Pelley admits the installation of the new system brought teething problems.

'When we transferred our records to Catsoft's product, the system would sometimes stop, or it would be painfully slow to input the data; on some occasions, it took up to four hours.' After sending its database of records off to Catsoft, however, the problem was discovered to be a couple of faulty records on the bank's old system. Since these bugs were corrected, the system has speeded up.

Pelley says the benefits from shifting to the new system will not be immediate. 'You have to adjust to a new system but, as long as the system's timing is okay, you don't really worry about improvements.'

(Source: Extracted from John Stokdyk, 'IT focus — Keeping Track of the Assets', *Accountancy Age* (30 July 1998))

Substantive procedures for property, plant and equipment

As we explained earlier, the performance of substantive procedures achieves the required reduction in audit risk of misstatements in property, plant and equipment balances, with inherent risk assessed as being moderate to high, and control risk not assessed at all (and thus taken as being high). Substantive procedures must, therefore, be designed and performed so as to achieve the desired low level of detection risk.

9 LEARNING OBJECTIVE

Design a substantive audit program for property, plant and equipment.

Designing substantive procedures

In the first audit, evidence must be obtained as to the fairness of the opening balances and the ownership of the assets comprising the balances. When the entity has previously been audited by another firm of auditors, this evidence may be obtained from a review of the predecessor auditor's working papers. If the entity has not been previously audited, the auditor must undertake an investigation of the opening balances. Information concerning opening balances obtained in the initial audit is usually recorded in the permanent audit file. This record is updated annually to record changes in the major assets, particularly property, including details of title deeds and registered charges such as mortgages.

In a recurring engagement, the auditor concentrates on the current year's transactions. The opening balances have been verified through the preceding year's audit, and changes in the balance are usually few. This contrasts with the audit of current assets, which are subject to numerous transactions and for which the audit effort is concentrated on the closing balance. The auditor relies on the inspection of documentary evidence in verifying additions and disposals, and on mathematical evidence in verifying depreciation.

Possible substantive procedures for property, plant and equipment balances, and the specific account balance audit objectives to which the tests relate, are shown in Table 12.6. Risk considerations usually result in greater emphasis being placed on the existence or occurrence and valuation or measurement assertions. We will explain each substantive procedure in a later section.

TABLE 12.6 *Possible substantive procedures for property, plant and equipment assertions*

		Account balance audit objective (from Table 12.5)				
Category	**Substantive procedure**	**EO3**	**C4**	**R2**	**VM3**	**D3**
Initial procedures	1. Perform initial procedures on fixed asset balances and records that will be subjected to further testing. (a) Trace opening balances for plant assets and related accumulated depreciation accounts to and from the prior year's working papers. (b) Review activity in the general ledger, accumulated depreciation and depreciation expense accounts, and investigate entries that appear unusual in amount or source. (c) Obtain entity-prepared schedules of additions and disposals and determine that they accurately represent the underlying accounting records by: • adding and cross-adding the schedules and reconciling the totals with increases or decreases in the related general ledger balances during the period; • testing the agreement of items on schedules with entries in related general ledger accounts.	✓	✓	✓	✓	✓
Analytical procedures	2. Perform analytical procedures. (a) Calculate ratios. (b) Analyse ratio results relative to expectations based on prior years results, industry data, budgeted amounts or other data.	✓	✓		✓	
Tests of details of transactions	3. Agree asset additions with supporting documentation.	✓		✓	✓	✓
	4. Agree asset disposals with supporting documentation.	✓	✓	✓	✓	✓
	5. Review repairs and maintenance and rental expense.		✓			✓
Tests of details of balances	6. Examine title documents and contracts.	✓		✓		
	7. Review provisions for depreciation.				✓	
	8. Consider the possibility of impairment.				✓	✓
	9. Inquire into the valuation of property, plant and equipment.				✓	✓
Disclosure	10. Compare the report presentation with applicable Accounting Standards. (a) Determine that property, plant and equipment assets and related expenses, gains and losses are properly identified and classified in the financial report. (b) Determine the appropriateness of disclosures pertaining to the cost, value, depreciation methods and useful lives of major classes of asset, the pledging of assets as collateral and the terms of lease contracts.					✓

Initial procedures

Before performing any of the other steps in the audit program, the auditor determines that the opening general ledger balances agree with the prior period's audit working papers. Among other functions, this comparison will confirm that any adjustments determined to be necessary at the conclusion of the prior audit and reflected in the prior period's published financial report were also properly booked and carried forward. Next, the auditor should test the mathematical accuracy of entity-prepared schedules of additions and disposals, and reconcile the totals with changes in the related general ledger balances for property, plant and equipment during the period. In addition, the auditor should test the schedules by vouching items on the schedules to entries in the ledger accounts, and tracing ledger entries to the schedules to determine that they are an accurate representation of the accounting records from which they were prepared. The schedules may then be used as the basis for several other audit procedures. Figure 12.2 illustrates an auditor's lead schedule for property, plant and equipment and accumulated depreciation.

FIGURE 12.2 *Property, plant and equipment asset and accumulated depreciation lead schedule*

Highlift Company
Property, plant and equipment and accumulated depreciation
Lead schedule
31 December 20X1

W/P ref: G
Prepared by: C.J.G. Date: 4/2/X2
Reviewed by: R.C.P. Date: 12/2/X2

			Asset cost					Accumulated depreciation				
W/P ref.	Acct. no.	Account title	Balance 31/12/X0	Additions	Disposals	Adjust-ments DR/(CR)	Balance 31/12/X1	Balance 31/12/X0	Provisions	Disposals	Adjust-ments (DR)/CR	Balance 31/12/X1
G-1	301	Land	450 000^				450 000					
G-1	302	Buildings	2 108 000^	125 000		㉑(25 000)	2 208 000	379 440^	84 320		㉑ (1 000)	462 760
G-3	303	Mach. and equip.	3 757 250^	980 000	370 000	㉑25 000	4 392 250	1 074 210^	352 910	172 500	㉑ 1 000	1 255 620
G-4	304	Furn. and fixtures	853 400^	144 000	110 000		887 400	217 450^	43 250	21 000		239 700
			7 168 650	1 249 000	480 000	0	7 937 650	1 671 100	480 480	193 500	0	1 958 080
			F	F	F	F	FF	F	F	F	F	FF

^ Traced to general ledger and 31/12/X0 working papers

F Footed

FF Cross-footed and footed

㉑ To reclassify cost and related accumulated depreciation for purchased addition recorded in Buildings account that should have been recorded in Machinery and Equipment account. See adjusting entry #21 on W/P AE-4.

Analytical procedures

Analytical procedures are less useful as a source of evidence as to property, plant and equipment balances than they are for current assets and liabilities. This is because the balance can vary substantially as the result of relatively few transactions of which the auditor is already likely to be aware. A comparison of the annual depreciation charge with the cost or written-down value of the relevant class of assets should yield a measure comparable to the depreciation rate. Such evidence could provide some of the required evidence as to the valuation assertion. Comparison of repairs and maintenance expense with that for prior years or with net sales may indicate the possibility that some maintenance expenditures have not been recorded or that they have been capitalised in error.

Tests of details of transactions

These substantive procedures cover three types of transaction related to property, plant and equipment: additions, disposals, and repairs and maintenance.

Agreeing additions

The auditor needs first to ascertain management's policy with regard to the distinction between capital and revenue expenditure. Most entities specify a cut-off value below which purchases are expensed regardless of their nature. A consistent policy also needs to be followed in distinguishing improvements, which prolong the life or enhance the usefulness of existing assets and repairs and maintenance, which are necessary for the asset to continue to function over its expected useful life. The auditor must ensure that additions are properly capitalised and that a consistent policy is being followed.

The recorded amounts should be vouched to supporting documentation in the form of authorisations in the minutes, suppliers' invoices and contracts. If there are numerous transactions, the vouching may be done on a test basis. In performing this test, the auditor ascertains that the amount capitalised includes installation, freight and similar costs, but excludes expenses included on the supplier's invoice, such as a year's maintenance charge. For construction in progress, the auditor may review the contract and documentation in support of construction costs. The auditor should physically inspect major items, ensuring that details of the asset inspected (such as its description and the manufacturer's serial number) agree with the documentation.

The auditor also needs to inquire about leases for property, plant and equipment entered into during the period. Lease agreements convey, to a lessee, the right to use assets, usually for a specified period of time. For accounting purposes, leases may be classified as either finance leases or as operating leases. The auditor should read the lease agreement to determine its proper accounting classification in accordance with AAS 17 (IAS 17), Accounting for Leases. When a finance lease exists, both an asset and a liability should be recognised in the accounts and financial report. The cost of the asset and the related liability should be recorded at the present value of the future minimum lease payments. The auditor should use recomputation to verify the accuracy of the entity's determination of the present value of the lease liability.

The vouching of additions provides evidence about the occurrence, rights and obligations, and measurement assertions. In addition, the examination of lease contracts pertains to the disclosure assertion, due to the disclosures that are required under AAS 17 (IAS 17).

Agreeing disposals

Evidence of sales, disposals and trade-ins should be available to the auditor in the form of cash remittance advices, written authorisations and sales agreements. Such documentation should be carefully examined to determine the accuracy and propriety of the accounting records, including the recognition of gain or loss, if any.

The following procedures may also be useful to the auditor in determining whether all disposals have been recorded:

- analysing the miscellaneous revenue account for proceeds from sales of property, plant and equipment;
- investigating the disposition of facilities associated with discontinued product lines and operations;
- tracing disposal work orders and authorisations for disposals to the accounting records;
- reviewing insurance policies for termination or reductions of coverage;
- inquiring of management as to disposals.

Inspection of the results of any physical inventory of plant and machinery undertaken by the entity provides further evidence that all disposals have been recorded.

Evidence that all disposals or retirements have been properly recorded relates to the occurrence, rights and obligations, and measurement assertions. Evidence supporting the validity of transactions that reduce property, plant and equipment relates to the completeness assertion.

Reviewing repairs and maintenance and rental expenses

The auditor's objective in reviewing repairs and maintenance expenses is to determine the propriety and consistency of the charges to this expense. The auditor should scan the individual charges, in excess of the entity's cut-off value for capitalisation, to ensure that they are properly expensed. This procedure is related to the examination of additions to ensure that they are properly capitalised.

This substantive procedure provides important evidence concerning the completeness assertion for property, plant and equipment because it reveals expenditures that should be capitalised. In addition, the analysis may reveal misclassifications in the accounts that relate to the disclosure assertion.

Rental expenses are reviewed to ensure that such rents relate to assets under operating leases. Documentary evidence needs to be tested for evidence of leases that should be accounted for as finance leases. This procedure provides evidence as to the completeness assertion in that all assets acquired under finance leases are properly accounted for as additions to property, plant and equipment.

Tests of details of balances

The auditor usually concludes that the closing balance is correctly stated — with respect to the assertions of existence, completeness, and rights and obligations — after having tested the opening balance with the prior year's working papers, and verified additions and disposals. However, the auditor may examine documentary evidence as to the existence and rights and obligations assertions of the recorded balance.

The principal test of balances relates to valuation and disclosure. These are testing the provision for depreciation, considering the need for provision for impairment and the appropriateness of any revaluation.

Examining title documents and contracts

The auditor may establish ownership of vehicles by examining registration certificates and insurance policies. For plant and equipment, the 'paid' invoice may be the best evidence of ownership. Evidence of ownership of freehold property is found in title deeds, property rates bills, mortgage payment receipts and fire insurance policies. The auditor can also verify ownership of freehold property by reviewing public records. When this form of additional evidence is desired, the auditor may seek the help of a solicitor. The examination of ownership documents contributes to the existence and rights assertion and obligations assertions for property, plant and equipment.

Reviewing provisions for depreciation

In this test, the auditor seeks evidence as to the reasonableness, consistency and accuracy of depreciation charges.

- *Reasonableness*: The auditor determines the reasonableness of depreciation provisions by considering such factors as the entity's past history in estimating useful lives and the remaining useful lives of existing assets. The auditor must also ensure that management has reviewed the depreciation rates during the year and adjusted the rates as necessary in accordance with AAS 4, Depreciation of Non-current Assets (IAS 16, Property, Plant and Equipment).

- *Consistency*: The auditor can ascertain the depreciation methods used by reviewing depreciation schedules prepared by the entity and inquiring of management. The auditor must then determine whether the methods in use are consistent with those used in the preceding year. On a recurring audit, this can be established by a review of the previous year's working papers.
- *Accuracy*: The auditor verifies accuracy through recalculation. Ordinarily, the auditor does this on a selective basis by recomputing the depreciation on major assets and testing depreciation taken on additions and disposals during the year.

These substantive procedures provide evidence about the valuation assertion.

Considering the possibility of impairment

The auditor must be satisfied that the carrying value of property, plant and equipment does not exceed the greater of their realisable value or value in use in accordance with ED 99 (IAS 36), Impairment of Assets.

The auditor may derive evidence of overvalued assets by observing obsolete or damaged units during a tour of the plant; identifying assets associated with discontinued activities but not yet disposed of; and inquiring of management as to budgets and forecasts for specific activities in relation to the carrying value of assets associated with those activities.

Where amounts have been written off the carrying value of any property, plant or equipment asset, the auditor must be satisfied, by inquiring of management as to future plans, that the write-down is reasonable.

Inquiring into the valuation

Management may also choose to revalue property, plant and equipment so as to reflect more fairly their value to the business. AAS 38, Revaluation of Non-current Assets (IAS 16, Property, Plant and Equipment) requires that any revaluation must be applied to a class of assets, not to individual assets within a class. Full valuations must be made or reviewed by an independent valuer. Interim valuations may be made by an internal valuer. The auditor would need to be satisfied as to the skill, competence and objectivity of the valuer, whether that valuer is independent or an employee of the entity. In particular, it would be necessary for the auditor to:

- sight a copy of the valuer's report;
- pay regard to the basis of valuation stated therein;
- consider its appropriateness as the basis for determining the carrying amount of that class of assets in the financial report (SAS 520; ISA 620).

This substantive procedure provides evidence about the valuation assertion and the disclosure assertion.

Disclosure

The financial report presentation requirements for property, plant and equipment are extensive. The financial report should show, for example, the depreciation expense for the year; the book value for major classes of property, plant and equipment; and the depreciation method(s) used. For assets carried other than at cost, information that must be disclosed comprises (1) the name and qualifications of the valuer and whether they are internal or independent, (2) the basis of valuation and (3) the date and amounts of the valuation. The auditor acquires evidence concerning these matters through the substantive procedures described in the preceding sections.

Property pledged as security for loans should be disclosed. The auditor may obtain information on pledging by reviewing the minutes, the register of charges and long-term contractual agreements; by confirming debt agreements; and by making inquiries of management. The auditor can determine the appropriateness of the entity's disclosures related to assets under lease by referring to the authoritative accounting pronouncements and the related lease agreements.

LEARNING CHECK

12.7 Transactions involving property, plant and equipment are infrequent and, where material, are usually subject to special treatment. For this reason, auditors rarely test controls over fixed asset transactions or the plant register, preferring to adopt a predominantly substantive approach.

12.8 The principal inherent risks are those for existence and valuation assertions, namely:
- that management has an incentive to overstate the existence and/or value of property, plant and equipment;
- that valuation requires considerable estimation and judgement.

12.9 Because property, plant and equipment transactions are few and the make-up of the balance is relatively constant, the auditor's substantive procedures concentrate on verifying transactions that reconcile the opening balance with the closing balance.

12.10 Valuation requires:
- a consideration of the reasonableness, consistency and accuracy of the year's depreciation provision;
- a consideration of the need for an impairment provision;
- verification of revaluations.

SUMMARY

Inventories and property, plant and equipment are the major non-monetary assets in most entities' financial reports. Misstatements in these balances are frequently a major cause of audit failure. There are many similarities in the audit of these balances, but also some significant differences. For both balances, the primary inherent risks are misstatements in the occurrence or existence and valuation or measurement assertions. In verifying the existence of inventories, the auditor relies on physical inspection, whether through observation of cyclical counts verifying perpetual inventory records or through attendance at annual physical inventory.

However, in verifying property, plant and equipment, the auditor relies on verifying changes in the recorded balance, including an inspection of additions. The auditor rarely inspects assets making up the balance, reflecting the incidence of transactions which are frequent for inventories, being a current asset, but infrequent for property, plant and equipment.

Given that inventory and property, plant and equipment are non-monetary assets, valuation of both is determined by the application of accounting procedures involving a high degree of judgement. For inventories, the auditor needs to understand the costing system to determine its appropriateness and its accuracy in accumulating cost data. For property, plant and equipment, the principal judgements involve estimating useful economic lives, residual value and the basis of depreciation. Again, the auditor needs to determine the appropriateness of the judgements made and the accuracy of the resulting computations. In both cases, the auditor needs to ensure that the accounting basis adopted complies with applicable Accounting Standards and that required disclosures are properly made in the financial report.

KEY TERMS

Cyclical inventory counts, p. 459
Finished goods, p. 456
Inventory count sheets, p. 460
Inventory master file, p. 458
Inventory tags, p. 460
Perpetual inventory records, p. 458
Physical inventory, p. 456
Plant register, p. 476
Production move orders, p. 458
Raw materials, p. 456
Work in process, p. 456

NOTE

1. The source of this account is the US Securities and Exchange Commission's Accounting Series, release no. 19.

FURTHER READING

Peress, Michael, 'Be Sceptical of Barter Transactions', *The CPA Journal* (January 1990), p. 56.

Sarasohn, L. & Luehlfing, M., 'Fixed Assets Don't Squeak', *Management Accounting* (US) (November 1996), pp. 29–36.

Windsor, Sean, 'The Use of Audit Sampling Techniques to Test Inventory', *Journal of Accountancy* (January 1991), pp. 107–11.

Review questions

12.1 Describe the alternative methods by which entities determine their inventory at the balance sheet date and the possible effect of each method on audit strategy.

12.2 Describe the functions involved in maintaining inventory records.

12.3 Identify procedures necessary for an effective inventory count.

12.4 Describe four tests of control applicable to the existence and occurrence assertions.

12.5 Explain why the assessment of control over inventory records is so important in verifying the valuation of manufactured inventory.

12.6 For the auditor's observation at the physical inventory, what steps should he or she perform? Why should the auditor take test counts?

12.7 Why does the auditor usually adopt a predominantly substantive audit strategy for property, plant and equipment assertions?

12.8 Explain why inherent risk for the valuation assertion for property, plant and equipment is usually assessed as being high.

12.9 Describe the purpose and contents of the plant register.

12.10 Discuss procedures that would be useful in ensuring that all disposals of property, plant and equipment have been recorded.

Discussion questions

12.1 Consider the impact the development of barcodes has had on the ability to maintain proper inventory records. Could any problems arise from reliance on barcodes?

12.2 Discuss the many different ways of identifying production overheads and methods of apportionment to determine the cost of inventory. Consider the audit implications of each method.

12.3 Many companies use standard costing as the basis for inventory costing. What audit procedures may be appropriate for establishing the fairness of the standard costs, for testing the maintenance of the standard cost records and for determining the disposition of variances?

12.4 Overhead is to be absorbed into the cost of inventory on the basis of the normal level of activity. What evidence is available to the auditor in verifying management's determination of that level of activity?

12.5 Is attendance at physical inventory more appropriately viewed as a test of controls or as a substantive procedure?

12.6 Consider the cut-off implications of physical inventory being before or after the year end and closing inventory being determined by adjusting the count by reference to purchases and sales records in the intervening period.

12.7 Consider the problems confronting the auditor in verifying both the rate and method of depreciation.

12.8 What steps can the auditor take to ensue that the disposal of fully depreciated assets is properly recorded? What are the implications if such assets are retained in the accounts?

12.9 One of the bases of valuation required by the proposed Accounting Standard on impairment is that of 'present value'. What does this involve? Why may it cause difficulties for auditors?

Professional application questions

★
BASIC
★★
MODERATE
★★★
CHALLENGING

12.1 (Inventory — computer information system) ★★

You are the auditor of Fenton Electronics Limited, which has recently installed a computerised barcode system to record goods received, sales and inventory quantities. The company is a retailer of electrical products.

1. When the goods are received, the goods received department:
   - either reads the barcode on the box containing the product or inputs the barcode number manually, and
   - manually inputs the number of items received (e.g. a box may contain 100 videotapes).

   The quantity of items received is added to the quantity of stock recorded on the computer.
2. When goods are sold to the customer, the barcode of the product is either read or input manually, and the computer produces the sales invoice using the selling price of the product, as recorded on the computer's standing data file. The quantity of items sold is deducted from the stock quantity recorded on the computer.

(continued)

3. Periodically, the stock is counted and these counts are compared with those on the computer. The stock quantities on the computer are amended when significant differences are found.
4. The system allows:
   - details of new products and the selling prices of products to be added or amended;
   - stock quantities to be amended from differences found at the stock count;
   - special prices to be charged to customers (e.g. where the product is damaged or discontinued).

   The main products that the company sells comprise:
   - slow-moving products, such as televisions, video recorders, video cameras and audio equipment;
   - fast-moving, low-value products, such as batteries, videotapes and audio tapes.

Required

(a) Describe the edit checks that should be incorporated into the computer system to ensure that details of goods received are correctly entered into the computer.

(b) (i) Suggest how frequently inventory should be test counted.

(ii) Describe the procedures the company should carry out to ensure the inventory quantities in the computer system are accurate.

(c) Describe the controls that should be used to ensure that the prices of the products on the computer file and on the products in the store are correct.

(ACCA Audit Framework — Paper 6, December 1994 — adapted)

12.2 (Physical inventory — substantive procedures) ★★

MOP Motors (MOP) sells car accessories such as seat covers, headlight protectors and towbars from six retail outlets spread across Sydney, Melbourne and Brisbane. MOP also has a main warehouse located at head office in Sydney.

MOP has about 250 stock lines active at any one time. The value of individual items ranges from 10 cents to $2500. Around 25 per cent of year-end stock is expected to be held at the warehouse, with the remainder spread relatively evenly across the six retail outlets. A full stocktake will be carried out at all locations at the year end.

The inventory system produces the following reports at the year end:

1. A complete stock listing, showing:
   - stock code;
   - total quantity held;
   - cost per unit;
   - total cost per stock item.

   The report also gives a breakdown of where stock items are held and the total value of items held at each location.
2. An ageing report of all stock lines, showing:
   - stock code;
   - total quantity held;
   - sales quantity over each of the previous three months;
   - month-by-month purchase details.

In addition, the system produces a stocksheet report for each location. It lists the description and stock code of each item held at that location, as per the perpetual records. Quantities are omitted because these are completed by the count team.

Required

(a) Performing test counts at the stocktake helps the auditor gather evidence about the existence and completeness assertions. In general, identify the populations from which samples must be selected to satisfy each of these assertions.

(b) In the case of MOP, describe how you would select samples to test the existence and completeness assertions at each location. State which assertion you would pay more attention to, and explain why.

(c) Explain how your test count sample sizes for a retail outlet would be affected if the following independent events occurred.

   (i) A higher value of stock was held at the outlet compared to that at other outlets.

   (ii) Stock thefts had occurred at the outlet over the previous few months.

   (iii) Your preliminary assessment of internal controls was that they were very good, but the manager decided no tests of control would be performed.

   (iv) The outlet had a history of only minor differences between the perpetual records and actual stock held compared with those at other outlets.

   (v) The branch auditors assigned to the stocktake were new to the job.

   (vi) Three out of five outlet staff, including the manager, had commenced work in the past three months.

(d) Briefly explain your answer in each case.

(Professional Year Programme of the ICAA — 1999, Accounting 2 Module — adapted)

12.3 (Physical inventory — substantive procedures) ★★

Your firm is responsible for auditing the financial statements of Hucknall Manufacturing Limited for the year ended 30 September 20X2. The company operates from a single site. Its sales are $5 million and the profit before tax is $110 000. There are no inventory records, so the inventory counts at the year end will be used to value the inventory in the financial statements. Because Monday 30 September is a normal working day, it has been decided that the inventory count should take place on Sunday 29 September when there is no movement of inventory.

The company has produced the following schedule to determine the value of inventory at 30 September 20X2 from that counted on 29 September 20X2.

		$	$
Value of inventory at 29.9.X2			583 247
Add	Cost of goods received on 30.9.X2	10 969	
	Production labour on 30.9.X2	3 260	
	Overheads relating to labour at 120%	3 912	18 141
Less	Cost of goods sold on 30.9.X2		(36 740)
Value of inventory at 30.9.X2			564 648

The company keeps basic accounting records on a microcomputer, using a standard software package. The following accounting procedures are used for sales, purchases and wages.

(*continued*)

1. The shipping department raises dispatch notes when the goods are sent to customers. Sales invoices are produced from the dispatch notes. Sales invoices are input into the computer, which posts them to the accounts receivable ledger and the general ledger;
2. When goods are received, a goods received note is prepared. Purchase invoices are matched with the goods received notes and purchase orders, and authorised by the chief executive officer. After the purchase invoices have been authorised, they are input into the computer, which posts them to the accounts payable ledger and the general ledger.
3. For the wages system, the hours worked for each employee are input into the computer, which calculates the gross wage and deductions (e.g. for tax, medical insurance, etc.) and the net pay. All employees are paid weekly.

Required

(a) Describe the audit procedures you should perform to verify the accuracy of the inventory count:

(i) before the inventory count, and

(ii) on the day of the inventory count.

Include details of the matters you should record in your working papers for follow-up at the final audit.

(b) Explain the substantive procedures you should perform to check the company's schedule (as shown on the previous page) which adjusts the value of inventory at 29 September to that at the company's year end of 30 September 20X2. (You are required to verify only the total value of inventory of $564 648 at 30 September 20X2. You are not required to describe the procedures necessary to verify the accuracy of the individual values of raw materials, work in progress and finished goods.)

(c) Describe the substantive procedures you should perform to check purchases cut-off at the year end.

(ACCA — Question 1, Paper 6, December 1998 — adapted)

12.4 (Inventory — substantive procedures) ★★

You are reviewing the audit files of Fifties Fashions Limited, a manufacturer and retailer of retro clothing. In your review of your audit assistant's work on inventory, you note the following:

1. In performing substantive analytical procedures, the audit assistant has used several management reports supplied by the management accountant. These provided detailed figures, which allowed the assistant to conduct tests such as inventory turnover by product line. The audit assistant followed up all results that differed from those expected, and obtained satisfactory explanations from management. Her overall conclusion was:

> 'Results of analytical review procedures concur with our knowledge of the client's business. Variations from expected results have been satisfactorily explained by the client. These results allow a significant reduction in the tests of details work.'

2. To audit the provision for obsolescence, the audit assistant obtained the aged inventory report as at the balance date. Because inventory comprises fashion items and thus becomes obsolete quickly, all inventory items over six months old were selected for testing. Any items appearing to be obsolete (e.g. items for which there were no recent orders) were checked to ensure they had been provided for. The audit assistant concluded that all testing showed satisfactory results, and that the provision for obsolescence appeared to be fairly stated.

Required

(a) Outline any queries you would raise with your audit assistant.

(b) Describe the additional audit procedures you believe need to be performed to ensure sufficient appropriate audit evidence is obtained for the two situations.

(Professional Year Programme of the ICAA — 1997, Accounting 2 Module — adapted)

12.5 (Fixed assets — substantive procedures) ★★

Shane Simpson, an external auditor, has been engaged to audit the financial statements of Parklane Constructions Limited for the year ended 31 December 20X1. Parklane's financial statements reflect a substantial amount of mobile construction equipment used in the company's operations. The equipment is accounted for in the subsidiary ledger. Shane has performed an evaluation of the internal control systems of the company and found it to be satisfactory.

Required

Identify the substantive procedures that Shane should use in examining mobile construction equipment and its related depreciation in Parklane's financial statements.

(AICPA — adapted)

12.6 (Property valuation — reliance on experts) ★★

Your client, FNP Limited, engaged the services of Z Limited (Z), a firm of real estate valuers, to perform a valuation of all real estate held by the company. As a result of this revaluation, property values on the balance sheet were significantly increased, leading to a material increase in net asset backing per share.

Required

(a) Describe the audit procedures that would be required with respect to the valuations performed by Z.

(b) Explain whether the procedures identified in (a) would change if employees of FNP had performed the valuations.

(c) Assume that you are not satisfied with the results of procedures performed. Explain what alternative procedures could be performed.

(Professional Year Programme of the ICCA — 1999, Advanced Audit Module — adapted)

12.7 (Inventory valuation — reliance on experts) ★★★

Your client is Estate Jewellers Pty Limited (EJ), a proprietary company that specialises in estate jewellery. EJ purchases pieces at auction, cleans and remodels them, and then sells them to the general public. This is the first year your firm has conducted the audit.

(continued)

At the year end, EJ expects to have around 2000 pieces of jewellery on hand, ranging from small items worth $50 to more expensive items worth over $10 000. No two items of jewellery are the same. Due to the complex nature of inventory, the audit partner has decided to engage an expert to provide a year-end valuation report. The expert is to use the client's (unpriced) inventory list and append his or her estimate of the (lower of cost or net realisable) value of each item. The partner intends to place full reliance on the expert's report to reach an opinion on EJ's inventory balance. Year-end stocktake attendance by audit staff is not planned.

Required

(a) When an auditor decides it is appropriate to rely on an expert's report in lieu of stocktake attendance, explain what should be documented in the audit working papers in relation to this decision.

(b) Outline the arguments for and against relying on the expert's report in lieu of attendance at EJ's stocktake.

(c) Explain what difference it would make to the level of reliance you would place on the expert's report if the scope of the expert's work was set by your firm and the expert's fee was paid by:

  (i) the audit firm;

  (ii) the client.

(d) It is now post balance date and you have arranged a meeting with the expert to discuss his report on EJ's inventory. Give examples of questions to ask the expert in this meeting to satisfy yourself that the report is appropriate for your purposes.

(Professional Year Programme of the ICAA — 1999, Accounting 2 Module — adapted)

12.8 (Property, plant and equipment — substantive procedures) ★★★

Your firm is the auditor of Daybrook Insurance Brokers Limited, which operates from a number of branches and provides insurance for the general public and businesses. The company obtains insurance from large insurance companies and takes a commission for its services. You have been asked to audit certain aspects of the company's property, plant and equipment for the year ended 30 June 20X2.

The company's main property, plant and equipment comprise:

- freehold land and buildings;
- microcomputers, printers and related equipment, which are used by staff;
- cars, which are provided to directors and salespeople who visit customers.

The company has been operating for a number of years, and it maintains details of its office equipment and cars on a computerised fixed asset register. The company uses the following depreciation rates:

- buildings (2 per cent per year oncost);
- office equipment (including computers) (10 per cent per year oncost);
- motor vehicles (i.e. cars) (25 per cent per year oncost).

You are concerned that the depreciation rate for the computers may be inadequate.

Required

(a) Describe how you would verify the ownership of freehold land and buildings, computers and cars.

(b) Explain how you would determine that the depreciation rate on the various assets is adequate.

(ACCA — Question 2, Paper 6, June 1995 — adapted)

Case studies

12.1 (Inventory — substantive procedures) ★★★

You are planning the audit of Munchees Limited, a manufacturing company which sells biscuits and snack foods to a large number of retailers nationally. You have turned your attention to the audit of inventory and have obtained the following information from client staff:

1. Year-end inventory is expected to be as follows:

	$000
Raw materials	850
Work in progress	525
Finished goods	1005
	2380

   This represents 20 per cent of total assets.
2. The company uses standard costing to value its inventory, which consists of approximately 150 product lines. At the year end, the relatively equal inventory value of each of these lines will be held.
3. The inventory is stored in approximately fifty warehouses nationally. The company has a policy of taking out short-term leases on unused warehouse space (to minimise rental costs), so the number of warehouses in use varies over time.
4. Goods are manufactured centrally at the Bigtown factory and then shipped out to the warehouses.
5. The recent launch of a new biscuit, Creamy Bix, resulted in poorer than expected sales. Consequently, the company has excess inventory in finished goods, amounting to $200 000. Their use-by date is six weeks after the balance date.
6. A new work-in-progress system was successfully introduced two months after the previous year end. Staff have commented on how this system is a great improvement.
7. Raw materials largely comprise bulk inventories of flour, rice and potatoes. These are held in large storage bins at the Bigtown factory.
8. Work in progress largely comprises biscuit dough, which is stored in several locations throughout the Bigtown factory — both in large sealed vats awaiting processing and in mixing bowls attached to the ten different production lines.
9. As in prior years, all warehouses and the Bigtown factory will be closed at the balance date, to allow a full physical inventory. A perpetual inventory system is used.
10. From your experience in prior years, you know that the company has a highly accurate budgeting system. Final figures rarely vary more than 3 per cent from budget.

Required

(a) Identify the key financial statement assertions for the audit of inventory at Munchees.

(b) Identify and discuss specific issues to be considered in relation to the audit for the existence, and valuation and measurement assertions for Munchees' inventory balance. Describe the audit procedures you would undertake to address these issues.

(Professional Year Programme of the ICCA — 1996, Accounting 2 Module — adapted)

12.2 (Property, plant and equipment — substantive procedures) ★★★

Your firm is auditing the financial statements of Newthorpe Manufacturing Limited for the year ended 30 June 20X1. You have been assigned to the audit of the company's property, plant and equipment, which comprise freehold land and buildings, plant and machinery, fixtures and fittings and motor vehicles.

The freehold land and buildings were purchased ten years earlier (in July 19X1) for $2 million. At the date of purchase, a valuer estimated that both the land and the buildings each had a value of $1 million. Depreciation has been charged since 19X1 on the buildings at 2 per cent per year on-cost. At 30 June 20X1 the accumulated depreciation is $200 000 before the revaluation.

A qualified valuer, who is not an employee of the company, valued the land and buildings at $5 million ($2.9 million for the land and $2.1 million for the buildings). These values will be incorporated into the financial statements as at 30 June 20X1.

The partner in charge of the audit is concerned at the large increase in the value of the land and buildings since they were purchased. She has asked you to check the reliability and accuracy of the valuation. She suggested that AUS 606 (ISA 620), Using the Work of an Expert could assist you in carrying out this work.

In addition, you have been asked to verify the existence and completeness of plant and machinery recorded in the company's computerised fixed asset register. The fixed asset register records the description of each fixed asset, the original cost, the depreciation charge and the accumulated depreciation.

Required

(a) Describe the audit work you will carry out to check whether the valuer has provided an accurate and independent valuation of the land and buildings.

(b) Describe the audit work you will carry out to check the existence and completeness of plant and machinery, as recorded in the company's fixed asset register.

(ACCA — Question 3, Paper 6, June 1997 — adapted)

chapter 13

chapter 13

Auditing cash and investments

Overview

LEARNING OBJECTIVES

After studying this chapter, you should be able to:

1. identify the audit objectives applicable to cash
2. discuss considerations relevant to determining the audit strategy for cash
3. design and execute an audit program for cash balances
4. explain procedures for confirming bank balances
5. describe the irregularity known as lapping and how the auditor can detect it
6. identify the audit objectives applicable to investments
7. describe control procedures applicable to investments
8. design and execute an audit program for investments
9. explain the special considerations applicable to the audit of investments in subsidiaries, associates and joint ventures.

Professional statements

AUSTRALIAN		INTERNATIONAL	
AUS 602	Using the Work of Another Auditor	ISA 600	Using the Work of Another Auditor
AAS 14	Accounting for Investments in Associates	IAS 28	Accounting for Investments in Associates
AAS 19	Accounting for Interests in Joint Ventures	IAS 31	Financial Reporting of Interests in Joint Ventures
AAS 20	Foreign Currency Translation	IAS 21	The Effects of Changes in Foreign Exchange Rates
AAS 21	Accounting for the Acquisition of Assets Including Business Entities	IAS 22	Business Combinations
AAS 24	Consolidated Financial Reports	IAS 27	Consolidated Financial Statements and Accounting for Investments in Subsidiaries
AAS 28	Statement of Cash Flows	IAS 7	Cash Flow Statements
AGS 1002	Bank Confirmation Requests		
AGS 1032	The Audit Implications of Accounting for Investments in Associates		

We have already described the internal control structures for transactions affecting both cash and investment assets in connection with the audits of sales and purchases in Chapters 10 and 11. In this chapter, we will be concerned primarily with the application of substantive audit procedures aimed at verifying these account balances. However, we will consider control procedures over the safekeeping of these assets: (1) the use of bank reconciliations in the case of cash and (2) the maintenance of an investment register.

For each of these account balances, we will:

- identify the audit objectives;
- describe controls over safekeeping;
- discuss considerations relating to the audit plan;
- explain applicable substantive procedures.

Special consideration will be given, in the audit of cash, to audit procedures designed to detect a fraud known as 'lapping' and to the audit of petty cash balances and imprest bank accounts.

A particular feature of the audit of investments is the special disclosure requirement for investments in subsidiaries, associates and joint ventures. It is usually in the form of a consolidated financial report. In this chapter we will also explain the additional audit responsibilities in verifying investments in group entities, and the responsibilities for the consolidated financial report.

CASH

Cash balances include cash on hand and at bank or on deposit at similar financial institutions. Cash on hand includes undeposited receipts and petty cash. Cash at bank includes cash held in current and savings accounts and in imprest accounts such as payroll bank accounts, which is available on demand. AAS 28, Statement of Cash Flows (IAS 7, Cash Flow Statements) has an intermediate category of investments referred to as cash equivalents. Cash equivalents are highly liquid investments readily convertible to known amounts of cash within three months. These are included with cash in the cash flow statement and may be included with cash on the balance sheet.

Other balances at bank that are not readily available and do not meet the definition of cash equivalents (such as debenture sinking fund cash and other accounts that have restrictions on their use) should ordinarily be classified as investments, rather than as part of cash balances. Unlike any other balance sheet account balance, cash may be either an asset or a liability. The latter arises where the bank or other institution with which the entity holds an account allows the entity to write cheques in excess of the balance in the account up to an agreed limit known as an overdraft.

Audit objectives

1 LEARNING OBJECTIVE
Identify the audit objectives applicable to cash.

We addressed internal control considerations and the related audit objectives for cash receipts and payments in Chapters 10 and 11. For cash receipts, you should refer to pages 377–9 for internal control considerations; to pages 387–8 for tests of control and dual-purpose tests; and to page 396 for a description of substantive tests of cash receipts cut-off. For cash payments, you should refer to pages 422 and 423 for control procedures; to page 431 for tests of control and dual-purpose tests; and to page 439 for substantive tests of payments cut-off. Table 13.1 includes only account balance audit objectives.

TABLE 13.1

Selected specific audit objectives for cash balances

Assertion category	Account balance audit objective
Existence	Recorded cash balances exist at the balance sheet date (**E1**).
Completeness	Recorded cash balances include the effects of all cash transactions that have occurred (**C1**). Year-end transfers of cash between banks are recorded in the proper period (**C2**).
Rights and obligations	The entity has legal title to all cash balances shown at the balance sheet date (**RO1**).
Valuation	Recorded cash balances are realisable at the amounts stated on the balance sheet and agree with supporting schedules (**V1**).
Disclosure	Cash balances are properly identified and classified in the balance sheet (**D1**). Lines of credit, loan guarantees and other restrictions on cash balances are appropriately disclosed (**D2**).

2 LEARNING OBJECTIVE

Discuss considerations relevant to determining the audit strategy for cash.

Developing the audit plan

Before planning the audit, it is necessary to consider the effectiveness of control procedures designed to ensure the correctness of the recorded balance by way of regular bank reconciliations and the use of imprest accounts. We will then consider materiality and risk, before identifying factors applicable to determining a strategy for the audit of cash.

Safekeeping of cash

Although the auditor adopts a predominantly substantive approach to the audit of cash balances, an understanding of procedures for maintaining accountability over cash is necessary in designing the substantive tests of details. The principal procedures are:

- independently performed bank reconciliations;
- the use of imprest accounts.

Bank reconciliations

In the audit of cash receipts (see Chapter 10) and cash payments (see Chapter 11), the auditor will have obtained an understanding of **bank reconciliations** and tested controls relating to their preparation and use. This involves an independent comparison of the balance shown on the bank statement with the balance recorded in the entity's records. The difference between the two is reconciled by listing outstanding deposits and unpresented cheques. Verifying the reconciliation of the bank account at the balance sheet date is an important substantive procedure. The extent of the auditor's procedures depends on whether there is an entity-prepared reconciliation for the auditor to verify.

Imprest accounts

An **imprest petty cash fund** is established by transferring a specified amount of cash, such as $200 or $500, to a petty cash box. When cash is paid out of the fund, an authorised voucher is placed in the petty cash box in its place. This voucher could be a supplier's invoice or a special petty cash voucher authorised by a responsible official. When the cash is getting low, the vouchers will be used as support for a cheque requisition to replenish the fund. On replenishment, the cash in the petty cash box will be restored to its imprest level. The following internal control features apply to the management of an imprest petty cash fund:

- The fund should be maintained at the imprest level; that is, cash in the fund plus vouchers for payments should always equal the imprest amount.
- The fund should be in the custody of one individual.
- The fund should be kept secure and stored in the safe when not in use.
- Payments from the fund should be for small amounts, and documentation should support each payment.
- The fund should not be mingled with other cash.
- Replenishment of the fund should be based on a review of supporting documentation.
- Upon payment, supporting documents should be stamped 'PAID' to prevent their reuse.

Certain bank accounts — typically payroll and dividend bank accounts — are sometimes also set up on an imprest basis. The **imprest bank account** is opened, or replenished with the net payroll, dividend, etc. When all cheques written on the account have been presented, the balance will be zero. Until such time, reconciliation can be achieved by agreeing the balance as per the bank statement with unpresented cheques. Internal controls over an imprest bank account include the following:

- An individual, such as a paymaster or assistant treasurer, should be authorised to sign cheques drawn on the account.
- Only payroll cheques, dividend cheques, etc. should be written against the account.
- Each pay/dividend period, a cheque for the total net amount payable should be deposited in the imprest bank account.
- The imprest bank account should be independently reconciled each month.

Materiality and risk

For many entities, cash balances represent only a small proportion of assets. However, the amount of cash flowing through the accounts over a period of time is usually greater than for any other account in the financial report. Moreover, cash is vital to the survival of the business as a going concern. The inability of an entity to pay its debts as they fall due because it has a shortage of cash can render a company insolvent, despite the profitability of its operations. Cash, therefore, has a materiality that is greater (relative to its balance) than any other account balance.

The high volume of transactions contributes to a significant level of inherent risk for cash balance assertions, particularly existence and completeness. In addition, the nature of cash balances makes them susceptible to theft, as evidenced by numerous kinds of fraudulent schemes involving cash. In contrast to receivables or inventories, however, the risks pertaining to the rights and obligations, valuation and disclosure assertions for cash are minimal, given the absence of complexities involving these assertions.

Audit strategy

Given the large volume of cash transactions and the small account balance, the audit strategy is invariably to concentrate on verifying the account balance. Moreover, given the significance of cash to an entity's liquidity, auditors tend to plan their procedures to detect much smaller levels of misstatements than for other accounts. The small balance means that it is usually more cost effective to assess inherent and control risks as being high, and to obtain the required overall reduction in audit risk by performing substantive tests of details of balances.

That is not to say that the verification of cash transactions is unimportant. It has a significant impact on recorded sales and purchase balances. We have already considered the assessment of control risk and the description of substantive tests of details of cash transactions in relation to sales and purchases. Nevertheless, even when the lower assessed level of control risk approach is applied in the audit of cash transactions, auditors tend to perform a significant level of substantive procedures in verifying cash balances.

In verifying cash, the auditor must remember that the closing balance may be an overdraft. The assertions of existence and completeness are thus equally important, given that the balance may be either an asset or a liability.

Substantive procedures for cash balances

Procedures described in this section exclude those for petty cash and imprest bank accounts. We will consider the audit of these two accounts separately (see pages 509 and 510).

Determining detection risk

As explained above, the significance of cash to the entity's liquidity and the fact that the balance is relatively small mean that the acceptable level of detection risk in verifying cash balances is invariably set as low.

3 LEARNING OBJECTIVE

Design and execute an audit program for cash balances.

Designing substantive procedures

Table 13.2 (page 500) lists possible substantive procedures to achieve the specific audit objectives for cash balances. The list is organised in accordance with the general framework for developing audit programs for substantive procedures, which we explained in Chapter 9. Note that several of the tests apply to more than one audit objective and that each objective is addressed by multiple possible procedures. Not all of the procedures will be performed in every audit. We will explain each of the procedures in a following section, including comments on when certain of the tests could be omitted and on how some tests can be tailored based on applicable risk factors.

Initial procedures

The starting point for verifying cash balances is to trace the current period's opening balances to the closing audited balances in the prior year's working papers. Next, the auditor should review the current period's activity in the general ledger cash accounts for any significant entries that are unusual in nature or amount and that may require investigation.

In addition, the auditor obtains any schedules that might have been prepared by the entity showing summaries of undeposited cash receipts at different locations and/or summaries of bank balances. The auditor should determine the mathematical accuracy of such schedules and check their agreement with related cash balances in the general ledger. This test provides evidence about the valuation assertion.

Analytical procedures

Cash balances do not normally show a stable or predictable relationship with other current or historical financial or operating data. However, the auditor can compare cash balances with amounts expected from cash flow forecasts.

Tests of details of transactions

As discussed previously, we described tests of details of cash receipt and payment transactions in Chapters 10 and 11. In this chapter, we will look at tests of transactions around the balance sheet date that assist in verifying the balance as at that date.

TABLE 13.2 *Possible substantive procedures for cash balance assertions*

Category	Substantive procedure	Cash balance audit objective (from Table 13.1)				
		E1	C#	RO1	V1	D#
Initial procedures	1. Perform initial procedures on cash balances and records that will be subjected to further testing. (a) Trace opening balances for cash on hand and in bank to prior year's working papers. (b) Review activity in general ledger accounts for cash and investigate entries that appear unusual in amount or source. (c) Obtain entity-prepared summaries of cash on hand and in bank, verify mathematical accuracy, and determine agreement with general ledger.				✓	
Analytical procedures	2. Perform analytical procedures by comparing cash balances with expected amounts.	✓	✓ 1		✓	
Tests of details of transactions	3. Perform cash cut-off tests. (*Note*: These tests may have been performed as part of the audit programs for accounts receivable and accounts payable.): (a) Observe that all cash received by the close of business on the last day of the fiscal year is included in cash and that no receipts of the subsequent period are included, or (b) Review the documentation such as daily cash summaries, duplicate deposit slips, and bank statements covering several days before and after the year-end date to determine proper cut-off. (c) Observe the last cheque issued and mailed on the last day of the fiscal year and trace to the accounting records to determine the accuracy of the cash payments cut-off, or (d) Compare dates on cheques issued for several days before and after the year-end date to the dates on which the cheques were recorded to determine proper cut-off.	✓	✓ 1			
	4. Trace bank transfers before and after the balance sheet date to determine that each transfer is properly recorded as a payment and a receipt in the same accounting period.	✓	✓ 2			
Tests of details of balances	5. Count undeposited cash on hand.	✓	✓ 1	✓	✓	
	6. Confirm bank balances.	✓	✓ 1	✓	✓	
	7. Confirm other arrangements with banks.	✓	✓ 1	✓	✓	✓ 1, 2
	8. Verify reconciliations as appropriate.	✓	✓ 1, 2	✓	✓	
	9. Obtain and use the subsequent period's statements to verify bank reconciliation items and look for evidence of window dressing.	✓	✓ 1, 2	✓	✓	
Disclosure	10. Compare report presentation with applicable Accounting Standards.					
	(a) Determine that cash balances are properly identified and classified.					✓ 1
	(b) Determine that bank overdrafts are reclassified as current liabilities.					✓ 1
	(c) Make inquiries of management, review correspondence with banks, and review minutes of board of directors meetings to determine matters requiring disclosure, such as lines of credit, loan guarantees, compensating balance agreements, or other restrictions on cash balances.					✓ 2

Cash cut-off tests

A proper cut-off of cash receipts and cash payments at the end of the year is essential to the proper statement of cash at the balance sheet date. Two **cash cut-off tests** are performed:

- a cash receipts cut-off test (see Chapter 10);
- a cash payments cut-off test (see Chapter 11).

The use of the subsequent period's bank statement (described below), is also helpful in determining whether a proper cash cut-off has been made. Cash cut-off tests are directed primarily at the financial report assertions of existence or occurrence and completeness.

Tracing bank transfers

Many entities maintain accounts with more than one bank. A company with multiple bank accounts may transfer money between bank accounts. Money may be transferred, for example, from a general bank account to a payroll bank account for payroll cheques that are to be distributed on the next pay day. When a bank transfer occurs, several days will elapse before the cheque clears the bank on which it is drawn. Thus, cash on deposit as per bank records will be overstated during this period because the cheque will be included in the balance of the bank in which it is deposited and will not be deducted from the bank on which it is drawn. Bank transfers may also result in a misstatement of the bank balance as per books if the payment and receipt are not recorded in the same accounting period.

Intentionally recording a transfer as a deposit in the receiving bank while failing to show a deduction from the account on which the transfer cheque is drawn is an irregularity known as **kiting**. Kiting may be used to conceal a cash shortage or overstate cash in bank at the report date.

The auditor identifies bank transfers by analysing the cash book for a few days either side of the balance sheet date, then enters these onto a **bank transfer schedule**. The schedule is then completed by determining, from applicable bank statements, the dates on which the bank recorded the transfers, as illustrated in Table 13.3.

TABLE 13.3 *Bank transfer schedule*

	Bank accounts			Payment date		Receipt date	
Cheque number	From	To	Amount of cheque ($)	Per books	Per bank	Per books	Per bank
4100	General	Payroll	50 000	31/12	3/1	31/12	2/1
4275	General	Branch 1	10 000	31/12	4/1	2/1	2/1
4280	General	Branch 2	20 000	2/1	2/1	31/12	31/12
B403	Branch 4	General	5 000	2/1	3/1	3/1	31/12

If we assume all cheques are dated and issued on 31 December, cheque 4100 in Table 13.3 has been handled properly because both book entries were made in December and both bank entries occurred in January. This cheque would be listed as an unpresented cheque in reconciling the general bank account at 31 December and as a deposit in transit in reconciling the payroll bank account. Cheque 4275 illustrates a transfer cheque in transit at the closing date. Cash per books is understated by $10 000 because the cheque has been deducted from the balance per books by the issuer in December, but has not been added to the Branch 1 account per books by the depositor until January. Thus, an adjusting entry is required at 31 December to increase the branch balance per books.

Cheques 4280 and B403 illustrate the likelihood of kiting because these December cheques were not recorded as payments per books until January, even though they were deposited in the receiving banks in December. Cheque 4280 results in a $20 000 overstatement of cash at bank because the receipt per books occurred in December, but the corresponding book deduction was not made until January. Cheque B403 may illustrate an attempt to conceal a cash shortage because the bank deposit occurred in December, presumably to permit the reconciliation of bank and book balances, and all other entries were made in January.

Kiting is possible when weaknesses in internal controls allow one individual to issue and record cheques (that is, improper segregation of duties) or when there is collusion between the individuals responsible for the two functions. In addition to tracing bank transfers, the auditor may detect kiting by:

- obtaining and using a subsequent period's bank statement (as discussed on page 507), because the kited cheque clearing in January will not appear on the list of unpresented cheques for December;
- performing a cash cut-off test, because the last cheque issued in December will not be recorded in the cheque register.

The tracing of bank transfers provides reliable evidence concerning the existence or occurrence and completeness assertions.

Tests of details of balances

There are five commonly used substantive tests for cash balances in this category:

1. counting cash on hand;
2. confirming bank balances;
3. confirming other arrangements with banks;
4. verifying bank reconciliations;
5. obtaining and using the subsequent period's bank statement.

Counting cash on hand

Cash on hand consists of undeposited cash receipts and change funds. To perform **cash counts** properly, the auditor should:

- control all cash and negotiable instruments held by the entity until all funds have been counted;
- insist that the custodian of the cash be present throughout the count;
- obtain a signed receipt from the custodian on return of the funds;
- ascertain that all undeposited cheques are payable to the order of the entity, either directly or through endorsement.

The control of all funds is designed to prevent transfers by entity personnel of counted funds to uncounted funds. The sealing of funds and the use of additional auditors are often required when cash is held in many locations. Having the custodian present and requiring his or her signature on return of the funds minimises the possibility, in the event of a shortage, of the custodian claiming that all cash was intact when released to the auditor for counting.

This procedure provides evidence of each of the financial report assertions except disclosure. It should be noted that the evidence about rights is weak because the custodian of the fund may have substituted personal cash to cover a shortage.

4 LEARNING OBJECTIVE

Explain procedures for confirming bank balances.

Confirming bank balances

It is customary for the auditor to obtain a **bank confirmation** for cash on deposit and loan balances at the balance sheet date. Figure 13.1 illustrates a 'Bank confirmation — audit request (general)'. The form requests information about account balances (whether of cash on deposit or of overdrafts and other loans) and accounts opened or closed in the year. The procedure for using the form, as explained in AGS 1002, Bank Confirmation Requests, is as follows:

- The request is prepared in triplicate for each bank with which the entity has an account, including those that may have a zero balance at the end of the year.
- It is signed by an authorised cheque signer of the entity and sent, together with a request letter also signed by an authorised signatory/signatories.
- The auditor should personally mail the request in the auditor's own return address envelope to assure the competency of the evidence from this procedure.
- The original is to be returned by the bank to the auditor with a copy to the entity.

FIGURE 13.1 *Bank confirmation — audit request (general)*

BANK CONFIRMATION — AUDIT REQUEST (GENERAL)

Instructions

Auditor

(a) Complete all known details in shaded areas before forwarding to the bank.
(b) If the space provided on the form is inadequate, please attach a statement giving the full details as required by the headings on the form.

Bank

(a) Ensure that the details supplied are as at the confirmation date shown below.
(b) Complete unshaded areas by listing information as called for under the relevant heading, from detail contained in the bank's records.
(c) Confirm details in the shaded areas as to correctness, and mark any variation in red on all copies. Also insert, in red, any information that may have been omitted by the customer/auditor.
(d) Three (3) copies of the form should be received by the bank. All completed copies of the Confirmation are to be signed, with the original returned direct to the auditor in the enclosed stamped addressed envelope. The duplicate is to be forwarded to the client and the triplicate retained by the bank.

To — Bank (name & address)	From — Customer (name & address)
Auditor (name & address) Contact Telephone	Customer's authorised signature Date
Confirmation date	Third party authority is attached. Yes ☐

1. CREDIT ACCOUNT BALANCES

Give details of all account balances in favour of the bank customer as at [/ /]. Include details of any current accounts, interest bearing deposits, foreign currency accounts, convertible certificates of deposit, money market deposits, etc. if not listed below.

Account Name	Account Number	Balance	Currency	Interest Rate

2. DEBIT ACCOUNT BALANCES

Give details of all account balances listed to the bank as at [/ /] by the bank customer in respect of overdraft accounts, bank loans, term loans, etc. and also repayment terms.

Account Name	Account Number	Balance and Currency	Overdraft Limit	Interest Rate	Repayment Terms (e.g. monthly, quarterly, etc.)

3. PROMISSORY NOTES/BILLS OF EXCHANGE HELD FOR COLLECTION ON BEHALF OF THE CUSTOMER

Maker/Acceptor	Amount	Due Date

(continued)

FIGURE 13.1 ***Bank confirmation — audit request (general)*** *(continued)*

4. CUSTOMER'S OTHER LIABILITIES TO THE BANK   CONFIRMATION DATE ______

List liabilities owed, including:

(a) bills discounted with recourse, endorsed drafts/notes, forward exchange contracts, letters of credit, liability in respect of shipping documents where customer's account not yet debited;

(b) data, name of beneficiary, amount and brief description of any guarantee, bonds or indemnities undertaken by the bank on behalf of the customer (with recourse) or given by the customer;

(c) other liabilities — give details.

Nature of liability	Amount	Currency	Due date

5. ITEMS HELD AS SECURITY FOR CUSTOMER'S LIABILITIES TO THE BANK

Indicate if securities relate to particular borrowings or liabilities to the bank and whether lodged in the customer's name. Also indicate details of any negative pledge arrangements.

If lodged by a third party, that party's authority to disclose details must be attached.

Description (include amount if applicable)

6. ACCOUNTS OPENED/CLOSED

List details of any accounts opened or closed during the twelve months prior to confirmation date / /

Account name	Account number	Account name	Account number

7. SEALED PACKETS, LOCKED BOXES, SECURITY PACKETS ETC.

Are sealed packets held on behalf of the customer? Yes ☐ No ☐

Are locked boxes held on behalf of the customer? Yes ☐ No ☐

Are security packets held on behalf of the customer? Yes ☐ No ☐

8. UNUSED LIMITS/FACILITIES

Please confirm details of all available unused limits/facilities at confirmation date.

Types of facility	Amount of facility	Amount of facility unused	Conditions of facility use

9. OTHER INFORMATION

Please confirm (see shaded area) and/or provide any other details (unshaded area) relating to any financial relationships not dealt with under any of the above headings.

This certificate has been completed from our records at __________ branch only. The bank and its staff are unable to warrant the correctness of that information and accordingly hereby disclaim all liability in respect of the same. The information contained herein is confidential and provided for private use in confirmation of our customer accounts for audit purposes only. It may not be used for any other purpose or by any other persons. In particular this is not a credit reference.

Authorising officer's signature	Name	Bank stamp	Date completed and returned
Telephone no.	Title		

The confirming of cash on deposit provides evidence primarily of the existence of cash at bank (because there is written acknowledgment that the balance exists) and of rights and obligations (because the balances are in the name of the entity). The response from the bank also provides some evidence for the valuation assertion for cash at bank, in that the confirmed balance is used in arriving at the correct cash balance at the balance sheet date. Furthermore, it contributes to the completeness assertion; however, it cannot be relied on entirely because the bank confirmation contains a disclaimer in favour of the bank. The bank cannot be held liable if the information supplied is incomplete or inaccurate.

The confirming of overdraft and loan balances provides evidence of:

- existence, because there is written acknowledgement that the loan balance exists;
- rights and obligations, because the loan is a debt of the entity;
- valuation, because the response indicates the amount of the loan balance.

This test also contributes to the completeness assertion in the same manner as for confirming deposit balances.

Confirming other arrangements with banks

The bank confirmation form also requests information as to other arrangements with the bank, such as bills of exchange held by the bank for collection, bills discounted with recourse, guarantees of loans to third parties and unused facilities.

The auditor should enter details of such arrangements as are believed to exist. The auditor's request for other information does not require the branch holding the account to make a detailed search of all of the bank's records, and the response must be interpreted in the light of the bank's disclaimer of responsibility. Nevertheless, the confirmation of other arrangements with banks is especially helpful in meeting the disclosure assertion. It also provides evidence for each of the other assertions. However, the evidence for the completeness assertion is limited to information known by the branch officer completing the confirmation.

Where the auditor believes there may be material accounts, agreements or transactions that he or she is unaware of, the auditor should contact the bank and request further information (AGS 1002.08).

Verifying bank reconciliations

When the entity prepares bank reconciliations on a regular basis that are expected to be reliable, the auditor will test the reconciliations prepared as at the balance sheet date. The test normally includes:

- comparing the closing bank balance with the balance confirmed on the bank confirmation form;
- verifying the validity of deposits in transit and unpresented cheques;
- establishing the mathematical accuracy of the reconciliation;
- vouching reconciling items such as bank charges and credits and errors to supporting documentation;
- investigating old items, such as cheques outstanding for a long period of time, and unusual items.

Verifying the validity of deposits in transit and unpresented cheques involves:

- tracing or test tracing entries in the bank statement for the last month of the fiscal year to the cash book or bank reconciliation at the beginning of the month, marking them off in the process;
- identifying deposits and cheques recorded in the cash book for the last month of the fiscal year, or in the reconciliation at the beginning of that month not marked as appearing on the bank statement, and tracing them through to the closing reconciliation;
- clearing the bank reconciliation to ensure that all applicable outstanding deposits and unpresented cheques are marked as having been traced from the cash book.

If there are large numbers of transactions, the test may be restricted to items over a certain amount.

The working paper for an auditor test of an entity-prepared bank reconciliation is illustrated in Figure 13.2.

FIGURE 13.2 *Review of entity-prepared bank reconciliation*

Bates Company
Bank Reconciliation-City-Bank-General
31/12/X1
(PBC)

A–1
Prepared by: C.J.W. Date: 15/1/X2
Reviewed by: A.C.E. Date: 18/1/X2

Acc. # 110 31/12/X1
Bank acc. no. 12345-642

Balance per bank				120262 47 ^
Deposits in transit:	Per books	Per bank		
	30-12	2-1	8425 15 ✓	
	31-12	7-1	17844 79 ✓	
				26269 94 ✗
Unpresented cheques:				
		1047	225 94 ✓	
		1429	21600 00 ✓	
		1435	47 25 ✓	
		1436	1428 14 ✓	
		1437	1000 00 ✓	
		1440	832 08 ✓	
		1441	41 08 ✓	(25174 49) ✗
Add NSF cheque-ZIM 28/12				200 00 ∅
Balance per books				121557 92 ✘
Adjusting entry-AJE ④				200 00
Balance as adjusted				121357 92
				To A
	Adjusting entry			
Dr. accounts receivable ZIM			200	
Cr. cash in bank				200
NSF cheque charged by bank 29/12				

^ Agreed to bank statement and bank confirmation
✓ Traced to January bank statement
✗ Footed
∅ Traced to statement and debit memoranda
✘ Traced to general ledger

When the entity does not prepare a bank reconciliation or when control risk over entity-prepared reconciliations is high (such as when it is prepared by the cashier), the auditor may prepare the bank reconciliation. When the auditor suspects possible material misstatements, the auditor may obtain the year-end bank statement directly from the bank for use in preparing the bank reconciliation, rather than relying on the copy of the bank statement held by the entity. This procedure will prevent the entity from making alterations to the data to cover any misstatements.

It is also necessary to verify deposits in transit and unpresented cheques by tracing them to the subsequent period's bank statement. When the next period's bank statement validates these and other reconciling items, the reliance that an auditor can place on a bank reconciliation is significantly enhanced.

Testing or preparing a bank reconciliation establishes the correct cash at bank balance at the balance sheet date. Thus, it is a primary source of evidence for the valuation assertion. This test also provides evidence for the existence, completeness, and rights and obligations assertions.

Obtaining and using the subsequent period's bank statement

The **subsequent period's bank statement** would normally be issued at the end of the month following the entity's financial year end. If the audit deadline does not permit waiting for the issue of this statement, then a special statement may be requested. The date should be at a point in time that will permit most of the year-end unpresented cheques to clear the bank — usually seven to ten business days following the end of the entity's fiscal year. The entity should be requested to instruct the bank to send a copy of the subsequent period's bank statement directly to the auditor. On receipt of the subsequent period's bank statement, the auditor should:

- trace all prior year dated cheques to the unpresented cheques listed on the bank reconciliation;
- trace deposits in transit on the bank reconciliation to deposits on the statement;
- scan the statement for unusual items.

The tracing of cheques is designed to verify the list of unpresented cheques. In this step, the auditor may also find that a prior period cheque not on the list of unpresented cheques has cleared the bank and that some of the cheques listed as unpresented have not cleared the bank. The former may be indicative of an irregularity known as kiting, which we explained earlier in connection with bank transfers (see page 501); the latter may be due to delays in the entity mailing the cheques or in the payees depositing the cheques. The auditor should investigate any unusual circumstances.

When the aggregate effect of uncleared cheques is material, it may indicate an irregularity known as **window dressing**. This is a deliberate attempt to enhance a company's apparent short-term solvency. (Assume that the entity's balances at the balance sheet date show current assets of \$800 000 and current liabilities of \$400 000. If \$100 000 of cheques to short-term creditors have been prematurely entered, then the correct totals are current assets of \$900 000 and current liabilities of \$500 000, which results in a 1.8:1 current ratio instead of the reported 2:1.) Window dressing is normally perpetrated by writing cheques on the last day of the financial year but not mailing them until several weeks later, when cleared funds are available at the bank to meet those cheques. If none of a sequence of cheques is presented for payment on the bank statement for more than two weeks after the balance sheet date, then the auditor should make inquiries of the treasurer. Recipients do not usually delay banking cheques once received, and it is normal for most cheques to clear the bank statement within a week of issue.

The tracing of deposits in transit to the subsequent period's bank statement is normally a relatively simple matter because the first deposit on that statement should be the deposit in transit shown on the reconciliation. When this is not the case, the auditor should determine the underlying circumstances for the time lag from the treasurer, and corroborate his or her explanations. Delays in depositing cash receipts could indicate the practice of a fraud known as lapping (see below).

In scanning the subsequent period's statement for unusual items, the auditor should be alert for such items as unrecorded bank debits and credits, and bank errors and corrections. Figure 13.2 (page 506) illustrates a deposit made prior to the year end that is returned by the drawer's bank after the year end, marked 'not sufficient funds' (NSF) and requiring adjustment.

By obtaining the subsequent period's statement directly from an independent source, the auditor secures a high degree of competent corroborating information about the validity of the year-end bank reconciliation and the existence, completeness, rights and obligations, and valuation assertions for cash in bank.

Disclosure

Cash should be correctly identified and classified in the balance sheet. Cash on deposit, for example, is a current asset, but debenture sinking fund cash is a long-term investment. In addition, there should be appropriate disclosure of arrangements with banks, such as lines of credit, compensating balances and contingent liabilities. Responses to questions 3 and 4 in the bank confirmation request illustrated in Figure 13.1 (pages 503–4) are matters that may require disclosure as contingent liabilities. A bank overdraft is normally reported as a current liability.

The auditor determines the appropriateness of the report presentation from a review of the draft of the entity's financial report and the evidence obtained from the foregoing substantive procedures. In addition, the auditor should review the minutes of meetings of the board of directors and inquire of management for evidence of restrictions on the use of cash balances.

Other issues

This section covers three topics: (1) testing to detect an irregularity known as lapping (or teeming and lading); (2) auditing impress petty cash funds; and (3) auditing imprest bank accounts.

5 LEARNING OBJECTIVE

Describe the irregularity known as lapping and how the auditor can detect it.

Detecting lapping

Lapping is an irregularity that results in the deliberate misappropriation of cash receipts, either temporarily or permanently, for the personal use of the individual perpetrating the unauthorised act. Lapping is usually associated with collections from customers, but it may also involve other types of cash receipt. Conditions conducive to lapping exist when the same individual handles cash receipts and maintains the accounts receivable ledger. The auditor should assess the likelihood of lapping in obtaining an understanding about the segregation of duties in the receiving and recording of collections from customers.

An example of lapping

Assume on a given day that cash register receipts totalled $600 and mail receipts opened by the defrauder consisted of one payment on account by cheque for $200 from customer A. The lapper would steal $200 in cash and destroy all evidence as to the mail receipt, except for the customer's cheque. The cash receipts journal entry would agree with the register ($600), and the deposit slip would show cash of $400 and customer A's cheque for $200. These facts can be tabulated as follows:

Actual receipts		Documentation		Cash receipts journal entry		Bank deposit slip	
Cash	$600	Cash tape	$600	Cash sales	$600	Cash	$400
Customer A's cheque	200		—		—	Customer A's cheque	200
	$800		$600		$600		$600

To conceal the shortage, the defrauder usually attempts to keep bank and book amounts in daily agreement so a bank reconciliation will not detect the irregularity. The defrauder also corrects the customer's account within three to four days of actual collection so any apparent discrepancy in the customer's account can be explained as a delay in receiving the money or in posting. To accomplish the latter, the amount stolen is shifted to another customer's account (customer B) several days later as follows:

Actual receipts		Documentation		Cash receipts journal entry		Bank deposit slip	
Cash	$500	Cash tape	$500	Cash sales	$500	Cash	$400
Customer B's cheque	300	Customer A's cheque	200	Customer A's cheque	200	Customer B's cheque	300
	$800		$700		$700		$700

The total shortage is now $300 — $200 from the first example plus $100 from the second example.

Auditing procedures

Tests to detect lapping are performed only when the control risk for cash receipts transactions is moderate or high. There are three procedures that should detect lapping:

1. *Confirm accounts receivable on a surprise basis at an interim date.* Confirming at this time will prevent the individual engaged in lapping from bringing the 'lapped' accounts up to date. Confirmation at the balance sheet date may be ineffective because the 'defrauder' may anticipate this procedure and adjust the 'lapped' accounts to their correct balances at this date.
2. *Make a surprise cash count.* The cash count will include coin, currency and customer cheques on hand. The auditor should oversee the deposit of these funds. Subsequently, the auditor should compare the details of the deposit shown on the duplicate deposit slip with cash receipts journal entries and postings to the customers' accounts.
3. *Compare details of cash receipts journal entries with the details of corresponding daily deposit slips.* This procedure should uncover discrepancies in the details such as those shown in the above two examples.

Auditing impress petty cash funds

The balance of petty cash is rarely material. Some auditors audit petty cash only if the total petty cash payments and replenishments throughout the year are material. Even then, the degree of misstatement would need to be substantial to have a material effect on the financial report. Other auditors, however, believe that entities expect the auditor to verify petty cash and that it is important for the auditor to be seen to audit petty cash.

Substantive procedures

In auditing petty cash, the auditor performs tests of details of transactions and tests of balances. The auditor will test a number of replenishing transactions, including reviewing supporting documentation, accounting for all pre-numbered receipts, and determining that the reimbursement cheque was for the correct amount. The test of balances involves counting the fund. The count is usually made on a surprise basis at an interim date rather than at the balance sheet date. The auditor may also count the fund at the balance sheet date, along with all other cash funds, to avoid the possibility that petty cash may be used to conceal a shortage elsewhere.

Auditing imprest bank accounts

As we explained above, an entity may use an imprest bank account for payroll and dividends.

Substantive procedures

The tests should include confirming the balance with the bank, reviewing the reconciliation prepared by the entity, and using the subsequent period's bank statement. The adjusted or true cash balance at the balance sheet date should be the imprest amount. The only reconciling items on the bank statement will be unpresented payroll or dividend cheques. Employees usually cash their pay cheques promptly, so all the unpresented cheques should clear the bank on the subsequent period's bank statement. Unpaid dividends are more likely to be a problem. However, larger entities with quoted share capital (which are more likely to experience unpresented dividend cheques) usually employ an independent share registrar — one of whose functions is to distribute dividends. In such cases, the entity pays the total dividend to the registrar in a single cheque, and it is the registrar's responsibility to pay individual dividends and to maintain records of unpresented dividend cheques.

LEARNING CHECK

13.1 A high volume of cash transactions results in a high inherent risk but controls over cash transactions are usually strong and are tested in connection with the audits of sales and purchases.

13.2 Regular bank reconciliations are an important control over the prevention and detection of fraud and error.

13.3 Cash balances are usually relatively small but significant, given their importance for liquidity, and auditors tend to adopt a predominantly substantive approach to the audit of cash balances.

13.4 Principal substantive audit procedures applied to balances are:
- counting cash;
- confirming balances with banks;
- testing the closing bank reconciliation;
- tracing outstanding items in the reconciliation to the next period's bank statement.

13.5 In counting cash, the auditor should control all cash funds and count them in the presence of the custodian.

13.6 Lapping is the concealment of the misappropriation of cash by the use of subsequent receipts, which is facilitated where one individual handles cash and maintains the accounts receivable ledger. The auditor should be alert to delays in crediting cheques to receivables and to discrepancies between duplicate deposit slips and cash receipts journal details.

13.7 Petty cash need not be audited where the petty cash transactions are immaterial, although many auditors still do so, as a matter of routine, by vouching reimbursements and counting the balance.

INVESTMENTS

An entity's investment balances involve the ownership of securities issued by other entities. The securities may be in the form of certificates of deposit, preferred and ordinary shares, corporate debentures or government bonds. Consideration is given here to only investments in ordinary shares and corporate debentures. Investments may be held for a variety of reasons, with the principal reasons being:

- to hold surplus funds or funds earmarked for a future purpose;
- to secure a long-term relationship with the other party.

A special category of this latter type of investment is investment for the purpose of acquiring influence or control over the activities of the other entity. Such entities may be classified as subsidiaries, associates or joint ventures, and are regarded as part of the economic entity. The financial report of the investing or 'parent' entity is required to include appropriate balances relating to these other entities, so as to present a consolidated picture of the group or reporting entity. The audit of such investments extends to the verification of the balances in group entity financial reports, which are consolidated with the parent entity's accounts. In the final section of this chapter we will explain the auditor's responsibilities in connection with consolidated accounts.

Investment transactions involve cash receipts, such as dividends and interest received on investments, and proceeds on their disposal. We considered control structure considerations for cash receipts in Chapter 10. Investment transactions also involve cash payments for the purchase of investments. We considered control structure considerations for payment transactions in Chapter 11. In this chapter, we will consider additional controls applicable to investing transactions only. We will discuss these controls in the course of discussing the development of the audit plan.

6 LEARNING OBJECTIVE

Identify the audit objectives applicable to investments.

Audit objectives

For each of the five categories of financial report assertion, Table 13.4 lists specific account balance audit objectives pertaining to accounts affected by investing transactions. In the following sections we will explain considerations and procedures relevant to meeting these objectives.

TABLE 13.4

Selected specific audit objectives for investments

Assertion category	Account balance audit objective
Existence	Recorded investment balances represent investments that exist at the balance sheet date (**E1**).
	Investment revenues, gains and losses resulted from transactions and events that occurred during the period (**E2**).
Completeness	All investments are included in the balance sheet investment accounts (**C1**).
	The profit and loss statement includes the effects of all investment transactions and events during the period (**C2**).
Rights and obligations	All recorded investments are owned by the reporting entity (**RO1**).
Valuation	Investments are reported on the balance sheet at valuation, lower of cost or net realisable value or cost, as appropriate for particular investments (**V1**).
	Investment revenues, gains and losses are reported at proper amounts (**V2**).
Disclosure	Investment balances are properly identified and classified in the financial report (**D1**).
	Appropriate disclosures are made concerning (1) related party investments, (2) the bases for valuing investments, and (3) the pledging of investments as collateral (**D2**).

Developing the audit plan

Before planning the audit, it is first necessary to consider the effectiveness of control structure components designed to ensure that investment transactions are properly supervised and that the investments are subject to adequate safeguards over misappropriation. We will then consider materiality and risk before identifying factors applicable to determining a strategy for the audit of investments.

Safekeeping of investments

7 LEARNING OBJECTIVE

Describe control procedures applicable to investments.

Because the purchase and sale of investments are often processed separately from other purchases and sales, and the certificates of title may be readily negotiable, entities holding substantial investment portfolios usually adopt specific control procedures over investments.

Control environment

The understanding of several control environment factors is relevant to the audit of the investments. The authority and responsibility for investing transactions, for example, should be assigned to a company officer such as the treasurer. This individual should be a person of integrity, with appropriate knowledge and skills, who realises the importance of observing all prescribed control procedures and who can assist other participating members of management in making initial and ongoing assessments of the risks associated with individual investments.

The information system must include provision for capturing the data required for each method of accounting for the various categories of investment in equity and debt securities, both at acquisition and subsequent reporting dates. Accounting personnel must be familiar with these requirements and capable of implementing them.

In addition, internal auditors and the audit committee of the board of directors should closely monitor the effectiveness of controls over investing activities.

Common documents and records

Title to investments is normally evidenced by a document such as a share or debenture certificate. Arrangements need to be made to ensure their safe custody. They may be held in a bank safe deposit box or directly by the bank or other financial institution as nominees for the entity. In addition, an important document specific to the investment cycle is the **broker's advice** or **contract note** issued by a broker specifying the exchange price of investing transactions; it is the primary source document for recording investing transactions.

Where substantial investments are held, a separate **investment subsidiary ledger** or **investment register** may be maintained. This records details of acquisitions and disposals, the receipt of interest and dividends, and market values.

Functions and related controls

Activities in the investing cycle include the following investing functions and related controls:

- Purchases and sales should be made in accordance with management's authorisations. The purchase and sale of investments intended to be retained as non-current assets would normally require board approval.
- Dividend and interest cheques must be promptly deposited intact, and the completeness of recorded investment income must be independently verified.
- Transactions should be recorded on the basis of appropriate supporting documentation, and the duties of recording of transactions and custody of the securities should be segregated.

- Securities should be stored in safes or vaults, with access restricted to authorised personnel. Periodically, relevant documents should be independently compared against recorded balances.
- Changes in value and in circumstances pertaining to the appropriate classification of investments should be periodically analysed.
- Management should undertake performance reviews to detect poor investment performance and/or erroneous reporting.
- Periodically, the classification of individual investments should be reviewed.

The auditor should obtain an understanding of the entity's laid down procedures to identify potential misstatements that could occur in investment balances and to design substantive procedures accordingly. If investment certificates are kept in the entity's safe and not independently verified, for example, then the audit program must call for physical inspection at or close to the balance sheet date.

Materiality, risk and audit strategy

Securities held as short-term investments may be material to an entity's short-term solvency, but income from such securities is seldom significant to the results of operations of entities outside the financial services sector. Securities held as non-current investments may be material to both the balance sheet and the profit and loss statement.

Many factors affect the inherent risk for investments. The volume of investing transactions is generally quite low. However, securities are susceptible to theft, and the accounting for investments can become complex. In addition, certain inherent risks are more challenging to address with controls, giving management an opportunity to manipulate the reporting for investments. Specifically, the proper classification of an investment may be contentious, which affects the valuation method, income effects and disclosure requirements applicable to the investment. Investments classified as current assets must be carried at the lower of cost and net realisable value. Falls in their market value must be recognised, but gains can be recognised only on realisation. For investments classified as being non-current, falls in value need be recognised only if they are expected to be permanent. Moreover, the entity may choose to carry such assets at valuation and thus recognise unrealised gains as increases in equity, although not as income.[1] Valuation of unquoted investments is subjective and may contribute to high levels of inherent risk for the valuation and disclosure assertions.

Closely related to investments are specialised financial instruments such as options, swaps and forward contacts. These are often called 'derivatives' because their value is derived from market determined prices such as security prices, foreign exchange rates and commodity prices. They are often used to manage exposure to risks associated with such markets. The Auditing and Assurance Standards Board recently issued an exposure draft (ED) originating with the International Auditing Practices Committee (IAPC) as detailed in the following 'Professional environment'.

The low volume of investing transactions means that it is generally most cost efficient to use the predominantly substantive approach in auditing investment balances. We assume this approach in this chapter. Recall, however, that with this approach, the auditor must obtain an understanding of the internal control structure applicable to investments as a basis for identifying potential misstatements before designing substantive procedures. As with cash, this mostly relates to controls over the custody of investment assets. However, it is also necessary to understand some of the special features of investment transactions.

PROFESSIONAL ENVIRONMENT

Auditing derivative financial instruments

The IAPC [exposure draft (ED)] recognises the following factors, in respect of derivative financial instruments in the current business environment, which may impact on audit risk:

- Derivative financial instruments are becoming more complex.
- The use of derivative financial instruments is becoming more commonplace.
- The accounting requirements for financial statement measures and disclosures are expanding.
- There is increasing use of service organisations to manage activities involving derivatives.
- Values may be volatile and impact on recorded amounts.
- Because of complexity, management may not fully understand the risks involved in using derivative instruments.
- The characteristics of derivative activities have resulted in increased business risks for many entities.

Further to the Australian audit guidance provided in AGS 1030, Derivatives in a Corporate Environment: A Guide for Auditors (issued in 1997), the IAPC ED relates audit considerations to a now more developed derivatives market.

In contrast to AGS 1030, which presents the audit considerations appropriate in a developing financial market (giving emphasis to particular products used in a corporate treasury segment of an entity), the IAPC ED takes a more holistic view of the use of derivatives by an entity. It recognises that derivative activities generally *support* the business activities of the entity, and therefore factors affecting the day-to-day operations of the business also have implications for derivative activities.

The auditor is reminded that it is in the context of the audit of the financial report *taken as a whole* that the auditor has responsibility to consider the appropriateness of management's assertions about derivatives in the preparation of the financial report.

The ED also uses definitions and assertions regarding financial instruments based on current accounting requirements. At the time when AGS 1030 was issued the accounting requirements were still in an early stage of development.

The IAPC ED applies a risk-based approach to auditing derivatives. It considers the relevant economic indicators (such as interest rates, inflation or exchange rates), firstly in the context of the relevant industry, and then as applicable to the individual entity, by taking into account the nature of its business and its control environment.

Its focus is on the nature of the derivative rather than on particular products, thereby recognising a dynamic financial market, which permits the introduction of new products to match situations.

The IAPC ED does not give detailed procedural guidance as provided in the Appendix to AGS 1030. In line with current audit methodology, it provides a framework for assessing and addressing audit risk relating to the entity's use of derivative financial instruments.

(Source: Extracted from the Auditing and Assurance Standards Board of the Australian Accounting Research Foundation, Australian Preface to the Proposed International Auditing Practice Statement, ED 76, Auditing Derivative Financial Instruments, September 2000)

Substantive procedures for investments

For most entities, investment transactions are infrequent, but individual transactions are usually for substantial amounts. Investment transactions rarely present cut-off problems so the auditor may perform many substantive procedures before or after the balance sheet date. Profit and loss statement balances relating to investments are usually verified at the same time.

Determining detection risk

Relevant inherent risk and control risk assessments can vary widely, owing to the variety of types of investment and circumstance across entities. However, the small number of transactions means that it is not usually cost effective to test controls. Acceptable detection risk is usually set as being low, and most evidence is obtained through the performance of substantive procedures.

8 LEARNING OBJECTIVE

Design and execute an audit program for investments.

Designing substantive procedures

Table 13.5 lists possible substantive procedures for investment balances and the specific audit objectives to which they relate. We will explain each of the procedures in a following section.

TABLE 13.5 *Possible substantive procedures for investment balance assertions*

		Investment balance audit objective (from Table 13.4)				
Category	**Substantive procedure**	**E#**	**C#**	**RO1**	**V#**	**D#**
Initial procedures	1. Perform initial procedures on investment balances and records that will be subjected to further testing: (a) Trace opening balances for investment accounts to prior year's working papers. (b) Review activity in all investment-related balance sheet and profit and loss statement accounts, and investigate entries that appear unusual in amount or source. (c) Obtain entity-prepared schedules of investments and determine that they accurately represent the underlying accounting records from which they are prepared by: • adding and cross-adding the schedules and reconciling the totals with the related subsidiary and general ledger balances; • testing the agreement of items on schedules with entries in related subsidiary and general ledger accounts.				✓ 1, 2	
Analytical procedures	2. Perform analytical procedures by analysing interest and dividend yields relative to expectations.	✓ 1, 2	✓ 1, 2		✓ 1, 2	
Tests of details of transactions	3. Vouch entries in investment and related profit and loss and equity accounts.	✓ 1, 2	✓ 1, 2	✓	✓ 1, 2	✓ 1
Tests of details of balances	4. Inspect and count securities on hand.	✓ 1	✓ 1	✓		✓ 1
	5. Confirm securities held by others.	✓ 1	✓ 1	✓		
	6. Recalculate investment revenue earned.	✓ 2	✓ 2		✓ 2	
	7. Review documentation concerning fair values.				✓ 1, 2	

(continued)

TABLE 13.5 *Possible substantive procedures for investment balance assertions (continued)*

Category	Substantive procedure	Investment balance audit objective (from Table 13.4)				
		E#	C#	RO1	V#	D#
Disclosure	8. Compare report presentation with the Corporations Law and applicable Accounting Standards:					
	(a) Determine that investment balances are properly identified and classified in the financial report.					✓ 1
	(b) Determine the appropriateness of disclosures concerning the valuation bases for investments, realised and unrealised gains or losses, related party investments, and pledged investments.					✓ 2

Initial procedures

The series of procedures in this category (as shown in Table 13.5) follows the pattern established for other major account balances. Firstly, the auditor verifies the agreement of opening investment balances with audited amounts in the prior year's working papers. Next, the auditor reviews the activity in investment-related accounts to identify entries that are unusual in nature or amount and that should be investigated. Then, the auditor checks entity-prepared schedules of investment additions and disposals in the period for mathematical accuracy and agreement with the underlying accounting records. The latter procedure includes determining that schedules and subsidiary investment ledgers agree with related general ledger control account balances. The schedules can then serve as the basis for additional substantive procedures.

Analytical procedures

It is rarely possible to obtain much evidence from the application of analytical procedures to investment balance sheet accounts. Current asset investments tend not to have any predictable relationship with other balances, while non-current investments are subject to so few transactions that it is easier to proceed directly to tests of details. Analytical procedures can be applied in comparing interest and dividend revenues to investment balances. Unexpected differences in interest or dividend yields may indicate misstatements; for example, a higher-than-expected rate of return may be found to have been caused by erroneous recording of the unrealised gain from an increase in the value of non-current securities in the profit and loss account rather than as a revaluation reserve.

Tests of details of transactions

Auditors usually vouch purchases and sales of investments by examining brokers' advices and evidence of appropriate approval. Purchases and sales of non-current investments, for example, should be vouched to authorisations in the minutes of directors meetings. These tests provide evidence about the occurrence of transactions, the transfer of ownership of securities, and the valuation of the securities at the transaction date. For sales, the auditor can verify the gain or loss recorded in the profit and loss account by referring to the carrying value in the investment register.

Evidence as to the completeness of recorded purchases is determined through verification of purchase and payment transactions, as we described in Chapter 11. Evidence as to the completeness of sales of investments is determined through verification of the existence of recorded investment assets as one of the tests of details of balances.

The auditor can vouch dividend and interest receipts to remittance advices accompanying the payment. A problem often arises as to completeness. Receipt of dividends is not always capable of being anticipated, and the misrecording or even misappropriation of a dividend payment may not be readily detected by the information system. Interest can normally be verified by analytical procedures. Dividends paid by quoted companies can normally be checked against reference works recording dividend payments. For substantial investments in unquoted companies, the auditor may need to verify dividends received against copies of the companies' financial reports.

Tests of details of balances

Tests of details of balances involve inspecting or confirming recorded investments, verifying income from investments and checking their market value.

Inspecting and counting securities on hand

Securities held at the entity's own premises should be inspected and counted at the same time as the count of cash and other negotiable instruments. In performing the test, the custodian of the securities should be present throughout the count, a receipt should be obtained from the custodian when the securities are returned, and the auditor should control all securities until the count is completed.

For securities stored for safekeeping in bank safety deposit boxes, the banks will generally seal the boxes on the nominated date of the count at the entity's request and will confirm to the auditor that there was no access to the box, other than by the auditor, until all locations have been counted. When the count is not made on the balance sheet date, the auditor should prepare a reconciliation from the date of the count to the report date by reviewing any intervening security transactions.

In inspecting securities, the auditor should observe such matters as:

- the certificate number on the document;
- the name of the owner (which should be the entity, either directly or through endorsement);
- the description of the security;
- the number of shares (or debentures);
- the par or face value of the shares (or debentures);
- the name of the issuer.

These data should be recorded as part of the auditor's analysis of the investment account. Figure 13.3 (page 518) illustrates an audit working paper for quoted equity securities. All securities should be checked against the records in the investment register and, for securities purchased in prior years, the details should be compared with those shown on the prior year's working papers. A lack of agreement between the certificate numbers may indicate unauthorised transactions for those securities.

This substantive procedure provides evidence about the existence, completeness, rights and obligations, and disclosure assertions.

Confirming securities held by others

Securities held by outsiders for safekeeping must be confirmed as of the date on which securities held by the entity are counted. The steps in the confirmation process for securities are identical to those for confirming receivables. Thus, the auditor must control the mailings and receive the responses directly from the custodian. The data confirmed are the same as the data that should be noted when the auditor is able to inspect the securities.

Securities may also be held by creditors as collateral against loans. In such cases, the confirmation should be sent to the indicated custodian. The confirmation of securities held by third parties provides evidence as to the existence or occurrence, and rights and obligations assertions. It will also furnish evidence about the completeness assertion if the confirmation response indicates more securities on hand than recorded.

Recalculating investment revenue earned

The auditor verifies income from investments by use of documentary evidence and recalculation. Dividends on all shares listed on stock exchanges and many others are included in dividend record books published by investment services. The auditor can independently verify the dividend revenue by referring to the declaration date, amount and the payment date as shown in the record book. The verification of dividend income is usually incorporated into the schedule of investments, as illustrated in Figure 13.3.

FIGURE 13.3 *Quoted equity securities working paper*

Williams Company
Quoted Equity Securities
31 December 20X1

W/P ref: H–2
Prepared by: A.E.R. Date: 3/1/X2
Reviewed by: R.C. 91 Date: 10/1/X2

Accounts 115 and 425

Description	CTF no.	Date acquired	No. of shares	Cost per share	Balance 1/1/X1	Purchases	Sales	Balance 31/12/X1	Market price at 31/12/X1 per share	Total	Dividend income
General Manufacturing	C2779	21/4/X0	900⋀	22.00	19 800✓			19 800✗ ^	24.50∀	22 050^	675ⓧ
Metropolitan Edison	M82931	21/9/X0	500	33.20	16 600✓		16 600∅	^			127ⓧ
Pacific Papers	54942	14/2/X1	200⋀	18.50		3 700∅		3 700✗ ^	17.00∀	3 400^	
Warrenton Corp.	7336	19/7/X0	400⋀	27.25	10 900✓			10 900✗ ^	29.25∀	11 700^	120ⓧ
					47 300✓	3 700	16 600	34 400		37 150	922
					F	F	F	FF to H–1		F	F To R–1

⋀ Examined stock etc. at Federal Trust Co.
✓ Traced to prior year's working papers
⋀ Traced to general ledger balance
F Added
FF Added and cross-added
^ Extension checked
∅ Vouched to broker's advices and board of directors authorisations
∀ Per market quotation in 2/1/X2 Stock Exchange Journal
ⓧ Dividend rates checked to Standard and Poors; dividends received traced to cash receipts journal.
Aggregate market value exceeded aggregate cost of securities at both beginning and end of year. Therefore, no allowance for declines in market value.

The auditor can verify the interest earned by examining the interest rates and payment dates indicated on the debenture certificate. This substantive procedure is directed primarily at the valuation and completeness assertions for interest revenue. However, it also provides evidence about the existence assertion for interest receivable.

Reviewing documentation concerning market values

Where held as current assets, quoted equity securities and marketable debt securities (such as ordinary shares, government bonds and corporate debentures) are normally valued at the lower of the aggregate cost or market value. Investments held as non-current assets are usually stated at the lower of the cost or impaired value, but may be carried at valuation. In any event, disclosure is also required of the valuation of quoted securities. The auditor should verify market quotations by referring to published security prices on stock exchanges. For infrequently traded securities, the auditor may need to seek advice from an independent broker as to the estimated market value at the balance sheet date. When market quotations are based on a reasonably broad and active market, they ordinarily constitute sufficient appropriate audit evidence as to the current market value of the securities.

Audited financial reports of the entity in which investments are held assist in the valuation of unquoted shares, debentures and similar debt obligations. Audited financial reports also represent appropriate evidence as to the adequacy of provisions against cost, if any. This substantive test relates to the valuation assertion.

Disclosure

To conform to the requirements of the Corporations Law and Accounting Standards, the presentation of investments in securities in the financial report requires the following:

- an analysis of investments as between current and non-current;
- a classification of investments into government and semi-government stocks and bonds, debentures, shares and share options;
- a recognition of dividends, interest and realised gains and losses in the profit and loss statement;
- a recognition of impairment write-offs in the profit and loss statement;
- disclosure of the basis and methods of accounting;
- disclosure of the market value of quoted investments;
- disclosure of any liens.

The foregoing substantive procedures should provide evidence of the first four of the above items. Inspection of the minutes, loan agreements and register of charges should reveal the existence of liens. In addition, the auditor should inquire of management as to its intent in holding the securities. On the basis of the evidence obtained, the auditor then determines whether the proposed report presentations and disclosures are appropriate.

Substantive procedures for consolidated financial reports

9 LEARNING OBJECTIVE

Explain the special considerations applicable to the audit of investments in subsidiaries, associates and joint ventures.

Where a company (or other entity) controls another company (or other entity), a consolidated financial report must be prepared for the economic entity. The economic entity comprises both the parent company and the controlled entities (unless the company or entity is itself a controlled entity) (AAS 24, Consolidated Financial Reports; IAS 27, Consolidated Financial Statements and Accounting for Investments in Subsidiaries). The auditor is required to report on the consolidated financial report. To do so, he or she must identify the controlled companies (or other entities) comprising the reporting entity, verify the amounts pertaining to the other companies (or entities) to be consolidated, and verify the accuracy of the preparation of the consolidated financial report.

Similar but less extensive disclosure requirements apply in respect of investments in associates (AAS 14 [IAS 28], Accounting for Investments in Associates) and in joint ventures (AAS 19, Accounting for Interests in Joint Ventures; IAS 31, Financial Reporting of Interests in Joint Ventures). The same audit procedures with respect to subsidiaries also apply to investments in associates and joint ventures. The parent entity and its subsidiaries, associates and joint ventures are referred to collectively as group entities.

Specific guidance for the audit of investments in associates is given in AGS 1032, The Audit Implications of Accounting for Investments in Associates. Much of this guidance is also relevant to the audit of subsidiaries and joint ventures.

Determining detection risk

Inherent risk is normally low for all related account balance assertions, except where the nature of the relationship with related entities is unusually complex. This gives rise to uncertainty as to the existence of control over the related entities, in which case the inherent risk for the completeness assertion may be high. Sometimes, too, the consolidation adjustments may be particularly complex and involve a significant degree of management estimation. This can happen with the consolidation of foreign group entities whose financial report may be prepared on accounting bases different from those appropriate to the parent entity, or with new acquisitions requiring determination of the fair value of their net assets at the date of acquisition. In such cases, the inherent risk as to the valuation or measurement assertion may be moderate.

Given the materiality of the amounts involved, the audit approach will be predominantly substantive. Little or no reliance will be placed on controls, which are unlikely to be strong. Detection risk will, therefore, be inversely related to the relevant inherent risk assessments.

A special problem arises where the accounts of one or more of the group entities are audited by another auditor, because it may be risky to rely on work performed by another person.

Designing substantive procedures

Table 13.6 shows a list of possible substantive procedures for the consolidated financial report, together with the assertions to which each test relates.

TABLE 13.6

Possible substantive tests of consolidated financial report assertions

Substantive procedure	Assertions				
	E	C	RO	V	D
Identify the reporting entity.	✓	✓	✓		
Verify the financial reports of other group entities.	✓	✓		✓	
Verify the consolidating adjustments.				✓	
Compare the report presentation with applicable Accounting Standards.					✓

Identifying the reporting entity

Where an entity has investments in entities that it controls (or over which it exercises significant influence), and where that entity is a reporting entity, it must prepare a consolidated financial report of the economic entity comprising the parent entity and its subsidiaries, associates and joint ventures. The auditor ensures that all entities included in the consolidated financial report are properly recognised as subsidiaries, associates or joint ventures of the parent entity, and that no such entities are excluded.

Control or influence by one entity over another is most likely to arise where the parent has an investment in another entity greater than 50 per cent for it to be accounted for as a subsidiary, or greater than 20 per cent for consideration to be given to accounting for it as an associate. For joint ventures, the relationship is determined by contractual arrangements with the other venturers. For such investments, the auditor verifies that the investment in those entities does provide the parent with the required degree of control or influence. For subsidiaries in which the parent entity does not own a majority of the voting rights, the auditor will need to obtain and verify management's explanation as to the basis on which control is secured.

The auditor also investigates the possibility that cumulative investments by the entity and its subsidiaries enable the economic entity to exercise control or significant influence over other entities. If, for example, the parent holds 15 per cent of the shares of another entity and one of its subsidiaries also holds 40 per cent, then that other entity is controlled by the group and is to be accounted for as a subsidiary. In obtaining an understanding of the business in the planning stage and in reviewing related party transactions, the auditor should be alert for evidence of the existence of control over other entities other than through ownership of voting rights. The auditor will need to obtain and verify an explanation as to why such entities are excluded from the consolidation.

This procedure provides evidence as to the existence and rights and obligations assertions with respect to entities consolidated as controlled entities, and as to the completeness assertion that all controlled entities are included in the consolidation.

Verifying the financial reports of other group entities

To verify the amounts included in the consolidated financial report, the auditor must obtain and verify the financial report of each group entity. Where the auditor is not also the auditor of another group entity, consideration must be given as to the extent of reliance to be placed on the work of the other auditor. AUS 602 (ISA 600), Using the Work of Another Auditor recommends that the principal auditor:

- obtain information regarding the professional competence of the other auditor;
- advise the other auditor of the independence requirements and obtain representation as to the other auditor's compliance;
- advise the other auditor of the reliance to be placed on his or her work and of any special requirements, such as identification of intercompany transactions;
- advise the other auditor as to applicable accounting and auditing requirements and obtain representation as to the other auditor's compliance;
- consider the findings of the other auditor.

Where the principal auditor is unable to rely on the work of the other auditor, the principal auditor has the statutory right of access, under the Corporations Law, to the accounting and other records of any entity controlled by the parent entity. The principal auditor can require any information and explanations necessary to report on the consolidated financial report from any officer or auditor of that entity.

This procedure provides evidence as to the existence assertion and the completeness assertion with respect to assets, liabilities and transactions with entities consolidated with those of the parent entity.

Verifying the consolidating adjustments

Consolidation adjustments fall into four categories: (1) acquisitions and disposals, (2) the elimination of inter-entity balances and transactions, (3) the standardisation of accounting policies, and (4) the translation of foreign currencies.

Acquisitions and disposals

On the acquisition of an interest in an associate or subsidiary, its assets are consolidated (directly or by way of equity accounting) in the group accounts at their fair value at the date of acquisition (AAS 21, Accounting for the Acquisition of Assets Including Business Entities; IAS 22, Business Combinations). The difference between the fair value of the parent entity's ownership interest in the net assets and the consideration paid constitutes purchased goodwill. It is important that the auditor verifies the amounts recorded as fair value. This involves testing management estimates and evaluating the work of experts. Of particular concern are valuations placed on intangibles not recorded in the books of the controlled entity. Adjustments on the disposal of a controlling interest must be verified against the carrying value of the controlled entity's net assets immediately prior to disposal.

Elimination of inter-entity balances and transactions

In the course of auditing each group entity, the auditor ensures that inter-entity transactions are properly identified and recorded. Where group entities are audited by other auditors, they must be requested to ensure that all such transactions are properly accounted for. At the year end, the auditor obtains an analysis of inter-entity balances, verifies their reconciliation with each other and ensures that they are properly eliminated. The auditor should also ensure that any inter-entity profit in assets held by any of the group entities is properly identified and eliminated on consolidation.

Standardisation of accounting policies

Where the financial reports of group entities have been prepared using accounting policies inconsistent with those of the reporting entity, appropriate adjustments must be made on consolidation. When auditing group entities or when communicating with other auditors of group entities, the auditor must identify any accounting policies inconsistent with those of the reporting entity, and verify the consolidating adjustment.

Translation of foreign currencies

Where a group entity's financial reports are prepared in a foreign currency, they must be translated for purposes of consolidation. The auditor must verify the exchange rates used, check the translations and ensure that the accounting treatment conforms to the requirements of AAS 20, Foreign Currency Translation (IAS 21, The Effects of Changes in Foreign Exchange Rates).

These substantive procedures provide evidence as to the existence, completeness and valuation assertions.

Comparison of report presentation with applicable Accounting Standards

The auditor should ensure that the disclosures in the consolidated financial report conform to the requirements of applicable Accounting Standards and the Corporations Law. Particular requirements are explanations as to why control exists over entities in which the parent entity's ownership interest is 50 per cent or less, and why control does not exist over entities in which the ownership interest is greater than 50 per cent.

LEARNING CHECK

13.8 Inherent risks in investments include the negotiability of documents of title and the proper classification of securities dependent on management intent. The principal controls relate to those over the safekeeping of securities and the maintenance of an investment register.

13.9 The infrequency of investment transactions leads to a predominantly substantive approach to their audit, which should include:
- a count of securities on hand and the confirmation of securities in safekeeping;
- verification of investment income;
- verification of market values.

13.10 The auditor is responsible for reporting on the consolidated financial report, including:
- identifying group entities;
- determining the reliability of group entity financial reports, especially where audited by other auditors, for the purpose of including them in the consolidated financial report;
- verifying consolidation adjustments.

SUMMARY

The verification of cash balances is an important part of a financial report audit. This is because even though the balances as of the balance sheet date may appear immaterial relative to other assets, the amount of cash flowing through the accounts during the audit period can be very material. In addition, cash is susceptible to misappropriation and is involved in many fraudulent schemes, including kiting and lapping. Thus, several types of substantive procedure to test cash balances are performed during most audits, including conducting cash cut-off tests, tracing bank transfers, counting cash on hand, confirming certain balances and other arrangements with banks, reviewing bank reconciliations, obtaining and using subsequent period bank statements, and determining the adequacy of management's disclosures for cash balances.

Investing transactions occur infrequently and internal control over the processing of transactions is generally good. However, because transactions are infrequent and usually individually significant, it is common for the auditor to use a predominantly substantive approach. Important among audit procedures is the physical inspection of certificates of title of investments, or their confirmation with independent custodians. The auditor also employs a predominantly substantive approach in verifying the consolidation of investments in group entities in the consolidated financial report of the economic entity.

KEY TERMS

Bank confirmation, p. 502
Bank reconciliations, p. 497
Bank transfer schedule, p. 501
Broker's advice, p. 512
Cash counts, p. 502
Cash cut-off tests, p. 501
Contract note, p. 512
Imprest bank account, p. 498
Imprest petty cash fund, p. 497
Investment register, p. 512
Investment subsidiary ledger, p. 512
Kiting, p. 501
Lapping, p. 508
Subsequent period's bank statement, p. 507
Window dressing, p. 507

NOTE

1. The process of accounting for investments is under review. The International Accounting Standards Committee's IAS 39, Financial Instruments: Recognition and Measurement requires remeasurement of all equity investments (except those in subsidiaries and associates) at fair value.

FURTHER READING

Braid, Michael, 'Counting the Cash', *The CPA Journal* (September 1979), pp. 82–4.

Carmichael, Douglas R., 'Audit Reporting Considerations for the New Statement of Cash Flows', *The CPA Journal* (June 1988), pp. 72–3.

Compton, John C. & Van Son, W. Peter, 'Check Truncation: The Auditor's Dilemma', *Journal of Accountancy* (January 1983), pp. 36–8.

Doppelt, Andrew B., 'The Telltale Signs of Money Laundering', *Journal of Accountancy* (March 1990), pp. 31–3.

Fensome, Martin, 'Statement of Auditing Practice AUP 1, Bank Confirmation Requests', *Australian Accountant* (August 1993) pp. 54–5; *Charter* (September 1993) pp. 32–3.

Locke, C., 'Auditing Issues — Bank Confirmation Requests', *Charter* (March 1998), pp. 76–7.

Mills, J., 'Controlling Cash in Casinos', *Management Accounting* (USA) (May 1996), pp. 38–40.

Morris, David M. & Fisher, Donna J., 'Investment vs Trading — A Misnomer', *The CPA Journal* (May 1990), pp. 28–37.

Patterson Jr. George F., 'New Guide on Auditing Investments', *Journal of Accountancy* (February 1997).

Pomeroy, Harlan, 'Restrictive Covenants: What the CPA Should Know', *Journal of Accountancy* (February 1981), pp. 61–8.

Sauls, Walter S., 'Developing a Kite-Detection System', *Internal Auditor* (December 1984), pp. 39–42.

Review questions

13.1 Explain the use and audit of imprest accounts.

13.2 Explain why the balance of cash on hand and at bank is always audited, and why a predominantly substantive approach is preferred.

13.3 Explain why it is important to trace transfers between bank accounts either side of the balance sheet date.

13.4 Describe the procedures for counting cash on hand.

13.5 Outline the procedures involved in verifying the bank reconciliation.

13.6 Explain lapping. Describe appropriate audit procedures to perform where it is suspected.

13.7 What substantive tests apply to the existence and valuation assertions for investment balances?

13.8 Explain the financial reporting principle underpinning the audit verification of the existence and completeness assertions with respect to entities consolidated into the group financial report.

13.9 Describe procedures to be undertaken where group entities are audited by other auditors.

Discussion questions

13.1 Why is it important for the auditor to identify and confirm all bank accounts operated by the entity during the year? How can the auditor be satisfied that all accounts have been confirmed?

13.2 Consider the implications of on-line banking with respect to control over banking transactions and the maintenance of cash and bank records.

13.3 Where petty cash transactions are quantitatively immaterial, discuss arguments for and against their audit by the independent auditor.

13.4 The effort involved in perpetrating a lapping fraud never justifies its rewards. Discuss.

13.5 Consider the audit implications of the introduction of paperless share trading and the elimination of share certificates.

13.6 Discuss the approach to ascertaining the value of investments in proprietary companies and in unquoted public companies.

13.7 Cash and investments now represent only part of the sum total of financial assets held by most companies. Apart from accounts receivable, what other financial assets may a company hold? Are there any specific accounting and audit requirements for them?

13.8 Discuss the problems associated with reliance on the work of other auditors. Should groups of entities be required to appoint a single firm of auditors?

Professional application questions

★
BASIC
★★
MODERATE
★★★
CHALLENGING

13.1 (Auditing petty cash) ★

The audit manager responsible for the audit of Tryms Limited, a sole trader of clothing, has asked you to consider the petty cash system and recommend what audit work may be necessary. You have found that petty cash is recorded in a handwritten analysed petty cash book and is not kept in an imprest system. From the petty cash book you have recorded the petty cash expenditure for each month as follows:

20X0	**$**
November	855
December	6243
20X1	
January	972
February	796
March	893
April	751
May	986
June	695
July	749
August	8634
September	948
October	849

Required

(a) Advise the audit manager as to the desirability of performing further substantive procedures on petty cash. Consider audit risk and materiality.

(b) Assume that the audit manager decides more work is necessary. Describe the testing you would perform to ensure that petty cash is fairly stated.

(ACCA Audit Framework — Paper 6(Y), December 1997 — adapted)

13.2 (Audit program for cash balances) ★

In the audit of Tyneside Manufacturing Limited, the audit senior, Andy Shearer, was responsible for the audit of cash. After performing a substantial amount of compliance testing, Andy determined that the control risk for cash balances was low. He performed testing of cut-off for cash balances at the end of the year and satisfied himself that cut-off had been correctly performed. He received confirmation directly from the bank for each of Tyneside's bank accounts. No bank accounts were opened or closed during the year.

Required

Prepare the audit program of substantive procedures to verify the bank balances of Tyneside Manufacturing.

(AICPA — adapted)

13.3 (Substantive procedures for cash balances) ★

Joplin Limited's financial year ends on 30 June 20X1 and the company's auditor, Hagan and Partners, conducts the annual audit during July and August. Hagan and Partners has prepared auditing procedures for the different phases of the audit engagement with Joplin. Included among the steps in the audit program for cash on deposit with Bonza Bank are the following:

1. Obtain a bank confirmation as at 30 June 20X1, directly with Bonza Bank.
2. Verify the client-prepared bank reconciliation for the month of June 20X1.
3. Obtain a copy of the bank statement for the month of July 20X1.

Required

(a) Explain why Hagan and Partners should obtain a bank confirmation directly from Bonza Bank.

(b) Describe what is involved in verifying the client-prepared bank reconciliation.

(c) Explain the purpose of obtaining the bank statement for the month of July.

(CIMA — adapted)

13.4 (Substantive procedures for investments) ★

Amber Reynolds, an audit senior, was given the task of auditing Eve Limited, an investment company. Her firm had not performed the audit before; however, from a discussion with the prior year's auditors, she found out that the following transactions occurred during the prior year:

- payment of debenture interest;
- accrual of debenture interest, payable at the year end;
- redemption of outstanding debentures;
- purchase of a portfolio of shares.

Amber has been asked to detail audit procedures for this year's audit based on the assumption that similar transactions will occur.

Required

(a) Identify a substantive procedure that Amber would need to perform to verify each of the above transactions, and the assertion to which each relates.

(b) Indicate the type of evidence obtained from each of the procedures noted in (a).

13.5 (Audit of consolidated financial reports) ★★

The Mighty Company Limited is a reporting entity of which your firm of accountants is the auditor. Mighty's consolidated financial report incorporates the financial reports of its four subsidiaries. Three subsidiaries are incorporated in Australia and audited by your firm. The fourth subsidiary is located in another country and audited by another firm of professional accountants.

Required

(a) Explain how you would verify the intercompany balances.

(b) Describe other audit adjustments you would expect to find and explain how you would verify each of them:

(i) where the subsidiary had been acquired prior to the financial year being audited;

(ii) where the subsidiary had been acquired during the financial year under audit.

(c) Describe the procedures necessary to determine the level of reliance to be placed on the audited financial report of the foreign subsidiary.

13.6 (Procedures to detect lapping) ★★

Toon World Limited (TW) is a manufacturer of children's toys. During the year it began to encounter cash flow difficulties. TW management hired an accounting firm to perform a special investigation to ascertain whether the company had any problems in its sales and collection cycle. The management performed a brief review and found accounts receivable collection problems. The audit partner decided that Alfred Bates (an audit senior) was the best person for this assignment. From an initial review, Alfred made the following notes:

Toon World Limited	**Prepared by:** Alfred Bates
Review of sales and collection	**Date:** 25/8/X1

The accounting department employs one bookkeeper who receives and opens all incoming mail. This bookkeeper is also responsible for depositing receipts, filing remittance advices on a daily basis, recording receipts in the cash receipts journal, and posting receipts in the individual customer accounts and the general ledger accounts. There are no cash sales. The bookkeeper prepares and controls the mailing of monthly statements to customers.

The concentration of functions and the receivable collection problems appears to indicate that a systematic defalcation of customers' payments through a delayed posting of remittances (lapping of accounts receivable) is present. I was surprised to find that no customers complained about receiving erroneous monthly statements.

Required

Outline the procedures that Alfred should perform to determine whether lapping exists.

(AICPA — adapted)

13.7 (Audit of investments) ★★

Your firm is the auditor of Jane's Charity for Pensioners. The charity was formed many years ago from a large gift by Jane, the income from which is used to pay pensions to needy individuals. The original gift has been invested in fixed interest stock and shares in listed companies. The trustees manage the charity, and the full-time administrator keeps the accounting and other records.

The draft summarised income and expenditure account for the year ended 30 September 20X1 and an extract from the balance sheet are given below, together with the audited figures for 20X0.

(continued)

Income and expenditure account for year ended 30 September

Income	**20X1**	**20X0**
	$	**$**
From fixed interest investments	44 200	41 900
From shares in listed companies	123 900	123 500
	168 100	165 400
Expenditure		
Payments to pensioners	141 300	144 300
Administration costs	21 600	20 500
Audit and accountancy	4 700	4 500
Sundry expenses	2 800	2 600
	170 400	171 900
Net (deficit) for the year	(2 300)	(6 500)

Extract from balance sheet at 30 September

Cost of investments		
Fixed interest investments	511 200	511 200
Shares in listed companies	1 445 600	1 262 700
	1 956 800	1 773 900

The following information has been provided:

1. During the year some shares were sold at a profit of $182 900 and the proceeds were re-invested in shares of other companies.
2. There were no purchases or sales of fixed interest investments in the year ended 30 September 20X1. In the year ended 30 September 20X0 some of the fixed interest investments were sold and others were purchased using the proceeds of sale.
3. The charity is managed by voluntary trustees who meet four times per year, and the administrator keeps the minutes of the meetings.
4. The administrator keeps the accounting records.
5. As auditor of the charity, you prepare the financial statements from the accounting records kept by the administrator and audit those financial statements. Your audit report is addressed to the trustees of the charity.

Required

Describe the audit work you would carry out:

(a) to verify income from investments. Your audit tests should verify that all the income from the investments has been received by the charity and included in the financial statements, including dividends from the shares in listed investments bought and sold during the year.

(b) to verify the ownership of the fixed interest investments and shares in listed companies.

(ACCA Audit Framework — Paper 6, December 1996 — adapted)

13.8 (Bank reconciliation — substantive procedures) ★★

Wombat Limited's financial report for the year ended 31 December 20X2 shows a balance of cash at bank of $166 830. As the staff member of Wombat's independent auditors assigned to the audit of cash, you obtain a copy of the company's bank statement that shows a balance of $183 759 and a copy of the bank reconciliation prepared by the company's cashier, which is reproduced below. You are aware that control risk over the bank reconciliation procedure is assessed as being moderate to high because the reconciliation is not independently prepared.

Wombat Limited
Bank Reconciliation 31 December 20X2

	$
Balance per bank statement 31 December 20X2	183 759.00
Deposits outstanding	
30 December	18 870.00
31 December	19 730.00
	38 600.00
	222 359.00
Unpresented cheques	
2696	250.00
2724	2 894.00
2725	5 690.00
2728	7 242.00
2729	19 000.00
2730	3 980.00
2731	535.00
2732	17 760.00
2733	2 556.00
	59 900.00
Cheque returned 'not sufficient funds' 29 December	162 450.00
Bank charges December	3 480.00
Balance per books 31 December 20X2	900.00
	$166 830.00

Required

Explain the substantive tests of details you will perform in verifying each item appearing on the reconciliation.

13.9 (Performing a bank reconciliation) ★★★

Your firm is the auditor of Newton Textiles Limited and you are auditing the financial statements for the year ended 31 December 20X0. The company has a turnover of $2.5 million and a profit before tax of $150 000. The company has supplied you with the following bank reconciliation at the year end. You have entered the 'date cleared' on the bank statement (the date on which the cheques and deposits appeared on January's bank statement).

				$	$
Balance per bank statement at 31 December 20X0					(9 865)
Add: deposits not credited					
CJ date		**Type**	**Date cleared**		
31 Dec.		ARL	3 Jan.	11 364	
24 Dec.		CS	3 Jan.	653	
27 Dec.		CS	4 Jan.	235	
28 Dec.		CS	5 Jan.	315	
29 Dec.		CS	6 Jan.	426	
30 Dec.		CS	7 Jan.	714	
31 Dec.		CS	10 Jan.	362	14 069
Less: uncleared cheques					
CJ date	**Cheque no.**	**Type**	**Date cleared**		
30 Dec.	2163	CP	3 Jan.	1 216	
31 Dec.	2164	APL	18 Jan.	10 312	
31 Dec.	2165	APL	19 Jan.	11 264	
31 Dec.	2166	APL	18 Jan.	9 732	
31 Dec.	2167	APL	20 Jan.	15 311	
31 Dec.	2168	APL	21 Jan.	8 671	
31 Dec.	2169	APL	19 Jan.	12 869	
31 Dec.	2170	APL	21 Jan.	9 342	
31 Dec.	2171	CP	3 Jan.	964	(79 681)
Balance per cash journal at 31 December 20X0					(75 477)

Notes:

- 'CJ date' is the date on which the transaction was entered into the cash journal.
- Type of transaction: ARL (accounts receivable receipt); CS (receipt from cash sales); APL (accounts payable payment); CP (cheque payment [for other expenses]).
- All cheques for accounts payable payments are written out at the end of the month.

Required

(a) List the matters that cause you concern on the client's bank reconciliation. Describe the investigations that you will carry out on these items.

(b) Explain what adjustments to the financial statements would be required from (a).

(ACCA Audit Framework — Paper 6(Y), December 1997 — adapted)

Case studies

13.1 (Substantive procedures for cash balances) ★★★

You have been asked by the financial controller, Thomas Tank, of Train Limited to carry out an investigation of a suspected fraud by the company's cashier. The cashier, Ralph Biggs, has left the firm without notice.

Train is a small company, and there were few controls and checks over Ralph's work because the company had employed him for a number of years. You are aware that the auditor found a discrepancy in the bank reconciliation for the company's year end of 30 June 20X0, and that Ralph left the day on which it was discovered. Thomas Tank has asked you to carry out the investigation, rather than the company's auditor. He is not happy with the auditor because he believes he should have found the fraud earlier or at least warned that there were control weaknesses.

Thomas says that Ralph was responsible for:

- receiving cash from customers for both credit and cash sales;
- making all payments, including purchase ledger payments and sundry payments;
- drawing the cash for wages;
- recording all receipts and payments in the cash book and preparing a bank reconciliation;
- making and approving petty cash payments and recording these transactions in the petty cash book.

The computerised sales and purchase ledgers are maintained by the staff in the sales and purchases accounting departments who post all transactions to these ledgers. Ralph used to send the sales ledger clerk a schedule showing the cash he had received. The remittance advices from customers were attached to this schedule, and they showed the invoices that were being paid.

The purchase ledger controller would inform Ralph of the payments he wished to make, and Ralph would then prepare the cheques, which Thomas signed. A remittance advice was attached to the payment that was sent to the supplier. Ralph would prepare the purchase and sales ledger control accounts each month and the reconciliation of these balances to the total balances on the respective ledgers.

For cash sales, the sales department raises a sales order, which is sent to the dispatch department which raises a dispatch note. The first copy of the dispatch note is given to the customer, the second copy is sent to the sales accounting department and the third copy is retained in the dispatch department. The sales accounting department then prices the invoice. The customer would pay the cash to Ralph, who retained a copy of the invoice for his records. Ralph would record the sales details in his analysed cashbook, and the month's cash sales were posted from the total in the cashbook to the nominal ledger.

The payroll department calculates the wages. Ralph would draw the cheque to pay the wages and receive the cash. The payroll department makes up the wage packets and pays the wages to employees. Ralph would retain any wages not given to employees.

Thomas is the authorised signatory for cheques; however, Ralph was the signatory when Thomas was on holiday.

Required

Describe what checks you would conduct to (a) determine whether a fraud has taken place and (b) quantify the loss. Consider:

(a) bank reconciliations;
(b) cash receipts;
(c) cash payments;
(d) petty cash.

(ACCA Audit Framework — Paper 3.4, December 1991 — adapted)

13.2 (Substantive procedures for investments) ★★★

You are performing the audit of Galway Limited for the financial year ended 30 June 20X0. Under the terms of a major loan contract, Galway is required to maintain certain financial ratios. If the ratios are breached, then the loan is immediately due for repayment. This would create significant cash flow problems. To comply with the loan covenant and maintain the ratios, Galway must continue to hold its 100 per cent shareholding in Mayo Limited as a long-term investment.

You have obtained a management representation letter from the client, which says in part that 'Galway Limited warrants for the period 1 July 20X0 to 30 June 20X1 that it intends to retain ownership of its entire parcel of ordinary shares in Mayo Limited. Galway has not entered into any discussions with any party, directly or indirectly, regarding the sale of these shares.'

On 24 July 20X0, you noted an article in the financial press which described the rumoured sale of the business assets of Mayo to a foreign investor.

Required

(a) Does the management representation letter from Galway regarding its shareholding in Mayo constitute sufficient appropriate audit evidence? Give reasons for your answer.

(b) Describe the procedures you need to perform in relation to this situation prior to signing the audit report.

(Professional Year Programme of the ICAA — 1997, Advanced Audit Module — adapted)

chapter 14

PART 5

Completing the audit, reporting and other services

PART 5

Part 5 completes the body of knowledge concerning auditing and provides a link to other assurance services provided by auditors and accountants. There are four chapters in this part. **Chapter 14** examines the matters of judgement crucial to the completion of an audit. Such matters require the professional expertise and skills of professional accountants, including their ability to identify risk areas, assess management representation, undertake reviews and analysis of audit findings, and competently communicate matters with management and the audit committee. The conclusions of such tasks are then reported in **Chapter 15**, where we will discuss compliance of statutory regulations and professional standards, alongside the different types of audit opinion pursuant to different matters of concern (such as limitations of audit, uncertainties or disagreement in accounting policies).

In **Chapter 16** we will broaden readers' auditing knowledge to include the concepts of the information economy, examining accounting, auditing and controls in an e-commerce environment. This chapter analyses the impact of e-commerce and looks at the range of audit and assurance services relevant to today's electronically enabled business world. In line with the mission of the book, **Chapter 17** looks beyond the external financial report audit and discusses internal, operational and public sector auditing. While these types of audit use similar concepts, this chapter provides readers with further insights into how auditing strategies and methods are adopted inside organisations and within the public sector.

chapter 14 Completing the audit

Overview

LEARNING OBJECTIVES

After studying this chapter, you should be able to:

1. describe the auditor's responsibilities with respect to events occurring after the end of the financial year
2. explain the different types of accounting treatment for events occurring after the end of the financial year
3. explain the procedures in ensuring that the going-concern basis is appropriate
4. explain the procedures in ensuring that all contingent liabilities have been properly identified and disclosed
5. describe and state the purpose of a management representation letter
6. indicate why analytical procedures are important in undertaking the overall review of the financial report
7. identify the steps in evaluating audit findings
8. indicate the appropriate communications with the entity at the conclusion of the audit.

Professional statements

AUSTRALIAN		INTERNATIONAL	
AUS 508	Inquiry Regarding Litigation and Claims	ISA 501	Audit Evidence — Additional Considerations for Specific Items, Part C: Inquiry Regarding Litigation and Claims
AUS 512	Analytical Procedures	ISA 520	Analytical Procedures
AUS 520	Management Representations	ISA 580	Management Representations
AUS 706	Subsequent Events	ISA 560	Subsequent Events
AUS 708	Going Concern	ISA 570	Going Concern
AUS 710	Communication to Management on Matters Arising from an Audit	ISA 1007	Communication with Management
AASB 1002	Events Occurring after Reporting Date	IAS 10	Contingencies and Events Occurring after Balance Sheet Date
AASB 1034	Information to be Disclosed in Financial Reports		

We discussed aspects of interim and year-end audit testing in previous chapters. In this chapter we are concerned with two important additional areas of activity in completing the financial report audit: firstly, completing the audit fieldwork, which pertains to all transactions and events up until the date on which the audit report is signed, and secondly, evaluating the audit findings and communicating with the entity.

The procedures performed in completing the audit fieldwork have a number of distinctive characteristics: (1) they do not pertain to specific transaction cycles or accounts; (2) they involve many subjective judgements by the auditor; and (3) they often involve issues that are potentially of high risk to the auditor. For these reasons they are usually performed by audit managers or other senior members of the audit team (and closely reviewed by audit partners) who have extensive audit experience with the entity.

Significant importance is also given to evaluating the findings and communicating with the entity. The manager and audit partner on the engagement are actively involved in this process, because it is important to ensure that the work is completed properly and that significant matters are considered in formulating the audit opinion. The communication with the entity also provides an important source of evidence to the entity that the auditor has appropriately performed his or her work.

The adage 'last but not least' applies to completing the audit. The decisions made by the auditor in this last stage are usually crucial to the ultimate outcome of the audit. Moreover, the conclusions reached by the auditor in completing the audit often have a direct impact on the opinion to be expressed on the entity's financial report.

In completing the audit, the auditor frequently works under tight time constraints, because entities usually seek the earliest possible date for the issue of the audit report. Despite potential problems with tight time deadlines, the auditor must take the time to make sound professional judgements and to express the opinion appropriate in the circumstances.

COMPLETING THE FIELDWORK

In completing the fieldwork, the auditor performs specific auditing procedures to obtain additional audit evidence. The specific audit evidence relates to reviewing for **subsequent events** that may have an impact on the financial report, considering factors that may have an impact on going-concern assumptions, reviewing for contingent liabilities, obtaining the **management representation letter** and performing analytical procedures. These procedures are performed at the end of the audit and not necessarily in the following sequence.

Undertaking a subsequent-events review

The auditor is responsible for designing specific procedures to identify subsequent events that may have an impact on the financial statements before the audit report is signed, as discussed in AUS 706 (ISA 560), Subsequent Events. Subsequent events, as described in AUS 706 (ISA 560), are both events occurring between the end of the period and the date of the audit report, and facts discovered after the date of the audit report.

In identifying subsequent events, the auditor needs to consider two separate issues. Firstly, the auditor must assess whether it is an event on which he or she has a responsibility to act (AUS 706; ISA 560). Secondly, if the auditor does have a responsibility to take action, he or she must consider the appropriate accounting treatment for the subsequent event (AASB 1002, Events Occurring after Reporting Date (IAS 10, Contingencies and Events Occurring after Balance Sheet Date)).

Auditing considerations of subsequent events

1 LEARNING OBJECTIVE

Describe the auditor's responsibilities with respect to events occurring after the end of the financial year.

Auditing Standards require the auditor to apply procedures designed to provide reasonable assurance that all significant events occurring up to the date of the audit report are identified (AUS 706.04; ISA 560.04). After the audit report has been signed the auditor does not have a responsibility to detect subsequent events.

Events occurring up to the date of the audit report

The auditor is required to perform procedures to identify and evaluate all events that may require adjustment or disclosure in the financial report up until the date on which the audit report is signed (identified by period 1 in Figure 14.1). This responsibility is discharged by the auditor in the following two ways: (1) by being alert for subsequent events in performing year-end substantive procedures (such as cut-off tests and the search for unrecorded liabilities); and (2) by performing the auditing procedures specified in AUS 706.05 (ISA 560.05) at or near the completion of the examination, which include:

- reviewing procedures that management has established to ensure that subsequent events are identified;
- reading minutes of the meetings of shareholders, the board of directors and audit and executive committees for the period after the balance sheet date, and inquiring about matters discussed at meetings for which minutes are not yet available;
- reading the entity's latest available interim financial report and, as considered necessary and appropriate, budgets, cash flow forecasts and other related management reports;
- inquiring (or adding to previous oral or written inquiries) of the entity's lawyers;
- inquiring of management as to whether any subsequent events have occurred that may affect the financial report. Examples of specific inquiries of management include: the current status of items that were accounted for on the basis of tentative, preliminary or inconclusive data; whether new commitments, borrowings or guarantees have been entered into; and whether sales of assets have occurred or are planned.

FIGURE 14.1

Subsequent-events time dimension

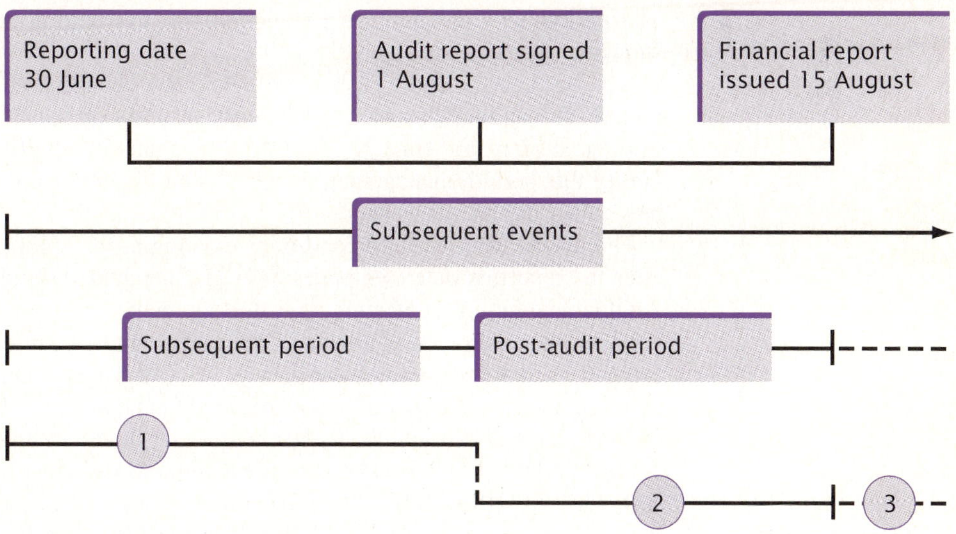

Period (1) Auditors have a responsibility to discover and evaluate all subsequent events that may have a material effect on the financial report.

Period (2) Auditors have a responsibility to examine only events that come to their attention.

Period (3) Auditors have a responsibility to examine only events that come to their attention and that existed at the date of the audit report.

If the audit procedures identify events that could affect the financial report, the auditor should carry out further procedures to assess whether such events are appropriately reflected in the financial report. At this point the auditor needs to consider the appropriate accounting treatment of the event, as discussed in AASB 1002 (IAS 10).

As part of the subsequent events review, the auditor will usually want to obtain a **solicitors' representation letter** and a management representation letter to gain some level of assurance on certain items. Subsequent events may also raise going-concern issues that the auditor needs to address. We discuss these issues later in this chapter.

Subsequent events are often issues that may cause a conflict between the management of the company and the auditor, probably because subsequent events of most interest to the auditor are usually events that have a negative impact on the financial report. Where the management does not amend the financial report when the auditor believes amendment to be necessary, the auditor should, in accordance with AUS 702 (ISA 700), issue a modified audit report (see Chapter 15).

Post-audit responsibilities for subsequent events

After the audit report has been signed the auditor has no responsibility to perform procedures to detect subsequent events or to make any inquiry regarding the financial report. This is one of the main reasons that the date on the audit report is important. However, if the auditor becomes aware of a fact after the audit report has been signed, it may be appropriate to take some type of action. The action the auditor should take depends on whether the fact is discovered after the date of the audit report but before the financial report has been issued or after the financial report has been issued (shown as periods 2 and 3 respectively on Figure 14.1).

Events occurring after the date of the audit report but before the financial report is issued

The period after the date of the audit report but before the financial report is issued is shown as period 2 on Figure 14.1. It is not uncommon for this period to comprise several weeks, because the auditor does not have much control over when the financial reports are issued. The auditor has no responsibility to make an inquiry or to perform auditing procedures during this time to discover any material after-balance-date events. However, during this period, management is responsible for informing the auditor of any events that may affect the financial report.

The events may relate to conditions existing at the reporting date or conditions existing after the reporting date (see pages 541–2). The auditor should consider the need to amend the financial report, conferring with management.

If the financial report is amended, the auditor must carry out any necessary auditing procedures, including extending the review of after-balance-date events, and reissue the audit report at the date of approval of the amended financial report. If management does not amend the financial report where the auditor believes it should be amended, and the audit report has not been released to the entity, then the auditor should issue a qualified report in accordance with AUS 702 (ISA 700). If the financial report has been released to the entity and management refuses to make the required amendments, then the auditor should act to prevent reliance on the audit report. He or she can do this by, for example, exercising the auditor's right to be heard at the general meeting at which the audited financial report is presented to members.

Facts discovered after the financial report is issued

An auditor has no responsibility to make an ongoing inquiry on the financial report after it has been issued (the period shown as period 3 on Figure 14.1 on page 539). This responsibility is essentially the same as that in period 2, when action by the auditor is required only if he or she becomes aware of an event. The key difference is that the only event that concerns the auditor in period 3 is something that he or she *missed* before signing the audit report and that has now come to light. This is in contrast to period 2 when the auditor must consider whether to take action in relation to *any* event of which he or she becomes aware. This limitation in period 3 ensures that there is an end point to the auditor's responsibilities in relation to a company's financial report for a particular year.

The main issue for the auditor to consider in assessing the impact of this event is to determine whether the auditor would have qualified the audit report if the event had been known at the date of the audit report. If the auditor would have qualified the audit report, then he or she should consider whether the financial report needs revision. If management does not agree to the revision, then the auditor should notify the persons ultimately responsible for the overall direction of the entity that he or she will act to prevent future reliance on the audit report.

The preferred result is the preparation of a revised financial report by the client and the issue of a revised audit report as soon as practicable. Again, prior to the issue of a revised audit report the auditor should extend the review of subsequent events up to the date of the issuance of the revised report. The new report should include an emphasis of matter paragraph referring to a note in the financial report that explains the revision of the previously issued financial report and the earlier audit report (see Chapter 15).

The new report should be dated not earlier than the date on which the revised financial report is approved. If the issue of the following period's financial report is imminent, then the revised financial report may not be issued. However, in these circumstances appropriate disclosures are required in the following period's report.

2 LEARNING OBJECTIVE

Explain the different types of accounting treatment for events occurring after the end of the financial year.

Accounting considerations

AASB 1002, Events Occurring after Reporting Date (IAS 10, Contingencies and Events Occurring after Balance Sheet Date) refers to events occurring after the reporting date but prior to the time of completion. The time of completion is the date of the directors' statement or the date on which the financial report is adopted. In auditing, the time of completion is extended to the date on which the audit report is signed, although the directors' statement and the audit report are usually signed on the same date.

The accounting issue that needs to be considered in determining the appropriate disclosure is whether the event relates to a condition existing at the reporting date or whether it relates to a condition occurring after the reporting date. The appropriate treatment for these events is outlined in AASB 1002 (IAS 10) and discussed in the following sections.

Conditions existing at the reporting date

The balance sheet and profit and loss account must be prepared on the basis of conditions existing at the reporting date. AASB 1002 (IAS 10) states that the financial report must reflect the financial effect of an event occurring after the reporting date that:

(a) provides additional evidence of conditions that existed at the reporting date; or

(b) reveals for the first time a condition that existed at the reporting date.

Estimates made in accounting are a common example of where evidence that comes to light after the end of the year may provide further information about the amount of the balance. Examples include the selling price of inventories after the end of the financial year, which provides evidence about the net realisable value at balance date, or the settlement of recorded year-end estimated liabilities relating to litigation.

Whether a condition existing at reporting date should be disclosed by way of a note or recognised in the financial statements primarily depends on whether it can be reliably measured.

Conditions arising after the reporting date

Where an event occurring after the reporting date provides new information that does not relate to conditions existing at the reporting date, the information should be disclosed by way of a note to the accounts if nondisclosure has the potential to adversely affect decisions about the allocation of scarce resources made by users of the financial report. This type of event does not give rise to adjustments to assets and liabilities because it does not relate to conditions that existed at the reporting date.

Examples of these types of events are:

- a fire or flood after the reporting date;
- a major currency re-alignment after the reporting date;
- the raising of additional share or loan capital;
- mergers or acquisitions after the reporting date.

Example of the difference between conditions existing at and arising after the reporting date

Assume that a major customer becomes bankrupt on 1 February 20X2. Also assume that the entity considered the customer's balance to be totally collectable in making its estimate of potentially uncollectable accounts in its 31 December 20X1 financial report. If, on review of the subsequent event, the auditor determines that the bankruptcy was attributable to the customer's deteriorating financial position (which existed, but was unknown to the entity, at the balance sheet date), then the entity should be asked to adjust the 31 December 20X1 financial report for the loss. If the auditor determines instead that the customer was financially sound at 31 December and that the bankruptcy resulted from a fire or similar catastrophe that occurred after the balance sheet date, then only disclosure in the notes to the 31 December financial report is needed.

3 LEARNING OBJECTIVE

Explain the procedures in ensuring that the going-concern basis is appropriate.

Considering the appropriateness of the going-concern assumption

The auditor would normally consider the appropriateness of the going-concern assumption in detail when completing the audit, but consideration of going concern should happen at all stages of the audit. Where financial reports are prepared on a **going-concern basis**, as is normally the case, the auditor must consider whether applying this basis is appropriate in the valuation and measurement of items appearing in the financial report and in the support of the directors' assertion as to solvency in the directors' declaration. AUS 708 (ISA 570), Going Concern requires the auditor to assess the risk of going-concern problems at the planning stage and again during the final review. Indications that continuance as a going concern should be questioned may be financial (such as material operating losses), operating (such as the loss of key management personnel) or other (such as changes in legislation). The period to be considered by such an assessment extends to the expected date of the auditor's report for the succeeding financial reporting period. This period is known as the 'relevant period'.

Where, at the planning stage, the risk of going-concern problems is assessed as being remote, no additional procedures are necessary to test for the existence of such problems. When a question arises regarding the going-concern basis, whether at the planning stage or subsequently, additional procedures may be necessary. The auditor performs most of these procedures during the period of completion of the audit (AUS 708.21; ISA 570.09), such as:

- reviewing subsequent events;
- analysing the latest interim financial information (for example, actual versus budgeted cash flow);

- examining compliance with the terms of debenture and loan agreements;
- reading the minutes of meetings of directors and other important committees;
- requesting information from the entity's solicitors;
- considering the effect of unfilled customer orders.

Where a going-concern problem is identified, the auditor will need to discuss with management its plans for alleviating the problem — for example, by raising additional finance, disposing of surplus assets or selling loss-making business operations. The auditor will need to obtain written representation concerning such plans and should consider their feasibility by analysing their effect on cash flow or other relevant forecasts. Where appropriate, the auditor will need to obtain written confirmation from third parties, such as banks or creditors, as to the existence of:

- their commitment to additional lending or to a scheme of reconstruction;
- their willingness to be identified in the financial report as having entered into such arrangements.

The auditor may modify the audit report of an entity in response to going-concern problems. We will discuss the types of reporting option available to the auditor in Chapter 15.

4 LEARNING OBJECTIVE

Explain the procedures in ensuring that all contingent liabilities have been properly identified and disclosed.

Reviewing for contingent liabilities

A contingency is an existing condition, situation or set of circumstances that involves uncertainty as to possible gain (contingent asset) or loss (**contingent liability**) that will be resolved when one (or more) future event(s) occurs or fails to occur. Contingent liabilities are the most common and therefore are the subject of the rest of this section. AASB 1034, Information to be Disclosed in Financial Reports requires disclosure in the notes of material contingent liabilities. Such liabilities include:

(a) liabilities of the entity which have not been recognised because:
   (i) of significant uncertainty as to whether a sacrifice of future economic benefits will be required (for example, a guarantee provided to a financier for a loan taken out by another entity, where default on that loan is uncertain as at the reporting date); or
   (ii) the amount of the liability cannot be measured reliably (for example, a claim for damages against the entity, where the entity is defending the claim even though professional advice indicates the defence is unlikely to succeed, and the amount of the claim cannot be measured reliably as at the reporting date due to the unique nature of the claim); and

(b) items that are not recognised as liabilities because of significant uncertainty as to whether an obligation presently exists.

When the conditional event meets the criteria for recognition of reliability of measurement and probability of occurrence, the obligation should be recognised as a liability in the financial report and thus is no longer a 'conditional' liability. When the conditional event does not meet the criteria for recognition, it may still meet the disclosure requirements as a contingent liability. Irrespective of whether conditional liabilities should be recognised as liabilities or otherwise described in the notes, they are of relevance to the auditor because they are unlikely to be recorded in the accounting records until the occurrence of the uncertain future event. Therefore, there is a risk that they will not be completely and properly disclosed. These obligations include potential liabilities from income tax disputes, product warranties, guarantees of obligations of others, and litigation and claims.

The auditor's concerns about contingent liabilities are not limited to completing the audit. However, the review will often be towards the end of the audit because the auditor needs the most complete information set available. During audit testing, and particularly in searching for unrecorded liabilities (see Chapter 11), the auditor should be alert to the possibility of contingent liabilities. Moreover, in reading the minutes of directors meetings and in reviewing contracts, the auditor should look for circumstances that may indicate contingencies that should be investigated. Contingencies that are often the highest risk to auditors are associated with litigation. The most appropriate audit procedure in relation to these types of contingency is inquiry of the entity's solicitor(s) by means of a solicitor's representation letter.

Solicitor's representation letter

A solicitor's representation letter is generally used to assist the auditor in obtaining the following audit evidence, as per AUS 508.02, Inquiry Regarding Litigation and Claims (ISA 501.32, Audit Evidence — Additional Considerations for Specific Items, Part C: Inquiry Regarding Litigation and Claims):

- whether all material legal matters have been identified;
- the probability of any material revenue or expense arising from such matters and the estimated amount thereof; and
- the adequacy of the accounting treatment of such matters, including their disclosure in the financial report.

Thus, the primary evidence obtained from solicitors' representation letters relates to contingencies. Despite the importance of these letters, management represents the initial source of information about the existence of such matters. Thus, the auditor should review and discuss procedures for identifying such matters, and obtain from management:

- a description and estimate of the financial consequences of legal matters; and
- an assurance (preferably in writing) of the completeness of such information.

Other auditing procedures — such as reading the minutes of meetings of directors; reviewing contracts, loan agreements (particularly those outside the normal course of business) and bank confirmations; and reviewing solicitors' fee accounts and correspondence — may also disclose litigation, claims and so on, as well as other contingent liabilities. The auditor should examine supporting documentation in the entity's files pertaining to all such matters that have come to his or her attention. It should be recognised, however, that the auditor normally does not possess sufficient legal skill to make an informed judgement on all these matters. Accordingly, the auditor needs the assistance of an outside specialist. A solicitor's representation letter to the entity's outside solicitor(s) is the auditor's primary means of obtaining corroborating information about management's assertions concerning the status of litigation, claims and unrecorded or contingent liabilities.

A solicitor's representation letter is shown in Figure 14.2. It should be prepared by management and sent by the auditor to each solicitor identified as having handled legal matters during the year. As shown in Figure 14.2, the letter should ask the solicitor to respond directly to the auditor.

If the response from the solicitor contains a material disagreement with management's original evaluation of a matter, then the auditor should seek discussions with management and the solicitor. If the disagreement is not resolved, then the auditor needs to consider its effect on the audit report.

If no response is received from the solicitor, then the auditor should ask management to contact the solicitor asking for a completion of the request or an explanation for the lack of response, to be sent to the auditor. If the auditor assesses the reasons given by the solicitor to be unacceptable, or if no response is obtained, then the auditor should consider alternative audit procedures to gain sufficient appropriate audit evidence. Where significant, appropriate audit evidence cannot be obtained, the lack or limitation of response would be considered a limitation on the scope of the auditor's work and the auditor would need to consider whether an 'except for' opinion or inability to form an opinion should be expressed (AUS 508.24; ISA 501.37).

FIGURE 14.2 *Solicitor's representation letter*

CLIENT COMPANY LIMITED
Letterhead

Messrs ABC & Co.
Solicitors
(Address)

Dear..

In connection with the preparation and audit of the financial report of the company and the following subsidiaries [and/or divisions]:

....

....

for the reporting period [date], we request that you provide to this company, at our cost, the following information:

1. Confirmation that you are acting for the company [and the above-named subsidiaries and/or divisions] in relation to the matters mentioned below and that the directors' descriptions and estimates of the amounts of the financial settlement (including costs and disbursements) which might arise in relation to those matters are in your opinion reasonable.

Name of company (subsidiary or division)	Directors' description of matter (including current status)	Directors' estimate of the financial settlement (inclusive of costs and disbursements)

2. Should you disagree with any of the information included in 1 above, please comment on the nature of your disagreement.
3. In addition to the above, a list of open files that you maintain in relation to the company [and the above-mentioned subsidiaries and/or divisions].
4. In relation to the matters identified under 2 and 3 above, we authorise you to discuss these matters with our auditors [name and address], if requested, and at our cost.

   It is understood that:

   (a) the company [and the above-named subsidiaries and/or divisions] may have used other solicitors in certain matters;

   (b) the information sought relates only to information relating to legal matters referred to your firm, (including branches or subsidiaries) which were current at any time during the above-mentioned reporting period, or have arisen since the end of the reporting period and up to the date of your response;

   (c) unless separately requested in writing, you are not responsible for keeping the auditors advised of any changes after the date of your reply;

   (d) you are required to respond only on matters referred to you as solicitors for the company (and the above-mentioned subsidiaries and/or divisions), not on those within your knowledge solely because of the holding of any office as director, secretary or otherwise of the company (and the above-mentioned subsidiaries and/or divisions), by a consultant, partner or employee of your firm;

   (e) your reply is sought solely for the information of, and assistance to, this company in connection with the audit of, and report with respect to, the financial report of the company (and the above-mentioned subsidiaries and/or divisions), and will not be quoted or otherwise referred to in any financial report or related documents of the company (and the above-mentioned subsidiaries and/or divisions), nor will it be furnished to any government agency or other person, subject to specific legislation requirements without the prior written consent of your firm.

Your prompt assistance in this matter will be appreciated.

Would you please forward a signed copy of your reply directly to our auditors [name] at [address] by [date].

Yours faithfully
CLIENT COMPANY LIMITED

per..

Secretary

(Source: Aus 508, Appendix)

In some cases, the solicitor's response may indicate significant uncertainty about the likelihood of an unfavourable outcome of litigation or claims, or the amount or range of potential loss. The matter may be in only the initial stage of litigation, for example, and there may be no historical experience of the entity in similar litigation. In this situation, the auditor may conclude that the financial report is affected by an inherent uncertainty that is not susceptible to reasonable estimation at the balance sheet date. If the uncertainty is adequately disclosed in the financial report, then the audit report should contain an unqualified opinion with an emphasis of matter section. If, in the auditor's opinion, the disclosure of the uncertainty is inadequate or unreliable, then the auditor would express an 'except for' or an adverse opinion on the basis of a disagreement with management (AUS 508.25). We will discuss the various reports in Chapter 15.

5 LEARNING OBJECTIVE

Describe and state the purpose of a management representation letter.

Obtaining the management representation letter

AUS 520.02 (ISA 580.02), Management Representations requires the auditor to obtain appropriate representations from management, which may be either oral or written. A written representation is better evidence than an oral representation and will often take the form of a representation letter from management. The objectives of such a letter are to:

- confirm oral representations given to the auditor;
- document the continuing appropriateness of such representations;
- reduce the possibility of misunderstandings concerning management's representations;
- impress upon management that it has the primary responsibility for the financial report.

The management representation letter may complement other auditing procedures (for example, in connection with (1) the completeness of identified contingent liabilities and related party transactions or (2) the existence of mitigating factors in the presence of going-concern problems). In some cases, however, a representation letter may be the primary source of audit evidence. When a client plans to discontinue a line of business, for example, the auditor may be unable to corroborate this event through other auditing procedures.

The auditor should be careful in placing too much reliance on management representation letters. Although the Auditing Standards state that the auditor may rely on representations under certain circumstances, the level of acceptable reliance has not been recently tested in the courts. Legal judgements in the past have not given much weight to management representations as audit evidence. The Kingston Cotton Mill case (*Re: Kingston Cotton Mill Company* (No. 2) (1896) 2 Ch. 279) suggested it was inappropriate for the auditor to rely on an inventory certificate signed by management in evaluating the quantity and value of inventory. In the Pacific Acceptance case (*Pacific Acceptance Corporation Ltd v. Forsyth and Others* (1970) 90 WN (NSW) 29) the auditors were criticised for relying on management representations excessively rather than examining documentary evidence. (*Note*: We discussed these cases in Chapter 3.) These cases provide a warning for auditors who rely on management representations too heavily when alternative sources of audit evidence are available.

Contents of a management representation letter

Written representations from management, where they pertain to financial report amounts directly, should be limited to matters that either individually or collectively are considered to be material to the financial report. Representation letters should be prepared on the entity's stationery, addressed to the auditor, signed by appropriate officers (usually the senior executive officer and the senior financial officer), and dated on the same date as the auditor's report. In many audits, the auditor will draft the representations, which subsequently become the responsibility of the officers who sign the letter. A management representation letter is illustrated in Figure 14.3.

FIGURE 14.3 *Management representation letter*

CLIENT COMPANY LIMITED
Canberra ACT

Independent Auditor — Date [as of audit report]

Dear ....

This representation letter is provided in connection with your audit of the financial report of Client Company Limited for the year ended 30 June 20X1 for the purpose of expressing an opinion as to whether the financial report gives a true and fair view of [or 'presents fairly'] the financial position and results of operations in accordance with [indicate relevant financial reporting framework].

We acknowledge our responsibility for the fair presentation of the report in accordance with [indicate relevant financial reporting framework].

We confirm, to the best of our knowledge and belief, the following representations:

- There have been no irregularities involving management or employees who have a significant role in the internal control system or who could have a material effect on the financial report.
- We have made available to you all books of account and supporting documentation and all minutes of meetings of shareholders and the board of directors; namely those held on 30 September 20X0 and 15 March 20X1, respectively.
- The financial report is free of material misstatements, including omissions.
- The company has complied with all aspects of contractual agreements that could have a material effect on the financial report in the event of non-compliance. There has been no non-compliance with requirements of regulatory authorities that could have a material effect on the financial report in the event of non-compliance.
- The following have been properly recorded and, when appropriate, adequately disclosed.
  (a) the identity of, and balances and transactions with, related parties;
  (b) losses arising from sale and purchase commitments;
  (c) agreements and options to buy back assets previously sold;
  (d) assets pledged as collateral.
- We have no plans or intentions that may materially alter the carrying value or classification of assets and liabilities reflected in the financial report.
- We have no plans to abandon lines of product or other plans or intentions that will result in any excess or obsolete inventory, and no inventory is stated at an amount in excess of net realisable value.
- The company has satisfactory title to all assets and there are no liens or encumbrances on the company's assets, except for those that are disclosed in Note X to the financial report.
- We have recorded or disclosed, as appropriate, all liabilities, both actual and contingent, and have disclosed in Note X to the financial report all guarantees that we have given to third parties.
- Other than ... described in Note X to the financial report, there have been no events subsequent to period end which require adjustment of or disclosure in the financial report or Notes thereto.
- The ... claim by XYZ Company has been settled for the total sum of XX which has been properly accrued in the financial report. No other claims in connection with litigation have been or are expected to be received.
- There are no formal or informal compensating balance arrangements with any of our cash and investment accounts. Except as disclosed in Note X to the financial report, we have no other line of credit arrangements.
- We have properly recorded or disclosed in the financial report the capital stock repurchase options and agreements, and capital stock reserved for options, warrants, conversions and other requirements.

Managing Director...

Principal Accounting Officer..

(Source: ISA 580, Management Representations — adapted)

Effects on the auditor's report

A management representation letter is not a substitute for any auditing procedures necessary to provide a reasonable basis for an opinion on the financial report. This evidence is judged to have relatively low reliability as a result of possible management bias. However, the refusal of management to furnish a written representation does constitute a limitation on the scope of the auditor's examination. In such circumstances, the auditor may express an 'except for' opinion or an inability to form an opinion (AUS 520.16; ISA 580.15). At the same time, the auditor may draw management's attention to the statutory and regulatory provisions that give the auditor access to records and information (s.310 of the Corporations Law). Furthermore, the auditor could consider that such refusal may have an additional effect on the audit report (s.308 of the Corporations Law).

Performing analytical procedures

6 LEARNING OBJECTIVE

Indicate why analytical procedures are important in undertaking the overall review of the financial report.

Analytical procedures are an important part of the completion of the audit. As stated in AUS 512.02 (ISA 520.02), Analytical Procedures:

> The auditor should apply analytical procedures at the planning and overall review stages of the audit.

In earlier chapters we explained and illustrated the application of analytical procedures in planning an audit and performing year-end substantive procedures. Analytical procedures involve the use of ratios and other comparative techniques. The objectives of using analytical review in the **overall review** is to corroborate conclusions formed during the audit on individual elements of financial information and to assist in arriving at the overall conclusion that the financial information as a whole is consistent with the knowledge of the entity's business. Analytical review procedures applied at the end of the audit are also a useful method in gaining assurance that the company will remain a going concern for the relevant period.

A variety of analytical procedures may be used. The procedures should be:

- applied to critical audit areas identified during the audit;
- based on financial report data after all audit adjustments and reclassifications have been recognised.

As in earlier applications of analytical procedures, entity data may be compared with expected entity results, available industry data and relevant non-financial data such as units produced or sold and the number of employees.

In carrying out an overall review, the auditor (often the audit senior in the first instance) reads the financial report and accompanying notes. In so doing, he or she considers the adequacy of the evidence gathered for unusual or unexpected balances and relationships that have been either anticipated in planning or identified during the audit through substantive procedures. Analytical procedures are then applied to the financial report to determine if any additional unusual or unexpected relationships exist. If such relationships exist, then the auditor should perform additional auditing procedures in completing the audit. The auditor is usually in a good position to critically evaluate the results of analytical procedures at the end of the audit, given his or her knowledge gained over the course of the audit. However, there is a risk that the auditor who has been responsible for a large amount of the audit fieldwork may be 'too close' to the audit work performed and may miss an unusual or unexpected relationship that would be recognised by someone who has not been so directly involved with the audit. For this reason, and because this review is so important, the partner or manager on the engagement would also review the analytical procedures. He or she should have a comprehensive knowledge of the entity's business and, as another advantage, would not have been directly involved with the audit fieldwork. Often, partners or managers pick up inconsistencies or problems because they have extensive business knowledge and because they can look at the figures more objectively than can someone who has done most of the fieldwork.

LEARNING CHECK

14.1 The auditor is required to identify and evaluate events occurring up to the date of the audit report. These events may relate to conditions that existed at balance date that may require an adjustment to the accounts or conditions that arose after the reporting date that could only result in disclosure by a note to the accounts.

14.2 The auditor should assess the appropriateness of the going-concern assumption during the final review. Additional audit procedures must be performed if there are any questions about the going-concern assumption.

14.3 Contingencies are existing situations that involve uncertainty about a possible gain or loss. Legal disputes are the primary source of contingencies; for this reason, a solicitor's representation letter is often obtained from the entity's outside solicitor(s) to corroborate information as to management's assertions in relation to the status of litigation or claims.

14.4 A management representation letter impresses upon management that it has the primary responsibility for the financial report. It may be the primary source of audit evidence, where appropriate audit evidence cannot reasonably be expected to exist.

14.5 Analytical procedures performed in completing the audit help the auditor to conclude that the financial information as a whole is consistent with his or her knowledge of the entity's business.

7 LEARNING OBJECTIVE

Identify the steps in evaluating audit findings.

EVALUATING THE FINDINGS

The auditor has the following two objectives in evaluating the findings: (1) determining the type of opinion to be expressed (which we will discuss in more detail in Chapter 15); and (2) determining whether the audit process has complied with the Auditing Standards. To meet these objectives, the auditor completes the following steps: makes the final assessment of materiality and audit risk; undertakes the **technical review** of the financial report; undertakes the final review(s) of working papers; and formulates an opinion and drafts the audit report.

Making the final assessment of materiality and audit risk

In formulating an opinion on the financial report, the auditor should assimilate all the evidence gathered during the examination. An essential prerequisite in deciding on the opinion to express is a final assessment of materiality and audit risk. The auditor should assess whether the aggregate of the uncorrected misstatements that have been identified during the audit is material. The aggregate of uncorrected misstatements comprises (AUS 306.13; ISA 320.13):

(a) specific misstatements identified by the auditor, including the net effect of uncorrected misstatements identified during the audit of previous periods that affect the current financial report; and
(b) the auditor's best estimate of other misstatements which cannot be specifically identified (i.e. projected errors).

The data that have been accumulated are then compared with the auditor's preliminary judgements concerning materiality that he or she made in planning the audit. Any adjustments in planning materiality that have been made during the course of the examination should be included in this assessment. If the aggregate level of uncorrected misstatements is material, then the auditor needs to consider reducing audit risk by extending audit procedures or requesting management to adjust the financial report.

In planning the audit, the auditor specifies an acceptable level of audit risk. As the aggregate level of uncorrected misstatement increases, the risk that the financial report may be materially misstated will also increase. When the auditor concludes that audit risk is at an acceptable level, he or she can proceed to formulate the opinion supported by the findings. However, if the auditor believes audit risk is not acceptable, then he or she should either perform additional substantive procedures or convince management to make the adjustments necessary to reduce the risk of material misstatement to an acceptable level. If management does not make the adjustments as required by the auditors, then the auditor may decide to issue a qualified audit report (AUS 306.15; ISA 320.15).

Undertaking the technical review of the financial report

This is a very important part of the audit and requires a high degree of technical knowledge, given the large number of professional and legislative requirements and the constantly changing nature of these requirements. The technical review includes matters pertaining to the form and content of each of the basic financial reports, in accordance with:

- the requirements of applicable Accounting Standards and other required disclosures;
- other matters as required by the Corporations Law;
- the official listing requirements of the Australian Stock Exchange (where this applies).

To assist in this process many public accounting firms have detailed financial report check lists, which are completed by the auditor who performs the initial review of the financial report. Once completed, the check list and financial statements are reviewed by the manager and partner in charge of the engagement. The completed check list and the findings of the reviewers should be included in the working papers. Prior to the release of the audit report on a publicly held client, there may also be a technical review of the report by a partner who was not a member of the audit team. This serves as a double check on the quality of the financial report presentation and disclosure.

If there are any problems with disclosure, they should be discussed with management. Usually, management will act on the auditor's advice in relation to technical aspects of disclosure. (Often, they will *seek* the auditor's advice in this area). Inevitably there will be disagreements, particularly associated with sensitive disclosure requirements such as directors' remuneration and related parties. If a disagreement about disclosure between management and the auditor cannot be resolved, then the auditor should consider issuing a qualified audit report (which we will discuss in Chapter 15).

Undertaking the final review(s) of working papers

In Chapter 6 we discussed the first-level review of working papers by a supervisor. The review is made to evaluate the work done, the evidence obtained and the conclusions reached by the person preparing the working paper. It is also conducted to ensure that the audit work meets an appropriate level of quality. The work performed undergoes more comprehensive reviews at the end of the audit fieldwork.

Often, the audit manager will review all of the audit working papers (including those reviewed by the audit senior) to ensure that the work has been performed properly. The manager will also sign all of the working papers reviewed to provide evidence of the review.

The manager's review of the working papers is designed to obtain assurance that:

- the work done by subordinates has been accurate and thorough;
- the judgements exercised by subordinates were reasonable and appropriate in the circumstances;
- the audit engagement has been completed in accordance with the conditions and terms specified in the engagement letter;

- all significant accounting, auditing and reporting questions raised during the audit have been properly resolved;
- the working papers support the auditor's opinion;
- the audit process has complied with the Auditing Standards and the firm's quality control policies and procedures.

Detailed check lists covering the above matters are commonly used in performing the review of working papers. The manager will also list queries raised while performing the review. The queries are generally addressed by the person who undertook the work and must be cleared by the manager before the audit is completed.

The review by the partner has similar objectives to the review performed by the manager. The extent of the partner review will depend on the partner, the type of engagement and the partner's confidence in the audit manager. Generally, the partner will not review all working papers, but will focus on sections of the audit that he or she perceives to be high risk. This assessment may come from the partner's knowledge of the client or from the final analytical review performed on the client.

As a further quality control some firms require a **second partner review** of the working papers by a partner who did not participate in the audit. The rationale for this review is that the objectivity of the reviewer may challenge matters approved by earlier reviewers. Thus, the review provides additional assurance that all Auditing Standards and the firm's quality control standards have been met in the engagement.

PROFESSIONAL ENVIRONMENT How effective are audit reviews?

While the audit review process is generally presumed to benefit audit quality, concerns have been expressed from time to time about the objectivity of such processes. Studies conducted by the auditing profession in the United States (such as the Cohen Commission) and by regulators such as the Securities and Exchange Commission (SEC) have publicly questioned the objectivity of auditors and audit review processes. Regulators in the United States have considered mandating that audit firms (and/or partners) be rotated periodically to mitigate the potential bias thought to arise from too much familiarity with a client.

The increasingly competitive audit environment — as well as encroaching regulatory and legal action — has prompted audit firms to re-examine and, in some cases, re-engineer the nature of their underlying review processes. Included in this new approach are these key features:

- a movement away from iterative reviews, in which the work of a junior auditor is sequentially reviewed by the audit senior, the audit manager and, finally, the engagement partner;
- a reduction in the number of reviews;
- a drastic reduction in the level of working paper documentation.

In practice, the re-engineered audit might look something like this. Following an emphasis on doing it right the first time (as stressed by the quality revolution in business management), partners and managers will be more directly involved in audit planning, risk assessments and decisions on where to focus audit effort. For low-risk clients, working papers may be reviewed only once (by a manager or partner) rather than receiving several reviews in the field. One Big Five firm in Canada is phasing in a 'review by interview' process whereby junior auditors are interviewed in the field by the reviewer and have to answer queries in real time. No written review notes are provided, and there is no opportunity to research issues or seek client assistance after the fact.

(Source: Extracted from K. Jamal, 'Great Expectations', *CA Magazine* (August 2000), pp. 43–44, 54 and 59)

Formulating an opinion and drafting the audit report

During the course of an audit engagement, a number of auditors perform a variety of audit tests. (The number of auditors will vary according to the size of the company being audited.) As the tests for each section of the audit are completed, the auditor is expected to summarise his or her findings. This summary should include: any proposed audit adjustments; any weaknesses in the system or problems that should be passed on to management; and a conclusion on the section of the audit completed. In completing the audit, the separate findings of each of the sections need to be summarised and evaluated so as to express an opinion on the financial report as a whole. The ultimate responsibility for these steps rests with the partner in charge of the engagement. In some cases, the audit manager makes the initial determinations, which are then carefully reviewed by the partner.

Before reaching a final decision on the audit opinion, the auditor should meet with management. At this meeting, the auditor reports the findings orally and attempts to provide a rationale for proposed adjustments and/or additional disclosures that have not been resolved. Management may attempt to defend its position. Agreement is generally reached on the changes to be made, and the auditor can proceed to issue an unqualified opinion. The potential threat of a qualified audit report and the negative signal it would send to investors is usually enough to ensure that management agrees with the auditor's opinion. However, when such an agreement is not obtained, the auditor may have to issue a qualified opinion. The auditor's opinion is communicated through an audit report. (We will discuss the various types of audit report in Chapter 15.)

8 LEARNING OBJECTIVE

Indicate the appropriate communications with the entity at the conclusion of the audit.

COMMUNICATING WITH THE ENTITY

Communication with the entity is an important part of the audit. It serves to highlight the problems found, suggest improvements in the client's system and give some evidence to the extent of work performed. AUS 710, Communication to Management on Matters Arising from an Audit (ISA 1007, Communication with Management) discusses the requirements of the auditor to communicate with management. According to the definition in AUS 710 (ISA 1007), management includes the governing body, audit committee, individual members of the governing body, officers and other persons having responsibility for planning and directing the activities of an entity. There are some special considerations in reporting to the audit committee, so we will consider the process in a separate section.

Communicating matters with management

AUS 710.02 (ISA 1007.17) states:

> The auditor should communicate significant matters relating to the audit, or identified as a result of the audit procedures performed, to an appropriate level of management on a timely basis.

In assessing the significance of each matter identified, the auditor should consider the nature of the matter, relevant characteristics of the entity and the potential for the matter to materially affect the financial report. Other matters that may be reported to management include (1) those that have resulted in the auditor assessing both the inherent risk and control risk as being high, and (2) irregularities, including fraud and non-compliance with legislative, regulatory or contractual requirements. However, the auditor has no duty to design audit procedures for identifying matters that may be appropriate to report to management (i.e. detection of fraud is not part of the requirements of a normal financial report audit). Sometimes, management may want the auditor to review certain parts of the accounting system or perform certain other procedures. These tasks are not considered part of the financial report audit; instead, they come under the category of 'assurance services' (which we will discuss in Chapter 16).

The extent and nature of communication with management has been considered in a number of legal cases. The case of *WA Chip and Pulp Co. Pty Limited v. Arthur Young & Co.* (1987) SACLC looked at the issue of whether detected irregularities immaterial to the audit need to be brought to management's attention. The court found that not only items material to the audit require reporting to management. The auditor should also consider warning and informing management of any matters that come to their attention that may be a cause for concern.

In drafting AUS 710 (originally AUP 35), consideration was given to the judgement by Rogers CJ in the AWA case (*AWA v. Daniels t/a Deloitte, Haskins & Sells & ORS* (1992) IO ACLC 933). In this case it was found that weaknesses discovered in the control system must be reported to management promptly and that significant matters must be reported not just to management but also to an appropriate level of management. Such matters may include:

- reasons for assessing the inherent risk and control risk as being high for specific financial report assertions, notably internal control weaknesses;
- irregularities, including fraud and non-compliance with laws and regulations;
- the selection and application of accounting policies for material unusual transactions or in controversial areas;
- accounting estimates on the basis of known past and current events and on future events;
- audit adjustments that have a material effect on the financial report;
- disagreements with operational management that could have a significant effect on the entity's financial report;
- difficulties encountered in performing the audit;
- any other matters, including those falling outside the scope of the audit (for example, inefficiencies), which may usefully be brought to management's notice.

Certain matters may be so significant that they require reporting to the audit committee or governing body. Less significant matters may be reported to a level of management with authority to take appropriate action, with a record of the discussion to be included in the working papers. Other matters may initially be communicated verbally, to save time and to clarify the situation before the matter is put in writing.

In preparing the **management letter**, to ensure that significant problems are highlighted without excluding trivial matters, the auditor may report major findings in the main body of the management letter, with an attached appendix detailing all other items found. This avoids the potential problem of the auditor excluding a matter that he or she thinks is trivial that management may later allege would have been of importance to them.

Preparing the management letter

During the course of an audit engagement, auditors observe many facets of the entity's business organisation and operations. At the conclusion of an audit, it is desirable to write a letter to management (known as a management letter) that contains recommendations for improving the efficiency and effectiveness of those matters noticed during the course of the audit. The principal purpose of such a letter is to advise management of weaknesses in the internal control structure. It also tangibly demonstrates the auditor's continuing interest in the welfare and future of the entity, as well as providing legal evidence of matters reported by the auditor to management (as required by AUS 710 (ISA 1007)). The issue of management letters has now become an integral part of the services rendered by many auditors. Problems identified with the client also provide the audit firm with the opportunity of performing 'other services' (including assurance services) in the areas of the client's system that need improvement.

The audit plan should contain a separate section on management letters. Where feasible, the plan should indicate areas of the entity's operations and controls that may be included in management letters. As the audit progresses, matters that are relevant to management letters should be noted in the audit working papers to ensure that they are not overlooked. Subsequently, the working papers should provide adequate documentation of the comments contained in the management letter. Such support will also be useful in any discussions with management about the comments. Management letters should be carefully prepared, well organised and written in a constructive tone. The auditor usually discusses the contents of the draft letter with the person responsible for the accounting system (usually the financial controller). In particular, the practicality of implementing the suggested changes to the existing system should be discussed. However, absence of agreement should not inhibit the inclusion of recommendations that the auditor considers desirable. To avoid misunderstanding, management letters should contain a paragraph advising management that the auditor's examination is made to form an opinion on the financial report and that the report to management should not be regarded as a statement of all matters of concern that may exist.

Prompt issue of management letters on completion of the audit creates a favourable impression and may encourage both an early and a positive response by management. Where the interim audit reveals material weaknesses in internal control, it may be desirable to issue a management letter on completion of that phase of the audit as well as on completion of the final audit.

The letter should request a written reply indicating the action taken or intended to be taken on the matters raised. If no response is received, then the auditor should consider whether to raise the matter directly with the audit committee. In any event, if management takes no action, then the auditor should consider raising the matter again in subsequent management letters, for example.

Communicating matters with the audit committee

The audit committee is part of the corporate governance structure to improve the credibility and objectivity of the accountability process. It also facilitates communication between the external auditor and the board of directors. The external auditor has a number of special responsibilities in his or her relations with the audit committee.

Audit Committees: Best Practice Guide[1] (produced by the Australian Accounting Research Foundation, the Australian Institute of Company Directors and the Institute of Internal Auditors) includes a number of specific responsibilities of the external auditor in his or her relationship with the audit committee. The auditor should communicate major issues that were discussed with management in connection with the appointment of the auditor. Any serious difficulties encountered in the performance of the audit should also be reported to the audit committee. This could include unreasonable delays in management providing information or representations and an unreasonable timetable for the completion of the audit. The auditor should also report any significant errors, problems or weaknesses revealed by the audit, and any areas of significant disagreement with management, the corrective actions taken and their current status. The general idea is that the audit committee, being a more independent body within the corporate structure, can follow up problems or difficulties encountered by the external auditor. The audit committee is also there to ensure that management does not exert undue influence on the auditor.

Appendix 1 of AUS 710 also details recommendations for auditors in their communications with audit committees. The auditor should inform management about significant matters affecting the audit of the financial report and material control weaknesses. The auditor should also report additional information regarding the scope and results of the audit that may assist the audit committee in overseeing the disclosure process for which management is responsible.

Currently, in Australia, audit committees are not a mandatory requirement for companies. Thus, there cannot be strict requirements for auditors to report to them. However, when there is an effective audit committee, the auditor should consider them in his or her assessment of the client's control structure. The auditor should also use them as much as possible in ensuring that the requirements of the financial statement audit are properly and objectively fulfilled.

PROFESSIONAL ENVIRONMENT — Should audit committees be mandatory?

Corporate governance, as defined by the Australian Stock Exchange (ASX), involves 'those monitoring and control mechanisms that are put in place by companies with the objective of enhancing shareholder value'.[1] Audit committees are one such corporate governance mechanism whereby companies have attempted to respond to the growing public pressure for greater accountability brought on by major corporate collapses. These committees have become mandatory requirements in countries such as the United States, the United Kingdom, Canada, Singapore and Israel.

Australian public companies are currently not required to form audit committees, either by statute or by ASX listing rules. (*Note*: The ASX does require disclosure of whether the company has an audit committee.)

... Consequently, the argument can be made that, as Australian listed companies are already required by ASX listing rules to disclose if they have an audit committee or not, they should also be required to disclose additional information such as the audit committee's composition, rights, functions and number of yearly meetings.[2] A proposal such as this could help improve the operation and performance of the committees in line with 'best practice' guidelines such as those issued by the Australian Accounting Research Foundation (AARF), Australian Institute of Company Directors (AICD), and the Institute of Internal Auditors (IIA) in 1997.[3]

If listed companies are required to make disclosures about such matters, they may not wish to disclose that, for example, they have an audit committee but it has no real rights or functions. Therefore, they could improve the way their audit committees operate so as not to be seen by financial statement users that their committees are used for nothing more than their 'image value'.

In weighing up the benefits and costs of compulsory audit committee formation, it must be recognised that there is 'a danger that legislators, regulators and others will expect too much of audit committees, and that they will be assigned responsibilities which, because of competence or time constraints, their members will be unable to satisfy. This will result in unfulfilled expectations and in undermining confidence in audit committees.'[4] Therefore, they may not prove to be the panacea that many have expected them to be, without adequate consideration of their limitations.

References

1. Australian Stock Exchange, *Disclosure of Corporate Governance Practices by Listed Companies*, 1994, p. 1.
2. Effective from 1 February 1993, sub-section 300(1) of the Corporations Law (formerly sub-section 307(2)) requires public companies, that are not wholly owned subsidiaries of another company or of a recognised company, to disclose in their annual directors' report the number of board committee meetings held during the year and each director's attendance at those meetings.
3. AARF, AICD and IIA, *Audit Committees: Best Practice Guide*, 1997.
4. Porter, B. and Gendall, P., *An International Comparison of the Development and Role of Audit Committees in the Private Corporate Sector*, Massey University Discussion Paper Series, 1993.

(Source: Extracted from P. Baxter & J. Pragasam, 'Audit Committees: One Size Fits All?', *Australian CPA* (April 1999), pp. 42–3)

LEARNING CHECK

14.6 The purposes of the auditor's final assessment of materiality and risk are to determine whether (1) the auditor's preliminary judgements concerning materiality have been met and (2) audit risk is at an acceptable level to warrant the expression of an unqualified opinion.

14.7 The technical review of the financial report includes a review of matters pertaining to the form and content of the financial report, in accordance with the requirements of applicable Accounting Standards and other required disclosures.

14.8 At the end of the audit the audit manager will perform a comprehensive review of the working papers to ensure the work has been performed properly. The partner will also review high-risk sections of the audit or may decide to look at the entire audit working papers as well.

14.9 In completing the audit, the auditor needs to summarise and evaluate the separate findings of each of the sections to express an opinion on the financial report as a whole. The type of audit opinion to be expressed is determined by the partner in charge of the engagement.

14.10 Significant matters identified as a result of audit procedures should be reported to an appropriate level of management.

SUMMARY

This chapter describes several key responsibilities of the auditor in completing an audit of a financial report. The two main differences in completing the audit from the work discussed in prior chapters is that completion does not pertain to a specific account balance or transaction class and that it has a high level of involvement of senior audit staff on the engagement. Steps performed in completing the fieldwork include performing the subsequent-events review, considering the applicability of the going-concern basis, obtaining evidence concerning contingent liabilities, obtaining the letter of management representations, and performing analytical procedures. Steps involved in evaluating the auditor's findings include making a final assessment of materiality and audit risk, making a technical review of the financial report, making a final review of the working papers, and formulating an opinion and drafting the audit report.

The auditor is required to communicate with the entity any internal control weaknesses found and may include (in the management letter) recommendations regarding the efficiency and effectiveness of the entity's operations. The auditor also has a duty to report other matters pertaining to the conduct of the audit to the audit committee when appropriate. The management letter is an important part of the audit reporting process because it provides more detail on matters that may be of more use to the daily functioning of the entity than the audit report (which we will discuss in Chapter 15).

The process of completing the audit, evaluating the findings and communicating with the entity is one of the most important stages of the audit process. Many of the successful legal cases against auditors related to deficiencies that occurred at this stage of the audit. It is therefore important that the partner and manager have significant involvement during this process. It is also crucial that this process is completed carefully and properly despite the fact that reporting deadlines will often impose significant time pressures.

KEY TERMS

Contingent liability, p. 543
Going-concern basis, p. 542
Management letter, p. 553
Management representation letter, p. 538
Overall review, p. 548
Second partner review, p. 551
Solicitor's representation letter, p. 540
Subsequent events, p. 538
Technical review, p. 549

NOTE

1. Australian Accounting Research Foundation, the Australian Institute of Company Directors and the Institute of Internal Auditors, *Audit Committees: Best Practice Guide*. Melbourne, 1997, pp. 22–3.

FURTHER READING

Cohen, Jeffrey R., Krishnamoorthy, Ganesh & Wright, Arnold M., 'Evidence on the Effect of Financial and Nonfinancial Trends on Analytical Review', *Auditing: A Journal of Theory and Practice* (Spring 2000), pp. 27–48.

Jiambalvo, James & Wilner, Neil, 'Auditor Evaluation of Contingent Claims', *Auditing: A Journal of Theory and Practice* (Fall 1985), pp. 1–11.

Kirk, Donald J., 'Experiences with the Public Oversight Board and Corporate Audit Committees', *Accounting Horizons* (March 2000), pp. 103–11.

Rau, Stephen E. & Moser, Donald V., 'Does Performing Other Audit Tasks Affect Going-Concern Judgements?', *Accounting Review* (October 1999), pp. 493–508.

Reimers, Jane L. & Fennema, M. G., 'The Audit Review Process and Sensitivity to Information Source Objectivity', *Auditing: A Journal of Theory and Practice* (Spring 1999), pp. 117–23.

Wright, Arnold & Ashton, Robert H., 'Identifying Audit Adjustments with Attention-Directing Procedures', *Accounting Review* (October 1989), pp. 710–28.

Review questions

14.1 What procedures should the auditor perform to identify subsequent events?

14.2 How would you define the two types of after-balance-date events? What are the potential accounting effects of each type?

14.3 What procedures should the auditor perform when a question arises regarding going concern?

14.4 What are the objectives of a management representation letter?

14.5 What should the auditor do when aggregate uncorrected misstatements are material?

14.6 What is the purpose of the final review of working papers?

Discussion questions

14.1 Explain the auditor's responsibility for identifying and acting on after-balance-date events. Is there an 'end point' to the auditor's responsibilities?

14.2 Can facts discovered after the issue of the financial report have an impact on the audit report? Discuss.

14.3 What is the possible effect on the audit report of a solicitor's failure to respond to a request for representation?

14.4 Can a management representation letter be a substitute for auditing procedures? Discuss.

14.5 Explain the purpose of the performance of analytical procedures at the end of the audit.

14.6 Describe the various steps required in evaluating the findings of the audit.

14.7 Discuss the audit partner's responsibilities in evaluating the findings of the audit.

14.8 Explain the purpose of preparing a management letter at the end of the audit.

14.9 Is a management letter required when only minor problems are discovered during the audit? Discuss.

14.10 Describe the responsibility of the auditor to communicate with the audit committee.

Professional application questions

★ BASIC
★★ MODERATE
★★★ CHALLENGING

14.1 (Management representation letter) ★

During the audit of the financial statements of Blackheath Manufacturing Limited (BM), the managing director, Mr S. Hill, and the auditor, Mr P. Wales, reviewed matters that were supposed to be included in a written management representation letter. Mr Hill prepared the management representation letter shown below after their discussion.

> **To: Mr P. Wales, FCA**
>
> In connection with your audit of the annual financial statements of Blackheath Manufacturing Limited for the year ended 30 June 20X2, for the purpose of expressing an opinion as to whether the financial statements give a true and fair view of the financial position and results of operations in conformity with generally accepted accounting principles, we confirm, to the best of our knowledge and belief, the following presentations made to you during the audit. There were no:
>
> - plans or intentions that may materially affect the carrying value or classification of assets and liabilities;
> - communications from regulatory agencies concerning non-compliance with, or deficiencies in, financial reporting practices;
> - agreements to repurchase assets previously sold;
> - other legal claims other than those already disclosed;
> - capital stock repurchase options or agreements, or capital stock reserved for options, warrants, conversions and other requirements;
> - compensating balance or other arrangements involving restrictions on cash balances.
>
> S. Hill
>
> Mr S. Hill
> Managing Director
> Blackheath Manufacturing Limited
> 27 August 20X2

Required

(a) Explain the purpose of a management representation letter.

(b) Identify the other matters that Mr Hill's representation letter should specifically address.

(AICPA — adapted)

14.2 (Subsequent events) ★★

In connection with the audit of Barlow Limited for the year ended 31 December 20X2, your audit partner became aware that certain events and transactions took place after 31 December 20X2 but before the issue of her audit report, dated 8 February 20X3. These events and transactions are detailed below. She asks you to consider whether any should have been adjusted in the financial report before she signed the audit report.

1. *3 January 20X3* — Barlow Limited received a shipment of raw materials from Thailand. The materials were sent free-on-board shipping point from the supplier during November 20X2.
2. *15 January 20X3* — The company settled and paid a personal injury claim of a former employee as a result of an accident that occurred in March 20X2. The company had not previously recorded a liability for the claim.
3. *25 January 20X3* — The company agreed to purchase for cash the outstanding share capital of Tuscan Limited. The acquisition is likely to double the sales volume of Barlow.
4. *1 February 20X3* — A plant owned by Barlow was damaged by a flood, resulting in an uninsured loss of inventory.
5. *5 February 20X3* — Barlow issued and sold to the general public \$300 000 in convertible debentures.

Required

For each of the five events/transactions, indicate to the audit partner the sorts of procedure that should have brought the matters to her attention and the form of disclosure that should have been required in the financial report (if any).

(AICPA — adapted)

14.3 (Contingencies/solicitor's representation letter) ★★

You are the auditor of Niagra Limited, a pharmaceutical company that has recently invented a new 'wonder drug' that apparently cures baldness. Sales for this drug have been remarkable and have led it to be the predominant product of this company. However, you read some newspaper reports that indicate there are serious side effects from using the drug and that legal actions had commenced against Niagra before the end of the financial year. The management of Niagra confirms these reports and gives you some indication of how the cases are expected to be resolved.

You decide that it would be wise to obtain a solicitor's representation letter to corroborate some of the information given to you by management on the status of these cases. The solicitors for Niagra refuse to supply you with the information you require. Apparently, the partner in charge of Niagra's work is on leave and not due to return until after the audit report is signed.

Required

(a) Explain the purpose of a solicitor's representation letter.

(b) Explain what you would do in the above situation.

14.4 (Final assessment of materiality/effect on audit report) ★★

You are nearing completion of the 31 December 20X1 audit of WEB Wholesalers Limited. The following figures have been extracted from the final draft financial report:

	$'000
Operating profit before income tax	5 722
Operating profit after income tax	3 541
Total revenue	718 635
Current assets	253 881
Non-current assets	216 752
Total assets	470 633
Current liabilities	103 333
Non-current liabilities	132 760
Total liabilities	236 093
Shareholders' equity	234 540

During your review of the audit files, you note the following items as recorded on the summary of audit differences:

1. WEB has been involved in a long-standing dispute with the taxation authorities in relation to the amount of sales tax payable on certain lines of merchandise. The case was resolved this year in favour of the taxation authorities. The court ruled that WEB, as well as paying the outstanding taxes, must pay a non-tax-deductible fine of $420 000.
2. Sales cut-off at one of WEB's stores was incorrect, resulting in a large sale of stock made in early January 20X2 being recorded in the 31 December 20X1 year end. The cost price of the inventory sold was $250 000. WEB marks up inventory by 40 per cent.
3. Purchases cut-off at the same store was also incorrect, resulting in a large purchase of stock made in late December not being recorded until January 20X2. The invoice price of the inventory purchased was $5 950 000.

You also note that the planning materiality level was set by the audit manager at $200 000.

Required

(a) Consider each above item independently. State whether the amounts involved would be considered to be material for the purpose of issuing an audit report. Give reasons.

(b) Explain the relevance, if any, of the planning materiality level to your decisions in (a). Explain your answer.

(Professional Year Programme of the ICAA — 1999, Advanced Audit Module — adapted)

14.5 (Subsequent events/post-audit discovery of facts) ★★★

The financial year of Brisbane Beer Limited ended on 31 December 20X3. Your audit report was signed on 24 February 20X4 and the financial statements were issued on 6 March. The following list describes events that occur or are discovered from the date of the balance sheet to 31 March 20X4. Assume each has a material effect on the financial report.

1. *15 January* — Inventory is sold at a price below the net realisable value at 31 December 20X3.
2. *20 January* — A major customer becomes bankrupt as a result of ongoing net losses.
3. *31 January* — The board of directors authorises the acquisition of a company as a subsidiary.
4. *10 February* — A fire destroys a major company warehouse.
5. *25 February* — A lawsuit is decided against the company for an accident that occurred on 10 October. The damages are three times higher than estimated on 31 December.
6. *28 February* — The board of directors authorises a two-for-one stock split.
7. *7 March* — A foreign government expropriates a major foreign subsidiary following the unexpected overthrow of the government.
8. *31 March* — A court rules that a minority group is the rightful legal owner of land on which an operating division is located.

Required

(a) Indicate your responsibilities for each of the above events.

(b) Indicate the type of disclosure (if any) that you would recommend in relation to each of the above events.

14.6 (Subsequent events/post-audit discovery of facts) ★★★

The financial year of Moorgate Limited ended on 30 June 20X2. Your audit report was signed on 25 August and the financial statements were issued on 10 September. Listed below are events that occurred or are discovered after the end of the financial year. Assume that each has a material effect on the financial report.

1. *1 August* — A lawsuit was filed against Moorgate for damages that allegedly occurred before 30 June. In the opinion of Moorgate's lawyers, there is a danger of a significant loss.
2. *15 August* — You discovered that debtor A of Moorgate went bankrupt on 10 August. The most recent sale had taken place on 25 May and no transactions had occurred since that date.
3. *1 September* — You discovered that a legal action commenced against Moorgate in relation to a faulty product sold in May 20X2.
4. *15 September* — A fire burnt down one of Moorgate's warehouses, resulting in a loss of 30 per cent of the inventory that was on hand at that date.
5. *30 September* — You discovered that debtor B of Moorgate went bankrupt on 15 July. Sales associated with this debtor occurred prior to the end of the year.
6. *30 September* — You discovered that debtor C of Moorgate went bankrupt on 25 September. The sale had taken place before the end of the year, but the amount had appeared collectable at the date on which the audit report was signed.

Required

(a) Indicate your responsibilities for each of the above events.

(b) Indicate the type of disclosure (if any) you would recommend in relation to each of the six events.

14.7 (Evaluating going-concern basis) ★★★

Consider the following independent situations, which all relate to the year ended 30 June 20X3.

1. Gregor is the sole director and proprietor of Greg's Gift Shop (GGS). GGS leases premises in a large shopping complex in the south of Adelaide. Greg received a preliminary notice in May 20X3 that the complex owners were planning a major redevelopment commencing later in the year. Greg's lease would be terminated around October 20X3 and at this stage it appears that no alternative premises will be offered. All necessary approvals have been obtained for the redevelopment project.
2. Frannie's Florist is in the same situation as Greg's Gift Shop, but at a different shopping complex. Council approval for the redevelopment project has not yet been granted at this complex.
3. Ms Gucci runs a beauty parlour in a shopping arcade in the suburbs of Melbourne. Her lease runs out on 31 December 20X3. Ms Gucci informed you at the planning stage of the audit that she does not intend to renew her lease. She will simply close the shop, sell what equipment she can, pay her outstanding accounts and retire.
4. ZX Limited is a subsidiary of an overseas electronic giant, ZY Limited. ZX has always made a loss and has always been financially supported by ZY. Each year, ZY signs a letter of support stating they will provide financial support for ZX in the next twelve months. You have such a letter on file this year. However, recent articles in the financial press suggest that ZY is in financial difficulties and may be subject to a hostile takeover bid.

Required

(a) Discuss whether there is a potential going-concern issue in each situation.

(b) Describe the additional procedures that you would perform (if any) in each situation.

(Professional Year Programme of the ICAA — 1999, Accounting 2 Module — adapted)

14.8 (Analytical procedures and going concern) ★★★

You have just completed preliminary analytical procedures of your client Asia On-Line Limited (AOL) which has a 31 March year end. AOL is involved in the development and design of new computer programs specifically for use on the Internet. The company was formed five years ago by a young entrepreneur, Ms Tang, with equity provided by her parents and a few friends. Ms Tang designed a program that was one of the first of its kind to assist users in the design of personalised web pages. The program was user friendly and cheaper than its competitors and therefore became very successful. The company has subsequently launched other Internet-related programs onto the market which have attracted, at best, moderate attention. Ms Tang has told you that she is in the final stages of a new program that will help users in purchasing products over the Internet. The product has involved substantial research and development over the past three years. She is extremely excited about this new product and believes that sales will reverse any past trading problems they have had. She has also told you that she has raised sufficient finance to enable finalisation and launch of the product within six months.

During the initial years where the company experienced rapid growth, all profits were reinvested to further research and development and to purchase an office block as the corporate headquarters. Office space not required by the company is rented out to tenants on normal commercial terms. Three small retail sites were also purchased that are used as outlets for the company's products as well as other computer software products. Ms Tang believes that she purchased these properties well and has told you that the market values are far in excess of the current book values.

The results of the ratio analysis undertaken as part of the analytical procedures were as follows:

Ratios	20X3	20X2	20X1
Days in debtors	45	33	28
Current ratio	0.62	0.73	1.01
Debt/equity ratio	2.03	1.94	1.72
Gross profit ratio	0.20	0.28	0.32
Net profit ratio	–0.05	–0.04	–0.02
Net assets per share	$2.87	$2.99	$3.25

Required

(a) Discuss AOL's overall financial position with reference to the ratio analysis undertaken as part of the analytical procedures.

(b) Nominate other factors listed above that may indicate that the company has going-concern problems.

(c) List factors that may exist to assist AOL with addressing this going-concern problem. Outline the information that you would need in relation to each factor identified.

(Professional Year Programme of the ICAA — 1999, Advanced Audit Module — adapted)

Case studies

14.1 (Subsequent events) ★★★

You are the supervisor on the audit of Golden $ Club, a large suburban club in New South Wales. As well as the usual club facilities such as poker machines, bars and a bistro, the club also operates a large gymnasium, an indoor heated pool and a restaurant.

The following dates are relevant to the current audit engagement:

Balance date	31 December 20X1
Financial report signed	15 February 20X2
Audit report signed	15 February 20X2
Annual report mailed to members	22 February 20X2

(*continued*)

You are aware that the following independent and material events have occurred:

1. On 5 February 20X2, the financial controller informs you that the board has recently received a letter from the assistant general manager, Mr T. The letter contains a confession: Mr T has been lodging fraudulent expense claims over the past five years, amounting to some $40 000. The financial controller's preliminary estimates indicate that this figure is materially correct; however, he believes it will take at least another two months before the exact figure is known. The police have been informed of the fraud and are searching for Mr T, who appears to have left the country.
2. On 8 January 20X2 the Federal Government announced that it intends to introduce legislation sometime in March, removing the current tax concessions enjoyed by clubs such as Golden $ Club. The changes will result in Golden $ Club being subject to the same tax rules that apply to companies. At present, the tax laws are such that Golden $ Club pays federal taxes only on net income from non-members, which represents about 10 per cent of total net income. The club's board of management, in conjunction with other clubs in the state, intends to lobby the government to reverse its decision. The board is confident the club's tax concessions will remain in place.
3. On 17 February 20X2, the financial controller informs you that on the previous day, a participant in one of the club's aerobics classes, Ms P, injured herself after slipping on the gym floor. Ms P is the spouse of one of the state's leading barristers. A preliminary letter has already been received from Mr P, stating that Ms P intends to take legal action to recover the cost of medical treatment, plus damages, from the club.
4. On 18 February 20X2, the financial controller informs you that a serious fire occurred in one of the club's kitchens during the New Year's Eve celebrations. Although covered by insurance, the fire caused extensive damage to the bistro area and the adjacent bar. Both the bistro and bar are expected to remain unserviceable until at least mid-March, resulting in an expected fall in revenue of around 7 per cent.
5. On 1 February 20X2 you read the minutes of a board meeting held on 15 January 20X2. The minutes note that merger discussions with the nearby bowling club are progressing smoothly and the matter will be put to a vote of members on 30 April 20X2. Costs associated with putting the issue to a vote (currently not included in the 31 December 20X1 financial report) are approximately $50 000.
6. On 23 February 20X2, the general manager informs you that on 18 February 20X2 the board decided to sell land it was holding as a long-term investment. It seems that a very generous offer was made by an overseas buyer. The contract is due to be signed on 25 February 20X2.
7. On 10 February 20X2, the board signed a contract for the upgrade of the club's air conditioning system. The upgrade is necessary to ensure compliance with workers compensation regulations. The first payment of $100 000 is due on 1 March 20X2. Work will be completed (and the final contract payment made) by 31 December 20X2.
8. On 31 January 20X2, the board decides that the club's restaurant will close permanently on 31 March 20X2. Although relatively well patronised, the restaurant has been losing around $10 000 per month and the board feels it can no longer justify keeping it open.

Required

(a) Explain what further evidence you would seek in relation to each of the above matters.

(b) Describe the action, if any, you would recommend to management in relation to the accounting treatment of each of the above items.

(Professional Year Programme of the ICAA — 1999, Advanced Audit Module — adapted)

14.2 (Communicating matters to management) ★★★

You have completed your audit of Balga Limited, a listed company, for the year ended 30 June 20X2. As at this date, Balga reported net assets of $5 million and sales revenue of $6 million. Materiality for the audit was set at $400 000.

During the audit you made note of the following potential management letter points:

1. Invoice number 697, issued on 1 May 20X2, contained incorrect prices. This resulted in the invoice being understated by $2500.
2. Inventory held at a third-party warehouse was found to be damaged and unsaleable; however, it was not written off. It is currently shown in the accounting records at its original cost of $25 000.
3. High turnover in the head office accounts department resulted in the bank account remaining unreconciled for three months. The problem was only resolved several weeks after the year end.
4. A minor fraud was perpetrated by warehouse staff, who acted in collusion with the stock controller to steal approximately $10 000 of stock during a six-month period. All employees involved in the fraud have since left the company. Additional controls have been put in place to prevent recurrence of the problem.
5. Unrecorded liabilities amounting to $5600 were discovered during the examination of cash payments made post balance date.
6. Two laser printers purchased by the marketing department were mistakenly posted to repairs and maintenance expense rather than fixed assets. The printers cost $8000 and depreciation of $2000 should have been charged in the year ending 30 June 20X2.
7. During testing of controls performed on payroll, it was noted that staff at one branch were verbally advising management of their annual leave requirements rather than completing the appropriate form.
8. During the review of prepayments, it was noted that Balga's lease for its office premises expired in March 20X2 and has not yet been renewed.

At the end of the audit the chairman of the board approached you and said: 'And another thing, don't waste the board's time by including all those trivial issues in the management letter. We only want to know about important things that may have a real impact on our operations, not irrelevant matters.'

Required

(a) Explain the risks of complying with the chairman's request. Describe how you could accommodate the chairman's request while minimising the risks for your firm of not reporting issues to the board.

(b) Assume each of the above items warrants disclosure in your management letter to Balga. Draft the management letter to the board.

(Professional Year Programme of the ICAA — 1998, Accounting 2 Module — adapted)

chapter 15 Reporting on financial reports

Overview

LEARNING OBJECTIVES

After studying this chapter, you should be able to:

1. outline the reporting standards for a financial statement audit
2. explain what is stated in the audit opinion of an audit report
3. prepare an unqualified audit report
4. outline the different types of qualified opinion
5. explain the various circumstances that give rise to audit qualifications
6. describe the various circumstances that require an emphasis of matter
7. explain the reporting requirements for consolidated accounts
8. explain reporting considerations for comparatives in a financial report
9. describe the effect of opening balances on the audit report
10. understand the requirements for audit and review reports on half-year accounts.

Professional statements

AUSTRALIAN		INTERNATIONAL	
AUS 212	Other Information in Documents Containing Audited Financial Reports	ISA 720	Other Information in Documents Containing Audited Financial Statements
AUS 510	Initial Engagements — Opening Balances	ISA 510	Initial Engagements — Opening Balances
AUS 702	The Audit Report on a General Purpose Financial Report	ISA 700	The Auditor's Report on Financial Statements
AUS 704	Comparatives	ISA 710	Comparatives
AUS 706	Subsequent Events	ISA 560	Subsequent Events
AUS 708	Going Concern	ISA 570	Going Concern
AUS 902	Review of Financial Reports	ISA 910	Engagements to Review Financial Statements
AASB 1001	Accounting Policies — Disclosure	IAS 1	Disclosure of Accounting Policies
		IAS 8	Net Profit or Loss for the Period, Fundamental Errors and Changes in Accounting Policies
AASB 1029	Half-year Accounts and Consolidated Accounts		
AGS 1016	Audit Review Reports — Half-year Accounts and Consolidated Account; and Addendum to AGS 1016		
APS 1	Conformity with Accounting Standards and UIG Consensus Views		

The final phase of the auditing process is reporting the findings. This chapter expands on the explanation of the audit report that we provided in Chapter 4.

To meet their reporting responsibilities, auditors must have a thorough understanding of the reporting requirements of Auditing Standards pertaining to audit reports. Firstly, they must know the required contents of the audit report expressing an unqualified opinion and the conditions that must be met for it to be issued. They must also understand the types of departure from an unmodified report, which may be due to an audit qualification or an **emphasis of matter**, and the circumstances in which each is appropriate. Lastly, they must be knowledgeable about their reporting responsibilities under the Corporations Law and other special reporting considerations. We will explain each of these topics in this chapter.

Throughout the chapter we assume that the auditor is reporting on an engagement to perform an attest audit, in accordance with Auditing Standards, to render an opinion as to whether management's general purpose **financial report** has been prepared in all material respects in accordance with an identified financial reporting framework. Chapter 1 contains a discussion on the different types of assurance engagement. Chapter 16 considers assurances associated with e-commerce and Chapter 17 explains the types of assurance associated with internal, operational and government auditing.

STANDARDS OF REPORTING

LEARNING OBJECTIVE 1

Outline the reporting standards for a financial statement audit.

Paragraph 2 of AUS 702, The Audit Report on a General Purpose Financial Report states that:

> The auditor should review and assess the conclusion drawn from the audit evidence obtained as the basis for expressing an opinion whether, in all material respects, the financial report is presented fairly in accordance with Accounting Standards and UIG Consensus Views and, where appropriate, relevant statutory and other requirements. The audit report should contain a clear written expression of opinion on the financial report taken as a whole.

Paragraph 2 of ISA 700, The Auditor's Report on Financial Statements contains a much briefer statement to allow for a variety of acceptable financial reporting frameworks and particular national statutory requirements:

> The auditor should review and assess the conclusions drawn from the audit evidence obtained as the basis for the expression of an opinion on the financial statements.

Financial report

A financial report on which an auditor reports means a general purpose financial report. It is intended to meet the information needs common to users who are unable to command the preparation of reports tailored to satisfy all of their information needs (APS 1, Conformity with Accounting Standards and UIG Consensus Views). The disclosure and presentation requirements for such reports are generally determined by **Accounting Standards** and **UIG Consensus Views**, and statutory and other requirements. The Corporations Law outlines the scope of the contents of a financial report (s.295), including:

- the financial statements for the year, including:
  - — the profit and loss statement for the year;
  - — a balance sheet as at the end of the year;
  - — a statement of cash flows for the year;

- notes to the financial statements, including:
  - disclosures required by regulations;
  - notes required by Accounting Standards;
  - any other information necessary to give a **true and fair view**;
- the directors' declaration that:
  - the financial statements and notes comply with Accounting Standards;
  - the financial statements and notes give a true and fair view;
  - in the directors' opinion, there are reasonable grounds to believe that the company will be able to pay its debts as and when they become due and payable;
  - in the directors' opinion, the financial statements and notes are in accordance with the law.

There is a conflict between the Corporations Law terminology of 'profit and loss statement' and 'balance sheet', and the Accounting Standards reference to 'statement of financial performance' and 'statement of financial position'. Most corporations are assumed to adopt the terminology of the Accounting Standards.[1]

Accounting Standards and UIG Consensus Views

The auditor is primarily commenting on whether the financial report is in accordance with Accounting Standards, which are the Australian Accounting Standards Board (AASB) Accounting Standards and the Australian Accounting Standards (AASs). The auditor must also ensure compliance with UIG Consensus Views.

The AASB Accounting Standards are required Standards for reporting entities that are companies by virtue of the Corporations Law (s.334). The AASs have been developed by the AASB and the former Public Sector Accounting Standards Board (PSASB) either jointly or exclusively. There are no significant differences between the two sets of Standards. As at 31 December 1999, only four AASs[2] (which relate to superannuation plans and government reporting) did not have an equivalent AASB Standard.

From 1 January 2000, the old PSASB was merged with the AASB. The AASB will now set all Standards for the Australian economy. Thus, there will be a gradual demise in the AASs, because new AASB Standards will be worded in such a way as to apply to both public and private sector entities.

UIG Consensus Views are not Accounting Standards; rather, they are the consensus views contained in abstracts issued by the Urgent Issues Group, a committee of the AASB. The UIG was established to provide timely guidance on financial reporting issues, for which differing opinions exist. In the audit opinion, the phrase 'other mandatory professional reporting requirements' includes reference to UIG Consensus Views.

International Accounting Standards (IASs)

Accounting Standards are, as far as possible, compatible with IASs. Where an IAS has been issued in respect of a subject that is not covered by an Accounting Standard, the AASB will consider the IAS as the basis for an Accounting Standard. The importance of IASs is expected to increase significantly over the next ten years. A new structure for the International Accounting Standards Committee (IASC) to improve its ability as a 'global standard setter' took effect from 1 January 2001.

Reporting requirements

Members of the Institute of Chartered Accountants in Australia (ICAA) and CPA Australia are required to take all reasonable steps within their power to ensure financial reports comply with the Accounting Standards and UIG Consensus Views, or that a **qualified opinion** is issued (APS 1.13). If general purpose financial reports are to provide a **fair presentation** (or give a true and fair view if a reporting entity is under the requirements of the Corporations Law) of the reporting entity's performance, financial position, and financing and investing, then the Accounting Standards and UIG Consensus Views must be consistently applied in their preparation and presentation of those reports (APS 1.06).

Consistency refers to both the application of policies in successive periods and the treatment of items of a similar nature. A change in accounting policies should be made only in response to new or changed statutory requirements or Accounting Standards, or in the interests of improved financial reporting. In accordance with AASB 1001, Accounting Policies — Disclosure (IAS 1, Disclosure of Accounting Policies), the summary of accounting policies shall refer to a note disclosing the nature, reason and financial effect of the change.

When dealing with matters not covered by a specific Statement of Accounting Standards (or relevant IAS), the auditor should use policies generally accepted by the accounting profession and business community. Moreover, the auditor should select and apply all accounting policies (especially when there is a choice between alternatives permitted from within specific Accounting Standards) with regard to relevance, reliability, materiality and substance over form.

Relevant statutory and other requirements

Where the audit is being conducted in accordance with statutory and other requirements such as the Corporations Law in Australia, the auditor usually has an additional responsibility to report on compliance with relevant sections of the regulations or statutory requirements. Reporting on such matters may be explicit or on an exception basis. The opinion on such requirements may be separated from the opinion on fair presentation in accordance with Accounting Standards and mandatory professional reporting requirements — that is, the report may be qualified with respect to other requirements, but unqualified as to presentation (or vice versa).

Part 2M.3, Division 3 of the Corporations Law prescribes the auditor's reporting duties. An auditor who conducts an audit of the financial report for a financial year or half year must form an opinion (s.307) on whether:

- the financial report is:
  - — in accordance with the law;
  - — complies with Accounting Standards;
  - — gives a true and fair view;
- he or she has been given all information, explanation and assistance necessary for the conduct of the audit;
- the financial records have been kept to enable the preparation and audit of the financial report;
- the records and registers have been kept as required by law.

The auditor must give reasons if, in his or her opinion, the financial report does not give a true and fair view. If the financial report does not comply with Accounting Standards, then the auditor must quantify the effect of that non-compliance to the extent that is practicable and give reasons if it is not practicable to quantify the effect fully (s.308[1], [2]).

The auditor's report must describe (s.308[3]) any defect or irregularity in the financial report. It must also report on an exception basis any deficiency, failure or shortcoming in respect of matters referred to above (s.307[b], [c] or [d]).

Directors' declaration

The financial statements on which the auditor is to report include the directors' declaration (s.295[4]). In reaching his or her opinion on the financial statements, the auditor will need to review the contents of this declaration. The requirements of the declaration are to state:

- that the financial statements and notes comply with Accounting Standards;
- the directors' opinion as to the truth and fairness of the view given by the financial statements and notes required by Accounting Standards;
- whether, in the directors' opinion, the company is able to pay its debts as they become due and payable;
- whether, in the directors' opinion, the financial statements and notes are in accordance with the Corporations Law.

No additional audit procedures are necessary to arrive at an opinion as to the directors' declaration. In particular, the auditor will have obtained evidence relating to the requirements as to after-balance-date events and the solvency declaration during the after-balance-date review and inquiry into **going concern** (see Chapter 14).

2
LEARNING OBJECTIVE

Explain what is stated in the audit opinion of an audit report.

Expression of opinion

AUS 702.21 requires a section within the report headed 'Audit Opinion' or 'Qualified Audit Opinion' (as appropriate), which should:

> ... clearly express the auditor's opinion as to whether the financial report is presented fairly in accordance with:
> (a) Accounting Standards and other mandatory professional reporting requirements; and
> (b) when appropriate, relevant statutory and other requirements.

Where the opinion is qualified, the auditor must also provide the reasons for the qualification and its effect on the information in the financial report (in quantified terms) wherever practicable. AUS 702 reiterates the requirement laid down in the London and General Bank case (see Chapter 3) that it is the duty of the auditor to convey information, not merely to arouse enquiry.

The auditor's opinion refers to the financial report as a whole. While the auditor performs the audit examination item by item, he or she must consider whether the impression created by the financial report taken as a whole is consistent with his or her intimate knowledge of the entity and its financial condition.

AUS 702 recommends that the auditor use the phrase '**presents fairly** in accordance with applicable Accounting Standards and other mandatory professional reporting requirements [and, when appropriate, relevant statutory and other requirements]' wherever possible. For audit reports prepared pursuant to the Corporations Law, the expression 'true and fair view' is used. (The majority of audits performed use this latter expression.)

ISA 700 also recommends the use of the term 'true and fair', although it allows the term 'presents fairly' as shown below (ISA 700.17):

> The auditor's report should clearly state the auditor's opinion as to whether the financial statements give a true and fair view (or are presented fairly, in all material respects) in accordance with the financial reporting framework and, where appropriate, whether the financial statements comply with statutory requirements.

ISA 700 notes that the two expressions are equivalent in its view.

Unfortunately, Auditing Standards for reporting have not always been consistent across national boundaries. The United Nations, in the report *The Role of Accounting Disclosure in the East Asian Crisis*, suggested that the Big Five firms should include in their audit reports any differences between national Accounting Standards and IASs and between national

Auditing Standards and ISAs.[3] This idea has developed even further, with the International Federation of Accountants (IFAC) deciding in 2000 to form a self-policing independent oversight board to examine audit reporting across national boundaries (see the 'Professional environment' below).

PROFESSIONAL ENVIRONMENT

IFAC forms self-policing independent oversight board

New York — The International Federation of Accountants (IFAC) has begun to pull together an independent oversight board that will monitor the federation's effort to create a global regulatory structure for firms that perform transnational audits.

The federation currently is in the polemic process of building a complex infrastructure that will try to induce the auditors of transnational corporations to meet IFAC standards of auditing, education and ethics. The regime will consist of a forum of accounting firms, a compliance committee, an ethical structure, education standards and a transnational auditing committee.

Once formed and duly mandated, the oversight board will serve the global public interest by bringing independent third-party scrutiny to all elements of the IFAC regime.

Though somewhat toothless in terms of disciplinary action, the [Public Oversight Board's] powers could be described as firm but gentle.

'By definition, an oversight board should not be an executive board,' said Peter W. Johnston, IFAC's chief executive. 'It has oversight, the power to comment, and certainly the power to influence. For any pronouncement by the board concerning regulators or IFAC or the profession, those who were involved would have to listen to the board and would have to take action in response to its recommendations. It will be powerful by virtue of being influential.'

The recently formed International Forum on Auditing Development — an already-active component of infrastructure — has met four times with the goal of promoting understanding among government regulators . . .

Compounding the complexity, the board will have to oversee the effectiveness of the IFAC regime in over 100 countries that regulate audits in as many different ways and have as many different definitions of public interest.

While trying to 'impose clear and unequivocal minimum guidelines for self-regulation of the profession,' the federation will not have the power to 'impose' anything without the agreement of national governments . . .

Johnston said he expects the board to have as many as seven members of impeccable integrity and professional qualification that will represent as many corners of the world. He would like them to be very prominent world citizens, particularly the chairman, whom he hopes will be a high-profile professional . . .

As the board begins to form, IFAC will ask the chairman to advise the federation on the best form, content and process of the board. IFAC members have recommended potential candidates for the board. Johnston hopes to have selected a chairman by year's end and an entire board selected by the middle of next year.

Ideally, he said, the [Forum of Firms] and the Compliance Committee and other elements of the regime will develop concurrently, and the several entities will contribute to each other's formation. The whole system is not expected to be up and running until 2003.

Although the IFAC will be encroaching on national turfs in a certain sense, its chief executive, Peter Johnston, believes that national regulators will welcome the regime because they recognise their own territorial limits in a world of transterritorial business. The oversight board will be the independent liaison through which the regulators can tell the federation whether its program is useful and effective.

Hoping to avoid any appearance of molding an oversight board to its own desires, the IFAC plans to appoint an initial chairperson of the board and then divest itself from the process as much as possible.

The IFAC is looking for potential board members who are specifically *not* accountants or auditors. Rather, it is looking for qualified individuals from the world's users of audit information, such as business leaders, investors and academics.

(Source: Extracted from G. Cheney, 'IFAC Forms Self-policing Independent Oversight Board', *Accounting Today* (23 October–5 November, 2000), p. 5)

3 LEARNING OBJECTIVE

Prepare an unqualified audit report.

Unqualified audit report

We introduced and discussed the concept of an **unqualified audit opinion** on a general purpose financial report in Chapter 4. We also provided an example of an unqualified audit report for CSR Limited on page 158, with a detailed discussion about each of the components on pages 156–9. An unqualified audit report will often be unmodified, but it may be 'modified' if an emphasis of matter section is required (which we will discuss in the next section).

The wording of the report is not standardised. AUS 702 (ISA 700) requires the report to reflect the individual circumstances relevant to each audit but adds that a measure of uniformity will improve the comparability of reports issued by different auditors and thus promote the reader's understanding. An example of an unqualified audit report is included in AUS 702, Appendix 1 and reproduced in Figure 15.1. The majority of unqualified reports will look similar to the one illustrated in Chapter 4 and the example in Figure 15.1. The illustration of an audit report in ISA 700 is similar in all material respects.

The basic elements of an unqualified audit report are:

- *a title*: This identifies the audit report and distinguishes it from other reports issued by management. The title includes the word 'independent' to indicate the nature of the audit.
- *an addressee*: The report is normally addressed to those who requested the audit and were ultimately responsible for the auditor's appointment (for example, the shareholders of a company or the members of a superannuation fund).
- *the scope*: This identifies the financial report audited, the name of the entity and the reporting period covered. It also restates the responsibilities of the governing body and the auditor. In essence, it describes the nature of the audit, stating that it was conducted in accordance with Auditing Standards.
- *the audit opinion*: An opinion is expressed that the financial report is presented fairly. The financial statements are identified and the opinion is linked to a financial reporting framework.
- *a signature*: The report is signed by the audit firm or the individual audit partner, as appropriate.
- *the auditor's address*: This specific location is where the auditor maintains an office.
- *the date on which the audit report is signed*: The audit report is dated after the financial report has been signed by the governing body. This date is important because the auditor has responsibility for subsequent events up to this date (see Chapter 14).

FIGURE 15.1

Example of an unqualified audit report

INDEPENDENT AUDIT REPORT

To [addressee]

Scope

We have audited the financial report of XYZ for the year ended 30 June 20X1 as set out on pages X to Y.[1] The [members of the governing body] are responsible for the financial report. We have conducted an independent audit of the financial report in order to express an opinion on it to [addressee].

Our audit has been conducted in accordance with Australian Auditing Standards to provide reasonable assurance whether the financial report is free of material misstatement. Our procedures included examination, on a test basis, of evidence supporting the amounts and other disclosures in the financial report, and the evaluation of accounting policies and significant accounting estimates. These procedures have been undertaken to form an opinion whether, in all material respects, the financial report is presented fairly in accordance with Accounting Standards and other mandatory professional reporting requirements [and relevant statutory and other requirements] so as to present a view which is consistent with our understanding of the [entity's] financial position, the result of its operations and its cash flows.

The audit opinion expressed in this report has been formed on the above basis.

Audit opinion

In our opinion, the financial report presents fairly in accordance with applicable Accounting Standards and other mandatory professional reporting requirements [and . . .][2] the financial position of XYZ as at 30 June 20X1 and the results of its operations and its cash flows for the year then ended.

Date.. Firm...

Address .... Partner...

[1] Or identify the individual components when appropriate.

[2] Cite relevant statutory and other requirements when appropriate.

(Source: AUS 702, Appendix 1)

LEARNING CHECK

15.1 Accounting Standards, UIG Consensus Views and statutory and other requirements determine the disclosure and presentation requirements of general purpose financial reports.

15.2 According to Australian Auditing Standards, an audit opinion on whether the financial statements are 'presented fairly' should be made in the audit report. For audit reports prepared pursuant to the Corporations Law, the expression 'true and fair view' is used instead.

15.3 An unqualified audit report means that the financial statements are presented fairly (or give a 'true and fair' view). An unqualified audit report is also unmodified if it does not require an emphasis of matter.

MODIFIED AUDIT REPORTS

An audit report may be modified as a result of (1) a qualified opinion or (2) an emphasis of matter. A qualified audit opinion means that a material matter affects the financial report and the auditor believes that matter precludes a statement that the whole financial report 'presents fairly' the financial position of the entity. We will discuss the various degrees of qualifications in the next section. An emphasis of matter relates to certain limited circumstances in which the audit report is unqualified but the auditor believes it is appropriate to draw attention to or emphasise a matter that is relevant to the users of the audit report. An audit report might have a qualification (relating to a separate issue) *and* an emphasis of matter, because one does not preclude the other. Other reporting mechanisms such as a management letter or report to a regulatory agency are not a substitute for modified audit reports.

4 LEARNING OBJECTIVE

Outline the different types of qualifed opinion.

Qualified audit report

Qualified opinions are expressed when circumstances exist that preclude the auditor from stating that the financial report is 'presented fairly'. The types of qualified opinion depend on the circumstances and the degree of the problem. The qualified opinions permitted by Auditing Standards are:

- an **'except for' opinion** (e.g. Figure 15.3 on page 577);
- an **adverse opinion** (e.g. Figure 15.4 on page 578); and
- an **inability to form an opinion** (e.g. Figure 15.5 on page 579).

The interpretation of what each of these reports means is shown in Table 15.1.

TABLE 15.1

Types of audit opinion and their interpretation

Type of opinion	Signal	Interpretation
Unqualified	Favourable	The financial report is properly drawn up in accordance with an identified financial reporting framework. Taken as a whole, it presents fairly the financial position, results of operations and cash flows of the entity.
'Except for'	Favourable, with a qualification	Except for the specific reservation, deficiency, shortcoming or scope limitation, the financial report is fairly presented.
Adverse	Unfavourable	The financial report is not fairly presented. It is misleading and is of no use.
Inability to form an opinion	Neither favourable nor unfavourable	The auditor is unable to express an opinion on the financial report owing to audit limitations.

The auditor makes a judgement within the framework of Auditing Standards and the financial reporting framework in determining whether a financial report is fairly presented. In deciding on the appropriate opinion, the auditor considers if there is (1) any disagreement with management, pertaining to the financial report, (2) conflict between applicable financial reporting frameworks or (3) sufficient appropriate evidence to have a reasonable basis for an opinion. The decision process in choosing from the various qualified audit reports is illustrated in Figure 15.2 on page 576.

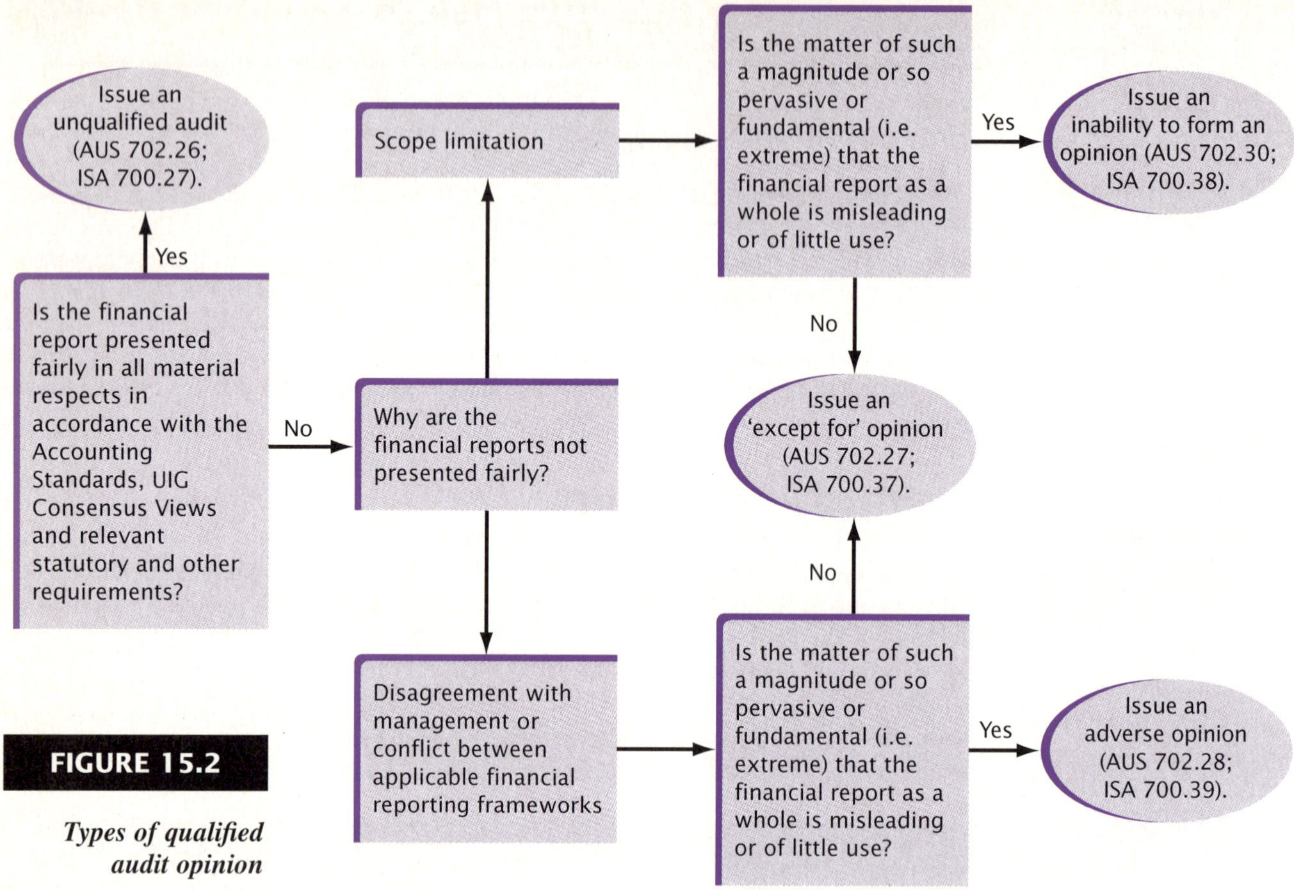

FIGURE 15.2

Types of qualified audit opinion

Materiality is an important consideration in arriving at an appropriate opinion because an unqualified opinion is appropriate when the matter is immaterial. When the effect is material, an 'except for' opinion is expressed. When the effect on the financial report is extremely material, the auditor is likely to issue an adverse opinion or an inability to form an opinion (depending on the circumstances). However, the auditor also needs to consider the concept of pervasiveness in determining whether an adverse opinion or inability to form an opinion should be issued. Pervasiveness relates to the number of financial report items affected by a circumstance. When a small number of items are affected, the auditor will usually render an 'except for' opinion because the effects can be adequately explained in the 'Qualification' section and the overall financial report will still be useful. Conversely, when a large number of items are affected, it may be impractical to attempt to explain all the effects in the 'Qualification' section, so the auditor will issue an inability to form an opinion or an adverse opinion.

Before issuing a qualified opinion of any kind, the auditor should do everything reasonably possible to express an unqualified opinion. Conversely, the auditor should not shirk from issuing a qualified opinion if necessary, particularly if he or she is in disagreement with management. As a consequence of the qualification, the format of the audit report is modified. A 'Qualification' section is inserted, following the 'Scope' section. It outlines the reasons for the opinion expressed and quantifies the effect thereof (AUS 702.19; ISA 700.40). The audit opinion section is headed 'Qualified audit opinion', in which reference is made to the qualification in the 'Opinion' section.

5 LEARNING OBJECTIVE

Explain the various circumstances that give rise to audit qualifications.

Circumstances that give rise to a qualification

We will now consider in more detail the circumstances that give rise to the qualified opinions discussed in the previous section. (We will present illustrative reports for many of the circumstances.) The issue of a qualified opinion may be necessary if there is:

- a disagreement with management (e.g. Figure 15.3);
- conflict between applicable financial reporting frameworks (e.g. Figure 15.4 on page 578);
- a scope limitation (e.g. Figure 15.5 on page 579).

Disagreement with management

The auditor may disagree with management over the appropriateness of the accounting policies selected; the method of their application, including consistency in the selection and application of accounting policies; the adequacy of disclosures in the financial report; or the compliance of the financial report with relevant statutory and other requirements.

Disagreements often relate to the application of Accounting Standards or the adequacy of disclosures of sensitive matters to the company. The method of application of Standards may relate to accounting estimates such as an appropriate provision for warranty or for doubtful debts. The subjectivity of these types of estimate often causes disagreements between the management and the auditor. Disagreements over the adequacy of disclosures may relate to the disclosure of litigation, significant plans of the company, or directors' benefits. Management may not want these disclosed for fear of detrimental market reactions or for strategic reasons.

The auditor must undertake all reasonable steps to overcome the cause of the disagreement. However, fairness of presentation is a matter of judgement, and occasional disagreements are the essence of an independent audit. Ultimately, the auditor should stick by his or her view on the appropriate treatment in the circumstances and ensure that the correct action is taken if management will not amend the accounts. In practice, a disagreement with management is the most common situation that results in a qualified audit report. An example of a disagreement with management resulting in an 'except for' opinion is shown in Figure 15.3.

FIGURE 15.3

Qualified audit report including an 'except for' opinion

INDEPENDENT AUDIT REPORT

Scope

(Section is not modified.)

Qualification

XYZ has not recognised interest earned but not received as at balance date. This is a departure from Australian Accounting Standard AAS 1, Profit and Loss or other Operating Statements which requires that all items of revenue arising during a period be taken into account in determining the profit for that period. The total interest earned but not received as at 30 June 20X1 was $xxx (20X0 — $xxx). In our opinion, this revenue should have been recognised in the year in which it was earned. Had this been done, the operating profit before income tax would be $xxx (20X0 — $xxx), after income tax and extraordinary items $xxx (20X0 — $xxx), total equity $xxx (20X0 — $xxx) and sundry debtors $xxx (20X0 — $xxx).

Qualified audit opinion

In our opinion, except for the effects on the financial report of the matter referred to in the qualification paragraph, the financial report presents fairly in accordance with applicable Accounting Standards and other mandatory professional reporting requirements [and . . . ,][1] the financial position of XYZ as at 30 June 20X1 and the results of its operations and its cash flows for the year then ended.

Date .... Firm ....

Address .... Partner ....

[1] Cite relevant statutory and other requirements when appropriate.

(Source: AUS 702, Appendix 2, Example 2 — adapted)

Conflict between applicable financial reporting frameworks

In unusual circumstances, the application of accounting policies in compliance with statutory and other requirements may not result in a fair presentation in accordance with the Accounting Standards and UIG Consensus Views. In this instance, the auditor should express an unqualified opinion in accordance with statutory and other requirements and a qualified opinion in accordance with the Accounting Standards and UIG Consensus Views. An example of this situation, resulting in an adverse opinion, is shown in Figure 15.4.

FIGURE 15.4

Qualified audit report including an adverse opinion

INDEPENDENT AUDIT REPORT

Scope

(Section is not modified.)

Qualification

Included in the financial report as a non-current asset is [parent entity's] investment in [subsidiary entity], recorded at a cost of $xxx. [Parent entity] has not presented a consolidated financial report which combines the financial report of [subsidiary entity] with that of [parent entity]. Although a consolidated financial report is not required by . . .,[1] it is required by Australian Accounting Standard AAS 24, Consolidated Financial Reports because [parent entity] has the capacity to dominate [subsidiary entity's] decision-making in relation to its financial and operating policies.

The audited financial report of [subsidiary entity] for the year ended 30 June 20X1 disclosed an operating loss and extraordinary items after income tax of $xxx (20X0 — $xxx) and a net liability position of $xxx (20X0 — $xxx). As there were no significant transactions between [parent entity] and [subsidiary entity] during the year and no significant inter-entity balances at balance date, had a consolidated financial report been presented, it would disclose an operating loss and extraordinary items after income tax attributable to members of [parent entity] of approximately $xxx (20X0 — $xxx) and a net liability position of approximately $xxx (20X0 — $xxx). In our opinion, the presentation of a consolidated financial report is fundamental to a proper appreciation of [parent entity's] financial position, the results of its operations and its cash flows.

Qualified audit opinion

In our opinion, the financial report of [parent entity] complies with . . .;[1] however, because of the effects of the matter discussed in the Qualification paragraphs, the financial report does not present fairly in accordance with applicable Accounting Standards and other mandatory professional reporting requirements the financial position of [parent entity] as at 30 June 20X1 and the results of its operations and its cash flows for the year then ended.

Date .... Firm ....

Address .... Partner ....

[1] Cite relevant statutory and other requirements.

(Source: AUS 702, Appendix 2, Example 3 — adapted)

Scope limitation

In undertaking an examination in accordance with Auditing Standards, the auditor is expected to obtain sufficient appropriate audit evidence to have a reasonable basis for expressing an opinion on the financial report. When the auditor cannot perform the necessary procedures or the procedures do not provide sufficient evidence, the auditor is said to have a scope limitation. Scope limitations may be imposed by the audit mandate or result from circumstances of the particular engagement.

The terms of the engagement may prohibit the auditor from carrying out specific audit procedures or restrict the type of opinion that the auditor may express. If the auditor judges that the outcome of such restrictions is an inability to form an opinion, then the audit engagement should be declined. The audit should also be declined when known limitations impinge on the auditor's legal duties and/or ethical or other professional responsibilities. Examples of scope limitations imposed during the course of the audit include a refusal to permit confirmation of receivables, sign a client representation letter or give the auditor access to the minutes of board of directors meetings.

Scope limitations also exist when, in the opinion of the auditor, the entity's accounting records are inadequate or the timing of the auditor's appointment means the auditor is unable to carry out a desirable audit procedure. The auditor should attempt to carry out reasonable audit procedures to overcome the scope limitation. The accounting records may be inadequate if some of the records for the year have been lost or destroyed (e.g. during a fire) during the year. An example of a restriction attributable to the timing of appointment is where the auditor is appointed after the year end and the stock count has already been performed.

When a scope limitation exists, the auditor should:

- give substantive reasons for the limitation in a qualification paragraph;
- express an 'except for' opinion or an inability to form an opinion.

The importance of the missing evidence and the materiality of the effects of the item(s) in question on the financial report are factors the auditor should consider in deciding whether to qualify an opinion or express an inability to form an opinion. When the scope limitation extends to many financial report items, there is a greater probability that a statement of inability to form an opinion will be necessary.

The wording of the 'Opinion' section should refer to the potential effects on the financial report of the items for which the auditor has not obtained audit satisfaction, rather than to the scope limitation itself. This is because the auditor's opinion relates to the financial report. A scope limitation resulting in an inability to form an opinion is illustrated in Figure 15.5.

FIGURE 15.5

Qualified audit report including the expression of an inability to form an opinion

INDEPENDENT AUDIT REPORT

Scope

(Section is not modified.)

Qualification

As stated in Note X to the financial statements, a fire at the [entity's] computer centre destroyed many of the accounting records. The fire occurred prior to the completion of our audit. As the remaining accounting records are not adequate to permit the application of necessary auditing procedures, we are unable to obtain all the information and explanations we require in order to form an opinion on the financial report.

Qualified audit opinion

In our opinion, because of the existence of the limitation on the scope of our work as described in the Qualification section, and the effects of such adjustments, if any, as might have been determined to be necessary had the limitation not existed, we are unable to and do not express an opinion as to whether the financial report is presented fairly in accordance with applicable Accounting Standards and other mandatory professional reporting requirements [and . . .][1] of the financial position of XYZ as at 30 June 20X1 and the results of its operations and its cash flows for the year then ended.

Date .... Firm ....

Address .... Partner ....

[1] Cite relevant statutory and other requirements when appropriate.

(Source: AUS 702, Appendix 2, Example 4 — adapted)

6 LEARNING OBJECTIVE

Describe the various circumstances that require an emphasis of matter.

An emphasis of matter

An auditor may add an 'emphasis of matter' section to an audit report while still expressing an unqualified opinion on the financial report. The purpose of this is to draw the attention of users of the audit report to relevant information. An emphasis of matter is not designed for any circumstance that is not quite material enough to result in a qualified 'except for' opinion. It is for very specific circumstances, which include (AUS 702.57–.65):

- **additional disclosures** with which the auditor concurs and that make the accounts true and fair;
- an **inherent uncertainty** (going concern or other) that is adequately disclosed;
- inconsistency with other information included with the audited financial report;
- the reissue of the financial report due to subsequent events.

ISA 700 allows an emphasis of matter for a broader range of circumstances than are detailed in AUS 702. It should be made clear that the contents of the 'Emphasis of matter' section do not constitute a qualification (for example, by use of an opening phrase such as, 'Without [further] qualification to the opinion expressed above, attention is drawn to . . .').

Additional disclosure

Additional disclosures requiring explanation in an 'Emphasis of matter' section are those that imply that the application of a particular Accounting Standard has resulted in the financial report being potentially misleading, but where the auditor considers the opinion should not be qualified because the additional disclosures not only are necessary to prevent users being misled, but also are wholly consistent with the objectives of a general purpose financial report.

The 'Emphasis of matter' section follows the 'Opinion' section of the audit report and is headed 'Application of Accounting Standard AASB xxx' and/or 'Application of Urgent Issues Group Consensus View xxx'. This section:

- draws attention to the additional disclosure;
- states that application of the particular Accounting Standard and/or UIG Consensus View has resulted, in the auditor's opinion, in a misleading financial report;
- provides reasons for additional disclosures;
- states the relevance and reliability of additional disclosures in meeting the objectives of a general purpose financial report (AUS 702.58).

Figure 15.6 on the right illustrates an audit report that includes an emphasis of matter due to additional disclosures. Rare circumstances would result in a modification to an audit report of this nature.

Inherent uncertainty (including going concern)

The term 'inherent uncertainty' applies to the outcome of any report item or disclosure contingent upon future events that is not capable of reasonable estimation at the date of the audit report. Uncertainties differ from accounting estimates in that the latter are generally capable of reasonable determination by auditors, and guidance on this matter is contained in AUS 516 (ISA 540), Audit of Accounting Estimates. Uncertainties may range from a single event (such as the outcome of a lawsuit) to multiple events (such as recurring operating losses and major financial problems that affect the ability of the entity to continue as a going concern).

Uncertainties present a special problem for the auditor because evidence of their resolution does not exist prior to completion of the examination. On the basis of available evidence, the auditor is responsible for determining whether the uncertainties are properly accounted for and disclosed. The auditor is not expected to predict the outcome of the uncertainties.

When the auditor considers that the inherent uncertainty is not adequately disclosed, it will constitute a disagreement with management and the appropriate form of qualification is either an 'except for' or an adverse opinion. In these situations there should be no emphasis of matter.

When an inherent uncertainty is adequately disclosed, an emphasis of matter is added to an unqualified opinion, as illustrated in Figure 15.7.

FIGURE 15.6

An audit report including an emphasis of matter due to additional disclosures

INDEPENDENT AUDIT REPORT

(Scope section is not modified.)

Opinion section expresses unqualified opinion.

(c) when read in the context of the section below, in accordance with applicable Accounting Standards and other mandatory professional reporting requirements.

Application of Accounting Standard AASB 10XX

Without qualification to the opinion expressed above, attention is drawn to the following matter. As required by the Corporations Law the company has, in the preparation of its balance sheet and profit and loss account, applied the ABC method of accounting for widgets in accordance with Accounting Standard AASB 10XX:

. . .

The directors are of the opinion, however, that application of the ABC method has not resulted in the financial statements giving a true and fair view of the matters required by Part 3.6 of the Corporations Law. The directors have therefore provided the additional disclosures in Note X which indicate that had the LMN method of accounting for widgets been adopted, the financial statements would, in the director's opinion, have given a true and fair view. The effect of adopting the LMN method rather than the ABC method is disclosed in Note X.

Because of [state the auditor's reasons in full], it is our opinion that:

(a) application of the ABC method in accordance with Accounting Standard AASB 10XX has, in this instance, resulted in the treatment of widgets leading to the balance sheet and profit and loss account being potentially misleading;
(b) the additional disclosures provided by the directors in Note X are necessary to ensure the financial statements as a whole are not misleading;
(c) the information in Note X, including application of the LMN method as the most appropriate alternative method, is relevant and reliable.

Date .... Firm ....

Address .... Partner ....

(Source: AUS 702, Appendix 4, Example 5 — adapted)

FIGURE 15.7

An audit report including an emphasis of matter due to an inherent uncertainty being adequately disclosed

INDEPENDENT AUDIT REPORT

(Scope section is not modified.)

(Opinion section expresses an unqualified opinion.)

Inherent uncertainty regarding litigation

Without qualification to the opinion expressed above, attention is drawn to the following matter. As indicated in Note X to the financial statements, XYZ is the defendant in litigation alleging infringement of certain patent rights and claiming royalties and damages amounting to $xxx. The [entity] has filed a counteraction for damages etc. amounting to $xxx, and preliminary hearings and discovery proceedings on both actions are in progress. As discussed in Note X, the circumstances of the case are such that the ultimate outcome of the litigation cannot presently be determined with an acceptable degree of reliability, and accordingly no provision for any liability that may result has been made in the financial statements.

Date .... Firm ....

Address .... Partner ....

(Source: AUS 702, Appendix 2, Example 1 — adapted; ISA 700.35)

Going concern

The most common inherent uncertainty the auditor needs to consider is in relation to going concern. The issue of going concern is significant enough to warrant a separate Auditing Standard — AUS 708 (ISA 570), Going Concern. The auditor is responsible for evaluating whether the entity has the ability to continue as a going concern for the relevant period (that is, from the date of the auditor's current report to the expected date of the auditor's report on the succeeding financial reporting period). We explained the procedures for evaluating going concern in Chapter 14. It is sufficient to note here that auditing procedures performed to achieve other audit objectives should enable the auditor to identify conditions and events that indicate, when considered in the aggregate, that there is substantial doubt about the entity's ability to continue as a going concern. When information is obtained contrary to the going-concern assumption, the auditor should consider management's plans for dealing with the adverse effects of the identified conditions and events. Management may plan to dispose of assets, borrow money or restructure debt, reduce or delay expenditure, or increase ownership equity.

If there is uncertainty that the entity will continue as a going concern that is adequately disclosed, then the auditor should issue an unqualified audit opinion with an emphasis of matter. If the circumstances are not adequately disclosed, then the auditor should issue an 'except for' opinion as a result of a disagreement with management. If it is highly improbable that the entity will continue as a going concern, then disclosure of the circumstances will not be enough and the auditor should express an adverse opinion. These reporting alternatives are shown in Figure 15.8 on the right.

Inconsistent other information

The audited financial report is often bound together with other unaudited statements and reports to comprise the entity's annual report. The inclusion of some of this other information, such as the directors' report, may be required by relevant regulations or statutes. The entity provides other information, such as a chairperson's report or a five-year financial summary, voluntarily. Much of this information is presented in a glossy format, designed to be easy to read (i.e. using colour, graphs, brief summaries etc.) and often meant to put a positive slant on the company's operations for the year. AUS 212, Other Information in Documents Containing Audited Financial Reports (ISA 720, Other Information in Documents Containing Audited Financial Statements) requires the auditor to obtain details of other information intended for inclusion in the annual report that may have a relationship with information in the audited financial report. The auditor should review this for inconsistency with the audited financial report and for material misstatements of fact, before signing the auditor's report. An inconsistency may cause a reader to doubt the reliability of the information in the audited financial report, while a misstatement of fact may cause harm to readers who mistakenly interpret the auditor's opinion as extending to the entire document.

When the auditor becomes aware of an inconsistency between the financial report being reported on and other information contained in the same document, he or she must determine whether the financial report or the other information needs revision. The matter should be discussed with management. If the financial report requires revision and management refuses to revise the report, then the auditor should express an 'except for' or adverse opinion. If the other information requires revision and management refuses to do so, then the auditor should include an emphasis of matter describing the material inconsistency. An emphasis of matter is more appropriate than a qualification because nothing is actually wrong in the financial report.

AUS 212 (ISA 720) also discusses material misstatements of fact. These misstatements concern matters not related to the financial report. If the auditor believes the other information contains a misstatement, then he or she must discuss the matter with management. After discussion, if the auditor is satisfied that there is a material misstatement of fact, then the auditor should notify the entity in writing and seek legal advice as to further appropriate action if management refuses to correct the misstatement.

FIGURE 15.8

Linking going concern considerations with types of audit opinion

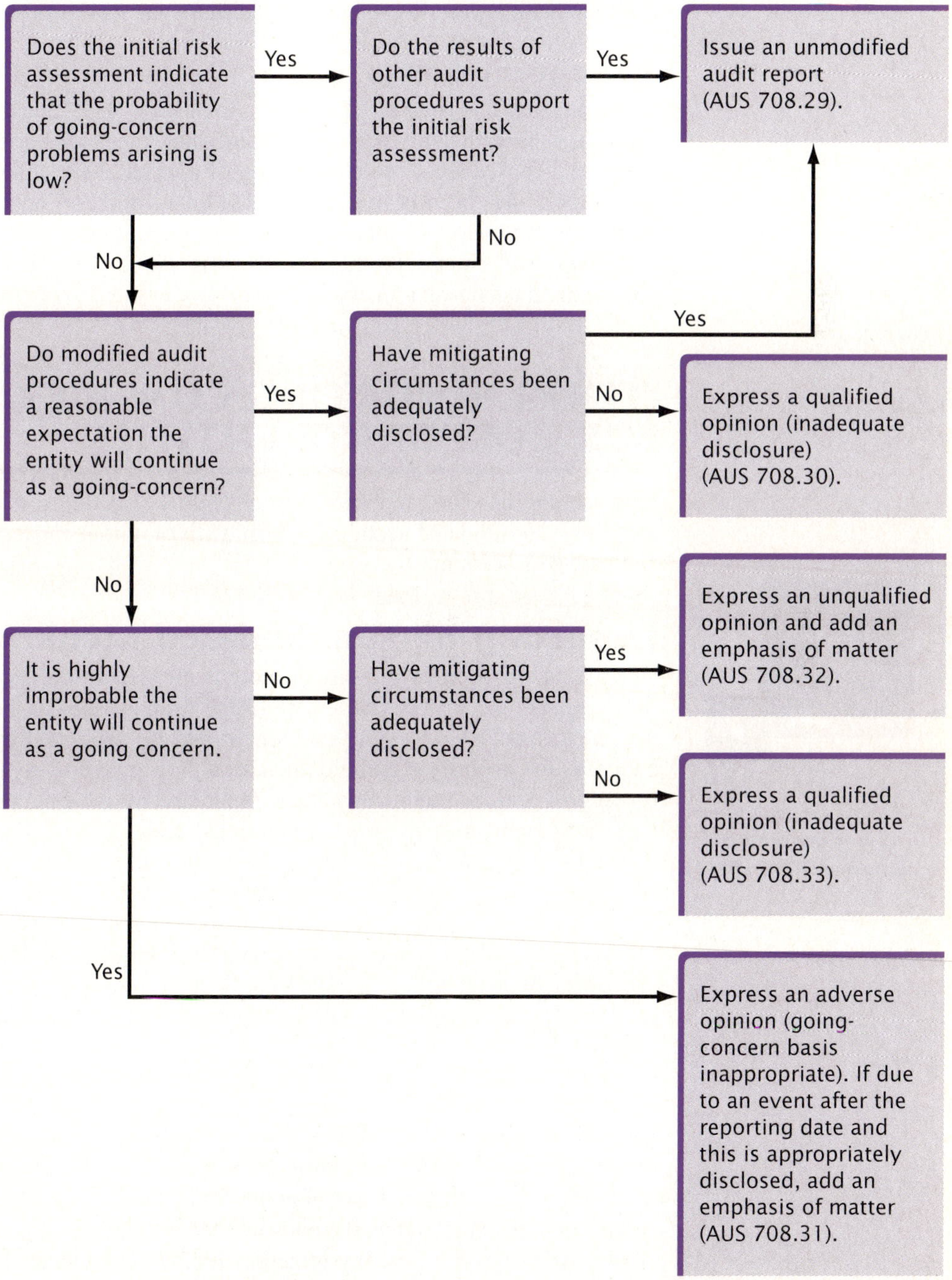

(Source: AUS 708, Appendix 1)

Inappropriateness of going concern as a result of new conditions after reporting date

If it is highly improbable that an entity will continue as a going concern due to an event that occurred after the reporting date (which provides new information that does not relate to conditions that existed at reporting date), and there has been adequate disclosure, then the audit report should include an emphasis of matter. However, if the disclosure is inadequate or amounts and other disclosures are unreliable, then the auditor should express a qualified audit report on the basis of a disagreement with management.

Subsequent events

We considered this issue in Chapter 14 (for which AUS 706 (ISA 560), Subsequent Events applies). It is sufficient here to say that when management prepares a revised financial report as a consequence of the discovery of a material fact after the financial report and the audit report have been issued, the revised financial report and the new audit report should include an 'Emphasis of matter' section. Reasons for the revision of the previously issued financial report, along with the earlier report issued by the auditor, should be included in a note to the financial statements.

OTHER REPORTING CONSIDERATIONS FOR CORPORATE ENTITIES

This section discusses reporting responsibilities relating to some specific circumstances, including: consolidated accounts; **comparatives**; initial engagements — opening balances; and half-year accounts.

7 LEARNING OBJECTIVE

Explain the reporting requirements for consolidated accounts.

Reporting on consolidated accounts

When a reporting entity has one or more controlled entities, it may be necessary for more than one auditing firm to participate in the examination. In the case of controlled entities that are companies, the other auditors would be appointed by the directors of the chief entity (as the majority shareholder or through the exercise of such other powers as provide for control over the other entity) and are required to issue a report on the controlled entity's financial statements under the Corporations Law.

The Corporations Law (s.323) provides the auditor of a reporting entity for which consolidated accounts are required with the right of access to the accounting records and registers of controlled entities and the right to require from their officers and auditors such information and explanation as is needed. In many cases, auditors build up a continuing formal relationship with other auditors. Such relationships may include inter-firm reviews, for example, of compliance with quality control procedures. Evaluation of the work of the other auditor need not be applied on each specific engagement. In the case of branches or divisions, the other auditor would be appointed by the principal auditor and thus act as an agent. The other auditor would therefore normally be one with whom the principal auditor has built up a formal relationship. Such relationships also commonly exist between auditors of chief and controlled entities where the chief entity recognises the advantages to itself when appointing auditors of controlled entities.

The opinion expressed on the consolidated accounts is the sole responsibility of the principal auditor. In order that the principal auditor may obtain the necessary assurance as to the accounts of controlled entities not audited by him or her, it is necessary that he or she undertake certain steps with respect to the work of the other auditor (see Chapter 13). The

AASB argues that the required reference to controlled entities audited by other auditors is unnecessary because the principal auditor accepts full responsibility for the opinion expressed on the group accounts, unless required by legislation or as part of a qualification.

If the auditor concludes that reliance cannot be placed on the work of another auditor and is unable to perform satisfactory alternative procedures, then he or she should qualify the audit report with respect to the limitation of the scope of the audit. If, for example, the auditor of a controlled entity does not cooperate fully with the auditor of a chief entity, then a qualification relating to the failure to receive adequate information and explanations would be required.

8 LEARNING OBJECTIVE

Explain reporting considerations for comparatives in a financial report.

Comparatives

Comparatives refer to amounts or disclosures of one or more prior periods that are presented on a comparative basis with those of the current period. Comparatives form an integral part of the current period's financial report. As such, reporting standards apply not only to the amounts and disclosures of the current period, but also to comparatives.

The auditor has a responsibility to obtain sufficient appropriate audit evidence to ensure that comparatives are not materially misstated (AUS 704.02 (ISA 710.02), Comparatives) and that (1) comparatives agree with those in the prior period financial report and (2) accounting policies used for comparatives are consistent with those of the current period. During the audit of the current year, the auditor should be alert to circumstances and events relating to the prior period financial report that will have an impact on the comparatives. The circumstances considered in AUS 704 (ISA 710) are (1) that the prior period opinion was qualified, (2) subsequent events, (3) a change of auditor and (4) that the prior period financial report is unaudited.

Qualified prior period report

It is possible that a prior period audit opinion was qualified while an unqualified opinion is expressed for the current year. However, the audit report for the current year will be qualified if (1) the matter that gave rise to a qualification for the prior period also results in a qualification of the audit report in the current period's financial information or (2) the unresolved matter, while not resulting in a qualification of the current period's financial information, is material in relation to amounts and disclosures in the current period.

Subsequent events

A material misstatement may be discovered in a prior period financial report on which the auditor previously expressed an unqualified opinion. In such circumstances, if the report has been revised and reissued with a new audit report, then the auditor should satisfy himself or herself that comparatives agree with the new financial report. If the prior period report is not revised, but the comparatives have been properly accounted for and disclosed in accordance with an identified financial reporting framework, then the auditor should express an unqualified opinion.

The auditor should express a qualified opinion if the prior period financial report is not revised and the misstatement has not been properly accounted for and is material in respect to the current period's amounts.

Change of auditor

Additional reporting requirements must be met when there has been a change in auditors during the period covered by the comparative financial reports. If the incoming auditor is unable to obtain sufficient appropriate audit evidence regarding the comparatives, then the current audit report is qualified on the basis of scope limitations. The successor auditor should refer to the predecessor's audit report in the 'Qualification' section and state:

- that the financial report of the prior period was audited by another auditor (and provide the name of the auditor);
- the date of the predecessor auditor's report;
- the type of opinion expressed by the predecessor;
- the substantive reasons if the report was qualified.

Unaudited prior period financial report

If the prior period report is unaudited, then the auditor has a responsibility to seek sufficient appropriate audit evidence to assess whether the comparatives are misstated. If there is persuasive evidence that there are no material misstatements, then an unqualified opinion should be expressed. If sufficient appropriate evidence is unavailable, then a statement of inability to form an opinion should be expressed on the comparatives. The auditor should also encourage disclosure in the financial report that the comparatives are unaudited.

9 LEARNING OBJECTIVE

Describe the effect of opening balances on the audit report.

Initial engagements — opening balances

In an **initial audit engagement** the auditor needs (AUS 510.02 (ISA 510.02), Initial Engagements — Opening Balances) to obtain sufficient appropriate audit evidence to ensure that:

- the opening balances do not contain misstatements that materially affect the current period's financial report;
- the prior period's closing balances have been correctly brought forward to the current period or, when appropriate, have been restated; and
- appropriate accounting policies are consistently applied or changes in accounting policies have been properly accounted for and adequately disclosed.

The auditor should obtain sufficient appropriate audit evidence in relation to the above matters. AUS 510 (ISA 510) suggests that reliance may be placed on the work of another auditor if the prior period financial report was audited by other auditors. Other procedures need to be performed if prior period accounts were unaudited. The sufficiency or lack thereof of appropriate audit evidence may lead to the following reporting conclusions:

- If the auditor is unable to obtain sufficient appropriate audit evidence, then there is a limitation on the scope of the audit work. Accordingly, he or she should express an 'except for' opinion or an inability to form an opinion.
- If material misstatements in opening balances affect the current period's financial report, then the auditor should express a qualified opinion.

10 LEARNING OBJECTIVE

Understand the requirements for audit and review reports on half-year accounts.

Half-year accounts

The Corporations Law prescribes that disclosing entities must (s.302):

- prepare a half-year financial report and directors' report;
- have the financial report audited or reviewed, and obtain an auditor's report;
- lodge the financial report, the directors' report and the auditor's report with the Australian Securities and Investment Commission (ASIC).

According to s.302 (b) of the Corporations Law, the half-year reports may be either audited or reviewed, although the majority of Australian companies opt for review. AGS 1016, Audit Review Reports — Half-year Accounts and Consolidated Account has been prepared to assist auditors in undertaking a review or audit of a half-year financial report. If the half-year report is audited, then the reporting requirements are covered by AUS 702 (ISA 700). If a review engagement is needed, then it should be performed in accordance with AUS 902, Review of Financial Reports (ISA 910, Engagements to Review Financial

Statements). There are no requirements for the auditor's report on a half-year report to be circulated to the entity's members. However, the auditor should encourage distribution of the report to members in the interests of effective communication. AASB 1029, Half-year Accounts and Consolidated Accounts specifies the required disclosures relating to the profit and loss account, the balance sheet and the statement of cash flows. For the purpose of preparing the half-year accounts or consolidated accounts, each half-year is to be treated as a discrete reporting period.

When a review is conducted instead of an audit, the Corporations Law requires that the company's auditor undertake it. In accordance with AUS 902 (ISA 910), a review of half-year accounts should be based on current knowledge of the entity. In undertaking the review, the auditor should consider aspects of the audit process relevant to the current audit for the forthcoming full-year financial statements.

The review must be conducted in accordance with the Auditing Standards applicable to review engagements. The limited nature of the review procedures employed provides a level of assurance that is less than given in an audit. A disclaimer that no audit opinion is expressed is included because no audit is performed.

The 'Scope' section clearly outlines that a review has been performed rather than an audit, and that negative rather than positive assurance is given (see Chapter 1). Instead of an 'Audit opinion' section, there is a 'Statement' section that provides a negative assurance (AGS 1016, Audit Review Reports — Half-year Accounts and Consolidated Account; and Addendum to AGS 1016 [Appendix 3]):

> Based on our review, which is not an audit, we have not become aware of any matter that makes us believe that the half-year financial report of XYZ Limited is not in accordance with . . .

Generally, the market has looked positively on the requirement to prepare audited or reviewed half-year reports. There are moves to continue to improve disclosure via requirements for more narrative disclosures and quarterly financial reports (see the 'Professional environment' below).

PROFESSIONAL ENVIRONMENT Reports for the marketplace

Companies are starting to spend more time poring over each other's annual reports to see just who is setting the best practice trends. And narrative disclosures, regarded by some as little more than public relations fluff, are now becoming more punchy and relevant.

The recent adoption by the Australian Stock Exchange (ASX) of Group of 100 (G100) guidelines on how to prepare reviews of operations and financial condition as the recommended template for better integration of narrative disclosure, will add greater impetus for companies to ensure their annual reports are understood by the marketplace.

Six points are highlighted by the G100 guidelines as being crucial to developing an understandable annual or half-year report. A good review of operations and financial condition must:

- be written in a clear style and as succinctly as possible;
- be in narrative form, supported by figures and graphics where these assist understanding of matters discussed;
- avoid the use of technical language as far as possible;
- be balanced and objective, dealing even-handedly with both positive and negative aspects of operations and financial condition;

- contain analytical description rather than replicating information in the financial statements; and
- discuss individual aspects and segments of the organisation in the context of a discussion of the organisation as a whole.

Bruce Brook, Pacific Dunlop Limited's group chief accountant and former president of the Group of 100, says the objective of the G100 document is to try to encourage companies to tell the story of the preceding year to shareholders in the annual report rather than make it just another statement of compliance with the Corporations Law.

'There is so much focus on the accounts and the notes to the accounts, but they're only one part of the picture,' he says. 'If you want to understand how a company is performing, what its current situation is and what the future prospects are, you can't rely exclusively on the balance sheet, profit and loss statement, the statement of cash flows and a set of notes.

'You need to have a discussion. You need words to explain a company's risk profile, the company's strengths and any potential exposures.'

Stuart Grant, former executive director of accounting policy at the Australian Securities and Investment Commission, is part of the team coordinating the Annual Report Awards.

'We're detecting a steady improvement in the quality of annual reporting. Companies are getting better at reporting to shareholders,' Grant says.

'Community attitudes also change over time, and in line with the change in community attitudes, our criteria by which the reports are judged become more stringent.

'As a result, some companies that previously received a gold medal award for their report might receive a bronze. It's not that the report is worse than the previous year's effort. It's just that requirements and expectations have changed and the report may not have met the new benchmarks.'

Stuart Grant argues that discussion and analysis [are] crucial to communicating with shareholders, but the recently issued Accounting Standards on concise financial statements make the mistake of requiring the information to be subject to audit.

... Quarterly reporting to shareholders, the Stock Exchange and market analysis is another way some companies are notifying the market of profit results.

BHP and Wesfarmers are two listed entities that report financial results to the market quarterly, and both companies believe it adds value to shareholder understanding of company peformance.

Keith Alfredson, a former Arthur Andersen audit partner, believes the practice of quarterly reporting will help companies keep the marketplace informed and aid compliance with the continuous disclosure regime.

He says the first quarter and third quarter announcements made by companies need not undergo reviews by external auditors in the same way as half-year and annual reports, but rather be subject to good corporate governance procedures.

'The companies might want to — as a corporate governance measure — run it by their audit committee to ensure that the numbers are right', he says.

'I think people will reject quarterly reporting if it requires a review by the auditors because they won't want to pay the cost. And I doubt whether the cost benefits for a full external audit review of quarterly reports are there.'

(Source: T. Roberts, 'Good Reports', *Charter* (June 1999), pp. 38–9)

LEARNING CHECK

15.4 The audit report may be modified as a result of (1) a qualified opinion or (2) an emphasis of matter.

15.5 The type of qualified opinion depends on the magnitude and pervasiveness of the matter(s). The available qualified opinions are:
- an 'except for' opinion;
- an adverse opinion;
- an inability to form an opinion.

15.6 The circumstances that may result in a qualified opinion are: (1) a disagreement with management; (2) a conflict between applicable financial reporting frameworks; and (3) insufficient appropriate audit evidence to form an opinion.

15.7 An 'Emphasis of matter' section is not a qualification and may be used only in specific circumstances, which include: the need for additional disclosures; inherent uncertainties (including going concern); inconsistent other information; and subsequent events.

15.8 The opinion expressed on the consolidated accounts of a company is the sole responsibility of the principal auditor.

15.9 For opening balances in initial engagements, an unqualified opinion is expressed if: there are no misstatements in opening balances; closing balances of prior periods have been correctly brought forward; and accounting policies are consistently applied.

15.10 An audit or a review report is required for half-year accounts. It is given to the directors for lodgement with the ASIC.

SUMMARY

Reporting the findings is the final phase of a financial report audit. The auditor must comply with relevant Auditing Standards when reporting on audited financial reports. The auditor's conclusion is heavily reliant on the work performed in completing the audit (see Chapter 14). Depending on the circumstances, the auditor may issue an unmodified audit report; a modified audit report that may be qualified and expresses one of three other types of opinion; or an unqualified audit report with an emphasis of matter. Given the signal it sends to users of the financial reports, a modified report (particularly a qualified report) should be issued only after careful consideration. When expressing a qualified opinion, the report must contain a clear statement as to the reasons for the qualification and the effect thereof. There are specific circumstances that allow the issuance of an emphasis of matter as part of the audit report.

There are special reporting considerations for reporting on consolidated accounts, comparatives in financial statements, initial engagements (opening balances) and half-year accounts. The auditor must exercise due care in conducting the audit so as to obtain a reasonable basis for an opinion and to express the opinion justified by the findings.

KEY TERMS

Accounting Standards, p. 568
Additional disclosures, p. 580
Adverse opinion, p. 575
Comparatives, p. 584
Consistency, p. 570
Emphasis of matter, p. 568
'Except for' opinion, p. 575
Fair presentation, p. 570
Financial report, p. 568
Going concern, p. 571
Inability to form an opinion, p. 575
Inherent uncertainty, p. 580
Initial audit engagements, p. 586
Presents fairly, p. 571
Qualified opinion, p. 569
True and fair view, p. 569
UIG Consensus Views, p. 568
Unqualified audit opinion, p. 573

NOTES

1. The International Accounting Standards' terminology is 'income statement' and 'balance sheet'.
2. The four AASs are: AAS 25, Financial Reporting by Superannuation Plans; AAS 27, Financial Reporting by Local Governments; AAS 29, Financial Reporting by Government Departments; and AAS 31, Financial Reporting by Governments.
3. Anonymous, 'International Brand: International Standards', *World Accounting Report*, (November 1998), p. 4.

FURTHER READING

Carcello, Joseph V., 'Going-Concern Opinions: The Effects of Partner Compensation Plans and Client Size', *Auditing: A Journal of Practice and Theory* (Spring 2000), pp. 67–77.

Chen, Charles J. P., 'An Emerging Market's Reaction to Initial Modified Audit Opinions: Evidence From the Shanghai Stock Exchange', *Contemporary Accounting Research* (Fall 2000), pp. 429–55.

Hatherly, David J., Innes, John & Brown, Tom, 'The Expanded Audit Report — An Empirical Investigation', *Accounting and Business Research* (Autumn 1991), pp. 311–19.

Nugent, Michael, 'Uncertain about What Type of Audit Report to Issue?', *Charter* (August 1997), pp. 84–5.

Picker, Ruth, 'AUS 702: Emphasis ... but no certainty?', *Australian Accountant* (March 1997), pp. 57–8.

Review questions

15.1 What are the professional reporting requirements for members of the ICAA and CPA Australia when auditing a set of financial reports?

15.2 What are the principal effects of the Corporations Law on the auditor's reporting requirements?

15.3 What are the contents of an unqualified audit report? Explain each section.

15.4 What are the three different types of qualified audit opinion? Explain each type.

15.5 Under what circumstances may the auditor decide to include an 'Emphasis of matter' section in his or her audit report?

15.6 What evidence does the auditor need to obtain in relation to opening balances on an initial engagement?

Discussion questions

15.1 What is the difference between the expressions 'true and fair' and 'presents fairly' in a report on a set of financial statements? In your opinion, which of the two provides the higher level of assurance?

15.2 What is meant by an unqualified audit opinion?

15.3 What is the difference between (a) a qualified and unqualified audit report, and (b) a modified and unmodified audit report?

15.4 It is widely acknowledged that materiality is an important consideration in auditing. Is materiality the only consideration for an auditor deciding whether to qualify a financial report? Discuss.

15.5 What does each of the three different qualified audit reports mean to users wanting to rely on the financial statements?

15.6 What circumstances may give rise to qualified opinions?

15.7 Why add an 'Emphasis of matter' section to an audit report? Does the matter need to be material to warrant such a section in the audit report?

15.8 Under what circumstances may the auditor decide to qualify the financial report as a result of a question over going concern? Does it matter whether the event that caused the going-concern problem occurred after the balance date?

15.9 What are the requirements for comparatives in the financial statements?

15.10 What are the requirements for assurance on half-yearly engagements prepared by an entity?

Professional application questions

★ BASIC
★★ MODERATE
★★★ CHALLENGING

15.1 (Effect of circumstances on audit opinion) ★

Assume that the following separate circumstances could be sufficiently material to require the expression of a qualified opinion:

1. Management wanted to reduce the provision for doubtful debts by $5 million. The auditor did not agree and felt that it should stay at its current level.
2. The auditor was engaged to audit the client after the entity's year end, so the auditor could not observe the stock count that was held at the year end.
3. The entity is a defendant in a major litigation (relating to a faulty product) that has not been settled as of the date of signing the audit report.
4. A fire in the company's office due to a faulty photocopier has destroyed all records of accounts receivable as at the year end.
5. The disclosure of director's benefits does not comply with AASB 1017 (IAS 24), Related Party Disclosures.
6. A new competitor in the market over the past year has raised serious concerns about the entity's ability to continue as a going concern.
7. The directors refused the auditor access to three months worth of the minutes of directors' meetings because they contained discussion of a highly confidential matter.
8. The company changed its method of depreciation from straight line to reducing balance, necessitating a restatement of prior years' statements.

Required

Indicate the effect of the above eight circumstances on the auditor's report.

15.2 (Effect of circumstances on audit opinion) ★★

Consider the following independent and material situations:

1. CareMore Limited is a charity that derives 50 per cent of its revenues from door-knocking campaigns conducted by volunteers. Internal controls over cash are strong from the time cash is delivered to CareMore's head office. In addition, you are satisfied you have obtained sufficient appropriate audit evidence on other account balances. However, you have been unable to ensure that all cash received is recorded upon its initial receipt by volunteers.
2. During the year Saints Limited sold an office block in the central business district of Adelaide. Part of the proceeds was invested in bank bills, pending reinvestment in a major capital works project. The terms of the arrangement with the bank are such that the interest on the bills is added to the principal at the end of each ninety-day term and the bills are automatically rolled over for another ninety days. Saints has refused to credit any of the interest to revenue, because it argues the interest has not yet been received into its working account and should not be taken up until this is the case.
3. One month before balance date, Figtree Limited had its computer system and backups sabotaged by a disgruntled ex-employee. Management have done their best to reconstruct the accounting records over the past couple of months but have been finding this increasingly difficult, because much of their time is taken up keeping the company afloat. Management prepared the year-end financial statements from what few accounting records remain. You have serious doubts as to the accuracy of these figures and have been unable to verify any of the material balances.

Required

Nominate the type of audit report you would issue in each of the above situations. Explain your answer, and outline what you would state in the qualification paragraph, if applicable.

(Professional Year Programme of the ICAA — 1998, Accounting 2 Module — adapted)

15.3 (Going-concern issues, audit opinion) ★★

Fly-by-Night Limited is a listed public company that manufactures highly sophisticated navigation equipment for defence force aircraft and Navy ships. The company has a 30 June 20X2 year end, and the statutory accounts are due to be signed one week after the board of directors meeting on 5 August 20X2. During the course of the audit, you become aware that the Commonwealth Government has reviewed its budget in an effort to reduce the growing deficit. As a result, defence expenditure has had major cuts.

One of the major projects to be scrapped as a result of these cuts is the planned upgrading of the navigation equipment for the Navy's submarine fleet. You are aware that the company's budget for this year includes a major subcontract to the Department of Defence and the Navy for this project.

The company has been experiencing cash flow difficulties and has recently applied for a significant increase to a borrowing facility that is already fully drawn. Management is adamant that the company will continue to be viable. If necessary, it claims it can resort to cutbacks in its future capital expenditure program, seek additional off-balance sheet financing and/or reschedule existing debt arrangements.

Required

(a) Explain the concept of going concern. Discuss the reporting options open to an auditor when going-concern issues arise.

(b) Discuss the potential audit report options in relation to Fly-by-Night.

(Professional Year Programme of the ICAA — 1996, Advanced Audit Module — adapted)

15.4 (Preparation of the audit report, comparative statements) ★★

You are an audit senior and your firm has recently been appointed the auditor of Newgrange Limited for the year ended 31 December 20X1. Newgrange is a large family-owned brewery that has never previously been audited. It requires an audit for this year because it recently borrowed significant funds and the bank has requested an audit. Your audit manager has asked you to investigate how the audit will be affected by the fact that Newgrange's comparatives and opening balances have never previously been audited.

Required

Prepare a memo to the audit manager explaining the differences between opening balances and comparatives. Outline the audit procedures that should be carried out on these figures as part of the audit of Newgrange.

15.5 (Effect of circumstances on audit opinion) ★★★

You are an audit manager finalising your 30 June 20X2 audits. The following independent and material matters have come to your attention:

1. The audit of the statutory records of Whale Limited, a reporting entity, revealed the following problems:
   - failure to update the members' register for changes in shareholders;
   - failure to obtain written consent from directors to act;
   - no preparation of minutes of directors' meetings in respect of the current year;
   - failure to hold the annual general meeting in the previous financial year.

   The company made no comment in respect of either the failure to keep properly updated statutory registers or the failure to hold an annual general meeting.
2. Shark Limited, a reporting entity, uses the last-in first-out basis in respect of valuation of closing inventories, which is one of the most significant balance sheet accounts. The difference between first-in first-out and last-in first-out has a material effect on the closing inventory balance.
3. ABC Limited is a holding company with a number of wholly owned subsidiaries. One of these, FX Limited, is a self-sustaining foreign subsidiary with manufacturing and distribution facilities throughout South-east Asia. The group accounts of ABC and its subsidiaries consist of the consolidated accounts of ABC and its subsidiaries and exclude the accounts of FX, which are attached separately. The consolidated accounts include a note stating that the directors believe it is misleading to consolidate FX because its operations are very different from those of the rest of the group and are carried out under substantially different conditions. The note includes details of inter-company balances and transactions.

Required

Discuss the audit issues to be considered in each of the above circumstances, and their likely impact on the audit opinion to be issued. Justify your answer with references to Auditing Standards and the Corporations Law, as appropriate.

(Professional Year Programme of the ICAA — 1996, Advanced Audit Module — adapted)

15.6 (Effect of circumstances on audit opinion) ★★★

You are an audit partner finalising your 30 June 20X1 audits. The following independent and material matters have come to your attention:

1. Food Fund Limited, a charity, is a non-reporting entity. As in prior years, you have performed the audit in accordance with its Articles of Association. The financial report is prepared by another firm of accountants on behalf of Food Fund's board of directors, because Food Fund does not have the in-house expertise to perform this function. During your review of the internal control structure, you noted that the company did not have sufficient controls over the collection of income to enable you to be satisfied that all income received was recorded. However, you have been satisfied that the company has correctly accounted for all income recorded.
2. Telken Limited is the chief entity of the Telken Limited Group, a reporting entity. Your firm did not act as auditor of either Telfast Limited or the Teldane Company — the entities controlled by Telken. You were unable to obtain the audit report for Telfast, although you do have a copy of the final draft audit report, and the other auditor's verbal assurance that an unqualified audit report was issued. In addition, despite receiving a copy of the audited report for the Teldane Company, you do not believe the financial report is suitable for consolidation with the other entities in the group. This is because the Teldane Company operates in Afghanistan, which has a vastly different accounting framework to that used in Australia. You have been able to quantify the financial effect of the required adjustments on the financial report of the Telken Group. However, management has refused to make the adjustments and has consolidated the existing version of Teldane's financial report.
3. Eureka Limited, a non-reporting entity, operates a small goldmine, which is run as a family business. The board consists of Mr Lawlor and his sister, Ms Lawlor, who are also the principal shareholders. As part of the final audit meeting, Ms Lawlor tells you: 'I reckon the vein we're currently mining will last eighteen months at the most — fourteen months at the least. After the gold is extracted, we are shutting up shop; we'll let the licence expire and retire to Kalgoorlie.' Ms Lawlor then shows you a surveyor's report backing up her assertion regarding the amount of gold in the vein. The financial report does not disclose this information.
4. Prime Trust is a reporting entity. Ms Ford, the finance director, refuses to adopt AASB 1017 (IAS 24), Related Party Disclosures on the grounds that it 'requires information to be disclosed to the public that should remain known only to the parties concerned'. This is consistent with her stance in prior years, which resulted in your issuing a qualified audit report. You are satisfied that the current financial report is materially correct in all regards, apart from the non-compliance with AASB 1017 (IAS 24).

Required

Identify the type of audit report to be issued for each of the above situations.

(Professional Year Programme of the ICAA — 1998, Advanced Audit Module — adapted)

15.7 (Preparation of the audit report — various circumstances) ★★★

Mike Brady, a registered company auditor, has completed the audit of the financial report of Trueline Limited as of and for the financial year ended 30 June 20X1. Mike also audited the financial statements for Trueline for the prior financial year. He drafted the following report for 30 June 20X1.

We have audited the balance sheet and statements of profit and loss, and cash flows for Trueline Limited as of 30 June 20X1. Our audit was made in accordance with generally accepted Accounting Standards and accordingly included such tests of the accounting records as we considered necessary in the circumstances.

In our opinion, the above-mentioned financial report is accurately and fairly presented in accordance with generally accepted accounting principles in effect at 30 June 20X1.

Mike Brady

Mike Brady, CPA

25 August 20X1

Other information

1. During the year, Trueline changed its method of accounting for long-term construction contracts. It properly reflected the effects of the change in the current year's financial statements and restated the prior year's statements. Mike is satisfied with Trueline's justification for making the change. The change is discussed in Note 24 to the financial statements.
2. Mike was unable to perform normal accounts receivable confirmation procedures, but he used alternative procedures to satisfy himself as to the validity of the receivables.
3. Trueline is the defendant in a litigation, of which the outcome is highly uncertain. If the case is settled in favour of the plaintiff, Trueline will be required to pay a substantial amount of cash that may require the sale of certain fixed assets. The litigation and possible effects have been properly disclosed in Note 26 to the financial statements.

Required

(a) Consider all the above facts and the pertinent requirements of AUS 702 (ISA 700), and then rewrite the audit report in an acceptable and complete format, incorporating any necessary departures from the unqualified report.

(b) Identify any items included in the 'Other information' section that would not affect the audit report. Explain why this is the case.

(AICPA — adapted)

15.8 (Preparation of the audit report — various circumstances) ★★★

You are the audit partner of Toon Park Limited, which operates amusement parks in every capital city in Australia. Toon Park is a reporting entity under the Corporations Law. Consider the impact of the following two situations on your audit report for the year ending 30 June 20X1:

1. The new financial controller has reconsidered the method used to review the useful lives of the amusement park assets and has determined that the old method is no longer appropriate. Accordingly, he has implemented a new policy for the current financial year, which is adequately disclosed in the accounts. However, you are not satisfied that this new policy is appropriate, because it extends the useful lives of the assets significantly, without apparent justification.

(*continued*)

2. Toon Park is also in a dispute with its bank, which has demanded full repayment of all loans outstanding within the next six months. Toon Park is unable to meet this repayment deadline without obtaining funding from another source. Although negotiations for re-financing from another bank are progressing well, no loan agreements have yet been signed. The uncertainty surrounding the loan has been adequately disclosed in Toon Park's financial statements.

Required

(a) Discuss the impact of the above events on the audit report you intend to issue for Toon Park for the year ending 30 June 20X1.

(b) Draft an audit report for Toon Park for the year ending 30 June 20X1.

(Professional Year Programme of the ICAA — 1996, Accounting 2 Module — adapted)

Case studies

15.1 (Effect of circumstances on audit opinion) ★★★

You are the audit manager on the 30 June 20X1 audit of Burra Limited, which is a copper mining company. The following material items have come to your attention:

1. Burra has sufficient reserves of copper to allow production to continue at current levels for at least five years. However, falling copper prices have led to the closure of two of the three other mines in the area. Burra has experienced a drop in net profit over the past twelve months — down from $5 million in 20X0 to $200 000 in 20X1. An additional note included in the financial report outlines these issues and management's plans for continuing operations over the next financial year.
2. You are about to finalise the audit of Burra. Management has provided you with a draft annual report (including financial statements) for your review. On perusing the annual report, you note that net profit per the directors' report is $1 million, as opposed to the net profit in the financial report of $200 000. The directors explain that the difference is due to a late adjustment and that the $1 million figure is correct. You do not agree with the adjustment. The directors do not see the discrepancy as a problem and refuse to make any adjustment to the annual report.
3. Once the copper has been removed from each mine, Burra must pay the costs of environmental restoration to return the area to its pre-mine condition. Burra raises a provision in the financial report to allow for the costs of this work. The Commonwealth Government has just passed new environmental legislation, which some industry analysts say is likely to significantly increase the cost of restoration. However, Burra's management state that they cannot accurately estimate the extent of the increase because no data are available on which to base the revision of the provision. Accordingly, the provision has been calculated in the same way as in prior years. You are uncertain as to whether the provision is properly valued.

Required

(a) Discuss how each of the above situations will affect Burra's audit report.

(b) Prepare Burra's audit report for the year ended 30 June 20X1.

(Professional Year Programme of the ICAA — 1998, Accounting 2 Module — adapted)

15.2 (Preparation of the audit report — various circumstances) ★★★

Hillgrove Limited engaged Lucy Chow to perform its audit for the year ended 31 December 20X2. The financial report for the previous year was audited by Charles Brown, who expressed an unqualified opinion.

Lucy Chow's audit working papers contain the following information that does not appear in the 31 December 20X2 financial report of Hillgrove:

1. During the year, Hillgrove changed its method of valuing inventory from the first-in first-out method to the weighted average method. Management made this change because it believes first-in first-out more clearly reflects net income by providing a closer matching of costs and revenues. The change had the effect of reducing inventory at 31 December 20X2 by $65 000. The effect of the change on prior years was immaterial. Lucy firmly supports the company's position.
2. The company refused to capitalise certain lease obligations for equipment acquired in 20X2. Capitalisation of the leases in accordance with AASB 1008 (IAS 17) would have increased assets and liabilities by $500 000 and $650 000 respectively. Lucy concludes that the leases should have been capitalised.
3. One director appointed in 20X2 was formerly a partner in Lucy's accounting firm. Lucy's firm provided financial consulting services to Hillgrove during 20X1 and 20X0, for which Hillgrove paid approximately $1600 and $9000 respectively.

Required

Prepare the audit report that Lucy Chow should issue for the year ended 31 December 20X2.

(AICPA — adapted)

chapter 16

E-commerce and auditing

Overview

LEARNING OBJECTIVES

After studying this chapter, you should be able to:

1. describe the business environment in the information economy
2. appreciate the nature of, development of and strategic issues relating to e-commerce
3. explain the nature and scope of audit and assurance services for an e-commerce environment
4. assess the audit risk and control matters in an e-commerce environment
5. discuss the objectives and approach of forensic auditing, with an emphasis on frauds on the Internet.

> ... No accountant can afford to ignore the influence of the Internet altogether. Developing a certain familiarity with the workings of the Internet and e-commerce should be high on the agenda of every accountant, in business or in practice.[1]

The **information economy** is ultimately based on the increased salience of information as a commercial tool.[2] How organisations use information resources is central to their management, control and competitiveness. The relevance of accountants to the business world depends not only on their ability to produce relevant financial information, but also on their ability to capture, comprehend, analyse, manage and use quality information. This also highlights the importance of information and **communication technologies** as key enabling tools in the process of commercial and technological change. In this chapter we will familiarise you with the nature, development and business models of electronic commerce (**e-commerce**), providing guidance for professional accountants in auditing, assurance and business advisory services. We will commence with a brief review of the current electronic business environment, leading to a more detailed description of e-commerce and various business models. Then, we will explain trends in the methods of auditing e-commerce business cycles. To approach the topic with a broad perspective, we will also highlight the risks associated with e-commerce and the types of assurance service currently offered by accounting firms. On-line and continuous auditing are also topics in this chapter. We will also explain some of the key audit risk and control considerations, based on AGS 1056, Electronic Commerce: Audit Risk Assessments and Control Considerations. This is the only auditing guidance available, so this summary offers a quick overview of the recommendations by the profession in Australia. In the final part of the chapter, we will discuss one of the major risks in e-commerce — cyber crime — and the approaches adopted in the assurance service of forensic auditing.

THE INFORMATION ECONOMY AND BUSINESS ENVIRONMENT

1 LEARNING OBJECTIVE

Describe the business environment in the information economy.

The development of the information economy is related to the process of business transformation within modern economies. Through the increased use of information and associated technologies by businesses and other users, new industrial structures, systems, patterns and trends emerge alongside new products and services. Complicated networks of enterprises replace the traditional entities, and business is performed using information and communication technologies. Customers, suppliers and other **intermediaries** are drawn together under processes conducted through the Internet, with an unlimited market space. Internal employees are less hierarchically managed, cross-functional relationships are used, and business innovation is enhanced through empowerment and knowledge management strategies. Businesses are linked by way of strategic partnerships and have direct access to global resources. Table 16.1 illustrates the different aspects of business transformation.

The information economy is not a synonym for the commercial evolution of the Internet.[3] Apart from reflecting the commercial impact of technology, the information economy is concerned with the use of information and communication technologies in business processes, including the continuous growth of innovative methods such as outsourcing and quality assurance services. It is a pragmatic phenomenon as a response to the needs of businesses and economies when knowledge and information are the key drivers to business success and survival.

TABLE 16.1

A profile of business transformation

Aspects of operations	Traditional economy	Information economy
Organisations	Inwardly focused entities	Extended network
Market	Distinctive marketplace	Unlimited market space
Infrastructure	Physical, hierarchical infrastructure	Integrated, digital infrastructure using communication technology
Resources	Functional, hierarchical use of resources	Shared use of **knowledge-based** resources
Business emphasis	Local outlook, visible returns	Global outlook, empowerment, enhanced relationships
Access	Arm's length operations	Direct, on-line operations in real time

A conceptual model of the information economy

A conceptual model developed by the Austin Centre for Research into Electronic Commerce[4] uses four layers of commercial activity that characterise such an information economy. Each layer illustrates the respective business motivations in the new information economy and reflects the commercial opportunities and challenges. Businesses transform to meet the needs of information economy, so as to maintain their competitive advantages. The four layers are: the infrastructure layer, the applications layer, the intermediary layer and the e-commerce layer.

The infrastructure layer

This layer consists of enterprises that supply products and services that aid the development of a network infrastructure based on the Internet. The infrastructure comprises Internet backbone and service providers, networking hardware and software, server and PC manufacturers, and security suppliers. These parties support the basic components of business transmission and provide the capability to process information.

The applications layer

The components of the applications layer are developed as the existing Internet protocol is built on to satisfy certain business uses, such as on-line business activities. They include parties such as Internet consultants, e-commerce applications, **multimedia applications**, web-development software, search engine software and on-line training.

The intermediary layer

Intermediaries in on-line business smooth and augment the market and transaction process by bringing together buyers and sellers through networks. They enable applications and infrastructure to be translated and used in business transactions. Examples of intermediaries are on-line travel agents, on-line brokers, on-line libraries and media publications providers, on-line advertising and electronic auctions.

The e-commerce layer

This layer represents the transactions of goods and services between businesses and consumers over the Internet. It includes electronic retailers, manufacturers selling on-line, fee/subscription-based enterprises, on-line entertainment and professional services.

Enterprises are not normally limited to a particular layer; instead, they operate across different layers. As technology and commercial activities converge, the above model conceptualises the development of an emerging Internet ecosystem which becomes the backbone of information economy. It signifies the evolution of the electronic business models in the development of on-line commerce. Figure 16.1 shows the conceptual model of commercial activity that characterises information economy.

FIGURE 16.1

Layers in an information economy

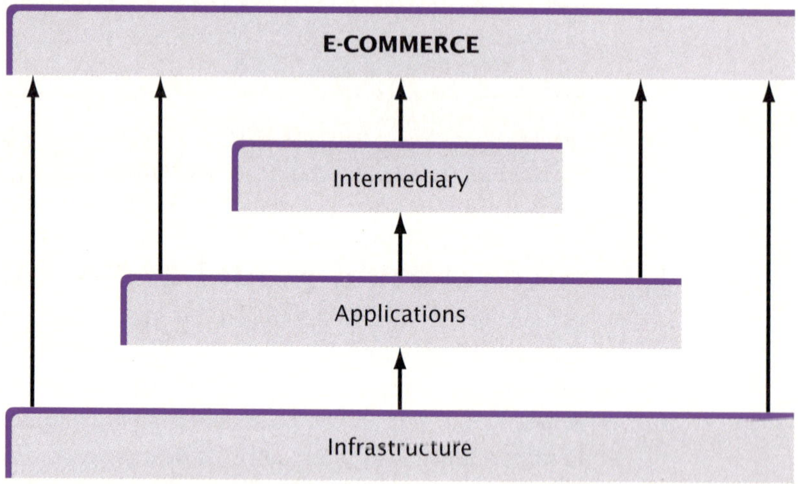

The information economy represents a fundamental change in the business environment globally. Its evolution is largely based on the impact of information and communication technology (notably through the development of the Internet) on commercial activity. The result is a reorganisation of economic activity involving increased use of information as a key resource and the wider deployment of technology. E-commerce has become the integral part of information economy, meaning that all aspects of business need to be re-designed. Existing businesses need to review existing business processes and explore how these could be improved by using the latest technologies. In this chapter we will focus on the impact of e-commerce and the implications for auditors and assurance service providers.

2 LEARNING OBJECTIVE

Appreciate the nature of, development of and strategic issues relating to e-commerce.

THE NATURE AND DEVELOPMENT OF E-COMMERCE

E-commerce builds on the structures of traditional commerce by adding the flexibilities offered by electronic networks. In turn, electronic networks create new opportunities so commercial transactions can be conducted more efficiently, involving more interactive activities among interested groups and using more innovative processes. In this section we will discuss the nature and development of e-commerce with a view to identifying the implications for auditors.

The evolution of e-commerce

With its fast-developing features, e-commerce has evolved through many forms and there is little agreement on what constitutes electronic commerce. For some time, large business enterprises have used e-commerce to conduct their **business-to-business** (B2B) transactions. **Electronic data interchange (EDI)** on private networks began in the 1960s, and banks have been using dedicated networks for **electronic funds transfer (EFT)** for almost as long. However, with the increased awareness and popularity of the Internet, e-commerce now also encompasses individual customers in **business-to-consumers** (B2C) transactions with businesses of all sizes.

E-commerce can be defined as the use of electronic networks to facilitate commercial transactions. It includes:

- on-line purchasing of tangible and intangible products, including on-line ordering (with or without on-line access to catalogues) and direct delivery to the customer, bypassing traditional retailers. Such activity includes the direct sale of intangible and digitised content of items where payment and delivery are made via the personal computer at home;
- on-line advertising and marketing for purposes of promoting sales;
- fund management and transfers via the Internet;
- on-line transactions and information transfers between **information aggregators** and intermediaries, including business-to-business transactions;
- on-line catalysts for commercial transactions such as telecommunications systems, facilitating hardware and software, Internet access services, information accreditation agencies and on-line service providers.

The extent of e-commerce activities

In March 2000, it was estimated that more than 300 million people had access to the Internet. The percentage of on-line users who have purchased over the Internet rose to 29 per cent in 1999 — up from 23 per cent in 1998. Conservative projections are that 54 per cent of on-line users will have practised e-commerce by 2003.[5]

Ernst & Young conducted a global study of Internet retailing (commonly called **e-tailing**) in November 1999, with over 4000 on-line consumers from Australia, Canada, France, Italy, the United Kingdom and the United States. Factors unique to Australia, such as the distance from major markets, meant that Australia was found to be at the early stage of e-commerce adoption and to have a much higher level of consumer concern about Internet security.

The Ernst & Young report revealed many common factors in e-tailing in all the responding countries, with the United States being the clear leader in the establishment and development of significant global and home-based e-tail businesses. On-line shopping more than doubled in the United States from 1998 to 1999 and rose by more than 50 per cent in Europe. Total annual on-line spending grows exponentially — up by around 500 per cent from 1997 to 1999. Countries in the earlier stage of e-tailing, such as Australia, are more inclined to defend their domestic markets as well as seeking further Internet-based export opportunities.

In Australia, nearly half of households have personal computers and 22 per cent are on line, but only 5 per cent of these households have made an Internet purchase. On the supply side, 72 per cent of Australian companies active on the Internet supplied goods and services outside Australia, reflecting a positive international outlook. On-line shopping in Australia has been confined to the high-income and high-education sector, which is spending about 8 per cent of its shopping dollars on line. That figure is expected to rise to 23 per cent over the next few years. The report also identifies that Australian e-tailers will need to further build customer relationships, using data gathered from transactions to personalise and customise offers to individual customers.[6]

A survey by the Organisation for Economic Cooperation and Development (OECD) noted the differences between assorted estimates of the level of e-commerce, which range between US$23 billion of transactions and US$1.5 trillion. It found that e-commerce is set to account for around 15 per cent of retail sales within major economies during the formative years of the new millennium.[7] E-commerce is one more channel for conducting business — among the traditional channels of mail, face-to-face contact and telephony — and all channels of commercial activities complement one another.

E-commerce enables new forms of business, as well as new ways of doing business. Amazon.com, for example, is a bookseller based in Seattle, Washington. The company has no physical stores, sells all its books via the Internet, and coordinates deliveries from the publishers directly so they do not have to maintain any inventory. Companies such as Kantara and software.net take this business style a step further. All of their products are electronic and can be stored on the same computers used for processing orders and serving the Web, so inventory of these companies is totally digital. Another example is AMP Inc. which offers its clients the opportunity to purchase electronic connectors and related components directly from its web-based catalogue, bypassing the need for EDI-based purchase orders and confirmations.

The relationship between e-commerce and information

Following on from the conceptual framework of the information economy (see page 601), e-commerce activities can be regarded as an integral process of the modern economy, which combines the layers of infrastructure, applications and intermediaries to achieve the optimum performance of business transactions. E-commerce has tremendous scope for strategic impact across an enterprise. The extent to which it is adopted across functions depends on the form and nature of the enterprise and the commercial environment within which it operates. The functions affected by e-commerce may include product development, resourcing, promotion, marketing, sales, contracting, financing, transaction processing, system procurement, transport and logistics, accounting and administration, financing, reporting and insurance. Thus, to appreciate its impact, we must understand the strategic implications of e-commerce.

The core of e-commerce lies in its commercial transaction cycle. Surrounding this core is the use of electronic methods to advertise and promote products, the facilitation of contracts, market intelligence and sales support. The full development of e-commerce requires giving users certain guarantees in respect of privacy, information security and integrity.

Managers of organisations need to assess the strategic impact of e-commerce. They must possess the business knowledge that helps them to assess the best strategy as well as gauge the knowledge of competitors and the changes in the markets. They will rely on the following core information resources to identify the relevant strategic implications:

- *Human resources and management* embody corporate knowledge, intellectual property and project/product-based knowledge. Having knowledge of its human resources can help an entity formulate policies relating to its work force, skilling, staff recruitment and retention policies, supporting structures.
- *Market and product knowledge* encompasses knowledge of the value chain concept, production costs, productivity, competitive dynamics, partnerships, market locations, operational strategies and workplace support.

- *Infrastructure and structural support* comprises support activities used in Porter's **value chain**.[8] An entity's infrastructure includes firm infrastructure such as accounts, finance and quality management; technology development and procurement; physical processes such as inventory; data storage; product development; hardware, software and electronic data links; and security systems.
- *The customer/supplier element* concerns all the entity's interactions with customers, prospective markets, suppliers and banks, along with its relationship enhancement programs and databases.

Business strategic issues

If anyone assumes all large enterprises are moving into e-commerce at the same speed, findings of a study by PricewaterhouseCoopers in 2000 indicate otherwise. The study report *Electronic Business Outlook for the New Millennium* reveals a clear divergence between organisations actively pursuing e-business to gain competitive advantage and those hesitating. The latter are 'waiting' for some concrete examples of successes, and are concerned about issues such as security. The study also found that many companies are focusing too narrowly on only certain areas, such as customer communications. These companies tend to ignore areas such as on-line relationships with vendors, suppliers and partners, as well as support for security, risk and compliance, privacy and technology development.[9]

It seems that to be sustainable in the information economy, businesses should develop an ongoing and viable business strategy in respect of the extent and nature of their e-commerce orientation. Below, we will discuss some business strategic issues.

Identifying the incentives for e-commerce

General inertia by management in implementing e-commerce is not always supported by an understanding of the real incentives for the business. The OECD study identified common incentives for engaging in e-commerce: transaction management, business efficiency, new market development, a reshaping of customer relationships, and access to new markets and market segments. But, the implementation of e-commerce systems is an expensive process. Web-based retail solutions may be less expensive and more appropriate for smaller enterprises with unsophisticated processes. For larger enterprises, incorporating e-commerce in their enterprise resource planning is costly, and the corresponding threat to profitability must be acknowledged. However, developments in infrastructure and computer devices are powerful enablers, allowing web designers and host and support enterprises to undertake a rich level of resource sharing, which in turn allows the expansion of more efficient handling of e-commerce activities and business growth.

Specific themes in e-commerce

To help managers evaluate their business positions, Merrill Lynch identified specific themes that tend to characterise electronic marketplaces.[10] These themes can be described as improved customer status, low entry barriers, the disintermediation of business processes, and the scaling of matters. Let us look at these in more detail in turn:

- Customers are powerful on the Internet because they can gather and demand information about rival products.
- Entry to the market is relatively easy, although a real cost is the cost of sustainable development.
- Intermediaries such as the distributor can be easily eliminated, to be replaced by new **informediaries**, who find products and aggregate resources for potential customers.
- Because the incremental cost of the incremental transaction is negligible, matters are scaled to allow for the incremental transaction.

Different business models of e-commerce

There are broadly two types of e-commerce: business-to-business and business-to-consumer. For purposes of simplicity, we will not discuss the public administration (e.g. the Australian tax aspect of e-commerce). The OECD estimates of e-commerce in the United States in 2003 are US$1331 billion of business-to-business transactions and US$108 billion of business-to-consumers transactions. The size of the former category of transactions has been estimated to be ten to twelve times the extent of the former between 1998 and 2003, but the two forms will become blurred over time.

Business-to-business applications include the sell side where goods or services are sold to business customers to create revenue. These applications provide the capability to integrate inventory and production systems with ease of use and access. The buy side focuses on helping enterprises make procurements, and these applications are designed primarily for internal staff so they can process spending and acquisitions more efficiently. Marketplace applications bring together both sell and buy sides, using a community of network and common resources.

Business-to-consumers commerce is considered secondary to business-to-business commerce in terms of volume. However, the market for the former is expected to take off when the Internet can be accessed by large numbers of low-cost and ubiquitous devices such as mobile phones and televisions. The impact of business-to-consumers applications can be seen in the volume of digital content available free of charge to the public. The offer of on-line content is mostly a complement to the physical form of businesses, with some providers offering additional advantages from on-line transacting. Common applications are travel reservations, banking, insurance, on-line securities trading and investment, and retail such as books, compact discs, apparel and cars. However, in many cases, e-commerce in consumer markets encounters impediments to its growth, including concerns regarding the security of payment, the potential for fraud, the privacy of personal data, and problems in assessing on-line merchants. The take-up in the market for business-to-consumer transactions has been slow, and its future development depends on a maturing of a generation who possess a strong familiarity with information and communication technologies.

Disintermediation and the emergence of informediaries

The Internet can effectively remove bottlenecks (as represented in the past by intermediaries such as distributors), so it stimulates **disintermediation** by decreasing search costs, reducing user entry barriers and automating activity. Enterprises are bypassing the need for sales representatives and costly house calls; for example, *Encyclopaedia Britannica* effectively disintermediated its door-to-door sales force when it offered its product free over the Internet. Internally, people can share information and corporate knowledge more readily and act on it more quickly through the Internet and intranet. Consequently, adjusting systems to take disintermediation into consideration may prove essential to sustaining a competitive advantage in the long term.

On the other hand, there is also the emergence of re-intermediation — an altered model of intermediation which uses the critical mass concept of information aggregators and providers (called 'informediaries'). An informediary is a web site that provides specialised, up-to-date information on behalf of producers of goods and services and potential customers. Informediaries gather, analyse and redistribute information using information and communication technologies. They create new services and add value to potential information users. They may even be able to organise exchanges and resales, on-line auctions, etc. Banks, travel agents and airlines, music stores and large publishing organisations offer services for sale as well as informediaries.

Small and medium-sized enterprises

Small and medium-sized enterprises (SMEs) are usually more innovative in applying e-commerce models. There are two kinds of SMEs in terms of e-commerce applications: (1) those SMEs whose existence depends on the Internet and, therefore, that generate all their sales and customer communications through this medium; and (2) those that are experimenting with the new distribution channel as a means of complementing their existing capabilities. Typically, SMEs face many problems in implementing and developing new technological systems. The most significant issue of implementation is the sheer cost of investment. Other problems include cultural factors (especially for family businesses that are used to doing business in conventional ways), the cost of and changes in infrastructure, the divergence of business applications and technology, a lack of knowledge and awareness, the uncertainty of benefits, the nature of the products to be sold on line, a lack of maturity of e-commerce, security, the absence of a legal framework concerning e-commerce, the cost of consumer access, and the lack of human resource. Below, the 'Professional environment' is an example of the business impact of e-commerce.

PROFESSIONAL ENVIRONMENT E-business as core business

A global research report, *The E-business Value Chain: Winning Strategies in Seven Global Industries*[11] reported that 57 per cent of business executives say e-business is transforming their company's role within their industry. E-business is changing nearly all that enterprises do, from the procurement of supplies to the delivery of products and services. New industry e-entrants, value-added services and delivery channels are shifting the boundaries within and between industries, altering the existing value chains.

The joint study by The Economist Intelligence Unit and KPMG reports the survey and interview results of 331 industry executives and forty-two interviewees from America, Europe and Asia. The report analyses a number of measures, including the level of senior management commitment, web site development and on-line revenues.

The report also indicates that the greatest e-business barrier lies within the organisation. The need to redesign business processes, the lack of e-business skills and the lack of integration between front-end and back-end systems are the three major hurdles in implementing an e-business strategy.

A high level of involvement by senior management has also been found to be crucial to the success of e-business strategy. More than half reported a high involvement of senior managers, while 42 per cent of the enterprises experienced inadequate support from the top. Opinions regarding integration or separation of the e-business unit and other functions were split. The major obstacle to e-business plans was the reluctance to cut out intermediaries, while the Internet offers cooperation between business partners.

According to the study, the top e-business goal is to provide value-added products and services to meet the escalating demands of customers and to keep goods and services from becoming commodities. Another top goal is reaching new customers, particularly overseas.

(Source: Adapted from 'The e-business value chain: winning strategies in seven global industries. A global study conducted by the Economist Intelligence Unit in cooperation with KPMG')

LEARNING CHECK

16.1 The information economy does not only concern technology, but also the use of information and communication technologies in business processes, including a continual growth of innovative methods.

16.2 The conceptual model of the information economy consists of four key layers: the infrastructure layer, the applications layer, the intermediary layer and e-commerce layer. The e-commerce layer combines all aspects of the information economy and uses both internal networks (intranets) and external networks (the Internet).

16.3 To identify the relevant strategic implications, e-commerce relies on core information resources such as those concerning human resources, management, market and product knowledge, infrastructural supports and customer/supplier relationships.

16.4 The implementation of e-commerce involves many strategic issues, which include satisfying various corporate objectives or incentives, identifying the extent of intermediation required, selecting different business models, and understanding the costs, constraints and benefits for the business concerned.

E-COMMERCE — AUDIT AND ASSURANCE SERVICES

3 LEARNING OBJECTIVE

Explain the nature and scope of audit and assurance services for an e-commerce environment.

In identifying the nature and extent of audit and assurance services for an e-commerce environment, we will consolidate the earlier discussions concerning the business process and strategies of e-commerce. Figure 16.2 denotes an e-commerce environment with the relevant business processes and related audit and assurance services. In the absence of any Auditing Standard specifically related to e-commerce, the wide-ranging applications of e-business may result in an unlimited scope in the demand for professional assurances.

An e-commerce environment

An e-commerce transaction can be effected through four main steps: information sharing, on-line submissions, fulfilment, and service and support. Each step involves a part of the business strategy and an operational process.

Information sharing

This step involves using the entity's infrastructure or information systems to effectively address the goals of the company and its customers. An enterprise can use the Internet to provide information about its products, services and related news, while also learning about its markets. On the other hand, this is the initial stage when customers get to know about the company and its products. A large number of web sites are aimed at the general public, but a significant number of sites are aimed at business markets. Intermediaries or informediaries and brokers often offer sites that allow buyers and sellers in a particular market to interact, trade information, bid and make sales.

Business processes and strategies

The entity designs a web site, including a web page, survey/enquiry forms, e-mail services that use network communities, and data monitor systems that track and follow up visitors and enquiries. It can identify its own niche market by gathering competitive information, evaluating the various incentives for embarking on e-commerce activities, and developing its implementation strategy.

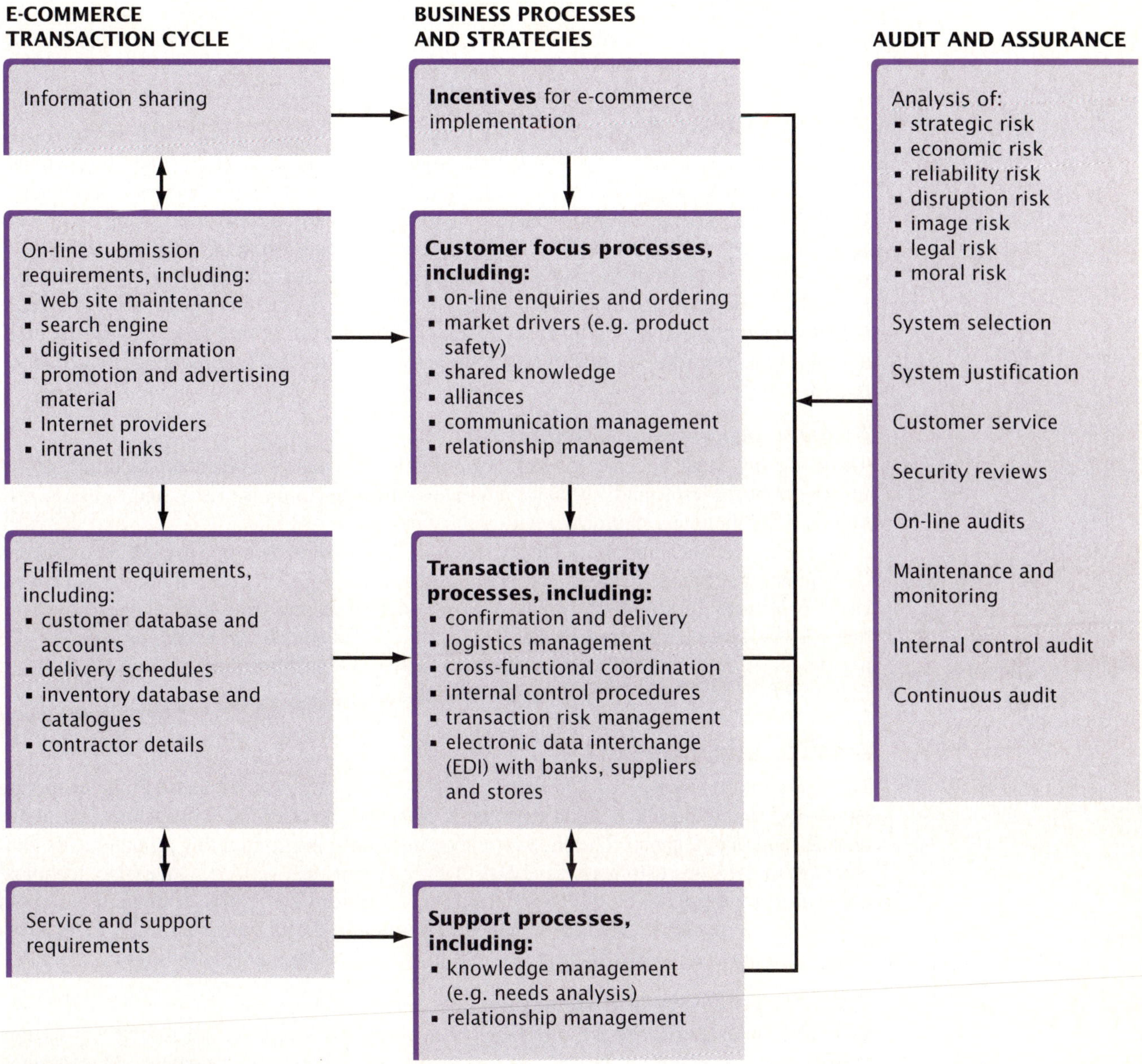

FIGURE 16.2

An e-commerce environment analysis

On-line submissions

This step involves potential customers electronically ordering either through the Internet or by e-mail. Thus, on-line submission refers to the ordering stage or transaction initiation stage. The entity gathers electronic forms (i.e. order forms) or digitised information. The web site maintenance and support systems must be reliable to handle electronic forms and the information secured therein. Other web sites and intranet (if applicable) search engines may also be incorporated within the web site, and the reliability of these links is essential to ensure that promotional and personal information is kept intact.

Business processes and strategies

The on-line submission and ordering process signifies the first impression of the company for customers. The entity must adhere to the concept of customer focus when using its intelligence on market drivers, ascertaining the level of shared knowledge, assessing the possibility of alliances and enhancing relationships with external parties. Moreover, this is the initial stage of a transaction and must be supported by sound communication technology.

Fulfilment

This step involves confirming orders, delivering goods and ensuring payment on accounts. This part of e-commerce activities is very much related to the effectiveness and efficiency of the entity's internal control systems. The entity has to confirm transactions with customers; update and interrogate the inventory database and customer database; use EDI to communicate with shippers, suppliers and distributors; provide delivery schedules; and print pro forma invoices and delivery notes. In some cases, the entity may need to prepare banking instructions and details to set up direct debits/credits. Other tasks may be the preparation of daily/weekly reports of sales/purchases activities and the updating of accounting records.

Business processes and strategies

The company must be able to maintain effective logistics management methods, cross-functional procedures, and sufficient internal controls to minimise risks, and to use EDI to interact with the bank regarding secured information.

Payment over the Internet is the most fluid and fast-developing aspect of e-commerce. Consumers and businesses can use credit cards, electronic cheques, digital cash (**micro-cash**) or electronic transfers to make payments. EDI is one technique, while some suppliers offer commerce-server software specifically designed to handle accepting web payments. Security and controls are the key issues in the fulfilment stage of an e-commerce transaction.

Service and support

This step entails a range of activities by the company to monitor and use the corporate knowledge and experience about customers, products, discrepancies in systems, customer services and maintenance. The supplier may enter into some contracting arrangements with other businesses or customers, as a part of the maintenance service. Otherwise, technical notes to track the features of 'frequently asked questions', common complaints, product shortages and discrepancies can be built in for product development projects. Enterprises often use maintenance and support services to enhance customer relationships.

Business processes and strategies

E-commerce systems should interface with corporate strategies regarding knowledge management, resource planning and customer relationship management. Management should continally monitor the features and performance of e-commerce activities, because opportunities and threats are changing rapidly — an environment that results from the development in information and communication technology.

Audit and assurance services

Electronic commerce provides organisations and enterprises with new tools and techniques for reducing costs, communicating more effectively, promoting and increasing sales, and improving operational efficiency and effectiveness. To keep pace with the electronic revolution in business, auditors must acquire an understanding of new technologies. New audit approaches should be developed to ensure the enterprises' e-commerce objectives are achieved in an adequate manner. For independent auditors, a client's e-commerce environment will most likely require electronic audit tools. Audit plans must be developed with a clear understanding of the e-commerce characteristics and their limitations. Internal auditors, on the other hand, must be fully involved in the e-commerce system from the outset of implementation to maintenance and support. Both types of auditor are also concerned with the reliability of the management and financial reports generated on the e-commerce transactions.

The e-commerce environment opens up enormous opportunities for professional accountants in the range of assurance services they can provide. Here, we will describe the types of audit and assurance service related to the e-commerce environment. Note, however, that the following discussions pertain to a scope beyond the financial report audit.

Risk analysis

Enterprises and organisations may choose to participate in different levels of e-commerce activities. Lower involvement is about a basic network presence, company promotion, and pre-and post-sales support. These services often rely on web hosting services, which are convenient and cheap for small enterprises. They typically provide the speed, reliability and scalability of the powerful web servers, but with minimal administrative support. The more advanced e-commerce services are used by expanding enterprises that are concerned with building a customer base and retaining relationships with existing customers. Control systems, technical support and an understanding of the technical aspects, together with legal and cultural developments, are essential.

At the information sharing stage, a professional accountant may add value by conducting a risk analysis. Security and operational issues are the key aspects of risk analysis. An enterprise initiating an e-commerce system must determine how it is going to assure the confidentiality of information such as prices, inventory quantities and other trading data of value to competitors. The integrity of the transaction details must be maintained so only authorised personnel have access to the identity of customers and users, and so the transmission of data is secured and not vulnerable to tampering.

The key operational concern is that investment in e-commerce should be justified from a cost and strategic perspective. Web site design issues such as speed, currency of information, follow-up of enquiries, excessive information, lack of resources, and an inability to protect customers from intruders are the related risks. Powell identifies a number of e-commerce risks: **strategic risk**, **economic risk**, **reliability risk**, **disruption risk**, **image risk**, **legal risk** and **moral risk**.[12] Strategic risk concerns the use of the Internet to gain a competitive advantage. Economic risk refers to the justifiable returns on the cost of investment in e-commerce. Reliability risk is about the adequacy of a well-tested and monitored e-commerce system. Disruption risk relates to the probability of the integrity of the system being disrupted. Image risk arises from the fear of hackers vandalising the web sites, and requires proof that security measures are competent and protected. Thus, legal compliance and attention to staff capability are necessary to overcome such risks in implementing e-commerce.

System selection and justification

The professional accountant or auditor should be involved during the early stages of the e-commerce project by performing reviews of the proposed internal control systems, carrying out pilot tests, assessing the e-commerce business model, and participating in project management. Specific areas for assessment include the proposed communication system, the network data generation and maintenance system, access controls, change authorisation and controls, physical controls and contingency planning. In reviewing the possible e-commerce business models, the accountant should ensure that the financial and operational feasibility of the proposed initiatives have been well researched and that the model details the financial resources needed to implement the staffing, technical and equipment requirements. The business model should also identify the strengths and weaknesses (or risks) of e-commerce, detailing the changes that the business processes will undergo and the expected timing or staging of those changes. The model should also consider working conditions, job specifications, and the physical layout of office and operational areas. The accountant should assess how well the emerging e-commerce model will interact with future business models or existing ones during the transitional period.

The accountant's project management tasks should include verifying that the organisation has established a skilled project team representing the company's and information technology personnel. The team must have a thorough understanding of the legal and security implications of the proposed system. Interactions with other business partners may also be essential when shared knowledge and linked networks are involved.

Customer service

Interactions with customers are an essential part of e-commerce. The accountant must verify that applications are as self-service oriented as possible. Customer service may include users' ability to:

- review the customer database to identify changes in personal information, banking instructions etc.;
- enter their own orders and receive confirmations;
- carry out claims on line speedily;
- propose changes to delivery dates and order quantities, with amended confirmations;
- review the transaction/account status;
- check shipment details;
- access accounts receivable details;
- search for, request and download on-line information and documentation;
- download reports.

The accountant should be able to review pricing and other procedures for follow-up inquiries by customers.

Security reviews

The accountant carrying out security reviews should examine procedures surrounding the confidentiality of data, transmission of information, periodical reconciliation procedures, authenticating procedures, and the arrangements with outside contractors such as information aggregators and brokers. He or she should also conduct server security reviews. Accountants may certify web-based information using products such as Webtrusts. The examination of on-line security is an ongoing procedure, which sometimes becomes part of the on-line auditing.

On-line audits

An on-line audit evaluates the likely acceptance of on-line sites or services among targeted users. It includes:

- on-line market analysis and overview;
- marketing and communication goals implementation;
- technology evaluation;
- on-line content audit;

- target audience identification and analysis;
- site upgrade and enhancement recommendations;
- ongoing competitive analysis;
- traffic monitoring and server log analysis.

The components of an on-line content audit comprise the review of the content or service offering, review of the competitors' content or service offering, a site review with the client, a joint audit with a review questionnaire, and recommendations for content or service improvements.

An on-line audit is appropriate both before and after a web site for on-line service is built. It involves checking each on-line activity against set goals to provide for specific and actionable recommendations in terms of communication, security and customer relationships.

The on-line auditor should be familiar with software copyright information and ensure compliance is achieved. Audit software is available in the market for auditors to integrate clients' systems with that of the auditor's so they can interact on line. Based on Microsoft Access, Audit Leverage is an example of a package designed for internal auditors. This audit software enables all audit work to be done on line.[13]

Maintenance and monitoring

The accountant's review should confirm that the enterprise is monitoring its web site performance in terms of criteria such as download time, transaction time, availability and access. Errors such as failed connection, missing information or pages, and broken links must be listed and investigated. The accountant may use or prepare comparative web performance statistics to evaluate overall performance. Also relevant is a review of other web information to ascertain its currency, the accuracy of management reports and data for analysis. The auditor may recommend a reference material repository. This is a part of the web site that contains information related to the business cycle, econometric reports and forecasts, industry trends, media releases and/or links to other relevant web sites. The presence of the repository may enhance customer relationships and maintain competitive advantage.

Internal control audit

This is a typical audit examination of the adequacy of internal controls within the e-commerce environment. The audit may encompass the control environment, the control features relating to transaction details and transmission security, risk assessment and controls to minimise such risks, information and communication technology, and the competency and sufficiency of human resources. The approach to this audit is similar to that for normal business, only the audit or examination focuses more on the risks associated with e-commerce.

Continuous audit

Continuous auditing was named one of the top five emerging issues for 1999, selected by the task force charged with defining the American Institute of Certified Public Accountants' Top Technology Lists.[14] The electronic revolution has created a demand for more timely assurance on a broader range of information than that provided by the annual audit of historical financial statements.

In a continuous audit, client information would be released in a very short time frame (via the Internet) and audit reports on that information would follow the release of the information almost immediately. Thus, a continuous audit is a process or method that enables independent auditors to provide written assurance on a subject matter using a series of auditors' reports issued simultaneously with, or a short time after, the occurrence of events underlying the subject matter. It would be conducted on continuous financial and non-financial information made available to users in formats defined by management.[15]

Auditors could be requested to continuously audit and report on:

- financial statements available on demand via a web site;
- specific financial information in conjunction with a debt covenant agreement;
- compliance with published policies and practices regarding e-commerce transactions (e.g. reliance on secure encrypted systems for credit card processing);
- the effectiveness of controls operating in key systems or processes.

A continuous audit presents a number of auditing issues. There would be little time for the auditor to gather audit evidence in verifying and substantiating the subject matter(s) concerned. The auditor could not rely on normal audit procedures such as obtaining independent confirmations and addressing material misstatements, so a reliable and well-controlled application system would be vital. The auditor would have to employ fully automated audit software such as IDEA or ACL to read, manipulate and generate the information required. Other conditions necessary to ensure a successful continuous audit would be:

- effective communication (and technology) between the client and the auditor;
- prior agreement as to the form, content and scope of the audit;
- a sound knowledge by the auditor of the operating systems employed by the client.

The above discussion examines the e-commerce environment in terms of the implications of e-commerce and the related strategies and business processes. We introduced e-commerce audit and assurance services to enable you to appreciate the emerging role of the accountant in this environment. The following 'Professional environment' is an example of the increasing involvement of accountants in on-line businesses.

PROFESSIONAL ENVIRONMENT

Use of auditors to verify privacy policies of on-line sellers

Expedia.com, the travel site owned by Microsoft, is the latest company to subject its privacy policies to an audit — in this case, by the firm PricewaterhouseCoopers. Expedia said that starting today, the PricewaterhouseCoopers seal, a small box with the company's logo, would appear next to its new privacy policy, along with a statement by PricewaterhouseCoopers attesting that Expedia practises what it preaches. 'This won't directly increase sales,' said Suzie LeVine, Expedia's marketing manager. 'But it will increase customer confidence in the site. And that, combined with all the services we provide, will increase sales.'

Analysts said E-loan, an on-line lending firm, was the first e-commerce company to post results of a privacy audit from one of the Big Five accounting firms, having done so with PricewaterhouseCoopers early last year. Chris Larsen, E-loan's chief executive, said the audit was a response to a controversy last year surrounding Microsoft and Truste, a nonprofit organisation that provides a seal to sites that meet its privacy standards.

Nonetheless, Mr Larsen said he 'completely lost faith in Truste after that', so he hired PricewaterhouseCoopers to perform an initial audit of E-loan's privacy practices and post the results on the E-loan web site. The effort cost roughly $250 000 in fees and staff time, an E-loan spokeswoman said. In addition, E-loan pays PricewaterhouseCoopers an additional $30 000 for each quarterly audit. As to what effect the audit has had on business, Mr Larsen said, 'It's hard to tell. People have been widely supportive of it, but I see it more as a prerequisite to doing business. Consumers have an expectation of privacy.'

(Source: Extracted from Bob Tedeschi, 'Some On-line Sellers are Hiring Prominent Auditors to Verify Their Privacy Policies and Increase Trust', *New York Times* (18 September 2000), p. 42)

4 LEARNING OBJECTIVE

Assess the audit risk and control matters in an e-commerce environment.

AUDIT RISK AND CONTROL CONSIDERATIONS

In view of the increasing likelihood that accountants and auditors will be working in an Internet-driven environment, in this section we will offer a framework for the conduct of auditing and assurance services in e-commerce. AGS 1056, Electronic Commerce: Audit Risk Assessments and Control Considerations (issued in August 2000) provides the backbone of this section. We will discuss audit planning, risk assessment, control considerations, and audit and assurance issues, complementing the discussions in Parts 2 and 3.

Audit planning

The key audit planning procedures identified in Chapter 6 also apply in an e-commerce environment, but the professional accountant should gain sufficient understanding of the client's business and its e-commerce activities to assess the risk and the necessary controls. Where other parties are involved (e.g. an outsourced party in the electronic transaction cycle), further considerations will be necessary to evaluate the security infrastructure.

Understanding the business

The professional accountant carrying out either a general purpose financial report audit or an assurance service must gain sufficient knowledge of the client to understand the events, transactions and practices that have an impact on the financial and management reports. AUS 304, Knowledge of the Business requires the professional accountant to make inquiries to identify the business strategy and e-commerce strategy, the business models (see page 606) that are employed, and the expertise of the personnel involved. The professional accountant must ensure that he or she possesses the required expertise before undertaking the professional engagement. It is also worthwhile for the auditor to note if management is aware of the commitment and the extent of implications of any of the company's e-commerce activities.

E-commerce activities

We explained different types of e-commerce activity in the earlier part of this chapter. The professional accountant should determine if management has thoroughly investigated the e-commerce strategy such that risks and opportunities have been adequately assessed. The risk related to particular industries may be higher than others. The size of the organisation and the scale of its operations also influence the scale of the e-commerce activities employed by the business. The professional accountant should document such matters concerning the e-commerce activities, and discuss with the management the likely impacts on the company's financial report, management controls and audit. Discussions should cover:

- the technical and information technology skills of personnel involved in e-commerce;
- the changes that are necessary in the infrastructure of the existing systems to accommodate all aspects of the e-commerce activities;
- for a new business system, whether it has been fully investigated and tested;
- the cost implications of e-commerce and of management's expectations of the amount invested in e-commerce;
- the particular business model(s) used by the business and an evaluation of the model(s);
- management's awareness of the cost of monitoring e-commerce activity and the risks involved, especially with respect to the management of customer data, and transaction and information security;

- documentation of interface issues, such as links with Internet providers, distributors, application software and the entire financial reporting system within the organisation;
- the development of a flow chart or detailed documentation of the transaction cycle (The professional accountant should acknowledge the complexity of the e-commerce system and examine any difficulties encountered during implementation.);
- monitoring of the performance of the e-commerce system through certain parameters with which management has agreed;
- the review of the above monitoring process, and the investigation of review results;
- making management aware of follow-up actions from complaints, and whether they improve the efficiency of the system.

Furthermore, if management needs to review matters such as the scale of its e-commerce and its connections with outsiders (e.g. strategic alliances), then the professional accountant is able to provide an advisory role.

Use of experts and outsourcing

Where the professional accountant is concerned about the required skills necessary to understand the client's systems fully, especially on the technical information technology infrastructure and control elements, he or she may employ an outside expert. AUS 206, Quality Control for Audit Work and AUS 606, Using the Work of an Expert provide guidance on the use of experts.

Similarly, if the client employs a third party to operate either a part of or the entire e-commerce system, AUS 404, Audit Implications Relating to Entities Using a Service Entity and AGS 1042, Reporting on Control Procedures at Outsourcing Entities provide some guidance in assessing the risks related to outsourcing. The auditor must review business continuity plans and outsourcing agreements.

Risk assessment

The client company should have a control framework in place that addresses the detailed business processes of an e-commerce transaction cycle (see page 609). The risks involved can be classified as either business risks or technology-related risks. Business risks for an e-commerce environment concern any failure of the business to maintain its viability through its e-commerce activities. Technology-related risks are threats which result from failures in technology delivery, such as a breach of the security of information or the inability of the system to produce complete, timely, reliable financial records and reports.

Client's business strategies and models

While the client is responsible for developing an adequate e-commerce strategy, the professional accountant is often approached for expert advice. The business strategies adopted by the client determine the nature and extent of the risks involved; for example, the client will determine the type of information to be processed through the Internet and the limits of third party access, which will affect the requirement for constant monitoring of the security of information. The issue of Internet traffic will also be influenced by the entity's opportunity, via the system, to obtain new markets.

The professional accountant is often consulted during an entity's planning, development and implementation of e-commerce. On the other hand, the adoption of different business e-commerce models (such as business-to-business or business-to-consumers), is based on the assumption that management understands the value chain of the business and the flow of information required.

Business risks

The business risks relating to e-commerce can be categorised as those relating to:

- business relationships (such as with trading partners, customers, suppliers and banks), as a result of open access and competitive information being available on the Internet. Management should ensure the accuracy of information, a positive company image, and the reliability of other business intelligence networks used by the system;
- transactions, as a result of threats to the fulfilment of transactions (such as problems with delivery and the recording, processing and updating of data);
- security, as a result of the threats of an inadequate security infrastructure, fraudulent activities, hackers' interference, abuses of privacy, computer crashes, loss of data, etc. Security controls and authorisation processes should be implemented to minimise these risks. However, some risks are inherent in the system owing to the capability of changing technology.

To address the above risks, management must implement certain control measures to safeguard the authenticity of transactions and the security of information processed through the Internet. We will describe detailed control considerations in the following section.

Control considerations

The primary purposes of the control measures are to prevent fraud and error, and to maintain the privacy and security of both customers and the information processed. These controls must be dynamic, and capable of ensuring flexible systems to operate and interface with one another with minimum disruption and risk of system failures. Also, the controls should ensure the authenticity of transactions and access. Auditors are concerned with the controls necessary to maintain proper records, thus ensuring the reliability of the financial reports and audit risk minimised. Professional accountants carrying out assurance services relating to e-commerce are required to understand the controls to assess the performance of the e-commerce activities, and to add value to the decision-making process of clients' management.

Security controls

The security of transactions through the Internet should be established by the implementation of various security measures. The types of security infrastructure reviewed by the professional accountant include:

- logical and physical security measures such as firewalls, encryption, physical controls over password issues, authorisation, etc. The IBM SecureWay Firewall version 4.1 for Windows NT, for example, offers a combination of advanced e-mail protection features alongside other firewall architectures (such as filtering, proxy and a circuit level gateway), to provide customers with a high level of security for controlling communication and business;
- internal and external security measures (the latter relating to interfaces with external parties, Internet security and virus protection);
- user profiles, including authorisation and review procedures for users, password security, and logical controls over access;
- information protection, which relates to all measures used to safeguard the integrity of files, virus protection, transmission security, and controls such as check digits, reasonableness check, etc.;
- privacy issues relating to customer information;
- potential liabilities arising from a breach of legislation, copyright issues, etc.

The professional accountant considers the various security measures to ensure that the controls are properly incorporated within the e-commerce system. Accountants should refer to AUS 214, Auditing in a CIS Environment and AGSs 1018, 1020 and 1022 concerning stand-alone microcomputers, on-line computer systems and database systems. The entity's information technology staff must carefully monitor additional interface controls between the Internet and intranet, along with the entire e-commerce design. The professional accountant may be involved in the development and design of the system with management to ensure proper safeguards are incorporated and documented.

Transaction integrity

The security infrastructure described above considers the information sharing and monitoring aspects of the e-commerce environment, while controls relating to transaction integrity safeguard the ordering or transaction initiation stage and the execution or fulfilment stage. Transaction integrity relates to the completeness, accuracy and reliability of the information provided for recording and processing financial records and annual financial statements.

Systems controls for transaction integrity include:

- controls for remote locations (controls on ordering, delivery, authorisation procedures and the accuracy of information);
- identity controls for authorised personnel or businesses;
- processing controls to ensure the completeness and accuracy of transactions and to identify irregularities;
- records controls such as reconciliations between systems and subsystems, timely and accurate reporting, and distribution controls;
- monitoring procedures to ensure all discrepancies are followed up immediately and resubmissions are processed;
- authenticity, accuracy and reasonableness controls on the customers database, inventory levels, catalogues and prices, etc., which should be similar to normal computer information system controls.

Process alignment

The auditor is concerned with the alignment process between the on-line shopfront and the internal reporting systems (or the back office systems) so the Internet transactions are captured accurately and completely in the organisation's reports. The auditor should ascertain, for example, when a transaction takes place through the Internet and is subsequently recognised in the system. He or she will need to review any disputed transactions and follow up system changes. Training of information technology staff for both on-line operations and back office systems is essential.

Electronic records

The verification procedures for transactions should include an examination of proper information policies and proper implementation of security controls to prevent unauthorised access or changes to the financial records. The auditor should consider the controls incorporated during system design — such as integrity checks, electronic date stamps using digital signatures, version controls on electronic evidence, and transmission controls on real-time transactions — to ensure they are regularly maintained and occasionally reviewed.

Audit and assurance issues

Owing to the nature of e-commerce, accountants and auditors concerned with financial reports will consider other key issues that may have an impact on their approach to the respective engagements. These issues include:

- information technology issues such as the technical competence of management and staff, the obsolescence of technology, system integrity and the overall complexity of the electronic environment;
- the combination of the three elements of internal control described in AUS 402 (the control environment, information systems and control procedures) into the e-commerce system. It is important for the auditor to understand the information technology security and system controls to minimise risks;
- frequent monitoring by management to ensure that irregular, improper, unusual and abnormal items are investigated, so the system can be improved and updated regularly. Furthermore, the company may experience different types of problem in various sectors, or different rates of growth, so it needs to scale its e-commerce operations and development to reflect the resources required;
- management's attitude to, awareness of, and actions regarding internal control and maintenance of the e-commerce environment;
- system failures either at the organisational level or from outsourced operations, which may have a significant impact on the organisation's earnings and reputation. The auditor should consider the risks relating to the business continuity aspects of the e-commerce environment;
- matters such as those affected by disintermediation (e.g. inventory held, overdue accounts, forecasts and budgets), the difficulties of relying on data produced for e-commerce, and going-concern issues;
- materiality issues, which involve not only quantitative measures but also qualitative matters. Auditors and accountants will consider the materiality of financial data on e-commerce without traditional benchmarks.
- the fact that many e-businesses report a financial loss during their initial stage of e-commerce. The auditor/professional accountant should consider the economic impact of the e-commerce activities, the integrity and reliability of the entity's financial data, and the viability of maintaining continuous on-line activities. He or she must use professional judgement to assess the appropriateness of the going-concern assumptions of the financial reports and the adequacy of disclosures.

CYBER CRIMES AND FORENSIC AUDITING

5
LEARNING OBJECTIVE

Discuss the objectives and approach of forensic auditing, with an emphasis on frauds on the Internet.

The portal giant Yahoo! was shut down for three hours on 6 February, 2000. The retailer Buy.com was hit the next day, hours after going public. By that evening, eBay, Amazon.com and CNN had gone dark. The mayhem continued the next morning, with online broker E*Trade and others having traffic to their sites virtually shut off. Was this the work of a super hacker? Even at the time of publication, law enforcement officials did not know, or would not tell. But what worries experts more than the identity of the culprit group is how easily these attacks have been orchestrated and executed. Someone could sit at home and, with a few keystrokes, disrupt e-commerce around the globe.[16]

The cyber world is a new arena for risk managers and businesses — one in which the risks are unclear yet dwarf exposures in the physical sense. **Distributed denial-of-service** attacks (DDOS), like the ones launched by hackers against Yahoo! and other sites in February 2000, are more than just tremendous business interruption losses. They are an emerging area of concern called downstream liability.[17] Some of the new e-commerce insurance policies offer coverage (up to US$25 million) at a price somewhere between 2 per cent to 3.5 per cent of the limits purchased, yet the potential policy holder must undergo an extensive audit of its computer systems, networks, on-line marketplaces, security measures and so on.

In this section we will offer a basic appreciation of (1) the extent and nature of electronic crimes that impose significant risks on e-commerce activities, and (2) the objectives of forensic auditing.

Cyber crimes and electronic crimes

The complexity of the information economy, the reliance of business on technology, and the increasing amount of interconnectivity among organisations are both a result of and a driver for e-commerce. These widespread developments have created opportunities for theft, fraud and other forms of exploitation by offenders both outside and inside organisations. As businesses grow, their networked systems become increasingly sophisticated and less dependent on human intervention. Monitoring individual behaviour becomes difficult and vulnerability to electronic crimes (**e-crimes**) grows as organisations are increasingly connected to, and reliant on, individuals and systems outside their control. Most are alert to the risks posed by electronic viruses such as the May 2000 'I love you' virus, which led to derivative viruses and is estimated to have cost businesses and governments more than US$10 billion.

Denial-of-service attacks, including the launch of viruses, can be perpetrated internally or externally. They disable network and e-commerce services. These attacks, like the ones on Yahoo!, use the large-scale communications bandwidth of an intermediary to overwhelm their victims' systems with meaningless service requests, thereby degrading or denying legitimate users any service. But criminals are doing much more — everything from stealing intellectual property and committing fraud to unleashing viruses and committing acts of cyber terrorism in which political groups or unfriendly governments disseminate crucial information. As the broadband technology catches on, the Internet will go from being the occasional dial-up service to being 'always on', much like the telephone. That concept may be beneficial to e-tailers, but could pose a real danger to consumers and e-commerce activities.

However, many organisations are still unaware of the extent to which they can be harmed by a wide variety of cyber or electronic crimes that may originate with their own employees or business partners. A recent survey of Fortune 500 companies by the US Federal Bureau of Investigation (FBI) and the Computer Security Institute found that financial losses from computer crime exceeded $360 million between 1997 and 1999. Of the survey respondents, 62 per cent reported computer security breaches within 1999 alone.[18]

Not all computer crimes are Internet related. E-crime perpetrators can be either external or internal, or they can be just computer-systems related. External attackers are either sophisticated 'crackers' who develop and use technology-based tools that facilitate illegal entry into a victim's network system or other technologies, or just 'cookbook' crackers. ('Cookbook' crackers, who lack the knowledge, skills and abilities to create and use more sophisticated tools, seek out such tools to launch attacks.) Internal attackers, on the other hand, can include dissatisfied current employees working alone or with other insiders or ex-employees. Some experts consider that organisations face greater risk from the fraudulent acts of their own employees or former employees with knowledge of their systems.

Electronic criminals commit their crimes using a wide variety of easily accessible tools, which are often available on the Internet. Such tools include:[19]

- *anonymous re-mailers*: These machines on the Internet are configured to receive and re-send traffic by replacing the original source address of the sender with the address of the anonymous re-mailer machine. Intruders use them to mask their identities.
- *Internet packet filters or 'sniffers'* : This software allows intruders to intercept network traffic.
- *nukers*: These software tools are used by intruders to destroy system log trails.
- *password crackers* : This software allows intruders to 'break' encrypted password files stolen from a victim's network server.
- *scanners*: Automated software can help intruders identify services running on network machines that may be able to be exploited.
- *spoofers*: Software can allow intruders to masquerade as other system users.
- *steganography*: This method of encrypting and hiding data in graphics or audio files is used by intruders to spy, steal or traffic in information via electronic dead drops, like a web page.
- ***Trojan programs***: The injection of unauthorised code into a legitimate program can cause it to perform unknown (and hidden) functions. Intruders use these programs to create undocumented 'backdoors' into network systems.

Forensic auditing

An effective investigative tool to help combat fraudulent claims, a forensic audit investigates the causes and effect of possibly fraudulent activities or system failures that may be the consequences of fraud. The forensic auditor looks for evidence of fraud and documents system failures, and identifies the extent of losses incurred. A forensic audit may be held in response to a claim against a company as a result of intentional or unintentional failures of e-commerce transactions. Forensic audits can also be employed for an insurer to evaluate the liability of a claim (e.g. a disability claim through a work-related accident; a system failure claim through a computer crash; and so on).

It is not uncommon for professional accountants to be engaged as forensic auditors. The accountant is experienced in identifying evidence and is able to evaluate losses such as loss of earnings. Typical materials reviewed in a forensic audit concerning e-commerce include all system documentations, log trailers, authorisation signatories, transaction reports and registers.

The auditor should be capable of understanding the network systems and should seek symptoms using specially designed programs (e.g. a data analysis program). A forensic audit involving the e-commerce environment may feature:

- comparing employee e-mails and addresses, log-on times and messages;
- searching for duplicate numbers on payments or receipts;
- scanning lists of suppliers, customers and inventory movements;
- analysing the sequence of transactions to identify the intervention by unauthorised personnel;
- finding users of the same addresses and signalling phantom users.

A proactive, critical approach to controlling e-commerce transactions is necessary to minimise risks. The auditor may be able to identify suspicious matters in the process, but the skilful evaluation of the results will demand professional judgement, competence and experience.

LEARNING CHECK

16.5 Auditors and accountants must understand the implications of the e-commerce transaction cycle, which includes information sharing, on-line submission, fulfilment of orders, service and support systems.

16.6 Different types of audit and assurance service available for e-commerce include those relating to risk analysis, system selection, customer service, security reviews, on-line audits on information quality, review of the maintenance and monitoring of e-commerce systems, internal control audits and continuous audits.

16.7 AGS 1056 summarises the audit risk assessments and control considerations for e-commerce. The process involves audit planning, risk assessment, control considerations, security controls, integrity controls, process alignment, electronic records and an understanding of the issues such as the competence of the IT staff, control elements, management attitude, and risk of system failures.

16.8 With the increasing concerns to combat cyber crimes, forensic auditing has been developed to investigate the causes and effects of electronic crimes, including cyber crimes. The accountant is experienced in identifying evidences to evaluate losses attributable to an identifiable occurrence of e-commerce.

SUMMARY

In this chapter we discussed the development of the information economy and the emerging significance of e-commerce. We presented a conceptual model of the information economy (with infrastructure, applications, intermediation and e-commerce layers), with the emergence of e-commerce as the highest level of an information economy, using all aspects of the economy in an integrated manner. We discussed the nature and development of e-commerce, highlighting the wide-ranging implications for business managers and accountants in terms of the changes in business processes and strategies, technological and organisational infrastructures, and the role of accountants in performing audit and other assurance services.

In the latter part of the chapter, we described the audit risk and control considerations to be undertaken by accountants and auditors in an e-commerce environment. The latest auditing guideline issued by the profession in Australia — AGS 1056, Electronic Commerce: Audit Risk Assessments and Control Considerations — was discussed. The considerations include planning matters, risk assessment, control issues such as security of data, transaction integrity, process alignment and electronic record maintenance. Furthermore, an overview of audit and assurance issues in relation to e-commerce highlighted the impact on the approach adopted by accountants in providing an assurance engagement service. In the final part of the chapter we looked at an inherent risk in e-commerce — cyber crimes. We discussed the nature and development of e-crimes, and explored the scope of forensic auditing and approaches in practice.

KEY TERMS

Business-to-business, p. 603
Business-to-consumers, p. 603
Communication technologies, p. 600
Disintermediation, p. 606
Disruption risk, p. 611
Distributed denial of service, p. 619
E-commerce, p. 600
E-crimes, p. 620
E-tailing, p. 603
Economic risk, p. 611
Electronic data interchange (EDI), p. 603
Electronic funds transfer (EFT), p. 603
Image risk, p. 611
Information aggregators, p. 603
Information economy, p. 600
Informediaries, p. 605
Intermediaries, p. 600
Knowledge-based, p. 601
Legal risk, p. 611
Microcash, p. 610
Moral risk, p. 611
Multimedia applications, p. 601
Reliability risk, p. 611
Strategic risk, p. 611
Trojan programs, p. 621
Value chain, p. 605

NOTES

1. Liz Fisher, 'E-commerce — A Threat or a Challenge?', *Accounting & Business*, (March 2000), pp. 20–1. A collection of e-commerce articles appeared in that issue of *Accounting & Business*, which is the journal of the Association of Chartered Certified Accountants (ACCA).
2. Colin Turner, *The Information E-conomy — Business Strategies for Competing in the Digital Age*, 1st edn. Kogan Page, London, 2000, pp. 1–5.
3. Colin Turner, *The Information E-conomy — Business Strategies for Competing in the Digital Age*, 1st edn. Kogan Page, London, 2000, p. 4.
4. Austin Center for Research in Electronic Commerce, *Report of the Internet Economy Indicators*. University of Texas, 1999. Web site: www.internetindicators.com
5. David Powell, 'Consuming e-commerce', *Australian CPA* (September 2000), pp. 4–3.
6. Ernst & Young, *Virtual Shopping in Australia: An Ernst & Young Special Report*. January 2000. Web site: www.ey.com/GLOBAL/
7. OECD, *The Economic and Social Impact of Electronic Commerce*. Paris, 1998.
8. M. Porter, *Competitive Advantage*. The Free Press, New York, 1985.
9. The Conference Board and PricewaterhouseCoopers, *Electronic Business Outlook for the New Millennium*. 2000. Web site: www.pwcglobal.com
10. Merrill Lynch, *E-commerce virtually here*. Global Securities Research and Economic Working Group, 1999. Web site: www.ml.com
11. The Economist Intelligence Unit and KPMG, *The E-business Value Chain: Winning Strategies in Seven Global Industries*. United States, September 2000. Web sites: www.store.eiu.com and www.kpmg.com
12. See Note 4.
13. An audit software developed by The Department Management Software for Internal Auditors, based on Microsoft Access. Web site: www.auditleverage.com/
14. American Institute of Certified Public Accountants and the Canadian Institute of Chartered Accountants, *Continuous Auditing* (Product 022510). 2000. The CICA's Auditing Standards Board commissioned a research report on the viability of 'continuous assurance services' and the significant issues that auditors may likely encounter when performing them. The AICPA supported the initiative and appointed members to the study group. The Australian Accounting Research Foundation formed a group of volunteers to review and provide comments on the materials developed.

15. See Note 14.
16. Ira Sager, 'First Yahoo! Then eBay. The Net's Vulnerability Threatens E-commerce and You', *Business Week* (21 February, 2000), pp. 36–42.
17. John Conley, 'Outwitting Cybercriminals', *Risk Management* (July 2000), pp. 18–26.
18. KPMG Forensic and Litigation Services, *E-commerce and Cyber Crime: New Strategies for Managing the Risks of Exploitation*. New York, 2000. Web site: www.kpmg.com

FURTHER READING

Australian Securities and Investment Commission, *Survey of On-line Trading Web sites*, August 2000.

Australian Securities and Investment Commission, Policy Statements: Policy Statement 107, Electronic Prospectuses; Policy Statement 118, Investment Advisory Services: Media, Computer Software and Internet Advice; Policy Statement 141, Offers of Securities on the Internet.

Attaway Sr, Morris C., 'What Every Auditor Needs to Know about E-commerce', *The Internal Auditor* (June 2000), pp. 56–60.

Ceniceros, Roberto, 'Understanding the Risks of E-commerce', *Business Insurance* (16 October 2000), p. 38.

Coderre, David G., 'Computer-assisted Fraud Detection', *The Internal Auditor* (August 2000), pp. 25–7.

Conley, John, 'Outwitting Cybercriminals', *Risk Management*, (July 2000), pp. 18–26.

Gatti, Joseph, 'Integrating Hotdata into CRM and E-business Systems', *Direct Marketing* (June 2000).

George, Alan, 'Big Five Auditors Squeezed between the US SEC and the E-conomy', *Middle East* (May 2000), pp. 22 and 31.

Groomer, S. Michael, 'Continuous Audits: The Wave of the Future', *Infotech Update* (July–August 1999), pp. 1 and 5.

Helms, Glenn L. and Lilly, Fred L., 'Case Study on Auditing in an Electronic Environment', *CPA Journal* (April 2000), pp. 52–4.

Huss, H. Fenwick, Jacobs, Fred A., Patterson, Denise A. and Park, Manyong, 'An Integrative Model of Risk Management in Auditing', *American Business Review*, (June 2000), pp. 113–22.

Kaplan, Jim, 'Software Compliance Auditing Resources', *Auditor on the Net* (Vol. 3, No. 1, 1996). Web site: www.kentis.com/archive

Kosiur, David, *Understanding Electronic Commerce*. Strategic Technology Series, Microsoft Press, Washington DC, 1997.

Longo, Joseph P., 'Cyber Enforcement in the Financial Services Sector'. Address to the Australian Competition and Consumers Commission's Global Commerce Conference, Sydney, 9 November, 1998. Joseph Longo is National Director, Enforcement of the Australian Securities and Investment Commission.

KPMG Forensic and Litigation Services, *E-commerce and Cyber Crime: New Strategies for Managing the Risks of Exploitation*. 2000.

PricewaterhouseCoopers, *Retail Industry's First E-Commerce Roadmap*, Retail Systems 2000, Chicago, 2000.

PricewaterhouseCoopers, *Business Information for Corporate General Counsel*, February 2000. Web site: www.pwcglobal.com

Turner, Colin, *The Information Economy, Business Strategies for Competing in the Digital Age*, Kogan Page, United Kingdom, 2000.

Williams, Kathy, 'Preparing Your Business for Secure E-commerce', *Strategic Finance* (September 2000), p. 21.

Review questions

16.1 What is the concept of the information economy? What does it mean for the transformation of business processes?

16.2 What is e-commerce? What does e-commerce encompass?

16.3 Select an e-commerce business process. How does it work?

16.4 Which different types of audit and assurance service are related to an e-commerce environment?

16.5 What factors need to be considered in planning a financial report audit of an e-commerce business? Explain each factor.

16.6 What are the typical risks in an e-commerce environment? How do these risks affect the auditor's work?

16.7 How do cyber crimes affect an e-business?

16.8 What are the typical approaches generally adopted by a forensic auditor?

Discussion questions

16.1 Why do you think Australia appears to be at an early stage of adopting e-commerce in business, relative to the rates of adoption in other developed countries?

16.2 Do you agree that the key factors for accountants in reviewing e-commerce activities are risks and security? Discuss how risks and security may affect the auditor in planning a financial report audit of an e-commerce client.

16.3 What key controls are necessary to safeguard security and transactions in an e-commerce environment?

16.4 What is meant by a forensic audit? Discuss (a) the significance of cyber crimes in affecting a company's business and (b) the common features of a forensic audit.

16.5 What is the impact of e-commerce on professional accountants? Discuss.

16.6 Do you think auditors face a higher level of uncertainties in an e-commerce environment?

16.7 How do you think the approaches to a financial report audit may change in an e-commerce environment?

16.8 Do you think auditors for an e-commerce business should take on an active role in detecting e-crimes?

Professional application questions

★ BASIC
★★ MODERATE
★★★ CHALLENGING

16.1 (Forensic audit) ★★

The Standard Publishing Insurance Company provides insurance covers for professional publishers. Australian Cyber-Publications Inc. (ACPI) recently filed a claim for the loss it incurred following a break-down of its computer network, in which its customers' files were lost. ACPI sells business publications (journals, magazines and news reports) to 1000 corporate customers via subscriptions through the Internet. The

(continued)

payment and delivery systems are also linked with the customers' files, held by the master e-commerce system. You are called in to conduct a forensic audit to establish the validity of the claim, and the extent to which it is appropriate.

Required

Explain the key considerations of the forensic audit you will conduct.

16.2 (Controls for electronic payment) ★★★

Traditional financial transactions contain characteristics to safeguard the parties' interests by incorporating certain controls. In an electronic payment system using the Internet, the expectations of confidentiality of identities, the integrity of transactional details, and the assurance that the parties of the contract are competent and trustworthy are pertinent to businesses.

Required

Using the following headings, identify the controls you would expect to find in an e-commerce system:

(a) Confidentiality of information;
(b) Transaction integrity;
(c) Authorisation of payments;
(d) Assurance of business credibility.

Case study

16.1 (Sales system controls) ★★★

Lorell's Bakery is a company which focuses on specialty cakes, chocolates and biscuits, with unique flavourings and ingredients for special occasions. The bakery sells only cakes and biscuits that have been baked within the past 24 hours. In 1999, 80 per cent of the company's customers were based locally while 20 per cent were from interstate Australia. Lorell Luk, the company's owner, notes that the local market is relatively stable and that she needs to expand her national market. Her goal is to increase national market share.

Ordering system

Orders from national or local customers are placed through the bakery's toll-free and local telephone numbers, with customers providing credit card information, delivery address and other relevant order information. To safeguard accuracy, the operator repeats the order to the customer, who has the option of receiving a fax confirmation. Orders are then sequentially numbered and entered into personal computers by ten data-entry operators. The computers are connected to a local area network (LAN).

After an order is entered, the computer system generates a production request for the twelve bakers working in three shifts and a mailing label. Four packers per shift pick and package the appropriate cakes/biscuits and place mailing labels on decorative boxes. These boxes are then delivered by carriers that guarantee a maximum two-day delivery. The company accepts orders 24 hours per day, seven days per week.

Each mailing label contains a barcode that is scanned to update the outstanding orders file. Information on filled orders is automatically deleted from the system. For quality control, an inspector periodically compares the packed goods with the order.

The e-commerce approach
On her accountant Michael Sleigh's advice, Lorell develops an electronic storefront system on the Internet. The web site provides a catalogue of available cakes/biscuits and chocolate, with different shapes, flavours and styles, and allows customers to place orders on line as well as by telephone.

The on-line customer completes an order form and provides the same information requested in a telephone order. The company sends the customer an e-mail confirmation when the order is filled, and provides information on the expected delivery date. Orders received at the electronic shopfront are maintained on a file that is used as input to the existing order-entry systems. Lorel hires Harry, a local college student majoring in information technology, to help develop the web site.

National sales increase beyond expectations and soon approximately 80 per cent of all sales are received through the Internet. The business experiences overall cost efficiencies, with no increase in the number of order takers. Harry, working four hours each week day, is responsible for maintaining the LAN and all of the programming for processing customer orders, preparing production requests, printing mailing labels, and transmitting credit card charges to the company's bank. Harry also serves as the weekend computer operator for nightly updating of files, printing reports and preparing backups. Alison, the LAN supervisor, performs these duties during the week. Each weekend, Harry takes the back-up disk home with him so the company always has a current copy of its files off site.

After some customer complaints about not receiving shipments, the packers start recording the number of shipments made during each shift on a summary sheet. The bookkeeper is responsible for comparing the number of shipments with the weekly sales summary report and investigating any differences. However, Harry finds that the bookkeeper frequently forgets to make the comparisons, so he does it himself.

When Harry graduates, Lorell hires him full time to write programs for an inventory control system and a system to automatically reconcile the credit card settlement report from the bank with the company's sales records. Lorell also asks him to develop programs to order supplies automatically by sending electronic data interchange records to the three baking ingredients suppliers and the decorative accessories supplier.

Lorell is aware that new and larger production facilities are now needed to accommodate the increased demand, so she approaches a local community bank for financial support. The bank requires the company to provide the audited financial statements. Lorell engages Michael Sleigh & Associates to conduct an audit of the financial statements as of 31 December 20X0. Michael tells Lorell that because so much significant information is transmitted, processed, maintained and accessed electronically, he needs information on the sales system's controls to plan and perform his audit.

Required
Draft a memorandum for Michael Sleigh to discuss with Lorell Luk concerning the audit and internal control implications of the sales systems.

(Based on G. L. Helms and Fred L. Lilly, *CPA Journal* (April 2000), pp. 52–4)

chapter 17

Internal, operational and government auditing

Overview

LEARNING OBJECTIVES

After studying this chapter, you should be able to:

1. define internal auditing and describe its objectives and scope
2. state the source and nature of Standards for the Professional Practice of Internal Auditing
3. define operational auditing and describe the phases of an operational audit
4. explain accountability in the public sector
5. explain the role of parliamentary committees in the accountability process
6. state the assertions, audit objectives and reporting requirements of financial statement audits in the public sector
7. describe the nature of performance auditing.

Professional statements

AUSTRALIAN		INTERNATIONAL	
Standards for the Professional Practice of Internal Auditing, Institute of Internal Auditors		Standards for the Professional Practice of Internal Auditing, Institute of Internal Auditors	
Code of Ethics, Institute of Internal Auditors		Code of Ethics, Institute of Internal Auditors	
AUS 106	Explanatory Framework for Standards on Audits and Audit-related Services	ISA 120	Framework of ISAs
AUS 604	Considering the Work of Internal Auditing	ISA 610	Considering the Work of Internal Auditing
AUS 806	Performance Auditing		
AUS 808	Planning for Performance Audits		
AUP 32	Audit Independence		

In Chapter 1 we introduced several types of auditing, such as financial report auditing, **internal auditing** and **operational auditing** (or **performance auditing**). Independent, internal or government auditors can perform these audits. So far, we have focused on financial report auditing undertaken by independent auditors. Now, we will direct our attention to internal auditors and to financial and operational auditing undertaken by government auditors in the public sector. For each type of auditing, we will consider the relevant objectives, scope and Auditing Standards. We will also refer to the Professional Guidance Statements of the Institute of Internal Auditors where appropriate.

INTERNAL AUDITING

As we explained in Chapter 7, internal auditing is an important part of the monitoring component of an entity's internal control structure, as well as providing other valuable services to an entity. However, alongside the auditing profession, internal auditing is undergoing change. A new Code of Ethics was approved in June 2000. The Institute of Internal Auditors also issued additional professional guidance statements, covering a wide range of subjects and including major changes to the Standards for the Professional Practice of Internal Auditing.

There are three levels of guidance statements. Level I (mandatory) guidance consists of core materials such as the definition of internal auditing, the Code of Ethics and the Standards for the Professional Practice of Internal Auditing. Level II (authoritative) guidance statements comprise practice advisories on various topics related to internal auditing, including Standard interpretations and applications in specific internal auditing environments. Level III guidance statements are development and practice aids, which include research studies, books and seminars.

LEARNING OBJECTIVE 1

Define internal auditing and describe its objectives and scope.

A definition of internal auditing

The Institute of Internal Auditors defines internal auditing as:

> ... an independent, objective assurance and consulting activity designed to add value and improve an organisation's operations. It helps an organisation accomplish its objectives by bringing a systematic, disciplined approach to evaluate and improve the effectiveness of risk management, control, and governance processes.

Several parts of this definition merit comment.

- 'Internal' indicates that such auditing is carried on within an organisation by employees of the organisation or by personnel contracted for the purpose.
- 'Independent and objective' suggests that internal auditing is an activity carried out without bias or prejudice, with unrestricted access to people, records, facilities and products. In undertaking the function, the internal auditor's judgements are not subordinated to those of management.
- 'Assurance and consulting activity designed to add value and improve operations' notes that the internal auditing function provides a certain level of assurance for subject matters that assist in better management decisions and operations. The activity is wide ranging and includes functions that are advisory or task oriented, the performance of which contribute to the overall value of the business by improving the efficiency of operations and the quality of management decisions.

- 'A systematic, disciplined approach to evaluate and improve the effectiveness of risk management, control and governance processes' refers to the structure and approach of internal auditing. The nature of internal auditing involves a search for facts and a systematic process of evaluating the results of operations, identifying risks, assessing the adequacy of controls, implementing improvements in control procedures and ensuring an effective governance structure.

The evolution of internal auditing

Internal auditing began as a one-person clerical function that consisted of primarily the independent verification of bills before payment. Over the years, it has evolved into a highly professional activity that extends beyond the appraisal of the efficiency and effectiveness of an entity's operations. Internal auditing has become a function that evaluates and improves an organisation's risk management, control and governance processes to add value to the organisation. These changes affect the efficiency and effectiveness of all phases within an organisation and are a governance process in themselves.

The growth and importance of internal auditing have led to the formation of an international professional organisation, which provides greater recognition for internal auditing and increases its status as a professional activity. The Institute of Internal Auditors (IIA) was incorporated in New York in 1941 and is now a worldwide organisation, with local chapters in over 100 countries. It is administered through regional groupings. National institutes have also been formed in some countries. In Australia, the first chapter of the IIA was established in Sydney in 1952. A national institute, the Institute of Internal Auditors — Australia (IIAA), was formed in 1986. It currently has seven chapters and a sub-branch. The IIAA is one element in the IIA's South Pacific region, which includes New Zealand, Papua New Guinea and the South Pacific Islands.

The IIA administered its first Certificate of Internal Auditor's Examination in 1972. The examination focuses on the knowledge and ability of the candidates in respect to the current practice of internal auditing. It consists of four parts:

1. *Internal audit process* (auditing 65–75 per cent; professionalism 10–20 per cent; fraud 10–20 per cent): The focus is on the theory and practice of internal auditing.
2. *Internal audit skills* (problem solving and evaluating audit evidence 45–60 per cent; data gathering, documentation and reporting 25–40 per cent; sampling and mathematics 10–20 per cent): The emphasis is on skills necessary to the practice of internal auditing.
3. *Management control and information technology* (management control 30–40 per cent; operations management 10–20 per cent; information technology 45–55 per cent): The focus is on business disciplines essential to the practice of internal auditing.
4. *The audit environment* (financial accounting 30–40 per cent; finance 20–30 per cent; managerial accounting 20–30 per cent; regulatory environment 10–20 per cent): This part covers the traditional topical areas such as finance, economics and financial accounting.

To become a certified internal auditor (CIA), an individual must pass the examination and have a minimum of two years experience as an internal auditor (or equivalent). Auditing experience in public accounting qualifies as work experience in internal auditing. To retain the CIA certificate, the individual must comply with the IIA's Standards and Code of Ethics. Although the CIA examinations concentrate on internal auditing, many of the principles are similar to those of external audits.

PROFESSIONAL ENVIRONMENT **Skills gap for internal auditors**

The role of internal auditor is changing rapidly. Internal auditing no longer means implementing systems and controls. Technology has brought with it a whole new set of issues for internal auditors to wrestle with: e-business, Internet/intranet security and information technology disaster recovery to name a few.

In May 2000, Arthur Andersen conducted a survey of sixty heads of internal audit of FTSE250 companies in the United Kingdom. The resulting report details the 'skills gap' internal audit departments face in dealing with information technology risks, as well as demonstrating a surprising lack of appetite among these departments for technological tools.

The survey confirms the trend of technological revolution. The largest single issue faced by 70 per cent of the responding heads of internal auditing is the significant increase in e-business activities. The survey found that 47 per cent of heads of internal auditing believe they have inadequate levels of information technology audit skills to meet their business' needs. Recruitment and retention of staff with these skills is one of the major challenges facing the profession over the next several years. The companies surveyed believe that only 38 per cent of the skills shortages will be closed by the use of specialist outside consultants. The remainder of the gap will be addressed through hiring, training and secondments.

The most widely used technological tools among internal audit departments are best practice databases and data analysis tools (69 per cent and 61 per cent respectively). Only 11 per cent of internal audit departments use data mining tools and only 13 per cent use electronic voting software. Companies' spending on internal auditing compared with that on external auditing is increasing, however. In 1998 the average ratio was 1.49 times more on internal than external auditing, but now it is 2.2 times.

(Source: Adapted from Arthur Andersen, 'Internal audit and technology in the new economy', (May 2000). See web site: www.arthurandersen.com)

The objectives and scope of internal auditing

The objective of internal auditing is to assist members of an organisation in the effective discharge of their responsibilities. In meeting this objective, internal auditing provides analyses, appraisals, recommendations, counsel and information concerning the activities that have been audited. The objectives of internal auditing include minimising risks and promoting effective governance and control throughout the organisation at a reasonable cost.

The scope of internal auditing should encompass the examination and evaluation of (a) the adequacy and effectiveness of the organisation's governance and internal control structure, and (b) the quality of performance in carrying out assigned responsibilities. Internal auditors should:

- review the reliability and integrity of financial and operating information and the means used to identify, measure, classify and report such information;
- review the systems established to ensure compliance with those policies, plans, procedures, laws and regulations that could have a significant impact on operations and reports, and determine whether the organisation is in compliance;

- assess risks within the business operations and those from outside the business which may affect the ongoing wellbeing of the enterprise as a whole;
- review the means of minimising risks and assist management in risk management processes;
- appraise the economy and efficiency with which resources are employed;
- review operations or programs to ascertain whether they are being carried out as planned, and whether results are consistent with established objectives and goals.

The last two activities relate to operational auditing. Internal auditing carries out its activities under the policies established by management and the board of directors of the organisation.

The purpose, authority and responsibility of internal auditing is usually formalised in a document (charter). The charter is normally drawn up in accordance with the needs of the organisation and should (1) clarify the purpose of the internal audit department, (2) specify the unrestricted scope of the work and (3) state that internal auditors have no authority or responsibility for the activities they audit. A survey conducted by Mathews, Cooper and Leung in 1995, however, indicated that 18 per cent of internal auditing units were still operating without the guidance of a formal charter.[1]

2 LEARNING OBJECTIVE

State the source and nature of Standards for the Professional Practice of Internal Auditing.

Standards for the Professional Practice of Internal Auditing

The IIA's board of directors voted in June 1999 to approve a new definition of internal auditing and a new Professional Practice Framework (PPF). Both were based on the recommendations of the Guidance Task Force, which was a special committee of the IIA charged with examining the adequacy of the existing Standards and guidance for the practice of internal auditing. The task force concluded that a significant gap existed between the existing Standards and current practice, and that a new framework was needed to carry the profession into the twenty-first century.

The newly adopted framework (Figure 17.1) calls for the development of three sets of Standards: attribute Standards, performance Standards and implementation Standards. Compliance is prescribed in the introduction to the Standards. Recognition is given to the international nature of the practice and membership of the profession.

FIGURE 17.1

Professional practices framework

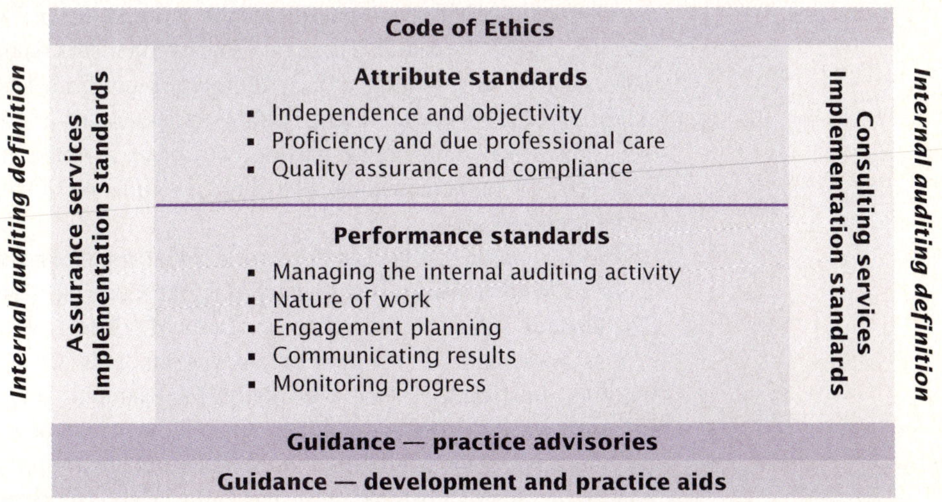

(Source: Institute of Internal Auditors)

The responsibility for compliance rests with the entity's head of internal audit, now called the Chief Audit Executive (CAE) — a new designation introduced by the performance Standards. The CAE is the person responsible for overseeing the entire internal audit service. He or she should be a member of the organisation's management, with a position of sufficient authority to ensure that the results of auditing activity are communicated to appropriate parties, that the internal auditing activity yields maximum value to the organisation, and that appropriate follow-up action has been taken.

Compliance is also required by the Standards in the Code of Ethics. All members agree to 'read and abide by the Code of Ethics' when they sign their membership application form.

Structure of the Standards

Internal auditing activities are performed in diverse legal and cultural environments, within organisations that vary in purpose, size and structure, and by persons within or outside the organisation. These differences may affect the practice of internal auditing in each environment. Thus, compliance with the Standards for the Professional Practice of Internal Auditing is essential if internal auditors are to meet their responsibilities. The purpose of the Standards is to:

1. delineate basic principles that represent the practice of internal auditing as it should be;
2. provide a framework for performing and promoting a broad range of value-added internal auditing activities;
3. establish the basis for the measurement of internal auditing performance;
4. foster improved organisational processes and operations.

The Standards for the Professional Practice of Internal Auditing are undergoing major revision. Exposure drafts have been issued and are available in English, Spanish and French. (Comments on the first set of Standards in exposure drafts closed on 20 September 2000, with part of the new Standards published in January 2001.)

The Standards consist of attribute Standards (the 1000 series), performance Standards (the 2000 series) and implementation Standards (still being prepared at the time of publication). The attribute Standards address the characteristics of organisations and individuals performing internal audit services. The performance Standards describe the nature of internal audit services and provide quality criteria against which the performance of these services can be measured. These two sets of Standards (summarised in Table 17.1 on page 635) apply to any assurance or auditing work performed by internal auditors. Implementation Standards that are unique to either an assurance or consulting engagement have also been developed. Thus, there will be one set of attribute and performance Standards and two sets of implementation Standards — one set for assurance work and one for consulting services.

The Standards are part of the professional practices framework (Figure 17.1), which includes the definition of internal auditing, the Code of Ethics, the Standards and guidance. The Code of Ethics calls for high standards of honesty, objectivity, diligence and loyalty.

It is reasonable to state that the above Standards are similar to those for independent auditors. Independence and objectivity, for example, are paramount to the discharge of internal auditing activities, and internal auditors should be free from interference in accomplishing their responsibilities. Internal auditors should possess the knowledge, skills and competencies needed to perform individual responsibilities. They should apply the care and skill expected of a reasonably prudent and competent internal auditor.

TABLE 17.1

Attribute and performance standards of the IIA

Attribute Standards	Performance Standards
1000 Purpose, Authority and Responsibility of Internal Auditing Activity	2000 Managing the Internal Auditing Activity
1100 Independence and Objectivity	2010 Planning
1110 Organisational Independence	2020 Communication and Approval
1120 Individual Objectivity	2030 Resource Management
1130 Impairments to Independence or Objectivity	2040 Policies and Procedures
1200 Proficiency and Due Professional Care	2050 Coordination
1210 Proficiency	2060 Reporting to Board and Senior Management
1220 Due Professional Care	2100 Nature of Work
1230 Continuing Professional Development	2110 Risk Management
1300 Quality Assurance and Compliance	2120 Control
1310 Assessment of the Quality Assurance Program	2130 Governance
1320 Internal Assessments	2200 Engagement Planning
1330 Independent Reviews	2210 Engagement Objectives
1340 Reporting on Quality Assurance and Compliance	2220 Engagement Scope
1350 Use of 'Conducted in accordance with the Standards'	2230 Engagement Resource Allocation
1360 Disclosure of Non-compliance	2240 Engagement Work Program
	2300 Performing the Engagement
	2310 Identifying Information
	2320 Analysis and Evaluation
	2330 Recording Information
	2340 Engagement Supervision
	2400 Communicating Results
	2410 Criteria for Communicating
	2420 Quality of Communications
	2430 Engagement Disclosure of Non-compliance with the Standards
	2440 Disseminating Results
	2500 Monitoring Progress
	2510 Management's Acceptance of Risks

Note: Embedded within the Standards are individual statements (with the prefix 'A') concerning assurance engagements.

The CAE should develop and maintain a quality assurance program designed to achieve compliance with the Standards and the Code of Ethics. The program should provide assurance that the internal auditing activity adds value and improves the organisation's operations. Further, the internal auditing activity's compliance with the Standards should be evaluated at least once every five years by a qualified, independent, external reviewer, using appropriate guidelines and tools.

The relationship between internal and external auditors

There is usually a close relationship between internal auditors and an entity's outside independent auditors. The work of internal auditors may be a supplement to, but not a substitute for, the work of independent auditors in a financial report audit. One of the responsibilities of the CAE is to coordinate the work of internal auditors with the work of the external auditor. It is not uncommon for the external auditor to review the internal auditing department's planned work program for the year to minimise duplication of effort or to seek direct assistance during a financial report audit (as explained in Chapter 4). AUS 604 (ISA 610), Considering the Work of Internal Auditing establishes standards and provides guidance to external auditors on obtaining an understanding of the activities of internal auditing and its effect on audit risk.

Although they have a close working relationship, internal and independent auditors have important differences, as outlined in Table 17.2.

TABLE 17.2

Organisational and functional differences between internal and independent auditors

	Internal auditors	Independent auditors
Employer	Companies and government units	Public practice entities
National organisations	IIAA	• Institute of Chartered Accountants in Australia (ICAA) • CPA Australia
Certifying designation	Certified internal auditor (CIA)	• Chartered accountant (CA) • Certified practising accountant (CPA)
Licence to practise	No	• Registered company/ independent auditor • Public practising certificate
Primary responsibility	To board of directors	To members
Scope of audits	All activities of an organisation	Primarily financial reports

Independent auditors are contractors. They provide a service for a fee and are independent from the entity they audit. In contrast, internal auditors work in a staff capacity, although they are independent from the rest of the entity. They report to the board of directors directly or its audit committee. Sometimes, the internal audit function is outsourced. In these instances, an independent auditor usually performs the internal audit function. In the study by Mathews, Cooper and Leung, 57 per cent of the chief executive officers surveyed reported that their organisations regularly outsourced some area of internal audit function. The study also showed that a significant portion of the outsourcing work was being obtained by the organisation's independent auditor.[2] Sometimes, concerns are expressed about the independence issue if the same audit practice is conducting both functions, as noted in AUS 604.08 (ISA 610):

> Internal auditing is part of the entity. Irrespective of the degree of internal auditing's autonomy and objectivity, it cannot achieve the same degree of independence as required of the external auditor when expressing an opinion on the financial report. The external auditor has sole responsibility for the audit opinion expressed, and that responsibility is not reduced by any use made of internal auditing. All judgements relating to the audit of the financial report are those of the external auditor.

AUP 32 Audit Independence states that:

> The provision of internal audit services by the external auditor of the same entity may place at risk the perception of the independence of the external auditor from the perspective of financial report users and other interested parties. ... For each engagement, the external auditor should not assume the role of management when undertaking internal audit services and any recommendations made by the auditors are for the implementation by management, rather than by the auditor. The external auditor should not accept any internal audit engagement which involves the auditor becoming part of the entity's internal control structure relating to the preparation of financial report information.

Graphically, the scope of the work of the independent auditor can be presented as a horizontal line. He or she primarily focuses on historical information when issuing an opinion on an entity's financial report. In contrast, there is no limit to the scope of work of the internal auditor, which may be presented as a vertical line. Internal auditors are concerned with the economy, efficiency and effectiveness of an entity's operational procedures and activities. The work is future oriented. However, both independent and internal auditors audit for compliance with (1) the control policies and procedures of an entity, (2) regulations and (3) the procedures necessary to safeguard the entity's assets. In these areas, the independent auditor relies on the work performed by internal auditors.

Independent audit reports have a standard format and audit opinions expressed are in accordance with specified circumstances. They are also widely distributed to members and third parties. In contrast, internal audit reports are distributed to primarily management and the audit committee, and their format varies considerably, depending on the nature of the audit being undertaken.

OPERATIONAL AUDITING

Operational auditing has been used in the past to evaluate a variety of activities that include management's performance, management's planning and quality control systems, and specific operating activities and departments. As suggested by its name, this type of auditing pertains to an entity's non-financial operations. It is the systematic process of gathering evidence to ascertain whether a process or operation is effectively and efficiently run.[3]

Internal auditors generally conduct operational audits of non-government units, although independent auditors are sometimes engaged.

3 LEARNING OBJECTIVE

Define operational auditing and describe the phases of an operational audit.

A definition of operational auditing

The IIA defines operational auditing as:[4]

> ... a systematic process of evaluating an organisation's effectiveness, efficiency and economy of operations under management's control, and reporting to appropriate persons the results of the evaluation along with recommendations for improvement.

The essential parts of this definition are as follows:

- 'Systematic process' refers, as in the case of a financial report audit, to a logical, structured and organised series of steps or procedures. This aspect includes proper planning, as well as obtaining and objectively evaluating evidence pertaining to the activity being audited.

- 'Evaluating an organisation's ... operations' is a process that should be based on established or agreed-upon criteria. In operational auditing, the criteria are often expressed in terms of performance standards established by management. However, in some cases, a government agency or industry may set the standards. These criteria frequently are less clearly defined than the criteria used in financial report audits. Operational auditing measures the degree of correspondence between actual performance and the criteria.
- 'Effectiveness, efficiency and economy of operations' refers to the primary purpose of operational auditing, which is to help the management of the audited organisation to improve this effectiveness, efficiency and economy. Thus, operational auditing focuses on the future, in direct contrast to a financial report audit, which has a historical focus.
- 'Reporting to appropriate persons' is about reporting to management or the individual or agency that requested the audit. Except when the audit is requested by a third party, the distribution of the report remains within the entity. In most cases, the board of directors or its audit committee receives copies of operational audit reports.
- 'Recommendations for improvement' are one of the most challenging aspects of this type of auditing. Unlike a financial report audit, an operational audit does not end with a report on the findings, but extends to making recommendations.

Phases of an operational audit

There are more phases in an operational audit than in a financial report audit. Figure 17.2 shows the similarities and differences in the phases between these two types of audit. We will explain each phase of an operational audit in the following sections.

FIGURE 17.2

The phases of financial report and operational audits

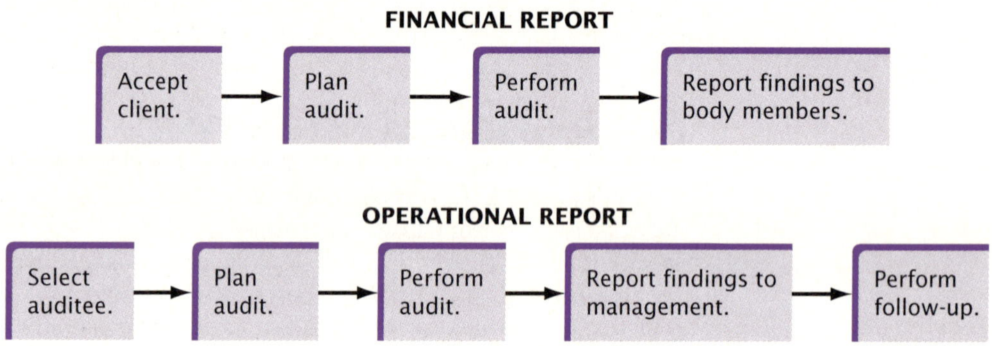

Selecting an auditee

Like many other activities within an entity, operational auditing is usually subject to budgetary or economic constraints. It is important, therefore, to put the resources for operational auditing to the best use. Selecting the auditee begins with a preliminary study (or survey) of potential auditees within an entity, to identify the activities that have the highest audit potential in terms of improving the effectiveness, efficiency and economy of operations. In essence, the preliminary study is a screening process that results in a ranking of potential auditees.

The starting point of the preliminary study is to obtain a comprehensive understanding of the entity's organisational structure and operating characteristics. In addition, the auditor should be knowledgeable about the industry in which the entity operates, and the nature and extent of applicable government regulations. Attention is next focused on the activity, unit or function that could be audited (referred to hereafter as the 'auditee'). The auditor obtains an understanding of the potential auditees by:

- reviewing background file data on each auditee;
- touring the auditee's facilities to ascertain how auditee objectives are accomplished;

- studying the relevant documentation about the auditee's operations (such as policies and procedure manuals, flow charts, performance and quality control standards and job descriptions);
- interviewing the auditee manager about specific problem areas (often called the 'entry interview');
- applying analytical procedures to identify trends and unusual relationships;
- conducting mini-audit probes (or tests) to confirm or clarify the auditor's understanding of potential problems.

The auditor should document his or her understanding of each auditee through completed questionnaires, flow charts and narrative memoranda. Based on this understanding, the auditor prepares a preliminary study report (or memorandum) which summarises the findings and includes a recommendation as to the auditee(s) that should be audited. The report is for the exclusive use of the internal auditing department. It is not a report for management.

Planning the audit

Careful audit planning is essential to both the effectiveness and efficiency of an operational audit. Planning is especially critical for this type of audit, given the diversity of operational audits. The cornerstone of audit planning is the development of an audit program. The program must be tailored to the circumstances found in the auditee in the preliminary study phase of the audit. As in the case of a financial report audit, the audit program contains a set of procedures designed to obtain evidence pertaining to one or more objectives. The evidence examined is usually based on samples of data. Thus, consideration should be given in audit planning to the use of statistical sampling techniques. In addition, the auditor should recognise when computer-assisted techniques will be cost efficient.

Audit planning also includes selecting the audit team and scheduling the work. The audit team must include auditors who have the technical expertise needed to meet the audit objective(s). The work should be scheduled in consultation with the auditee to obtain the maximum cooperation from the auditee's personnel during the audit.

Performing the audit

During the audit, the auditor makes an extensive search for facts pertaining to the problems identified in the auditee during the preliminary study. Undertaking the audit is the most time-consuming phase of an operational audit. This phase is often referred to as 'making the in-depth audit'.

In an operational audit, the auditor relies on primarily inquiry and observation. A common approach is to develop a questionnaire for the auditee and to use it as a basis for interviewing auditee personnel. Based on these inquiries, the auditor expects to obtain opinions, comments and suggested solutions to the problems. Effective interviewing is indispensable in an operational audit. Through his or her observation of auditee personnel, the auditor may be able to detect inefficiencies and other conditions that are contributing to the problem(s).

The auditor must also use analysis in an operational audit. This involves the study and measurement of actual performance in relation to some criteria. The criteria may be internally developed by the entity (such as stated productivity goals and budgets) or externally generated (in the form of industry standards or derived by the auditor from previous audits of similar activities). Analysis provides a basis for determining the degree to which the auditee is meeting specified objectives.

The work done, the findings and the recommendations should be documented in working papers. As in a financial report audit, the working papers represent the primary support for the auditor's report. The audit senior (or auditor in charge) normally has the responsibility for reviewing the working papers both during and on completion of the examination. Reviews during the audit are helpful in monitoring progress, whereas the review at the end of the audit ensures the overall quality of the work.

Reporting the findings

The audit report is the final product of an operational audit. It is unique, varying for each auditee. It does not contain the familiar standardised language of an audit report of a financial audit. However, the following are among the common features:

- *A statement of the objectives and scope of the audit* : It is usual to outline the objectives of the engagement in a letter to the auditee. These may include: (1) to document, analyse and report on the status of current operations; (2) to identify areas that require attention; and (3) to recommend corrective action or improvements. The scope of the audit could identify the activities or units being audited and the specific financial and operational conditions to be evaluated.
- *A general description of the work done* : This section of the report will indicate: (1) the personnel interviewed; (2) the specific documents, files, reports, systems and procedures selected for evaluation; (3) the analysis of data; (4) the development of recommendations for improvement; and (5) the discussions held with appropriate unit management personnel. Discussions serve several important purposes, including giving the auditor an opportunity to test the accuracy of the findings and the appropriateness of the recommendations, and enabling the auditor to obtain the auditee's comments for inclusion in the report. The initial draft may be revised.
- *A summary of findings*: All significant findings are included in the report for consideration by readers.
- *Recommendations for improvement* : The recommendations included are, in the judgement of the auditor, likely to improve the operations of the organisation. They may differ in relation to difficulty of implementation, urgency, visibility of benefits and required additional resources (e.g. facilities, equipment and personnel). They may simply suggest the need for further study of the problems.
- *Comments of the auditee* : The inclusion of the auditee's comments is optional. Ordinarily, they are included only when the auditee disagrees with the findings and the recommendations. The auditor's findings are meant to result in constructive criticism, so when writing the report, the auditor should be sensitive to the recipient's reactions. When the language used by the auditor in the report is less threatening, the response of the recipient is likely to be more positive. Ordinarily, copies of operational auditing reports are sent to senior management and to the audit committee.

Performing follow-up work

The **follow-up phase** of an operational audit requires the auditor to follow up on the auditee's response to the audit report. Ideally, the policies of the entity should require the manager of the audited unit to respond to the report in writing within a specified time period. However, the follow-up should extend to determining the adequacy of the measures taken by the auditee in implementing the recommendations. The IIA Standards state that internal auditors should follow up to ascertain that appropriate action has been taken on the report findings. The absence of an appropriate response to the auditor should be communicated to senior management.

The involvement of an independent auditor

Based on their expertise and experience, independent auditors are qualified to perform operational audits. An operational audit engagement is a distinct form of management advisory service. The following observations may be made about operational audits:

- Independent accountants are increasingly being asked to provide this service for both private sector and government clients.
- This type of service provides independent evaluation and advice to boards of directors, senior management and elected officials who are being held to high standards of responsibility and stewardship.
- The experience gained in public accounting in the diagnostic and fact-finding aspects of financial auditing and management advisory services provides an excellent background for performing operational audits.

LEARNING CHECK

17.1 Internal auditing is an independent, objective assurance and consulting activity designed to add value and improve an organisation's operations. It helps an organisation accomplish its objectives by bringing a systematic, disciplined approach to evaluating and improving the effectiveness of its risk management, control and governance processes.

17.2 The IIA professional practices framework (which is being revised) consists of three levels of guidance. Level I (mandatory) consists of core materials: the Definition of Internal Auditing, the Code of Ethics and the Standards for the professional practice of internal auditing. Level I materials are being finalised, following the end of the period for comment on the exposure drafts on 20 September 2000. Level II (authoritative) materials are in development and consist of practice advisories representing best practices. Level III (development and practice) comprises other development materials endorsed by the IIA.

17.3 The Standards consist of attribute Standards, performance Standards (including assurance Standards) and implementation Standards. Detailed implementation Standards applicable to assurance engagements and consulting services performed by internal auditors have also been developed.

17.4 To become a certified internal auditor (CIA), a candidate must pass the CIA examination and have a minimum of two years experience as an internal auditor (or the equivalent). Internal auditors are expected to comply with IIA Standards and the Code of Ethics.

17.5 Irrespective of internal auditing's degree of autonomy and objectivity, it cannot achieve the same degree of independence as that of the external auditor when expressing an opinion on the financial report. There are similarities and differences between the internal auditor and the independent auditor, but both normally complement one another in terms of their scope of work and findings.

17.6 Operational auditing is a systematic process of evaluating an organisation's effectiveness, efficiency and economy of operations. The phases of an operational audit are: (1) selecting the auditee; (2) planning the audit; (3) performing the audit examination; (4) reporting the findings; and (5) undertaking the follow-up.

AUDITORS IN THE PUBLIC SECTOR

Auditing in the public sector is an expanding area of activity. It extends to all tiers (federal, state and local) of government. The principles of auditing theory and practice in the private sector are applicable to auditing in the public sector. However, there are some variations in audit approach, which are primarily due to the different environment in which the public sector entities operate.

4 LEARNING OBJECTIVE

Explain accountability in the public sector.

The requirements of public accountability

A knowledge of the parliamentary system is necessary to comprehend the process of **accountability** in the public sector. Figure 17.3 shows a typical structure of a parliamentary system in a democratic state. (The framework for the Commonwealth Parliament is indicated and discussed hereafter, but the principles also apply at the state level.)

FIGURE 17.3

Outline of a parliamentary system and the accountability process

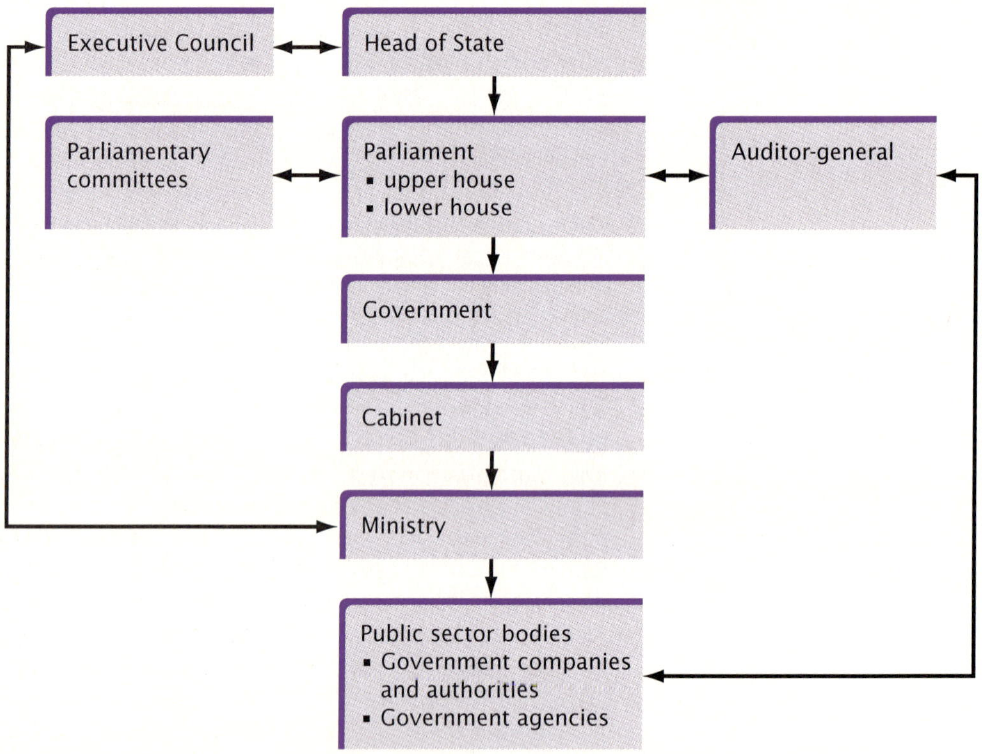

The legislature comprises the head of state (the governor-general in Australia) and the two houses of Parliament — the upper house (the Senate) and the lower house (the House of Representatives). To become law, a legislative Bill has to be passed by both houses.

The party that wins a majority of seats in the lower house performs the role of government. The leader of the majority party is appointed as the prime minister by the head of state. The prime minister chooses members of his or her party to serve as ministers. The government is responsible for policy direction and for the acquisition and allocation of public resources to matters of state. Ministers are responsible for a particular government portfolio and have two roles: (1) as Cabinet members, responsible for the administration of their 'ministry', and (2) as members of the Executive Council in an advisory capacity to the head of state.

Government services are provided through agencies, government authorities and companies or other controlled entities.

- ***Agencies***: Agencies are government departments, parliamentary departments, or prescribed agencies. They are established by proclamation of the head of state. Each department has a chief executive who is responsible to a minister. The minister is responsible for the overall formation of the department's policy and administration. Central agencies comprise the Department of the Prime Minister and Cabinet and the Treasury. Each agency has extensive responsibility for policy advice and direction.
- *Authorities*: A government authority is a body corporate that is created for a public purpose by an Act. The authority is independent of other government operations and may be partly self-funding. Each authority has a governing board or committee whose composition is prescribed in the Act.
- *State-owned companies*: These companies are incorporated in accordance with the Corporations Law in which the state has a controlling interest. They provide essential services and are profit oriented.
- *Controlled entity*: This type of entity is controlled by a government authority or a state-owned company.

The process of accountability starts with Parliament allocating resources to the agencies, approving the terms and use to which these resources are put, and specifying the expected outcomes of the programs or initiatives. The process ends with these agencies reporting back to Parliament on the use of allocated resources, and the results achieved. The auditor-general is the independent auditor who undertakes the audit and reporting function. He or she provides an assurance to Parliament that public resources have been appropriately used. In this regard, parliamentary committees play a crucial role in the accountability process.

5
LEARNING OBJECTIVE
Explain the role of parliamentary committees in the accountability process.

Parliamentary committees

Parliamentary committees are set up by Parliament or by statute for a particular reason. A purpose of the committee may be to review the expenditure of public finances (e.g. the Public Accounts Committee) or to review agency budgets (e.g. the Senate Estimates Committee). A committee may consist of representatives from both houses of Parliament.

In Australia, the committee that examines the reports of the Commonwealth Auditor-General is the Joint Committee of Public Accounts and Audit (JCPAA). This committee comprises members and senators, including the chairperson of the House of Representatives Standing Committee on Expenditure.

The JCPAA owes its existence and authority to the *Public Accounts and Audit Committee Act 1951* (Cwlth) (the PAAC Act). It is the Commonwealth Parliament's watchdog, helping to ensure that government agencies are held to account for their use of public money. The duties of the committee are to:

- examine the accounts of the receipts and expenditure of the Commonwealth;
- examine the financial affairs of Commonwealth authorities and inter-government bodies;
- examine all reports of the auditor-general laid before the houses of Parliament;
- report to both houses of Parliament matters pertaining to accounts, statements and reports which the committee feels should be brought to the attention of the Parliament;
- report desirable alterations to the method of keeping public accounts in the mode of receipt, control, issue or payment of public moneys;
- inquire into matters referred to it by either house of Parliament.

The JCPAA holds public inquiries and examines all the reports of the auditor-general. The auditor-general provides the JCPAA with formal submissions, briefings and information as appropriate. An audit observer (from the Office of the Auditor-General) responsible for the department or body under review is present at all inquiries. The auditor-general (and senior staff) may meet with the committee to discuss the implications of all findings.

Auditor-general

The auditor-general (in both state and Commonwealth spheres) is an independent officer of Parliament who audits and reports to Parliament on the activities and performance of government agencies, authorities, companies and their controlled entities. Independence is an essential attribute, because it lends credibility to the work of the auditor-general. (Hereafter, we will discuss the Commonwealth auditor-general, although the functions of this office at both Commonwealth and state levels is essentially similar.)

The *Auditor-General Act 1997* (Cwlth) provides for the appointment of an auditor-general for the Commonwealth of Australia and defines the functions of the role. The terms and conditions of the auditor-general's appointment and the powers prescribed in the Act support his or her independence.

The auditor-general is appointed by the governor-general on the recommendation of the responsible minister for a term of ten years. The proposed recommendation is initially referred to the JCPAA. On approval by the JCPAA, the proposal is put to the governor-general. This consultative process enhances the independence of the auditor-general.

The auditor-general can be removed from office only under specified conditions. These are:

- if both houses of Parliament in the same parliamentary session request that the governor-general remove the auditor-general on the grounds of misbehaviour or physical or mental incapacity; or
- if the auditor-general becomes bankrupt.

The auditor-general may resign by giving the governor-general a signed resignation notice.

Australian National Audit Office

The Australian National Audit Office (ANAO) is established to assist the Commonwealth Auditor-General carry out his or her functions. The staff of the audit office are persons appointed under the *Public Service Act 1922* (Cwlth). In carrying out the auditor-general's functions, ANAO staff can be directed by only the auditor-general or other staff authorised to give such direction.

The auditor-general's capacity and ability to obtain the required information enhances the independence of the audit. (Information-gathering powers are prescribed by the Act.) The auditor-general has the power to direct a person in writing to provide any information, to attend and give any evidence before the auditor-general (or an authorised official), and to produce any document(s) under his or her control or custody. The auditor-general can obtain information orally, in writing or under oath if necessary. There are significant penalties for providing false and misleading information. The auditor-general also has access to premises occupied by the Commonwealth, a Commonwealth authority or a Commonwealth company. In addition, he or she has free access to any document (or other property) and the right to examine, make copies of, or take extracts from any document.

The auditor-general's freedom of access to relevant premises and documents, and his or her information-gathering powers are not limited by any other law unless expressly stated.

International affiliations

The ANAO is a member of two international audit institutions:

- the International Organisation of Supreme Audit Institutions (INTOSAI);
- the Asian Organisation of Supreme Audit Institutions (ASOSAI).

The INTOSAI was formed in 1953 and has a membership of 170 Supreme Audit Institutions (SAIs). It holds a triennial congress — referred to as the International Congress of Supreme Audit Institutions (INCOSAI) — which is a useful medium for the SAIs to exchange ideas and experiences. The INTOSAI publishes the *International Journal of Government Auditing* and has established committees and working groups to study and report on various issues of interest to members. The regional working groups that promote the interests of INTOSAI are:

- the Organisation of Latin American and Caribbean Supreme Audit Institutions (OLACEFS);
- the African Organisation of Supreme Audit Institutions (AFROSAI);
- the Arab Organisation of Supreme Audit Institutions (ARABOSAI);
- the Asian Organisation of Supreme Audit Institutions (ASOSAI);
- the South Pacific Association of Supreme Audit Institutions (SPASAI);
- the Caribbean Organisation of Supreme Audit Institutions (CAROSAI);
- the European Organisation of Supreme Audit Institutions (EUROSAI).

Audit mandates

Government auditors perform their duties in accordance with **audit mandates**, which specify the type of audit required and what to audit. Audit mandates also state the functions and powers needed to carry out the audit and to report. These mandates are usually embodied in legislation, but in some cases they are determined by arrangement or contract.

The Commonwealth Parliament has passed a number of Acts that provide a legislative framework for the performance, propriety and accountability of Commonwealth entities. These are:

- the *Financial Management and Accountability Act 1997*, which provides for the proper use and management of public money, public property and other Commonwealth resources;
- the *Commonwealth Authorities and Companies Act 1997*, which provides regulations for certain aspects of the financial affairs of Commonwealth authorities, and stipulates rules for reporting and accountability. It also contains reporting requirements for Commonwealth companies in addition to the requirements of the Corporations Law;
- the *Auditor-General Act 1997*, which provides for the appointment of the Commonwealth Auditor-General and sets out the functions of the office.

The auditor-general undertakes financial statement audits and performance audits of Commonwealth agencies, authorities and companies (see below).

6 LEARNING OBJECTIVE

State the assertions, audit objectives and reporting requirements of financial statement audits in the public sector.

Financial statement audits

The audit objective is to express an opinion on the financial statements of the entity under examination. The auditor-general is responsible for financial statement audits of government controlled entities. The financial statements and the auditor's report are included in the annual report of an entity, which is presented to Parliament. In this way, management is held accountable for the entity's performance.

The auditor-general must state whether the financial statements have been prepared in accordance with the orders of the Commonwealth Minister for Finance and whether they give a true and fair view of matters required by those orders. Reasons must be provided if the auditor-general is not of that opinion. The auditor-general must quantify the financial effect where possible, and disclose it if there is non-compliance with the orders of the Minister for Finance.

The auditor-general must report on an exception basis if:

- he or she did not obtain all the necessary information and explanations, stating the particulars of the shortcomings;
- proper accounting records have not been kept;
- records have not been retained for at least seven years;
- records have not been made available for inspection.

For consolidated financial statements, the auditor-general must report:

- the name of a subsidiary for which he or she has not acted as an auditor or audited the financial statements;
- whether he or she has not examined those financial statements and the auditor's report on them;
- the name of the subsidiary for which the financial statements have been qualified;
- the deficiency, if the financial statements were not appropriate for consolidation;
- whether there was any deficiency in the procedures and methods used in arriving at amounts for consolidation.

In undertaking financial statement audits, the government auditor determines audit objectives on the basis of assertions that we discussed in Chapter 5, restated here:

- *Existence or occurrence* : An asset or liability exists and pertains to the entity at a given date. A transaction or event took place which pertains to an entity.
- *Rights and obligations*: The beneficial ownership of assets or a liability is incident on the entity.
- *Completeness* : There are no unrecorded assets, liabilities or transactions.
- *Valuation or measurement*: An asset or liability is recorded at the appropriate value. A transaction is recorded in the proper amount and in the correct period.
- *Disclosure* : An item is identified, classified, disclosed and described in accordance with acceptable accounting policies and applicable legal requirements.

One important consideration in the audit of government agencies is the legal framework within which the agencies exist. Another is the standard of probity and propriety (ethics) expected of public officials. The following additional assertions relate to these features:

- *Compliance* : The agency complies with all relevant legislation and financial and other administrative directives of the executive and Parliament. Compliance pertains to applicable legislation, applicable administrative requirements, ministerial directives and financial directives or agreements.
- *Probity*: There is no material fraud or dishonesty in management actions.
- *Propriety*: Management decisions and actions are appropriate in regard to the stewardship of public moneys.

7 LEARNING OBJECTIVE

Describe the nature of performance auditing.

Performance auditing

The ANAO defines a performance audit as:[5]

> ... an independent and systematic examination of the management of an organisation, program or function for the purposes of:
> - forming an opinion about:
>   - —whether the organisation, program or function is being managed in an economical, efficient and effective manner;
>   - —the adequacy of internal procedures for promoting and monitoring economy, efficiency and effectiveness;
> - suggesting ways by which management practices, including procedures for monitoring performance, might be improved.
>
> It may include a review of:
> - the use of human, financial and other resources;
> - information systems, performance measures and monitoring arrangements;
> - procedures followed by entities for remedying identified deficiencies.

The objective of a performance audit of a Commonwealth public sector entity is to provide assurance to Parliament, the executive, boards, management and the community on the economy, efficiency and effectiveness of that entity's administration. Performance auditing does not involve a review of government policy decisions. Such a review impinges on the role of the executive and Parliament. Auditors, may however, examine actions taken in the course of administering a program, then review information leading to policy decisions.

The terms 'economy', 'efficiency' and 'effective' are defined in AUS 806, Performance Auditing as follows:

- 'Economy' is the acquisition of the appropriate quality and quantity of resources at the appropriate times and at the lowest cost.
- 'Efficiency' is using resources to maximise output for a given input, or to minimise input for any given quantity and quality of output.
- 'Effectiveness' refers to the achievement of the objectives or other intended results of operations, programs or activities.

The auditor-general has a mandate to conduct a performance audit of all government agencies, authorities and companies other than government business enterprises. For government business enterprises, performance audits may be undertaken by the auditor-general where requested by the relevant minister, the Minister for Finance or the JCPAA. General performance audits are concerned with common aspects of administration (e.g. the use of government credit cards, protective security measures, the procurement of resources, and fraud prevention and detection). Such audits are conducted in more than one entity, with particular operational aspects examined across a number of entities. These are therefore distinguished from the performance audits of an individual entity.

Phases of a performance audit

We will now describe the steps of performance auditing in the public sector. These are identical to operational auditing described earlier. Although operational and performance auditing have a common ground, we will emphasise the peculiar features of public sector entities in terms of performance auditing.

The size of a department or agency generally precludes an overall performance audit. Thus, performance audits generally focus on a function, activity, program or operation of an auditee. The major steps in a performance audit are:

- selecting an auditee;
- planning the audit;
- performing the audit;
- reporting on the audit;
- following up.

Selecting an auditee

Care should be exercised in choosing an activity or operation for audit, so as to select those that will yield the most benefit in terms of economy, efficiency and effectiveness. During the selection process, the auditor should consider the materiality of a specific program or operation, the complexity or diversity of its systems (or recent changes to its systems), possible control weaknesses or inefficient practices, evidence of deficiencies, public interest as indicated by parliamentary debates and media coverage, political sensitivity or perceived national importance of the program.

An auditee may be identified by a preliminary study, of which the objective is to become familiar with the auditee's objectives, organisational structure, operating facilities, control systems, operational activity and personnel. The preliminary study will aid in audit planning and assist the auditor in deciding whether to continue with the audit. In undertaking the preliminary study, the auditor should:

- review legislative, ministerial or policy documents;
- assess if objectives are measurable and determine if any performance measures are in use;
- review operations, procedures and resources to obtain an understanding of administrative processes;
- identify performance indicators and determine if these are valid;
- identify any external constraints that prevent objectives being achieved.

An outcome of a preliminary study is a recommendation to either proceed with or terminate the audit. If the decision is to proceed, discussions are held with the auditee to explain the scope and objectives of the performance audit. If the decision is not to proceed, the results of the preliminary study may be reported to Parliament. Sometimes, a performance audit may be undertaken in response to a request by the Parliament or the JCPAA, or as a result of findings of other audits undertaken by the ANAO.

Where a preliminary study has not been undertaken, the auditor seeks an opening interview with appropriate senior personnel of the auditee. The ANAO stipulates that the objectives of this interview are to:

> - allow the audit team to meet key staff of the audited body;
> - further explain the type of audit to be conducted, and the objectives, scope, timing and methods to be employed;
> - provide an opportunity for the audited body to comment/make suggestions for ANAO consideration;
> - establish suitable liaison arrangements at both the management and working levels, including arrangements for progressive advice and discussion of tentative findings;
> - ensure the audited body clearly understands the audit processes, including the description of access powers and safeguards on confidentiality;
> - outline the responsibilities of the audited body and clarify any queries or misunderstandings;
> - make administrative arrangements for the audit team, such as office accommodation, access to buildings, personnel, files, systems and data.[6]

Planning the audit

An audit plan should:

- identify the auditee, the activity and the functional areas on which the audit will focus;
- specify audit objectives and determine the audit scope (boundaries) and issues to be examined;
- establish time budgets and allocate staff resources. Staff should have the required expertise and sufficient experience to undertake the audit. There may be a need to use a multidisciplinary team;
- specify the use of consultants or experts. If the required expertise is not available in-house, then consultants or other auditee assistance may be hired;
- consider using auditee staff as part of the audit team during the planning phase. However, the impact of the auditee assistance on independence must be considered;
- identify an audit method. The use of statistical sampling techniques and computer-assisted audit techniques may be considered;
- arrange for progress reviews of the audit;
- set the completion date and reporting requirements.

During the planning phase, the auditee management is informed in writing of the type of audit to be conducted, and of the timing and duration of the audit. Details are also provided about the audit team and the contact person.

Performing the audit

Performing an audit may involve establishing audit criteria, obtaining evidence and analysing audit findings. Audit criteria consist of standards against which auditee representations may be evaluated. They may be obtained from previous audit files or from other performance audits. Alternatively, they may be developed from various sources such as enabling legislation, entity operating and procedure manuals, agency policies, directives and guidelines, ANAO publications and publications of private sector auditors.

Evidence must be gathered as outlined in the audit work program. This should be relevant to stated audit objectives and meet acceptable audit standards. Evidence obtained during a preliminary survey forms part of the total evidence gathered for the examination phase of the audit.

Audit findings are evaluated against criteria developed initially. Recommendations for the improvement of such aspects as procedures and systems flow from the evaluation. The development and evaluation of audit findings take place during various phases of the performance audit. The preliminary findings may be discussed on an informal basis with the auditee. If these are challenged, then the auditor may seek further evidence.

Developed findings are then assessed in terms of their cause and effect. Cause forms the basis of the recommendation. There may be several causes of each finding and they may be external to the entity. The effect may be quantitative or qualitative. The effect demonstrates the need for corrective action and justifies a recommendation in cost–benefit terms.

An exit interview is held at the conclusion of an audit. Provisional audit findings are conveyed to the auditee during this interview. The auditee has an opportunity to comment on the audit findings and correct any misunderstandings or misinterpretations. The auditee may also provide additional written comments after the interview. These are considered in the preparation of the proposed audit report.

Reporting on the audit

The ANAO reporting standards specify that the basic purposes of audit reports are to:

- explain clearly the scope and objectives of the audit;
- present findings and conclusions objectively;
- present only findings and conclusions adequately supported by evidence;
- include recommendations for any remedial action and information on the underlying causes;
- present critical comments in perspective and draw out lessons for future improvement;
- identify issues needing further study or consideration;
- recognise management-initiated improvements;
- recognise the views of the audited body and, where appropriate, state reasons for any disagreements by the ANAO.[7]

Performing follow-up work

After the report has been tabled in Parliament, the auditee is expected to implement the auditor's recommendations. This compliance may be followed up through the Department of Finance, parliamentary review or the ANAO.

The auditee is expected to submit quarterly reports through the appropriate minister to the Minister for Finance on corrective action taken in response to the recommendations. The ANAO receives copies of these reports for information. The ANAO may systematically follow up on the audit through an annual review of the auditee's progress in responding to performance audit findings.

Auditing Standards

We considered the Auditing Standards and Auditing Guidance Statements prepared by the Auditing and Assurance Standards Board in Chapter 1. Compliance with these Standards is mandatory whenever an audit or an audit-related service is undertaken. This provides an assurance of a uniform quality of service. Here, we refer to specific Standards applicable to performance audits:

- AUS 806, Performance Auditing;
- AUS 808, Planning Performance Audits.

These Standards are to be read in conjunction with AUS 106, Explanatory Framework for Standards on Audits and Audit-related Services (ISA 120, Framework of ISAs).

Section 24 of the Auditor-General Act requires the auditor-general to set Auditing Standards with which auditors must comply in performing financial statement and performance audits of the Commonwealth public sector. Having regard to the Auditing Standards issued by the Australian Accounting Research Foundation (AARF) and noting the commonality in Standards expected of auditors in both the private and public sectors, the auditor-general determined that the ANAO Standards should incorporate those Codified Auditing Standards and Auditing Guidance Statements issued by the accounting bodies. Accordingly, by notification in Commonwealth Gazette No. GN6 on 11 February 1998, the auditor-general adopted these Auditing Standards (AUSs) and Auditing Guidance Statements (AGSs) as the ANAO Standards.

As the internationally recognised leader in public sector auditing, the INTOSAI issued a set of Auditing Standards in 1992 (revised in 1995). These Standards do not have any mandatory application, but reflect 'best practice' consensus among SAIs.

LEARNING CHECK

17.7 The process of accountability starts with the Commonwealth Parliament making an allocation of resources to agencies and approving the terms of their use. The process ends with agencies reporting back to Parliament on the use of these resources and the results they have achieved. Agencies are government departments, parliamentary departments or prescribed agencies.

17.8 The auditor-general is an independent officer of the Parliament who audits and reports to Parliament on the activities and performance of government agencies, authorities and their controlled entities. Parliamentary committees play a crucial role in the accountability process. The *Auditor-General Act 1997* (Cwlth) sets out the terms and conditions of the appointment of the Commonwealth auditor-general. It also prescribes the role's general functions and powers. The Commonwealth auditor-general performs his or her duties in accordance with audit mandates contained in enabling legislation or determined by arrangement or contract. He or she undertakes financial statement audits and performance audits.

17.9 The purpose of a performance audit is to provide an assurance that an entity's activities have been carried out economically, efficiently and effectively.

17.10 The ANAO Auditing Standards have been notified by the Commonwealth auditor-general in the Commonwealth Gazette. The Auditing Standards (AUSs) and Auditing Guidance Statements (AUGs) were adopted as the ANAO Auditing Standards. The INTOSAI has issued Auditing Standards for the benefit of member SAIs.

SUMMARY

Internal and operational audits are a significant part of the professional practice of auditing. They involve independent and internal auditors. Certain Auditing Standards must be met for each type of audit. The auditor-general is the independent auditor undertaking audits of government agencies and government controlled companies, which are performed in accordance with audit mandates included in relevant Acts. The principal types of audit performed by the auditor-general are financial statement audits and performance audits. The ANAO has adopted the codified pronouncements issued by the AARF as the ANAO Auditing Standards. The INTOSAI has issued Auditing Standards that reflect 'best practice' consensus among SAIs.

KEY TERMS

NOTES

1. C. M. H. Mathews, B. J. Cooper & P. A. Leung, *Profile of Internal Audit in Australia 1995 — The Complete Study*. Deloitte Touche Tohmatsu, Melbourne, 1995.
2. See note 1.
3. Douglas Ziegenfuss, 'The Rebirth of Operational Auditing', *New Accountant* (November/December 1998), pp. 21–4.
4. Darwin J. Casler & James R. Crockett, *Operational Auditing: An Introduction*. Institute of Internal Auditors, Altamonte Springs, Florida, 1982, p. 14.
5. Australian National Audit Office, *General Guidance on the Conduct of Performance Audits*. Canberra, 1998, p. 6.
6. See Note 5, p. 10.
7. See Note 5, pp. 12–13.

FURTHER READING

American Institute of Certified Public Accountants, Special Committee on Operational and Management Auditing, *Operational Auditing Engagements*. New York, 1982.

Auditor General Act 1997 (Cwlth) No. 151, 1997.

Australian National Audit Office, Auditing Standards. Canberra, 1998.

Australian National Audit Office, *General Guidance on Conduct of Performance Audits*. Canberra, 1998.

Australian National Audit Office web site: http://www.anao.gov.au

Commonwealth Authorities and Companies Act 1997 (Cwlth) No. 153.

Financial Management and Accountability Act 1997 (Cwlth) No. 154.

Institute of Internal Auditors, *Professional Internal Auditing Standards: Standards for the Professional Practice of Internal Auditing and Statement of Responsibilities of Internal Auditors*. Florida, 30 June 2000.

Rollason, Berrie, 'The External–Internal Audit Connection', *Australian Internal Auditor* (Vol. 2, No. 3, 1996), pp. 12–13.

APPENDIX 17A

The IIA Code of Ethics — a summary

The purpose of the IIA Code of Ethics is to promote an ethical culture in the profession of internal auditing. A code of ethics is necessary and appropriate for the profession of internal auditing, given that the profession is founded on the trust placed in its objective assurance about risk management, control and governance. The Code of Ethics extends beyond the definition of internal auditing to include two essential components:

1. principles that are relevant to the profession and practice of internal auditing;
2. rules of conduct that describe behavioural norms expected of internal auditors. These rules are an aid to interpreting the principles in practical applications, and are intended to guide the ethical conduct of internal auditors.

The Code of Ethics, together with the IIA professional practices framework and other relevant pronouncements, provides guidance to internal auditors serving others. 'Internal auditors' refers to IIA members, recipients of or candidates for IIA professional certifications, and those who provide internal audit services as defined by the IIA. The Code of Ethics applies to both individuals and entities that provide internal auditing services. Breaches of the code will be evaluated and administered according to by-laws and administrative guidelines.

Internal auditors are expected to apply and uphold the following four principles:

1. integrity
2. objectivity
3. confidentiality
4. competency.

For each of the four principles, rules of conduct apply.

1. *Integrity*

   Perform work with honesty, diligence, and responsibility.

   Observe the law and make relevant disclosures.

   Not be a party to any illegal activity or in acts that are discreditable to the profession.

   Respect and contribute to the legitimate and ethical objectives of the organisation.

2. *Objectivity*

   Not participate in any activity or relationship that may impair unbiased assessments, or in conflict with the interests of the organisation.

   Not accept anything that may impair professional judgement.

   Disclose all material facts, the non-disclosure of which may distort the reporting of activities.

3. *Confidentiality*

   Be prudent in the use and protection of information acquired.

   Not use information for any personal gain or in a manner that is contrary to the law or detrimental to the ethical objectives of the organisation.

4. *Competency*

   Engage in only those services for which one has the necessary knowledge, skills and experience.

   Perform internal auditing services in accordance with the Standards for the Professional Practice of Internal Auditing.

   Continually improve the proficiency and the effectiveness and quality of services.

(Source: Institute of Internal Auditors)

Review questions

17.1 Is internal auditing a management or an accounting function? Explain.

17.2 What is the objective of internal auditing? Is the scope of internal auditing limited to audits of financial information?

17.3 What are the elements of an internal audit? Use an example of an investment company that invests for depositors as trustees.

17.4 What are the roles of the Australian National Audit Office (ANAO)? Obtain the latest ANAO annual report and make a summary. What issues are highlighted?

17.5 What are the differences between a financial statement audit for the public sector and a financial report audit for a business?

Discussion questions

17.1 Is it still true to say that internal auditing is part of internal control within an organisation? Explain your answer.

17.2 How do internal auditors review the governance process of an organisation?

17.3 What are the differences between the independence of an internal auditor and that of an independent auditor? Can an internal auditor be truly independent?

17.4 How do the phases of an operational audit differ from those of a financial report audit?

17.5 How does the notion of 'accountability' apply to public sector auditing?

17.6 What are the duties and powers of the Commonwealth Auditor-General?

17.7 What additional assertions must the Commonwealth Auditor-General consider when performing the audit of a public sector entity?

17.8 What is the meaning of 'economy, efficiency and effectiveness' in performance audits? Provide examples in your answer.

Professional application questions

★ BASIC
★★ MODERATE
★★★ CHALLENGING

17.1 (Role of internal auditing) ★

The managing director of Startrack Software Limited, a new dot.com company listed in the Australian Stock Exchange, received a letter from the company's external auditors which noted:

> We are very concerned that you do not have an internal audit function within your company. The establishment of an internal audit function is a key aspect of any firm's control structure. We recommend that you either set up your own internal audit function or arrange with an accounting firm to perform the work for you.

(continued)

The managing director was unimpressed by this comment. He rang the external auditors and said that Startrack did not need an internal audit function because he trusted all of his employees and he was completely confident that they would not be involved in any fraudulent acts against the company.

Required

Explain to the managing director of Startrack Software why it is important for the company to establish an internal audit function.

17.2 (Reliance on internal audit) ★★

Internal auditors are ethically bound to be honest, objective and diligent in performing their duties. Much of their work relates to the review and testing of internal control structures. Often, it appears to the management of a company that the internal and external audit functions perform a considerable amount of similar work. When management first initiates an internal audit function, it sometimes expects that much of the audit testing required by the external auditors should be eliminated, thereby reducing audit costs.

Required

(a) Explain the factors that determine the usefulness of an internal audit function to the external auditor.

(b) Describe the likely impact, if any, of the existence of an internal audit function on the annual audit fees of the external auditor.

17.3 (Establishment of internal audit) ★★

You are the external audit manager of Oppex Retailer Limited, a large public company. Over the past two years Oppex has expanded rapidly as a result of several acquisitions of smaller entities. The directors have been concerned about their fiduciary role in taking on the responsibility for the newer and much larger group. Last year, on the advice of your firm, Oppex set up an independent audit committee. One of the committee's recommendations was to establish an internal audit department, and the directors have asked your firm to assist by performing the internal audit function on behalf of the company.

Required

(a) Advise the directors of Oppex in relation to the establishment of the internal audit department and your firm's role.

(b) Discuss how the performance of the internal audit function may have an impact on your independence as an external auditor.

(Professional Year Programme of the ICAA — 1998, Advanced Auditing Module — adapted)

17.4 (Operational Auditing) ★★

You are an audit manager in a medium-sized firm of chartered accountants called Price Young. The audit partner in charge of staff development, Felicity Young, has asked you to organise a staff training day on 'operational auditing'. She explains to you that internal audit work has been a significant growth area for Price Young. Many companies in recent years have outsourced their internal audit departments and requested tenders for external contractors. Price Young has been very active and quite successful in tendering for this work.

Felicity says that the lack of knowledge within the firm in relation to operational auditing was a current problem. This area of work has comprised a large amount of the internal audit work the firm has recently won. Consequently, the firm would like you to train the staff on some of the basic concepts of operational auditing, addressing the following questions:

1. What are the similarities and differences between the phases of an operational audit and the phases of a financial statement audit?
2. What is involved in carrying out a preliminary study?
3. What are the key factors in undertaking the examination?
4. What are the essential elements of the report on audit findings?
5. What is the nature and extent of the follow-up carried out for the audit?

Required

Address each of the above questions in preparing your training session 'presentation'.

17.5 (Role of the auditor-general) ★★

The Commonwealth auditor-general is responsible for financial statement audits of Commonwealth agencies, authorities and companies. Some people argue that there is no need for an auditor-general with a monopoly over these types of service. They argue that it would be a much better system if audits of public sector entities were opened up to public tendering.

Required

(a) Describe the role of the Commonwealth auditor-general.

(b) Evaluate the above argument.

17.6 (Performance audit) ★★

You are an audit supervisor at Jones and Partners. The Department of Health has just appointed Jones and Partners to carry out a performance audit on all public, private and repatriation hospitals in New South Wales. The broad objective of the audit is to obtain detailed information on the types of patient using hospitals, by age and sex. The audit will eventually form part of a larger Commonwealth study on hospital use and costs. Its immediate purpose is to help the state government in planning and funding hospital systems, by providing data to be compared against international benchmark standards. The state government plans to place a high level of reliance on the report of Jones and Partners.

Your key contact is Ms Jeffreys, the director-general of the Department of Health. She has arranged for you to obtain full cooperation from the head of each hospital to be included in the audit.

As agreed in your terms of engagement, Jones and Partners will collect the data, audit it and prepare a report on its findings. The report is to be addressed to the director-general and completed within six months.

Required

(a) Discuss the differences (and similarities) between a performance audit and an attest audit carried out on a financial report under the Corporations Law.

(b) Explain the level of assurance that will be expressed in your report to the director-general.

(c) Discuss the type of report to be issued to the director-general.

(Professional Year Program of the ICAA — 1997, Advanced Auditing Module — adapted)

17.7 (Objectives and scope of internal audit) ★★★

You are an audit senior within an accounting firm. Your firm recently won a tender to provide internal audit services to New Nordic Limited, a bakery that specialises in making bread for the restaurant trade. New Nordic operates two bakeries — one in the north of the city and one in the south. Both bakeries also operate a fleet of delivery trucks.

For the past three months, many of New Nordic's customers have been complaining about slower-than-usual delivery times for products. Some customers have had to resort to buying bread from supermarkets when deliveries have not arrived as scheduled.

Management believes the problem is due to a combination of a 50 per cent increase in sales volumes and the outdated manual system used for scheduling deliveries. It has asked you to outline the audit strategy you intend to adopt to investigate and resolve this problem.

Required

Outline the key steps you will undertake in your capacity as internal auditor for this assignment.

(Professional Year Programme of the ICAA — 1997, Advanced Auditing Module — adapted)

Case studies

17.1 (Role of internal audit) ★★★

Parkland Limited is a manufacturer of indoor and outdoor spa pools. It has been operating for a number of years. The managing director of the company, Mr Brad Reed, has always been very conscious about maintaining a good system of internal control within the company. The company has had an internal audit department almost from the time it began operations ten years ago. The department currently comprises the internal audit manager and four internal auditors.

The external auditors have always been very impressed with the internal audit function and have often relied on the work of the internal auditors in the past. After completing the current year's audit, the external auditors raised a concern in their management letter about the amount of non-audit work performed by the internal audit department — it had increased to about 30 per cent of the total hours worked. In the management letter, the external auditors cited some examples of the types of non-audit work that was being performed.

1. The internal audit manager had replaced the financial controller for about four months while she was on long-service leave. The internal audit manager's position was not replaced during this time.
2. The group accountant responsible for the budget consulted heavily with the internal audit department in the preparation of the budget. The group accountant also discussed variances to the budgeted figures in detail with the internal audit department.
3. The bank reconciliation had been a problem for Parkland for a number of years. There were always significant unexplained variances. It was eventually discovered that the cash receipts officer, who also prepared the bank reconciliation, had perpetrated a serious fraud for a number of years. Mr Reed decided that the most sensible approach in future was for the internal audit department to prepare the bank reconciliations.

4. One of the internal auditors was recently involved in the design, installation and initial operation of a new computer system. The auditor was primarily concerned with the design and implementation of internal accounting controls and the computer application controls for the new system. The auditor also conducted testing of the controls during the test runs.

Required

(a) Define objectivity as it relates to the internal audit function.

(b) For each of the above four situations, explain whether the objectivity of Parkland's internal audit department has been materially impaired.

17.2 (Performance audits) ★★★

An International Fisheries Conference was held in the United States some six months ago in response to international concern regarding the status of the world's marine resources. The southern bluefin tuna was a fish species singled out as being under threat due to poor management of catch limits. Approximately 90 per cent of this tuna catch occurs in Australian waters, contributing $50 million per year to Australian gross domestic product and employing several hundred people, directly and indirectly.

As a result of the findings of the conference, the Australian media have been highly critical of the Commonwealth Government's management of fish resources, particularly southern bluefin tuna. The media have highlighted the terms of the United Nations Convention on the Laws of the Sea (UNCLOS), which states that management of fish resources can be removed from a country's control if it can be shown that those resources are not managed in an ecologically sustainable manner. Australia is a signatory to this convention. The disclosure of the terms of UNCLOS has prompted an outcry from local tuna fishing operators, who claim that the government's mismanagement will cost them their livelihood.

The Commonwealth Fisheries Department is responsible for managing southern bluefin tuna stock in Australia. As part of its responsibilities, the department gathers data on stock levels, and issues and monitors fishing licences. It was established under the *Fisheries Administration Act 1991* (Cwlth). Included in the legislated objectives of the department is objective 7, which states that it 'should maximise economic efficiency in the fishing industry while meeting the objective of ecologically sustainable development'.

Given the data revealed at the International Fisheries Conference, the Commonwealth Government is concerned whether the department is achieving this objective. To allay public and industry concerns regarding southern bluefin stocks, the Director of the National Audit Office has engaged your firm to carry out a performance audit on the Commonwealth Fisheries Department.

Your firm's two broad objectives are as follows:

1. Report on the steps that the department is taking to achieve objective 7 in relation to southern bluefin tuna.
2. Provide an opinion as to how effective these steps have been in meeting that objective.

You have held a preliminary meeting with the department's director-general, who told you that the following management strategies are used to achieve objective 7:

- Input controls, which impose restrictions on the type and/or amount of fishing (as a means of limiting catches), include limits on the number of fishing operators and the size and number of vessels.

(*continued*)

- Data maintained at the department include fishing operators by state, and the size and number of vessels. Data are updated annually based on information supplied by the operators.
- Output controls, which directly limit the size of fish catches, include setting quotas and issuing licences that specify the tonnage of each fish species that may be caught.
- The department records the total tonnage permissible per species per year, broken down into state regions. This is reconciled to the tonnage allowed per licence and quotas in each state.
- Stock assessment is conducted, which involves annually estimating the remaining fish stocks (by species). The estimates are used to set the following year's quotas and licence conditions.
- The department records the results of aerial and radar surveys of fish stocks. These surveys are carried out annually in each state.
- Each fishing vessel must maintain logbooks as a condition of the licence. These logbooks detail the type and tonnage of fish caught, the percentage of the catch sold and the price realised for the catch.
- The examination of logbooks (completed on a quarterly basis) to ensure completeness. The data from the logbooks are entered into a database and consolidated to provide information such as total catch and waste levels. The department keeps the logbooks as proof that the licence conditions have been met.
- Investment reports detail the level of investment in the fishing industry overall and the return achieved from this investment.
- Data are maintained on the average cost of each vessel, and then used in calculating the return achieved (using price data obtained from the logbooks). Details as to the cost of each vessel are updated annually based on information supplied by the fishing operators.

Required

(a) Explain what type of audit mandate has established the performance audit of the department.

(b) Identify and discuss the factors that you would consider in assessing the inherent risk and control risk for the performance audit of the department.

(c) List the factors that you would consider in assessing materiality for the performance audit of the department.

(Professional Year Programme of the ICAA — 1998, Advanced Auditing Module — adapted)

chapter 18

PART 6

Future directions

PART 6

This part consists of a single chapter that captures the latest trend in the fields of auditing and assurance, which have continued to evolve. **Chapter 18** reiterates the important development of information technology by alerting readers to advances in financial software and in the mobile Internet. Following the discussion of the principles of independence in Chapter 2, this chapter also reviews the latest developments in the debate of audit independence and the implications of firm restructuring. While quality benchmarking remains a pivotal issue, the introduction of value reporting and the continuing attention drawn to environmental auditing highlight the possibility of more imminent changes in the practice of auditing and assurance.

chapter 18

Contemporary issues in auditing and assurance

Overview

LEARNING OBJECTIVES

After studying this chapter, you should be able to:

1. appreciate the latest developments in financial software and the mobile Internet and their impact on auditors' work
2. describe the current developments in auditor independence
3. discuss the recent restructuring relating to accounting firms
4. review some non-audit benchmarks applicable to auditors
5. define value reporting
6. describe the meaning of and Standards for environmental auditing.

Professional statements

AUSTRALIAN		INTERNATIONAL	
AUS 214	Auditing in a CIS Environment	ISA 401	Auditing in a CIS Environment
AUS 304	Knowledge of the Business	ISA 310	Knowledge of the Business
AUS 902	Review of Financial Reports	ISA 910	Engagements to Review Financial Statements
AGS 1036	The Consideration of Environmental Matters in the Audit of a Financial Report	IAPS 1010	The Consideration of Environmental Matters in the Audit of Financial Statements
AUP 32	Audit Independence		

Over the past couple of decades, the concept of auditing has been changing significantly in response to an increasing public demand for a much broader role of audit and assurance services. As we discussed in Chapter 1, no longer are the traditional audit functions sufficient to define the role and conduct of today's and tomorrow's audit and assurance services. In this last chapter, we will identify additional contemporary issues in the path of this development, looking at how some of the key factors such as information and communication technology and quality benchmarks are having an impact on the work of professional accountants. Major advances in information technology (such as the advent of expert financial software, doing business on the Internet, and new certification standards for electronic commercial activities) are already a feature of accountants' and auditors' work. Furthermore, auditors in both the public and private sectors are increasingly required to report on and review non-financial matters such as environmental compliance and ISO Standards. These new arenas, together with the change in emphasis in traditional auditing practices, have presented the professional accountant with a spectrum of new challenges. In this chapter we will provide a broad overview of the key issues facing auditors in the future, and a brief exploration of current research and developments in the profession.

INFORMATION TECHNOLOGY

LEARNING OBJECTIVE 1

Appreciate the latest developments in financial software and the mobile Internet and their impact on auditors' work.

Information technology is rapidly changing the global business market. It is altering not only the way in which business is conducted, but also the way in which information is accessed. These developments present auditors and accountants with a major challenge. Fundamental to the ability to deal with the pace of change in professional practice is an ability to manage change itself — to capitalise on the opportunities presented, and to recognise real and potential threats.

We dealt with key considerations of information technology and e-commerce elsewhere in this book (see Chapter 16 in particular). Here, we will focus on the advances being made in **financial software** and the **mobile Internet**. By the time this textbook is in the marketplace, auditors will undoubtedly have to deal with other new matters.

Advances in financial software

An organisation's financial systems are the most important software it operates. However, although technological advancements are typically widely reported, developments in financial software are often less publicised. This possibly is fuelled by the traditional perception that financial software — affording a means to record transactions, finalise annual accounts and perhaps to write management reports — is understood by only accountants. The reality is, however, that reliable financial software is crucially important to anyone concerned with managing finances efficiently and effectively, whether they are accountants, financial controllers, managers, business advisers or auditors. It is a prerequisite not only for business success but also for survival, because every organisation now does business by computer. Financial software is needed to keep track of business performance, access significant business data, identify problems, evaluate plans and formulate strategies.

A recent survey conducted of more than 600 chief financial officers of large and small government and private enterprises in Australia and New Zealand over a period of three years (1995–97) identified a continuing high degree of volatility in financial systems.[1] It found that an abnormally high number of organisations were changing their financial software and that many had lowered their expectations as to how long their software would last. The survey results showed, for example, that one third of the market had recently changed its financial system software, and about another third was doing so. Only about one third of the market had remained stable, uncertain about what to do in this regard. The average life span of an organisation's core financial systems was found to be 5.6 years, compared with 7.7 years for previous systems.

This abnormal degree of volatility means that auditors and accountants, to be effective, must not only understand the rationale for changes in clients' financial systems (and the factors that influence such changes) but also appreciate the technological differences they may confront and be able to adjust their advice and approach accordingly. Contemporary organisations need to be able to react sooner, access information more quickly and report it faster.

Information technology has been both a cause and effect of changes that have occurred in the business world over the past ten years or so. There are three major developments, each a consequence of the previous one. Firstly, desktop computers have proliferated to the point that they are now an indispensable business tool. Secondly, these computers have been networked to each other and to larger computers. Thirdly, the focus of larger computers has changed from providing information to a few individuals to providing information across the organisation. As these changes have accelerated, they have demanded more from the technology that spawned them. The whole 'client–server' revolution — the key trend in information technology in the 1990s —was driven by the need for information systems to more closely reflect changed business imperatives. It is simply not possible to use the modern business model with old technology. Businesses and governments need access to timely business information, which can be delivered only by systems that integrate corporate data with end-user systems. It is therefore not surprising that businesses continue to look for new software to satisfy their needs.

The three primary reasons for changes in financial software are:

1. poor support by the software supplier (e.g. in providing expert advice, in supporting the implementation process, and in providing maintenance and upgrading services);
2. outmoded technology (e.g. where the supplier has not kept up to date with technological advances);
3. the supplier going out of business.

An investigation conducted into a range of accounting software (such as ACCPAC and Visual Accounting), including the respective **audit trails**, controls and reporting functions, revealed some shortcomings.[2] Some packages, for example, retained journal data only until they were posted. However, such shortcomings have now been rectified and most systems retain journals for a year or longer. In addition, they now all assign sequential transaction numbers for identification, and print journals in transaction number order. Notwithstanding these recent improvements, some concerns about audit trails and controls still exist.

To provide adequate financial services and audits to clients, professional accountants must be aware of the business needs of their clients (and, therefore, of the limitations and strengths of financial software being used or being considered to meet those needs). Matters that accountants and auditors need to consider can be classified into the following categories:

- clients' business needs in terms of financial software;
- considerations when implementing financial software;
- audit trails in financial software;
- necessary internal control features of financial software.

Here, we will briefly discuss each of these matters.

Clients' business needs in terms of financial software

It is imperative that any financial system be reliable. Auditors must, therefore, be aware when a client's financial software presents problems (such as errors occurring due to functional limitations, a failure to detect errors or, simply, inadequate information being produced from clumsy data processing mechanisms). Quite often, accountants and auditors become involved in providing essential advice for the selection and implementation of financial software. CPA Australia is often contacted by companies for advice on financial packages.

Experience has shown that many organisations make mistakes by opting to use complicated spreadsheet models rather than commonsense. Failure to prioritise their system requirements has meant that some businesses have not focused on the major feature (or limitations) of a financial package. One chief financial officer, for example, chose a complex spreadsheet model with complicated weightings only to discover that the selected package could not import files from various company databases, and that it was very weak in its ability to support multiple operating sites.

What one company considers a key feature may not necessarily be of crucial importance for others. Desirable features include flexible reporting, a single point of data entry, reliability and accessibility by spreadsheet, integrated moduling, end-user access, flexibility in structure, on-line analysis, and the ability to work on different scales or levels of operation. Table 18.1 lists the top ten buying criteria specified by the chief financial officers in Australia, based on one research study.[3]

TABLE 18.1

Top ten buying criteria

Order of importance	Criterion
1	Flexible reporting
2	Single point of data entry
3	Proven reliability
4	Accessible by spreadsheet
5	Integrated modules
6	End-user access
7	Flexible accounts structure
8	On-line analysis
9	Suitable for Australian conditions
10	Scalable

(Source: Graeme Philipson, 'Change at the Coalface', *Accounting Software in Australia*. Australian Society of Certified Practising Accountants (now CPA Australia) 1997, p. 18)

Considerations when implementing financial software

Once financial software is chosen as a prospective purchase (or identified as being preferable), the management of the business should develop a full list of the key issues to be addressed, so all parties concerned can consider them in detail. These parties include the vendor, the accountants, the auditor and other system analysts. The list of issues should be ranked in terms of importance. As we have already stressed in this chapter, flexible and timely financial management information systems are no longer a luxury — they are a necessity.

Factors to consider include those detailed below:

- *Reporting capabilities* : The most important issue for accountants and auditors in their use of financial software is to be able to extract information. This entails consideration of the system's report writing capabilities and, often, the client's executive information system requirements. Another issue is the ability to download data into spreadsheets.
- *Integration with other systems* : It is important that data from client financial systems are able to interface with audit software and other expert analysis systems. Integration facilities may also mean that the financial software can interface with (or extract information from) other operating systems such as inventory control, production management and credit control management files.
- *Flexibility and adaptability* : A financial system must be capable of flexible reporting, conversion or automatic adaptation to new environments such as those that involve different versions of a software, different currencies or multiple applications.
- *User friendly* : Ease of use is crucial to ensure that new software can be taught to and applied by staff (including non-financial personnel) as quickly and easily as possible. End-user requirements should be explained.
- *Timeliness and time pressure*: The new software needs to be able to respond quickly to changing demands and regular reporting requirements such as the end-of-month reporting. It needs also to be able to identify discrepancies quickly and to cope with a high volume of transactions.
- *Accessibility of data* : Different levels of data access must be specified and controlled. There must be ease of interrogation.
- *Expandability and upgradability*: Information technology is continuing to develop rapidly, so all financial software must be capable of future expansion. Its facilities must be able to be upgraded to meet both increasing technological demands and an increasing volume of data processing.
- *Data integrity and security* : The auditor must be satisfied with the physical security and data integrity within the system. They must be built into every phase of the operation and every function. This is the part of the system where audit trails exist and where internal controls are established to maintain the integrity and reliability of the information.
- *Reliability* : The system must be reliable in terms of its hierarchical security options, support mechanisms, information loads and so on.
- *Cost*: The issue of cost involves value for money, ensuring that the software does what is needed and that it provides assurance for future support and maintenance. Other issues that need to be considered are the limitations on existing resources, the implementation cost and budgetary constraints.

Audit trails in financial software

The audit trail is an essential element in ensuring the reliability of financial software. Apart from the considerations we raised in Parts 2 and 3, the auditor needs to be aware of the following issues:

- An audit trail should provide a means of tracing a transaction from its origin to the financial statements, and vice-versa. Establishing a source document field (which accepts the identity of any source document, enabling an authorised user to look up the transaction by referring to that identity) is an additional useful feature. A look-up screen is also helpful for auditors.
- While most accounting software provides a listing of ledgers, some modules still do not have ledgers, preventing the accounting package from transferring all the transactions in accounts receivable, accounts payable and inventory to the general ledger. A continuing

audit trail deficiency is the inability to trace entries easily from the ledger accounts to their original journal source.

- An audit trail that shows the flow of data among the various modules in an accounting package enables the auditor to examine either summary data or subsidiary modules. This depends on the availability of ledger modules and proper referencing or identification. An additional advantage is the possibility of using several modules at the same time, using Windows technology.

Necessary internal control features of financial software

In terms of internal control, the following are some essential features of which auditors must be aware:

- The Windows environment supports only passwords for access controls. The assignment of different passwords to individual users is a better control than a shared task password system. Password systems should require users to select hard-to-guess passwords, preferably with a minimum length of six characters (made up of a combination of alphabetic and numeric characters and other keyboard symbols).
- An ineffective program control exists when accounting software is not written in a compiler-based language. Those failing to use the compiled programming code rely on the programming ignorance of users, which is a risky security method.
- An effective way of protecting data files from exposure to unauthorised entry is to use encryption. However, while it may be an effective safeguard, encryption has drawbacks: firstly, storing encrypted data requires additional space and more processing time, and secondly, the higher the level of encryption, the more costly its implementation.
- Proper input controls ensure data input errors can be detected. Some data filters for account identifiers are code checks and check digits. However, a wrong but valid identification code depends on a visual check of the accuracy of code checks. Therefore, a screen confirmation must be in place to ensure its effectiveness. Check digits should also use audible checks.
- Processing controls can be established with electronic check lists that guide users in the proper sequence of operations. Interim print-outs can be made for checking purposes. Electronic archiving, however, is superior to hard copy, not only because access is easier, cheaper and can be controlled, but also because it is easier to store duplicates in alternative locations for security. A warning should be provided where the sequential checks are violated.
- Other controls — such as output controls, controls over changes to accounts without transactions, and reporting capabilities — are essential concerns for the auditor. Commonly found controls include date–time stamps on output, access logs, authorisation for master file changes, and so on. A reporting capability now being used is the 'drill-down' method. This entails firstly viewing an account balance, 'drilling down' to the details and, after selecting an item in the account, 'drilling down' even further to the underlying journal entry, and then to an on-line image of a transaction document.

Technology continues to change. It is essential, therefore, that auditors possess a general awareness of the contemporary developments in financial software if they are to provide effective advice on the selection and implementation of accounting programs. Financial software suppliers have completely rewritten their systems in recent years to take advantage of new technologies. A few years ago, for example, most practising accountants who used accounting software switched from DOS to the Windows environment. While some DOS accounting products continue to sell at a very modest price, most developers are either no longer updating their DOS products (choosing to continue them for as long as they keep selling) or abandoning them. Development efforts now focus on the Windows platform and some are written in Visual Basic. Demonstrating how fast Windows technology is moving, Microsoft NT is becoming the platform of choice for accounting programs. Developers have recognised that NT has the reliability and robustness needed for applications as mission-critical as accounting processes. At the time of writing, financial software has been developed for enterprise solutions and small business accounting. Other integrated software for customer relationship management (CRM), human resources, manufacturing and e-business has also become mainstream.

The mobile Internet

The Internet is transforming traditional financial practices and services into a range of cheap commercial enterprising activities that are delivered quickly and easily accessed. The Internet provides an information-on-demand medium for electronic trading, the transmission of reports and documents, advanced software access, and virtual designs of goods and services.

Companies can deliver and use knowledge to produce relevant outcomes to suit immediate needs. On-line shopping and trading are already becoming a threat to many traditional market leaders. Chapter 16 provided an account of electronic commercial activity and the role of professional accountants, outlining the risks and issues such as security and certification. In this chapter we will discuss the latest development in the Internet and communication technology — the mobile Internet and the emergence of mobile commerce, (m-commerce).

The world's two fastest growing sectors — mobile technology and the Internet with broadband services — have converged into an opportunity that no organisation can afford to ignore. The revolution is called the mobile Internet, and it will have an immense impact on telecommunication systems, Internet service providers and any organisation wishing to transact in the new information economy. The mobile phone has moved away from being solely a telephony service, towards being a unique personal identifier and assistant. A wireless portal will be the norm for telecommunication systems and, soon, everyone and everything will become 'connected'. Some predict that within three years there will be more wireless connections to the Internet than fixed connections, and that the majority of e-commerce transactions will terminate or originate on a wireless device. A recent KPMG study[4] on the mobile Internet listed examples of the global market trends:

- Of current mobile traffic volume, 3 per cent of second-generation mobile phones already offer basic data services. By 2003, more consumers will access the Internet via mobile phones than by personal computers.
- The market for m-commerce in Europe alone is estimated to be worth 23 million Euro by 2003, compared with a mere 300 million Euro in 1998.
- The popularity of wireless devices for voice communications and the subsequent substitution of fixed telephones will accelerate the adoption of broadband mobile services.
- Mobile Internet-enabled laptops will free people from their desks, creating mobile offices, mobile application hosting and m-commerce.

Mobile Internet applications already exist in countries such as Japan and the United States. Table 18.2 provides a summary of mobile Internet applications on page 670.

TABLE 18.2

Mobile Internet applications

Services	Device	Available in:
Lifestyle applications		
Remote access	E-mail, web browsers, televisions	Australia, Japan, Europe, the United States
Information services	News, weather, stock prices, horoscopes, lottery, sports, train timetables, horse racing, public emergency	Australia, Japan, Europe, the United States
Directory services	Restaurants, film sessions, television programs, hotels, telephone directories, town listings, dictionaries, recipes	Australia, Japan, Europe, the United States
Location-based services	Automatic teller machines, navigators	Australia, Japan, Europe, the United States
Entertainment	Network games, karaoke, gambling, chat, jokes	Japan, Europe, Australia, the United States
Interactive services	Banking, stock trading, ticket booking, on-line shopping, insurance, car rental, billing	Australia, Europe, Japan, the United States
Telematics	Remote automative diagnostics	Europe
Telemetry	Vending machines, ticket machines, car parking	Japan
Mobile professional and business applications		
Videoconferencing	Videoconferencing	Australia (in 2002), Japan
Remote access	E-mail, calendaring, shared scheduling, job postings, procedures manuals, corporate directories, bulletins, document sharing	Australia, Japan, Europe, the United States
Sales force and field automation	Customer account records, contact management, order entry/status, call scheduling, tracking, product/stock availability, delivery scheduling, on-site claims, loan/credit applications, interest rate information	—
Operations and maintenance	Remote machinery diagnostics, fleet tracking	—
E-tailing	Credit card authorisation, debit acceptance, smart cards, electronic funds transfer, identity verification	—

Survival of businesses in the mobile Internet economy will require a redevelopment of vision and a reorientation by businesspeople and managers with respect to the new technology. Speed, critical resource management, a solid customer base, and marketing and personalised services are key ingredients for survival. It is difficult to predict the ultimate impact on the functions of accountants and auditors, but professional accountants need to grasp the ongoing evolution in the role of operating systems such as financial management, customer support, reporting, risks and security measures for m-commercial transactions. Accountants may be required, for example, to provide assurance services in terms of:

- information risk management for clients in their management of technology and the security implications of mobile Internet-enhanced transactions;
- taxation advice on telecommunication operations on a global basis;
- the design, testing and implementation of customer support and billing systems;
- financing decisions in the telecommunication industry, and in any likely mergers and acquisitions.

CURRENT ISSUES OF THE PROFESSION

The independent external audit is a fundamental element of the world's capital market system. A report of the Public Oversight Board of the US Securities and Exchange Commission[5] sums up the importance of the audit function as follows:

> The independent audit fills an essential role for the investing public and creditors by enhancing the reliability of an operation's published financial statements and giving assurance of that reliability to users of those financial statements. Strengthening the professionalism of the auditor requires an environment in which boards of directors and management of client companies have high expectations about the auditing firm's integrity, objectivity and professional expertise in which the auditor, in meeting these obligations recognises an overriding public responsibility.

While the fundamental role of independent auditing has not changed, the profession has witnessed a shift in audit approach, public expectations and the role of auditors, with the broadening perspective of the assurance framework (see Chapter 1). A major response to this shift is the debate on auditor independence, which is a key feature of professionalism (see Chapter 2). In this chapter, we will provide a further update on contemporary issues relating to the profession.

2 LEARNING OBJECTIVE

Describe the current developments in auditor independence.

A framework for auditor independence

In Chapter 2 we discussed (1) the Ruling of Auditor Independence proposed by the US Securities and Exchange Commission in June 2000 and (2) the latest International Federation of Accountants' (IFAC) exposure draft on auditor independence issued around the same time. The Securities and Exchange Commission's proposal, which gave rise to immense objections from the Big Five firms, advocated a restrictive 'independence by appearance' approach; on the other hand, the IFAC proposal adopts a more conceptual approach to auditor independence.

In November 2000 following extensive negotiations with the American Institute of Certified Practising Accountants (AICPA) and representatives of the accounting profession, the Securities and Exchange Commission voted unanimously to adopt amendments to the rules governing relations between independent auditors and clients. The new rules embody a more moderate approach to issues of concern arising from the June 2000 proposal. The amended provisions allow firms to offer two consulting services, information technology consulting and internal auditing, subject to certain restrictions. Except for non-financial, operational audits, an audit firm can, for example, perform as much as 40 per cent of a client's internal auditing. This restriction does not apply to companies with less than $200 million in assets.[6]

In January 2001 the US Independence Standards Board (ISB) also issued an exposure draft for a conceptual framework for auditor independence. The exposure draft contains the concepts and basic principles that will guide the ISB in its future Standard setting. The ISB argues that the need for a framework arose from the confusion and debates about independence rules and regulations (many in the form of interpretations) that apply to public companies and their auditors in the United States. The framework, similar to the IFAC framework that we described in Chapter 2, defines auditor independence and identifies its goals. The ISB model involves three steps: (1) identify threats to the auditor's independence and consider their significance; (2) evaluate the effectiveness of potential safeguards, including restrictions; and (3) determine an acceptable level of independence risk.

Under the ISB framework, the goal of independence is 'to support user reliance on the financial reporting profession and to enhance capital market efficiency'. The goal looks beyond the immediate benefit of the auditor's independence — that is, unbiased audit decisions — to the broader targets of user reliance on the financial reporting process and enhanced capital market efficiency.

The framework, in identifying five types of threats to the auditor's independence, follows the approach of European Standard setters. It includes, for example, the following threats:

- *self-interest* — the threat that arises when an auditor acts in his or her own emotional, financial or other personal self-interest;
- *self-review* — the threat of bias arising when an auditor audits his or her own work or the work of a colleague;
- *advocacy* — the threat that arises when an auditor acts as an advocate for or against an audit client's position or opinion rather than as an unbiased attestor;
- *familiarity (or trust)* — the threat that arises when an auditor is being influenced by a close relationship with an audit client;
- *intimidation* — the threat that arises when an auditor is being, or believes that he or she is being, overtly or covertly coerced by an audit client or by another interested party.

Some of these categories may overlap. In addition, although some involve conscious acts by an auditor in his or her own self-interest, others may result from subconscious biases. Once an auditor identifies such threats and evaluates their significance, he or she should analyse potential safeguards. These safeguards should include procedures firms can perform to protect auditor independence, such as:

- a second partner's review;
- consultation with designated professionals in the firm;
- disclosure to the audit committee of client;
- restrictions on an auditor's relationships with an audit client (e.g. prohibitions on owning the stock of an audit client and on assigning to an audit client firm professionals whose family members are employed in certain positions at the client).

Standard setters must analyse the significance of threats and the effectiveness of potential safeguards to ensure that their standards sufficiently reduce independence risk.

One of the most controversial aspects of the auditor independence debate is the role that 'appearance' should play in setting Standards. The 'appearance' concept, although not well defined, is ingrained in the existing independence literature. Everyone who has undertaken an introductory auditing course knows that auditors must be independent in both fact and appearance. But what does it mean to 'appear' independent? Whose perceptions count?

The ISB exposure draft, in its discussion of the definition and goal of independence, specifies that the Board and other Standard setters should consider the perceptions of investors and other users of financial information.

The framework defines auditor independence as 'freedom from those factors that compromise, or can reasonably be expected to compromise, an auditor's ability to make unbiased audit decisions'. While the Board understands that the framework does not provide easy answers to specific independence questions, it supplies a structure and method for analysing issues. The framework recognises that auditor independence is a means to an end, not the ultimate goal. Quality audits and reliable and credible information that contribute to efficient capital markets are the objectives.

Perhaps one of the most significant concerns of the ISB is if a Standard that enhances auditor independence slightly would discourage qualified people from entering the profession, thereby reducing audit quality. The ISB concluded that prohibiting former firm partners and other professionals from accepting jobs with audit clients could significantly reduce the profession's appeal and reduce the possibility of long-term improvements in financial management of clients. It accepts that mandating safeguards would achieve the same independence benefits without the adverse consequences.[7]

3 LEARNING OBJECTIVE

Discuss the recent restructuring relating to accounting firms.

Restructuring of accounting firms

In recent years, the profession has witnessed many inter-firm mergers, restructuring, splitting and consolidations. In March 2000, three of the Big Five firms — PricewaterhouseCoopers, Ernst & Young and KPMG — were selling off their most profitable operations, their consulting businesses, in deals worth billions of US dollars. Many in the profession were questioning the firms' motives when the prospects for management and technology consultants had rarely seemed brighter. Besides, the sudden desire to downsize came less than two years after the Big Five were determined to grow through various amalgamations. Reasons for the 'great consulting sell-off' were argued to include a number of factors, including the desire to make money when market valuations were high.

Others referred to the increasing regulatory scrutiny by the US Securities and Exchange Commission in its run-up to the new independence rulings. A spokesman from one of the Big Five Australasian operations explained that the Commission's stance had restricted the firms from taking at-risk positions with audit clients. The Big Five have expanded services beyond the traditional auditing and tax, gained enormous market power in consulting, and entered equity and joint venture arrangements with clients. Many companies, including dot.com businesses, are registering with the US Securities and Exchange Commission, whose rules apply far beyond the US borders and had become the catalyst for accounting firm restructurings. As the independence issue became more pressing, Ernst & Young, KPMG and PricewaterhouseCoopers were floating or selling their consulting firms.

Unlike some competitors, Arthur Andersen maintained its consulting arm as an essential part of the organisation, following the decision by Andersen Consulting (now Accenture) to split from Arthur Andersen. It maintains its desire to develop a **multidisciplinary practice**.

In Australia, the potential of multidisciplinary practices is illustrated by comments in an issues paper released by the Law Council of Australia in October 2000:

> For example, a boutique operation specialising in elder law could provide integrated services such as financial retirement planning, estate planning, investment counselling, conveyancing, social security assistance and health-related services.

So far, the Law Society of New South Wales and the New South Wales government are the only bodies that allow law firms to become incorporated bodies with the freedom to choose how and with whom they practise. Would the development of multidisciplinary practices lead to law firms competing aggressively against accounting firms and their legal arms?

In Europe, accounting firms have bought big law firms and created giant partnerships, while multidisciplinary practices were debated in the United States but rejected by a 75 per cent vote by the law profession. In Australia, accounting firms have legal departments in which non-partner lawyers are employed. It will be, therefore, some time before one can notice if the accounting profession is influenced by the creation of these partnerships.[8]

As the Big Five firms were undergoing restructuring, the smaller firms took on another trend. The smaller accounting firms have been seen to be subjects of **consolidation** by organisations. Following the example of American Express in mid-1998, there were many consolidations in which small to medium-sized accounting firms joined to compete with the Big Five. In the United States, for example, there was the H&R Block acquisition of McGladrey & Pullen. In the United Kingdom, the first consolidator of accounting firms, the Tenon Group, was floated in March 2000. In Australia, the consolidator Stockford floated its conglomerate of more than thirty accounting firms in November 2000. Another chartered accountant firm in the Melbourne suburb of South Yarra used a pooled development fund as a vehicle for a 'roll-up' and floated fifteen accounting firms in twelve months. And the list continues . . .

Our aim in this chapter is not to analyse current trends and issues in depth, but to alert readers to the contemporary scene of the profession. Nevertheless, critics of the consolidation model of accounting firms argue that few large firms will be able to secure and retain the market share they need to effectively control the economics of the industry. Large firms cannot offer products or services that smaller firms could not match through strategic alliances and as members of robust global networks. Also, American Express Tax and Business Services has lost US$100 million on its consolidation business, while the share price performance of consolidators in general lack lustre.

While the consolidators have reported losses, the most profitable firms in the accounting industry have not been big firms. Smaller firms also tend to have lower relative fixed costs, with lower break-even points.[9] It is believed that there will be further evolution in the forms of accounting firms' restructuring, possibly towards a model that gives more recognition to the intellectual capital of financial service providers.

QUALITY BENCHMARKING AND THE AUDITOR

4
LEARNING OBJECTIVE

Review some non-audit benchmarks applicable to auditors.

There is a strong view that the self-regulatory Standards and regulations that ensure the quality of the professional services prevail in the profession. These self-regulatory controls include:

- high education entry requirements;
- rigorous induction programs;
- character checking upon entry to the profession;
- compulsory public practice induction;
- compulsory continuing professional development;
- extensive ethical rulings and codes of conduct;
- separate public practice registration;
- compulsory quality review programs
- compulsory professional indemnity insurance;
- adherence to detailed and mandatory Auditing Standards and auditing pronouncements.

These controls set a minimal list of mechanisms and standards with which professional accountants and auditors must comply. However, as auditors expand their services and as their roles become more complicated, it is expected that they must not only keep abreast of current demands in quality delivery applicable to businesses, but also have the ability to assess the impact of such standards on their own work. In this section, we will focus on some of the **benchmarks** of which auditors and professional accountants must be aware.

The ISO 9000 series

The ISO 9000 series comprises a collection of Standards for quality management published by the International Organisation for Standardisation (ISO). They define a framework of minimum requirements for the implementation of quality systems to be used in contractual situations.

The Standards in the ISO 9000 series have been adopted worldwide as suitable criteria for the assessment and registration of companies by independent accredited third party organisations. In brief, the ISO 9000 series comprises quality systems models for quality assurance and management standards. (Much information is available on the ISO 9000 home page.)

TABLE 18.3

ISO series

Number	Name
ISO 9001 (1994)	Quality Systems — Model for Quality Assurance in Design, Development, Production, Installation and Servicing
ISO 9002 (1994)	Quality Systems — Model for Quality Assurance in Production, Installation and Servicing
ISO 9003 (1994)	Quality Systems — Model for Quality Assurance in Final Inspection and Test
ISO 9000–1 (1994)	Quality Management and Quality Assurance Standards — Part 1: Guidelines for Selection and Use
ISO 9000–4 (1994)	Quality Management and Quality Systems Elements — Guidelines

The advantage of the ISO 9000 series is evident when selecting, implementing and monitoring a new management system. The series uses tracking features such as internal quality audits, corrective action and management review processes. Companies that operate in accordance with ISO Standards are better able to satisfy expectations and clearly identify the resulting advantages of their operations. A certified quality management system can:

- optimise organisational structure and operational integration;
- improve awareness of organisational objectives;
- improve communications and quality of information;
- better define responsibilities and authorities;
- improve traceability to the causes of quality problems;
- improve the use of time and other resources;
- formalise systems to ensure consistent quality and punctual delivery;
- enhance documented systems to provide useful reference and training;
- improve relationships with customers and suppliers;
- enhance the ability to bid for ISO 9000 contracts;
- provide for continual quality assessment by experienced professionals;
- ensure improved records are available in the case of litigation.

A number of publications explain ISO 9000 quality systems, including those that provide a compliance guide and explain operational procedures. Accounting firms are well placed to capitalise on their understanding of and familiarity with quality system requirements.[10] They have the opportunity to build on their audit skills to become a practice that provides ISO registration services.

Many larger international audit firms are attempting to become accredited ISO 9000 registrars, because this represents a significant financial investment. (KPMG, for example, has obtained accreditation by the ISO and its authorised agents to provide accreditation service to its clients.) The accreditation process involves setting up focus groups to determine what clients want, hiring the necessary staff, advertising and undertaking the cost of the accreditation. The issue, however, raises 'conflict of interest' considerations. Accounting firms need to decide whether to provide consulting services related to ISO 9000 or whether to offer the registration service. Providing both services would put a firm in a conflict of interest.

If a company decides to go through the ISO registration process, the compliance audit may be quite exhaustive. A distinctive feature of ISO 9000 registration is that a third party conducts the registration process. These quality system registrars use common evaluation parameters and work under strict guidelines established by the ISO although there are some differences in how registrars interpret the Standards and use the measurement techniques. For auditors who are involved in ISO audits, the following issues are relevant:

- There must be a quality manual which documents the organisation's structure, responsibilities, procedures, processes, resources and reporting framework. The auditor will look for objective evidence of an effective quality system such as effective communication of organisational philosophies, proper controls over processes, a management monitoring system and so on.
- The inspection and testing method must be designed in a way that is suitable for the organisational structure and its operations. The auditor should be made aware of the issues relating to the operations and industry standards.
- The criteria used by auditors to assess the effectiveness of a quality system are (1) proper documentation and communication mechanisms that enable the system to be well understood by the work force, (2) proper implementation of the system and (3) an objective evaluation of the effectiveness of the system.

Total quality management and the auditor

With auditors becoming increasingly involved in auditing an entire business, ISO 9000 can be very useful in helping auditors to identify and review issues that have an impact on quality management in an organisation. Arguably, the primary consideration in **total quality management** is its sustainability. Recent research into this issue (and the applicability of ISO 9000)[11] has led to the design of a tool to audit issues that have a negative impact on sustainability. Based on work carried out in different manufacturing organisations, the sustainability of total quality management was found, for example, to rely on factors such as continual improvement, organisational behaviour, human resources management, industrial relations and the labour process. These factors reflect a variety of perspectives within business operations. The issues found to have an impact on such factors were analysis of strengths, weaknesses, opportunities and threats (SWOT), competitors, quality and performance standards, new technologies, industrial relations, management–worker relationship, policies design, the positioning of quality functions and resources, functional boundaries, communication, job flexibility, the supervisory structure, the improvement infrastructure, and education and training.

In providing various types of assurance review, auditors are generally able to assist management in pinpointing the matters that have a negative impact on the total quality management of an organisation. Furthermore, they may be able to use the Standards specified in ISO 9000 as audit tool benchmarks to provide the necessary level of assurance for effectiveness.

An understanding of the total business process is one of the strengths that financial accountants and auditors can build on as they add value for their employers and clients. Most accountants and auditors are good at analysing situations in organisations, constructing detailed work plans, explaining complex situations to clients from a variety of backgrounds and keeping confidences. Auditors can also perform ISO audits or assist clients in achieving ISO registration/performance.

According to Barthelemy and Zairi,[12] quality auditing has progressed from a practice solely concerned with tools used to detect non-conformance (non-compliance) to one concerned with using instruments geared towards continual improvement. They postulate that it now encapsulates a much more dynamic approach, being more focused on innovation and best practice than on minimum levels of performance.

Undoubtedly, auditing is an important function for the effective deployment of quality systems such as ISO 9000. Not only is it conducted to ensure total compliance with set procedures and agreed standards at all times and at all stages during the productive and organisational process, but it also helps to develop the organisation by providing mechanisms for continual improvement, innovation and the fostering of a problem-solving culture. The steps involved in quality auditing are shown in Figure 18.1.

FIGURE 18.1

The steps in quality auditing

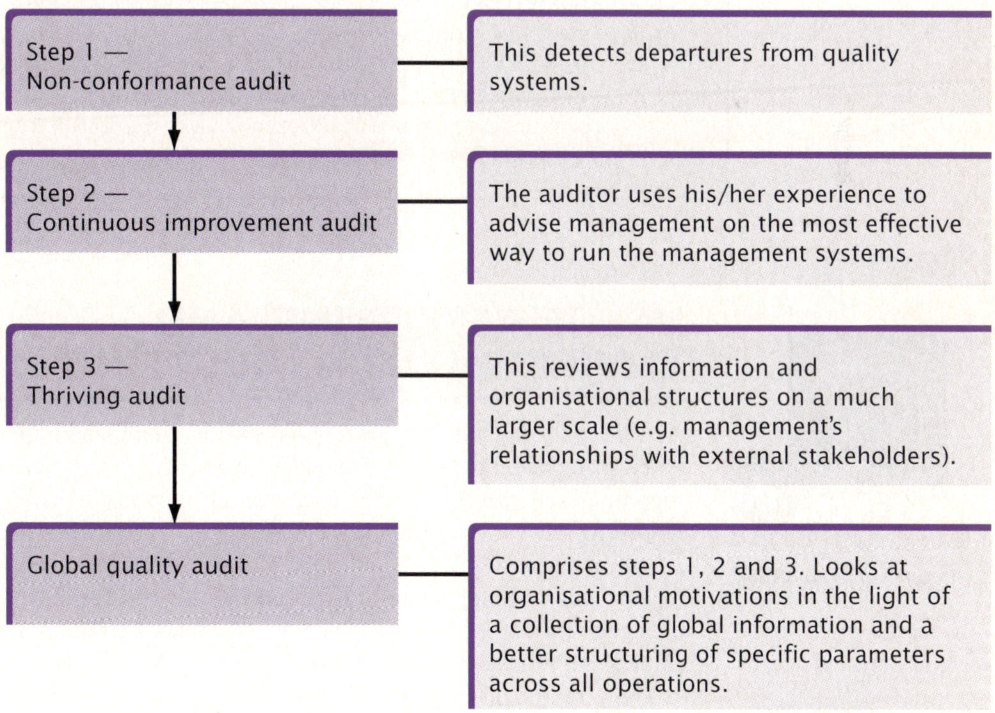

Although the scenario presented in Figure 18.1 may be well outside the scope of the traditional external auditor, the current diversification of services provided by auditors and the growing prominence of the concept of adding value to client services indicate that such a trend (or similar developments) may be an issue in the future.

LEARNING CHECK

18.1 Advances in financial software and the mobile Internet are the key drivers of today's business systems management. Professional accountants and auditors must be aware of the needs and characteristics of their clients' systems and the methods of implementation of suitable financial software, with particular emphasis on minimising risks and ensuring the availability of audit trails and internal controls. The mobile Internet combines the two fastest growing technologies: information and telecommunication technologies. It has become an important business application tool.

18.2 Accountants not only have to deal with the changing business models driven by technologies, but are also confronted with new rules for auditor independence and market conditions. The latest proposal for auditor independence is based on a conceptual framework of threats and safeguards.

18.3 Professional firms are undergoing different types of restructuring as a response to market conditions such as stringent regulatory restrictions, competition, the development of multidisciplinary practices and firm consolidations.

18.4 Audit of quality management refers to the audit activities that help management to design, implement, monitor and improve quality within their organisations. Under the concept of total quality management, auditors are required to understand the entire business, in order to be able to add value to management in terms of continual improvements.

18.5 Certification under ISO 9000 requires registered auditors to carry out appropriate quality audits, and certified organisations to provide a quality assurance to general users. ISO 9000 standards are universally accepted as the benchmark for quality assurance. An ISO 9000 audit requires the examination of a framework of audit procedures, as well as the verification of adherence to certain Standards in documentation, operation controls and communication.

VALUE REPORTING AND ENVIRONMENTAL AUDITING

5 LEARNING OBJECTIVE

Define value reporting.

As we reported earlier, the profession is keen to emphasise the role of independent auditing in ensuring capital market efficiency. However, value can only be realised if financial reports are effectively communicated to the markets. Methods of corporate valuation and reporting are evolving rapidly, but traditional accounting models are insufficient to be relied on to provide a full picture of corporate health. It is also vital for corporate management to communicate with investors adequately, to maximise total shareholder returns. The challenge for corporations is to enable the capital market to move its focus from short-term earnings to long-term value creation.

The concept of using shareholder value, which is underpinned by information on key value-creating activities, is not new. The Centre of Innovation in Corporate Responsibility (CICR) looks at maximising sources of value by integrating corporate social responsibility with strategic management.[13] The Blue Ribbon Committee report *Improving the Effectiveness of Corporate Audit Committees* — produced in response to concerns expressed by the US Securities and Exchange Commission about the quality of financial reports — refers to 'quality financial reports' through integrity and transparency, effective interrelationships between the boards and the shareholders.[14] Also, the Turnbull Report, which was endorsed by the London Stock Exchange for all listed companies in the United Kingdom, also refers to the inseparable nature of risk management and value creation.[15]

On the other hand, books have been written about the **value reporting** revolution and value-added reporting and research.[16] Many investors use shareholder values to support their investment decisions, build valuation models and assess future cash flows. Shareholder values are also used at corporate level to drive strategy and resource allocation. Value reporting is expected to receive an increasing amount of attention in the future of financial reporting and audits.

PricewaterhouseCoopers has devised a value reporting model, which will facilitate a top–down process of reporting and enable companies to communicate the internal workings of the company to investors in a language they use and understand. The key aspects of the proposed value reporting framework are:

- a comprehensive set of company specific financial and non-financial measures;
- both historical and predictive indicators;
- shareholder value-creation activities.

The model comprises a shareholder value metric and a value scorecard, which does not focus on operational matters but on key value-creating activities of the business as a whole, as long-term measures. The model is underpinned by four key elements:

1. the use of prospective indicators;
2. cash flow-oriented information instead of traditional earnings;
3. non-financial indicators such as customer retention, employee satisfaction and community support;
4. greater transparency to satisfy investors' demand for more information.

The concept of value reporting is supported by research. The Swedish Stock Exchange carried out research to determine the views of global investors and analysts on their information needs. The results of that survey show some key insights into best practice reporting, which includes:

- the extent of free cash flow;
- earnings per share;
- market leadership (or ranking in market);
- industry information (gross growth in comparison);
- corporate strategy and visions;
- objectives versus results;
- segmental analysis by business;
- quality management;
- key business activities;
- management activities;
- bad news;
- challenges, risks and uncertainties.

To develop a value reporting best practice model, PricewaterhouseCoopers advises the following summary features:

1. a market overview — the competitive, regulatory and macro-economic environments;
2. a value strategy — goals, objectives, governance and organisation;
3. managing for value — financial performance, financial position, risk management and segmental information;
4. a value platform — innovation, branding, customer relationships, supply chain management, people management and reputation (social, environmental and ethical).[17]

Value reporting, together with concepts such as shareholder (or stakeholder) value and the development of the triple bottom line concept,[18] can be said to become significant aspects of the role of professional accountants in the future.

6 LEARNING OBJECTIVE

Describe the meaning of and Standards for environmental auditing.

Developments in environmental auditing

While auditing has gradually evolved into a much broader concept of performance review, the recent development in **environmental auditing** is a response to a growing concern by businesses with controlling their environmental performance more effectively and complying with environmental regulations. A single and universally accepted definition of environmental auditing does not exist, possibly as a result of the evolving nature of the function.[19]

Notwithstanding the differing views, the definition of environmental auditing that is most widely accepted by businesses comes from the 1989 International Chamber of Commerce (ICC) position paper on environmental auditing:[20]

> [Environmental auditing is] a management tool comprising a systematic, documented, periodic and objective evaluation of how well environmental organisation, management and equipment are performing with the aim of helping to safeguard the environment by:
> (1) facilitating management control of environmental practices;
> (2) assessing compliance with company policies, which would include meeting regulatory requirements.

It is significant that environmental auditing, as described above, holds a fundamental contradiction. The ICC states that it is an internal management tool for company use only — that is, that it is not for publication or public disclosure/scrutiny. Yet, the ICC also states that it wishes to establish environmental auditing as a credible and trustworthy instrument in the mind of the public. Convincing the public of the credibility of company environmental audits requires transparency of purpose and information. This can be achieved by publication of audit reports. On the other hand, obtaining a full and frank appraisal of a company's environmental performance raises privacy considerations during the audit process, to the exclusion of external company stakeholders.

It has recently been suggested by Hillary[21] that the use of self-regulatory environmental management tools such as environmental auditing could become a more powerful force for environmental improvement — that is, people could use such tools to bargain to secure better environmental protection. Environmental auditing is certainly beginning to establish a higher global profile. In its 1986 position paper requiring compulsory auditing, the US Environmental Protection Agency stated that it may request, under certain conditions, internal and potentially incriminating environmental audit reports. The European Union adopted a more holistic approach to environmental protection, with the Commission of European Communities releasing its consultation paper on an environmental auditing scheme in 1990.[22] The scheme entailed the operation of an environmental management accounting system (EMAS), which requires mandatory verification by independent accredited verifiers for sites registering with the scheme. This process gives some credibility to environmental performance efforts made by companies.

Hillary suggested that environmental auditing should be an umbrella term under which different audit scopes exist. The following twelve types of environmental audit were identified:

- an activity audit;
- an associate audit;
- a compliance audit;
- an environmental management systems (EMS) audit;
- an energy audit;
- an issues audit;
- an occupational health and safety audit;
- a process safety audit;
- a site audit;
- a supplier/customer/contractor audit;
- a waste audit.

While the above list is not exhaustive, it indicates the broad range of environmental aspects that may be subject to the audit process. (In due diligence assessments, for example, the auditor may also be concerned with insurance liability audits, pre-acquisition and merger audits, and divestiture and pre-sale audits — all of which have a direct relationship with environmental matters.) The twelve types of audit are not exclusive of one another.

Standards for environmental auditing

Recent initiatives have sought to structure and formalise environmental auditing. The British Standard Institution developed in 1992 and reissued in 1994 a British Standard specifying an environmental management system — BS 7750, which includes environmental auditing for the environmental management system and the environmental performance of an organisation. Both BS 7750 and, more generally, any environmental management accounting systems outline environmental auditing as part of wider management systems, and provide guidelines on how to conduct an environmental audit. The broad principles are similar to those outlined in ISO 10011, Quality Systems Auditing Standards.

The ISO 14000 series

At the international level, the ISO developed a suite of twenty standards in the field of environmental management (the ISO 14000 series). This series was published in 1994. In terms of environmental auditing, the following three standards are applicable:

1. ISO 14011–1, Guidelines for Environmental Auditing — Audit Procedures. Part 1: Auditing of Environmental Management Systems;
2. ISO 14011–2, Guidelines for Environmental Auditing — Audit Procedures. Part 2: Compliance Audits;
3. ISO 14011–3, Guidelines for Environmental Auditing — Audit Procedures. Part 3: Audit of an Environmental Statement.

In addition, ISO 14001 contains a requirement for organisations to maintain programs and procedures for periodic environmental management system audits. The purpose of an environmental management system audit is to determine whether an organisation's environmental management system conforms to the ISO 14001 specification, and whether it has been properly implemented and maintained. In Australia, s.299 (1) of the Corporations Law requires companies, registered schemes and disclosing entities to disclose their performance in relation to environmental regulations in annual reports for years ending on or after 1 July 1998. Following the amendment to the Corporations Law, the Australian Securities and Investment Commission issued its Practice Note 68, New Financial Reporting and Procedural Requirements in November 1998, listing details of the information required. It specifies:

- that the requirements will normally apply where an entity is licensed or subject to conditions under environmental legislation or regulations;
- that the requirements are not related to financial disclosures specifically such as contingent liabilities, and that accounting concepts of materiality are not applicable;
- that the information provided cannot be reduced or eliminated because the information has been provided to a regulatory authority for the purposes of any environmental legislation; and
- that the information will generally be less technical than information provided in any compliance reports to an environmental regulator.

AGS 1036, The Consideration of Environmental Matters in the Audit of a Financial Report also provides some practical assistance concerning the impact of such factors as pollution, hazardous waste, and compliance with environmental laws and regulations on financial statement accruals, the impairment of assets, disclosures and so on. There is also increasing international awareness and adoption of environmental reporting, as shown in the following 'Professional environment'.

PROFESSIONAL ENVIRONMENT An international survey

KPMG Environmental Consulting, in cooperation with the University of Amsterdam, has published the most comprehensive survey of environmental reports ever conducted. The survey covers top companies in nineteen countries and reports on the environmental performance of many different sectors of industry. It found, for example, that 15 per cent of banks, insurance companies and securities companies produce an annual environmental report. The growing interest in companies' non-financial performance has encouraged companies to produce environmental reports of high quality.

Environmental reporting is now mandatory in several countries, including Australia under s.299(1)f of the amended Corporations Law. In addition, a National Pollutant Inventory has been created (similar to US and proposed EU models), which requires 3000 to 5000 Australian companies to report their emissions and inventories for specific chemicals.

Through its International Network of over 150 environmental consultants in more than twenty-five countries, KPMG was able to assess the state of environmental reporting among the *Fortune* top 250 multinational companies in the world and the top 100 companies in eleven countries, including Australia, the USA and several European countries.

The results of the survey show that:

- the number of companies with an environmental report or health, safety and environment (HSE) report increased from 13 per cent in 1993 to 17 per cent in 1996 to 24 per cent in 1999;
- compared with the rate in 1996, the rate of publishing external environmental and HSE reports increased in 1999 in all countries except the United States;
- companies in Germany published most reports in 1999 (36 per cent), followed by Sweden (34 per cent);
- four countries published fewer reports than the average of 24 per cent (Belgium, Finland, Australia and France), but they are catching up fast;
- industrial sectors (chemicals, forestry, pulp and paper, utilities, oil and gas, pharmaceuticals), are leading in reporting publicly on environmental issues. Lagging behind are sectors including finance, insurance and securities, trade and retail;
- progress against plans and targets for environmental reporting improved from 26 per cent in 1996 to 53 per cent in 1999;
- 18 per cent of the reports in 1999 were independently verified, often combining the expertise of environmental experts and financial accountants;
- 15 per cent of Australia's top companies published an environmental report in 1999, compared to 5 per cent in 1996.

(Source: Adapted from 'KPMG International Survey of Environmental Reporting 1999')

International codes of environmental conduct

A number of international codes of environmental conduct set out essential environmental management elements. These include:

- the Valdez Principles, developed by the Coalition for Environmentally Responsible Economics (CERES), in 1990;
- the ICC Charter for Sustainable Development;
- the UK Chemical Industries Association Responsible Care Programs.

The Valdez Principles were launched after the Exxon Valdez oil tanker disaster in Alaska. The CERES requires signatory companies to undertake annual environmental audits and make public the findings of these audits. The ICC Charter for Sustainable Development comprises sixteen principles for environmental management in achieving sustainable economic development. The Responsible Care Programs have been developed by many national chemical industry associations in the United States, Canada and the United Kingdom. All are voluntary in nature.

Voluntary business environmental codes may include environmental auditing components, which could be either the Valdez Principles, the ICC Charter for Sustainable Development or the Responsible Care principles. In practice, however, these have not been as widely supported by industry as might have been intended. Nonetheless, there are many different approaches to environmental auditing that can be taken. For environmental management systems and auditing programs to be effective, some of the characteristics of a corporate culture are required:

- top management commitment and board-level support;
- communication of relevant information to all levels of management and line management;
- agreement at all levels that the program is valuable;
- leadership, with direct access to the company's board and a competent audit team;
- environmental audit programs that fit comfortably into existing management systems.

Furthermore, the International Auditing Practice Committee has suggested that conduct of environmental management system audits requires the following:

- knowledge of the industry;
- knowledge of environmental issues, including environmental science and technologies;
- established auditing and verification philosophies and techniques;
- management systems and practices, including internal controls;
- environmental laws and regulations.

The IAPC suggests that environmental management system auditing probably presents a wider range of unique issues for the auditor than does financial statement auditing. To respond to these effectively, auditors who are and may be involved in certain environmental operations need to be knowledgeable about the environmental systems standards of environmental management accounting systems and ISO 14001, especially when the environmental audit is part of the audit scope.

Such an environmental audit may result in the recruitment of on-site personnel in an audit team, although an inability to be objective may sometimes mitigate the advantages offered by having inside site knowledge and work force credibility. Nonetheless, leading environmental auditing programs nowadays also include a person with detailed knowledge of the facility to be audited.

The occurrence of environmental auditing will increase in businesses in response to the increasing adoption of ISO Standards, the greater demands by stakeholders in business for accountability on environmental issues, and a growing sophistication in society's understanding of environmental threats and opportunities. The auditors of the twenty-first century must be aware of this development and equip themselves with the necessary skills to establish the relevance and value of their services. As a first step, they must be familiar with the legislative requirements in this area. To this end, a sample list of relevant environmental (Commonwealth and Victorian) laws is provided in Appendix 18A to provide a broad overview.

The latest developments in auditing and assurance (as discussed above) reflect the broadening role of accountants in value creation, as well as their social role.

LEARNING CHECK

18.6 Value reporting refers to reporting by organisations on matters that are not confined to financial information, but are key value drivers. These value drivers are based on adding shareholder value, aligning with corporate strategies, communicating non-financial matters to investors, and reporting on value creation activities and other indicators.

18.7 Environmental auditing does not have a standard definition. It is generally considered to be a management tool comprising a systematic, documented, periodic and objective evaluation of how well an organisation (including its management and equipment) is performing with respect to environmental issues.

18.8 The aim of the environmental audit is to help to safeguard the environment by facilitating effective management control and environmental practices, and by assessing compliance with company and regulatory requirements.

18.9 The development of environmental auditing has given rise to a range of potential audit and assurance services, covering different environmentally related operations related to issues such as energy, occupational health and safety, waste, contaminated sites and other activities such as the production of environmental products (e.g. chemicals).

18.10 The ISO 14000 series has been published as a set of guidelines for environmental auditing procedures. Organisations also adopt voluntary environmental practices. Examples are (1) adhering to environmental codes, (2) developing an environmentally friendly culture and (3) implementing an environmental management accounting system to identify, control and monitor risk areas.

SUMMARY

In this chapter we aimed to provide an overview of some of the current issues that may affect the role of professional accountants and auditors in the foreseeable future. Where since the fifth edition issues have become a significant matter to be discussed in depth, such as electronic commerce, they are explored independently in this text as a separate chapter. Issues such as information technology, the role of the profession as represented by the accounting firms, benchmarking, value reporting and environmental auditing continue to shape the work of professional accountants. We reviewed developments in information technology, with specific emphasis on the significance of financial software and the mobile Internet. Auditors and professional accountants must be familiar with the characteristics and technical features of financial software to ensure their suitability for clients and employers. The convergence of the Internet and telecommunication technologies also provides an insight into possible future business applications. Readers should appreciate the changing nature of the work of professional accountants, but some external factors must not be ignored. We further examined the role of the profession, with the latest development of the independence framework, and also covered the trend of restructuring by accounting firms in the face of some changing market conditions (such as legal backing for multi-disciplinary practices and competition).

We discussed audit quality benchmarking — elaborating on the issues of non-audit standards such as the ISO 9000 series — and introduced the concept of the total quality management audit. This approach focuses on auditing the business as a whole, with the inclusion of value-added services such as certification. While highlighting the impact of quality auditing, we also recognised the increasing attention given to value reporting — a form of business reporting that goes beyond the financial statements. Value reporting has formed the basis for the development of environmental auditing. The future of business reporting and auditing may well be underpinned by a demand of shareholder (or stakeholder) values, sustainability and long-term accountability.

KEY TERMS

Audit trail, p. 665
Benchmarking, p. 675
Consolidation, p. 674
Environmental auditing, p. 680
Financial software, p. 664
Mobile Internet, p. 664
Multidisciplinary practice, p. 673
Total quality management, p. 676
Value reporting, p. 679

NOTES

1. The publication *Accounting Software in Australia* was published by the *CFO Magazine*, with the ASCPA (now CPA Australia) in 1997. The publication reported on the findings of Strategic Research (the research arm of the company Strategic Publishing Group) from its recent survey of more than 600 chief financial officers in Australia and New Zealand on the use of accounting software.
2. H. M. Courtney, C. L. Prachyl & T. Glandon, 'Guide to Accounting Software', *Journal of Accountancy*, (March 1998), pp. 44–61.
3. See Note 1.
4. KPMG, 'Creating the New World Wireless Operator', *Mobile Internet — Any Place, Any Time, Everything*. Sydney, pp. 1–14. See web site www.kpmg.com.au/mobileinternet/html
5. Advisory Panel on Auditor Independence, *Strengthening the Professionalism of the Independent Auditor*, Report to the Public Oversight Board of the US Securities and Exchange Commission Practice Section. American Institute of Certified Public Accountants, Stamford, 1994.
6. 'Highlights', *Journal of Accountancy* (Vol. 191, No. 1, January 2001). See web site www.aicpa.org/pubs/jofa/jan2001/about.html
7. Susan McGrath, Arthur Siegel, Thomas W. Dunfee, Alan S. Glazer & Henry R. Jaenicke, 'A Framework for Auditor Independence — The ISB Lays a Foundation for Future Guidance', *Journal of Accountancy* (January 2000). See www.aicpa.org/pubs/jofa/jan2001/mcgrath.htm
8. Nick Tabakoff, 'Giant firms, small plans', *Business Review Weekly*, (24 March 2000), p. 3139.
9. Summary based on Ric Payne, 'Consolidation's Fatal Flaws', *Business Review Weekly* (8 December 2000), p. 2550; T. Thomas, 'The One-stop Shop Is Just Around the Corner', *Business Review Weekly* (3 November 2000), p. 1923. Also, based on search results from the *Australian Financial Review* and *Business Review Weekly* on movements of consolidators of accounting firms for 2000.
10. One such view is expressed in M. O'Sullivan, 'Registering an Advantage', *CA Magazine* (March 1997).
11. B. G. Dale, 'Total Quality Management Sustaining Audit Tool: Description and Use', *Total Quality Management* (December 1997).
12. J. L. Barthelemy & M. Zairi, 'Making ISO 9000 Work: The Role of Auditing', *Total Quality Management* (Vol. 6, No. 3, 1994), pp. 44–7. This article refers to quality audits which progress from non-conformance auditing into global auditing.

13. This is referred to in the President's message in the Centre for Innovation in Corporate Responsibility, *Triple Bottom Line*, Volume 1. Washington DC, 1999.
14. The Blue Ribbon Committee was charged by the New York Stock Exchange and the National Association of Securities Dealers in 1998 to review the effectiveness of corporate audit committees. Its report contained three conclusions: (1) quality financial reporting can only result from effective interrelationships among corporate boards, audit committees, financial management, the internal auditor and the external auditor; (2) integrity and transparency of financial reporting drives investor confidence; and (3) strengthening oversight in the financial reporting process of public companies will reduce instances of outright fraud.
15. The Turnbull Report, with the title *Internal Control: Guidance for Directors on the Combined Code 1999*, was submitted by the chairman, Nigel Turnbull, at the request of the London Stock Exchange. The Turnbull Report is the latest development of government endorsing corporate governance guidelines for listed companies.
16. Robert Eccles, Robert H. Herz & David Phillips, *The Value Reporting Revolution: Moving beyond the Earnings Game*. John Wiley and Sons, New York, 2001. Also, Ahmed Riahi-Belkaoui, *Value Added Reporting and Research — State of the Art*, Quorum Books, Westport, Conneticut, 1999.
17. This is a summary of a full major report by PricewaterhouseCoopers (see www.pricewaterhousecoopers.com/). The report contains the following sections: the pressure for change, the information gap, the value reporting framework, best practices and client extranet. The value reporting framework is a registered trademark.
18. The triple bottom line concept has been reported in a number of articles, such as by John Elkington in *Australian CPA* (March 1999) and by by Doug Holmes, 'Sustainable Development Reporting: An Australian Experience' *Australian CPA* (March 1999), pp. 15–21.
19. The fact that a universally accepted definition does not exist was reported by the International Auditing Practice Committee, *The Audit Profession and the Environment*. United States, 1995. L. B. Cahill (in *Environmental Audits*, 6th edn, Government Institutes, Rockville, Maryland, 1992) suggested that the lack of definition may be due to the evolving nature of environmental auditing.
20. International Chamber of Commerce, *Environmental Auditing*. Paris, 1989.
21. R. Hillary, 'Environmental Auditing: Concept, Methods and Developments', *International Journal of Auditing* (Vol. 2, March 1998), pp. 71–85.
22. Commission of European Communities, Council Regulation EEC no. 1836/93 (29 June 1993), which allowed voluntary participation by companies in the industrial section in EMAs.

FURTHER READING

Blondell, J., 'Way to Go', *Charter* (June 1998), pp. 20–2.

Bragg, S., 'Environmental Auditing: Practical Implementation'. Paper presented at the Environmental Strategies for Business: the European Dimension course, Imperial College, London, 29 June to 3 July 1992.

British Standards Institution, *Specification for Environmental Management Systems*, British Standard 7750. London, 1992, 1994.

Business International, *Managing the Environment: the Greening of European Business*. London, 1990.

Chemical Industries Association, *Responsible Care*. London, 1989.

Clements, K., 'Environmental Auditing for Industry: A European Perspective', *European Environment* (Vol. 1, No. 3, 1991), pp. 1–4.

Coalition for Environmentally Responsible Economics, *The 1990 CERES Guide to the Valdez Principles*. Boston, 1990.

Confederation of British Industry, *Narrowing the Gap: Environmental Auditing Guidelines for Business*. London, 1990.

Dale, B. G., 'Total Quality Management Sustaining Audit Tool: Description and Use', *Total Quality Management* (December 1997).

Dowson, J., 'Environmental Management Systems Certification — an Assessor's View', in R. Hillary (ed.), *Environmental Management Systems and Cleaner Production*. John Wiley and Sons, Chichester, 1997.

Elkington, J., Knight, P. & Hailes, J., *The Green Business Guide*. Victor Gollancz, London, 1991.

Environment Business, 'Industrial Environmental Auditing — Environmental Performance Evaluation', Supplement to *Environment Business*, (September 1990).

Environmental Protection Agency, 'Environmental Auditing Policy Statement', *Federal Register* (Vol. 51, No. 131, 1986), pp. 25.04–10.

Hillary, R., 'Environmental Auditing — the Management Option for the 1990s'. Paper presented at the Disaster '92 Conference, Disaster Prevention and Limitation Unit, University of Bradford, Sheffield, 8–9 September 1992.

Hillary, R., 'Motivation in Environmental Auditing: A Company Survey'. Unpublished MSc thesis, Imperial College of Science, Technology and Medicine, University of London, London, 1991.

Institute of Chartered Accountants, *Vision 2020. Task Force Report*. Sydney, 1998.

International Standards Organisation. 'Environmental Management: TC 207 Steer a Course Resolutely Forward', *ISO Bulletin* (Vol. 25, No. 12, December 1994).

Lewis, R. & Moriyama, H., 'Environmental Audits: Don't Pay for Pollution', *Acquisitions Monthly* (March 1990), pp. 26–7.

Muysken, J., 'WebTrust: Assurance and E-commerce', *Australian CPA* (August 1998), pp. 56–7.

APPENDIX 18A

Overview of Australian environmental legislation

The following list is indicative of current environmental legislation in Australia.

COMMONWEALTH ACTS
Agricultural and Veterinary Chemicals Act 1988
Agricultural and Veterinary Chemicals (Administration) Act 1992
Australian Heritage Commission Act 1975
Endangered Species Protection Act 1992
Environment Protection (Impact of Proposals) Act 1974
Environment Protection (Nuclear Codes) Act 1978
Environment Protection (Sea Dumping) Act 1981
Explosives Act 1961
Fisheries Act 1952–1988
Great Barrier Reef Marine Park Act 1975
Hazardous Waste (Regulation of Exports and Imports) Act 1989
Industrial Chemicals (Notification and Assessment) Act 1990
Ozone Protection Act 1988
Petroleum (Submerged Lands) Act 1967
Protection of the Sea (Prevention of Pollution from Ships) Act 1983
Resource Assessment Commission Act 1989
Trade Practices Act 1974
Quarantine Act 1908
World Heritage Properties Conservation Act 1983

(*continued*)

VICTORIAN ACTS

Air quality

Aerial Spraying Control Act 1966

Clean Air Act 1958

Environmental Protection (Ozone Layer) Act 1989

Hazardous substances

Agricultural Chemicals Act 1958

Dangerous Goods Act 1958

Drugs, Poisons and Controlled Substances Act 1981

Fertilisers Act 1974

Nuclear Activities (Prohibitions) Act 1983

Land use

Building Control Act 1981

Catchment and Land Protection Act 1994

Conservation, Forest and Lands Act 1987

Crown Land (Reserves) Act 1978

Drainage of Land Act 1975

Extractive Industries Act 1966

Land Conservation Act 1970

Mines Act 1958

Soil Conservation and Land Utilisation Act 1958

Urban Land Authority Act 1979

Pollution and waste

Environment Protection (Motor Vehicle Emission Control) (Unleaded Petrol) Regulations 1985

Environment Protection (Prescribed Waste Regulation) 1987

Environment Protection (Scheduled Premises and Exemptions) Regulations 1987

Prescriptive and empowering Acts

Administrative Appeals Tribunals Act 1984

Environmental Protection Act 1970

Environmental Effects Act 1978

Local Government Act 1958

Water quality

Catchment and Land Protection Act 1994

Marine Act 1988

Petroleum (Submerged Lands) Act 1982

Pollution of Waters by Oil and Noxious Substances Act 1986

Water Act 1989

Discussion questions

18.1 How do information and telecommunication technologies affect professional accountants? Illustrate by examining possible assurance and audit services for clients.

18.2 Accounting firms have been responding to various professional matters such as auditor independence. What are some of the professional issues that have had an impact on the operation of accounting firms? Discuss.

18.3 What is meant by value reporting? How do you think the concept of value reporting might have influenced the auditor's role in environmental audits?

18.4 The boundaries between disciplines appear to overlap one another. What do you think about the trend of multi-disciplinary practice and the development of conglomerates among firms?

18.5 What benchmarks are available for an environmental auditor? Discuss.

Professional application questions

★ BASIC
★★ MODERATE
★★★ CHALLENGING

18.1 (Audit trails in financial software) ★

An experienced (albeit elderly) audit partner was heard to make the following statement:

> 'I do not know why all this fuss is being made about audit trails when clients are implementing a new system. If advances in technology mean that there is less documentation, surely that must be a good thing. I think that there is a problem if auditors cannot audit a set of financial statements produced by a computer system without needing reams of paper. Especially with such auditing tools as analytical review now available to assist in auditing balances.'

Required

Comment on the partner's statement. In particular, address some of the problems from a lack of an audit trail which can be caused by advances in technology.

18.2 (Implementing financial software) ★★

A significant part of the modern auditor's role is often to assist clients with implementing financial software. The nature of this assistance can vary quite significantly, from design assistance to review of controls after completion. This sometimes raises issues of independence when it is perceived that the auditor has been too heavily involved in the process of assisting the client with the implementation of new software.

Required

(a) Discuss whether assistance in implementing new software is part of the role of the auditor or the management consultant.

(b) Discuss some of the key issues that need to be addressed when implementing a new information system.

18.3 (Mobile Internet) ★★

Your partner was approached by various clients who wished to gain some knowledge about using web-enhanced technology in their multimedia operations. Your partner asked each of his audit staff to describe an aspect of audit/assurance as a demonstration to the clients. You are given the task of describing the control elements in a mobile Internet-enhanced system.

Required

Write a memorandum to your partner, listing the matters that he should include in his presentation to the clients.

18.4 (ISO 9000) ★★

The beginnings of ISO 9000 go back to military manufacturing standards implemented during World War II. Since that time, it has been a process traditionally associated with the manufacturing industry. In recent years, service areas have been significantly more interested in ISO 9000 registration. The Report of the Special Committee on Assurance Services (Elliott Report) in the United States identified this registration as being a potential growth area for CPAs. This interest was evidenced by the AICPA becoming the first professional membership association in the United States to earn ISO 9001 certification by the International Organisation of Standards.

Required

(a) Explain ISO 9000 registration.

(b) Discuss why the accounting profession may consider itself to be best placed to provide ISO 9000 registration and audit services.

18.5 (Environmental auditing) ★★★

Environmental auditing is becoming a more important issue in financial reporting and also in relation to auditing requirements. The British Standard Institution developed a Standard (BS 7750) that included some guidance on environmental auditing.

> BS 7750 is a specification for an environmental management system. The system is used to describe the company's environmental management system, evaluate its performance and to define policy, practices, objectives and targets; and provides a catalyst for continuous improvement. The concept is similar to the use of ISO 9000 for quality systems, with the methods to be used open to definition by the company. The Standard provides the framework for development and assessment of the resultant environmental management system.
>
> BS 7750 was developed as a response to concern about environmental risks and damage (both real and potential). Compliance with the Standard is voluntary for companies, and complements required compliance with statutory legislation.

Required

(a) Explain the meaning of environmental auditing.

(b) List some other Standards that have been issued in relation to environmental auditing.

(c) Describe the types of task that may be involved in environmental auditing.

Glossary

Access controls Procedures designed to prevent unauthorised access to computer systems, including access to data files and programs

Account balance materiality The minimum misstatement that can exist in an account balance for it to be materially misstated

Account balances The difference between the summed dollar amounts of debits and credits recorded in a particular account contained within the general ledger

Accountability The responsibility of an entity to report on its use of resources allocated for a specific purpose. This accountability is determined through independent examination

Accounting estimate An approximation of a financial report item in the absence of exact measurement

Accounting Standards The Australian Accounting Standards issued by the Australian Accounting Research Foundation on behalf of the accounting bodies (i.e. the ICAA and CPA Australia), and applicable Accounting Standards issued by the Australian Accounting Standards Board

Accounts payable ledger A ledger recording details of transactions by supplier, and showing the balance owed

Accounts payable master file A computer file containing details of suppliers, details of transactions with suppliers, and the balance owed

Accounts receivable master file A computer file containing details of customers, details of transactions with customers, and the balance owed

Accounts receivable subsidiary ledger A ledger recording details of transactions by customer and showing the balance owed

Accounts receivable trial balance A listing of individual customer balances at a particular date on the accounts receivable master file or accounts receivable subsidiary ledger

Actual assessed level of control risk Assessed control risk for each assertion based on the evidence obtained from the study and an evaluation of the entity's internal control structure

Additional disclosures Disclosures made by the governing body of an entity in addition to applicable Accounting Standards to ensure that financial statements present a true and fair view

Adverse opinion An audit opinion stating that the financial report is adversely presented

Aged trial balance An accounts receivable trial balance in which customer balances are analysed by the period since each sales transaction was entered

Agencies A term commonly used to refer collectively to government departments, departments of parliament or prescribed agencies

Agency theory A theory that presupposes that when investors entrust their resources to managers (as agents), all parties involved in the relationship will act rationally and will attempt to maximise their benefits. The agent is the source of the demand for the audit. This theory is also known as the 'stewardship monitoring hypothesis'.

Aggregate likely misstatements The total likely misstatements in all accounts

Agreed-upon procedure engagement *See* 'Agreed-upon procedures'

Agreed-upon procedures Specific audit procedures performed by the auditor as agreed with the client. An agreed-upon procedures engagement provides a report of factual findings to the parties who have agreed to the specified procedures to be performed

Alleged audit failures Allegations where the auditor appears to have failed in performing audit functions

Analytical evidence Audit evidence obtained through applying analytical procedures. This involves considering or comparing relationships that exist in the entity's financial information.

Analytical procedures Procedures that involve the study and comparison of relationships among data

Analytical procedures risk The risk that analytical procedures will not detect the misstatements in an assertion

Application controls Controls that apply to the processing of specific types of transaction, such as invoicing customers, paying suppliers and preparing payroll. For computerised information system activities, application controls refer to control procedures that provide reasonable assurance that the recording, processing and reporting of data are properly performed for specific applications.

Application programs A set of instructions that enable the computer to perform specific data processing tasks

Articles of association The legal documents of a corporate entity that regulate its internal management

Assertion Statement made by management in a financial report that pertains to economic actions and events

Assessing control risk The process of evaluating the effectiveness of the design and operation of an entity's internal controls in preventing or detecting material misstatements in the financial report

Assurance The level of satisfaction with respect to the reliability of the information provided. The degree of satisfaction is determined by the nature and extent of procedures performed by the assurance provider, the results of the procedures and the objectivity of the evidence obtained.

Assurance engagement framework A framework of professional assurance services provided by accountants that incorporates audit engagements, review engagements and engagements to perform agreed-upon procedures and compilations

Attest audit An audit engagement in which an auditor expresses a positive opinion on written assertions provided by the audit client

Attest service *See* 'Attest audit'

Attestation An opinion expressed by an auditor on written assertions of another party when an audit or a review engagement is undertaken

Attestation risk The risk that an auditor may provide an incorrect audit opinion in an attest audit or a review engagement

Attribute sampling A sampling approach to determine the proportion of the population exhibiting a particular attribute, such as items in a transaction class whose processing deviates from laid down control procedures

Audit assurance An assurance provided by auditing procedures as to the reliability of management's representations in the financial statements

Audit committee A committee of non-executive directors responsible for overseeing external financial reporting

Audit evidence Information obtained by the auditor in arriving at the conclusions on which the audit opinion is based

Audit expectation gap The gap that exists between what users expect of an auditor and the service that auditors provide. This gap is due, in part, to the unreasonable expectations of users (which often exceed acceptable standards) and, in part, to the inadequate performance of auditors.

Audit independence The planning and performing of an audit, and the reporting of audit findings, with integrity and objectivity

Audit manager Staff member in charge of an audit. The audit manager coordinates and supervises the execution of the audit work program and is responsible for client liaison.

Audit mandate An authority to undertake an audit and provide a report. The mandate may prescribe the nature of the audit and the type of report expected.

Audit memoranda Written data in narrative form prepared by the auditor

Audit planning The preparation of an overall audit strategy for the expected conduct and scope of the audit

Audit program A detailed description of tests of control and substantive procedures that are planned to be performed

Audit risk The risk that an auditor may give an inappropriate opinion on the financial information that is materially misstated

Audit risk model A model that expresses the relationships among audit risk components. It simply states that audit risk = inherent risk × control risk × detection risk.

Audit rotation A practice whereby auditors are appointed for a fixed term of five or seven years, during which they cannot be removed from office. At the end of this term, the auditors must be replaced by those from another firm.

Audit team A group of people responsible for an audit, comprising a partner, a manager, an audit senior and staff assistants

Audit trail A chain of evidence provided by coding, cross-references and documentation that connects account balances and other summary results with original transaction data

Auditing An independent examination of financial or non-financial information for the purpose of providing an assurance on the credibility of that information to intended users

Auditing procedures Methods and techniques used by the auditor to gather and evaluate audit evidence

Auditing Standards Standards that contain the basic principles and essential procedures, together with related guidance, promulgated by the profession for the practice of auditing

Auditor liability A legal obligation of an auditor for committing a wrong or for not fulfilling a contract

Authorised price list A list of selling prices for each product approved by the responsible official

Bank confirmation Written confirmation of the balance at bank and other matters received directly by the auditor from the entity's bank

Bank reconciliations Schedules agreeing the balance of cash at bank per the entity's records with the balance shown on the statement of accounts received from the bank. The most common reconciling items are outstanding deposits and unpresented cheques.

Bank transfer schedule Schedule prepared by the auditor listing bank transfers for a few days either side of the balance sheet date, and the dates recorded in the books and the bank statements

Batch entry/batch processing Processing method whereby data are accumulated by classes of transaction and are entered and processed in batches

Benchmarking Critical comparison with a well-founded base or a similar case

'Big Five' The largest five international accountancy firms in the world. Prior to the merging of Coopers & Lybrand and Price Waterhouse, they were known as the 'Big Six' and included KPMG, Coopers & Lybrand, Price Waterhouse, Ernst & Young, Deloitte Touche and Arthur Andersen.

Block selection Selection of sampling units from a population by random or haphazard selection of characteristics held by clusters of sampling units, such as the initial letter of customers' names or the date at which the transaction occurred

Broker's advice A note issued by an investment broker detailing the execution of instructions to purchase or sell listed investments, and specifying the exchange price

Business-to-business Electronic commercial transactions between businesses (e.g. wholesaler and retailers)

Business-to-consumers Electronic commercial transactions between businesses and consumers

Cash counts Audit procedure of counting cash on hand and agreeing the balance with the books

Cash cut-off tests Audit procedure verifying the agreement of cash receipts recorded in the books at close of business on the balance sheet date with the physical movement of cash

Cash receipts cut-off test A substantive procedure designed to obtain reasonable assurance that cash receipts are recorded in the accounting period in which they are received

Cash receipts journal A journal recording cash receipt transactions for posting to the ledgers

Causal relationship A relationship where one matter causes another to happen

Cheque register A journal recording cheque payment transactions for posting to the ledgers. It is also referred to as a payments journal.

Cheque requisition A form authorising the issue of a cheque with details of the payee and amount

Cheque summary A computer-produced listing of cheques

Clock card A form entered by each employee into a special time clock that records the start and finish times each day of the week. It is used as a basis for preparing weekly payroll.

Common law Unwritten law formulated, developed and administered by the courts

Communication technologies Technologies that encompass communication channels (e.g. video conferencing and the mobile Internet)

Comparatives Amounts or disclosures of one or more prior periods that are presented on a comparative basis with those of the current period

Compilation engagement An accounting engagement in which an auditor prepares a financial report from the information provided by the client. No audit is performed.

Completeness An assertion pertaining to financial information that all transactions and accounts have been presented in the financial report

Compliance audit An audit that involves obtaining and evaluating evidence to determine whether certain financial and operating activities of an entity conform to specified conditions, rules or regulations

Components of financial reports Specific components of a financial report, such as an account balance (e.g. accounts receivable and accounts payable), which may be audited and reviewed

Comprehensive auditing Auditing that occurs when an auditor undertakes a range of audit and audit-related services within an audit mandate for a client. It encompasses the elements of a financial report audit, a compliance audit and a performance audit.

Computer-assisted audit techniques Techniques that involve using the computer in performing auditing procedures

Conceptual framework for auditing A theoretical framework that supports the key elements of an audit, using logical concepts

Concurring partner A partner, other than the audit engagement partner, who also reviews the audit files. In addition, he or she may sign the audit report.

Confirmation of accounts payable Written inquiry of suppliers, requesting confirmation of the balance owed at confirmation date

Confirmations Written responses by knowledgeable third parties to specific requests for factual information

Confirming A form of inquiry that enables the auditor to obtain information directly from an independent source outside the entity

Conflict of interest Situations in which users of the financial report may seek outcomes that may not be consistent with those sought by the management of the entity

Conformance role The auditor's function in ensuring that the organisation conforms to policies, procedures and statutory matters

Consistency The application of similar accounting policies and accounting methods over successive periods, and the identical treatment of items of a similar nature

Consolidation A merger of firms to consolidate types of service (as described in Chapter 18)

Contingency fee A fee paid on the basis of an outcome

Contingent liability A potential liability that becomes an actual liability when one or more future event(s) occurs or fails to occur

Continuous audit Audit assurance services provided in an ongoing manner so any new information placed on the Internet is validated for accuracy continuously

Contract note Another name for a broker's advice

Contractual relationship A relationship between two contracting parties

Contributory negligence The failure of the plaintiff to meet certain required standards of care

Control environment The overall attitude, awareness and actions of management regarding internal control and its importance in the entity

Control procedures Those policies and procedures, in addition to the control environment, that management has established to ensure, as far as possible, that specific entity objectives will be achieved

Control risk A risk that a material misstatement will not be prevented or detected on a timely basis by an entity's internal control structure

Corporate governance The framework of how directors and management perform their respective duties of conformance to add and create shareholder value

Corroborating information Evidence obtained by an auditor in support of transactions recorded in the accounting records of an entity

Counting Making a count of tangible resources or accounting for all pre-numbered documents

Credibility An assurance on the relevance and reliability of information

Credit memo A form for granting credit to customers for returned or damaged goods

Current file A file that contains corroborating information pertaining to the execution of the current year's audit program

Customer order An official purchase order issued by a customer

Cut-off tests Tests performed on transactions around the year end to ensure the completeness and occurrence of transactions

Cyclical inventory counts Periodic inventory counts that count, over a year, all or most inventory items

Damages An amount awarded as compensation for the losses suffered by plaintiff(s) in a legal action

Database A single common direct access file for all applications using common data

Deep pockets theory The perception by some that auditing firms are targets for litigation claims because they have the financial resources to withstand large claims made against them

Deontology A doctrine that holds that actions and motivations are inspired by a sense of moral obligation

Deposit slip A listing of bank notes, coins and individual cheques for deposit with the bank, a copy of which is receipted by the bank teller and retained by the entity

Design effectiveness of control procedures The ability of control procedures to prevent or correct misstatements

Detection risk A risk that the auditor's substantive procedures will collectively fail to detect a material misstatement

Deviation The failure to apply a control properly and consistently, or its application by an unauthorised employee

Deviation rate The proportion of a sample of transactions tested that have not been processed in accordance with laid down control procedures

Difference estimation A sampling approach where the amount being estimated is the absolute value of the difference between the recorded and the audited amount

Direct reporting audit An audit engagement in which an auditor expresses an opinion on an accountability matter for which the responsible party has not made a written assertion

Disclosure An assertion that components of a financial report are disclosed in accordance with a financial reporting framework

Discovery sampling A type of attribute sampling that is used to determine a specified probability of finding at least one example of an occurrence in a population

Disintermediation Doing away with intermediaries between businesses

Dispatch notes Forms authorising the release of goods from store and their delivery to the customer

Disruption risk Risk of network functioning being disrupted

Distributed denial of service A malicious virus that prevents network stations from being operative

Documentary evidence Information about financial transactions contained in documents such as source documents, agreements, contracts, various types of form, invoices and statements

Documentation of the control risk Documentation of the basis for the assessment of control risk as being less than high, or the conclusion that control risk is high

Documenting the understanding Documenting a description of the internal control structure in the form of completed internal control questionnaires, flow charts or narrative memoranda

Documents Items such as invoices, cheques and time tickets that provide evidence of the occurrence of transactions and the applicable price, nature and terms

Dollar unit sampling A statistical sampling plan based on attribute sampling, which identifies dollars making up the population as the sampling unit

Dual-purpose test A test that serves as both a test of control and a test of details of transactions

Due care Not being negligent — that is, planning and performing an audit and issuing an audit opinion with skill and competence, having regard to the needs of users

E-commerce Commercial transactions conducted by electronic means, including through the Internet

E-crimes Criminal or fraudulent activities carried out via the Internet

E-tailing Retailing through electronic means or the Internet

Economic risks Risk of loss incurred as a result of economic downturn or market conditions

Electronic data interchange (EDI) The electronic exchange of data between trading entities

Electronic evidence Any information produced or maintained by electronic means that an auditor uses to form an opinion about an assertion

Electronic funds transfer (EFT) Funds being transferred via the Internet and intranet

Embedded audit facility Procedures written directly into the program of specific computer applications enabling auditor intervention to capture or process data for audit purposes. *See* 'Integrated test facility' and 'Systems control audit file'

Emphasis of matter A paragraph highlighting a matter in an unqualified audit report following an audit opinion in specified circumstances

Employee earnings master file Computer file containing details of wage payments, including a cumulative record of wages paid

Encryption A means whereby a plain text message is changed into an unintelligible message by using a cipher system that replaces letters with coded symbols

Engagement letter A letter (contract) stating the scope and terms of the audit engagement

Enhancing role Services by the professional accountant that add value to the organisation

Environmental audit An audit that responds to the growing concern of businesses to control their environmental performance more effectively and to comply with a range of environmental regulations

Environmental auditing *See* 'Environmental audit'

Errors Unintentional mistakes, or omissions of amounts or disclosures in financial reports

'Except for' opinion An audit opinion that the financial report is fairly presented except for a specified matter

Existence An assertion pertaining to a financial report that assets or liabilities exist at a given date

Expected deviation rate The deviation rate that the auditor expects to be present in the population

Expected error The error that the auditor expects to be present in the population

Expert systems Computer models that incorporate the knowledge of human experts to assist others in performing functions or making decisions

Experts Specialists in areas other than auditing who may be consulted or called on to assist in the audit

Extent of substantive procedures The number of items or sample size to which a particular test or procedure is applied

Extent of tests of control The extent to which the tests of control are applied. These are directly affected by the auditor's planned assessed level of control risk; more extensive testing will be needed for a low assessed level of control risk than for a moderate assessed level of control risk.

External auditors Individual practitioners or members of public accounting firms who render professional auditing services to clients

Fair presentation A financial report presented fairly in accordance with a financial reporting framework

Financial report A general purpose financial report intended to meet the information needs common to users who are unable to command the preparation of reports tailored so as to satisfy all of their information needs

Financial report assertions *See* 'Assertions'

Financial report audit An audit that enables an auditor to express an opinion as to whether the financial report is prepared, in all material respects, in accordance with an identified financial reporting framework

Financial report materiality The aggregate level of materiality determined for each financial statement

Financial reporting review panel A high level committee that could liase with (1) Standard setting bodies on the setting of Standards to eliminate undesirable practices, and (2) professional bodies on the quality of accounting and audit work

Financial software Computer programs that provide financial management tools

Finished goods Manufactured inventory that is available for sale

Flow chart A schematic diagram using standardised symbols, interconnecting flow lines and annotations that portray the steps involved in processing information through the information system

Follow-up phase The final phase in an operational or performance audit, whereby the auditor follows up on the auditee's response to the recommendations made in the audit report

Forensic audit Audit assurance services to establish the validity of forensic evidences

Foreseeability The reasonable occurrence of an event that will have an impact on a person's decision

Fraud Any act that involves the use of deception to obtain an illegal advantage

General controls Controls that apply to computer information systems as a whole. They include controls related to such matters as data centre organisation, hardware and systems software acquisition and maintenance, and backup and recovery procedures. These controls are sometimes referred to as environmental controls.

General purpose financial reports Reports that look to the independent auditor's report for assurance that the two primary qualities that make accounting information useful for decision-making — namely, relevance and reliability — have been met

Generalised audit software Audit software that auditors use under a variety of data organisation and processing methods

Going concern An entity that envisages no major curtailment of its operations in the foreseeable future, and that assumes its ongoing viability by being able to pay off its debts

Going-concern basis An assumption that an entity will continue in the future unless evidence is available to the contrary

Goods received note A form issued by the receiving department detailing the description and quantity of the goods delivered by a supplier

Government auditors Public sector auditors who audit the accounts of municipalities and state and federal governments, and who report their audit findings to respective parliaments

Haphazard selection Selection of sampling units from a population by chance

Illegal acts Acts that involve non-compliance with laws and regulations

Image risk Same as reputational risk — that is, the risk of damaging the good impression of a company

Imprest bank account Bank account funded with a sum sufficient to meet the payment of special purpose cheques such as wages or dividends

Imprest petty cash fund Petty cash fund maintained at a constant level via replenishment with the value of vouchers paid out of the fund

Inability to form an opinion Circumstances in which no audit opinion can be formed

Independence Ability to withstand pressure from management influence when conducting an audit or providing audit-related services, such that one's professional integrity is not compromised

Independent checks The verification of work previously performed by other individuals or departments, or the proper valuation of recorded amounts

Information aggregators Providers of secondary and aggregated information for users. Also known as informediaries.

Information economy The state of economic affairs, with a primary focus on the sourcing, contexts and type of information used by the markets

Information hypothesis A hypothesis that posits that the demand for auditing is a result of investors wanting reliable information that can be used effectively in decision-making. Unlike the agency theory (see page 691), the emphasis is not so much on the agent as on the reliability of the information.

Information processing controls Controls that address risks related to the authorisation, completeness and accuracy of transactions

Information system The methods and records established to identify, assemble, analyse, calculate, classify, record and report transactions and other events that affect an entity, and to maintain accountability for assets, liabilities, revenues and expenditures

Informediaries Parties who act as information agents. They are information aggregators and disseminators who provide specialised services, using information analyses, to customers.

Inherent limitations The reasons (such as cost versus benefit and management override) that an entity's internal control structure can provide only reasonable assurance to management and the board of directors regarding the achievement of an entity's objectives

Inherent risk A material misstatement that could occur in the absence of internal controls

Inherent uncertainty An outcome of any report item or disclosure contingent on future events that cannot be reasonably estimated

Initial audit engagement The first audit of an entity by the particular audit firm

Initial engagements *See* 'Initial audit engagement'

Input controls Procedures that provide assurance that data received for processing have been properly authorised, that they are complete and that they have been correctly converted into machine readable form

Input devices Input equipment that enables users to enter data into a computer system

Inquiring Either oral or written inquiry by the auditor

Inspecting Careful scrutiny or detailed examination of documents and records, and the physical examination of tangible resources

Insurance hypothesis A view that posits that managers and professional participants in financial activities seek to use an auditor as a means of insurance — that is, as a means of shifting financial responsibility if any losses are expected from litigation

Integrated test facility (ITF) A type of test of control that requires using a fictitious entity and entering fictitious transactions for that entity with the regular transactions, and then comparing the result with the expected output

Interim audit work Audit work performed prior to balance sheet date. Typically, this involves performing tests of control and tests of details of transactions

Intermediaries Those who act between buyers and sellers

Internal audit An independent appraisal function established within an organisation to examine and evaluate the activities of the entity as a service to the entity

Internal auditing *See* 'Internal audit'

Internal auditors Those engaged as in-house employees of an organisation who are responsible for providing independent audit appraisals of the organisation's activities

Internal control Management's philosophy and operating style and all the policies and procedures adopted by management to assist in achieving the entity's objectives, including the safeguarding of assets, the prevention and detection of fraud and error, the accuracy and completeness of the accounting records, and the timely preparation of reliable financial information

Internal control evaluation check lists Lists that enumerate the types of potential misstatement that could occur in specific assertions

Internal control questionnaire A series of questions about accounting and control policies and procedures that the auditor considers necessary to prevent material misstatements in the financial report

Internal control structure The control environment, information system and control procedures maintained by management to assist in ensuring that the conduct of the business is orderly and efficient

Internationalisation of the profession The increasing acceptance by the accounting profession of International Standards, and the growing support across countries for the elimination of barriers to the practice of accountancy

Inventory count sheets Pre-prepared sheets for recording inventory description and quantity as counted. These are usually pre-numbered.

Inventory master file A computer file containing details of inventory items, their movement and the quantity on hand

Inventory tags Three-part, tie-on tags for recording the inventory count of each item

Investment register Subsidiary ledger recording individual investments in shares and debentures. Entries show purchases and sales, the cost of each bundle purchased, and the quantity and cost of the balance owned.

Investment subsidiary ledger Another name for an investment register

Irregularities Actions that comprise fraud and other illegal acts, acts that contravene the constitution of the entity, intentional (but not fraudulent) misstatements, and unintentional errors

Joint and several liability An obligation of two or more persons. Each is liable severally and all are liable jointly. A plaintiff may sue one or more jointly or severally.

Kiting An irregularity overstating the cash balance by intentionally recording a bank transfer as a deposit in the receiving bank while failing to show a deduction from the bank account on which the transfer cheque is drawn

Knowledge-based An intelligence system that is based on examining and aggregating relevant information and provides logical responses

Known misstatements Uncorrected errors specifically identified through substantive tests of details of transactions and balances

Lapping An irregularity concealing the misappropriation of cash by using subsequent cash receipts to conceal the original misappropriation

Lead schedule A summary working sheet that is supported by individual working papers

Legal risk Risk of being sued or incurring legal costs

Likely misstatement The total of uncorrected errors, projected uncorrected errors and estimated errors

Low-balling A practice whereby a bid price of an audit service is quoted at an unreasonably low level so as to win the bid, with any 'losses' subsequently recovered through other means

Lower assessed level of control risk approach An audit strategy based on the assumption that control risk is medium to low for an assertion

Management The individuals who control and are responsible for the resources invested within an entity

Management letter A letter written to the management of an entity by an auditor. It contains recommendations for improving the efficiency and effectiveness of significant matters that were noticed during the course of an audit

Management representation letter A letter that contains representations from management to an auditor

Management responsibility statement A statement provided by management in the annual report stating that management is responsible for the preparation of the financial report

Material account balance The size of the recorded account balance that is considered significant

Materiality In respect to accounting information, an omission, misstatement or non-disclosure that could adversely affect the decisions of the user in given circumstances

Mathematical evidence Audit evidence that results from recomputations by the auditor and comparisons of those results with client computations

Mean-per-unit method A sampling method where the amount being estimated is the average value of each sampling unit

Measurement An assertion that a transaction or event is recorded at the proper amount

Memorandum of association A legal document comprising the constitution of a corporate entity

Microcash Normally operated in banks and financial institutions, cash transactions that are monitored through electronic units being transferred between parties

Minutes of meetings The minutes of meetings of the board of directors and other executive committees of an entity

Mobile Internet The operations of functions using both the Internet and mobile communication technologies

Modified audit report An audit report that contains a qualified opinion and/or an emphasis of matter

Monthly customer statement A listing of transactions with each customer that have occurred since the date of the previous statement, which shows the closing balance due. This statement is sent to the customer

Moral risk Risk of harming others

Multidisciplinary practice (MDP) Professional firms that provide a wide range of services such as legal, accounting, banking, etc. within a single framework, with such services being of different disciplines

Multimedia applications Applications of electronic transactions that use multimedia

Narrative memorandum Written comments concerning the auditor's consideration of the internal control structure

Nature of substantive procedures The type and effectiveness of the auditing procedures to be performed. The types of substantive procedure are analytical procedures, tests of details of transactions and tests of details of balances.

Necessary controls Control procedures that are likely to prevent or detect specific potential misstatements

Negative assurance A statement of assurance that declares that nothing has come to the auditor's attention that indicates that the assertions are not presented fairly in accordance with identified criteria

Negligence Not exercising due care

Nonattest service A service that does not result in the expression of an opinion, negative assurance, a summary of findings, or any other form of assurance by the public accountant. Most non-attest services are those provided in respect to traditional accounting and taxation, management consulting or advice, and insolvency and business recovery.

Non-audit services Services that are not audit related. Examples are accounting, management consulting, and insolvency and business recovery

Non-sampling risk The component of audit risk that is not due to examining only a portion of the data, such as through the use of inappropriate procedures or the misinterpretation of evidence

Non-statistical sampling The use of judgement to determine sample size and to interpret the results

'No transaction' claim A claim by a client against an auditor for the failure of a risky venture in which the client has invested on advice that was provided by an auditor

Obligations Assertions that liabilities are the obligations of the entity

Observing The act of watching or witnessing the performance of some activity or process

Occurrence An assertion pertaining to financial information that transactions did occur

On-line auditing Audit assurance services provided through the Internet on the information transmitted on line

On-line entry/batch processing A processing system whereby transactions are entered as they occur, and undergo edit and validation checks, but they are accumulated for subsequent processing

On-line entry/on-line processing A processing system whereby master files are updated concurrently with data entry, and a transaction log is produced that consists of a chronological record of all transactions

Operating effectiveness of the control procedures The extent to which laid down control procedures are being complied with

Operating system A supervisory program that performs general functions required for the operation of the computer as it executes specific tasks

Operational auditing A systematic process of evaluating an organisation's effectiveness, efficiency and economy of operations under management's control, and then reporting to appropriate persons the results of the evaluation

Opinion shopping A practice whereby an audit client invites another firm of accountants to offer a second opinion on a disagreement the client's management has with the auditor over a proposed accounting treatment. This action can pressure the auditor to issue an unqualified audit report so as not to lose the audit to the second firm.

Oral evidence Responses to oral inquiries of officers and key employees of the entity

Organisational controls Controls that relate to the management philosophy and operating style and to organisational structure control environment factors. These controls provide assurance that there is appropriate segregation of duties within the computerised information service department and between it and user departments.

Output controls Controls of computer output that provide assurance that the processing result is correct and that only authorised personnel receive the output

Outsourcing The method of hiring external expertise in the discharge of certain organisational functions such as internal audit, control reviews, etc.

Overall review An overall review of a financial report so as to arrive at the conclusion that the financial information as a whole is consistent with the auditor's knowledge of the entity's business

Parallel simulation A method of testing controls that simulates the entity's processing of real data. Actual entity data are processed using auditor controlled software. The output is then compared with the entity's actual output.

Partner A member of a partnership of public practitioners. A partner has the overall and final responsibility of an audit engagement.

Pay slips Forms that indicate the make-up of an employee's current period's net pay, and that show the hours worked, gross wages and the payroll deductions

Payment transactions file A computer file containing details of payments made

Payments journal A journal recording cheque payment transactions for posting to the ledgers. Also referred to as a cheque register

Payroll register A journal recording details of the computation and amount of wages paid to each employee

Payroll transactions file A computer file recording details of wage payments to employees

Performance audit An independent and systematic examination of the management of an organisation, program or function for the purpose of (1) forming an opinion on whether it is being managed in an economical, efficient and effective manner, and (2) determining whether the internal procedures for promoting and monitoring economy, efficiency and effectiveness are adequate

Performance auditing *See* 'Performance audit'

Permanent file A permanent file that contains data useful in an audit on many future engagements

Perpetual inventory records Records of the movement of inventory items and of the quantity on hand

Personnel authorisation form A form issued by the personnel department indicating the job classification, wage rate and authorised payroll deductions for each employee

Personnel data master file A computer file containing details of employees, such as wage rate and date of hiring

Personnel file A record maintained by the personnel department recording details of employees such as wage rates and date of hiring

Phases of an audit The progressive steps in the conduct of an audit. These are (1) accepting the engagement, (2) planning the audit, (3) performing the audit and (4) providing an audit report

Physical controls Controls that limit access to assets and important records

Physical evidence Audit evidence obtained from physical examination or inspection of tangible assets

Physical inventory The process of ascertaining inventory quantities by count, weight or measurement

Planned acceptable level of detection risk A quantitative or judgemental measure of detection risk for each assertion, which is arrived at after inherent risk and control risk are assessed

Planned assessed level of control risk A quantitative or judgemental measure of control risk based on assumptions about the effectiveness of the design and operation of relevant controls

Planned detection risk A detection risk that is considered tolerable. *See* also 'Planned acceptable level of detection risk'

Planned level of substantive procedures Substantive procedures necessary to achieve the planned detection risk

Planning materiality Materiality determined during the planning phase of the audit

Plant register A record of plant and equipment items containing such information as description, supplier, serial number and location, as well as cost and depreciation charges that reconcile with the control account in the general ledger

Population Transactions in a transaction class or items making up an account balance that the auditor believes to be consistent as far as the likelihood of deviation or misstatement of the type being sought is concerned

Positive assurance An audit opinion providing a high level of assurance as to whether the assertions are presented in accordance with established or stated criteria

Predecessor auditor An auditor who has since been replaced by a current auditor

Predominantly substantive approach A preliminary audit strategy based on the assumption that the assessed level of control risk for an assertion is high

Preliminary assessment of control risk An assessment for the purpose of obtaining a reasonable expectation as to the effectiveness of controls such that the detailed audit program can be designed under the appropriate audit strategy

Preliminary audit strategy An audit strategy based on certain assumptions such as an assessed level of control risk, the extent of understanding of internal control structure, the tests of control to be performed and the planned level of substantive procedures to be performed

Presents fairly As used in the audit opinion, the term recommended by AUS 702. 'Fairly' communicates to the user that the auditor has applied judgement when considering the application of the financial reporting framework.

Privity of contract The contractual relationship that exists between two or more contracting parties

Probability-proportional-to-size sampling A statistical sampling plan based on attribute sampling which identifies dollars making up the population as the sampling unit. It is also known as 'dollar unit sampling'.

Procedures to obtain an understanding Procedures performed to obtain knowledge of an entity's internal control structure

Processing controls Controls that provide an assurance that computer processing has been performed as intended for a particular application

Production move orders Documents authorising the requisitioning of materials and labour for the purpose of manufacturing

Professional ethics The written code of ethics put forward by a professional body

Professional indemnity insurance An insurance taken by a professional person to indemnify the assured against loss resulting from the proven negligence of the professional person

Professional judgement An exercise of an opinion by an accountant or auditor that is based on the assumption that he or she has the professional skills and expertise to exercise due professional care and to be objective in providing advice or opinions on matters presented to him or her

Projected error Population error based on the projection of the error rate in the sample tested

Projections Prospective financial information prepared on the basis of hypothetical assumptions about future events and management actions that are not necessarily expected to take place. A projection can also be a combination of a best estimate and hypothetical assumptions.

Proper authorisation Procedures that ensure that transactions are authorised by personnel acting within the scope of their authority

Proportionate liability An arrangement whereby the plaintiff's loss is divided among the defendants according to their share of responsibility

Proximity Closeness in space, time or relationships, where the occurrence of events is foreseeable. It applies within an expected range of relationships.

Public interest In the interest of the community or the people as a whole

Purchase journal A journal recording approved suppliers' invoices for posting to the accounts receivable ledger

Purchase orders Forms showing the description of the goods, the quantity ordered and other relevant data. The order is signed by the purchasing officer.

Purchase requisitions Forms issued by authorised personnel in user departments detailing goods and services required

Purchase transactions file A computer file listing details of all purchase transactions

Purchases cut-off test A substantive test of details of transactions designed to obtain reasonable assurance that purchase transactions occurring near the balance sheet date are recorded in the accounting period in which the transactions occurred and that the corresponding entries for inventories are made in the same period

Qualified audit opinion Audit opinions, with reservations or disclaimers, or any opinion other than an unqualified opinion

Qualified opinion *See* 'Qualified audit opinion'

Quality assurance programs Systematic programs in which all procedures are subject to different quality checks and reporting mechanisms to ensure adherence to standards of quality

Random selection Selection of sampling units from a population by the use of random number tables or computer-generated random numbers

Ratio estimation A sampling method for which the amount being estimated is the ratio of the difference between recorded and audited values

Raw materials Materials purchased from suppliers to be used in the manufacture of finished goods

Reasonable care and skill Professionalism or due professional care and competence reasonably expected of a professional person (as opposed to a layperson) under the circumstances of the case. The professional is expected to have considered all facts (and their reliability) to arrive at a responsible and well-informed opinion of the matter.

Records The primary accounting records of an entity, in the form of journals and ledgers

Recurring engagement An audit of an entity previously audited by the same auditor

Related party transactions Transactions consummated by related parties (that is, by parties who are involved in an economic action or event to the extent that 'arms length' bargaining of terms is not possible)

Reliability risk Risk of unreliable information being used or transmitted

Remittance advice A form accompanying cash or cheques paid by a customer, indicating the customer's details and the items being paid

Reperforming Recalculating or reconciling financial data. This process also involves redoing certain aspects of the processing of selected transactions.

Report of factual findings A report provided by an auditor who performs specific procedures requested by the client. No opinion is expressed. The user forms his or her own conclusion.

Representation letter A document containing replies (usually by management) to inquiries made by the auditor

Review An assurance service in which an auditor provides a moderate level of assurance. It is a lower level of assurance than that provided in an audit. The outcome of a review is a statement of negative assurance.

Review engagement *See* 'Review'

Review partner *See* 'Concurring partner'

Rights An assertion that assets are rights of the entity

Risk assessment The evaluation of probable or possible losses or failures in regard to a range of matters about which there is uncertainty

Risk of incorrect acceptance Risk that arises when the sample in a substantive test of details supports the conclusion that the recorded account balance is not materially misstated when it is materially misstated

Risk of incorrect rejection Risk that arises when the sample in a substantive test of details supports the conclusion that the recorded account balance is materially misstated when it is not materially misstated

Risk of overreliance The risk of assessing control risk as being too low

Risk of underreliance The risk of assessing control risk as being too high

Risk-based approach An approach that enables the auditor to focus on those areas of the audit that require the highest level of assurance

Risk management The minimisation of exposure of risks in businesses. This involves the techniques of identifying potential risks, estimating the probability of occurrence, minimising damages, and generally managing a business' risk profile

Roll-forward testing Analytical procedures or tests of details of transactions performed on transactions that occur between the date of testing (when testing is done before the end of the year) and the balance date

Rough cash book A listing of details of cheques and other cash received in the mail prepared by employees opening the mail

SME Small and medium-sized enterprises

Sales cut-off test A substantive procedure designed to obtain reasonable assurance that sales and accounts receivable are recorded in the accounting period in which the transactions occurred, and that the corresponding entries for inventories and cost of goods sold are made in the same period

Sales invoice Form detailing goods or services supplied to a customer and the amount owed

Sales journal A journal listing completed sales transactions

Sales order A form showing the description of the goods, the quantity ordered and other relevant data. The order is signed by the clerk accepting the order

Sales return cut-off test A substantive procedure designed to obtain reasonable assurance that sales returns are accounted for in the period in which the original sales transaction occurred

Sales transactions file A computer file listing details all sales transactions

Sampling interval The interval between successive sampling units selected for testing where systematic selection is being applied

Sampling risk The possibility that a properly drawn sample may, by chance, not be representative of the population

Sampling unit Items making up a transaction class or account balance out of which the sample is to be selected for testing

Second partner review A review of working papers by an audit partner who did not participate in the audit

Segregation of duties Procedures that ensure individuals do not perform incompatible duties

Selective testing The examination of specific items within a population based on the auditor's knowledge of the business and the characteristics of the population being tested

Self-regulatory The characteristic of an organisation or profession that governs its behaviour through self-imposed codes and regulations

Sequential sampling A type of attribute sampling that permits a halt to sampling if a certain number of occurrences are observed

Solicitor's representation letter A letter of audit enquiry to the entity's solicitor as a means of obtaining corroborating information about management's assertions concerning the status of litigation, claims and unrecorded or contingent liabilities

Standard format of audit reports The prescribed format, principles and wording of audit reports in accordance with Auditing Standards

Statistical sampling Sampling that uses probability theory to determine sample size and to interpret the results

Stewardship A concept whereby servants (i.e. management/officers) are entrusted with certain responsibilities to conduct the business so as to serve the best interests of the shareholders

Strategic risk Risk of adopting a strategy that is inappropriate and incapable of achieving specific goals

Stratification Subdivision of a population, such as by monetary value. The subpopulations need to be defined so sampling units can belong only to one stratum.

Subsequent events Events occurring between the period end and the date of the audit report, and facts discovered after the date of the audit report

Subsequent period's bank statement The first bank statement issued after the balance sheet date that is used by the auditor to verify the existence of outstanding deposits and unpresented cheques listed on the bank reconciliation as at the balance sheet date

Substantive procedures Procedures that provide evidence as to the fairness of management's financial report assertions

Successor auditor An auditor who has been appointed to take over an audit from previous auditors

Suppliers' invoices Forms issued by the supplier detailing goods or services supplied and the amount owed

Sustainability A situation where development can be maintained and its progress can be monitored, to ensure ongoing viability and relevance

Systematic selection Selection of sampling units from a population at regular intervals known as the sampling interval

Systems control and audit file An embedded audit facility that enables auditors to specify parameters of interest, such as transactions meeting specified criteria, which are then recorded on a special audit file for subsequent review by the auditors

Technical review A review by a partner or manager to ensure that the form and content of the financial report is in accordance with Accounting Standards, the Corporations Law and Australian Stock Exchange requirements (where applicable)

Teleology A doctrine that holds that actions are right or wrong only in terms of their ability to bring about desired ends

Termination notice A form issued by the personnel department on an employee's termination of employment

Test data approach A method of testing controls in a computerised information systems environment. The auditor prepares fictitious transactions and has these tested using the entity's software. The output from processing test data is then compared with the auditor's expected output.

Tests of control Audit tests performed to provide evidence about the effectiveness of the design and operations of internal controls

Tests of details of balances Substantive procedures to obtain evidence directly about an account balance rather than about the individual transactions that are debited and credited to the account

Tests of details of transactions Tests to obtain evidence of a sample or all of the individual debits or credits in an account, to reach a conclusion about the account balance

Third parties Parties other than a contracting party

Time budget The estimated amount of time required at each staff level (partner, manager, senior and staff assistants) to complete each part of the audit

Timing of substantive procedures The time at which substantive procedures are performed relative to the balance sheet date

Timing of tests of control The time at which tests of control are performed and the part of the accounting period to which they relate

Tolerable error The maximum error in the population that the auditor can accept as being consistent with the conclusion that sample results confirm achievement of the audit objective

Tolerable misstatement A level of misstatement that can exist in an account balance for it to be materially misstated

Tort A breach of duty other than under contract, leading to liability for damages (or compensation)

Total quality management (TQM) A management tool that oversees the entire the operation and identifies wherever efficiency can be enhanced

Tracing Following through a transaction from source documents to accounting records

Transaction class A grouping or classification of like transactions. When grouping sales transactions, for example, the reference is to a sales class.

Transaction walk-through review Tracing one or a few transactions within each major class of transaction through the transaction trail to identify and observe the related control policies and procedures

Transactions Exchanges of assets and services between an entity and outside parties, as well as the transfer or use of assets and services within an entity

Trojan programs Computer programs that are installed for pretence to conceal some real purpose

True and fair view A term that is synonymous with 'fairly presented'. It is used when expressing a fair opinion on financial reports when required by the Corporations Law.

UIG Consensus Views Consensus views contained in the abstracts issued by the Urgent Issues Group

Underlying accounting data Information about economic actions and events contained in the accounting records of an entity

Unqualified audit opinion An audit opinion stating that a financial report is fairly presented in accordance with a financial reporting framework

Unqualified audit report *See* 'Unqualified audit opinion'

Utilitarianism A doctrine that holds that actions should be directed towards providing the greatest good for the greatest number of people

Value chain A chain of activities within a composite function that, when put together, adds overall value to the users

Value reporting Reports that review matters beyond financial figures and that examine the overall performance of organisations in social, environmental and economic terms

Valuation An assertion that assets and liabilities are recorded at appropriate carrying value

Variable sampling A sampling approach to determine the value of the population, such as the difference between recorded and audited values of items making up an account balance

Vouching Selecting entries in the accounting records, and obtaining and inspecting the documentation that served as the basis for entries

'Watchdog' role The auditor's role in providing an overall assurance that the financial affairs of the entity are in order and that there are no material facts that the auditor considers would have affected the affairs of the company significantly

Window dressing A deliberate attempt to enhance some aspect of a company's apparent short-term solvency, such as by misstating the cut-off of cash receipts or payments

Work in process Part-manufactured products consisting of materials, direct labour and overhead applied to the stage of completion

Work in progress *See* 'Work in process'

Working papers Documentation stored on paper, film or in electronic media containing audit evidence in support of the audit opinion

Write-off authorisation memo A form signed by an appropriate official authorising the write-off of bad debts

Written representations Signed statements by responsible and knowledgeable individuals that have a bearing on one or more of management's assertions

Year-end work Audit work performed at or near the balance date. This typically involves the performance of substantive procedures.

Index